Bengt Jonsson Joachim Parrow (Eds.)

CONCUR '94: Concurrency Theory

5th International Conference
Uppsala, Sweden, August 22-25, 1994
Proceedings

Springer-Verlag
Berlin Heidelberg New York
London Paris Tokyo
Hong Kong Barcelona
Budapest

Series Editors

Gerhard Goos
Universität Karlsruhe
Postfach 69 80
Vincenz-Priessnitz-Straße 1
D-76131 Karlsruhe, Germany

Juris Hartmanis
Cornell University
Department of Computer Science
4130 Upson Hall
Ithaca, NY 14853, USA

Volume Editors

Bengt Jonsson
Department of Computer Systems, Uppsala University
P.O. Box 325, S-751 05 Uppsala, Sweden

Joachim Parrow
Swedish Institute of Computer Science
P.O. Box 1262, S-164 28 Kista, Sweden

CR Subject Classification (1991): F.3, F.1, D.3

ISBN 3-540-58328-7 Springer-Verlag Berlin Heidelberg New York
ISBN 0-387-58329-7 Springer-Verlag New York Berlin Heidelberg

CIP data applied for

Printed in Germany

Typesetting: Camera-ready by author
SPIN: 10475388 45/3140-543210 - Printed on acid-free paper

Preface

CONCUR'94 is the fifth in the annual series of conferences on theory of concurrency. The first two CONCUR conferences in 1990 and 1991 were held in Amsterdam, The Netherlands; in 1992 the venue was New York, USA and in 1993 it was Hildesheim, Germany. The proceedings have been published in the Springer-Verlag Lecture Notes in Computer Science series as volumes 458, 527, 630 and 715.

This year we received 108 submissions, from which the Programme Committee chose 29 for presentation at the conference in Uppsala and inclusion in these proceedings. I would here like to thank the members of the Programme Committee and the referees for their important and sometimes very difficult and strenuous work.

CONCUR'94 is organized jointly by the Swedish Institute of Computer Science, Uppsala University, and the Royal Institute of Technology in Stockholm. Financial support has generously been provided by Ericsson Telecom, Telia Research, The Wenner-Gren Scientific Foundation, The Swedish National Board for Industrial and Technical Development, The Swedish Research Council for Engineering Sciences, and The Swedish Natural Science Research Council.

I also want to thank Mads Dam, Patrik Ernberg, Lars-åke Fredlund, Maria Hultström, Hans Höök, Björn Lisper, Daniel Lundström, Fredrik Orava, and José-Luis Vivas for invaluable help with innumerable tasks in public relations, fundraising, and with the processing of submissions resulting in this volume. The Organizing Committee at the Department of Computer Systems at Uppsala University, chaired by Bengt Jonsson, is at this moment busy organizing the conference with great zeal and deserves profound gratitude from me and from all conference participants.

Stockholm, June 1994 Joachim Parrow

Programme Committee

Ralph-Johan Back
Jos Baeten
Eike Best
Ed Clarke
Mads Dam
Rob van Glabbeek
Cliff Jones
Bengt Jonsson (Org. Com. Chair)
Kim Larsen
Ugo Montanari
Mogens Nielsen
Catuscia Palamidessi
Joachim Parrow (Prog. Com. Chair)
Scott Smolka
Bernhard Steffen
Colin Stirling
P.S. Thiagarajan
Frits Vaandrager
Pierre Wolper
Zhou Chaochen

CONCUR'94 Referees

P.A. Abdulla
L. Aceto
T. Amtoft
H.R. Andersen
A. Asperti
J.C.M. Baeten
T. Basten
J. Bergstra
K. Bernstein
E. Best
J. Blanco
F. de Boer
R.N. Bol
D.J.B. Bosscher
A. Bouali
J. Bradfield
F. van Breugel
G. Bruns
O. Burkart
H.-D. Burkhard
M. Butler
L. Campora
S. Campos
I. Castellani
A. Cheng
S. Christensen
I. Christoff
L. Christoff
E.M. Clarke
A. Classen
R. Cleaveland
J. Coenen
A. Corradini
G. Costa
M. Dam
D. Dams
P. Degano
J. Desel
R. Devillers
M. Droste
J. Engelfriet
J.J. Elbro
E.A. Emerson
U.H. Engberg
L.-H. Eriksson
P. Ernberg
J. Esparza
A. Fantechi
G. Ferrari
J. Fischer
H. Fleischhack
W. Fokkink
N. De Francesco
L.-å. Fredlund
R. Gerber
S. German
R. Gerth
A. Geser
H. Geuvers
R. van Glabbeek
S. Gnesi
J.Chr. Godskesen
R. Gorrieri
J.F. Groote
J. Gunawardena
A. Gupta
V. Gupta
H. Hansson
C. Hermida
S. Hodges
M. Huhn
C. Huizing
H. Huttel
D. Van Hung
S.P. Iyer
A. Jeffrey
C.T. Jensen
S. Jha
C. Jones
B. Jonsson
R. Langerak
K. Larsen
I. Lee
H.-G. Linde-Göers
B. Lisper
G. Luettgen
L. Kempe
A. Kiehn
M. Kindahl
E. Kindler
H. Korver
M. Koutny
R. Kuiper
K. Lodaya
W. Marrero
S. Martini
A. Masini
S. Mauw
K. McMillan
J.-J.Ch. Meijer
A. Merceron
E. Moggi
F. Moller
U. Montanari
F. Morando
M. Morley
P.D. Mosses
M. Mukund
H. Mulder
D. Murphy
K. Namjoshi
V. Natarajan
R. Nederpelt
R. De Nicola
P. Niebert
M. Nielsen
F. Nielson
S.-O. Nyström
B.E. Olivier
C. Palamidessi
P. Panangaden
B. Pfitzmann
S. Prehn
C. Priami
P. Quaglia
S. Rajasekaran
R. Ramanujam
P. Rambags
G. Reggio
R. Ch. Riemann
P. Rosolini
F. Rossi
J.J.M.M. Rutten
D. Sangiorgi
V. Sassone
R. Segala
K. Sere
A. Skou
S. Smolka
M. Sohoni
O. Sokolsky
P.H. Starke
B. Steffen
C. Stirling
K. Sunesen
T. Thielke
P.S. Thiagarajan
Y.-K. Tsay
E. Tumlin
A. Uselton
F. Vaandrager
A. Valmari
J.J. Vereijken
C. Verhoef
B. Victor
I. Virbitskaite
J.L. Vivas
W. Vogler
J.J. van Wamel
Wang Ji
Wang Yi
H. Wehrheim
C. Weise
P. Wolper
J. von Wright
S.-H. Wu
Q. Xu
T. Yoneda
S. Yuen
S. Zhang
Zhou Chaochen
A. Zwarico
J. Zwiers

Contents

Geometry of Interaction
(Abstract)

Jean-Yves GIRARD
CNRS, Laboratoire de Mathématiques Discrètes
Marseille, France

Geometry of Interaction is based on the idea that the ultimate explanation of logical rules is through the cut-elimination procedure. This is achieved by means of a pure geometric interpretation of normalization :

- proofs are operators on the Hilbert space describing I/O dependencies
- cut-elimination is the solution of an I/O equation

$$U(x \oplus \sigma(a)) = y \oplus a$$

(the cut σ expressing a feedback of some output of the proof U to some input of U)

- termination is nilpotency of the operator σU
- execution is expressed by

$$RES(U, \sigma) := (1 - \sigma^2)U(1 - \sigma U)^{-1}(1 - \sigma^2)$$

This interpretation is available for full linear logic, which means, using translations for all constructive logics, in particular for typed λ-calculi. It also works for untyped calculus, *modulo* a slight weakening of the hypotheses, expressing the absence of deadlock.

Geometry of Interaction expresses a pure local asynchronous form of execution. Among the distinguished features of this execution, let us mention the distinction between public and private data. By the way there are two ways to combine operators in a way respecting privacy, and these two ways correspond to the two conjunctions of linear logic.

A Compositional Semantics for Statecharts using Labeled Transition Systems*

Andrew C. Uselton and Scott A. Smolka

Department of Computer Science
State University of New York at Stony Brook
Stony Brook, NY 11794 USA**

We characterize the statecharts *step semantics* of Pnueli and Shalev as a mapping Ψ from an inductively defined algebra of *statecharts terms* to a domain of *labeled transition systems* (LTSs). Statecharts equivalence $=_{SC}$, i.e. LTS isomorphism, is shown not to be a congruence and hence the step semantics is not compositional. We define a new semantic mapping $\Psi_{>}$ to a domain of LTSs with a richer label structure, and show that LTS isomorphism in this domain is the largest congruence contained in $=_{SC}$.

1 Introduction

Statecharts [Har87] is a highly structured and economical description language for complex, reactive systems [Pnu86, HP85], such as communication protocols and digital control units. Statecharts extend conventional state transition diagrams with three elements dealing with the notions of *hierarchy*, *concurrency* and *communication*. Hierarchy is achieved by embedding one statechart in the state of another statechart. Concurrency is supported by a (mainly) synchronous operation of statechart composition permitting a broadcast-style of communication among the constituent statecharts.

It is important to have a *formal semantics* for statecharts so that their behavior can be precisely and unambiguously understood, and safety-critical properties of systems can be formally verified. As pointed out in [HGdR89, Per93] this is no easy task due to the richness of the language and the fact that it is a visual language.

Figure 1(a), which depicts an example statechart S, demonstrates the main features of statecharts. The most prominent ingredients of a statechart are *states*, drawn as rectangles, and *transitions*, drawn as arrows. Each state has a *name*, and states may contain or be *refined* by other states. Refinement in statecharts may be viewed as embedding one finite-state automaton (FSA) in the state of another, and FSAs can be composed in parallel (indicated by the dotted lines separating them). Each FSA has an initial or *default* state, indicated by the

* Research supported in part by NSF Grants CCR-9120995 and CCR-9208585, and AFOSR Grant F49620-93-1-0250.

** E-mail: `uselton@cs.sunysb.edu`, `sas@cs.sunysb.edu`,

The set of primitive events is used to construct *labels* for the transitions. For each element $\pi \in \Pi$ there is a *negative event* $\overline{\pi}$ used to test for the absence of that event, and $\overline{\Pi} = \{\overline{\pi} \mid \pi \in \Pi\}$. A label l has a *trigger* and an *action*. The trigger of a label is a subset of $\Pi \cup \overline{\Pi}$ and the action is a subset of Π. A label l with trigger τ and action α is written τ/α, and we use the functions $trigger(l) = \tau$ and $action(l) = \alpha$.

Traditionally, sets τ and α are denoted in a statechart by listing their elements. For example, the label $\{a, \overline{b}\}/\{c, d\}$ is written $a\overline{b}/cd$. The set of labels generated by events Π is $\mathcal{L}(\Pi) = 2^{\Pi \cup \overline{\Pi}} \times 2^{\Pi}$. Without loss of generality we assume that $trigger(l) \cup action(l)$ does not contain contradictory events as in $a/\overline{a}$ or $a\overline{a}/b$, and that events in $action(l)$ do not duplicate events in $trigger(l)$, as in a/a.

For a statechart $(\Pi, N, \mathcal{T}, r)$ the set of names N is equipped with the functions $children_N : N \rightarrow 2^N$, and $type_N : N \rightarrow \{and, or\}$, and the partial function $default_N : N \rightarrow N$. When the context is clear we drop the subscript N on these functions. Let $\searrow \subset N \times N$ be the "child of" relation defined by $n \searrow n'$ if $n' \in children(n)$; then $\searrow+$ and $\searrow*$ are the transitive and reflexive, transitive closures of $\searrow$, respectively.

The names in N are organized in a tree-like structure. By this we mean that $\forall n \in N.\ r \searrow* n$ (r is the root), and if $n_1 \searrow n$ and $n_2 \searrow n$ then $n_1 = n_2$ (each state has a unique "parent"). If $type(n) = and$ then the children of n are combined in parallel and we call n an *and*-state. If $type(n) = or$ then the children of n are combined sequentially as in a traditional FSA, and we call n an *or*-state. By convention an *and*-state never has a child that is also an *and*-state. For every *or*-state n with $children(n) \neq \emptyset$, $default(n) \in children(n)$ gives the "initial state" of n's FSA.

In a statechart $(\Pi, N, \mathcal{T}, r)$ the set $\mathcal{T}$ of transitions is a finite subset of $N \times \mathcal{L}(\Pi) \times N$. A transition $t \in \mathcal{T}$ has a *source*, a *label*, and a *target*. For a transition $t = (n, l, n')$, $source(t) = n$, $target(t) = n'$, and $label(t) = l$. Furthermore, $trigger(t) = trigger(label(t))$, $action(t) = action(label(t))$, and n and n' must be siblings in an *or*-state.[3] That is, there is some n'' with $type(n) = or$ and $n, n' \in children(n'')$.

We refer to the tuples defined above as SPS (for Syntax of Pnueli and Shalev). The step semantics of statecharts given in [PS91] is defined in terms of SPS tuples. In the next section we give an inductively defined syntax for the *statecharts algebra* SA and relate it to the tuples of SPS. To do so we first need to define when two statecharts are isomorphic.

Two statecharts $(\Pi_1, N_1, \mathcal{T}_1, r_1)$ and $(\Pi_2, N_2, \mathcal{T}_2, r_2)$ are isomorphic, written $(\Pi_1, N_1, \mathcal{T}_1, r_1) \equiv_{\mathrm{SPS}} (\Pi_2, N_2, \mathcal{T}_2, r_2)$, if $\Pi_1 = \Pi_2$ and there is a bijection h :

[3] In [PS91] the source and the target of a transition are *sets* of states in $children^+(n)$ for some n. All of the results of this paper are valid for statecharts with this generalized *multilink* variety of transition.

$N_1 \to N_2$ such that $h(r_1) = r_2$ and for $n, n' \in N_1$ and $l \in \mathcal{L}(\Pi_1)$ we have:

$$(n, l, n') \in \mathcal{T}_1 \text{ if and only if } (h(n), l, h(n')) \in \mathcal{T}_2$$
$$type_{N_1}(n) = type_{N_2}(h(n))$$
$$\{h(c) \mid c \in children_{N_1}(n)\} = children_{N_2}(h(n))$$

and whenever either side is defined:

$$h(default_{N_1}(n)) = default_{N_2}(h(n))$$

Thus we do not distinguish between statecharts that differ only in the choice of names for the states.

3 An Inductively Defined Syntax for Statecharts

Statecharts are constructed from components that themselves resemble (smaller) statecharts, and this leads to the idea of defining operations on statecharts that construct complex statecharts from collections of simpler ones. This section presents an algebra SA of *statecharts terms.*

We assume that there is an inexhaustible supply of *state names* $\mathcal{N}$ and *event names* $\mathcal{E}$. (Thus, for a given statechart $(\Pi, N, \mathcal{T}, r)$, $N \subset \mathcal{N}$ and $\Pi \subset \mathcal{E}$.) The signature of SA consists of two types of operators, a k-place sequential composition operator representing *or*-states (i.e. FSA-like structures having k states) and a binary parallel composition operator representing *and*-states. More specifically, for $n \in \mathcal{N}$, $p_1, \ldots, p_k \in$ SA, $K = \{1, \ldots, k\}$, and finite $T \subset K \times \mathcal{L}(\mathcal{E}) \times K$,

$$[n\!:\!(p_1, \ldots, p_k), T]$$

is an *or*-term corresponding to an SPS *or*-state. n is the name of the state and terms $p_1, \ldots, p_k$ and transition set T are respectively the states and transitions of the FSA underlying n.

For $n \in \mathcal{N}$ and $p_1, p_2 \in$ SA,

$$[n\!:\!(p_1, p_2)]$$

is an *and*-term corresponding to an SPS *and*-state with name n and children p_1 and p_2 in parallel.

For $p = [n : (p_1, \ldots, p_k), T]$ or $p = [n : (p_1, p_2)]$ we define the function $name : \mathrm{SA} \to \mathcal{N}$ by: $name(p) = n$. The function $names(p)$ gathers all the names occurring within p (but not $name(p)$):

$$names([n\!:\!(p_1, \ldots, p_k), T] = \bigcup_{1 \le i \le k} \{name(p_i)\} \cup names(p_i)$$
$$names([n\!:\!(p_1, p_2)]) = \bigcup_{1 \le i \le 2} \{name(p_i)\} \cup names(p_i)$$

The *well-formed* terms of SA are such that the name used in constructing an SA-term is always a **new** name; i.e. $name(p) \notin names(p)$, and in both $[n : (p_1, \ldots, p_k), T]$ and $[n : (p_1, p_2)]$ each name $n_i = name(p_i)$ is distinct. As before we assume that labels are neither contradictory nor redundant.

The function ϕ : SA $\rightarrow$ SPS translates a well-formed SA-term into an SPS tuple. ϕ is inductively defined over SA as follows:

base case: Let $p = [n : (), \emptyset]$. Then $\phi(p) = (\emptyset, \{n\}, \emptyset, n)$, with $children_{\{n\}}(n) = \emptyset$ and $type_{\{n\}}(n) = or$.

***or*-term:** Let $p = [n : (p_1, \ldots, p_k), T]$, $k > 0$, and for $1 \leq i \leq k$, let $\phi(p_i) = (\Pi_i, N_i, \mathcal{T}_i, n_i)$. Also let $events(T) \subset \mathcal{E}$ be all the event names that occur in the transitions of T:

$$events(T) = \{\pi \in \mathcal{E} \mid \exists t \in T.\, \pi \in trigger(t), \overline{\pi} \in trigger(t), \pi \in action(t)\}$$

Then $\phi(p) = (\Pi, N, \mathcal{T}, n)$ with:
- $\Pi = \bigcup_{1 \leq i \leq k} \Pi_i \cup events(T)$,
- $N = \{n\} \cup \bigcup_{1 \leq i \leq k} N_i$,
- $type_N(n) = or$,
- $children_N(n) = \bigcup_{1 \leq i \leq k} \{name(p_i)\}$,
- $default_N(n) = name(p_1)$,
- $\mathcal{T} = \{(name(p_i), l, name(p_j) \mid (i, l, j) \in T\} \cup \bigcup_{1 \leq i \leq k} \mathcal{T}_i$.

***and*-term:** Let $p = [n : (p_1, p_2)]$, and for $1 \leq i \leq 2$, let $\phi(p_i) = (\Pi_i, N_i, \mathcal{T}_i, n_i)$. Also $N_- = \{n_i \mid 1 \leq i \leq 2, type_{N_i}(n_i) = and\}$. Then $\phi(p) = (\Pi, N, \mathcal{T}, n)$ with:
- $\Pi = \Pi_1 \cup \Pi_2$,
- $N = (\{n\} \cup N_1 \cup N_2) \setminus N_-$,
- $type_N(n) = and$,
- $children_N(n) = \bigcup_{1 \leq i \leq 2} \begin{cases} n_i & type_{N_i}(n_i) = or \\ children_{N_i}(n_i) & type_{N_i}(n_i) = and \end{cases}$
- $\mathcal{T} = \mathcal{T}_1 \cup \mathcal{T}_2$.

Parallel composition is binary in SA but not in SPS. ϕ handles this difference by removing the artificial nesting of *and*-terms.

We use $\Pi(p)$, $N(p)$, and $\mathcal{T}(p)$ to denote the projection functions on the SPS tuple $\phi(p)$, i.e. $\phi(p) = (\Pi(p), N(p), \mathcal{T}(p), name(p))$.

Two SA-terms p and p' are isomorphic, written $p \equiv_{SA} p'$, if $\phi(p) \equiv_{SPS} \phi(p')$. Thus the parenthesization of *and*-states, the order (after the default) of terms in an *or*-state, and the choice of names are unimportant.

Lemma 1. *ϕ is surjective.*

Theorem 2. *$\equiv_{SA}$ is a congruence for the operators of* SA.

Remark. If we redefine ϕ to be a function from the quotient algebra $\mathrm{SA}/\equiv_{\mathrm{SA}}$ to $\mathrm{SPS}/\equiv_{\mathrm{SPS}}$ then ϕ is a bijection between the two varieties of statecharts syntax. With this in mind we henceforth use the two syntaxes interchangeably.

4 The Step Semantics of Statecharts

In [PS91], Pnueli and Shalev define the *step semantics* for statecharts in terms of a set of *configurations*, or global states, and a set of *steps*, or semantic transitions between configurations. In this section, we characterize the step semantics of [PS91] as a mapping $\Psi : \mathrm{SA} \to \mathbf{LTS}$, where **LTS** is a domain of *labeled transition systems*. An element of **LTS** is a four-tuple $(Q, \Sigma, q_0, \longrightarrow)$, where Q is the set of states, Σ is the alphabet, $q_0 \in Q$ is the start state, and $\longrightarrow \subseteq Q \times \Sigma \times Q$ is the transition relation. A transition $(q, \sigma, q') \in \longrightarrow$ is usually written $q \overset{\sigma}{\longrightarrow} q'$.

Two LTSs $\mathcal{I}_1 = (Q_1, \Sigma_1, q_1, \longrightarrow_1)$ and $\mathcal{I}_2 = (Q_2, \Sigma_2, q_2, \longrightarrow_2)$ are isomorphic, written $\mathcal{I}_1 \equiv \mathcal{I}_2$, if there is a bijection h between their states such that $h(q_1) = q_2$ and for $q, q' \in Q_1$ and $\sigma \in \Sigma_1 \cup \Sigma_2$: $q \overset{\sigma}{\longrightarrow}_1 q'$ if and only if $h(q) \overset{\sigma}{\longrightarrow}_2 h(q')$.

To define the mapping Ψ, we first need to define, for a given SA-term p, the entities $\mathrm{C}(p)$, $\Sigma(p)$, $\Delta(p)$, and $\longrightarrow_p$. To do so, assume that $\phi(p)$ is the statechart given by $(\Pi, N, \mathcal{T}, r)$.

$\mathrm{C}(p)$ is the set of *configurations* of p and will be the state set of the LTS $\Psi(p)$. A configuration is a subset of N telling which *and*- and *or*-states "have control." Each configuration follows the *and/or* structure of $\phi(p)$ from r to the leaves of N. Thus a configuration always includes r; if an *and*-state is included then all of its children are included; and if an *or*-state with a non-empty set of children is included then exactly one of its children is included. $\mathrm{C}(p)$ is given by the inductively defined function $\mathrm{C} : \mathrm{SA} \to 2^{\mathcal{N}}$.

$$
\begin{aligned}
\mathrm{C}([n : (), \emptyset]) &= \{\{n\}\} \\
\mathrm{C}([n : (p_1, \ldots, p_k), T]) &= \textstyle\bigcup_{1 \le i \le k} \{\{n\} \cup q_i \mid q_i \in \mathrm{C}(p_i)\} \\
\mathrm{C}([n : (p_1, p_2)]) &= \{\{n\} \cup q_1 \cup q_2 \mid q_1 \in \mathrm{C}(p_1), q_2 \in \mathrm{C}(p_2)\}
\end{aligned}
$$

$\Delta(p)$ is the *initial configuration* of p, and will represent the initial state of $\Psi(p)$. $\Delta(p)$ is the unique configuration that always chooses the default of an *or*-state, and is defined analogously to $\mathrm{C}(p)$.

$$
\begin{aligned}
\Delta([n : (), \emptyset]) &= \{n\} \\
\Delta([n : (p_1, \ldots, p_k), T]) &= \{n\} \cup \Delta(p_1) \\
\Delta([n : (p_1, p_2)]) &= \{n\} \cup \Delta(p_1) \cup \Delta(p_2)
\end{aligned}
$$

$\Sigma(p) = 2^{\Pi(p)} \times 2^{\Pi(p)}$ will constitute the alphabet of $\Psi(p)$ and resembles the syntactic labels except that there are no negative events. The first set in an element $\sigma \in \Sigma$ is the *input* to which a statechart in a given configuration *reacts*.

The second set is the *output* the statechart produces upon reacting to the input. We sometimes write σ as an input/output pair σ_i/σ_o.

$\longrightarrow_p \subseteq \mathrm{C}(p) \times \Sigma(p) \times \mathrm{C}(p)$ is the set of *steps* of p and will be the transition relation of $\Psi(p)$. To define $\longrightarrow_p$, it is first necessary to identify the *admissible transition sets* of p, intuitively, the subset of $\mathcal{T}(p)$ that may be taken together from a given configuration on a given input. The following definitions are needed to define which sets $T \subseteq \mathcal{T}(p)$ are admissible sets.

Orthogonal: Two transitions t_1 and t_2 are orthogonal, written $t_1 \perp t_2$ if there is an *and*-term $p' = [n : (p_1, p_2)]$ in p with $t_1 \in \mathcal{T}(p_1)$ and $t_2 \in \mathcal{T}(p_2)$.

Consistent: For a set of transitions $T \subseteq \mathcal{T}(p)$ the set of all transitions orthogonal to every transition in T is given by the function *consistent* : $2^{\mathcal{T}(p)} \longrightarrow 2^{\mathcal{T}(p)}$ such that $\mathit{consistent}(T) = \{t \in \mathcal{T}(p) \mid \forall t' \in T.\, t \perp t'\}$.

Relevant: For a configuration $q \in \mathrm{C}(p)$ the relevant transitions are given by the function *relevant* : $2^{N(p)} \longrightarrow 2^{\mathcal{T}(p)}$ such that $\mathit{relevant}(q) = \{t \in \mathcal{T}(p) \mid \mathit{source}(t) \in q\}$.

Triggered: For a set of events $Ev \subseteq \Pi(p)$ the set of transitions triggered by Ev is given by the function *triggered* : $2^{\Pi(p)} \longrightarrow 2^{\mathcal{T}(p)}$ such that

$$\mathit{triggered}(Ev) = \left\{ t \in \mathcal{T}(p) \;\middle|\; \begin{array}{l} \pi \in \mathit{trigger}(t) \Rightarrow \pi \in Ev \\ \overline{\pi} \in \mathit{trigger}(t) \Rightarrow \pi \notin Ev \end{array} \right\}$$

Actions: The set of output actions generated by a set of transitions $T \subseteq \mathcal{T}(p)$ is given by the function *actions* : $2^{\mathcal{T}(p)} \longrightarrow 2^{\Pi(p)}$ such that $\mathit{actions}(T) = \bigcup_{t \in T} \mathit{action}(t)$.

Enabled: A set of transitions $T \subseteq \mathcal{T}(p)$ in a configuration $q \in \mathrm{C}(p)$ and with input $\sigma_i \subseteq \Pi(p)$ enables the set of transitions given by the function *enabled* : $\mathrm{C}(p) \times 2^{\overline{\Pi}(p)} \times 2^{\mathcal{T}(p)} \longrightarrow 2^{\mathcal{T}(p)}$ such that

$$\mathit{enabled}(q, \sigma_i, T) = \mathit{relevant}(q) \cap \mathit{consistent}(T) \cap \mathit{triggered}(\sigma_i \cup \mathit{actions}(T))$$

When a configuration q and input σ_i are understood we treat *enabled* as a function from $2^{\mathcal{T}(p)}$ to $2^{\mathcal{T}(p)}$.

Inseparable: A set of transitions T is *inseparable* (for a given configuration and input) if

$$\forall T' \subseteq T.\ \mathit{enabled}(T') \cap (T - T') \neq \emptyset$$

Admissible transition sets: The admissible transition sets of a statechart in configuration q with input σ_i are given by the function *steps* : $\mathrm{C}(p) \times 2^{\Pi(p)} \longrightarrow 2^{\mathcal{T}(p)}$ such that

$$\mathit{steps}(q, \sigma_i) = \{T \subseteq \mathcal{T}(p) \mid T \text{ is inseparable and } \mathit{enabled}(q, \sigma_i, T) = T\}$$

Next configuration: For $T \in \mathit{steps}(q, \sigma_i)$ the next configuration q' is given by the function *next* : $\mathrm{C}(p) \times 2^{\Pi(p)} \times 2^{\mathcal{T}(p)} \longrightarrow \mathrm{C}(p)$ such that

$$\mathit{next}(q, \sigma_i, T) = q - \left(\bigcup_{t \in T} \{n \in q \mid \mathit{source}(t) \searrow\!\!* \, n\} \right) \cup \left(\bigcup_{t \in T} \Delta(p_{\mathit{target}(t)}) \right)$$

where $p_{target(t)}$ should be understood to be such that $name(p_{target(t)}) = target(t)$.

Each admissible transition set T of p gives rise to a step and $\longrightarrow_p$ may be defined as:

$$\longrightarrow_p = \left\{ (q, \sigma_i/\sigma_o, q') \;\middle|\; \begin{array}{l} q \in \mathrm{C}(p), \sigma_i \in 2^{\Pi(p)}, T \in steps(q, \sigma_i), \\ \sigma_o = actions(T), \text{ and } q' = next(q, \sigma_i, T) \end{array} \right\}$$

The mapping $\Psi : \mathrm{SA} \to \mathbf{LTS}$ is now given by $\Psi(p) = (\mathrm{C}(p), \Sigma(p), \Delta(p), \longrightarrow_p)$, and two statecharts p and p' are semantically equal, written $p =_{\mathrm{SC}} p'$, if $\Psi(p) \equiv \Psi(p')$.

Remark. The example of Section 1 demonstrates that $=_{\mathrm{SC}}$ is not a congruence.

An *implicit step* is any step $q \xrightarrow{\sigma_i/\sigma_o} q'$ resulting from an admissible set T for which there is another step $q \xrightarrow{\sigma_i'/\sigma_o} q'$ also resulting from T such that $\sigma_i' \subset \sigma_i$. That is, σ_i has more events in it than strictly necessary.

5 A Compositional Semantics for Statecharts

In this section we present $\Psi_>$, a new semantic mapping for statecharts terms which we show to be compositional. $\Psi_>$ will be such that $\Psi_>(p) = (\mathrm{C}(p), \mathcal{W}(p), \Delta(p), \longrightarrow_p)$ where $\mathrm{C}(p)$ (the configurations of p) and $\Delta(p)$ (the initial configuration of p) are as before. The semantic alphabet is given a new definition, and is now called $\mathcal{W}(p)$, the set of *words* of p. We still use $\longrightarrow_p$ for the transition relation of $\Psi_>(p)$ and give it an inductive definition over the syntax of SA that excludes the implicit steps from Section 4. We refer to the new semantic domain as $\mathbf{LTS}_>$, and thus $\Psi_> : \mathrm{SA} \to \mathbf{LTS}_>$.

The semantic alphabet $\mathcal{W}(p)$ uses both primitive and negative events, and we let $\Lambda(p) = \Pi(p) \cup \overline{\Pi(p)}$. Negation is treated as an operator such that for $\lambda \in \Lambda : \overline{\overline{\lambda}} = \lambda$. $\mathcal{W}(p) \subset 2^{\Lambda(p)} \times 2^{\Lambda(p) \times \Lambda(p)}$ has elements $(w, >_w)$ that consist of a set of primitive and negative events w together with an irreflexive, transitive ordering relation $>_w$ called the *causal ordering* of w.

The function $\psi : \mathcal{L}(\Pi(p)) \to \mathcal{W}(p)$ constructs a word from a syntactic label. Let τ/α be a label. Then $\psi(\tau/\alpha) = (\tau \cup \alpha, \{(\lambda, \lambda') \mid \lambda \in \tau, \lambda' \in \alpha\})$. We often write just w for $(w, >_w)$. For a word w we have $trigger(w) = \{\lambda \in w \mid \nexists \lambda'.\ \lambda' >_w \lambda\}$, i.e. the maximal elements of w, and $action(w) = \{\lambda \in w \mid \exists \lambda'.\ \lambda' >_w \lambda\}$, i.e. all the rest.

We require every word $(w, >_w) \in \mathcal{W}(p)$ to have an irreflexive, transitive ordering $>_w$ in order to support the causality requirement of [PS91]. For example the (non-)word $(w, >_w) = (\{a, b\}, \{(a, b), (b, a)\})$ has a loop: $a >_w b$ and $b >_w a$, and we forbid such orderings in $\mathcal{W}(p)$.

$\longrightarrow_p \subseteq \mathrm{C}(p) \times \mathcal{W}(p) \times \mathrm{C}(p)$ is the set of steps of p and again will be the transition relation of $\Psi_>(p)$. $\longrightarrow_p$ is defined inductively over the syntax of p and will require two rules of inference for *or*-terms (**or**$_1$ and **or**$_2$) and two rules of inference for *and*-terms (**and**$_1$ and **and**$_2$). In the base case $p = [n : (), \emptyset)]$ we have $\longrightarrow_p = \emptyset$.

For an *or*-term $p = [n : (p_1, \ldots, p_k), T]$ the steps of $\longrightarrow_p$ are defined in terms of the syntactic transitions T and the steps of the $\longrightarrow_{p_i}$ $(1 \le i \le k)$. Recall that $K = \{1, \ldots, k\}$ and let $q_i, q_i' \in \mathrm{C}(p_i)$, for some $i \in K$. The rules for $\longrightarrow_p$ are:

$$(i, l, j) \in T \quad \Longrightarrow \quad \{n\} \cup q_i \xrightarrow{\psi(l)}_p \{n\} \cup \Delta(p_j) \qquad (\mathbf{or}_1)$$

$$q_i \xrightarrow{w}_{p_i} q_i' \quad \Longrightarrow \quad \{n\} \cup q_i \xrightarrow{w}_p \{n\} \cup q_i' \qquad (\mathbf{or}_2)$$

Rule **or**$_1$ can be used to infer the steps of p due to the syntactic transitions in T, and rule **or**$_2$ is for the steps due to internal behavior in the "active" component p_i.

Consider next the rules for *and*-terms and let $p = [n : (p_1, p_2)]$ be an *and*-term. Furthermore, let $q_1 \xrightarrow{w_1}_{p_1} q_1'$ and $q_2 \xrightarrow{w_2}_{p_2} q_2'$ be steps of p's components. There are four cases to consider in determining how, and if, w_1 and w_2 will *synchronize*; i.e. produce a step of p labeled by w, where w is the *synchronizing word* for the combined step:

1. w_1 and w_2 *conflict*, written $w_1 \sharp w_2$. Global consistency forbids w_1 and w_2 synchronizing. The conflict relation is defined by

$$\exists \lambda \in w_1 . \overline{\lambda} \in w_2 \Rightarrow w_1 \sharp w_2$$

2. w_1 and w_2 are *consistent*, meaning $\neg(w_1 \sharp w_2)$ and written $w_1 \sim w_2$, and the input to the statechart is sufficient to trigger both steps *independently.* The synchrony hypothesis requires that the two words synchronize.
3. One of the words, say w_1, *triggers* the other, written $w_1 \rightsquigarrow w_2$. The synchrony hypothesis requires q_2 to take its w_2 step if q_1 takes its w_1 step (though non-determinism is allowed if w_1 triggers more than one step of q_2). The triggering relation is defined by

$$w_1 \sim w_2 \text{ and } \mathit{trigger}(w_2) \subseteq w_1 \Longrightarrow w_1 \rightsquigarrow w_2$$

4. In the remaining case, w_1 is triggered by the input, but w_2 is not; nor does w_1 trigger w_2.

In each case the words w_1 and w_2 will be used to construct the synchronizing word w. Rule **and**$_1$ handles cases 2 and 3 in which both components take a step, while rule **and**$_2$ handles cases 1 and 4 in which only one of the components takes a step. In **and**$_2$, we will need to consider all the w_2's that p_2 can *initially* perform in configuration q_2. The function $initials_p : \mathrm{C}(p) \rightarrow 2^{\mathcal{W}(p)}$ is defined such that

$$initials_p(q) = \{w \in \mathcal{W}(p) \mid q \xrightarrow{w}_p\}$$

where $q \xrightarrow{w}_p$ stands for $\exists q'.\ q \xrightarrow{w}_p q'$ (similarly $q \not\xrightarrow{w}_p$ will be used below for $\nexists q'.\ q \xrightarrow{w}_p q'$).

In **and**$_1$, it is incorrect, in general, to construct the synchronizing word w by taking the point-wise union and transitive closure as in the function $\uplus$: $\mathcal{W}(p) \times \mathcal{W}(p) \rightarrow 2^{\mathcal{A}(p)} \times 2^{\mathcal{A}(p) \times \mathcal{A}(p)}$ given by

$$(w, >) \uplus (w', >') = (w \cup w', (> \cup >')^+)$$

(R^+ is the transitive closure of a relation R.) Consider $\psi(a/b)$ and $\psi(b/a)$: their point-wise union is the non-word $(\{a, b\}, \{(a, b), (b, a)\})$ mentioned above, and $\psi(a/b) \uplus \psi(b/a) = (\{a, b\}, \{(a, a), (a, b), (b, a), (b, b)\})$ is reflexive and therefore also not a word.

Causality forbids two transitions from triggering each other. In the case of $\psi(a/b)$ and $\psi(b/a)$ there are *two* ways they can synchronize: either an input a triggers both, and the synchronizing word is $(\{a, b\}, \{(a, b)\})$, or an input b triggers both, and the synchronizing word is $(\{a, b\}, \{(b, a)\})$.

Let $(w_\uplus, >_\uplus) = (w_1, >_1) \uplus (w_2, >_2)$ in the following. The function $\oplus : \mathcal{W}(p) \times \mathcal{W}(p) \rightarrow 2^{\mathcal{W}(p)}$ gives all the *maximal synchronizing* words contained in $(w_\uplus, >_\uplus)$ and is defined by

$$(w_1, >_1) \oplus (w_2, >_2) = \{(w_\uplus, >) \in \mathcal{W}(p) \mid \forall >'.\ > \subset >' \subseteq >_\uplus \Rightarrow (w, >') \notin \mathcal{W}(p)\}$$

In **and**$_2$, the synchronizing word w conflicts with every $w_2 \in initials_{p_2}(q_2)$. We thus define the set of *minimal distinguishing* words for a non-empty set $W \subset \mathcal{W}(p)$, given by the function $\sharp : 2^{\mathcal{W}(p)} \rightarrow 2^{\mathcal{W}(p)}$:

$$\sharp(W) = \{(w', \emptyset) \in \mathcal{W}(p) \mid \forall (w, >) \in W.\ w' \sharp\ w \text{ and } u \subset w' \Rightarrow \exists (v, >) \in W.\ u \sim v\}$$

Also, $\sharp\ (\emptyset) = \{(\emptyset, \emptyset)\}$.

Let $q_1, q_1' \in \mathrm{C}(p_1)$ and $q_2, q_2' \in \mathrm{C}(p_2)$. The rules for an *and*-term $p = [n : (p_1, p_2)]$ are now given by:

$$\left.\begin{array}{l} q_1 \xrightarrow{w_1}_{p_1} q_1' \\ q_2 \xrightarrow{w_2}_{p_2} q_2' \\ w \in w_1 \oplus w_2 \end{array}\right\} \Longrightarrow \{n\} \cup q_1 \cup q_2 \xrightarrow{w}_p \{n\} \cup q_1' \cup q_2' \qquad (\mathbf{and}_1)$$

$$\left.\begin{array}{l} q_1 \xrightarrow{w_1}_{p_1} q_1' \\ w_1 \rightsquigarrow w' \Rightarrow q_2 \not\xrightarrow{w'}_{p_2} \\ w \in w_1 \oplus w_2 \\ \quad w_2 \in \sharp(initials_{p_2}(q_2)) \end{array}\right\} \Longrightarrow \{n\} \cup q_1 \cup q_2 \xrightarrow{w}_p \{n\} \cup q_1' \cup q_2 \qquad (\mathbf{and}_2)$$

There is also a symmetric rule **and**$_2'$ in which p_2 takes a step but not p_1.

To illustrate our rules consider again Figure 1(a). State B has steps $\{E\} \xrightarrow{\psi(a/b)}_B \{F\}$ and $\{F\} \xrightarrow{\psi(a)}_B \{E\}$ while state C has $\{G\} \xrightarrow{\psi(b/c)}_C \{H\}$ and $\{H\} \xrightarrow{\psi(b)}_C \{G\}$ all by rule **or**$_1$. For state A in configuration $\{E, G\}$ **and**$_1$ gives the step $\{E, G\} \xrightarrow{w}_A \{F, H\}$ where (the only) $w \in \psi(a/b) \oplus \psi(b/c)$ is $(\{a, b, c\}, \{(a, b), (b, c), (a, c)\})$. **and**$_2$ does not give $\{E, G\} \xrightarrow{\psi(a/b)}_A$, since $\psi(a/b) \rightsquigarrow \psi(b/c)$. In state $\{F, H\}$ there is a step $\{F, H\} \xrightarrow{w}_A \{E, G\}$ for $w = (\{a, b\}, \emptyset)$ by **and**$_1$ and a step $\{F, H\} \xrightarrow{w}_A \{F, G\}$ for $w = (\{\overline{a}, b\}, \emptyset)$. The latter is from **and**$_2$ since $initials_B(\{F\}) = \{\psi(a)\}$ and $\{\overline{a}\}$ is the only element of $\sharp(\{\psi(a)\})$.

As in Section 4, two SA-terms p_1 and p_2 are semantically equal, written $p_1 \simeq p_2$, if $\Psi_>(p_1) \equiv \Psi_>(p_2)$.

Theorem 3. *$\simeq$ is a congruence for the operators of* SA. *That is, for* SA*-terms* $p, p' : p \simeq p' \Rightarrow \forall X[\cdot].\ X[p] \simeq X[p']$.

Proof sketch: By structural induction on $X[\cdot]$. Let $p \simeq p'$ and let $h : \mathrm{C}(p) \rightarrow \mathrm{C}(p')$ be a bijection witnessing this fact. For the empty context $[\cdot]$ the result holds trivially.

For $X[\cdot] = [n : (p_1, \ldots, [\cdot]_i, \ldots, p_k), T]$ $(k > 0, 1 \leq i \leq k)$ define the new bijection $h' : \mathrm{C}(X[p]) \rightarrow \mathrm{C}(X[p'])$ such that for $j \neq i$, $q_j \in \mathrm{C}(p_j)$ and $q = \{n\} \cup q_j$ we have $h'(q) = q$, and for $q_i \in \mathrm{C}(p)$ and $q = \{n\} \cup q_i$ we have $h'(q) = \{n\} \cup h(q_i)$. Clearly $h'(\Delta(X[p])) = \Delta(X[p'])$.

By **or**$_1$, for each transition $(g, l, j) \in T$ there is a step $q_g \xrightarrow{\psi(l)}_{X[p]} q_j$ iff $h'(q_g) \xrightarrow{\psi(l)}_{X[p']} h'(q_j)$. By **or**$_2$, $q_i \xrightarrow{w}_p q_i'$ leads to the step $q \xrightarrow{w}_{X[p]} q'$ iff $h(q_i) \xrightarrow{w}_{p'} h(q_i')$ leads to the step $h'(q) \xrightarrow{w}_{X[p']} h'(q')$. This yields $X[p] \simeq X[p']$ as desired.

For $X[\cdot] = [n : ([\cdot], p_2)]$, configurations of $X[p]$ are of the form $q = \{n\} \cup q_1 \cup q_2$, $q_i \in \mathrm{C}(p_i)$, $i = 1, 2$. Then $h'(q) = \{n\} \cup h(q_1) \cup q_2$. By **and**$_1$, $q_1 \xrightarrow{w_1}_p q_1'$ and $q_2 \xrightarrow{w_2}_{p_2} q_2'$ lead to a step $q \xrightarrow{w}_{X[p]} q'$ with $w \in w_1 \oplus w_2$ iff $h(q_1) \xrightarrow{w_1}_{p'} h(q_1')$ and $q_2 \xrightarrow{w_2}_{p_2}$ lead to the step $h'(q) \xrightarrow{w}_{X[p']} h'(q')$.[4]

By **and**$_2$, $q_1 \xrightarrow{w_1}_p q_1'$ and $\not\exists w'.(w_1 \rightsquigarrow w' \,\&\, q_2 \xrightarrow{w'}_{p_2})$ leads to a step $q \xrightarrow{w}_{X[p]} q'$ with $w_2 \in \sharp(initials_{p_2}(q_2))$ and $w \in w_1 \oplus w_2$ iff $h(q_1) \xrightarrow{w_1}_{p'} h(q_1')$

[4] It is here that a similar argument for the step semantics would fail. The semantic alphabet $\Sigma(p)$ would treat some steps as identical even though they *should* synchronize differently. A hypothetical synchronizing function $\oplus'$ as in $\sigma_i/\sigma_o \oplus' \sigma_i'/\sigma_o'$ cannot distinguish between, for instance, steps $\{D, F\} \xrightarrow{ab/cd}_A \{E, G\}$ of A and $\{B'\} \xrightarrow{ab/cd}_{A'} \{E'\}$ of A'. The argument works for the steps of $\Psi_>$ exactly because the necessary *and* sufficient condition for triggering a step is preserved by $\oplus$.

(and $\not\exists w'.(w_1 \rightsquigarrow w' \;\&\; q_2 \xrightarrow{w'}_{p_2})$ leads to the step $h'(q) \xrightarrow{w}_{X[p']} h'(q')$. The argument for $q_2 \xrightarrow{w_2}_{p_2} q'_2$ and $\not\exists w'.(w_2 \rightsquigarrow w' \;\&\; q_1 \xrightarrow{w'}_{p})$ is similar. Thus $X[p] \simeq X[p']$, and $\simeq$ is a congruence for the operators of SA.

□

Theorem 4. *$\simeq$ is the largest congruence contained in $=_{\mathrm{SC}}$.*

Proof sketch:

If this were not the case, there would be some equivalence $\approx$ intermediate between $=_{\mathrm{SC}}$ and $\simeq$, i.e. $\simeq \subset \approx \subset =_{\mathrm{SC}}$, that is a congruence. Thus for some statecharts p and p' we would have $p \not\simeq p'$, but $p \approx p'$ and $p =_{\mathrm{SC}} p'$. A case analysis shows that any time $p =_{\mathrm{SC}} p'$ but $p \not\simeq p'$ we have a situation analogous to that in Figure 2 where there is not enough synchronization information in the semantic alphabet. A similarly constructed parallel context $X[\cdot]$ yields $X[p] \not\approx X[p']$. Thus $\approx$ cannot be a congruence.

□

The semantic mapping $\Psi_>$ for SA-terms agrees with the semantics of [PS91]. It meets the requirements of the synchrony hypothesis, causality, and global consistency, while distinguishing between statecharts only when necessary for compositionality. Furthermore, given the LTS $\Psi_>(p)$ for SA-term p, the LTS $\Psi(p)$ of the step semantics can be easily generated as follows. The configurations Q and initial configuration q_0 are the same. For each step $q \xrightarrow{w}_p q'$ of $\Psi_>(p)$ there are steps $q \xrightarrow{\sigma_i/\sigma_o}_p q'$ for each $\sigma_i \subseteq \Pi$ with $\sigma_i \sim w$, $\mathit{trigger}(w) \subseteq \sigma_i$, and $\sigma_o = \mathit{action}(w)$. Finally, for the implicit steps, in which the configuration does not change because nothing was triggered by the input, we have: For statechart p and configuration q if $\exists \sigma_i \subseteq \Pi.\ \forall q \xrightarrow{w}_p q'.\ (\mathit{trigger}(w) \subset \sigma_i \Rightarrow w \sharp \sigma_i)$ then $q \xrightarrow{\sigma_i/\emptyset}_p q$.

6 Conclusion

We have presented an algebra SA of statechart terms which we have shown to be in one-to-one correspondence with the syntax of [PS91]. We also defined the semantic mapping $\Psi_>$ on SA-terms that respects the semantics of [PS91] while preserving enough synchronization information to guarantee compositionality. Thus, interpreting statecharts in the semantic domain **LTS**$_>$ allows one to use the syntactic hierarchy of statecharts as a design hierarchy.

The ideas presented in this paper fit into a larger ongoing project aimed at establishing a process-algebraic version of statecharts. The idea is to structure statecharts as an algebra SA with a compositional semantics; show that the statecharts process algebra SPA corresponds to the algebra SA; and finally give a sound and (relatively) complete axiomatization of SPA. The present paper achieves the first of these objectives, and [US94] achieves the second. The third objective is partly achieved in [US93] and an extended version of that paper is in preparation.

References

[Har87] D. Harel. Statecharts: A visual formalism for complex systems. *Science of Computer Programming*, 8:231–274, 1987.

[HGdR89] C. Huizing, R. Gerth, and W. P. de Roever. Modeling statecharts behavior in a fully abstract way. In *Proc. 13th CAAP*, number 299 in Lecture Notes in Computer Science, pages 271–294. Springer Verlag, 1989.

[HP85] D. Harel and A. Pnueli. On the development of reactive systems. In *Logic and Models of Concurrent Sytems*, number 133 in NATO ASI series, pages 477–498, Berlin, 1985. Springer-Verlag.

[HPSS87] D. Harel, A. Pnueli, J. P. Schmidt, and R. Sherman. On the formal semantics of statecharts. *Proc. 2nd IEEE Symposium on Logic in Computer Science*, pages 54–64, 1987.

[HRdR92] J. J. M. Hooman, S. Ramesh, and W. P. de Roever. A compositional axiomatization of statecharts. *Theoretical Computer Science*, 101:289–335, July 1992.

[Mar91] F. Maraninchi. The Argos language: graphical representation of automata and description of reactive systems. In *IEEE Workshop on Visual Languages*, 1991.

[Mar92] F. Maraninchi. Operational and compositional semantics of synchronous automaton composition. In *Proceedings of CONCUR '92 – Third International Conference on Concurrency Theory*, 1992.

[Per93] A. Peron. *Synchronous and Asynchronous Models for Statecharts.* PhD thesis, Universita di Pisa-Genova-Udine, 1993.

[Pnu86] A. Pnueli. Applications of temporal logic to the specification and verification of reactive systems: A survey of current trends. In et. al. de Baker, editor, *Current Trends in Concurrency*, number 224 in Lecture Notes inComputer Science, pages 510–584, 1986.

[PS91] A. Pnueli and M. Shalev. What is in a step: On the semantics of statecharts. In *Theoretical Aspects of Computer Software*, number 526 in Lecture Notes inComputer Science, pages 244–264, 1991.

[US93] A. C. Uselton and S. A. Smolka. State refinement in process algebra. In *Proceedings of the North American Process Algebra Workshop*, Ithaca, New York, August 1993. Available as TR 93-1369, Department of Computer Science, Cornell University.

[US94] A. C. Uselton and S. A. Smolka. A process algebraic semantics for statecharts via state refinement. In *Proceedings of IFIP Working Conference on Programming Concepts, Methods and Calculi (PROCOMET)*, June 1994. To appear.

On the Decidability of Non-Interleaving Process Equivalences[1]

Astrid Kiehn
Institut für Informatik, TU München
email: kiehn@informatik.tu-muenchen.de

Matthew Hennessy
Cognitive and Computing Sciences, University of Sussex
email: matthewh@cogs.succsex.ac.uk

Abstract. We develop decision procedures based on proof tableaux for a number of non-interleaving equivalences over processes. The processes considered are those which can be described in a simple extension of *BPP*, Basic Parallel Processes, obtained by omitting the restriction operator from *CCS*. Decision procedures are given for both *strong* and *weak* versions of *causal bisimulation, location equivalence* and *ST-bisimulation.*

1 Introduction

This paper is concerned with the development of automatic verification techniques for process description languages. Typically if P and Q are process descriptions we wish to develop decision procedures for checking if P and Q are semantically equivalent. If P and Q are expressions from *process algebras* or given in terms of *labelled transition systems* then there are already a number of software systems which can automatically check for such semantic identities, [9, 19]. The main semantic equivalences handled by these tools are variations on *bisimulation equivalence*, [18], and there is also the major restriction that the processes to be checked must be finite state.

More recently techniques have been developed for handling certain kinds of infinite state processes. For example in [8] it was shown that *strong bisimulation* is decidable for context-free processes while [6] contains a similar result for so-called Basic Parallel Processes, *BPP*; these correspond essentially to the processes generated by the standard syntax of *CCS* without the restriction operator. The decision procedures are not particularly efficient but at least they open up the possibility of the development of feasible proof techniques for classes of infinite state processes. The recent thesis, [5], provides an excellent overview. The basic underlying idea is the use of proof tableaux to compare the behaviour of processes. Extending a tableau corresponds to "unwinding" the processes in order to compare their future possible behaviours. By restricting in various subtle ways the methods allowed for extending tableaux one can ensure that they are always finite. If in addition only a finite number of tableaux can be produced from a given pair of process descriptions then, provided the specific tableau method is sound for a particular equivalence, we

1 This work has been supported by the ARC project *An Algebraic Theory for Distributed Systems*

have a decision procedure for that equivalence. This approach has been applied successfully to a number of infinite state languages but mostly for *strong bisimulation equivalence*. We wish to investigate the extent to which these techniques can also be used to develop decision procedures for *non-interleaving* semantic equivalences, [10, 20, 12].

We already know of one result of this kind. In [4] a decision procedure, based on a tableaux method, is presented for *distributed bisimulation* $\sim_d$, [3], over the language *BPP*. However the soundness of the procedure depends crucially on a separation property which is part and parcel of the underlying transition system. The procedure could be adapted if we had a cancellation property

$P \mid Q \sim P \mid R$ implies $Q \sim R$

where | represents the binary parallel composition of processes. But most (if not all other) standard non-interleaving equivalences such as *causal bisimulation*, [10], *ST-bisimulation*, [20] or *location equivalence*, [1] do not have this property. So we show how to extend the more recent technique developed in [7], to yield decision procedures for

- *location equivalence*
- *causal bisimulation*
- *ST-bisimulation*

over *BPP*. We also show how the method can be adapted to provide in addition decision procedures for weak versions of each of these equivalences over a large subclass of *BPP*, essentially those processes which can never evolve into states which are *divergent*. Moreover we show that this property is itself decidable for *BPP* processes.

Each of these three equivalences were originally defined using very different metalanguages for expressing and emphasising different intentional features of the behaviour of processes. In [16] it is shown how at least the first two can be expressed in a uniform framework and here we show that this framework can also be used to express *ST-bisimulation*. This is central to our work. We develop one decision procedure based on a tableau method for *local cause bisimulation* which from [16] is known to be equivalent to *location equivalence*, [2]. We then show how very simple modifications lead to a decision procedures for *global cause bisimulation*, which is known to be equivalent to *causal bisimulation* [10], and to our version of *ST-bisimulation*. Finally we show how further modifications can be made so as to deal with weak versions of these three equivalences.

We now briefly outline the remainder of the paper. In the next section we define the language, BPP_l, essentially the language of [6] extended with sets of causes. We also define *weak local cause bisimulation* and state some of its properties which we require. In the next section we develop some orderings on processes which are used in the semantic tableaux which in turn are explained in Section 4. This section gives the decision procedure for *local cause bisimulation* over BPP_l. The last section shows how to adapt this procedure to *causal bisimulation* and *ST-bisimulation* and to the weak version of these equivalences for *h-convergent* processes.

In this extended abstract most of the proofs are omitted. They will be contained in the full version of the paper.

2 Local Cause Bisimulation

As usual there is a countable set of atomic actions, $Act = \{a, b, c, \ldots, \bar{a}, \bar{b}, \bar{c}, \ldots\}$, ranged over by a, an invisible action τ not in Act and Act_τ, ranged over by μ, is used to denote $Act \cup \{\tau\}$. If X denotes a set of variables, ranged over by x, then the *standard* set of processes, $CCS(X)$, is obtained from the abstract syntax

$$t := nil \quad | \quad \mu.t \quad | \quad t+t \quad | \quad t \,|\, t \quad | \quad x \quad | \quad rec\, x.\, t$$

In order to describe the non-interleaving theories of processes we extend this syntax by introducing a countable set of *causes*, $\mathcal{C}$, which we assume have the form $\{l_1, l_2, \ldots\}$. These will be used in three different ways to describe the three different equivalences discussed in the paper. However for each of the equivalences we use exactly the same extended syntax:

$$T ::= \Gamma \rhd t \quad | \; T \,|\, T$$

where $t \in CCS(X)$, and Γ is a *cause set*, i.e. a finite subset of $\mathcal{C}$. We use $\mathcal{CS}$ to denote the set of possible cause sets which can occur in a term, i.e. $\mathcal{CS}$ is the collection of finite subsets of $\mathcal{C}$. Let $BPP_l\;(X)$ denote the set of extended processes. As usual the variable x in $rec\, x.\, t$ acts as a *binder* which leads in the standard manner to *free* and *bound* occurrences of variables and a closed process is one with no free occurrence of any variable. We also assume that all occurrences of x in $rec\, x.\, t$ are *guarded*, (see [18] for a formal definition). We use $p, q, \ldots$ to range over CCS, the set of closed processes of $CCS(X)$ and $P, Q \ldots$ to range over BPP_l, the set of closed processes in $BPP_l\;(X)$. For $T \in BPP_l\;(X)$ let $cau(T)$ be the set of causes, i.e. elements of $\mathcal{C}$, occurring in T and $cs(T)$, the set of *cause sets* of T, i.e. the set of subsets of $\mathcal{C}$ occurring in T. Obviously $cau(T) = \{\, l \in \Gamma \mid \Gamma \in cs(T)\,\}$. Within $BPP_l\;(X)$ we represent a CCS processes p as $\emptyset \rhd p$.

Throughout the paper we will use a structural congruence, $\equiv$, over extended processes. This is defined to be the least syntactic congruence generated by the equations

$$X \mid Y = Y \mid X$$
$$X \mid (Y \mid Z) = (X \mid Y) \mid Z$$
$$\Gamma \rhd (X \mid Y) = \Gamma \rhd X \mid \Gamma \rhd Y$$
$$\Gamma \rhd (X + Y) = \Gamma \rhd X + \Gamma \rhd Y$$

In other words we work modulo the commutativity and associativity of $|$ and we assume that $\Gamma \rhd$ distributes over the two operators $|$ and $+$.

In this section we give a transition system which formalises the "local causality" between the actions of processes. The natural bisimulation equivalence defined using this transition system is the same as location equivalence, at least for the processes in CCS, [16]. The transition system is given in Figures 1 and 2 and it defines two relations over processes from BPP_l. $P \xrightarrow[\Gamma, l]{a} {}^{(lc)}\, Q$ means that process P can perform the visible action a, the causes of this action being all the causes in Γ and all future actions which have this occurrence of a as a cause will have l in their set of causes. On the other hand $P \xrightarrow{\tau}^{(lc)} Q$ means that P can perform an internal computation and be transformed into Q. Notice also that each visible action, resulting from the application of the rule (LG1), introduces a new cause l. So as a computation proceeds the actions occurring in the computation are recorded as distinct causes in the cause sets of the process. The characteristic τ rule for local cause transitions is the rule for communication (L4). This means that the causes of communications are not accumulated in the cause sets. (L4) uses the somewhat non-standard notation $P[\emptyset/l]$ to denote the result of replacing each cause set Γ occurring in P by the cause set $\Gamma - \{l\}$. More generally we will use $P[\Delta/l]$ to denote the result of replacing each Γ containing l in P by $(\Gamma - \{l\}) \cup \Delta$.

The use of the structural congruence in the rules (LG5) and ($L6$) enables us to have a relatively simple set of defining rules for the transition systems. For example there is no rule which immediately applies to terms of the form $\Gamma \rhd (a.p \mid Q)$ by virtue of its syntactic form. But (LG3) can be applied to $\Gamma \rhd a.p \mid \Gamma \rhd Q$ and since $\Gamma \rhd (a.p \mid Q) \equiv \Gamma \rhd a.p \mid \Gamma \rhd Q$ the rule (LG5) can be used to infer the same transition for $\Gamma \rhd (a.p \mid Q)$.

For every extended process P, every visible action a, location l and cause set Γ let $Der_{\Gamma,l}(P, a)$ be defined as $\{Q \mid P \xrightarrow[\Gamma,l]{a}^{(lc)} Q\}$. Because we assume that processes are guarded these sets are always finite. For exactly the same reason the set of τ-derivatives, $Der(P, \tau) = \{Q \mid P \xrightarrow{\tau}^{(lc)} Q\}$, is finite.

For all $a \in Act$, $\Gamma \in \mathcal{P}(\mathcal{C})$, $l \in \mathcal{C}$ let $\xrightarrow[\Gamma,l]{a}^{(lc)} \subseteq (\ BPP_l \ \times \ BPP_l\ )$ be the least binary relations which satisfy the following axiom and rules.

(LG1) $\quad \Gamma \rhd a.p \xrightarrow[\Gamma,l]{a}^{(lc)} \Gamma \cup \{l\} \rhd p \quad l \notin \Gamma$

(LG2) $\quad P \xrightarrow[\Gamma,l]{a}^{(lc)} P',\ l \notin cau(Q)$ implies $P + Q \xrightarrow[\Gamma,l]{a}^{(lc)} P'$, $\ Q + P \xrightarrow[\Gamma,l]{a}^{(lc)} P'$

(LG3) $\quad P \xrightarrow[\Gamma,l]{a}^{(lc)} P',\ l \notin cau(Q)$ implies $P \mid Q \xrightarrow[\Gamma,l]{a}^{(lc)} P' \mid Q$

(LG4) $\quad \Gamma \rhd p[rec\,x.\ p/x] \xrightarrow[\Gamma,l]{a}^{(lc)} P'$ implies $\Gamma \rhd rec\,x.\ p \xrightarrow[\Gamma,l]{a}^{(lc)} P'$

(LG5) $\quad P \equiv P',\ P \xrightarrow[\Gamma,l]{a}^{(lc)} Q,$ implies $P' \xrightarrow[\Gamma,l]{a}^{(lc)} Q$

Fig. 1. Visible Local Cause Transitions

Let $\xrightarrow{\tau}{}^{(lc)} \subseteq (BPP_l \times BPP_l)$ be the least binary relation defined by the following axiom and rules.

(L1) $\Gamma \triangleright \tau.p \xrightarrow{\tau}{}^{(lc)} \Gamma \triangleright p$

(L2) $P \xrightarrow{\tau}{}^{(lc)} P'$ implies $P + Q \xrightarrow{\tau}{}^{(lc)} P'$
$Q + P \xrightarrow{\tau}{}^{(lc)} P'$

(L3) $P \xrightarrow{\tau}{}^{(lc)} P'$ implies $P \mid Q \xrightarrow{\tau}{}^{(lc)} P' \mid Q$

(L4) $P \xrightarrow[\Gamma,l]{a}{}^{(lc)} P',\ Q \xrightarrow[\Delta,k]{\bar{a}}{}^{(lc)} Q'$ implies $P \mid Q \xrightarrow{\tau}{}^{(lc)} P'[\emptyset/l] \mid Q'[\emptyset/k]$

(L5) $\Gamma \triangleright p[rec\, x.\ p/x] \xrightarrow{\tau}{}^{(lc)} P'$ implies $\Gamma \triangleright rec\, x.\ p \xrightarrow{\tau}{}^{(lc)} P'$

(L6) $P \equiv P',\ P \xrightarrow{\tau}{}^{(lc)} Q,$ implies $P' \xrightarrow{\tau}{}^{(lc)} Q$

Fig. 2. Invisible Local Cause Transitions

Definition 1 Local Cause Equivalence.
A symmetric relation $R \subseteq BPP_l \times BPP_l$ is called a *local cause bisimulation* iff $R \subseteq G(R)$ where
$(P, Q) \in G(R)$ iff
(*i*) $P \xrightarrow{\tau}{}^{(lc)} P'$ implies $Q \xrightarrow{\tau}{}^{(lc)} Q'$ for some $Q' \in BPP_l$ with $(P', Q') \in R$
(*ii*) $P \xrightarrow[A,l]{a}{}^{(lc)} P', l = new(cau(P) \cup cau(Q))$,
implies $Q \xrightarrow[A,l]{a}{}^{(lc)} Q'$ for some $Q' \in BPP_l$ with $(P', Q') \in R$.
Two processes P and Q are *local cause equivalent*, $P \sim_{lc} Q$, iff there is a local cause bisimulation R such that $(P, Q) \in R$.

Note that this definition uses the function new which when applied to a finite set of causes Γ returns the least cause l, in the ordering $l_0, l_1, \ldots$ not in Γ. We refer the reader to [16] for a proof that $\sim_{lc}$ coincides with *location equivalence* over CCS as defined in [2].

Our decision procedure depends on certain properties of the transition semantics which we now discuss. The first states that the equivalence is largely independent of the location sets of a process; it is preserved by uniformed renaming of cause sets. A (uniform) cause set renaming is a any function $\pi: \mathcal{CS} \longrightarrow \mathcal{CS}$.

Lemma 2. *Let $P, Q, R \in$ BPP$_l$ and let $\pi : cs(P) \longrightarrow cs(Q)$ be a cause set renaming which is bijective over $cs(P)$. Then*

1. $P \sim_{lc} Q$ if and only if $\pi(P) \sim_{lc} \pi(Q)$

2. $P \sim_{lc} Q$ *implies* $P \mid R \sim_{lc} Q \mid R$.

In general processes in BPP_l are not finite-state in this transition system but the state space of any process has a finite basis, i.e. every element of a state space can be viewed as a polynomial over a finite set of generators. For any process $t \in CCS(X)$ we associate the set of generators, $Gen(t)$, defined as follows.

$$Gen(t) = \begin{cases} \{x\} & \text{if } t \text{ is } x \\ \{nil\} & \text{if } t \text{ is } nil \\ \{t\} \cup Gen(t_1) \cup Gen(t_2) & \text{if } t \text{ is } t_1 + t_2 \\ \{t\} \cup Gen(t_1) & \text{if } t \text{ is } \mu.t_1 \\ Gen(t_1) \cup Gen(t_2) & \text{if } t \text{ is } t_1 \mid t_2 \\ \{t\} \cup Gen(t_1)[rec\, x.\, t_1/x] & \text{if } t \text{ is } rec\, x.\, t_1 \end{cases}$$

In this definition the two operators $+$ and $\mid$ are treated unequally. The reason for this is that we will show how to represent any process as the "parallel product" of generators as opposed to a "choice product". We use $\prod_{i \in I} p_i$ to denote the "parallel product" $p_{i_1} \mid p_{i_2} \mid \ldots \mid p_{i_k}$ where I is the finite index set $\{i_1, \ldots i_k\}$. Since we are working with respect to structural congruence $\equiv$, which includes the associativity and commutativity of $\mid$, this notation is consistent. But first an important syntactic property of the function Gen:

Lemma 3. *For every* CCS *term* u *and closed* CCS *term* p, $Gen(u[p/x]) \subseteq Gen(p) \cup Gen(u)[p/x]$.

For an extended process P we use $Gen(P)$ to denote $Gen(pure(P))$ where $pure(P)$ is the *CCS* process obtained by erasing all cause sets from P. The next lemma shows that the generators of extended processes are closed under transitions.

Lemma 4. *If* $P \xrightarrow{\tau}{}^{(lc)} Q$ *or* $P \xrightarrow[\Gamma,l]{a}{}^{(lc)} Q$ *then* $Gen(Q) \subseteq Gen(P)$.

It is very easy to see that the set of generators of any extended process P is finite and therefore the previous lemma gives us a representation theorem for the "state space" of processes reachable from P. If we ignore cause sets then every such state is equivalent to a parallel product of the generators of P. This is summarised in the next proposition.

Proposition 5. *Let* $p \in$ CCS.

1. *The set* $Gen(p)$ *is finite.*
2. *There is a set of generators* $\{p_i \mid i \in I\} \subseteq Gen(p)$ *such that* $p \equiv \prod_{i \in I} p_i$.
3. *If* G *is a set of generators,* $P \in \mathrm{BPP}_l$ *then the following holds:* $Gen(P) \subseteq G$ *and* $P \xrightarrow[\Gamma,l]{a}{}^{(lc)} Q$ *or* $P \xrightarrow{\tau}{}^{(lc)} Q$ *imply* $Gen(Q) \subseteq G$.

This result also shows that the class of processes we consider may be represented by Petri nets. To construct a net equivalent to P we use as places the elements of $Gen(P)$ and the transitions between places are defined using the operational semantics of *CCS*. The initial marking is determined by parallel product of P elements of $Gen(P)$. This representation will be used to decide h-convergence in Section 5.

3 Ordering Processes

In this section we develop two distinct orderings on extended processes which will be used in the decision procedure. Both are based on orderings on vectors of natural numbers.

Let $\mathbb{N}^k$ represent the set of vectors of length k of natural numbers. We use $\alpha, \beta, \ldots$ to range over these vectors with α_i denoting the i-component. The vectors can be lexicographically ordered in the standard way by

$$\alpha \sqsubset_{lex} \beta \text{ if there is a } j \text{ such that } \alpha_j < \beta_j \text{ and } \alpha_k = \beta_k \text{ for all } k < j.$$

This is a total and well-founded ordering on $\mathbb{N}^k$ and it can be used to induce a similar ordering on the set of *CCS* processes obtained from a finite set of generators.

For the moment let G be a finite set of *CCS* processes which we call generators and let us assume that they are totally ordered as $g_1 < g_2 < \ldots < g_k$. This may be any subset of *CCS* but in the next section where we are trying to decide whether or not P and Q are equivalent we will choose as G the set $Gen(P) \cup Gen(Q)$; from Lemma 5 we know that any process derived from P or Q will also be a parallel product of elements from G, or polynomial over G. Therefore we are interested in terms which are polynomials over G. For such a polynomial p let $\alpha_i(p)$ be the number of occurrences of g_i in p and let $\alpha(p) \in \mathbb{N}^{|G|}$ be the vector $\langle \alpha_1(p), \alpha_2(p), \ldots \rangle$. This enables us to define a total well-founded ordering on polynomials over G by

$$p \sqsubset_{lex} q \text{ if } \alpha(p) \sqsubset_{lex} \alpha(q).$$

This ordering can be in turn lifted to a subclass of extended terms, called *G-parforms* provided we first order cause sets.

Now $\mathcal{C}$ is ordered as $l_1 < l_2 < l_3 < \ldots$ and this extends naturally to cause sets, finite subsets of $\mathcal{C}$, again lexicographically. Let

$\{l_{n_1}, \ldots l_{n_k}\} < \{l_{m_1}, \ldots l_{m_{k'}}\}$, where $i < j$ implies $n_i < n_j$ and $m_i < m_j$, if there exists some j such that
1. $n_i = m_i$ for every $i < j$
2. if $j \leq n_k$ then $n_j < m_j$.

This is a total well-founded ordering on cause sets.

Definition 6. If G is a finite set of generators then a *G-parform* is any extended term of the form $\prod_{j \in J} \Gamma_j \rhd p_j$, where each p_j is a polynomial over G, which satisfies

1. $i \neq j$ implies $\Gamma_i \neq \Gamma_j$
2. $i < j$ implies $\Gamma_i < \Gamma_j$

Lemma 7. *For every extended process P such that $Gen(P) \subseteq G$ there is a G-parform Q such that $P \equiv Q$.*

Since the set of generators G is fixed for the remainder of the paper we will refer to G-parforms as simply parforms and we use $pf(P)$ to denote the parform to which P can be reduced. This is a slight abuse of notation as P may be reduced to two parforms which are not syntactically identical. But they will be equivalent up to the associativity and commutativity of | and therefore they are "essentially" the same.

We now extend the ordering $\sqsubset_{lex}$ to parforms. For any parform P of the form $\prod_{i\in I} \Gamma_i \rhd p_i$ and any cause set Γ the vector $\Gamma(P)$ is defined as follows:

$$\Gamma(P) = \begin{cases} \alpha(p_i), & \Gamma = \Gamma_i \\ \mathbf{0} & \text{otherwise} \end{cases}$$

(Here $\mathbf{0}$ is the vector which consists only of 0s.) Note that this is well-defined for parforms since every cause set appears at most once in these terms. This notation is used in the following definition.

Definition 8. Let P, Q be *G-parforms*. $P \sqsubset_{lex} Q$ if and only if there is a Γ such that $\Gamma(P) \sqsubset_{lex} \Gamma(Q)$ and for every $\Delta < \Gamma$, $\Delta(P) = \Delta(Q)$.

Proposition 9. *The relation $\sqsubset_{lex}$ is a total well-founded ordering on the set of* G-parforms.

Proposition 10. *Let P, Q, R be* parforms *with $cs(P) = cs(Q)$ and $P \sqsubset_{lex} Q$. Then*

1. $pf(P \mid R) \sqsubset_{lex} pf(Q \mid R)$,
2. *if $\pi\colon cs(P) \longrightarrow cs(Q)$ preserves the natural order on $\mathcal{CS}$ then $\pi(P) \sqsubset_{lex} \pi(Q)$.*

This is the first ordering required in the decision procedure. The second also comes from an ordering on $\mathbb{N}^k$:

for $\alpha, \beta \in \mathbb{N}^k$ let $\alpha \leq \beta$ if $\alpha_i \leq \beta_i$ for every $1 \leq i \leq k$.

However we first use this ordering to induce an ordering on *words* over $\mathbb{N}^k$:

If each $v, w \in (\mathbb{N}^k)^*$ let $v \preceq w$ whenever there is an injection $f : \{1, \ldots, |v|\} \rightarrow \{1, \ldots, |w|\}$ such that $i_1 < i_2$ implies $f(i_1) < f(i_2)$ and $v[i] \leq w[f(i)]$.

where $w[i]$ denotes the ith letter of w. The main property of this ordering is given by

Theorem 11. *Let $(u_i)_{i\in\mathbb{N}}$, $u_i \in (\mathbb{N}^k)^*$ be an infinite sequence of words over $\mathbb{N}^k$. Then there exists some $i, j \in \mathbb{N}$ such that $u_i \preceq u_j$.*

We now lift this ordering on words over $\mathbb{N}^k$ to *G-parforms* by associating in a systematic manner a word over $\mathbb{N}^k$ with each *G-parform.* If P is the G-parform $\prod_{i\in I} \Gamma_i \rhd p_i$ where $i_1 < i_2$ implies $\Gamma_{i_1} < \Gamma_{i_2}$ then let $\omega(P)$ denote the word $\alpha(p_1)\alpha(p_2)\ldots\alpha(p_{|I|})$.

Definition 12. For any pair of extended processes $P, Q \in BPP_l$ with G-parforms P', Q' let $P \preceq Q$ if $\omega(P') \preceq \omega(Q')$.

Example 1.

$$\{1\} \rhd (a.p) \mid \{1,2\} \rhd (b.nil \mid a.p)$$
$$\preceq$$
$$\{1\} \rhd (a.p \mid a.p) \mid \{1,2\} \rhd (c.nil) \mid \{2\} \rhd (a.p \mid b.nil \mid c.nil).$$

because $\alpha(a.p) \leq \alpha(a.p \mid a.p)$, $\alpha(b.nil \mid a.p) \leq \alpha(a.p \mid b.nil \mid c.nil)$.

There is an alternative characterisation of this ordering:

Proposition 13. *$P \preceq Q$ iff $Q \equiv Q_1 \mid Q_2$ and there is a cause set bijection $\pi: cs(P) \longrightarrow cs(Q)$ preserving the natural order on $\mathcal{CS}$ such that $Q_1 \equiv \pi(P)$.*

4 The Decidability Algorithm

In order to decide for two processes $P, Q \in BPP_l$, where $cs(P) = cs(Q)$, whether they are local cause equivalent we build up a tableau $T(P = Q)$. A tableau $T(P = Q)$ is a proof tree whose root is labelled $P = Q$ and whose proper nodes (there are also intermediate nodes, see below) are labelled with expressions of the form $P' = Q'$ where P', Q' are extended processes whose generators are in $Gen(P) \cup Gen(Q)$ and which satisfy $cs(P') = cs(Q')$. Each rule for extending a tableau has the form

$$\frac{P = Q}{P_1 = Q_1, \ldots, P_n = Q_n}$$

with possible side conditions. Intuitively the premise of such a rule can be viewed as a goal to achieve while the consequents represent sufficient subgoals to be established. All nodes in the proof tree are either terminal or nonterminal and a proof tree can be extended by applying one of the rules to a nonterminal node, thereby introducing n new nodes. It may be that the application of a rule will violate the condition that labels must be of the form $R = S$ with $cs(R) = cs(S)$. In such cases we can simply add a $\Gamma \triangleright nil$ factor to R for each $\Gamma \in cs(S) \setminus cs(R)$ and similarly for S. Extended processes are considered up to $\equiv$.

A node is terminal if it has one of the following forms:

- $P = Q$ where $P \equiv Q$; in which case the node is *successful*
- $P = Q$ where either
  1. there is some action a and some l with $Der_{\Gamma,l}(P, a) = \emptyset$ and $Der_{\Gamma,l}(Q, a) \neq \emptyset$ or $Der_{\Gamma,l}(P, a) \neq \emptyset$ and $Der_{\Gamma,l}(Q, a) = \emptyset$
  2. or $Der(P, \tau) = \emptyset$ and $Der(Q, \tau) \neq \emptyset$ or $Der(P, \tau) \neq \emptyset$ and $Der(Q, \tau) = \emptyset$.

  In this case the terminal node is called *unsuccessful*.

The rules are similar in nature to those used in [6] but a little more complicated. **UNWIND** replaces a label P = Q with a collection of intermediate nodes each labelled by expressions of the form $S = T$ where S, T are *finite sets* of identities between extended processes. In turn the rule **SUM** can be applied to each of these nodes labelled by $S = T$ to obtain once more nodes properly labelled by expressions $P' = Q'$ where P', Q' are extended processes. Note that in the development of a tableau each application of **UNWIND** is necessarily followed by an application of **SUM**.

The two **SUB** rules allow us to replace one subprocess by another provided suitably relabelled versions of them appear higher up in the proof tree. However the replacement can only be made under special circumstances refered to in the side conditions of the rules. A node **n** *dominates* another node **m** if

(UNWIND)
$$\frac{P = Q}{\{Der_{\Gamma,l}(P,a) = Der_{\Gamma,l}(Q,a)\} \quad Der(P,\tau) = Der(Q,\tau)}$$

where $l = new(cau(P)) = new(cau(Q))$

(SUM)
$$\frac{\{P_1,\ldots,P_n\} = \{Q_1,\ldots,Q_m\}}{\{P_i = Q_{f(i)}\}_{\{1,\ldots,n\}} \quad \{P_{g(j)} = Q_j\}_{\{1,\ldots,m\}}}$$

where f and g are mappings $f : \{1,\ldots n\} \longrightarrow \{1,\ldots m\}$
and $g : \{1,\ldots,m\} \longrightarrow \{1,\ldots,n\}$

(SUBL)
$$\frac{\pi(P_1) \mid P_2 = Q}{\pi(P_1') \mid P_2 = Q}$$

where π is order preserving and bijective on $cs(P_1)$ and there is
a dominated node labelled $P_1 = P_1'$ or $P_1' = P_1$ with $pf(P_1') \sqsubset_{lex} pf(P_1)$

(SUBR)
$$\frac{Q = \pi(P_1) \mid P_2}{Q = \pi(P_1') \mid P_2}$$

where π is is order preserving and bijective on $cs(P_1)$ and there is
a dominated node covered $P_1 = P_1'$ or $P_1' = P_1$ with $pf(P_1') \sqsubset_{lex} pf(P_1)$

Fig. 3. The Tableau Rules

- **m** appears higher up in the proof tree than **n**
- the rule **UNWIND** has been applied to the node **m**.

The side condition dictates that in order to apply a **SUBL** rule, for example, to a node **n**

1. it must be labelled by an equation of the form $\pi(P_1) \mid P_2 = Q$ where π is some order preserving cause set renaming which is bijective when restricted to $cs(P_1)$,
2. it must dominate a node **m** labelled by $P_1 = P_1'$ or $P_1' = P_1$,
3. in the label on the dominated node it must be the case that $pf(P_1') \sqsubset_{lex} pf(P_1)$.

The result of applying the rule is the generation of a new node labelled by $\pi(P_1') \mid P_2 = Q$. Note that as a result of the application of the rule the lexicographical order of the process in decreased. This order, $\sqsubset_{lex}$, is defined as in the last section using as the finite set G the set $Gen(P) \cup Gen(Q)$, where $P = Q$ labels the root of the tree, and is based on some fixed ordering on G.

There is a further constraint on use of the **SUB** rules or rather on the development of a proof tree: the two **SUB** rules have precedence over **UNWIND** and

SUM in that the latter two may only be applied if **SUBL** and **SUBR** are not applicable. This extra condition does not apply to the node **n** to which a **SUB** is being applied but to the entire proof tree above **n**.

A proof tree is developed for $P = Q$ by starting with a root labelled by $P = Q$ and systematically applying **UNWIND, SUM** and the **SUB** rules to non-terminal nodes, subject to this constraint. A proof tree is said to be *successful* if every leaf is a successful terminal node. An example of a complete tableau is as follows:

Example 2. Let $P = rec\,x.\,(a.x \mid b)$ and $Q = rec\,x.\,(b \mid a.x) + a.P \mid b$ with $P \sqsubset_{lex} Q$. To decide $P \sim_{lc} Q$ we develop a tableau $T(P = Q)$. Initially, rule **UNWIND** is applied yielding the two nodes labelled

$$\{\{1\} \rhd P \mid b\} = \{b \mid \{1\} \rhd Q, \{1\} \rhd P \mid b\} \text{ and}$$
$$\{a.P \mid \{1\} \rhd nil\} = \{\{1\} \rhd nil \mid a.Q,\, a.P \mid \{1\} \rhd nil\}.$$

For these two nodes the tableau is extended for the first node by

$$\dfrac{\textbf{(SUM)}\quad \{\{1\} \rhd P \mid b\} = \{b \mid \{1\} \rhd Q, \{1\} \rhd P \mid b\}}{\dfrac{\textbf{(SUBR)}\quad \{1\} \rhd P \mid b = b \mid \{1\} \rhd Q}{\{1\} \rhd P \mid b = b \mid \{1\} \rhd P} \qquad \{1\} \rhd P \mid b = \{1\} \rhd P \mid b}$$

and for the second by

$$\dfrac{\textbf{(SUM)}\quad \{a.P \mid \{1\} \rhd nil\} = \{\{1\} \rhd nil \mid a.Q,\, a.P \mid \{1\} \rhd nil\}}{\dfrac{\textbf{(UNWIND)}\quad a.P \mid \{1\} \rhd nil = \{1\} \rhd nil \mid a.Q}{\dfrac{\textbf{(SUM)}\quad \{\{2\} \rhd P \mid \{1\} \rhd nil\} = \{\{1\} \rhd nil \mid \{2\} \rhd Q\}}{\dfrac{\textbf{(SUBR)}\quad \{2\} \rhd P \mid \{1\} \rhd nil = \{1\} \rhd nil \mid \{2\} \rhd Q}{\{2\} \rhd P \mid \{1\} \rhd nil = \{1\} \rhd nil \mid \{2\} \rhd P}}} \qquad \mathbf{A}}$$

where **A** is $a.P \mid \{1\} \rhd nil = a.P \mid \{1\} \rhd nil$ and empty cause sets have been omitted. Since all terminal nodes are successful the tableau is successful, hence $P \sim_{lc} Q$.

Theorem 14. *Let $P, Q \in \mathrm{BPP}_l$. Every tableau for $P = Q$ is finite.*

Proof. Let $X = Gen(P) \cup Gen(Q)$. If the tableau is not finite then —as it is finitely branching— it must contain an infinite path. By Proposition 10 every application of a **SUB** rule preserves the order $\sqsubset_{lex}$ and since this order is well-founded this infinite path can not eventually only consist of applications of **SUB**. So there are infinitely many nodes, $(\mathbf{n}_i)_{i \in \mathbb{N}}$ along a path to which rule **UNWIND** is applied. Let $(U_i = V_i)_{i \in \mathbb{N}}$ denote the sequence of labels on these nodes.

We now consider the words over $\mathbb{N}^{|X|}$ generated by each pair U_i, V_i, $\omega(U_i), \omega(V_i)$ respectively. In fact it will be convenient to use words over the slightly larger set $\mathbb{N}^{|X|+1}$ and identify any vector $\alpha \in \mathbb{N}^{|X|}$ as the vector in $\mathbb{N}^{|X|+1}$ obtained by setting the last component to 0. If we then encode the equality symbol $=$ as a vector $\beta \in \mathbb{N}^{|X|+1}$ with $\beta(i) = 0$ for each generator position (i.e. for $i \leq |X|$) and $\beta(|X| + 1) = 1$ for the new component then $U_i = V_i$ can be represented as the word

$\omega(U_i)\beta\omega(V_i)$ over the alphabet $\mathbb{N}^{|X|+1}$. For convenience let ω_i denote this word which labels the node n_i.

Now consider two nodes $\mathbf{n_j}, \mathbf{n_k}$, where $j < k$, which are labelled by the equations $U_j = V_j$ and $U_k = V_k$ respectively. We show, by contradiction, that $\omega_j \not\preceq \omega_k$. Suppose this is not the case, i.e. $\omega_j \preceq \omega_k$ and therefore both $U_j \preceq V_k$ and $V_j \preceq U_k$. Since $\sqsubset_{lex}$ is a total order we can assume without loss of generality that $U_j \sqsubset_{lex} V_j$. By Proposition 13 we know that $U_k \equiv \pi(U_j) \mid R$ for some cause set renaming π which is bijective when restricted to $cs(U_j)$. But we now have all of the conditions necessary to apply the rule **SUBL** to the node $\mathbf{n_k}$. But by construction we know that **UNWIND** has been applied, which contradicts the condition that **UNWIND** can only be applied when a **SUB** rule is not applicable.

We have shown that $\omega_j \not\preceq \omega_k$ for any pair of nodes $\mathbf{n_j}, \mathbf{n_k}$ on the infinite subpath. We therefore have an infinite sequence of words over $\mathbb{N}^{|X|+1}$, namely $(\omega_i)_{i \in \mathbb{N}}$ with the property that $i < j$ implies $\omega_i \not\preceq \omega_j$. This contradicts Theorem 11.

Hence there is no infinite path in the tableau.

Proposition 15 Completeness.
Let $P, Q \in \mathrm{BPP}_l$. If $P \sim_{lc} Q$ then there is a successful tableau $T(P = Q)$.

Proposition 16 Soundness. *If a tableau $T(P = Q)$ is successful then $P \sim_{lc} Q$.*

Proof. The proper nodes induce a local cause bisimulation.

Theorem 17. *Local cause equivalence is decidable on all BPP_l processes.*

5 Other Equivalences

Reflecting on the decidability algorithm of the last section we observe that it depends on very few properties of the *local causes* transition system or the semantic equivalence. The only direct use of the *local causes* transition system is to determine the sets of derivatives $Der_{\Gamma,l}(P, a)$ and $Der(P, \tau)$ which are required to be finite. Thus the algorithm can be applied to other equivalences based on causes and cause sets provided they have the properties described in Lemma 2 and they have finite derivative sets. In the following we consider two such candidates namely global cause equivalence and ST equivalence. We then go on to outline how the algorithm can also be adapted to decide the corresponding weak equivalences for a large subclass of BPP_l.

Global cause equivalence $\sim_{gc}$ is an alternative formulation of causal bisimulations, [10], [11], based on cause sets; see [16] for a detailed exposition and a proof that it does indeed coincide with causal bisimulation. Global cause equivalence is defined in the standard way, as a maximal bisimulation, but the underlying transition is a variation on that given in Section 2. It is obtained from the transition rules given in Figure 1 and Figure 2 replacing the rule for communication (L4) with

$$\text{(L4')} \quad P \xrightarrow[\Gamma,l]{a}{}^{(gc)} P', \quad Q \xrightarrow[\Delta,k]{\bar{a}}{}^{(gc)} Q' \quad \text{implies} \quad P \mid Q \xrightarrow{\tau}{}^{(gc)} P'[\Delta/l] \mid Q'[\Gamma/k].$$

The intuition behind this rule is that a communication establishes causal links between the communicating partners. This is formalised by the injection of a copy of the partner's causes relevant for the communication. The equivalence is then defined in the same way as local cause equivalence, by replacing all lc indices by gc in Definition 1. Like local causality $\sim_{gc}$ is preserved by bijective cause set renamings (Lemma 2). Moreover $\sim_{gc}$ satisfies sufficient equations to ensure that extended processes can be transformed to *parforms* and moreover the derivative sets in the underlying transition system remain finite. Therefore the proofs of completeness and soundness of the tableau method remain valid if $\sim_{lc}$ is replaced by $\sim_{gc}$ and we have:

Theorem 18. *Global cause equivalence, and therefore causal bisimulation, is decidable over* BPP_l .

ST equivalence is not motivated by localities or causes. Instead it takes the view that actions are non-atomic and uses an underlying transition system based on subactions consisting of the *starting* and the *finishing* of actions. However this type of operational semantics can easily be formulated as another variation on the *local cause* transition system. The transition system for visible moves consists of the rules in Figure 1 where the axiom for prefixing is replaced by the two new axioms

$$\text{(LG1a)} \qquad \emptyset \rhd a.p \xrightarrow[\emptyset,l]{a}{}^{(st)} \{l\} \rhd a.p,$$

$$\text{(LG1b)} \qquad \{k\} \rhd a.p \xrightarrow[\{k\},l]{a}{}^{(st)} \emptyset \rhd p.$$

while invisible transition are derived with the standard transition system for τ-transitions as presented for example in [18]. Here the start of action a is simulated by performing action a with cause set $\emptyset$ while the end of a is simulated by a with the cause set $\{l\}$. Note that in (LG1b) the l cause is superfluous as it is not inserted into the term. It is simply there to ensure that transitions and terms of the ST transition system fit the general schema of our cause based operational semantics. Let $\sim_{st}$ be the bisimulation equivalence obtained in the standard way from this transition system. In this extended abstract we omit the proof that this coincides with ST bisimulation as defined in [20]. But once more this formulation ensures that the requirements for the applicability of the decision procedure are satisfied and we obtain:

Theorem 19. *ST equivalence is decidable on all* BPP_l *processes.* □

Let us now consider the weak versions of local cause, global cause and ST equivalence. These are obtained by abstracting from internal moves. We only outline the development for *local cause equivalence* but it can be easily adapted for the other two. The weak local cause transitions are defined as follows:

For $a \in Act$ let $\xRightarrow[\Gamma,l]{a}{}^{(lc)}$ be the least relation which satisfies

- $P \xrightarrow[\Gamma,l]{a}{}^{(lc)} Q$ implies $P \xRightarrow[\Gamma,l]{a}{}^{(lc)} Q$
- $P \xRightarrow[\Gamma,l]{a}{}^{(lc)} Q'$ and $Q' \xrightarrow{\tau}{}^{(lc)} Q$ implies $P \xRightarrow[\Gamma,l]{a}{}^{(lc)} Q$
- $P \xrightarrow{\tau}{}^{(lc)} P'$ and $P' \xRightarrow[\Gamma,l]{a}{}^{(lc)} Q$ implies $P \xRightarrow[\Gamma,l]{a}{}^{(lc)} Q$

We also use $\xRightarrow{\epsilon}{}^{(lc)}$ to denote the reflexive transitive closure of $\xrightarrow{\tau}{}^{(lc)}$.

Based on these transitions weak local cause equivalence is defined in the standard way:

Definition 20 Weak Local Cause Equivalence.
A symmetric relation $R \subseteq BPP \times BPP$ is called a *weak local cause bisimulation* iff $R \subseteq G(R)$ where $(p,q) \in G(R)$ iff
(*i*) $p \overset{\varepsilon}{\Longrightarrow}^{(lc)} p'$ implies $q \overset{\varepsilon}{\Longrightarrow}^{(lc)} q'$ for some $q' \in BPP_l$ with $(p',q') \in R$
(*ii*) $p \underset{\Gamma,l}{\overset{a}{\Longrightarrow}}^{(lc)} p', l = new(cau(p) \cup cau(q))$, implies $q \underset{\Gamma,l}{\overset{a}{\Longrightarrow}}^{(lc)} q'$
for some $q' \in BPP_l$ with $(p',q') \in R$.
Two processes p and q are *weak local cause equivalent*, $p \approx_{lc} q$, iff there is a local cause bisimulation R such that $(p,q) \in R$.

It is fairly easy to see how in principle the tableau algorithm has to be adapted in order to handle this new equivalence. The modification concerns the unwinding of processes and the sets of derivatives to be compared. These sets of derivatives are now defined by:

$$WDer_{\Gamma,l}(P,a) = \{Q \mid P \underset{\Gamma,l}{\overset{a}{\Longrightarrow}}^{(lc)} Q\},$$
$$WDer(P,\varepsilon) = \{Q \mid P \overset{\varepsilon}{\Longrightarrow}^{(lc)} Q\}.$$

Unfortunately although we assume that processes are *guarded* these sets may still be infinite. So if we are to adapt the basic decision procedure we must restrict our attention to a subclass where these are guaranteed to be finite.

A process $P \in BPP_l$ is said to be *convergent* if there is no infinite sequence

$$P = P_1 \overset{\tau}{\longrightarrow}^{(lc)} P_2 \overset{\tau}{\longrightarrow}^{(lc)} P_3 \overset{\tau}{\longrightarrow}^{(lc)} \ldots$$

and *h-convergent* if Q is convergent whenever $P \to P_1 \to P_2 \ldots P_n \to Q$ where $P_i \to P_{i+1}$ stands for $P_i \overset{\tau}{\longrightarrow}^{(lc)} P_{i+1}$ or $P_i \underset{\Gamma,l}{\overset{a}{\longrightarrow}}^{(lc)} P_{i+1}$ for some a, Γ. Intuitively this means P will never evolve to a process which can diverge internally.

Theorem 21. *The predicate* h-convergent *is decidable over* BPP_l .

Proposition 22. *If $P \in \mathrm{BPP}_l$ and P is h-convergent then $WDer_{\Gamma,l}(P,a)$, $WDer(P,\tau)$ and $Der(P,\varepsilon)$ are finite for all $l \in \mathcal{C}$, $\Gamma \in \mathcal{CS}$ and $a \in Act$.*

(WeakUNWIND)

$$\frac{P = Q}{\{WDer_{\Gamma,l}(P,a) = WDer_{\Gamma,l}(Q,a)\} \quad WDer(P,\varepsilon) = WDer(Q,\varepsilon)}$$

where $l = new(cau(P)) = (cau(Q))$

Fig. 4. Modified Tableau Rule for Weak Equivalences

So we adapt our decision procedure to decide $\approx_{lc}$ for *h-convergent* processes by replacing the rule **UNWIND** with **WeakUNWIND** given in Figure 4. As in the strong case one can show that tableaux generated by the new rules will be sound and that the algorithm is complete. With the modified rule the proofs in Section 4 can be easily modified to obtain:

Theorem 23. *Weak local cause equivalence is decidable on h–convergent* BPP_l *processes.*

Moreover by changing in an appropriate manner the definition of the sets of derivatives the decision also works for weak versions of the other two equivalences and therefore we also obtain:

Theorem 24. *Weak global cause equivalence and weak ST equivalence are decidable on h–convergent* BPP_l *processes.* □

6 Conclusions

In this paper we have generalised the method of deciding bisimulation equivalence for basic parallel processes of [6] for three well-known non-interleaving equivalences. We have followed closely the general strategy of that paper but because of the complex nature of the equivalences, considerable modifications were required. The main difficulty was in finding a condition for the replacement of one process by a simpler one which at the same time guaranteed the termination of the tableaux. The chosen solution, which uses cause set bijections, enabled us to guarantee termination employing the standard theorem by Higman, [17], from formal language theory.

We also considered decidability of the corresponding weak equivalences but our results only apply to a subclass of processes, namely those which can never diverge. For arbitrary BPP processes these problems are still open, as it is for weak bisimulation equivalence. However at least we have shown that the subclass of processes we can handle is decidable.

The results presented here also apply to Petri nets as basic parallel processes correspond exactly to a certain class of Petri nets (cf. [13]). For global cause equivalence and ST-equivalence the method given here can be directly transferred (cf. the Petri net representation in Section 2). In fact in the case of global cause equivalence our results can be seen as a generalisation of Vogler's work for safe nets and history preserving bisimulation ([22, 21]) as these two equivalences coincide (see [16]). Note that in general bisimulation equivalence is not decidable for arbitrary Petri nets ([14]).

In this paper we have completely ignored questions of complexity. But the result that history preserving bisimulation for safe nets is DEXPTIME complete, [15], indicate that the complexity of our decision procedures is fairly high.

References

1. G. Boudol, I. Castellani, M. Hennessy, and A. Kiehn. A theory of processes with localities. In *Proceedings of CONCUR 92.*
2. G. Boudol, I. Castellani, M. Hennessy, and A. Kiehn. Observing localities. *Theoretical Computer Science*, (114):31–61, 1993.
3. I. Castellani and M. Hennessy. Distributed bisimulations. Report 5/87, University of Sussex, 1987. Also in JACM 1989.
4. S. Christensen. Distributed bisimilarity is decidable for a class of infinite–state systems. In *Proceedings of CONCUR 92*, number 630 in Lecture Notes in Computer Science, 1992.

1. $\sigma \twoheadrightarrow \sigma' \Rightarrow \sigma\rho \twoheadrightarrow \sigma'\rho$
2. $\sigma \neq \lambda \wedge \rho \neq \lambda \wedge \sigma\rho \twoheadrightarrow \lambda \Rightarrow \sigma \twoheadrightarrow \lambda \wedge \rho \twoheadrightarrow \lambda$

Proof. 1. From the definition of the edges we infer $\sigma \xrightarrow{a} \sigma' \Rightarrow \sigma\rho \xrightarrow{a} \sigma'\rho$, which can be generalized using induction on the number of transitions.
2. Proof by induction on the number of transitions in the sequence $\sigma\rho \twoheadrightarrow \lambda$. If $\sigma\rho \rightarrow \lambda$ in one step, then either σ or ρ equals λ. If $\sigma\rho \rightarrow \sigma_1 \ldots \rightarrow \lambda$ in $n+1$ steps, either $\sigma = \lambda$, in which case the implication is trivially true, or σ is of the form $X\xi$, where X has a summand $a\eta$ and $\sigma_1 = \eta\xi\rho$. Now there are two cases. The first case is $\eta\xi = \lambda$. Then $\sigma \rightarrow \lambda$ and $\rho = \sigma_1 \twoheadrightarrow \lambda$ in n transitions. The second case is $\eta\xi \neq \lambda$, then we can apply the induction hypothesis to $\eta\xi$ and ρ. □

Definition 4. A graph is regular if it is bisimilar to a graph with a finite set of nodes. Let S be a specification and $X \in V_S$, then X is regular if $gr_S(X)$ is regular. A specification is regular if all variables in V_S are regular.

Two alternative characterizations of regularity follow directly from the definition.

Proposition 5. (i) *A graph is regular if and only if there is no infinite sequence* $s_0 \rightarrow s_1 \rightarrow s_2 \rightarrow \ldots$ *such that* $s_i \not\leftrightarrow s_j$ *for* $i \neq j$, *where* s_0 *is the root of the graph.* (ii) *A graph is regular if and only if there is no infinite sequence* $s_0 \twoheadrightarrow s_1 \twoheadrightarrow s_2 \twoheadrightarrow \ldots$ *such that* $s_i \not\leftrightarrow s_j$ *for* $i \neq j$, *where* s_0 *is the root of the graph.*

Refer to [8] for a proof of the following proposition, which gives a correspondence between regular and linear specifications.

Proposition 6. *A specification S is regular if and only if there is a linear specification T such that* $V_S \subset V_T$ *and for all* $X \in V_S$ $gr_S(X) \leftrightarrow gr_T(X)$.

3 Normed Processes and the Reachability Relation

3.1 Normed Processes

A weakly normed process (or normed process for short) is a process which may terminate in a finite number of steps.[1]

Definition 7. A node s in a graph is normed, notation $s\downarrow$, if s is a termination node, or there is a termination node t such that $s \twoheadrightarrow t$. A node that is not normed is called (strongly) perpetual[2], notation $s\Uparrow$. A graph is normed if its root node is normed. If S is a specification and $\sigma \in V_S^*$ then we say that σ is normed if $gr_S(\sigma)$ is normed.

[1] A strongly normed process is a process which may terminate at any point during its execution. We will not use this notion in this paper.

[2] A process is called weakly perpetual if it is not strongly normed.

Proposition 8. *Let S be a specification and $\sigma, \rho \in V_S^*$ then*

$$\sigma\rho\downarrow \Leftrightarrow \sigma\downarrow \wedge \rho\downarrow$$

Proof. If σ or ρ is a termination node, and thus equal to λ, the proposition is clearly true. Now suppose $\sigma \twoheadrightarrow \lambda$ and $\rho \twoheadrightarrow \lambda$, then use Proposition 3.1 to derive $\sigma\rho \twoheadrightarrow \lambda$. For proving the other implication, suppose $\sigma\rho \twoheadrightarrow \lambda$ then we can use Proposition 3.2 to derive $\sigma \twoheadrightarrow \lambda$ and $\rho \twoheadrightarrow \lambda$. □

Proposition 9. *Let $\sigma, \rho \in V_S^*$ such that $\sigma\Uparrow$, then $gr_S(\sigma\rho) \leftrightarrows gr_S(\sigma)$.*

Proof. Construct a bisimulation by relating $\eta\xi$ to η for all $\eta, \xi \in V_S^*$ for which η is perpetual. □

In a given state, we can count the minimal number of transitions needed to terminate. This is called the norm of the state.

Definition 10. The norm of a node s is inductively defined by

$$norm(s) = \begin{cases} \infty & \text{if } s\Uparrow \\ 0 & \text{if } s\downarrow \text{ and } s \text{ is a termination node} \\ 1 + \min\{norm(t) | s \rightarrow t\} & \text{if } s\downarrow \text{ and } s \text{ is not a termination node} \end{cases}$$

Proposition 11. *For all nodes s and t $s \leftrightarrows t$ implies $norm(s) = norm(t)$.*

Proof. If both s and t are perpetual, then it is clear. Because s and t are bisimilar, it is impossible that s is perpetual and t is normed or vice versa. If s and t are normed, use induction on the norm. □

Given a specification S we can calculate the normed variables in the following way. Define a sequence of sets of variables N_i inductively by

$$N_0 = \emptyset$$
$$N_{i+1} = N_i \cup \{X \mid \exists_{a\sigma \subset X, \sigma \in V_S^*} \forall_{Y \in \sigma}\, Y \in N_i\}$$

Now set $N = \cup_{i \geq 0} N_i$ then N can be computed effectively.

Theorem 12. *The set N contains exactly all normed variables of V_S. There is some $i \geq 0$ such that $N_i = N_{i+1}$ and for this value $N = N_i$.*

Proof. It is clear from the construction that N contains only normed variables. In order to see that N contains all normed variables, we suppose that X is the variable such that $X\downarrow$, $X \notin N$ and $X \twoheadrightarrow \lambda$ with a minimal number of transitions. We consider two cases. If $X \rightarrow \lambda$, then X has a summand a for some $a \in A$ and thus $X \in N_1$, which is a contradiction. If $X \rightarrow X_0 \ldots X_n \twoheadrightarrow \lambda$, then $(X_0 \ldots X_n)\downarrow$ and thus $X_0 \twoheadrightarrow \lambda, \ldots X_n \twoheadrightarrow \lambda$. These variables all need at least one less transition to reach λ than X, so they are elements of N. But by the definition of N this would imply that $X \in N$, which again gives a contradiction.

Finally, since the N_i are an increasing sequence of subsets of V_S and V_S is finite, there are only finitely many different sets N_i and therefore there exists an i such that $N_i = N_{i+1}$, which implies that $N_{i+k} = N_i$ for all k. □

Now we complete the proof of Theorem 20. Let T be the subtree formed by all descendants of node $\langle 0,0\rangle$. T must be infinite because it contains all nodes $\langle n,0\rangle$ (Lemma 25). T is finitely branching, therefore by König's Lemma it contains an infinite branch. Let B be the lowest infinite branch, that is, the infinite branch with nodes $\langle i,p_i\rangle$ such that for all i if $\langle i,q\rangle$ is on an infinite branch, then $q \geq p_i$.

Since for every i there is a unique p_i such that $\langle i,p_i\rangle \in B$, we may consider B as a function mapping i to p_i.

We claim that for infinitely many $i \geq 0$ we have $\langle i,0\rangle \in B$. Suppose that this is not the case, then for all n greater than some value k the nodes $\langle n,0\rangle$ are not in B.

Such a node $\langle n,0\rangle$ is a descendant of a node $\langle k+1,j\rangle$ with $j < |\sigma_j|$. Since there are infinitely many such n and finitely many such j, at least one node $\langle k+1,j\rangle$ must have infinitely many descendants $\langle n,0\rangle$. That node is therefore the root of an infinite subtree and we apply König's Lemma to find an infinite branch B' in this subtree. B' can be extended to an infinite branch in T, which contradicts the fact that B is the lowest infinite branch.

Now find the first j such that there is an $i < j$ with $L(\langle i,0\rangle) = L(\langle j,0\rangle)$ and $\langle i,0\rangle,\langle j,0\rangle \in B$. By Corollary 24 there is a reachability sequence $L(\langle i,0\rangle)\overset{\rho_0}{\hookrightarrow}\ldots\overset{\rho_q}{\hookrightarrow}L(\langle j,0\rangle)$. Since j is minimal, this sequence is a minimal cycle. Moreover, $L(\langle j,0\rangle)L(\langle j,1\rangle)\ldots L(\langle j,|\sigma_j|-1\rangle)$ is equal to $L(\langle i,0\rangle)\rho_q\ldots\rho_0 L(\langle i,1\rangle)\ldots L(\langle i,|\sigma_i|-1\rangle)$.

We can repeat this construction, finding the first $j' > j$ such that there is an i' satisfying $j < i' < j'$ and $L(\langle i',0\rangle) = L(\langle j',0\rangle)$, giving us another occurrence of a minimal cycle $L(\langle i',0\rangle)\overset{\xi_0}{\hookrightarrow}\ldots\overset{\xi_{q'}}{\hookrightarrow}L(\langle j',0\rangle)$, with $L(\langle j',0\rangle)L(\langle j',1\rangle)\ldots L(\langle j',|\sigma_{j'}|-1\rangle)$ is equal to $L(\langle i',0\rangle)\xi_{q'}\ldots\xi_0 L(\langle i',1\rangle)\ldots L(\langle i',|\sigma_{i'}|-1\rangle)$.

Repeating this construction infinitely often produces infinitely many occurrences of minimal cycles. Since there are only finitely many minimal cycles (Proposition 17), some minimal cycle occurs at least twice. Say $X\overset{\rho_0}{\hookrightarrow}\ldots\overset{\rho_q}{\hookrightarrow}X$ with occurrences $L(\langle i,0\rangle)\overset{\rho_0}{\hookrightarrow}\ldots\overset{\rho_q}{\hookrightarrow}L(\langle j,0\rangle)$ and $L(\langle i',0\rangle)\overset{\rho_0}{\hookrightarrow}\ldots\overset{\rho_q}{\hookrightarrow}L(\langle j',0\rangle)$. Setting $\rho = \rho_q\ldots\rho_0$, we know

$$\begin{aligned}
&L(\langle i,0\rangle) = L(\langle j,0\rangle) = L(\langle i',0\rangle) = L(\langle j',0\rangle) = X,\\
&L(\langle j,0\rangle)L(\langle j,1\rangle)\ldots L(\langle j,|\sigma_j|-1\rangle) = L(\langle i,0\rangle)\rho L(\langle i,1\rangle)\ldots L(\langle i,|\sigma_i|-1\rangle), \text{ and}\\
&L(\langle j',0\rangle)L(\langle j',1\rangle)\ldots L(\langle j',|\sigma_{j'}|-1\rangle) = L(\langle i',0\rangle)\rho L(\langle i',1\rangle)\ldots L(\langle i',|\sigma_{i'}|-1\rangle)
\end{aligned}$$

We consider two cases. First let $\rho = \lambda$, then

$$L(\langle j,0\rangle)\ldots L(\langle j,|\sigma_j|-1\rangle) = L(\langle i,0\rangle)\ldots L(\langle i,|\sigma_i|-1\rangle)$$

and thus $\sigma_i = \sigma_j$ which implies $\sigma_i \leftrightarrows \sigma_j$. Thus we have found i and j as promised at the start of the proof.

The second case is $\rho \neq \lambda$. Since there are no normed stacking cycles and cycle $X\overset{\rho_0}{\hookrightarrow}\ldots\overset{\rho_q}{\hookrightarrow}X$ is stacking, it must be a perpetual cycle. This means that $\rho\Uparrow$.

Consequently (Proposition 9),

$$\begin{array}{l} L(\langle j,0\rangle)L(\langle j,1\rangle)\ldots L(\langle j,|\sigma_j|-1\rangle) = \\ L(\langle i,0\rangle)\rho L(\langle i,1\rangle)\ldots L(\langle i,|\sigma_i|-1\rangle)\leftrightarrows \\ L(\langle i,0\rangle)\rho = \\ L(\langle i',0\rangle)\rho\leftrightarrows \\ L(\langle i',0\rangle)\rho L(\langle i',1\rangle)\ldots L(\langle i',|\sigma_{i'}|-1\rangle) = \\ L(\langle j',0\rangle)L(\langle j',1\rangle)\ldots L(\langle j',|\sigma_{j'}|-1\rangle) \end{array}$$

and thus $\sigma_j \leftrightarrows \sigma_{j'}$, and again we have found i and j as promised. This concludes the proof of Theorem 20. □

5 Linearization

A specification in GNF can be transformed into a linear specification if the conditions from the main theorem in the previous section are met. In this section we will give an effective linearization method. The idea behind the method is simply to get rid of anything following a perpetual variable and introduce new process variables corresponding to sequences of old ones. If this procedure converges, it yields a linear BPA-specification equivalent to the original one.

First we need some additional definitions.

Definition 26.

1. If σ is a non empty sequence of variables, then $[\sigma]$ denotes a fresh process variable.
2. If S is a specification, then $[S]$ is the collection of equations derived from S by replacing every summand $aXY\sigma$ by $a[XY\sigma]$.
3. The operator $*$ concatenates a sequence of variables to a process definition. It is defined as follows.

$$(a_0\sigma_0 + \ldots + a_n\sigma_n) * X\sigma = a_0\sigma_0 * X\sigma + \ldots + a_n\sigma_n * X\sigma$$

$$a\rho * X\sigma = \begin{cases} a\rho X\sigma & \text{if } \rho\downarrow \\ a\rho & \text{if } \rho\Uparrow \end{cases}$$

Definition 27. A specification S is reduced if for every summand $aX_0 \ldots X_n$ $(n > 0)$ $(X_0 \ldots X_{n-1})\downarrow$.

Definition 28. The reduction $red(S)$ of a specification S is derived from S by replacing all summands $aX_0 \ldots X_n$ $(n > 0)$ for which there exists $0 \leq i < n$ with $(X_0 \ldots X_{i-1})\downarrow$ and $X_i\Uparrow$ by $aX_0 \ldots X_i$.

A specification S can be linearized by calculating a sequence of equivalent specifications S_i $(i \geq 0)$. If S is regular, only a finite number of specifications must be calculated in order to reach a linear S_i. The specifications are defined as follows.

$$\begin{array}{ll} S_0 & = red(S) \\ S_{i+1} & = [S_i] \cup \{[XY\sigma] = Def_{red(S)}(X) * Y\sigma \mid \\ & \qquad X, Y \in V_S, \sigma \in V_S^*, \exists_{a\in A, Z\in V_{S_i}} aXY\sigma \subset Z, [XY\sigma] \notin V_{S_i}\} \end{array}$$

We will not present a detailed proof of the correctness of this method. We will only give the main steps of the proof.

It is easy to verify that every S_i is a reduced specification. Furthermore, by constructing a bisimulation, we have for all $X \in V_S$ and $i \geq 0$, $gr_S(X) \leftrightarrow gr_{S_i}(X)$.

Finally we have that S is regular if and only if for some $i \geq 0$ $S_i = S_{i+1}$. We will only sketch the proof. Suppose that $S_i = S_{i+1}$, then $S_i = [S_i]$, so there are no summands $aXY\sigma$ and thus S_i is linear, which implies that S is regular. For the other implication, suppose that all S_i are different, then there is an infinite sequence

$$X \rightarrow_{S_1} [\sigma_1] \rightarrow_{S_2} [\sigma_2] \rightarrow_{S_3} \ldots$$

such that $[\sigma_{i+1}] \in V_{S_{i+1}}$ and $[\sigma_{i+1}] \notin V_{S_i}$ for $i \geq 0$. This sequence can be transformed into an infinite sequence

$$X \rightarrow_S \sigma_1' \rightarrow_S \sigma_2' \rightarrow_S \ldots$$

of which infinitely many sequences σ_i' are not bisimilar. This contradicts regularity of S.

6 Example

We will apply the results from the previous sections to a simple example. Consider the following specification.

$$\begin{aligned} A &= aBCD \\ B &= bB + b \\ C &= cAC + c \\ D &= d \end{aligned}$$

Clearly the variables B, C and D are normed and since $aBCD$ is a summand of A, A is normed too. Next we derive a reachability sequence. Since $B\downarrow$, we have $A \overset{D}{\hookrightarrow} C$ and since $A\downarrow$, we have $C \overset{C}{\hookrightarrow} A$. Thus we have a reachability cycle $A \overset{D}{\hookrightarrow} C \overset{C}{\hookrightarrow} A$. This cycle is clearly stacking, and because $ACD\downarrow$ it is a normed cycle. Now we may conclude that the specification is not regular. Indeed we have an infinite sequence

$$A \twoheadrightarrow ACD \twoheadrightarrow ACDCD \twoheadrightarrow \ldots$$

Now consider a slightly modified system, which is derived from the previous system by deleting summand c of C. This makes C perpetual.

$$\begin{aligned} A &= aBCD \\ B &= bB + b \\ C &= cAC \\ D &= d \end{aligned}$$

The variables B and D are normed, while A and C are perpetual. We can find three minimal cycles

$$B \overset{\lambda}{\hookrightarrow} B$$
$$A \overset{D}{\hookrightarrow} C \overset{C}{\hookrightarrow} A$$
$$C \overset{C}{\hookrightarrow} A \overset{D}{\hookrightarrow} C$$

The first cycle is not stacking. The second and third cycle (which are in fact equal) are not normed, because $(ACD)\Uparrow$ and $(CDA)\Uparrow$. Following the main theorem, we conclude that the specification is regular. Now we can apply the linearization procedure and get for S_0 the reduction of S:

$$\begin{aligned} A &= aBC \\ B &= bB + b \\ C &= cA \\ D &= d \end{aligned}$$

For S_1 we obtain:

$$\begin{aligned} A &= a[BC] \\ B &= bB + b \\ C &= cA \\ D &= d \\ [BC] &= bBC + bC \end{aligned}$$

Already S_2 is a linear specification:

$$\begin{aligned} A &= a[BC] \\ B &= bB + b \\ C &= cA \\ D &= d \\ [BC] &= b[BC] + bC \end{aligned}$$

7 Conclusions

We have proved that regularity of BPA systems is decidable. The question whether it is decidable that a single process variable defines a regular process is still open. We conjecture that it is decidable. A simple example shows that this question is more complicated than regularity of a complete BPA system. Consider the specification

$$\begin{aligned} X &= aYZ \\ Y &= bYc + d \\ Z &= eZ \end{aligned}$$

Then it is easy to show that X and Y are irregular, so the specification as a whole is irregular. If we would change the definition of Z into

$$Z = cZ$$

then the complete specification is still irregular (since Y is still irregular), but now X is regular. The reason is clearly that the normed stacking tail c^n of Y is reduced to a regular perpetual process c^∞ by appending Z.

From this example we conclude that it is necessary to take the actual values of the atomic actions into account when deciding regularity of a single process variable. This probably leads to a more complex decision procedure than the one presented in this paper. Since the reachability relation and normedness are completely independent of the actual atomic actions, only the presence of any atomic action plays a role in the decision prodedure presented here.

We do not think that the restriction to complete systems is a problem in practical applications. In most cases one is interested in the linearization of a complete system. Specifications in languages such as PSF [6] only consider complete systems, without singling out a specific variable.

We claim that the techniques described in this paper easily extend to BPA_δ (which results from BPA by adding the special process constant δ for unsuccessful termination). A more interesting topic for future research is the question whether there are extensions of BPA with some operator for parallelism, on which regularity is also decidable.

References

1. J.C.M. Baeten, J.A. Bergstra & J.W. Klop, Decidability of bisimulation equivalence for processes generating context-free languages, Proc. PARLE 87 (J.W. de Bakker, A.J. Nijman, P.C. Treleaven, eds.), LNCS 259, pp. 93-114, 1987.
2. J.C.M. Baeten & W.P. Weijland, Process algebra, Cambridge Tracts in Theoretical Computer Science 18, Cambridge University Press, 1990.
3. J.A. Bergstra & J.W. Klop, Process theory based on bisimulation semantics, Linear time, branching time and partial order in logics and models for concurrency (J.W. de Bakker, W.P. de Roever, G. Rozenberg, eds.), LNCS 354, pp. 50-122, 1989.
4. S. Christensen, H. Hüttel & C. Stirling, Bisimulation equivalence is decidable for all context-free processes, Proc. CONCUR'92 (W.R. Cleaveland, ed.), LNCS 630, pp. 138-147, 1992.
5. S. Christensen, Y. Hirschfeld & F. Moller, Bisimulation equivalence is decidable for basic parallel processes, Proc. CONCUR'93 (E. Best, ed.), LNCS 715, pp. 143-157, 1993.
6. S. Mauw & G.J. Veltink, A process specification formalism, Fundamenta Informaticæ XIII, pp. 85-139, 1990.
7. S. Mauw & G.J. Veltink, Algebraic specification of communication protocols, Cambridge Tracts in Theoretical Computer Science 36, Cambridge University Press, 1993.
8. R. Milner, A complete inference system for a class of regular behaviours, JCSS 28, pp. 439–466, 1984.
9. D.M.R. Park, Concurrency and automata on infinite sequences, Proc. 5th GI Conf. (P. Duessen, ed.), LNCS 104, pp. 167-183, 1981.

A Fast Algorithm for Deciding Bisimilarity of Normed Context-Free Processes

Yoram Hirshfeld* Faron Moller†

University of Edinburgh

Abstract

Until recently, algorithms for deciding bisimulation equivalence between normed context-free processes have all been nondeterministic. The optimal such algorithm, due to Huynh and Tian, is in $\Sigma_2^{\mathrm{P}} = \mathrm{NP}^{\mathrm{NP}}$: it guesses a proof of equivalence and validates this proof in polynomial time using oracles freely answering questions which are in NP. Hirshfeld, Jerrum and Moller have since demonstrated that this problem is actually decidable in polynomial time. However, this algorithm is far from being practical, giving a $O(n^{13})$ algorithm, where n is (roughly) the size of the grammar defining the processes, that is, the number of symbols in its description. In this paper we present a deterministic algorithm which runs in time $O(n^4 v)$ where v is the norm of the processes being compared, which corresponds to the shortest distance to a terminating state of the process, or the shortest word generated by the corresponding grammar. Though this may be exponential, it still appears to be efficient in practice, when norms are typically of moderate size. Also, the algorithm tends to behave well even when the norm is exponentially large. Furthermore, we believe that the techniques may lead to more efficient polynomial algorithms; indeed we have not been able to find an example for which our optimised algorithm requires exponential time.

1 Introduction

There are many formalisms for handling the problem of describing and analyzing processes. Possibly foremost among these are algebraic systems such as regular expressions, algebraic grammars and process algebras. There are also many automated tools built upon these formalisms, exploiting the fact that properties of finite-state processes are typically decidable. In particular the equivalence problem is decidable regardless of what reasonable semantic notion of equivalence is chosen. However, realistic systems, which typically involve infinite entities such as counters or real-time aspects, are not finite-state, and in practice these

*The first author is on Sabbatical leave from The School of Mathematics and Computer Science, Tel Aviv University.

†The second author is supported by Esprit Basic Basic Research Action No.7166 "CONCUR2" and is currently at the Swedish Institute of Computer Science.

are only partially modelled by finite-state approximations. There has thus been much interest lately in the study of the decidability of important properties, such as the equivalence and model checking problems, for various classes of infinite-state systems. However, these results are generally negative, such as the classic result regarding the undecidability of language equivalence over context-free grammars.

In the realm of process algebra, a fundamental idea is that of bisimilarity [13], a notion of equivalence which is strictly finer than language equivalence. This theoretical notion is put into practice particularly within Milner's Calculus of Communicating Systems (CCS) [11]. This equivalence is undecidable over the whole calculus CCS. However, Christensen, Hüttel and Stirling recently proved the remarkable result that bisimilarity is in fact decidable over the class of context-free processes [3], those processes which can be defined by context-free grammars in Greibach normal form. Previously this result was shown by Baeten, Bergstra and Klop [1] for the simpler case of normed context-free processes, those defined by grammars in which all variables may rewrite to finite words. It has also been demonstrated that no other equivalence in Glabbeek's linear-time/branching-time spectrum [4] is in fact decidable over this class [6], even over the subclass of normed processes, which places bisimilarity in a favourable light indeed.

Viewed less as a theoretical question, decidability is only half of the story of a property of systems; in order to be applicable the decision procedure must be computationally tractable as well. The techniques of [1, 3] require extensive searches making these unsuitable for implementation. Though there has been little success in simplifying the technique of [3] for general context-free processes, there have been several simplifications to the proof of [1] for normed processes [2, 5, 9] which exploit certain decomposability properties enjoyed within this subclass but not in general. However, the best of these techniques still yields an algorithm which is both exponential-time in the size of the problem as well as being nondeterministic, requiring oracles to provide correct answers to apparently intractable search problems.

Recently Huynh and Tian have shown that this problem lies in $\Sigma_2^{\mathrm{P}} = \mathrm{NP}^{\mathrm{NP}}$ [10]: they have an algorithm which given a proof of the equivalence of two processes validates this proof in polynomial time using oracles freely answering questions which are in NP. Being nondeterministic, this technique is still far from being efficiently implementable. More recently Hirshfeld, Jerrum and Moller have shown that this problem is decidable in polynomial time [7]. However, this algorithm is equally far from being practical, giving a $O(n^{13})$ algorithm, where n is (roughly) the size of the grammar defining the processes, that is the number of symbols in its description.

In this paper we present a deterministic algorithm for deciding bisimilarity of normed context-free processes which runs in time $O(n^4 v)$ where v is the norm of the processes being compared, which corresponds to the shortest distance to a terminating state of the process, or the shortest word generated by the corresponding grammar. Though this may be exponential, the algorithm still appears to be efficient in practice, when norms are typically of moderate size. Also, the algorithm tends to behave well even when the norm is exponentially large. Furthermore, we believe that the techniques may lead to more efficient polynomial algorithms; indeed we have not been able to find an example for which our optimised algorithm requires exponential time.

The remainder of the paper is organised as follows. In Section 2 we provide preliminary definitions for our framework; in particular we define (normed) context-free processes and bisimilarity, and provide several established results concerning these notions. In Section 3 we provide the definitions and results which underlie our algorithm. Then in Section 4 we present first our basic algorithm, based on the results of the previous section, as well as a more efficient implementation, and provide an analysis of the complexity of the algorithm. Finally in Section 5 we review our achievements, relate the work to other existing results, and describe some further applications of the techniques.

2 Context-Free Processes

In this section we review the various established definitions and results on which we shall base our study. Firstly, we define our notion of a process as follows.

Definition 2.1 *A* process *is (a state in) a* labelled transition system, *a 4-tuple* $(S, A, \longrightarrow, \alpha_0)$ *where*

- S *is a set of* states;
- A *is some set of* actions;
- $\longrightarrow \subseteq S \times A \times S$ *is a* transition relation, *written* $\alpha \xrightarrow{a} \beta$ *for* $(\alpha, a, \beta) \in \longrightarrow$. *We shall extend this definition by reflexivity and transitivity to allow* $\alpha \xrightarrow{s} \beta$ *for* $s \in A^*$; *and*
- $\alpha_0 \in S$ *is the* initial state.

The norm *of a process state* $\alpha \in S$, *written* norm(α), *is the length of the shortest transition sequence from that state to a terminal state, that is, a state from which no transitions evolve. A process is* weakly normed *iff its initial state has a finite norm, and it is* normed *iff all of its states have finite norm.*

The class of processes in which we shall be interested is a subclass of those generated by context-free grammars, as defined for example in [8] as follows.

Definition 2.2 *A* context-free grammar (CFG) *is a 4-tuple* (V, T, P, S), *where*

- V *is a finite set of* variables;
- T *is a finite set of* terminals;
- $P \subseteq V \times (V \cup T)^*$ *is a finite set of* production rules, *written* $X \rightarrow \alpha$ *for* $(X, \alpha) \in P$. *We shall assume that some rule* $X \rightarrow \alpha$ *exists in* P *for each variable* $X \in V$; *and*
- $S \in V$ *is the* start symbol.

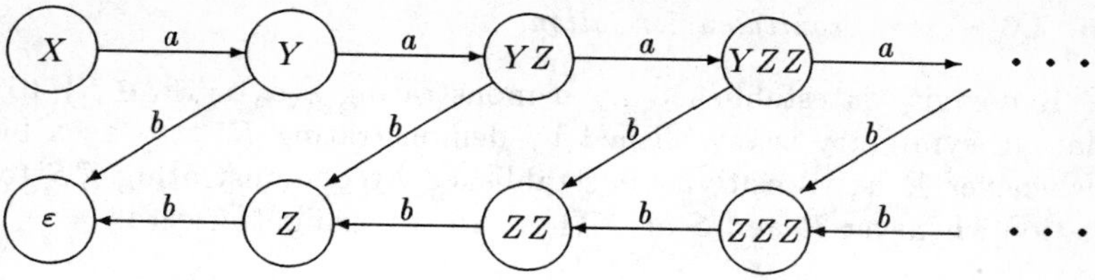

Figure 1: The context-free process $X \rightarrow aY,\ Y \rightarrow aYZ,\ Y \rightarrow b,\ Z \rightarrow b$

The norm *of a variable $X \in V$, written* norm(X), *is the length of the shortest string of terminals which can be generated from X. A CFG is* weakly normed *iff its start symbol has a finite norm, and it is* normed *iff all of its variables have finite norm.*

A grammar is in Greibach normal form (GNF) *iff each of its production rules is of the form $X \rightarrow a\alpha$ where $a \in T$ and $\alpha \in V^*$. If each such α is of length at most k, then it is in k-GNF.*

The class of CFGs in GNF corresponds to the class of processes defined by guarded systems of recursive equations over the basic process algebra (BPA) of [1]. Every CFG in GNF in this sense defines a (context-free) process as follows.

Definition 2.3 *With the CFG (V, T, P, S) in GNF we associate the process $(V^*, T, \longrightarrow, S)$ where there are no transitions leading from ε, and $X\sigma \stackrel{a}{\longrightarrow} \alpha\sigma$ iff $X \rightarrow a\alpha$ is a production in P.*

The class of context-free processes *is exactly that class of processes generated by CFGs in GNF.*

As an example, consider the CFG given by the GNF rules $X \rightarrow aY$, $Y \rightarrow aYZ$, $Y \rightarrow b$ and $Z \rightarrow b$. This grammar defines the process depicted in Figure 1. This process (as well as its defining grammar) is normed, with norm$(X) = 2$ and norm$(Y) =$ norm$(Z) = 1$.

Clearly every normed CFG in GNF gives rise to a normed process. We can also see immediately the following basic fact regarding processes.

Lemma 2.4 norm$(\alpha\beta)$ = norm(α) + norm(β).

The notion of process equivalence in which we are interested is bisimulation equivalence [13] as defined as follows.

Definition 2.5 *Let $(S, A, \longrightarrow, s_0)$ be a process. A relation $\mathcal{R} \subseteq S \times S$ is a* bisimulation *iff whenever $(\alpha, \beta) \in \mathcal{R}$ we have that*

- *if $\alpha \stackrel{a}{\longrightarrow} \alpha'$ then $\beta \stackrel{a}{\longrightarrow} \beta'$ for some β' with $(\alpha', \beta') \in \mathcal{R}$; and*
- *if $\beta \stackrel{a}{\longrightarrow} \beta'$ then $\alpha \stackrel{a}{\longrightarrow} \alpha'$ for some α' with $(\alpha', \beta') \in \mathcal{R}$.*

α and β are bisimilar, *written $\alpha \sim \beta$, iff $(\alpha, \beta) \in \mathcal{R}$ for some bisimulation $\mathcal{R}$.*

Lemma 2.6 $\sim$ *is an equivalence relation.*

Proof Reflexivity is established by demonstrating $\{(\alpha,\alpha) : \alpha \in S\}$ to be a bisimulation; symmetry is established by demonstrating $\mathcal{R}^{-1}$ to be a bisimulation whenever $\mathcal{R}$ is; transitivity is established by demonstrating $\mathcal{RS}$ to be a bisimulation whenever $\mathcal{R}$ and $\mathcal{S}$ are. These are all straightforward. □

The main result on which we shall build regarding this process class, originally proved in [1], is given by the following.

Theorem 2.7 *Bisimilarity is decidable for normed context-free processes.*

What we provide in this paper is a procedure of relatively low complexity for deciding bisimilarity of normed context-free processes. Specifically, we fix a CFG $G = (V, T, P, S)$ in GNF, and decide whether two given states α and β of the process $(V^*, T, \longrightarrow, S)$ given by Definition 2.3 are bisimilar.

We shall rely on the following established results concerning bisimilar processes.

Lemma 2.8 *If* $\alpha \sim \beta$ *and* $\alpha \xrightarrow{s} \alpha'$ *for* $s \in A^*$ *then* $\beta \xrightarrow{s} \beta'$ *such that* $\alpha' \sim \beta'$.

Proof Suppose that $\mathcal{R}$ is a bisimulation relating α and β, and that

$$\alpha = \alpha_0 \xrightarrow{a_1} \alpha_1 \xrightarrow{a_2} \cdots \xrightarrow{a_p} \alpha_p = \alpha'.$$

Then we must have that

$$\beta = \beta_0 \xrightarrow{a_1} \beta_1 \xrightarrow{a_2} \cdots \xrightarrow{a_p} \beta_p = \beta'$$

with $(\alpha_i, \beta_i) \in \mathcal{R}$ for $0 \le i \le p$. Hence $(\alpha', \beta') \in \mathcal{R}$ so $\alpha' \sim \beta'$. □

Lemma 2.9 $\alpha \sim \beta$ *implies* $\mathrm{norm}(\alpha) = \mathrm{norm}(\beta)$.

Proof Suppose that $\mathrm{norm}(\alpha) > \mathrm{norm}(\beta)$. Let s be chosen such that $\beta \xrightarrow{s} \varepsilon$ and $\mathrm{length}(s) = \mathrm{norm}(\beta)$. Clearly we cannot have that $\alpha \xrightarrow{s} \varepsilon$ so we cannot have that $\alpha \sim \beta$. □

The technique underlying our algorithm exploits properties of the sequential composition and decomposition of processes, as outlined in the following few facts. Firstly, we have a basic congruence result.

Lemma 2.10 *If* $\alpha \sim \beta$ *and* $\alpha' \sim \beta'$ *then* $\alpha\alpha' \sim \beta\beta'$.

Proof It is straightforward to show that $\Big\{(\alpha\alpha', \beta\beta') : \alpha \sim \beta,\ \alpha' \sim \beta'\Big\}$ is a bisimulation. □

More importantly, motivated by [12] we have a unique prime decomposition result for weakly normed (and hence normed) processes. To demonstrate this we first prove a cancellation lemma.

Lemma 2.11 *If $\alpha\gamma \sim \beta\gamma$ and γ is weakly normed, then $\alpha \sim \beta$.*

Proof It is straightforward to show that $\left\{(\alpha,\beta) : \alpha\gamma \sim \beta\gamma,\ \mathrm{norm}(\gamma) < \infty\right\}$ is a bisimulation. □

Notice that this fact fails to hold when γ is not weakly normed. For example, given $X \longrightarrow a$ and $Y \longrightarrow aY$ we have that $XY \sim XXY$ but $X \not\sim XX$.

Definition 2.12 *α is* prime *(wrt $\sim$) iff $\alpha \neq \varepsilon$ and $\alpha \sim \beta\gamma$ implies $\beta = \varepsilon$ or $\gamma = \varepsilon$.*

Theorem 2.13 *Weakly normed processes have unique (up to $\sim$) prime decompositions.*

Proof Existence is established by induction on the norm.

For uniqueness, suppose that $\alpha_1 \cdots \alpha_p \sim \beta_1 \cdots \beta_q$ are prime decompositions and that we have established the uniqueness of prime decompositions for all α with $\mathrm{norm}(\alpha) < \mathrm{norm}(\alpha_1 \cdots \alpha_p)$.

If $p = 1$ or $q = 1$ then we immediately have our result.

Otherwise suppose that $\alpha_1\alpha_2 \cdots \alpha_p \xrightarrow{a} \alpha_1'\alpha_2 \cdots \alpha_p$ is a norm-reducing transition, that is, $\mathrm{norm}(\alpha_1'\alpha_2 \cdots \alpha_p) < \mathrm{norm}(\alpha_1\alpha_2 \cdots \alpha_p)$.

Then $\beta_1\beta_2 \cdots \beta_q \xrightarrow{a} \beta_1'\beta_2 \cdots \beta_q$ with $\alpha_1'\alpha_2 \cdots \alpha_p \sim \beta_1'\beta_2 \cdots \beta_q$, so by induction we must have that $\alpha_p \sim \beta_q$,

Hence by Lemma 2.11 we have that $\alpha_1 \cdots \alpha_{p-1} \sim \beta_1 \cdots \beta_{q-1}$ from which our result then follows by Lemma 2.10. □

One further result concerning bisimilarity which we rely on pertains to *Caucal bases*, otherwise known as *self-bisimulations* [2].

Definition 2.14 *For any binary relation $\mathcal{B}$ over processes, let $\overset{\mathcal{B}}{\equiv}$ be the congruence closure of $\mathcal{B}$ wrt sequential composition. $\mathcal{B}$ is a* Caucal base *iff whenever $(\alpha,\beta) \in \mathcal{B}$ we have that*

- *if $\alpha \xrightarrow{a} \alpha'$ then $\beta \xrightarrow{a} \beta'$ for some β' with $\alpha' \overset{\mathcal{B}}{\equiv} \beta'$; and*
- *if $\beta \xrightarrow{a} \beta'$ then $\alpha \xrightarrow{a} \alpha'$ for some α' with $\alpha' \overset{\mathcal{B}}{\equiv} \beta'$.*

Lemma 2.15 *If $\mathcal{B}$ is a Caucal base, then $\overset{\mathcal{B}}{\equiv}$ is a bisimulation, so $\overset{\mathcal{B}}{\equiv} \subseteq \sim$.*

Proof We demonstrate that if $\alpha \overset{\mathcal{B}}{\equiv} \beta$ then the two clauses given by Definition 2.5 hold true. The proof of this we carry out by induction on the depth of inference of $\alpha \overset{\mathcal{B}}{\equiv} \beta$.

If $\alpha \overset{\mathcal{B}}{\equiv} \beta$ follows from $(\alpha,\beta) \in \mathcal{B}$, then the result follows from $\mathcal{B}$ being a Caucal base.

If $\alpha \overset{\mathcal{B}}{\equiv} \beta$ follows by one of the congruence closure conditions, then the result easily follows by induction. □

3 Basic Definitions and Results

In this section we provide the results underlying the correctness of our algorithm. We start by assuming that we have a normed CFG (V, T, P, S) in GNF. The basic idea is to exploit the unique prime decomposition theorem by decomposing process terms sufficiently far to be able to establish or refute the equivalence which we are considering. Further, we try to construct these decompositions by a refinement process which starts with an overly generous collection of candidate decompositions. This is the motivation behind the following definitions.

Definition 3.1

- *A* base *is a collection of pairs* (X, α) *where* $X \in V$ *and* $\alpha \in V^*$ *satisfy* $\mathrm{norm}(X) = \mathrm{norm}(\alpha)$.
- *A base* $\mathcal{B}$ *is* full *iff whenever* $X \sim Y\beta$ *then* $(X, Y\gamma) \in \mathcal{B}$ *for some* $\gamma \sim \beta$. *In particular,* $(X, X) \in \mathcal{B}$ *for all* $X \in V$.
- *The relation* $\equiv_{\mathcal{B}}$ *generated by* $\mathcal{B}$ *is defined recursively by:*
  - $\varepsilon \equiv_{\mathcal{B}} \varepsilon$; *and*
  - $X\alpha \equiv_{\mathcal{B}} Y\beta$ *iff for some* γ,
    - $(X, Y\gamma) \in \mathcal{B}$ *and* $\gamma\alpha \equiv_{\mathcal{B}} \beta$; *or*
    - $(Y, X\gamma) \in \mathcal{B}$ *and* $\alpha \equiv_{\mathcal{B}} \gamma\beta$,

Hence we are proposing that a base $\mathcal{B}$ consist of pairs (X, α) representing candidate decompositions, that is, such that $X \sim \alpha$. The relation $\alpha \equiv_{\mathcal{B}} \beta$, being defined recursively, is thus easily decidable in time $O(\mathrm{norm}(\alpha))$. The importance of fullness then is given by the following property.

Proposition 3.2 *If* $\mathcal{B}$ *is full, then* $\sim\ \subseteq\ \equiv_{\mathcal{B}}$.

Proof By induction on the norm. For the base case we know by definition that $\varepsilon \equiv_{\mathcal{B}} \varepsilon$.

Suppose then that $X\alpha \sim Y\beta$ and that $E \sim F$ implies $E \equiv_{\mathcal{B}} F$ whenever $\mathrm{norm}(E) < \mathrm{norm}(X\alpha)$.

First suppose that $\mathrm{norm}(X) \leq \mathrm{norm}(Y)$. By unique decomposition we have that $X\gamma' \sim Y$ for some γ'. Hence by fullness of $\mathcal{B}$ we have that $(Y, X\gamma) \in \mathcal{B}$ for some $\gamma \sim \gamma'$. Thus $X\alpha \sim Y\beta \sim X\gamma\beta$ so $\alpha \sim \gamma\beta$. But then by induction we have that $\alpha \equiv_{\mathcal{B}} \gamma\beta$, and so $X\alpha \equiv_{\mathcal{B}} Y\beta$.

By a symmetric argument we can show that if $\mathrm{norm}(X) > \mathrm{norm}(Y)$ then $X\alpha \equiv_{\mathcal{B}} Y\beta$. □

We can relax the definition of fullness of a base slightly while maintaining the validity of Proposition 3.2 by only requiring one of (X, Y) and (Y, X) to be in the base whenever $X \sim Y$. This will give us a slight increase in efficiency.

Now we have the task of discovering a full base which contains only semantically sound decomposition pairs. To do this, we start with a full but finite (and indeed small) base which we refine iteratively whilst maintaining fullness. This refinement is as follows.

Definition 3.3 *Given a base $\mathcal{B}$, define the subbase $\widehat{\mathcal{B}} \subseteq \mathcal{B}$ by:*
$(X, \alpha) \in \widehat{\mathcal{B}}$ *iff* $(X, \alpha) \in \mathcal{B}$ *and*

- *if* $X \xrightarrow{a} \beta$ *then* $\alpha \xrightarrow{a} \gamma$ *with* $\beta \equiv_{\mathcal{B}} \gamma$; *and*
- *if* $\alpha \xrightarrow{a} \gamma$ *then* $X \xrightarrow{a} \beta$ *with* $\beta \equiv_{\mathcal{B}} \gamma$.

Lemma 3.4 *If $\mathcal{B}$ is full then $\widehat{\mathcal{B}}$ is full.*

Proof If $X \sim Y\beta$, then by fullness of $\mathcal{B}$ we have $(X, Y\gamma) \in \mathcal{B}$ for some $\gamma \sim \beta$. If $X \xrightarrow{a} \sigma$ then $Y\gamma \xrightarrow{a} \delta$ with $\sigma \sim \delta$ and thus by Proposition 3.2 $\sigma \equiv_{\mathcal{B}} \delta$. Similarly if $Y\gamma \xrightarrow{a} \delta$ then $X \xrightarrow{a} \sigma$ with $\sigma \sim \delta$ and thus $\sigma \equiv_{\mathcal{B}} \delta$. Hence $(X, Y\gamma) \in \widehat{\mathcal{B}}$. □

So we can iteratively apply this refinement to our finite full base, and be guaranteed that the process will stabilize at some base $\mathcal{B}$ for which we shall demonstrate that $\equiv_{\mathcal{B}} \; = \; \sim$. This last result will follow from Proposition 3.2 as well as the following.

Proposition 3.5 *If $\widehat{\mathcal{B}} = \mathcal{B}$ then $\equiv_{\mathcal{B}} \; \subseteq \; \sim$.*

Proof $\equiv_{\mathcal{B}}$ is contained in $\overset{\mathcal{B}}{\equiv}$, the congruence generated by $\mathcal{B}$, so $\mathcal{B}$ must be a self-bisimulation. Hence our result follows from Lemma 2.15. □

We are thus simply left now with the task of constructing our initial base $\mathcal{B}_0$. This is achieved as follows.

Definition 3.6 *For each X and Y with* $\text{norm}(X) \geq \text{norm}(Y)$ *fix some* $[X]_{\text{norm}(Y)}$ *such that* $X \xrightarrow{s} [X]_{\text{norm}(Y)}$ *in* $\text{length}(s) = \text{norm}(Y)$ *norm-reducing steps.*
Let $\mathcal{B}_0$ be the collection of all such $(X, Y[X]_{\text{norm}(Y)})$ *pairs.*

Lemma 3.7 *$\mathcal{B}_0$ is full.*

Proof If $X \sim Y\beta$, then $\text{norm}(X) \geq \text{norm}(Y)$, so $(X, Y\gamma) \in \mathcal{B}_0$ for some γ such that $X \xrightarrow{s} \gamma$ in $\text{length}(s) = \text{norm}(Y)$ norm-reducing steps. But this norm-reducing transition sequence can only be matched by $Y\beta \xrightarrow{s} \beta$. But then we must have that $\gamma \sim \beta$, so $\mathcal{B}_0$ is full. □

Notice that $\mathcal{B}_0$ contains at most n^2 pairs, where n is the number of variables X in the grammar. However, we can order the variables as $X_1, X_2, \ldots, X_n$ such that $\text{norm}(X_i) \leq \text{norm}(X_j)$ whenever $i \leq j$ and then set

$$\mathcal{B}_0 \;=\; \left\{ (X_j, X_i[X_j]_{\text{norm}(X_i)}) : 1 \leq i \leq j \leq n \right\}$$

Then this $\mathcal{B}_0$ will be of size $\frac{n(n+1)}{2}$ and can be shown to be full by the slightly relaxed definition using the same proof above.

Definition 3.8 *Let* $\mathcal{B}_{i+1} = \widehat{\mathcal{B}_i}$, *and let* $\mathcal{B}$ *be the first* $\mathcal{B}_{i+1} = \mathcal{B}_i$.

We thus finally have our desired base $\mathcal{B}$, and we are left to prove our promised characterisation theorem.

Theorem 3.9 $\equiv_{\mathcal{B}} \; = \; \sim$.

Proof Immediate from Proposition 3.2 and Proposition 3.5. □

We have now accomplished our goal of defining a deterministic procedure for deciding bisimilarity between normed processes: we simply iterate our refinement procedure on our finite initial base $\mathcal{B}_0$ until it stabilizes at our desired base $\mathcal{B}$, and then we test for $\equiv_{\mathcal{B}}$. However, we have not given an explicit algorithm for performing this procedure, so we cannot as yet remark in much detail on its complexity. This task is left for the next section.

4 The Algorithm

In this section we describe our basic algorithm, and then provide modifications for improving its efficiency. To start with, we fix the problem domain: let (V, T, P, X_s) be a CFG in k-GNF, with

$$V = \{X_1, X_2, \ldots, X_m\}$$
$$P = \left\{ X_i \rightarrow a_{ij}\alpha_{ij} \; : \; 1 \leq i \leq m, \; 1 \leq j \leq l_i \right\}$$

and such that the indices on the nonterminals and productions are ordered so that $\mathrm{norm}(X_i) \leq \mathrm{norm}(X_{i+1})$ for each $1 \leq i < m$, and that the first rule for each nonterminal generates a norm-reducing transition so that $\mathrm{norm}(X_i) > \mathrm{norm}(\alpha_{i1})$. (We can compute the norms of the variables by solving simple linear equations and thus rearrange our grammar into this form efficiently.) Let l be the maximum value of l_i, that is, the maximum number of rules associated with a single nonterminal, and hence the maximum number of transitions evolving from any given state. Our complexity will be expressed in terms of $n = klm$ which is roughly the size of the grammar $|G|$, that is, the number of symbols used to describe the grammar, as well as the largest norm $v = \mathrm{norm}(X_m)$ expressed by the grammar nonterminals.

We want to decide, given $\alpha, \beta \in V^*$, whether or not $\alpha \sim \beta$. To do so, we start by computing $\mathcal{B}$ as in the previous section, and then determine if $\alpha \equiv_{\mathcal{B}} \beta$. The algorithm thus has three phases: the first phase computes the initial base $\mathcal{B}_0$; the second phase computes the final base $\mathcal{B}$ by iterating the refinement operation until it stabilizes; and the third phase decides if the two processes in question are related by $\equiv_{\mathcal{B}}$. Notice that to decide several process equivalences defined over the same CFG, we need only perform the first two phases once.

The second and third phases simply require us to be able to compute the relation $\equiv_{\mathcal{B}}$ which is straightforward from its definition taking time which is linear in the norm of the processes being compared. The only issue worth commenting on at this point is the definition of $\mathcal{B}_0$. In order to compute $\mathcal{B}_0$ we must compute $[X_i]_p$, a term derived from X_i through $p \leq \text{norm}(X_i)$ norm-reducing steps. In particular, these steps will be fixed as those given by the first rule for each X_i. A function for defining $[\alpha]_p$ for $p \leq \text{norm}(\alpha)$ is thus given as follows.

Definition 4.1

$$[\alpha]_0 \stackrel{\text{def}}{=} \alpha;$$

$$[X_i\alpha]_p \stackrel{\text{def}}{=} \begin{cases} [\alpha]_{p-\text{norm}(X_i)} & \textit{if } p \geq \text{norm}(X_i); \\ [\alpha_{i1}]_{p-1}\alpha & \textit{if } p < \text{norm}(X_i). \end{cases}$$

Some fundamental properties of this definition are summarized as follows.

Lemma 4.2

1. *For* $p \leq \text{norm}(\alpha)$, $\alpha \stackrel{a_1 a_2 \cdots a_p}{\longrightarrow} [\alpha]_p$ *in* p *norm-reducing steps.*
2. $[\alpha]_{\text{norm}(\alpha)} = \varepsilon$.
3. *For* $p \leq \text{norm}(\alpha)$ *and* $p + q \leq \text{norm}(\alpha\beta)$, $[[\alpha]_p\beta]_q = [\alpha\beta]_{p+q}$.
4. $\text{length}([\alpha]_p) \leq (j-1)(k-1) + \text{length}(\alpha)$, *where* j *is the maximum index of a nonterminal appearing in* α *(or* 1, *if* $\alpha = \varepsilon$*).*
   In particular, $\text{length}([X_i]_p) \leq (i-1)(k-1) + 1$
5. *Computing* $[\alpha]_p$ *takes at most* $(j-1)k + \text{length}(\alpha)$ *steps, where* j *is the maximum index of a nonterminal appearing in* α *(or* 1, *if* $\alpha = \varepsilon$*).*
   In particular, $[X_i]_p$ *takes at most* $(i-1)k + 1$ *steps to compute.*

Proof

1. By induction on p.
   Firstly, if $p = 0$ then the result is immediate.
   Otherwise let $\alpha = X_i\beta$.
   If $p \geq q = \text{norm}(X_i)$ then
   $$\alpha \stackrel{a_1 \cdots a_q}{\longrightarrow} \beta \stackrel{a_{q+1} \cdots a_p}{\longrightarrow} [\beta]_{p-q} = [\alpha]_p.$$
   If $p < \text{norm}(X_i)$ then
   $$\alpha \stackrel{a_1}{\longrightarrow} \alpha_{i1}\beta \stackrel{a_2 \cdots a_p}{\longrightarrow} [\alpha_{i1}\beta]_{p-1} = [\alpha]_p.$$
2. By induction on $\text{norm}(\alpha)$.
   If $\alpha = \varepsilon$ then the result is immediate.
   Otherwise let $\alpha = X_i\beta$.
   Then $[\alpha]_{\text{norm}(\alpha)} = [\beta]_{\text{norm}(\beta)} = \varepsilon$.

3. By induction on $\mathrm{norm}(\alpha\beta)$.

   Firstly, if $p = 0$ then the result is immediate.

   Otherwise let $\alpha = X_i\gamma$.

   If $p \geq \mathrm{norm}(X_i)$ then

$$[[\alpha]_p\beta]_q = [[\gamma]_{p-\mathrm{norm}(X_i)}\beta]_q = [\gamma\beta]_{p+q-\mathrm{norm}(X_i)} = [\alpha\beta]_{p+q}.$$

   If $p + q < \mathrm{norm}(X_i)$ then

$$[[\alpha]_p\beta]_q = [[\alpha_{i1}]_{p-1}\beta]_q = [\alpha_{i1}\beta]_{p+q-1} = [\alpha\beta]_{p+q}.$$

   If $p < \mathrm{norm}(X_i) \leq p + q$ then

$$\begin{aligned}[[\alpha]_p\beta]_q &= [[\alpha_{i1}]_{p-1}\gamma\beta]_q = [\alpha_{i1}\gamma\beta]_{p+q-1} \\ &= [[\alpha_{i1}]_{\mathrm{norm}(X_i)-1}\gamma\beta]_{p+q-\mathrm{norm}(X_i)} = [\gamma\beta]_{p+q-\mathrm{norm}(X_i)} = [\alpha\beta]_{p+q}.\end{aligned}$$

4. By induction on p.

   Firstly, if $p = 0$ then the result is immediate.

   Otherwise let $\alpha = X_i\beta$.

   If $p \geq \mathrm{norm}(X_i)$ then

$$\begin{aligned}\mathrm{length}([\alpha]_p) &= \mathrm{length}([\beta]_{p-\mathrm{norm}(X_i)}) \\ &\leq (j-1)(k-1) + \mathrm{length}(\alpha) - 1 \qquad \text{(by induction.)}\end{aligned}$$

   If $p < \mathrm{norm}(X_i)$ then

$$\begin{aligned}\mathrm{length}([\alpha]_p) &= \mathrm{length}([\alpha_{i1}]_{p-1}\beta) \\ &\leq (i-2)(k-1) + k + \mathrm{length}(\alpha) - 1 \qquad \text{(by induction)} \\ &\leq (j-1)(k-1) + \mathrm{length}(\alpha).\end{aligned}$$

5. By induction on p.

   Firstly, if $p = 0$ then the result is immediate.

   Otherwise let $\alpha = X_i\beta$.

   If $p \geq \mathrm{norm}(X_i)$ then computing $[\alpha]_p$ takes one more step than computing $[\beta]_{p-\mathrm{norm}(X_i)}$, which by induction takes at most $(j-1)k + (\mathrm{length}(\alpha) - 1)$ steps to compute, which gives us our result.

   If $p < \mathrm{norm}(X_i)$ then computing $[\alpha]_p$ takes one more than computing $[\alpha_{i1}]_{p-1}$, which, since α_{i1} is a sequence of at most k nonterminals with smaller norm — and hence indices — than X_i, by induction takes at most $(i-2)k + k$ steps to compute, which gives us our result.

□

Our basic algorithm for computing $\alpha \sim \beta$ then takes the following form.

relation $\mathcal{B}$, rather than recomputing it each time, and converge on the final relation in this fashion.

We can use the following definition to compute testpairs.

$$TP(\varepsilon, \varepsilon) \;=\; \emptyset;$$

$$TP(X_i\alpha, X_j\beta) \;=\; \begin{cases} \{\,(i,j)\,\} \cup TP\Big([X_i]_{\mathrm{norm}(X_j)}\alpha, \beta\Big) & \textit{if } i \geq j; \\ \{\,(j,i)\,\} \cup TP\Big(\alpha, [X_j]_{\mathrm{norm}(X_i)}\beta\Big) & \textit{if } i < j. \end{cases}$$

Note that we needn't retain any information apart from the indices of the related variables. Again, this computation is potentially exponential. However, our aim is to avoid needing to make it overly often.

The algorithm then is as follows.

0. Compute the required testpair sets:

   for $i \;=\; 1$ *to* m *do*

   for $j \;=\; i$ *to* m *do*

$$\begin{aligned} TS(j,i) = \Big\{ \{\, TP(\alpha_{jq},\ \alpha_{ip}[X_j]_{\mathrm{norm}(X_i)}) \;:\; a_{jq} = a_{ip},\ 1 \leq q \leq l_j \,\} \\ :\ 1 \leq p \leq l_i \Big\} \\ \cup \Big\{ \{\, TP(\alpha_{jq},\ \alpha_{ip}[X_j]_{\mathrm{norm}(X_i)}) \;:\; a_{jq} = a_{ip},\ 1 \leq p \leq l_i \,\} \\ :\ 1 \leq q \leq l_j \Big\} \end{aligned}$$

1. Initialize the base indices $\mathcal{I} = \mathcal{I}_0$:

$$\mathcal{I} \;=\; \Big\{\, (j,i) \;:\; 1 \leq i \leq j \leq m \,\Big\};$$

2. Iterate the refinement procedure:

   Unmatched $\;=\; \emptyset$;

   repeat

   $\mathcal{I} \;=\; \mathcal{I} \setminus$ *Unmatched*;

   Unmatched $\;=\; \emptyset$;

   for each $(j,i) \in \mathcal{I}$ *do*

   if $\forall\, T \in TS(j,i)\ \exists S \in T$ *such that* $S \setminus \mathcal{I} \;\neq\; \emptyset$

   then Unmatched $=$ *Unmatched* $\cup \Big\{\, (j,i) \,\Big\}$;

   until Unmatched $\;=\; \emptyset$;

3. Return $\alpha \equiv_{\mathcal{B}} \beta$, where $\mathcal{B} = \{\, (X_j, X_i[X_j]_{\mathrm{norm}(X_i)}) \;:\; (j,i) \in \mathcal{I} \,\}$.

The initial phase 0 computes all necessary testpairs that have to be computed by the algorithm. The set $TS(j,i)$ represents the condition under which we may have $X_j \equiv_{\mathcal{B}} X_i[X_j]_{\text{norm}(X_i)}$: each element T of $TS(j,i)$ represents different ways in which a particular transition of one can be matched by a transition of the other, so there must be one of these, that is some S in T, which contains only testpairs which are related by the base, so that $S \setminus \mathcal{I} = \emptyset$. This explains the iteration procedure in phase 2.

Notice that the sets $TS(j,i)$, containing only pairs of variable indices, are all small. Thus beyond the initial phase zero, the algorithm executes in polynomial time.

To further cut down on the work carried out in the initialization phase zero, we can further adopt some degree of *memoizing*. Instead of recursing through two processes by stepping forward an amount equal to the minimum of the norms of the leading variables, we can keep track of what testpoint states (X, α) where $\text{norm}(X) \geq \text{norm}(\alpha)$ we have met before, and step forward in the algorithm by $\text{norm}(\alpha)$ distance. Indeed we have failed to find any examples which yield an exponential number of steps using this final implementation scheme, which gives us confidence that the technique is of practical value.

5 Conclusions

We have presented a deterministic algorithm for deciding bisimilarity of normed context-free processes. This algorithm is an improvement on previously existing nondeterministic — and hence exponential — algorithms as its complexity is kept to a minimum, though it might still be exponential in its worst case. The running time is $O(n^4 v)$ where v is the norm of the processes being compared. However, we have attempted to avoid this worse case, and we suspect that our final algorithm, if not already polynomial, would stand up against any polynomial-time algorithm which might be proposed.

This problem has actually been demonstrated to be polynomial [7]. However, the bound demonstrated there is $O(n^{13})$, which makes for an impractical procedure. It is hoped that the techniques presented here may lead to better polynomial algorithms.

References

[1] J.C.M. Baeten, J.A. Bergstra and J.W. Klop. Decidability of bisimulation equivalence for processes generating context-free languages. In Proceedings of PARLE'87, J.W. de Bakker, A.J. Nijman and P.C. Treleaven (eds), *Lecture Notes in Computer Science* 259, pp93–114. Springer-Verlag, 1987.

[2] D. Caucal. Graphes canoniques des graphes algébriques. *Informatique Théorique et Applications (RAIRO)* 24(4), pp339–352, 1990.

[3] S. Christensen, H. Hüttel and C. Stirling. Bisimulation equivalence is decidable for all context-free processes. In Proceedings of CONCUR'92, W.R. Cleaveland (ed), *Lecture Notes in Computer Science* 630, pp138–147. Springer-Verlag, 1992.

[4] R.J. van Glabbeek. The linear time-branching time spectrum. In Proceedings of CONCUR'90, J. Baeten and J.W. Klop (eds), *Lecture Notes in Computer Science* 458, pp278–297. Springer-Verlag, 1990.

[5] J.F. Groote. A short proof of the decidability of bisimulation for normed BPA processes. *Information Processing Letters* 42, pp167–171, 1991.

[6] J.F. Groote and H. Hüttel. Undecidable equivalences for basic process algebra. *Information and Computation*, 1994.

[7] Y. Hirshfeld, M. Jerrum and F. Moller. A polynomial algorithm for deciding bisimilarity of normed context-free processes. Department of Computer Science Research Report ECS-LFCS-94-286. University of Edinburgh, 1994.

[8] J.E. Hopcroft and J.D. Ullman. **Introduction to Automata Theory, Languages, and Computation**. Addison Wesley, 1979.

[9] H. Hüttel and C. Stirling. Actions speak louder than words: proving bisimilarity for context-free processes. In Proceedings of LICS'91, IEEE Computer Society Press, pp376–386, 1991.

[10] D.T. Huynh and L. Tian. Deciding bisimilarity of normed context-free processes is in Σ_2^P. *Journal of Theoretical Computer Science* 123, pp183–197, 1994.

[11] R. Milner. **Communication and Concurrency**. Prentice Hall, 1989.

[12] R. Milner and F. Moller. Unique decomposition of processes. *Journal of Theoretical Computer Science* 107, pp357–363, 1993.

[13] D.M.R. Park. Concurrency and Automata on Infinite Sequences. *Lecture Notes in Computer Science* 104, pp168–183. Springer Verlag, 1981.

Model-Based Verification Methods and Tools (Abstract)

J. C. Fernandez
VERIMAG, France

J. Sifakis
VERIMAG, France

R. de Simone
INRIA, France

We describe established verification methods in the framework of communicating concurrent systems, focusing on model-based approaches implemented by existing tools for automatic verification.

Such tools can be sorted by several features: input description language, specification style for properties (temporal logic *vs* operational behaviour), type of interpretation (linear time *vs* branching time). In contrast, most share the same modeling into labeled transition systems. In addition to the techniques of model-checking (or satisfaction of a temporal logic formula by a model) and model comparison (by behavioural equivalence or behavioural inclusion), we also present several methods for model simplification (abstraction, quotient minimisation,...). In all cases we face the issues of algorithmic complexity, of expressivity, and also of clarity and simplicity of usage.

We end with an extensive description of the verification tools ALDEBARAN and AUTO developed in our groups, followed by a tentative hands-on session for the attendees.

New Results on the Analysis of Concurrent Systems with an Indefinite Number of Processes

Mahesh Girkar Robert Moll
Department Of Computer Science
University of Massachusetts
Amherst, MA 01003

Abstract

In this paper we extend some of the results presented by German and Sistla in [4]. Their framework for concurrent systems, at a certain level of abstraction, is suitable for modeling a number of resource-oriented problems in concurrency in which there is a unique control process (called the *synchronizer*) and an arbitrary number of identical user processes [13, 2]. Communication between processes is via synchronous actions in the style of Milner's Calculus of Communicating Systems [12]. In the first part of the paper, we consider certain "specialized" execution semantics instead of the "general" execution semantics considered in [4]. These semantics are aimed at "restricting" communications between processes that would otherwise be possible. Without such restrictions, it is not possible to model problems in which there is a need to distinguish processes based on either the current states of the user processes, or their indices, *etc.* In contrast to the work done in [4], we show that the reachability problem for each of the specialized execution semantics we consider is undecidable. As a consequence, both deadlock detection and the *Model Checking* problem for the synchronizer when reasoning with logics such as Linear temporal logic LTL [4], Linear Temporal Logic without the nexttime operator LTL/X [8], and Restricted Temporal Logic RTL [14] are also undecidable.

In the second part of the paper we consider the problem of detecting whether there are infinitely many model sizes k such that some execution of k user processes and the synchronizer deadlocks, assuming unrestricted execution semantics, and we show that this problem is decidable. This result extends a known result, namely, that detecting a single instance of deadlock in such a model, is decidable [4]. We say that models exhibit "strong stability" if and only if there are a "bounded" number of model sizes for which a potential deadlock exists, and thus we show that that detecting strong stability is decidable. We also consider a framework in which we allow an arbitrary number of synchronizers to participate in an execution, and show that strong stability is decidable in this case as well.

1 Introduction

Most formal models for concurrent systems provide a means for describing, and ultimately, detecting such phenomenon as deadlock, starvation and liveness. In a resource oriented model, for example, such as that presented in [13, 2], processes are entities executing operations which request and release resources. These resources are controlled by one or many finite state devices called synchronizers. In such a model, properties such as deadlock and liveness can be expressed naturally using temporal logic. In general, a proof that establishes such a property depends on the model having a fixed number of processes. Even when the number of processes increases in a "uniform" way, the task of proving that the model still possesses desirable properties must be performed all over again.

We adopt the framework described in [4], which can describe concurrency problems that fit within the realm of resource–oriented models and which can account for an increasing number of identical processes. This framework consists of a unique control process (*synchronizer*) and several identical user processes. Communication between processes is via synchronous actions in the style of Milner's Calculus of Communicating Systems [12]. The synchronizer states are annotated with subsets of atomic propositions that are true in that state. Linear Temporal Logic, LTL, is the smallest class of temporal formulas that can be constructed using these propositions, the standard boolean connectives, and the temporal operators X (nexttime), and U (until). Linear Temporal Logic without the nexttime operator, LTL/X, is LTL without X. RTL is even simpler — it contains only one temporal operator, $+$ (meaning "eventually"). Every RTL formula is also an LTL/X formula, and every LTL/X formula is an LTL formula. Given a temporal formula in any of these logics, and given an infinite sequence of subsets of atomic propositions, there is a well–defined semantics for defining when such a sequence is a "witness" for that formula. The *Model checking* problem is the problem of deciding if there is a $k > 0$, and an infinite execution of k user processes and the synchronizer, such that the sequence of subsets of atomic propositions that appear along the states of the synchronizer in this execution are a witness for the validity of the temporal formula.

German and Sistla [4] show that model checking when reasoning with LTL (and hence with LTL/X and RTL), and deadlock detection is decidable. However, in their framework, the execution semantics allows all transitions that can be made; *i.e.* there is no policy which is used to "filter" out transitions that may not be of interest. Reasoning about problems such as the *Gas–Station Customer* problem [2] and concurrency problems in which priority schemes can be assigned for transitions depending upon states of the processes are not easy to describe in this framework. In the Gas–Station Customer problem, user processes are *Customers* who queue to pump gas. The *Pump* is modeled as a synchronizer. Each customer pays money to an *Operator* (a second synchronizer), pumps gas, collects any left–over money from the *Operator*, and departs. The *Operator* and *Pump* exchange information to keep track of the customers being serviced; otherwise, we could encounter problems such as one customer collecting left–over money belonging to another one, etc. Thus, such problems require an indexing scheme to distinguish user processes. Other concurrency problems, such as a the *producer–consumer problem* in which "producing" has more priority than "consuming" need a different semantic.

One way to describe these semantics would be to use an indexed version of LTL, namely $ILTL$ [4]. $ILTL$ is a fairly powerful logic that can express a large number of complicated global properties regarding an execution, and hence can be used to describe these specialized execution semantics. But model checking when reasoning with $ILTL$ is undecidable [4]. To circumvent this problem, we considered an alternate approach. Instead of using $ILTL$, we check whether we can determine properties of interest for certain simple specialized execution semantics directly. The property that we consider is the *reachability criterion* — namely, is there a $k > 0$, such that some execution in a model of size k will cause the synchronizer to reach some given final state. We consider three simple execution semantics and show that this problem is undecidable for all three semantics. As a corollary, we obtain the following result:

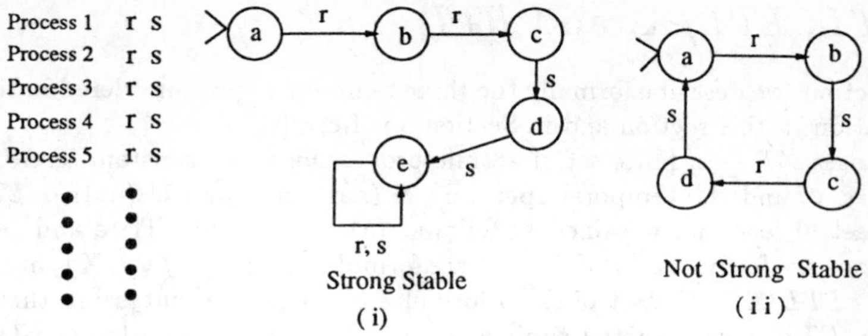

Figure 1: Strong Stability Examples

Deadlock detection, as well as Model Checking [4] with respect to logics such as LTL, LTL/X, and RTL, with these execution semantics is undecidable.

In the second part of the paper, we define the concept of strong stability for this framework. If a concurrent system exhibits strong stability, then there exists an effectively obtainable bound k such that model instances of size k or greater never deadlock. We show that for the general execution semantics considered by German and Sistla, strong stability is decidable. This generalizes the following result in [4]: detecting a single instance of deadlock is decidable.

To distinguish between a single instance of deadlock and strong stability, consider the following examples. In Figure 1, an arbitrary number of identical processes request resource "r" followed by resource "s". For these processes, we consider two different synchronizers. In (i), a potential deadlock exists with one process in the system (after executing request "r" for the first process, the synchronizer cannot satisfy the request for resource "s"); however two or more processes will never deadlock. For the synchronizer in (ii), deadlock exists if and only if there are an odd number of processes. Thus, the first model is strong stable, whereas the second is not. In both models, deadlock can be detected using the procedure outlined in [4]; but that procedure cannot be used directly to ascertain whether the model is strong stable.

Thus concurrent behavior when an infinite number of processes are present may result in phenomena such as deadlock occurring infinitely often. Strong stability is the concept we use to assess such behavior.

We also consider a setting where a potentially arbitrary number of synchronizers interact with an indefinite number of user processes. Such a framework would be useful to analyze problems such as the Gas–Station Customer Problem in which the number of pumps increases. As a designer of such concurrent systems, one would like to be assured that additional pumps will not cause deadlock. We show that if we do not restrict the execution semantics, then detecting strong stability is decidable for this case.

Other work related to our research is that of Kurshan [10], Kurshan and McMillan [11], Wolper and Lovinfosse [15], Clarke, Browne, and Grumberg [1], and Apt and Kozen [7].

2 *LTL*, *LTL*/X, and *RTL*

In this section, we describe formally the three temporal logics considered in this paper. The notation in this section and in Section 3 is from [4].

LTL uses $\mathcal{AP}$ — a finite set of atomic propositions, the constant **True**, the connectives $\neg$, $\vee$, and the temporal operators **X** (nexttime) and **U** (until). *LTL* is the smallest set of formulas obtained as follows: (a) the constant **True** and the atomic propositions are formulas; (b) if f and g are formulas, then $\neg f$, $f \vee g$, $\mathbf{X}f$, and $f\mathbf{U}g$ are formulas. *LTL*/**X** is the set of *LTL* formulas obtained without using the nexttime operator. *RTL* is constructed similarly, except it has only one temporal operator, namely + (or "eventually"). Thus, if f and g are *RTL* formulas, then $\neg f$, $f \vee g$, and $+f$ are also *RTL* formulae. Any *RTL* formula can be expressed in *LTL*/**X**, since the eventually operator is a weaker form of the until operator ($+f \equiv \mathbf{True}\mathbf{U}f$).

An *interpretation* is a pair (t, i) where $t = t_0, t_1, \ldots$ is a finite or infinite sequence of subsets of $\mathcal{AP}$ and i is a nonnegative integer. $(t, i) \models f$ is used to denote that the interpretation satisfies a formula f. $\models$ is defined inductively as follows for temporal formulas as follows (Items 1,2,3 and 4 refer to all the three logics, 5 refers to *LTL* and *LTL*/*X*, and 6 refers *RTL*):

1. $(t, i) \models \mathbf{True}$
2. $(t, i) \models A$, where $A \in \mathcal{AP}$, *iff* $A \in t_i$.
3. $(t, i) \models \neg f$ *iff* $(t, i) \not\models f$.
4. $(t, i) \models f \vee g$ *iff* $(t, i) \models f$ or $(t, i) \models g$.
5. $(t, i) \models \mathbf{X}f$ *iff* $(t, i+1) \models f$.
6. $(t, i) \models (f\mathbf{U}g)$ *iff* there exists $k \geq i$ such that $(t, k) \models g$, and for all $j, i \leq j < k, (t, j) \models f$.
7. $(t, i) \models (+f)$ *iff* there exists $k \geq 0$ such that $(t, k) \models f$.

Finally, we say that $t \models f$ *iff* $(t, 0) \models f$. In words, if $t \models f$, we say that the temporal formula f is *valid* for the sequence of subsets of atomic propositions that appear in t. We use the words "sequence of subsets of atomic propositions" and "interpretation" interchangeably.

3 The Concurrency Model

Our model for concurrency consists of a unique *synchronizer* process and many identical *user* processes [4]. We first describe the alphabet used by the processes to interact with each other. Intuitively, the alphabet provides a mechanism for synchronization between two processes. It is thus useful to model operations which request/release a resource. A communication alphabet $\sum$ is a union of mutually disjoint sets $\sum^+, \sum^-$, and ϵ. ϵ is used to represent internal process transitions. $\sum^+(\sum^-)$ is the set of action (complements of the action) symbols. Thus, if $c \in \sum^+$, then its complement $\overline{c} \in \sum^-$. Each member of $\sum$ is a communication symbol.

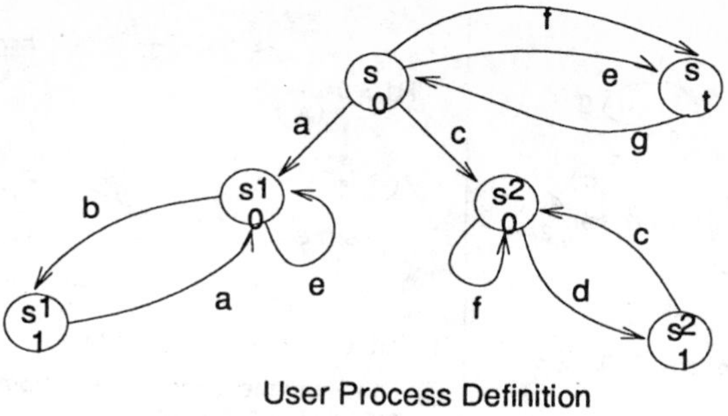

Figure 3: User process definition for Transformation τ_2

synchronizer is reachable in an execution for some $(P^k, \mathcal{S}), k > 0$, using execution semantic $\mathcal{E}_2$.

The process definition in Figure 3 tracks the register values of the counter machine in the following way: Every increment of a register value, say register $R1$, such that the new value is encountered for the first time in a sequence of transitions in the counter machine, brings a "new" indexed user process to state s_0^1. Such a process can never go back to state s_0, and hence can participate only in keeping track of the value in register $R1$. Thus, a process in state s_0 has necessarily a larger index than a process in any of the states $s_0^1, s_1^1, s_0^2, s_1^2$.

It is now straightforward to prove the following theorem:

Theorem 4 *Let M be any counter machine and let $(P, \mathcal{S}) = \tau_2(M)$. Then, there is a path in M which reaches s_f if and only if state s_f is reachable in an execution for some $(P^k, \mathcal{S}), k > 0$ using execution semantic $\mathcal{E}_2$. Hence the reachability problem with execution semantic $\mathcal{E}_2$ is undecidable.*

6 Assigning Priorities to Communication Symbols

Let T be any total ordering on the set of communication symbols in Σ^+. According to execution semantic $\mathcal{E}_3$, when the synchronizer is in a state s, it always communicates using the highest priority communication symbol (as given by T), provided there is some user process which has a complementary symbol for this communication; otherwise, it tries to communicate using the second highest priority communication symbol, and so on.

Again, determining reachability of a certain state in the synchronizer with semantic $\mathcal{E}_3$ is undecidable. For this, we assume that our counter machine is "deterministic". Every such counter machine has the following property: there are at most two transitions out of every state of the counter machine; in this case, these two transitions are labeled by mutually exclusive conditions $R1 = 0$ and $R1 > 0$, or by mutually exclusive conditions $R2 = 0$ and $R2 > 0$; (if there is only one edge out of a state which is labeled by one of these conditions, we can always add the other mutually exclusive condition out of this state which leads to a new state s_{new} such that there are no edges directed out of s_{new}; clearly, this does not affect the set of paths in the

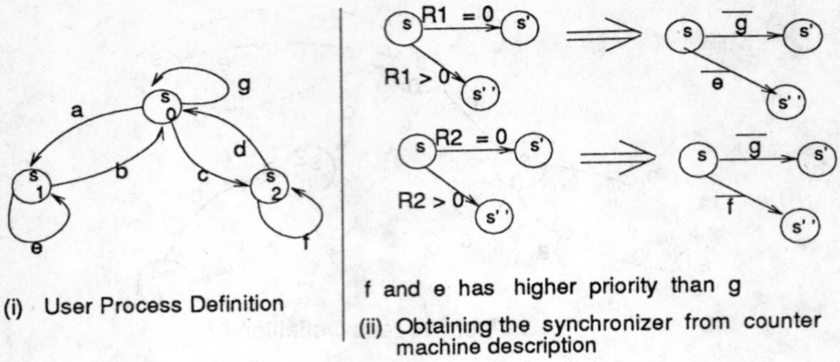

Figure 4: Counter Machine to Concurrent System — Transformation τ_3

counter machine that lead to a designated final state of interest). We also assume that there are no ϵ transitions.

Using transformations which simulate deterministic turing machines by deterministic 4–counter machines, and deterministic 4–counter machines by deterministic 2–counter machines, it is undecidable for an arbitrary deterministic 2–counter machine whether a certain designated state is reachable [6]. We now give transformation τ_3 from an arbitrary deterministic 2–counter machine M to a concurrent system, which will prove that the reachability problem in concurrent systems with execution semantic $\mathcal{E}_3$ is undecidable.

The user process definition corresponding to M is shown in Figure 4(i). The synchronizer construction is similar to that in τ_1 except for states that have 2 edges labeled with mutually exclusive conditions. In this case, the transformation is as shown in Figure 4(ii).

Consider any total priority scheme for communication symbols $\{a, b, c, d, e, f, g\}$ which gives e and f higher priority than g (the other symbols can be in any order). Note that out of every state of the synchronizer, there are at most two outgoing edges; if there is only one edge out of a state of the synchronizer, it is labeled by either $\overline{a}, \overline{b}, \overline{c}, \overline{d}$. If there are two edges out of a state, then they are labeled either $\overline{e}$ or $\overline{g}$, or $\overline{f}$ or $\overline{g}$. Since the priorities of e and f are higher than g, clearly, the transition $s \xrightarrow{\overline{g}} s'$ is made in the synchronizer instead of $s \xrightarrow{\overline{e}} s'$ if and only if there is no user process is in state s_1. A similar results holds for making a transition $s \xrightarrow{\overline{g}} s'$ instead of $s \xrightarrow{\overline{f}} s'$. With these observations, it is easy to prove the following theorem:

Theorem 5 *There is a path in the counter machine M which reaches state s_f if and only if there is a $k > 0$, and a concurrent execution that respects $\mathcal{E}_3$ in system $(P^k, \mathcal{S})$, where P and $\mathcal{S}$ are constructed using τ_3, which reaches state s_f. Hence, the reachability problem with execution semantic $\mathcal{E}_3$ is undecidable.*

7 Deadlock and Model Checking with $\mathcal{E}_1$, $\mathcal{E}_2$ and $\mathcal{E}_3$

We now show that the problem of determining reachability in a synchronizer can be reduced to determining if there is a deadlock (a finite execution which cannot be extended) or determining if a temporal formula holds for some concurrent execution (model checking). Since the reachability problem is undecidable under the execution semantics $\mathcal{E}_1$, $\mathcal{E}_2$ and $\mathcal{E}_3$, it follows that detecting deadlock or checking the model for the validity of a temporal formula are also undecidable.

We assume that the user processes are such that (a) two user processes cannot communicate, and (b) user processes do not have edges labeled ϵ. From the results for the specialized execution semantics discussed earlier, the reachability problem in the synchronizer with such user processes is undecidable.

First consider the case when there is one synchronizer and arbitrary number of user processes under the execution semantics $\mathcal{E}_1$, $\mathcal{E}_2$ and $\mathcal{E}_3$. To reduce the reachability problem to deadlock detection, consider having epsilon labeled self loops for every state of the synchronizer except the state s_f, which we need to check for reachability. Also, eliminate any edges out of s_f. Clearly, in this case, a system will deadlock if and only if s_f is reachable.

To reduce the reachability problem to model checking, consider a labeling which labels all states except s_f by atomic proposition R and labels s_f by atomic proposition J. The temporal formula $+J$ asserts that "eventually", J holds, and can be expressed in LTL, LTL/X and RTL. We can augment the above construction so that if there is an execution that reaches s_f, then that execution can always be made infinite by adding a self loop around s_f which is labeled by ϵ. Clearly, this formula holds in the above concurrent system if and only if in the counter machine M there is a path which reaches state s_f. Using these observations, and the previously proved theorems, we get the following theorem:

Theorem 6 *Given an arbitrary concurrent system $(P, \mathcal{S})$ the reachability problem, deadlock detection problem, and the model checking problem for formulas in LTL, LTL/X and RTL are undecidable if one adopts execution semantics $\mathcal{E}_1$, $\mathcal{E}_2$, or $\mathcal{E}_3$.*

8 Strong Stability

In this section, we assume that concurrent systems $(P, \mathcal{S})$ respect the generalized execution semantics. The problem of detecting whether there is any instance of deadlock in a concurrent system of the form $(P, \mathcal{S})$ is decidable [4]. We now consider the following generalization of this problem: Are there infinitely many model sizes k, such that some concurrent execution of $(P^k, \mathcal{S})$ deadlocks? Such an analysis is useful as it differentiates concurrent systems in which there are infinite model sizes that deadlock (infinitely many failures) from those that have only finitely many model sizes that deadlock (a bounded number of failures). We also consider this same problem in a scenario where we allow arbitrary number of synchronizers to participate in an execution.

Definition 1 *If there are only finitely many k's such that $(P^k, \mathcal{S})$ has a deadlock configuration, then $(P, \mathcal{S})$ is* strong stable.

Theorem 7 *Strong Stability is decidable.*

We sketch the proof of Theorem 7. We assume that there are no self-loops in either the user process or the synchronizer. If so, we do the following transformation:

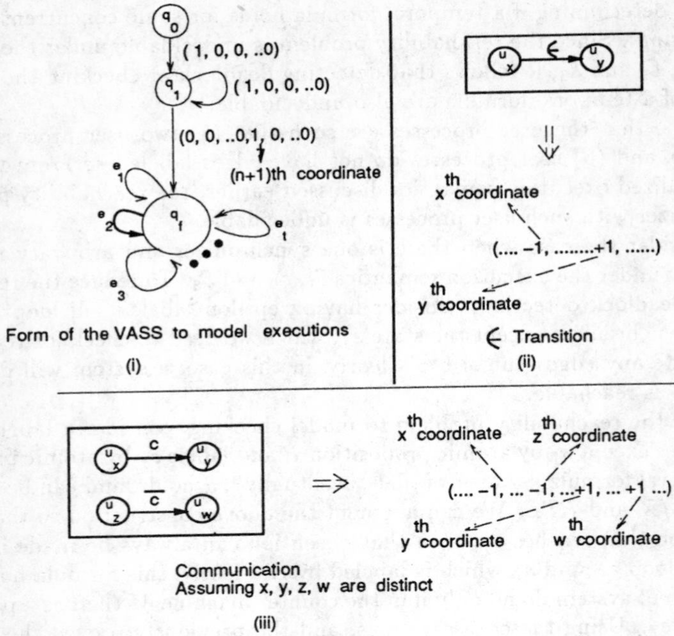

Figure 5: Vass Construction

(i) if $s \xrightarrow{\epsilon} s$ then, we remove this loop; and (ii) if $s \xrightarrow{c} s$ where c is a communication symbol, then we replace this self-loop by a sequence of two edges $s \xrightarrow{c} s_{new} \xrightarrow{\epsilon} s$, where s_{new} is a new state. Clearly, there is a deadlock in $(P^k, \mathcal{S})$ if and only if there is a deadlock in $(P'^k, \mathcal{S}')$, where P' and $\mathcal{S}'$ are obtained using the above rules.

We build a VASS [9] (Vector Addition System with States) which "mimics" concurrent executions that arise in $(P, \mathcal{S})$.

We first define a VASS formally. A VASS is a finite state automaton in which labels on each arcs are n-tuples of integers. A configuration of the VASS is an ordered pair (q, v) where q in a state and v is a point in Z^n. Starting with an initial configuration (q, x), a path from q in the automaton induces a sequence of configurations. A new vector is obtained from the previous configuration by a component-wise vector addition of the label on the arc "traveled" and the vector in the previous configuration. A configuration (q', y) is r-reachable from (q, x) *iff* there is a path from the initial configuration (q, x) to (q', y) (denoted by $(q', y) \in r(q, x)$). Such a path is an r-path from (q, x) to (q', y). A configuration (q', y) is R-reachable from (q, x), *iff* there is a path from (q, x) to (q', y) such that all vectors along the path (including x and y) are non-negative in all components (denoted by $(q', y) \in R(q, x)$). Such a path is an R-path from (q, x) to (q', y). The *Reachability Problem* for VASSes is the problem of deciding, for an arbitrary q, q', x and y, if $(q', y) \in R(q, x)$. This problem is decidable [9].

A VASS is constructed from a concurrent system as follows (see Figure 5):

First, suppose the user process description has states $u_1, u_2, \ldots, u_n$ and the synchronizer description has states $s_1, s_2, \ldots, s_m$. Assume that u_1 is the start state of the user processes, and s_1 is the start state of the synchronizer. (If there are more than one start states in either the user process description or the synchronizer description, we can always add a new start state and edges from this new start state to the original start states labeled by ϵ. This does not affect the analysis to be presented.)

The VASS for this concurrent system has $n + m$ dimensions. The first n coordinates keep track of the number of user processes in states $u_1, u_2, \ldots u_n$; the last m coordinates keep track of the states of the synchronizer (Note: we can do without these last m coordinates. However, it becomes easier to modify this description when we deal with an arbitrary number of synchronizers participating in an execution).

The states and edges of the VASS are as shown in Figure 5(i). There is an initial start state q_0. The transition from q_0 to q_1 "prepares" at least one user process to execute with the synchronizer. This edge is labeled with the vector that has +1 in the first coordinate (representing start state u_1) and zero in all other coordinates.

To prepare an arbitrary number of user processes, we add a self–loop for state q_1 that is labeled with the same vector as the one from q_0 to q_1.

From q_1, we jump nondeterministically to state q_f with a vector that is 0 in all coordinates except the $(n+1)$th coordinate (the $(n+1)$th coordinate represents start state s_1 of the synchronizer). This vector prepares the synchronizer for execution.

Finally, there are several self–loops around q_f. Each self–loop is labeled by vectors that represent either (a) an internal transition of either a user process or the synchronizer process; or (b) a communication between processes (two user processes or a user process and the synchronizer).

Figure 5(ii) shows how an internal transition of a user process can be represented. If this transition is from state u_x to u_y $(1 \leq x, y \leq n)$, then the vector has a -1 in the xth coordinate, +1 in the yth coordinate, and zero in all other coordinates. The -1 acts as a guard, checking whether there is any user process in state u_x; if so, then, provided an internal transition from u_x to u_y occurs, this transition is simulated by decreasing the number of user processes in state u_x by 1 and increasing the number of user processes in state u_y by 1. Figure 5(iii) shows how to represent a communication between a user process in state u_x and another in state u_z. After communicating, the process in state u_x moves to state u_y, and the process in state u_z moves to u_w. The vector for such a communication (provided x, y, z, and w are distinct) has -1 in the xth and zth coordinate,+1 in the yth and wth coordinate, and zero in all other coordinates. For the special case $x = z$ and $y \neq w$, the vector has -2 in the xth coordinate, +1 in the yth and wth coordinate, and zero in all other coordinates. Other special cases can be handled similarly. Internal transitions of the synchronizer, and a communication between the synchronizer and a user process are also handled similarly, except now we use the last m coordinates as well as the first n coordinates in forming the required vector.

It is easy to prove that R–paths in the VASS correspond to concurrent executions of $(P, \mathcal{S})$. Also, by construction, deadlock occurs in the system if and only we reach a configuration of the form (q_f, v), where the vector v is such that vector addition of v with any vector on any self–loop around q_f makes one of the coordinates negative. Coordinates of such a vector satisfies a certain condition. This condition states precisely that the global state reached with this execution is such that no process can do an ϵ transition, nor can they communicate with each other via some complementary pair of communication symbols.

For example, suppose there is an edge labeled ϵ out of state $u_i, 1 \leq i \leq n$. If a concurrent execution of $(P^k, \mathcal{S})$ is such that there is at least one user process in state u_i in the final global state, then, clearly, this execution can be extended (it has not deadlocked). In this case, the R–path corresponding to this execution will be such that the final vector v along this path will have its ith coordinate (recall that this coordinate counts the number of user processes in state u_i) greater than zero. A similar condition on the coordinates of the final vector can be obtained if the concurrent execution can be extended by a communication. For each state in either the user process or the synchronizer process in which a process can do an ϵ–transition, and, for each pair of states in which the two processes in these states can communicate, we can obtain conditions of this form which state that a concurrent execution can be extended.

Let C be the disjunct of these conditions. Then, $\neg C$, gives us the precise condition that states that a concurrent execution has deadlocked. Condition $\neg C$ can be expressed by using boolean operators $\vee$ and $\wedge$ over *atomic conditions* of the form $v[i] = 1$, $v[i] > 0$, and $v[i] = 0$, where $v[i]$ refers to the ith coordinate of v, and is called a *positive* condition in [4].

German and Sistla [4] show that in a VASS, starting with a certain initial configuration, it is decidable whether a certain state can be reached with a vector that satisfies any condition of this form. This proves that the deadlock detection problem in these systems is decidable. However, this result does not readily extend to strong stability. To prove the decidability of strong stability, we need to prove that the problem stated in Theorem 8 is decidable. The proof follows by adapting Kosaraju's proof for decidability of the reachability problem in a VASS [9] to the problem of detecting whether there are infinitely many vectors satisfying a given positive condition that can be reached by R–paths from a given initial configuration. A detailed proof can be found in [5].

Theorem 8 *Let V be a VASS and p any positive condition. It is decidable whether there are infinitely many configurations (q_f, v_f) for a state q_f such that (q_f, v_f) is R–reachable from initial configuration (q_0, v_0), and v_f satisfies condition p.*

Since deadlock can be expressed by a positive condition, by construction, if there are infinitely many vectors satisfying this condition that reach state q_f in the VASS, then there are infinitely many sizes of the system that deadlock. Thus, using Theorem 8, we get the result stated in Theorem 7.

We now consider the case where we allow an arbitrary number of identical synchronizers to participate in an execution. Such an analysis is useful from a theoretical point of view as indicated by problems such as the Gas–Station Customer problem with an increasing number of pumps. Even though a "real" instance of this problem cannot be modeled using a "generalized" execution semantics, a liberal version of this problem could be modeled by the machinery developed so far. A designer of such a liberal version would want to check if there are infinitely many instances of deadlock situations with increasing number of synchronizers. We show that strong stability is decidable in this setting. First, it is easy to modify the construction above to account for this fact. In this case, the VASS will have self loops around state q_0 and q_f to account for more than one synchronizer. For such a VASS, we say the system is strong stable if and only if there are infinitely many system sizes k such that, for some $j > 0$, there is an execution of j user processes and k synchronizers that deadlocks. Note that now we need infinitely many configurations arising out of the last m coordinates, which represent the number of synchronizers in each of the m synchronizer states. It is easy to modify the proof of Theorem 8 to reflect this fact. We thus get the following theorem:

Theorem 9 *Strong Stability is decidable for the case where we allow arbitrary number of synchronizers.*

9 Conclusion

We have shown that certain specialized execution semantics which restrict the class of legal concurrent executions, make the problem of detecting deadlock and model checking undecidable. These execution semantics are aimed as restricting transition sequences that are otherwise possible. We have formulated questions regarding strong stability for a very basic concurrency model in which a synchronizer controls resources and processes request resources from the synchronizers. We have shown for our model that strong stability is decidable. The proof follows from the fact that infinite R–reachability, suitably formulated, is decidable for VASSes.

There are several problems, such as the *Dining–Philosopher* problem, in which all processes are identical and there is no synchronizer process. Moreover, a process can communicate with other processes that are within a finite "distance" away from it. For example, in the Dining–Philosophers problem, a philosopher can communicate only with philosophers on his left and right — a distance of one away. This setting is different from a similar setting analyzed by German and Sistla [4]. In their setting, all processes are identical, but a process can communicate with all other processes. Assuming such communications, German and Sistla show that the problem of model checking is decidable, and, given a temporal formula, it can be validated in time polynomial in the size of the process description and the size of the formula. In a forthcoming paper, we show that, as with the choice of protocols $\mathcal{E}_1, \mathcal{E}_2$, and $\mathcal{E}_3$ presented here, the bounded distance communication protocol also makes reachability undecidable.

References

[1] Browne M. C., Clarke E. M., and Grumberg O. Reasoning About Networks With Many Identical Finite State Processes. *Information and Computation*, 81:13–31, August 1986.

[2] Buy U., and Moll R. Liveness Analysis and the Automatic Generation of Concurrent Programs. *Proceedings of the DIMACS Workshop on Computer–Aided Verification*, pages 535–550, 1990.

[3] German S., and Sistla A. P. Reasoning With Many Processes. *Proc. Symp. on Logic in Computer Science*, pages 138–152, June 1987.

[4] German S., and Sistla A. P. Reasoning About Systems With Many Processes. *JACM*, 39(3):675–735, July 1992.

[5] Girkar M. *New Results in the Analysis of Concurrent Systems.* Phd. Thesis, University of Massachussetts, Amherst, 1994.

[6] Hopcroft J. E., and Ullman J. D. *Introduction to Automata Theory, Languages, and Computation.* Addison–Welsey Publishing Company, 1979.

[7] Apt K., and Kozen D. Limits to Automatic Program Verification. *Information Processing Letters*, 22:307–309, May 1986.

[8] Kaivola R., and Valmari A. The Weakest Compositional Semantic Equivalence Preserving Nexttime–less Linear Temporal Logic. *CONCUR*, pages 207–221, 1992.

[9] Kosaraju S. R. Decidability Of Reachability In Vector Addition Systems. *Proceedings of the 16th ACM Symposium on Theory of Computing*, pages 267–281, 1982.

[10] Kurshan R. P. Modelling Concurrent Programs. *Proceedings of Symposium in Applied Mathematics*, 31:45–57, 1985.

[11] Kurshan R. P., and McMillan K. A Structural Induction Theorem For Processes. *Proc. Symp. on Eigth ACM Symposium on Principles of Distributed Computing*, pages 239–247, August 1989.

[12] Milner R. A Calculus Of Communication Systems. *LNCS 92*, 1980.

[13] Ramamritham K. Synthesizing Code For Resource Controllers. *IEEE Transactions on Software Engg*, 11(8):774–783, August 1985.

[14] Sistla A. P., and Zuck L. D. Reasoning in a Restricted Temporal Logic. *Information and Computation*, 102(2):167–195, February 1993.

[15] Wolper P., and Lovinfosse V. Verifying Properties Of Large Sets Of Processes With Network Invariants. *Intl. Workshop on Automatic Verification Methods for Finite State Systems*, pages 69–80, June 1989.

Verification of Nonregular Temporal Properties for Context-Free Processes*

Ahmed Bouajjani** † Rachid Echahed*** † Riadh Robbana** †

Abstract. We address the problem of the specification and the verification of processes with infinite-state spaces. Many relevant properties for such processes involve constraints on numbers of occurrences of events (truth of propositions). These properties are nonregular and hence, they are not expressible neither in the usual logics of processes nor by finite-state ω-automata. We propose a logic called PCTL that allows the description of such properties. PCTL is a combination of the branching-time temporal logic CTL with Presburger arithmetic. Mainly, we study the decidability of the satisfaction relation between *context-free processes* and PCTL formulas. We show that this relation is decidable for a large fragment of PCTL. Furthermore, we study the satisfiability problem for PCTL. We show that this problem is highly undecidable (Σ_1^1-complete), even for the fragment where the satisfaction relation is decidable, and exhibit a nontrivial fragment where the satisfiability problem is decidable.

1 Introduction

The logical framework for the specification and verification of processes has been extensively developed during the last decade. Logics of processes, including temporal logics [Pnu77, GPSS80, Wol83, CES83, EH83], dynamic logics [FL79, Str82] and fixpoint calculi [Pra81, Koz83, Var88], have been proposed as specification formalisms. Important efforts have been devoted to the study of the expressiveness of these logics as well as their decision problems. There are two decision problems concerning logics of processes that are addressed in these works. The first one is the *satisfaction problem* which consists in deciding whether some given process, modeled by a Kripke structure, satisfies some given specification expressed by a formula. The second one is the *satisfiability problem* which consists in deciding whether some given formula is satisfiable, i.e., there exists some Kripke structure that satisfies the considered formula.

The majority of the works done in this area consider propositional logics that express *regular* properties of processes, i.e., properties that correspond to sets of infinite sequences or trees (according to the underlying semantics of the logic) that are definable by finite-state ω-automata [Buc62, Rab69]. Several works have established the links between logics of processes and finite-state automata [Str82, SE84, VW86, Tho87, Niw88, Var88]. These works show in particular that the *regular* logics of processes are expressive enough for the specification of *finite-state* processes (modeled by finite-state Kripke structures). Moreover, the decidability of the satisfiability problem for these logics has been shown

* Partially supported by the ESPRIT-BRA project REACT.
** VERIMAG-SPECTRE, Miniparc-Zirst, Rue Lavoisier, 38330 Montbonnot St-Martin, France.
*** LGI-IMAG, BP53, 38041 Grenoble cedex, France.
† Ahmed.Bouajjani@imag.fr, Rachid.Echahed@imag.fr, Riadh.Robbana@imag.fr

[GPSS80], [Wol83], [Str82], [SE84], and their satisfaction problem has been widely investigated in the case of finite-state processes, leading to automatic verification techniques as model-checking [QS82], [CES83], [VW86], [EL86].

Recently, intensive investigations have been consecrated to the extension of the specification and verification methods successfully used for finite-state processes, in order to deal with processes having infinite state spaces. One of the most important directions of these investigations concerns processes that generate *context-free* sets of computation sequences [BBK87]. Important results have been obtained concerning the comparison between these processes w.r.t. behavioural equivalences [BBK87, GH91, CHS92]. Mainly, it has been shown that bisimulation equivalence is decidable for all context-free processes [CHS92]. However, very few results have been obtained concerning the extension of the logical framework to the specification and verification of context-free processes. As far as we know, the existing results in this topic concern the extension of the model-checking technique of the μ-calculus to context-free processes [BS92]. So, this work, even it is a nice and interesting extension of the existing verification methods, it allows unfortunatly to verify only the regular properties of context-free processes whereas a wide class of the relevant properties of such processes are nonregular. For instance, in the specification of a communication protocol, we may require that

1. *between the beginning and the ending of every session, there are exactly the same numbers of requests and acknowledgements.*
2. *during every session, the number of acknowledgements never exceeds the number of requests.*

Actually, as these examples show, significant properties of context-free processes are essentially temporal properties involving constraints on *numbers of occurrences* of some events (or numbers of states satisfying some state property). For this reason, we propose in this paper a new temporal logic that allows to express such properties. This logic, called PCTL (for Presburger Computation Tree Logic) is a combination of Presburger arithmetic with the branching-time temporal logic CTL [CES83]. In PCTL, we dispose of *occurrence variables* that can be associated with state formulas and then used to express constraints on the number of occurrences of states satisfying these formulas. The constraints are expressed in the language of Presburger arithmetic. For instance, in the formula $[x : \pi].\varphi$, we associate the state formula π with the variable x. Then, x counts the number of occurrences of π along each computation sequence starting from the current state. Using this notation, the properties informally described above can be expressed in PCTL by:

1. $\forall\Box\,(\text{BEGIN} \Rightarrow [x, y : \text{REQ}, \text{ACK}].\ \forall\Box\,(\text{END} \Rightarrow (x = y)))$
2. $\forall\Box\,(\text{BEGIN} \Rightarrow [x, y : \text{REQ}, \text{ACK}].\ (x \geq y)\forall\mathcal{U}\text{END})$

Then, it can be observed that PCTL allows to characterize a large class of nonregular languages. These languages can be context-free as in the examples above, but also non context-free (context-sensitive). The existing logics that can express nonregular properties are extensions of the propositional dynamic logic with nonregular programs [HPS83]. However, concerning these logics, the works that have been done address only the satisfiability problem and never consider the satisfaction problem nor the verification topic. Moreover, most of the presented results for these logics are negative (high undecidability results) [HPS83, HP84] and the positive ones are somewhat restrictive [KP83, HR90].

Our aim in this paper is to present a study of the two decision problems concerning PCTL: mainly, its satisfaction problem for context-free processes in order to provide an automatic verification method for these processes, and also its satisfiability (and dually validity) problem.

First, we show that the satisfaction problem is undecidable for the full PCTL and even non recursively enumerable. Actually, this undecidability result is not due to the fact that we are dealing with context-free processes but rather to the expressive power of PCTL. However, we show that surprisingly, by a slight syntactic restriction, we get a fragment of PCTL where the satisfaction problem for context-free processes becomes decidable. This fragment, called PCTL$^+$, contains the most significant nonregular PCTL properties, as for instance the properties (1) and (2) given above. Our decision procedure is based on a reduction of the satisfaction problem, given a context-free process and a PCTL$^+$ formula, to the validity problem of Presburger formulas. At our knowledge, this is the first result that allows to verify automatically nonregular properties for context-free processes.

On the other hand, we show that the satisfiability problem for PCTL and even for PCTL$^+$ is highly undecidable, more precisely Σ_1^1-complete, and then, the validity problem for these logics is Π_1^1-complete. Nevertheless, we exhibit a nontrivial fragment of PCTL$^+$, containing for instance the properties (1) and (2) above, where the validity problem is decidable.

The remainder of this paper is organized as follows: In Section 2, we recall some basic definitions and results and introduce some notations. In Section 3 we define the context-free processes. The logic PCTL is defined in Section 4. The satisfaction problem for PCTL and the fragment PCTL$^+$ is considered in Section 5, and Section 6 is dedicated to the satisfiability problem for PCTL and its fragments. Finally, concluding remarks are given in Section 7. For lack of space, all the proofs are omitted here and given in the full paper.

2 Preliminaries

We recall in this section some well-known notions that are necessary for the understanding of the paper and introduce some notations.

2.1 Presburger arithmetic

Presburger arithmetic is the first order logic of integers with addition, subtraction and the usual ordering. Let us recall briefly the definition of this logic.

Let $\mathcal{V}$ be a set of variables. We use $x, y, \ldots$ to range over variables in $\mathcal{V}$. Consider the set of terms defined by

$$t ::= 0 \mid 1 \mid x \mid t - t \mid t + t$$

Integer constants ($k \in \mathbb{Z}$) and multiplication by constants (kt) can be introduced as abbreviations. The set of Presburger formulas is defined by

$$f ::= t \leq t \mid \neg f \mid f \vee f \mid \exists x.\ f$$

Classical abbreviations can be used as the boolean connectives as conjunction ($\wedge$), implication ($\Rightarrow$) and equivalence ($\Leftrightarrow$) as well as the universal quantification ($\forall$). The semantics of these formulas is defined in the standard way. Given a formula f with free variables $x_1, \ldots, x_n$, and a valuation $E : \mathcal{V} \rightarrow \mathbb{Z}$, we denote by $||f||(E)$ the truth value of f for the valuation E. We say that a formula is satisfiable if there exists some valuation E such that $||f||(E)$ is true. It is well known that the satisfiability problem for Presburger formulas is decidable (e.g., see [BJ74] for a decision procedure).

2.2 Sequences, languages and grammars

Let Σ be a finite alphabet. We denote by Σ^* (resp. Σ^ω) the set of finite (resp. infinite) sequences over Σ. Let $\Sigma^\infty = \Sigma^* \cup \Sigma^\omega$.

Given a sequence $\sigma \in \Sigma^\infty$, $|\sigma| \in \{0, 1, \ldots, \omega\}$ denotes the length of σ. Let ϵ denotes the empty sequence, i.e., the sequence of length 0. Let $\Sigma^+ = \Sigma - \{\epsilon\}$. For every $a \in \Sigma$, $|\sigma|_a$ is the number of occurrences of a in σ. In the sequel, we write $a \in \sigma$ to denote the fact that a appears in the sequence σ. For every $i \in \mathbb{N}$ such that $i \leq |\sigma|$, $\sigma(i)$ is the ith element of σ.

A context-free grammar (CFG) over Σ in Greibach normal form (GNF) is a tuple $G = (\Sigma, N, \mathit{Prod}, Z)$ where N is a set of nonterminals, *Prod* is a set of productions of the form $A \rightarrow a \cdot \alpha$ where $a \in \Sigma$ and $\alpha \in N^*$, and Z is the starting symbol. Elements of Σ are sometimes called terminal symbols. Given a production $p \in \mathit{Prod}$, we denote by $\mathit{lhs}(p)$ the left hand side of p and by $\mathit{rhs}(p)$ its right hand side. We adopt standard notations for the derivation relation ($\Longrightarrow$) and its reflexive-transitive closure ($\stackrel{*}{\Longrightarrow}$). We use subscripts to indicate if necessary the set of productions or the sequences of productions used in the derivation. We denote by $L(G)$ the language generated by the grammar G (i.e., the set of sequences $\sigma \in \Sigma^*$ such that $Z \stackrel{*}{\Longrightarrow} \sigma$). For more details concerning the theory of formal languages, see for instance [Har78].

2.3 Kripke strutures

A Kripke structure over the alphabet Σ (KS for short) is a tuple $K = (\Sigma, S, \Pi, R)$ where S is a countable set of states, $\Pi : S \rightarrow \Sigma$ is a labelling function and $R \subseteq S \times S$ is a transition relation.

We write $s \rightarrow_R s'$ to denote the fact that $(s, s') \in R$. We write $s \not\rightarrow_R$ when there is no state s' such that $(s, s') \in R$. An *infinite computation sequence* of K from a state s is a sequence $s_1 s_2 \cdots$ such that $s = s_1$ and $\forall i \geq 1.\ s_i \rightarrow_R s_{i+1}$. A *finite computation sequence* of K starting from s is a sequence $s_1 \cdots s_n$ such that $s = s_1$, $\forall i.\ 1 \leq i < n.\ s_i \rightarrow_R s_{i+1}$, and $s_n \not\rightarrow_R$. We denote by $\mathcal{C}(K, s)$ the set of finite and infinite computation sequences of K starting from s. We say that K is *finite-branching* if for each state $s \in S$, the set $\{s' : s \rightarrow_R s'\}$ is finite.

3 Context-Free Processes

The definition we adopt for context-free processes is very close to the definition of BPA (Basic Process Algebra) processes [BBK87]. The difference between the two definitions is that the operational semantics of BPA processes is given by means of edge-labelled graphs (i.e., labelled transition systems) whereas the semantics of our context-free processes is defined using state-labelled graphs (i.e., Kripke structures). We choose this semantics because our aim is to consider context-free processes as models for the temporal logic PCTL introduced in the next section which is interpreted on KS's.

Let *Prop* be a finite set of atomic propositions. We consider from now on that the alphabet Σ is 2^{Prop}. We call the elements of Σ *state labels*. We use $P, Q, \ldots$ to denote atomic propositions and we use the letters $a, b, \ldots$ to range over elements of Σ. Let *Var* be a set of variables. We use $A, B, \ldots$ to range over variables in *Var* and greek letters $\alpha, \beta, \ldots$ to range over sequences in Var^*. Then, consider the set of terms $\mathcal{T}$ defined by the following grammar:

$$t ::= a \mid A \mid t + t \mid t \cdot t \mid \epsilon$$

Intuitively, the operator "+" stands for nondeterministic choice whereas "$\cdot$" is the sequential composition operator ; ϵ (the empty sequence) represents the idle process. In the sequel, we identify the terms $\epsilon \cdot t$ and $t \cdot \epsilon$ with the term t, for any term t.

Syntactically, a context-free process (CFP for short) is defined by a finite system of equations $\Delta \stackrel{\text{def}}{=} \{A_i = t_i \ : \ 1 \leq i \leq n\}$ where all the A_i's are distinct variables and all the variables occurring in the terms t_i are in the (finite) set $Var_\Delta = \{A_1, \ldots, A_n\}$.

A term $t \in \mathcal{T}$ is *guarded* if every variable occurrence in t is within the scope of a state label $a \in \Sigma$. A CFP $\Delta = \{A_i = t_i \ : \ 1 \leq i \leq n\}$ is guarded (GCFP) if every term t_i is guarded.

We define the operational semantics of CFP's by associating with each system Δ a Kripke structure $\mathcal{K}_\Delta$ representing its computation graph. This structure is given by $\mathcal{K}_\Delta = (\Sigma, S_\Delta, \Pi_\Delta, R_\Delta)$ where

- $S_\Delta = \Sigma \times \mathcal{T}$,
- $\forall \langle a, t \rangle \in S_\Delta .\ \Pi_\Delta(\langle a, t \rangle) = a$,
- $R_\Delta \subseteq S_\Delta^2$ is the smallest relation such that
  1. $\langle a, a' \rangle \rightarrow_{R_\Delta} \langle a', \epsilon \rangle$,
  2. "$A = t$" $\in \Delta$ and $\langle a, t \rangle \rightarrow_{R_\Delta} \langle a', t' \rangle$ implies $\langle a, A \rangle \rightarrow_{R_\Delta} \langle a', t' \rangle$,
  3. $\langle a, t_1 \rangle \rightarrow_{R_\Delta} \langle a', t_1' \rangle$ implies $\langle a, t_1 + t_2 \rangle \rightarrow_{R_\Delta} \langle a', t_1' \rangle$,
  4. $\langle a, t_1 \rangle \rightarrow_{R_\Delta} \langle a', t_1' \rangle$ implies $\langle a, t_2 + t_1 \rangle \rightarrow_{R_\Delta} \langle a', t_1' \rangle$,
  5. $\langle a, t_1 \rangle \rightarrow_{R_\Delta} \langle a', t_1' \rangle$ implies $\langle a, t_1 \cdot t_2 \rangle \rightarrow_{R_\Delta} \langle a', t_1' \cdot t_2 \rangle$.

Clearly, for any variable $A \in Var_\Delta$ and any $a \in \Sigma$, the set of reachable states from $\langle a, A \rangle$ is in general infinite.

Kripke structures such as $\mathcal{K}_\Delta$ (i.e., defined as above from CFP's), are called context-free Kripke structures (CFKS's).

A GCFP $\Delta = \{A_i = t_i \ : \ 1 \leq i \leq n\}$ is in Greibach normal form (GNF), if every term t_i is either ϵ or in the form $\sum_{j=1}^{n_i} a_j^i \alpha_j^i$ where $n_i \geq 1$, the α_j^i's are sequences in Var_Δ^* and, for every A in the α_j^i's, "$A = \epsilon$" $\notin \Delta$. Then, we denote by $\mathcal{S}(\Delta)$ the set of *transition rules* $A_i \mapsto t$ where, either $A_i = \epsilon \in \Delta$ and $t = \epsilon$, or $A_i = \sum_{j=1}^{n_i} a_j^i \alpha_j^i$ and $t = a_j^i \alpha_j^i$ for some $j \in \{1, \cdots, n_i\}$.

It has been shown (see [BBK87]) that every GCFP can be transformed into GNF preserving bisimilarity. Notice that, for every GCFP, the structure $\mathcal{K}_\Delta$ is finite-branching.

4 Presburger CTL

The logic Presburger CTL (PCTL) is an extension of the branching-time temporal logic CTL [CES83] where constraints on numbers of occurrences of state properties can be expressed using Presburger formulas.

Recall that *Prop* is a finite set of atomic proposition and that $\Sigma = 2^{Prop}$. Recall also that we use letters $P, Q, \ldots$ to range over elements of *Prop*, letters $x, y, \ldots$ to range over variables in $\mathcal{V}$ and $f, g, \ldots$ to range over Presburger formulas. First, consider the set of *state formulas* given by:

$$\pi ::= P \mid \neg\pi \mid \pi \vee \pi$$

The set of formulas of PCTL is defined by:

$$\varphi ::= P \mid f \mid \neg\varphi \mid \varphi \vee \varphi \mid \widetilde{\exists} x.\varphi \mid [x : \pi].\varphi \mid \varphi \forall\mathcal{U} \varphi \mid \varphi \exists\mathcal{U} \varphi$$

We consider as abbreviations the usual boolean connectives as conjunction ($\wedge$), implication ($\Rightarrow$) and equivalence ($\Leftrightarrow$). In addition, we use the universal quantification $\widetilde{\forall} x.\varphi = \neg\widetilde{\exists} x.\neg\varphi$ and the following standard abbreviations: $\forall\Diamond\varphi = \mathsf{true}\forall\mathcal{U}\varphi$, $\exists\Diamond\varphi = \mathsf{true}\exists\mathcal{U}\varphi$, $\forall\Box\varphi = \neg\exists\Diamond\neg\varphi$ and $\exists\Box\varphi = \neg\forall\Diamond\neg\varphi$. We write $[x_1, \ldots, x_n : \pi_1, \ldots, \pi_n].\varphi$ or $[x_i : \pi_i]_{i=1}^{n}.\varphi$ for $[x_1 : \pi_1]. \cdots .[x_n : \pi_n].\varphi$.

The operators $\exists\mathcal{U}$ and $\forall\mathcal{U}$ are the classical CTL *until* operators with existential and universal path quantification. The Presburger formulas f are used to express constraints on the numbers of occurrences of states satisfying some state formulas. Then, we call these formulas *occurrence constraints.* The operator $\widetilde{\exists}$ corresponds to the usual existential quantification over integers. We distinguish (even syntactically) between the PCTL operator $\widetilde{\exists}$ and the Presburger existential quantifier $\exists$ that may be used locally in some occurrence constraint f. In the formula $[x : \pi].\varphi$, the variable x is associated with the state formula π, and then, starting from the current state, x represents the number of occurrences of states satisfying π. The variable x can be used in the occurrence constraints appearing in φ. For instance, the formula $[x : \pi].\exists\Diamond(P \wedge x \leq 5)$ expresses the fact that from the current state, say s, there exists some reachable state s' where P holds and such that the path relating s to s' contains less than 5 states satisfying π. From now on, we refer to the variables x as *occurrence variables.* The construction "$[x : \pi]$" in the formula above binds the variable x in the subformula $\exists\Diamond(P \wedge x \leq 5)$. So, a variable x may be bound by either the quantifier $\exists$, or by the quantifier $\widetilde{\exists}$, or by the construction "$[x : \pi]$". Then, every variable appearing in some formula is either *bound* or *free.* We denote by $\mathcal{F}(\varphi)$ the set of variables occurring free in φ. A formula φ is *closed* if all the variables occurring in it are bound (i.e., $\mathcal{F}(\varphi) = \emptyset$), otherwise φ is *open.* We assume without loss of generality that each variable occurring in any PCTL formula is bound at most once.

The formal semantics of PCTL is defined by a satisfaction relation between the states of a KS over Σ and the formulas. First, let us define a satisfaction relation for state formulas. Let K be a KS over Σ. The satisfaction relation $\models$ for state formulas is defined for any state s and atomic proposition P by $s \models P$ iff $P \in \Pi(s)$, and extended straightforwardly to boolean combinations of atomic propositions. Now, let us consider the general case. Since the formulas may be open, the satisfaction relation is defined w.r.t. a valuation E of the variables. Along a computation sequence, the valuation changes according to the satisfaction, at the visited states, of the state formulas associated with the occurrence variables. We define a *state formulas association* as a function γ that associates state formulas with variables in $\mathcal{V}$.

For any function F from $\mathcal{V}$ to some target set T (F stands for either a valuation E or a state formula γ), we denote by $\mathcal{D}(F)$ the set of variables x such that $F(x)$ is defined. We denote also by $F[x \leftarrow \tau]$ where $\tau \in T$, the function F' such that $\mathcal{D}(F') = \mathcal{D}(F) \cup \{x\}$ and which associates τ with x and coincides with F on all the other variables.

Given a state formulas association γ and a valuation E, we define, for every sequence $\sigma \in S^\infty$ and every two ranks $i, j \in I\!N$ such that $i, j \leq |\sigma|$, the valuation

$$E^{[i,j]}_{(\sigma,\gamma)} = E[x \leftarrow E(x) + |\{k \in \{i, \ldots, j\} \; : \; \sigma(k) \models \gamma(x)\}|]_{x \in \mathcal{D}(\gamma)}.$$

Now, given a state formulas association γ and a valuation E, the satisfaction relation $\models$ for all PCTL formulas is inductively defined for any state s by:

$$
\begin{array}{ll}
s \models_{(E,\gamma)} P & \text{iff } P \in \Pi(s) \\
s \models_{(E,\gamma)} f & \text{iff } \|f\|(E') = \mathsf{true} \text{ where} \\
 & \quad E' = E[x \leftarrow E(x) + \text{if } s \models \gamma(x) \text{ then } 1 \text{ else } 0]_{x \in \mathcal{D}(\gamma)} \\
s \models_{(E,\gamma)} \neg\varphi & \text{iff } s \not\models_{(E,\gamma)} \varphi \\
s \models_{(E,\gamma)} \varphi_1 \vee \varphi_2 & \text{iff } s \models_{(E,\gamma)} \varphi_1 \text{ or } s \models_{(E,\gamma)} \varphi_2 \\
s \models_{(E,\gamma)} \exists x.\varphi & \text{iff } \exists k \in \mathbb{Z}.\ s \models_{(E',\gamma)} \varphi \text{ where } E' = E[x \leftarrow k] \\
s \models_{(E,\gamma)} [x : \pi].\varphi & \text{iff } s \models_{(E',\gamma')} \varphi \text{ where } E' = E[x \leftarrow 0] \text{ and } \gamma' = \gamma[x \leftarrow \pi] \\
s \models_{(E,\gamma)} \varphi_1 \forall\mathcal{U} \varphi_2 & \text{iff } \forall \sigma \in \mathcal{C}(K,s). \\
 & \quad \exists i \in I\!N.\ 1 \leq i \leq |\sigma|.\ \sigma(i) \models_{(E'(i),\gamma)} \varphi_2 \text{ and} \\
 & \quad \forall j \in I\!N.\ 1 \leq j < i.\ \sigma(j) \models_{(E'(j),\gamma)} \varphi_1, \text{ where } E'(k) = E^{[1,k-1]}_{(\sigma,\gamma)} \\
s \models_{(E,\gamma)} \varphi_1 \exists\mathcal{U} \varphi_2 & \text{iff } \exists \sigma \in \mathcal{C}(K,s). \\
 & \quad \exists i \in I\!N.\ 1 \leq i \leq |\sigma|.\ \sigma(i) \models_{(E'(i),\gamma)} \varphi_2 \text{ and} \\
 & \quad \forall j \in I\!N.\ 1 \leq j < i.\ \sigma(j) \models_{(E'(j),\gamma)} \varphi_1, \text{ where } E'(k) = E^{[1,k-1]}_{(\sigma,\gamma)}
\end{array}
$$

The CTL operators $\exists\bigcirc$ (there is some successor state) and $\forall\bigcirc$ (all the successors) can be defined in PCTL by: $\exists\bigcirc\varphi = [x : \mathsf{true}].\exists\Diamond((x = 2) \wedge \varphi)$ and $\forall\bigcirc\varphi = \neg\exists\bigcirc\neg\varphi$.

Then, clearly PCTL subsumes the logic CTL. Moreover, it can express properties that can not be expressed in the usual propositional temporal logics [GPSS80, Wol83, EH83], dynamic logics [FL79, Str82] and fixpoint calculi [Koz83, Var88]. Indeed, these logics can express only regular properties, i.e., properties that can be defined by finite-state automata (on infinite trees or sequences) [VW86, Tho87, Niw88] whereas PCTL can express nonregular properties.

For example, we can express the fact that between the beginning and the ending of some communication protocol session, there are exactly the same numbers of requests and acknowledgements. This is done by the formula:

$$\forall\Box\,(\text{BEGIN} \Rightarrow [x, y : \text{REQ}, \text{ACK}].\ \forall\Box\,(\text{END} \Rightarrow (x = y))) \tag{1}$$

We can require in addition that during every such session, the number of acknowledgements never exceeds the number of requests. This is done by:

$$\forall\Box\,(\text{BEGIN} \Rightarrow [x, y : \text{REQ}, \text{ACK}].\ (x \geq y)\forall\mathcal{U}\text{END}) \tag{2}$$

The conjunction of the two formulas (1) and (2) expresses the fact that, in every computation sequence, the subsequence between any pair of consecutive BEGIN and END is in the language of well-balanced parentheses (semi-Dyck set) with REQ (resp. ACK) as a left (resp. right) parenthesis. Now, we can express the stronger property that every subsequence between two consecutive BEGIN and END is actually in the language

$\{\text{REQ}^n \cdot \text{ACK}^n \ : \ n \geq 1\}$. This is done by the formula:

$$\widetilde{\forall} n.\ \forall\Box\,(\text{BEGIN} \Rightarrow$$
$$[x, y, z : \text{REQ}, \text{ACK}, \text{END}].$$
$$\forall\Box\,((\text{ACK} \wedge (x = n) \wedge (y = 1)) \Rightarrow \forall\Box\,((\text{END} \wedge (z = 1)) \Rightarrow (x = n) \wedge (y = n)))) \quad (3)$$

Then, as the examples above show, we can characterize in PCTL a large class of nonregular languages. These languages can be context-free as in (1), (2) and (3), but also context-sensitive using a conjunction of more than two occurrence constraints concerning different sets of occurrence variables. For instance, we can consider languages as $\{\pi_1^n \cdots \pi_k^n \ : \ n \geq 1\}$ or $\{\pi_1^n \cdot \pi_2^m \cdot \pi_1^n \cdot \pi_2^m \ : \ n, m \geq 1\}$.

In the formulas (1), (2) and (3), the constraints concern the numbers of occurrences of some propositions in every fixed computation sequence, independently from the other sequences. Actually, we can express also in PCTL properties involving global constraints on the whole set of computation sequences. For instance, consider the *uniform inevitability* property that says: there exists some rank n such that every computation sequence (of length greater than n) satisfies some proposition P at rank n. This property has been shown in [Eme87] to be non expressible by finite-state infinite-tree automata. We can express this property in PCTL by:

$$\widetilde{\exists} n.\ [x : \mathsf{true}].\ \forall\Box((x = n) \Rightarrow P) \tag{4}$$

Now, we introduce fragments of PCTL that are considered in the next section for decidability issues. The main fragment we consider is called PCTL$^+$ and is obtained by the following definition:

$$\varphi ::= P \mid f \mid \neg\varphi \mid \varphi \vee \varphi \mid \widetilde{\exists} x.\varphi \mid [x : \pi].\varphi \mid \varphi \forall\mathcal{U} \pi \mid \pi \exists\mathcal{U} \varphi$$

as well as the abbreviations introduced previously (hence, the operators $\exists\bigcirc$ and $\forall\bigcirc$ are definable in PCTL$^+$). Thus, the difference with PCTL is that in the formulas of the form $\varphi_1 \forall\mathcal{U} \varphi_2$ (resp. $\varphi_1 \exists\mathcal{U} \varphi_2$), the subformula φ_2 (resp. φ_1) must be a state formula.

Notice that we still can express in PCTL$^+$ significant nonregular properties. For instance, all the formulas (1), (2), (3) and (4) given above are PCTL$^+$ formulas.

Then, we consider two fragments of PCTL$^+$ called PCTL$^+_\exists$ and PCTL$^+_\forall$. The fragment PCTL$^+_\exists$ (resp. PCTL$^+_\forall$) is the positive fragment (i.e., negations appear only in state formulas and occurrence constraints) where only existential (resp. universal) path quantification is used. Formally, PCTL$^+_\exists$ is defined by:

$$\varphi ::= \pi \mid f \mid \varphi \vee \varphi \mid \varphi \wedge \varphi \mid \widetilde{\exists} x.\varphi \mid \widetilde{\forall} x.\varphi \mid [x : \pi].\varphi \mid \exists\Box\pi \mid \pi \exists\mathcal{U} \varphi$$

whereas PCTL$^+_\forall$ is defined by:

$$\varphi ::= \pi \mid f \mid \varphi \vee \varphi \mid \varphi \wedge \varphi \mid \widetilde{\exists} x.\varphi \mid \widetilde{\forall} x.\varphi \mid [x : \pi].\varphi \mid \forall\Box\varphi \mid \varphi \forall\mathcal{U} \pi$$

Of course, all the abbreviations introduced previously can be used. So, we can enrich the syntax of PCTL$^+_\exists$ (resp. PCTL$^+_\forall$) by the formulas $\exists\Diamond\varphi$ and $\exists\bigcirc\varphi$ (resp. $\forall\Diamond\pi$ and $\forall\bigcirc\varphi$). It can be seen that the negation of every formula in PCTL$^+_\forall$ is a PCTL$^+_\exists$ formula. This is due to the following fact that can easily be shown using PCTL semantics:

$$\varphi \forall\mathcal{U} \pi \Leftrightarrow (\neg\exists\Box\neg\pi) \wedge \neg(\neg\pi \exists\mathcal{U} \neg\pi \wedge \neg\varphi) \tag{5}$$

Notice that all the formulas (1), (2), (3) and (4) given above are in PCTL$^+_\forall$.

5 The Satisfaction Problem

The satisfaction problem corresponds to the question whether some given state in some CFKS satisfies some given formula. We show that the satisfaction problem is undecidable for PCTL. However, it turns out that this problem is actually decidable for PCTL$^+$.

5.1 Undecidability for full PCTL

Let us start with the undecidability results. We adopt the notations of [Rog67] for the elements of the arithmetical hierarchy. The class Σ_1 corresponds to the class of the recursively enumerable sets whereas Π_1 is the class of the complements of Σ_1 sets.

Proposition 5.1 *(Undecidable cases) The problems* $s \models_{(E,\gamma)} \phi\exists\mathcal{U}\pi$, *and* $s \models_{(E,\gamma)} \pi\forall\mathcal{U}\phi$, *where* $s \in S_\Delta$ *for some GCFP* Δ *and* ϕ *is a boolean combination of atomic propositions and occurrence constraints, are* Σ_1*-complete.*

The result above is obtained by a reduction of the halting problem of 2-counter machines. Actually, the proof uses only finite-state KS's. Then, the undecidability of the satisfaction problem for the formulas of the form $\phi\exists\mathcal{U}\pi$ and $\pi\forall\mathcal{U}\phi$ does not come from the fact that we are dealing with CFKS's but rather from the expressive power of PCTL. Now, by Proposition 5.1, and since negation is allowed in PCTL, we obtain

Theorem 5.1 *(Undecidability for PCTL) The problem* $s \models_{(E,\gamma)} \varphi$ *where* $s \in S_\Delta$ *for some GCFP* Δ *and* φ *is a PCTL formula, is not recursively enumerable.*

5.2 Decidability Results

Now, it remains to consider formulas of the forms $\pi\exists\mathcal{U}\varphi$ and $\varphi\forall\mathcal{U}\pi$. Using the fact (5), it is sufficient to consider the satisfaction problem for the formulas of the forms $\exists\Box\pi$ and $\pi\exists\mathcal{U}\varphi$. We show that the satisfaction problem for this kind of formulas is decidable. More generally, we show that this problem is decidable for all the formulas of PCTL$^+$. Our decision procedure is based on a reduction of the satisfaction problem between GCFP's and PCTL$^+$ formulas to the validity problem of Presburger formulas.

Let Δ be a GCFP. Without loss of generality, we consider the satisfaction problem for states of the form $s = \langle a, A\rangle$ where A is a variable in Var_Δ. To take into account states of the general form $s = \langle a, t\rangle$, it suffices to consider an additional equation $X = t$ where X is a fresh variable and consider the new state $s' = \langle a, X\rangle$. Moreover, we can assume that Δ is in GNF. Indeed, as we have already said in Section 3, every state in any GCFP has a bisimulation equivalent state in some GCFP in GNF and we can prove that bisimilar states satisfy the same PCTL formulas.

Satisfaction of $\exists\Box\pi$ formulas

Let us start with the satisfaction problem in the relatively simple case of the formulas $\exists\Box\pi$. Suppose that we are interested in the problem $s \models_{(E,\gamma)} \exists\Box\pi$ where $s = \langle a, A\rangle$.

Since Δ is in GNF, all the reachable states from s by R_Δ are of the form $\langle b, \alpha\rangle$ where $b \in \Sigma$ and $\alpha \in Var_\Delta^*$. Let us define a Δ-circuit as a sequence $\langle a_1, B_1 \cdot \beta_1\rangle \cdots \langle a_n, B_n \cdot \beta_n\rangle$ where $n \geq 2$, for every $i \in \{1, \ldots, n-1\}$, $\langle a_i, B_i \cdot \beta_i\rangle \rightarrow_{R_\Delta} \langle a_{i+1}, B_{i+1} \cdot \beta_{i+1}\rangle$ and

$B_1 = B_n$. Notice that β_1 and β_n may be different. We say that a Δ-circuit is *elementary* if it does not contain another Δ-circuit.

Now, it is easy to see that $s \models_{(E,\gamma)} \exists\Box\pi$ holds in two cases. The first one is when there exists some finite computation sequence σ (without Δ-circuits) starting from s and satisfying continuously π. The second case corresponds to the existence of some infinite computation sequence starting from s that have some finite prefix $\sigma = \mu\nu$ where μ does not contain any Δ-circuit and ν is an elementary Δ-circuit, such that π is satisfied continuously in σ. Thus, since the structure $\mathcal{K}_\Delta$ is finite-branching (and even it is actually infinite), a finite exploration of this structure allows to decide whether $s \models_{(E,\gamma)} \exists\Box\pi$.

Actually, the problem $s \models_{(E,\gamma)} \exists\Box\pi$ can be reduced to the satisfaction problem for formulas of the form $\pi\exists\mathcal{U}\varphi$. Indeed, let us reconsider the two cases when $s \models_{(E,\gamma)} \exists\Box\pi$ holds. In the first case, we must have $s \models_{(E,\gamma)} \pi\exists\mathcal{U}(\pi \wedge \neg\exists\bigcirc\mathsf{true})$. Concerning the second case, in order to express the existence of a reachable Δ-circuit from s, we need to enrich the set of atomic propositions *Prop* by new propositions P_B for every variable $B \in Var_\Delta$, and replace in Δ each equation $B = \sum_{i=1}^{n} b_i \cdot \beta_i$ by the equation $B = \sum_{i=1}^{n} (b_i \cup \{P_B\}) \cdot \beta_i$. Then, we must have $s \models_{(E,\gamma)} \bigvee_{B \in Var_\Delta} (\pi\exists\mathcal{U}(P_B \wedge (\pi\exists\mathcal{U}(\pi \wedge P_B))))$.

Satisfaction of $\pi\exists\mathcal{U}\varphi$ formulas

Let us consider now the interesting case of formulas of the form $\pi\exists\mathcal{U}\varphi$. In order to present the essence of our technique, we consider at a first step formulas without nesting of the $\exists\mathcal{U}$ operator neither the $\widetilde{\exists}$ quantifier nor $\exists\Box\pi$ formulas. The general case is presented later. So, let $\varphi = \pi_1\exists\mathcal{U}(\pi_2 \wedge f)$ and suppose that we are interested in the problem $s \models_{(E,\gamma)} \varphi$ where $s = \langle a, A\rangle$.

First, let us get rid of the case where "$A = \epsilon$" $\in \Delta$. In that case, our problem reduces to the trivial problem of checking whether $\langle a, \epsilon\rangle \models_{(E,\gamma)} \pi_2 \wedge f$.

Now, by definition of the satisfaction relation, the fact that $\langle a, A\rangle \models_{(E,\gamma)} \pi_1\exists\mathcal{U}(\pi_2 \wedge f)$ means that there exists some computation sequence starting from $\langle a, A\rangle$ which has a nonempty *finite prefix* $\sigma = \sigma(1)\cdots\sigma(n)$ such that $\sigma(n) \models \pi_2$ and $\forall j \in \{1,\ldots,n-1\}$. $\sigma(j) \models \pi_1$ and $\|f\|(E^{[1,n]}_{(\sigma,\gamma)}) = \text{true}$. Let $\mathsf{PREF}(\langle a, A\rangle)$ be the set of nonempty finite prefixes of computation sequences starting from $\langle a, A\rangle$.

By abuse of notation, we represent each state s by its label $\Pi_\Delta(s)$, and then, we can consider computation sequences as sequences in Σ^∞ and admit the notation $b \models \pi$ where $b \in \Sigma$ and π is a state formula.

Then, the set $\mathsf{PREF}(\langle a, A\rangle)$ is generated by the CFG such that the set of nonterminal symbols is $Var_\Delta \cup \{[B] : B \in (\{Z\} \cup Var_\Delta)\}$, $[Z]$ is the starting symbol ($Z \notin Var_\Delta$) and the set of productions is $\{B \rightarrow b \cdot \beta : \text{"}B \mapsto b \cdot \beta\text{"} \in \mathcal{S}(\Delta)\} \cup \{[B] \rightarrow b \cdot B_1 \cdots B_{i-1} \cdot [B_i] : \text{"}B \mapsto b \cdot B_1 \cdots B_n\text{"} \in (\{Z \mapsto a \cdot A\} \cup \mathcal{S}(\Delta))$ and $0 \leq i \leq n\}$.

Moreover, let $L(\pi_1\mathcal{U}\pi_2)$ be the set of sequences $\sigma(1)\cdots\sigma(n)$ in Σ^+ such that for every $j \in \{1,\ldots,n-1\}$, $\sigma(i) \models \pi_1$ and $\sigma(n) \models \pi_2$. Clearly, this set is regular. Since the intersection of a context-free language with a regular one is context-free, the language $\mathsf{PREF}(\langle a, A\rangle) \cap L(\pi_1\mathcal{U}\pi_2)$ is context-free and then, it is generated by some context-free grammar in GNF $\mathcal{G} = (\Sigma, \mathcal{N}, \mathcal{P}, \mathcal{Z})$. Thus, we obtain

$$\langle a, A\rangle \models_{(E,\gamma)} \varphi \text{ iff } \exists\sigma \in L(\mathcal{G}) \text{ and } \|f\|(E^{[1,|\sigma|]}_{(\sigma,\gamma)}) = \text{ true} \qquad (6)$$

Now, we construct a Presburger formula Ω which is valid if and only if there exists some sequence $\sigma \in L(\mathcal{G})$ such that $\|f\|(E^{[1,|\sigma|]}_{(\sigma,\gamma)})$ is true. Consider the derivation

$$\omega \Longrightarrow_{p_1} \sigma_1\omega_1 \cdots \Longrightarrow_{p_n} \sigma_n\omega_n \Longrightarrow_{p_{n+1}} \sigma \tag{7}$$

where ω and the ω_i's are nonempty sequences of nonterminals and σ and the σ_i's are sequences in Σ^+.

First, let us define the sets of variables that are involved in Ω. With every state label $b \in \Sigma$ we associate a variable u_b. Let U be the set of such variables. The variable u_b stands for the number of occurrences of b in the sequence σ of (7). Furthermore, let $\Upsilon(f)$ be the set of state formulas π such that there exists some occurrence variable $x \in \mathcal{F}(f)$ such that $\gamma(x) = \pi$. With every $\pi \in \Upsilon(f)$, we associate a variable v_π. Let V be the set of such variables. The variable v_π stands for the number of occurrences of state labels satisfying π in σ. Finally, with every production $p \in \mathcal{P}$, we associate a variable w_p which stands for the number of applications of p in (7). Let W be the set of the w_p's.

Since the grammar $\mathcal{G}$ is in GNF, the number of occurrences of any state label b in σ (represented by u_b) is the addition of all the w_p's such that p is a production applied in (7) generating b (has b in its right-hand side). This fact is expressed, for every $b \in \Sigma$, by the formula $\Theta^b_{\mathcal{P}}(U, W)$:

$$(0 \leq u_b) \wedge u_b = \sum w_p \quad \text{for every } p \in \mathcal{P} \text{ such that } b \in rhs(p).$$

Then, we relate each variable v_π to the variables in U using the formula $\Psi^\pi_{\mathcal{P}}(U, V)$:

$$(0 \leq v_\pi) \wedge v_\pi = \sum u_b \quad \text{for every } b \in \Sigma \text{ such that } b \models \pi.$$

Now, we have to define the constraints on the variables in W. For this aim, we need some additional notations and definitions. We say that a sequence of productions $\delta \in \mathcal{P}^*$ is *elementary* if all its productions apply to different nonterminals, i.e., $\forall p \in \mathcal{P}.\ |\delta|_p \leq 1$. Given a nonterminal B, a sequence $\omega \in \mathcal{N}^+$ and a set of productions $\mathcal{P}' \subseteq \mathcal{P}$, we define $\Pi^B_{(\mathcal{P}',\omega)}$ to be the set of elementary sequences δ on $\mathcal{P}'$ such that $\exists \mu \in (\Sigma \cup \mathcal{N})^*$, $\exists \nu \in \mathcal{N}^*$, $\omega \overset{*}{\Longrightarrow}_\delta \mu B \nu$. Notice that the set $\Pi^B_{(\mathcal{P}',\omega)}$ is finite. We define also $\mathcal{R}(\mathcal{P}', \omega)$ to be the set of the reachable nonterminals from ω using the productions in $\mathcal{P}'$, i.e., $\mathcal{R}(\mathcal{P}', \omega) = \{B \in \mathcal{N} \ :\ \Pi^B_{(\mathcal{P}',\omega)} \neq \emptyset\}$.

First of all, the constraints on W must express the fact that any occurrence of a nonterminal appearing along the derivation (7) must be reduced so that only terminal symbols (elements of Σ) remain in the final produced chain σ. Thus, for any nonterminal B, the number of the B-reductions, i.e., applications of some productions p such that $lhs(p) = B$ (B-productions), must be equal to the number of the B-introductions, i.e., the number of the occurrences of B in ω and in the right-hand sides of the applied productions. This fact is expressed by the Presburger formula $\Gamma^B_{(\mathcal{P},\omega)}(W)$:

$$\sum_{p \in \mathcal{P}} |lhs(p)|_B \cdot w_p = |\omega|_B + \sum_{p \in \mathcal{P}} |rhs(p)|_B \cdot w_p$$

However, some valuations validating $\bigwedge_{B \in \mathcal{N}} \Gamma^B_{(\mathcal{P},\omega)}(W)$ may assign to some variable w_p a non null value while p is not necessarily involved in the derivation (7). Indeed, consider some valuation E that validates $\bigwedge_{B \in \mathcal{N}} \Gamma^B_{(\mathcal{P},\omega)}(W)$ and suppose that it corresponds to the derivation (7). Consider also some nonterminal B which does not appear in ω neither in any ω_i in (7). Now, assume that there is some production $p = B \rightarrow b \cdot B$ in $\mathcal{P}$. We can define another valuation E' which assigns to w_p any strictly positive integer and coincides with E on the other variables. Clearly, the new valuation E' validates also $\bigwedge_{B \in \mathcal{N}} \Gamma^B_{(\mathcal{P},\omega)}(W)$. However, this valuation must be discarded since the number of the b's calculated from E' using the formula $\Theta^b_{\mathcal{P}}(U, W)$ does not correspond necessarily to a value that can be obtained from some existing derivation of the grammar $\mathcal{G}$.

Thus, we must express in addition, the fact that for any nonterminal B, there exists some B-production p with $w_p > 0$ if and only if B appears in ω or in the ω_i's. This is done by the formula $\Xi^B_{(\mathcal{P},\omega)}(W)$:

$$\sum_{p \in \mathcal{P}} |lhs(p)|_B \cdot w_p > 0 \Leftrightarrow \bigvee_{\delta \in \Pi^B_{(\mathcal{P},\omega)}} \bigwedge_{p \in \delta} w_p > 0$$

Finally, consider the formula $\Phi_{(\mathcal{P},\omega)}(U, V, W)$ defined by

$$(\bigwedge_{p \in \mathcal{P}} w_p \geq 0) \wedge (\bigwedge_{B \in \mathcal{N}} \Gamma^B_{(\mathcal{P},\omega)} \wedge \Xi^B_{(\mathcal{P},\omega)}) \wedge (\bigwedge_{b \in \Sigma} \Theta^b_{\mathcal{P}}) \wedge (\bigwedge_{\pi \in \Upsilon(f)} \Psi^\pi_{\mathcal{P}})$$

Then, the Presburger formula Ω is

$$\exists U.\, \exists V.\, \exists W.\, \Phi_{(\mathcal{P},\mathcal{Z})} \wedge f[e(x)/x]_{x \in \mathcal{F}(f)}$$

where $e(x) =$ if $x \in \mathcal{D}(\gamma)$ then $v_{\gamma(x)} + E(x)$ else $E(x)$ and $f[e(x)/x]$ denotes the formula obtained from f by substituting each occurrence of the variable x by the expression $e(x)$. Then, we prove the following result:

Proposition 5.2 *The formula Ω is valid iff $\exists \sigma \in L(\mathcal{G})$ such that $\|f\|(E^{[1,|\sigma|]}_{(\sigma,\gamma)}) = true$.*

By (6) and Proposition 5.2. and since the validity problem in Presburger arithmetic is decidable, we can decide whether $\langle a, A\rangle \models_{(E,\gamma)} \pi_1 \exists\mathcal{U}(\pi_2 \wedge f)$. This result can be easily extended to any formula of the form $\pi\exists\mathcal{U}\phi$ where ϕ is a boolean combination of π's (state formulas) and f's (occurrences constraints).

Proposition 5.3 *(Decidable cases) The problems $s \models_{(E,\gamma)} \pi\exists\mathcal{U}\phi$, and $s \models_{(E,\gamma)} \phi\forall\mathcal{U}\pi$, where $s \in S_\Delta$ for some GCFP Δ and ϕ is a boolean combination of state formulas and occurrence constraints, are decidable.*

Satisfaction of PCTL$^+$ formulas

Let us consider now the general case of PCTL$^+$ formulas. Following the same lines as in the previous section, we show that the satisfaction problem for any given state in any CFKS and any given PCTL$^+$ formula is reducible to the validity problem in Presburger arithmetic.

So, consider a PCTL$^+$ formula φ and suppose that we are interested in the problem $\langle a, A\rangle \models_{(E,\gamma)} \varphi$. First of all, we transform the formula φ into a *normal form* defined by:

$\varphi ::= \bigvee\bigwedge(\pi \wedge \phi)$

$\phi ::= \phi \wedge \phi \mid \psi$

$\psi ::= f \mid \neg\psi \mid \widetilde{\exists} x.\phi \mid \exists\Box\pi \mid [x : \pi].(\widetilde{\pi} \wedge \phi)$ where $\widetilde{\pi} \in \{\pi, \neg\pi\} \mid \exists\bigcirc(\pi\exists\mathcal{U}(\pi \wedge \phi))$

Notice that in the case of a formula $[x : \pi].(\tilde{\pi} \wedge \phi)$, the state formula $\tilde{\pi}$ is either *equal* to the formula π which is associated with x, or *equal* to $\neg\pi$.

This normal form is obtained using distributivity laws and facts concerning temporal operators like (5) and the fact that $\pi\exists\mathcal{U}\varphi \Leftrightarrow \varphi \vee (\pi \wedge \exists\bigcirc(\pi\exists\mathcal{U}\varphi))$. Then, let us assume that φ is in normal form.

We get rid of the formulas $\exists\Box\pi$ that appears in φ using the fact that their satisfaction is reducible to the satisfaction of formulas in the form $\pi\exists\mathcal{U}\phi$ (see Section 5.2).

So, we can consider a "simplified" normal form which is defined by the syntax given above where the case of $\exists\Box\pi$ formulas is removed.

Let $\varphi = \bigvee_{i=1}^{n} \bigwedge_{j=1}^{m_i} (\pi_i^j \wedge \phi_i^j)$. Clearly, solving the problem $\langle a, A\rangle \models_{(E,\gamma)} \varphi$ reduces to solve the satisfaction problem for each subformula ϕ_i^j.

Then, consider the problem $\langle a, A\rangle \models_{(E,\gamma)} \phi$ where ϕ is one of the subformulas ϕ_i^j of φ. Let *height* be the function that associates with each such a formula its height measured as the number of nested $\exists\mathcal{U}$ operators, and let $h = height(\phi)$. Recall that in the case without nesting of $\exists\mathcal{U}$ operators, (i.e., $h = 1$) presented in Section 5.2, to solve the problem $\langle a, A\rangle \models_{(E,\gamma)} \pi_1\exists\mathcal{U}(\pi_2 \wedge f)$, we reason on the set of nonempty prefixes of the computation sequences starting from $\langle a, A\rangle$ (see the assertion (6)). Now, in the general case, we have to reason on (at most) h prefixes of each computation sequence starting from $\langle a, A\rangle$. For this, we define the CFG $\mathcal{G}_{(A,\phi)} = (\Sigma, \mathcal{N}, \mathcal{P}, \mathcal{Z})$ where

- $\mathcal{N} = \{[i, B, j] \ : \ B \in Var_\Delta,\ i, j \in \{1, \ldots, h+1\},\ i \leq j\}$,
- $\mathcal{Z} = [1, A, h+1]$,
- $\mathcal{P} = \{[i, B, j] \rightarrow b \cdot [i_1, B_1, i_2] \cdots [i_k, B_k, j] \ : \ i_1 \leq i_2 \leq \ldots \leq i_k \leq j$ and $i_1 \in \{i, i+1\}$, "$B \mapsto b \cdot B_1 \cdots B_k$" $\in \mathcal{S}(\Delta)$ where $B_i \in Var_\Delta$, for $1 \leq i \leq k\} \ \cup$ $\{[i, B, j] \rightarrow b \ : \ j \in \{i, i+1\}$ and "$B \mapsto b$" $\in \mathcal{S}(\Delta)\}$.

For every $k \in \{1, \ldots, h+1\}$, let $\mathcal{N}_k = \{[i, B, j] \in \mathcal{N} \ : \ i = k\}$ and let $\mathcal{P}_k = \{p \in \mathcal{P} :$ $lhs(p) \in \mathcal{N}_k\}$. It can be seen that every computation sequence σ starting from $\langle a, A\rangle$ can be written $\sigma = a \cdot \mu_1 \cdots \mu_h \nu$ such that $\mathcal{Z} \stackrel{+}{\Longrightarrow}_{\mathcal{P}_1} \mu_1\omega_1 \stackrel{+}{\Longrightarrow}_{\mathcal{P}_2} \mu_1\mu_2\omega_2 \cdots \stackrel{+}{\Longrightarrow}_{\mathcal{P}_h} \mu_1 \cdots \mu_h\omega_h$ where $\forall i.\ 1 \leq i \leq h.\ \omega_i \in (\bigcup_{k=i+1}^{h+1} \mathcal{N}_k)^*$.

We associate each subsequence μ_k with the kth level of $\exists\mathcal{U}$ nesting in the formula ϕ. Notice that the sequences μ_k are nonempty. Indeed, to deal with the satisfaction of a formula $\pi\exists\mathcal{U}\varphi$ at some level k, we distinguish (by taking the normal form of the formula) the case when it is satisfied immediatly at the current state (if φ is) and the case when it is satisfied farther on some outgoing computation sequence (then, the current state must satisfy $\pi \wedge \exists\bigcirc(\pi\exists\mathcal{U}\varphi)$). In the last case, to check the satisfaction of $\exists\bigcirc(\pi\exists\mathcal{U}\varphi)$, we proceed, as in Section 5.2, by reducing this problem to the validity of a Presburger formula that expresses constraints on the derivations of $\mathcal{G}_{(A,\phi)}$ such that, there exists some generated nonempty sequence μ_k where π is continuously satisfied, except in its last state where φ must be satisfied. This last state of μ_k is actually the initial state concerning the level $k+1$ and so on.

So, we construct a Presburger formula Ω which is valid if and only if $\langle a, A\rangle \models_{(E,\gamma)} \phi$. This formula is built by nesting the formulas that constraint the derivations of $\mathcal{G}_{(A,\phi)}$ at each level k. Let us define the set of variables that are involved in Ω. For every $k \in \{1, \ldots, h\}$, and every $b \in \Sigma$, we define a variable u_b^k that stands for the number of occurrences of b in the subsequence μ_k. For every π we define a variable v_π^k standing for the number of states in μ_k which satisfy π. We consider also for every $p \in \mathcal{P}$ a variable

w_p standing for the number of applications of p. Let U_k be the set of the u_b^k's, V_k be the set of the v_π^k's and W_k be the set of the w_p's such that $p \in \mathcal{P}_k$.

Now, for every $k \in \{1, \ldots, h\}$ and $b \in \Sigma$, consider the Presburger formula $\Theta_{\mathcal{P}}^{(b,k)}$:

$$(0 \leq u_b^k) \wedge u_b^k = \sum w_p \text{ for every } p \in \mathcal{P}_k \text{ such that } b \in \mathit{rhs}(p)$$

and let $\Psi_{\mathcal{P}}^{(\pi,k)}$ be the formula

$$(0 \leq v_\pi^k) = \sum u_b^k \text{ for every } b \in \Sigma \text{ such that } b \models \pi.$$

The constraints on the variables W consist in those expressed by the formulas Γ and Ξ defined in Section 5.2 and, in addition, some contraints expressing the fact that the computation sequence must be *consistent* with the state formulas involved in ϕ. Given $k \in \{1, \ldots, h\}$ and a state formula π, let $\mathsf{COND}_{\mathcal{P}}^{(\pi,k)}$ be the formula defined by:

$$\begin{array}{ll} \sum w_p = 0 & \text{for every } p \in \mathcal{P}_k \text{ such that } p = \text{“}[k, B, k] \rightarrow b \cdot \beta\text{”} \\ & \text{for some } B \in \mathit{Var}_\Delta,\ \beta \in \mathcal{N}^*, \text{ and } b \not\models \pi \end{array}$$

and $\mathsf{REACH}_{\mathcal{P}}^{(\pi,k)}$ be the formula defined by:

$$\begin{array}{ll} \sum w_p = 0 & \text{for every } p \in \mathcal{P}_k \text{ such that either } p = \text{“}[k, B, k+1] \rightarrow b\text{”} \\ & \text{or } p = \text{“}[k, B, i] \rightarrow b \cdot [k+1, B', j] \cdot \beta\text{”} \\ & \text{for some } B, B' \in \mathit{Var}_\Delta,\ i, j \geq k+1,\ \beta \in \mathcal{N}^*, \text{ and } b \not\models \pi \end{array}$$

The constraints $\mathsf{COND}_{\mathcal{P}}^{(\pi_1,k)}$ and $\mathsf{REACH}_{\mathcal{P}}^{(\pi_2,k)}$ are used to express the fact that, to satisfy some formula $\exists\bigcirc(\pi_1 \exists\mathcal{U}(\pi_2 \wedge \psi))$ at some level k, necessarily, all the states in the sequence μ_k, except the last one, must satisfy π_1 and its last state must satisfy π_2. Notice that the constraints $\mathsf{COND}_{\mathcal{P}}^{(\pi_1,k)}$ and $\mathsf{REACH}_{\mathcal{P}}^{(\pi_2,k)}$ have been expressed in the case $h = 1$ considered in Section 5.2 by the fact that the set of the (nonempty) prefixes of computation sequences $\mathsf{PREF}(\langle a, A \rangle)$ was restricted by intersection with $L(\pi_1 \mathcal{U} \pi_2)$.

Now, let $E' = E[x \leftarrow E(x) + (\text{if } a \models \gamma(x) \text{ then } 1 \text{ else } 0)]_{x \in \mathcal{F}(\phi) \cap \mathcal{D}(\gamma)}$. Then, we define the formula Ω as $[\![\phi]\!]_1^{(E',\gamma)}$ where for every $k \in \{1, \ldots, h\}$, and for every valuation F, and every state formula association η,

- $[\![\neg\psi]\!]_k^{(F,\eta)} = \neg[\![\psi]\!]_k^{(F,\eta)}$,
- $[\![\psi_1 \wedge \psi_2]\!]_k^{(F,\eta)} = [\![\psi_1]\!]_k^{(F,\eta)} \wedge [\![\psi_2]\!]_k^{(F,\eta)}$,
- $[\![f]\!]_k^{(F,\eta)} = f[F(x)/x]_{x \in \mathcal{F}(f)}$,
- $[\![\widetilde{\exists} x.\psi]\!]_k^{(F,\eta)} = \exists x.[\![\psi]\!]_k^{(F,\eta)}$,
- $[\![[x : \pi].(\pi \wedge \psi)]\!]_k^{(F,\eta)} = [\![\psi]\!]_k^{(F',\eta')}$ where $F' = F[x \leftarrow 1]$ and $\eta' = \eta[x \leftarrow \pi]$,
- $[\![[x : \pi].(\neg\pi \wedge \psi)]\!]_k^{(F,\eta)} = [\![\psi]\!]_k^{(F',\eta')}$ where $F' = F[x \leftarrow 0]$ and $\eta' = \eta[x \leftarrow \pi]$,
- $[\![\exists\bigcirc(\pi_1 \exists\mathcal{U}(\pi_2 \wedge \psi))]\!]_k^{(F,\eta)} =$
  $\exists U_k.\, \exists V_k.\, \exists W_k.$
  $(\bigwedge_{p \in \mathcal{P}_k} w_p \geq 0) \wedge (\bigwedge_{X \in \mathcal{N}_k} \Gamma_{(\mathcal{P},\Xi)}^X \wedge \Xi_{(\mathcal{P},\Xi)}^X) \wedge$
  $(\bigwedge_{b \in \Sigma} \Theta_{\mathcal{P}}^{(b,k)}) \wedge (\bigwedge_{\pi \in \Upsilon(f)} \Psi_{\mathcal{P}}^{(\pi,k)}) \wedge$
  $(\mathsf{COND}_{\mathcal{P}}^{(\pi_1,k)} \wedge \mathsf{REACH}_{\mathcal{P}}^{(\pi_2,k)}) \wedge$
  $[\![\psi]\!]_{k+1}^{(F',\eta)}$ where $F' = F[x \leftarrow v_{\eta(x)}^k + F(x)]_{x \in \mathcal{F}(\psi) \cap \mathcal{D}(\eta)}$.

Notice that in the definition above of the function $[\![\cdot]\!]_k^{(F,\eta)}$, we consider that F associates with each variable an *expression* (actually a sum of constants and variables) an not necessarily an integer value. For instance, in the last case, $F' = F[x \leftarrow v^k_{\eta(x)} + F(x)]_{x \in \mathcal{F}(\psi) \cap \mathcal{D}(\eta)}$ associates with each variable in $\mathcal{F}(\psi) \cap \mathcal{D}(\eta)$ the *expression* $v^k_{\eta(x)} + F(x)$. In the case of $[\![f]\!]_k^{(F,\eta)}$, for every variable $x \in \mathcal{F}(f)$, the expression $F(x)$ is substituted to each occurrence of x in f.

Then, we prove that $\langle a, A\rangle \models_{(E,\gamma)} \phi$ if and only if the Presburger formula Ω is valid, and hence, we obtain the following decidability result:

Theorem 5.2 *The problem $s \models_{(E,\gamma)} \varphi$ where $s \in S_\Delta$ for some GCFP Δ and φ is a PCTL$^+$ formula, is decidable.*

6 The Satisfiability Problem

We consider now the satisfiability problem for PCTL, i.e., the problem to know, given some PCTL formula φ, whether there exists some state s in some KS that satisfies φ.

First, we show that when we consider KS's without any restriction, the satisfiability problem is Σ^1_1-complete for PCTL as well as for PCTL$^+$ (see [Rog67] for an exposition of the analytical hierarchy). This makes the validity problem for PCTL, and also for PCTL$^+$, to be highly undecidable (Π^1_1-complete). Furthermore, we consider the satisfiability problem with CFKS's, i.e., KS's that correspond to some context-free process. Indeed, to check that some process specification is consistent (satisfiable), we are more interested by its satisfiability by some KS that corresponds to some process than by its satisfiability by any KS. We show, that when we restrict ourselves to the class of CFKS's, the satisfiability problem for PCTL$^+$ becomes semi-decidable (Σ_1-complete). This is due to the fact that the set of GCFP's over Σ is recursively enumerable and the satisfaction problem for PCTL$^+$ by CFKS's is decidable (see Theorem 5.2). Then, we have the following undecidability results

Theorem 6.1 *(Undecidability results)*

1. *The satisfiability problems for PCTL and PCTL$^+$ are Σ^1_1-complete.*
2. *The satisfiability problem for PCTL$^+$ with CFKS's is Σ_1-complete.*

Finally, we show that the satisfiability problem for PCTL$^+_\exists$ is actually decidable, and hence, the validity problem for PCTL$^+_\forall$ is also decidable.

Theorem 6.2 *The satisfiability problem for PCTL$^+_\exists$ is decidable.*

The proof of Theorem 6.2 is based on Theorem 5.2 and the fact that, since only existential path quantification is allowed in PCTL$^+_\exists$, we can show that a PCTL$^+_\exists$ formula is satisfiable if and only if it is satisfiable by some state in the *finite* Kripke structure $K = (\Sigma, S, \Pi, R)$ such that, for every $a \in \Sigma$, there are exactly two states s_a and s'_a such that $\Pi(s_a) = \Pi(s'_a) = a$, $s'_a \not\to_R$ and s_a is related by R with all the other states in S.

7 Conclusion

We propose in this paper a logical framework for the specification and the verification of processes with infinite state spaces. We provide mainly a recursive verification procedure for nonregular properties w.r.t. context-free processes. This procedure concerns properties that are definable in an expressively powerful logic PCTL combining a classical temporal logic (CTL) with Presburger arithmetic. The arithmetical part of the logic allows to express constraints on numbers of occurrences of state formulas. Naturally, our decidability results still hold if we consider any decidable extension of Presburger arithmetic.

The work we present can be extended straightforwardly to the specification and verification of *timed processes* with a discrete time domain: For instance, time "ticks" can be seen as occurrences of some particular event (corresponding to the truth of some special atomic proposition) and then, time constraints can be expressed as any other occurrence constraints. Moreover, we can also consider the notion of *duration* of a state formula, i.e., time during which the fixed state formula holds [CHR91]. Indeed, in the case of a discrete time domain, the notion of duration coincides with the notion of number of occurrences at states where time ticks appear. In this framework, the results of this paper extend some results given in [BES93].

References

[BBK87] J.C.M. Baeten, J.A. Bergstra, and J.W. Klop. Decidability of Bisimulation Equivalence for Processes Generating Context-Free Languages. Tech. Rep. CS-R8632, 1987. CWI.

[BES93] A. Bouajjani, R. Echahed, and J. Sifakis. On Model Checking for Real-Time Properties with Durations. In *8th Symp. on Logic in Computer Science*. IEEE, 1993.

[BJ74] G.S. Boolos and R.C. Jeffrey. *Computability and Logic*. Cambridge Univ. Press, 1974.

[BS92] O. Burkart and B. Steffen. Model Checking for Context-Free Processes. In *CONCUR'92*. Springer-Verlag, 1992. LNCS 630.

[Buc62] J.R. Buchi. On a Decision Method in Restricted Second Order Arithmetic. In *Intern. Cong. Logic, Method and Philos. Sci.* Stanford Univ. Press, 1962.

[CES83] E.M. Clarke, E.A. Emerson, and E. Sistla. Automatic Verification of Finite State Concurrent Systems using Temporal Logic Specifications: A Practical Approach. In *10th ACM Symp. on Principles of Programming Languages*. ACM, 1983.

[CHR91] Z. Chaochen, C.A.R. Hoare, and A.P. Ravn. A Calculus of Durations. *Information Processing Letters*, 40:269–276, 1991.

[CHS92] S. Christensen, H. Hüttel, and C. Stirling. Bisimulation Equivalence is Decidable for all Context-Free Processes. In *CONCUR'92*. Springer-Verlag, 1992. LNCS 630.

[EH83] E.A. Emerson and J.Y. Halpern. 'Sometimes' and 'Not Never' Revisited : On Branching versus Linear Time Logic . In *POPL*. ACM, 1983.

[EL86] E.A. Emerson and C.L. Lei. Efficient Model-Checking in Fragments of the Propositional μ-Calculus. In *First Symp. on Logic in Computer Science*, 1986.

[Eme87] E.A. Emerson. Uniform Inevitability is Tree Automaton Ineffable. *Information Processing Letters*, 24, 1987.

[FL79] M.J. Fischer and R.E. Ladner. Propositional Dynamic Logic of Regular Programs. *J. Comp. Syst. Sci.*, 18, 1979.

[GH91] J.F. Groote and H. Hüttel. Undecidable Equivalences for Basic Process Algebra. Tech. Rep. ECS-LFCS-91-169, 1991. Dep. of Computer Science, Univ. of Edinburgh.

[GPSS80] D. Gabbay, A. Pnueli, S. Shelah, and J. Stavi. On the Temporal Analysis of Fairness. In *7th Symp. on Principles of Programming Languages*. ACM, 1980.

[Har78] M.A. Harrison. *Introduction to Formal Language Theory*. Addison-Wesley Pub. Comp., 1978.

[HP84] D. Harel and M.S. Paterson. Undecidability of PDL with $L = \{a^{2^i} \mid i \geq 0\}$. *J. Comp. Syst. Sci.*, 29, 1984.

[HPS83] D. Harel, A. Pnueli, and J. Stavi. Propositional Dynamic Logic of Nonregular Programs. *J. Comp. Syst. Sci.*, 26, 1983.

[HR90] D. Harel and D. Raz. Deciding Properties of Nonregular Programs. In *31th Symp. on Foundations of Computer Science*, pages 652–661. IEEE, 1990.

[Koz83] D. Kozen. Results on the Propositional μ-Calculus. *Theo. Comp. Sci.*, 27, 1983.

[KP83] T. Koren and A. Pnueli. There Exist Decidable Context-Free Propositional Dynamic Logics. In *Proc. Symp. on Logics of Programs*. Springer-Verlag, 1983. LNCS 164.

[Niw88] D. Niwinski. Fixed Points vs. Infinite Generation. In *LICS*. IEEE, 1988.

[Pnu77] A. Pnueli. The Temporal Logic of Programs. In *FOCS*. IEEE, 1977.

[Pra81] V.R. Pratt. A Decidable Mu-Calculus: Preliminary Report. In *FOCS*. IEEE, 1981.

[QS82] J-P. Queille and J. Sifakis. Specification and Verification of Concurrent Systems in CESAR. In *Intern. Symp. on Programming, LNCS 137*, 1982.

[Rab69] M.O. Rabin. Decidability of Second Order Theories and Automata on Infinite Trees. *Trans. Amer. Math. Soc.*, 141, 1969.

[Rog67] H. Rogers. *Theory of Recursive Functions and Effective Computability*. McGraw-Hill Book Comp., 1967.

[SE84] R.S. Streett and E.A. Emerson. The Propositional μ-Calculus is Elementary. In *ICALP*. Springer-Verlag, 1984. LNCS 172.

[Str82] R.S. Streett. Propositional Dynamic Logic of Looping and Converse is Elementary Decidable. *Information and Control*, 54, 1982.

[Tho87] W. Thomas. On Chain Logic, Path Logic, and First-Order Logic over Infinite Trees. In *2nd Symp. on Logic in Computer Science*, 1987.

[Var88] M.Y. Vardi. A Temporal Fixpoint Calculus. In *POPL*. ACM, 1988.

[VW86] M.Y. Vardi and P. Wolper. Automata-Theoretic Techniques for Modal Logics of Programs. *J. Comp. Syst. Sci.*, 32, 1986.

[Wol83] P. Wolper. Temporal Logic Can Be More Expressive. *Inform. and Control*, 56, 1983.

Pushdown Processes: Parallel Composition and Model Checking

Olaf Burkart[1] and Bernhard Steffen[2]

[1] Lehrstuhl für Informatik II, RWTH Aachen,
Ahornstraße 55, 52056 Aachen, Germany.
E-mail: burkart@informatik.rwth-aachen.de

[2] Fakultät für Mathematik und Informatik, Universität Passau,
Innstraße 33, 94015 Passau, Germany.
E-mail: steffen@fmi.uni-passau.de

Abstract. In this paper, we consider a strict generalization of context-free processes, the *pushdown processes*, which are particularly interesting for three reasons: First, in contrast to context-free processes that do not support the construction of distributed systems, they are *closed under parallel composition* with finite state systems. Second, they are the *smallest* extension of context-free processes allowing parallel composition with finite state processes. Third, they can be *model checked* by means of an elegant adaptation to pushdown automata of the second order model checker introduced in [BuS92]. As arbitrary parallel composition between context-free processes provides Turing power, and therefore destroys every hope for automatic verification, pushdown processes can be considered as the appropriate generalization of context-free processes for frameworks for automatic verification.

1 Introduction

Over the past decade model-checking has emerged as a powerful tool for the automatic analysis of concurrent systems. Whereas model-checking for finite-state systems is well-established (cf. e.g. [EL86, CES86, Lar88, SW89, Win89, Cle90, CS92]), the theory for infinite systems is a current research topic. Bradfield and Stirling [Bra91, BrS91] observed that tableaux-based model-checking covers general infinite-state systems. However, their method is not effective. Therefore much work has focused on *context-free processes*, a subclass of the infinite-state systems. In particular, in [BuS92] an iterative model-checking algorithm is developed that decides the *alternation-free* part of the modal mu-calculus for *context-free* processes. Moreover, in [HS93] it is shown how this can be done using tableaux-based techniques. However, it is currently not known, which classes of infinite-state processes still allow *automatic* verification. In a landmark paper Muller and Schupp [MS85] proved that the Monadic Second Order Logic (MSOL) is decidable for pushdown transition graphs, which are a strict generalization of context-free processes with respect to bisimulation semantics. As a consequence, the model checking problem on pushdown transition graphs is decidable for the full modal mu-calculus, since this logic can be interpreted in MSOL. However, their decision procedure is non-elementary and thus not applicable to practical problems. Finally, an automata theoretic approach to model checking for infinite state systems has been proposed in [PI93]. There macro processes, which generalize pushdown processes, are checked against specifications expressed using Büchi automata on infinite strings. As these are linear-time properties, Purushothaman's results do not cover the branching-time model checking problem considered here.

In this paper we investigate *pushdown processes*, i.e. pushdown transition graphs in the context of process theory. We develop a new algebraic representation of pushdown processes by means of *Pushdown Process Algebra* (PDPA) expressions and present a model checking algorithm that decides the alternation-free mu-calculus in exponential time.

Pushdown processes are a particularly interesting generalization of context-free processes because of the following facts.

- In contrast to context-free processes that do not support the construction of distributed systems, pushdown processes are closed under parallel composition with finite state systems. This is shown in Section 2.3 by providing a kind of expansion theorem in the sense of [Mil89]. In fact, it will be shown that the implied 'representation explosion' is no worse than the standard 'state explosion' for finite state systems.
- Pushdown processes are the smallest extension of context-free processes allowing parallel composition with finite state processes, which is a consequence of Theorem 12 stating that every pushdown process is bisimilar to a (relabelled) parallel composition of a context-free process (namely a stack) with a finite process.

Our iterative model-checking algorithm decides the *alternation-free* part of the modal mu-calculus for pushdown processes. As in the case of context-free processes, the point of our algorithm is to consider a *second order* variant of the standard iterative model-checking techniques. It determines *property transformers* for the *fragments*[3] of the pushdown automaton, which describe the set of formulas that are valid at the start state of a fragment relative to the set of formulas that are valid at the end states of the fragment. The number of end states of a fragment, which actually coincides with the number of states of the finite control of the underlying pushdown automaton, determines the arity of the corresponding property transformer. Our new equation system-based algorithm elegantly realizes the corresponding computation. After the determination of these property transformers, the model-checking problem can be solved simply by checking whether the formula under consideration is a member of the set of formulas that results from applying the property transformer associated with the initial fragment of the pushdown automaton to the set of formulas that are valid at the end states.

[3] Intuitively, fragments should be interpreted as 'incomplete portions'. They are formally defined in the next section.

The next section introduces PDPA systems which serves as a finite representation of pushdown processes. We establish that pushdown processes are the smallest generalization of context-free processes that is closed under parallel composition with finite-state systems. Subsequently, Section 3 presents our logic and Section 4 develops our model-checking algorithm. The final section contains conclusions and directions to future work.

2 Modelling Pushdown Processes

In this section we introduce the notion of a *pushdown process*. It will be used to finitely represent infinite state behaviours, which themselves are modelled by *labelled transition graphs*:

Definition 1. A *labelled transition graph* is a triple $\mathcal{L} = (\mathcal{S}, Act, \rightarrow)$, where $\mathcal{S}$ is a set of *states*, Act is a set of *actions* and $\rightarrow \subseteq \mathcal{S} \times Act \times \mathcal{S}$ is the *transition relation*.

Intuitively, a labelled transition graph encodes the operational behaviour of a process. The set $\mathcal{S}$ represents the set of states the process may enter, Act the set of actions the process may perform and $\rightarrow$ the state transitions that may result upon execution of the actions.

In the remainder of the paper we use $s \xrightarrow{a} s'$ in lieu of $(s, a, s') \in \rightarrow$, and we write $s \xrightarrow{a}$ when there is an s' such that $s \xrightarrow{a} s'$. If $s \xrightarrow{a} s'$ then we call s' an *a-derivative* of s. A labelled transition graph is said to be *finite-state*, when $\mathcal{S}$ and Act are finite.

2.1 Syntax and Semantics of Pushdown Processes

To model pushdown processes we consider the class of guarded recursive PDPA (Pushdown Process Algebra) processes. PDPA process expressions are given by the abstract syntax

$$E ::= \mathbf{0} \mid a \mid [q, \gamma] \mid E_1 + E_2 \mid E\ ; (E_1, \ldots, E_n)$$

where $\mathbf{0}$ represents the empty process, a ranges over a set of *atomic actions* Act, q over a set of *states* Q and γ over finite words of a set of *stack symbols* Γ. Expressions of the form $[q, \gamma]$ are called *fragments*. Moreover, if a fragment is of the form $[q, Z]$ with $Z \in \Gamma$ we call it *simple*. As usual, the operator $+$ is nondeterministic choice while $E\ ; (E_1, \ldots, E_n)$ means the sequential composition of processes where n is called the *arity*. In the remainder of the paper we assume that ';' has higher precedence than '+' and we abbreviate $E_1, \ldots, E_n$ by $\widetilde{E}$ if the E_i are of no special interest. Henceforth, we restrict our attention to *guarded* process expressions, i.e. process expressions where every fragment occurs within the scope of an atomic action.

A *PDPA process* is now defined by a finite system Δ of recursive process equations

$$\Delta = \{\, [q_i, Z_i] =_{\text{df}} E_i \mid 1 \leq i \leq k \,\}$$

where the $[q_i, Z_i]$ are distinct simple fragments, the E_i are guarded PDPA expressions and all fragments occurring are elements of $Q \times \Gamma^*$ for sets Q and Γ. One fragment (generally $[q_1, Z_1]$) is singled out as the *root*, the starting point of the computation. The *arity* of the PDPA process is defined as the cardinality of Q. This notion is motivated by the fact that the property transformers describing the semantics of pushdown processes have exactly this arity. Finally, given a relation R, we write $\Delta_1 R \Delta_2$ in order to express the fact that the roots of Δ_1 and Δ_2 are related by R. – It should be noted that pushdown processes, i.e. guarded recursive PDPA processes, are *finitely branching*, i.e. for every E there are only finitely many E' with $E \xrightarrow{a} E'$.

Definition 2. Any PDPA process Δ with $Q = \{ q_1, \ldots, q_n \}$ defines a labelled transition graph. The transition relations are given as the least relations satisfying the following rules:

$$a \xrightarrow{a} \mathbf{0}, a \in Act \qquad \frac{E \xrightarrow{a} E'}{E + F \xrightarrow{a} E'} \qquad \frac{F \xrightarrow{a} F'}{E + F \xrightarrow{a} F'}$$

$$\frac{E \xrightarrow{a} E'}{[q, Z] \xrightarrow{a} E'} \; [q, Z] =_{\mathrm{df}} E \in \Delta \qquad \frac{[q, Z] \xrightarrow{a} E}{[q, Z\gamma] \xrightarrow{a} E \; ; ([q_1, \gamma], \ldots, [q_n, \gamma])}$$

$$\frac{E \xrightarrow{a} E'}{E \; ; (\widetilde{E}) \xrightarrow{a} E' \; ; (\widetilde{E})} \qquad \frac{E_1 \xrightarrow{a} E_1'}{\mathbf{0} \; ; (E_1) \xrightarrow{a} E_1'} \qquad \frac{E_i \xrightarrow{a} E_i'}{[q_i, \epsilon] \; ; (E_1, \ldots, E_n) \xrightarrow{a} E_i'}$$

BPA (Basic Process Algebra) processes and regular processes can be seen as special cases of PDPA processes. A *BPA process* is a PDPA process where Q contains only one state q. As usual, the fragment $[q, \gamma]$ is then identified with the string γ and a simple fragment is called a variable. Even more, the sequential composition of arity one $E \; ; (F)$ is written as $E \cdot F$ or simply as EF. Such processes are also called *context-free* (cf. e.g. [CHS92]). A *regular process* is a BPA process where each sequential composition is a so called *prefixing* $a \cdot X$, also written as $a.X$. Note that the Z_i play the role of the nonterminals of a context-free or regular grammar in these cases.

The name *pushdown* process algebra originates from the fact that classical nondeterministic pushdown automata without ϵ-moves and final states directly induce a pushdown process. They are defined as follows:

Definition 3. A *pushdown automaton* is a 6-tuple $(Q, Act, \Gamma, \delta, q_1, Z_1)$, where Q is a finite set of states, Act is a finite set of *actions*, Γ is finite set of *stack symbols*, $q_1 \in Q$ is the initial state, $Z_1 \in \Gamma$ is the initial stack symbol and δ is a mapping from $Q \times Act \times \Gamma$ to finite subsets of $Q \times \Gamma^*$.

Definition 4. Let $\mathcal{P} = (Q, Act, \Gamma, \delta, q_1, Z_1)$ be a pushdown automaton with $Q = \{ q_1, \ldots, q_n \}$. The *pushdown process induced by* $\mathcal{P}$ is the process system $\Delta(\mathcal{P})$ with

$$[q, Z] = \sum_i a_i \; ; [q_i', \beta_i] \in \Delta(\mathcal{P}) \quad \text{iff} \quad \delta(q, a_i, Z) \ni (q_i', \beta_i)$$

In order to capture when two processes are said to exhibit the same behaviour we use the well-known *bisimulation equivalence* [Mil89]:

Definition 5. A binary relation R between processes is a *bisimulation* if whenever $(P, Q) \in R$ then for each $a \in Act$ we have:

1. $P \xrightarrow{a} P'$ implies $\exists\, Q'.\, Q \xrightarrow{a} Q' \;\wedge\; (P', Q') \in R$
2. $Q \xrightarrow{a} Q'$ implies $\exists\, P'.\, P \xrightarrow{a} P' \;\wedge\; (P', Q') \in R$

Two processes P and Q are said to be *bisimulation equivalent* or *bisimilar*, written $P \sim Q$, if $(P, Q) \in R$ for some bisimulation R.

It is well known that each regular process possesses only a finite number of equivalence classes wrt. bisimulation – a regular process is therefore also called a *finite-state system* – whereas BPA processes have in general an infinite number of equivalence classes. Moreover, in [CM90] it is shown that pushdown processes are strictly more expressive with respect to the bisimulation semantics than context-free processes.

2.2 A Greibach-like Normal Form for Pushdown Processes

In the following sections we establish that each pushdown process is induced by some pushdown automaton, which additionally can be assumed to push at most 2 symbols onto the stack during a transition step.

We start by reviewing the usual BPA laws in the context of pushdown processes. These generalized BPA-laws, accordingly called *PDPA-laws*, are given in Figure 1. They are easily shown to be sound with respect to bisimilarity.

$$
\begin{array}{ll}
A1: & E_1 + E_2 = E_2 + E_1 \\
A2: & (E_1 + E_2) + E_3 = E_1 + (E_2 + E_3) \\
A3: & E_1 + E_1 = E_1 \\
A4: & (E_1 + E_2); (\widetilde{F}) = E_1; (\widetilde{F}) + E_2; (\widetilde{F}) \\
A5: & (E_1; (\widetilde{F})); (\widetilde{G}) = E_1; (F_1; (\widetilde{G}), \ldots, F_k; (\widetilde{G})) \\
A6: & [q, Z\gamma] = [q, Z]; ([q_1, \gamma], \ldots, [q_n, \gamma])
\end{array}
$$

Fig. 1. The PDPA laws

Proposition 6. *All the PDPA laws are valid up to* $\sim$.

In [BBK87] it is shown that any guarded BPA system can effectively presented in *Greibach Normal Form* (GNF), which only allows equations of the form $X = \sum_i a_i.\alpha_i$. This result is further strengthened in [Hüt91] by proving that the length of the string $a_i.\alpha_i$ can be bound by 3. Systems with this property are said to be in *3-GNF*. Here we present the analogous result for PDPA systems.

Definition 7. A pushdown process Δ is said to be in *Pushdown Normal Form* (PDNF) if all equations are of the form $[q, Z] = \sum_i a_i \cdot [q'_i, \beta_i]$.

The following theorem is proved in [BuS94]:

Theorem 8. *If Δ is a guarded system of PDPA equations, we can effectively construct a system Δ' in PDNF such that $\Delta \sim \Delta'$.*

2.3 Parallel Composition

We now introduce a binary CSP-like parallel operator $||$ for processes (cf. [Hoa88]). Intuitively, the parallel composition $P \parallel Q$ of two processes requires the synchronization of the actions common to both component alphabets and allows the interleaving of the others.

Definition 9. The *parallel composition* $P \parallel Q$ of two processes P, Q behaves as follows:

$$\frac{P \xrightarrow{a} P'}{P \parallel Q \xrightarrow{a} P' \parallel Q}\ a \notin Act(Q) \qquad \frac{Q \xrightarrow{a} Q'}{P \parallel Q \xrightarrow{a} P \parallel Q'}\ a \notin Act(P)$$

$$\frac{P \xrightarrow{a} P',\ Q \xrightarrow{a} Q'}{P \parallel Q \xrightarrow{a} P' \parallel Q'}$$

Theorem 10 [Expansion Theorem]. *Given a pushdown process P and a regular process R, we can effectively construct a pushdown process P' such that $P' \sim P \parallel R$*

The proof of this theorem is given in [BuS94], and an automata theoretic variant of this result, which also applies to macro processes, can be found in [PI93].

Example: We illustrate the construction by means of the process management system `PMS` consisting of the parallel composition of the "process handler" `PH` and the "controller" `C`.

$$\begin{aligned}\mathtt{PH} &= \{\ X_0 = \mathtt{create}.X_1,\ X_1 = \mathtt{create}.X_1X_1 + \mathtt{term}\ \}\\ \mathtt{C}\ &\doteq \{\ Y_0 = \mathtt{create}.Y_1,\ \ Y_1 = \mathtt{create}.Y_1 + \mathtt{shutdown}.Y_2,\ Y_2 = \mathbf{0}\ \}\end{aligned}$$

Here the process handler `PH` can be interpreted as a system that allows to create processes via the action `create` and to terminate active processes via the action `term`. The process management system offers its service until it is 'shut-down' by the controller `C` via the action `shutdown`, which causes the process management system to deadlock after having terminated all active processes. A pushdown process, bisimilar to this system, can be defined as follows:

$$\begin{aligned}\mathtt{PMS} = \{\ &[Y_0, X_0] = \mathtt{create}.[Y_1, X_1],\\ &[Y_1, X_1] = \mathtt{create}.[Y_1, X_1X_1] + \mathtt{term}.[Y_1, \epsilon] + \mathtt{shutdown}.[Y_2, X_1],\\ &[Y_2, X_1] = \mathtt{term}.[Y_2, \epsilon]\ \ \}\end{aligned}$$

Figure 2 shows the labelled transition graphs of the parallel components as well as the labelled transition graph of the overall system.

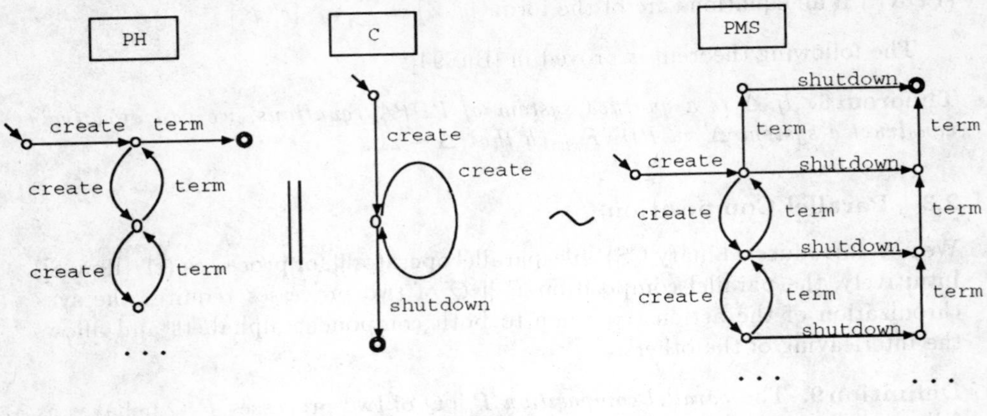

Fig. 2. The Process Management System example

2.4 Parallel Decomposition and moderate Pushdown Processes

The heart of this section is a Chomsky-Schützenberger like representation theorem for pushdown processes, which states that each pushdown process can be represented as the relabelled parallel composition of a regular and a context-free process. This result allows us to further constrain the process format, which is essential for the presentation of our algorithm.

Definition 11. The behaviour of a relabelled process $P[\varphi]$ with relabelling function $\varphi : Act \rightarrow Act'$ is determined by the transition rule:

$$\frac{P \xrightarrow{a} P'}{P[\varphi] \xrightarrow{\varphi(a)} P'[\varphi]}$$

Now the proof of the following theorem is straightforward (cf. [BuS94]).

Theorem 12. *For any pushdown process Δ_{PD} there exist a regular process Δ_R, a BPA process Δ_{CF} and a relabelling $[\varphi]$ such that*

$$\Delta_{PD} \quad \sim \quad (\Delta_R \parallel \Delta_{CF})\,[\varphi]$$

Thus pushdown processes form the smallest extension of context-free processes being closed under parallel composition with regular processes.

Using the well-known 3-GNF for BPA processes the representation theorem implies that every pushdown process can effectively be rewritten in a way that each fragment $[q, \gamma]$ appearing on a right-hand side has length at most 2.

Definition 13. A pushdown process Δ is said to be *moderate* if each equation is of the form $[q, Z] = \sum_i a_i \ .[q'_i, \beta_i]$ with $|\beta_i| \leq 2$ for each i.

Corollary 14. *If Δ is a guarded system of PDPA equations, we can effectively find a moderate system Δ' such that $\Delta \sim \Delta'$.*

3 Specifying Behavioural Properties

The logic we consider is the alternation-free fragment of the modal mu-calculus [Koz83, Lar88], i.e. the fragment which does not contain *alternating fixed points* [EL86]. For algorithmic simplicity, however, we represent formulas by means of *hierarchical (mutually recursive) equational systems* (cf. [CS91, CS92]), which are equally expressive as this fragment (cf. [CKS92]).

3.1 Syntax and Semantics of Basic Formulas

Let *Var* be a (countable) set of variables, and *Act* be a set of actions. In what follows, X will range over *Var*, and a over *Act*. Then the syntax of *basic* formulas is given by the following grammar.[4]

$$\Phi ::= tt \mid ff \mid X \mid \Phi \vee \Phi \mid \Phi \wedge \Phi \mid \langle a \rangle \Phi \mid [a]\Phi$$

The formal semantics appears in Figure 3. It is given with respect to a labelled transition system $(\mathcal{S}, Act, \rightarrow)$, and an environment ρ mapping variables to subsets of $\mathcal{S}$, where $\rho\,[\,S/X\,]$ is the environment resulting from ρ by updating the binding of X to S.

$[\![tt]\!]\rho = \mathcal{S}$	$[\![\Phi_1 \vee \Phi_2]\!]\rho = [\![\Phi_1]\!]\rho \cup [\![\Phi_2]\!]\rho$
$[\![ff]\!]\rho = \emptyset$	$[\![\Phi_1 \wedge \Phi_2]\!]\rho = [\![\Phi_1]\!]\rho \cap [\![\Phi_2]\!]\rho$
$[\![X]\!]\rho = \rho(X)$	$[\![\langle a \rangle \Phi]\!]\rho = \{\, s \mid \exists\, s'.\ s \xrightarrow{a} s' \wedge s' \in [\![\Phi]\!]\rho \,\}$
	$[\![[a]\Phi]\!]\rho = \{\, s \mid \forall\, s'.\ s \xrightarrow{a} s' \Rightarrow s' \in [\![\Phi]\!]\rho \,\}$

Fig. 3. The Semantics of Basic Formulas.

Intuitively, the semantic function maps a formula to the set of states for which the formula is "true". Accordingly, all states satisfy tt, while no state satisfies ff. Furthermore s satisfies X if s is an element of the set bound to X in ρ. The propositional constructs are interpreted in the usual fashion: s satisfies $\Phi_1 \vee \Phi_2$ if it satisfies one of the Φ_i and $\Phi_1 \wedge \Phi_2$ if it satisfies both of them. The constructs $\langle a \rangle$ and $[a]$ are *modal operators*; s satisfies $\langle a \rangle \Phi$ if it has an a-derivative satisfying Φ, while s satisfies $[a]\Phi$ if each of its a-derivatives satisfy Φ.

3.2 Syntax and Semantics of Hierarchical Equational Systems

By themselves, basic formulas do not provide much expressive power because they may only describe properties about a finite part of a system's behaviour.

[4] In order to simplify our presentation, we only assume the atomic propositions tt and ff here. However, an extension covering arbitrary *atomic propositions*, which are consistent with the representation of the transition system under consideration, is straightforward.

To remedy this lack of expressiveness, formulas may also be defined using *hierarchical equational systems.*

Definition 15.

- An *(equational) block* has one of two forms, $\texttt{min}\{Eq\}$ or $\texttt{max}\{Eq\}$, where Eq is a list of (mutually recursive) equations $(X_1 = \Phi_1, \ldots, X_n = \Phi_n)$ in which each Φ_i is a basic formula and the X_i are all distinct.
- An *equational system* $\Theta = (B_1, \ldots, B_m)$ is a list of equational blocks where the variables appearing on the left-hand sides of the blocks, denoted by $Var(\Theta)$, are all distinct.
- An equational system $\Theta = (B_1, \ldots, B_m)$ is *hierarchical* if the existence of a left-hand-side variable of a block B_j in a right-hand-side formula of a block B_i implies $i \leq j$.

To define the semantics of an hierarchical equational system (HEQ) Θ, we first define the semantics of an individual block. Let $Eq = (X_1 = \Phi_1, \ldots, X_n = \Phi_n)$ be a list of equations. Then, given a fixed environment ρ, we may build a function $f^\rho_{Eq} : \mathfrak{P}(\mathcal{S})^n \rightarrow \mathfrak{P}(\mathcal{S})^n$ as follows. Let $\widetilde{S} = (S_1, \ldots, S_n) \in \mathfrak{P}(\mathcal{S})^n$, and let $\rho_{\widetilde{S}} = \rho[S_1/X_1, \ldots, S_n/X_n]$ be the environment that results from ρ by updating the binding of X_i to S_i. Then $f^\rho_{Eq}(\widetilde{S}) = (\llbracket\Phi_1\rrbracket\rho_{\widetilde{S}}, \ldots, \llbracket\Phi_n\rrbracket\rho_{\widetilde{S}})$.

$\mathfrak{P}(\mathcal{S})^n$ forms a complete lattice, where the ordering, join and meet operations are the pointwise extensions of the set-theoretic inclusion $\subseteq$, union $\cup$ and intersection $\cap$, respectively. Moreover, for any equation list Eq and environment ρ, f^ρ_{Eq} is monotonic with respect to this lattice and therefore, according to Tarski's fixed-point theorem [Tar55], has both a *greatest* fixed point, νf^ρ_{Eq}, and a *least* fixed point, μf^ρ_{Eq}. In general, these may be characterized as follows.

$$\nu f^\rho_{Eq} = \bigcup\{\, \widetilde{S} \mid \widetilde{S} \subseteq f^\rho_{Eq}(\widetilde{S}) \,\}, \qquad \mu f^\rho_{Eq} = \bigcap\{\, \widetilde{S} \mid f^\rho_{Eq}(\widetilde{S}) \subseteq \widetilde{S} \,\}$$

Blocks $\texttt{max}\{Eq\}$ and $\texttt{min}\{Eq\}$ are now interpreted as the "greatest" fixed point of Eq, respectively the least, yielding *environments* in the following fashion.

$$\llbracket\texttt{max}\{Eq\}\rrbracket\rho = \rho_{\nu f^\rho_{Eq}}, \qquad \llbracket\texttt{min}\{Eq\}\rrbracket\rho = \rho_{\mu f^\rho_{Eq}}$$

Given ρ, we finally define the relative semantics of an hierarchical equational system $\Theta = (B_1, \ldots, B_m)$ in terms of the following sequence of environments: $\rho_m = \llbracket B_m\rrbracket\rho, \ldots, \rho_1 = \llbracket B_1\rrbracket\rho_2$ as $\llbracket\Theta\rrbracket\rho = \rho_1$.

The development of what it means for a state in a labelled transition system to satisfy a basic formula Φ whose variables are "bound" by an hierarchical equational system Θ is now straightforward: we say that Φ is *closed* with respect to Θ if every variable in Φ is a member of $Var(\Theta)$, and we refer to Θ as *closed* if each right-hand side in each block in Θ is closed with respect to Θ. Henceforth, the set of all closed hierarchical equational systems is denoted with $\mathrm{L}\mu_1$.

It turns out that it is sufficient to deal with the case where Φ is a variable and moreover, that $\llbracket\Theta\rrbracket\rho$ does not depend on ρ for closed equational systems Θ (cf. [BuS92]). Thus when Θ is closed, we omit reference to ρ. Furthermore, we abbreviate $s \in [\![X_1]\!]_{[\Theta]}$ with $s \models \Theta$, when X_1 is the first variable in the first block of Θ. Finally, given a process expression E we write $E \models \Theta$ if the state labelled E in the underlying transition graph satisfies Θ. The generalization for a set of hierarchical equational systems $M \subseteq \mathrm{L}\mu_1$ is written as $E \models M$, meaning $E \models \Theta$ for all $\Theta \in M$.

Instead of associating with each formula the set of states of the transition graph which satisfy this formula, we can alternatively associate the set of all valid formulas to a given state. This 'dual' viewpoint is essential for our algorithm. Henceforth, we write $\mathrm{L}\mu_1(P)$ for the set of formulas which are valid at the start state of the process P.

In the remainder of the paper we will only consider a minimal equational block B. Maximal equational blocks are dealt with in a dual way and the extension to hierarchical equational systems is straightforward.

4 Verifying Behavioural Properties

Our algorithm is an extension of the second order model checker presented in [BuS92], which allows us to deal with fragments of PDPA processes. The heart of the algorithm consists of determining *property transformers* for each fragment of the PDPA process under consideration, which provide a compositional and sound description of the logical behaviour of the pushdown process.

In Section 4.1 we establish that using property transformers provides a sound basis for model-checking. This follows from the second-order formulation of the semantics of processes in terms of its valid formulas. Subsequently, we present our model-checking algorithm (cf. Section 4.2). The effectiveness of our method is a consequence of the fact that it suffices to deal with the part of a property transformer which concerns the subformulas of the property to be investigated.

4.1 Second Order Semantics

The validity of a formula is defined with respect to single states. This notion cannot directly be adapted to fragments: the truth value at the start state might not be the same in different contexts, i.e. for different continuations[5]. However, if two continuations satisfy the same sets of formulas, then so does the start state of the fragment in these both contexts. This observation is the key to the *second order semantics* of [BuS92]: It is consistent with usual semantics to view a process as a *property transformer*, i.e. as a function which yields the set of formulas valid at the start state, relative to the assumption that the tuple of sets of formulas to which the transformer is applied are valid at the end states. Complete proofs to these results can be found in [BuS94].

---

[5] Note that we are dealing with forward-modalities. Thus the validity of formulas "propagates" backward.

Definition 16 [Property Transformer]. Let P be a process of arity z and $M_1, \ldots, M_z \subseteq \mathrm{L}\mu_1$. Then we interpret P as the function $[\![P]\!] : \mathfrak{P}(\mathrm{L}\mu_1)^z \rightarrow \mathfrak{P}(\mathrm{L}\mu_1)$, called the *property transformer* of P, which is defined as follows.

$$\Phi \in [\![P]\!](M_1, \ldots, M_z) \text{ iff } \forall\, P_1, \ldots, P_z \in \mathcal{P}. \quad (\forall_{1 \leq i \leq z}.\ \ P_i \models M_i\,) \implies P\ ;\ (P_1, \ldots, P_z) \models \Phi$$

That the second order semantics is consistent with the usual semantics of processes in terms of its valid formulas, is a consequence of the following theorem.

Theorem 17. *Let $P, P_1, \ldots, P_z$ be processes where P has arity z and let $\Phi \in \mathrm{L}\mu_1$ be a closed hierarchical equational system. Then we have:*

$$P; (P_1, \ldots, P_z) \models \Phi \qquad \Longleftrightarrow \qquad \Phi \in [\![P]\!](\mathrm{L}\mu_1(P_1), \ldots, \mathrm{L}\mu_1(P_z))$$

Corollary 18 [Consistency of Second Order Semantics]. *Given a process P of arity z and a closed hierarchical equational system $\Phi \in \mathrm{L}\mu_1$, we have:*

$$P \models \Phi \qquad \Longleftrightarrow \qquad \Phi \in [\![P]\!](\underbrace{\mathrm{L}\mu_1(0), \ldots, \mathrm{L}\mu_1(0)}_{z\ times}),$$

The point of the second order semantics is its *compositionality* with respect to sequential composition:

Theorem 19 [Compositionality of Second Order Semantics].
Given a process P of arity z and processes $P_1, \ldots, P_z$ of arity z', we have:

$$[\![P\ ;\ (P_1, \ldots, P_z)]\!] = [\![P]\!] \circ ([\![P_1]\!], \ldots, [\![P_z]\!])$$

4.2 The Model-Checking Algorithm

In this section, we generalize the model-checking algorithm of [BuS92] in order to deal with *pushdown* processes. This algorithm, which assumes a process representation in terms of a moderate PDNF, consists of three steps:

1. Constructing a *recursive function scheme* Θ_{PT} with respect to the PDPA process and the minimal equational block B of interest: The appropriate solution of this scheme, called the *PT-equational system*, yields the property transformers for each fragment of the pushdown process restricted to the subformulas of B.
2. Solving of the PT-equational system Θ_{PT} by component-wise computation of a *property transformer* for each fragment of the pushdown process: essentially, we proceed as in the finite-state case (cf. [CKS92]), except for
   - the domain for the iteration, which is second order here, i.e. it consists of property transformers.
   - the handling of fragments. They are dealt with by applying the currently valid approximation of their property transformers.

The computation of the *component property transformers* (CPT) consists of two phases: the initialization and the fixpoint computation.
The initialization of the CPTs depends on whether we process a *min* or a *max*-block: a CPT is initialized with the maximal transformer in case X is a *max*-variable and with the minimal transformer otherwise. This reflects the fact that *max*-variables are initially assumed to be satisfied by all states and *min*-variables by none.
The fixpoint computation is done by standard fixpoint iteration. The evaluation of the right-hand sides during the fixpoint computation simply consists of functional composition and the application of the meet and join operations of the lattice of all CPT's (cf. [BuS92]).

3. Deciding the model-checking problem: Having the predicate transformers at hand, the model-checking problem can be solved by checking whether the considered formula is a member of the set of formulas that results from applying the property transformer associated with the root fragment of the PDPA process to the tuple of sets of formulas that are valid for a terminated (deadlocked) state.

Constructing the PT-Equational System: The first step of the algorithm consists of constructing an equational system for the property transformers of interest. The construction embodies the behavioural structure of the given PDPA process and the semantics of the given formula, respectively.

Let Δ be a moderate pushdown process with arity n, i.e. $|Q| = n$, and let for simplicity $B = \mathtt{min}\ \{ X_i = \Phi_i \mid 1 \leq i \leq m \}$ be a single closed minimal equational block with left-hand side variables $\mathcal{X} = \{ X_i \mid 1 \leq i \leq m \}$, where X_1 represents the property to be investigated. – The extension to arbitrary hierarchical equational systems is straightforward.

To solve the model-checking problem we are mainly interested in computing the *semantic* property transformers $\Pi_{[q,Z]} =_{\mathrm{df}} [\![[q, Z]]\!]_{|\mathcal{X}} : \mathfrak{P}(\mathcal{X})^n \rightarrow \mathfrak{P}(\mathcal{X})$ of simple fragments restricted to the variables of B. For the sake of clarity, we split such a property transformer into its *component property transformers* (CPT) $\Pi^X_{[q,Z]} : \mathfrak{P}(\mathcal{X})^n \rightarrow \mathbb{B}$. Given $X \in \mathcal{X}$, $\Pi^X_{[q,Z]}$ is defined by $\Pi^X_{[q,Z]} =_{\mathrm{df}} \chi^X \circ \Pi_{[q,Z]}$, where χ^X denotes the predicate characterizing the membership of X and $\mathbb{B}$ is the Boolean lattice over $\{0, 1\}$. Note that the CPTs $\Pi^X_{[q,Z]}$ for a given $[q, Z]$ are equivalent to $\Pi_{[q,Z]}$, as $\Pi_{[q,Z]} = \bigcup_{X \in \mathcal{X}} \delta_X \circ \Pi^X_{[q,Z]}$, where $\delta_X(0) = \emptyset$ and $\delta_X(1) = \{X\}$.

Let now $\perp^{(n)}$ denote the least CPT which maps every element of $\mathfrak{P}(\mathcal{X})^n$ to 0, $\top^{(n)}$ the greatest CPT which maps every element of $\mathfrak{P}(\mathcal{X})^n$ to 1 and $\chi_n^{X \in j} : \mathfrak{P}(\mathcal{X})^n \rightarrow \mathbb{B}$ be the predicate characterizing whether X is a member of the j-th argument. Then the PT-equational system Θ_{PT} is built by means of the rules specified in Figure 4. The obtained PT-equational system consists of three parts: a set of PT-equations related to the property represented by the minimal equational block B, a set of PT-equations handling the assumptions at the end states of fragments and a set of PT-equations defining the property transformers of non-simple fragments by applying the PDPA law $A6$.

Property related equations

$$
\begin{array}{llll}
t^X_{[q,Z]} & = \top^{(n)} & \in \Theta_{PT}, \text{ if } & X = tt \in B \\
t^X_{[q,Z]} & = \bot^{(n)} & \in \Theta_{PT}, \text{ if } & X = ff \in B \\
t^X_{[q,Z]} & = t^{X'}_{[q,Z]} & \in \Theta_{PT}, \text{ if } & X = X' \in B \\
t^X_{[q,Z]} & = t^{X'}_{[q,Z]} \sqcup t^{X''}_{[q,Z]} & \in \Theta_{PT}, \text{ if } & X = X' \vee X'' \in B \\
t^X_{[q,Z]} & = t^{X'}_{[q,Z]} \sqcap t^{X''}_{[q,Z]} & \in \Theta_{PT}, \text{ if } & X = X' \wedge X'' \in B \\
t^X_{[q,Z]} & = \sqcup \{ t^{X'}_{[q',\beta]} \mid [q,Z] \xrightarrow{a} [q',\beta] \} & \in \Theta_{PT}, \text{ if } & X = \langle a \rangle X' \in B \\
t^X_{[q,Z]} & = \sqcap \{ t^{X'}_{[q',\beta]} \mid [q,Z] \xrightarrow{a} [q',\beta] \} & \in \Theta_{PT}, \text{ if } & X = [a] X' \in B
\end{array}
$$

Equations related to assumptions

$$
t^X_{[q_i,\epsilon]} = \chi_n^{X \in i} \in \Theta_{PT}
$$

Decomposition equations

$$
t^X_{[q,Z_1 Z_2]} = t^X_{[q,Z_1]} \circ (t_{[q_1,Z_2]}, \ldots, t_{[q_n,Z_2]}) \in \Theta_{PT}, \text{ if } t^X_{[q,Z_1 Z_2]} \text{ occurs in some property related equation}
$$

Fig. 4. The rules for constructing Θ_{PT}

The Fixpoint Iteration: Due to the fact that we consider a minimal equational block B we have to compute the *minimal* fixpoint of the constructed PT-equational system. This is done using a standard fixpoint algorithm as outlined in Figure 5. The central procedure **compfix** updates the component property transformers $t^X_{[q,Z]}$ until consistency is reached. It uses the auxiliary functions **rhs**, which delivers the right-hand side term of a given PT-variable, and **eval**, which evaluates a PT-term with respect to a given environment. After the fixpoint computation the algorithm completes by applying the computed property transformer associated with the root fragment $[q_1, Z_1]$ to the n-tuple where each component is the set of variables valid for the empty process. The overall model-checking algorithm can then be summarized as follows:

procedure solve(B, Δ)
BEGIN
Construction of the PT-equational system Θ_{PT}.
compfix;
Let $\Upsilon^{X_1}_{[q_1,Z_1]}$ be the component property transformer associated with $[q_1, Z_1]$ after termination of the fixpoint computation and
let X_{nil} be the set of variables of B which are valid for the empty process **0**.
RETURN $\Upsilon^{X_1}_{[q_1,Z_1]}(X_{nil}, \ldots, X_{nil})$;
END

procedure compfix
BEGIN
  /* **Initialization** */
  Let $\widetilde{t}$ be the vector of PT-variables which occur on a left-hand side in an equation of Θ_{PT}.

  $\rho.old = \emptyset, \quad \rho.new = [\,\widetilde{\bot^{(n)}}/\widetilde{t}\,];$

  /* **Fixpoint Computation** */
  WHILE $\rho.new \neq \rho.old$ DO
    $\rho.old := \rho.new$
    $\rho.new = [\,\mathbf{eval}(\mathbf{rhs}(\widetilde{t}), \rho.old)/\widetilde{t}\,];$
  OD
END

Fig. 5. The Algorithm for Computing the Fixpoint of Θ_{PT}.

Correctness and Complexity: The procedure **solve** consists of the construction of Θ_{PT}, the fixpoint computation accomplished by a call to **compfix** and a final computation of $\Upsilon^{X_1}_{[q_1,Z_1]}(X_{nil}, \ldots, X_{nil})$. It always terminates, since the number of simple fragments is finite and the procedure **compfix** is monotonic on the finite lattice $\mathfrak{P}(\mathcal{X})^{|Q|} \to \mathfrak{P}(\mathcal{X})$. Moreover, upon termination of **compfix**, a single application of $\Upsilon^{X_1}_{[q_1,Z_1]}$ suffices to decide whether the formula represented by X_1 is valid for the overall system, i.e. at the start state of the process defined by the PDPA equation system. This is a consequence of the following stronger property, whose rather involved proof can be found in [BuS94].

Theorem 20 [Coincidence]. *Let Θ_{PT} be the PT-equational system obtained from a pushdown process Δ and a closed minimal equational block B. Moreover, let the* algorithmic *property transformer $\Upsilon^X_{[q,Z]}$ be the value of $t^X_{[q,Z]}$ after termination of the procedure* **compfix**. *Then we have*

$$\forall\, X \in \mathcal{X}, q \in Q, Z \in \Gamma.\ \ \Upsilon^X_{[q,Z]} \;=\; \Pi^X_{[q,Z]}$$

Now the correctness of the algorithm is an easy corollary.

Corollary 21 [Correctness]. *The algorithm computes the set of all variables of B which are valid at the start state of the process defined by Δ.*

$$X \in \Upsilon_{[q_1,Z_1]}(X_{nil}, \ldots, X_{nil}) \quad\Longleftrightarrow\quad [q_1, Z_1] \models X$$

Considering its complexity, it turns out that the worst case time complexity of our model-checking algorithm is quadratic in the size of the PDPA system and exponential in the size of the formula as well as in the cardinality of the arity. The proof of this theorem can also be found in the full version [BuS94].

Theorem 22 [Complexity]. *Let Δ be a moderate PDPA process system and B be a closed minimal equational block. Measuring the size of Δ as the number of summands in all right-hand side expressions the worst-case time complexity of* **solve** *is*

$$O(\ |Q| * |\Delta|^2 * |B|^2 * 4^{|B|*|Q|}\ )$$

5 Conclusions and Future Work

We have shown that pushdown processes, which strictly generalize context-free processes, 1) form the smallest extension closed under parallel composition with finite state systems, and 2) can be model checked by means of an elegant adaptation to pushdown automata of the second order model checker introduced in [BuS92]. In fact, pushdown processes turn out to be the appropriate generalization of context-free processes for the automatic verification of distributed systems: any nontrivial parallel composition involving context-free processes requires at least the more general structure of pushdown processes.

Concerning future work, we hope that the presented characterization theorems for pushdown processes may help to solve the still open problem whether bisimulation equivalence is decidable for pushdown processes or not.

Acknowledgements

We would like to thank Hardi Hungar and the anonymous referees for their constructive comments and suggestions.

References

[BBK87] J.C.M. Baeten, J.A. Bergstra, and J.W. Klop. Decidability of Bisimulation Equivalence for Processes Generating Context-Free Languages. Technical Report CS-R8632, CWI, September 1987.

[Bra91] J.C. Bradfield. *Verifying Temporal Properties of Systems with Applications to Petri Nets.* PhD thesis, University of Edinburgh, 1991.

[BrS91] J.C. Bradfield and C. Stirling. Local Model Checking for Infinite State Spaces. Technical Report ECS-LFCS-90-115, LFCS, Edinburgh, Jun 1991.

[BuS92] O. Burkart and B. Steffen. Model Checking for Context-Free Processes. In *CONCUR '92, LNCS 630*, pages 123–137. Springer, 1992.

[BuS94] O. Burkart and B. Steffen. Composition, Decomposition and Model Checking of Pushdown Processes. Technical Report MIP-9402, Universität Passau, 1994.

[CES86] E.M. Clarke, E.A. Emerson, and A.P. Sistla. Automatic Verification of Finite State Concurrent Systems Using Temporal Logic Specifications. *ACM Transactions on Programming Languages and Systems*, 8(2):244–263, 1986.

[CHS92] S. Christensen, H. Hüttel, and C. Stirling. Bisimulation Equivalence is Decidable for all Context-Free Processes. In *CONCUR '92, LNCS 630*, pages 138–147. Springer, 1992.

[CKS92] R. Cleaveland, M. Klein, and B. Steffen. Faster Model Checking for the Modal Mu-Calculus. In *CAV '92, LNCS 663*, pages 410–422, 1992.

[Cle90] R. Cleaveland. Tableau-Based Model Checking in the Propositional Mu-Calculus. *Acta Informatica*, 27:725–747, 1990.

[CM90] D. Caucal and R. Monfort. On the Transition Graphs of Automata and Grammars. In *Graph-Theoretic Concepts in Computer Science, LNCS 484*, pages 311–337. Springer, 1990.

[CS91] R. Cleaveland and B. Steffen. Computing Behavioural Relations, Logically. In *ICALP '91, LNCS 510*, pages 127–138. Springer, 1991.

[CS92] R. Cleaveland and B. Steffen. A Linear-Time Model-Checking Algorithm for the Alternation-Free Modal Mu-Calculus. In *CAV '91, LNCS 575*, pages 48–58. Springer, 1992.

[EL86] E.A. Emerson and C.-L. Lei. Efficient Model Checking in Fragments of the Propositional Mu-Calculus. In *Proc. 1th Annual Symp. on Logic in Computer Science*, pages 267–278. IEEE Computer Society Press, 1986.

[Hüt91] H. Hüttel. *Decidability, Behavioural Equivalences and Infinite Transition Graphs.* PhD thesis, University of Edinburgh, Dec 1991. CST-86-91.

[Hoa88] C.A.R. Hoare. *Communicating Sequential Processes.* Prentice–Hall, 1988.

[HS93] H. Hungar and B. Steffen. Local Model-Checking for Context-Free Processes. In *ICALP '93, LNCS 700*, pages 593–605, 1993.

[Koz83] D. Kozen. Results on the Propositional μ-Calculus. *Theoretical Computer Science*, 27:333–354, 1983.

[Lar88] K.G. Larsen. Proof Systems for Hennessy–Milner Logic with Recursion. In *CAAP '88, LNCS 299*, pages 215–230. Springer, 1988.

[Mil89] R. Milner. *Communication and Concurrency.* Prentice–Hall, 1989.

[MS85] D.E. Muller and P.E. Schupp. The Theory of Ends, Pushdown Automata, and Second-Order Logic. *Theoretical Computer Science*, 37:51–75, 1985.

[PI93] S. Purushothaman Iyer. A Note on Model Checking Context-Free Processes. In *NAPAW '93*, 1993. To appear in LNCS.

[SW89] C. Stirling and D. Walker. Local Model Checking in the Modal Mu-Calculus. In *TAPSOFT '89, LNCS 351*, pages 369–383. Springer, 1989.

[Tar55] A. Tarski. A Lattice-Theoretical Fixpoint Theorem and its Applications. *Pacific Journal of Mathematics*, 5:285–309, 1955.

[Win89] G. Winskel. A Note on Model Checking the Modal Mu-Calculus. In *ICALP '89, LNCS 372*, pages 761–772. Springer, 1989.

Local Model Checking for Parallel Compositions of Context-Free Processes

Hardi Hungar

Computer Science Department
University Oldenburg
D-26111 Oldenburg, Germany
hungar@informatik.uni-oldenburg.de

Abstract.
Decidability of modal logics is not limited to finite systems. The alternation-free mu-calculus can be model checked for sequential systems given in a context-free form (or even a more general one). But the parallel composition of such systems introduces undecidabilities. Nevertheless, several instances can be handled as it is shown in this paper. The known model check techniques prove to be not extendable to parallel compositions. A new tableau system is introduced which is complete in the sequential case and for parallel compositions involving at most one infinite system. The verification of a queue which results from the parallel composition of two (context-free) stacks demonstrates its ability to cope with nontrivial compositions of infinite systems, too.

1 Introduction

Context-free processes (CFPs) are in general infinite state systems which nevertheless allow model checking of alternation-free mu-calculus formulae [5, 12]. This also holds for even larger classes of processes, i.e. pushdown processes (PDPs) [6] and higher-order pushdown processes (HOPDPs) [11]. These classes are rather powerful: CFPs are essentially the elements of BPA [1], PDPs have additionally a finite control and are themselves generalized by HOPDPs. But the classes are not closed under parallel compositions. Only finite processes may be run in parallel with a pushdown process (first-order or higher-order). This may be considered unsatisfactory, but already two CFPs plus a finite control can simulate a Turing-machine, thus destroying decidability of the model checking problem.

Yet there are several instances of this problem which can be handled, i.e. parallel compositions of processes which provably satisfy a modal specification. But the known model check techniques can not readily handle those cases, they are restricted to the sequential case. Of course one could try to adopt any modular reasoning principle, which breaks down a property of a parallel composition to assertions about its components, and then use sequential model checking. But this would ignore the structure of the processes used in the parallel composition. Instead, in this paper an approach is developed which copes directly with the parallel composition of CFPs (and PDPs).

The model checking algorithms for CFPs compute, for each position in the process, the set of subformulae of the formula in question which are valid at that position. Within definitions of nonatomic actions one assumes a set of subformulae valid at the end state of the definition, and the computation is done once for each assumption. That it is enough to know the subformulae valid at the end is the main observation underlying these algorithms. But within a parallel composition with synchronization on actions, also the environment and its current state have to be incorporated. Trying this it becomes soon apparent that it is not sufficient to know which subformulae are true for the continuation of the process.

Instead of representing the continuation of a sequential process by the set of formulae valid for it, I propose to use a (regular) set of process terms for that purpose. This has the advatage to be able to compute further step by step the parallel composition with the environment when one process reaches its continuation part, and it again allows a finite representation of the possibly infinite set of continuations. The use of continuation grammars is inspired by the application of Büchi's regular canonic systems [4] for parsing context-free grammars.

First, I show that a sound and complete tableau system in the style of [12] may also be based on regular continuations instead of formula sets. Then I extend the system in a natural way to cope with parallel compositions with synchronization on common actions, and I demonstrate its power by applying it to the parallel composition of two stacks (given by CFPs) which together form a queue (which could not be modeled by CFPs, or even HOPDPs). There are no general completeness results for the parallel tableau system because of the undecidability of the model checking problem. But if at most one process in the parallel composition is infinite, every valid assertion can be derived.

Related Work

The first model check procedures for the mu-calculus were limited to finite state systems cf. [10, 7, 9, 8, 14, 16, 17]. Bradfield and Stirling gave a tableau system for the full mu-calculus which can deal with infinite state systems, but the system is in general not effective, i.e. the set of successful tableaux is not decidable. Burkart and Steffen [5] presented an effective procedure deciding alternation-free formulae in context-free processes and extended it to pushdown processes [6]. A tableau system for CFPs can be found in [12] and extensions to the more powerful class of higher-order pushdown processes in [11].

All the dedicated tableau systems, including the one given in this paper, could be viewed as specific effective variants of Bradfield's and Stirling's system. The problem in finding these variants is to come up with representations of infinite sets of states which allow to create and decide a sufficiently large set of successful tableaux. And usually, the form of successful tableaux depends on the representation, i.e. each variant has its own structural success criteria.

2 Processes and Formulae

2.1 Context-Free Processes

Other than in [5, 12], I take BPA terms [1] to represent context-free processes. The definitions are fairly standard. I would like to point out that I do not require recursion to be guarded. Modifications to the proof systems necessary to cope with unguarded recursion have already been presented in [11].

Definition 1. A *process term* is generated by the following production rules.

$$t ::= \mathbf{0} \mid a \mid p \mid t + t \mid t \cdot t\,,$$

where a is from a set of *atomic actions* Act and p from a set of *identifiers* Idf. Additionally, there is an empty term ϵ. $\mathcal{T}(p_1, \ldots, p_n)$ denotes the set of nonempty terms with identifiers among $\{p_1, \ldots, p_n\}$. The *alphabet* $\alpha(t)$ of a term t is the set of occuring atomic actions.

A term is in *normal form* iff for every subterm $t_1 \cdot t_2$, either $t_1 \in Act$ or $t_1 \in Idf$.

Definition 2. A *context-free process* (CFP) is a term t_0 together with a set of definitions $p_i = t_i$, $i = 1, \ldots, n$ where $t_j \in \mathcal{T}(p_1, \ldots, p_n)$ for all $j = 0, \ldots, n$. Each CFP has an *alphabet* which includes the union of the alphabets of the terms t_j.

A CFP defines a transition system.

Definition 3. A *transition system* is a set of states and a binary relation on the set of states for every $a \in Act$. One of the states is the distinguished *start state*. I write $s \stackrel{a}{\to} s'$ if the pair (s, s') is an element of the relation of the action a.

Definition 4. The transition system defined by a CFP (with the notations of Definition 2) has $\mathcal{T}(p_1, \ldots, p_n)$ plus ϵ as its set of states and t_0 as the start state. For each a in its alphabet, the following set of rules defines the transition relation.

$$\frac{-}{a \stackrel{a}{\to} \epsilon} \qquad \frac{t_i \stackrel{a}{\to} t}{p_i \stackrel{a}{\to} t} \qquad \frac{t_1 \stackrel{a}{\to} t_1'}{t_1 + t_2 \stackrel{a}{\to} t_1'} \qquad \frac{t_2 \stackrel{a}{\to} t_2'}{t_1 + t_2 \stackrel{a}{\to} t_2'}$$

$$\frac{t_1 \stackrel{a}{\to} t_1'}{t_1 \cdot t_2 \stackrel{a}{\to} t_1' \cdot t_2}\; t_1 \neq \epsilon \qquad \frac{t_1 \stackrel{a}{\to} \epsilon}{t_1 \cdot t_2 \stackrel{a}{\to} t_2}$$

Note that no transition origins at ϵ or $\mathbf{0}$. I will interpret mu-calculus formulae in those transition systems. Since this interpretation is invariant under bisimulation, the set of states may actually be changed. The tableau system is easier to formulate if all occuring terms are in normal form.

Fact 5 *Every term can be transformed into a normal form term (according to Definition 1 which generates a bisimular transition system. This can be done by using the associativity of "·" and its distributivity from the right over "+". If t and t' are normal form terms, then I write $t;t'$ for the normal form term bisimilar to $t \cdot t'$.*

As an example for this consider $(a\cdot(p+c)\cdot\tilde{a})$, which is not in normal form, and its normal form equivalent $(a\cdot(p\cdot\tilde{a}+c\cdot\tilde{a}))$. Interpreting terms as directed graphs where edges are labeled with atomic actions or identifiers (+ is branching, concatenation), a normal form term will give a tree, whereas an arbitrary term might give a dag.

I will consider parallel compositions of processes, but only top-level parallelism. Parallel processes have to synchronise on actions from the intersection of their alphabets, other actions occur interleaved. The (straightforward) formal definition is as follows.

Definition 6. A *parallel process* is either a CFP or a parallel composition $\pi_1 \parallel \pi_2$ of two parallel processes π_1 and π_2 . Its alphabet is the union of both alphabets, and its transition system is the product of both component transition systems with synchronisation on the common actions, i.e.

$$\frac{\pi_1 \xrightarrow{a} \pi_1'}{\pi_1 \parallel \pi_2 \xrightarrow{a} \pi_1' \parallel \pi_2}\ (a \notin \alpha(\pi_2)) \qquad \frac{\pi_2 \xrightarrow{a} \pi_2'}{\pi_1 \parallel \pi_2 \xrightarrow{a} \pi_1 \parallel \pi_2'}\ (a \notin \alpha(\pi_1))$$

$$\frac{\pi_1 \xrightarrow{a} \pi_1' \ ,\ \pi_2 \xrightarrow{a} \pi_2'}{\pi_1 \parallel \pi_2 \xrightarrow{a} \pi_1' \parallel \pi_2'}\ (a \in \alpha(\pi_1) \cap \alpha(\pi_2))$$

2.2 Mu Calculus

The following negation–free syntax defines a sublanguage of the mu-calculus, which in spite of being as expressive as the full mu-calculus allows a simpler technical development.

$$\phi ::= \mathit{ff} \mid \mathit{tt} \mid X \mid \phi \wedge \phi \mid \phi \vee \phi \mid [a]\phi \mid \langle a\rangle\phi \mid \ \nu X.\phi \mid \mu Y.\phi$$

In the above, $a \in \mathit{Act}$, and $X, Y \in \mathit{Var}$, where Var is a set of variables. Only *closed*, *alternation free* formulae will be used, i.e. every variable is bound by a ν or μ, and no ν-subformula has a free variable which, in the context of the whole formula, is bound by a μ, and vice versa.

Given a transition system, the semantics of a formula is a subset of its states. A transition system satisfies a formula if its start state belongs to this set. The formal semantics of formulae is given in the appendix. The *closure* $CL(\phi)$ of a formula ϕ is the set of all its subformulae with each free variable replaced (iteratively) by the corresponding fixpoint subformula, e.g. $CL(\nu X.\phi) = \{\nu X.\phi\} \cup CL(\phi[\nu X.\phi/X])$.

3 The Problem

Consider the following example of a parallel composition of essentially two stacks.

$$r \parallel s \text{ where}$$

$$r = p\cdot\bar{c}\cdot r\,, \qquad p = (a\cdot(p+c)\cdot\tilde{a}) + (b\cdot(p+c)\cdot\tilde{b})$$
$$s = c\cdot q\cdot s\,, \qquad q = (\tilde{a}\cdot(q+\bar{c})\cdot\bar{a}) + (\tilde{b}\cdot(q+\bar{c})\cdot\bar{b})$$

$r \parallel s$ is an unbounded queue which works as follows. First, it may do an arbitrary (possibly infinite) number of a or b steps. This corresponds to pushing a number of values into the queue. After every a or b, it may do a c, after which all as and bs received so far are forwarded as $\tilde{a}$s and $\tilde{b}$s to the second component, in reversed order. This forwarding is terminated by a $\bar{c}$, after which the second component may output the as and bs as $\bar{a}$s and $\bar{b}$s in the same order they were received by the first component. The first component may concurrently receive further input.

This process defines – as CFPs may in general – an infinite transition system, even after factoring out bisimilar states. The known techniques to verify sequential CFPs only consider the terms $t_0, \ldots, t_n$ and their subterms. Whenever the definition of an identifier has to be considered (when an assertion of the form $p_i\cdot t$ **sat** $[a]\phi$ or $p_i\cdot t$ **sat** $\langle a\rangle\phi$ is encountered), the reasoning is split: One proves the formula for t_i assuming that a set of formulae is valid at the end of t_i, and verifies this assumption for t. Only a finite set of assertions has to be considered because all relevant assumptions belong to the closure of the formula under investigation.

If we tried to extend this sort of reasoning to parallel compositions of CFPs, we would not expect the same finiteness property to hold. Maybe stronger assertions would have to be made about intermediate states. In any case, we can not hope for a complete proof system, because already by adding a finite process to the queue above we would get a Turing-machine. But how the proof system should work, even if it is incomplete, is hard to imagine. In the sequential case, it is obvious what to do when a term is reduced to ϵ. One just has to check whether the remaining formula belongs to the set of assumptions. But in a parallel composition, one might end up with an assertion of the form

$$\epsilon \text{ assuming } \phi \parallel t \text{ assuming } \psi \textbf{ sat } \theta\,,$$

meaning

> "Every process t_1 satisfying ϕ run in parallel with any process $t\cdot t_2$ where t_2 satisfies ψ must satisfy θ."

So one would have to evaluate parallel compositions of combinations of process terms and processes specified by formulae, for which sensible reasoning principles seem hard to conceive.

The solution I choose is to replace the formula representations of the continuations by term grammars generating sets of continuation terms. Remembering that Büchi's regular canonical systems [4] can be used to describe intermediate prefix terms during the construction of a right derivation in a context-free grammar, it is plausible to use regular grammars to describe suffixes of the "left derivations" of process terms, which are generated during the proof. Using the production rules

$$U ::= \tilde{a}{\cdot}U \mid \tilde{b}{\cdot}U \mid \tilde{a}{\cdot}\bar{c}{\cdot}r \mid \tilde{b}{\cdot}\bar{c}{\cdot}r$$
$$V ::= \bar{a}{\cdot}V \mid \bar{b}{\cdot}V \mid s$$
$$W ::= \bar{a}{\cdot}W \mid \bar{b}{\cdot}W \mid \bar{a}\cdot s\,,$$

a finite proof that the queue satisfies

$$\nu X.([-]X \wedge [a]\mu Y.(([\tilde{a},\tilde{b},\bar{b},c,\bar{c}]Y \wedge \langle\tilde{a},\tilde{b},\bar{b},c,\bar{c}\rangle Y) \vee (\langle\bar{a}\rangle tt \wedge [\tilde{a},\tilde{b},\bar{b},c,\bar{c}]f\!f)))$$

can be formulated as shown below. The formula expresses that whenever an a is pushed into the queue and no further input is made, after a finite number of internal steps and outputs the queue will be able to output an a and no other outputs or internal steps are possible. In the formula, $[-]$ is used as a shorthand for a box including all atomic actions, meaning the conjunction of all single box formulae, whereas $\langle\tilde{a},\tilde{b},\bar{b},c,\bar{c}\rangle\ldots$ means the same as the disjunction of the respective formulae.

The following abbreviations are used: ν stands for the formula itself, μ for the minimal fixpoint subformula, $[\!\langle\tilde{a},\tilde{b},\bar{b},c,\bar{c}\rangle\!]\mu$ for $[\tilde{a},\tilde{b},\bar{b},c,\bar{c}]\mu \wedge \langle\tilde{a},\tilde{b},\bar{b},c,\bar{c}\rangle\mu$, and $\bar{a}!$ for $\langle\bar{a}\rangle tt \wedge [\tilde{a},\tilde{b},\bar{b},c,\bar{c}]f\!f$.

A term involving U, V or W represents the set of terms resulting from replacing these symbols by terms from the respective regular language, i.e. the set of process terms which result from *finitely* many expansions of the regular nonterminals. Note the difference between nonterminal symbols and declared identifiers: P whith the only production rule $P ::= a \cdot P$ denotes the empty set of processes, whereas p defined by $p = a \cdot p$ is the process a^ω. If the term t in an assertion t **sat** ϕ contains regular nonterminals, the assertion is meant to be valid if all process terms generated by regular expansion from t satisfy ϕ.

The assertion to be proved is

$$r \parallel s \textbf{ sat } \nu\,.$$

This can be generalized to

$$r \parallel V \textbf{ sat } \nu\,.$$

I.e. it suffices to prove ν for a set of terms containing $r \parallel s$. Now the fixpoint formula gets unfolded and both conjuncts have to be proven. Here, I consider only the first conjunct,

$$r \parallel V \textbf{ sat } [-]\nu\,.$$

The second is in fact a special case of an assertion occuring later. $[-]\nu$ splits into eight conjuncts, one for each atomic actions. Only those for $a, b, \bar{a}, \bar{b}$ require nontrivial tableaux. $\bar{a}$ and $\bar{b}$ appear after unfolding V, resulting in a recurrence of $r \parallel V$ **sat** ν. Since a maximal fixpoint has been unfolded, this recurrence counts as a proof. The other possible actions are a and b. Applying the appropriate production rule for U, they lead to

(•) $$(p+c) \cdot U \parallel V \textbf{ sat } \nu .$$

Again, both conjuncts within ν have to be proven.

I will start with $[-]\nu$. As above, $\bar{a}$ and $\bar{b}$ lead to immediate recurrence, whereas via a and b the previous assertion – $(p+c) \cdot U \parallel V$ **sat** ν – recurs. The fifth possible action for $(p+c) \cdot U \parallel V$ is c, which produces

$$U \parallel q \cdot s \textbf{ sat } \nu .$$

Further $\tilde{a}$ or $\tilde{b}$ actions will reduce to (apart from recurrences of $U \parallel (q+\bar{c}) \cdot V$ **sat** ν)

$$\bar{c} \cdot r \parallel (q+\bar{c}) \cdot V \textbf{ sat } \nu .$$

Here, the only possible action, namely $\bar{c}$, lets $r \parallel V$ **sat** ν recur.

Now to the second conjunct necessary to prove (•) i.e.

$$(p+c) \cdot U \parallel V \textbf{ sat } [a]\mu .$$

An a yields

$$(p+c) \cdot \tilde{a} \cdot U \parallel V \textbf{ sat } \mu .$$

The three rules for V generate

$$(p+c) \cdot \tilde{a} \cdot U \parallel \bar{a} \cdot V \textbf{ sat } \mu \qquad (p+c) \cdot \tilde{a} \cdot U \parallel \bar{b} \cdot V \textbf{ sat } \mu \qquad (p+c) \cdot \tilde{a} \cdot U \parallel s \textbf{ sat } \mu .$$

Since $(p+c) \cdot \tilde{a} \cdot U \parallel \bar{a} \cdot V$ **sat** $\bar{a}!$ holds, unfolding of μ can prove the first assertion. The second is reduced to $(p+c) \cdot \tilde{a} \cdot U \parallel V$ **sat** μ. This is the recurrence of a minimal fixpoint assertion. Other than with maximal fixpoints, not every recurrence counts as a proof. Here, a regular nonterminal has been expanded. Since only finite expansions are considered, this corresponds to an inductive step of the form:

> "A term generated by $n+1$ expansion steps satisfies μ, if all terms generated by n steps satisfy μ."

Therefore, this recurrence is "good". The third assertion reduces to

$$(p+c) \cdot \tilde{a} \cdot U \parallel c \cdot q \cdot s \textbf{ sat } [\![\langle \tilde{a}, \tilde{b}, \bar{b}, c, \bar{c} \rangle]\!]\mu .$$

A c followed by an $\tilde{a}$ gives $U \parallel (q+\bar{c}) \cdot \bar{a} \cdot s$ **sat** μ, which generalizes to

$$U \parallel (q+\bar{c}) \cdot W \textbf{ sat } \mu .$$

The first two production rules of U give

$$\tilde{a} \cdot U \parallel (q+\bar{c}) \cdot W \textbf{ sat } \mu \qquad \tilde{b} \cdot U \parallel (q+\bar{c}) \cdot W \textbf{ sat } \mu ,$$

which immediately recur. The other rules produce $\tilde{a} \cdot \bar{c} \cdot r \parallel (q+\bar{c}) \cdot W$ **sat** μ and $\tilde{b} \cdot \bar{c} \cdot r \parallel (q+\bar{c}) \cdot W$ **sat** μ, which both reduce (via $\bar{c} \cdot r \parallel (q+\bar{c}) \cdot W$ **sat** μ) to

$$r \parallel W \textbf{ sat } \mu .$$

Three rules for W yield the cases

$$r \parallel \bar{a} \cdot W \textbf{ sat } \bar{a}! \qquad r \parallel \bar{b} \cdot W \textbf{ sat } [\![\tilde{a}, \tilde{b}, \bar{b}, c, \bar{c}]\!]\mu \qquad r \parallel \bar{a} \cdot s \textbf{ sat } \bar{a}! \,.$$

The first and third are obviously valid, and the second recurs to $r \parallel W$ **sat** μ, again via expanding a nonterminal.

The proof above is a description of a successful tableau which establishes the validity of $r \parallel s$ **sat** ν. In the next section, I will first define the tableau system for (sequential) CFPs and prove its completeness. Only in Section 5 I will present the system dealing with parallel compositions which will allow a completely formal proof of the assertion.

4 A New Tableau System for CFPs

As already explained in the previous section, the assertions may now contain nonterminals from a regular grammar.

Definition 7. Let a set *Reg* of *nonterminal symbols* be given which is disjoint to *Act* and *Idf*. The set of *regular process terms* is given by

$$r ::= t \mid t; U \,,$$

where $U \in Reg$ and t is a process term in normal form. A *regular production* is of the form

$$U ::= r \,.$$

If $t; U$ is a regular term and $U ::= r$ is one of a given set of productions, then

$$t; U \mapsto t; r \,.$$

The step from $t; U$ to $t; r$ is called *(regular) unfolding* and the step from $t; r$ to $t; U$ is called *(regular) folding*. The *language* of a regular term is the set of all process terms which can be generated by finitely many unfolding steps, i.e.

$$\mathcal{L}(r) =_{\mathrm{df}} \{ t \mid r \mapsto^* t \} \,.$$

Note that regular process terms are all in normal form. This is not an absolute necessity, but it facilitates the formulation of the tableau rules for formulae of the form $[a]\phi$ or $\langle a \rangle \phi$. I can not simply use the notion of $t \xrightarrow{a} t'$, even after generalizing it to regular process terms, mainly because of unguarded recursion, which may introduce infinitely many successors to a node in the tableau. To avoid this, a simplified way of computing a-successors, which works for normal form terms, is included in the tableau system. In this way, one can keep track of the intermediately generated process terms. There is a success criterion which allows to cut off the potentially infinite generation process in certain good cases.

$$\frac{r \ \mathbf{sat}\ \phi \wedge \psi}{r \ \mathbf{sat}\ \phi \qquad r \ \mathbf{sat}\ \psi} \qquad \frac{r \ \mathbf{sat}\ \phi \vee \psi}{r \ \mathbf{sat}\ \phi} \qquad \frac{r \ \mathbf{sat}\ \phi \vee \psi}{r \ \mathbf{sat}\ \psi}$$

$$\frac{r \ \mathbf{sat}\ \nu X.\phi(X)}{r \ \mathbf{sat}\ \phi(\nu X.\phi(X))} \qquad \frac{r \ \mathbf{sat}\ \mu Y.\phi(Y)}{r \ \mathbf{sat}\ \phi(\mu Y.\phi(Y))}$$

$$\frac{r + r' \ \mathbf{sat}\ [a]\phi}{r \ \mathbf{sat}\ [a]\phi \qquad r' \ \mathbf{sat}\ [a]\phi} \qquad \frac{r + r' \ \mathbf{sat}\ \langle a\rangle\phi}{r \ \mathbf{sat}\ \langle a\rangle\phi} \qquad \frac{r + r' \ \mathbf{sat}\ \langle a\rangle\phi}{r' \ \mathbf{sat}\ \langle a\rangle\phi}$$

$$\frac{a \cdot r \ \mathbf{sat}\ [a]\phi}{r \ \mathbf{sat}\ \phi} \qquad \frac{a \cdot r \ \mathbf{sat}\ \langle a\rangle\phi}{r \ \mathbf{sat}\ \phi} \qquad \frac{p_i \cdot r \ \mathbf{sat}\ [a]\phi}{t_i; r \ \mathbf{sat}\ [a]\phi} \qquad \frac{p_i \cdot r \ \mathbf{sat}\ \langle a\rangle\phi}{t_i; r \ \mathbf{sat}\ \langle a\rangle\phi}$$

$$\frac{U \ \mathbf{sat}\ \phi}{r_1 \ \mathbf{sat}\ \phi \quad \ldots \quad r_n \ \mathbf{sat}\ \phi} \ (U ::= r_1, \ \ldots \ , U ::= r_n \text{ are all productions of } U) \qquad \frac{r' \ \mathbf{sat}\ \phi}{r \ \mathbf{sat}\ \phi} \ (r \mapsto r')$$

Fig. 1. Tableau Rules for Sequential Processes

Definition 8. Let a set of definitions $D =_{\mathrm{df}} \{p_1 = t_1, \ldots, p_n = t_n\}$ and a set of regular productions be given. An *assertion* has the form r **sat** ϕ, where r is a regular term containing only defined identifiers. It is *valid* iff for all $t \in \mathcal{L}(r)$ the CFP consisting of D and t satisfies ϕ.

The tableau system is formulated with respect to a fixed set of definitions $p_i = t_i$ and a set of regular productions $U ::= r$.

Figure 1 contains the rules of the tableau system. They are "upside-down" proof rules, i.e. the assertion above the line is valid if all assertions below the line are valid. For a tableau constructed according to these rules to count as a proof of the assertion at its root, all its leaves have to satisfy one of the success criteria given in the next definition.

Definition 9. A leaf is *recurring* if there is a predecessor which is labeled with the same assertion as the leaf. A tableau is *successful* if it is finite and all *leaves* are *successful*. *Successful leaves* are

1. labeled with r **sat** tt, or
2. labeled with r **sat** $[a]\phi$ where r is of the form ϵ, $\mathbf{0}$, or $b \cdot r'$ with $b \neq a$,
3. recurring, labeled with r **sat** $\nu X.\phi$, and on the connecting path the maximal fixpoint gets unfolded, or

4. recurring, labeled with r **sat** $[a]\phi$, and on the connecting path only rules dealing with $+$, process expansion and regular folding are applied, or
5. recurring and more regular unfolding steps than folding steps are done on the connecting path.

An assertion is *derivable* if it has a successful tableau.

It is easy to see that all rules are backwards sound, i.e. the assertion above the line is valid if all assertions below are valid. E.g. the folding rule $\dfrac{r' \textbf{ sat } \phi}{r \textbf{ sat } \phi} (r \mapsto r')$ is sound, because the set of process terms which can be generated from r contains the terms which can be generated from r'.

Leaves of the form in the first or second clause of the previous definition are obviously valid, but the recurring leaves require an argument. The third clause captures *ν-recurrence*. Roughly, it formalizes the argument

$$(S \subseteq [\![\phi(\nu X.\phi)]\!] \Leftarrow S \subseteq [\![\nu X.\phi]\!]) \Rightarrow S \subseteq [\![\nu X.\phi]\!]$$

(which is valid for maximal fixpoints): The tableau establishes the backward implication on the left, therefore the formula on the right holds, i.e. the leaf is valid. The fourth clause only deals with unguarded recursion. Otherwise, no such leaves would occur. It relies on the fact that if $[a]\phi$ is false, there must be an a-transition to a state where ϕ does not hold. But after the first cycle, all possible a-successors will be examined in different branches of the tableau. The fifth clause makes use of the finiteness condition for the language of a regular term. Its correctness translates to "if, for all n, all process terms generated in $n+1$ steps satisfy ϕ whenever all process terms generated in n steps satisfy ϕ, then all finitely generated terms satisfy ϕ." Note the special case where a regular nonterminal has an empty language. The assertion might trivially recur, as in the case where $U ::= U$ is the only production, but also the assertion is always valid in this case.

This completes a sketch of the proof of the first half of the following theorem.

Theorem 10. *The tableau system is sound and complete for CFPs.*

To argue for the completeness of the system, I will refer to the system from [12] which is known to be complete. The formula continuations from that system have to be replaced by regular nonterminals. Since in that system, continuations are introduced only at process expansions, this will be done here, too. The main point of the proof is that for any relevant formula continuation, there is an equivalent regular continuation.

Let a CFP with definitions $p_1 = t_1, \ldots, p_n = t_n$ and main term t_0 be given. The regular productions are of the form

$$U ::= t$$

for subterms $p \cdot t$ of t_0 , or

$$U ::= t; V$$

for subterms $p \cdot t$ of $t_1, \ldots, t_n$. Since the t_i are assumed to be in normal form, each subterm of the form $p \cdot t$ extends to the "end" of t_i , i.e. it is not part of left side of a sequential composition. $U ::= \epsilon$ occurs if there is some p at one of the ends of t_0 . There are also productions of the form $U ::= V$.

Which nonterminals and which productions actually make up the grammar depends on the formula to be proved. Let ϕ be the formula in question. In the following, lowercase greek letters will denote elemnts of the closure of ϕ , and capital greek letters will denote subsets of it. For any Ψ there is one nonterminal U_Ψ . The language of U_Ψ will consist of all possible continuations which satisfy every $\psi \in \Psi$. For every Θ and every $t \in \mathcal{T}(p_1, \ldots, p_n)$, let

$$[\![t]\!](\Theta) =_{\mathrm{df}} \{ \psi \mid \forall t'.t' \textbf{ sat } \Theta \Rightarrow t; t' \textbf{ sat } \psi \} .$$

The productions are

$$\begin{array}{ll} U_\Psi ::= t & \text{where } \Psi = \{ \psi \mid t \textbf{ sat } \psi \} \\ U_\Psi ::= t; U_\Theta & \text{where } \Psi = [\![t]\!](\Theta) \\ U_\Psi ::= U_\Theta & \text{where } \Psi \subset \Theta . \end{array}$$

The nonterminals U_Ψ allow to express every continuation of an identifier which occurs at the beginning of a regular term in the constructed tableau. This means that whenever a regular term $p \cdot t; U_\Theta$ is encountered, there is a production rule $U_\Psi ::= t; U_\Theta$ which can be applied to fold $t; U_\Theta$. The completeness proof now roughly follows the pattern of the proof of the completeness result of [12] (this proof is contained in the full version of that paper which is not yet published). The nonterminals U_Ψ play the role of the formula continuations Ψ .

5 A Tableau System for Parallel Processes

The tableau rules can easily be generalized to deal with parallel processes. The rules dealing with $\wedge, \vee, \nu, \mu$ remain exactly the same, only that parallel terms are allowed. All other rules, except the two rules removing $[a]$ resp. $\langle a \rangle$, apply to exactly one parallel component, e.g. we have the rule

$$\frac{r + r' \parallel r'' \textbf{ sat } \langle a \rangle \phi}{r \parallel r'' \textbf{ sat } \langle a \rangle \phi} .$$

To remove $[a]$ or $\langle a \rangle$, all parallel components with a in their alphabet must do an a-transition, e.g.
if a is in both alphabets,

$$\frac{a \cdot r \parallel a \cdot r' \textbf{ sat } [a]\phi}{r \parallel r' \textbf{ sat } \phi} \qquad \frac{a \cdot r \parallel a \cdot r' \textbf{ sat } \langle a \rangle \phi}{r \parallel r' \textbf{ sat } \phi} ,$$

and, if a is only in the alphabet of the left component,

$$\frac{a \cdot r \parallel r' \textbf{ sat } [a]\phi}{r \parallel r' \textbf{ sat } \phi} \qquad \frac{a \cdot r \parallel r' \textbf{ sat } \langle a\rangle\phi}{r \parallel r' \textbf{ sat } \phi} .$$

The success criteria are also straightforward adaptations of the sequential ones. Only regular recurrence gets more complicated. It is not necessary to require that in every component, more unfolding than folding steps do occur. It is e.g. sufficient that on the paths to every leaf recurring to a fixed node, one and the same component gets unfolded more often than folded. This condition is satisfied by a tableau proving the assertion of Section 3. But other conditions are also acceptable. They are formulated in the following definition.

Definition 11.

- A set $D \subseteq \mathcal{Z}^k$ is *decreasing* iff for any $\mathbf{n} \in \mathcal{N}^k$, there is no infinite sequence $(\mathbf{d}_i)_{i \in \mathcal{N}}$, $\mathbf{d}_i \in D$ with
$$\forall l.\ \mathbf{n} + \Sigma_{i=0}^{l} \mathbf{d}_i \in \mathcal{N}^k .$$
- For a path π in a tableau for a term with k parallel components, let $d_{\pi,j}$ be the number of folding steps minus the number of unfolding steps in the jth component on the path π, and let $\mathbf{d}_\pi$ denote $(d_{\pi,1}, \ldots, d_{\pi,k})$.
- Let a node in a tableau and a set of leaves recurring to that node be given, and let Π be the set of paths from the node to the recurring leaves. The set of leaves form a *regular decreasing set* if $\{\mathbf{d}_\pi \mid \pi \in \Pi\}$ is decreasing.

Note that it is decidable whether a finite set in $\mathcal{Z}^k$ is decreasing. The most common cases will be that one component is decreased on each path or that on each path, at least one is decreased and none is increased.

Definition 12. A leaf in a parallel tableau is *successful* if it is

1. labeled with an assertion whose formula part is tt, or
2. labeled with the formula $[a]\phi$ and one of the parallel components with a in its alphabet is of the form ϵ, $\mathbf{0}$, or $b \cdot r'$ with $b \neq a$,
3. recurring, labeled with a maximal fixpoint formula, and on the connecting path the maximal fixpoint gets unfolded, or
4. recurring, labeled with $[a]\phi$, and on the connecting path only rules dealing with $+$, process expansion and regular folding are applied, or

A parallel tableau is *successful* if it is finite and there is a function assigning every leaf which is not successful to one of its predecessors with the same assertion s.t. for each node the set of assigned leaves forms a regular decreasing set.

The arguments for the soundness of the parallel tableau system are nearly the same as the ones for the sequential system. Note that it is sufficient that box recurrence happens in one parallel component. Suppose that due to unguarded recursion in one component, some $[a]$ can not be removed. Then, regardless of the other components, branches for all possible a-transitions of that component are generated when only that component is treated by the process expansion rule. With regular decreasing nodes, the argument is as follows. As in the sequential case, we take an element t of the regular language which is generated by the term in the recurring assertion. t is generated by some of number of unfolding steps in each parallel component, giving a vector $\mathbf{n} \in \mathcal{N}^k$. The validity of the formula for t relies on its validity for terms generated by $\mathbf{n} + \mathbf{d}_\pi$ unfolding steps, where π is a path to an assigned leaf. That the set of vectors $\mathbf{d}_\pi$ is decreasing guarantees that this gives a well-founded inductive argument.

As already explained, there can be no general completeness result. But I can show completeness in the case where only one parallel component is infinite and all other components are finite processes. A finite process is a CFP with only tail end recursion in its definitions, or, in other words, no general sequential composition but action prefixing instead.

Theorem 13. *If at most one component of a parallel composition is infinite, the parallel tableau system is complete.*

The proof of the result is a generalization of the sequential completeness proof. Continuations are only used for the infinite component. The regular sets are further split according to the different truth values of the closure formulae for the different states the environment may have at that time. I.e. if the parallel composition with at least one state of the environment yields different sets of valid formulae for two continuations, they have to be distinguished. Since the environment has finitely many (non bisimular) states, still a finite set of continuation sets are sufficient.

If at most one component of a parallel composition is infinite, the composition is equivalent to a pushdown process [6]. Model checking algorithms, both global and local ones, complete for pushdown processes are already known [6, 11]. So the completeness of the parallel system is no big surprise. But nevertheless this demonstrates the adequateness of the rules. Further evidence is provided by the example from Section 3, where a nontrivial property of a parallel composition of infinite state systems is proved. The proof sketch in that section can indeed be formalized by a successful tableau. The property is nontrivial in that it relies on the correct interaction of both infinite state systems.

6 Conclusion

I have presented a local model checking technique which can handle nontrivial parallel compositions of infinite state system. It is complete if at most one component has infinitely many states, but it may successfully be applied even in other cases.

Several questions naturally arise. There are standard ones like whether the method can be extended to the full mu calculus or what the complexity of an implementation would be. But the most interesting, and probably the most difficult one is: Are there further sufficient or even necessary and sufficient criteria for tractable problems? A hint may be that by using regular continuations of single processes, only finite information is kept which may later be exploited to compute continuations of the parallel composition.

Another challenge is to design a system capable of handling unbounded parallelism.

Acknowledgement

I would like to thank Bernhard Steffen for introducing me to the model check problem of context-free processes and Olaf Burkart for convincing me of the advantages of an algebraic notation for processes. Special thanks are due to Hans Langmaack for extensively covering the parsing theory of context-free languages in his lectures.

References

1. Bergstra, J.A., and Klop, J.W., *Process theory based on bisimulation semantics.* LNCS 354 (eds de Bakker, de Roever, Rozenberg) (1988), 50–122.
2. Bradfield, J.C., *Verifying temporal properties of systems.* Birkhäuser, Boston (1992).
3. Bradfield, J.C., and Stirling, C. P., *Verifying temporal properties of processes.* Proc. CONCUR '90, LNCS 458 (1990), 115-125.
4. Büchi, J.R., *Regular canonical systems.* Archiv f. math. Logik und Grundlagenforschung **6** (1964) 91–111.
5. Burkart, O., and Steffen, B., *Model checking for context-free processes.* CONCUR '92, LNCS 630 (1992), 123–137.
6. Burkart, O., and Steffen, B., *Pushdown processes: Parallel composition and model checking.* Tech. Rep. Aachen/Passau (1994), 17 p.
7. Clarke, E.M., Emerson, E.A., and Sistla, A.P., *Automatic verification of finite state concurrent systems using temporal logic specifications.* ACM TOPLAS **8** (1986), 244–263.
8. Cleaveland, R., *Tableau-based model checking in the propositional mu-calculus.* Acta Inf. **27** (1990), 725-747.
9. Cleaveland, R., and Steffen, B., *A linear-time model-checking algorithm for the alternation-free modal mu-calculus.* CAV 91, LNCS 575 (1992), 48–58. (1986), 1–32.
10. Emerson, E.A., and Lei, C.-L., *Efficient model checking in fragments of the propositional mu-calculus.* 1st LiCS (1986), 267–278.
11. Hungar, H. *Local model checking of higher-order processes,* Technical Report, Oldenburg (1994), 13p.
12. Hungar, H., and Steffen, B., *Local model checking for context-free processes.* ICALP '93, LNCS 700 (1993), 593-605.
13. Kozen, D., *Results on the propositional μ-calculus.* TCS **27** (1983), 333–354.
14. Larsen, K. G., *Proof systems for satisfiability in Hennessy-Milner logic with recursion.* TCS **72** (1990), 265-288.
15. Larsen, K.G., *Efficient local correctness checking.* CAV '92.
16. Stirling, C. P., and Walker, D. J., *Local model checking in the modal mu-calculus.* TAPSOFT '89, LNCS 351 (1989), 369-383.

17. Winskel, G., *A note on model checking the modal mu-calculus.* ICALP '89, LNCS 372 (1989), 761–772.

A Semantics of mu-Calculus Formulae

Formulae are interpreted with respect to a fixed (possibly infinite) transition system with set of states $\mathcal{S}$ and an environment $e : Var \rightarrow 2^{\mathcal{S}}$.

$$\begin{aligned}
[\![X]\!]e &= e(X) \\
[\![\phi_1 \vee \phi_2]\!]e &= [\![\phi_1]\!]e \cup [\![\phi_2]\!]e \\
[\![\phi_1 \wedge \phi_2]\!]e &= [\![\phi_1]\!]e \cap [\![\phi_2]\!]e \\
[\![[a]\phi]\!]e &= \{\, s \mid \forall s'.\, s \stackrel{a}{\rightarrow} s' \Rightarrow s' \in [\![\phi]\!]e \,\} \\
[\![\langle a \rangle\phi]\!]e &= \{\, s \mid \exists s'.\, s \stackrel{a}{\rightarrow} s' \wedge s' \in [\![\phi]\!]e \,\} \\
[\![\nu X.\phi]\!]e &= \bigcup \{S' \subseteq \mathcal{S} \mid S' \subseteq [\![\phi]\!]e[X \mapsto S']\} \\
[\![\mu X.\phi]\!]e &= \bigcap \{S' \subseteq \mathcal{S} \mid S' \supseteq [\![\phi]\!]e[X \mapsto S']\}
\end{aligned}$$

Intuitively, the semantic function maps a formula (with free variables) to the set of states for which the formula is "true". Accordingly, a state s satisfies X if s is an element of the set bound to X in e. Since $[\![\phi]\!]e$ does not depend on e for a closed ϕ, this definition assigns a unique set of states to each closed formula.

The Logical Structure of Concurrent Constraint Programming Languages (Abstract)

Prakash Panangaden
McGill University
(Joint work with N. Mendler, P. Scott and R. Seely)

The Concurrent Constraint Programming paradigm has been the subject of growing interest as the focus of a new paradigm for concurrent computation. Like logic programming it claims close relations to logic. In fact these languages *are* logics in a certain sense that we make precise. In recent work it was shown that the denotational semantics of determinate concurrent constraint programming languages forms a categorical structure called a hyperdoctrine which is used as the basis of the categorical formulation of first order logic. What this connection shows is the combinators of determinate concurrent constraint programming can be viewed as logical connectives. In the present work we extend these ideas to the operational semantics of these languages and thus make available similar analogies for the indeterminate concurrent constraint programming languages. We also describe a linear extension of concurrent constraint programming and discuss hyperdoctrines for such languages. The discussion concludes with an examination of the prospects for understanding other formalisms for concurrent computation in the same way. One need never have heard of a hyperdoctrine in order to follow the talk.

Countable Non-Determinism and Uncountable Limits*

Pietro Di Gianantonio[1], Furio Honsell[1], Silvia Liani[1]
and Gordon D. Plotkin[2]

[1] Dipartimento di Matematica e Informatica, Università di Udine
via Zanon, 6, I 33100 Udine
[2] Department of Computer Science, University of Edinburgh
Kings Buildings, Mayfield Road Edinburgh EH9 3JZ

Abstract. In this paper we address the problem of solving recursive domain equations using *uncountable limits* of domains. These arise for instance, when dealing with the ω_1-continuous function-space constructor and are used in the (generative) denotational semantics of programming languages which feature non-deterministic fair constructs implemented with unbounded choice. It is well known that such features cannot be modeled using just Scott-continuous functions; they can be modeled conveniently, instead, using functions which satisfy the weaker continuity property of ω_1-continuity. Surprisingly, the category of cpo's and ω_1-continuous embeddings is not ω_0-cocomplete. Hence the standard technique of Adámek and Koubek for solving reflexive domain equations involving these constructs fails. This phenomenon was not noticed before in the literature. We discuss two alternative methods that can be used to solve the required domain equations. The first one is an application of the method of Adámek and Koubek to a different category. The second one, instead, is a genuine extension of their method and amounts to considering cones instead of limits. We put both methods on solid categorical grounds and discuss some applications. Finally we utilise the second method in order to give a model for the untyped λ-calculus whose theory is precisely the $\boldsymbol{\lambda\beta\eta}$ theory. Thus we show that ω_1-lambda models are *complete* for the $\lambda\beta\eta$-calculus.

* Work partially supported by MURST 40% & 60% grants, by EEC/HCM Network "Lambda Calcul Typé", by EEC Science Research Project MASK and by an SERC Senior Fellowship.

1 Introduction

This paper deals with the domain-theoretic constructions needed to provide *generative* semantics, implemented using unbounded choice, for *fair* non-deterministic programming languages. Following [8], by a *generative* semantics we mean one which provides denotations only for *fair* executions. Generative semantics, in this sense, is opposed to the more widely studied *restrictive* semantics, (see e.g. [3]), where fair executions are isolated within a larger domain of *all* executions. We will not elaborate on the problematic notion of *fairness*. For our purposes a "naive" definition of the *fair behaviour* of a non-deterministic program suffices. Namely: a non-deterministic program exhibits weakly fair behaviour if during its execution no subprocess is forever denied its turn for execution in case it is continuously enabled. As customary in the generative approach, see e.g. [2], we model *fair choice* constructs by reducing them to constructs which make use of unbounded (but countable) non-deterministic choice operators. Hence we discuss constructions which accommodate, in effect, programs with random assignments. The practical motivations for investigating fairness are clear. Here, we would like to mention, however, only a foundational significance of random assignment, which is recalled, perhaps, less often. As shown by Chandra, [4], only flow diagrams with random assignment can count as the *universal model* of non-deterministic computations. This is, of course, if we consider *divergence* as well as *termination* sets.

The paper is organised as follows. We start by recalling briefly, in Sections 2 and 3, some of the main issues that arise in the denotational semantics of languages involving unbounded (but countable) non-determinism. We use the simple non-deterministic *guarded command language* $\mathcal{GC}$, introduced by Dijkstra [5], extended with random assignment. We illustrate, in particular, the relation between uncountable non-determinism and fair choice and show that Scott-continuous functions are not adequate for modelling uncountable non-determinism. Following [2] we introduce the notion of ω_1-continuity and then introduce the "fairness" category $\mathbf{CPO_1}$. In Section 4 we address the issue of solving recursive domain equations in $\mathbf{CPO_1}$. First we show that the standard categorical techniques, based on embeddings [10], do not apply in this case, by proving that the corresponding category of embeddings $\mathbf{CPO_1^E}$ is not ω_0-cocomplete. Then, we give a construction, somewhat "by hand", which, nevertheless, provides a solution to a particular equation which cannot be dealt with by the standard methods. In Section 5 we show how this construction can be put on solid categorical grounds. In particular we give two methods which generalise appropriately the technique of [1] and allow us to solve recursive domain equations involving several domain constructors, including $\rightarrow_{\omega_1}$ (exponentiation in $\mathbf{CPO_1}$) and, for the first method, $\mathcal{P}^\omega$ the countable powerdomain constructor (introduced in [8] where it is written as $\mathcal{P}_1$). It is an open question as to whether this powerdomain satisfies condition A (see below) needed for the application of the second method. Finally in Section 6 we utilise the second method to find a particular solution of the domain equation $D \cong [D \rightarrow_{\omega_1} D]$ in order to define a model for the untyped lambda calculus whose theory is exactly the theory $\boldsymbol{\lambda\beta\eta}$.

2 Unbounded non-determinism and fairness

Dijkstra's *guarded command language*, $\mathcal{GC}$, is an imperative language featuring a particular kind of command, the *guarded* command, that can be used to implement *finitary non-determinism*. See Appendix A for the definition and semantics of $\mathcal{GC}$.

The *random assignment* command $x := ?$ is added to $\mathcal{GC}$ in order to achieve *countable non-determinism*; it sets x to an arbitrary natural number. As is well-known, this command allows countable sets of possible outputs even under the assumption of program termination. König's lemma does not apply to this context; representing the computation history of a non-deterministic program using a generating tree, the random assignment command allows programs whose generating tree may not be finitely branching, and hence can have an infinite number of nodes without having an infinite path (all computations terminate).

The $\mathcal{GC}$-language has *weakly fair iteration* if, for every iteration cycle, each guard B_i that is continuously enabled will not be indefinitely postponed. Clearly the assumption of fairness implies unbounded non-determinism. More precisely: under the assumption of fairness, we can construct an appropriate non-deterministic program which exhibits the same behaviour as the random assignment command:

$$x := 0; b := \mathit{true};$$
$$\mathbf{do}\ b \rightarrow x := x + 1 \ \square\ b \rightarrow b := \mathit{false}\ \mathbf{od}$$

The simulation can go also the other way. By using the unbounded choice operator, we can simulate fair computations. More precisely the weakly fair iteration command:

$$\mathbf{do}\, B_1 \rightarrow C_1 \ \square\ \cdots\ \square\ B_n \rightarrow C_n\, \mathbf{od}$$

is simulated by the following statement:

$$\begin{array}{l} \mathbf{do}\,(B_1 \vee \ldots \vee B_n) \rightarrow x_1 := ?; \ldots; x_n := ?; \\ \qquad\qquad\qquad\qquad \mathbf{do}\ B_1 \wedge (x_1 > 0) \rightarrow x_1 := x_1 - 1; C_1 \\ \qquad\qquad\qquad\qquad \square\ \ldots \\ \qquad\qquad\qquad\qquad \square\ B_n \wedge (x_n > 0) \rightarrow x_n := x_n - 1; C_n \\ \qquad\qquad\qquad\qquad \mathbf{od} \\ \mathbf{od} \end{array}$$

where $x_1, \ldots, x_n$ do not occur in the B_i or C_i.

This connection between fairness and unbounded (but countable) non-determinism motivates the study of non-deterministic languages with unbounded choice operators. Thus, generative semantics for fair processes (i.e. involving only and all fair computations) can be given by simulation via semantics for countable non-determinism, rather than through a difficult direct analysis of fairness properties.

3 Scott-continuity vs. ω_1-continuity

In order to define the denotational semantics of the language $\mathcal{GC}$ we need to introduce a *domain of denotations* for non-deterministic computations. For this purpose we consider the *Plotkin powerdomain* of the flat cpo $S_\perp$, where S is a countable set of stores (states of computations); see [2] for more details.

Definition 1. i) The powerdomain $\mathcal{P}(S_\perp)$ is the set $\{A \subseteq S_\perp \mid A \neq \emptyset, A \text{ finite or } \perp \in A\}$ partially ordered by:

$$A \sqsubseteq B \text{ iff } A = B \vee (\perp \in A \wedge A \setminus \{\perp\} \subseteq B)$$

ii) Given a function $f : S \rightarrow \mathcal{P}(S_\perp)$, its extension is $f^+ : \mathcal{P}(S_\perp) \rightarrow \mathcal{P}(S_\perp)$, where $f^+(A) = \bigcup_{a \in A \setminus \{\perp\}} f(a) \cup \{\perp \mid \perp \in A\}$.

The denotational semantics of $\mathcal{GC}$ is given by a function

$$\mathcal{C} : Com \rightarrow (S \rightarrow \mathcal{P}(S_\perp))$$

When we extend the language $\mathcal{GC}$ with the atomic command $x := ?$ we need to give a different powerdomain capable of accommodating unbounded (but countable) non-determinism. We need, in fact, a richer set of points including countable sets of total values.

Definition 2. [2] The powerdomain $\mathcal{P}^\omega(S_\perp)$ is the set $\{A \subseteq S_\perp \mid A \neq \emptyset\}$ partially ordered by: $A \sqsubseteq B$ iff $A = B \vee (\perp \in A \wedge A \setminus \{\perp\} \subseteq B)$.

It is easy to prove that $\mathcal{P}^\omega(S_\perp)$ is a cpo with $\{\perp\}$ as least element. The meaning function: $\mathcal{C} : Com \rightarrow (S \rightarrow \mathcal{P}^\omega(S_\perp))$ is the obvious extension of the previous one, using a least fixed-point for iteration and with the further clause:

$$\mathcal{C}[\![x := ?]\!]s = \{[x \mapsto n]s \mid n \in I\!N\}$$

As pointed out in [2] there are essential failures of Scott continuity in a (compositional) denotational semantics for this form of unbounded non-determinism. We now give an example of this phenomenon. Consider the command:

$$\textbf{do } x = 0 \rightarrow x :=?; \, x := x + 1 \;\Box\; x > 1 \rightarrow x := x - 1 \textbf{ od}$$

Its semantics is given by the least fixed-point of an operator F which is monotone but not Scott-continuous; F is defined by:

$$F(f)(s) = \begin{cases} \{s\} & \text{if } s(x) = 1 \\ f^+(\{[x \mapsto n+1]s \mid n \in I\!N\}) & \text{if } s(x) = 0 \\ f^+(\{[x \mapsto x-1]s\}) & \text{if } s(x) > 1 \end{cases}$$

To check the non continuity of F observe that the n-th approximation of its fixed-point, with $n \geq 2$, is given by:

$$F^{(n)}(s) = \begin{cases} \{[x \mapsto 1]s\} \cup \{\perp\} & \text{if } s(x) = 0 \\ \{[x \mapsto 1]s\} & \text{if } 0 < s(x) \leq n \\ \{\perp\} & \text{otherwise} \end{cases}$$

The ω-th approximation of the fixed-point is therefore:

$$F^{(\omega)}(s) = \bigsqcup_{n<\omega} F^{(n)}(s) = \begin{cases} \{[x \mapsto 1]s\} \cup \{\bot\} & \text{if } s(x) = 0 \\ \{[x \mapsto 1]s\} & \text{if } 0 < s(x) \end{cases}$$

However $F^{(\omega)}$ is not the fixed-point of F; to obtain the fixed-point we need to add an $\omega + 1$ step since: $F^{(\omega+1)} = F(F^{(\omega)}) = \lambda s.\{[x \mapsto 1]s\} = F(F^{(\omega+1)})$.

The command considered always terminates, but since it is unknown how many iterations are necessary to finish the command when the input is 0, every finite approximation $F^{(n)}$ can diverge for input 0 and since $F^{(\omega)}$ is the pointwise sup of the finite approximations also $F^{(\omega)}$ can diverge for input 0.

It is possible to construct examples of iterative commands whose semantics are obtained iterating the application of the associated functionals for any recursive ordinal. For example the semantics of the command:

$$\textbf{do } x < y \rightarrow y := y - 1 \;\square\; 1 < x \rightarrow x := x - 1;\ y :=?\ \textbf{od}$$

is obtained after $\omega \times \omega$ steps.

These are instances of the many non-Scott-continuity phenomena which arise when dealing with unbounded choice. Other examples are: the non-continuity of $\lambda f.f^{+}$ or the fact that there is no continuous compositional semantics for this language, see [2]. Therefore, in order to discuss the denotational semantics for unbounded choice we follow the solution of Apt and Plotkin and consider spaces of functions which satisfy a weaker continuity condition, ω_1-continuity. All functionals arising in the problematic cases are in fact continuous w.r.t. to this weaker notion of continuity.

Definition 3. i) Let A be a partial order, and let κ be a cardinal number. A *κ-chain* in A is a monotone map from κ to A.
ii) A partial order A is *κ-complete* if it has lubs of all κ-chains.
iii) Let A, B be partial orders and let $f : A \rightarrow B$ be a function. Then f is *κ-continuous* if it preserves lubs of κ-chains.

We are led to study the following categories:

Definition 4. The *fairness* category $\mathbf{CPO_1}$ has as objects the ω_0- and ω_1-complete partial orders with a least element, and as morphisms the ω_1-continuous functions. We will use also the subcategory $\mathbf{CPO}$ having the same objects as $\mathbf{CPO_1}$ and as morphisms the functions which are both ω_0- and ω_1-continuous.

Both $\mathbf{CPO_1}$ and $\mathbf{CPO}$ are Cartesian closed categories with the usual Cartesian product and pointwise-ordered function spaces. In $\mathbf{CPO_1}$ least fixed-points of morphisms, such as F, are obtained by iteration through all the countable ordinals:

Proposition 5. *Let $f : D \rightarrow D$ be a morphism in $\mathbf{CPO_1}$ For every ordinal $\beta \leq \omega_1$ define $f^{(\beta)}$ in D by $f^{(0)} = \bot_D$, $f^{(\beta+1)} = f(f^{(\beta)})$, $f^{(\lambda)} = \bigsqcup_{\beta<\lambda} f^{(\beta)}$ (λ a limit ordinal). Then $f^{(\omega_1)}$ is the least fixed-point of f.*

4 Solving recursive domain equations

In this section we discuss reflexive domain equations in $\mathbf{CPO_1}$ and the difficulties in applying the traditional techniques developed in category theory for solving them. Finally, we outline how to overcome these difficulties in the special case of $D \cong [D \to D]$.

If we want to give a denotational semantics for a language featuring higher-order procedures together with unbounded choice, we need to solve reflexive equations on $\mathbf{CPO_1}$ involving $\to_{\omega_1}$ as domain constructor. Also if we consider languages with a parallel constructor, to be interpreted via interleaving and resumptions, we need to solve reflexive domain equations, involving the powerdomain constructor $\mathcal{P}^\omega$ for countable non-determinism extending that considered above on flat cpos. We are therefore led to investigate the theory of reflexive domain equations in $\mathbf{CPO_1}$. Traditionally, reflexive domain equations are handled in one of the two following ways.

The first method works in any category $\mathbf{C}$ with colimits of ω_0-chains. It proceeds by analogy with the solution of fixed-point equations $x = f(x)$ in cpos, given by $Fix_f = \bigsqcup_n f^n(\bot)$ and justified by the existence of chain-lubs and by the continuity of f. What one does in the categorical setting is to construct the solution of the equation $X \cong F(X)$ as $Fix_F = colim\ \Delta$ where $\Delta = \langle F^n(X_0), F^n(e)\rangle_{n\in\omega}$ is the ω-chain constructed starting from an object X_0 and a morphism
$e : X_0 \to F(X_0)$. This is justified by the existence of colimits and by the continuity of the endofunctor F (meaning that it preserves the colimits of ω_0-chains), see [10]. (Strictly speaking, the analogy between categories and partial orders would lead us to take X_0 as the initial object. This is often done, but here the extra generality will prove useful.)

The second method for solving recursive domain equations in category theory has been developed by Adámek & Koubek [1] and used in [8]. It allows one to solve a larger class of equations than the first method and it is based on the fact that, under a stronger assumption of cocompleteness of the category, a weaker requirement for the functor can be required. In particular, this method allows one to find a fixed-point solution also for functors which are only ω_1-continuous, i.e. which preserve the colimits of ω_1-chains. The least fixed-point is obtained in this case as the colimit of a suitable ω_1-chain.

Both approaches are based on the subcategory of embeddings:

Definition 6. Let $\mathbf{CPO^E}$ ($\mathbf{CPO_1^E}$) be the subcategory of $\mathbf{CPO}$ ($\mathbf{CPO_1}$) having the same objects and whose morphisms from D to E are the *embedding* functions from D to E. Embeddings are the morphisms $e : D \to_{(\omega_1)} E$ for which there exists a morphism $p : E \to_{(\omega_1)} D$, called a *projection* such that: $p \circ e = id_D$ and $e \circ p \sqsubseteq id_E$; $\langle e, p\rangle$ is an (ω_1-)*embedding-projection* pair (or (ω_1-)*ep* pair).

Given an embedding e there exists a unique function p satisfying the above conditions and conversely. Restricting to embeddings allows one to consider loc-

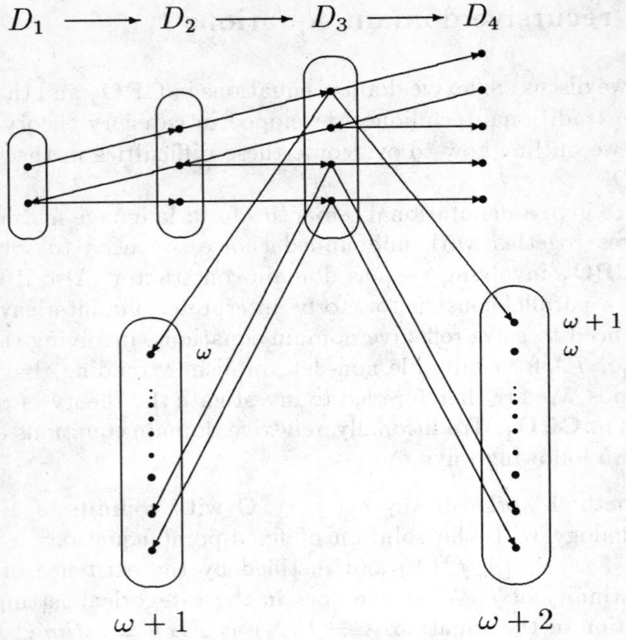

Fig. 1. Counterexample

ally monotone functors of mixed variance, such as $\rightarrow_{\omega_1}$, as covariant functors on the subcategory of embeddings, see [10, 8] for more details.

Not surprisingly if we consider the category $\mathbf{CPO_1^E}$ the first method, above, fails to produce a solution of the simple reflexive equation $D \cong [D \rightarrow_{\omega_1} D]$. For the $\rightarrow_{\omega_1}$ constructor is *not* continuous. But, much more surprisingly, also the second method fails since the category $\mathbf{CPO_1^E}$ is not ω_0-cocomplete (i.e. it does not have colimit for every ω_0-chain), contrary to what has been claimed in [8]. For a counterexample, define an ω_0-chain $\langle D_n, e_n \rangle_{n \in I\!N^+}$ in the category $\mathbf{CPO_1^E}$, see Fig.1, as follows: we take D_n to be the set of natural numbers $\{0, 1, \ldots, n\}$ with the obvious linear order: $0 \sqsubseteq 1 \sqsubseteq \ldots \sqsubseteq n$; then we define the embedding $e_n : D_n \rightarrow_{\omega_1} D_{n+1}$ in the following way:

$$e_n(m) = \begin{cases} m & \text{if } m < n \\ n+1 & \text{if } m = n \end{cases}$$

Notice that this chain would be the one constructed according to both methods outlined above in order to solve in $\mathbf{CPO_1^E}$ the recursive domain equation $D \cong D_\perp$, starting from the domains $D_1 = \{0, 1\}$ and $D_2 = \{0, 1, 2\} = (D_1)_\perp$ and the morphism $e_1 : D_1 \rightarrow_{\omega_1} D_2$ defined as above.

This chain does not have a colimit. For, consider the two cones having as vertices $\omega + 1 = \{1, 2, \ldots, \omega\}$ and $\omega + 2 = \{1, 2, \ldots, \omega, \omega + 1\}$, respectively, and whose embeddings $e^1_n : D_n \to \omega + 1$ and $e^2_n : D_n \to \omega + 2$, for $n > 0$, are defined by:

$$e^1_n(m) = \begin{cases} m & \text{if } m < n \\ \omega & \text{if } m = n \end{cases} \qquad e^2_n(m) = \begin{cases} m & \text{if } m < n \\ \omega + 1 & \text{if } m = n \end{cases}$$

Now suppose, for the sake of contradiction, that $\mu : D_n \to D$ $(n > 0)$ is the colimit (D being the vertex) of the above chain. Then there is a mediating embedding $e : D \to \omega + 1$, and one can easily show that e is an isomorphism. So, if the colimit exists it is $\omega + 1$. Therefore there must be a mediating morphism from $\omega + 1$ to $\omega + 2$. Unfortunately, such a mediating morphism does not exist. In fact there is only one possible embedding e' from $\omega + 1$ to $\omega + 2$, for which necessarily, $e'(\omega) = \omega$. But this means that the diagram does not commute, so we have a contradiction.

Nevertheless the classical domain equation: $D \cong [D \to_{\omega_1} D]$, can still be solved non-trivially. The mathematical construction might seem ad hoc, but it amounts to the construction of an inverse limit. It will be fully generalised and put on firm categorical ground in the next section.

In order to provide a non-trivial solution we start from a given cpo D_0 and an ω_1-ep pair $\langle e_{0,1}, p_{1,0} \rangle$, where $e_{0,1}$ in $[D_0 \to_{\omega_1} [D_0 \to_{\omega_1} D_0]]$ and $p_{1,0}$ in $[[D_0 \to_{\omega_1} D_0] \to_{\omega_1} D_0]$.

A chain $\langle D_\beta, \langle e_{\alpha,\beta}, p_{\beta,\alpha} \rangle \rangle_{\alpha<\beta\leq\omega_1+1}$ of cpos and ω_1-ep pairs is defined by induction on β in the following way:

- let $\beta = 1$. We define $D_1 = [D_0 \to_{\omega_1} D_0]$ and $e_{0,1}$, $p_{0,1}$ are the functions given above.
- Let $\beta = \beta' + 2$. We define:
  - $D_\beta = [D_{\beta'+1} \to_{\omega_1} D_{\beta'+1}]$
  - $e_{\beta'+1,\beta} = \lambda\, d_{\beta'+1} .\, e_{\beta',\beta'+1} \circ d_{\beta'+1} \circ p_{\beta'+1,\beta'}$
  - $p_{\beta,\beta'+1} = \lambda\, d_\beta .\, p_{\beta'+1,\beta'} \circ d_\beta \circ e_{\beta',\beta'+1}$

  and for $\alpha \leq \beta'$ we define:
  - $e_{\alpha,\beta} = e_{\beta'+1,\beta} \circ e_{\alpha,\beta'+1}$
  - $p_{\beta,\alpha} = p_{\beta'+1,\alpha} \circ p_{\beta,\beta'+1}$
- Let $\beta = \lambda$ be a limit ordinal. We define:
  - $D_\beta = \{\langle d_0, \ldots, d_\alpha, \ldots \rangle_{\alpha<\beta} \mid d_\alpha \in D_\alpha \;\&\; \forall\, \alpha' < \alpha\; d_{\alpha'} = p_{\alpha,\alpha'}(d_\alpha)\}$
  - $e_{\alpha,\beta} = \lambda d_\alpha . \langle p_{\alpha,0}(d_\alpha), \ldots, d_\alpha, e_{\alpha,\alpha+1}(d_\alpha), \ldots \rangle$
  - $p_{\beta,\alpha} = \lambda\, \vec{d} \,.\, d_\alpha$
- Let $\beta = \lambda + 1$ with λ limit ordinal. We define:
  - $D_\beta = [D_\lambda \to_{\omega_1} D_\lambda]$
  - $e_{\lambda,\beta} = \lambda\, \vec{d} \,.\, \lambda\, \vec{d'} \,.\, \bigsqcup_{\alpha<\lambda} e_{\alpha,\lambda}(d_{\alpha+1}(d'_\alpha))$
  - $p_{\beta,\lambda} = \lambda f . \langle f^{(0)}, \ldots, f^{(\alpha)}, \ldots \rangle$

  where we define:

  * $f^{(\alpha+1)} = p_{\lambda,\alpha} \circ f \circ e_{\alpha,\lambda}$
  * $f^{(\gamma)} = p_{\gamma+1,\gamma}(f^{(\gamma+1)})$ for $\gamma = 0$ or γ a limit ordinal smaller than λ

and for $\alpha < \lambda$ we define:

- $e_{\alpha,\lambda+1} = e_{\lambda,\lambda+1} \circ e_{\alpha,\lambda}$
- $p_{\lambda+1,\alpha} = p_{\lambda,\alpha} \circ p_{\lambda+1,\lambda}$

Note. Observe that for λ a limit ordinal $\langle e_{\beta,\lambda} \rangle_\beta : \langle D_\beta, e_{\alpha,\beta} \rangle_{\alpha<\beta<\lambda} \rightarrow D_\lambda$ is a cone in the category $\mathbf{CPO_1^E}$ but it is not necessarily the colimit.

Theorem 7. *$e_{\omega_1,\omega_1+1} : D_{\omega_1} \cong [D_{\omega_1} \rightarrow_{\omega_1} D_{\omega_1}]$ is an isomorphism with inverse p_{ω_1+1,ω_1} and therefore D_{ω_1} is a non-trivial solution of the recursive domain equation $D \cong [D \rightarrow_{\omega_1} D]$.*

The previous theorem is a straightforward consequence of Theorem 16 bellow.

5 Two methods for solving domain equations

In this section we discuss two general methods which can be used to solve a large class of domain equations obtained using non-ω_0-continuous domain constructors which satisfy some ω_1-continuity conditions.

The first method, is an appropriate application of the method of Adámek and Koubek [1], and consists in *changing the category* under consideration and then applying the following theorem:

Theorem 8. *Let $\mathbf{C}$ be a category having colimits of both ω_0- and ω_1-chains and let $F : \mathbf{C} \rightarrow \mathbf{C}$ be an ω_1-continuous functor. Suppose $e : D \rightarrow F(D)$ is a morphism. Then a chain $\langle D_\beta, e_{\alpha,\beta} \rangle_{\alpha<\beta\leq\omega_1+1}$ can be constructed by induction on β as follows:*

- $D_0 = D$, $D_1 = F(D_0)$ *and* $e_{0,1} = e$
- *for* $\beta = \beta' + 2$
  - $D_\beta = F(D_{\beta'+1})$
  - $e_{\beta'+1,\beta} = F(e_{\beta',\beta'+1})$
  - $e_{\alpha,\beta} = e_{\beta'+1,\beta} \circ e_{\alpha,\beta'+1}$ *(for $\alpha \leq \beta'$)*
- *for $\beta = \lambda$ a limit ordinal, $\langle e_{\alpha,\beta} \rangle_\alpha : \langle D_\alpha, e_{\alpha,\gamma} \rangle_{\alpha<\gamma<\beta} \rightarrow D_\beta$ is a colimiting cone*
- *for $\beta = \lambda + 1$ with λ a limit ordinal,*
  - $D_\beta = F(D_\lambda)$ *and*
  - *$e_{\lambda,\lambda+1}$ is the mediating morphism between the colimiting cone $\langle e_{\alpha+1,\lambda} \rangle_\alpha : \langle D_{\alpha+1}, e_{\alpha+1,\gamma+1} \rangle_{\alpha<\gamma<\lambda} \rightarrow D_\lambda$ and the cone $\langle F(e_{\alpha,\lambda}) \rangle_\alpha : \langle D_{\alpha+1}, e_{\alpha+1,\gamma+1} \rangle_{\alpha<\gamma<\lambda} \rightarrow F(D_\lambda)$*
  - $e_{\alpha,\lambda+1} = e_{\lambda,\lambda+1} \circ e_{\alpha,\lambda}$ *(for $\alpha < \lambda$)*

We have that $e_{\omega_1,\omega_1+1} : D_{\omega_1} \rightarrow F(D_{\omega_1})$ is an isomorphism and $e_{0,\omega_1} = e^{-1}_{\omega_1,\omega_1+1} \circ F(e_{0,\omega_1}) \circ e$

The idea in this case is to solve recursive domain equations using the category $\mathbf{CPO^E}$ instead of the category $\mathbf{CPO^E_1}$. This is possible because, although we use non-continuous functions, it is not always necessary to consider non-continuous embeddings in order to solve a recursive domain equation. The category **CPO** has ω_0- and ω_1-colimits and so, as shown in [8], $\mathbf{CPO^E}$ has ω_0- and ω_1-colimits and locally ω_1-continuous functors in **CPO** yield ω_1-continuous functors on $\mathbf{CPO^E}$. All the functors we use in the construction of recursive domains, i.e. $+, \times, \rightarrow_{\omega_1}, \mathcal{P}^\omega$, are locally ω_1-continuous and restrict to functors on **CPO** and so we may solve recursive domain equations using them in $\mathbf{CPO^E}$.

Using this first method, therefore, we have to restrict ourselves to continuous embeddings. This condition, however, is too restrictive if we want to define a non-initial solution of $D \cong [D \rightarrow_{\omega_1} D]$ obtained starting from a domain D_0 and a non-continuous embedding $e_0 : [D_0 \rightarrow_{\omega_1} [D_0 \rightarrow_{\omega_1} D_0]]$. Such a recursively defined domain will be used in Section 6 in order to give a minimal model for the λ-calculus. Hence, in order to produce a general construction which includes that solution, we present a second method for defining fixed-points of functors, which yields limits obtained also starting from non-continuous embeddings.

This second method can be seen as a generalisation of the solution proposed by Adámek and Koubek. With respect to their solution we ask for a weaker requirement on the category and functors. In particular we can apply this construction also to categories such as $\mathbf{CPO^E_1}$ which do not have colimits of ω_0-chains.

Definition 9. Given a category **C** we say that a functor $F : \mathbf{C} \rightarrow \mathbf{C}$ *satisfies condition A* if for every chain Δ in **C**, such that $\Delta = \langle D_\alpha, f_{\alpha,\beta}\rangle_{\alpha<\beta<\lambda}$, where λ is a countable limit ordinal, $D_{\alpha+1} = F(D_\alpha)$ and $f_{\alpha+1,\beta+1} = F(f_{\alpha,\beta})$ there exists a cone $\mu : \Delta \rightarrow D_\lambda$ and a morphism $f_\lambda : D_\lambda \rightarrow F(D_\lambda)$ such that for all $\alpha < \lambda$ $f_\lambda \circ \mu_{\alpha+1} = F(\mu_\alpha)$, i.e. the diagram in Fig.2 commutes.

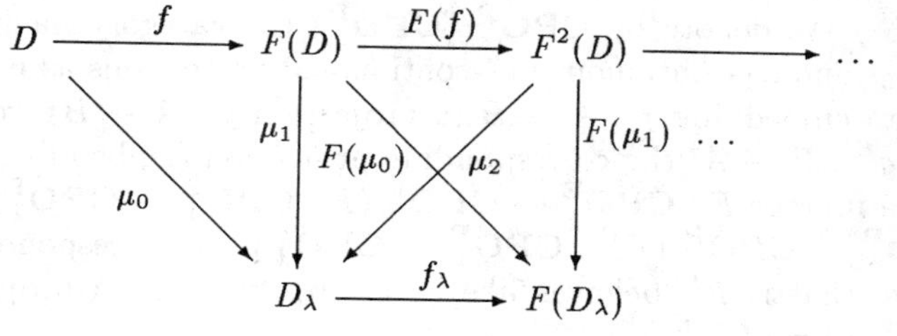

Fig. 2. Diagram for condition A

Proposition 10. *In a category* **C** *having colimits for every* ω_1*-chain, if a functor* $F : \mathbf{C} \rightarrow \mathbf{C}$ *is* ω_1*-continuous, satisfies condition A and there is an object* D_0 *and* *a morphism* $e : D_0 \to F(D_0)$, *then* F *has a fixed-point* $i : D \cong F(D)$ *and there exists a morphism* $e : D_0 \to D$ *such that:* $e = i^{-1} \circ F(e) \circ e_0$.

Proof. Under the specified conditions it is possible to construct an ω_1-chain $\langle D_\beta, e_{\alpha,\beta}\rangle_{\alpha<\beta<\omega_1}$ in the following way:

- $D_1 = F(D_0)$ and $e_{0,1} = e$
- for $\beta = \beta' + 2$
  - $D_\beta = F(D_{\beta'+1})$
  - $e_{\beta'+1,\beta} = F(e_{\beta',\beta'+1})$
  - $e_{\alpha,\beta} = e_{\beta'+1,\beta} \circ e_{\alpha,\beta'+1}$ (for $\alpha \leq \beta$)
- for $\beta = \lambda$ a limit ordinal, $\langle e_{\alpha,\beta}\rangle_\alpha : \langle D_\alpha, e_{\alpha,\gamma}\rangle_{\alpha<\gamma<\beta} \to D_\beta$ is the cone whose existence is assured by the existence condition A.
- for $\beta = \lambda + 1$ with λ a limit ordinal,
  - $D_\beta = F(D_\lambda)$ and
  - $e_{\lambda,\lambda+1}$ is the morphism whose existence is assured by condition A.
  - $e_{\alpha,\lambda+1} = e_{\lambda,\lambda+1} \circ e_{\alpha,\lambda}$ (for $\alpha < \lambda$)

If we consider now the colimiting cone $\langle e_{\alpha,\omega_1}\rangle_\alpha : \langle D_\alpha, e_{\alpha,\beta}\rangle_{\alpha<\beta<\omega_1} \to D_{\omega_1}$ and the unique morphism i between the cones $\langle e_{\alpha+1,\omega_1}\rangle_{\alpha<\omega_1}$ and $\langle F(e_{\alpha,\omega_1})\rangle_{\alpha<\omega_1}$ it is easy to prove that $i : D_{\omega_1} \to F(D_{\omega_1})$ is an isomorphism and obviously the equation $e_{0,\omega_1} = i^{-1} \circ F(e_{0,\omega_1}) \circ e_0$ holds. □

We want to apply Proposition 10 in order to prove that the functors which are unary compositions of basic functors $+, \times, \to_{\omega_1}$ admit a fixed-point. In order to do so we now consider the category $\mathbf{CPO_1^E}$. As shown in [8] $\mathbf{CPO_1^E}$ has colimits for every ω_1-chain and the domain constructors $+, \times, \to_{\omega_1}$ and their compositions, are functors preserving ω_1-colimits (since they are locally ω_1-continuous). So it remains to prove that the unary compositions of the basic functors satisfy condition A.

To do that we need to establish some properties concerning ω_0-chains.

Notation i) We denote by $\mathbf{CPO^P}$ ($\mathbf{CPO_1^P}$) the category having cpo's as objects and ω_0- and ω_1-continuous (ω_1-continuous) projections as morphisms.

ii) Given an embedding $f : A \to B$ (a projection $g : A \to B$) we denote by $f^P : B \to A$ ($g^E : B \to A$) the corresponding projection (embedding).

iii) Given a functor $F : \mathbf{CPO^E} \to \mathbf{CPO^E}$ ($F : \mathbf{CPO_1^E} \to \mathbf{CPO_1^E}$) we denote by $F^P : \mathbf{CPO^P} \to \mathbf{CPO^P}$ ($F^P : \mathbf{CPO_1^P} \to \mathbf{CPO_1^P}$) the corresponding functor on projections, that is F^P behaves like F on objects, and on projections it is defined by: $F^P(g) = (F(g^E))^P$.

Proposition 11. *The category* $\boldsymbol{CPO_1}$ *has all inverse limits of chains.*

Proposition 12. *In* $\boldsymbol{CPO_1}$ *the countable limit construction preserves projections. That is, suppose* $\Delta = \langle D_n, p_n\rangle_{n\in\mathbb{N}}$ *is a chain of morphisms and* $\xi : D_\omega \to \Delta$ *is its limit in* $\boldsymbol{CPO_1}$. *Then if each* p_n *is a projection each* ξ_n *is also a projection.*

Lemma 13. *For every unary composition* $F : \mathbf{CPO}_1^E \to \mathbf{CPO}_1^E$ *of the basic functors and for every* ω_0*-chain of projections* $\Delta = \langle D_n, p_n \rangle_{n \in \mathbb{N}}$*, in* $\mathbf{CPO}_1$ *let* $F^P\Delta$ *indicate the* ω_0*-chain* $\langle F^P(D_n), F^P(p_n)\rangle_{n\in\mathbb{N}}$ *and let* $\varphi : D_\omega \to \Delta$ *and* $\xi : D_{F\omega} \to F^P\Delta$ *be the limits in* $\mathbf{CPO}_1$ *of* Δ *and* $F^P\Delta$ *respectively. Clearly* $F^P(\varphi) : F^P(D_\omega) \to F^P\Delta$ *is a cone. Let* p_ω *be the unique function* $p_\omega : F^P(D_\omega) \to D_{F\omega}$ *making the two cones commute:*

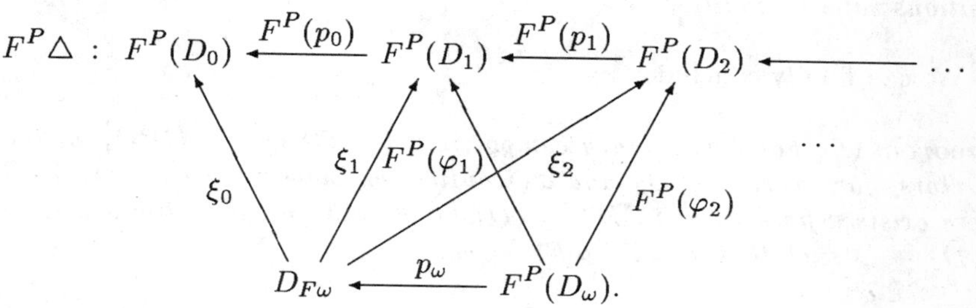

Then the following properties hold:

i) $p_\omega = \bigsqcup_{n\in\mathbb{N}} \xi_n^E \circ F^P(\varphi_n)$

ii) $F^P(\varphi_m) \circ \bigsqcup_{n\in\mathbb{N}} ((F^P(\varphi_n))^E \circ \xi_n) = \xi_m$

iii) p_ω *is a projection and*

$p_\omega^E = \bigsqcup_{n\in\mathbb{N}} (F^P(\varphi_n))^E \circ \xi_i$

Proposition 12 and Lemma 13 immediately yield the corresponding results for all the countable ordinals.

Proposition 14. *Every unary composition* $F : \mathbf{CPO}_1^E \to \mathbf{CPO}_1^E$ *of the basic functors satisfies the following property: given a chain of projections* $\Delta = \langle D_\alpha, p_{\beta,\alpha}\rangle_{\alpha<\beta<\lambda}$ *such that* λ *is a countable limit ordinal,* $D_{\alpha+1} = F(D_\alpha)$ *and* $p_{\beta+1,\alpha+1} = F(p_{\beta,\alpha})$ *let* $\xi : D_\lambda \to \Delta$ *be a limiting cone in* $\mathbf{CPO}_1$ *and let* $p_\lambda : F^P(D_\lambda) \to D_\lambda$ *be the unique morphism making the diagram in Fig.3 commute. Then we have:*

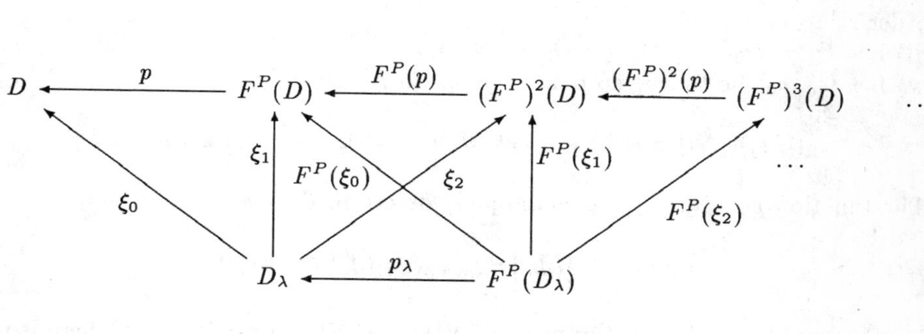

Fig. 3. *Diagram of projections*

i) $p_\lambda = \bigsqcup_{\alpha<\lambda} \xi^E_{\alpha+1} \circ F^P(\xi_\alpha)$

ii) p_λ *is a projection and* $p^E_\lambda = \bigsqcup_{\alpha\in\lambda} (F^P(\xi_\alpha))^E \circ \xi_{\alpha+1}$

By using the previous propositions one has immediately that:

Corollary 15. *In the category* $\boldsymbol{CPO^E_1}$ *the functors* $+, \times, \to_{\omega_1}$ *and their compositions satisfy condition A.*

We can finally conclude:

Theorem 16. *For every unary composition* $F : \boldsymbol{CPO^E_1} \to \boldsymbol{CPO^E_1}$ *of the basic functors, for every cpo* D_0 *and* ω_1*-continuous embedding* $e_0 : D_0 \to F(D_0)$ *there exists a fixed-point* $i : D \cong F(D)$ *for* F *and an* ω_1*-continuous embedding* $e : D_0 \to D$ *such that:* $e = i^{-1} \circ F(e) \circ e_0$.

6 A minimal model for the λ-calculus

In this section we utilise the construction of Section 4 in order to define a cpo D_{ω_1} satisfying the equation $D_{\omega_1} \cong [D_{\omega_1} \to_{\omega_1} D_{\omega_1}]$, which provides a minimal model for the $\lambda\beta\eta$-calculus. That is, an equation $M = N$ is true in the model if and only if M and N are $\beta\eta$-convertable. This result is interesting because it shows that the $\lambda\beta\eta$-calculus is *complete* w.r.t. to the class of reflexive domain models in $\mathbf{CPO_1}$, i.e. the class of domains satisfying the above domain equation. By *completeness* we mean that the class of λ-equalities which hold in all such models is exactly the theory $\boldsymbol{\lambda\beta\eta}$; see [9] for a more detailed account of this issue. The "completeness" problem for reflexive domain models of Scott continuous functions is a longstanding open problem.

The construction of D_{ω_1} is as follows:

Definition 17. i) Let T be the term model for the pure $\lambda\beta\eta$-calculus, i.e. the elements of T are the equivalence classes $[M]$ of pure λ-terms under $\beta\eta$-conversion.
ii) Let D_0 be the flat cpo obtained by adding $\bot$ to the set T with the obvious order relation.
iii) Let $D_1 = D_0 \to_{\omega_1} D_0$ $(= D_0 \to_\omega D_0)$,
iv) Let $\langle e_0, p_0\rangle$ be the ω_1-ep pair from D_0 to D_1 given by:

$$e_0([M])([N]) = [MN], \quad e_0([M])(\bot) = \bot \quad \text{and } e_0(\bot)(d_0) = \bot$$

The function $p_0 : D_1 \to_{\omega_1} D_0$ is uniquely determined by e_0:

$$p_0(f) = \bigsqcup\{d_0 \mid \forall d'_0.\ e_0(d_0)(d'_0) \sqsubseteq f(d'_0)\}$$

in other words: $p_0(f) = [M]$ if $\forall[N].f([N]) = [MN]$ and $p_0(f) = \bot$ if there is no such term $[M]$.

The function p_0 is not continuous but only ω_1-continuous. This is the only place where ω_1-continuity plays an essential role.

Using the machinery presented in Section 4 it is now possible to build a chain $\langle D_\beta, \langle e_{\alpha,\beta}, p_{\beta,\alpha}\rangle\rangle_{\alpha<\beta\le\omega_1+1}$ such that $e_{\omega_1,\omega_1+1} : D_{\omega_1} \cong D_{\omega_1} \to_\omega D_{\omega_1}$.

Given an environment $\rho : Var \to D_{\omega_1}$ we write $[\![M]\!]_\rho$ for the denotation of M in D_{ω_1} (relative to ρ).

Notation. For every function σ : Var $\to \Lambda$ and λ-term M with free variables $\{x_1, \ldots, x_n\}$, we write M_σ for the term $M[\sigma(x_1)/x_1, \ldots, \sigma(x_n)/x_n]$, moreover we write $[\sigma]$ for the environment such that $[\sigma](x) = e_{0,\omega_1}[\sigma(x)]$.

Proposition 18. *For every λ-term M and for every function $\sigma : Var \to \Lambda$ the following equality holds: $p_{\omega_1,0}([\![M]\!]_{[\sigma]}) = [M_\sigma]$*

Proof. By induction on the structure of M.

i) the case where M is a variable is immediate.

ii) for an application, $M \equiv NP$ we calculate:

$$\begin{aligned} p_{\omega_1,0}([\![NP]\!]_{[\sigma]}) &= p_{\omega_1,0}(e_{\omega_1,\omega_1+1}([\![N]\!]_{[\sigma]})([\![P]\!]_{[\sigma]})) \\ &\sqsupseteq p_{\omega_1,1}([\![N]\!]_{[\sigma]})(p_{\omega_1,0}([\![P]\!]_{[\sigma]})) \\ &\sqsupseteq e_0(p_{\omega_1,0}([N_\sigma]))(p_{\omega_1,0}([P_\sigma])) \\ &= e_0([N_\sigma])([P_\sigma]) \quad \text{(by induction hypothesis)} \\ &= [(NP)_\sigma] \end{aligned}$$

and since D_0 is flat, equality holds.

iii) For an abstraction, $M \equiv \lambda x.N$ we have:

$$\begin{aligned} p_{\omega_1,0}([\![\lambda x.N]\!]_{[\sigma]}) &= p_{\omega_1,0}(p_{\omega_1+1,\omega_1}(\lambda d : D_{\omega_1}.[\![N]\!]_{[\sigma][d/x]})) \\ &= p_0(f) \end{aligned}$$

where $f = \lambda d_0 : D_0.p_{\omega_1,0}([\![N]\!]_{[\sigma][e_{0,\omega_1}(d_0)/x]})$. But now, for any term P we have:

$$\begin{aligned} f([P]) &= p_{\omega_1,0}([\![N]\!]_{[\sigma][e_{0,\omega_1}([P])/x]}) \\ &= p_{\omega_1,0}([\![N]\!]_{[\sigma[P/x]]}) \\ &= [N_{\sigma[P/x]}] \quad \text{(by induction hypothesis)} \\ &= [(\lambda x.N)_\sigma P] \end{aligned}$$

And from this $[(\lambda x.N)_\sigma] = p_0(f)$. □

We now have:

Theorem 19. *The $\lambda\beta\eta$-theory induced by D_{ω_1} is the minimal λ-calculus theory, i.e. the theory* $\boldsymbol{\lambda\beta\eta}$.

Proof. We need to prove that for every pair of terms M, N:

$$\vdash_{\beta\eta} M = N \ \text{ iff } \ \forall \rho.[\![M]\!]_\rho = [\![N]\!]_\rho$$

Since D_{ω_1} is a model, the implication from left to right is straightforwards. Suppose, instead, that $\forall \rho.[\![M]\!]_\rho = [\![N]\!]_\rho$. Then taking $\rho(x) = x$ for all x in Var, and using Proposition 18 we calculate:

$$[M] = [M_\rho] = p_{\omega_1,0}\,([\![M]\!]_{[\rho]}) = p_{\omega_1,0}\,([\![N]\!]_{[\rho]}) = [N_\rho] = [N]$$

and so $\vdash_{\beta\eta} M = N$. □

The previous theorem *cannot* be generalised to arbitrary theories. There is no reflexive model in $\mathbf{CPO_1}$ for the theory considered in [9]; this can be shown by a similar argument to that given there for the Scott-continuous case.

Acknowledgements

We would like to thank Marco Forti, Cosimo Laneve, Alex Simpson and Piero Zanchi for the several discussions on the subject. We thank Paul Taylor for the "Commutative Diagrams" Latex package.

References

1. ADÁMEK, J., KOUBEK, V., *Least Fixed-Point of a Functor*, Journal of Computer and System Sciences Vol.**19**, No.**2**, 1979, 163-178.
2. APT, K.R., PLOTKIN, G.D., *Countable Non-Determinism and Random Assignment*, Journal of the ACM Vol.**33**, No.**4**, 1986, 724-767.
3. COSTA G., *Metric characterisation of fair computations in CCS*, Lecture Notes in Computer Science, Vol.**186**, Springer-Verlag, Berlin/New York, 1985, 239-251.
4. CHANDRA, A.K., *Computable Non-Deterministic Functions*, in "Proceedings. 19th Annual Symposium on Mathematical Foundations of Computer Science". IEEE, New York, 1978, 127-131.
5. DIJKSTRA, E.W., *A Discipline of Programming*, Prentice-Hall, Englewood Cliffs, New York, 1976.
6. PARK, D., *On the Semantics of Fair Parallelism*, in "Proceedings. Winter School on Formal Software Specification", Lecture Notes in Computer Science, Vol.**86**, Springer-Verlag, Berlin/New York, 1980, 504-526.
7. PLOTKIN, G.D., *A Powerdomain Construction*, SIAM J. Comput. Vol.**5**, No.**3**, 1976, 452-487.
8. PLOTKIN, G.D., *A Powerdomain for Countable Non-Determinism*, in "Proceedings. 9th ICALP", M. Nielsen and E.M. Schmidt Eds., Lecture Notes in Computer Science, Vol.**140**, Springer-Verlag, Berlin/New York, 1982, 418-428.
9. RONCHI DELLA ROCCA, S., HONSELL, F., *An Approximation Theorem for Topological Lambda Models and the Topological Incompleteness of Lambda Calculus*, Journal of Computer and System Sciences Vol. **45**, No. **1**, 1992, 49-75.
10. SMYTH, M.B., PLOTKIN, G.D., *The Category-Theoretic Solution of Recursive Domain Equations*, SIAM J. Comput. Vol.**11**, No.**4**, 1982, 761-783.

AppendixA: The language $\mathcal{GC}$

The language $\mathcal{GC}$ is a language featuring assignment, command composition, and two non-deterministic commands: non-deterministic selection and non-deterministic multitest loop, which iterates as long as at least one of its guards is true. The set *Com* of *commands* of the language $\mathcal{GC}$, ranged over by C, is generated by the following abstract syntax grammar:

$$C ::= x := E \mid C_1; C_2 \mid \mathbf{if}\, G\, \mathbf{fi} \mid \mathbf{do}\, G\, \mathbf{od}$$

$$G ::= G_1 \,\square\, G_2 \mid B \rightarrow C$$

Here G ranges over the set *GCom* of *guarded commands* and x ranges over identifiers. The set *Exp* of *expressions*, ranged over by E, and the set *BExp* of *boolean expressions*, ranged over by B are assumed given The grammar is extended with extra clause $C ::= x :=?$, when dealing with unbounded non-determinism.

The denotational semantics of $\mathcal{GC}$ is defined as follows, assuming functions $\mathcal{E} : Exp \rightarrow (S \rightarrow Val)$ and $\mathcal{B} : BExp \rightarrow (S \rightarrow \{tt, ff\})$[3]:

$$\mathcal{C}[\![x := E]\!]s = \{[\mathcal{E}[\![E]\!]s \mapsto x]s\}$$

$$\mathcal{C}[\![C_1; C_2]\!] = (\mathcal{C}[\![C_2]\!])^+ \circ \mathcal{C}[\![C_1]\!]$$

$$\mathcal{C}[\![\mathbf{if}\, B_1 \rightarrow C_1 \,\square\, \cdots \,\square\, B_n \rightarrow C_n\, \mathbf{fi}]\!]s$$

$$= \begin{cases} \{s\} & \text{if } \mathcal{B}[\![B_i]\!]s = ff, \text{ for } i = 1, \ldots, n \\ \bigcup\{\mathcal{C}[\![C_i]\!]s \mid \mathcal{B}[\![B_i]\!]s = tt\} & \text{otherwise} \end{cases}$$

$$\mathcal{C}[\![\mathbf{do}\, B_1 \rightarrow C_1 \,\square\, \cdots \,\square\, B_n \rightarrow C_n\, \mathbf{od}]\!] = f$$

where $f : S \rightarrow \mathcal{P}(S_\perp)$ is the least function satisfying the recursive specification:

$$f(s) = \begin{cases} \{s\} & \text{if } \mathcal{B}[\![B_i]\!]s = ff, \text{ for } i = 1, \ldots, n \\ f^+(\bigcup\{\mathcal{C}[\![C_i]\!]s \mid \mathcal{B}[\![B_i]\!]s = tt\}) & \text{otherwise} \end{cases}$$

[3] For simplicity, the semantics of non-deterministic selection command does not cause failure when each guard fails.

SProc Categorically

J.R.B. Cockett and D.A. Spooner

University of Calgary,
Department of Computer Science,
2500 University Drive N.W.,
Calgary, Canada T2N 1N4

Abstract. We provide a systematic reconstruction of Abramsky's category **SProc** of synchronous processes [Abr93]: **SProc** is isomorphic to a span category on a category of traces. The significance of the work is twofold: It shows that the original presentation of **SProc** in mixed formulations is unnecessary — a simple categorical description exists. Furthermore, the techniques employed in the reconstruction suggest a general method of obtaining process categories with structure similar to **SProc**. In particular, the method of obtaining bisimulation equivalence in our setting, which represents an extension of the work of Joyal, Nielsen and Winskel [JNW93], has natural application in many settings.

1 Introduction

In [Abr93], Abramsky proposed a new paradigm for the semantics of computation, *interaction categories*, where the following substitutions are made:

Denotational semantics	Categories	Interaction categories
Domains	objects	Interface specifications
Continuous functions	maps	Communicating Processes
Functional composition	composition	Interaction

This paradigm shift, away from the classical approach to modeling computation, provided by domain theory, had an immediate effect. The problem of finding fully abstract models for programming languages — a problem that had dogged the semantics community for two decades — suddenly became tractable [AJM93]: game theoretic interaction categories could be constructed in a relatively straightforward manner to capture the key operational aspects of computation. It was a construction that had eluded the classical methods and was brought into reach by the simple trick of passing to the much richer semantic settings provided by interaction categories.

In effect, Abramsky had used ideas from concurrency to solve a problem in programming semantics. Furthermore, in providing a "process" based semantics for programming, he raised the possibility that these two disparate aspects of computing could be unified. Such a unified view, he realized, would facilitate the transfer of ideas between the two areas and enhance their mutual development.

Up to that time the concurrency community had regarded processes to be structured objects whose morphisms were simulations. This view made inaccessible a fundamental and very basic verification technique of modern programming: type checking. In the interaction category paradigm, a processes is a map between interface specifications and type checking is the demonstration that a process respects the constraints imposed by its interfaces.

To realize the benefits of a having type system for concurrency, Abramsky [Abr93] introduced the interaction category of *synchronous processes*, **SProc**, and its sister the interaction category of *asynchronous processes*, **ASProc**. In describing **SProc** Abramsky employed a wide range of methodologies: Aczel's theory of non-well-founded sets, linear type theory, category theory, and concurrency theory. While this helped to focus the ideas of a wide community, it did not provide a clear understanding of the required categorical foundation for the construction. In this paper we present a categorical reconstruction of **SProc** and, more importantly, introduce the techniques employed.

The main conceptual tool in this reconstruction, that of systems of *open maps*, which we call *cover systems*, is not new. The recognition of their relationship to bisimulation, however, is recent (see Joyal, Nielsen, and Winskel [JNW93]). A cover system on a category is a compositional class of maps, including all isomorphisms, which is closed to pulling back along arbitrary maps. A span of cover maps from one object to another can be viewed as a witness to a bisimulation. This view provides a unified framework for describing bisimulation in a number of categorical models of concurrency, among which are labelled transition systems, labelled event structures, and transition systems with independence.

Cover systems can also be used to induce a congruence on span categories. From a category with a cover system $(\mathbf{X}, \mathcal{X})$, we construct the quotiented span category $Proc(\mathbf{X}, \mathcal{X})$, which we call the category of processes: this construction is 2-functorial. The main results of the paper concern the manner in which **SProc** arises as such a process category. We exhibit, in fact, three different (but related) categories and their cover systems for which **SProc** is the resulting process category.

The relationship of interaction categories to span categories is already implicit in Abramsky's work when he refers to the bicategories of Carboni and Walters [CW87]. We maintain that the explicit reconstruction of this aspect of **SProc** is of considerable interest as it indicates much more clearly the categorical foundation required.

2 SProc Recounted

Abramsky presents **SProc** as an example of an interaction category [Abr93]. The objects of this category are safety specifications for concurrent systems, given as sets of permissible traces, maps are given by processes (i.e. transition systems modulo strong bisimulation), and composition is given by *interaction*.

The category is presented in the style of a linear type theory emphasizing the similarity to other examples of interaction categories (e.g. Games and Strategies [AJ92]). Linear negation $\perp$ and multiplicative conjunction $\otimes$ are defined on the objects (types) of **SProc**, inducing multiplicative disjunction $A \oplus B \stackrel{\text{def}}{=} (A^\perp \otimes B^\perp)^\perp$ and linear implication $A \multimap B \stackrel{\text{def}}{=} A^\perp \oplus B$. A satisfaction relation $\models$ is introduced between processes and types, allowing a morphism $p : A \longrightarrow B$ to be defined by a process p for which $p \models A \multimap B$.

As we are not concerned here with the linear type structure of **SProc**, we take a more direct description of the category. We will, however, follow Abramsky in choosing synchronization trees, in terms of non-well-founded sets, as canonical representatives of processes. Thus, the synchronization trees over a label set Σ are the largest solution to the (non-well-founded) set equation:

$$ST_\Sigma = \mathcal{P}(\Sigma \times ST_\Sigma).$$

We will use the process notation $p \stackrel{a}{\longrightarrow} q$ to represent $(a, q) \in p$.

For any set X and function $f : X \longrightarrow Y$, let $(X^*, \epsilon, \cdot)$ denote the free monoid on X and $f^* : X^* \longrightarrow Y^*$ the unique homomorphic extension of f. Given any process p on the label set Σ we can construct a macro process with labels in Σ^* whose transitions correspond to sequences of transitions in p:

$$M(p) = \{(\epsilon, p)\} \cup \{(x \cdot s, q) \mid p \stackrel{x}{\longrightarrow} p' \wedge (s, q) \in M(p')\}.$$

We shall write $p \stackrel{s}{\Longrightarrow} q$ to mean $(s, q) \in M(p)$. The finite sequences of visible actions (or traces) of a synchronization tree are:

$$traces(p) = \{s \in \Sigma^* \mid \exists q.\, p \stackrel{s}{\Longrightarrow} q\}.$$

SProc can now be defined as follows:

- The objects A are pairs

$$(\Sigma_A, S_A \subseteq \Sigma_A^*),$$

  where S_A is a non-empty and prefix closed set of traces over alphabet Σ_A.
- The morphisms $p : A \longrightarrow B$ are synchronization trees $p \in ST_{\Sigma_A \times \Sigma_B}$ such that:

$$fst^*(traces(p)) \subseteq S_A \wedge snd^*(traces(p)) \subseteq S_B.$$

- Composition is given by a combination of synchronous product and restriction, following SCCS [Mil83]:

$$p; q = \{((a, c), p'; q') \mid \exists b.\, p \stackrel{(a,b)}{\longrightarrow} p' \wedge q \stackrel{(b,c)}{\longrightarrow} q'\}.$$

- Identities are synchronous buffers, or wires, through which information flows unchanged instantaneously:

$$1_A = \{((a, a), 1_{A \backslash a}) \mid a \in S_A\}.$$

Where $A\backslash s$ is given by

$$A\backslash s = (\Sigma_A,\ \{t \mid s \cdot t \in S_A\}), \quad \text{if } s \in S_A.$$

That is the permitted behaviors after (performance of) the trace s.

Although parallel composition combined with restriction is not an associative operation in process algebra, the typed framework provided by **SProc** is enough to make it so. **SProc** provides a model of full second-order linear logic (it is a compact closed category with additional structure); it also supports *delay* monads, which allow asynchrony to be built upon synchrony following Milner[Mil83].

3 A Category of Traces

The first step in reconstructing **SProc** is to construct a category whose objects are trace specifications and whose maps are simply homomorphisms. We show how this can be done for lextensive categories with list arithmetic (see Cockett [Coc90]). A lextensive category has finite limits, finite coproducts, and the property that in the following diagram

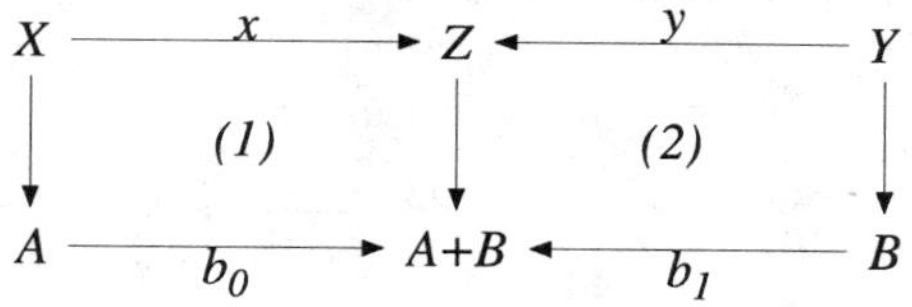

(1) and (2) are pullbacks exactly when the top row is a coproduct (see Carboni, Lack and Walters [CLW92], or Cockett [Coc93]). It is important to realize that, foundationally, this is all the structure that is required: although we shall need some extra ingredients to carry through the subsequent construction of processes, the remaining ingredients are a matter of choice rather than axiomatization.

Let **C** be a lextensive category with a list constructor $((\_)^*, \epsilon, cons)$. A subobject $s : S \longrightarrow \Sigma^*$ in **C** is a *trace specification* provided maps q and e exists such that

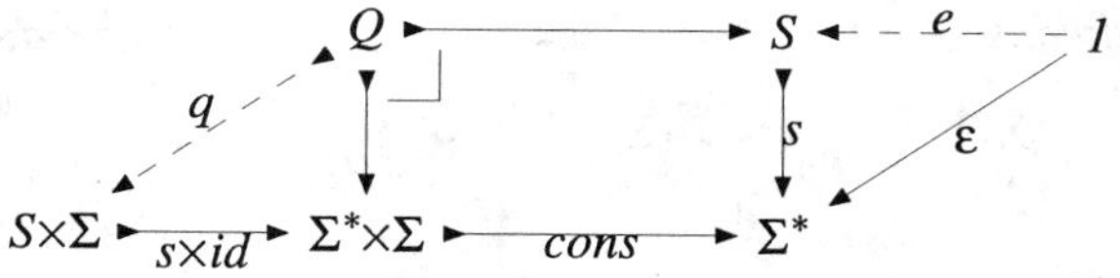

(1)

commutes. The object Σ^* is understood as the finite sequences over "alphabet" Σ — this is described in [Coc90], where it is also shown that the functor $(\_)^*$ preserves pullbacks. The object Q corresponds to the non-ϵ sequences of S, and the existence of q means that S is prefix-closed; the existence of e means S contains ϵ.

Definition 3.1 *Trace(C) is the category whose objects are trace specifications and whose maps $f : A \longrightarrow B$ are pairs (f_Σ, f_S) for which*

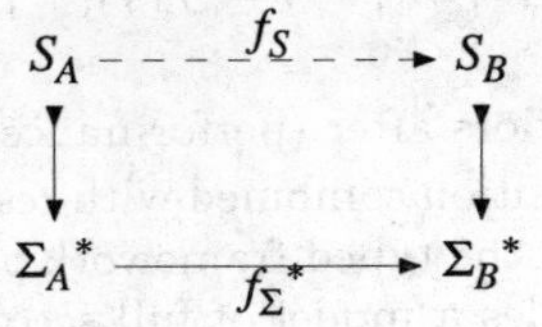

$$
\begin{array}{ccc}
S_A & \overset{f_S}{\dashrightarrow} & S_B \\
\downarrow & & \downarrow \\
\Sigma_A{}^* & \underset{f_\Sigma{}^*}{\longrightarrow} & \Sigma_B{}^*
\end{array}
$$

commutes.

$Trace(\mathbf{C})$ may be viewed as the category of models of a higher-order sketch (see Power and Wells [PW92]) involving the list functor in $\mathbf{C}$. It is perhaps unexpected to find that:

Proposition 3.2 *Trace(C) is a lextensive category.*

Proof. Initial and final objects are given by $\epsilon_0 : 1 \longrightarrow 0^*$ and $id_1 : 1^* \longrightarrow 1^*$, respectively, where 0 is initial and 1 is final in $\mathbf{C}$.

The pullback of $f : A \longrightarrow B$ and $g : C \longrightarrow B$ is given componentwise in $\mathbf{C}$, using the fact that $(\_)^*$ preserves pullbacks:

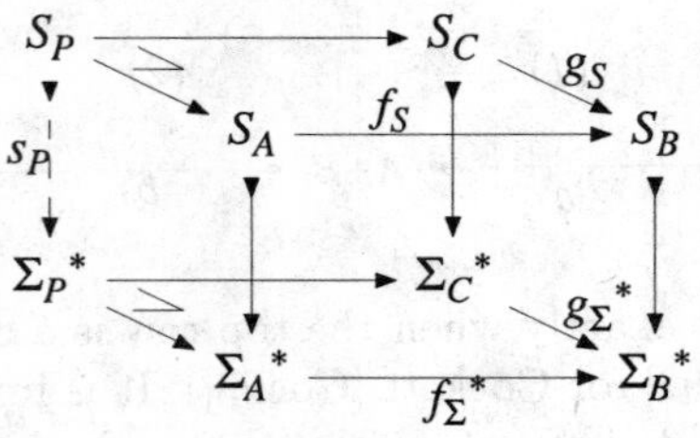

For coproducts it is worth shifting attention to the arrow $q : Q \longrightarrow S \times \Sigma$ by which a trace can be equivalently specified. The coproduct is then given by:

$$
\begin{array}{ccccc}
Q_A & \overset{b_0}{\longrightarrow} & Q_A + Q_B & \overset{b_1}{\longleftarrow} & Q_B \\
{\scriptstyle q;s\times id;cons}\downarrow & & \downarrow & & \downarrow{\scriptstyle q;s\times id;cons} \\
\Sigma_A{}^* & \underset{b_0{}^*}{\longrightarrow} & (\Sigma_A + \Sigma_B)^* & \underset{b_1{}^*}{\longleftarrow} & \Sigma_B{}^*
\end{array}
$$

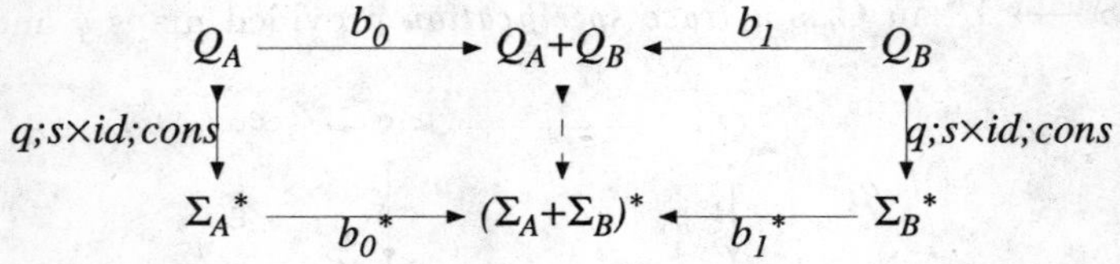

from which the fact that it is extensive follows immediately. $\square$

It is worth noting that the definition given by Abramsky for $A \otimes B$ in **SProc** is precisely the product in $Trace(\mathbf{Set})$. Clearly, the objects of **SProc** are the objects of this category. That the maps in Abramsky's formulation of **SProc** come from another source is unnecessary, as we shall see.

4 Cover Systems

Let $\mathbf{X}$ be a category with pullbacks. A collection $\mathcal{X}$ of the maps of $\mathbf{X}$ is a *cover system* provided it contains all isomorphisms, is closed to composition, and is closed to pulling back along arbitrary maps — i.e. if $x \in \mathcal{X}$ and the following is a pullback, then $y \in \mathcal{X}$:

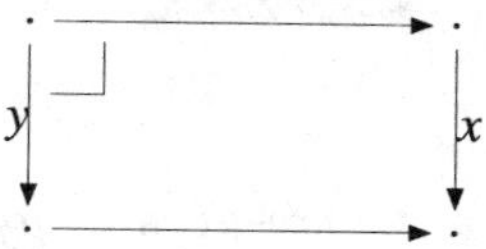

In any category the class of isomorphisms $\mathcal{I}$ and the class of retractions $\mathcal{R}$ are cover systems which are preserved by all functors. In a regular category, the class $\mathcal{E}$ of regular epimorphisms is a cover system.

A commuting square $h; f = k; g$ in a category with a cover system $\mathcal{X}$ is an *$\mathcal{X}$-pullback* provided the induced map x to the inscribed pullback is in $\mathcal{X}$:

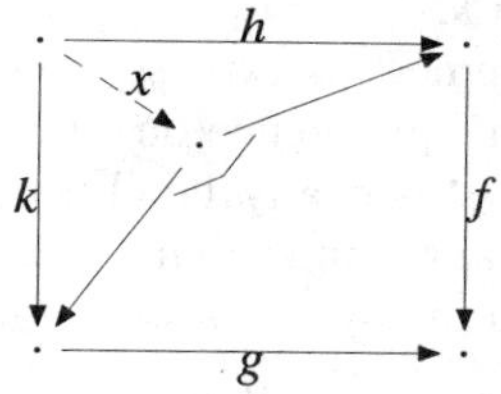

In the category of models of a sketch, one obtains a cover system by considering those model morphisms for which a chosen naturality square is an $\mathcal{X}$-pullback.

The latter technique will be motivated through a series of related examples. The first demonstrates how one obtains the standard notion of strong bisimulation on labelled transition systems via spans of cover maps. The subsequent examples of deterministic transition systems and trace specifications will be used later in the reconstruction of **SProc**.

4.1 Transition Systems

Given a lextensive category $\mathbf{C}$, we define the category $Tran(\mathbf{C})$ as the category of models in $\mathbf{C}$ of the following sketch:

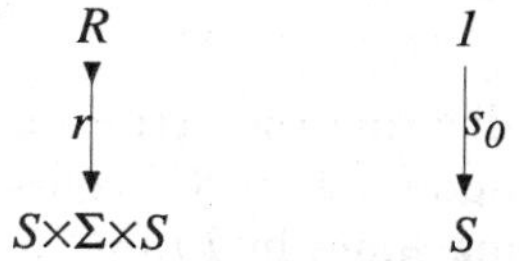

$Tran(\mathbf{Set})$ is the category of labelled transition systems presented by Winskel [Win87]: the objects are structures

$$(\Sigma,\ S,\ s_0 \in S,\ R \subseteq S \times \Sigma \times S)$$

and morphisms $A \longrightarrow B$ are pairs of functions

$$(\sigma : S_A \longrightarrow S_B, \; \lambda : \Sigma_A \longrightarrow \Sigma_B)$$

which preserve transitions and initial states.

If $\mathcal{C}$ is a cover system on $\mathbf{C}$ then the maps $f : A \longrightarrow B$ of $Tran(\mathbf{C})$ for which

$$
\begin{array}{ccccc}
R_A & \xrightarrow{\quad r \quad} & S_A \times \Sigma_A \times S_A & \xrightarrow{\;p_0;p_0\;} & S_A \\
{\scriptstyle f_R}\downarrow & & & & \downarrow{\scriptstyle f_S} \\
R_B & \xrightarrow{\quad r \quad} & S_B \times \Sigma_B \times S_B & \xrightarrow{\;p_0;p_0\;} & S_B
\end{array}
$$

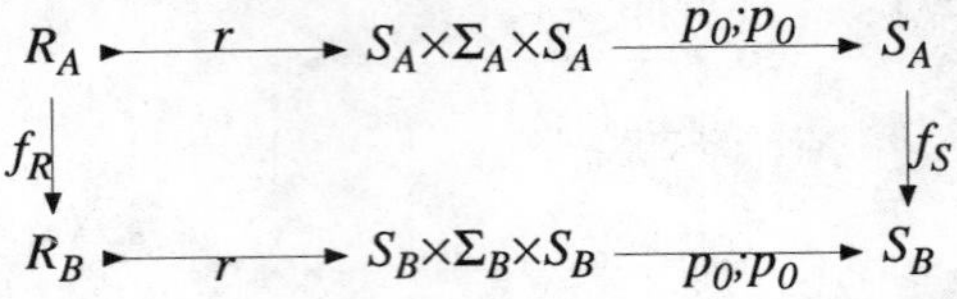

is a $\mathcal{C}$-pullback form a cover system we will call $\exists^{(Tran(\mathbf{C}),\mathcal{C})}$, or simply $\exists^{\mathcal{C}}$ if $Tran(\mathbf{C})$ is understood.

For $Tran(\mathbf{Set})$, a map $f : A \longrightarrow B$ of $\exists^{\mathcal{I}}$ has the property that each transition from a state $f(s)$ of B is the image (via f) of a unique transition from state s of A, while $\exists^{\mathcal{E}}$ has the weaker property that each transition from $f(s)$ is the image of at least one transition from s.

In [JNW93], the cover system $\exists^{\mathcal{E}}$ is expressed via a path lifting property, and is shown to yeild bisimulation equivalence on the objects of $Tran(\mathbf{Set})$: taking the fibre category $Tran(\mathbf{Set})_{\Sigma}$ over any label set Σ and the restriction $\exists^{\mathcal{E}}_{\Sigma}$ of $\exists^{\mathcal{E}}$ to the maps of the fibre, transition systems A and B are strongly bisimilar if and only if there exists a span of $\exists^{\mathcal{E}}_{\Sigma}$ maps with endpoints A and B:

$$
\begin{array}{ccc}
 & R & \\
{\scriptstyle f}\swarrow & & \searrow{\scriptstyle g} \\
A & & B
\end{array}
$$

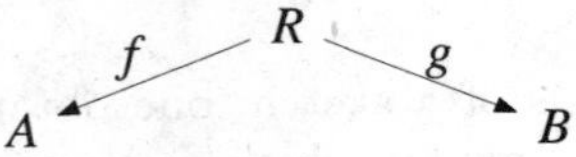

To see this choose any state r of the "relation" R; if $f(r)\xrightarrow{x}s'$ in A then there exists r' such that $f(r') = s'$ and $r\xrightarrow{x}r'$ in R, so $g(r)\xrightarrow{x}g(r')$ in B. As maps f and g preserve initial states, all reachable states of A and B "appear" in the relation R.

4.2 Deterministic Transition Systems

A closely related, yet simpler, example is given by deterministic labelled transition systems. Let $DTran(\mathbf{C})$ be the category of models in $\mathbf{C}$ of the following sketch:

$$
\begin{array}{ccc}
 & P & \\
{\scriptstyle m}\swarrow & & \searrow{\scriptstyle \alpha} \\
S \times \Sigma & & S \xleftarrow{\;s_0\;} 1
\end{array}
$$

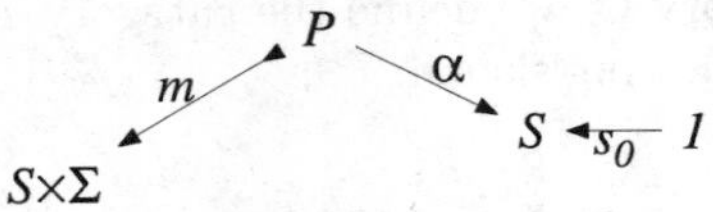

m is a permission relation, indicating the actions available at each state, and α determines the state change upon action. Of course $DTran(\mathbf{C})$ is just the full subcategory of deterministic machines in $Tran(\mathbf{C})$.

A cover system $\exists^{\mathcal{C}}$ is similarly obtained on $DTran(\mathbf{C})$ by considering those maps for which the square associated with $m; p_0$ is a $\mathcal{C}$-pullback. Considering a fibre $DTran(\mathbf{C})_{\Sigma}$, we find that $\exists^{\mathcal{R}}_{\Sigma}$ and $\exists^{\mathcal{I}}_{\Sigma}$ coincide, which is not unexpected as bisimulation and language equivalence coincide for such deterministic objects.

4.3 Trace Specifications

Recall the map $q : Q \longrightarrow S \times \Sigma$ of diagram 1 which represents the non-ϵ traces of an object of $Trace(\mathbf{C})$. Corresponding to each $f : A \longrightarrow B$ is an induced map $f_Q : Q_A \longrightarrow Q_B$, giving the following naturality square in $\mathbf{C}$:

$$
\begin{array}{ccccc}
Q_A & \xrightarrow{\ q_A\ } & S_A \times \Sigma_A & \xrightarrow{\ p_0\ } & S_A \\
{\scriptstyle f_Q}\big\downarrow & & & & \big\downarrow{\scriptstyle f_S} \\
Q_B & \xrightarrow{\ q_B\ } & S_B \times \Sigma_B & \xrightarrow{\ p_0\ } & S_B
\end{array}
$$

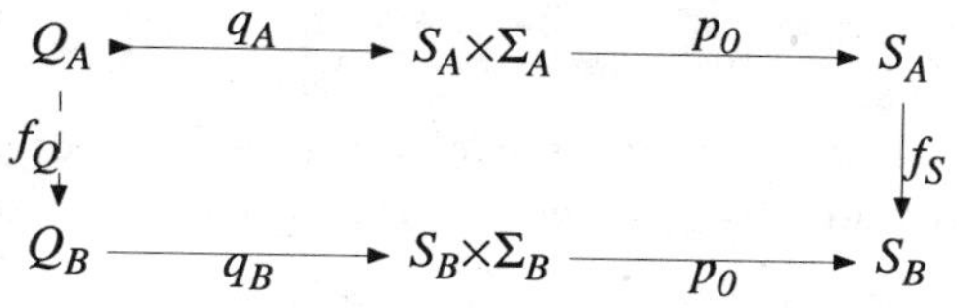

If $\mathcal{C}$ is a cover system on $\mathbf{C}$ then $\exists^{\mathcal{C}}$ is the cover system on $Trace(\mathbf{C})$ consisting of those $f : A \longrightarrow B$ for which this square is a $\mathcal{C}$-pullback.

In $Trace(\mathbf{Set})$, a map $f : A \longrightarrow B$ of $\exists^{\mathcal{I}}$ has the property that each extension of a trace $f(t)$ in B is the image of a unique extension of trace t in A, while $\exists^{\mathcal{E}}$ has the more generous property that for each extension of $f(t)$ there exists a corresponding extension of t. We will see that $\exists^{\mathcal{E}}$ yields the notion of bisimulation required to reconstruct **SProc**

It is interesting to note that when one considers only a fibre $Trace(\mathbf{C})_\Sigma$, both $\exists^{\mathcal{R}}_\Sigma$ and $\exists^{\mathcal{I}}_\Sigma$ coincide with the isomorphisms $\mathcal{I}_\Sigma$ — a consequence of the properties of trace specifications. Later we will see that nondeterminism is recaptured in such deterministic settings through the construction of "processes".

5 Processes as Spans

A fruitful way of regarding a process on a category such as $Trace(\mathbf{C})$ is as a *span*, that is a pair of maps with a common domain:

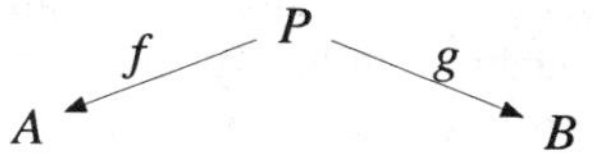

One should regard the endpoints A and B as interface specifications, and thus the legs f and g deterimine how actions in the apex P determine (visible) actions simultaneously at each interface.

From any category $\mathbf{X}$ with pullbacks one can form the bicategory of spans in $\mathbf{X}$: the objects are those of $\mathbf{X}$; the 1-cells $A \longrightarrow B$ are spans in $\mathbf{X}$, which we will write as $P_{(f,g)}$; and 2-cells $P_{(f,g)} \longrightarrow P'_{(f',g')}$ are given by maps $h : P \longrightarrow P'$ such that

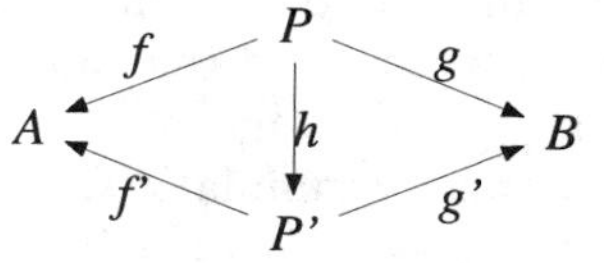

commutes in **X**. 1-cell composition is given by pullback, and is thus determined only to isomorphism — i.e. $P_{(f,g)}; Q_{(h,k)}$ is $R_{(p;f,\, q;k)}$, where:

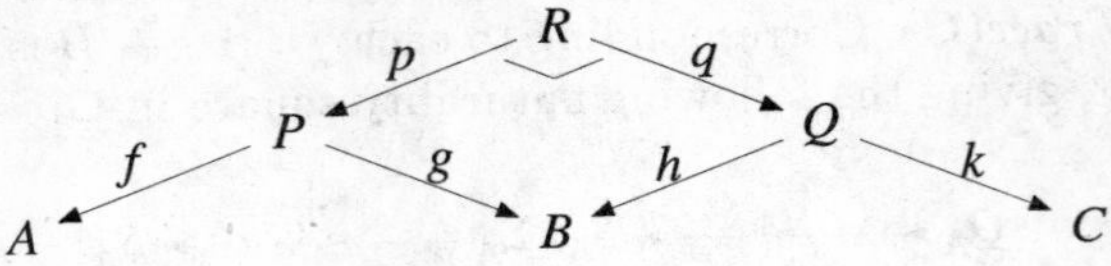

A cover system $\mathcal{X}$ on **X** induces a congruence $\sim_{\mathcal{X}}$ (or $\mathcal{X}$-bisimulation) on spans, taking $P_{(f,g)}$ and $Q_{(h,k)}$ as equal when there exist maps x and y of $\mathcal{X}$ such that

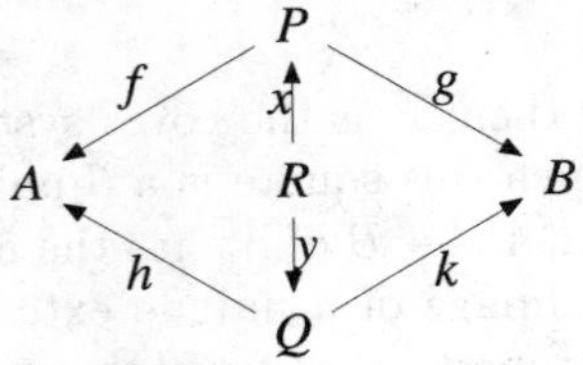

commutes in **X**. Quotienting 1-cells by $\sim_{\mathcal{X}}$ gives a category $Proc(\mathbf{X}, \mathcal{X})$ of processes up-to the specified equivalence.

Certainly the simplest example of this construction is a category of relations: for **E** a regular category, $Proc(\mathbf{E}, \mathcal{E})$ is usually written $Rel(\mathbf{E})$.

Just as relations constructed from the functions of **Set**, the processes constructed from the traces of $Trace(\mathbf{Set})$ may exhibit nondeterminism: the CCS agents $a.(b.0 + c.0)$ and $a.b.0 + a.c.0$ can be seen as maps $1 \longrightarrow A$ of **SProc**, with $A = \{\epsilon, a, a \cdot b, a \cdot c\} \subseteq \{a, b, c\}^*$. These are represented respectively by the following spans:

where $A' = \{\epsilon, a_1, a_2, a_1 \cdot b, a_2 \cdot c\}$ distinguishes the a-action which preceeds b from the a-action which preceeds c. Clearly the latter process alone commits to performing either b or c upon performance of an a.

Although the cover system on $Trace(\mathbf{C})$ required to reconstruct **SProc** is $\exists^{\mathcal{R}}$ (or $\exists^{\mathcal{E}}$ when **C** is regular), $\exists^{\mathcal{I}}$ plays an important role as well and it is worth commenting on the processes which result. For example, with $A = \{\epsilon, a\} \subseteq \{a\}^*$ and $A' = \{\epsilon, a_1, a_2\} \subseteq \{a_1, a_2\}^*$, the following spans

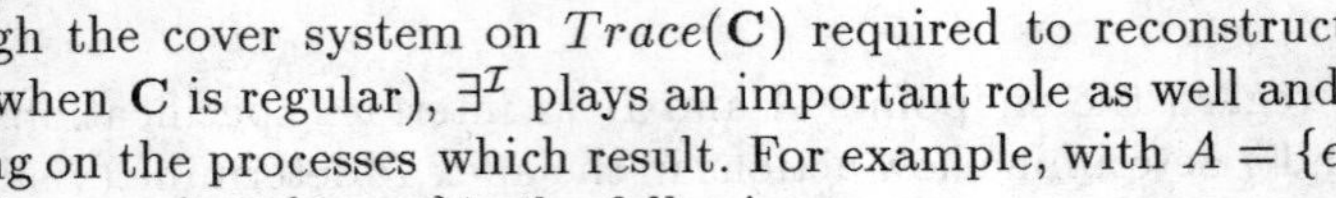

represent distinct processes. In fact, $\exists^{\mathcal{I}}$ distinguishes processes with different amounts of nondeterminism — even when that nondeterminism is not visible.

The application of cover systems to morphisms in span categories reveals a subtlety in the relationship between bisimulation and cover maps, as bisimulation is traditionally viewed as being specific to a label set while cover maps are independent of labelling. As we have seen the category $Trace(\mathbf{C})$ is fibred over $\mathbf{C}$, so it is possible to recapture the notion of (labelled) bisimulation implied by the cover system. However, that information may not be enough to reconstruct the cover system: in particular, for $Trace(\mathbf{C})$ with the cover system $\exists^{\mathcal{R}}$, traces over the same label set are bisimilar only if they are isomorphic.

The construction of processes can in fact be viewed as a 2-functor $Proc : \mathbf{Cov} \longrightarrow \mathbf{Cat}$, where $\mathbf{Cov}$ is the 2-category for which:

- objects $(\mathbf{X}, \mathcal{X})$ are categories with cover systems;
- 1-cells $F : (\mathbf{X}, \mathcal{X}) \longrightarrow (\mathbf{Y}, \mathcal{Y})$ are functors $F : \mathbf{X} \longrightarrow \mathbf{Y}$ which take $\mathcal{X}$-pullbacks to $\mathcal{Y}$-pullbacks;
- and 2-cells $\alpha : F \Longrightarrow G : (\mathbf{X}, \mathcal{X}) \longrightarrow (\mathbf{Y}, \mathcal{Y})$ are natural transformations $\alpha : F \Longrightarrow G$ whose naturality squares are $\mathcal{Y}$-pullbacks.

For a functor F of $\mathbf{Cov}$, $Proc(F)$ applies F to each leg of a span,

$$FA \xleftarrow{\;Ff\;} FP \xrightarrow{\;Fg\;} FB$$

and for $\alpha : F \Longrightarrow G$, $Proc(\alpha)_A$ is as follows:

$$FA \xleftarrow{\;=\;} FA \xrightarrow{\;\alpha_A\;} GA$$

Consequently, one can show that:

Proposition 5.1 *If $\boldsymbol{C}$ is lextensive with cover system $\mathcal{C}$ then $Proc(\boldsymbol{C}, \mathcal{C})$ is compact-closed. Furthermore, if coproducts in $\boldsymbol{C}$ preserve $\mathcal{C}$ then $Proc(\boldsymbol{C}, \mathcal{C})$ has finite biproducts.*

Coproducts in $Trace(\mathbf{C})$ preserve $\exists^{\mathcal{C}}$ whenever coproducts in $\mathbf{C}$ preserve $\mathcal{C}$, so in particular $Proc(Trace(\mathbf{C}), \exists^{\mathcal{I}})$ and $Proc(Trace(\mathbf{C}), \exists^{\mathcal{R}})$ are compact-closed with finite biproducts. It is also easy to see that if $\mathbf{C}$ is regular then $\exists^{\mathcal{E}}$ is preserved by coproducts (as coequalizers and coproducts commute), so $Proc(Trace(\mathbf{C}), \exists^{\mathcal{E}})$ is compact-closed with biproducts.

Note that the choice of $\mathbf{Cat}$ as the endpoint of $Proc$ is certainly not optimal. Of course choosing an appropriate 2-category will involve an abstract characterization of a "process category": if done correctly, one would hope that $Proc$ was part of a 2-adjunction.

6 SProc Reformulated

This section demonstrates that **SProc** can be obtained as an instance of the general construction of the previous section. Specifically,

Proposition 6.1 ***SProc*** *is isomorphic to $Proc(Trace(\boldsymbol{Set}), \exists^{\mathcal{E}})$.*

The proof of this statement makes use of the coinduction principle for non-well-founded sets: two synchronization trees are equal exactly when they are bisimilar. First note that the construction $A\backslash s$ on the objects of **SProc** can be extended to a construction on the spans of $Trace(\mathbf{Set})$ as follows: [1]

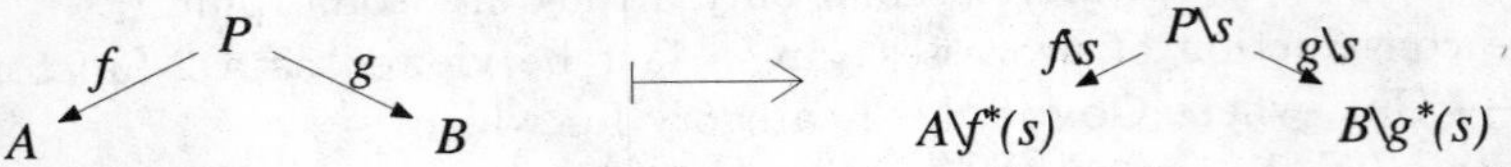

The isomorphism is given by a functor F which constructs the synchronization tree of a span. It is defined to have identity effect on objects, and has the following effect on arrows:

$$P_{(f,g)} \quad \stackrel{F}{\longmapsto} \quad \{((f(x), g(x)), F(P_{(f,g)}\backslash x)) \mid x \in S_P\}$$

It is easily seen that $P_{(f,g)} : A \longrightarrow B$ implies $F(P_{(f,g)}) : A \longrightarrow B$. That identities and composition are preserved is witnessed by the following bisimulations:

$$\{(id_{A\backslash s},\ F(A_{(id,id)}\backslash s)) \mid s \in S_A\}$$
$$\{(F(P_{(f,g)}\backslash r_0^*(s)); F(Q_{(h,k)}\backslash r_1^*(s)),\ F((P_{(f,g)}; Q_{(h,k)})\backslash s)) \mid s \in S_R\}$$

where $(R,\ r_0,\ r_1)$ is a pullback of g and h in $Trace(\mathbf{Set})$ (i.e. $R_{(r_0;f,\ r_1;k)}$ is the composite of $P_{(f,g)}$ and $Q_{(h,k)}$). Finally, if $C_{(c,d)}$ is a span of cover maps equating $P_{(f,g)}$ and $Q_{(h,k)}$, then the following is a bisimulation equating $F(P_{(f,g)})$ and $F(Q_{(h,k)})$:

$$\{(F(P_{(f,g)}\backslash c^*(s)),\ F(Q_{(h,k)}\backslash d^*(s)) \mid s \in S_C\}$$

As the categories in question have the same objects and F has identity effect on objects, it is enough to show that F is full and faithful.

To show that F is full we construct a span $G(p)$ from a map p in **SProc**, and then show $p = F(G(p))$. First form the traces of a synchronization tree, but with the labels separated:

$$G_S(p) = \{\epsilon\} \cup \{(a, q) \cdot s \mid p \stackrel{a}{\longrightarrow} q \ \wedge\ s \in G_S(q)\}.$$

The span $G(p)$ associated to process $p : A \longrightarrow B$ is then:

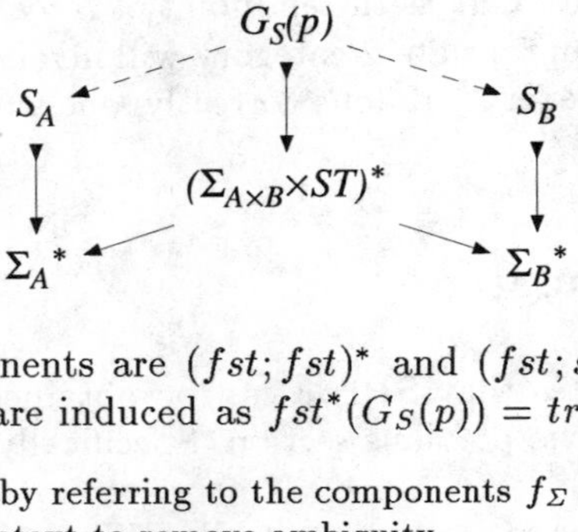

where the lower components are $(fst; fst)^*$ and $(fst; snd)^*$, respectively, and the upper components are induced as $fst^*(G_S(p)) = traces(p)$. It follows from

[1] We will abuse notation by referring to the components f_Σ of a map f of $Trace(\mathbf{Set})$ also as f, relying on context to remove ambiguity.

this definition that $F(G(p)\backslash(a,q)) = F(G(q))$, consequently the relation below is a bisimulation.

$$\{(p,\ F(G(p))) \mid p \in arrows(\mathbf{SProc})\}$$

To see that F is faithful, suppose $F(P_{(f,g)}) = F(Q_{(h,k)})$. The span $C_{(c,d)}$ below,

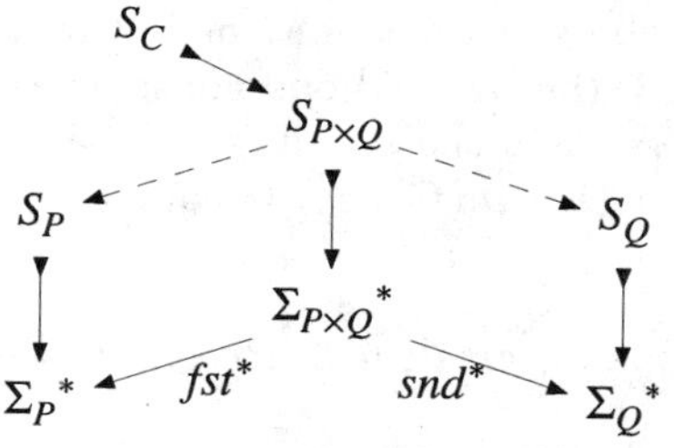

where $S_C = \{s \mid \langle f,g\rangle^*(fst^*(s)) = \langle h,k\rangle^*(snd^*(s))\}$, equates $P_{(f,g)}$ and $Q_{(h,k)}$. Clearly $c; f = d; h$ and $c; g = d; k$. To see that $c \in \exists_{\mathcal{E}}$, suppose $s \cdot x \in S_P$. Then $F(P) \overset{s}{\Longrightarrow} F(P\backslash s)$ and $F(P\backslash s) \overset{f(x),g(x)}{\longrightarrow} F(P\backslash s \cdot x)$. An induction on s shows that

$$\exists t \in S_Q.\ \langle f,g\rangle^*(s) = \langle h,k\rangle^*(t) \ \wedge\ F(Q) \overset{t}{\Longrightarrow} F(Q\backslash t) \ \wedge\ F(P\backslash s) = F(Q\backslash t)$$

So $y \in \Sigma_Q$ exists such that $\langle f,g\rangle(x) = \langle h,k\rangle(y)$ and $F(Q\backslash t) \overset{h(y),k(y)}{\longrightarrow} F(Q\backslash t \cdot y)$. Then, as $S_C \subseteq S_{P\times Q}$, there exists $u \in S_C$ for which $fst^*(u) = s \cdot x$, as required.

7 SProc Revisited

This section outlines how **SProc** is obtained through our construction starting with either $DTran(\mathbf{C})$ or $Tran(\mathbf{C})$ as base categories. Although simpler than the formulation presented above, each reformulation is most easily seen with the previous one in hand. We begin by developing a general result concerning the 2-functor $Proc$.

We say that a cover system $\mathcal{X}$ is *left-factor closed* if f is an $\mathcal{X}$-map whenever both $f; g$ and g are $\mathcal{X}$-maps. Examples of left-factor closed cover systems are the isomorphisms $\mathcal{I}$ of any category and $\exists^{\mathcal{I}}$ as defined for any of the categories $Trace(\mathbf{C})$, $DTran(\mathbf{C})$ or $Tran(\mathbf{C})$.

A span whose legs belong to a left-factor closed cover system $\mathcal{X}$ is an isomorphism in $Proc(\mathbf{X}, \mathcal{X}')$ for any cover system $\mathcal{X}'$ containing $\mathcal{X}$:

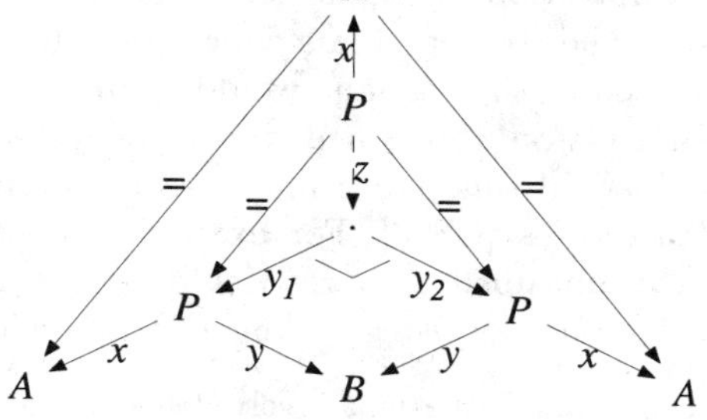

Consequently,

Lemma 7.1 *If* $(\eta, \epsilon) : F \Longrightarrow G : (\boldsymbol{X}, \mathcal{X}) \longrightarrow (\boldsymbol{Y}, \mathcal{Y})$ *is a* ***Cov****-adjunction*[2] *such that* $\eta_X \in \mathcal{X}'$ *and* $\epsilon_Y \in \mathcal{Y}'$ *for left-factor closed cover systems* $\mathcal{X}' \subseteq \mathcal{X}$ *and* $\mathcal{Y}' \subseteq \mathcal{Y}$*, then* $Proc(\boldsymbol{X}, \mathcal{X})$ *is equivalent to* $Proc(\boldsymbol{Y}, \mathcal{Y})$.

An adjunction (actually a coreflection) of the require form exists between $Trace(\mathbf{C})$ and $DTran(\mathbf{C})$: the right adjoint constructs the traces of a transition system in the standard way, and the counit is an $\exists^{\mathcal{I}}$-map at each component. As $\exists^{\mathcal{I}} \subseteq \exists^{\mathcal{C}}$ for any $\mathcal{C}$, $Proc(DTran(\mathbf{C}), \exists^{\mathcal{C}})$ is equivalent to $Proc(Trace(\mathbf{C}), \exists^{\mathcal{C}})$. Thus,

Proposition 7.2 ***SProc*** *is equivalent to* $Proc(DTran(\boldsymbol{Set}), \exists^{\mathcal{E}})$.

An appropriate adjuction exists which relates $DTran(\mathbf{C})$ and $Tran(\mathbf{C})$ as well: the left adjoint makes a transition system deterministic by adding (target) state information to the labels; the unit and counit are also $\exists^{\mathcal{I}}$-maps. Therefore,

Proposition 7.3 ***SProc*** *is equivalent to* $Proc(Tran(\boldsymbol{Set}), \exists^{\mathcal{E}})$.

Each of these alternate formulations has the advantage of admitting finite presentation of many infinite trace specifications. As specifications of allowable interaction, however, the objects of $DTran(\mathbf{C})$ — being deterministic — are clearly preferable to those of $Tran(\mathbf{C})$.

8 Conclusion

The fact that **SProc** arises as the processes of trace specifications, deterministic transitions systems, and transition systems, is not altogether surprising: these afterall are very standard models for interleaved concurrency. It does, however, illustrate a considerable latitude in the choice of starting point when constructing a specific process category.

Abramsky's category **ASProc** [AGN93] is similarly obtained. In this setting, the monads of delay occur at the level of the base category $Trace(\mathbf{C})$, $DTran(\mathbf{C})$, or $Tran(\mathbf{C})$. These monads are special in that the associated Kleisli categories have finite limits, allowing the construction of compact-closed process categories. It is interesting to note that pullbacks and products in these Kleisli categories give the notions of composition and parallel "product" that one expects for asynchronous processes. The cover systems which provide weak equivalence are obtained indirectly, related to the way one would compute weak bisimulation in terms of strong bisimulation on a modified transition system.

The methods described in this paper may also be applied to obtain rather different interaction categories [CS93]. For example, categories of games and strategies [AJ92] can be obtained as a restricted process category of a basic category of games and homomorpisms — the restriction concerns the legs of

[2] The functors and natural transformations involved belong to **Cov**.

the spans which must satisfy certain conditions. This construction can also be performed from a variety of starting points rather than, as originally presented, via traces.

Acknowledgements

The second author is grateful for the support of his former supervisor Graham Birtwistle, and both authors are grateful for the support of NSERC. Many thanks to Rick Blute and Tom Fukushima, who provided valuable comments on an earlier draft.

References

[Abr93] Abramsky, S., *Interaction Categories (Extended Abstract).* Theory and Formal Methods Workshop, Springer Verlag, 1993.

[AGN93] Abramsky, S., S. Gay and R. Nagarajan, *Constructing and verifying typed processes.* Available by FTP, 1993.

[AJ92] Abramsky, S., and R. Jagadeesan. *Games and Full Completeness for Multiplicative Linear Logic.* Imperial College Technical Report DoC 92/24, 1992.

[AJM93] Abramsky, S., Jagadeesan, R., and Malacaria, P. *Games and full abstraction for PCF: preliminary annnouncement.* Unpublished.

[Acz88] Aczel, P., *Non-well-founded sets.* CLSI Lecture Notes 14, Center for the Study of Language and Information, 1988.

[CLW92] Carboni, A., S. Lack and R.F.C. Walters, *Introduction to extensive and distributive categories.* Manuscript, March 1992.

[CW87] Carboni, A. and R.F.C. Walters, *Cartesian bicategories I.* Journal of Pure and Applied Algebra, 49:11–32, 1987.

[Coc90] Cockett, J.R.B., *List-arithmetic open categories: Locoi.* Journal of Pure and Applied Algebra, 66:1–29, 1990.

[Coc93] Cockett, J.R.B., *Introduction to distributive categories.* Mathematical Structures in Computer Science, 3:277–307, 1993.

[CS93] Cockett J.R.B. and D. Spooner, *The category of Protocols.* Presented at Dägstuhl, 1993.

[JNW93] Joyal, A., M. Nielsen and G. Winskel, *Bisimulation and open maps.* Proceedings of the Eighth Symposium on Logic in Computer Science, IEEE, 1993.

[Mil83] Milner, R., *Calculi for synchrony and asynchrony.* Theoretical Computer Science, 25:267–310, 1983.

[PW92] Power, A.J. and C.Wells, *A formalism for the specification of essentially algebraic structures in 2-categories.* Mathematical Structures in Computer Science, 2:1-28, 1992.

[Win87] Winskel, G., *A Compositional Proof System on a Category of Labelled Transition Systems.* Information and Computation 87:2–57.

From Timed Graphs to Hybrid Automata (Abstract)

Costas Courcoubetis
Institute of Computer Science, FORTH
and University of Crete, Greece

We discuss various automata-theoretic formalisms for the specification and verification of real-time systems. We start with the general formalism of the hybrid automata as a model and specification language for hybrid systems. This is an extension of the traditional automata on infinite words in which the behavior of variables is governed in each state by a set of differential equations. Then we introduce the models of the timed automata and the integration graphs as special cases of the hybrid automata. We discuss the complexity of important verification issues related to the above models such as reachability and model-checking, and we survey the related algorithms.

Hierarchical Models of Synchronous Circuits (Abstract)

David Dill
Stanford University

We seek a behavioral model of synchronous circuit operation which generalizes Mealy machines in several ways:

- It should allow the expression of nondeterministic behavior.
- It should allow parallel composition of machines and hiding of output signals.
- It should not restrict bidirectional communication between machines.
- It should deal reasonably with zero-delay cycles, which can be present in unrestricted communication graphs.
- It should provide a preorder that precisely captures the proper relationship between implementation and specification behaviors.
- It should allow the computation of the "most general environment" of a circuit.

Surprisingly, given the attention that has been paid to switching theory over the years, no adequate model exists meeting these criteria. Devising such a model is more challenging than we had expected. This talk is a description of several of the specific problems that arise, along with solutions to some of them.

The Observational Power of Clocks

Rajeev Alur[1] Costas Courcoubetis[2*] Thomas A. Henzinger[3**]

[1] AT&T Bell Laboratories, Murray Hill, NJ, USA.
[2] Department of Computer Science, University of Crete, Greece.
[3] Department of Computer Science, Cornell University, Ithaca, NY, USA.

Abstract. We develop a theory of equivalences for timed systems. Two systems are equivalent iff external observers cannot observe differences in their behavior. The notion of equivalence depends, therefore, on the distinguishing power of the observers. The power of an observer to measure time results in untimed, clock, and timed equivalences: an untimed observer cannot measure the time difference between events; a clock observer uses a clock to measure time differences with finite precision; a timed observer is able to measure time differences with arbitrary precision.

We show that the distinguishing power of clock observers grows with the number of observers, and approaches, in the limit, the distinguishing power of a timed observer. More precisely, given any equivalence for untimed systems, two timed systems are k-clock congruent, for a nonnegative integer k, iff their compositions with every environment that uses k clocks are untimed equivalent. Both k-clock bisimulation congruence and k-clock trace congruence form strict decidable hierarchies that converge towards the corresponding timed equivalences. Moreover, k-clock bisimulation congruence and k-clock trace congruence provide an adequate and abstract semantics for branching-time and linear-time logics with k clocks.

Our results impact on the verification of timed systems in two ways. First, our decision procedure for k-clock bisimulation congruence leads to a new, symbolic, decision procedure for timed bisimilarity. Second, timed trace equivalence is known to be undecidable. If the number of environment clocks is bounded, however, then our decision procedure for k-clock trace congruence allows the verification of timed systems in a trace model.

1 Introduction

At the center of every theory of concurrency lies a notion of equivalence between systems: it indicates what aspects of a system behavior are considered to be observable. In the case of untimed systems, a variety of equivalences have been promoted—most notably, perhaps, bisimilarity and trace equivalence—and

* Supported in part by the ESPRIT BRA project REACT.
** Supported in part by the National Science Foundation under grant CCR-9200794 and by the United States Air Force Office of Scientific Research under contract F49620-93-1-0056.

although there may be no agreement as to which equivalence is most appropriate, the relationship between different equivalences is well understood (see, for example, [13]). This is not the case for timed systems, where the introduction of time as a continuous quantity makes the question of what is observable even more subtle. This paper studies the relationship between several equivalences on timed systems that are induced by different capabilities of an observer to measure time.

A timed system always proceeds in one of two ways—by performing an action or by letting a certain amount of real time pass (see, for example, [4, 8, 12, 16]). The observability of actions and time delays are orthogonal issues, and as we are interested in the latter, we settle the former by studying the common untimed equivalences of bisimilarity (Section 3) and trace equivalence (Section 4).

From time-abstract and timed equivalences There are two extreme capabilities of an observer to measure time: (1) it may not be able to measure the duration of any delay, or (2) it may be able to measure the exact real-numbered duration of every delay. The first assumption leads to *time-abstract* (or *untimed*) *equivalences*; the second assumption, to *timed equivalences.* Both assumptions, however, have drawbacks. Time-abstract equivalences, on one hand, are unrealistically weak, because they do not admit timed systems themselves as observers; that is, time-abstract equivalences are not congruences under parallel composition. Timed equivalences, on the other hand, are unrealistically strong—what system can observe a delay of duration π?—uncomfortably strong—timed trace equivalence, for example, is undecidable—and, as we will demonstrate, unnecessarily strong.

To resource-bounded observational congruences We focus on the resources that an observer needs to distinguish timed systems and define a sequence of congruences that lie between time-abstract and timed equivalences. A *clock* is a resource that measures the length of a time interval with finite (integer) precision. The assumption that the observer has k clocks to measure time leads to ***k*-*clock congruences.*** We show that the k-clock congruences form, in both the bisimulation and trace worlds, a strict infinite hierarchy between the corresponding time-abstract and timed equivalences; that is, the distinguishing power of an observer increases with the number of clocks it uses. Alternatively, if every process has one clock, then the distinguishing power of an environment increases with the number of environment processes.

Decision procedures are known for time-abstract and timed bisimilarity and for time-abstract trace equivalence [2, 4, 14, 15, 17]. We present algorithms for deciding the k-clock congruences. In the bisimulation world, where the k-clock hierarchy collapses at $2n + 1$ clocks for a given pair of systems with n clocks, we obtain a new algorithm for deciding timed bisimilarity; unlike the decision procedure of [14], our algorithm can be executed symbolically. In the trace world, where the timed equivalence is undecidable, we obtain an algorithm for checking the correctness of substitutions in a hierarchical verification process. In both worlds, our results can be used to replace a timed system with a simpler system, provided the number of environment clocks is bounded.

Via automata, games, and logics Clocks provide a clean and general paradigm for specifying timed systems: clocks have been added to such diverse languages as temporal logic [5], ω-automata [4], and process algebra [11]. We develop our results using the model of *timed automata* (Section 2). A timed automaton operates with finite control—a finite set of control locations and a finite set of real-valued clocks. All clocks proceed at the same rate and measure the amount of time that has elapsed since they were started (or reset). Each automaton transition may compare some of the clock values with integer constants and reset some of the clocks. This model of timed automata has been widely and successfully used for the specification and verification of real-time systems [1, 3, 4, 6, 7, 9, 11, 12].

Our results on bisimulation equivalences in Section 3 are obtained by studying bisimulation games. We define *time-abstract* (or *untimed*), *k-clock*, and *timed bisimulation games*. Suppose that Player I attempts to distinguish two systems, while Player II tries to show bisimilarity. In a timed game, Player II must match a delay of Player I with a delay of the same duration; in a time-abstract game, Player II can match a delay of Player I with a delay of arbitrary duration; in a k-clock game, Player I may choose, in addition to a delay, any constraints on the values of k clocks, and Player II can match the delay of Player I with a delay of arbitrary duration as long as the clock constraints are satisfied.

We also provide logical characterizations of the k-clock congruences. For this purpose, we add clock variables to modal logics and prove Hennessy-Milner-like theorems. In the bisimulation world, two systems are k-clock congruent iff they cannot be distinguished by branching-time formulas with k clocks; in the trace world, iff they cannot be distinguished by linear-time formulas with k clocks. The limit of all k-clock congruences provides, then, an adequate and abstract semantics for clock logics. While in general this limit—*untimed bisimulation congruence* and *untimed trace congruence*—is weaker than the corresponding timed equivalence, it surprisingly coincides with the corresponding timed equivalence on initial system states, in which all clock values are 0.

Related work The relationship between timed bisimilarity and untimed bisimulation congruence is studied also in [10]. There, it is shown that timed bisimilarity coincides with untimed bisimulation congruence provided that the observer can compare clock values with arbitrary rational constants; indeed, in this scenario a single observer clock suffices. Furthermore, it is proved that if the observer is required to compare clock values with multiples of $1/n$, then the observational power grows with n, yielding a strict hierarchy of equivalences based on the time granularity of the observer. By contrast, we assume that the observer clocks have the same granularity as the system clocks and show that the power of the observer increases with the number of clocks it uses.

2 Timed Transition Systems

A *labeled transition system* consists of a set Q of states, a set L of labels, and a family $\{\xrightarrow{\alpha}\ \subseteq Q^2 \mid \alpha \in L\}$ of transition relations, one for each label in L.

The transition relation can be extended to finite words over L: for a word $\overline{\alpha} = \alpha_0\alpha_1\cdots\alpha_n$ in L^* and two states q and q', define $q \xrightarrow{\overline{\alpha}} q'$ iff there exist states $q_0, q_1, \ldots, q_{n-1}$ such that $q \xrightarrow{\alpha_0} q_0 \xrightarrow{\alpha_1} \cdots \xrightarrow{\alpha_{n-1}} q_{n-1} \xrightarrow{\alpha_n} q'$.

Let the *time domain* $\mathbb{R}_{\geq 0}$ be the set of nonnegative real numbers. A *timed transition system* is a labeled transition system with $\mathbb{R}_{\geq 0} \subseteq L$; that is, the label set includes all time increments, and the transition relation $\xrightarrow{\delta}$, for a time increment δ, represents a delay of duration δ. We define timed transition systems by timed automata.

Timed automata A *timed automaton* A is a tuple (Σ, Γ, V, E), where Σ is a finite input alphabet, Γ is a finite set of clocks, V is a finite set of locations, and E is a finite set of edges. Each edge is a tuple $(s, \sigma, \mu, \lambda, s')$ that represents a transition from location $s \in V$ to location $s' \in V$ on the input symbol $\sigma \in \Sigma$. The edge constraint μ is a boolean combination of atomic formulas of the form $x \leq c$ or $c \leq x$, for a clock x and a nonnegative integer c. The reset set $\lambda \subseteq \Gamma$ specifies the clocks that are reset,

A *state* of the timed automaton A is a pair (s, ν) consisting of a location $s \in V$ and a clock mapping $\nu\colon \Gamma \mapsto \mathbb{R}_{\geq 0}$ that assigns a time value to each clock. All clocks are initialized to zero: the state (s, ν) is *initial* iff $\nu(x) = 0$ for each clock x. We write Q_A for the state set of A, and Q_A^0 for the set of initial states of A. The timed automaton A proceeds from state to state in two ways.

- *Time successor.* For every time increment $\delta \in \mathbb{R}_{\geq 0}$ and every state (s, ν), let $(s, \nu) \xrightarrow{\delta} (s, \nu + \delta)$, where $\nu + \delta$ is the clock mapping that assigns the value $\nu(x) + \delta$ to each clock x.
- *Transition successor.* For every input symbol σ, every state (s, ν), and every edge $(s, \sigma, \mu, \lambda, s')$ such that ν satisfies the edge constraint μ, let $(s, \nu) \xrightarrow{\sigma} (s', \nu[\lambda := 0])$, where $\nu[\lambda := 0]$ is the clock mapping that assigns the value 0 to each clock $x \in \lambda$, and the value $\nu(x)$ to each clock $x \notin \lambda$.

We associate two labeled transition systems with the timed automaton A.

1. First, we observe both input symbols and time increments. The *timed transition system* of A, denoted by $\mathcal{S}_t(A)$, consists of the state set Q_A, the label set $\mathbb{R}_{\geq 0} \cup \Sigma$, and the transition relations $\xrightarrow{\alpha}$, for $\alpha \in \mathbb{R}_{\geq 0} \cup \Sigma$.
2. Second, we observe input symbols and hide time increments. For every input symbol σ and every pair of states $q, q' \in Q_A$, define $q \stackrel{\sigma}{\Rightarrow} q'$ iff $q \xrightarrow{\delta\sigma\delta'} q'$ for some time increments $\delta, \delta' \in \mathbb{R}_{\geq 0}$. The *time-abstract* (or *untimed*) *transition system* of A, denoted by $\mathcal{S}_u(A)$, consists of the state set Q_A, the label set Σ, and the transition relations $\stackrel{\sigma}{\Rightarrow}$, for $\sigma \in \Sigma$.

Given two timed automata $A = (\Sigma, \Gamma, V, E)$ and $A' = (\Sigma, \Gamma', V', E')$ over the same input alphabet Σ and disjoint sets Γ and Γ' of clocks, the *parallel composition* $A \otimes A'$ is the timed automaton $(\Sigma, \Gamma \cup \Gamma', V \times V', E'')$ such that $((s_1, s_1'), \sigma, \mu \wedge \mu', \lambda \cup \lambda', (s_2, s_2')) \in E''$ iff $(s_1, \sigma, \mu, \lambda, s_2) \in E$ and $(s_1', \sigma, \mu', \lambda', s_2') \in E'$. The timed transition system of $A \otimes A'$, then, represents the product of the timed transition systems of A and A': for all states $q_1, q_2 \in Q_A$, $q_1', q_2' \in Q_{A'}$, and all labels $\alpha \in \mathbb{R}_{\geq 0} \cup \Sigma$, we have $(q_1, q_1') \xrightarrow{\alpha} (q_2, q_2')$ for $\mathcal{S}_t(A \otimes A')$ iff $q_1 \xrightarrow{\alpha} q_2$ for $\mathcal{S}_t(A)$ and $q_1' \xrightarrow{\alpha} q_2'$ for $\mathcal{S}_t(A')$.

Equivalences and congruences on timed automata We define equivalence relations on systems as equivalence relations on system states: two systems are equivalent iff the initial states of the disjoint union of both systems are equivalent. Consider two equivalence relations $\equiv_1$ and $\equiv_2$ on the states of timed automata.

- We write $\equiv_1 \subseteq \equiv_2$, and call $\equiv_2$ *weaker than* $\equiv_1$ (on all states), iff for every timed automaton A and every pair of states $q, q' \in Q_A$, if $q \equiv_1 q'$ then $q \equiv_2 q'$.
- We write $\equiv_1 \subseteq_{init} \equiv_2$, and call $\equiv_2$ *weaker than* $\equiv_1$ *on initial states*, iff for every timed automaton A and every pair of initial states $q, q' \in Q_A^0$, if $q \equiv_1 q'$ then $q \equiv_2 q'$.

Notice that it may happen that $\equiv_2$ is weaker than $\equiv_1$, but $\equiv_1$ and $\equiv_2$ coincide on initial states. We say that $\equiv_2$ is *strictly weaker than* $\equiv_1$, written $\equiv_1 \prec \equiv_2$, iff $\equiv_2$ is weaker than $\equiv_1$ on all states and $\equiv_2 \not\subseteq_{init} \equiv_1$; that is, $\equiv_1$ distinguishes two $\equiv_2$-equivalent initial states.

The congruence induced by an equivalence relation on systems depends on the choice of operators used to build complex systems from simple systems. We study the parallel composition operator $\otimes$ on timed automata. For a given alphabet Σ, let TA_Σ denote the set of timed automata over Σ, and for $k \geq 0$, let TA_Σ^k denote the set of timed automata over Σ with at most k clocks. An equivalence relation $\equiv$ is a *congruence* iff whenever $q \equiv q'$ for two states q and q' of a timed automaton $A \in \mathrm{TA}_\Sigma$, then for all timed automata $B \in \mathrm{TA}_\Sigma$ and all initial states $q_0 \in Q_B^0$, the equivalence $(q, q_0) \equiv (q', q_0)$ holds for the product automaton $A \otimes B$. The congruence *induced by* the equivalence relation $\equiv$ is the weakest congruence relation that is stronger than $\equiv$.

If an equivalence relation $\equiv$ is not a congruence, then there are two $\equiv$-equivalent states q and q' of a timed automaton A—the *observed* automaton—and there is an initial state q_0 of a timed automaton B—the *observer* automaton—such that $(q, q_0) \not\equiv (q', q_0)$ for the product automaton $A \otimes B$. The observer automaton B, then, distinguishes the two states q and q' of the observed automaton A. Notice that our definition requires the observer automaton to be in the class TA_Σ of the observed automaton. Furthermore, the clock constraints of B compare clock values to integer constants; that is, the observer automaton has the same granularity for counting time as the observed automaton.

Region equivalence Emptiness checking and model checking algorithms for timed automata are based on an equivalence relation that partitions the states of a timed automaton A into so-called regions [1, 4]. Two clock mappings ν and ν' for A are region equivalent, written $\nu \equiv_r \nu'$, iff

1. Corresponding clock values agree on the integer parts: for every clock x, either $\lfloor \nu(x) \rfloor = \lfloor \nu'(x) \rfloor$, or both $\nu(x)$ and $\nu'(x)$ exceed the largest constant that is compared with x by the edge constraints of A;
2. Corresponding clock values agree on the ordering of the fractional parts: (*i*) for every clock x, $\langle \nu(x) \rangle = 0$ iff $\langle \nu'(x) \rangle = 0$, where $\langle \delta \rangle = \delta - \lfloor \delta \rfloor$; and (*ii*) for every pair x and y of clocks, $\langle \nu(x) \rangle \leq \langle \nu(y) \rangle$ iff $\langle \nu'(x) \rangle \leq \langle \nu'(y) \rangle$.

Two states (s, ν) and (s', ν') of A are *region equivalent* iff $s = s'$ and $\nu \equiv_r \nu'$; two states that belong to different timed automata are not region equivalent. An equivalence class of Q_A induced by $\equiv_r$ is called a *region*.

Two observations about region equivalence are in order. First, there are only finitely many regions (linear in the number of locations and edges, and singly exponential in the number of clocks and the length of edge constraints). Second, region equivalence is a congruence.

3 Bisimulation Equivalences

Consider a labeled transition system $\mathcal{S}$ with state set Q and label set L. An equivalence relation $\equiv \subseteq Q^2$ is a *bisimulation* for $\mathcal{S}$ iff $q_1 \equiv q_2$ implies for every label $\alpha \in L$ that

- If $q_1 \xrightarrow{\alpha} q_1'$, then there exists a state q_2' such that $q_1' \equiv q_2'$ and $q_2 \xrightarrow{\alpha} q_2'$;
- If $q_2 \xrightarrow{\alpha} q_2'$, then there exists a state q_1' such that $q_1' \equiv q_2'$ and $q_1 \xrightarrow{\alpha} q_1'$.

Two states q and q' are *bisimilar* with respect to $\mathcal{S}$ iff there exists a bisimulation $\equiv$ for $\mathcal{S}$ such that $q \equiv q'$; that is, bisimilarity with respect to $\mathcal{S}$ is the weakest bisimulation for $\mathcal{S}$.

Bisimulation can be viewed as a game between two players. Let q_1 and q_2 be two states of $\mathcal{S}$.

- *Move of Player I.* Player I chooses a side $i \in \{1,2\}$, a label $\alpha \in L$, and a state q_i' such that $q_i \xrightarrow{\alpha} q_i'$.
- *Move of Player II.* Let $j \in \{1,2\}$ such that $i \neq j$. Player II chooses a state q_j' such that $q_j \xrightarrow{\alpha} q_j'$. If no such state exists, Player I wins the game. Otherwise, the game continues on the two states q_1' and q_2'.

Thus, at every step Player I chooses a move, and Player II responds with a matching move. The goal of Player I is to distinguish the two starting states q and q' by enforcing a situation in which Player II cannot find a matching move. The starting states are bisimilar iff Player I cannot distinguish them; that is, iff Player I does not have a winning strategy.

The weakest bisimulation for $\mathcal{S}$ can be computed by an iterative approximation procedure that repeatedly refines a partition of the state set Q until a bisimulation is obtained. The initial partition Π_0 contains a single equivalence class. Now consider the partition Π_i after the i-th refinement. For two subsets $\pi, \pi' \subseteq Q$, and a label $\alpha \in L$, let $pre_\alpha(\pi, \pi')$ be the set of states $q \in \pi$ such that $q \xrightarrow{\alpha} q'$ for some $q' \in \pi'$. If there are two equivalence classes $\pi, \pi' \in \Pi_i$ and a label $\alpha \in L$ such that both $pre_\alpha(\pi, \pi')$ and $\pi - pre_\alpha(\pi, \pi')$ are nonempty, then we obtain the new partition Π_{i+1} by splitting π into the two equivalence classes $pre_\alpha(\pi, \pi')$ and $\pi - pre_\alpha(\pi, \pi')$. If no such splitting is possible, then the current partition is the weakest bisimulation for $\mathcal{S}$.

The iterative approximation procedure is a semidecision procedure for bisimilarity iff each partition is computable; that is, the label set is finite and the equivalence classes can be represented in an effective manner that supports the operations *pre* and set difference. The iterative approximation procedure is a decision procedure for bisimilarity iff it is a semidecision procedure that terminates. In the case of timed transition systems, the state set is infinite and, therefore, termination is not necessarily guaranteed.

3.1 Timed bisimilarity

Two states q and q' of a timed automaton A are *timed bisimilar*, written $q \equiv_{tb} q'$, iff q and q' are bisimilar with respect to the timed transition system $\mathcal{S}_t(A)$. If timed bisimulation is viewed as a game, whenever Player I takes a transition step, Player II must match it with a transition on the same input symbol; and whenever Player I lets time δ elapse, Player II must let time δ elapse, too.

Example 1. Consider a timed automaton with the single location s, the single clock x, and the single edge from s to itself labeled with the input symbol σ and the edge constraint $x = 1$. A state of the automaton is fully specified by the value $\delta \in \mathbb{R}_{\geq 0}$ of the clock x. Two states δ and δ' are timed bisimilar iff either $\delta = \delta'$ or both $\delta, \delta' > 1$. ■

A few observations about timed bisimilarity are in order. First, Example 1 shows that, unlike in the case of region equivalence, the number of equivalence classes of timed bisimilarity can be infinite. Indeed, the relations $\equiv_{tb}$ and $\equiv_r$ are incomparable; none is weaker than the other. Second, timed bisimilarity is a congruence. Third, timed bisimilarity is decidable: there is an EXPTIME algorithm to decide if two given states of a timed automaton are timed bisimilar [14].

3.2 Untimed bisimilarity

Two states q and q' of a timed automaton A are *untimed bisimilar*, written $q \equiv_{ub} q'$, iff q and q' are bisimilar with respect to the untimed transition system $\mathcal{S}_u(A)$. If untimed bisimulation is viewed as a game, Player II must match a transition step of Player I with a transition on the same input symbol, but whenever Player I lets time δ elapse, Player II may let any amount of time elapse.

Two states δ and δ' of Example 1 are untimed bisimilar iff either both $\delta, \delta' \leq 1$ or both $\delta, \delta' > 1$. Indeed, untimed bisimilarity always has finitely many equivalence classes, and each equivalence class is a union of regions [2, 10]. It follows that region equivalence is an untimed bisimulation ($\equiv_r \prec \equiv_{ub}$). Moreover, every timed bisimulation is an untimed bisimulation ($\equiv_{tb} \prec \equiv_{ub}$).

The iterative approximation procedure decides, in EXPTIME, if two given states of a timed automaton are untimed bisimilar: (1) every equivalence class that is computed by repeated refinement of the initial partition is a union of regions and, therefore, can be represented by a formula involving linear inequalities over the clock variables; (2) termination is guaranteed, because $\equiv_{ub}$ has finitely many equivalence classes.

The following example shows that untimed bisimilarity is not a congruence.

Example 2. Figure 1 shows a timed automaton A with two clocks x and y. The input alphabet is the singleton set $\{\sigma\}$. The two initial states $(s, \overline{0})$ and $(u, \overline{0})$

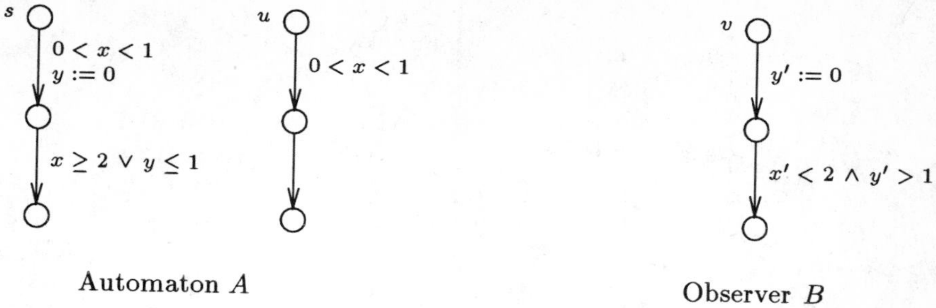

Fig. 1. Example 2

are untimed bisimilar. Now consider the product of A with the observer B with the two clocks x' and y'. The two states $((s,\overline{0}),(v,\overline{0}))$ and $((u,\overline{0}),(v,\overline{0}))$ of the product automaton $A \otimes B$ are not untimed bisimilar. ■

3.3 Untimed bisimulation congruence

We now study the congruence induced by the untimed bisimulation $\equiv_{ub}$. The number of clocks of an observer increases its power to distinguish states. Consider, for instance, Example 2 again. The two states $(s,\overline{0})$ and $(u,\overline{0})$ can be distinguished using two clocks, but they cannot be distinguished by an observer with a single clock: for all timed automata B with one clock and all initial states q of B, the two states $((s,\overline{0}),q)$ and $((u,\overline{0}),q)$ of the product automaton are untimed bisimilar.

This observation prompts us to define a sequence of congruences. Let k be a nonnegative integer and let A be a timed automaton in TA_Σ. Two states q and q' of A are *k-clock congruent*, written $q \approx_{ub}^k q'$, iff for all timed automata $B \in \mathrm{TA}_\Sigma^k$ and all initial states q'' of B, the equivalence $(q,q'') \equiv_{ub} (q',q'')$ holds for the product automaton $A \otimes B$. Untimed bisimulation congruence is the intersection of all k-clock congruences: two states q and q' of A are *untimed bisimulation congruent*, written $q \approx_{ub} q'$, iff $q \approx_{ub}^k q'$ for all $k \geq 0$.

The k-clock congruences $\approx_{ub}^k$ can also be characterized using games. We modify the untimed game by introducing a set of environment clocks. If there are k environment clocks, then the state of the environment is represented by a k-tuple of real numbers. The game is played, instead of on states of a timed automaton, on pairs of the form (q,ν), where q is an automaton state and ν is a k-tuple of reals that provides time values for the environment clocks. We call such a pair an *augmented state*. With each time move, Player I chooses, in addition to a time increment, a constraint on the environment clocks. Player II may then choose any time increment provided it satisfies the clock constraint chosen by Player I.

Formally, a *k-clock move* α is a triple (σ,μ,λ), where σ is an input symbol, μ is a constraint on the environment clocks, and $\lambda \subseteq \{1,\ldots,k\}$ is a reset set.

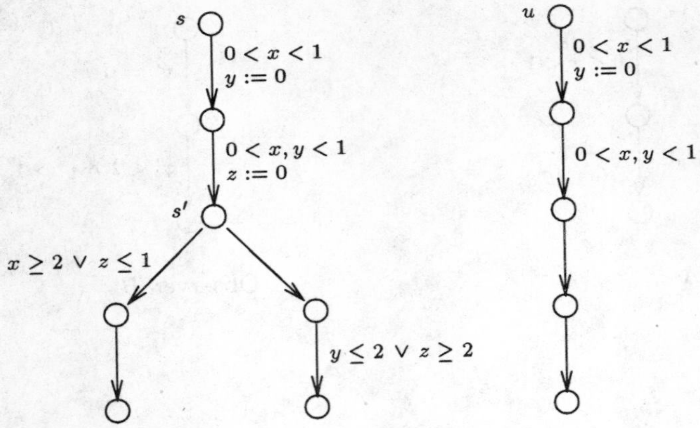

Fig. 2. Example 3

Given a timed automaton A, we thus obtain the *k-clock transition system* $\mathcal{S}_u^k(A)$. The states of $\mathcal{S}_u^k(A)$ are the augmented states $Q_A \times \mathbb{R}_{\geq 0}^k$; the labels of $\mathcal{S}_u^k(A)$ are the k-clock moves; and for each k-clock move, let $(q,\nu) \xrightarrow{\alpha} (q',\nu')$ iff there is a time increment δ such that $q \xrightarrow{\delta\sigma} q'$, and $\nu+\delta$ satisfies μ, and $\nu' = (\nu+\delta)[\lambda := 0]$.

The following lemma characterizes all k-clock congruences as bisimulations for k-clock transition systems.

Lemma 1. *Two states q and q' of a timed automaton A are k-clock congruent iff the augmented states $(q,\overline{0})$ and $(q',\overline{0})$ are bisimilar with respect to the k-clock transition system $\mathcal{S}_u^k(A)$.*

We can show that each equivalence class of $\approx_{ub}$ (and, hence, of $\approx_{ub}^k$ for each k) is a union of regions. It follows that the number of equivalence classes of untimed bisimulation congruence is finite and, thus, untimed bisimulation congruence differs from timed bisimilarity. Later, we will see that the two relations $\approx_{ub}$ and $\equiv_{tb}$ coincide on all *initial* states.

Theorem 2. *Untimed bisimulation congruence is strictly weaker than region equivalence ($\equiv_r \prec \approx_{ub}$), and is weaker than timed bisimilarity ($\equiv_{tb} \subseteq \approx_{ub}$).*

An infinite hierarchy of congruences Example 2 shows that 1-clock congruence is strictly weaker than the 2-clock congruence. By generalizing this example, we obtain a strict hierarchy of congruences; that is, each additional clock gives additional distinguishing power to an observer.

Example 3. Consider the timed automaton shown in Figure 2. It uses the three clocks x, y, and z. Consider the initial states $(s,\overline{0})$ and $(u,\overline{0})$. Using three environment clocks x', y', and z', we now show that Player I can distinguish these two states. Player I always moves on the right hand side. It resets y' in its first move, and resets z' in the second move. In the third move, it requires the environment clocks to satisfy the constraint $x' < 2 \wedge z' > 1$. This forces Player II to choose the left branch from location s'. In the fourth move, Player I uses the constraint $y' > 2 \wedge z' < 2$ to move to the final location on right hand side, and Player II cannot match this move.

On the other hand, it is not difficult to check that with only two environment clocks, Player I cannot distinguish $(s, \overline{0})$ and $(u, \overline{0})$. ■

Theorem 3. *The equivalence relations* $\approx_{ub}^{k}$, *for* $k \geq 0$, *form a strict hierarchy* $(\equiv_{ub} = \approx_{ub}^{0} \succ \approx_{ub}^{1} \succ \approx_{ub}^{2} \succ \cdots \succ \approx_{ub})$.

The hierarchy of k-clock congruences collapses if we choose the natural numbers as time domain. In this case, a single observer clock suffices to distinguish any two noncongruent states $(\equiv_{ub} \succ \approx_{ub}^{1} = \approx_{ub})$.

Deciding k-clock congruence We now outline an algorithm for deciding k-clock congruence. The iterative approximation procedure on the k-clock transition system $\mathcal{S}_u^k(A)$ is not effective, as the number of possible k-clock moves is infinite. This is because the integer constants in a constraint on the environment clocks may be arbitrarily large.

We therefore modify the k-clock game in three ways. First, since the objective of Player I is to limit the possible choices of Player II, we require Player I to choose the tightest possible constraints on the environment clocks. Second, we require Player I to reset every environment clock when it reaches the value 1. Third, we allow Player I to employ ϵ-moves to reset a clock without choosing an input symbol. Formally, a *bounded k-clock ϵ-move* is of the form (σ, μ, λ), where $\sigma \in \Sigma \cup \{\epsilon\}$, the clock constraint μ is a conjunction of atomic constraints, one for each environment clock x, of the form $x < 1$ or $x = 1$, and the reset set λ contains the clock x iff μ contains the conjunct $x = 1$. We obtain the *bounded k-clock transition system* $\hat{\mathcal{S}}_u^k(A)$ with the state set $Q_A \times [0, 1]^k$ and with the bounded k-clock ϵ-moves as labels. The following lemma shows that this modification of the k-clock transition system for A does not change the induced bisimulation.

Lemma 4. *For all* $k \geq 0$, *all states* q *and* q' *of a timed automaton* A, *and all* k*-tuples* $\nu, \nu' \in [0, 1]^k$ *such that* ν *and* ν' *are region equivalent, the augmented states* (q, ν) *and* (q', ν') *are bisimilar with respect to the bounded* k*-clock transition system* $\hat{\mathcal{S}}_u^k(A)$ *iff they are bisimilar with respect to the* k*-clock transition system* $\mathcal{S}_u^k(A)$.

The k-clock congruence $\approx_{ub}^{k}$ can be computed, then, by iterative approximation on the bounded k-clock transition system $\hat{\mathcal{S}}_u^k(A)$. The procedure is effective, because the number of bounded k-clock ϵ-moves is finite (exponential in k) and each equivalence class that is computed is a union of extended regions (i.e., regions that contain both system and environment clocks); termination is guaranteed, because the number of extended regions is finite. The complexity of the algorithm is quadratic in the number of extended regions, and therefore exponential in both k and in the description of the timed automaton A.

Theorem 5. *Given two states* q *and* q' *of a timed automaton* A *and a nonnegative integer* k, *it can be decided in EXPTIME if* $q \approx_{ub}^{k} q'$.

Deciding untimed bisimulation congruence Suppose that two states q and q' of a timed automaton A with n clocks are not untimed bisimulation congruent. In the full paper, we show that Player I needs at most $2n+1$ environment clocks to distinguish q and q'. Roughly speaking, this is because with $2n+1$ clocks, Player I can always keep an environment clock identical to each system clock on both sides of the game.

Lemma 6. *Let A be a timed automaton with n clocks. Two states of A are untimed bisimulation congruent iff they are $(2n+1)$-clock congruent.*

It follows that for any given timed automaton, the hierarchy of k-clock congruences collapses. This property, in conjunction with our decision procedure for k-clock congruence, allows us to decide untimed bisimulation congruence.

Theorem 7. *Given two initial states q and q' of a timed automaton A, it can be decided in EXPTIME if $q \approx_{ub} q'$.*

Deciding timed bisimilarity We have already seen that the relations $\equiv_{tb}$ and $\approx_{ub}$ are different: two states can be untimed bisimulation congruent but not timed bisimilar. Surprisingly, both relations coincide on initial states.

To see this, we introduce environment clocks in the timed game. We thus obtain a k-clock game on augmented states in which Player II must always choose the same time increment as Player I. In this game, the values of the environment clocks are identical on both sides; consequently, the state of the game is given by two augmented states of the form (q, ν) and (q', ν). If the game is started on initial states, then initially an environment clock is identical to each system clock, and provided there are enough environment clocks, this invariant can be maintained throughout the game. An augmented state (q, ν) in which each system clock equals some environment clock can be represented by a triple (s, γ, ν), where s is the location of q and γ is a mapping from system clocks to environment clocks. The following lemma is proved by induction on the number of moves in a game.

Lemma 8. *If Player I wins the timed game with environment clocks starting from the augmented states (s, γ, ν) and (s', γ', ν), then for all environment clock mappings ν', Player I wins the untimed game with environment clocks starting from (s, γ, ν) and (s', γ', ν').*

In other words, for augmented states in which all system clocks equal environment clocks, the timed game is equivalent to the untimed game. On initial states, untimed bisimulation congruence coincides therefore with timed bisimilarity.

Theorem 9. *Consider a timed automaton A with n clocks and two initial states q and q'. The following statements are equivalent:*

1. *The states q and q' are $(2n+1)$-clock congruent ($q \approx_{ub}^{2n+1} q'$).*
2. *The states q and q' are untimed bisimulation congruent ($q \approx_{ub} q'$).*
3. *The states q and q' are timed bisimilar ($q \equiv_{tb} q'$).*

This result gives us an EXPTIME iterative approximation algorithm for deciding timed bisimilarity of initial states (i.e., timed bisimilarity of initialized systems). Since the iterative approximation algorithm can be executed symbolically, by representing equivalence classes as formulas, we expect it to be more practical and flexible than the algorithm of [14].

3.4 Branching-time logics with clocks

The bisimilarity of states of a labeled transition system can be characterized by a modal next-state logic called Hennessy-Milner logic or, equivalently, by the branching-time temporal logic CTL: two states are bisimilar iff they satisfy the same CTL formulas.

In this section, we give a logical characterization of both k-clock congruence and untimed bisimulation congruence. For this purpose, we extend CTL with clock variables, thus obtaining the real-time logic TCTL [1]. The clock variables are bound by reset quantifiers, and they can be compared with nonnegative integer constants (the original definition of TCTL uses a freeze quantifier, which is equivalent to the reset quantifier). We use the modal operators $\exists\bigcirc\,\sigma.$ ("at the possible next input symbol σ") and $\exists\Diamond$ ("eventually along some word"); since we consider only finite words in this paper, the operator $\exists\Box$ is not useful.

Formally, the formulas of TCTL$^\Diamond$ are defined inductively as

$$\phi \;::=\; x \leq c \mid c \leq x \mid \neg\phi \mid \phi_1 \wedge \phi_2 \mid \exists\bigcirc\,\sigma.\,\phi \mid \exists\Diamond\,\sigma.\,\phi \mid (x := 0).\,\phi$$

for clocks x, nonnegative integers c, and input symbols σ. Given a timed transition system with the state set Q and the label set $\mathbb{R}_{\geq 0} \cup \Sigma$, every formula of TCTL$^\Diamond$ defines a subset of Q. Let q be a state and let ν be a clock mapping. Then $q \models \phi$ iff $q \models_\emptyset \phi$ for the empty clock mapping $\emptyset$, and

- $q \models_\nu \exists\bigcirc\,\sigma.\,\phi$ iff there exist a state q' and a time increment δ such that $q \xrightarrow{\delta\sigma} q'$ and $q' \models_{\nu+\delta} \phi$;
- $q \models_\nu (x := 0).\,\phi$ iff $q \models_{\nu[x:=0]} \phi$.

The logic TCTL$^\circ$ is the fragment of TCTL$^\Diamond$ without the eventuality operator $\exists\Diamond$.

Example 4. Recall the timed automaton A of Figure 1. Let ϕ be the TCTL$^\circ$-formula

$$(x := 0).\,\exists\bigcirc\,\sigma.\,(y := 0).\,\exists\bigcirc\,\sigma.\,(x < 2 \wedge y > 1).$$

Then $(s, \overline{0}) \not\models \phi$ and $(u, \overline{0}) \models \phi$. Thus the formula ϕ distinguishes the locations s and u. On the other hand, let ψ be the formula

$$((x := 0).\,\exists\bigcirc\,\sigma.\,\exists\bigcirc\,\sigma.\,x < 2) \wedge (\exists\bigcirc\,\sigma.\,(x := 0).\,\exists\bigcirc\,\sigma.\,x > 1).$$

Both states $(s, \overline{0})$ and $(u, \overline{0})$ satisfy ψ. Indeed, no TCTL$^\Diamond$-formula that uses only one clock variable can distinguish the states $(s, \overline{0})$ and $(u, \overline{0})$. ■

The logics TCTL° and $\mathrm{TCTL}^{\diamond}$ induce equivalence relations on the states of a timed automaton: two states q and q' are $\mathrm{TCTL}^{\diamond}$-equivalent iff they satisfy the same $\mathrm{TCTL}^{\diamond}$-formulas. We prove that TCTL°-equivalence and $\mathrm{TCTL}^{\diamond}$-equivalence coincide with each other and with untimed bisimulation congruence.

First we observe that the equivalence induced by $\mathrm{TCTL}^{\diamond}$ is weaker than region equivalence [1]: if two augmented states (q, ν) and (q', ν') are region equivalent, then for all $\mathrm{TCTL}^{\diamond}$-formulas ϕ, $q \models_{\nu} \phi$ iff $q' \models_{\nu'} \phi$. By induction on the number of moves that an observer needs to distinguish two augmented states in the k-clock game, we can show that if two augmented states are not bisimilar with respect to a k-clock transition system, then they can be distinguished by a TCTL°-formula with at most k clock variables. On the other hand, if two augmented states are bisimilar with respect to a k-clock transition system, then we can prove, by induction on the structure of formulas, that they satisfy the same k-clock formulas of $\mathrm{TCTL}^{\diamond}$. This leads to a logical characterization of k-clock congruence.

Theorem 10. *Consider a timed automaton A and two states q and q'. The following statements are equivalent:*

1. *The states q and q' are k-clock congruent ($q \approx_{ub}^{k} q'$).*
2. *For all $\mathrm{TCTL}^{\diamond}$-formulas ϕ with at most k clock variables, $q \models \phi$ iff $q' \models \phi$.*
3. *For all TCTL°-formulas ϕ with at most k clock variables, $q \models \phi$ iff $q' \models \phi$.*

It follows that untimed bisimulation congruence is an adequate and abstract semantics for both TCTL° and $\mathrm{TCTL}^{\diamond}$.

4 Trace Equivalences

In the full paper, we develop the theory of trace equivalences for timed systems as carefully as the theory of bisimulation equivalences. Here we present only a few highlights.

Given a labeled transition system $\mathcal{S}$ with state set Q and label set L, and a state $q \in Q$, define the *language* $\mathcal{L}(\mathcal{S}, q)$ as the set $\{\overline{\alpha} \in L^* \mid \exists q'.\, q \xrightarrow{\overline{\alpha}} q'\}$ of finite words over L that are generated by $\mathcal{S}$ starting from q. Two states q and q' are *trace equivalent* with respect to $\mathcal{S}$ iff $\mathcal{L}(\mathcal{S}, q) = \mathcal{L}(\mathcal{S}, q')$. It is well-known that trace equivalence is strictly weaker than bisimilarity.

Timed trace equivalence Two states q and q' of a timed automaton A are *timed trace equivalent*, written $q \equiv_{tt} q'$, iff q and q' are trace equivalent with respect to the timed transition system $\mathcal{S}_t(A)$. That is, two states are timed trace equivalent iff they generate the same timed words—i.e., sequences of input symbols and time increments.

As expected, timed trace equivalence is strictly weaker than timed bisimilarity, but incomparable to region equivalence and incomparable to untimed bisimilarity. While timed trace equivalence is a congruence, it is computationally intractable. The undecidability proof for $\equiv_{tt}$ follows the proof that the language inclusion problem for timed automata over infinite words is undecidable [4].

Theorem 11. *The problem of deciding if two initial states of a timed automaton are timed trace equivalent is undecidable.*

Untimed trace equivalence Two states q and q' of a timed automaton A are *untimed trace equivalent*, written $q \equiv_{ut} q'$, iff q and q' are trace equivalent with respect to the untimed transition system $\mathcal{S}_u(A)$. That is, two states are untimed trace equivalent iff they generate the same untimed words—i.e., sequences of input symbols (all time increments are hidden).

Untimed trace equivalence is strictly weaker than region equivalence. Indeed, for all states q, the untimed language $\mathcal{L}(\mathcal{S}_u(A), q)$ can be characterized as a regular set over regions [4]. The problem of deciding untimed trace equivalence can then be reduced to the problem of deciding the language equivalence of two finite automata over regions.

Theorem 12. *There is an EXPSPACE algorithm that decides if two states of a timed automaton are untimed trace equivalent.*

Untimed trace equivalence is not a congruence. Hence we study the congruence induced by the equivalence relation $\equiv_{ut}$.

***k*-clock trace congruences** As before, we consider a sequence of congruences. Let $k \geq 0$ and let A be a timed automaton in TA_Σ. Two states q and q' of A are *k-clock trace congruent*, written $q \approx_{ut}^k q'$, iff for all timed automata $B \in \mathrm{TA}_\Sigma^k$ and all initial states q'' of B, the equivalence $(q, q'') \equiv_{ut} (q', q'')$ holds for the product automaton $A \otimes B$. That is, two states are k-clock trace congruent iff in all environments with at most k clocks, they generate the same untimed words.

Lemma 13. *Two states q and q' of a timed automaton are k-clock trace congruent iff the augmented states $(q, \overline{0})$ and $(q', \overline{0})$ are trace equivalent with respect to the k-clock transition system $\mathcal{S}_u^k(A)$.*

As in the case of bisimulation, each additional clock increases the distinguishing power of an observer. Recall, for instance, Example 2. The initial states $(s, \overline{0})$ and $(u, \overline{0})$ generate different untimed words in the presence of an observer with two clocks and, therefore, are not 2-clock trace congruent. Both states, however, are bisimilar with respect to the 1-clock transition system $\mathcal{S}_u^1(A)$ and, hence, also 1-clock trace congruent.

Theorem 14. *The equivalence relations $\approx_{ut}^k$, for $k \geq 0$, form a strict hierarchy ($\equiv_{ut} = \approx_{ut}^0 \succ \approx_{ut}^1 \succ \approx_{ut}^2 \succ \cdots$).*

The k-clock trace congruences can be decided by a technique similar to the decision procedure for the k-clock bisimulation congruences. First, we show that $q \approx_{ut}^k q'$ iff the augmented states $(q, \overline{0})$ and $(q', \overline{0})$ are trace equivalent with respect to the bounded k-clock transition system $\hat{\mathcal{S}}_u^k(A)$. Then we decide trace equivalence with respect to $\hat{\mathcal{S}}_u^k(A)$ by constructing an equivalent finite automaton over extended regions.

Theorem 15. *Given two states q and q' of a timed automaton A and a nonnegative integer k, it can be decided in EXPSPACE if $q \approx_{ut}^k q'$.*

Untimed trace congruence Untimed trace congruence is the intersection of all k-clock trace congruences: two states q and q' of a timed automaton A are *untimed trace congruent*, written $q \approx_{ut} q'$, iff $q \approx_{ut}^{k} q'$ for all $k \geq 0$.

Theorem 16. *Untimed trace congruence is strictly weaker than region equivalence, is the same as timed trace equivalence on initial states, and is weaker than timed trace equivalence on all states.*

However, unlike in the case of bisimulation, timed trace congruence is still undecidable.

Theorem 17. *The problem of deciding if two initial states of a timed automaton are timed trace congruent is undecidable.*

It follows that the verification of timed systems in a trace model is computationally intractable. The decision procedures for k-clock trace congruences are therefore all the more important: they can be used for the compositional verification of timed systems in the trace model, provided the number of environment clocks is bounded.

Linear-time logics with clocks If we extend linear temporal logic with clock variables, we obtain the real-time logic TPTL [5]. Since we consider only finite words, we omit the temporal operator $\Box$. The formulas of TPTL$^\circ$ are defined inductively as

$$\phi \ ::= \ x \leq c \mid c \leq x \mid \neg\phi \mid \phi_1 \wedge \phi_2 \mid \bigcirc\sigma.\,\phi \mid (x := 0).\,\phi$$

for clocks x, nonnegative integers c, and input symbols σ. Every formula ϕ of TPTL$^\circ$ defines a set of timed words. We write $q \models \phi$ iff ϕ defines a superset of the timed language $\mathcal{L}(\mathcal{S}_t(A), q)$.

As in the branching-time case, two states of a timed automaton can be distinguished by a TPTL$^\circ$-formula iff they are not untimed trace congruent. However, unlike in the branching-time case, if two states can be distinguished by a TPTL$^\circ$-formula, then they can be distinguished already by a TPTL$^\circ$-formula that uses a single clock variable.

Theorem 18. *Consider two states q and q' of a timed automaton A. The following statements are equivalent:*

1. *The states q and q' are untimed trace congruent ($q \approx_{ut} q'$).*
2. *For all* TPTL$^\circ$*-formulas ϕ, $q \models \phi$ iff $q' \models \phi$.*
3. *For all* TPTL$^\circ$*-formulas ϕ with at most 1 clock variable, $q \models \phi$ iff $q' \models \phi$.*

Further Work

(1) We studied timed and untimed equivalences and k-clock congruences in the bisimulation and trace cases. Corresponding relations can, of course, be defined for any equivalence relation on labeled transition systems, say, failures equivalence.

(2) We restricted ourselves to finite behaviors of systems, thus omitting liveness constraints. In the context of trace equivalences in particular, one typically considers automata on infinite words with acceptance conditions [4], and the full temporal logic TPTL [5]. We expect our results to generalize in a straightforward way.

(3) Our subject was the *distinguishing* power of clocks as observers. A complementary topic is the *expressive* power of clocks as specifiers. For example, it not difficult to show that if we measure the expressive power of timed automata by their ability to define languages of timed words, then the class of automata with $k + 1$ clocks is more expressive than the class of automata with at most k clocks. Similarly, the expressive power of TPTL-formulas strictly increases with the number of clock variables.

References

1. R. Alur, C. Courcoubetis, and D. Dill. Model checking in dense real time. *Information and Computation*, 104:2–34, 1993.
2. R. Alur, C. Courcoubetis, N. Halbwachs, D. Dill, and H. Wong-Toi. Minimization of timed transition systems. In *3rd CONCUR*, 340–354. Springer LNCS 630, 1992.
3. R. Alur, C. Courcoubetis, and T. Henzinger. Computing accumulated delays in real-time systems. In *5th CAV*, 181–193. Springer LNCS 697, 1993.
4. R. Alur and D. Dill. A theory of timed automata. *Theoretical Computer Science*, 126:183–235, 1994.
5. R. Alur and T. Henzinger. A really temporal logic. *J. ACM*, 41:181–204, 1994.
6. R. Alur, T. Henzinger, and M. Vardi. Parametric real-time reasoning. In *25th ACM STOC*, 592–601, 1993.
7. C. Courcoubetis and M. Yannakakis. Minimum and maximum delay problems in real-time systems. In *3rd CAV*, 399–409. Springer LNCS 575, 1991.
8. T. Henzinger, Z. Manna, and A. Pnueli. Temporal proof methodologies for real-time systems. In *18th ACM POPL*, 353–366, 1991.
9. T. Henzinger, X. Nicollin, J. Sifakis, and S. Yovine. Symbolic model checking for real-time systems. In *7th IEEE LICS*, 394–406, 1992.
10. K. Laren and Y. Wang. Time-abstracting bisimulation: implicit specifications and decidability. In *Mathematical Foundations of Programming Semantics*, 1993.
11. N. Lynch and F. Vaandrager. Action transducers and timed automata. In *3rd CONCUR*, 436–455. Springer LNCS 630, 1992.
12. X. Nicollin, J. Sifakis, and S. Yovine. From ATP to timed graphs and hybrid systems. In *Real Time: Theory in Practice*, 549–572. Springer LNCS 600, 1991.
13. R. van Glabbeek. *Comparative Concurrency Semantics and Refinement of Actions.* PhD thesis, Vrije Universiteit te Amsterdam, 1990.
14. K. Čerāns. Decidability of bisimulation equivalence for parallel timer processes. In *4th CAV*, 302–315. Springer LNCS 663, 1992.
15. K. Čerāns, J. Godskesen, and K. Larsen. Timed modal specification: theory and tools. In *5th CAV*, 253–267. Springer LNCS 697, 1993.
16. Y. Wang. Real-time behavior of asynchronous agents. In *1st CONCUR*, 502–520. Springer LNCS 458, 1990.
17. M. Yannakakis and D. Lee. An efficient algorithm for minimizing real-time transition systems. In *5th CAV*, 210–224. Springer LNCS 697, 1993.

A Dynamic Approach to Timed Behaviour

Jeremy Gunawardena*

Department of Computer Science,
Stanford University, Stanford, CA 94305, USA.

Abstract. In classical applied mathematics time is treated as an independent variable. The equations which govern the behaviour of a system enable one to determine, in principle, what happens at a given time. This approach has led to powerful techniques for calculating numerical quantities of interest in engineering. The temporal behaviour of reactive systems, however, is difficult to treat from this viewpoint and it has been customary to rely on logical rather than dynamic methods. In this paper we describe the theory of min-max functions, [6, 11, 15], which permits a dynamic approach to the time behaviour of a restricted class of reactive systems. Our main result is a proof of the Duality Conjecture for min-max functions of dimension 2.

1 Introduction

In classical applied mathematics time is treated as an independent variable. The equations which govern the behaviour of a system enable one to determine, in principle, what happens at a given time. A convenient abstract formulation of this approach is the idea of a dynamical system, (S, F), where S is a set and $F : S \to S$ is a self-map of S, [5]. The basic problem in dynamical systems is to understand the behaviour of the sequence

$$x,\ F(x),\ F^2(x),\ \cdots \tag{1}$$

for different $x \in S$. If the elements of S are thought of as states of the system then $F^s(x)$ tells us the state at time s if the system is started in state x at time 0. Although it is now well understood that an analytic (closed form) solution for $F^s(x)$ is only possible in very isolated special cases, there has been much progress in understanding the asymptotic behaviour of the system. That is, in understanding what happens when $s \to \infty$. The dynamic approach has led to powerful techniques for calculating quantities of interest in applications.

The temporal behaviour of reactive systems, however, is difficult to treat from a dynamic viewpoint: time is usually a dependent variable—packets are timestamped in a distributed system—and it has been customary to rely on logical rather than dynamic methods. This has resulted in the development of several theories of timed behaviour: various species of timed process algebra, timed I/O

* Current address: Hewlett-Packard Laboratories, Filton Road, Stoke Gifford, Bristol BS12 6QZ; jhcg@hplb.hpl.hp.com

automata, real time temporal logics and timed Petri nets. (An overview of these approaches may be found in [17].) They have been used to specify and to reason about the behaviour of real time systems but, for the most part, it has not been easy to use them to calculate the numbers that an engineer would like to know: throughput, latency, cycle time, minimum buffer capacity, etc.

In this paper we shall show that for a restricted class of reactive systems it is possible to use dynamic methods and that numerical quantities of interest in applications can be calculated. Our approach is built on the theory of min-max functions which was first introduced in [9] following earlier work in [15]. (For a discussion of the history of this area, see [6, §1].) The following two definitions introduce the basic idea.

Let $a \vee b$ and $a \wedge b$ denote the maximum (least upper bound) and minimum (greatest lower bound) of real numbers respectively: $a \vee b = \max(a, b)$ and $a \wedge b = \min(a, b)$. It is well known that these operations are associative and commutative and that each distributes over the other. Furthermore, addition distributes over both maximum and minimum:

$$h + (a \vee b) = h + a \vee h + b, \qquad h + (a \wedge b) = h + a \wedge h + b. \tag{2}$$

In expressions such as these $+$ has higher binding than $\wedge$ or $\vee$.

Definition 1. *A min-max expression, f, is a term in the grammar:*

$$f := x_1, x_2, \cdots \mid f + a \mid f \wedge f \mid f \vee f$$

where $x_1, x_2, \cdots$ are variables and $a \in \mathbf{R}$.

For example, $x_1 + x_2 \wedge x_3 + 2$ and $x_1 \vee 2$ are forbidden but $x_1 - 1 \vee x_2 + 1$ is allowed. The numbers which appear in a min-max expression are called parameters.

Definition 2. *A min-max function of dimension n is any function, $F : \mathbf{R}^n \to \mathbf{R}^n$, each of whose components, $F_i : \mathbf{R}^n \to \mathbf{R}$, is a min-max expression of n variables $x_1, \cdots, x_n$.*

As described above, the main problem in the theory of min-max functions is to study the asymptotic behaviour of the sequence (1) where S is Euclidean space of n dimensions and F is a min-max function of dimension n. To understand what needs to be calculated, it is helpful to consider the applications in which min-max functions arise. They were introduced to deal with the problem of defining the speed of an asynchronous digital circuit, [10]. In the absence of a clocking mechanism, a design engineer needs some measure by which circuits performing the same function can be compared in speed of operation. The behaviour of certain asynchronous circuits can be represented by a min-max function in which the state, $\mathbf{x} \in \mathbf{R}^n$, is a vector whose component x_i indicates the time at which a transition occurs on the i-th input wire. (The circuit is thought of as a closed system with the outputs fed back to the inputs. The dimension n is hence equal to the number of input wires.) A transition on a wire is a change in logic level from 1 to 0 or vice versa. The min-max function describes how the state changes; the parameters in the function being estimated from the internal gate delays in the circuit. If the circuit is in state $\mathbf{x}$ then $F(\mathbf{x})$ records the times at which the next transitions occur on the wires. It is easy to calculate the average time to the next transition over a sample of s state changes:

$$\frac{F^s(\mathbf{x}) - F^{s-1}(\mathbf{x}) + \cdots + F(\mathbf{x}) - \mathbf{x}}{s} = \frac{F^s(\mathbf{x}) - \mathbf{x}}{s}.$$

If we now let s tend to ∞ we see that the asymptotic average time to the next transition is given by the vector quantity

$$\lim_{s \to \infty} \frac{F^s(\mathbf{x})}{s}. \tag{3}$$

We refer to this asymptotic average, when the limit (3) exists, as the cycle time vector of the system. It appears to depend on $\mathbf{x}$ and hence to be a property not only of the system but also of where the system is started from. However, one of the first things that we shall learn about min-max functions is that (3), when it exists, is independent of the choice of $\mathbf{x}$ and is therefore characteristic of the system. This brings us to the main problem of this paper: when does the limit (3) exist and how can we calculate it when it does?

Before proceeding further we should clarify the implications for asynchronous circuits. Burns was the first to define a timing metric for asynchronous circuits, [2], and it can be shown that, under his assumptions, [2, §2.2.2], the cycle time vector as defined here has the simple form $(h, h, \cdots, h)$ where h is Burns's cycle period. The circuits considered by Burns are characterised by the fact that they only require maximum timing constraints. The corresponding min-max function F is max-only: $\wedge$ does not appear in any F_i. The theory of such functions is now well understood, as we shall discuss below. Burns was unable to give a rigorous definition of a timing metric for systems with both maximum and minimum constraints and he pointed out via an example, [2, §4.5], that his methods fail for such systems. Our work extends the theory to deal with this more general case.

We should also point out that min-max functions have been used to study timing problems in synchronous circuits as well, [16]. However, in this application area the critical problem is to calculate a fixed point of F: a vector $\mathbf{x}$ where $F(\mathbf{x}) = \mathbf{x}$. In related work we have given a necessary and sufficient condition for the existence of a fixed point for any min-max function, [11, Theorem 12]. In this paper we shall concentrate on the cycle time problem. A careful discussion of the applications to both asynchronous and synchronous timing problems is given in [10].

Having discussed how the application area naturally suggests the main problem of this paper, we shall step back slightly to explain how the theory of min-max functions fits into current theoretical research.

In concurrency theory, min-max functions can be thought of as describing systems which are timed analogues of untimed conflict free systems. To see why this is the case we note that a conflict free system may be identified with an

{AND, OR} automaton, [8, §3]. In this event-based view, we are only concerned with whether or not an event occurs. When we add time to the picture, we need to know when the event will occur. It is clear that AND causality, in which an event has to wait for all the events in a set, translates naturally into a maximum timing constraint, while OR causality, in which an event has to wait only for the first event of a set, translates into a minimum timing constraint. A treatment along these lines appears in [9, §3].

The identification of conflict freedom with {AND, OR} causality is consistent with other well-known descriptions of conflict freedom such as persistence in Petri nets, [13], Keller's conditions for labelled transition systems, [12, §1.3], confluence in CCS, [14, Chapter 11], and conflict freedom in event structures, [18]. A precise statement of this appears in [7]. The mathematical theory of untimed conflict free systems is simple and has been known in essence for many years. There is only one theorem, which asserts that a certain poset is a semi-modular lattice, [7]. In contrast, the mathematical theory of timed conflict free systems, which is to say the theory of min-max functions, has already revealed some deep results and contains many open problems. We note in passing that it has been shown that timed marked graphs and, more generally, timed persistent Petri nets, have an interesting mathematical theory, [3], but the connection between this work and the theory of min-max functions has not yet been determined.

Of more immediate relevance to min-max functions is the work on max-plus algebra, [1, §3]. This is relatively unfamiliar in concurrency theory but deserves to be more widely known. It allows us to reduce the special case of a max-only function (or, dually, a min-only function) to a linear problem which can be dealt with by classical matrix methods. To see why this is so, note that, because $\vee$ is associative and commutative, any max-only function in the variables $x_1, \cdots, x_n$ can be reduced to the canonical form:

$$F_i(x_1, \cdots, x_n) = (a_{i1} + x_1 \vee \cdots \vee a_{in} + x_n), \tag{4}$$

where $a_{ij} \in \mathbf{R} \cup \{-\infty\}$. (The $-\infty$ merely serves as a zero for $\vee$; additive operations involving $-\infty$ work in the obvious way.) Now comes a very beautiful trick, which is due to Cuninghame-Green, [4]: redefine the operations on $\mathbf{R} \cup \{-\infty\}$ so that $+$ becomes $\vee$ and $\times$ becomes $+$. This new algebra is called max-plus algebra, [1, Definition 3.3]. The equation (4) can now be rewritten as

$$F(\mathbf{x}) = A\mathbf{x}$$

where $\mathbf{x}$ is considered as a column vector, $A = (a_{ij})$ is the matrix of parameter values and matrix multiplication is used on the right hand side.

The basic dynamical problem, of determining $F^s(\mathbf{x})$, now has an easy solution: it is simply the matrix product $A^s\mathbf{x}$ in max-plus algebra. More importantly, we can also show that the limit (3) exists and calculate it explicitly. We postpone further discussion of how to do this to §2. The theory of min-max functions can now be understood as a non-linear generalisation of max-plus algebra. The theory begins, in effect, where [1] ends.

We can now return to the cycle time problem which was enunciated above. What progress has been made towards solving it? In earlier work we identified and stated the Duality Conjecture, [11, §2], whose affirmative resolution would not only show that the limit (3) always exists but would also give a simple formula for calculating it. We also showed that if the Duality Conjecture were true then we could give a simple proof of Olsder's fixed point criterion for separated functions—the main result of [15]—as well as deduce several other powerful results. The Conjecture appears, therefore, to capture a fundamental property of min-max functions. The main result of the present paper, Theorem 9, is a proof of the Duality Conjecture for functions of dimension 2. This is the first rigorous evidence that the Conjecture is true in generality. Unfortunately, the proof does not extend to higher dimensions.

The rest of the paper falls into two parts. In the first part we state the elementary properties of min-max functions, recall the linear theory for max-only functions and state the Duality Conjecture. The second part gives the proof in dimension 2.

The author is very grateful to Professor Geert-Jan Olsder for his encouragement and hospitality during a visit to the University of Delft during which the details of the proof presented here were first worked out. The work described in this paper was undertaken as part of project STETSON, a joint project between Hewlett-Packard Laboratories and Stanford University on asynchronous hardware design.

2 Basic properties and the linear theory

In this section we study some of the elementary properties of min-max functions and show, in particular, why the limit (3) is independent of **x**. We then discuss the special case of max-only functions using the linear methods of max-plus algebra. This leads us to the Duality Conjecture via the important concept of projections. Proofs are omitted for reasons of space.

We shall frequently use numerical operations and relations and apply them to vectors. These should always be assumed to be applied to each component separately. Hence $\mathbf{u} \leq \mathbf{v}$ means $u_i \leq v_i$ for each i. Similarly, $(\bigwedge_l \mathbf{a}_l)_i = \bigwedge_l (\mathbf{a}_l)_i$. Let $\mathbf{c}(h) = (h, h, \cdots, h)$ denote the vector each of whose components has the same value h.

The first useful property of a min-max function of dimension n is that it is monotone:

$$\mathbf{u} \leq \mathbf{v} \implies F(\mathbf{u}) \leq F(\mathbf{v}). \tag{5}$$

Second, F is homogeneous, in the sense that, for any $h \in \mathbf{R}$,

$$F(\mathbf{u} + \mathbf{c}(h)) = F(\mathbf{u}) + \mathbf{c}(h). \tag{6}$$

This follows easily from (2), [6, Lemma 2.3]. The third and final elementary property is not quite so obvious. Let $|\mathbf{u}|$ denote the l^∞, or maximum, norm on vectors in $\mathbf{R}^n$: $|\mathbf{u}| = \bigvee_{1 \leq i \leq n} |u_i|$, where $|u_i|$ is the usual absolute value on real numbers.

Lemma 3. *(Non-expansive property.) Let F be a min-max function of dimension n. If $\mathbf{u}, \mathbf{v} \in \mathbf{R}^n$ then $|F(\mathbf{u}) - F(\mathbf{v})| \leq |\mathbf{u} - \mathbf{v}|$.*

It is important to note that F is not contractive. That is, there is no $0 < \lambda < 1$ such that $|F(\mathbf{u}) - F(\mathbf{v})| \leq \lambda|\mathbf{u} - \mathbf{v}|$. If there were, then the Contraction Mapping Theorem would imply that F had a unique fixed point and that $F^s(x)$ converges to it as $s \to \infty$. The dynamic behaviour of F is more complicated than that. However, suppose that the limit (3) exists at some point $\mathbf{x} \in \mathbf{R}^n$. Then it follows immediately from the non-expansive property that (3) exists everywhere in $\mathbf{R}^n$ and has the same value.

Definition 4. *Let F be a min-max function. If the limit (3) exists somewhere, it is called the cycle time vector of F and denoted by $\chi(F) \in \mathbf{R}^n$.*

When does the cycle time vector exist? Let us begin to answer this by considering the special case of a max-only function. Suppose that F is a max-only function of dimension n and that A is the associated $n \times n$ matrix in max-plus algebra. For example, the following max-only function of dimension 3

$$\begin{aligned} F_1(x_1, x_2, x_3) &= x_2 + 2 \vee x_3 + 5 \\ F_2(x_1, x_2, x_3) &= x_2 + 1 \\ F_3(x_1, x_2, x_3) &= x_1 - 1 \vee x_2 + 3 \end{aligned} \tag{7}$$

has the associated max-plus matrix

$$\begin{pmatrix} -\infty & 2 & 5 \\ -\infty & 1 & -\infty \\ -1 & 3 & -\infty \end{pmatrix}. \tag{8}$$

We recall that the precedence graph of A, [1, Definition 2.8], denoted $\mathcal{G}(A)$, is the directed graph with annotated edges which has nodes $\{1, 2, \cdots, n\}$ and an edge from j to i if, and only if, $A_{ij} \neq -\infty$. The annotation on this edge is then the real number A_{ij}. We shall denote an edge from j to i by $i \leftarrow j$. A path in this graph has the usual meaning of a chain of directed edges: a path from i_m to i_1 is a sequence of nodes $i_1, \cdots, i_m$ such that $i_j \leftarrow i_{j+1}$ for $1 \leq j < m$. A circuit is a path which starts and ends at the same node: $i_1 = i_m$. This includes the possibility that $m = 1$. A circuit is elementary if the nodes $i_1, \cdots, i_{m-1}$ are all distinct. A path or circuit is upstream from node i if there is a path in $\mathcal{G}(A)$ from some node on the path or circuit to node i. The weight of a path p, $|p|_\mathsf{w}$, is the sum of the annotations on the edges in the path:

$$|p|_\mathsf{w} = \sum_{j=1}^{m-1} A_{i_j i_{j+1}}.$$

The length of a path, $|p|_\ell$, is the number of edges in the path: $|p|_\ell = m - 1$. If g is a circuit, the ratio $|g|_\mathsf{w}/|g|_\ell$ is the cycle mean of the circuit, [1, Definition 2.18].

Definition 5. *Let $\boldsymbol{\mu}(A) \in (\mathbf{R} \cup \{-\infty\})^n$ be defined by*

$$\mu_i(A) = \bigvee \{\ |g|_{\mathsf{w}}/|g|_{\ell}\ \mid g \text{ a circuit in } \mathcal{G}(A) \text{ upstream from node } i\}.$$

It is not difficult to check that in calculating $\mu_i(A)$ it is only necessary to consider elementary circuits, of which there are only finitely many. By convention, $\bigvee \emptyset = -\infty$. Because each component expression of a max-only function must be non-empty, it follows that each row of the associated max-plus matrix must have an entry not equal to $-\infty$. There is, therefore, always some circuit upstream from any node. Hence, for any matrix associated to a max-only function, $\boldsymbol{\mu}(A) \in \mathbf{R}^n$. The precedence graph of example (8) is shown below

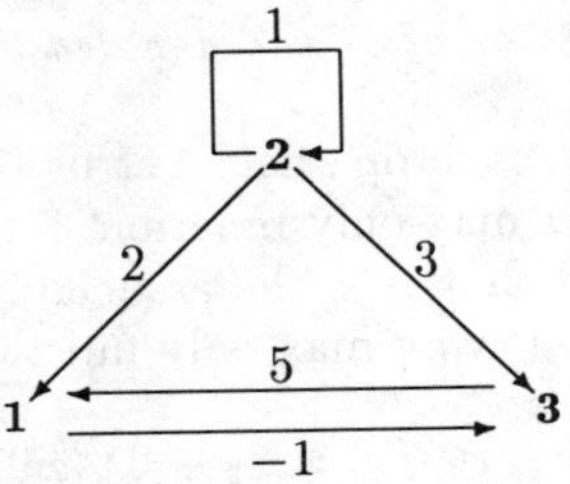

and the reader should have no difficulty in showing that $\boldsymbol{\mu}(A) = (2, 1, 2)$. The significance of $\boldsymbol{\mu}(A)$ is revealed by the following result whose proof may be found in [11, Proposition 2.1].

Proposition 6. *Let F be a max-only function and A the associated matrix in max-plus algebra. The limit (3) exists and $\boldsymbol{\chi}(F) = \boldsymbol{\mu}(A)$.*

We now want to consider a general min-max function. Before doing so we need to make some remarks about duality. Let f be a min-max expression. By similar arguments to those used to find the canonical form (4) it is easy to see that f can be placed in conjunctive form:

$$f = f_1 \wedge f_2 \wedge \cdots \wedge f_k,$$

where the f_i are distinct max-only expressions in canonical form. (This expression can be made unique, up to permutation of the f_i, by throwing out redundant terms, [6, Theorem 2.1], although one has to be careful to define "redundant" correctly. The resulting expression is called conjunctive normal form. Although normal forms were used to state the Duality Conjecture in [11] it is not essential to use them and we shall not do so in this paper.) By a dual argument, we can also put f into disjunctive form:

$$f = g_1 \vee g_2 \vee \cdots \vee g_l,$$

where the g_i are distinct min-only expressions in canonical form. Note that expressions in conjunctive form have parameters in $\mathbf{R} \cup \{-\infty\}$ while those in disjunctive form have parameters in $\mathbf{R} \cup \{+\infty\}$.

There is a simple algorithm for moving back and forth between conjunctive and disjunctive form which we shall need to use in §3. We explain it here by working through an example. Consider the min-max expression of 2 variables,

$$f = (a + x_1 \vee b + x_2) \wedge c + x_1, \tag{9}$$

where $a, b, c \in \mathbf{R}$. This is effectively in conjunctive form but to be more precise we should write f as

$$(a + x_1 \vee b + x_2) \wedge (c + x_1 \vee -\infty + x_2).$$

To express f in disjunctive form we go back to the initial min-max expression (9) and rewrite each individual term $a_i + x_i$ (where $a_i \neq -\infty$) in disjunctive form. This gives

$$((a + x_1 \wedge +\infty + x_2) \vee (+\infty + x_1 \wedge b + x_2)) \wedge (c + x_1 \wedge +\infty + x_2).$$

We now use the distributivity of $\wedge$ over $\vee$ to interchange the order of the two operations and get

$$((a \wedge c) + x_1 \wedge +\infty + x_2) \vee (c + x_1 \wedge b + x_2), \tag{10}$$

which is in disjunctive form.

Now suppose that F is an arbitrary min-max function of dimension n. Each component of F can be placed in conjunctive form as above:

$$F_k(\mathbf{x}) = (A^k_{11} + x_1 \vee \cdots \vee A^k_{1n} + x_n) \wedge \cdots \wedge (A^k_{\ell(k)1} + x_1 \vee \cdots \vee A^k_{\ell(k)n} + x_n), \tag{11}$$

where $A^k_{ij} \in \mathbf{R} \cup \{-\infty\}$. Here $\ell(k)$ is the number of conjunctions in the component F_k. We can now associate a max-plus matrix A to F by choosing, for the k-th row of the matrix, one of the $\ell(k)$ conjunctions in (11): $A_{kj} = A^k_{i_k j}$ where $1 \leq i_k \leq \ell(k)$ specifies which conjunction is chosen in row k.

Definition 7. *The matrix A constructed in this way is called a max-only projection of F. A set of max-only projections is the collection of all such matrices from a single conjunctive form such as (11). Dually, a set of min-only projections is constructed from a disjunctive form.*

Sets of max-only projections are not unique. However, if we use conjunctive normal form then it follows from [6, Theorem 2.1] that the corresponding set of normal max-only projections is uniquely defined for any function F. Sets of projections can be quite large: the function (11) has $\prod_{1 \leq i \leq n} \ell(i)$ distinct max-only projections.

At this point an example may be helpful. Consider the min-max function of dimension 2:

$$\begin{aligned} F_1(x_1, x_2) &= (a + x_1 \vee b + x_2) \wedge c + x_1 \\ F_2(x_1, x_2) &= (t + x_1 \wedge u + x_2) \end{aligned} \tag{12}$$

where $a, b, c, t, u \in \mathbf{R}$. F_1 is already in conjunctive form while F_2 is in disjunctive form. We first put F_2 into conjunctive form using the algorithm discussed above:

$$F_2(x_1, x_2) = (t + x_1 \vee -\infty + x_2) \wedge (-\infty + x_1 \vee u + x_2)$$

and then read off a set of max-only projections:

$$\{ \begin{pmatrix} a & b \\ t & -\infty \end{pmatrix}, \begin{pmatrix} a & b \\ -\infty & u \end{pmatrix}, \begin{pmatrix} c & -\infty \\ t & -\infty \end{pmatrix}, \begin{pmatrix} c & -\infty \\ -\infty & u \end{pmatrix} \} . \tag{13}$$

Dually, we can put F_1 into disjunctive form—an exercise already performed in (10):

$$F_1(x_1, x_2) = ((a \wedge c) + x_1 \wedge +\infty + x_2) \vee (c + x_1 \wedge b + x_2)$$

and read off a set of min-only projections:

$$\{ \begin{pmatrix} a \wedge c & +\infty \\ t & u \end{pmatrix}, \begin{pmatrix} c & b \\ t & u \end{pmatrix} \} . \tag{14}$$

We hope this has clarified these important constructs. For the remainder of the paper we shall use the letter A for max-plus matrices and the letter B for min-plus matrices. It will also be convenient to introduce the notation $\boldsymbol{\eta}(B)$ to indicate the vector which is "dual" to $\boldsymbol{\mu}(A)$. In other words, $\boldsymbol{\eta}(B)$ is the vector of minimum upstream cycle means in $\mathcal{G}(B)$.

Let F be any min-max function of dimension n and let P and Q be sets of max-only and min-only projections, respectively, of F. It is clear from the construction above that, for any $A \in P$, $F(\mathbf{x}) \leq A\mathbf{x}$ for all $\mathbf{x} \in \mathbf{R}^n$. It follows from (5) that $F^s(\mathbf{x}) \leq A^s\mathbf{x}$ for all $s \geq 0$. Now choose $\epsilon > 0$. It then follows from Proposition 6 that, for all sufficiently large s, $F^s(\mathbf{x})/s \leq \boldsymbol{\mu}(A) + \mathbf{c}(\epsilon)$. Since this holds for any max-only projection in P, and there are only finitely many such, we see that $F^s(\mathbf{x})/s \leq (\bigwedge_{A \in P} \boldsymbol{\mu}(A)) + \mathbf{c}(\epsilon)$ for all sufficiently large s. By a dual argument applied to the min-only projections of F, we can conclude that

$$(\bigvee_{B \in Q} \boldsymbol{\eta}(B)) - \mathbf{c}(\epsilon) \leq \frac{F^s(\mathbf{x})}{s} \leq (\bigwedge_{A \in P} \boldsymbol{\mu}(A)) + \mathbf{c}(\epsilon). \tag{15}$$

for all sufficiently large s.

Conjecture 8. *(The Duality Conjecture.) Let F be any min-max function and let P and Q be any sets of max-only and min-only projections, respectively, of F. Then,*

$$\bigvee_{B \in Q} \boldsymbol{\eta}(B) = \bigwedge_{A \in P} \boldsymbol{\mu}(A). \tag{16}$$

The significance of this should be clear. It implies that any min-max function has a cycle time and gives us a formula for computing it. It is worth working through an example to see how the numbers come out. We reproduce below the details for example (12) whose projections were worked out above. The $\boldsymbol{\mu}(A)$ of the max-only projections of (12), in the order in which they are listed in (13), are shown below as column vectors:

$$\begin{pmatrix} a \vee (b+t)/2 \\ a \vee (b+t)/2 \end{pmatrix}, \begin{pmatrix} a \vee u \\ u \end{pmatrix}, \begin{pmatrix} c \\ c \end{pmatrix}, \begin{pmatrix} c \\ u \end{pmatrix}.$$

So the right hand side of (16) is

$$\begin{pmatrix} (a \vee (b+t)/2) \wedge (a \vee u) \wedge c \\ (a \vee (b+t)/2) \wedge u \wedge c \end{pmatrix}. \tag{17}$$

The $\eta(B)$ of the min-only projections, in the same order as they appear in (14), are:

$$\begin{pmatrix} a \wedge c \\ u \wedge a \wedge c \end{pmatrix}, \begin{pmatrix} c \wedge (b+t)/2 \wedge u \\ c \wedge (b+t)/2 \wedge u \end{pmatrix},$$

and so the left hand side of (16) is

$$\begin{pmatrix} (a \wedge c) \vee (c \wedge (b+t)/2 \wedge u) \\ (u \wedge a \wedge c) \vee (c \wedge (b+t)/2 \wedge u) \end{pmatrix}. \tag{18}$$

The reader will have no trouble confirming that (17) and (18) are identical. The calculation gives little hint as to why the numbers come out to be the same. We shall try and understand this in the next section. Before moving on, we note that since ϵ was arbitrary, (15) already tells us that

$$\bigvee_{B \in Q} \eta(B) \leq \bigwedge_{A \in P} \mu(A). \tag{19}$$

The next section is devoted to showing that the reverse inequality also holds, at least when F has dimension 2.

3 The Duality Conjecture in dimension 2

Theorem 9. *If F is any min-max function of dimension 2 then $\bigvee_{B \in Q} \eta(B) = \bigwedge_{A \in P} \mu(A)$.*

The proof of this occupies the entire section. We begin with some preparatory remarks and notation, which are tailored to dimension 2. If A is a 2×2 matrix in max-plus algebra,

$$A = \begin{pmatrix} a & b \\ c & d \end{pmatrix},$$

with $a, b, c, d \in \mathbf{R} \cup \{-\infty\}$, then the maximum upstream cycle mean of component 1 is

$$\mu_1(A) = \begin{cases} a \vee (b+c)/2 \vee d & \text{if } b \neq -\infty \\ a & \text{otherwise} \end{cases}. \tag{20}$$

This equation is valid even when a, b, c, d take on the value $-\infty$; the point of the second formula being that, if $b = -\infty$, then node 2 is no longer upstream of node 1. In all other cases, the first formula gives the correct answer. A similar dual equation holds for $\eta_1(B)$.

Now suppose that we have some expression of the form $e = \bigwedge_{i\in\mathcal{L}}(a_i \vee b_i \vee c_i)$ where $\mathcal{L}$ is some finite index set and $a_i, b_i, c_i \in \mathbf{R} \cup \{-\infty\}$. In what follows we shall want to rewrite expressions like this "the other way round", as a maxima of minima. Let $\mathsf{P}^n(\mathcal{L})$ denote the set of partitions of $\mathcal{L}$ into n disjoint pieces:

$$\mathsf{P}^n(\mathcal{L}) = \{\{U_1, \cdots, U_n\} \mid U_i \subseteq \mathcal{L},\ \mathcal{L} = U_1 \cup \cdots \cup U_n \text{ and } U_i \cap U_j = \emptyset \text{ for } i \neq j\}.$$

By distributivity, it follows easily that

$$e = \bigvee_{\{S,T,U\}\in\mathsf{P}^3(\mathcal{L})} \bigwedge_{i\in S} a_i \wedge \bigwedge_{i\in T} b_i \wedge \bigwedge_{i\in U} c_i. \tag{21}$$

In this equation we rely on the convention that $\bigwedge\emptyset = +\infty$. If both $-\infty$ and $+\infty$ appear in one of the partition terms (for instance, if S contains an index i with $a_i = -\infty$ and $U = \emptyset$) then the $-\infty$ will "win" and the corresponding partition will not contribute to the final maximum.

Let F be a min-max function of dimension 2 and let us use x and y in place of the variables x_1 and x_2. We may write F in conjunctive form in the following way:

$$\begin{array}{l} F_1(x,y) = \bigwedge_{1\le i\le n_1}(a_i + x \vee b_i + y) \\ F_2(x,y) = \bigwedge_{1\le j\le n_2}(c_j + x \vee d_j + y), \end{array} \tag{22}$$

where $a_i, b_i, c_j, d_j \in \mathbf{R} \cup \{-\infty\}$. It will be convenient to identify the sets $I_1, I_2 \subseteq \{1, \cdots, n_1\}$ and $J_1, J_2 \subseteq \{1, \cdots, n_2\}$ where

$$\begin{array}{l} I_1 = \{i \mid b_i = -\infty\}\ \ I_2 = \{i \mid a_i = -\infty\} \\ J_1 = \{j \mid d_j = -\infty\}\ J_2 = \{j \mid c_j = -\infty\}. \end{array}$$

Because not both a_i and b_i can be $-\infty$, and similarly for c_j and d_j, these sets satisfy the restrictions

$$I_1 \cap I_2 = \emptyset \text{ and } J_1 \cap J_2 = \emptyset. \tag{23}$$

This method of indexing F is convenient because it allows us to write down the max-only projections quite simply as:

$$A(i,j) = \begin{pmatrix} a_i & b_i \\ c_j & d_j \end{pmatrix},$$

where (i,j) runs over the index set $\{1, \cdots, n_1\} \times \{1, \cdots, n_2\}$. (It is useful to picture this index set as a rectangular region of lattice points in the plane. Most of the assertions that we shall make regarding subsets of it can be easily visualised in this way.) Let P denote the corresponding set of max-only projections. If we apply the dualising algorithm used on example (9) to construct a disjunctive form for F then we can read off a set of min-only projections. Let Q denote this set. Let R be the first component of the right hand side of (16): $R = \bigwedge_{A\in P} \mu_1(A)$. Similarly, let L be the first component of the left hand side: $L = \bigvee_{B\in Q} \eta_1(B)$. We established in (19) that $L \leq R$. We shall now show that $R \leq L$. It is clear that if we can do this for the first component of any min-max function of dimension 2 then we will have proved Theorem 9. A few final pieces of notation are required: if $X \subseteq A \times B$, then $\pi_1 X$ and $\pi_2 X$ will denote the projections of X onto A and B, respectively. If X, A are sets then $A \backslash X = \{a \in A \mid a \notin X\}$. If $X \subseteq A$ then $\overline{X} = A \backslash X$ when A is clear from the context.

We can now begin the proof in earnest. Using (20) and (21) we can rewrite R "the other way round" by the method discussed above. If

$$\{S, T, U\} \in \mathsf{P}^3(\{1, \cdots, n_1\} \times \{1, \cdots, n_2\})$$

it will be convenient to introduce the auxiliary function

$$\rho(S, T, U) = \bigwedge_{p \in \pi_1 S} a_p \wedge \bigwedge_{(q,r) \in T} \frac{b_q + c_r}{2} \wedge \bigwedge_{u \in \pi_2 U} d_u. \tag{24}$$

We may then write

$$R = \bigvee_{\{S,T,U\} \in \mathsf{P}^3(\{1,\cdots,n_1\} \times \{1,\cdots,n_2\})} \rho(S, T, U) \tag{25}$$

where we must assume that $\pi_1 T \cap I_1 = \pi_1 U \cap I_1 = \emptyset$ because of (20). We may further disregard those partitions which make a contribution of $-\infty$ to the maximum. So we may finally assume that the partitions in (25) satisfy the restrictions

$$\begin{array}{c} \pi_1 S \cap I_2 = \emptyset \\ \pi_1 T \cap I_1 = \pi_2 T \cap J_2 = \emptyset \\ \pi_2 U \cap J_1 = \pi_1 U \cap I_1 = \emptyset. \end{array} \tag{26}$$

It is easy to deduce from these equations and the fact that $\{S, T, U\}$ is a partition, that $I_1 \times \{1, \cdots, n_1\} \subseteq S$. (This is where a picture comes in handy.) In particular,

$$I_1 \subseteq \pi_1 S. \tag{27}$$

We want to compare (25) with L. To compute L we need the set Q of min-only projections which are obtained by dualising (22). The dualisation amounts to writing the component expressions of F "the other way round". We leave it to the reader to check that the resulting min-only projections can be indexed as

$$B(X, Y) = \begin{pmatrix} \bigwedge_{p \in X} a_p & \bigwedge_{q \in \overline{X}} b_q \\ \bigwedge_{r \in Y} c_r & \bigwedge_{u \in \overline{Y}} d_u \end{pmatrix}, \tag{28}$$

where $X \subseteq \{1, \cdots, n_1\}$ and $Y \subseteq \{1, \cdots, n_2\}$ are any subsets satisfying the restrictions:

$$\begin{array}{c} I_1 \subseteq X \subseteq \{1, \cdots, n_1\} \backslash I_2 \\ J_1 \subseteq Y \subseteq \{1, \cdots, n_2\} \backslash J_2. \end{array} \tag{29}$$

Min-only matrices must have entries in $\mathbf{R} \cup \{+\infty\}$ and it is clear that the restrictions in (29) will guarantee this. It is largely for this purpose that the subsets I_1, I_2 and J_1, J_2 were introduced.

Lemma 10. *With the details above, suppose that for each partition $\{S, T, U\}$ satisfying the restrictions in (26), it is possible to find X, Y satisfying the restrictions in (29) such that*

$$\rho(S, T, U) \leq \eta_1 B(X, Y).$$

Then $R \leq L$.

Proof: With the restrictions in (26) and (29), we have

$$R = \bigvee_{S,T,U} \rho(S, T, U) \leq \bigvee_{X,Y} \eta_1 B(X, Y) = L.$$

QED

All we have done so far is book-keeping. The main part of the argument is still to come. The crux of the proof hinges on the nature of the set T. If we think about the form of $\eta_1 B(X, Y)$, as calculated from (the dual version of) (20), then the part played by T is the set $\overline{X} \times Y$. This differs from T in being a product subset, or rectangle, in $\{1, \cdots, n_1\} \times \{1, \cdots, n_2\}$. It is this clue which gives rise to the argument which follows. The idea is to replace the partition (S, T, U) by a new partition (S', T', U') which still satisfies (26) but for which $\rho(S, T, U) \leq \rho(S', T', U')$. The new partition will have T' rectangular. Such partitions can be dealt with relatively simply. Rectangularisation is thus the crucial step.

Choose some partition $\{S, T, U\}$ satisfying (26). We first need to deal with the possibility that $T = \emptyset$. Assume that this is so. It follows from (24) that

$$\rho(S, \emptyset, U) = \bigwedge_{p \in \pi_1 S} a_p \wedge \bigwedge_{u \in \pi_2 U} d_u.$$

Now suppose further that $\pi_2 U = \{1, \cdots, n_2\}$. It follows from (26) that $J_1 = \emptyset$. Let $X = \pi_1(S)$ and $Y = \emptyset$. It follows from (26) and (27) that X, Y satisfy (29). Since $Y = \emptyset$, the corresponding matrix $B(X, Y)$, shown in (28), has $+\infty$ in the bottom left corner. If $\overline{X} \neq \emptyset$, it follows from (20) that,

$$\eta_1 B(X, Y) = \bigwedge_{p \in X} a_p \wedge \bigwedge_{u \in \overline{Y}} d_u$$

and it is clear that $\rho(S, \emptyset, U) = \eta_1 B(X, Y)$. If $\overline{X} = \emptyset$ then certainly $\rho(S, \emptyset, U) \leq \eta_1 B(X, Y)$ since the latter omits the contribution from U. In either case we are done. Now suppose that $\pi_1 S \neq \{1, \cdots, n_1\}$. It then follows from (26) that $\pi_2 U = \{1, \cdots, n_2\}$ and we have already done this case. So we may assume that $\pi_1 S = \{1, \cdots, n_1\}$ and hence that $I_2 = \emptyset$. Let $X = \{1, \cdots, n_1\}$, which certainly satisfies (29), and let Y be any subset of $\{1, \cdots, n_2\}$ which satisfies (29). We can always choose such a subset in view of (23). Because $\overline{X} = \emptyset$, it follows from (20) that $\eta_1 B(X, Y) = \bigwedge_{p \in X} a_p$. Hence $\rho(S, \emptyset, U) \leq \eta_1 B(X, Y)$ and once again we are done. This deals with all the possibilities when $T = \emptyset$.

Now assume that $T \neq \emptyset$. Suppose that we can find $u \in \pi_1 T$ and $v \in \pi_2 T$ such that $(u,v) \notin T$. Then either $(u,v) \in S$ or $(u,v) \in U$. If $(u,v) \in S$ then let $D \subseteq \{1,\cdots,n_1\} \times \{1,\cdots,n_2\}$ be the set $D = \{x \in T \mid \pi_1 x = u\}$. Evidently, $D \neq \emptyset$. Construct a new partition $\{S',T',U'\}$ such that $S' = S \cup D$, $T' = T \setminus D$ and $U' = U$. It is clear that this is still a partition of $\{1,\cdots,n_1\} \times \{1,\cdots,n_2\}$. We need to check that it satisfies (26). Since T has got smaller, it follows that T' cannot violate (26) and, of course, U has not changed. As for S, it is easy to see that $\pi_1 S' = \pi_1 S$, so that S also satisfies (26). We thus have a good partition. Furthermore, since T' has got smaller while $\pi_1 S' = \pi_1 S$ and $\pi_2 U' = \pi_2 U$, it is easy to see that $\rho(S,T,U) \leq \rho(S',T',U')$. If $(u,v) \in U$ then we move elements from T to U and a similar argument works. We can now carry on constructing new partitions in this way. Since T is finite and strictly decreases each time, the process can only stop in two ways. Either we end up with $T = \emptyset$, which we have already dealt with, or we find that we can no longer choose (u,v) satisfying the requirements above. But it must then be the case that $T = \pi_1 T \times \pi_2 T$. Hence we may assume that T is non-empty and rectangular. The importance of this stems from the following elementary fact whose proof should be clear.

Lemma 11. *With the above details, if T is rectangular, then*

$$\bigwedge_{(q,r)\in T} (b_q + c_r)/2 = ((\bigwedge_{q\in\pi_1 T} b_q) + (\bigwedge_{r\in\pi_2 T} c_r))/2.$$

The remainder of the argument resembles the case when $T = \emptyset$. Suppose first that $\pi_2 U = \{1,\cdots,n_2\}$ so that $J_1 = \emptyset$. Let $X = \pi_1 S$ and $Y = \emptyset$. As before, these satisfy (29). The corresponding $B(X,Y)$ has $+\infty$ in the bottom left corner. It follows from (20) that $\rho(S,T,U) \leq \eta_1 B(X,Y)$ since the latter simply omits the contribution coming from T, if $\overline{X} \neq \emptyset$, and from both T and U, if $\overline{X} = \emptyset$. Now suppose that $\pi_1 S = \{1,\cdots,n_1\}$ so that $I_2 = \emptyset$. Let $X = \{1,\cdots,n_1\}$, which certainly satisfies (29), and choose any Y which also satisfies (29), which we may always do by (23). The corresponding $B(X,Y)$ has $+\infty$ in the top right corner. It follows from (20) that $\rho(S,T,U) \leq \eta_1 B(X,Y)$ since the latter omits the contributions from both T and U. Now let $\overline{X} = \pi_1 T$. If $X \not\subseteq \pi_1 S$ then it follows from (26) that $\pi_2 U = \{1,\cdots,n_2\}$, which we have already considered. So we may assume that $X \subseteq \pi_1 S$ and so $\bigwedge_{p\in\pi_1 S} a_p \leq \bigwedge_{p\in X} a_p$. Furthermore, it is easy to see that X satisfies (29). Let $Y = \pi_2 T$ and suppose that $\overline{Y} \not\subseteq \pi_2 U$. Then, in a similar way, it must be the case that $\pi_1 S = \{1,\cdots,n_1\}$, which we have also considered. Hence, we may also assume that $\overline{Y} \subseteq \pi_2 U$ and so $\bigwedge_{u\in\pi_2 U} d_u \leq \bigwedge_{u\in\overline{Y}} d_u$. Furthermore, Y also satisfies (29). But now, $\rho(S,T,U) \leq \eta_1 B(X,Y)$ because in the latter the contribution from $\overline{X} \times Y$ is equal to that from T by Lemma 11, while the other contributions have got larger. This completes the proof of Theorem 9.

The argument we have presented is straightforward once the details of the book-keeping have been mastered. A similar approach can be attempted in higher dimensions, albeit at the cost of vastly increased book-keeping. It is not the book-keeping that defeats this, however. It turns out that Lemma 10 is no longer of any use. There is an example in dimension 3 such that, for a given partition of the form $\{S, T, U\}$ (but now requiring 8 entries), there is no single min-plus matrix satisfying the conditions of Lemma 10. Different min-plus matrices are required for different values of the parameters in F. This does not happen in dimension 2 as we have just seen. Attempting to force through a proof along these lines runs into a wall of technical difficulties in higher dimensions. It seems clear that some new ideas are required to make further progress on the Duality Conjecture.

4 Conclusion

The dynamic approach that we have sketched here has already succeeded in calculating numerical quantities of importance in engineering applications. It also presents an attractive collection of mathematical problems which are easy to formulate but difficult to prove. We have studied one such problem, perhaps the most fundamental one, in this paper. Other open problems are discussed in [6, 11].

It is interesting to speculate on how the theory could be extended to deal with a broader class of reactive systems. It is well known that digital circuits such as latches exhibit a variety of oscillatory behaviour (for example, metastability). These are outside the repertoire of min-max functions. It is also well known that the next stage of behavioural complexity in dynamical systems is non-periodic behaviour such as chaos, [5]. Is it possible to model metastability by chaos in a suitable dynamical system? Because of the great progress that has been made towards developing numerical measures of chaos (Liapunov exponents, entropy, etc), this could open up a new chapter in the study of metastability. In order to explore some of these possibilities we have tried to exploit the analogy between untimed systems with $\{\mathsf{AND}, \mathsf{OR}\}$ causality and timed systems described by min-max functions. By extending the untimed models to include NOT, or negation, [7, 8], we are hoping to understand how the theory of min-max functions may be extended to deal with timed conflict. There are many difficulties with developing a consistent theory along these lines, [7], and it still remains to be seen whether this will provide a foundation for a dynamic theory in the presence of conflict.

References

1. F. Baccelli, G. Cohen, G. J. Olsder, and J.-P. Quadrat. *Synchronization and Linearity.* Wiley Series in Probability and Mathematical Statistics. John Wiley and Sons, 1992.
2. S. M. Burns. *Performance Analysis and Optimization of Asynchronous Circuits.* PhD thesis, California Institute of Technology, 1990.
3. J. Campos, G. Chiola, and M. Silva. Ergodicity and throughput bounds of Petri nets with unique consistent firing count vector. *IEEE Transactions on Software Engineering*, 17(2):117–125, 1991.

4. R. A. Cuninghame-Green. Describing industrial processes with interference and approximating their steady-state behaviour. *Operational Research Quarterly*, 13(1):95–100, 1962.
5. R. L. Devaney. *An Introduction to Chaotic Dynamical Systems*. Addison-Wesley Publishing Company, Inc., 1989.
6. J. Gunawardena. Min-max functions. To appear in *Discrete Event Dynamic Systems*.
7. J. Gunawardena. The Muller unfolding. In preparation.
8. J. Gunawardena. A generalized event structure for the Muller unfolding of a safe net. In E. Best, editor, *CONCUR'93 - 4th International Conference on Concurrency Theory*, pages 278–292. Springer LNCS 715, 1993.
9. J. Gunawardena. Periodic behaviour in timed systems with {AND, OR} causality. Part I: systems of dimension 1 and 2. Technical Report STAN-CS-93-1462, Department of Computer Science, Stanford University, February 1993.
10. J. Gunawardena. Timing analysis of digital circuits and the theory of min-max functions. In *TAU'93, ACM International Workshop on Timing Issues in the Specification and Synthesis of Digital Systems*, September 1993.
11. J. Gunawardena. Cycle times and fixed points of min-max functions. To appear in the Proceedings of the *11th International Conference on Analysis and Optimization of Systems*, Sophia-Antipolis, France, June 1994.
12. R. M. Keller. A fundamental theorem of asynchronous parallel computation. In T. Y. Feng, editor, *Parallel Processing*, pages 102–112. Springer LNCS 24, 1975.
13. L. H. Landweber and E. L. Robertson. Properties of conflict-free and persistent Petri nets. *Journal ACM*, 25(3):352–364, 1978.
14. R. Milner. *Communication and Concurrency*. International Series in Computer Science. Prentice-Hall, 1989.
15. G. J. Olsder. Eigenvalues of dynamic max-min systems. *Discrete Event Dynamic Systems*, 1:177–207, 1991.
16. T. Szymanski and N. Shenoy. Verifying clock schedules. In *Digest of Technical Papers of the IEEE International Conference on Computer-Aided Design of Integrated Circuits*, pages 124–131. IEEE Computer Society, 1992.
17. J. Vytopil, editor. *Formal Techniques in Real-Time and Fault-Tolerant Systems*. Springer LNCS 571, 1991.
18. G. Winskel. Event structures. In W. Brauer, W. Reisig, and G. Rozenberg, editors, *Advances in Petri Nets*. Springer LNCS 255, 1987.

Note to the reader

Copies of [6]-[11] are available by ftp from hplose.hpl.hp.com, (15.254.100.100). Use "anonymous" as user name and refer to "/pub/jhcg/README" for more information.

Algebras of Processes of Timed Petri Nets [1]

Józef Winkowski

Instytut Podstaw Informatyki PAN
ul. Ordona 21, 01-237 Warszawa, Poland
phone: +48 22 362841, fax: +48 22 376564, email: wink@wars.ipipan.waw.pl

Abstract. Processes of timed Petri nets are represented by labelled partial orders with some extra features. These features reflect the execution times of processes and allow to combine processes sequentially and in parallel. The processes can be represented either without specifying when particular situations appear (free time-consuming processes), or together with the respective appearance times (timed time-consuming processes). The processes of the latter type determine the possible firing sequences of the respective nets.

1 Motivation and introduction

Petri nets are a widely accepted model of concurrent systems. Originally they were invented for modelling those aspects of system behaviours which can be expressed in terms of causality and choice. Recently a growing interest can be observed in modelling real-time systems, which implies a need of a representation of the lapse of time. To meet this need various solutions has been proposed known as timed Petri nets.

For the usual Petri nets there exist precise characterisations of behaviours. Among them occurrence nets as described in [Wns 87] and in [MMS 92], and algebras of processes as in [DMM 89] seem to be most adequate.

In the case of timed Petri nets the situation is less advanced since the existing semantics either do not reflect properly concurrency (cf. [GMMP 89] for a review) or they oversimplify the representation of the lapse of time (as in [BG 92]). Besides, the presence of the concept of time in the model gives rise to a variety of problems as those of performance evaluation, and this creates a need of new formal tools.

In this paper we try to build the needed tools by representing the behaviour of a timed net by an algebra of structures called concatenable weighted pomsets. These structures correspond to concatenable processes of [DMM 89] with some extra information about the lapse of time. If the lapse of time is represented only in terms of delays between situations then we call such structures free time-consuming processes. If also the time instants at which situations arise are given then we call them timed time-consuming processes.

[1] This work has been partially supported by the Polish grant No. 2 2047 92 03

There are natural homomorphisms from the algebra of timed time-consuming processes of a net to the algebra of its free time-consuming processes and from the algebra of free time-consuming processes to an algebra whose elements reflect how much time the respective processes take. More precisely, to each free time-consuming process there corresponds a table of least possible delays between its data and results (a delay table) such that the tables corresponding to the results of operations on processes (a sequential and a parallel composition) can be obtained by composing properly the tables corresponding to components.

The delay tables which correspond to processes generalize in a sense the concept of execution time. The representation of execution time by a number is not adequate enough when we have to do with processes consisting of independent components. For example, for a process $\alpha \otimes \beta$ which consists of independent components α and β the execution time cannot be represented by a number since it may vary depending on when the components α and β start. At the same time, the table of least possible delays between causally related initial and terminal situations is unique.

An important property of free time-consuming processes and their delay tables is that they do not depend on when the respective data appear. Due to this property one can compute how a process of this type proceeds in time for any given combination of appearance times of its data. The combination which is given plays here the role of a marking. This marking is timed in the sense that not only the presences of tokens in places but also the respective appearance times (which need not be the same) are given.

The possibility of computing how a free time-consuming process applies to a given timed marking allows us to find the corresponding timed process. The possibility of finding timed processes of a net allows us to see which of them can be chosen and to define the possible firing sequences of the net.

The paper exploits some ideas of [Wi 80] and [Wi 92]. It is an improved version of [Wi 93]. Results are presented in it without proofs. The respective proofs will be given in a more complete paper.

2 Concatenable weighted pomsets

Processes of timed nets will be represented by partially ordered multisets (pomsets in the terminology of [Pra 86]) with some extra arrangements of minimal and maximal elements (similar to those in concatenable processes of [DMM 89]), and with some extra features (weights) and properties. Let V be a set of labels.

2.1. Definition. A *concatenable weighted labelled partial order* (or a *cwlp-order*) over V is $\mathcal{A} = (X, \leq, d, e, s, t)$, where:

(1) $(X, \leq)$ is a finite partially ordered set with a subset X_{min} of minimal elements and a subset X_{max} of maximal elements such that each maximal chain has an element in each maximal antichain,

(2) $d : X \times X \to \{-\infty\} \cup [0, +\infty)$ is a *weight function* such that $d(x, y) = -\infty$ iff $x \leq y$ does not hold, $d(x, x) = 0$, and $d(x, y)$ is the maximum of sums $d(x, x_1) + ... + d(x_n, y)$ over all maximal chains $x \leq x_1 \leq ... \leq x_n \leq y$ from x to y whenever $x \leq y$,

(3) $e : X \to V$ is a *labelling function*,

(4) $s = (s(v) : v \in V)$ is a family of enumerations of the sets $e^{-1}(v) \cap X_{min}$ (an *arrangement of minimal elements*),

(5) $t = (t(v) : v \in V)$ is a family of enumerations of the sets $e^{-1}(v) \cap X_{max}$ (an *arrangement of maximal elements*). □

By an enumeration of a set we mean here a sequence of elements of this set in which each element of this set occurs exactly once.

The property of the order in (1) is known in the theory of Petri nets as K-density. It is assumed in order to guarantee that each maximal antichain of a cwlp-order $\mathcal{A}$ defines a decomposition of $\mathcal{A}$ into components such that $\mathcal{A}$ could uniquely be reconstructed from these components (cf. 2.5). The property (2) implies that for $x \leq y$ there exists a maximal chain $x \leq x_1 \leq ... \leq x_n \leq y$ from x to y which is *critical* in the sense that $d(x, y) = d(x, x_1) + ... + d(x_n, y)$. Together with (1) it implies also that the weight function is determined uniquely by specifying its values for x, y such that y is an immediate successor of x.

The interpretation of a cwlp-order as a representation of a process will be given in section 4.

2.2. Definition. A cwlp-order $\mathcal{A} = (X, \leq, d, e, s, t)$ is said to be *isomorphic* to other one $\mathcal{A}' = (X', \leq', d', e', s', t')$ if there exists an isomorphism from $\mathcal{A}$ to $\mathcal{A}'$, that is a bijection $b : X \to X'$ such that $x \leq y$ iff $b(x) \leq' b(y)$, $d'(b(x), b(y)) = d(x, y)$, $e'(b(x)) = e(x)$, $s'(v) = b(s(v))$, and $t'(v) = b(t(v))$, where $b(x_1...x_n)$ denotes $b(x_1)...b(x_n)$, for all $x, y \in X$ and $v \in V$. □

2.3. Definition. A *concatenable weighted pomset* (or a *cw-pomset*) over V is an isomorphism class of cwlp-orders over V. □

The cw-pomset which is the isomorphism class of a given cwlp-order $\mathcal{A} = (X, \leq, d, e, s, t)$ is written as $[\mathcal{A}]$ and $\mathcal{A}$ is called its *instance*. The restriction of $\mathcal{A}$ to X_{min} with t replaced by s and that to X_{max} with s replaced by t are instances of cw-pomsets written respectively as $\partial_0([\mathcal{A}])$ and $\partial_1([\mathcal{A}])$ and called the *source* and the *target* of $[\mathcal{A}]$. If $X = X_{min} = X_{max}$ then $\leq$ reduces to the identity and we call $[\mathcal{A}]$ a *symmetry*. If also $t = s$ then $[\mathcal{A}] = \partial_0([\mathcal{A}]) = \partial_1([\mathcal{A}])$ and $[\mathcal{A}]$ becomes a *trivial symmetry* or, equivalently, a *multiset* of elements of V with the multiplicity of each $v \in V$ given by *cardinality*$(e^{-1}(v) \cap X)$. By *cwpomsets*(V), *symmetries*(V), *trivsym*(V) we denote respectively the set of cw-pomsets, the set of symmetries, and the set of trivial symmetries over V.

Examples of cw-pomsets of which one is a symmetry are shown in figure 1. In the graphical representation we omit arrows which follow from the transitivity of order and weights which follow from the assumed properties of weight function. The arrangements of minimal and maximal elements are shown by endowing the labels of minimal elements with subscripts and the labels of maximal elements with superscripts, where each subscript (resp.: superscript) denotes the position of the corresponding element in the respective enumeration.

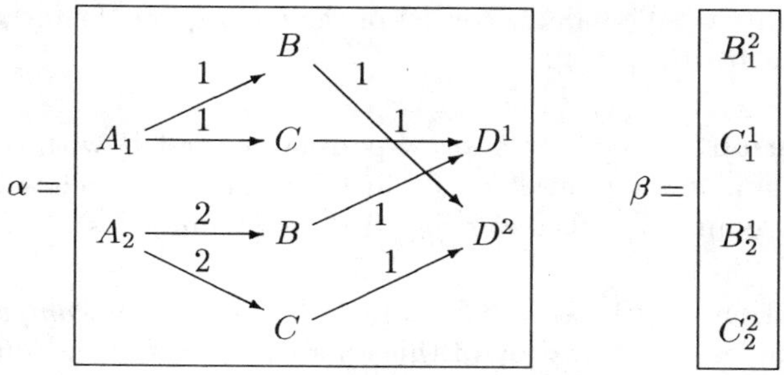

Figure 1

To each permutation p of a sequence $1, ..., n$ there corresponds an operation I_p, called after [DMM 89] an *interchange*, which to each n-tuple $(a_1, ..., a_n)$ of trivial symmetries $a_i = [(X_i, \leq_i, d_i, e_i, s_i, t_i)]$ assigns the symmetry $I_p(a_1, ..., a_n)$ $= [(X, \leq, d, e, s, t)]$, where X is a disjoint union of (suitable copies of) $X_1, ... X_n$, $\leq$ is the identity on X, $e(x) = e_i(x)$ for $x \in X_i$, $s(v) = s_1(v)...s_n(v)$ (the concatenation of $s_1(v), ..., s_n(v)$), and $t(v) = s_{p(1)}(v)...s_{p(n)}(v)$ (the concatenation of $s_{p(1)}(v), ..., s_{p(n)}(v)$). By $*$ and I_* we denote respectively the permutation $1 \mapsto 2, 2 \mapsto 1$ and the corresponding interchange.

Let $\mathcal{A} = (X, \leq, d, e, s, t)$ be a cwlp-order and let $cuts(\mathcal{A})$ denote the set of all maximal antichains of $\mathcal{A}$. Each maximal antichain $Y \in cuts(\mathcal{A})$ defines the subsets

$$\downarrow Y = \{x \in X : x \leq y \text{ for some } y \in Y\}$$

and

$$\uparrow Y = \{x \in X : y \leq x \text{ for some } y \in Y\}.$$

Given two maximal antichains $Y, Y' \in cuts(\mathcal{A})$, we write $Y \sqsubseteq Y'$ if $\downarrow Y \subseteq \downarrow Y'$.

2.4. Proposition.; The relation $\sqsubseteq$ is a partial order on the set $cuts(\mathcal{A})$ such that $cuts(\mathcal{A})$ with this order is a lattice. □

2.5. Proposition. For each $Y \in cuts(\mathcal{A})$ the order $\leq$ is the transitive closure of the union of its restrictions to the subsets $\downarrow Y$ and $\uparrow Y$. □

2.6. Proposition. For each $Y \in cuts(\mathcal{A})$ and for all $x \in \downarrow Y$ and $y \in \uparrow Y$ the weight $d(x, y)$ is given by the formula $d(x, y) = max(d(x, z) + d(z, y) : z \in Y)$. □

2.7. Proposition. For each $Y \in cuts(\mathcal{A})$ the restrictions of $\mathcal{A}$ to $\downarrow Y$ and $\uparrow Y$ with a family $r = (r(v) : v \in V)$ of enumerations of the sets $e^{-1}(v) \cap Y$ playing the role of arrangement of maximal elements of $\downarrow Y$ and of arrangement of minimal elements of $\uparrow Y$ are cwlp-orders, written respectively as $head_{Y,r}(\mathcal{A})$ and $tail_{Y,r}(\mathcal{A})$. □

The cw-pomset $[\mathcal{A}]$ is said to consist of the cw-pomset $[head_{Y,r}(\mathcal{A})]$ followed by the cw-pomset $[tail_{Y,r}(\mathcal{A})]$.

2.8. Proposition. For every two cw-pomsets α and β with $\partial_0(\beta) = \partial_1(\alpha)$ there exists a unique cw-pomset $\alpha;\beta$ which consists of α followed by β. This cw-pomset is a symmetry whenever α and β are symmetries. □

The operation $(\alpha, \beta) \mapsto \alpha;\beta$ is called the *sequential composition* of cw-pomsets. Examples of application of this operation are shown in figure 2.

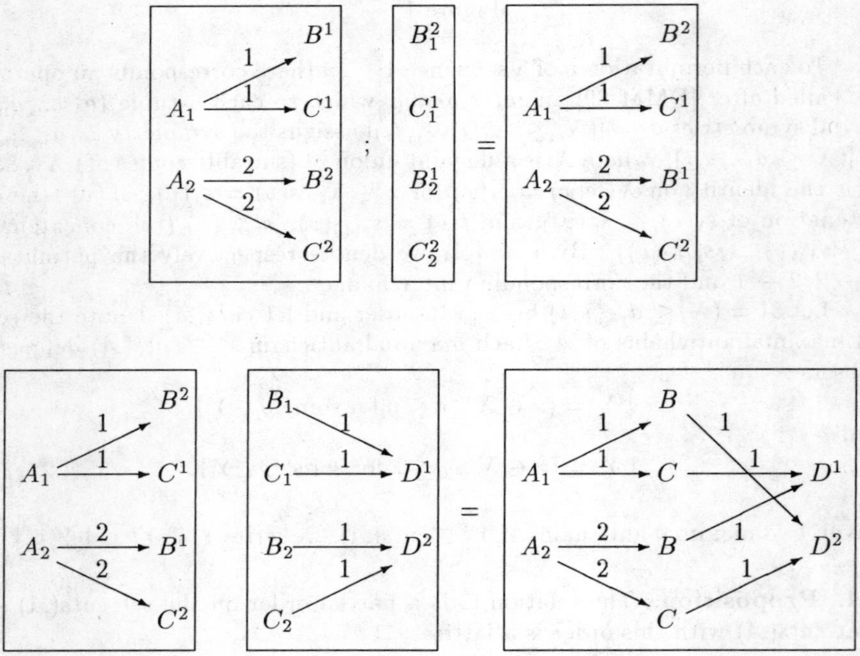

Figure 2

2.9. Proposition. The sequential composition is defined for all pairs (α, β) of cw-pomsets with $\partial_0(\beta) = \partial_1(\alpha)$, it is associative and such that $\partial_0(\alpha;\beta) = \partial_0(\alpha)$, $\partial_1(\alpha;\beta) = \partial_1(\beta)$, and $\partial_0(\alpha);\alpha = \alpha;\partial_1(\alpha) = \alpha$ for all cw-pomsets α,β. □

Another operation on cw-pomsets can be introduced with the aid of *splittings*, where a splitting of a cwlp-order $\mathcal{A} = (X, \leq, d, e, s, t)$ is a partition $p = (X', X'')$ of X into two disjoint subsets X', X'' which are *independent* in the sense that x', x'' are incomparable whenever $x' \in X'$ and $x'' \in X''$, each $s(v)$ is $(s(v)|X')(s(v)|X'')$, the concatenation of the restrictions of $s(v)$ to X' and X'', and each $t(v)$ is $(t(v)|X')(t(v)|X'')$, the concatenation of the restrictions of $t(v)$ to X' and X''.

Let $\mathcal{A} = (X, \leq, d, e, s, t)$ be a cwlp-order and let $splittings(\mathcal{A})$ denote the set of splittings of $\mathcal{A}$.

2.10. Proposition. For each $p = (X', X'') \in splittings(\mathcal{A})$ the restrictions of $\mathcal{A}$ to X' and X'' with arrangements of minimal elements given respectively by $s|X' = (s(v)|X' : v \in V)$ and $s|X'' = (s(v)|X'' : v \in V)$, and arrangements of maximal elements given respectively by $t|X' = (t(v)|X' : v \in V)$ and $t|X'' = (t(v)|X'' : v \in V)$, are cwlp-orders, written respectively as $left_p(\mathcal{A})$ and $right_p(\mathcal{A})$. □

The cw-pomset $[\mathcal{A}]$ is said to consist of the cw-pomset $[left_p(\mathcal{A})]$ accompanied by the cw-pomset $[right_p(\mathcal{A})]$.

2.11. Proposition. For every two cw-pomsets α and β there exists a unique cw-pomset $\alpha \otimes \beta$ which consists of α accompanied by β. This cw-pomset is a symmetry whenever α and β are symmetries. □

The operation $(\alpha, \beta) \mapsto \alpha \otimes \beta$ is called the *parallel composition* of cw-pomsets. An example of application of this operation is shown in figure 3.

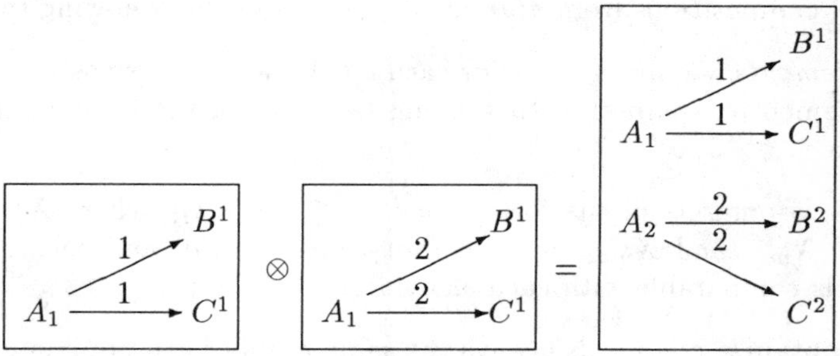

Figure 3

2.12. Proposition. The parallel composition is defined for all pairs (α, β) of cw-pomsets, it is associative, and has a neutral element *nil*, where *nil* is the unique cw-pomset with the empty instance. □

2.13. Proposition. The parallel composition is *functorial* in the sense that

$$\alpha;\beta \otimes \gamma;\delta = (\alpha \otimes \gamma);(\beta \otimes \delta)$$

whenever $\alpha;\beta$ and $\gamma;\delta$ are defined. □

2.14. Proposition. The parallel composition is *coherent* in the sense that

$$I_p(u_1, ..., u_n); \alpha_{p(1)} \otimes ... \otimes \alpha_{p(n)} = \alpha_1 \otimes ... \otimes \alpha_n; I_p(v_1, ..., v_n)$$

for all $\alpha_1, ..., \alpha_n \in cwpomsets(V)$ with $\partial_0(\alpha_i) = u_i$ and $\partial_1(\alpha_i) = v_i$, and for each permutation p of the sequence $1, ..., n$. □

2.15. Proposition. The subset of symmetries is closed w.r. to the compositions and interchanges. □

2.16. Theorem. The structure

$$CWPOMSETS(V) = (cwpomsets(V), \partial_0, \partial_1, ;, \otimes, nil, I_*)$$

is a symmetric strict monoidal category (the *monoidal category of cw-pomsets over V*) with cw-pomsets playing the role of morphisms, trivial symmetries playing the role of objects, and I_* playing the role of a natural transformation from $(\alpha, \beta) \mapsto \alpha \otimes \beta$ to $(\alpha, \beta) \mapsto \beta \otimes \alpha$. It contains $SYMMETRIES(V)$, the subcategory of symmetries with the members of $symmetries(V)$ playing the role of morphisms. □

2.17. Proposition. Each cw-pomset α can be obtained with the aid of interchanges and compositions from *atomic* cw-pomsets of the following two types:

(1) *one-element* cw-pomsets, one for each $v \in V$, written also as v, namely the one-element cw-pomset with v being the label of the only element of its instance,

(2) *prime* cw-pomsets of the form $\pi = [(X, \leq, d, e, s, t)]$, where $X = X_{min} \cup X_{max}$, X_{min} and X_{max} are nonempty and disjoint, and each element of X_{min} is comparable with each element of X_{max}.

In order to obtain α one needs always the same number $|\alpha|(\pi)$ of copies of each prime cw-pomset π. □

By $|\alpha|$ we denote the multiset of prime processes which are needed to construct a cw-pomset α. By $atomic(V)$, $oneelement(V)$, $prime(V)$ we denote respectively the set of atomic, one-element, and prime cw-pomsets over V. For each subset P of cw-pomsets over V by $closure(P)$ we denote the least subset of $cwpomsets(V)$ that contains P and is closed w.r. to interchanges and compositions.

2.18. Theorem. The monoidal category $CWPOMSETS(V)$ and its subcategory $SYMMETRIES(V)$ are generated respectively by the set $atomic(V)$ of atomic cw-pomsets and the subset $oneelement(V)$ of one-element cw-pomsets in the sense that

$$cwpomsets(V) = closure(atomic(V))$$
$$symmetries(V) = closure(oneelement(V)) \quad \square$$

Following the line of [DMM 89] it is possible to show that the properties formulated here of the monoidal category of cw-pomsets characterize this category up to isomorphism.

3 Tables

Tables of delays between situations of processes (delay tables) are matrix-like objects with a special indexing of rows and columns.

3.1. Definition. A *table* over a set V of labels is a triple $F = (I, J, f)$, where $I, J : V \to \{0, 1, ...\}$ and f is a function which assigns a weight $f(m, n) \in \{-\infty\} \cup [0, +\infty)$ to each pair of indices m, n such that $m = (u, i)$ and $n = (v, j)$ with $u, v \in V$, $1 \leq i \leq I(u)$ and $1 \leq j \leq J(v)$. $\square$

Functions I, J can be regarded as multisets of elements of V. For each table $F = (I, J, f)$ we have two tables $\partial_0'(F) = (I, I, \delta(I))$ and $\partial_1'(F) = (J, J, \delta(J))$, where $\delta(K)$ denotes the function with $\delta(K)(m, n) = 0$ for $n = m$ and $\delta(K)(m, n) = -\infty$ otherwise. If $J = I$ and there exist permutations φ_v of $1, ..., I(v)$ such that $f(m, n) = 0$ for $m = (u, i)$ and $n = (v, j)$ with $v = u$ and $j = \varphi_u(i)$), and $f(m, n) = -\infty$ for the remaining m, n, then we call F a *table symmetry*. In particular, if all φ_v are identities then we say that F is a *trivial* table symmetry and identify it with the multiset with the multiplicity $I(v) = J(v)$ of each $v \in V$. For $I = J = 0$ we have the *empty* table nil'. By $tables(V)$, $tsymmetries(V)$, and $trivtsym(V)$ we denote respectively the set of tables, the set of table symmetries, and the set of trivial table symmetries over V. An example of a table which corresponds to the tc-process α in figure 1 is shown in figure 4 (where each pair of the form (x, k) is written as xk).

$tab(\alpha)$ =

	$D1$	$D2$
$A1$	2	2
$A2$	3	3

Figure 4

For each permutation p of $1, ..., n$ we have an *interchange* I_p' which assigns to each n-tuple $(F_1, ..., F_n)$ of trivial symmetries $F_k = (I_k, I_k, \delta(I_k))$ a symmetry

$F = (I, I, f)$, where $I(v) = I_1(v) + ... + I_n(v)$ and $f(m,n) = -\infty$ except for $m = (u,i)$ and $n = (u, p(i))$, where $f(m,n) = 0$. In particular, for $*$ denoting the permutation $1 \mapsto 2, 2 \mapsto 1$ we have the interchange I'_*.

For each pair (F, F') of tables $F = (I, J, f)$ and $F' = (I', J', f')$ such that $\partial'_0(F') = \partial'_1(F)$ we have the unique table $F;' F' = (I, J', g)$ with $g(m,n)$ denoting the maximum of sums $f(m,k) + f'(k,n)$ over all $k = (v,j)$ with $v \in V$ and $1 \leq j \leq J(v)$.

The operation $(F, F') \mapsto F;' F'$ is called the *sequential composition* of tables. An example of application of this operation is shown in figure 5.

	B1	B2	C1	C2
A1	1	$-\infty$	1	$-\infty$
A2	$-\infty$	2	$-\infty$	2

$;'$

	D1	D2
B1	1	$-\infty$
B2	$-\infty$	1
C1	1	$-\infty$
C2	$-\infty$	1

$=$

	D1	D2
A1	2	$-\infty$
A2	$-\infty$	3

Figure 5

For each pair (F, F') of tables $F = (I, J, f)$ and $F' = (I', J', f')$ we have the unique table $F \otimes' F' = (I + I', J + J', h)$ with $h(m,n) = f(m,n)$ for $m = (u,i)$ and $n = (v,j)$ such that $u, v \in V$ and $1 \leq i \leq I(v)$ and $1 \leq j \leq J(v)$, $h(m,n) = f'(m', n')$ for $m = (v, i + I(v))$ and $n = (v, j + J(v))$ and $m' = (v,i)$ and $n' = (v,j)$ such that $u, v \in V$ and $1 \leq i \leq I'(v)$ and $1 \leq j \leq J'(v)$, and $h(m,n) = -\infty$ for the remaining m, n.

The operation $(F, F') \mapsto F \otimes' F'$ is called the *parallel composition* of tables. An example of application of this operation is shown in figure 6.

	B1	C1
A1	1	1

$\otimes'$

	B1	C1
A1	2	2

$=$

	B1	B2	C1	C2
A1	1	$-\infty$	1	$-\infty$
A2	$-\infty$	2	$-\infty$	2

Figure 6

3.2. Theorem. The structure

$$TABLES(V) = (tables(V), \partial'_0, \partial'_1, ;', \otimes', nil', I'_*)$$

is a symmetric strict monoidal category (the *monoidal category of tables* over V) with tables playing the role of morphisms, trivial table symmetries playing the role of objects, and I'_* playing the role of a natural transformation from $(\alpha, \beta) \mapsto \alpha \otimes' \beta$ to $(\alpha, \beta) \mapsto \beta \otimes' \alpha$. It contains $TSYMMETRIES(V)$, the subcategory of table symmetries with the members of $tsymmetries(V)$ playing the role of morphisms. □

To each cw-pomset $\alpha = [(X, \leq, d, e, s, t)]$ over V there corresponds the unique table $tab(\alpha) = (I, J, f)$ with

$$I(v) = length(s(v)) = cardinality(e^{-1}(v) \cap X_{min})$$
$$J(v) = length(t(v)) = cardinality(e^{-1}(v) \cap X_{max})$$

for all $v \in V$, and with $f(m,n) = d((s(u))(i), (t(v))(j))$ for $m = (u,i)$ and $n = (v,j)$ such that $u, v \in V$ and $1 \leq i \leq I(u)$ and $1 \leq j \leq J(v)$.

3.3. Theorem. The correspondence $\alpha \mapsto tab(\alpha) : CWPOMSETS(V) \rightarrow TABLES(V)$ is a homomorphism. The restriction of this homomorphism to the subcategory of symmetries is an isomorphism from this subcategory to the subcategory of table symmetries. □

4 Processes and their delay tables

In general, by a process we mean here a finite partially ordered complex of time-consuming acts which transform some entities into some other entities. A process of this type, called a *time-consuming process*, can be represented by a cw-pomset $[(X, \leq, d, e, s, t)]$, where:

- elements of X represent the entities which take part in the process,
- the partial order $\leq$ specifies the causal succession of entities, i.e. how the entities cause each other,
- the weight function d specifies the least possible delays with which entities appear after their causal predecessors,
- the labelling function e specifies the meanings of entities,
- s and t are respectively an arrangement of entities which the process receives from its environment and an arrangement of entities which the process delivers to its environment.

It may be given either without specifying when its entities appear (a free time-consuming process), or together with the respective appearance times (a timed time-consuming process). In the first case the labelling function e specifies only the proper meaning of each entity from a given set V of meanings. In the second case e specifies an extended meaning which consists of the proper meaning and of the respective appearance time.

Let V be a set of meanings.

4.1. Definition. A *free time-consuming process* (or a *free tc-process*) over V is (a process which can be represented by) a cw-pomset over V. □

By $ftcprocesses(V)$ we denote the set of free tc-processes over V. Being identical with $cwpomsets(V)$ this set defines $FTCPROCESSES(V)$, the *monoidal category of free tc-processes* over V. According to 3.3, to each free tc-process α in this set there corresponds the table $tab(\alpha) \in tables(V)$, called the *delay table* of α.

4.2. Proposition. The correspondence $\alpha \mapsto tab(\alpha) : ftcprocesses(V) \rightarrow tables(V)$ is a homomorphism. □

4.3. Definition. A *timed time-consuming process* (or a *timed tc-process*) over V is (a process which can be represented by) a cw-pomset $\alpha = [(X, \leq, d, e, s, t)]$ over $V \times (-\infty, +\infty)$ such that $e = e_{proper} \times e_{time} : X \rightarrow V \times (-\infty, +\infty)$, i.e. $e(x) = (e_{proper}(x), e_{time}(x))$ with $e_{proper}(x) \in V$ and $e_{time}(x) \in (-\infty, +\infty)$ for $x \in X$, where for all $x \in X - X_{min}$ we have

$$e_{time}(x) = max(e_{time}(y) + d(y, x) : y \leq x, y \neq x). \ \Box$$

By $ttcprocesses(V)$ we denote the set of timed tc-processes over V.

4.4. Proposition. The set $ttcprocesses(V)$ is closed w.r. to the compositions and interchanges. □

Being a closed subset of $cwpomsets(V \times (-\infty, +\infty))$, the set $ttcprocesses(V)$ defines a subcategory of the monoidal category $CWPOMSETS(V \times (-\infty, +\infty))$, written as $TTCPROCESSES(V)$ and called the *monoidal category of timed tc-processes* over V. To each timed tc-process $\alpha = [(X, \leq, d, e, s, t)]$ in this set there corresponds the free tc-process $free(\alpha) = [(X, \leq, d, e_{proper}, s, t)]$ in $ftcprocesses(V)$ and the delay table $tab(free(\alpha))$ in $tables(V)$.

4.5. Proposition. The correspondence

$$\alpha \mapsto free(\alpha) : ttcprocesses(V) \rightarrow ftcprocesses(V)$$

is a homomorphism. □

Timed tc-processes can be obtained by applying free tc-processes to *families of time sequences* of the form $M = (M(v) : v \in V)$, where each $M(v)$ is a finite sequence of time instants. Each such a family M represents the fact that entities with the respective meanings appear at specified time instants and it defines $st(M) = (length(M(v)) : v \in V)$, a *multiset of meanings*, and $timed(M) = (occ(t, M(v)) : v \in V)$, a *multiset of timed meanings*, where $occ(t, M(v))$ denotes the number of occurrences of the time instant t in the sequence $M(v)$.

4.6. Proposition. For each free tc-process α over V and each family $M = (M(v) : v \in V)$ of time sequences such that for each $v \in V$ the length of $M(v)$ coincides with the multiplicity of v in $\partial_0(\alpha)$ there exists a unique timed tc-process $timed(M, \alpha)$ over V whose instance $\mathcal{B}$ can be obtained from an instance $\mathcal{A} = (X, \leq, d, e, s, t)$ of α by replacing the labelling function e by e', where $e'_{proper}(x) = e(x)$ and $e'_{time}(x) = (M(v))(i)$ (the i-th element of $M(v)$)

for $x \in X_{min}$ and $x = (s(v))(i)$ (the i-th element of $s(v)$), and $e'_{proper}(x) = e(x)$ and $e'_{time}(x) = max(e'_{time}(y) + d(y,x) : y \leq x, y \neq x)$ for $x \in X - X_{min}$. The source $\partial_0(timed(M,\alpha))$ of this process is compatible with the multiset $timed(M)$ of timed meanings in the sense that it defines the same multiset. The correspondence $(M,\alpha) \mapsto timed(M,\alpha)$ is surjective in the sense that each timed tc-process over V is of the form $timed(M,\alpha)$ for some α and M. □

5 Processes of timed nets

Let $N = (Pl, Tr, pre, post, D)$ be a timed place/transition Petri net with a set Pl of places of infinite capacities, a set Tr of transitions, input and output functions $pre, post : Tr \rightarrow Pl^+$, where Pl^+ denotes the set of multisets of places, and with a duration function $D : Tr \rightarrow [0, +\infty)$. The multiset $pre(\tau)$ represents a collection of tokens, $pre(\tau, p)$ tokens in each place p, which must be consumed in order to execute a transition τ. The multiset $post(\tau)$ represents a collection of tokens, $post(\tau, p)$ tokens in each place p, which is produced by executing τ. The non-negative real number $D(\tau)$ represents the duration of each execution of τ. We assume that $pre(\tau) \neq 0$, $post(\tau) \neq 0$, $D(\tau) \neq 0$ for all transitions τ, and that $pre(\tau)$, $post(\tau)$, $D(\tau)$ determine τ uniquely.

A distribution of tokens in places is represented by a marking $\mu \in Pl^+$, where $\mu(p)$, the multiplicity of p in μ, represents the number of tokens in p. If many executions of transitions are possible for the current marking but there is too few tokens to start all these executions then a conflict which thus arises is resolved in an indeterministic manner. We assume that it takes no time to resolve conflicts: when an execution of a transition can start, it starts immediately, or it is disabled immediately. Finally, we admit many concurrent nonconflicting executions of the same transition.

The behaviour of N can be described by characterizing the possible processes of N, where a process is either an execution of a transition, or a presence of a token in a place, or a combination of such processes. Formal definitions are as follows.

5.1. Proposition. For $\tau \in Tr$ there exists a unique prime free tc-process $fproc(\tau)$ over Pl such that $fproc(\tau) = [(X, \leq, d, e, s, t)]$, where

(1) $X = X_{min} \cup X_{max}$ with X_{min} and X_{max} disjoint and such that the cardinality of $(e^{-1}(p) \cap X_{min})$ is $pre(\tau, p)$ and the cardinality of $(e^{-1}(p) \cap X_{max})$ is $post(\tau, p)$ for all $p \in Pl$,

(2) $d(x, x') = D(\tau)$ for all $x \in X_{min}$ and $x' \in X_{max}$. □

5.2. Definition. A *free tc-process* of N is a member of

$$closure(oneelement(Pl) \cup fproc(Tr))$$

where $fproc(Tr)$ denotes the set of all free tc-processes $fproc(\tau)$ with $\tau \in Tr$. □

By $fbeh(N)$ we denote the set of free tc-processes of N. Being closed w.r. to the compositions and interchanges this set defines a subcategory $FBEH(N)$ of the monoidal category $FTCPROCESSES(Pl)$. We call this subcategory the *algebra of free tc-processes* of N.

5.3. Proposition. For each $\tau \in Tr$ with $fproc(\tau) = [(X, \leq, d, e, s, t)]$ as in 5.1 there exist timed tc-processes, called *timed copies* of $fproc(\tau)$, which are of the form $\alpha = [(X, \leq, d, e', s, t)]$, where

(1) $e'_{proper} = e$,

(2) $e'_{time}(x') = max(e'_{time}(x) + D(\tau) : x \in X_{min})$ for all $x' \in X_{max}$. □

5.4. Definition. A *timed tc-process* of N is a member of

$$closure(oneelement(Pl) \cup tproc(Tr))$$

where $tproc(Tr)$ denotes the set of all timed copies of free tc-processes $fproc(\tau)$ with $\tau \in Tr$. □

By $tbeh(N)$ we denote the set of timed tc-processes of N. Being closed w.r. to the compositions and interchanges, this set defines a subcategory $TBEH(N)$ of the monoidal category $TTCPROCESSES(Pl)$. We call this subcategory the *algebra of timed tc-processes* of N.

From 4.6 it follows that, being relatively small, the algebra of free tc-processes of N determines uniquely the much larger algebra of timed tc-processes of N. Nevertheless, we cannot avoid completely dealing with timed tc-processes since they are needed in order to formulate important concepts and problems. In particular, only in the case of timed tc-processes we can express that a process excludes another process due an earlier enabling of a transition, and only from timed tc-processes we are able to reconstruct classical firing sequences.

To be more precise, we start with an observation.

5.5. Proposition. Let α be any timed tc-process of N, let $\mathcal{A} = (X, \leq, d, e, s, t)$ be any instance of this process, and let u be an instant of time. Let $X(u)$ be the set of $x \in X$ such that $e_{time}(y) \leq u$ whenever $y = x$ or y is a direct predecessors of x (which implies $X_{min} \subseteq X(u)$). Let $Y(u)$ be the subset of those elements of $X(u)$ which are maximal in $X(u)$. Then $Y(u)$ is a maximal antichain. □

The set $X(u)$ represents the entities which appear not later than at u or are results of prime components of α which start not later than at u (for instance, in the example in figure 7 the set $X(u)$ consists of $A_1 at3$, $Bat4$, $Cat4$, $A_2 at1$, $Bat3$, $Cat3$, $D^2 at4$). By restricting $\mathcal{A}$ to $X(u)$ we obtain a set $\alpha|u$ of timed tc-processes of the form $[head_{Y(u),r}(\mathcal{A})]$, a multiset $\mu_{\alpha,u}$ of timed meanings, where

$\mu_{\alpha,u}(v)$ is the number of elements of $Y(u)$ with the label v, and a multiset $\Theta_{\alpha,u}$ of prime free tc-processes, where $\Theta_{\alpha,u}(\pi)$ is the number $|free(\alpha')|(\pi)$ of copies of π in $free(\alpha')$ for any $\alpha' \in \alpha|u$ (cf. 2.17). The set $\alpha|u$ and the multisets $\mu_{\alpha,u}$, $\Theta_{\alpha,u}$ do not depend on the choice of instance of α. The multiset $\mu_{\alpha,u}$ may be regarded as a *timed marking* whose each item $\mu_{\alpha,u}(p,t)$ represents an appearance of a token in place p at time instant t. The multiset $\Theta_{\alpha,u}$ may be regarded as a multiset of transitions represented by prime free tc-processes of $\Theta_{\alpha,u}$.

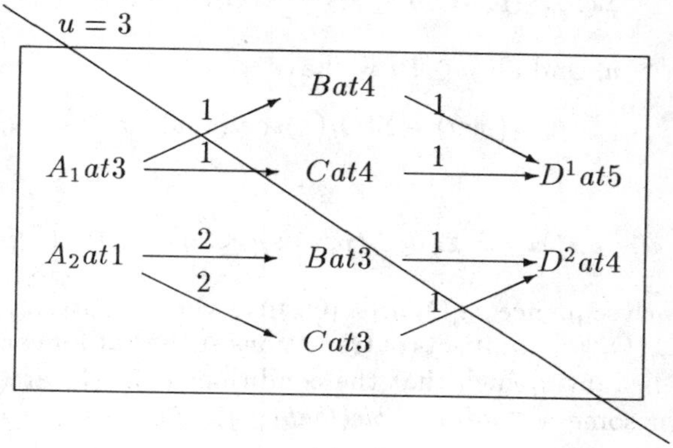

Figure 7

By considering all possible time instants u, including $-\infty$, we obtain for each $\alpha \in tbeh(N)$ a sequence $-\infty = u_0 < u_1 < \ldots < u_n < u_{n+1} = +\infty$ such that $\alpha|u$, $\mu_{\alpha,u}$, $\Theta_{\alpha,u}$ are constant and respectively equal to some α_i,μ_i,Θ_i on each interval $[u_i, u_{i+1})$. In this manner to α a sequence $fs(\alpha) = \mu_0[\Theta_1)\mu_1 \ldots [\Theta_n)\mu_n$ there corresponds which may be regarded as a candidate for a possible firing sequence of N.

Whether indeed $fs(\alpha)$ is a possible firing sequence depends on whether the process α cannot or can be excluded by another process due to an earlier enabling of a transition, and it can be reflected with the aid of concepts of dominance and admissibility.

Given two timed tc-processes α and β, we say that β *dominates* α if there exists a time instant u_0 such that $\Theta_{\alpha,u} = \Theta_{\beta,u}$ and $\Theta_{\alpha,u} = \Theta_{\alpha,u_0}$ and $\Theta_{\beta,u} < \Theta_{\beta,u_0}$ for $u < u_0$. Given any set P of timed tc-processes, a member α of P is said to be *admissible* in this set if there is no $\beta \in P$ which dominates α. Thus P determines a subset $admissible(P)$ of its admissible members.

With these concepts we are able to say which timed tc-processes of the considered net N are realizable and to describe how they define firing sequences of N. Namely, a timed tc-process α of N can be realized, and thus $fs(\alpha)$ is a possible firing sequence, iff α is admissible.

Thus we obtain a set $admissible(tbeh(N))$ of admissible timed tc-processes of N such that only members of this set can be realized in N, and firing sequences of N can be defined as $fs(\alpha)$ for admissible α. This is justified by the following fact.

5.6. Theorem. If $fs(\alpha) = \mu_0[\Theta_1\rangle\mu_1 ... [\Theta_n\rangle\mu_n$ for some $\alpha \in admissible(tbeh(N))$ then for each $i = 1, ..., n$ there exists a time instant u_i such that

(1) u_i is the earliest instant of time such that, for all $p \in Pl$,

$$\Sigma(\mu_{i-1}(p, u) : u \leq u_i) \geq pre(\tau, p),$$

(2) Θ_i is a maximal multiset of transitions such that, for all $p \in Pl$,

$$\Sigma(\mu_{i-1}(p, u) : u \leq u_i) \geq \Sigma(\Theta_i(\tau)pre(\tau, p) : \tau \in Tr),$$

(3) for all $u > u_i$ and all $p \in Pl$ we have

$$\mu_i(p, u) = \mu_{i-1}(p, u) + \Sigma(\Theta_i(\tau)post(\tau, p) : \tau \in Tr, u_i + D(\tau) = u)$$

and

$$\Sigma(\mu_i(p, u) : u \leq u_i) = \Sigma(\mu_{i-1}(p, u) : u \leq u_i) - \Sigma(\Theta_i(\tau)pre(\tau, p) : \tau \in Tr).$$

Conversely, each sequence $\mu_0[\Theta_1\rangle\mu_1 ... [\Theta_n\rangle\mu_n$, where $\mu_0, \mu_1, ..., \mu_n$ are timed markings and $\Theta_1, ..., \Theta_n$ are multisets of transitions such that for each $i = 1, ..., n$ there exists a time instant u_i such that the conditions (1) - (3) are satisfied, is of the form $fs(\alpha)$ for some $\alpha \in admissible(tbeh(N))$. □

6 Closing remarks

The representation of the behaviours of timed Petri nets in terms of processes and their delay tables seems to be conceptually simple due to its algebraic nature. In this representation nets can be viewed as sets of atomic generators of their behaviours considered as subalgebras of a monoidal category. Processes which constitute such behaviours determine in a natural way their execution times in the form of delay tables rather than of single numbers. This seems to be adequate for many applications and allows the parallel composition of processes to be a bifunctor.

The descriptions of behaviours of timed Petri nets in terms of processes have this advantage over descriptions in terms of firing sequences that the behaviours of large nets can be obtained by combining the behaviours of their components. This follows from the simple observation that such descriptions are compositional in the sense that

$$fbeh(N) = closure(fbeh(N_1) \cup ... \cup fbeh(N_k))$$

and

$$tbeh(N) = closure(tbeh(N_1) \cup ... \cup tbeh(N_k))$$

whenever N consists of subnets $N_1, ..., N_k$ which possibly share places but have mutually disjoint sets of transitions.

Moreover, the descriptions in terms of processes are more economical than the descriptions in terms of firing sequences since one process can represent a set of firing sequences.

References

[BG 92] Brown, C., Gurr, D., *Timing Petri Nets Categorically* , Springer LNCS 623, Proc. of ICALP'92, 1992, pp.571-582

[DMM 89] Degano, P., Meseguer, J., Montanari, U., *Axiomatizing Net Computations and Processes*, in the Proceedings of 4th LICS Symposium, IEEE, 1989, pp.175-185

[GMMP 89] Ghezzi, C., Mandrioli, D., Morasca, S., Pezze, M., *A General Way to Put Time in Petri Nets*, Proc. of the 5th Int. Workshop on Software Specifications and Design, Pittsburgh, May 1989, IEEE-CS Press

[MMS 92] Meseguer, J., Montanari, U., Sassone, V., *On the Semantics of Petri Nets*, Springer LNCS 630, Proc. of CONCUR'92, 1992, pp.286-301

[Pra 86] Pratt, V., *Modelling Concurrency with Partial Orders*, International Journal of Parallel Programming, Vol.15, No.1, 1986, pp.33-71

[Wi 80] Winkowski, J., *Behaviours of Concurrent Systems*, Theoretical Computer Science 12, 1980, pp.39-60

[Wi 92] Winkowski, J., *An Algebra of Time-Consuming Computations*, Institute of Computer Science of the Polish Academy of Sciences, Technical Report 722, December 1992

[Wi 93] Winkowski, J., *A Representation of Processes of Timed Petri Nets*, Institute of Computer Science of the Polish Academy of Sciences, Technical Report 728, August 1993

[Wns 87] Winskel, G., *Petri Nets, Algebras, Morphisms and Compositionality*, Information and Computation 72, 1987, pp.197-238

Operational Semantics for the Petri Box Calculus*

Maciej Koutny,** Javier Esparza*** and Eike Best†

Abstract. The Petri Box Calculus (PBC), based on Milner's CCS, has been developed to provide a compositional semantics of high level programming constructs in terms of a class of Petri nets with interfaces, called Petri Boxes. In this paper we present a structural operational semantics for Box expressions which provide the syntax for the PBC. We show that the use of equations in addition to action rules leads to a uniform theory consisting essentially of a single action rule, a set of context rules, and a set of equations. To capture what is basically the standard Petri net transition rule, we introduce an overbarring and underbarring technique which is related to that used in the event systems due to Boudol and Castellani. We define step sequence rules and show their consistency and completeness with respect to the counterparts from net theory. The results hold also for expressions involving unguarded recursion.

Keywords: Petri nets, process algebra, step sequences, structured operational semantics.

1 Introduction

The Petri Box Calculus (PBC) [2, 3, 15] is a net-based model for specifying concurrent systems which has been developed with two aims in mind: (i) to serve as the semantic domain of a compositional semantics of high level concurrent programming languages [4, 16]; and (ii) to support a compositional semantics in terms of Petri nets and their associated causal partial order behaviour [2, 3, 5, 15, 22]. The PBC can be seen as a bridge between high-level programming constructs, e.g. blocks, variables, recursion and critical sections, and more primitive concepts of Petri net theory, such as local states and transitions.

The PBC basically consists of a syntactic domain of Box expressions, and a semantic domain of Petri Boxes. There exists a semantic homomorphism from Box expressions to Boxes; its properties are described in [3]. Boxes are Petri nets equipped with an interface. They behave like black boxes extended with a communication facility and can be combined appropriately at their interfaces.

* Work done within the Esprit Basic Research Action 3148 DEMON and the Esprit Basic Research Working Group 6067 CALIBAN.

** Dept. of Computing Science, University of Newcastle upon Tyne, NE1 7RU, U.K.

*** Dept. of Computing Science, University of Edinburgh, EH9 3JZ, U.K.

† Institut für Informatik, Universität Hildesheim, Marienburger Platz 22, D - 31141 Hildesheim, Germany.

Box expressions, on the other hand, are an extension and modification of CCS [24] with asynchronous multilabel communication; they are like a generalised asynchronous version of SCCS [6, 11], not unlike the multiparty interaction of Smolka et al. [28], but contrasting somewhat with Milne's CIRCAL [23].

In this paper we give a step sequence operational semantics of Box expressions in the Plotkin style [27]. In doing so we define *marked expressions* which can be used to represent Petri Boxes with markings (Box expressions correspond to unmarked Petri Boxes). The net semantics of Petri Boxes corresponding to marked expressions serves as a guideline in the development of the appropriate inference rules. Moreover, we formulate a number of 'equalities' on marked expressions which are derived from the structural isomorphism holding for the corresponding Petri Boxes with markings (called marked Boxes). The main technical result is that the operational semantics defined for Box expressions is fully consistent with the standard Petri net semantics of the corresponding Boxes. This bisimulation-like result holds for all marked expressions; in particular, we do not assume that recursion or the branches of a choice must be guarded.

The paper is structured as follows. Section 2 introduces the syntax of Box expressions, their intended meaning, and the semantic model of Petri Boxes without repeating the details which can be found in [3, 19]. The next section defines the notion of a marked expression, which relates to the notion of a Box expression roughly like the notion of a marked net relates to that of an unmarked net. It ends with the introduction of equations on marked expressions which correspond to the structural isomorphism on the corresponding marked Boxes. Section 4 defines the structured operational semantics of marked expressions in terms of step sequences (multisets of concurrent occurrences of actions or sequences thereof). The consistency and completeness results are formulated in Section 5. The paper ends with a brief comparison with related work.

The proofs of all the results can be found in [19].

2 Box Expressions and Petri Boxes

We define a set $\mathcal{A}$ of primitive action names. The communication capabilities of Box expressions are expressed using communication labels, which are finite multisets[1] of action names. The set of communication labels is denoted by $\mathcal{L}$. We assume that there exists a 'conjugation' bijection, $\widehat{\ }: \mathcal{A} \to \mathcal{A}$, such that $\widehat{a} \neq a$ and $\widehat{\widehat{a}} = a$ for all $a \in \mathcal{A}$. Intuitively, a communication label like $\{a, b\}$ expresses a capability to synchronise with an action $\widehat{a}$ and an action $\widehat{b}$.

The syntax of Box expressions E is given in Table 1.[2] When α is a singleton multiset, $\alpha = \{a\}$, we sometimes leave out the enclosing set brackets. We adopt

[1] We use standard operations on multisets: sum, $+$, difference, $\setminus$, and k–multiple of a multiset, $k \cdot \alpha$.

[2] We use $a, b, c, \ldots$ to denote action names, $\alpha, \alpha_1, \alpha_2, \ldots$ to denote communication labels, X to denote variable, and E, F, G to denote Box expressions.

the usual notions of a free and bound variable, and of a closed expression. Table 2 shows examples of closed Box expressions.[3]

Table 1. Box expressions

$E ::= \alpha \mid$	basic action	$(\alpha \in \mathcal{L})$
$X \mid$	variable	
$E;E \mid$	sequence	
$E \,\square\, E \mid$	choice	
$E \| E \mid$	concurrent composition	
$[E * E * E] \mid$	iteration	
$[a : E] \mid$	scoping	$(a \in \mathcal{A})$
$\mu X.E$	recursion	

The basic semantics of Box expressions is given by means of a mapping $Box(.)$ that takes a Box expression E and produces a labelled (possibly infinite) arc-weighted Petri net,[4] called a *Box*, whose labelling indicates an interface at which it can be composed. Every Box has one or more places labelled e (for entry) and one or more places labelled x (for exit). Other places are labelled by $\emptyset$ and are called internal. Transitions are labelled either by communication labels in $\mathcal{L}$, or by variable names. If the communication label is $\emptyset$ then the transition is called internal and treated as the τ in CCS; otherwise the transition belongs to the communication interface. Appendix B shows Boxes corresponding to the expressions in Table 2.

Table 2. Examples of Box expressions

$E_1 = (a;b) \,\square\, c$	$E_2 = [a : (\{a,b\} \| \{\hat{a},\hat{a}\}) \| \{a,c\}]$	$E_3 = \mu X.((a;X) \,\square\, b)$
$E_4 = \mu X.((X;a) \,\square\, a)$	$E_5 = \mu X.(a \| X)$	$E_6 = [a \,\square\, b * c * d]$

The construct $\mu X.E$ denotes recursion [1, 24]. Sequence and choice are standard; the $\square$ is used to denote what is essentially the + in CCS [24] and the comma (,) in COSY [18]. The iterative construct $[E * F * G]$ means 'perform E once, then perform zero or more repetitions of F, then perform G once'. The basic expression $E = \alpha$ means 'execute a single action with communication capabilities α and terminate'. The concurrent composition operator is basically a disjoint union and hence differs from its counterparts in CCS and COSY, and is similar to the $\|_\emptyset$ in TCSP [17]. For instance, $a \| \widehat{a}$ can perform the $\{a\}$ and $\{\widehat{a}\}$ actions, but no synchronised action (in contrast to $a.nil | \widehat{a}.nil$ in CCS).

Synchronisation can only be achieved through the scoping operator; below we explain the scoping construct $[a : E]$ in terms of its intended semantics, $Box([a : E]) = [a : Box(E)]$.
Scoping of a Box $Box(E)$ may add/remove transitions to/from it according to certain criteria applied to the labels of transitions. It consists of two consecutive

[3] Note that [3] also defines explicit synchronisation and restriction operators which we here combine into a single scoping operator.

[4] Actually, an equivalence class thereof; but for the purposes of this paper, we may ignore this distinction.

steps, synchronisation and restriction. The synchronisation step is a 'repeated application' of the basic CCS synchronisation mechanism, i.e. synchronisation over pairs $(a, \hat{a})$ of conjugate action names. For instance, in E_2, the subexpression $\{a, b\}$ can synchronise with $\{\hat{a}, \hat{a}\}$ (as it were, using the a of $\{a, b\}$ coupled with one of the $\hat{a}$'s) and $\{\hat{a}, \hat{a}\}$ can also synchronise with $\{a, c\}$ (using the other $\hat{a}$ coupled with the a of $\{a, c\}$). This yields a three-way synchronisation. The resulting transition is labelled $\{b, c\}$ (action names participating in the synchronisation are deleted) and inherits the connectivity from the transitions corresponding to $\{a, b\}$, $\{\hat{a}, \hat{a}\}$ and $\{a, c\}$. In the restriction step all transitions that have at least one a or $\hat{a}$ in their label are removed. Thus the transition labelled by $\{b, c\}$ is a transition of $Box(E_2)$ because it survives the restriction (see also Section 4).

Although the syntactic substitution $E[X \leftarrow F]$ lies outside the signature of our process algebra, it is needed to formalise the rewriting of recursive terms. To ensure that it is consistent with transition refinement in the domain of Boxes [2], i.e. that $Box(E[X \leftarrow F]) = Box(E)[X \leftarrow Box(F)]$ holds,[5] we use two simple rules. The first says that any bound variable names may need to be changed to avoid clashes. The other deals with the problem caused by substitutions like $[a : a\|X][X \leftarrow \hat{a}]$ and $[b : b\|X][X \leftarrow \hat{a}]$. These should result in expressions generating the same Box, but if we were to perform a 'dumb' substitution, the resulting expressions, $[a : a\|\hat{a}]$ and $[b : b\|\hat{a}]$, would violate this. The reason is that scoping binds the name of the action name it involves. [19] defines consistent re-naming of action names, which allows changing bound action names to avoid name clashes, where a and $\hat{a}$ are bound in E if they occur in a scoping context $[a : E]$. For our example, we re-name a to c, which results in $[c : c\|X][X \leftarrow \hat{a}] = [c : c\|\hat{a}]$ satisfying $Box([c : c\|\hat{a}]) = Box([b : b\|\hat{a}])$. We will treat as syntactically equivalent any two Box expressions which can be shown equal by changing bound variables and/or by consistent re-naming of action names.

3 Marked Expressions and Equations

Dealing with the behaviour of a Box expression amounts to axiomatising the transition rule of the corresponding Petri net with the initial marking that places one token on each e–labelled place and no tokens elsewhere. In a typical process algebra treatment, the action rule $E \xrightarrow{a} F$ involves a change in the structure of E; for instance, $a.nil + b.nil \xrightarrow{a} nil$. However, the transition rule of Petri nets involves the modification of a net's marking, but not of its structure. There are, therefore, two natural approaches to axiomatising the transition rule: (i) the occurrence of a transition in a Petri net leads to a modification of its structure (as well as of its marking); and (ii) the action rule for Box expressions does not change the structure of the expression. We here have adopted the latter alternative since otherwise we would have lost the compositionality of the translation from expressions to Boxes, and we would have to define a non-standard transi-

[5] $Box(E)[X \leftarrow Box(F)]$ denotes a simultaneous transition refinement in which all transitions labelled X in $Box(E)$ are replaced by $Box(F)$.

tion rule for Petri nets. Moreover, we believe that (ii) leads to a rather elegant treatment of the iteration construct (see Sections 5 and 6).

To capture changes of the state of an evolving Box expression, we introduce the overbarring and underbarring of its subexpressions. This yields what we call a *marked expression*. The overbarred subexpression $\overline{E}$ means that E is enabled (or is in its initial state) and may subsequently occur, while $\underline{E}$ means that E is in its final state. For instance, $\overline{(a;b)\square c}$ means 'the whole expression $(a;b)\square c$ is enabled', while $(\overline{a};b)\square c$ means 'the overbarred subexpression a is enabled'. On the other hand, $(\underline{a};b)\square c$ informally means 'the underbarred subexpression a has just occurred and is now in its final state'.

Table 3 presents the syntax of marked expressions D.[6] For example, $(\underline{a};b)\square c$ is derived syntactically from $(\underline{E};E)\square E$, $(D;E)\square E$, $D\square E$ and D. Notice that $\overline{\mu X.E}$ is a marked expression, and therefore marked expressions comprise recursively defined processes. The notions of a bound variable, etc., are defined as for Box expressions.

Table 3. Marked expressions (E is a Box expression and $a \in \mathcal{A}$)

$$\begin{array}{llll} D ::= \overline{E} & \mid \underline{E} & \mid D;E & \mid E;D \mid \\ \quad D\square E & \mid E\square D & \mid D\|D & \mid [a:D] \mid \\ \quad [D*E*E] & \mid [E*D*E] & \mid [E*E*D] & \end{array}$$

The mapping $Box(.)$ is extended in a compositional way to marked expressions. For a marked expression D, $Box(D)$ is a marked Box which is the Petri Box $Box(\lfloor D\rfloor)$ with an added marking, where $\lfloor D\rfloor$ is obtained from D by leaving out all overbars and underbars.[7] We add the marking by a straightforward modification of the definition of $Box(.)$ given in [3]; one only has to mark the entry (exit) places in the subnets corresponding of overbarred (underbarred) subexpressions. [19] formally defines marked Boxes and the required extension to the $Box(.)$ mapping (see also Appendix A). In Appendix B we show two marked Boxes, $Box((\overline{a}\|\underline{b});c)$ and $Box((\underline{a};b)\square c)$

The operational semantics of marked expressions will be defined in the SOS style [27], with the structure of an executed marked expression being left unchanged. A change of state will be indicated by replacing some overbars by underbars. E.g., we will have a transition from $(\overline{a};b)\square c$ to $(\underline{a};b)\square c$.

Inference rules are not sufficient to ensure that a marked expression is capable of executing exactly the same actions as the corresponding Box. For example, $Box(\overline{(a;b)}\square c)$ enables a transition labelled with a, yet $\overline{(a;b)}\square c$ cannot mimic this using the inference rules alone. We deal with this problem by defining a relation $\equiv$ on marked expressions which identifies (some of) the expressions generating the same Box. For example, using the equation $\overline{E;F}\equiv\overline{E};F$ we will be able to rewrite $\overline{(a;b)}\square c$ to $(\overline{a};b)\square c$ and after that use inference rules to derive a transition. As another example, the equation $\underline{E};F \equiv E;\overline{F}$ essentially means that if E has just finished, F is enabled and can occur. In the same way as other

[6] We will use D, H, J to denote marked expressions.

[7] $\lfloor D\rfloor$ can be seen as a representation of the structure of the expression D.

equations, it corresponds to a structural equality on the corresponding marked Boxes. For instance, $Box((\underline{a}; b) \Box c) = Box((a; \overline{b}) \Box c)$. The equation $\underline{E}; F \equiv E; \overline{F}$ is a means of capturing the equality of Box markings on the level of marked expressions.

Tables 4 shows a set of basic equations that match the operators of the syntax. We then define $\equiv$ to be the least congruence on marked expressions satisfying the basic equations. The application of the equations in Table 4 to marked expressions does not lead out of their syntax, which can be shown by structural induction.

Table 4. Equations for marked expressions (E, F, G are Box expressions; D, H are marked expressions)

Operator	*Equation(s)*	
Sequence	$E; \underline{F} \equiv \underline{E; F}$	ES1
	$\underline{E}; F \equiv E; \overline{F}$	ES2
	$\overline{E; F} \equiv \overline{E}; F$	ES3
Choice	$E \Box \underline{F} \equiv \underline{E \Box F}$	EC1
	$\overline{E \Box F} \equiv E \Box \overline{F}$	EC2
	$\underline{E} \Box F \equiv \underline{E \Box F}$	EC3
	$\overline{E \Box F} \equiv \overline{E} \Box F$	EC4
Concurrent composition	$\underline{E} \Vert \underline{F} \equiv \underline{E \Vert F}$	ECC1
	$\overline{E \Vert F} \equiv \overline{E} \Vert \overline{F}$	ECC2
Iteration	$[E * F * \underline{G}] \equiv \underline{[E * F * G]}$	EI1
	$[\underline{E} * F * G] \equiv [E * \overline{F} * G]$ $\equiv [E * \underline{F} * G]$ $\equiv [E * F * \overline{G}]$	EI2
	$\overline{[E * F * G]} \equiv [\overline{E} * F * G]$	EI3
Scoping	$[a : \underline{E}] \equiv \underline{[a : E]}$	ESc1
	$\overline{[a : E]} \equiv [a : \overline{E}]$	ESc2
Recursion	$\overline{\mu X.E} \equiv \overline{E[X \leftarrow \mu X.E]}$	ER

There is a subtle point concerning the use of the expansion equation for recursion, ER. One might think of replacing it by $\mu X.E \equiv E[X \leftarrow \mu X.E]$ (without overbars), which corresponds to a structural identity in the Box model. However, this would be inconsistent with the usual treatment of recursion in other process algebras[8] and, furthermore, allowing $\mu X.E \equiv E[X \leftarrow \mu X.E]$ would yield too many identifications. For instance, we would have

$$\overline{\mu X.(a; X)} \equiv \overline{a; \mu X.(a; X)} \equiv \overline{a; a; \mu X.(a; X)}$$

[8] Recursion is not unfolded unnecessarily; e.g. in CCS $\mu X.a.X \xrightarrow{a} a.a.a.a.\mu X.a.X$ is not allowed.

while only the first equivalence, but not the second, may be derived from ER. As it stands, the equivalence classes of $\equiv$ are finite, provided that recursion is guarded [19]. An unguarded recursion may lead to an infinite equivalence class:

$$\overline{\mu X.(a \,\square\, X)} \equiv \overline{a \,\square\, \mu X.(a \,\square\, X)} \equiv a \,\square\, \overline{\mu X.(a \,\square\, X)} \equiv \cdots$$

One may wonder why all equations except ER are symmetric with respect to overbarring and underbarring. The reason is simplicity. A symmetric version of ER would do no harm; it is just unnecessary. The set of equations in Table 4 is minimal in a sense which will be made precise at the end of Section 5.

The following result clarifies the relationship between the equivalences on marked expressions: structural (defined by Table 4) and that induced by the *Box*(.) mapping.

Proposition 1 [19]. *If $D \equiv H$ then $Box(D) = Box(H)$. Moreover, if $H = \overline{\lfloor D \rfloor}$ and $Box(D) = Box(H)$ then $D \equiv H$.* □

Note that $Box(D) = Box(H)$ and $\lfloor D \rfloor = \lfloor H \rfloor$ does not, in general, imply $D \equiv H$.

4 Generating Step Sequences

The model of Boxes separates concurrent composition (basically a disjoint union) from synchronisation. This could lead to a formal overhead if a single action interleaving semantics of marked expressions was to be defined. Originally for this reason, we have decided to work directly with an operational semantics for step sequences. The decision has been rewarding, because it led to the development of simpler rules (in particular, that for scoping).

Let D and H be two marked expressions and γ be a finite non-empty multiset of communication labels. By means of inference rules, we shall define a relation

$$D \xrightarrow{\gamma} H$$

which is informally intended to mean: 'D may execute the step γ and become H'. The general form of γ is $\gamma = \{\alpha_1, \ldots, \alpha_k\}$, where each α_j $(1 \leq j \leq k)$ is a communication label. Informally, γ denotes a concurrently enabled multiset of such communication labels or, in Petri net terminology, a 'step' of the Box underlying D and H. For example, $\underline{(\overline{a}; b)} \,\square\, c$ enables the step $\gamma = \{\{a\}\}$ which contains a single action, and $(\overline{\{a,d\}}; b) \| \overline{\{c,c\}}$ enables $\gamma = \{\{a,d\},\{c,c\}\}$. The Box associated to the latter contains two concurrently enabled transitions, one labelled by $\{a,d\}$ and the other labelled by $\{c,c\}$.

Table 5 shows a set of inference rules (and a single axiom, RB) that match the operators of the syntax. Note that our operational semantics is split into a behavioural part, viz. the basic and scoping rules, and a structural part, viz. the contextual rules.

In the rule RSc for scoping, we use the following notation: A finite non-empty multiset of communication labels $\gamma_i = \{\alpha_1, \ldots, \alpha_k\}$, where $1 \leq i \leq m$, is

Table 5. Inference rules for marked expressions (E, F, G are Box expressions; D, H are marked expressions; γ, δ, γ_i are finite non-empty multisets of communication labels; syn_a is defined in the text)

Operator	*Inference rule(s)*	
Basic action	$\overline{\alpha} \xrightarrow{\{\alpha\}} \underline{\alpha}$	RB
Sequence	$\dfrac{D \xrightarrow{\gamma} H}{D; E \xrightarrow{\gamma} H; E}$	RS1
	$\dfrac{D \xrightarrow{\gamma} H}{E; D \xrightarrow{\gamma} E; H}$	RS2
Choice	$\dfrac{D \xrightarrow{\gamma} H}{D \,\square\, E \xrightarrow{\gamma} H \,\square\, E}$	RC1
	$\dfrac{D \xrightarrow{\gamma} H}{E \,\square\, D \xrightarrow{\gamma} E \,\square\, H}$	RC2
Concurrent composition	$\dfrac{D \xrightarrow{\gamma} D' ,\ H \xrightarrow{\delta} H'}{D \Vert H \xrightarrow{\gamma+\delta} D' \Vert H'}$	RCC1
	$\dfrac{D \xrightarrow{\gamma} D'}{D \Vert H \xrightarrow{\gamma} D' \Vert H}$	RCC2
	$\dfrac{H \xrightarrow{\gamma} H'}{D \Vert H \xrightarrow{\gamma} D \Vert H'}$	RCC3
Iteration	$\dfrac{D \xrightarrow{\gamma} H}{[D * F * G] \xrightarrow{\gamma} [H * F * G]}$	RI1
	$\dfrac{D \xrightarrow{\gamma} H}{[E * D * G] \xrightarrow{\gamma} [E * H * G]}$	RI2
	$\dfrac{D \xrightarrow{\gamma} H}{[E * F * D] \xrightarrow{\gamma} [E * F * H]}$	RI3
Scoping	$\dfrac{D \xrightarrow{\gamma_1 + \cdots + \gamma_m} H ,\ \gamma_1, \ldots, \gamma_m \in syn_a}{[a : D] \xrightarrow{\{\gamma_1 \ominus a, \ldots, \gamma_m \ominus a\}} [a : H]}$	RSc

defined to belong to syn_a if it determines a step of transitions that can survive the scoping on a, and yield a transition of $[a : D]$. For this to be the case, the number of a's must balance the number of $\widehat{a}$'s, because otherwise there would still be something to be removed by the implicit restriction operator, and also due to the underlying multiway synchronisation the number of the $(a, \widehat{a})$ pairs must be equal to $k - 1$. Therefore, either both numbers are zero, in which case $k = 1$ and γ contains a single transition of the body D which involves neither a nor $\widehat{a}$ (and therefore survives restriction); or $k \geq 2$ and both numbers are nonzero and equal to $k - 1$; then each transition α_j contains at least one a or $\widehat{a}$, and the α_j's can be synchronised to yield a single transition of $[a : D]$. Formally, $\gamma_i = \{\alpha_1, \ldots, \alpha_k\} \in syn_a$ if the balancing condition

$$\sum_{j=1}^{k} \alpha_j(a) = \sum_{j=1}^{k} \alpha_j(\widehat{a}) = k - 1$$

holds[9] and, furthermore, if $k \geq 2$ then, for all j, $\alpha_j(a) + \alpha_j(\widehat{a}) \geq 1$. Moreover,

$$\gamma_i \ominus a = (\alpha_1 + \cdots + \alpha_k) \setminus (k - 1) \cdot \{a, \widehat{a}\}$$

is used to denote the label of the resulting synchronisation transition. For the example E_2 in Section 2, $k = 3$, $m = 1$ and $\gamma_1 = \{\{a, b\}, \{\widehat{a}, \widehat{a}\}, \{a, c\}\}$. Such a γ_1 belongs to syn_a since there are two each of a and $\widehat{a}$, and each communication label contains a least one of them. Moreover,

$$\gamma_1 \ominus a = (\{a, b\} + \{\widehat{a}, \widehat{a}\} + \{a, c\}) \setminus 2 \cdot \{a, \widehat{a}\} = \{b, c\}.$$

The rule RSc assumes that D can execute a multiset of transitions which can be partitioned onto a number of γ_i's which can survive scoping, as described above. Since after scoping each γ_i gives rise to a transition $\gamma_i \ominus a$, the resulting step $\{\gamma_1 \ominus a, \ldots, \gamma_m \ominus a\}$ can be executed by $[a : D]$.

One can show, by structural induction, that applying the rules in Table 5 to marked expressions does not lead out of the syntax. In a similar way, one may show that if $D \xrightarrow{\gamma} H$ then $\lfloor D \rfloor = \lfloor H \rfloor$. Note that the rule for scoping does not affect steps which do not contain any $a, \widehat{a}$ – labels. Indeed, if $D \xrightarrow{\gamma} H$, where $\gamma = \{\alpha_1, \ldots, \alpha_k\}$ and $\alpha_i(a) + \alpha_i(\widehat{a}) = 0$, for all i, then by setting $\gamma_i = \{\alpha_i\}$ for $i = 1, \ldots, k$, we obtain: $\gamma_i \in syn_a$ for all i, and $[a : D] \xrightarrow{\gamma} [a : H]$.

4.1 Examples

We show derivations for expressions from Table 2 based on the inference rules and equations in Tables 4 and 5, indicating which inference rules and equations

---

[9] $\alpha_j(a)$ denotes the multiplicity of the a in α_j.

have been applied. We first deduce that $\overline{E_1} = \overline{(a;b)\,\Box\, c}$ can make an a-move followed by a b-move:

$$
\begin{array}{rcll}
\overline{E_1} & \equiv & \overline{(a;b)}\,\Box\, c & \text{EC4} \\
 & \equiv & (\overline{a};b)\,\Box\, c & \text{ES3} \\
 & \xrightarrow{\{\{a\}\}} & (\underline{a};b)\,\Box\, c & \text{RB RS1 RC1} \\
 & \equiv & (a;\overline{b})\,\Box\, c & \text{ES2} \\
 & \xrightarrow{\{\{b\}\}} & (a;\underline{b})\,\Box\, c & \text{RB RS2 RC1} \\
 & \equiv & \underline{(a;b)}\,\Box\, c & \text{ES1} \\
 & \equiv & \underline{(a;b)\,\Box\, c} & \text{EC3}
\end{array}
$$

By applying the rule for scoping, we show that $\overline{E_2}$ can do a $\{b,c\}$-move:

$$
\begin{array}{rcl}
\overline{E_2} & \equiv & [a : \overline{(\{a,b\} \| \{\widehat{a},\widehat{a}\}) \| \{a,c\}}]\ \text{ESc2} \\
 & \equiv & [a : (\overline{\{a,b\}} \| \overline{\{\widehat{a},\widehat{a}\}}) \| \overline{\{a,c\}}]\ \text{ECC1}(\times 2) \\
 & \xrightarrow{\{\{b,c\}\}} & [a : (\underline{\{a,b\}} \| \underline{\{\widehat{a},\widehat{a}\}}) \| \underline{\{a,c\}}]\ \text{RB}(\times 3)\ \text{RCC1}(\times 2)\ \text{RSc}
\end{array}
$$

The third derivation shows that $\overline{E_3}$ can make an a-move and a b-move.

$$
\begin{array}{rcll}
\overline{E_3} & \equiv & \overline{(a;E_3)\,\Box\, b} & \text{ER} \\
 & \equiv & (\overline{a};E_3)\,\Box\, b & \text{EC4 ES3} \\
 & \xrightarrow{\{\{a\}\}} & (\underline{a};E_3)\,\Box\, b & \text{RB RS1 RC1} \\
 & \equiv & (a;((a;E_3)\,\Box\,\overline{b}))\,\Box\, b & \text{ES2 ER EC2} \\
 & \xrightarrow{\{\{b\}\}} & (a;((a;E_3)\,\Box\,\underline{b}))\,\Box\, b & \text{RB RC2 RS2 RC1} \\
 & \equiv & \underline{(a;((a;E_3)\,\Box\, b))\,\Box\, b} & \text{EC1 ES1 EC3}
\end{array}
$$

The last expression in this derivation is final in the sense that it has the form of an underbarred Box expression. As it stands, there is no equation that would allow this last expression to be folded back to $\underline{E_3}$. Had we also included a symmetric counterpart of ER, then we would have been in a position to do this. We also note that $\overline{E_3}$ can make an infinite sequence of a-moves since

$$\overline{E_3} \equiv (\overline{a};E_3)\,\Box\, b \xrightarrow{\{\{a\}\}} (\underline{a};E_3)\,\Box\, b \equiv (a;\overline{E_3})\,\Box\, b.$$

The next example is similar to that discussed in [1] and shows a non-tail-end recursive expression not directly expressible in CCS. It shows that the marked expression $\overline{E_4}$ can make two successive a-moves. By induction, it can be shown that $\overline{E_4}$ can make an arbitrary number of successive a-moves. But the argument cannot be used to show that it can do an infinite sequence of a-moves; in fact it cannot. This may be contrasted with the previous example.

$$\begin{array}{rcll}
\overline{E_4} & \equiv & \overline{(E_4;a)\,\Box\, a} & \text{ER} \\
 & \equiv & (\overline{E_4};a)\,\Box\, a & \text{EC4 ES3} \\
 & \equiv & (((E_4;a)\,\Box\,\overline{a});a)\,\Box\, a & \text{ER EC2} \\
 & \xrightarrow{\{\{a\}\}} & (((E_4;a)\,\Box\,\underline{a});a)\,\Box\, a & \text{RB RC2 RS1 RC1} \\
 & \equiv & (((E_4;a)\,\Box\, a);\overline{a})\,\Box\, a & \text{EC1 ES2} \\
 & \xrightarrow{\{\{a\}\}} & (((E_4;a)\,\Box\, a);\underline{a})\,\Box\, a & \text{RB RS2 RC1} \\
 & \equiv & \underline{(((E_4;a)\,\Box\, a);a)\,\Box\, a} & \text{ES1 EC3}
\end{array}$$

As the next example, one can prove by induction that $\overline{E_5}$ can do a γ_n-move, for every $n \geq 1$, where $\gamma_n = n \cdot \{\{a\}\}$. We only show the inductive step: Suppose that $\overline{E_5} \equiv D$ and $D \xrightarrow{\gamma_n} H$. Then

$$\begin{array}{rcll}
\overline{E_5} & \equiv & \overline{a\|\mu X.(a\|X)} & \text{ER} \\
 & \equiv & \overline{a}\|D & \text{ECC2 Ind.Hyp.} \\
 & \xrightarrow{\{\{a\}\}+\gamma_n} & \underline{a}\|H & \text{RB Ind.Hyp. RCC1}
\end{array}$$

The last example shows the way iteration is dealt with.

$$\begin{array}{rcll}
\overline{E_6} & \equiv & [\overline{a}\,\Box\, b * c * d] & \text{EI3 EC4} \\
 & \xrightarrow{\{\{a\}\}} & [\underline{a}\,\Box\, b * c * d] & \text{RB RC1 RI1} \\
 & \equiv & [a\,\Box\, b * \overline{c} * d] & \text{EC3 EI2} \\
 & \xrightarrow{\{\{c\}\}} & [a\,\Box\, b * \underline{c} * d] & \text{RB RI2} \\
 & \equiv & [a\,\Box\, b * \overline{c} * d] & \text{EI2} \\
 & \xrightarrow{\{\{c\}\}} & [a\,\Box\, b * \underline{c} * d] & \text{RB RI2} \\
 & \equiv & [a\,\Box\, b * c * \overline{d}] & \text{EI2} \\
 & \xrightarrow{\{\{d\}\}} & [a\,\Box\, b * c * \underline{d}] & \text{RB RI3} \\
 & \equiv & \underline{E_6} & \text{EI3}
\end{array}$$

5 The main results

We now discuss the relationship between the operational semantics of marked expressions and the Petri net semantics of the corresponding Boxes, aiming at establishing a close correspondence between these two semantic models. It should be noted that we do not place any restrictions (such as guardedness) on the expressions involved.

Let $\mathcal{B}$ and $\mathcal{B}'$ be two marked Boxes, and let $\gamma = \{\alpha_1, \ldots, \alpha_n\}$ be a non-empty multiset of communication labels. We will denote

$$\mathcal{B} \xrightarrow{\gamma} \mathcal{B}'$$

if there is a set of concurrently enabled transitions (a step) $\{t_1, \ldots, t_n\}$ in $\mathcal{B}$, whose occurrence[10] leads to $\mathcal{B}'$, and whose labels are respectively $\alpha_1, \ldots, \alpha_n$. (In particular, the unmarked nets underlying $\mathcal{B}$ and $\mathcal{B}'$ are equal.)

[10] According to the step occurrence rule of Petri nets [25].

Theorem 2 (Consistency of the inference rules). *Let D and H be marked expressions. If $D \xrightarrow{\gamma} H$ then $Box(D) \xrightarrow{\gamma} Box(H)$.* □

Together with Proposition 1, this ensures the consistency of the operational semantics for marked expressions, based on structural equations and inference rules, with the standard step sequence Petri net semantics of marked Boxes. Theorem 2 can be proved by a rather straightforward induction on the structure of the expression D. The proof of completeness is more involved. We cannot obtain a result of the form '$Box(D) \xrightarrow{\gamma} Box(J)$ implies $D \xrightarrow{\gamma} J$', because on the expression level, before the step γ can be made, the D may need to be first subjected to a $\equiv$ – transformation.

Theorem 3 (Completeness of the inference rules). *Let D be a marked expression and $Box(D) \xrightarrow{\gamma} \mathcal{B}$. Then there are marked expressions H and J such that $Box(J) = \mathcal{B}$ and $D \equiv H \xrightarrow{\gamma} J$.* □

This theorem has a nontrivial proof; in particular, if D involves an unguardedly recursive expression. The proof (and all others) can be found in [19]. The two theorems establish a step sequence based bisimulation between marked expressions and the corresponding marked Boxes.

Remark. Leaving out any of the equations in Table 4 would render the last theorem false. Thus we have chosen a minimal set of structural equations which ensure a full consistency between the operational and Petri net semantics of marked expressions.

6 Concluding Remarks

The approach presented in this paper is related to other existing studies on the relationship between algebraic and net-theoretic models of concurrency. Petri nets have been used to provide a non-interleaving semantics for languages based on CCS or TCSP in, for example, [7, 8, 9, 10, 12, 13, 14, 26, 29, 30]. In general, all these papers were taking as a starting point a CCS-like notation with its standard interleaving semantics and then provided a translation of algebraic terms into Petri nets so that the standard interleaving (or a postulated non-interleaving) semantics of terms and the standard Petri net semantics of corresponding nets would match. Our situation in this respect was rather different as we started from both the language (Box expressions) and its denotational semantics (Petri Boxes obtained via the $Box(.)$ mapping) and had to find an operational semantics of the former consistent with the net semantics of the latter.

We do not provide here a detailed account of the various approaches proposed in the literature over the past decade; the interested reader is referred to, e.g., [7, 9]. Instead, we will mention the relationship between our work and that due to Boudol and Castellani, and Degano, De Nicola and Montanari. Boudol and Castellani [7] treat only finite (recursion-free) terms and use so-called 'marked terms' which resemble our marked expression. The feature they share is that as an expression evolves, its structure does not change. In the case of marked terms, the execution of an action marks that action within the expression as 'used'. This should be contrasted with the way marked expressions are defined here, as there the only information which is kept after the execution of an action is the resulting marking. Another important issue is the treatment of recursion in [9], where recursion is performed by 'eager' unfolding which, in the same way as ER, removes the need for a separate inference rule for recursion.

This paper shows a (bisimulation-like) consistency between the operational (SOS rules and equations) and denotational (Petri Box) semantics in terms of step sequences of an algebraic notation given by the Box model. This result and the fact that we do not place any restrictions on recursion (such as guardedness) compares favourably with the results obtained by others. The algebra of processes we use is richer than those usually treated elsewhere. In particular, by having an explicit iteration operator we can specify and deal smoothly with a class of infinite processes without having to resort to a general recursion. By using over- and underbarring we can define a simple rule for iteration, whereas this can cause problems in the usual treatment of iteration [21] where one 'unwinds' iteration each time it is (re)entered:

$$(a; b; c)^* \xrightarrow{a} b; c; (a; b; c)^*.$$

It is also worth noting that over- and underbarring render unnecessary the **skip** process in the treatment of the sequential composition. Finally, a partial order operational semantics of Box expressions is described in [20], but the completeness result obtained there holds only for processes involving guarded recursion.

Acknowledgements

We would like to thank Raymond Devillers for his detailed comments on the earlier versions of this paper. It is also a pleasure to acknowledge many fruitful discussions with other DEMON and CALIBAN members, and the useful comments made by the referees.

References

1. J.C.M.Baeten and W.P.Weijland: Process Algebra. Cambridge Tracts in Theoretical Computer Science (1990).
2. E.Best, R.Devillers and J.Esparza: General Refinement and Recursion Operators in the Box Calculus. Proc. of STACS-93, Springer-Verlag Lecture Notes in Computer Science Vol. 665, 130-140 (1993).
3. E.Best, R.Devillers and J.Hall: The Petri Box Calculus: a New Causal Algebra with Multilabel Communication. Advances in Petri Nets (ed. G.Rozenberg), Springer-Verlag Lecture Notes in Computer Science Vol.609, 21-69 (1992).
4. E.Best and R.P.Hopkins: $B(PN)^2$ – a Basic Petri Net Programming Notation. Proc. of PARLE-93, Springer-Verlag Lecture Notes in Computer Science Vol. 694, 379-390 (1993).

5. E.Best and H.G.Linde-Göers: Compositional Process Semantics of Petri Boxes. Proc. of MFPS (Mathematical Foundations of Programming Semantics), Springer-Verlag Lecture Notes in Computer Science (1993).
6. G.Boudol: Notes on Algebraic Calculi of Processes. In: Logics and Models of Concurrent Systems. K.R.Apt (ed.), 261-304 (1985).
7. G.Boudol and I.Castellani: Flow Models of Distributed Computations: Event Structures and Nets. Rapport de Recherche, INRIA, Sophia Antipolis (July 1991).
8. F.De Cindio, G.De Michelis, L.Pomello and C.Simone. Milner's Communicating Systems and Petri Nets. In: Selected Papers of 3rd European Workshop on Applications and Theory of Petri Nets, IF 66 (Springer-Verlag, Heidelberg), 40-59 (1983).
9. P.Degano, R.De Nicola and U.Montanari: A Distributed Operational Semantics for CCS Based on C/E Systems. Acta Informatica 26 (1988).
10. P.Degano, R.De Nicola and U.Montanari: Partial Order Derivations for CCS. In: Proc. FCT, Lecture Notes in Computer Science Vol.199, Springer Verlag, 520-533 (1985).
11. R. de Simone: Higher-level Synchronising Devices in MEIJE-SCCS. Theoretical Computer Science Vol.37, 245-267 (1985).
12. R.J. van Glabbeek and F.V.Vaandrager: Petri Net Models for Algebraic Theories of Concurrency. Proc. PARLE'87, Lecture Notes in Computer Science Vol.259, Springer Verlag, 224-242 (1987).
13. U.Goltz: On Representing CCS Programs by Finite Petri Nets. Arbeitspapiere der GMD Nr.290 (February 1988).
14. U.Goltz and A.Mycroft: On the Relationships of CCS and Petri Nets. In: J.Paredaens (ed.), Proc. 11th ICALP, Lecture Notes in Computer Science Vol.154, Springer Verlag, 196-208 (1984).
15. J.Hall: General Recursion. DEMON Technical Report, Computing Laboratory, The University of Newcastle upon Tyne (June 1991).
16. J.Hall, R.P.Hopkins and O.Botti: A Petri Box Semantics of occam. Advances in Petri Nets (ed. G.Rozenberg), Springer-Verlag Lecture Notes in Computer Science Vol.609, 179-214 (1992).
17. C.A.R.Hoare: Communicating Sequential Processes. Prentice Hall (1985).
18. R.Janicki and P.E.Lauer: Specification and Analysis of Concurrent Systems: the COSY Approach. Volume 26 in Springer Verlag's Monographs on Theoretical Computer Science Series (1992).
19. M.Koutny, J.Esparza and E.Best: Operational Semantics for the Petri Box Calculus. Hildesheimer Informatik-Berichte 13/93 (October 1993).
20. M.Koutny: Partial Order Semantics of Box Expressions. Proc. of 15th International Conference on Application and Theory of Petri Nets, Lecture Notes in Computer Science, Springer (1994).
21. W.Li and P.E. Lauer: Using the Structural Operational Approach to Express True Concurrency. Technical Report 85-01, Department of Computer Science and Systems, McMaster University (1985).
22. H.G.Linde-Göers: Compositional Branching Processes of Petri Boxes. Ph.D. Thesis, Universität Hildesheim (October 1993).
23. G.J.Milne: CIRCAL and the Representation of Communication, Concurrency and Time. ACM ToPLaS 7/2, 270-298 (April 1985).
24. R.Milner: Communication and Concurrency. Prentice Hall (1989).
25. M.Nielsen and P.S.Thiagarajan: Degrees of Nondeterminism and Concurrency. Proc. of 4th Conf. on Foundations of Software Technology and Theoretical Com-

puter Science, Springer-Verlag Lecture Notes in Computer Science Vol.181 (eds. M.Joseph and R.Shyamasundar), 89-117 (1984).
26. E.R.Olderog: Operational Petri Net Semantics for CCSP. In: G. Rozenberg (ed.), Advances in Petri Nets 1987, Springer-Verlag Lecture Notes in Computer Science, Vol. 266, 196-223 (1987).
27. G.Plotkin: A Structural Approach to Operational Semantics. Report DAIMI FN-19, Århus University, Computer Science Department, Århus, Denmark (1981).
28. Y.-J.Joung and S.A.Smolka: Efficient, Dynamically Structured Multiparty Interaction. Proc. of 28th Annual Allerton Conference on Communication, Control, and Computing (1990).
29. D.Taubner: Finite Representations of CCS and TCSP by Automata and Petri Nets. Lecture Notes in Computer Science, Vol. 369, Springer Verlag (1989).
30. G.Winskel: Petri Nets, Algebras, Morphisms and Compositionality. Info. Control 72, 197-238 (1987).

A Construction of Marked Boxes

A labelled Petri net is a tuple $\Sigma = (S, T, W, \lambda)$ where (S, T, W) is a (possibly infinite) weighted Petri net: S is the set of places, T is the set of transitions, and the connection mapping is given by $W : ((S \times T) \cup (T \times S)) \rightarrow \mathbf{N}$. The labelling mapping λ has the domain $S \cup T$; for each $s \in S$, $\lambda(s) \in \{e, \emptyset, x\}$, and for each $t \in T$, $\lambda(t)$ is a communication label or a variable name. We require that for every transition t there are s and s' such that $W(s,t) > 0$ and $W(t,s') > 0$. We also define ${}^\bullet\Sigma = \{s \in S \mid \lambda(s) = e\}$ and $\Sigma^\bullet = \{s \in S \mid \lambda(s) = x\}$. A marked net is a tuple (S, T, W, λ, M) where $M : S \rightarrow \mathbf{N}$ is a marking.

In [3], a Petri Box is defined as a labelled net $\Sigma = (S, T, W, \lambda)$ such that: (1) ${}^\bullet\Sigma$ and $\Sigma^\bullet$ are non-empty; (2) for every $s \in {}^\bullet\Sigma$, ${}^\bullet s$ is empty, and (3) for every $s \in \Sigma^\bullet$, $s^\bullet$ is empty. We define a *marked Box* to be a marked net $\Sigma = (S, T, W, \lambda, M)$ satisfying (1–3).

The $Box(.)$ mapping for marked expressions is defined compositionally. For example, $Box(\overline{E}) = \overline{Box(E)}$ and $Box(D;E) = Box(D);Box(E)$, where the two operations involving Boxes are defined in the following way.

Let $\Sigma = (S, T, W, \lambda)$ be a Petri Box. Then $\overline{\Sigma} = (S, T, W, \lambda, M_e)$, where M_e is a marking defined by $M_e(s) = 1$ if $s \in {}^\bullet\Sigma$, and $M_e(s) = 0$ otherwise.

Let $\Sigma_1 = (S_1, T_1, W_1, \lambda_1, M_1)$ be a marked Box and $\Sigma_2 = (S_2, T_2, W_2, \lambda_2)$ be a disjoint Petri Box.
Then $\Sigma_1; \Sigma_2 = \Sigma$, where Σ is a marked net satisfying the following (below $S = S_1 \cup S_2 \cup (\Sigma_1^\bullet \times {}^\bullet\Sigma_2) \setminus (\Sigma_1^\bullet \cup {}^\bullet\Sigma_2)$ is the set of places of Σ):

$$\Sigma = (S, T_1 \cup T_2, W_1 \cup W_2 \cup W, \lambda_1 \cup \lambda_2 \cup \lambda, M_1 \cup M).$$

The domains of W_i, λ_i and M_1 are suitably truncated. The λ and M are defined by taking $M(S \cap S_2) = \{\emptyset\}$ and for $s = (s_1, s_2) \in S \setminus (S_1 \cup S_2)$, $\lambda(s) = \emptyset$ and $M(s) = M_1(s_1)$. Finally, $W(t,s)$ is defined by (the $W(s,t)$ is symmetrical):

$$W(t,s) = \begin{cases} W_i(t, s_i) & t \in T_i,\ s = (s_1, s_2) \in S \setminus (S_1 \cup S_2)\ (i = 1, 2) \\ 0 & t \in T_i,\ s \in S \cap (S_1 \cup S_2) \setminus S_i \qquad (i = 1, 2) \end{cases}$$

The other operations on marked Boxes are introduced in [19] a similar way as the corresponding notions defined for Petri Boxes in [2, 3].

B Examples of Petri Boxes

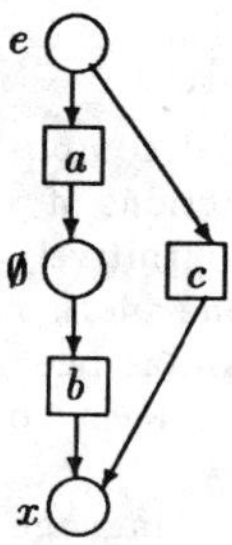

$Box(E_1)$

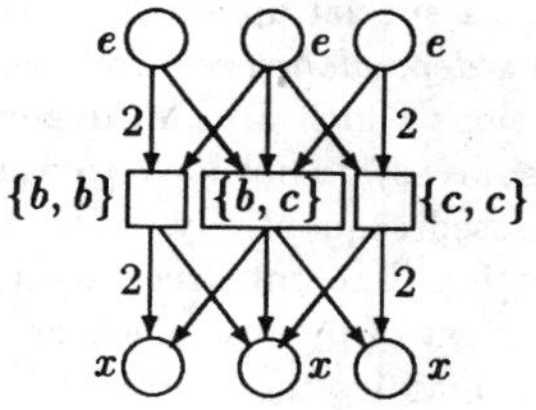

$Box(E_2)$

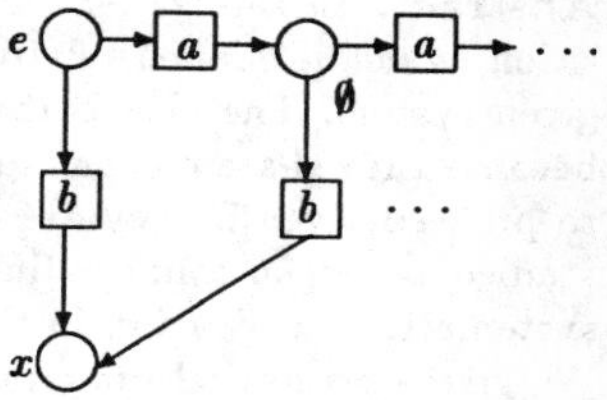

$Box(E_3)$

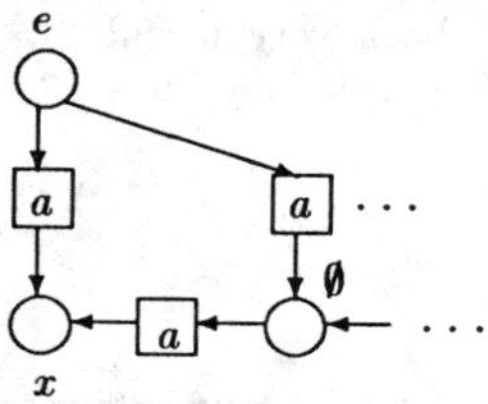

$Box(E_4)$

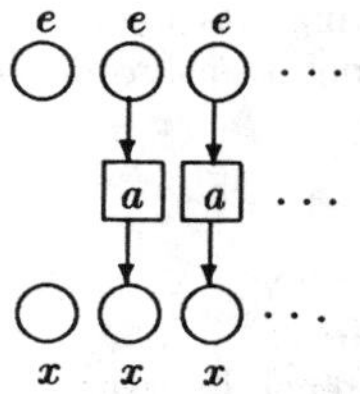

$Box(E_5)$

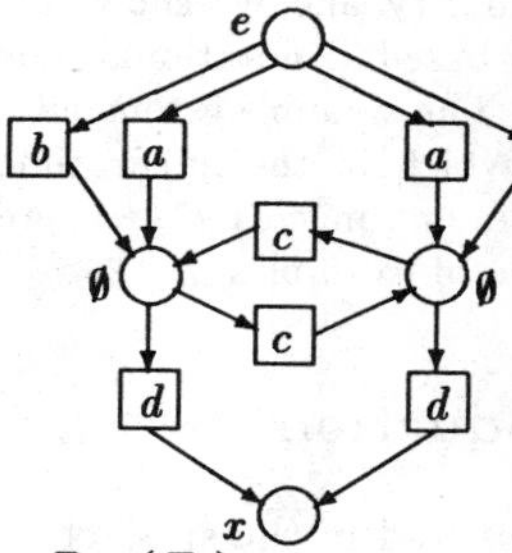

$Box(E_6)$

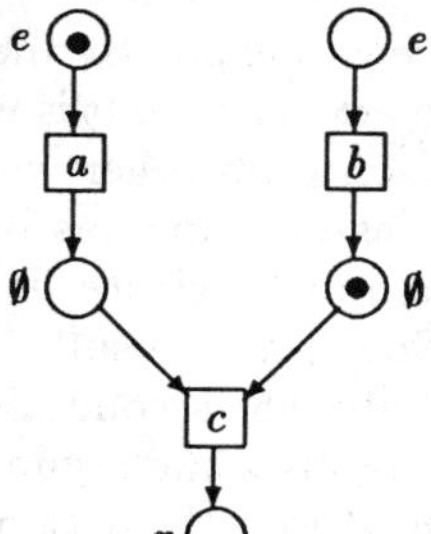

$Box((\overline{a}\|\underline{b});c)$

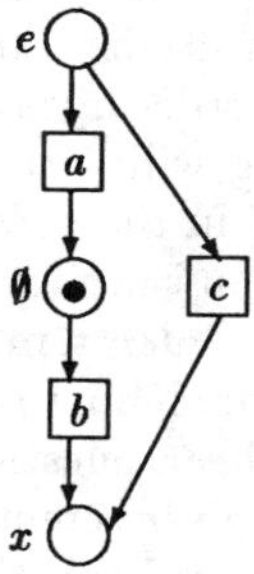

$Box((\underline{a};b)\,\square\,c) = Box((a;\overline{b})\,\square\,c)$

Weak Sequential Composition in Process Algebras

Arend Rensink and Heike Wehrheim*

Institut für Informatik, University of Hildesheim
Postfach 101363, D–31113 Hildesheim, Germany
{rensink,wehrheim}@informatik.uni-hildesheim.de

Abstract. In this paper we study a special operator for sequential composition, which is defined relative to a *dependency relation* over the actions of a given system. The idea is that actions which are *not* dependent (intuitively because they share no common resources) do not have to wait for one another to proceed, even if they are composed sequentially. Such a notion has been studied before in a linear-time setting, but until recently there has been no systematic investigation in the context of process algebras.
We give a structural operational semantics for a process algebraic language containing such a sequential composition operator, which shows some interesting interplay with choice. We give a complete axiomatisation of strong bisimilarity and we show consistency of the operational semantics with an event-based denotational semantics developed recently by the second author. The axiom system allows to derive the *communication closed layers law*, which in the linear time setting has been shown to be a very useful instrument in correctness preserving transformations. We conclude with a couple of examples.

1 Introduction

We are interested in the subject of sequential versus concurrent behaviour in process algebra. In the usual interleaving semantics, two actions that are specified as occurring in parallel will be modelled as occurring in either of the two possible orders; the parallelism is deemed unobservable and hence not explicitly modelled. On the other hand, if an ordering is specified between two actions then it is usually assumed that this ordering will actually be realised in practice, in other words the actions will indeed occur in the specified order. The first assumption has been the subject of much debate, and in fact a whole branch of computer science dealing with non-standard, *partial order* semantics has been developed as a result of dropping this assumption and modelling parallelism more faithfully. The second assumption, however, has hardly been questioned. Yet there are actually some arguments against it. If one postulates an inherent notion of *dependency* among the actions performed by a system, then one can imagine that only *dependent* actions will actually be executed in the specified order, whereas *independent* actions can be performed in either order even if they are actually composed in sequence. For instance, in compiler optimisation, if neither of two sequentially composed assignment statements depends on

* Research partially supported by the HCM Cooperation Network "EXPRESS" (Expressiveness of Languages for Concurrency), the Esprit Basic Research Working Group 6067 (CALIBAN) and a Graduiertenförderungsstipendium of the University of Hildesheim

the other then a compiler is free to reorder them. There is a similar connection to *serialisability* in data bases.

The idea of a dependency relation over the actions of a system can already be found in *trace theory* as developed by Mazurkiewicz [14]. Zwiers et al. have also exploited this idea in [13, 21, 10]. In both cases however, the models used are *linear-time*, which is to say that the points in time at which choices are made are not represented in the model. We aim at extending this idea to branching-time semantics, in particular to strong bisimulation. In this effort we are guided by an existing partial-order denotational model developed by one of the authors (Wehrheim [20]). Other partial-order models in which an explicit notion of (in)dependency plays a role are e.g. Shields, [17], Bednarczyk [5], Stark [18], but there dependency is defined on the level of *events*, i.e., *occurrences* of actions, rather than actions themselves. The resulting concept is much more concrete than the one we present here.

We postulate a dependency relation over the actions and develop an operational semantics (Section 2) based on a *weak* notion of sequential composition, which takes dependency into account. The resulting semantics has some surprising features. In particular, the occurrence of an action may resolve choices that are in some sense in the "future" of the system. In Section 3, our semantics is shown to adhere to a well-studied format for SOS rules, the so-called *GSOS format* (cf. [7]). As a consequence we can apply existing (meta-level) theory to derive that strong bisimilarity is a congruence. We also develop a complete axiomatisation for bisimilarity. In Section 4, we show consistency of our operational semantics with the partial-order denotational semantics of [20] mentioned above. (Historically we *started out* with the denotational model, and the operational semantics was developed as a justification of it.) Most of the features that give rise to complications in the operational semantics are completely natural in the denotational model. In Section 5 we discuss some examples where the notion of weak sequential composition is used to good advantage. Among others, we recapture the *communication closed layers law* advocated in the work of Zwiers et al., extended to take synchronisation into account. Finally, Section 6 contains some concluding remarks.

For lack of space, all proofs have been omitted.

2 Language and Operational Semantics

We assume a global set of actions *Act* with a reflexive and symmetric relation $D \subseteq Act \times Act$ called *dependency*. The inverse notion of *independency* is defined by $a\ I\ b$ iff $\neg(a\ D\ b)$. The *dependency class* of a given action is denoted $[a]_D := \{\, b \mid b\ D\ a \,\}$, extended to $[A]_D := \bigcup_{a \in A}[a]_D$; similarly $[a]_I := \{\, b \mid b\ I\ a \,\}$ and $[A]_I := \bigcap_{a \in A}[a]_I$. The language **L** studied in this paper is generated by the following grammar:

$$B ::= \mathbf{0}_P \mid a \mid B + B \mid B \cdot B \mid B \parallel_A B$$

where $a \in Act$ and $P, A \subseteq Act$. We will also use the *alphabet* $\alpha(B)$ of a term B, recursively defined as follows:

$$\begin{aligned} \alpha(\mathbf{0}_P) &:= \varnothing \\ \alpha(a) &:= \{a\} \quad \text{where } a \in Act \\ \alpha(B * C) &:= \alpha(B) \cup \alpha(C) \quad \text{where } * \in \{+, \cdot, \parallel_A\} \end{aligned}$$

The operators of **L** have been taken from existing languages (CCS [15], CSP [12], ACP [4]) but some of them will get a non-standard interpretation. The basic new idea is the effect of dependency on sequential composition: in our semantics, independent actions never have to wait for one another to proceed even if they are sequentially composed. Actions from the second operand C of a term $B \cdot C$ are able to "overtake" B if they are independent of B. We will call such actions *permissible according to* B. Even if B is "deadlocked" in the sense of not being able to perform any action itself, it may still permit actions of C. Note that if all actions are dependent, our notion of sequential composition reduces to the standard one. The index P in the deadlock constants $\mathbf{0}_P$ explicitly represents the permissible actions, i.e. the actions for which $\mathbf{0}_P$ acts like successful termination rather than proper deadlock. We use auxiliary notations $\mathbf{0} = \mathbf{0}_\varnothing$ (no actions are permitted; complete deadlock) and $\mathbf{1} = \mathbf{0}_{Act}$ (all actions are permitted; complete termination).

As regards the rest of the language: the term a executes a and then terminates successfully. $B + C$ denotes the *choice* between B and C, which can not only be resolved in the usual way, by the first action of B or C, but also by actions of processes that (sequentially) follow the choice. For instance, if $a\ D\ c$ and $a\ I\ b$ then $(a+b) \cdot c$ denotes a process that either executes a or b and afterwards c (as usual) or can start with c after which the choice between a and b is resolved and only b is left to be performed. The family of operators $\{\|_A\}_{A \subseteq Act}$ stand for TCSP-like *parallel composition* with synchronisation on actions of A, with the additional requirement (important in the partial order semantics) that dependent actions of parallel components have to be executed in a nondeterministically chosen order rather than (truly) concurrently.

We now formalise these intuitions operationally. First consider sequential composition. Examples of operational rules for normal sequential composition are the following from Baeten and Weijland [4] (for a detailed discussion see [3]):

$$\frac{B \xrightarrow{a} B'}{B \cdot C \xrightarrow{a} B' \cdot C} \qquad \frac{B \xrightarrow{a} \surd}{B \cdot C \xrightarrow{a} C}$$

where $B \xrightarrow{a} \surd$ denotes that B can terminate successfully by executing a. The rules state that either B has not terminated yet, in which case the sequential composition can only execute actions of B, or B terminates and afterwards C starts. In contrast to this, our weak sequential composition allows execution of actions of C if these actions are independent of B. In a first attempt to capture this operationally, instead of the second rule above we propose

$$\frac{C \xrightarrow{a} C' \quad a \in [\alpha(B)]_I}{B \cdot C \xrightarrow{a} B \cdot C'}$$

This works satisfactorily with terms like $a \cdot b$ where $a\ I\ b$: we can derive $a \cdot b \xrightarrow{b} a \cdot \mathbf{1}$. However if $a\ D\ c$ and $b\ I\ c$ then $c \in [\alpha(a+b)]_D$, hence the above rule would not allow to derive the desired transition $(a+b) \cdot c \xrightarrow{c} b$. We see that the effect of dependencies is more subtle than allowed for by the above rule. In particular, the first operand may actually change as a consequence of "permitting" actions. To capture this effect we define a transition-like *permission* relation $B \overset{a}{\cdots\rightarrow} B'$, expressing that B permits a and changes into B'. The rules for this relation are given in Table 1.

Table 1. Permission relation

action	$\dfrac{a\ I\ b}{b \overset{a}{\dashrightarrow} b}$	deadlock	$\dfrac{a \in P}{0_P \overset{a}{\dashrightarrow} 0_P}$
choice	$\dfrac{B \overset{a}{\dashrightarrow} B' \quad C \overset{a}{\not\dashrightarrow}}{B+C \overset{a}{\dashrightarrow} B'}$	$\dfrac{C \overset{a}{\dashrightarrow} C' \quad B \overset{a}{\not\dashrightarrow}}{B+C \overset{a}{\dashrightarrow} C'}$	$\dfrac{B \overset{a}{\dashrightarrow} B' \quad C \overset{a}{\dashrightarrow} C'}{B+C \overset{a}{\dashrightarrow} B'+C'}$
sequential composition	$\dfrac{B \overset{a}{\dashrightarrow} B' \quad C \overset{a}{\dashrightarrow} C'}{B \cdot C \overset{a}{\dashrightarrow} B' \cdot C'}$	parallel composition	$\dfrac{B \overset{a}{\dashrightarrow} B' \quad C \overset{a}{\dashrightarrow} C'}{B \parallel_A C \overset{a}{\dashrightarrow} B' \parallel_A C'}$

The most interesting permission rules are those for choice: if only one of the operands permits an action a then the choice can thereby be resolved. The sequential and parallel composition of processes only permit actions if both components do. The following property reflects some of the intuitions behind the permission relation:

Proposition 1. $B \overset{a}{\dashrightarrow} B' \Rightarrow a \in [\alpha(B')]_I$.

Ordinary transitions are defined in Table 2. Note especially the second rule of sequential composition, which states that $B \cdot C$ can execute actions from C if they are permitted by B. It is now straightforward to derive the transition $(a+b)\cdot c \xrightarrow{c} b \cdot \mathbf{1}$ discussed above (where $a\ D\ c\ I\ b$). We define *transition-permission systems* as the natural extension of labelled transition systems to our setting.

Table 2. Transition relation

action	$\dfrac{}{a \xrightarrow{a} \mathbf{1}}$	choice: $\dfrac{B \xrightarrow{a} B'}{B+C \xrightarrow{a} B'}$	$\dfrac{C \xrightarrow{a} B'}{B+C \xrightarrow{a} B'}$
sequential composition	$\dfrac{B \xrightarrow{a} B'}{B \cdot C \xrightarrow{a} B' \cdot C}$	$\dfrac{B \overset{a}{\dashrightarrow} B' \quad C \xrightarrow{a} C'}{B \cdot C \xrightarrow{a} B' \cdot C'}$	
parallel composition	$\dfrac{B \xrightarrow{a} B' \quad a \notin A}{B \parallel_A C \xrightarrow{a} B' \parallel_A C}$	$\dfrac{C \xrightarrow{a} C' \quad a \notin A}{B \parallel_A C \xrightarrow{a} B \parallel_A C'}$	$\dfrac{B \xrightarrow{a} B' \ C \xrightarrow{a} C' \ a \in A}{B \parallel_A C \xrightarrow{a} B' \parallel_A C'}$

Definition 2 (transition-permission system). For a term $B \in \mathbf{L}$, the *transition-permission system* of B, $tps(B)$, is defined by $\langle Act, \mathbf{L}, \rightarrow, \dashrightarrow, B\rangle$.

3 Axiomatisation of Bisimilarity

To interpret the operational semantics we define an equivalence relation over tps's. Two terms are then regarded to describe the same behaviour if the tps's generated by the operational semantics are equivalent. The equivalence relation we choose for this purpose is the standard (strong) *bisimilarity*.

Definition 3 (bisimilarity). Let $T_i = \langle Act, S_i, \rightarrow_i, \dashrightarrow_i, q_i\rangle$ be tps's for $i = 1, 2$. A *bisimulation relation* is a binary relation $\rho \subseteq S_1 \times S_2$ such that $q_1\ \rho\ q_2$ and whenever $s_1\ \rho\ s_2$ [resp. $s_2\ \rho\ s_1$] then

1. $s_1 \xrightarrow{a} s_1'$ implies $s_2 \xrightarrow{a} s_2'$ for some $s_2' \rho^{-1} s_1'$ [resp. $s_2' \rho s_1'$];
2. $s_1 \overset{a}{\dashrightarrow} s_1'$ implies $s_2 \overset{a}{\dashrightarrow} s_2'$ for some $s_2' \rho^{-1} s_1'$ [resp. $s_2' \rho s_1'$].

If a bisimulation relation exists, we call T_1 and T_2 *bisimilar*, denoted $T_1 \sim T_2$.

This notion is lifted to terms as usual: $B \sim C$ iff $tps(B) \sim tps(C)$. We establish that bisimilarity is a congruence with respect to the operators of our language. For this purpose, rather than giving a direct proof we derive the result from existing meta-theory. In the past few years we have seen the development of theory relating the *format* of SOS rules to properties of the resulting operational semantics. Typically, the kind of property proved in this way is the congruence of certain equivalence relations with respect to operations defined by the SOS rules; in particular, this is done for strong bisimilarity in the seminal paper by Bloom, Israel and Meyer [7]. In order to apply this general theory, we have to reinterpret permissions $\overset{a}{\dashrightarrow}$ as transitions with special labels, e.g., $\xrightarrow{\hat{a}}$, where for all $a \in Act$, $\hat{a}$ is a new label not in Act. Hence $\xrightarrow{\lambda}$ denotes a "proper" transition if $\lambda \in Act$ and a permission if $\lambda = \hat{a}$ for some $a \in Act$. We state without proof that with this modification, the SOS rules in Tables 1 and 2 all satisfy the GSOS format defined in [7]. Hence the following is a direct consequence of [7, Theorem 5].

Theorem 4 (congruence). $\sim$ *is a congruence over* $\mathbf{L}$.

Now for an axiomatisation of bisimilarity. The unusual behaviour of weak sequential composition forces some modifications to the standard axioms for bisimilarity. For instance, the axiomatisation of ACP [6] contains the rule $(x+y)z = xz + yz$ (where juxtaposition is sequential composition). For weak sequential composition however, this is not valid: for instance, if $a\ I\ c\ I\ b$ then $(a+b)\cdot c \xrightarrow{c} (a+b)\cdot \mathbf{1}$ which can still do both a and b; however, if $a\cdot c + b\cdot c \xrightarrow{c} B$ then either $B = a\cdot\mathbf{1}$ or $B = b\cdot\mathbf{1}$, neither of which can do both a and b. It follows that $(a+b)\cdot c \not\sim a\cdot c + b\cdot c$.

Aceto, Bloom and Vaandrager [1] have developed a general method for deriving complete axiomatisations for strong bisimilarity directly from GSOS rules. Unfortunately, it turns out that this part of the existing SOS meta-theory is not directly applicable to our system in its current form. One problem lies in the fact that although our language can only describe finite behaviour, still in a technical sense it allows infinite computations to be specified: for instance, if $a\ I\ b$ then $b \xrightarrow{\hat{a}} b \xrightarrow{\hat{a}} \cdots$. This means that the technique of [1] fails to induce a normal form. Nevertheless, a complete axiomatisation does exist, as we show below. Unfortunately, to obtain normal forms we need auxiliary operators not in $\mathbf{L}$. In particular, we introduce a new family of *prefix operators* for all $a \in Act$, which we denote by juxtaposition, i.e. aB prefixes B with $a \in Act$. The operational semantics of prefix is given in Table 3. Note in particular the difference between the prefix aB and the sequential composition $a \cdot B$, for instance if $B \xrightarrow{b} B'$ where $a\ I\ b$: the latter then allows $a\cdot B \xrightarrow{b} a \cdot B'$ which cannot be matched by aB.

Apart from prefix, Table 3 defines auxiliary operators needed to axiomatise sequential composition and synchronisation. Unlike prefix, these other auxiliaries appear only temporarily and can always be removed by rewriting. $\Vert\!\!\_{A}$ is the standard *left merge* from ACP, adapted to our notion of synchronisation and extended to deal with permissions. $|_A$ is the relevant version of the *communication merge*. $\bar{\cdot}$ and $\bar{\cdot}$,

Table 3. Operational semantics of auxiliary operators

prefix	$\dfrac{}{aB \xrightarrow{a} B}$	$\dfrac{a\, I\, b \quad B \stackrel{b}{\dashrightarrow} B'}{aB \stackrel{b}{\dashrightarrow} aB'}$
left sequential	$\dfrac{B \xrightarrow{a} B'}{B \mathbin{\underset{\cdot}{-}} C \xrightarrow{a} B' \cdot C}$	$\dfrac{B \stackrel{a}{\dashrightarrow} B' \quad C \stackrel{a}{\dashrightarrow} C'}{B \mathbin{\underset{\cdot}{-}} C \stackrel{a}{\dashrightarrow} B' \mathbin{\underset{\cdot}{-}} C'}$
right sequential	$\dfrac{B \stackrel{a}{\dashrightarrow} B' \quad C \xrightarrow{a} C'}{B \mathbin{\underset{\cdot}{\overset{\shortmid}{-}}} C \xrightarrow{a} B' \cdot C'}$	$\dfrac{B \stackrel{a}{\dashrightarrow} B' \quad C \stackrel{a}{\dashrightarrow} C'}{B \mathbin{\underset{\cdot}{\overset{\shortmid}{-}}} C \stackrel{a}{\dashrightarrow} B' \mathbin{\underset{\cdot}{\overset{\shortmid}{-}}} C'}$
left merge	$\dfrac{B \xrightarrow{a} B' \quad a \notin A}{B \mathbin{\|\!\lfloor}_A C \xrightarrow{a} B' \mathbin{\|}_A C}$	$\dfrac{B \stackrel{a}{\dashrightarrow} B' \quad C \stackrel{a}{\dashrightarrow} C'}{B \mathbin{\|\!\lfloor}_A C \stackrel{a}{\dashrightarrow} B' \mathbin{\|\!\lfloor}_A C'}$
communication merge	$\dfrac{B \xrightarrow{a} B' \quad C \xrightarrow{a} C' \quad a \in A}{B \mathbin{|}_A C \xrightarrow{a} B' \mathbin{\|}_A C'}$	$\dfrac{B \stackrel{a}{\dashrightarrow} B' \quad C \stackrel{a}{\dashrightarrow} C'}{B \mathbin{|}_A C \stackrel{a}{\dashrightarrow} B' \mathbin{|}_A C'}$

called *left sequential* and *right sequential*, serve a similar purpose with respect to sequential composition as left and communication merge with respect to synchronisation: in $B \mathbin{\underset{\cdot}{-}} C$, intuitively the first action comes from B whereas in $B \mathbin{\underset{\cdot}{\overset{\shortmid}{-}}} C$ it should come from C.

The language obtained by extending $\mathbf{L}$ with the above auxiliary operators is denoted $\mathbf{L}^+$. Before we can give the axiomatisation of $\mathbf{L}^+$ we still need some more machinery in the form of functions over $\mathbf{L}^+$. First of all, $\pi\colon \mathbf{L}^+ \to \mathbf{2}^{Act}$ returns the *permissible actions* of a term, intuitively those actions for which a permission relation can be deduced. Second, we define the *residue* of a term after permitting a

Table 4. Permissible actions and residue

$\pi(\mathbf{0}_P) := P$	$res_a(\mathbf{0}_P) := \mathbf{0}_P$
$\pi(a) := [a]_I$	$res_a(b) := b$
$\pi(B+C) := \pi(B) \cup \pi(C)$	$res_a(B+C) := \begin{cases} res_a(B) + res_a(C) & \text{if } a \in \pi(B) \cap \pi(C) \\ res_a(B) & \text{if } a \in \pi(B) \setminus \pi(C) \\ res_a(C) & \text{if } a \in \pi(C) \setminus \pi(B) \end{cases}$
$\pi(B * C) := \pi(B) \cap \pi(C)$	$res_a(B * C) := res_a(B) * res_a(C) \quad (* \in \{\cdot, \mathbin{\underset{\cdot}{-}}, \mathbin{\underset{\cdot}{\overset{\shortmid}{-}}}, \|_A, \mathbin{\|\!\lfloor}_A, \mathbin{|}_A\})$
$\pi(aB) := [a]_I \cap \pi(B)$	$res_a(bB) := b\, res_a(B)$

given action, as a family of functions $res_a\colon \mathbf{L}^+ \to \mathbf{L}^+$ for every $a \in Act$. Intuitively, if a is permitted by B then $res_a(B)$ corresponds to the remainder of B after that permission, i.e., $B \stackrel{a}{\dashrightarrow} res_a(B)$. The residue can unfortunately not be dealt with by adding it as yet another auxiliary operator to $\mathbf{L}^+$, basically because it cannot be captured operationally. The following lemma formalises the intuitions underlying π and res. It is proved by induction on the structure of B.

Lemma 5. *For all* $B \in \mathbf{L}^+$, $B \stackrel{a}{\dashrightarrow} B'$ *if and only if* $a \in \pi(B)$ *and* $B' = res_a(B)$.

Finally, we come to the axiomatisation of $\mathbf{L}^+$. It is given in Table 5.

The equations for choice, C1–4, form an important part of our equational theory, in that over the sublanguage consisting of just deadlock, prefix and choice, all bisimilarities can be proved using these equations only. This is stated in the following theorem, which slightly extends the standard result in that we have a family of

Table 5. Axioms for bisimulation

$x + y = y + x$	C1	$x \parallel_A y = x \mathbin{\lfloor\!\lfloor}_A y + y \mathbin{\lfloor\!\lfloor}_A x + x \mid_A y$	P
$x + (y + z) = (x + y) + z$	C2	$(x + y) \mathbin{\lfloor\!\lfloor}_A z = (x \mathbin{\lfloor\!\lfloor}_A z) + (y \mathbin{\lfloor\!\lfloor}_A z)$	PL1
$x + x = x$	C3	$ax \mathbin{\lfloor\!\lfloor}_{A \setminus \{a\}} y = a(x \parallel_A y)$	PL2
$x + \mathbf{0}_{\pi(x) \cap P} = x$	C4	$ax \mathbin{\lfloor\!\lfloor}_{A \cup \{a\}} y = \mathbf{0}_{\pi(ax) \cap \pi(y)}$	PL3
$a = a\mathbf{1}$	A	$\mathbf{0}_P \mathbin{\lfloor\!\lfloor}_A x = \mathbf{0}_{P \cap \pi(x)}$	PL4
$x \cdot y = x \mathbin{\overset{\cdot\;}{-}} y + x \mathbin{\overset{\;\cdot}{-}} y$	S	$x \mid_A y = y \mid_A x$	PC1
$(x + y) \mathbin{\overset{\cdot\;}{-}} z = (x \mathbin{\overset{\cdot\;}{-}} z) + (y \mathbin{\overset{\cdot\;}{-}} z)$	SL1	$(x + y) \mid_A z = x \mid_A z + y \mid_A z$	PC2
$ax \mathbin{\overset{\cdot\;}{-}} y = a(x \cdot y)$	SL2	$ax \mid_{A \cup \{a\}} ay = a(x \parallel_A y)$	PC3
$\mathbf{0}_P \mathbin{\overset{\cdot\;}{-}} x = \mathbf{0}_{P \cap \pi(x)}$	SL3	$ax \mid_{A \cup \{a\}} by = \mathbf{0}_{\pi(ax) \cap \pi(by)}$ if $a \neq b$	PC4
$x \mathbin{\overset{\;\cdot}{-}} (y + z) = x \mathbin{\overset{\;\cdot}{-}} y + x \mathbin{\overset{\;\cdot}{-}} z$	SR1	$ax \mid_{A \setminus \{a\}} y = \mathbf{0}_{\pi(ax) \cap \pi(y)}$	PC5
$x \mathbin{\overset{\;\cdot}{-}} ay = a(res_a(x) \cdot y)$ if $a \in \pi(x)$	SR2	$\mathbf{0}_P \mid_A x = \mathbf{0}_{P \cap \pi(x)}$	PC6
$x \mathbin{\overset{\;\cdot}{-}} ay = \mathbf{0}_{\pi(x) \cap \pi(ay)}$ if $a \notin \pi(x)$	SR3		
$x \mathbin{\overset{\;\cdot}{-}} \mathbf{0}_P = \mathbf{0}_{\pi(x) \cap P}$	SR4		

deadlock constants $\mathbf{0}_P$ instead of just a single one (corresponding to our $\mathbf{0}_\varnothing$—note that if we restrict $\mathbf{L}$ to $\mathbf{0}_\varnothing$ then indeed we cannot derive any permissions any more).

Theorem 6. *If* $\mathbf{L}_t^+$ *(for* tree language *denotes the fragment of* $\mathbf{L}^+$ *consisting of deadlock, prefix and choice, then C1–4 are complete for bisimilarity in* $\mathbf{L}_t^+$.

The other equations in our system basically allow to reduce every term to this fragment $\mathbf{L}_t^+$; the above completeness result then carries over to the entire language. The interesting operator is once more weak sequential composition, axiomatised in S–SR4. We follow the standard technique (cf. [1]) of splitting the operator into the two auxiliary ones $\overset{\cdot\;}{-}$ and $\overset{\;\cdot}{-}$ introduced above. The former is relatively easy to capture equationally. Note in particular that here we do have the distributivity over choice discussed at the beginning of this section. Right sequential is more complex: especially, if the second operand is a prefix term then we have to distinguish whether or not the first operand *permits* the prefixed action (SR2 and 3); and as the first operand may change as a consequence of this permission, we also need the *residue*. It is here, therefore, that we need the functions π and *res*.

Let T^+ denote the theory in Table 5. We first need to show that all the equations of T^+ are sound modulo bisimilarity, and then that they induce normal forms which are terms of $\mathbf{L}_t^+$. Together with Theorem 6, this establishes completeness. For the soundness proof we need that π and *res* are well-defined modulo the given equations.

Proposition 7. *If $B = C$ is an instance of one of the equations in Table 5, then on the one hand, $\pi(B) = \pi(C)$, and on the other, $res_a(B) = res_a(C)$ is an instance of the same equation.*

Now we state the required soundness property.

Theorem 8 (soundness). *If $T^+ \vdash B = C$ then $B \sim C$.*

Next, we show that all terms of $\mathbf{L}^+$ can be rewritten to *normal forms* in $\mathbf{L}_t^+$.

Theorem 9 (normalisation). *If $C \in \mathbf{L}^+$ then $T^+ \vdash B = C$ for some $B \in \mathbf{L}_t^+$.*

The final completeness result just collects the previous theorems.

Corollary 10 (completeness). *For all* $B, C \in \mathbf{L}^{+}$, $B \sim C$ *iff* $T^{+} \vdash B = C$.

In order to work with the proof system in practise, one would need to prove a lot of auxiliary equations first. At this point we merely mention that sequential composition is associative and that $\mathbf{1} \cdot B = B$ for all $B \in \mathbf{L}$. This allows us, respectively, to write series of sequential compositions without parentheses and to get rid of spurious left-over $\mathbf{1}$'s in many derivations; for instance, if $a\ D\ b\ D\ c$ then $a \cdot b \cdot c \xrightarrow{a} \mathbf{1} \cdot b \cdot c = b \cdot c \xrightarrow{b} \mathbf{1} \cdot c = c$, instead of arriving at either $(\mathbf{1} \cdot \mathbf{1}) \cdot c$ or $\mathbf{1} \cdot (\mathbf{1} \cdot c)$.

4 Denotational Semantics

Besides the operational semantics we will also define a denotational semantics for the language $\mathbf{L}$ which is shown to be consistent with the operational semantics. More precisely, we will show that the transition-permission system of a term B derived via the operational semantics is bisimilar to the transition-permission system obtained from the denotational semantics of B. The model we use for this purpose was introduced in Wehrheim [20], where it is discussed and motivated in detail.

The models are sets of partial runs, implicitly ordered by prefix. We will use a global set of events $\mathbf{E}$, assumed to be closed under pairing: $(\mathbf{E} \cup \{*\}) \times (\mathbf{E} \cup \{*\}) \subseteq \mathbf{E}$, where $* \notin \mathbf{E}$ is a special symbol. A *directed acyclic graph* is an ordered subset of $\mathbf{E}$ where the (reflexive and cycle-free) ordering represents the *causal relation* between events. Runs are represented by *labelled dags with permission sets*, or *P-dags* for short, where the dag part supplies information about the *past* behaviour up to a certain point, and the permission set consists of all actions that are independent of the *future* behaviour.

Definition 11 (labelled P-dag). A *labelled P-dag* is a tuple $u = \langle E, \leq, l, P \rangle$ where

- $E \subseteq \mathbf{E}$ is a set of *events*;
- $\leq \subseteq E \times E$ is a reflexive and cycle-free *flow relation*;
- $l: E \longrightarrow Act$ is a *labelling function*, and
- $P \subseteq Act$ is a *permission set* (P-set).

We use u, v, w to range over P-dags, and E_u, $\leq_u$ etc. to denote the components of a P-dag u. The labelling function extends the dependency relation to events: $e\ D_u\ e'$ iff $l_u(e)\ D\ l_u(e')$. u is called *D-compatible* if precisely all dependent events are ordered, i.e., $\leq_u \cup \geq_u = D_u$. The set of all D-compatible P-dags is denoted $\mathbf{PD}_D$. The P-dags we use in our semantics will always be D-compatible. If $f: E_u \longrightarrow E$ is an injective function, then $f(u) := \langle f(E_u), f(\leq_u), l_u \circ f^{-1}, P \rangle$ defines the image of u under f. Two dags u and v are said to be *dag-equal* (denoted $u =_{dg} v$) if $\langle E_u, \leq_u, l_u \rangle = \langle E_v, \leq_v, l_v \rangle$, and *compatibly labelled* iff $l_u|_{E_u \cap E_v} = l_v|_{E_u \cap E_v}$.

Now we define some P-dag constants and operators. The following constants will be used to represent the maximal runs of the processes $\mathbf{0}_P$ and a:

$$
\begin{aligned}
\varepsilon_P &:= \langle \varnothing, \varnothing, \varnothing, P \rangle \\
e_a &:= \langle \{e\}, \{(e,e)\}, \{(e,a)\}, Act \rangle \ .
\end{aligned}
$$

The operators to be considered are union and weak sequential composition of P-dags. Union is only defined for compatibly labelled P-dags and sequential composition is only defined if the event sets are disjoint and the first operand permits the events of the second to happen. The latter idea is captured by the notion of *enabling*: we say that u *enables* v (denoted $u \vdash v$) if $E_u \cap E_v = \varnothing$ and $P_u \supseteq l_v(E_v)$.

$$u \cup v := \langle E_u \cup E_v, \leq_u \cup \leq_v, l_u \cup l_v, P_u \cap P_v \rangle \quad \text{if } l_u|_{E_u \cap E_v} = l_v|_{E_u \cap E_v}$$
$$u \cdot v := \langle E_u \cup E_v, \leq_u \cup \leq_v \cup ((E_u \times E_v) \cap D), l_u \cup l_v, P_u \cap P_v \rangle \quad \text{if } u \vdash v.$$

Finally, we define a *smoothening* and a *prefix relation* over P-dags, as follows:

$$u \sqsubseteq v :\Leftrightarrow E_u = E_v \wedge \leq_u \subseteq \leq_v \wedge l_u = l_v \wedge P_u = P_v$$
$$u \preccurlyeq v :\Leftrightarrow E_u \subseteq E_v \wedge \leq_u = \leq_v \cap (E_v \times E_u) \wedge \ell_u = \ell_v|_{E_u} \wedge P_u = P_v \setminus [l(E_v \setminus E_u)]_D$$

Intuitively, $u \sqsubseteq v$ states that v augments u with some additional ordering (for instance to make it D-compatible), whereas $u \preccurlyeq v$ states that u is a sub-behaviour of v, that is, the computation can be carried on after u and may evolve into v.

Definition 12 (P-dag structure). A *P-dag structure* is a non-empty prefix closed set of compatibly labelled P-dags. The set of P-dag structures is denoted **PDS**.

The above operators are now lifted to P-dag structures, and used to model the operators of **L**. To model the behaviour of terms $B \|_A C$, we rely on *label-preserving bijections* from the A-labelled events of the left hand operand to the A-labelled events from the right hand operand. Such bijections establish which events synchronise with one another. If u and v are P-dags then $[u \rightarrow_A v]$ denotes the space of label-preserving bijections from $\{ e \in E_u \mid l_u(e) \in A \}$ to $\{ e \in E_v \mid l_v(e) \in A \}$; if $f : u \rightarrow_A v$ then the following functions map the events from u resp. v to their synchronisations:

$$\hat{f}_1 : e \mapsto \begin{cases} (e, f(e)) & \text{if } f(e) \text{ is defined} \\ (e, *) & \text{otherwise} \end{cases} \qquad \hat{f}_2 : e \mapsto \begin{cases} (f^{-1}(e), e) & \text{if } f^{-1}(e) \text{ is defined} \\ (*, e) & \text{otherwise.} \end{cases}$$

As a consequence, synchronising u and v is a matter of finding an $f : u \rightarrow_A v$ and constructing $\hat{f}_1(u) \cup \hat{f}_2(v)$. Unfortunately, in general this is not D-compatible; the ordering has to be augmented. In the end therefore, we model the synchronisation of u and v according to f by all $w \in \mathbf{PD}_D$ such that $\hat{f}_1(u) \cup \hat{f}_2(v) \sqsubseteq w$.

The denotational semantics of **L** is now given by the function $[\![\cdot]\!] : \mathbf{L} \times \mathbf{E} \rightarrow \mathbf{PDS}$ inductively defined in Table 6. The second argument of the function is only used to ensure disjointness of sets of events.

Consider again $B = (a + b) \cdot c$ where $a \; I \; b \; I \; c$ and $a \; D \; c$. This yields the following P-dag structure (where $\rightarrow$ denotes prefix, and we have left out the events, which in this case does not matter since there is only one occurrence of every action):

$$
\begin{array}{ccccc}
\varepsilon_{\{b\}} & \rightarrow & \boxed{a}\{b\} & \rightarrow & \boxed{a \rightarrow c}\{a, b, c\} \\
\varepsilon_\varnothing & \rightarrow & \boxed{b}\{b\} & & \\
& \searrow & \boxed{c}\{a, c\} & \rightarrow & \boxed{\begin{smallmatrix}b\\c\end{smallmatrix}}\{a, b, c\}
\end{array}
$$

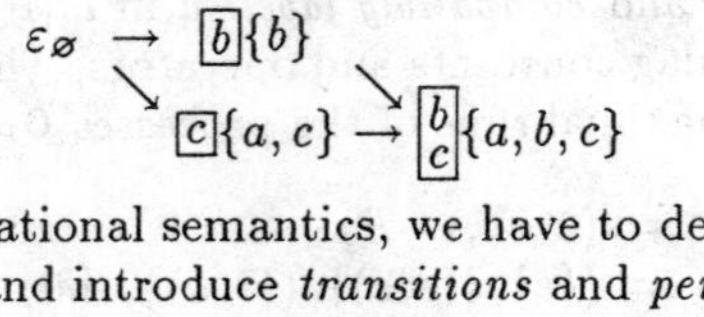

To relate this to the operational semantics, we have to define a notion of *state* over the denotational model, and introduce *transitions* and *permissions* over them. Here

Table 6. P-dag structure semantics for **L**

$$\llbracket 0_P \rrbracket_e := \{\varepsilon_P\}$$
$$\llbracket a \rrbracket_e := \{\varepsilon_{[a]_I}, e_a\}$$
$$\llbracket B + C \rrbracket_e := \llbracket B \rrbracket_{(e,*)} \cup \llbracket C \rrbracket_{(*,e)}$$
$$\llbracket B \cdot C \rrbracket_e := \{\, u \cdot v \mid u \in \llbracket B \rrbracket_{(e,*)}, v \in \llbracket C \rrbracket_{(*,e)}, u \vdash v \,\}$$
$$\llbracket B \parallel_A C \rrbracket_e := \{\, w \in \mathbf{PD}_D \mid u \in \llbracket B \rrbracket_e, v \in \llbracket C \rrbracket_e, f\colon u \to_A v, \hat f_1(u) \cup \hat f_2(v) \sqsubseteq w \,\}$$

we encounter the interesting situation that the P-dags themselves are not suitable to represent states. For instance, in the example above we see that the P-dag structure does not have a smallest element, and there is no natural notion of initial state. Instead, we use *nonempty sets of dag-equal P-dags* as states: if $\mathcal{P} \in \mathbf{PDS}$ then

$$s \xrightarrow{a}_{\mathcal{P}} s' :\Leftrightarrow \exists e \in \mathbf{E}.\ s' = \{\, u \in \mathcal{P} \mid \exists v \in s.\ v \preccurlyeq u \wedge E_u = E_v \cup \{e\} \wedge l_u(e) = a \,\}$$
$$s \cdots\!\!\xrightarrow{a}_{\mathcal{P}} s' :\Leftrightarrow s' = \{\, u \in s \mid a \in P_u \,\}$$

For the above example, this yields the following transitions (permissions are ignored):

$$\{\varepsilon_{\{b\}}\} \to \{\boxed{a}\{b\}\} \to \{\boxed{a \to c}\{a,b,c\}\}$$
$$\{\varepsilon_{\{b\}}, \varepsilon_\varnothing\} \to \{\boxed{b}\{b\}\}$$
$$\{\varepsilon_\varnothing\} \to \{\boxed{c}\{a,c\}\} \to \{\boxed{\begin{smallmatrix}b\\c\end{smallmatrix}}\{a,b,c\}\}$$

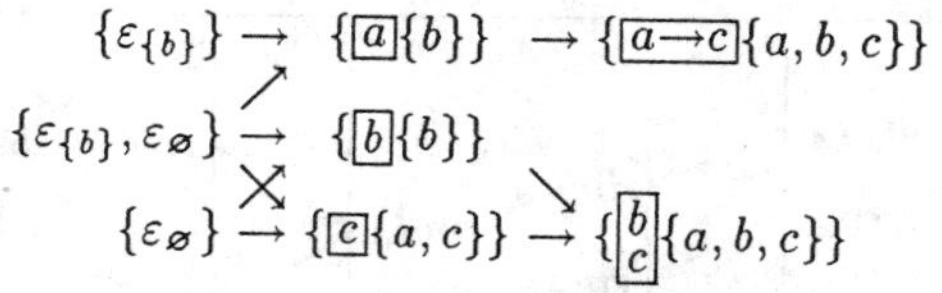

In general, therefore, the states of $\mathcal{P}$ are subsets of $[u]_{=_{dg}} \cap \mathcal{P}$; a natural initial state of a given P-dag structure $\mathcal{P}$ is then $[\varepsilon_\varnothing]_{=_{dg}} \cap \mathcal{P}$. Hence for a P-dag structure $\mathcal{P}$, the transition-permission system of $\mathcal{P}$ is defined by

$$tps(\mathcal{P}) := \langle Act, \{\, s \mid \exists u.\ \varnothing \subset s \subseteq [u]_{=_{dg}} \cap \mathcal{P} \,\}, \to_{\mathcal{P}}, \cdots\!\to_{\mathcal{P}}, [\varepsilon_\varnothing]_{=_{dg}} \cap \mathcal{P}\rangle\ .$$

The next theorem states the consistency of operational and denotational semantics.

Theorem 13. *For all $B \in \mathbf{L}$ and $e \in \mathbf{E}$, $tps(B) \sim tps(\llbracket B \rrbracket_e)$.*

5 Examples

We discuss some small examples from the world of protocols, in which our notion of weak sequential composition and the interaction with choice are essential.

5.1 Connection Release Phase

We consider a small protocol for connection-oriented data transfer between two parties. The example is inspired by Goltz and Götz [11]. The protocol consists of three phases: *connection establishment, data transfer* and *connection release*. Here we concern ourselves only with the interaction between the data transfer and release phases. We start by a specification of the form $Prot = Data \cdot Rel$, which reflects the idea that after connection release, no data can be transferred any more. However, it can in general not be ruled out that *some* actions from the data phase take place only after the release phase has started. Let us assume that data is only transferred from party A to party B, and the transfer of one data item consists of two actions, $dreq_A$ and $dind_B$ for *data request* and *data indication* taking place at A and B, respectively. The release phase, on the other hand, can be initiated by either A or B by a *release request* $rreq_A$ or $rreq_B$, is indicated at the other end by a *release indication* $rind_B$ or $rind_A$, and confirmed by a *release confirm* $rcnf_A$ or $rcnf_B$. The corresponding processes are specified as follows:

$$\begin{aligned} Data &= \mathbf{1} + dreq_A \cdot dind_B \\ Rel &= rreq_A \cdot rind_B \cdot rcnf_A + rreq_B \cdot rind_A \cdot rcnf_B \ . \end{aligned}$$

(We have modelled just one possible data transfer; in the next example we will see a somewhat more involved data phase.) The four possible interactions are depicted in Fig. 1 below. Note that in scenario (4), the data indication $dind_B$ can take place before or after the release request $rreq_B$; however, after a release confirm, no data can arrive any more.

Fig. 1. Possible interactions of data and release phase

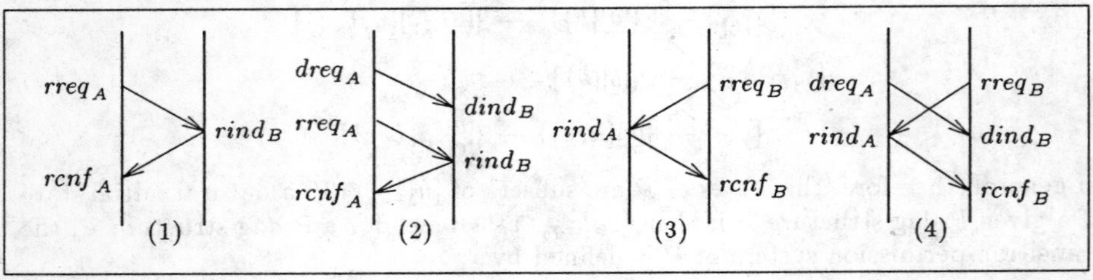

Consider the dependencies between the actions. The local actions of each party are dependent with the exception of $dind_B$ and $rreq_B$; the idea here is that party B cannot know if there is a data indication coming or not, and hence this cannot influence whether or not B will request release. In addition, each indication should be dependent on the corresponding request, and the confirmation on the indication. Now we can analyse the behaviour of this protocol. Its first transition is either a data request (by A) or a release request (by A or B). If it is a data request then

$$Prot = Data \cdot Rel \xrightarrow{dreq_A} dind_B \cdot Rel$$

which corresponds to scenario (2) or (4) of Fig. 1. Which of these two is chosen depends on who initiates the release. Note that both $rreq_A$ and $rreq_B$ are already enabled in $dind_B \cdot Rel$. In fact, $dind_B$ can be delayed even further:

$$dind_B \cdot Rel \xrightarrow{rreq_B} dind_B \cdot rind_A \cdot rcnf_B \xrightarrow{rind_A} dind_B \cdot rcnf_B$$

At this stage, however, the data indication must take place. On the other hand, if the first action of *Prot* is the release request from B, then (because $res_a(Data) = Data$) the choice in the data phase is not resolved by this and up to bisimilarity we get

$$Prot \xrightarrow{rreq_B} Data \cdot rind_A$$

corresponding to scenario (3) or (4) in Fig. 1. The next action will decide between these two possibilities: it is either $dreq_A$ or $rind_A$, the latter of which *does* decide the choice in *Data*, i.e., $Data \cdot rind_A \xrightarrow{rind_A} \mathbf{1}$.

Note in particular that the non-right-distributivity of choice over (weak) sequential composition is important here: the alternative protocol $Rel + dreq_A \cdot dind_A \cdot Rel$, obtained by distributing *Rel* over the choice in *Data*, is different from *Prot*, since in this new protocol, an initial $rreq_B$-action resolves the choice and $dreq_A$ may be refused afterwards. The denotational model of *Prot* looks as follows (where we have left out the permission sets and hence the states collapse to their underlying dags):

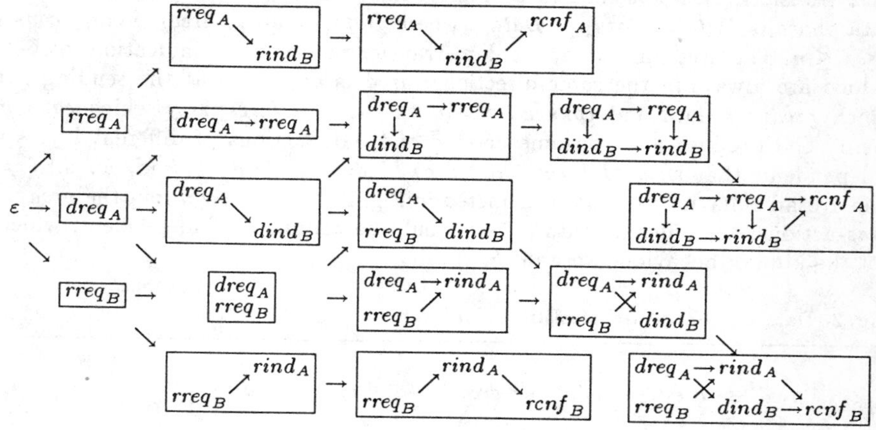

5.2 Communication Closed Layers

An algebraic law that has been applied quite successfully in a linear time setting is the *communication closed layers* law (CCL), advocated for instance by Zwiers et al. in [13, 21, 10]. As mentioned in the introduction, this law has actually been one of the motivations for the present work. In our setting, CCL can be formulated as follows:

$$\begin{pmatrix} (B_1 \parallel_{A_1} C_1) \\ \cdot \\ (B_2 \parallel_{A_2} C_2) \end{pmatrix} = \begin{pmatrix} B_1 \\ \cdot \\ B_2 \end{pmatrix} \parallel_{A_1 \cup A_2} \begin{pmatrix} C_1 \\ \cdot \\ C_2 \end{pmatrix} . \tag{1}$$

Each pair B_i, C_i is thought to form a *layer* of an ongoing algorithm or protocol, in which information is exchanged between the components B_i and C_i using two different mechanisms: interference due to dependencies between actions, and synchronisation over A_i. Both kinds of interference are however ruled out between components of *different* layers: if $i \neq j$ then

- different components of different layers are mutually independent; i.e., $\alpha(B_i) \setminus A_i$ is independent of $\alpha(C_j) \setminus A_j$;
- different layers do not synchronise; i.e., $\alpha(B_i) \cap A_j = \varnothing$ and $\alpha(C_i) \cap A_j = \varnothing$.

These conditions constitute the requirement of *communication closedness*, which is necessary for (1) to hold. Recall that $A_1 \; I \; A_2 \iff \forall a_1 \in A_1, a_2 \in A_2 . \, a_1 \; I \; a_2$; then the formal statement of CCL is as follows.

Theorem 14 (CCL). *If $B_i, C_i \in \mathbf{L}$ and $A_i \subseteq Act$ for $i = 1, 2$ and for all $i \neq j$, $(\alpha(B_i) \setminus A_i)\ I\ (\alpha(C_j) \setminus A_j)$ and $\alpha(B_i) \cap A_j = \alpha(C_i) \cap A_j = \varnothing$, then*

$$(B_1 \parallel_{A_1} C_1) \cdot (B_2 \parallel_{A_2} C_2) = (B_1 \cdot B_2) \parallel_{A_1 \cup A_2} (C_1 \cdot C_2)$$

An interesting special case is $B \cdot C = B \parallel_{\varnothing} C = C \cdot B$, which holds if $\alpha(B)\ I\ \alpha(C)$ (obtained by setting $B_1 = B$, $B_2 = C_1 = \mathbf{1}$, $C_2 = C$ and $A_1 = A_2 = \varnothing$). By induction one can extend Theorem 14 to $m > 1$ layers of $n > 1$ components each.

Here we show an application of CCL. Consider a data phase consisting of $n \geq 1$ data transfers, each specified in a "logical layer" $Data_n$. The specification of the data phase is $Data = Data_1 \cdots Data_n$, where $Data_i = prod \cdot dreq_i \cdot dind_i \cdot cons$ for $1 \leq i \leq n$. The $dreq_i$ and $dind_i$ are data transfer requests and indications as before (which are always in the same direction), *prod* is an action at the sending party which *produces* data and *cons* an action at the receiving party which *consumes* them. The produce and consume actions and data actions of different layers are independent; that is, $prod\ I\ cons$ and $dreq_j\ I\ dreq_i\ I\ dind_j\ I\ dind_i$ for all $i \neq j$. The overall behaviour of *Data* is depicted in Fig. 2. Note that without the *prod*- and *cons*-actions, the different data phases would be completely independent, which is not the kind of behaviour we want to specify.

Fig. 2. Data transfer phase consisting of *n* layers

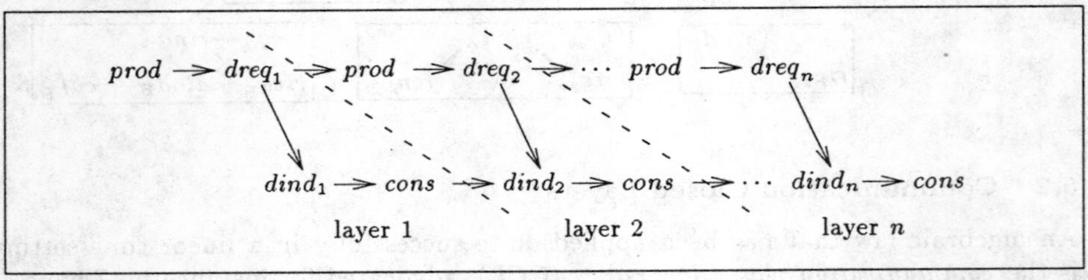

Now we want to transform this specification to one which is composed "vertically", that is, in which the roles of the sending and receiving parties and that of the channel are distinguished. First we do this to the separate data layers:

$$Data'_i = ((prod \cdot dreq_i) \parallel_{\varnothing} (dind_i \cdot cons)) \parallel_{dreq_i, dind_i} (dreq_i \cdot dind_i)\ .$$

It is easy to see that $Data_i$ can be rewritten to $Data'_i$ using the equations P–PC6 and C4. Now we introduce auxiliary names $Send_i = prod \cdot dreq_i$, $Rec_i = dind_i \cdot cons$ and $Chan_i = dreq_i \cdot dind_i$, allowing us to write

$$Data = ((Send_1 \parallel_{\varnothing} Rec_1) \parallel_{dreq_1, dind_1} Chan_1) \cdots ((Send_n \parallel_{\varnothing} Rec_n) \parallel_{dreq_n, dind_n} Chan_n)\ .$$

If $i \neq j$ then one the one hand, $\alpha(Send_i \parallel_{\varnothing} Rec_i) \setminus \{dreq_i, dind_i\} = \{prod, cons\}\ I\ \varnothing = \alpha(Chan_j) \setminus \{dreq_j, dind_j\}$, and on the other, $\alpha(Data_i) \cap \{dreq_j, dind_j\} = \varnothing$. Hence the conditions of CCL are fulfilled, implying

$$Data = \begin{pmatrix} (Send_1 \parallel_{\varnothing} Rec_1) \\ \vdots \\ (Send_n \parallel_{\varnothing} Rec_n) \end{pmatrix} \parallel_A \begin{pmatrix} Chan_1 \\ \vdots \\ Chan_n \end{pmatrix}$$

where $A = \bigcup_{i=1}^{n} \{dreq_i, dind_i\}$. The left hand side can in turn be subjected to CCL, since $\alpha(Send_i)\ I\ \alpha(Rec_j)$ for all $i \neq j$; hence we have

$$Data = \left(\begin{pmatrix} Send_1 \\ \vdots \\ Send_n \end{pmatrix} \|_{\varnothing} \begin{pmatrix} Rec_1 \\ \vdots \\ Rec_n \end{pmatrix} \right) \|_A \begin{pmatrix} Chan_1 \\ \vdots \\ Chan_n \end{pmatrix}$$

This is indeed the structure we were aiming at: there are now clearly recognisable subterms describing the behaviour of sender, receiver and channel.

6 Conclusions

The work reported here is part of an ongoing project in which the connection between such concepts as causality and action refinement is investigated. In this paper we have succeeded in "downgrading" the notion of causality to the operational idea that an action may "overtake" any term of which it is independent, even if it is specified as taking place only after that term, resulting in a weakened notion of sequential composition, the consequences of which we have discussed in some detail.

In the literature, this idea has so far been considered primarily in a linear time setting; see especially Mazurkiewicz [14]. In the process algebraic setting of this paper it has some surprising consequences, especially for the combination of sequential composition and choice. In this respect, we have investigated only one of a number of possible alternatives, driven by considerations based on the existing partial-order model of Wehrheim [20]. In a sense, the operational semantics forms the "projection" of a partial-order denotational semantics to an interleaving setting, retaining, however, some independence information that is more commonly associated with non-interleaving models. When we set out, it was not clear that this could be done at all; and in fact, many of the aspects that are unusual in the operational, interleaving point of view, such as the moment at which choices are resolved, are completely natural in the denotational, partial order model.

Note that the linear time model of Janssen, Poel and Zwiers [13] and Fokkinga, Poel and Zwiers [10], which is used as denotational model for a language similar to ours (especially also including weak sequential composition), does not lend itself easily to a compositional operational characterisation, since deadlocking runs are simply thrown out (for instance, they have the equivalent of $B \cdot \mathbf{0}_{\varnothing} = \mathbf{0}_{\varnothing}$).

Since the rules of our operational semantics fit into the GSOS format known from the literature, we could immediately use existing SOS theory to show that the operational semantics defines a unique transition relation—which is not self-evident, given the fact that it features negative premises—and that (strong) bisimilarity is a congruence for all the operators of our language. Since we had in no way worked towards that result, we regard this as an interesting "proof of the pudding," both for the SOS theory and for our own semantics. We have moreover given a complete axiomatisation of the language with respect to bisimilarity. In this respect however, the existing SOS theory, although yielding useful hints, was not directly applicable.

The usefulness of the notion of weak sequential composition has been demonstrated by two small examples from the area of protocol design. The first of these shows that in some situations, the interplay with choice we have specified is exactly what one wants. As part of the second example, we have extended the *communication closed layers law*, known from the linear time setting, to our language. This example does not involve the choice operator (although it does contain synchronisation and in that sense goes beyond the usual linear time applications); we conjecture that to put CCL to maximal benefit in the context of process algebra, it should be generalised somehow to include choices between layers.

The language we have considered in this paper may be changed or extended in several ways. The interplay between weak sequential composition and choice, which is the central issue of this paper, can conceivably be simplified – although we stress once more that our approach is very natural in the denotational model. In fact the peculiarities (if they should be called such) of the operational characterisation might as well be attributed to the interleaving nature of this characterisation, raising the immediate question if some partial-order operational semantics would not be more appropriate. Another suggestion (thanks to one of the referees) is that the problems we envisage to solve with weak sequential composition could alternatively be tackled with *prioritised parallel composition*. This is an interesting subject for study, although it is perhaps questionable if any simplification could be obtained this way, the interplay of priority and choice itself being a very nontrivial issue.

Possible language extensions to be investigated are: ordinary ("strong") sequential composition, renaming, recursion and action refinement. Adding strong sequential composition would have the advantage that action prefix is no longer an auxiliary operator. (Note that we can simulate strong sequential composition using a total dependency relation, but since this relation is global we would then lose the weak version.) Adding renaming is straightforward. In the denotational semantics, adding recursion is also straightforward (using standard fixpoint techniques). Hence once more we have a measuring stick for the operational case. The operational characterisation however turns out to be problematic, mainly due to the fact that we cannot define *guardedness* in the usual way. Usually process variables are said to be guarded if they are in the scope of a prefixing operator or, more generally, if they only occur on *sleeping positions* (Vaandrager [19]), corresponding to operands which are not tested by the rules of the operational semantics. However, our rules for sequential composition test both arguments and in fact there are no operators at all in our language which have a sleeping position. This will be the subject of further research. Finally, we plan to investigate the consistent extension of dependencies to action refinement. This has already been done in the denotational model (see [20]). The operational characterisation will probably not be easier than for the "ordinary" case without dependencies; it remains to be seen if the existing techniques (see e.g. Aceto and Hennessy [2], Degano and Gorrieri [9], Rensink [16]) are applicable.

Acknowledgement. Thanks are due to Frits Vaandrager for some very helpful suggestions regarding the operational semantics.

References

1. L. Aceto, B. Bloom, and F. Vaandrager. Turning SOS rules into equations. In *Seventh Annual IEEE Symposium on Logic in Computer Science*, pages 113–124. IEEE, Com-

puter Society Press, 1992. Full version available as CWI Report CS-R9218, June 1992, Amsterdam. To appear in the LICS 92 Special Issue of Information and Computation.

2. L. Aceto and M. Hennessy. Towards action-refinement in process algebras. *Information and Computation*, 103:204–269, 1993.
3. J. C. M. Baeten and F. W. Vaandrager. An algebra for process creation. In *J.W. de Bakker, 25 Jaar Semantiek — Liber Amicorum*. Stichting Mathematisch Centrum, Amsterdam, Apr. 1989. Also availabe as: Report CS-R8907, CWI, Amsterdam.
4. J. C. M. Baeten and W. P. Weijland. *Process Algebra*. Cambridge University Press, 1990.
5. M. A. Bednarczyk. *Categories of Asynchronous Systems*. PhD thesis, University of Sussex, Oct. 1987. Available as Report 1/88, School of Cognitive and Computing Sciences, University of Sussex.
6. J. A. Bergstra and J. W. Klop. Algebra of communicating processes with abstraction. *Theoretical Comput. Sci.*, 37(1):77–121, 1985.
7. B. Bloom, S. Istrail, and A. R. Meyer. Bisimulation can't be traced. In *Fifteenth Annual Symposium on the Principles of Programming Languages*, pages 229–239. ACM, 1988. Preliminary Report.
8. J. W. de Bakker, W.-P. de Roever, and G. Rozenberg, editors. *Linear Time, Branching Time and Partial Order in Logics and Models for Concurrency*, volume 354 of *Lecture Notes in Computer Science*. Springer-Verlag, 1989.
9. P. Degano and R. Gorrieri. An operational definition of action refinement. Technical Report TR–28/92, Università di Pisa, 1992. To appear in Information and Computation.
10. M. Fokkinga, M. Poel, and J. Zwiers. Modular completeness for communication closed layers. In E. Best, editor, *Concur '93*, volume 715 of *Lecture Notes in Computer Science*, pages 50–65. Springer-Verlag, 1992.
11. U. Goltz and N. Götz. Modelling a simple communication protocol in a language with action refinement. Draft version, 1991.
12. C. A. R. Hoare. *Communicating Sequential Processes*. Prentice-Hall, 1985.
13. W. Janssen, M. Poel, and J. Zwiers. Actions systems and action refinement in the development of parallel systems. In J. C. M. Baeten and J. F. Groote, editors, *Concur '91*, volume 527 of *Lecture Notes in Computer Science*, pages 298–316. Springer-Verlag, 1991.
14. A. Mazurkiewicz. Basic notions of trace theory. In de Bakker et al. [8], pages 285–363.
15. R. Milner. *Communication and Concurrency*. Prentice-Hall, 1989.
16. A. Rensink. *Models and Methods for Action Refinement*. PhD thesis, University of Twente, Enschede, Netherlands, Aug. 1993.
17. M. W. Shields. Concurrent machines. *The Computer Journal*, 28(5):449–465, 1985.
18. E. W. Stark. Concurrent transition systems. *Theoretical Comput. Sci.*, 64:221–269, 1989.
19. F. W. Vaandrager. Expressiveness results for process algebras. Report CS–R9301, Centre for Mathematics and Computer Science, 1993. Available by ftp: ftp.cwi.nl, pub/CWIreports/AP.
20. H. Wehrheim. Parametric action refinement. Hildesheimer Informatik-Berichte 18/93, Institut für Informatik, Universität Hildesheim, Nov. 1993. To be presented at PROCOMET '94, San Miniato, June 1994.
21. J. Zwiers. Layering and action refinement for timed systems. In J. W. de Bakker, C. Huizing, W.-P. de Roever, and G. Rozenberg, editors, *Real-Time: Theory in Practice*, volume 600 of *Lecture Notes in Computer Science*. Springer-Verlag, 1991.

Efficient parallelism vs reliable distribution: a trade-off for concurrent computations*

Paris C. Kanellakis[1], Dimitrios Michailidis[1] and Alex A. Shvartsman[2]

[1] Department of Computer Science, Brown University, Box 1910
Providence, RI 02912-1910, USA

[2] Digital Equipment Corporation, 30 Porter Road, LJ02/I11
Littleton, MA 01460-1446, USA

Abstract. Concurrent computations should combine efficiency with reliability, where efficiency is usually associated with parallel and reliability with distributed computing. Such a desirable combination is not always possible, because of an intuitive trade-off: efficiency requires removing redundancy from computations whereas reliability requires some redundancy. We survey a spectrum of algorithmic models (from fail-stop, synchronous to asynchronous and from approximate to exact computations) in which reliability is guaranteed with small trade-offs in efficiency. We illustrate a number of cases where optimal trade-offs are achievable. A basic property of all these models, which is of some interest in the study of concurrency, is that "true" read/write concurrency is necessary for fault tolerance. In particular, we outline (from [14]) how algorithms can be designed so that, in each execution, the total "true" concurrency used can be closely related to the faults that can be tolerated.

1 Introduction

A basic problem of massively parallel computing is that the unreliability of inexpensive processors and their interconnection may eliminate any potential efficiency advantage of parallelism. Here, we overview an investigation of fault models and parallel computation models under which it is possible to achieve algorithmic efficiency (i.e., speed-ups close to linear in the number of processors) despite the presence of faults.

There is an intuitive trade-off between reliability and efficiency because reliability usually requires *introducing redundancy* in the computation in order to detect errors and reassign resources, whereas gaining efficiency by massively parallel computing requires *removing redundancy* from the computation to fully utilize each processor. Thus, even allowing for some abstraction in the model of parallel computation, it is not obvious that there are any non-trivial fault models that allow near-linear speed-ups. So it was somewhat surprising when in [15] we demonstrated that it is possible to combine efficiency and fault tolerance for

* Research supported in part by ONR grant N00014-91-J-1613 and by ONR contract N00014-91-J-4052 ARPA Order 8225.

many basic algorithms expressed as concurrent-read concurrent-write parallel (CRCW) random access machines (PRAMs [12]).

The [15] fault model allows *any pattern of dynamic fail-stop no restart processor errors, as long as one processor remains alive*. The fault model was applied to all CRCW PRAMs in [22, 34]. It was extended in [16] to include *processor restarts*, and in [36] to include *arbitrary static memory faults*, i.e., arbitrary memory initialization, and in [14] to include *restricted memory access* patterns through controlled memory access. Concurrency of reads and writes is an essential feature that accounts for the necessary redundancy so it can be restricted but not eliminated. Also, as shown in [15], it suffices to consider COMMON CRCW PRAMs (all concurrent writes are identical) in which the atomically written words need only contain a constant number of bits.

The work we survey makes two key assumptions. The first provides the means of saving "correct" state (as the core of fault tolerance) and the second highlights the importance of "true" concurrency (as a source of redundancy for fault tolerance). We assume:

1. Processor faults do not affect memory.
2. Processors can read and write memory concurrently, CRCW.

These two assumptions are essential for deterministic algorithms with *dynamic faults*. *Static* or initial memory can be contaminated [36]. *Static* or initial processor faults can be handled with EREW algorithms [14]. For dynamic behavior there is a trade-off between concurrency and fault tolerance, which we overview here (see [14] for the full details).

A central algorithmic primitive in our work is the *Write-All* operation [15]. Iterated *Write-All* forms the basis for the algorithm simulation techniques of [22, 34] and for the memory initialization of [36]. Therefore, improved *Write-All* solutions lead to improved simulations and memory clearing techniques.

The *Write-All* problem is: *using P processors write 1s into all locations of an array of size N, where $P \leq N$*. When $P = N$ this operation captures the computational progress that can be naturally accomplished in one time unit by a PRAM. We say that *Write-All completes at the global clock tick at which all the processors that have not fail-stopped share the knowledge that 1's have been written into all N array locations*. Requiring completion of a *Write-All* algorithm is critical if one wishes to iterate it, as pointed out in [22] which uses a certification bit to separate the various iterations of (Certified) *Write-All*. The *Write-All* completes in all algorithms presented here.

Under dynamic failures, efficient deterministic solutions to *Write-All*, i.e., increasing the fault-free $O(N)$ work by small polylog(N) factors, are desirable. The first such solution was algorithm W of [15] which has (to date) the best worst-case work bound $O(N + P \log^2 N / \log\log N)$ for $1 \leq P \leq N$. This bound was first shown in [21] for a different version of the algorithm and in [24] the basic argument was adapted to algorithm W. The strongest lower bound to date for *Write-All* was derived in [21], namely $\Omega(N + P \log N)$ work is required for $1 \leq P \leq N$.

Let us now describe the contents of this survey, with some pointers to the literature. We focus on upper bounds. In Section 2 we present a synthesis of parallel computation and fault models. This synthesis includes most of the models proposed to date (see [18]). It links the work on fail-stop no-restart errors, to fail-stop errors with restarts, where both detectable and undetectable restarts are considered.

The detectable restart case has been examined, using a slightly different formalism in [6, 16]. It represents an intermediate level on asynchrony for which we have many interesting algorithmic techniques.

The undetectable restart case is equivalent to the most general general model of asynchrony that has received a fair amount of attention in the literature. An elegant deterministic solution for *Write-All* in this case appeared in [3]. The proof in [3] is existential, because it uses a counting argument. It has recently been made constructive in [28].

For some important early work on asynchronous PRAMs we refer to [7, 8, 13, 21, 22, 25, 26, 27, 29]. In the last three years, randomized asynchronous computation has been examined in depth in [4, 5, 20]. These analyses involve randomness in a central way. They are mostly about off-line or *oblivious* adversaries, which cause faults during the computation but pick the times of these faults before the computation.

Although, we will not survey this interesting subject here we would like to point-out that one very promising direction involves combining techniques of randomized asynchronous computation with randomized information dispersal [30]. Randomized algorithms often achieve better practical performance than deterministic ones, even when their analytical bounds are similar. Future developments in asynchronous parallel computation will employ randomization as well as the array of deterministic techniques surveyed here.

The work on fault-tolerant and efficient parallel shared memory models has also been applied to distributed message passing models; see [1, 9, 10].

In Section 3 we examine an array of algorithms for the *Write-All* problem. These employ a variety of deterministic techniques and are extensible to the computation of other functions (see Section 6). In Section 4 we examine the problem of approximate *Write-All*, which has a work optimal solution. We also provide a randomized solution for this problem, which uses random choices to improve on the work bounds (which become linear). In Section 5 we overview the trade-off between concurrency and fault tolerance for *Write-All*. We apply the resulting concurrency minimization techniques to all functions computable in the fail-stop models, without or with restarts (Section 6). Throughout or exposition we present a number of open questions, which delimit the present state-of-the-art.

2 Fault-Tolerant Parallel Computation Models

In this section we detail a hierarchy of fail-stop models of parallel computation, define relevant complexity measures and characterize *robust* algorithms.

2.1 Fail-Stop PRAMs

The parallel random access machine (PRAM) of Fortune and Wyllie [12] combines the simplicity of a RAM with the power of parallelism, and a wealth of efficient algorithms exist for it; see surveys [11, 19] for the rationale behind this model and the fundamental algorithms. We build our models of fail-stop PRAMs as extensions of the PRAM model.

1. There are Q *shared* memory cells, and the input of size $N \leq Q$ is stored in the first N cells. Except for the cells holding the input, all other memory is cleared, i.e., contains zeroes. Each memory cell can store $\Theta(\log N)$ bits. All processors can access shared memory. We assume they "know" the input size N, i.e., the $\log N$ bits describing it can be part of their finite state control. We assume that each processor also has a constant size *private* memory, that only it can access.
2. There are $P \leq N$ initial processors with unique identifiers (PIDs) in the range $1, \ldots, P$. Each processor "knows" its PID and the value of P, i.e., these can be part of its finite state control.
3. The processors that are active all execute synchronously as in the standard PRAM model [12]. Although processors proceed in synchrony and an observer outside the PRAM can associate a "global time" with every event, the processors do not have access to "global time", i.e., processors can try to keep local clocks by counting their steps and communicating through shared memory but the PRAM does not provide a "global clock".
4. Processors stop without affecting memory. They may also restart, depending on the power of a *fault-inducing adversary.*

In the study of fail-stop PRAMs, we consider three main types of failure-inducing adversaries. These form a hierarchy, based on their power. Note that, each adversary is more powerful than the preceding ones and that the last case can be used to simulate *fully asynchronous* processors [3].

Fail-stop failures: adversary causes processors to stop during the computation; there are no restarts.

Fail-stop failures, detectable restarts: adversary causes stop failures; subsequently to a failure, the adversary might restart a processor and a restarted processor "knows" of the restart.

Fail-stop failures, undetectable restarts: adversary causes stops and restarts, but a restarted processor does not necessarily "know" of the restart.

A major characteristic of these adversary models is that they are *dynamic and worst-case*. The adversaries have full information about the structure and the dynamic behavior of the algorithms whose execution they interfere with, while being completely unknown to the algorithms.

In the case of *randomized algorithms* we assume that the adversary has full information about any random choices (when they are made), but cannot a priori predict what the random bits will be before they are chosen.

We formalize failures as follows. A failure pattern F is syntactically defined as a set of triples $<tag$, PID, $t>$ where *tag* is either **failure** indicating processor failure, or **restart** indicating a processor restart, PID is the processor identifier, and t is the time indicating when the processor stops or restarts. This time is a "global time", that could be assigned by an observer (or adversary) outside the machine. The *size* of the failure pattern F is defined as the cardinality $|F|$, where $|F| \leq M$ for some parameter M.

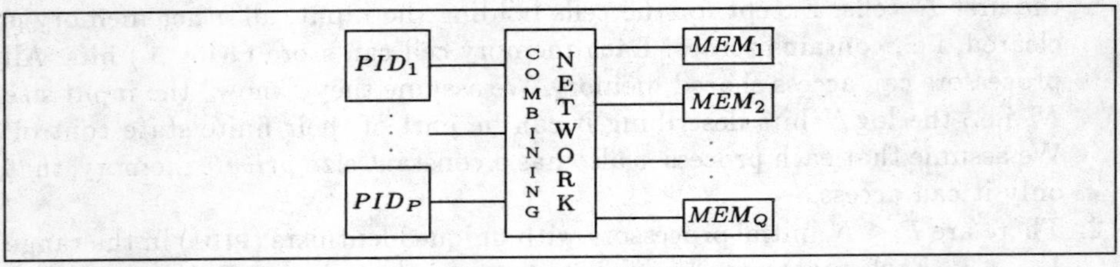

Fig. 1. An architecture for a fail-stop multiprocessor.

Remark on (un)detectable restarts. One way of realizing detectable restarts is by modifying the finite state control of the PRAM. Each instruction can have two parts, a *green* and a *red* part. The green part gets executed under normal conditions. If a processor fails then all memory remains intact, but in the subsequent restart the next instruction red part is executed instead of the green part. For example, the model used in [6, 16] can be realized this way. The undetectable restarts adversary can also be realized in a similar way by making the algorithm weaker. For undetectable restarts algorithms have to have identical red and green parts. For example, the fully asynchronous model of [3] can be realized this way.

The abstract model we are studying can be realized in the architecture in Fig. 1. There are P *fail-stop* processors [32]. There are Q shared memory cells. These semiconductor memories can be manufactured with built-in fault tolerance using replication and coding techniques [31]. Processors and memory are interconnected via a synchronous network [33]. A combining interconnection network well suited for implementing synchronous concurrent reads and writes is in [23] and can be made more reliable by employing redundancy [2].

2.2 Measures of Efficiency

We use a generalization of the standard *Parallel-time* $\times$ *Processors* product to measure work of an algorithm when the number of processors performing work fluctuates due to failures or delays [15, 16]. In the measure we account for the *available processor steps* and we do not charge for time steps during which a processor was unavailable due to a failure.

Definition 1. Consider a parallel computation with P initial processors that terminates in time τ after completing its task on some input data I of size N and in the presence of the fail-stop error pattern F. If $P_i(I,F) \leq P$ is the number of processors completing an instruction at step i, then we define $S(I,F,P)$ as: $S(I,F,P) = \sum_{i=1}^{\tau} P_i(I,F)$.

Definition 2. A P-processor PRAM algorithm on any input data I of size $|I| = N$ and in the presence of any pattern F of failures of size $|F| \leq M$ uses *available processor steps* $S = S_{N,M,P} = \max_{I,F}\{S(I,F,P)\}$.

The available processor steps measure S is used in turn to define the notion of algorithm *robustness* that combines fault tolerance and efficiency:

Definition 3. Let $T(N)$ be the best sequential (RAM) time bound known for N-size instances of a problem. We say that a parallel algorithm for this problem is a *robust parallel algorithm* if: for any input I of size N and for any number of initial processors P ($1 \leq P \leq N$) and for any failure pattern F of size at most M with at least one surviving processor ($M < N$ for fail-stop model), the algorithm completes its task with $S = S_{N,M,P} \leq c\, T(N) \log^{c'} N$, for fixed c, c'.

For arbitrary failures and restarts, the completed work measure S depends on the size N of the input I, the number of processors P, and the size M of the failure pattern F. The ultimate performance goal is to perform the required computation at a work cost as close as possible to the work performed by the best sequential algorithm known. Unfortunately, this goal is not attainable when an adversary succeeds in causing too many processor failures during a computation.

Consider a *Write-All* solution, where it takes a processor one instruction to recover from a failure. If an adversary has a failure pattern F with $|F| = \Omega(N^{1+\varepsilon})$ for $\varepsilon > 0$, then work will be $\Omega(N^{1+\varepsilon})$ regardless of how efficient the algorithm is otherwise.

This illustrates the need for a measure of efficiency that is sensitive to both the size of the input N, and the size of the failure pattern $|F| \leq M$. We thus also introduce the *overhead ratio* σ that amortizes work of the essential work and failures:

Definition 4. A P-processor PRAM algorithm on any input data I of size $|I| = N$ and in the presence of any pattern F of failures and restarts of size $|F| \leq M$ has *overhead ratio* $\sigma = \sigma_{N,M,P} = \max_{I,F}\left\{\frac{S(I,F,P)}{|I|+|F|}\right\}$.

When $M = O(P)$ as in the case of the stop failures without restarts, S properly describes the algorithm efficiency, and $\sigma = O(\frac{S_{N,M,P}}{N})$. When F can be large relative to N and P with restarts enabled, σ better reflects the efficiency of fault-tolerant algorithms. We can generalize the definition of σ in Def. 4 in terms of the ratio $\frac{S(I,F,P)}{T(I)+|F|}$, where $T(I)$ is the time complexity of the best known sequential solution for a particular problem.

Processor Issues. We have chosen to consider only the failure models where the processors do not write any erroneous or maliciously incorrect values to shared memory. While malicious processor behavior is often considered in conjunction with message passing systems, it makes less sense to consider malicious behavior in tightly coupled shared memory systems.

The fail-stop model with undetectable restarts and dynamic adversaries is the most general fault model we deal with. It can be viewed as a model of parallel computation with arbitrary asynchrony.

Memory Issues. In our models we assume that $\log N$-bit word parallel writes are performed atomically in unit time. The algorithms in such models can be modified so that this restriction is relaxed. The algorithms that assume word atomicity can be mechanically compiled into algorithms that assume only the bit atomicity.

A much more important assumption in many *Write-All* solutions was the initial state of additional auxiliary memory used (typically of $\Omega(P)$ size). The basic assumption has been that: *The $\Omega(P)$ auxiliary shared memory is cleared or initialized to some known value.*

While this is consistent with definitions of PRAM such as [12], it is nevertheless a requirement that fault-tolerant systems ought to be able to do without. Interestingly there is an efficient deterministic procedure that solves the *Write-All* problem even when the shared memory is *contaminated*, i.e., contains arbitrary values, see [36].

Interconnect Issues. In the absence of failures, any P-processor CREW (concurrent read exclusive write) or EREW (exclusive read exclusive write) PRAM can simulate a P-processor CRCW PRAM with only a factor of $O(\log P)$ more parallel work [19]. However, a more severe difference exists between CRCW and CREW PRAMs (and thus also EREW PRAMs) when the processors are subject to failures.

The choice of CRCW (concurrent read, concurrent write) model used here is justified because of a lower bound [15] that shows that the CREW (concurrent read, exclusive write) model does not admit efficient fault-tolerant algorithms.

Theorem 5 [15]. *Given any deterministic or randomized N-processor* CREW PRAM *algorithm for the* Write-All *problem (where $P = N$), the adversary can force fail-stop errors that result in $\Omega(N^2)$ steps being performed, even if the processors can read and locally process all shared memory at unit cost.*

However we would still like to control memory access concurrency. We define measures that gauge the concurrent memory accesses of a computation.

Definition 6. Consider a parallel computation with P initial processors that terminates in time τ after completing its task on some input data I of size N in the presence of fail-stop error pattern F. If at time i ($1 \leq i \leq \tau$), P_i^{R} processors perform reads from N_i^{R} shared memory locations and P_i^{W} processors perform writes to N_i^{W} locations, then we define:

(i) the *read concurrency* ρ as: $\rho = \rho_{I,F,P} = \sum_{i=1}^{\tau} (P_i^{\text{R}} - N_i^{\text{R}})$, and

(ii) the *write concurrency* ω as: $\omega = \omega_{I,F,P} = \sum_{i=1}^{\tau} (P_i^{\text{W}} - N_i^{\text{W}})$.

For a single read from (write to) a particular memory location, the read (write) concurrency ρ (ω) for that location is simply the number of readers (writers) minus one. For example, if only one processor reads from (writes to) a location, then ρ (ω) is 0, i.e., no concurrency is involved.

The concurrency measures ρ and ω are cumulative over a computation and a function of the individual computation (not only N, P, M as is S).

For the algorithms in the EREW model, $\rho = \omega = 0$, while for the CREW model, $\omega = 0$. Thus our measures capture one of the key distinctions among the EREW, CREW and CRCW memory access disciplines.

3 Exact Write-All Algorithms

3.1 Dynamic Faults and Algorithm W

Algorithm W of [15] is an efficient fail-stop *Write-All* solution (Fig. 2) when the failures are dynamically determined by an on-line adversary. It uses full binary trees for processor enumeration, processor allocation, and progress measurement. Active processors synchronously iterate through the following four phases:

W1: *Processor enumeration.* All the processors traverse bottom-up the processor enumeration tree. A version of parallel prefix algorithm is used resulting in an overestimate of the number of live processors and an enumeration of the live processors.

W2: *Processor allocation.* All the processors traverse the progress measurement tree top-down using a divide-and-conquer approach based on processor enumeration and are allocated to un-written input cells.

W3: *Work phase.* Processors work at the leaves reached in phase W2. Each leaf of the progress tree is associated with a list L of input data that is sequentially processed (for optimality the size of L is $\log N$).

W4: *Progress measurement.* All the processors traverse bottom-up the progress tree using a version of parallel prefix and compute an underestimate of the progress of the algorithm.

Algorithm W achieves optimality when parameterized on L using a progress tree with $N/\log N$ leaves and $\log N$ input data associated with each of its leaves. By optimality we mean that for a range of processors the work is $O(N)$. A complete description of the algorithm can be found in [15]. Martel [24] gave a tight analysis of algorithm W.

Theorem 7 [15, 24]. *Algorithm W is a robust parallel Write-All algorithm with* $S = O(N + P\log^2 N/\log\log N)$, *where* N *is the input array size and the initial number of processors* P *is between* 1 *and* N.

```
forall processors PID=1..P parbegin
   Phase W3: Visit leaves based on PID to work on the input data
   Phase W4: Traverse the progress tree bottom up to measure progress
   while the root of the progress tree is not N do
      Phase W1: Traverse counting tree bottom up to enumerate processors
      Phase W2: Traverse the progress tree top down to reschedule work
      Phase W3: Perform rescheduled work on the input data
      Phase W4: Traverse the progress tree bottom up to measure progress
   od
parend
```

Fig. 2. A high level view of algorithm W.

The above bound is tight for algorithm W. This upper bound was first shown in [21] for a different algorithm. The data structuring technique [21] might lead to even better bounds for *Write-All*. The best lower bound to date is $\Omega(N + P \log N)$.

Note that, in a "snapshot" model, where all memory can be read and locally processed in unit time but where writes are accounted as before, algorithm W is optimal in $\Theta(N + P \log N / \log\log N)$ [15, 16].

Open Problem A: Is there an optimal algorithm for *Write-All* in the fail-stop no restart model, e.g., with $\Omega(N + P \log N)$ work?

3.2 Dynamic Faults, Detected Restarts, and Algorithm V

Algorithm W has efficient work when subjected to arbitrary failure patterns without restarts and it can be extended to handle restarts. However, since accurate processor enumeration is impossible if processors can be restarted at any time, the work of the algorithm becomes inefficient even for some simple adversaries. On the other hand, the second phase of algorithm W does implement efficient top-down divide-and-conquer processor assignment in $O(\log N)$ time when permanent processor PIDs are used. Therefore we produce a modified version of algorithm W, that we call V. To avoid a restatement of the details, the reader is referred to [16].

V uses the optimized algorithm W data structures for progress estimation and processor allocation. The processors iterate through the following three phases based on the phases W2, W3 and W4 of algorithm W:

- V1: Processors are allocated as in the phase W2, but using the permanent PIDs. This assures load balancing in $O(\log N)$ time.
- V2: Processors perform work, as in the phase W3, at the leaves they reached in phase V1 (there are $\log N$ array elements per leaf).
- V3: Processors continue from the phase V2 progress tree leaves and update the progress tree bottom up as in phase W4 in $O(\log N)$ time.

The model assumes re-synchronization on the instruction level, and a wrap-around counter based on the PRAM clock implements synchronization with respect to the phases after detected failures [16]. The work and the overhead ratio of the algorithm are as follows:

Theorem 8 [16]. *Algorithm V using $P \leq N$ processors subject to an arbitrary failure and restart pattern F of size M has work $S = O(N + P\log^2 N + M\log N)$ and overhead ratio $\sigma = O(\log^2 N)$.*

One problem with the above approach is that there could be a large number of restarts and a large amount of work. Algorithm V can be combined with algorithm X of the next section or with the asymptotically better algorithm of [3] to provide better bounds on work.

3.3 Dynamic Faults, Undetected Restarts, Algorithms X and Y

When the failures cannot be detected, it is still possible to achieve sub-quadratic upper bound for any dynamic failure/restart pattern. We present *Write-All* algorithm X with $S = O(N \cdot P^{\log \frac{3}{2}}) = N \cdot P^{0.59}$ [6, 16]. This simple algorithm can be improved to $S = O(N \cdot P^{\epsilon})$ using the method in [3]. We present X for its simplicity and in the next section a (possible) deterministic version of [3].

Algorithm X utilizes a progress tree of size N that is traversed by the processors independently, not in synchronized phases. This reflects the local nature of the processor assignment as opposed to the global assignments used in algorithms V and W. Each processor searches for work in the smallest subtree that has work that needs to be done. It performs the work, and moves to the next subtree.

```
01 forall processors PID=0..P-1 parbegin
02    Perform initial processor assignment to the leaves of the progress tree
03    while there is still work left in the tree do
04       if subtree rooted at current node u is done then move one level up
05       elseif u is a leaf then perform the work at the leaf
06       elseif u is an interior tree node then
07          Let u_L and u_R be the left and right children of u respectively
08          if the subtrees rooted at u_L and u_R are done then update u
09          elseif only one is done then go to the one that is not done
10          else move to u_L or u_R according to PID bit values
11       fi fi
12    od
13 parend
```

Fig. 3. A high level view of algorithm X.

The algorithm is given in Fig. 3. Initially the P processors are assigned to the leaves of the progress tree (line 02). The *loop* (lines 03-12) consists of a multi-way decision (lines 04-11). If the current node u is marked done, the processor moves up the tree (line 04). If the processor is at a leaf, it performs work (line 05). If the current node is an unmarked interior node and both of its subtrees are done, the interior node is marked by changing its value from 0 to 1 (line 08). If a single subtree is not done, the processor moves down appropriately (line 09). For the final case (line 10), the processors move down when neither child is done. Here the processor PID is used at depth h of the tree node: based on the value of the hth most significant bit of the binary representation of PID, bit 0 will send the processor to the left, and bit 1 to the right.

The performance of algorithm X is characterized as follows:

Theorem 9 [6, 16]. *Algorithm X with P processors solves the Write-All problem of size N ($P \leq N$) in the fail-stop restartable model with work $S = O(N \cdot P^{\log \frac{3}{2}})$. In addition, there is an adversary that forces algorithm X to perform $S = \Omega(N \cdot P^{\log \frac{3}{2}})$ work.*

The algorithm views undetected restarts as delays, and it can be used in the asynchronous model where it has the same work [6]. Algorithm X could also be useful for the case without restarts, even though its worst-case performance without restarts is no better than algorithm W.

A family of randomized *Write-All* algorithms was presented by Anderson and Woll [3]. The main technique in these algorithms is abstracted in Fig. 4. The basic algorithm in [3] is obtained by randomly choosing the permutation in line 03. In this case the expected work of the algorithm is $O(N \log N)$, for $P = \sqrt{N}$ (assume N is a square).

```
01 forall processors PID = 1..√N parbegin
02   Divide the N array elements into √N work groups of √N elements
03   Each processor obtains a private permutation π_PID of {1, 2, ..., √N}
04   for i = 1..√N do
05     if π_PID[i]th group is not finished then
06       perform sequential work on the √N elements of the group
07       and mark the group as finished
08     fi
09   od
10 parend
```

Fig. 4. A high level view of the algorithm Y.

We propose the following way of determinizing the algorithm (see [17]): Given $P = \sqrt{N}$, we choose the smallest prime m such that $P < m$. Primes are sufficiently dense, so that there is at least one prime between P and $2P$, so that the complexity of the algorithms is not distorted when P is not a prime. We then construct the multiplication table for the numbers $1, 2, \ldots m-1$ modulo m. Each row of this table is a permutation and this structure is a group. Processor with PID i uses the ith permutation as its schedule.

This table need not be pre-computed, as any item can be computed directly by any processor with the knowledge of its PID, and the number of work elements W it has processed thus far as $(PID \cdot w)$ **mod** m.

The most interesting open problems in this area arise in the model of dynamic faults, undetected restarts.

Open Problem B: What is the performance of deterministic algorithm Y? We conjecture that it uses $O(N \log N)$ work.

Open Problem C: The major open problem for the case of undetectable restarts is whether there is a robust *Write-All* solution, i.e., one with work $N \cdot \text{polylog}(N)$. Also, whether there is a solution with $\sigma = \text{polylog}(N)$.

3.4 Algorithms for Initial Faults

An assumption made by all of the above algorithms is that global memory is initially clear. It turns out that this assumption is not critical for the existence of efficient *Write-All* algorithms.

Algorithm Z of [36] is an efficient *Write-All* algorithm for the case that the global memory may be contaminated (i.e., set to arbitrary initial values). It works by combining a *bootstrap* approach with algorithm W. The algorithm makes a number of iterations.

At the beginning, all processors clear a small initial segment of memory. In subsequent iterations the memory cleared in the previous step is used to execute W in order to clear a bigger memory segment. By an appropriate choice of the relationship between the sizes of consecutive segments of clear memory the algorithm can be made to terminate in $O(\log N / \log\log N)$ iterations resulting in a *Write-All* solution that has work $S = O(N + P \log^3 N / (\log\log N)^2)$ *without any initialization assumptions.*

Looking at another variation of *Write-All*, [14] consider the case of *static* processor faults. This is the situation where all the processor faults occur at the beginning of the execution of the *Write-All* algorithm and no processors are allowed to fail once the algorithm has begun executing.

It turns out that this is a much simpler case that does not require any concurrent memory accesses. Algorithm E of [14] solves the *Write-All* problem with static faults optimally with work $S = O(N + P' \log P)$, where $P' \leq P$ is the number of live processors at the beginning of the execution. Like Z this algorithm makes no assumptions about the initial memory contents.

Although much is known about handling static faults, an interesting open problem remains.

Open Problem D: Prove the $\Omega(N + P \log N)$ lower bound on *Write-All* on a CRCW PRAM with initial faults only (the previous lower bounds make use of dynamic faults [21]).

4 Approximate Write-All Algorithms

So far we have required that all array locations be set to 1; this is the *exact Write-All* problem. In this section we relax the requirement that all locations be set to 1 and instead require that only a fraction of them be written into. For any $0 < \varepsilon < \frac{1}{2}$ we define the *approximate Write-All* problem, denoted AWA(ε), as the problem of initializing at least $(1-\varepsilon)N$ array locations to 1.

We can interpret the exact *Write-All* as a computation of a function, where the result of an exact *Write-All* algorithm is a single vector value (with all locations set to 1), whereas the approximate *Write-All* would correspond to the computation of a relation, where the result could be one of several different vectors (with any $(1-\varepsilon)N$ locations set to 1).

4.1 Computing Approximate Write-All Optimally

Here we show that computing some relations robustly is easier than computing functions robustly.

Consider the majority relation $\mathcal{M}$: Given a binary array $x[1..N]$, $x \in \mathcal{M}$ when $|\{x[i] : x[i] = 1\}| > \frac{1}{2}N$. Dwork observed that the $\Omega(N \log N)$ lower bound of [21] on solving exact *Write-All* using N processors also applies to determining membership in $\mathcal{M}$ in the presence of failures. It turns out that $O(N \log N)$ work is also sufficient to compute a member of the majority relation.

Let's parameterize the majority problem in terms of the approximate *Write-All* problem by using the quantity ε such that $0 < \varepsilon < \frac{1}{2}$. As discussed above we would like to initialize at least $(1-\varepsilon)N$ array locations to 1. Surprisingly, algorithm W has the desired property:

Theorem 10 [18]. *Given any constant ε such that $0 < \varepsilon < \frac{1}{2}$, algorithm W solves the AWA(ε) problem with $S = O(N \log N)$ using N processors.*

If we choose $\varepsilon = 1/2^k$ (k a constant) and iterate this *Write-All* algorithm $\log\log N$ times, the number of unvisited leaves will be $N\varepsilon^{\log\log N} = N(\log N)^{\log \varepsilon}$ $= N(\log N)^{-k} = N/\log^k N$. Thus we can get even closer to solving the *Write-All* problem:

Theorem 11 [18]. *For each constant k, there is a robust AWA($\frac{1}{\log^k N}$) algorithm that has work $S = O(N \log N \log\log N)$.*

4.2 Linear Work Using Randomization

We close our exposition of AWA with an observation that illustrates the power of randomization (vs determinism). As shown in [21], deterministic *Write-All* solutions have a work lower bound of $\Omega(N \log N)$ when the number of active processors is N. This is true even for approximate *Write-All*. There is, however, a simple randomized *Write-All* algorithm for the approximate case that requires linear work, under a slightly weaker survivability assumption.

This simple probabilistic algorithm consists of having each processor pick independently at random one of the N locations and set it to 1. If the number of locations that must be written is $N' = \alpha N$ for some constant $0 < \alpha < 1$ this method results in a CRCW Monte-Carlo algorithm with linear expected work.

This algorithmic method has been used in [25, 27]. (For a definition of Monte-Carlo probabilistic algorithms see [19]). Let us first present an analysis without faults.

Lemma 12. *Let N be the size of an array initialized to 0 and let $P \leq N$ be the number of processors of a fault-free CRCW PRAM. If at each parallel step each processor sets to 1 an array location chosen independently uniformly at random, then the expected work required to set to 1 a number $N' < N$ of locations is $O(N \log \frac{N}{N-N'})$ and the expected number of parallel steps is $O(\frac{N}{P} \log \frac{N}{N-N'})$.*

Proof. Since the random choices are independent we consider these choices as if they occured sequentially. Let W_i be the random variable denoting the number of trials needed to go from i to $i+1$ array locations set to 1, $0 \leq i \leq N'-1$. Then the work of the algorithm is $W = W_0 + \cdots + W_{N'-1}$. Each of the W_i's is geometrically distributed with success probability $\frac{N-i}{N}$ so that $E(W_i) = \frac{N}{N-i}$. Then the expected work of the algorithm (expected number of choices needed) is

$$\begin{aligned} E(W) &= \sum_{i=0}^{N'-1} E(W_i) \\ &= \sum_{i=0}^{N'-1} \frac{N}{N-i} \\ &= N(H_N - H_{N-N'}) \\ &= N \ln \frac{N}{N-N'} + O(\frac{1}{N}) \\ &= O(N \log \frac{N}{N-N'}) \end{aligned}$$

where H_i is the ith harmonic number. Since the choices are independent P such choices can be made at each parallel step so that the expected number of parallel steps is $E(T) = \frac{E(W)}{P} = O(\frac{N}{P} \log \frac{N}{N-N'})$. □

Clearly, if we allow any number of processor failures, then an adversary can fail enough processors that no *Write-All* algorithm, not even randomized, can terminate in constant parallel time. If we make the additional assumption, however, that the number of surviving processors is linear in the size of the input, then the randomized algorithm given above requires only constant parallel steps.

Theorem 13. *The approximate Write-All problem of size N where the number of locations to be written is αN and the number of surviving processors is at least βN, for some constants $0 < \alpha, \beta < 1$ can be solved probabilistically on a CRCW PRAM with expected $O(N)$ work in expected $O(1)$ parallel steps.*

Proof. From the above theorem for $N' = \alpha N$ we obtain

$$E(W) = N \ln \frac{1}{1-\alpha} + O(\frac{1}{N}) = O(N)$$

and the expected number of parallel steps is

$$E(T) = \frac{1}{\beta} \ln \frac{1}{1-\alpha} + O(\frac{1}{N^2}) = O(1).$$

□

Note that the assumption that βN processors survive is only needed to obtain the bound on the expected number of parallel steps. The expected work does not depend on any survivability assumptions. To have a termination condition in the algorithm we stop the processors after a constant, e.g., $kE(T)$ number of rounds.

Open Problem E: The constant-time randomized algorithm described above is of the Monte-Carlo variety, i.e., it may fail to accomplish its task within the stated bounds. It is an open question whether there is a Las Vegas randomized algorithm (i.e., one that always succeeds) with similar performance bounds.

5 Minimizing Concurrency

Among the key lower bound results is the fact that no efficient fault-tolerant CREW PRAM *Write-All* algorithms exist [15] — if the adversary is dynamic then any P-processor solution for the *Write-All* problem of size N will have (deterministic) work $\Omega(N \cdot P)$. Thus memory access concurrency is necessary to combine efficiency and fault tolerance. However, while most known solutions for the *Write-All* problem indeed make heavy use of concurrency, the goal of minimizing concurrent access to shared memory is attainable.

5.1 Minimizing Concurrency: Processor Priority Trees

We gave a *Write-All* algorithm in [14] in which we bound the *total amount of concurrency* used in terms of the *number of dynamic processor faults* of the actual algorithm run. The algorithm is an extension of algorithm W and its key new ingredient is the organization of all processors that need to access a common memory location into a *processor priority tree* (PPT).

In the rest of our discussion we assume that T is a memory location that needs to be accessed by $p \leq P$ processors simultaneously. We concentrate here on concurrent writes and treat concurrent reads in the next section.

A PPT is a binary tree whose nodes are associated with processors based on a processor numbering. All levels of the tree but the last are full and the leaves of the last level are packed as left as possible. PPT nodes are numbered from 1 to p in a breadth-first left-to-right fashion where the parent of the ith node has index $\lfloor i/2 \rfloor$ and its left/right children have indices $2i$ and $2i+1$, respectively. Processors are also numbered from 1 to p and the ith processor is associated with the ith node. *Priorities* are assigned to the processors based on the level they are at. The root has the highest priority and priorities decrease according to the distance from the root. Processors at the same level of the tree have the same priority, which is lower than that of their parents.

Processor priorities are used to determine when a processor can write to the common memory location T. All the processors with the same priority attempt to write to T concurrently but *only if higher priority processors have failed to do so*. To accomplish this the processors of a PPT concurrently execute algorithm CW, shown in Fig. 5. Starting at the root (highest priority) and going down the tree one level at a time, the processors at each level first read T and then concurrently update it iff it contains an old value. This implies that if level i processors effect the write, all processors at higher levels must have failed.

```
forall processors ID = 1..p parbegin
  --Processors write a new value to location T as follows
  for i = 0 .. ⌊log p⌋ do  --For each level i of processor priority tree
    if 2^i ≤ ID < 2^(i+1) then  --The processors at level i
      READ location T
      if T does not contain new value then
        WRITE new value to T
    fi fi
  od
parend
```

Fig. 5. Pseudocode for the controlled write (CW) algorithm.

Whereas unrestricted concurrent writes by $p \leq P$ processors take only one step to update T, a PPT requires as many steps as there are levels in the tree, i.e., $O(\log p)$. The following lemma is instrumental in bounding the write concurency.

Lemma 14 [14]. *If algorithm* CW *is executed in the presence of a failure pattern F, then its write concurrency ω is no more than the number of failures $|F|$.*

A *Write-All* algorithm with controlled write concurrency can be obtained by incorporating PPTs into the four phases of algorithm W. This is done by replacing each concurrent write in these phases by an execution of CW. We allow $\lfloor \log P \rfloor + 1$ steps for each execution of CW, thus slowing down each iteration of the original algorithm W by a $O(\log P)$ factor. The resulting algorithm is known as W_{CW} [14].

PPTs are organized and maintained as follows. At the outset of the algorithm and at the beginning of each execution of phase W1 each processor forms a PPT by itself. As processors traverse bottom up the trees used by algorithm W they may encounter processors coming from the sibling node. In this case the two PPTs are *merged* to produce a larger PPT at the common parent of the two nodes. In order to be able to use Lemma 14 to bound the overall write concurrency of the algorithm, we must guarantee that a newly constructed PPT has no processors that have already been accounted for as dead in the above lemma. Such processors are those that are above the PPT level that effected the write. In order to accomplish this we *compact* PPTs before merging to eliminate these processors.

To compact and merge two PPTs, the processors of each PPT store in the memory location they are to update the size of the PPT, the index of the level that effected the write and a timestamp along with the new value to be stored in this location. A timestamp in this context is just a sequence number that need not exceed N (see [15]). Since there can be at most P processors, $O(\log N) + O(\log N) + O(\log P) + O(\log\log P) = O(\log N)$ bits of information need to be stored for the new value, the timestamp, the size of the tree and the level index.

After the $\log P$ steps of CW, the processors of each of the two PPTs to be merged read concurrently the information stored in the two memory locations they updated and compute the size of the resulting PPT, which is the sum of the two sizes read less the number of the certifiably dead processors above the levels that effected the writes. By convention, when two PPTs are merged the processors of the left PPT are added to the bottom of the right one. The timestamp is needed so that processors can check whether the values they read are current (i.e., there is some PPT at the sibling node and merging has to take place) or old. This process is illustrated in Fig. 6.

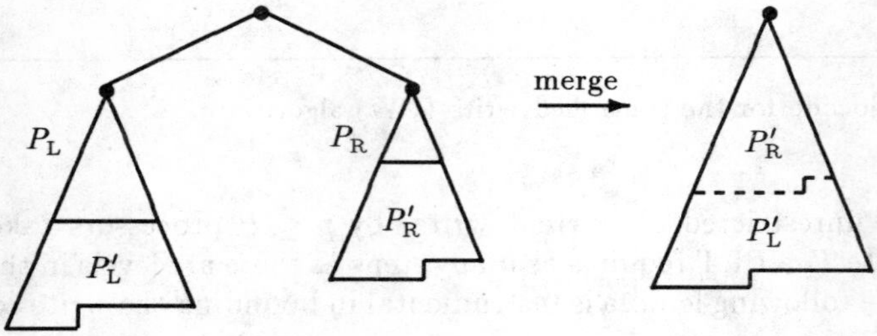

Fig. 6. Merging and compacting two PPTs.

Further details of algorithm W_{CW} are provided in [14]. The following theorem describes its performance.

Theorem 15 [14]. *Algorithm* W_{CW} *is a robust algorithm for the Write-All problem with* $\omega \leq |F|$ *and work* $S = O(N \log N \log P + P \log P \log^2 N / \log\log N)$, *where* $1 \leq P \leq N$.

5.2 Controlling Read/Write Concurrency

Algorithm CW can be extended to also handle concurrent reads. The basic idea here is to replace concurrent reads by broadcasts through each PPT. The broadcasts are performed in an elaborate way that allows us to control read concurrency without degrading CW's performance. It relies on the observation that each level of a PPT contains one more processor than all the levels above it. This allows us to use levels $0, \ldots, i-1$ to broadcast to level i in constant time.

```
01 --Code executed by each of the p processors in the PPT
02 Initialize B[ID]  --broadcast location for processor ID
03 for i = 0...⌊log p⌋ do  --for each level i of the PPT
04    if 2^i ≤ ID < 2^(i+1) then  --if the processor is at level i
05       READ B[ID]
06       if B[ID] has not been updated then
07          READ (value, level) from T
08          if T contains some old value then
09             level := i  --level i effects the write
10             WRITE (newvalue, level) to T
11          else if 2^level ≤ ID − 2^i + 1 < 2^i then
12             ID := ID − 2^i + 1  --replace the processor that was to update B[ID]
13    fi fi fi fi
14    if ID < 2^(i+1) and ID + 2^(i+1) ≤ p then  --if the processor's level is ≤ i
15       WRITE newvalue to B[ID + 2^(i+1)]  --broadcast to level i + 1
16    fi
17 od
```

Fig. 7. High level view of algorithm CR/W for the controlled read/write. ID is the position of the processor in the PPT and *newvalue* is the value to be written.

Algorithm CR/W: A high level view of this algorithm, that we call CR/W, is given in Fig. 7. The broadcast takes place through a shared memory array (B in Fig. 7). Such an array is used by each PPT so that processors can communicate with each other based on their positions in the PPT; $B[k]$ stores values read by the kth processor of the PPT. This allows processors to communicate without requiring them to know each other's identity. These arrays can be stored in a segment of memory of size P for all the PPTs (see [14]).

Each processor on levels $0, \ldots, i-1$ is associated with exactly one processor on each of levels $i, i+1, \ldots$. Specifically, the jth processor of the PPT is responsible for broadcasting to the jth (in a left-to-right numbering) processor of each level below its own. The algorithm proceeds in $\lfloor \log p \rfloor + 1$ iterations that correspond to the PPT levels. At iteration i, each processor of level i reads its B location (line 5). If this location has not been updated, then the processor reads T directly (lines 6–7).

Since a PPT level has potentially more live processors than all the levels above it combined, there is in general at least one processor on each level that reads T since no processor at a higher level is assigned to it. If a level is full, this processor is the rightmost one (the root of the PPT for level 0). As long as there are no failures this is the only direct access to T. Concurrent accesses can occur only in the presence of failures. In such a case several processors on the same level may fail to receive values from processors at higher levels, in which case they will access T directly incurring concurrent reads.

A processor that needs to read T directly first checks whether it contains the value to be written (line 8) and then writes to it (line 10) if it does not. As can be seen from the figure, whenever processors update T they write not only the new value for T but also the index of the level that effected the write.

If a processor P_k that accesses T directly verifies that T has the correct value and the failed processor that should have broadcast to P_k is at or below the level that effected the write, then P_k assumes the position of the failed processor in the PPT (lines 11–12). This effectively moves failed processors towards the leaves of the PPT and plays an important role in establishing the bound on the read concurrency. Failed processors are moved towards the leaves only if they are not above the level that effects the write since processors above this level will be eliminated by compaction as was done in the previous section.

Algorithms CR1 and CR2: In addition to CR/W we use two simpler algorithms when all the processors of a PPT need to read a common memory location but no write is involved.

The *first* of them, referred to as CR1, is similar to CR/W but without the write step (lines 8–10). It is also simpler than CR/W in that processors that are found to have failed are pushed towards the bottom of the PPT irrespective of the level they are at. This algorithm is used for bottom-up traversals during W.

The *second* algorithm, referred to as CR2, uses a simple top-down broadcast through the PPT. Starting with the root each processor broadcasts to its two children; if a processor fails then its two children read T directly. Thus the processors of level i are responsible to broadcast only to processors of level $i+1$. No processor movement takes place. This algorithm is used for top-down traversals during W.

Clearly, all three of CR/W, CR1, and CR2 require $O(\log P)$ time for PPTs of at most P processors.

Algorithm $W_{CR/W}$: Incorporating algorithms CR/W, CR1, and CR2 along with the techniques of PPT compaction and merging into W results in a *Write-All* algorithm that controls both read and write concurrency. The details of this algorithm, known as $W_{CR/W}$, can be found in [14]. The following theorem provides bounds on the performance of $W_{CR/W}$.

Theorem 16 [14]. *Algorithm* $W_{CR/W}$ *is a robust algorithm for the Write-All problem with* $S = O(N \log N \log P + P \log P \log^2 N / \log\log N)$, *read concurrency* $\rho \leq 7\,|F| \log N$, *and write concurrency* $\omega \leq |F|$, *where* $1 \leq P \leq N$.

By taking advantage of parallel slackness and by clustering the input data into groups of size $\log N \log P$, we can obtain a modification of algorithm $W_{CR/W}$ that has a non trivial processor optimality range. The modified algorithm, known as $W^{opt}_{CR/W}$, is described in [14]. Its performance is characterized by the following theorem:

Theorem 17 [14]. *Algorithm* $W^{opt}_{CR/W}$ *is a robust algorithm for the Write-All problem with* $S = O(N + P\frac{\log^2 N \log^2 P}{\log\log N})$, *write concurrency* $\omega \leq |F|$, *and read concurrency* $\rho \leq 7\,|F| \log N$, *where* $1 \leq P \leq N$.

The algorithm can be further extended to handle arbitrary initial memory contents [14]. It is also possible to reduce the maximum *per step* memory access concurrency by polylogarithmic factors by utilizing a general pipelining technique. Finally, [14] established a lower bound showing that no robust *Write-All* algorithm exists with write concurrency $\omega \le |F|^{\varepsilon}$ for $0 \le \varepsilon < 1$.

6 General Computations with Minimal Concurrency

In this section we will work our way from the simplest to the most complicated functions with robust solutions.

6.1 Constants, Booleans and Write-All

Solving a *Write-All* problem of size N can be viewed as computing a constant vector function. Constant scalar functions are the simplest possible functions (e.g., simpler than boolean OR and AND).

At the same time, it appears that the *Write-All* problem is a more difficult (vector) task than computing scalar boolean functions such as multiple input OR and AND. One of the known lower bounds applies to the model with *memory snapshots*, i.e., processors can read and process the entire shared memory in unit time [15]. For the snapshot model there is a sharp separation between *Write-All* and boolean functions. Clearly, any boolean function can be computed in constant time and $O(N)$ work in the snapshot model, while we have a lower bound result for any *Write-All* solution in the snapshot model requiring work $\Omega(N\frac{\log N}{\log\log N})$.

6.2 General Parallel Assignment

Consider computing and storing in an array $x[1..N]$ the values of a vector function f that depend on PIDs and the initial values of the array x. Assume each of the N scalar components of f can be computed in $O(1)$ sequential time. This is the *general parallel assignment* problem.

forall processors $PID = 1..N$ **parbegin**
    shared integer array $x[1..N]$;
    $x[PID] := f(PID, x[1..N])$
parend

In [15] a general technique was shown for making this operation robust using the same work as required by *Write-All*. We modify the assignment so that it remains correct when processors fail and when multiple attempts are made to execute the assignment (assuming the surviving processors can be reassigned to the tasks of faulty processors). This is done using binary version numbers and two generations of the array:

forall processors $PID = 1..N$ **parbegin**
    shared integer array $x[0..1][1..N]$;
    bit integer v;
    $x[v+1][PID] := f(PID, x[v][1..N])$;
    $v := v + 1$
parend

Here, bit v is the current version number or tag (mod 2), so that $x[v][1 \ldots N]$ is the array of current values. Function f will use only these values of x as its input. The values of f are stored in $x[v+1][1 \ldots N]$ creating the next generation of array x. After all the assignments are performed, the binary version number is incremented (mod 2).

At this point, a simple transformation of any *Write-All* algorithm, with the modified *general parallel assignment* replacing the trivial "$x[i] = 1$" assignment, will yield a robust N-processor algorithm:

Theorem 18. *The asymptotic work complexities of solving the general parallel assignment problem and the Write-All problem are equal.*

6.3 Any PRAM Step

The original motivation for studying the *Write-All* problem was that it captured the essence of a single PRAM step computation. It was shown in [22, 34] how to use the *Write-All* paradigm in implementing general PRAM simulations. The generality of this result is somewhat surprising.

Fail-stop faults: An approach to such simulations is given in Fig. 8. The simulations are implemented by robustly executing each of the cycles of the PRAM step: instruction fetch, read, compute, and write cycles, and next instruction address computation. This is done using two generations of shared memory, "current" and "future", and by executing each of these cycles in the *general parallel assignment* style, e.g., using algorithm W.

Using such techniques it was shown in [22, 34] that if $S_w(N, P)$ is the efficiency of solving a *Write-All* instance of size N using P processors, and if a linear amount of clear memory is available, then any N-processor PRAM step can be deterministically simulated using P fail-stop processors and work $S_w(N, P)$. If the *Parallel-time* $\times$ *Processors* of an original N-processor algorithm is $\tau \cdot N$, then the work of the fault-tolerant simulation will be $O(\tau \cdot S_w(N, P))$.

By using algorithm $\mathrm{W}^{\mathrm{opt}}_{\mathrm{CR/W}}$ we obtain efficient PRAM simulations on fail-stop PRAMs whose concurrency depends on the number of failures. In particular, we obtain the following:

Theorem 19 [14]. *Any N processor, τ parallel time EREW PRAM algorithm can be simulated on a fail-stop P-processor CRCW PRAM using work $O(\tau \cdot (N + \frac{P \log^2 P \log^2 N}{\log \log N}))$ so that the write concurrency of the simulation is $\omega \le |F|$ and the read concurrency is $\rho \le 7|F| \log N$, for any fail-stop failure pattern F and $1 \le P \le N$.*

The work bound of this theorem also holds for simulations of non-EREW PRAM algorithms but the concurrency bounds depend on the concurrency of the simulated algorithm. If ω_0 and ρ_0 are the write and read concurrencies of the simulated algorithm, respectively, then for the simulation we have $\omega \le |F| + \omega_0$ and $\rho \le 7|F| \log N + \rho_0\, O(\log N)$. Alternatively, we can maintain the same concurrency bounds at the expense of increasing the work by a logarithmic factor by first converting the original algorithm into an equivalent EREW algorithm [19].

When the full range of simulating processors is used ($P = N$) optimality is not achievable. In this case customized transformations of parallel algorithms (such as prefix and list ranking algorithms [25, 35]) may improve on the oblivious simulations.

```
forall processors PID=1..P parbegin  --Simulate N fault-prone processors
  The PRAM program for N processors is in shared memory (read-only)
  Shared memory has two generations: current and future;
  Initialize N simulated instruction counters to start at the first instruction
  while there is a simulated processor that has not halted do
    --Tentative computation: Fetch instruction; Copy registers to scratchpad
      Perform read cycle using current memory
      Perform the compute cycle using scratchpad
      Perform write cycle into future memory
      Compute next instruction address
    --Reconcile memory and registers: Copy future locations to current
  od
parend
```

Fig. 8. Simulations using *Write-All* primitive.

Fail-stop faults with detectable restarts: For the model with detectable restarts we have the following simulation theorem:

Theorem 20. *Any N processor, τ parallel time EREW PRAM algorithm can be simulated on a fail-stop P-processor CRCW PRAM with detectable restarts using work $O(\tau \cdot (N \log P + P \log P \log^2 N) + |F| \log N \log P)$ and overhead ratio $\sigma = O(\log^2 N \log P)$ so that the write concurrency of the simulation is $\omega \leq |F|$ and the read concurrency is $\rho \leq 7|F| \log N$, for any failure/restart pattern F and $1 \leq P \leq N$.*

Proof. To obtain this result we use algorithm $\mathrm{W_{CR/W}}$ with $\log N$ elements clustered at each leaf of the progress tree and then apply the analysis of algorithm V [16]. This algorithm differs from $\mathrm{W_{CR/W}}$ for the no-restarts model in that a failed processor upon restarting waits until the beginning of the next W1 phase. This gives rise to the $|F| \log N \log P$ term in the work bound. □

Note that the above algorithm is not optimal and the work may be unbounded since F may be arbitrarily large.

Open Problem F: It is open whether there exist robust simulations that achieve both limited concurrency and bounded work for the detectable restart model.

Fail-stop faults with undetectable restarts: When the failures are undetectable, deterministic simulations become difficult due to the possibility of processors delayed due to failures writing stale values to shared memory. Fortunately, for fast polylogarithmic time parallel algorithms we can solve this problem by using polylogarithmically more memory. We simply provide as many "future" generations of memory as there are PRAM steps to simulate. Processor registers are stored in shared memory along with each generation of shared memory.

Prior to starting a parallel step simulation, a processor uses binary search to find the newest simulated step. When reading, a processor linearly searches past generations of memory to find the latest written value. In the result below we use the existential algorithm [3].

Theorem 21. *Any N-processor, $\log^{O(1)} N$-time, Q-memory* PRAM *alg. can be determin. executed on a fail-stop P processor* CRCW PRAM *$(P \leq N)$ with undetectable restarts, and using shared memory $Q \cdot \log^{O(1)} N$. Each N-processor PRAM step is executed in the presence of any pattern F of* failures *and* undetected restarts *with $S = O(N^{1+\varepsilon})$, for any positive ε.*

Open Problem G: It is open whether there exist (robust) PRAM simulations with limited concurrency for the undetectable restart model.

The fail-stop model with undetectable restarts is clearly the most challenging model, both from a technical and from a practical point of view. The simulation result above is considerably weaker than what is achievable for the other models. This is an area where the application of randomized techniques (e.g., [4, 5, 20]) is most promising.

References

1. M. Ajtai, J. Aspnes, C. Dwork, O. Waarts, "The Competitive Analysis of Wait-Free Algorithms and its Application to the Cooperative Collect Problem", *to appear in PODC*, 1994.
2. G. B. Adams III, D. P. Agrawal, H. J. Seigel, "A Survey and Comparison of Fault-tolerant Multistage Interconnection Networks", *IEEE Computer*, 20, 6, pp. 14-29, 1987.
3. R. Anderson, H. Woll, "Wait-Free Parallel Algorithms for the Union-Find Problem", *Proc. of the 23rd ACM Symp. on Theory of Computing*, pp. 370-380, 1991.
4. Y. Aumann and M.O. Rabin, "Clock Construction in Fully Asynchronous Parallel Systems and PRAM Simulation", in *Proc. of the 33rd IEEE Symposium on Foundations of Computer Science*, pp. 147-156, 1992.
5. Y. Aumann, Z.M. Kedem, K.V. Palem, M.O. Rabin, "Highly Efficient Asynchronous Execution of Large-Grained Parallel Programs", in *Proc. of the 34th IEEE Symposium on Foundations of Computer Science*, pp. 271-280, 1993.
6. J. Buss, P.C. Kanellakis, P. Ragde, A.A. Shvartsman, "Parallel algorithms with processor failures and delays", Brown Univ. TR CS-91-54, August 1991.
7. R. Cole and O. Zajicek, "The APRAM: Incorporating Asynchrony into the PRAM Model," in *Proc. of the 1989 ACM Symp. on Parallel Algorithms and Architectures*, pp. 170-178, 1989.
8. R. Cole and O. Zajicek, "The Expected Advantage of Asynchrony," in *Proc. 2nd ACM Symp. on Parallel Algorithms and Architectures*, pp. 85-94, 1990.

9. R. DePrisco, A. Mayer, M. Yung, "Time-Optimal Message-Efficient Work Performance in the Presence of Faults," *to appear in PODC*, 1994.
10. C. Dwork, J. Halpern, O. Waarts, "Accomplishing Work in the Presence of Failures" in *Proc. 11th ACM Symposium on Principles of Distributed Computing*, pp. 91-102, 1992.
11. D. Eppstein and Z. Galil, "Parallel Techniques for Combinatorial Computation", *Annual Computer Science Review*, 3 (1988), pp. 233-83.
12. S. Fortune and J. Wyllie, "Parallelism in Random Access Machines", *Proc. the 10th ACM Symposium on Theory of Computing*, pp. 114-118, 1978.
13. P. Gibbons, "A More Practical PRAM Model," in *Proc. of the 1989 ACM Symposium on Parallel Algorithms and Architectures*, pp. 158-168, 1989.
14. P. C. Kanellakis, D. Michailidis, A. A. Shvartsman, "Controlling Memory Access Concurrency in Efficient Fault-Tolerant Parallel Algorithms", *7th Intl Workshop on Distributed Algorithms*, pp. 99-114, 1993. An extended version appears as TR CS-94-23, Brown University.
15. P. C. Kanellakis and A. A. Shvartsman, "Efficient Parallel Algorithms Can Be Made Robust", *Distributed Computing*, vol. 5, no. 4, pp. 201-217, 1992; prelim. vers. in *Proc. of the 8th ACM PODC*, pp. 211-222, 1989.
16. P. C. Kanellakis and A. A. Shvartsman, "Efficient Parallel Algorithms On Restartable Fail-Stop Processors", in *Proc. of the 10th ACM Symposium on Principles of Distributed Computing*, 1991.
17. P. C. Kanellakis and A. A. Shvartsman, "Robust Computing with Fail-Stop Processors", in *Proc. of the Second Annual ONR Workshop on Ultradependable Multicomputers*, Office of Naval Research, pp. 55-60, 1991.
18. P. C. Kanellakis and A. A. Shvartsman, "Fault Tolerance and Efficiency in Massively Parallel Algorithms", in *Foundations of Dependable Computing*, vol. II, chapter 2.2, G. Koob, C. Lau (editors), Kluwer, 1994 (to appear).
19. R. M. Karp and V. Ramachandran, "A Survey of Parallel Algorithms for Shared-Memory Machines", in *Handbook of Theoretical Computer Science* (ed. J. van Leeuwen), vol. 1, North-Holland, 1990.
20. Z. M. Kedem, K. V. Palem, M. O. Rabin, A. Raghunathan, "Efficient Program Transformations for Resilient Parallel Computation via Randomization," in *Proc. 24th ACM Symp. on Theory of Comp.*, pp. 306-318, 1992.
21. Z. M. Kedem, K. V. Palem, A. Raghunathan, and P. Spirakis, "Combining Tentative and Definite Executions for Dependable Parallel Computing," in *Proc 23d ACM. Symposium on Theory of Computing*, pp. 381-390, 1991.
22. Z. M. Kedem, K. V. Palem, and P. Spirakis, "Efficient Robust Parallel Computations," *Proc. 22nd ACM Symp. on Theory of Computing*, pp. 138-148, 1990.
23. C. P. Kruskal, L. Rudolph, M. Snir, "Efficient Synchronization on Multiprocessors with Shared Memory," in *ACM Trans. on Programming Languages and Systems*, vol. 10, no. 4, pp. 579-601 1988.
24. C. Martel, personal communication, March, 1991.
25. C. Martel, A. Park, and R. Subramonian, "Work-optimal Asynchronous Algorithms for Shared Memory Parallel Computers," *SIAM Journal on Computing*, vol. 21, pp. 1070-1099, 1992
26. C. Martel and R. Subramonian, "On the Complexity of Certified Write-All Algorithms", to appear in *Journal of Algorithms* (a prel. version in the *Proc. of the 12th Conference on Foundations of Software Technology and Theoretical Computer Science*, New Delhi, India, December 1992).

27. C. Martel, R. Subramonian, and A. Park, "Asynchronous PRAMs are (Almost) as Good as Synchronous PRAMs," in *Proc. 32d IEEE Symposium on Foundations of Computer Science*, pp. 590-599, 1990.
28. J. Naor, R.M. Roth, "Constructions of Permutation Arrays for Ceratin Scheduling Cost Measures", manuscript, 1993.
29. N. Nishimura, "Asynchronous Shared Memory Parallel Computation," in *Proc. 3rd ACM Symp. on Parallel Algor. and Architect.*, pp. 76-84, 1990.
30. M.O. Rabin, "Efficient Dispersal of Information for Security, Load Balancing and Fault Tolerance", *J. of ACM*, vol. 36, no. 2, pp. 335-348, 1989.
31. D. B. Sarrazin and M. Malek, "Fault-Tolerant Semiconductor Memories", *IEEE Computer*, vol. 17, no. 8, pp. 49-56, 1984.
32. R. D. Schlichting and F. B. Schneider, "Fail-Stop Processors: an Approach to Designing Fault-tolerant Computing Systems", *ACM Transactions on Computer Systems*, vol. 1, no. 3, pp. 222-238, 1983.
33. J. T. Schwartz, "Ultracomputers", *ACM Transactions on Programming Languages and Systems*, vol. 2, no. 4, pp. 484-521, 1980.
34. A. A. Shvartsman, "Achieving Optimal CRCW PRAM Fault Tolerance", *Information Processing Letters*, vol. 39, no. 2, pp. 59-66, 1991.
35. A. A. Shvartsman, *Fault-Tolerant and Efficient Parallel Computation*, Ph.D. dissertation, Brown University, Tech. Rep. CS-92-23, 1992.
36. A. A. Shvartsman, "Efficient Write-All Algorithm for Fail-Stop PRAM Without Initialized Memory", *Information Processing Letters*, vol. 44, no. 6, pp. 223-231, 1992.

On Unifying Assumption–Commitment Style Proof Rules for Concurrency

Qiwen Xu[1]*, Antonio Cau[2]** and Pierre Collette[3]***

[1] Department of Computer Science, Åbo Akademi, Lemminkainenkatu 14, SF-20520 Turku, Finland,

[2] Institut für Informatik und Praktische Mathematik, Christian-Albrechts-Universität zu Kiel, Preußerstr. 1-9, D-24105 Kiel, Germany,

[3] Unité d'Informatique, Université Catholique de Louvain, Place Sainte-Barbe 2, B-1348 Louvain-la-Neuve, Belgium

Abstract. Assumption–Commitment paradigms for specification and verification of concurrent programs have been proposed in the past. We show that two typical parallel composition rules for shared variable and message passing programs [8, 12] which hitherto required different formulations are instances of one general rule mainly inspired by Abadi & Lamport's composition theorem [1].

1 Introduction

Compositional methods support the verify-while-develop paradigm (an interesting account is given in [15]). However, compared to sequential programs, concurrent programs are much harder to specify and verify. In order to obtain tractable proof rules for concurrency, *assumption–commitment* (sometimes also called *rely–guarantee*), as against monolithic, specification paradigms have been proposed, in which a component is verified to satisfy a commitment under the condition that the environment satisfies an assumption. Such proof systems have been studied for concurrent programs communicating through shared variables [8, 17, 18, 19], as well as through message passing (as in `OCCAM` for example) [12, 14, 20]. Although historically these two systems were developed independently, it has been noticed from the beginning that the proof rules (recalled in Sect. 3) look remarkably similar. Nevertheless, there is a puzzling difference. Indeed, suppose the processes P_1 and P_2 satisfy the assumption-commitment pairs A_1–C_1 and A_2–C_2 respectively. Then, in the case of shared variable concurrency, $P_1||P_2$ satisfies the assumption-commitment pair A–C if the following premises hold:

$$A \vee C_1 \rightarrow A_2 \qquad A \vee C_2 \rightarrow A_1 \qquad C_1 \vee C_2 \rightarrow C$$

* Partially supported by ESPRIT Project 6021 (REACT) and Finnish Akademi Project IRENE.

** Partially supported by ESPRIT Project 6021 (REACT).

*** Supported by National Fund for Scientific Research (Belgium).

But in the case of message passing concurrency, the corresponding premises are:

$$A \wedge C_1 \rightarrow A_2 \qquad A \wedge C_2 \rightarrow A_1 \qquad C_1 \wedge C_2 \rightarrow C$$

In this paper, we take the convention that operators $\vee$ and $\wedge$ bind more closely than $\rightarrow$ (and than $\leftrightarrow$, used in latter sections). Intuitively, the use of disjunction for shared variable programs and conjunction for message passing programs can be understood from the following observations:

- In [8, 17, 18, 19], assumptions and commitments are constraints on atomic steps; a step of $P_1 \| P_2$ is either a step of P_1 *or* a step of P_2.
- In [12, 14, 20], assumptions and commitments are predicates on communication traces; a trace of $P_1 \| P_2$ is both a trace of P_1 *and* a trace of P_2.

This topic has not caught too much attention, largely because the two worlds of concurrency did not meet until recently the effort of writing a comprehensive book on verification of concurrent programs [16] which contains both systems has been undertaken. For this effort it becomes desirable to build a connection between the two rules, especially to obtain a rule which applies to *mixtures* of shared variable and communication based concurrency.

In the meantime, there has been a number of efforts on general methods for composing assumption-commitment specifications, such as Abadi & Lamport's composition theorem [1] and its reformulation in [6] at the semantical level, and the systems in [10, 5, 2] at the proof theoretic level. Abadi & Lamport's composition theorem is particularly powerful, and it is speculated in [1] that it can be applied to several verification methods.

In this paper, we show that the proof rules for the two styles of concurrency are special instances of a new general rule for parallel composition; the latter is based on Abadi & Lamport's composition theorem. In Sect. 2 we first illustrate with two examples the semantics for both shared variable and message passing concurrency. Section 3 presents the two specific assumption–commitment rules for the two types of concurrency. Section 4 gives the general assumption-commitment parallel composition rule. In Sect. 5 we prove that the specific rules are instances of the general rule. We conclude the paper with a short discussion in Sect. 6.

2 Computations

A concurrent process is by definition run together with some other processes. When we consider one process in particular, we call it component, and call the other processes its environment. The execution of a process is modeled by interleaving its atomic actions with those from the environment. A behavior is a sequence

$$\sigma : \sigma_0 \xrightarrow{a_1} \sigma_1 \xrightarrow{a_2} \sigma_2 \xrightarrow{a_3} \cdots$$

where each σ_i is a state, a_i denotes an agent, and the sequence is either infinite or ends in a state σ_m for some $m \geq 0$. The length $|\sigma|$ of a behavior σ is the number of transitions in it. For any finite k, such that $0 \leq k \leq |\sigma|$, $\sigma|_k$ is the prefix of σ of length k and σ_k is the $(k+1)$-th state of σ.

Agents are used to distinguish actions performed by the environment from those performed by the component. Consequently, in principle two agents suffice: the environment and the component in question. However, allowing arbitrary sets of agents eases the composition problem: in the compositional approach, semantic parallel composition is basically the set-intersection of behaviors of its composing processes [1]. Proof theoretically, a parallel composition rule can be formulated with logical conjunction which corresponds to set intersection.

In this paper, we do not wish to adopt a specific semantics. However, to illustrate that set intersection, as semantical operator, corresponds to parallel composition, we outline a possible semantics with help of simple examples.

Consider the concurrent program $x := x + 1 \parallel x := x + 2$ first. As one of the many possibilities, we choose $\{a\}$ and $\{b\}$ as the agent sets for the first and second process respectively. All other agents, e.g. $\{c, d\}$ are considered to be agents from the outside environment. A state η is a mapping from program variables to values; $\eta\surd$ indicates that this is a terminated state, in which the symbol "$\surd$" is pronounced as "tick", adopting an early convention introduced by Hoare. Some typical behaviors from the viewpoints of $x := x + 1$ and $x := x + 2$ are respectively:

$x := x + 1$	$x := x + 2$
$0 \xrightarrow{c} 5 \xrightarrow{a} 6\surd$	$0 \xrightarrow{d} 5 \xrightarrow{a} 6$
$0 \xrightarrow{d} 5 \xrightarrow{a} 6$	$0 \xrightarrow{b} 2$
$0 \xrightarrow{c} 5 \xrightarrow{a} 6 \xrightarrow{b} 8$	$0 \xrightarrow{b} 2\surd$
$0 \xrightarrow{c} 5 \xrightarrow{a} 6\surd \xrightarrow{b} 103\surd$	$0 \xrightarrow{c} 5 \xrightarrow{a} 6 \xrightarrow{b} 8$
$0 \xrightarrow{c} 5 \xrightarrow{a} 6 \xrightarrow{b} 8\surd$	$0 \xrightarrow{c} 5 \xrightarrow{a} 6 \xrightarrow{b} 8\surd$

To support compositionality when defining the semantics of one process, the information of the other process should not be used; b-transitions are thus arbitrary from the point of view of $x := x + 1$. Note also our treatment of the termination flag $\surd$: it is allowed to be raised only if the component has finished executing its code, but it can also be raised later when an arbitrary number of subsequent environment transitions have been performed.

Only the matching behaviors of $x := x + 1$ and $x := x + 2$ are retained in the semantics of their parallel composition. Thus, typical behaviors of the program $x := x + 1 \parallel x := x + 2$ are:

$$0 \xrightarrow{d} 5 \xrightarrow{a} 6$$
$$0 \xrightarrow{c} 5 \xrightarrow{a} 6 \xrightarrow{b} 8$$
$$0 \xrightarrow{c} 5 \xrightarrow{a} 6 \xrightarrow{b} 8\surd$$

When considering the effect of $x := x + 1 \parallel x := x + 2$ as a whole program, it should not matter which process is responsible for which state transition. In general, $[\![\mu : P]\!]$ is the set of behaviors in which transitions from P are labeled by *any* agent in the set μ and transitions from the environment are labeled by *any* agent in the set $\overline{\mu}$. Formally speaking, let $\sigma \simeq_\mu \sigma'$ denote that one behavior can be derived from the other by changing some occurrence of μ–agents by other μ–agents and some occurrence of $\overline{\mu}$–agents by other $\overline{\mu}$–agents. Then, $[\![\mu : P]\!]$ is closed with respect to $\simeq_\mu$ (μ-abstraction [1]). Returning to the above example, other behaviors of the parallel composition are:

$$0 \xrightarrow{d} 5 \xrightarrow{b} 6$$
$$0 \xrightarrow{c} 5 \xrightarrow{a} 6 \xrightarrow{a} 8$$
$$0 \xrightarrow{c} 5 \xrightarrow{b} 6 \xrightarrow{b} 8$$
$$0 \xrightarrow{d} 5 \xrightarrow{a} 6 \xrightarrow{a} 8\surd$$
$$0 \xrightarrow{d} 5 \xrightarrow{b} 6 \xrightarrow{b} 8\surd$$

Let $S^{\simeq_\mu}$ denote the closure of a set of behaviors S under μ-abstraction. Then, for any choice of μ, μ_1, and μ_2 such that $\mu = \mu_1 \cup \mu_2$ and $\mu_1 \cap \mu_2 = \emptyset$, the semantics of parallel composition is defined as

$$[\![\mu : P_1 \parallel P_2]\!] = ([\![\mu_1 : P_1]\!] \cap [\![\mu_2 : P_2]\!])^{\simeq_\mu}$$

We now consider OCCAM-like programs. In OCCAM, only local variables are allowed and processes communicate by passing messages over named channels. In a semantics, communication traces, which are sequences of records containing channel names and communicated values, are included. Therefore, a state now maps program variables to values and a special variable h (called history variable) to communication traces. Consider the program

$$P_1 \stackrel{\text{def}}{=} a?x; b!x^2; c?y \qquad \parallel \qquad P_2 \stackrel{\text{def}}{=} b?z; c!z^3$$

It consists of two processes: the first process receives a number, calculates its square, then passes the result to the second process; after receiving a value, the second process calculates its cube and sends the result back to the first process. As one of the possibilities, we simply use process names P_1 and P_2 as the agents when the transition is an *output* communication from that process (internal computation steps, which are not present in this simple example, can be labeled in the same way). Assume the overall environment process has the name P_e. Without being verbose as in the previous example, we only give one interesting behavior of their parallel composition, in which the variables are ordered as (h, x, y, z) and $<>$ stands for the empty trace:

$$(<>, 0, 0, 0) \xrightarrow{P_e} (<(a, 3)>, 3, 0, 0) \xrightarrow{P_1} (<(a, 3)(b, 9)>, 3, 0, 9)$$
$$\xrightarrow{P_2} (<(a, 3)(b, 9)(c, 729)>, 3, 729, 9)\surd$$

3 Specific Assumption–Commitment Proof Rules

In this section, we review the specific assumption–commitment proof rules for the parallel composition of respectively shared variable and OCCAM-like programs. We only consider verification of weak total correctness, i.e., partial correctness plus the fact that the program does not perform an infinite number of actions. Total correctness for concurrent programs additionally requires that no deadlock occurs; however, coping with deadlock-freedom requires a more sophisticated model [7] than the one presented in Sect. 2.

Specifications are tuples $(p,\ A,\ C,\ q)$, in which state predicates p and q are respectively pre and post conditions while, in order to achieve compositionality, the A–C pair describes the interaction between the component and the environment. In shared variable concurrency, programs interact by interleaved atomic updates of a shared state, and therefore, the A–C pair describes the possible state changes by the environment and the component respectively; in message passing concurrency, programs interact by joint communications, and thus the A–C pair describes communication traces.

The informal interpretation for a process P to satisfy a specification tuple $(p,\ A,\ C,\ q)$ is as follows: for any behavior σ of P

I) if precondition p holds initially in σ, and A holds over any prefix of σ, then C holds after the transition extending that prefix,

II) if precondition p holds initially in σ and A holds over σ, then
- P performs only a finite amount of transitions,
- if σ is a terminated behavior, then the final state satisfies postcondition q

3.1 Shared Variable Programs

In this setting, A and C are binary state predicates. The convention is to use unprimed variables to refer to the state before and primed variables to refer to the state after the transition. For example, $(\eta, \eta') \models x' \geq x$ if the value of x in η' is greater than or equal to the value of x in η. For any behavior σ, define

- ⋆ A holds over σ iff $(\sigma_i, \sigma_{i+1}) \models A$ for any environment transition (σ_i, σ_{i+1}) in σ

and

- ⋆ C holds over σ iff $(\sigma_i, \sigma_{i+1}) \models C$ for any component transition (σ_i, σ_{i+1}) in σ

The parallel composition rule for shared variable programs is:

$$\frac{\begin{array}{lll} P_1\ \underline{sat}\ (p,\ A_1,\ C_1,\ q_1) & A \vee C_1 \rightarrow A_2 & \\ P_2\ \underline{sat}\ (p,\ A_2,\ C_2,\ q_2) & A \vee C_2 \rightarrow A_1 & C_1 \vee C_2 \rightarrow C \end{array}}{P_1 \parallel P_2\ \underline{sat}\ (p,\ A,\ C,\ q_1 \wedge q_2)}$$

The assumption A_1 specifies the state changes that the component process P_1 can tolerate from its environment. Both state changes by process P_2 (for which C_2 is guaranteed) as well as state changes of the overall environment (for which A is assumed) must be viewed as state changes by the environment of P_1. Since those state changes are *interleaved* in the execution model (see Sect. 2), the condition

$A \vee C_2 \rightarrow A_1$ is precisely the one needed to ensure that the assumption of process P_1 is respected by its environment. Similar arguments also hold for process P_2. Finally, if both C_1 and C_2 are guaranteed, then the condition $C_1 \vee C_2 \rightarrow C$ ensures that C is guaranteed for the state changes by $P_1 \| P_2$

Example: Consider the problem [9, 13] of finding the index of the first positive number in an integer array $X(1, \ldots, n)$. The following program consists of two parallel processes, one searching the odd and the other the even positions. A global variable k is used to store the index found. Initially, k is set to $n+1$ and is not changed if there are no positive numbers in the array. Two local search pointers i and j are used. At each position, a process checks whether its search pointer is still below k (otherwise it terminates) and then a process advances the pointer or sets k to the value of the pointer depending on the current value of the array at that position.

$$i := 1;$$
$$\textsf{do}\ \ \langle i < k \wedge X[i] > 0 \rightarrow k := i \rangle\ \Box\ \langle i < k \wedge X[i] \leq 0 \rightarrow i := i + 2 \rangle\ \textsf{od}$$

$$j := 2;$$
$$\textsf{do}\ \ \langle j < k \wedge X[j] > 0 \rightarrow k := j \rangle\ \Box\ \langle j < k \wedge X[j] \leq 0 \rightarrow j := j + 2 \rangle\ \textsf{od}$$

The brackets "$\langle$" and "$\rangle$" indicate that the alternatives separated by "$\Box$" are executed atomically. The first process satisfies the specification:

$$p: \quad k = n + 1$$
$$A_1 : (k' = k \vee (k' < k \wedge X(k') > 0)) \wedge X' = X \wedge i' = i$$
$$C_1 : (k' = k \vee (k' < k \wedge X(k') > 0)) \wedge X' = X \wedge j' = j$$
$$q_1 : \ (X(k) > 0 \vee k = n + 1) \wedge (\forall u.\ odd(u) \wedge X(u) > 0 \rightarrow k \leq u)$$

Condition A_1 expresses that the environment does not change the array, nor the local search pointer i; moreover, if k is changed, it can only be decreased and the new index corresponds to a positive number in the array. Condition C_1 describes what the component guarantees, matching the assumption of the second process. Post condition q_1 says that the final value of k is either $n+1$ or points to a positive number in the array, and that if there are positive numbers at odd positions then the final value of k is smaller than or equal to the smallest index of them.

Similarly, the second process satisfies the specification:

$$p: \quad k = n + 1$$
$$A_2 : (k' = k \vee (k' < k \wedge X(k') > 0)) \wedge X' = X \wedge j' = j$$
$$C_2 : (k' = k \vee (k' < k \wedge X(k') > 0)) \wedge X' = X \wedge i' = i$$
$$q_2 : \ (X(k) > 0 \vee k = n + 1) \wedge (\forall v.\ even(v) \wedge X(v) > 0 \rightarrow k \leq v)$$

With the parallel composition rule for shared variables, we can infer that the parallel composition of both processes satisfies:

$$p: \ k = n + 1$$
$$A : k' = k \wedge X' = X \wedge i' = i \wedge j' = j$$
$$C : true$$
$$q: \ (X(k) > 0 \vee k = n + 1) \wedge (\forall w.\ X(w) > 0 \rightarrow k \leq w)$$

The postcondition indicates that k has the index of the first positive number if there exists one.

3.2 OCCAM-like Programs

In this setting, A and C are predicates over the history variable h. In any state of a behavior, h stores all the communications performed so far. The projections of the history onto channels a, and both a and b for example are denoted by h_a and h_{ab} respectively. For any behavior σ, define

- ⋆ A holds over σ iff $\sigma_i \models A$ for any state σ_i in σ

and

- ⋆ C holds over σ iff $\sigma_i \models C$ for any state σ_i in σ

When restricting to an OCCAM-like model, one has the following parallel composition rule [14, 20]:

$$\frac{\begin{array}{lll} P_1 \ \underline{sat}\ (p,\ A_1,\ C_1,\ q_1) & A \wedge C_1 \rightarrow A_2 & p \wedge A \rightarrow A_1 \wedge A_2 \\ P_2 \ \underline{sat}\ (p,\ A_2,\ C_2,\ q_2) & A \wedge C_2 \rightarrow A_1 & C_1 \wedge C_2 \rightarrow C \end{array}}{P_1 \parallel P_2 \ \underline{sat}\ (p,\ A,\ C,\ q_1 \wedge q_2)}$$

Suppose process P_1 has two input channels a and b, with channel a from the overall environment and channel b from P_2. Assume (by A) that the overall environment either sends nothing or number 2 on channel a, and suppose process P_2 guarantees (by C_2) to send nothing or number 5 on channel b. Then the combined information process P_1 may assume is the *conjunction* of the two: the only possible message on channel a is 2 and the only possible message on channel b is 5. This motivates the condition $A \wedge C_2 \rightarrow A_1$.

Example: Consider the simple program $P_1 \stackrel{\text{def}}{=} a?x; b!x^2; c?y \parallel P_2 \stackrel{\text{def}}{=} b?z; c!z^3$ again. Assume the input value on channel a, if there is one, to be 3. This is expressed by letting A be the predicate $h_a \preceq < (a, 3) >$, where $\preceq$ denotes prefix relation. Then we know that the value passed to process P_2 is 9, and the value sent back to P_1 is 729. The program satisfies the specification

$$\begin{array}{ll} p: h_{abc} = <>, & q: x = 3 \wedge y = 729 \wedge z = 9, \\ A: h_a \preceq < (a, 3) >, & C: h_b \preceq < (b, 9) > \wedge\ h_c \preceq < (c, 729) > \end{array}$$

and this can be proved by using the parallel composition rule. Indeed, P_1 satisfies

$$\begin{array}{ll} p: \ h_{abc} = <>, & \\ A_1: h_a \preceq < (a, 3) > \wedge\ h_c \preceq < (c, 729) >, & q_1: x = 3 \wedge y = 729, \\ & C_1: h_b \preceq < (b, 9) >, \end{array}$$

and P_2 satisfies

$$\begin{array}{ll} p: \ h_{abc} = <>, & q_2: z = 9, \\ A_2: h_b \preceq < (b, 9) >, & C_2: h_c \preceq < (c, 729) > . \end{array}$$

Conclusion. Instead of surprising, the difference between the two parallel composition rules is probably what one would have expected. In short, this is due to different interaction mechanisms and different specified properties. However, this difference has for a long time cast doubts on whether it is possible to unify the two styles of concurrency, and in particular to have one general rule for both cases.

4 A General Rule

For a general rule to work, the assumption–commitment specifications cannot be restricted to the specific properties illustrated in the previous section. Now, specifications are built using temporal predicates directly (temporal merely in the sense that they are interpreted over behaviors). The notation $\sigma \models \varphi$ indicates that behavior σ satisfies predicate φ. A temporal predicate φ is a *safety* predicate iff for any behavior σ:

$$\sigma \models \varphi \qquad \text{iff} \qquad \text{for any finite } k \text{ such that } 0 \leq k \leq |\sigma| : \sigma|_k \models \varphi$$

A state predicate p is lifted to a temporal predicate by defining $\sigma \models p$ as $\sigma_0 \models p$. The boolean connectors $\wedge$, $\vee$, $\rightarrow$, and $\leftrightarrow$ are also extended to temporal operands in the obvious way. For instance,

$$\sigma \models \varphi_1 \rightarrow \varphi_2 \qquad \text{iff} \qquad \text{if } \sigma \models \varphi_1 \text{ then } \sigma \models \varphi_2$$

An assumption-commitment specification is of the form $\mu : (E, < M^S, M^R >)$ where μ is a set of agents and E, M^S, M^R are temporal predicates. The assumption about the environment is described by E, which is restricted to be a safety predicate. The commitment is divided into a safety predicate M^S and a remaining predicate M^R. Liveness should be described by M^R, but for the soundness of the composition rule it is not necessary to insist on M^R to be a pure liveness predicate. The intended meaning of a specification is that a valid behavior satisfies the commitment provided that it satisfies the assumption. However, to eliminate the danger of circular reasoning when composing specifications without imposing extra conditions about specification predicates (as in [1] e.g.), we employ a slightly more complicated interpretation, based not only on logical implication $\rightarrow$ but also on a temporal operator $\hookrightarrow$. This so-called 'spiral' interpretation is used widely in message passing concurrency [12, 14, 20]; in shared variable concurrency, this interpretation is equivalent (as proved in [7]) to the one based on logical implication only [18, 19]. Let :

$$\sigma \models \varphi_1 \hookrightarrow \varphi_2 \qquad \text{iff} \qquad \begin{array}{l} \text{for any finite } k \text{ such that } 1 \leq k \leq |\sigma| : \\ \text{if } \sigma|_{k-1} \models \varphi_1 \text{ then } \sigma|_k \models \varphi_2 \end{array}$$

We then define :

$$\models P \ \underline{sat} \ \mu : (E, \ < M^S, M^R >)$$
iff
$$\text{for all } \sigma \text{ in } [\![\mu : P]\!] \ : \ \sigma \models (E \hookrightarrow M^S) \wedge (E \rightarrow M^R)$$

Therefore, for any behavior of P,

I′) if any prefix of σ satisfies E, then M^S holds after the transition extending that prefix, and

II′) if σ satisfies E, then σ also satisfies M^R.

A specification $\mu:(E, < M^S, M^R >)$ should also be μ–abstract: formally, for two behaviors σ and σ' such that $\sigma \simeq_\mu \sigma'$, this implies the following:

$$\sigma \models (E \hookrightarrow M^S) \wedge (E \rightarrow M^R) \quad \text{iff} \quad \sigma' \models (E \hookrightarrow M^S) \wedge (E \rightarrow M^R)$$

A syntactic composition rule for assumption–commitment specifications is:

$$\frac{\begin{array}{ll} \mathit{init}(E \rightarrow E_1 \wedge E_2) & \text{(PG1)} \\ E \wedge M_1^S \wedge M_2^S \rightarrow E_1 \wedge E_2 & \text{(PG2)} \\ M_1^S \wedge M_2^S \rightarrow M^S & \text{(PG3)} \\ E \wedge M_1^R \wedge M_2^R \rightarrow M^R & \text{(PG4)} \\ P_i \ \underline{sat} \ \mu_i : (E_i, \ < M_i^S, M_i^R >) & \text{(PG5)} \end{array}}{P_1 \parallel P_2 \ \underline{sat} \ \mu : (E, \ < M^S, M^R >)}$$

where $\mu = \mu_1 \cup \mu_2$, $\mu_1 \cap \mu_2 = \emptyset$, and operator *init* is defined as

$$\sigma \models \mathit{init}\,\varphi \qquad \text{iff} \qquad \sigma_0 \models \varphi$$

Our formulation is based mainly on [1] and the subsequent investigation [7] of it. Recently we were informed about an early paper by Barringer and Kuiper [3] that we did not notice when the current research was conducted. They already suggested to divide commitments into safety and liveness parts, and used a similar interpretation for the correctness formula. Moreover, our rule above is also similar to theirs. However, they only studied shared variable concurrency in that paper, and subsequently restricted the assumptions to state transitions as those used in the shared variable rule. The latest work by Abadi and Lamport [2] also uses 'spiral' interpretation. Instead of agents, the index variables in the TLA formulas seem to have played a similar role.

Informally, the soundness of our rule can be understood as follows. The first thing to observe is that both E_1 and E_2 hold as long as (i.e., will not become false before) E does. If E holds initially, then by PG1, E_1 and E_2 also hold. Suppose a transition is made (either by P_1, P_2 or the overall environment) leading to a new state. Then from PG5 it follows that M_1^S and M_2^S hold in the behavior up to the second state, and therefore, if E holds also up to the second state then from PG2 it follows that E_1 and E_2 hold too. We can repeat the argument over the next transition until all finite prefixes are considered. Because E, E_1 and E_2 are safety predicates, the complete (possibly infinite) behavior also satisfies E_1 and E_2 if it satisfies E. Now proving the soundness of the rule becomes straightforward: if any prefix of a behavior satisfies E, then we have just indicated that it satisfies E_1 and E_2, and consequently it follows from PG5 and PG3 that M^S holds after one more transition; if any complete behavior satisfies E, then we know that it satisfies E_1 and E_2, and therefore it follows from PG5 and PG4 that M^R also holds. A formal proof is given below.

Proof (Soundness of the general rule).
We want to prove $\models P_1 \parallel P_2$ $\underline{sat}$ $\mu : (E, \ < M^S, M^R >)$ under the assumption that PG1–PG5 are valid. We first establish a lemma (which only relies on PG1 and PG2):

i) $\models E \wedge (E_1 \hookrightarrow M_1^S) \wedge (E_2 \hookrightarrow M_2^S) \rightarrow E_1 \wedge E_2$. Let us assume $\sigma \models E$ and $\sigma \models (E_1 \hookrightarrow M_1^S) \wedge (E_2 \hookrightarrow M_2^S)$; since E_1 and E_2 are safety predicates, we only have to prove $\sigma|_k \models E_1 \wedge E_2$ for any finite k such that $0 \leq k \leq |\sigma|$. This proceeds by induction on k.

(a) base: $k = 0$

(1) $\sigma \models E$	assumption
(2) $\sigma\|_0 \models E$	E is safety, (1)
(3) $\sigma\|_0 \models E_1 \wedge E_2$	(2), PG1

(b) induction: assume $\sigma|_{k-1} \models E_1 \wedge E_2$.

(1) $\sigma \models E$	assumption
(2) $\sigma\|_k \models E$	E is safety, (1)
(3) $\sigma \models (E_1 \hookrightarrow M_1^S) \wedge (E_2 \hookrightarrow M_2^S)$	assumption
(4) $\sigma\|_{k-1} \models E_1 \wedge E_2$	ind. hyp.
(5) $\sigma\|_k \models M_1^S \wedge M_2^S$	(3), (4)
(6) $\sigma\|_k \models E_1 \wedge E_2$	(2), (4), PG2

We have $[\![\mu : P_1 \parallel P_2]\!] = ([\![\mu_1 : P_1]\!] \cap [\![\mu_2 : P_2]\!])^{\simeq_\mu}$. Because the specification $\mu : (E, \ < M^S, M^R >)$ is μ–abstract, we only have to check that for any behavior $\sigma \in [\![\mu_1 : P_1]\!] \cap [\![\mu_2 : P_2]\!]$, the following ii) and iii) hold

ii) $\sigma \models E \hookrightarrow M^S$. For any finite k such that $1 \leq k \leq |\sigma|$, we assume $\sigma|_{k-1} \models E$ and prove $\sigma|_k \models M^S$.

(1) $\sigma\|_{k-1} \models E$	assumption
(2) $\sigma \in [\![\mu_1 : P_1]\!] \cap [\![\mu_2 : P_2]\!]$	assumption
(3) $\sigma \models (E_1 \hookrightarrow M_1^S) \wedge (E_2 \hookrightarrow M_2^S)$	(2), PG5
(4) $\sigma\|_{k-1} \models (E_1 \hookrightarrow M_1^S) \wedge (E_2 \hookrightarrow M_2^S)$	(3), $E_i \hookrightarrow M_i^S$ are safety
(5) $\sigma\|_{k-1} \models E_1 \wedge E_2$	(1), (4), i)
(6) $\sigma\|_k \models M_1^S \wedge M_2^S$	(3), (5)
(7) $\sigma\|_k \models M^S$	(6), PG3

iii) $\sigma \models E \rightarrow M^R$. We assume $\sigma \models E$ and prove $\sigma \models M^R$.

(1) $\sigma \models E$	assumption
(2) $\sigma \in [\![\mu_1 : P_1]\!] \cap [\![\mu_2 : P_2]\!]$	assumption
(3) $\sigma \models (E_1 \hookrightarrow M_1^S) \wedge (E_2 \hookrightarrow M_2^S)$	(2), PG5
(4) $\sigma \models E_1 \wedge E_2$	(1), (3), i)
(5) $\sigma \models (E_1 \rightarrow M_1^R) \wedge (E_2 \rightarrow M_2^R)$	(2), PG5
(6) $\sigma \models M_1^R \wedge M_2^R$	(4), (5)
(7) $\sigma \models M^R$	(1), (6), PG4

□

5 Unification Proof

Having established the general rule, the remaining part of this paper is to show that the two rules for shared variable and OCCAM-like programs are special cases of it. To match the schema of the general rule, we have to map the tuple $(p,\ A,\ C,\ q)$ to a specification of the form $\mu : (E, < M^S, M^R >)$, so that points I′) and II′) of the general rule in Sect. 4 capture the points I) and II) of the specific rules in Sect. 3. It clearly appears from the comparison of these points that:

- E is the conjunction of p (lifted to a temporal predicate: $\sigma \models p$ iff $\sigma_0 \models p$) with another temporal predicate that captures the meaning of A.
- M^S is a temporal predicate that captures the meaning of C.
- M^R is the conjunction of the temporal predicates fin_μ and $post\ q$, where

$\sigma \models fin_\mu$	iff	the number of μ transitions in σ is finite
$\sigma \models post\ q$	iff	q holds for any terminated (ticked) state of σ

We shall be more precise about the temporal predicates that capture the meaning of A and C when we come to the two particular proof rules. We first list a number of useful algebraic properties of the operators *init*, *post* and *fin*. These operators can be viewed as functions from predicates to predicates. Like usual functional operators, we assume they bind more closely than boolean connectors.

$$\models init\ t_1 \rightarrow init\ t_2 \quad \text{if} \quad \models t_1 \rightarrow t_2 \tag{I1}$$
$$\models init\ (t_1 \wedge t_2) \leftrightarrow init\ t_1 \wedge init\ t_2 \tag{I2}$$
$$\models init\ (t_1 \rightarrow t_2) \leftrightarrow (init\ t_1 \rightarrow init\ t_2) \tag{I3}$$
$$\models fin_{\mu_1} \wedge fin_{\mu_2} \leftrightarrow fin_{\mu_1 \cup \mu_2} \tag{F1}$$
$$\models post\ q_1 \wedge post\ q_2 \leftrightarrow post\ (q_1 \wedge q_2) \tag{Q1}$$

5.1 Shared Variable Concurrency

In order to transform binary state predicates A and C of Sect. 3.1 into temporal predicates, we introduce a new temporal operator *links*. Let μ be a set of agents and r be a binary state predicate:

$\sigma \models links_\mu\ r$
iff
for any transition $\sigma_i \xrightarrow{\delta} \sigma_{i+1}$ such that $\delta \in \mu$, $(\sigma_i, \sigma_{i+1}) \models r$.

Operator *links* enjoys the following algebraic properties:

$$\models links_\mu\ r_1 \rightarrow links_\mu\ r_2, \quad \text{if} \quad \models r_1 \rightarrow r_2 \tag{L1}$$
$$\models links_{\mu_1}\ r \wedge links_{\mu_2}\ r \leftrightarrow links_{\mu_1 \cup \mu_2}\ r \tag{L2}$$
$$\models init\ (links_\mu\ r) \tag{IL}$$

Since environment and component transitions in $[\![\mu : P]\!]$ are labeled with agents in $\overline{\mu}$ and μ respectively, the second conjunct of E is $links_{\overline{\mu}}\ A$ whereas M^S is the predicate $links_\mu C$. In summary, the specification tuples (p, A_1, C_1, q_1),

(p, A_2, C_2, q_2), and $(p, A, C, q_1 \wedge q_2)$ of the shared variable rule are mapped respectively to:

$$\mu_1 : (E_1, < M_1^S, M_1^R >) \quad \text{where} \quad \begin{cases} E_1 \stackrel{\text{def}}{=} p \wedge links_{\overline{\mu_1}}\ A_1 \\ M_1^S \stackrel{\text{def}}{=} links_{\mu_1}\ C_1 \\ M_1^R \stackrel{\text{def}}{=} post\ q_1 \wedge fin_{\mu_1} \end{cases}$$

$$\mu_2 : (E_2, < M_2^S, M_2^R >) \quad \text{where} \quad \begin{cases} E_2 \stackrel{\text{def}}{=} p \wedge links_{\overline{\mu_2}}\ A_2 \\ M_2^S \stackrel{\text{def}}{=} links_{\mu_2}\ C_2 \\ M_2^R \stackrel{\text{def}}{=} post\ q_2 \wedge fin_{\mu_2} \end{cases}$$

$$\mu : (E, < M^S, M^R >) \quad \text{where} \quad \begin{cases} E \stackrel{\text{def}}{=} p \wedge links_{\overline{\mu}}\ A \\ M^S \stackrel{\text{def}}{=} links_{\mu}\ C \\ M^R \stackrel{\text{def}}{=} post\ (q_1 \wedge q_2) \wedge fin_{\mu} \end{cases}$$

We then derive the shared variable rule from the general one by showing that the premises in the general rule (listed on the left side of the table below) are implied by the premises in the shared variable rule (listed on the right side and labeled by PS1–PS3).

$\models init(E \rightarrow E_1 \wedge E_2)$	$\models A \vee C_1 \rightarrow A_2$	(PS1)
$\models E \wedge M_1^S \wedge M_2^S \rightarrow E_1 \wedge E_2$	$\models A \vee C_2 \rightarrow A_1$	(PS2)
$\models M_1^S \wedge M_2^S \rightarrow M^S$	$\models C_1 \vee C_2 \rightarrow C$	(PS3)
$\models E \wedge M_1^R \wedge M_2^R \rightarrow M^R$		

In particular, the use of *disjunction* in PS1 (and similarly for PS2, PS3) is due to the following fact:

$$\star \text{ if } \models A \vee C_1 \rightarrow A_2 \text{ then } \models links_{\overline{\mu}}\ A \wedge links_{\mu_1}\ C_1 \rightarrow links_{\overline{\mu_2}}\ A_2$$

This follows directly from L1, L2, and the observation $\overline{\mu_2} = \overline{\mu} \cup \mu_1$ (because $\mu = \mu_1 \cup \mu_2$ and $\mu_1 \cap \mu_2 = \emptyset$).

Premise 1: $\models init(E \rightarrow E_1 \wedge E_2)$

(1)	$\models init\ E \leftrightarrow init\ p$	definition, I2, IL
(2)	$\models init\ E_1 \leftrightarrow init\ p$	definition, I2, IL
(3)	$\models init\ E_2 \leftrightarrow init\ p$	definition, I2, IL
(4)	$\models init\ E \rightarrow init\ E_1 \wedge init\ E_2$	(1)–(3)
(5)	$\models init(E \rightarrow E_1 \wedge E_2)$	(4), I2, I3

Premise 2: $\models E \wedge M_1^S \wedge M_2^S \rightarrow E_1 \wedge E_2$.
We prove $\models E \wedge M_1^S \rightarrow E_2$. The proof of $\models E \wedge M_2^S \rightarrow E_1$ is similar.

(1)	$\models links_{\overline{\mu}}\ A \rightarrow links_{\overline{\mu}}\ A_2$	PS1, L1
(2)	$\models links_{\mu_1}\ C_1 \rightarrow links_{\mu_1}\ A_2$	PS1, L1
(3)	$\models links_{\overline{\mu}}\ A_2 \wedge links_{\mu_1}\ A_2 \rightarrow links_{\overline{\mu_2}}\ A_2$	$\overline{\mu} \cup \mu_1 = \overline{\mu_2}$, L2
(4)	$\models links_{\overline{\mu}}\ A \wedge links_{\mu_1}\ C_1 \rightarrow links_{\overline{\mu_2}}\ A_2$	(1)–(3)
(5)	$\models E \wedge M_1^S \rightarrow E_2$	(4), definitions

Premise 3: $\models M_1^S \wedge M_2^S \rightarrow M^S$.

(1)	$\models \mathit{links}_{\mu_1}\, C_1 \rightarrow \mathit{links}_{\mu_1}\, C$	PS3, L1
(2)	$\models \mathit{links}_{\mu_2}\, C_2 \rightarrow \mathit{links}_{\mu_2}\, C$	PS3, L1
(3)	$\models \mathit{links}_{\mu_1}\, C \wedge \mathit{links}_{\mu_2}\, C \;\rightarrow\; \mathit{links}_{\mu}\, C$	$\mu_1 \cup \mu_2 = \mu$, L2
(4)	$\models \mathit{links}_{\mu_1}\, C_1 \wedge \mathit{links}_{\mu_2}\, C_2 \;\rightarrow\; \mathit{links}_{\mu}\, C$	(1)–(3)
(5)	$\models M_1^S \wedge M_2^S \rightarrow M^S$	(4), definitions

Premise 4: $\models E \wedge M_1^R \wedge M_2^R \rightarrow M^R$. We prove $\models M_1^R \wedge M_2^R \rightarrow M^R$.

(1)	$\models \mathit{post}\; q_1 \;\wedge\; \mathit{post}\; q_2 \;\rightarrow\; \mathit{post}\; (q_1 \wedge q_2)$	Q1
(2)	$\models \mathit{fin}_{\mu_1} \;\wedge\; \mathit{fin}_{\mu_2} \;\rightarrow\; \mathit{fin}_{\mu}$	$\mu_1 \cup \mu_2 = \mu$, F1
(3)	$\models M_1^R \wedge M_2^R \rightarrow M^R$	(1), (2), definitions

5.2 Message Passing Concurrency

In order to transform the trace predicates A and C of Sect. 3.2 into temporal predicates, we apply the usual 'always' operator $\Box$ of temporal logic. Notice that, since states record communication traces, trace predicates can be viewed as state predicates. For any trace predicate r, let:

$$\sigma \models \Box\, r \qquad \text{iff} \quad \sigma_i \models r, \;\; \text{for any finite } i \text{ such that } 0 \leq i \leq |\sigma|$$

The 'always' operator enjoys the following properties:

$$\models \Box\, r_1 \;\rightarrow\; \Box\, r_2, \quad \text{if} \quad \models r_1 \rightarrow r_2 \qquad (\Box 1)$$

$$\models \Box\, (r_1 \wedge r_2) \;\leftrightarrow\; \Box\, r_1 \wedge \Box\, r_2 \qquad (\Box 2)$$

$$\models \mathit{init}\; \Box\, r \;\leftrightarrow\; \mathit{init}\; r \qquad (\text{IA})$$

Thus, the second conjunct of E is $\Box\, A$, and M^S is $\Box\, C$. The specification tuples (p, A_1, C_1, q_1), (p, A_2, C_2, q_2), and $(p, A, C, q_1 \wedge q_2)$ of the OCCAM rule are mapped respectively to:

$$\mu_1 : (E_1, < M_1^S, M_1^R >) \qquad \text{where} \quad \begin{cases} E_1 \stackrel{\text{def}}{=} p \wedge \Box A_1 \\ M_1^S \stackrel{\text{def}}{=} \Box C_1 \\ M_1^R \stackrel{\text{def}}{=} \mathit{post}\; q_1 \wedge \mathit{fin}_{\mu_1} \end{cases}$$

$$\mu_2 : (E_2, < M_2^S, M_2^R >) \qquad \text{where} \quad \begin{cases} E_2 \stackrel{\text{def}}{=} p \wedge \Box A_2 \\ M_2^S \stackrel{\text{def}}{=} \Box C_2 \\ M_2^R \stackrel{\text{def}}{=} \mathit{post}\; q_2 \wedge \mathit{fin}_{\mu_2} \end{cases}$$

$$\mu : (E, < M^S, M^R >) \qquad \text{where} \quad \begin{cases} E \stackrel{\text{def}}{=} p \wedge \Box A \\ M^S \stackrel{\text{def}}{=} \Box C \\ M^R \stackrel{\text{def}}{=} \mathit{post}\; (q_1 \wedge q_2) \wedge \mathit{fin}_{\mu} \end{cases}$$

In the same vein as before, we derive the `OCCAM` rule by showing that its premises imply those of the general rule:

$$
\begin{array}{ll}
\models init(E \rightarrow E_1 \wedge E_2) & \models A \wedge C_1 \rightarrow A_2 \quad \text{(PM1)} \\
\models E \wedge M_1^S \wedge M_2^S \rightarrow E_1 \wedge E_2 & \models A \wedge C_2 \rightarrow A_1 \quad \text{(PM2)} \\
\models M_1^S \wedge M_2^S \rightarrow M^S & \models C_1 \wedge C_2 \rightarrow C \quad \text{(PM3)} \\
\models E \wedge M_1^R \wedge M_2^R \rightarrow M^R & \models p \wedge A \rightarrow A_1 \wedge A_2 \quad \text{(PM4)}
\end{array}
$$

The use of conjunction in PM1 (and similarly for PM2, PM3) is due to the fact:

$$\star \text{ if } \models A \wedge C_1 \rightarrow A_2 \text{ then } \models \Box A \wedge \Box C_1 \rightarrow \Box A_2$$

which follows directly from □1 and □2.

Premise 1: $\models init(E \rightarrow E_1 \wedge E_2)$

$$
\begin{array}{lll}
(1) & \models init\ E \leftrightarrow init\ (p \wedge A) & \text{definition, I2, IA} \\
(2) & \models init\ E_1 \leftrightarrow init\ (p \wedge A_1) & \text{definition, I2, IA} \\
(3) & \models init\ E_2 \leftrightarrow init\ (p \wedge A_2) & \text{definition, I2, IA} \\
(4) & \models init\ E \rightarrow init\ E_1 \wedge init\ E_2 & \text{(1)–(3), I1, PM4} \\
(5) & \models init(E \rightarrow E_1 \wedge E_2) & \text{(4), I2, I3}
\end{array}
$$

Premise 2: $\models E \wedge M_1^S \wedge M_2^S \rightarrow E_1 \wedge E_2$. We prove $\models E \wedge M_1^S \rightarrow E_2$. The proof of $\models E \wedge M_2^S \rightarrow E_1$ is similar.

$$
\begin{array}{lll}
(1) & \models \Box A \wedge \Box C_1 \rightarrow \Box A_2 & \Box 1,\ \Box 2,\ \text{PM1} \\
(2) & \models E \wedge M_1^S \rightarrow E_2 & \text{(1), definitions}
\end{array}
$$

Premise 3: $\models M_1^S \wedge M_2^S \rightarrow M^S$.

$$
\begin{array}{lll}
(1) & \models \Box C_1 \wedge \Box C_2 \rightarrow \Box C & \Box 1,\ \Box 2,\ \text{PM3} \\
(2) & \models M_1^S \wedge M_2^S \rightarrow M^S & \text{(1), definitions}
\end{array}
$$

Premise 4: $\models E \wedge M_1^R \wedge M_2^R \rightarrow M^R$. Same as for the shared variable case.

6 Discussion

Cliff Jones is probably the first person who noticed the similarity (and of course the obvious difference) between the two proof rules for shared variable and `OCCAM`-like concurrent programs. Furthermore, he remarked in [9], "the extension of a modal logic to cover binary relations may yield some interesting insights. In particular, more general forms of rely- and guarantee- conditions should be definable, and perhaps some unification of proof methods found".

This paper has made one step in exactly this direction. Although the general rule does not contain any modal operators directly, we base it on temporal logic, because the formulae are interpreted over, in principle, possibly infinite behaviors. To facilitate the derivations of the two rules for shared variable and `OCCAM`-like concurrent programs, we (inspired by Jones' recent work, e.g., [10]) have chosen application–oriented temporal operators which are defined semantically. It is possible to use a standard temporal logic (e.g., [11]) instead, but then the derivations in this paper would become less straightforward.

Being a unified rule, the general rule can be used for both shared variable and message passing concurrency, and as a matter of fact, for any other model which satisfies the general properties we have discussed. However, most of the applications that we are aware of in concurrency are based on one single communication model. In such cases, the direct use of a general rule is not recommended: it is much more effective to use the specialized rules for specific verification tasks. The general rule, on the other hand, may be useful in models in which shared variable concurrency and message passing concurrency are jointly combined. For example, the distributed mutual exclusion algorithm reported in [4] uses both shared variables and message passing, and therefore it could be a good test for our general rule. It must be noted, however, that understanding a complicated algorithm is always a difficult task, and a formal verification is certain to be a challenge, to which a good method can only provide a (relatively) effective tool, but never a ready solution.

Acknowledgement We are grateful to Willem-Paul de Roever for repeatedly drawing our attention to the problem, much encouragement, and extensive comments. We thank Cliff Jones for a careful reading and comments which led to a major restructuring of the presentation. A discussion with Job Zwiers, and comments from the anonymous referees were also very helpful.

References

1. M. Abadi and L. Lamport. Composing specifications. ACM Trans. on Program. Lang. Syst., 15:73–132, 1993.
2. M. Abadi and L. Lamport. Conjoining specifications. Digital Equipment Corporation Systems Research Center, Research Report 118, 1993.
3. H. Barringer and R. Kuiper. Hierarchical development of concurrent systems in a temporal logic framework. In S.D. Brookes, A.W. Roscoe and G. Winskel eds., Proc. of Seminar on Concurrency 1984, LNCS 197, Springer-Verlag, 1985.
4. M. Ben-Ari. Principles of Concurrent and Distributed Programming. Chapter 11. Prentice Hall, 1990.
5. P. Collette. Application of the composition principle to Unity–like specifications. In M.-C. Gaudel and J.-P. Jouannaud eds., Proc. of TAPSOFT 93, LNCS 668, Springer-Verlag, 1993.
6. P. Collette. An explanatory presentation of composition rules for assumption-commitment specifications. Information Processing Letters, 50:31–35, 1994.
7. P. Collette and A. Cau. Parallel composition of Assumption–Commitment specifications: a unifying approach for shared variable and distributed message passing concurrency. Technical Report 94-03, Université Catholique de Louvain, 1994.
8. C.B. Jones. Development methods for computer programs including a notion of interference. DPhil. Thesis, Oxford University Computing Laboratory, 1981.

9. C.B. Jones. Tentative steps towards a development method for interfering programs. ACM Trans. Program. Lang. Syst., 5(4):596–619, 1983.
10. C.B. Jones. Interference resumed. In P. Baile ed., Australian Software Engineering Research, 1991.
11. Z. Manna and A. Pnueli. The Temporal Logic of Reactive and Concurrent Systems, specification, Vol. I. Springer-Verlag, 1991.
12. J. Misra and M. Chandy. Proofs of Networks of Processes. IEEE SE, 7(4):417-426, 1981.
13. S. Owicki and D. Gries. An axiomatic proof technique for parallel programs. Acta Inform., 6:319–340, Springer-Verlag, 1976.
14. P.K. Pandya and M. Joseph. P-A logic - a compositional proof system for distributed programs. Distributed Computing, 5:37–54, 1991
15. W.-P. de Roever. The quest for compositionality. Proc. of IFIP Working Conf., The Role of Abstract Models in Computer Science, North-Holland, 1985.
16. W.-P. de Roever, J. Hooman, F. de Boer, Y. Lakhneche, Q. Xu and P. Pandya. State-Based Proof Theory of Concurrency: from noncompositional to compositional methods. Book manuscript, 350 pages, Christian-Albrechts-Universität zu Kiel, Germany, 1994.
17. C. Stirling. A generalization of Owicki-Gries's Hoare logic for a concurrent while language. Theoretical Computer Science, 58:347–359, 1988.
18. K. Stølen. A method for the development of totally correct shared-state parallel programs. In J.C.M. Baeten and J.F. Groote eds., Proc. of CONCUR 91, LNCS 527, Springer-Verlag, 1991.
19. Q. Xu and J. He. A theory of state-based parallel programming: Part 1. In J. Morris and R. Shaw eds., Proc. of BCS FACS 4th Refinement Workshop, Cambridge, Springer-Verlag, 1991.
20. J. Zwiers, A. de Bruin and W.-P. de Roever. A proof system for partial correctness of Dynamic Networks of Processes. Proc. of the Conference on Logics of Programs 1983, LNCS 164, Springer-Verlag, 1984.

Liveness and Fairness in Duration Calculus*

Jens Ulrik Skakkebæk

Department of Computer Science
Technical University of Denmark, Bldg. 344
DK-2800 Lyngby, Denmark
E-mail: jus@id.dtu.dk

Abstract. This paper embeds durations in an interval temporal logic proposed by Venema. The resulting logic, DCL, is a conservative extension of the original Duration Calculus with two extra chopping operators. In contrast to the original Duration Calculus, DCL can be used to specify and verify abstract liveness and fairness properties of systems. In fact, it is shown that durations are useful for specifying such properties on a dense time domain.
The example of a simple oscillator is used to illustrate specification and verification of a simple liveness property. Fairness is illustrated using a Round-Robin scheduler with preemption. The relationship with linear time Temporal Logic is discussed and illustrated using an example of a resource allocator.

1 Introduction

Liveness is a well-established, *abstract* notion that specifies delay-insensitive progress properties of systems. It is used in specifications to avoid giving specific bounds on delays. An often used interpretation of liveness is that "something good" eventually happens [10]. As an example, it might be required of an oscillating system that it will not become stable.

An important application of liveness is *fairness*, which is used in specifications of concurrent systems to define progress in subcomponents of the system. For example, given two processes wanting to execute on a shared processor, a fair scheduler will ensure that each process eventually will execute on the processor.

In concrete designs of real-time systems, the system designer will obviously use *concrete* liveness which is expressed using fixed bounds. For example, a concrete specification of the oscillating system might require that it changes state within, say, 5 seconds. Such properties can be classified as *safety properties* which specify that "something bad" does not happen.

The Duration Calculus (DC) [27] was introduced to reason about safety properties of real-time systems. It is an extension of a dense-time version of Moszkowski's discrete-time Interval Temporal Logic (ITL) [3, 14]. It was the first real-time formalism to introduce the concept of an integrating (duration)

* The work was partially funded by ESPRIT BRA 7071 Provably Correct Systems (ProCoS).

operator, which is convenient for reasoning about intermittent system behaviors. Examples of applications can be found in [6, 16, 18]. As a simple illustration, formulas of DC can express that the oscillator may in any period of 8 seconds only spend 5 seconds in a certain state.

Classical temporal logics (such as linear time Temporal Logic (TL) [13]) and infinite-time ITL [17] can express properties of arbitrarily large intervals (using arbitrarily distant interval endpoints). In contrast, classical ITL/DC fixes a finite observation interval and defines properties of *sub-intervals*; and thereby loses the ability to specify abstract liveness properties. For instance, it is impossible to express that the oscillator *eventually* will have spent 5 seconds in a state. A *process scheduler* is an instance of an oscillating system where it is useful to express such properties.

Examples as these motivate an interest in extending DC to allow for specification of abstract liveness. Previously, Zhou [25] has investigated the possibility of introducing *infinite* intervals for this purpose. However, it is no longer meaningful to evaluate duration measures over such intervals. Special care must be taken to distinguish between finite and infinite intervals, which causes the approach to lose some appeal.

We have been inspired by Venema [24] to introduce modal operators which quantify over both *super-intervals* and sub-intervals. That is, properties are specified over an infinite number of finite intervals instead of over infinite intervals. This way, no special restrictions have to be placed on the evaluation of the duration measures.

DC is extended by changing the base logic [5] from ITL to the modal interval logic CDT of Venema. CDT is a logic of *three* chopping operators: One corresponds to the DC chopping operator, another searches for an interval in the past, and the third likewise in the future. CDT is a simple and conservative extension of ITL: Dense-time ITL is obtained from CDT by omitting the two extra chopping operators from the syntactic and semantic definitions.

In Section 2 the basic interval logic (IL) is presented. IL is a syntactic modification of CDT. Section 3 defines the Duration Calculus with Liveness (DCL) which is an extension of IL with the duration operator.

The calculus is illustrated in Section 4 by the example of a simple delay-insensitive oscillator. The example shows how timed specifications can be shown to satisfy (imply) untimed abstract liveness specifications. A time-restricted Round-Robin scheduler is in Section 5 shown to satisfy an abstract fairness specification.

Using the three chopping operators, we can define operators in DCL with meanings very similar to operators of TL. It is illustrated in Section 6 how such operators can be used to specify a simple resource allocator, using the same style of specification as in TL, albeit in a simpler way.

Durations have been included in Temporal Logic, Temporal Logic of Actions (TLA), Metric Temporal Logic, and branching time temporal logic (CTL). Also a uniform model for DC, TL, and TLA has been proposed. These approaches are discussed in Section 7.

2 Interval Logic

The following sections present the syntax and semantics of Interval Logic (IL).
IL is a syntactic modification of dense-time CDT [24].

2.1 Syntax

The syntax of a formula A in IL is:

$$A ::= P \mid \lceil \rceil \mid \neg A \mid A_1 \vee A_2 \mid A_1 \,;A_2 \mid A_1 \vartriangleleft A_2 \mid A_1 \vartriangleright A_2$$

where P ranges over *atomic propositions*, $\lceil \rceil$ denotes a *point interval*, $;$, $\vartriangleleft$, and
$\vartriangleright$ the *chopping* operators, and $\neg$ and $\vee$ the usual propositional connectives.

Note, that we for reasons of readability have chosen a different syntax than
used in CDT: Let A and B be formulas. $A\,;B$ corresponds to CDT's A **C** B,
$A \vartriangleleft B$ to B **D** A, and $A \vartriangleright B$ to B **T** A. Thus, the order of arguments to $\vartriangleleft$ and
$\vartriangleright$ is reversed with respect to **D** and **T**. $\lceil \rceil$ is written π in CDT. Informally, we
can illustrate the chopping operators by simple diagrams:

$$\begin{array}{l}
\quad\quad\quad\quad\quad \vdash\text{---} A \text{----}\vdash\text{---} B \text{----}\vdash \\
A\,;B \quad\quad\quad \vdash\rule{4cm}{0.4pt}\dashv
\end{array}$$

$$\begin{array}{l}
\quad\quad\quad\quad \vdash\text{-------------} B \text{-------------}\dashv \\
A \vartriangleleft B \quad\quad \vdash\text{---} A \text{----}\vdash\rule{4cm}{0.4pt}\dashv
\end{array}$$

$$\begin{array}{l}
\quad\quad\quad\quad \vdash\text{-------------} A \text{--------------}\dashv \\
A \vartriangleright B \quad\quad \vdash\rule{4cm}{0.4pt}\vdash\text{---} B \text{----}\dashv
\end{array}$$

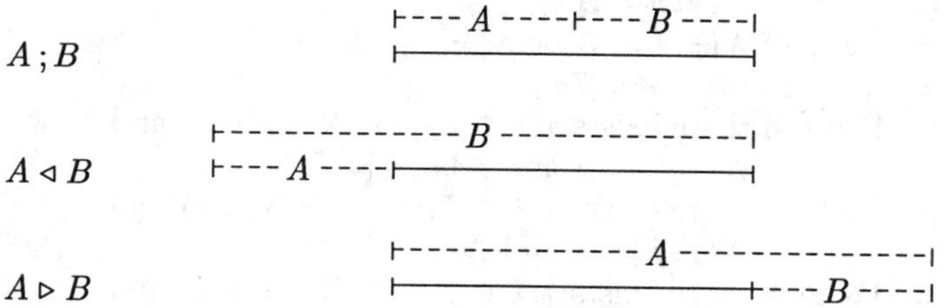

where the full-drawn lines indicate the observation interval and the dotted lines
indicate formula scopes.

2.2 Semantics

Let $\mathcal{T}$ be a set and $\le$ be a *total* ordering relation on $\mathcal{T}$. Intuitively, $\mathcal{T}$ is the set
of time points. Define $\mathcal{I}_\mathcal{T}$ over $\mathcal{T}$ to be the set of *possible intervals*:

$$\mathcal{I}_\mathcal{T} \,\hat{=}\, \{[b, e] \mid b, e \in \mathcal{T} \wedge b \le e\}$$

and define a *ternary* reachability relation $\mathcal{R}_\mathcal{T}$ over $\mathcal{T}$:

$$([b_1, e_1], [b_2, e_2], [b_3, e_3]) \in \mathcal{R}_\mathcal{T} \text{ iff } b_1 = b_3 \text{ and } e_1 = b_2 \text{ and } e_2 = e_3$$

where, say, $\mathcal{R}_\mathcal{T}(i, j, k)$ is informally depicted as:

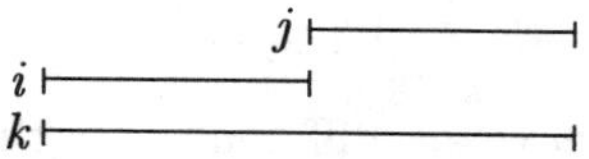

Furthermore, the subset of point intervals of a set is defined as:

$$Point(\mathcal{I}_\mathcal{T}) \mathrel{\widehat{=}} \{i \mid i \in \mathcal{I}_\mathcal{T} \land (\exists\, b \in \mathcal{T} : i = [b, b])\}$$

Let $\mathcal{P}$ denote the domain of proposition names and let P denote an element of $\mathcal{P}$. Let the *valuation* $\mathcal{V}_\mathcal{T}$ associate with each proposition P a subset of $\mathcal{I}_\mathcal{T}$:

$$\mathcal{V}_\mathcal{T} : \mathcal{P} \rightarrow 2^{\mathcal{I}_\mathcal{T}}$$

where $2^{\mathcal{I}_\mathcal{T}}$ denotes the domain of all subsets of $\mathcal{I}_\mathcal{T}$.

A *model* $\mathcal{M}_\mathcal{T}$ over the domain $\mathcal{T}$ is a tuple:

$$\mathcal{M}_\mathcal{T} \mathrel{\widehat{=}} (\mathcal{I}_\mathcal{T}, \mathcal{R}_\mathcal{T}, \mathcal{V}_\mathcal{T})$$

In the following, let i, j, k denote intervals and A, B, C denote formulas.

Truth of a formula is relative to an interval in a model. We write $\mathcal{M}_\mathcal{T}, i \models A$ to denote that the formula A is *true at i in* $\mathcal{M}_\mathcal{T}$.

The meaning of a formula is recursively defined:

$$\begin{array}{ll}
\mathcal{M}_\mathcal{T}, i \models P & \text{iff } i \in \mathcal{V}_\mathcal{T}(P) \\
\mathcal{M}_\mathcal{T}, i \models \neg A & \text{iff } \mathcal{M}_\mathcal{T}, i \not\models A \\
\mathcal{M}_\mathcal{T}, i \models A \lor B & \text{iff } \mathcal{M}_\mathcal{T}, i \models A \text{ or } \mathcal{M}_\mathcal{T}, i \models B \\
\mathcal{M}_\mathcal{T}, i \models \lceil\rceil & \text{iff } i \in Point(\mathcal{I}_\mathcal{T}) \\
\mathcal{M}_\mathcal{T}, i \models A ; B & \text{iff there exists } j, k \in \mathcal{I}_\mathcal{T} \text{ s.t. } \mathcal{R}_\mathcal{T}(j, k, i) \text{ and} \\
 & \quad \mathcal{M}_\mathcal{T}, j \models A \text{ and } \mathcal{M}_\mathcal{T}, k \models B \\
\mathcal{M}_\mathcal{T}, i \models A \lhd B & \text{iff there exists } j, k \in \mathcal{I}_\mathcal{T} \text{ s.t. } \mathcal{R}_\mathcal{T}(j, i, k) \text{ and} \\
 & \quad \mathcal{M}_\mathcal{T}, j \models A \text{ and } \mathcal{M}_\mathcal{T}, k \models B \\
\mathcal{M}_\mathcal{T}, i \models A \rhd B & \text{iff there exists } j, k \in \mathcal{I}_\mathcal{T} \text{ s.t. } \mathcal{R}_\mathcal{T}(i, k, j) \text{ and} \\
 & \quad \mathcal{M}_\mathcal{T}, j \models A \text{ and } \mathcal{M}_\mathcal{T}, k \models B
\end{array}$$

An IL formula A is *$\mathcal{T}$-valid* (written $\models_\mathcal{T} A$) iff $\mathcal{M}_\mathcal{T}, i \models A$ for every interval $i \in \mathcal{I}_\mathcal{T}$ in every model $\mathcal{M}_\mathcal{T}$.

2.3 Derived Operators

We can define the remaining propositional operators $\land$, $\Rightarrow$, and $\Leftrightarrow$ in the usual way. We assume $\neg$ to bind stronger than $;$, $\lhd$, and $\rhd$, which again bind stronger than $\land$, $\lor$, $\Rightarrow$, and $\Leftrightarrow$. It is also straight forward to define the usual truth constants from the existing operators:

$$\begin{array}{l}
\mathit{true} \mathrel{\widehat{=}} \lceil\rceil \lor \neg\lceil\rceil \\
\mathit{false} \mathrel{\widehat{=}} \lceil\rceil \land \neg\lceil\rceil
\end{array}$$

Shorthands are defined for useful temporal formulas:

$$\begin{array}{ll}
\Diamond A \mathrel{\widehat{=}} (\mathit{true} ; A ; \mathit{true}) \rhd \mathit{true} & \quad \textit{eventually} \\
\Box A \mathrel{\widehat{=}} \neg \Diamond \neg A & \quad \textit{always}
\end{array}$$

Note that the operators defined above are different from the original DC operators: Here $\Diamond A$ means that A must eventually hold on some sub-interval to the right of the left endpoint of the observation interval. Let $\textcircled{\scriptsize D}$ denote the original DC eventuality operator: $\textcircled{\scriptsize D}A \mathrel{\widehat{=}} \mathit{true}\,;A\,;\mathit{true}$. Then: $\textcircled{\scriptsize D}A \Rightarrow \Diamond A$. Using $\triangleleft$ instead of $\triangleright$, we may also specify past operators corresponding to the future operators $\Diamond$ and $\Box$.

The future *followed by* operator is defined as:

$$A \rightarrow B \mathrel{\widehat{=}} \Box(A \Rightarrow ((A \triangleright \neg\lceil\rceil) \vee (\mathit{true} \triangleright B)))$$

where the right hand side holds if either A holds on a non-point future extension or B holds on an immediately following interval.

2.4 Proof System

The proof system shown below is a subset of the CDT proof system by Venema [24]. For our purposes, we assume $\mathcal{T}$ to be dense.

Axioms. All instances of propositional tautologies are tautologies in IL.
We assume $\mathcal{T}$ to be dense:

$$\neg\lceil\rceil \Rightarrow \neg\lceil\rceil\,;\neg\lceil\rceil \qquad \textit{dense}$$

The chopping operators distribute over disjunction:

$$\left.\begin{array}{ll} (A \vee B) \otimes C \Leftrightarrow A \otimes C \vee B \otimes C & \vee\otimes r\!-\!\mathit{dist} \\ A \otimes (B \vee C) \Leftrightarrow A \otimes B \vee A \otimes C & \vee\otimes l\!-\!\mathit{dist} \end{array}\right\} \quad \text{where } \otimes \in \{\,;\,,\triangleleft,\triangleright\}.$$

An interval is a non-point interval iff it has a non-point initial, respectively final, sub-interval:

$$\begin{array}{ll} \neg\lceil\rceil\,;\mathit{true} \Leftrightarrow \neg\lceil\rceil & \neg\lceil\rceil\,; \\ \mathit{true}\,;\neg\lceil\rceil \Leftrightarrow \neg\lceil\rceil & ;\neg\lceil\rceil \end{array}$$

$\lceil\rceil$ is a unit of ;:

$$\begin{array}{ll} \lceil\rceil\,;A \Leftrightarrow A & \lceil\rceil\,; \\ A\,;\lceil\rceil \Leftrightarrow A & ;\lceil\rceil \end{array}$$

and from one side also of $\triangleleft$ and $\triangleright$:

$$\begin{array}{ll} \lceil\rceil \triangleleft A \Leftrightarrow A & \lceil\rceil\triangleleft \\ A \triangleright \lceil\rceil \Leftrightarrow A & \triangleright\lceil\rceil \end{array}$$

The local chopping operator is associative:

$$A\,;(B\,;C) \Leftrightarrow (A\,;B)\,;C \qquad ;\mathit{assoc}$$

Derivation Rules. We employ Modus Ponens and the rule of *Generalisation:*

> If A is a theorem of the proof system, then for $\otimes \in \{\,;\,,\triangleleft,\triangleright\}$ so are $\neg(\neg A \otimes \mathit{true})$ and $\neg(\mathit{true} \otimes \neg A)$.

Soundness and Completeness. A proof of soundness of CDT is sketched in [24]. A sketchy proof of completeness of CDT is also found in this paper. A completeness proof of a very similar logic is described in detail in [22, 23].

2.5 Useful Lemmas

The following lemmas turn out to be useful in later DCL proofs: False is a zero for the chopping operators (where $\otimes \in \{;, \lhd, \rhd\}$):

$$\begin{array}{ll} \mathit{false} \otimes A \Leftrightarrow \mathit{false} & \mathit{false}\otimes \\ A \otimes \mathit{false} \Leftrightarrow \mathit{false} & \otimes\, \mathit{false} \end{array}$$

Prefix properties extend to the right super-interval:

$$A\,;\mathit{true} \Rightarrow (A\,;\mathit{true}) \rhd \mathit{true} \qquad ;\mathit{true}\rhd$$

3 Duration Calculus with Liveness

Duration Calculus with Liveness (DCL) is a first-order extension of dense IL with *duration measures*.

3.1 Syntax

Let $\mathcal{S}$ denote the set of Boolean *atomic states* and let $S \in \mathcal{S}$. A *state* s is defined recursively:

$$s ::= S \mid \neg s \mid s_1 \vee s_2$$

where $\neg$ and $\vee$ are the usual propositional operators[2]. Intuitively, the meaning of a state is a function from $\mathcal{T}$ to $\{0, 1\}$.

Let *Fun* denote the set of function symbols and let $f \in \mathit{Fun}$. Also let x denote a *variable* name and let $\mathcal{X}$ be the set of variable names. A *term* r is defined as:

$$r ::= x \mid \int s \mid f(r_1, \ldots, r_n)$$

where $\int s$ is a *duration*. Intuitively, a duration is a measure of the type $\mathcal{I}_\mathcal{T} \to \mathbb{R}_+$. Although f may be any function of the right type, we most often use the classical arithmetic operators: $+$, $-$, $*$, and $/$ (with their obvious interpretations).

We define the propositions of IL to be *predicates* in DCL. Let *Term* denote the set of all possible terms and let *Pred* be the set of all predicate symbols:

$$P \mathrel{\widehat{=}} \{p(r_1, \ldots, r_n) \mid p \in \mathit{Pred} \wedge \bigwedge_i^n r_i \in \mathit{Term}\}$$

Often used predicates are the classical comparison operators ($=$, $<$, and $>$) with their usual notation and meaning.

---

[2] Note, that we overload the propositional symbols: They are used both to combine states and formulas.

Formulas are extended with quantifiers over variables:

$$A ::= P \mid \lceil\rceil \mid \neg A \mid A_1 \vee A_2 \mid A_1 ; A_2 \mid A_1 \lhd A_2 \mid A_1 \rhd A_2 \mid (\forall x : A)$$

This concludes the syntactic definitions. Useful shorthand operators are:

ℓ	$\widehat{=} \int 1$	Length
$\lceil s \rceil$	$\widehat{=} \int s = \ell \wedge \ell > 0$	(s holds almost everywhere on a non-point interval)

3.2 Semantics

We fix the meaning of predicates and functions by associating an n-place predicate $\underline{p}$ with each predicate symbol p and with each function symbol f an n-place function $\underline{f}$ closed on the reals.

An *interpretation* $\mathcal{J}$ associates with each state a function from $\mathcal{T}$ to $\{0, 1\}$:

$$\mathcal{J} : \mathcal{S} \rightarrow (\mathcal{T} \rightarrow \{0, 1\})$$

and a *value assignment* σ associates a real value with each variable:

$$\sigma : \mathcal{X} \rightarrow \mathbb{R}$$

Note that we assume that the state functions are *finitely variable*: In any interval, the function will only have a finite number of discontinuity points.

The meaning of a state s at time t in an interpretation $\mathcal{J}$ is written $\mathcal{J}[\![s]\!](t)$ and is defined recursively:

$$\begin{aligned}
\mathcal{J}[\![S]\!](t) &= \mathcal{J}(S)(t) \\
\mathcal{J}[\![\neg s]\!](t) &= 1 - \mathcal{J}[\![s]\!](t) \\
\mathcal{J}[\![s_1 \vee s_2]\!](t) &= \begin{cases} 0 \text{ } \textit{if } \mathcal{J}[\![s_1]\!](t) = 0 \textit{ and } \mathcal{J}[\![s_2]\!](t) = 0 \\ 1 \textit{ otherwise} \end{cases}
\end{aligned}$$

Let $\mathcal{J}[\![r]\!](i, \sigma)$ denote the meaning of the term r determined by the interval i and value assignment σ in the interpretation $\mathcal{J}$. The meaning of a term is defined recursively:

$$\begin{aligned}
\mathcal{J}[\![x]\!](i, \sigma) &= \sigma(x) \\
\mathcal{J}[\![\textstyle\int s]\!](i, \sigma) &= \textstyle\int_b^e \mathcal{J}[\![s]\!](t)\, dt, \text{ where } i = [b, e] \\
\mathcal{J}[\![f(r_1, \ldots, r_n)]\!](i, \sigma) &= \underline{f}(\mathcal{J}[\![r_1]\!](i, \sigma), \ldots, \mathcal{J}[\![r_n]\!](i, \sigma))
\end{aligned}$$

where $x \in \mathcal{X}$ and $f \in \mathit{Fun}$. The expression $\int_b^e \mathcal{J}[\![s]\!](t)\, dt$ employs the Riemann integral to compute the duration of a state function s over an interval[3]. The meaning of a formula is extended with the value assignment: We write $\mathcal{M}_{\mathcal{T}}, i, \sigma \models A$

[3] The Riemann integral is the familiar notion of integration and applies to functions that are continuous over the interval, except for a finite number of discontinuity points.

to denote that A is true at i in $\mathcal{M}_\mathcal{T}$ for value assignment σ and extend the IL valuation $\mathcal{V}_\mathcal{T}$ with σ:

$$\mathcal{V}_\mathcal{T}(p(r_1,\ldots,r_n))(\sigma) \mathrel{\widehat{=}} \{i \mid \underline{p}(\mathcal{J}[\![r_1]\!](i,\sigma),\ldots,\mathcal{J}[\![r_n]\!](i,\sigma))\}$$

Using this modified definition of $\mathcal{V}_\mathcal{T}$ it is straightforward to extend the meaning of the propositional operators shown in Section 2.2. For instance:

$$\mathcal{M}_\mathcal{T}, i, \sigma \models P \text{ iff } i \in \mathcal{V}_\mathcal{T}(P)(\sigma)$$

The meaning of a universal quantifier is:

$$\mathcal{M}_\mathcal{T}, i, \sigma \models (\forall\, x : A) \text{ iff for all valuations } \sigma' \text{ which are } x\text{-equivalent with } \sigma,\ \mathcal{M}_\mathcal{T}, i, \sigma' \models A$$

where σ and σ' are x-equivalent iff $\sigma(y) = \sigma'(y)$ for all variables y different from x.

A DCL formula A is $\mathcal{T}$-*valid* (written $\models_\mathcal{T} A$) iff $\mathcal{M}_\mathcal{T}, i, \sigma \models A$ for every possible interval $i \in \mathcal{I}_\mathcal{T}$ and value assignment σ in every model $\mathcal{M}_\mathcal{T}$.

3.3 Proof System

Axioms. The proof system for DCL is an extension of the proof system for IL with the axioms shown below (we assume the usual first order axioms and inference rules):

- We include the four axioms of DC. Let s_1 and s_2 be states and let r_1 and r_2 be non-negative reals:

$$\begin{array}{rl} \int 0 = 0 & Ax1 \\ \int s \geq 0 & Ax2 \\ \int s_1 + \int s_2 = \int(s_1 \wedge s_2) + \int(s_1 \vee s_2) & Ax3 \\ (\int s = r_1)\,;(\int s = r_2) \Leftrightarrow (\int s = r_1 + r_2) & Ax4 \end{array}$$

  and add three extra axioms to relate $\int$ to $\lhd$, $\rhd$, and $\lceil\,\rceil$:

$$\begin{array}{rl} (\int s = r_1) \lhd (\int s = r_1 + r_2) \Leftrightarrow (\int s = r_2) & Ax5 \\ (\int s = r_1 + r_2) \rhd (\int s = r_2) \Leftrightarrow (\int s = r_1) & Ax6 \\ (\ell = 0) \Leftrightarrow \lceil\,\rceil & Ax7 \end{array}$$

  From classical DC we have two axioms which formalize finite variability:

$$\begin{array}{ll} \lceil s \rceil\,; \mathit{true} \vee \lceil \neg s \rceil\,; \mathit{true} \vee \lceil\,\rceil & \mathit{InitTrichot} \\ \mathit{true}\,; \lceil s \rceil \vee \mathit{true}\,; \lceil \neg s \rceil \vee \lceil\,\rceil & \mathit{FinalTrichot} \end{array}$$

- A couple of extra axioms are needed to move existential quantification in and out of chopped sub-formulas[4]:

$$\begin{array}{ll} (\exists\, x : A) \otimes B \Leftrightarrow (\exists\, x : A \otimes B) & \otimes\exists\, l \\ B \otimes (\exists\, x : A) \Leftrightarrow (\exists\, x : B \otimes A) & \otimes\exists\, r \end{array}$$

  where $\otimes$ is one of ;, $\lhd$, or $\rhd$ and x does not occur free in B.

[4] These formulas can be viewed as a two-dimensional generalisation of the (one-dimensional) *Barcan formula* of classical, modal logic [7]: $(\forall\, x : \Box A) \Rightarrow (\Box \forall\, x : A)$.

- Let a *duration free* formula be a formula which does not contain any duration measures as sub-terms and let C be a such a duration free formula. C can then be moved in and out of chopped formulas:

$$\left.\begin{array}{ll} (A \wedge C) \otimes B \Leftrightarrow C \wedge A \otimes B & \textit{durfree}\otimes \\ A \otimes (B \wedge C) \Leftrightarrow C \wedge A \otimes B & \otimes\textit{durfree} \end{array}\right\} \text{ where } \otimes \in \{\,;, \triangleleft, \triangleright\}.$$

Soundness and Completeness. It is straightforward to show soundness by showing soundness of each axiom and each derivation rule. The original DC extension has been shown relative complete to Interval Temporal Logic [4]. It is therefore likely that the above DCL extension can be shown relative complete to IL.

3.4 Useful Lemmas

The next sections require the following lemmas: $\triangleright$ is left monotone:

$$(\Box(A \Rightarrow B) \wedge A \triangleright C) \Rightarrow B \triangleright C \qquad \triangleright\, \textit{Mono l}$$

An interval can be extended to an arbitrarily large super-interval:

$$\begin{array}{ll} (\forall x : \ell > x \triangleright \textit{true}) & \ell\triangleright \\ (\forall x : \textit{true} \triangleright \ell > x) & \triangleright\ell \end{array}$$

We can also show that if a state is true almost everywhere for any future interval, then it is impossible to construct a future interval in which this is not true:

$$\Box(\textstyle\int s = \ell) \Rightarrow \neg(\textstyle\int s \neq \ell \triangleright \textit{true}) \qquad ;\neq$$

and the closely related lemma which we will use in later proofs:

$$\Box\neg\lceil s\rceil \Rightarrow \Box \textstyle\int \neg s = \ell \qquad \neg\textstyle\int\Rightarrow$$

4 Liveness: A Simple Oscillator

We consider a specification of an oscillator with output z. A delay insensitive specification uses abstract liveness:

$$\textit{Spec} \mathrel{\widehat{=}} \Diamond\lceil z\rceil \wedge \Diamond\lceil\neg z\rceil$$

A timed implementation of this ensures that z alternates within a specified delay δ:

$$\begin{array}{l} \textit{Impl}_1 \mathrel{\widehat{=}} \Box(\lceil z\rceil \Rightarrow \ell \leq \delta) \\ \textit{Impl}_2 \mathrel{\widehat{=}} \Box(\lceil\neg z\rceil \Rightarrow \ell \leq \delta) \\ \textit{Impl} \ \mathrel{\widehat{=}} \textit{Impl}_1 \wedge \textit{Impl}_2 \end{array}$$

We want to show that the timed implementation satisfies the delay insensitive specification:

$$Th \mathrel{\widehat{=}} Impl \Rightarrow Spec$$

and start by proving the lemma:

$$Lem1 \mathrel{\widehat{=}} (\forall x \geq 0 : \Box(\textstyle\int s = \ell) \Rightarrow (\ell > x \wedge \lceil s \rceil) \triangleright true)$$

by contradiction:

$$\begin{array}{lll}
 & \Box(\int s = \ell) \wedge \neg((\ell > x \wedge \lceil s \rceil) \triangleright true) & ;\neq, deMorgan \\
\Rightarrow & \neg((\int s \neq \ell) \triangleright true \vee ((\ell > x \wedge \int s = \ell) \triangleright true)) & \triangleright \vee - dist \\
\Rightarrow & \neg((\int s \neq \ell \vee (\ell > x \wedge \int s = \ell)) \triangleright true) & prop \\
\Rightarrow & \neg((\int s \neq \ell \vee \ell > x) \triangleright true) & \triangleright \vee - dist \\
\Rightarrow & \neg(\ell > x \triangleright true \vee \int s \neq \ell \triangleright true)) & \ell\triangleright \\
\Rightarrow & \neg(true \vee \int s \neq \ell \triangleright true) & prop \\
\Rightarrow & false &
\end{array}$$

where *prop* denotes a proof step using simple propositional reasoning.

We can then show $Impl_2 \Rightarrow \Diamond\lceil z \rceil$ by contradiction:

$$\begin{array}{lll}
 & Impl_2 \wedge \neg \Diamond\lceil z \rceil & def \\
\Rightarrow & Impl_2 \wedge \Box\neg\lceil z \rceil & \neg\int\Rightarrow \\
\Rightarrow & Impl_2 \wedge \Box(\int \neg z = \ell) & Lem1 \\
\Rightarrow & Impl_2 \wedge (\ell > \delta \wedge \lceil \neg z \rceil) \triangleright true & def \\
\Rightarrow & \Box(\lceil \neg z \rceil \Rightarrow \ell \leq \delta) \wedge (\ell > \delta \wedge \lceil \neg z \rceil) \triangleright true & \triangleright Mono\ l \\
\Rightarrow & (\ell > \delta \wedge \ell \leq \delta) \triangleright true & FOL \\
\Rightarrow & false \triangleright true & false\triangleright \\
\Rightarrow & false &
\end{array}$$

where the *FOL* comment in a proof step indicates the use of rules of first-order predicate logic. We can similarly show $Impl_1 \Rightarrow \Diamond\lceil \neg z \rceil$.

Observe that *Spec* will not guarantee a *balanced* implementation: The time spent in the z state could be infinitesimal compared to the time spent in $\neg z$. It even allows a *Zeno*-like behaviour of the duration, where, say, for every visit in z, the time spent in z could be half the time spent in the previous visit to z.

Balanced behaviours can be specified using durations:

$$\Box((\textstyle\int z = \int \neg z) \triangleright true)$$

i.e. the oscillator eventually has visited each of the states for equal amounts of time.

Non-Zenoness of the scheduler may also be specified. Let $\delta \in \mathbb{R}_+$ be some chosen constant:

$$\Box((\textstyle\int z > \delta) \triangleright true)$$

which always requires the oscillator to *eventually* have spent δ in z.

5 Fairness: A Scheduler

To illustrate the use of abstract fairness in system specifications, we use an example inspired by [26]: The task is to schedule a set of processes on a single processor. For this, a Round-Robin scheduler with preemption is used: Processes are served on a first-come-first-served basis and an executing process is preempted after continuously executing for a period of δ time-units if other processes are waiting to execute on the shared processor. A context switch takes at most γ time-units.

Each process p_i is defined by two states which describe the condition of the process: The process is *ready* (indicated by the state $p_i.rdy$), if the process needs more process time and is *running* (indicated by $p_i.run$) if it is executing on the processor.

The scheduler is required to be abstractly fair towards each process:

$$Spec \mathrel{\hat{=}} \lceil p_i.rdy \land \neg p_i.run \rceil \Rightarrow \Diamond \lceil p_i.run \rceil$$

Two *assumptions* are made about the behavior of a process:

$$Asm \mathrel{\hat{=}} Asm_1 \land Asm_2$$

A process is always ready when it is running:

$$Asm_1 \mathrel{\hat{=}} \Box(\lceil p_i.run \rceil \Rightarrow \lceil p_i.rdy \rceil)$$

A process enters the ready state before it starts running. Once a process is ready, it will remain ready until it is assigned process time:

$$\begin{aligned} Asm_2 \mathrel{\hat{=}}\ & (\lceil \neg p_i.rdy \rceil \rightarrow \lceil p_i.rdy \land \neg p_i.run \rceil) \land \\ & (\lceil p_i.rdy \land \neg p_i.run \rceil \rightarrow \lceil p_i.run \rceil) \end{aligned}$$

The scheduler is of type Round-Robin with a limit on execution time and on context switches:

$$Impl \mathrel{\hat{=}} RoundRobin \land LimitExec \land ContSwitch$$

The scheduler is of type Round-Robin. That is, ready processes waiting to execute are not overtaken by later processes:

$$\begin{aligned} RoundRobin \mathrel{\hat{=}} \Box \textstyle\bigwedge_{j \neq i} \neg(& \lceil p_j.rdy \land \neg p_j.run \rceil \land \\ & (\lceil \neg p_i.rdy \lor p_i.run \rceil ; \lceil \neg p_i.run \rceil ; \lceil p_i.run \rceil)) \end{aligned}$$

If other processes are ready, a process may only execute for a period of δ:

$$LimitExec \mathrel{\hat{=}} \Box \textstyle\bigwedge_{i \neq j} (\lceil p_i.run \land p_j.rdy \rceil \Rightarrow \ell \leq \delta)$$

A context switch takes at most γ:

$$ContSwitch \mathrel{\hat{=}} \Box(\lceil \textstyle\bigvee_i p_i.rdy \land \bigwedge_j \neg p_j.run \rceil \Rightarrow \ell \leq \gamma)$$

For simplicity, in the following we consider the less general case of two processes p_1 and p_2 running on a shared processor. Let $2Spec$ and $2Impl$ denote the (obvious) specialization of Spec and Impl to the two process case. The goal is to prove the formula:

$$2Impl \Rightarrow 2Spec$$

Below is a sketch of the proof. To avoid trivial repetitions, only the proof for process p_1 is shown:

$$2Impl \Rightarrow (\lceil p_1.rdy \wedge \neg p_1.run \rceil \Rightarrow \Diamond \lceil p_1.run \rceil)$$

First, observe that (using *InitTrichot*):

$$\lceil \neg p_2.rdy \rceil\, ; true \vee \lceil p_2.run \rceil\, ; true \vee \lceil p_2.rdy \wedge \neg p_2.run \rceil\, ; true \vee \lceil\, \rceil$$

Each of the first three cases need to be considered; the first is:

$$Lem_1 \mathrel{\widehat{=}} \lceil p_1.rdy \wedge \neg p_1.run \rceil \wedge \lceil \neg p_2.rdy \rceil\, ; true \Rightarrow \Diamond \lceil p_1.run \rceil$$

which is proved as follows:

$$\begin{array}{lll}
 & \lceil p_1.rdy \wedge \neg p_1.run \rceil \wedge \lceil \neg p_2.rdy \rceil\, ; true & Asm_1 \\
\Rightarrow & \lceil p_1.rdy \wedge \neg p_1.run \wedge \neg p_2.run \rceil\, ; true & ; true \triangleright \\
\Rightarrow & (\lceil p_1.rdy \wedge \neg p_1.run \wedge \neg p_2.run \rceil\, ; true) \triangleright true & ContSwitch, Asm_2 \\
\Rightarrow & (\ell \leq \gamma\, ; (\lceil p_1.run \rceil \vee \lceil p_2.run \rceil)\, ; true) \triangleright true & \triangleright \vee\, l{-}dist,\ ; \vee -dist \\
\Rightarrow & (\ell \leq \gamma\, ; \lceil p_1.run \rceil\, ; true) \triangleright true \vee & \\
 & (\ell \leq \gamma\, ; \lceil p_2.run \rceil\, ; true) \triangleright true & RoundRobin, Asm_2 \\
\Rightarrow & (\ell \leq \gamma\, ; \lceil p_1.run \rceil) \triangleright true \vee false \triangleright true & prop, false \triangleright \\
\Rightarrow & (true\, ; \lceil p_1.run \rceil\, ; true) \triangleright true & defs \\
\Rightarrow & \Diamond \lceil p_1.run \rceil &
\end{array}$$

The proof of the second case:

$$Lem_2 \mathrel{\widehat{=}} \lceil p_1.rdy \wedge \neg p_1.run \rceil \wedge \lceil p_2.run \rceil\, ; true \Rightarrow \Diamond \lceil p_1.run \rceil$$

is quite similar to the first; and the proof of the third case:

$$Lem_3 \mathrel{\widehat{=}} \lceil p_1.rdy \wedge \neg p_1.run \rceil \wedge \lceil p_2.rdy \wedge \neg p_2.run \rceil\, ; true \Rightarrow \Diamond \lceil p_1.run \rceil$$

uses the second lemma. The proofs of Lem_2 and Lem_3 are omitted here due to space limitations.

6 Relation to Temporal Logic

It is interesting to compare the expressiveness DCL with other (timed and untimed) formalisms which are used to reason about both liveness and safety properties of dynamic systems. Such a formalism is the (untimed) linear time Temporal Logic (TL) [13]. This formalism was chosen here, since it is well-known and has successfully been used for more than a decade.

Below is shown informally how the intuition of the operators of the point-based TL can be encoded in DCL. The use of the operators is illustrated with an example from TL. For a formal, model-theoretic connection, we refer to the work on TLD [20].

6.1 Operators

We can define a number of (potentially) useful operators, which resemble the operators used in TL. Apart from $\Diamond$ and $\Box$ we can define the usual future operators:

$$\begin{array}{lll} \bigcirc A & \mathrel{\widehat{=}} \mathit{true} \rhd A & \text{next} \\ A \mathcal{U} B & \mathrel{\widehat{=}} ((\boxed{\text{D}} A \vee \lceil\rceil) ; B) \rhd \mathit{true} & \text{until} \\ A \mathcal{W} B & \mathrel{\widehat{=}} \Box\, A \vee A \mathcal{U} B & \text{waiting for} \end{array}$$

where $\boxed{\text{D}} A \mathrel{\widehat{=}} \neg(\mathit{true} ; \neg A ; \mathit{true})$ is the original DC operator which means that A must hold for all sub-intervals, and $\bigcirc A$ indicates that A must hold in some extension of the observed interval.

The past operators can be defined equivalently using $\lhd$.

6.2 Example: Resource Allocator

The following example is taken from Manna and Pnueli [13] and illustrates specifications with abstract fairness.

We specify the behavior of a resource allocator managing a resource shared by N processes. Let r_i be a state denoting the request for the resource by process i and let g_i denote that process i is granted access to the shared resource.

Mutual exclusion is specified as in TL:

$$\mathit{Mutex} \mathrel{\widehat{=}} \Box(\lceil \Sigma_i g_i \leq 1 \rceil \vee \lceil\rceil)$$

where it in DCL is necessary to include the point interval inside $\Box$.

As in TL, abstract fairness is easily specified as follows:

$$\mathit{Prog} \mathrel{\widehat{=}} \Box \Diamond \lceil \neg r_i \wedge \neg g_i \rceil$$

The implementation is specified by an automaton describing the protocol for accessing and releasing the shared resource.

$$\begin{array}{ll} \mathit{Prot}_1 & \mathrel{\widehat{=}} \lceil \neg g_i \rceil \Rightarrow \lceil \neg g_i \rceil \mathcal{W} \lceil r_i \wedge \neg g_i \rceil \\ \mathit{Prot}_2 & \mathrel{\widehat{=}} \lceil r_i \rceil \Rightarrow \lceil r_i \rceil \mathcal{W} \lceil r_i \wedge g_i \rceil \\ \mathit{Prot}_3 & \mathrel{\widehat{=}} \lceil g_i \rceil \Rightarrow \lceil g_i \rceil \mathcal{W} \lceil \neg r_i \wedge g_i \rceil \\ \mathit{Prot}_4 & \mathrel{\widehat{=}} \lceil \neg r_i \rceil \Rightarrow \lceil \neg r_i \rceil \mathcal{W} \lceil \neg r_i \wedge \neg g_i \rceil \\ \mathit{Prot} & \mathrel{\widehat{=}} \Box(\mathit{Prot}_1 \wedge \mathit{Prot}_2 \wedge \mathit{Prot}_3 \wedge \mathit{Prot}_4) \end{array}$$

To guarantee fairness, it is necessary to require that a process does not overtake the other processes an infinite number of times. In the current example, the choice was made to limit each overtaking to one for each process. In TL, 1-Bounded overtaking is given by the formula:

$$\mathit{Bnd} \mathrel{\widehat{=}} \Box(\lceil r_i \rceil \Rightarrow \lceil \neg g_j \rceil \mathcal{W} \lceil g_j \rceil \mathcal{W} \lceil \neg g_j \rceil \mathcal{W} \lceil g_i \rceil) \text{ for every } i, j,\ j \neq i$$

Alternatively, in DCL we can specify this in a slightly simpler manner:

$$\mathit{Bnd}' \mathrel{\widehat{=}} \Box(\neg(\lceil r_i \rceil \wedge \lceil g_j \rceil ; \lceil \neg g_j \rceil ; \lceil g_j \rceil)) \text{ for every } i, j,\ j \neq i$$

which is equivalent to:

$$\mathit{Bnd}'' \mathrel{\widehat{=}} (\lceil r_i \rceil \wedge \lceil g_j \rceil ; \lceil \neg g_j \rceil) \rightarrow \lceil \neg g_j \rceil \text{ for every } i, j,\ j \neq i$$

7 Related Work

Recently, a unifying model was invented to combine the Duration Calculus with Temporal Logic and the Temporal Logic of Actions (TLA) [11]. This unifying work has resulted in the logic called Temporal Logic with Durations (TLD) [20]. TLD formulas are constructed using combinators of DC, TL, and TLA, and can also specify liveness properties. However, the syntax and semantics of TLD is a major extension of DC and is for the single purpose of expressing liveness unnecessarily complicated.

The introduction of the Duration Calculus inspired duration extensions of existing temporal logics. $TL_{\int}$ [8] is a semantic and axiomatic extension of TL with a duration operator $\int A$, where A is a formula of TL. The semantics is somewhat different from DC's: The value of $\int A$ at time t is the sum of lengths of periods in the interval $[0, t]$ in which A holds.

Lakhneche and Hooman [9] have introduced durations in Metric Temporal Logic (MTL). The meaning of the MTL-$\int$ term $\int^r A$ denotes the accumulated time within the next r time-units in which the formula A is true. As in the original MTL, formulas are evaluated in both finite and infinite intervals. Durations are ensured to be evaluated in finite intervals by the subscription of $\int$ with the real-valued term denoting the length of the evaluation interval. As an example, the balanced oscillator is specified: $\exists\, r \cdot \Box(\int^r z = \int^r \neg z)$.

The branching time logic Timed CTL has also been extended with durations [1]. The resulting logic is called Duration Temporal Logic (DTL). Instead of a duration operator, DTL assigns duration variables to formulas which record the durations of the formulas. For instance, the balanced oscillator could be expressed as: $[x : z, y : \neg z].\forall \Diamond(x = y)$ where x and y are duration variables which record the durations of z resp. $\neg z$.

An integrating operator is defined within TLA^+ [12]. In contrast to DC and $TL_{\int}$ where the integrating operator is a part of the syntax, in TLA^+ it is encoded within the logic.

In [2] Brien specializes Tarski's calculus of relations [21] to a relational calculus on sets of time intervals, called the Time-Interval Calculus (TIC). A formula in TIC denotes the set of intervals on which it holds. TIC is closely related to Venema's CDT: Given a CDT formula A, let $[A] \mathrel{\widehat{=}} \{i \mid \mathcal{M}_{\mathcal{T}}, i \models A\}$. The *truncation operators* $\searrow$ and $\swarrow$ of TIC then correspond to the chopping operators $\lhd$ and $\rhd$ such that $[A \lhd B] = [A] \searrow [B]$ and $[A \rhd B] = [A] \swarrow [B]$.

8 Discussion

We have shown how abstract liveness conveniently can be introduced into DC by an addition of two extra chopping operators which extend beyond the interval in which the formula is evaluated. These operators have a simple and familiar semantics and conservatively extend the original logic.

In process scheduling, usually no assumptions are made about execution speeds of processes being constant, nor are any assumptions made about the relationship between execution speeds. To guarantee *fair* scheduling, it is required that the processes execute with a *positive* speed. In discrete temporal logics, this is sufficient to capture the intuition behind fairness. As shown in the oscillator example, however, for dense time this definition still enables unbalanced behaviours. To avoid this, we must require that the *accumulated* running time of each process eventually reaches a threshold. We have demonstrated how such balance conditions are elegantly specified using durations.

Observe the informal relationship with Temporal Logic. By changing the concept of validity from universal quantification over intervals in a model to an initial interval, the semantics can be tied even closer to the semantics of TL.

Recently, effort has gone into providing mechanized proof support for DC [19]. Specifically, a Gentzen style sequent system for DC has been implemented in the Prototype Verification System (PVS) [15] of SRI International to produce a DC proof assistant. Some of the DCL lemmas have been proven correct in an ad-hoc DCL extension of the proof assistant. In general, it is expected that the assistant can be extended to assist in a sequent formulation of DCL proofs.

Acknowledgements

I'm grateful to Natarajan Shankar, who directed my attention to the work of Venema. The specification of balanced scheduler is due to Anders P. Ravn, who also contributed with many suggestions. The helpful discussions with Kirsten M. Hansen, Michael R. Hansen, Tony Hoare, Jozef Hooman, Hans Henrik Løvengreen, Ben Moszkowski, Hans Rischel, and Morten U. Sørensen were also greatly appreciated.

References

1. A. Bouajjani, R. Echahed, and J. Sifakis. On model checking for real-time properties with durations. In *IEEE Symposium on Logic in Computer Science, Montreal, Canada.* IEEE Computer Society Press, June 1993.
2. S.M. Brien. A time-interval calculus. In *Mathematics of Program Construction*, volume 669 of *Lecture Notes in Computer Science*, pages 67–79. Springer-Verlag, June/July 1992.
3. J. Halpern, B. Moszkowski, and Z. Manna. A hardware semantics based on temporal intervals. In J. Díaz, editor, *10th ICALP. Automata, Languages and Programming*, volume 154 of *Lecture Notes in Computer Science*, pages 278–291. Springer-Verlag, 1983.
4. M. R. Hansen and Zhou Chaochen. Semantics and completeness of duration calculus. In W.-P. de Roever J. W. de Bakker, C. Huizing and G. Rozenberg, editors, *Real-Time: Theory in Practice, REX Workshop*, volume 600 of *Lecture Notes in Computer Science*, pages 209–225. Springer-Verlag, 1992.
5. M. R. Hansen and Zhou Chaochen. Lecture notes on the logical foundation of Duration Calculus. In Manuscript, 1994.
6. M. R. Hansen, Zhou Chaochen, and J. Staunstrup. A real-time duration semantics for circuits. In *TAU 1992 ACM/SIGDA Workshop on Timing Issues in the Specification and Synthesis of Digital Systems*, March 1992.

7. G.E. Hughes and M.J. Cresswell. *An Introduction to Modal Logic*. Routledge, 1968.
8. Y. Kesten and A. Pnueli. Age before beauty. Technical report, Department of Applied Mathematics, Weizmann Institute of Science, 1992.
9. Y. Lakhneche and J. Hooman. Metric temporal logic with durations. To appear in Theoretical Computer Science special issue on Hybrid Systems, 1994.
10. L. Lamport. What good is temporal logic? In R.E.A. Mason, editor, *Information Processing 83*, pages 657–668, Paris, 1983. North-Holland.
11. L. Lamport. The Temporal Logic of Actions. Research Report 79, Digital Equipment Corporation, Systems Research Center, December 1991.
12. L. Lamport. Hybrid systems in TLA^+. In *Workshop on Theory of Hybrid Systems*, volume 736 of *Lecture Notes in Computer Science*, pages 77–102. Springer-Verlag, October 1992.
13. Z. Manna and A. Pnueli. *The Temporal Logic of Reactive and Concurrent Systems: Specification*. Springer-Verlag, 1992.
14. B. Moszkowski. A temporal logic for multilevel reasoning about hardware. *IEEE Transactions on Computers*, 18(2):10–19, 1985.
15. S. Owre, N. Shankar, and J. M. Rushby. *User Guide for the PVS Specification and Verification System, Language, and Proof Checker (Beta Release)*. Computer Science Laboratory, SRI International, Menlo Park, CA 94025, USA, February 1993. Three volumes.
16. A.P. Ravn, H. Rischel, and K. M. Hansen. Specifying and verifying requirements of real-time systems. *IEEE Trans. Software Engineering*, 19(1):41–55, Jan. 1993.
17. R. Rosner and A. Pnueli. A choppy logic. In *IEEE Symposium on Logic in Computer Science*, pages 306–313. IEEE Computer Society Press, June 1986.
18. J.U. Skakkebæk, A.P. Ravn, H. Rischel, and Zhou Chaochen. Development of provably correct systems. In *IEEE Workshop on Real-Time Systems*, pages 116–121, June 1991.
19. J.U. Skakkebæk and N. Shankar. A Duration Calculus proof checker: Using PVS as a semantic framework. Technical Report SRI-CSL-93-10, Computer Science Laboratory, SRI International, Menlo Park, CA 94025, USA, December 1993.
20. M.U. Sørensen, O.E. Hansen, and H.H. Løvengreen. Combining temporal specification techniques. In *First International Conference on Temporal Logic*, Lecture Notes in Artificial Intelligence. Springer-Verlag, July 1994. To appear.
21. A. Tarski. On the calculus of relations. *Journal of Symbolic Logic*, 6(3):73–88, 1941.
22. Y. Venema. Two-dimensional modal logics for relational algebras and temporal logic of intervals. Technical Report LP-89-03, Institute for Language, Logic and Information, University of Amsterdam, 1989.
23. Y. Venema. Expressiveness and completeness of an interval tense logic. *Notre Dame Journal of Formal Logic*, 31(4):529–547, 1990.
24. Y. Venema. A modal logic for chopping intervals. *Journal of Logic Computation*, 1(4):453–476, 1991.
25. Zhou Chaochen. Infinite duration calculus, August 1992. Personal notes.
26. Zhou Chaochen, M.R. Hansen, A.P. Ravn, and H. Rischel. Duration specifications for shared processors. In *Symposium on Formal Techniques in Real-Time and Fault-Tolerant Systems*, volume 571 of *Lecture Notes in Computer Science*, pages 21–32. Springer-Verlag, January 1992.
27. Zhou Chaochen, C. A. R. Hoare, and A. P. Ravn. A calculus of durations. *Information Processing Letters*, 40(5):269–276, December 1991.

A Symbolic Semantics for the π-calculus - Extended Abstract -

Michele Boreale and Rocco De Nicola

Dipartimento di Scienze dell'Informazione
Università di Roma "La Sapienza"
Email: michele@dsi.uniroma1.it, denicola@vm.cnuce.cnr.it

Abstract. Symbolic transition systems are used as a basis for giving a new semantics of the π-calculus. This semantics is more amenable to automatic manipulation and sheds new light on the logical differences among different forms of bisimulation over dynamic process algebras. Symbolic transitions have the form $P \xrightarrow{\phi,\,\alpha} P'$, where, intuitively, ϕ is a *boolean constraint* over names that has to hold for the transition to take place, and α is a π-calculus action; e.g., $[x = y]\alpha.P \xrightarrow{[x=y],\,\alpha} P$ says that action α can be performed under any interpretation of names satisfying $x = y$. A symbolic bisimulation is defined on top of the symbolic transition system and it is shown that it captures the standard ones. Finally, a complete proof system is defined for symbolic bisimulation.

1 Introduction

The π-calculus [MPW92] is a widely studied process description language with primitives for expressing the exchange of channels names (or simply *names*) among processes. The exchanged names can also be tested for identity and this can be exploited to control instructions flow. These features permit a natural description of systems with dynamic linking.

Like traditional static process algebras, the π-calculus has undergone severe scrutiny and semantics for it have been proposed, relying on the standard notions of bisimulation [MPW92, PS93] and testing [Hen91, BD92]. However, theoretical studies to support equivalence checking have just begun; in [San93], with efficiency motivations, a new form of π-calculus bisimulation, called *open*, is proposed and studied.

In this paper, building on previous work by Hennessy and Lin on static value-passing process algebras [HL92, HL93], we provide a framework that yields alternative "efficient" characterization for various π-calculus bisimulation-based equivalences and a complete proof system to reason about them. An additional advantage of this framework is that it sheds light on the conceptual differences among known different forms of π-calculus bisimulation. Our attention will be confined to strong bisimulations, but we do not see any serious obstacle in extending our results to the weak ones.

The basic theory of bisimulation for the π-calculus has been introduced in [MPW92]. The fundamental notion is that of *ground* bisimulation; it has the same conceptual simplicity of the CCS one and suggests a natural strategy for equivalence checking. However, due to name passing, the definition-based verification technique runs into serious efficiency problems. On input actions, a case analysis on the received names is needed to check that receiving equal names leads to "equivalent" states. To see this, consider the processes $P = a(y).P'$ and $Q = a(y).Q'$; here the input prefix operator $a(y).R$ is used to describe receipt of a name at channel a and its substitution for the formal parameter y within R. To check that P and Q are ground bisimilar, following the definition we would have to verify that P' and Q' are bisimilar for all possible instantiations of y with a name occurring free in P and Q or with a fresh name. Of course, performing multiple checks for each input action may lead to exponential explosion.

Input prefix also introduces another problem: it does not preserve ground bisimulation equivalence. This leads to considering the maximal induced *congruence* as the closure under name-substitutions of the ground equivalence [MPW92]. Checking for congruence of two terms by relying on the original definition would consist in performing several (one for each "relevant" substitution) ground equivalence checks.

A simple example is sufficient to appreciate that, when verifying π-calculus bisimulation with such straightforward techniques, many performed checks are indeed useless.

Consider the two processes

$$P_1 = a(y).P \text{ and } P_2 = a(y).([y = z]P + [y \neq z]P)$$

where y and z are distinct and the $+$ operator stands for external choice. Here, both *match* $[z = y]$, and *mismatch* operators $[z \neq y]$, are used; $[z = y]P$ stands for a process that behaves like P if z and y are syntactically equal and is blocked otherwise, while $[z \neq y]P$ has exactly the opposite meaning.

It should be immediate to establish that P_1 and P_2 are equivalent. But, checking their equivalence by directly relying on the actual definition, requires checking that P and $[y = z]P + [y \neq z]P$ are bisimilar when y is replaced by z or by each of the free names of P. This could be very costly; it is however evident that, beside y, z is the only name that matters.

A significant gain in efficiency could be obtained by finding a systematic way to prune non-essential cases when performing the case analysis. To this aim, the idea pursued in this paper is that of setting up a framework where case analysis can be performed *symbolically*. First, a new transition system for the π-calculus is introduced, where the logical constraints that make a transition possible are made explicit. Then, a new bisimulation, which we refer to as *symbolic*, is defined, that performs the case-analysis directly on these logical constraints. It will be proved that symbolic bisimulation can be used to establish the standard ones.

The symbolic transitions are of the form $P \xrightarrow{\phi, \alpha} P'$, where ϕ is a *boolean constraint* over names that has to hold for the transition to take place, and α is a standard π-calculus action. A typical symbolic transition is $[x = y]\alpha.P \xrightarrow{[x=y], \alpha} P$, saying that action α can be performed under any interpretation of names satisfying $x = y$. A boolean constraint is in general built from the basic constraints

$[x = y]$ via the standard boolean connectives.

Symbolic bisimulation is defined on the top of the symbolic transition system, in a way that is parametric over the language of boolean constraints. This leads to distinct symbolic equivalences $\simeq^{\phi}$, depending on the boolean constraint ϕ. Informally, to verify $P \simeq^{\phi} Q$, it is required to find, for each symbolic move $P \xrightarrow{\psi, \alpha} P'$ of P, a case-partition of the condition $\phi \wedge \psi$, such that each subcase entails a matching symbolic move for Q. As an example, the equivalence $P_1 \simeq^{true} P_2$ of the above mentioned processes is readily verified by partitioning condition *true* as $\{[z = y], [z \neq y]\}$; this is sufficient because each of these two conditions entails that $[y = z]P + [y \neq z]P$ is equal to P. Actually, as we shall explain, the appropriate case analysis can be determined automatically.

Symbolic bisimulation is related to the standard ones by the following completeness theorem:

$P \simeq^{\phi} Q$ if and only if

for each name-substitution σ satisfying ϕ, $P\sigma$ is ground equivalent to $Q\sigma$

where a name-substitution σ *satisfies* ϕ if the result of applying σ to ϕ is a tautology; here, $P\sigma$ denotes the result of applying σ to P .

The above statement tells us that each symbolic equivalence $\simeq^{\phi}$ is the closure of the ground equivalence under all name-substitutions satisfying ϕ. Thus, for example, the congruence (i.e. the closure w.r.t. *all* substitutions) will be recovered as the symbolic bisimulation $\simeq^{true}$. Ground bisimulation equivalence of two specific processes P and Q will be instead recovered as a symbolic bisimulation $P \simeq^{\phi(P,Q)} Q$, where $\phi(P, Q)$ is a constraint imposing that all free names in P and Q be distinct.

In the paper, we also present a proof system to reason about symbolic bisimulation. The statements derivable within the system are of the form $\phi \rhd P = Q$ and the system is sound and complete in the sense that $\phi \rhd P = Q$ is derivable if and only if $P \simeq^{\phi} Q$. By taking advantage of the symbolic transitional semantics, the proof of completeness is, by and large, a symbolic version of the classical completeness proof for strong bisimulation over CCS [Mil89]. Additional complications are however introduced by the fact that the boolean condition ϕ may also constraint the communication capabilities of processes.

The symbolic characterization of the standard equivalences has also an additional advantage; it sheds new light on the conceptual difference between different forms of bisimulations for the π-calculus. Actually, in [MPW92], two forms of ground bisimulations (each inducing a different congruence) were introduced, the *early* form and the *late* one. Intuitively, they correspond to two different instantiation strategies for the formal parameter of input actions: in the first strategy (early), the instantiation is performed at the moment of inferring the input action, while in the other (late) it is performed later, when a communication is actually inferred. In open bisimulation [San93], the instantiation is delayed as much as possible; this yields an equivalence much stronger than the early and late ones. Our symbolic formulation indicates that each of the mentioned strategies corresponds to a different degree of generality in performing case-analysis.

Besides [San93], our work mainly relates to three papers: [HL92], [HL93] and [PS93]. In [HL92], the notion of symbolic bisimulation is introduced within a syntax-free framework, where *symbolic transition graphs* are considered; a polynomial-time verification algorithm is given and, for a version of CCS with value-passing, a completeness result similar to ours is proved. For the same value-passing language, a sound and complete proof system is presented in [HL93]. In [PS93], for the same name-passing language considered here, late and early ground bisimulation and the induced congruences are equipped with four distinct algebraic proof systems; efficiency considerations are absent.

The present paper may be viewed as the extension of [HL92] and [HL93] to a name-passing calculus, for which "efficient" characterizations of different bisimulation-based equivalences are obtained. A more detailed comparison with these and other papers is deferred to Section 5. Here we want only to stress the main reason that makes this extension non-trivial. The blurring of values and channel names, a distinctive feature of the π-calculus, allows names to appear both in the actions, in the processes and in the constraints; this gives rise to a subtle interplay between name-scoping and boolean constraining. This interplay is best revealed in the symbolic SOS rules for one of the name-binders of the π-calculus, the *restriction* operator (y). In $(y)P$, the name y is declared to be *new*, i.e. different from any other name; therefore, when we have $P \xrightarrow{\phi,\,\alpha} P'$ as a premise of an inference rule for $(y)P$, in the conclusion we have to discard from ϕ every assumption requiring y to be equal to other names, thus obtaining a new constraint $(y)\phi$, not containing y.

Throughout the paper, the early case will be treated in full detail, while the necessary changes of definitions and arguments for the simpler late case will be indicated time by time. The rest of the paper is organized as follows. In Section 2, after introducing the π-calculus and the standard notions of bisimulation equivalences, the symbolic transitional semantics and symbolic bisimulation are presented. Correctness and completeness of the latter w.r.t. standard bisimulations are also discussed. Section 4 presents the proof system and the corresponding theorems of soundness and completeness. Section 5 contains conclusions, comparisons with related work and suggestions for future research. Due to lack of space, proofs are just sketched; detailed proofs can be found in the full version of the paper [BD94].

2 Symbolic Semantics

In this section the π-calculus [MPW92] and its standard bisimulations will be briefly reviewed; then the new symbolic semantics will be introduced.

2.1 The π-calculus and its standard bisimulation semantics

Definition 1. *(Syntax)* Let $\mathcal{N}$ be a countable set and x, y range over it, let ϕ range over the language BF of *Boolean Formulae*:

$\phi ::= true \mid [x = y] \mid \neg\phi \mid \phi \wedge \phi$

and let α range over *actions*:

$$\alpha ::= \tau \, (silent\ move) \mid x(y) \, (input) \mid \overline{x}y (free\ output)$$

Let X range over a countable set of *process variables* and consider the language of *agent terms* built by means of *agent variables, inaction, action prefix, summation, boolean guard, restriction, parallel composition* and *recursion* in the following way:

$$P ::= X \mid \mathbf{0} \mid \alpha.P \mid P + P \mid \phi P \mid (y)P \mid P|P \mid recX.P$$

A *process* is an agent term where each occurrence of any agent variable X lies within the scope a $recX.$ operator. We let π denote the set of processes.

We fix now some basic notations. We shall use $false$ as an abbreviation for $\neg true$, $[x \neq y]$ as an abbreviation for $\neg[x = y]$ and $\phi_1 \vee \phi_2$ as an abbreviation for $\neg(\neg\phi_1 \wedge \neg\phi_2)$. *Evaluation* of a boolean formula into the set $\{true, false\}$ is defined in the expected way, once we set that for any two distinct names x and y, $[x = x]$ evaluates to $true$ and $[x = y]$ evaluates to $false$. We will write $\phi = true$ ($\phi = false$) if ϕ evaluates to $true$ ($false$); $n(\phi)$ will denote the set of names occurring in ϕ.

We use the *bound output action* $\overline{x}(y).P$, $x \neq y$, as a shorthand for $(y)(\overline{x}y.P)$. If $\alpha = x(y)$ or $\alpha = \overline{x}y$ or $\alpha = \overline{x}(y)$, we let $subj(\alpha) = x$ and $obj(\alpha) = y$. The π-calculus has two kinds of name *binders*: input prefix $x(y).P$ and restriction $(y)P$ bind the name y in P; consequently, the notions of *free names, fn(.), bound names, bn(.)* and *α-equality*, $\equiv$, over both process terms, formulae and actions, are the expected ones (we define $fn(\phi) = n(\phi)$ for a boolean formula ϕ). We let $n(.) = fn(.) \cup bn(.)$.

Substitutions, ranged over by σ, ρ, are functions from $\mathcal{N}$ to $\mathcal{N}$; for any $x \in \mathcal{N}$, $\sigma(x)$ will be written as $x\sigma$. Given a substitution σ and $V \subseteq_{fin} \mathcal{N}$, we define:

- $V\sigma = \{x\sigma \mid x \in V\}$
- $dom(\sigma) = \{x \mid x\sigma \neq x\}$
- $range(\sigma) = dom(\sigma)\sigma$
- $n(\sigma) = dom(\sigma) \cup range(\sigma)$

In the rest of the paper we confine ourselves to *finite* substitutions, i.e. those σ s.t. $n(\sigma)$ is finite. If t is either an action, a formula or a process term, $t\sigma$ denotes the result of applying the substitution σ to t, i.e. the expression obtained from t by simultaneously replacing each $x \in fn(t)$ with $x\sigma$. A set $\{x_1/y_1, \ldots, x_n/y_n\} = \{\tilde{x}/\tilde{y}\}$, with the x_i's pairwise distinct, will denote the following substitution σ: $x\sigma = y_i$ if $x = x_i$ for some $i \in \{1, \ldots, n\}$, $x\sigma = x$ otherwise. We also define $fn(\sigma) = n(\sigma)$; in this way, function $fn(\,.\,)$ is defined over both names, actions, processes, formulae and substitutions.

Unless otherwise stated, we will let $x, y, \ldots$ range over $\mathcal{N}$, $\alpha, \beta, \ldots$ over the set of actions (including derived bound output), $\phi, \psi, \ldots$ over BF, $P, Q, \ldots$ over π and $\rho, \sigma, \ldots$ over substitutions.

The standard "concrete" transitional semantics of π is given in Table 1. By following [PS93] we also include the (non-structural) `Alpha` rule, that permits freely α-renaming actions and processes; this rule often avoids tedious side conditions in the proofs. With our transitional semantics, the definition of (standard)

$$\texttt{Act}\frac{-}{\alpha.P \xrightarrow{\alpha} P}$$

$$\texttt{Sum}\frac{P_1 \xrightarrow{\alpha} P_1'}{P_1 + P_2 \xrightarrow{\alpha} P_1'} \qquad \texttt{Par}\frac{P_1 \xrightarrow{\alpha} P_1'}{P_1 \mid P_2 \xrightarrow{\alpha} P_1' \mid P_2}\ bn(\alpha) \cap fn(P_2) = \emptyset$$

$$\texttt{Com}\frac{P_1 \xrightarrow{\overline{x}z} P_1',\ P_2 \xrightarrow{x(y)} P_2'}{P_1 \mid P_2 \xrightarrow{\tau} P_1' \mid P_2'\{z/y\}} \qquad \texttt{Close}\frac{P_1 \xrightarrow{\overline{x}(y)} P_1',\ P_2 \xrightarrow{x(y)} P_2'}{P_1 \mid P_2 \xrightarrow{\tau} (y)(P_1' \mid P_2')}$$

$$\texttt{Res}\frac{P \xrightarrow{\alpha} P'}{(y)P \xrightarrow{\alpha} (y)P'}\ y \notin n(\alpha) \qquad \texttt{Open}\frac{P \xrightarrow{\overline{x}y} P'}{(y)P \xrightarrow{\overline{x}(y)} P'}\ x \neq y$$

$$\texttt{Guard}\frac{P \xrightarrow{\alpha} P'}{\phi P \xrightarrow{\alpha} P'}\ \phi = true \qquad \texttt{Rec}\frac{P[recX.P/X] \xrightarrow{\alpha} P'}{recX.P \xrightarrow{\alpha} P'}$$

$$\texttt{Alpha}\frac{P \xrightarrow{\alpha} P'}{Q \xrightarrow{\beta} Q'}\ P \equiv Q,\ \alpha.P' \equiv \beta.Q'$$

Symmetric versions of **Sum**, **Par**, **Com** and **Close** are omitted.

Table 1. Standard SOS for π.

early ground bisimulation equivalence $\dot{\sim}$ and early bisimulation congruence $\sim$ can be given as follows:

Definition 2. *(Early Bisimulation)*

- A symmetric relation $\mathcal{R} \subseteq \pi \times \pi$ is a ground early bisimulation iff $(P, Q) \in \mathcal{R}$ and $P \xrightarrow{\alpha} P'$ with $bn(\alpha) \cap fn(P, Q) = \emptyset$, imply
  - if α is not an input action, then $\exists\, Q'$: $Q \xrightarrow{\alpha} Q'$ and $(P', Q') \in \mathcal{R}$.
  - if $\alpha = x(y)$, then $\forall z \in fn(P, Q, y)\ \exists\, Q' : Q \xrightarrow{\alpha} Q'$ and $(P'\{z/y\}, Q'\{z/y\}) \in \mathcal{R}$.
- $\dot{\sim} = \cup\{\mathcal{R} \mid \mathcal{R}$ is a ground early bisimulation $\}$.
- $P \sim Q$ iff $\forall \sigma.\ P\sigma \dot{\sim} Q\sigma$.

The *late* version of the above definition is obtained by replacing the input-clause (the second clause of the first item) by the stronger:

- if $\alpha = x(y)$, then $\exists Q' : Q \xrightarrow{\alpha} Q'$ and $\forall\, z \in fn(P, Q, y)\ (P'\{z/y\}, Q'\{z/y\}) \in \mathcal{R}$.

It turns out [MPW92] that late bisimulation is strictly finer than early bisimulation.

2.2 Symbolic semantics

Before introducing the symbolic semantics, we need to fix some additional notation for boolean formulae and substitutions.

Definition 3. *(Basic Definitions)*

- $\sigma \models \phi$ stands for $\phi\sigma = true$;
- $\phi \models \psi$ stands for $\forall\ \sigma$: $\sigma \models \phi$ implies $\sigma \models \psi$;
- $[\alpha = \beta]$ stands for

$$\begin{array}{ll} [x = z] & \text{if for some } y\ (\alpha = x(y) \text{ and } \beta = z(y)) \text{ or} \\ & (\alpha = \overline{x}(y) \text{ and } \beta = \overline{z}(y)); \\ [x = z] \wedge [y = w] & \text{if } \alpha = \overline{x}y \text{ and } \beta = \overline{z}w; \\ \mathit{true} & \text{if } \alpha = \beta = \tau; \\ \mathit{false} & \text{otherwise.} \end{array}$$

- $\bigvee D$, where $D = \{\phi_1, \ldots, \phi_n\} \subseteq_{fin} BF$, $n > 0$, is the boolean formula $\phi_1 \vee \ldots \vee \phi_n$. A similar notation will be used for $\bigwedge D$. Furthermore, we let $\bigvee \emptyset$ denote *false* and $\bigwedge \emptyset$ denote *true*.
- The boolean formula $(y)\phi$ is defined by structural induction on ϕ as follows:

$$\begin{array}{rll} (y)\mathit{true} &= \mathit{true} & \\ (y)[w_1 = w_2] &= [w_1 = w_2] & \text{if } y \notin \{w_1, w_2\} \\ (y)[y = y] &= \mathit{true} & \\ (y)[y = w] &= (y)[w = y] = \mathit{false} & \text{if } y \neq w \\ (y)\neg\phi &= \neg(y)\phi & \\ (y)(\phi_1 \wedge \phi_2) &= (y)\phi_1 \wedge (y)\phi_2 & \end{array}$$

The symbolic transitional semantics of π is presented in Table 2. We comment on the rules. Each symbolic rule is the counterpart of a concrete one. Intuitively, the boolean condition ϕ in $P \xrightarrow{\phi,\alpha} P'$ is a constraint over the free names of P that has to hold for the transition to take place. The rule $\phi - \mathtt{Act}$ says that $\alpha.P$ can perform α unconditionally. In $\phi - \mathtt{Com}$ and $\phi - \mathtt{Close}$, the condition of matching channels ($[x = w]$) is moved into the boolean condition of the resulting symbolic transition; this is necessary to infer symbolic transitions such as: $(x(y).\mathbf{0}) \,|\, (\overline{w}\langle y\rangle.\mathbf{0}) \xrightarrow{[x=w],\,\tau} \mathbf{0} \,|\, \mathbf{0}$. The rule $\phi - \mathtt{Res}$ reveals the interplay between name-scoping and constraining: in $(y)P$, the name y is declared to be *new*, i.e. different from any other name; thus the rule says that, given a symbolic transition $P \xrightarrow{\phi,\alpha} P'$ as a premise, under the assumption that y is new, we have to discard every assumption about the identity of y from ϕ in the conclusion; as a result, the new constraint $(y)\phi$ that does not contain y is obtained. An example of derivation is:

$$\phi - \mathsf{Res}\frac{P \xrightarrow{[y=z]\vee[z=w],\,\tau} P'}{(y)P \xrightarrow{\mathit{false}\vee[z=w],\,\tau} (y)P'}$$

where z and w are different from y (note that $\mathit{false} \vee [z = w]$ is equivalent to $[z = w]$). A similar comment holds for $\phi - \mathtt{Open}$. The other inference rules should be self-explanatory.

$$\phi - \texttt{Act} \frac{-}{\alpha.P \stackrel{true,\,\alpha}{\longrightarrow} P}$$

$$\phi - \texttt{Sum} \frac{P_1 \stackrel{\phi,\,\alpha}{\longrightarrow} P_1'}{P_1 + P_2 \stackrel{\phi,\,\alpha}{\longrightarrow} P_1'} \qquad \phi - \texttt{Par} \frac{P_1 \stackrel{\phi,\,\alpha}{\longrightarrow} P_1'}{P_1 \mid P_2 \stackrel{\phi,\,\alpha}{\longrightarrow} P_1' \mid P_2} bn(\alpha) \cap fn(P_2) = \emptyset$$

$$\phi - \texttt{Com} \frac{P_1 \stackrel{\phi_1,\,\overline{x}z}{\longrightarrow} P_1',\ P_2 \stackrel{\phi_2,w(y)}{\longrightarrow} P_2'}{P_1 \mid P_2 \stackrel{\phi_1 \wedge \phi_2 \wedge [x=w],\,\tau}{\longrightarrow} P_1' \mid P_2'\{z/y\}} \qquad \phi - \texttt{Close} \frac{P_1 \stackrel{\phi_1,\,\overline{x}(y)}{\longrightarrow} P_1',\ P_2 \stackrel{\phi_2,\,w(y)}{\longrightarrow} P_2'}{P_1 \mid P_2 \stackrel{\phi_1 \wedge \phi_2 \wedge [x=w],\,\tau}{\longrightarrow} (y)(P_1' \mid P_2')}$$

$$\phi - \texttt{Res} \frac{P \stackrel{\phi,\,\alpha}{\longrightarrow} P'}{(y)P \stackrel{(y)\phi,\,\alpha}{\longrightarrow} (y)P'} y \notin n(\alpha) \qquad \phi - \texttt{Open} \frac{P \stackrel{\phi,\,\overline{x}y}{\longrightarrow} P'}{(y)P \stackrel{(y)\phi,\,\overline{x}(y)}{\longrightarrow} P'} x \neq y$$

$$\phi - \texttt{Guard} \frac{P \stackrel{\psi,\,\alpha}{\longrightarrow} P'}{\phi P \stackrel{\phi\wedge\psi,\,\alpha}{\longrightarrow} P'} \qquad \phi - \texttt{Rec} \frac{P[recX.P/X] \stackrel{\phi,\,\alpha}{\longrightarrow} P'}{recX.P \stackrel{\phi,\,\alpha}{\longrightarrow} P'}$$

$$\phi - \texttt{Alpha} \frac{P \stackrel{\phi,\,\alpha}{\longrightarrow} P'}{Q \stackrel{\phi,\,\beta}{\longrightarrow} Q'} P \equiv Q,\ \alpha.P' \equiv \beta.Q'$$

Symmetric versions of $\phi - \texttt{Sum}$, $\phi - \texttt{Par}$, $\phi - \texttt{Com}$ and $\phi - \texttt{Close}$ are omitted.

Table 2. Symbolic SOS for π.

We are now set to introduce symbolic bisimulation for the π-calculus. For a variant of CCS with value passing, symbolic bisimulation has been introduced in [HL92]. The underlying intuition is that of establishing equivalence of, say, P and Q under a condition ϕ, by matching, under ϕ, symbolic transitions of P, $P \stackrel{\psi,\alpha}{\longrightarrow} P'$, by *sets* of symbolic transitions of Q. More precisely, the condition $\phi \wedge \psi$, is partitioned into a set D of subcases, each of which entails a matching transition for Q. Due to the treatment of restricted names in the π-calculus, here we have to take into account the case when the performed action is a bound output $\overline{x}(y)$. In this case, we impose, by adding an extra condition, that the name y be different from any known name in subsequent reasoning.

Definition 4. *(ϕ-decomposition)* Given ϕ and a finite set of formulae $D = \{\phi_1, \ldots, \phi_n\}$, we say that D is a *ϕ-decomposition* iff $\phi \models \bigvee D$.

Definition 5. *(Symbolic Early Bisimulation)*

– A family $\mathcal{F} = \{R_\phi \mid \phi \in BF\}$ of symmetric binary relations over π, indexed over the set BF of boolean formulae, is a *family of symbolic early*

bisimulations (FSEB) iff for each ϕ, $(P,Q) \in R_\phi$ and $P \xrightarrow{\psi,\alpha} P'$, with $bn(\alpha) \cap fn(P,Q,\phi) = \emptyset$, imply:
there exists a χ-decomposition D, such that for each $\phi' \in D$, there is a symbolic transition $Q \xrightarrow{\psi',\beta} Q'$ with $\phi' \models (\psi' \wedge [\alpha = \beta])$ and $(P',Q') \in R_{\phi'}$, where:

$$\chi = \begin{cases} \phi \wedge \psi \wedge \bigwedge_{z \in fn(P,Q,\phi)} [y \neq z] & \text{if } \alpha \text{ is a bound output action } \overline{x}(y) \\ \phi \wedge \psi & \text{otherwise.} \end{cases}$$

– $P \simeq^\phi Q$ iff there exists a FSEB $\{R_\psi | \, \psi \in BF\}$ such that $(P,Q) \in R_\phi$.

Note that, on input actions, no multiple instantiation of the formal parameter is required; instead, a single instantiation with a *fresh* name suffices (the "freshness" condition is $bn(\alpha) \cap fn(P,Q,\phi) = \emptyset$ [1]). The case analysis on the received value is now embodied in the decomposition D; by performing this decomposition in an appropriate way, the number of cases to deal with is in general much smaller than that arising with the original definition (as shown, e.g., by the example about the processes P_1, P_2 in the Introduction).

Actually, the appropriate decomposition can be determined automatically. In [HL92], an algorithm is presented to check symbolic bisimulation between two finite *standard* symbolic transition graphs. A symbolic graph is standard if the bound name of each bound action transition does not occur free in any ancestor-node of the transition. This amounts to requiring that only *new* names are used for bound actions when generating the graph. Given two such graphs G_1 and G_2, the algorithm calculates, in a time polynimial with the sizes of the graphs, the *most general boolean expression* under which the two graphs are equivalent, i.e. a boolean ϕ such that if $G_1 \simeq^\psi G_2$, then $\phi \models \psi$. Therefore, the equivalence problem for graphs is reduced to the implication problem for boolean expressions. Now, altough a π-calculus process, even if finite, has in general infinitely many α-equivalent transitions (due to the $\phi - \mathtt{Alpha}$ rule), it is easy to see that only finitely many of them need to be considered when performing verificaton. More precisely, it is enough to consider a transition for each α-equivalence class of transitions. Starting from a π-calculus term, we can thus generate a graph that represents it and that, at least for finite processes, is finite. In order for the graph to be standard, we have also to take care of using fresh names for input and bound output transitions (by resorting, e.g., to a fresh name generator). By introducing minor modifications (that take into account the extra conditions due to bound output when determining the decomposition), we can then use Hennessy and Lin' algorithm to calculate the most general boolean expression of two π-calculus processes represented by finite symbolic transition graphs.

Symbolic Late Bisimulation is obtained by simply adding the condition $bn(\alpha) \cap n(\bigvee D) = \emptyset$ to the first item of the Definition 5: this amounts to imposing that no alternative of the decomposition depends on the "value" of the formal parameter $bn(\alpha)$, i.e. to forbidding case-analysis on the actual value of $bn(\alpha)$. The

[1] $fn(\psi)$ need not to be considered because we have $fn(\psi) \subseteq fn(P)$.

above discussion on automatic verification extends to the late case as well, by considering the late version of Hennessy and Lin' algorithm.

The following lemma, that relates standard and symbolic transitional semantics, is crucial to establish correctness and completeness of symbolic bisimulations.

Lemma 6. (Correspondence between Symbolic and Concrete SOS)

1. *If* $P \xrightarrow{\phi,\alpha} P'$*, with* $bn(\alpha) \cap fn(P,\sigma) = \emptyset$ *, and* $\sigma \models \phi$*, then* $P\sigma \xrightarrow{\alpha\sigma} P'\sigma$*.*
2. *If* $P\sigma \xrightarrow{\alpha} P'$*, with* $bn(\alpha) \cap fn(P,\sigma) = \emptyset$ *, then there exists a symbolic transition* $P \xrightarrow{\phi,\beta} P''$*, with* $\sigma \models \phi$*,* $\beta\sigma = \alpha$ *and* $P''\sigma = P'$*.*

PROOF: By transition induction on $P \xrightarrow{\phi,\alpha} P'$ and $P\sigma \xrightarrow{\alpha} P'$. □

In order to state both the the correctness and the completeness theorems, it is useful to have the following definition:

Definition 7. *(Closing* $\dot\sim$ *under* ϕ*)*For each $\phi \in BF$, let relation $\sim^\phi$ be: $P \sim^\phi Q$ iff $\forall\sigma$ such that $\sigma \models \phi$, $P\sigma \dot\sim Q\sigma$.

Theorem 8. (Correctness of Symbolic Bisim.) $P \simeq^\phi Q$ *implies* $P \sim^\phi Q$*.*

PROOF: Sketch. Consider the relation $\mathcal{R} = \{(P\sigma, Q\sigma) | \exists\phi.\sigma \models \phi$ and $P \simeq^\phi Q\}$. It is not difficult, by exploiting Lemma 6, to show that $\mathcal{R} \subseteq \dot\sim$. Precisely, one shows that $\mathcal{R}$ is a *Bisimulation up to Injective Substitutions*; in this proof technique, the clauses of usual bisimulation are weakened so to permit that matching transitions lead to states that are in the relation provided that some injective substitution is applied to them (in the present case, this is useful for bound output transitions). Details on the technique can be found in the full version of this paper [BD94] or in [San94]. □

3 Completeness of Symbolic Bisimulation

To prove the completeness theorem, we shall rely on the fact that only a suitable finite set of name-substitutions is "relevant" when working with fixed collection of processes and formulae. All the remaining substitutions are, in fact, *variants* of the considered ones, i.e. they can be obtained by injective renaming. This is a distinctive property of the π-calculus, since it relies on the blurring of names and variables.

Theorem 9. (Completeness of Symbolic Bisim.) $P \sim^\phi Q$ *implies* $P \simeq^\phi Q$*.*

PROOF: Sketch. We show that $\{\sim^\phi | \phi \in BF\}$ is a family of symbolic bisimulations. Suppose that $P \sim^\phi Q$ and that $P \xrightarrow{\psi,\alpha} P'$. We sketch here only the case $\alpha = \tau$. We have to find a decomposition of $\phi \wedge \psi$, such that each subcase entails a matching symbolic transition for Q. Fix any σ s.t. $\sigma \models \phi \wedge \psi$. From Lemma

6 applied to $P \xrightarrow{\psi,\alpha} P'$, we obtain that $P\sigma \xrightarrow{\tau} P'\sigma$. Hence, by definition of $\sim^{\phi}$, there is a transition $Q\sigma \xrightarrow{\tau} Q' \dot{\sim} P'\sigma$. Again from Lemma 6, we obtain that there exists a transition $Q \xrightarrow{\phi_\sigma,\tau} Q_\sigma$, with $Q_\sigma\sigma = Q' \dot{\sim} P'\sigma$ and $\sigma \models \phi_\sigma$.

Now, let $V = fn(P, Q, \phi \wedge \psi)$. The idea is to consider a *finite* set of substitutions, $S = \{\sigma_1, \ldots, \sigma_k\}$, such that each substitution σ satisfying $\phi \wedge \psi$ is a variant over V of some σ_i. These are obtained as the set of those σ's satisfying $\phi \wedge \psi$ with $n(\sigma) \subseteq V \cup Y$, where Y is a suitably large finite set of names disjoint from V (Y represents a reserve of fresh names). Then, we decompose $\phi \wedge \psi$ into a set $D = \{\psi_1, \ldots, \psi_k\}$, one subcase for each $\sigma_i \in S$; more precisely $\psi_i = \chi(\sigma_i, V) \wedge \phi_{\sigma_i}$, where $\chi(\sigma_i, V)$ is a certain formula satisfied exactly by the the variants of σ_i over V. Now, for each $i \in \{1, \ldots, k\}$, from $P'\sigma_i \dot{\sim} Q_{\sigma_i}\sigma_i$ and from the fact that ψ_i is satisfied only by variants of σ_i, we can conclude that $P' \sim^{\psi_i} Q_{\sigma_i}$ (in fact, variant substitutions "behave the same" w.r.t. $\dot{\sim}$). Furthermore, by exploiting the fact that for each variant σ of σ_i, $\sigma_i \models \phi \wedge \psi$ implies $\sigma \models \phi \wedge \psi$, we can conclude that D is a $\phi \wedge \psi$-decomposition.

The cases when α is an input or α is bound output are more involved, because we have to take into account the possibility of case-analysis also over the formal parameter $bn(\alpha)$. □

We end the section by showing that also ground bisimulation $\dot{\sim}$ can be characterized in terms of the symbolic one.

Theorem 10. *$P \dot{\sim} Q$ iff $P \simeq^{\phi} Q$, where $\phi = \bigwedge_{x,y \in fn(P,Q),\, x,y \text{ distinct}} [x \neq y]$.*

Proof: The theorem follows immediately from the correctness and completeness theorems for symbolic bisimulation and from the fact that $\dot{\sim}$ is closed under injective substitutions . □

4 The Proof System

Let us now consider the *finite* fragment of the calculus, i.e. the calculus without the *recX.* operator zand discuss an equational axiomatization of symbolic bisimulation over it. It is well known that decidable axiomatizations cannot exist for the full language. The statements derivable within the system are guarded equations of the form $\phi \rhd P = Q$, to be read as "under ϕ, P equals Q". In the sequel, we will write $\phi \rhd P = Q$ to mean that the equation $\phi \rhd P = Q$ is derivable within the proof system. Furthermore, we will abbreviate "$true \rhd P = Q$" simply as "$P = Q$".

The inference rules and the new relevant axioms of the proof system are presented in Table 3 and Table 4. The standard inference rules for reflexivity, symmetry and transitivity and the usual laws for Summation, Restriction and Alpha-conversion (see [MPW92]) have been omitted in this shortened version for lack of space. Our proof system can be viewed as the result of merging that of [HL93] and [PS93]. More precisely, all of the inference rules, but the *Res* rule, are taken from [HL93], while the axioms are taken from [PS93].

$$(Congr)\quad \frac{\phi \rhd P = Q}{\phi \rhd P' = Q'} \qquad \text{where } P' = Q' \text{ stands for either of } \tau.P = \tau.Q,\ \overline{x}y.P = \overline{x}y.Q,\ \psi P = \psi Q,\ P + R = Q + R,\ P|R = Q|R.$$

$$(Res)\quad \frac{\phi \rhd P = Q}{(y)\phi \rhd (y)P = (y)Q}$$

$$(Inp)\quad \frac{\phi \rhd \sum_{i\in I} \tau.P_i = \sum_{i\in I} \tau.Q_i}{\phi \rhd \sum_{i\in I} x(y).P_i = \sum_{i\in I} x(y).Q_i} \quad y \notin n(\phi)$$

$$(Guard)\quad \frac{\phi \wedge \psi \rhd P = Q,\ \phi \wedge \neg\psi \rhd Q = \mathbf{0}}{\phi \rhd \psi P = Q}$$

$$(False)\quad \frac{-}{false \rhd P = Q}$$

$$(Cut)\quad \frac{\phi_1 \rhd P = Q,\ \phi_2 \rhd P = Q}{\phi \rhd P = Q} \qquad \phi \models \phi_1 \vee \phi_2$$

$$(Axiom)\quad \frac{-}{true \rhd P = Q} \qquad \text{for each axiom } P = Q$$

Table 3. Inference Rules of the Proof System

The *Cut* rule permits case analysis on ϕ: it says that if ϕ can be split into two subcases ϕ_1 and ϕ_2, and for each subcase we can prove $P = Q$, then $P = Q$ is derivable under ϕ. The *Res* rule exhibits the same kind of logical "hiding" of the bound name y as the rules $\phi - \texttt{Res}$ and $\phi - \texttt{Open}$ of the transitional semantics. The other rules and axioms should be self-explanatory; anyway, we refer the reader to [PS93, HL93] for explanations on their intuitive meaning.

Soundness is straightforward to prove by exploiting the correctness and completeness of symbolic bisimulation w.r.t. the standard one.

Theorem 11. (Soundness of the Proof System)$\phi \rhd P = Q$ *implies* $P \sim^{\phi} Q$.

The actual proof of completeness relies on a "customized" notion of head normal form. Each process term has a provably equivalent head normal form.

$(Subst)$ $[x = y]\alpha.P = [x = y]\alpha\{x/y\}.P$

$(Res2)$ $(y)(\phi P) = ((y)\phi)(y)P$

(Exp)
Suppose $P \equiv \sum_{i \in I} \phi_i \alpha_i.P_i$ and $Q \equiv \sum_{j \in J} \psi_i \beta_i.Q_i$.
Suppose that no α_i (resp. β_j) binds a name free in Q (resp. P).

$$P \mid Q = \sum_{i \in I} \phi_i \alpha_i.(P_i \mid Q) + \sum_{j \in J} \psi_j \beta_j.(P \mid Q_j) + \sum_{\alpha_i \; opp \; \beta_j} (\phi_i \wedge \psi_j \wedge [x_i = y_j])\tau.R_{ij}$$

where $\alpha_i \; opp \; \beta_j$ and R_{ij} are defined as follows:
1. $\alpha_i = \overline{x_i} z$ and $\beta_j = y_j(y)$; then $R_{ij} = P_i \mid Q_j\{z/y\}$
2. $\alpha_i = \overline{x_i}(y)$ and $\beta_j = y_j(y)$; then $R_{ij} = (y)(P_i \mid Q_j)$
3. The converse of 1.
4. The converse of 2.

Table 4. Relevant Axioms of the Proof System.

Definition 12. *(Head Normal Forms)* A process P is in *head normal form (HNF)* if it is of the form $\sum_{i \in I} \phi_i S_i$, where:

- $\{\phi_i \mid i \in I\}$ is a *true*-decomposition such that $\phi_i \wedge \phi_j = false$ for each $i, j \in I$ with $i \neq j$;
- each S_i is of the form $\sum_{j \in J_i} \alpha_j.P_j$.

Theorem 13. (Complet. of the Proof System) *$P \simeq^\phi Q$ implies $\phi \rhd P = Q$.*

Proof: Sketch. The proof is by induction on the depth of P and Q under ϕ. If $P \simeq^\phi Q$, we can suppose, without loss of generality, that both P and Q are in HNF. We then split the condition ϕ into a decomposition D such that for each subcase $\psi \in D$:

1. under ψ, both $P = \sum_{i \in I} \alpha_i.P_i$ and $Q = \sum_{j \in J} \beta_j.Q_j$, that is P and Q are equal to some head normal form in the sense of [Mil89].
2. under ψ, all the free names appearing in some α_i or some β_j, can be treated as *constants*. More precisely, for any to such name x and y, if not $\phi \models [x = y]$ then $\phi \models [x \neq y]$.

By exploiting the above facts, the symbolic transitional semantics and the inductive hypothesis, one can show that P and Q are equal under ψ, i.e. $\psi \rhd P = Q$. Since this holds for each subcase $\psi \in D$, we can conclude by applying the *Cut* rule that $\phi \rhd P = Q$. □

A sound and complete proof system for late bisimulation can be obtained by replacing the *Inp* rule of the considered system with the simpler rule:

$$(Inp - L)\frac{\phi \rhd P = Q}{\phi \rhd x(y).P = x(y).Q} \; y \notin n(\phi).$$

5 Conclusions and Related Work

A symbolic transitional semantics for the π-calculus has been introduced and, on top of it, a notion of symbolic bisimulation has been defined, amenable to efficient checking. Symbolic bisimulation has then been related to the standard bisimulations of the π-calculus. A consequence of this is that more efficient checking of early and late bisimulations is possible. A sound and complete proof system for symbolic bisimulation has then been provided.

The symbolic characterization of the bisimulations has another major benefit: it sheds new light on the logical difference between various π-calculus bisimulations, based on different instantiation strategies, such as early, late and open. It is not difficult to see that different instantiation strategies correspond to different degrees of generality in the case analysis. Indeed, early bisimulation is the most general (and natural) one, since no restriction is imposed on the case-decomposition D. Late bisimulation is obtained by adding the requirement that the formal parameter of the input action ($bn(\alpha)$) does not appear in D, i.e. by forbidding case-analysis on the actual value of the formal parameter. Open bisimulation [San93] is only defined over the language without negation (hence essentially without mismatch $[x \neq y]$). It appears, but this needs to to be worked out in full detail, that open bisimulation can be obtained from the early symbolic one by completely omitting case analysis; this amounts essentially to requiring that D be a singleton. Extending open bisimulation to a language with mismatch is an interesting open problem of [San93]. It could be solved within our symbolic framework. It appears that a meaningful "conservative" extension of open bisimulation to the richer language can be obtained by requiring a limited form of case-analysis.

The original idea of symbolic bisimulation has been presented in [HL92]. There, a polynomial verification algorithm is proposed for a class of symbolic transition graphs and a theorem relating symbolic bisimulations to concrete bisimulations over a version of CCS with value-passing is presented. In [HL93], the same language has then been equipped with a sound and complete proof system. The results obtained by Hennessy and Lin are the direct inspiration of our work but they cannot be directly extended to the π-calculus for two main reasons:

1. the blurring of the distinction between variables, values and channels proper of the π-calculus;
2. the absence of a specific language for boolean constraints in the work by Hennessy and Lin.

It is easier to deal with a static value-passing process algebra, because channel names are neatly separated from the exchanged values and thus channels do not appear in the constraints. Of course, this is no longer true in a name-passing calculus, where a subtle interplay between name-scoping and boolean constraining is present. An example of such interplay is offered by the symbolic SOS rules for the restriction operator.

The symbolic framework of [HL92] and [HL93] is parametrised on the language of boolean constraints, in other words they do not have a specific language for boolean constraints. In order to establish the relationship between symbolic and concrete bisimulation, they just assume the existence of an extremely expressive language, capable of describing any given collection of environments (associations of variables with values). This is admittedly [HL92] a very strong requirement. It is at least not obvious, in presence of non-trivial types of values, that such a language exists. Here, we had to consider a *specific* language (BF) and had to deal with name substitutions rather than environments. Indeed, it must be said that our solution heavily depends on the specific features of the π-calculus: only finitely many substitutions are important when dealing with a fixed set of constraints and processes. This property does not hold for languages that, besides names, permit exchanging other kinds of values (e.g. integers) and make use of predicates (e.g. $\leq$) over them.

In [PS93], the ground equivalence and the corresponding congruence, for the early and late cases, are separately axiomatized, via four distinct algebraic proof systems. Confining ourselves to one specific form of bisimulation (either early or late), the main differences between our proof system and theirs can be summarized as follows. They consider the ground equivalence and the congruence separately; in our framework, all the equivalences obtainable as substitution-closure of the ground one (including, as particular cases, the ground equivalence itself and the congruence) are considered at once. As a consequence, it is possible to reason about each such equivalence, just by selecting the appropriate ϕ. Furthermore, at least when considering late ground equivalence, we gain in efficiency. If it has to be proven that $x(y).P$ is ground bisimilar to $x(y).Q$, within our framework it just suffices to derive $\phi \rhd P = Q$, for some ϕ not containing y and not stronger than the constraint given by our characterization of $\dot{\sim}$ in terms of $\simeq^{\phi}$. Within the framework of [PS93], it is instead needed to apply the input-prefix rule:

$$IP: \frac{\forall z \in fn(P, Q, y).\ P\{z/y\} = Q\{z/y\}}{x(y).P = x(y).Q}$$

whose premise *always* requires as many sub-proofs as the cardinality of $fn(P, Q, y)$. This example shows that making reasoning assumptions explicit can often avoid a number of useless checks. An accurate comparison between the two approaches w.r.t. efficient deduction strategies would be interesting.

Finally, our work is somewhat related to [Dam93] and to [FMQ94], where different kinds of symbolic transitional semantics for the π-calculus have been presented. In [Dam93], a symbolic semantics is used as a basis for developing a model checker; first-order (rather than boolean) formulae are utilized; in the operational rules for the restriction operator, the "hiding" of a name y in a formula is modeled using an existential quantifier $\exists y$. The aim of [FMQ94] is to define a general framework, within which the different kinds of instantiation strategies (such as early, late, open) can be described just by instantiating certain parameters. The problem of efficiently representing the considered equivalences is not tackled.

References

[BD92] M. Boreale and R. De Nicola. Testing equivalence for mobile processes. Technical Report SI 92 RR 04, Dipartimento di Scienze dell'Informazione Università "La Sapienza", Roma, 1992. Extended abstract appeared in: R. Cleaveland (ed.), *Proceedings of CONCUR '92, LNCS 630* , Springer-Verlag. Full version to appear in *Information and Computation.*

[BD94] M. Boreale and R. De Nicola. A symbolic semantics for the π-calculus. Technical Report SI 94 RR 04, Dipartimento di Scienze dell'Informazione Università "La Sapienza", Roma, 1994.

[Dam93] M. Dam. Model checking mobile processes. In E. Best, editor, *Proceedings of CONCUR '93, LNCS 715.* Springer-Verlag, Berlin, 1993.

[FMQ94] G. Ferrari, U. Montanari, and P. Quaglia. The π-calculus with explicit substitutions. Technical report, Università di Pisa, 1994. Accepted to *MFCS'94*.

[Hen91] M. Hennessy. A model for the π-calculus. Technical report, University of Sussex, 1991.

[HL92] M. Hennessy and H. Lin. Symbolic bisimulations. Technical report, University of Sussex, 1992.

[HL93] M. Hennessy and H. Lin. Proof systems for message-passing process algebras. In E. Best, editor, *Proceedings of CONCUR '93, LNCS 715.* Springer-Verlag, Berlin, 1993.

[Mil89] R. Milner. *Communication and Concurrency.* Prentice-Hall, 1989.

[MPW92] R. Milner, J. Parrow, and D. Walker. A calculus of mobile processes, part 1 and 2. *Information and Computation*, 100, 1992.

[PS93] J. Parrow and D. Sangiorgi. Algebraic theories for name-passing calculi. Technical report, University of Edinburgh, 1993. To appear in *Information and Computation.*

[San93] D. Sangiorgi. A theory of bisimulation for the π-calculus. In E. Best, editor, *Proceedings of CONCUR '93, LNCS 715.* Springer-Verlag, Berlin, 1993.

[San94] D. Sangiorgi. On the bisimulation proof method. Technical report, University of Edinburgh, 1994. In preparation.

On Bisimulation in the π-calculus

David Walker

Department of Computer Science
University of Warwick
Coventry CV4 7AL, U.K.

Abstract

Results concerning bisimulation equivalences in the (polyadic) π-calculus are presented. It is shown that on the restriction-free fragment of the calculus, open bisimilarity coincides with dynamic barbed bisimilarity in all (restriction-free) π-contexts, and also with barbed bisimilarity in the class of contexts obtained by adding a new operator. It is further shown that the first characterization does not extend to the full π-calculus, but that by introducing a distinction-indexed family of new operators, an analogue of the second result can be obtained for indexed open bisimilarity.

1 Introduction

The main purpose of this paper is to present some results concerning bisimulation equivalences in the π-calculus [6, 5]. We begin by setting the results in context.

Labelled transition systems provide natural models for process languages. Of particular importance are systems whose points are terms of a language and whose transition relations are defined by rules systematized by term structure. On such systems equivalence relations may be defined to underpin algebraic theories of agent behaviour. Among the most well-developed theories are those founded on *bisimulation* equivalences [3]. On a system with points $P, Q, \ldots$ and transition relations $\{\xrightarrow{\alpha} \mid \alpha \in L\}$, *bisimilarity* is the largest symmetric relation $\sim$ such that whenever $P \sim Q$, $\alpha \in L$ and $P \xrightarrow{\alpha} P'$, then $Q \xrightarrow{\alpha} Q'$ with $P' \sim Q'$.

The π-calculus is a process calculus in which one may naturally express systems which have evolving structure. Its basic entities are *names*. Agents interact by using names; and by mentioning names in interactions, they may pass to one another the ability to interact with other agents. Two families of transition rules have been studied [6, 7]. In the *late* system, instantiation of names occurs when an interaction is inferred; in the *early* system, when an input is inferred. The standard definition above applied to the early system gives rise to *early bisimilarity*. Using the late system, both early bisimilarity and the slightly stronger *late bisimilarity* arise naturally, though in each case the standard definition must be modified to take account of name instantiation after input transitions. Much standard process calculus theory extends to these equivalences. An important point, however, is that the equivalences are not preserved by name instantiation and thus not by the input prefix operators of the calculus. *Late congruence* and *early congruence* are defined by requiring the corresponding bisimilarity under all name instantiations. These equivalences, and related families indexed by *distinctions* (relations which record that certain names may not be identified), underpin appropriate generalizations of the standard theory.

An alternative presentation of π-calculus dynamics was introduced in [4, 5]. A *structural congruence* on terms is used to support a direct definition of *reduction* (interaction).

This, in conjunction with *observability relations*, then underlies *barbed bisimilarity* [8] and a family of *barbed congruences* each determined by a set of contexts in which agents' behaviour may be observed under reduction. The definition of barbed bisimilarity is such that it applies directly to a wide variety of calculi, and in particular to calculi of higher-order agents in which agents themselves may be passed in communications. It is the basis for the study in [10] of encodings of higher-order agents in the π-calculus and of λ-calculus in π-calculus. Further, barbed bisimilarity is consonant with standard theory. In particular, for CCS agents barbed bisimilarity in all CCS-contexts coincides with bisimilarity [8], and for π-calculus agents, barbed bisimilarity in all π-contexts coincides with early congruence [10].

Another bisimulation equivalence on π-calculus agents, *open bisimilarity*, was introduced in [11]. It differs from the late and early bisimilarities by allowing name instantiation at any point, not only on input transitions. Consequently, on the restriction-free fragment of the π-calculus it is a congruence relation and is strictly stronger than late congruence. Furthermore, it has a simple axiomatization and a useful algorithmic characterization [11]. To give a faithful treatment of the restriction operator, the appropriate definition on the full calculus involves a distinction-indexed family of relations.

The results of [11] provide evidence of the technical importance of open bisimilarity. Here we study the relation further and in particular seek alternative characterizations of it in the framework on barbed bisimulation. We consider first the restriction-free fragment of the calculus. We pursue two directions. First, recalling that early congruence coincides with barbed bisimilarity in all restriction-free π-contexts, we investigate whether the stronger open bisimilarity can be characterized as the barbed congruence determined by some natural enrichment of the set of contexts. We show that by adding a new operator, which allows a tuple of names representing a substitution to be received using a specified name and applied to its agent operand, this result is achieved. Secondly, we show that modifying the definition of barbed bisimilarity by incorporating the principal idea of *dynamic bisimilarity* [9] gives another characterization of open bisimilarity as *dynamic barbed congruence* with respect to restriction-free π-contexts (and also with respect to contexts which may contain in addition the new operator). Turning to the full calculus, where open bisimilarity is defined as a distinction-indexed family of relations, we first exhibit agents which are not open D-bisimilar for any distinction D but which are dynamic barbed bisimilar in all π-contexts. Thus a coincidence of the second kind mentioned above does not hold in the presence of restriction. However, we show that by suitably indexing the new operator mentioned above, the analogue of the first characterization result above does hold for the full calculus.

All of the results hold for both the strong and the weak versions of the equivalences. We consider here only the weak versions as the proofs are invariably more difficult. Technical preliminaries are collected in section 2. The restriction-free fragment is considered in section 3 and the full calculus in section 4. The final section contains some concluding remarks.

Acknowledgment I am grateful to Davide Sangiorgi for helpful comments and suggestions relating to this work.

2 Preliminaries

In this section we recall briefly some material on the (polyadic) π-calculus [6, 5], barbed bisimilarity [8, 10] and open bisimilarity [11]. For undefined terms and explanation we refer to these papers.

We assume an infinite set N of *names* x, y, z, a partition S of N into a set of infinite *(subject) sorts* and a *sorting* $\Sigma : \mathsf{S} \longrightarrow \mathsf{S}^*$. For $S \in \mathsf{S}$, $\Sigma(S)$ is the *object sort* associated with S. The *agents* of the version of the π-calculus studied here are the expressions given as follows which *respect* the sorting Σ:

$$P \ ::= \ \Sigma_{i \in I} M_i \, \pi_i . P_i \ \mid \ P \mid Q \ \mid \ (\nu\, x)P \ \mid \ A(\tilde{y})$$

Here the indexing set I in the guarded summation is finite and π ranges over the *prefixes* $x(\tilde{y})$ and $\overline{x}\tilde{y}$ (in which $\tilde{y}$ is a tuple of names and x is the *subject*) and τ. Also, M ranges over *match sequences* of the form $[x_1 = y_1] \cdots [x_n = y_n]$ where $n \geq 0$. This form of guarded summation plays a central rôle in completeness proofs in [11]. We write $\mathbf{0}$ for an empty sum and abbreviate $M\,\pi.\mathbf{0}$ to $M\,\pi$. In the prefix $x(\tilde{y})$ the occurrences of the names $\tilde{y}$ are binding; the occurrence of x in $(\nu\, x)$ is also binding. We write $\mathrm{fn}(P)$ for the set of *free names* of P, and $\mathrm{n}(P)$ for the set of all names occurring in P. Each *agent constant* A has a defining equation $A(\tilde{x}) \stackrel{\mathrm{def}}{=} P$ where $\mathrm{fn}(P) \subseteq \tilde{x}$. We assume that defining equations are such that $\mathrm{fn}(P)$ is finite for each P we consider. In building certain contexts to examine the behaviour of these agents, we shall consider infinite families $\{A_i(\tilde{x}_i) \stackrel{\mathrm{def}}{=} P_i\}_i$ of mutually-recursive agent constant definitions. In all such cases $\mathrm{fn}(P_i)$ will be coinfinite in each sort. (See the Conclusion for a discussion of this point.) We regard as identical agents which differ only in their bound names. We write Π for the set of all π-calculus agents, and $\Pi^{\widehat{\nu}}$ for those agents which contain no occurrence of a restriction operator $(\nu\, x)$. A *substitution* is a sort-respecting mapping σ, ρ from N to N. We write $P\sigma$ for the agent obtained from P by applying the substitution σ. We write $\{\tilde{y}/\tilde{x}\}$ for the substitution which maps each component of $\tilde{x}$ to the corresponding component of $\tilde{y}$ and is otherwise the identity. A *distinction* is a finite, symmetric and irreflexive sort-respecting relation on names. We often abbreviate an expression describing a distinction by omitting from it pairs whose presence may be inferred by symmetry. A substitution σ *respects* a distinction D if $(x, y) \in D$ implies $x\sigma \neq y\sigma$.

The behaviour of agents may be given either by means of labelled transition relations or via a reduction relation. Two labelled transition systems, *late* [6] and *early* [7], have been studied. Here we employ the early system in the polyadic setting. In it there are three kinds of action: input actions of the form $x\tilde{y}$; output actions of the form $\overline{x}(\nu\, \tilde{z})\tilde{y}$, where the set $\tilde{z}$ of bound names of the action (which is omitted when it is empty) satisfies $\tilde{z} \subseteq \tilde{y}$; and the action τ representing communication between agents. If α is not an output action then the set $\mathrm{bn}(\alpha)$ of bound names of α is empty. The transition rules are as follows where $\mathrm{n}(\alpha)$ is the set of names occurring in the action α. The third and fourth have symmetric forms.

1. $\ldots + M x(\tilde{y}).P + \ldots \stackrel{x\tilde{z}}{\longrightarrow} P\{\tilde{z}/\tilde{y}\}$ provided $M = [x_1 = x_1] \cdots [x_n = x_n]$.
2. $\ldots + M\,\pi.P + \ldots \stackrel{\pi}{\longrightarrow} P$ if π is $\overline{x}\tilde{y}$ or τ and $M = [x_1 = x_1] \cdots [x_n = x_n]$.
3. If $P \stackrel{\alpha}{\longrightarrow} P'$ then $P \mid Q \stackrel{\alpha}{\longrightarrow} P' \mid Q$ provided $\mathrm{bn}(\alpha) \cap \mathrm{fn}(Q) = \emptyset$.
4. If $P \stackrel{\overline{x}(\nu \tilde{z})\tilde{y}}{\longrightarrow} P'$ and $Q \stackrel{x\tilde{y}}{\longrightarrow} Q'$ then $P \mid Q \stackrel{\tau}{\longrightarrow} (\nu\, \tilde{z})(P' \mid Q')$ provided $\tilde{z} \cap \mathrm{fn}(Q) = \emptyset$.
5. If $P \stackrel{\alpha}{\longrightarrow} P'$ and $x \notin \mathrm{n}(\alpha)$ then $(\nu\, x)P \stackrel{\alpha}{\longrightarrow} (\nu\, x)P'$.
6. If $P \stackrel{\overline{w}(\nu \tilde{z})\tilde{y}}{\longrightarrow} P'$ and $x \in \tilde{y} - (\tilde{z} \cup \{w\})$ then $(\nu\, x)P \stackrel{\overline{w}(\nu \tilde{z} x)\tilde{y}}{\longrightarrow} P'$.

7. If $P\{\tilde{y}/\tilde{x}\} \xrightarrow{\alpha} P'$ and $A(\tilde{x}) \stackrel{\text{def}}{=} P$ then $A(\tilde{y}) \xrightarrow{\alpha} P'$.

We write $\Longrightarrow$ for the reflexive and transitive closure of $\xrightarrow{\tau}$, $\stackrel{\alpha}{\Longrightarrow}$ for the composition $\Longrightarrow\xrightarrow{\alpha}\Longrightarrow$, and $\stackrel{\widehat{\alpha}}{\Longrightarrow}$ for $\Longrightarrow$ if $\alpha = \tau$ and $\stackrel{\alpha}{\Longrightarrow}$ otherwise.

An alternative formulation of π-calculus dynamics is given by the reduction relation $\longrightarrow$ and the observability relation $\downarrow$ of [4, 5]. Regarding *structurally-congruent* [4] agents as identical, the *reduction relation* is defined by the following rules:

1. $(\overline{x}\tilde{z}.\, P + \ldots) \mid (x(\tilde{y}).\, Q + \ldots) \longrightarrow P \mid Q\{\tilde{z}/\tilde{y}\}$.
2. If $P \longrightarrow P'$ then $P \mid Q \longrightarrow P' \mid Q$.
3. If $P \longrightarrow P'$ then $(\nu\, x)P \longrightarrow (\nu\, x)P'$.

P is *observable at* x, $P \downarrow_x$, if x occurs free and unguarded (i.e. not beneath a prefix) in subject position in P. Also, P is *weakly observable at* x, $P \Downarrow_x$, if for some P', $P \Longrightarrow P'$ and $P' \downarrow_x$. The relation $\xrightarrow{\tau}$ of the labelled transition system agrees [4] up to structural congruence with the reduction relation $\longrightarrow$.

Several bisimulation equivalences on π-calculus agents have been considered. We give the definitions of those to be studied further here. As explained in the Introduction we consider only the weak versions of the equivalences.

Definition 1 *Early bisimilarity* is the largest symmetric relation $\dot{\approx}_e$ such that whenever $P \dot{\approx}_e Q$ and $P \xrightarrow{\alpha} P'$ then for some Q', $Q \stackrel{\widehat{\alpha}}{\Longrightarrow} Q'$ and $P' \dot{\approx}_e Q'$.

Agents P and Q are *early congruent*, $P \approx_e Q$, if $P\sigma \dot{\approx}_e Q\sigma$ for each substitution σ.

Extending to the weak polyadic setting techniques used in the strong monadic case [6, 7], and recalling that we work here with guarded summation, we have that early bisimilarity is preserved by all π-calculus operators except input prefix (the latter as it is not preserved by instantiation of names). Further, early congruence is the largest relation included in it which is preserved by all π-calculus operators.

Definition 2 *Barbed bisimilarity* is the largest symmetric relation $\dot{\approx}_b$ such that whenever $P \dot{\approx}_b Q$ then

1. if $P \downarrow_x$ then $Q \Downarrow_x$, and
2. if $P \longrightarrow P'$ then for some Q', $Q \Longrightarrow Q'$ and $P' \dot{\approx}_b Q'$.

If $\mathbf{C}$ is a set of contexts then P and Q are *barbed* $\mathbf{C}$*-congruent*, $P \approx_b^{\mathbf{C}} Q$, if $\mathcal{C}[P] \dot{\approx}_b \mathcal{C}[Q]$ for each context $\mathcal{C}[\cdot]$ in $\mathbf{C}$.

Barbed bisimilarity and congruence were introduced in [8]. Early congruence and barbed $\mathbf{\Pi}$-congruence coincide on Π where $\mathbf{\Pi}$ is the set of contexts built from the π-calculus operators [8, 10].

Definition 3 On $\Pi^{\widehat{\nu}}$, *open bisimilarity* is the largest symmetric relation $\approx$ such that whenever $P\sigma \xrightarrow{\alpha} P'$ then for some Q', $Q\sigma \stackrel{\widehat{\alpha}}{\Longrightarrow} Q'$ and $P' \approx Q'$.

Open bisimilarity was introduced, using the late transition system in the setting of the monadic π-calculus, in [11]. The relation is a congruence on $\Pi^{\widehat{\nu}}$ and is strictly stronger than early congruence. In the presence of the restriction operator $(\nu\, x)$, the definition of open bisimilarity must be altered to take into account that scope extrusion may limit allowable name instantiations. The definition is given in section 4.

3 The Restriction-free Fragment

We consider first the restriction-free fragment $\Pi^{\widehat{\nu}}$. We shall assume, purely for convenience in some constructions, that $\Sigma(S) = ()$ for some subject sort S. No result depends on this assumption.

We first introduce a new family of operators. Let S_* be a new sort and extend the sorting by allowing a name of sort S_* to carry any tuple $x_1y_1 \ldots x_ny_n$ such that x_i and y_i have the same sort in S for each i. Thus the extended sorting, no longer a function, relates S_* and $(S_1S_1 \ldots S_nS_n)$ for any $n \geq 0$ and $S_1, \ldots, S_n \in$ S. Then for $s : S_*$ define a unary operator $s \lhd \cdot$ by the following rules where $s\,\widetilde{xy}$ abbreviates the input action $s\,x_1y_1 \ldots x_ny_n$:

1. $s \lhd P \xrightarrow{s\,\widetilde{xy}} s \lhd P\{\widetilde{y}/\widetilde{x}\}$ provided the x_i are distinct, and

2. if $P \xrightarrow{\alpha} P'$ then $s \lhd P \xrightarrow{\alpha} s \lhd P'$.

Thus $s \lhd P$ may either receive at s a tuple of names representing a substitution which is applied to P, or evolve as P. In either case the principal operator remains unchanged. We have $\mathrm{fn}(s \lhd P) = \mathrm{fn}(P) \cup \{s\}$ and for a substitution ρ, $(s \lhd P)\rho = s\rho \lhd P\rho$. Note that we forbid S_* from appearing in objects sorts. It may be useful in some circumstances to relax this restriction. Further, since the extended sorting does not associate a unique object sort with S_*, we do not use names of sort S_* in positive subject position thereby avoiding the kind of 'object mismatch' occurring in the agent expression $s(z_1, z_2).\,P \mid \overline{s}\,x_1y_1x_2y_2.\,Q$.

Let $\Pi^{\widehat{\nu}+}$ be the set of agents built from the π-calculus operators except restriction together with the $s \lhd \cdot$ operators. Open bisimilarity, $\approx$, on $\Pi^{\widehat{\nu}+}$ is defined as on $\Pi^{\widehat{\nu}}$. The following notation will be useful.

Definition 4 We define:

1. $\mathbf{\Pi}$ is the set of contexts built from the operators of the π-calculus.
2. $\mathbf{\Pi}^{\widehat{\nu}}$ is the set of contexts in $\mathbf{\Pi}$ in which no restriction operator $(\nu\, x)$ occurs.
3. $\mathbf{\Pi}^{\widehat{\nu}+}$ is the set of contexts built from the $s \lhd \cdot$ operators together with the operators of the π-calculus except restriction.

We first show that $\approx$ is a congruence on $\Pi^{\widehat{\nu}+}$.

Lemma 1 If $P \approx Q$ then $\mathcal{C}[P] \approx \mathcal{C}[Q]$ for $\mathcal{C}[\cdot] \in \mathbf{\Pi}^{\widehat{\nu}+}$.

Proof: The proof is by induction on $\mathcal{C}[\cdot]$ and mainly involves extending to the weak early polyadic setting techniques used to establish congruence results in the strong late monadic case [6]. We show only how to treat the new operator. To establish that $P \approx Q$ implies $s \lhd P \approx s \lhd Q$ it suffices to show that $\mathcal{S} = \{\langle s \lhd P, s \lhd Q\rangle \mid P \approx Q,\, s \in \mathsf{N}\}$ is an open bisimulation. Suppose $P \approx Q$, ρ is a substitution and $(s \lhd P)\rho = s\rho \lhd P\rho \xrightarrow{\alpha} R$. Then either $\alpha = s\rho\,\widetilde{xy}$ and $R = s\rho \lhd P\rho\sigma$ where $\sigma = \{\widetilde{y}/\widetilde{x}\}$, or $R = s\rho \lhd P'$ where $P\rho \xrightarrow{\alpha} P'$. In the first case $(s \lhd Q)\rho \xrightarrow{\alpha} R' = s\rho \lhd Q\rho\sigma$ and since $\approx$ is preserved by substitution so $P\rho\sigma \approx Q\rho\sigma$, $R\mathcal{S}R'$. In the second case $Q\rho \stackrel{\widehat{\alpha}}{\Longrightarrow} Q'$ with $P' \approx Q'$ and so $(s \lhd Q)\rho \stackrel{\widehat{\alpha}}{\Longrightarrow} R' = s\rho \lhd Q'$ and $R\mathcal{S}R'$. □

An important lemma in π-calculus relates action and substitution: if $P \xrightarrow{\alpha} P'$ then $P\rho \xrightarrow{\alpha\rho} P'\rho$; and if $P\rho \xrightarrow{\beta} P''$ and ρ is one-one, then for some α and P' with $\alpha\rho = \beta$ and

$P'\rho = P''$, $P \xrightarrow{\alpha} P'$. (We assume that bound names are fresh.) With the addition of the $s \lhd \cdot$ operators the second statement remains true but the first does not. To see the latter suppose $P = s \lhd \overline{x}z$, $\alpha = s\,xy$ and $\rho = \{x/z\}$. Then $P \xrightarrow{\alpha} P' = s \lhd \overline{y}z$. But $P\rho = s \lhd \overline{x}x$, $\alpha\rho = \alpha$ and $P\rho \xrightarrow{\alpha} P'' = s \lhd \overline{y}y \neq P'\rho$. However, the result holds if ρ is one-one. Indeed we have:

Lemma 2

1. Suppose $P \xrightarrow{\alpha} P'$ and that if $\alpha = s\,\widetilde{x}\widetilde{y}$ with $s : S_*$ then ρ is one-one on $\widetilde{x}$ and there is no $z \in \mathrm{fn}(P) - \widetilde{x}$ such that $z\rho \in \widetilde{x\rho}$. Then $P\rho \xrightarrow{\alpha\rho} P'\rho$.
2. Suppose $P\rho \xrightarrow{\beta} P''$ and ρ is one-one. Then for some α and P' with $\alpha\rho = \beta$ and $P'\rho = P''$, $P \xrightarrow{\alpha} P'$.

Proof: 1. By induction on inference. We consider only the case $P = s \lhd R$. There are two subcases.
(a) Suppose $\alpha = s\,\widetilde{x}\widetilde{y}$ and $P' = s \lhd R\sigma$ where $\sigma = \{\widetilde{y}/\widetilde{x}\}$. Noting that ρ is one-one on $\widetilde{x}$, let $\sigma' = \{\widetilde{y\rho}/\widetilde{x\rho}\}$. We claim that for all $z \in \mathrm{fn}(R)$, $z\sigma\rho = z\rho\sigma'$ and hence that $R\sigma\rho = R\rho\sigma'$. For if $z \in \widetilde{x}$, say $z = x_i$, then $z\sigma\rho = y_i\rho$ and $z\rho\sigma' = (x_i\rho)\sigma' = y_i\rho$, and if $z \notin \widetilde{x}$ then by the side condition $z\rho \notin \widetilde{x\rho}$ and so $z\sigma\rho = z\rho = z\rho\sigma'$. Now $P\rho = s\rho \lhd R\rho \xrightarrow{\alpha\rho} s\rho \lhd R\rho\sigma'$ and by the above, $R\rho\sigma' = R\sigma\rho$. Hence $s\rho \lhd R\rho\sigma' = P'\rho$.
(b) Suppose $P' = s \lhd R'$ where $R \xrightarrow{\alpha} R'$. By induction hypothesis $R\rho \xrightarrow{\alpha\rho} R'\rho$ and so $P\rho \xrightarrow{\alpha\rho} s\rho \lhd R'\rho = P'\rho$.
2. By induction on inference. Again we consider only the case $P = s \lhd R$ and again there are two subcases.
(a) Suppose $\beta = s\rho\,\widetilde{x}\widetilde{y}$ and $P'' = s\rho \lhd R\rho\sigma$ where $\sigma = \{\widetilde{y}/\widetilde{x}\}$. Since ρ is one-one there are unique $\widetilde{z}, \widetilde{w}$ such that $\widetilde{z\rho} = \widetilde{x}$ and $\widetilde{w\rho} = \widetilde{y}$. Let $\alpha = s\,\widetilde{z}\widetilde{w}$ so that $\alpha\rho = \beta$. Then $P \xrightarrow{\alpha} P' = s \lhd R\sigma'$ where $\sigma' = \{\widetilde{w}/\widetilde{z}\}$. Since ρ is one-one the condition that there is no $v \in \mathrm{fn}(P) - \widetilde{z}$ such that $v\rho \in \widetilde{x}$ holds. Hence by the argument in part 1, $R\sigma'\rho = R\rho\sigma$ and so $P'\rho = P''$.
(b) Suppose $P'' = s\rho \lhd R''$ where $R\rho \xrightarrow{\beta} R''$. By induction hypothesis $R \xrightarrow{\alpha} R'$ with $\alpha\rho = \beta$ and $R'\rho = R''$. So $P \xrightarrow{\alpha} P' = s \lhd R'$ and $P'\rho = P''$. □

We now formulate a useful sufficient condition for a relation to be an open bisimulation on $\widehat{\Pi^\nu}$. Its utility (see Theorem 1) lies in the fact that it allows consideration to be restricted to a finite number of substitutions and a finite number of actions.

Lemma 3 Suppose that $\mathcal{S}$ is closed under one-one substitutions and that whenever $P\mathcal{S}Q$ there are a finite U with $\mathrm{fn}(P,Q) \subseteq U$ and a finite V containing at least twice as many names of each sort as U with $V \cap U = \emptyset$ such that for each partial $\sigma : U \rightharpoonup U \cup V$,

1. if $P\sigma \xrightarrow{\alpha} P'$ with $\alpha = \overline{x}\widetilde{y}$ or τ, then $Q\sigma \xRightarrow{\widehat{\alpha}} Q'$ with $P'\mathcal{S}Q'$, and
2. if $P\sigma \xrightarrow{x\widetilde{y}} P'$ with $\widetilde{y} \subseteq U \cup V$, then $Q\sigma \xRightarrow{x\widetilde{y}} Q'$ with $P'\mathcal{S}Q'$.

Then $\mathcal{S}$ is an open bisimulation on $\widehat{\Pi^\nu}$.

Proof: Suppose $P\mathcal{S}Q$ and let U and V be as in the statement. Let θ be a substitution and assume without loss of generality, since $\mathrm{fn}(P,Q) \subseteq U$, that $z\theta = z$ if $z \notin U$. Then by the choice of V we can express θ as $\sigma\rho$ where $\sigma : U \rightharpoonup U \cup V$ and ρ is one-one with $z\rho = z$ if $z \notin U \cup V$.

(i) Suppose $P\theta \xrightarrow{\alpha} P'$ where $\alpha = \overline{x}\tilde{y}$ or τ. Then since $P\theta = P\sigma\rho$ and ρ is one-one, by the second part of the previous lemma $P\sigma \xrightarrow{\beta} P''$ with $\beta\rho = \alpha$ and $P''\rho = P'$. Since $P\mathcal{S}Q$ and $\sigma : U \rightharpoonup U \cup V$, $Q\sigma \stackrel{\widehat{\beta}}{\Longrightarrow} Q''$ with $P''\mathcal{S}Q''$. Then since ρ is one-one, by the first part of the previous lemma $Q\theta \stackrel{\widehat{\alpha}}{\Longrightarrow} Q' = Q''\rho$. Hence since $\mathcal{S}$ is closed under one-one substitutions, $P'\mathcal{S}Q'$.

(ii) Suppose $P\theta \xrightarrow{x\tilde{y}} P'$. Since $P\theta = P\sigma\rho$ and ρ is one-one, by the second part of the previous lemma $P\sigma \xrightarrow{x'\tilde{z}} P''$ where $x'\rho = x$, $\tilde{z}\rho = \tilde{y}$ and $P''\rho = P'$. By choice of V we can associate with each $y \in \tilde{y}$ such that $y \notin U \cup V \cup \rho''(U \cup V)$ a distinct $y' \in V$ of the same sort with $y' \notin \sigma''(U) \cup \tilde{z}$. Let $\tilde{w}$ be $\tilde{z}$ but with each such y replaced by y'. Then $P\sigma \xrightarrow{x'\tilde{w}} P'''$ where $P'''\{\tilde{z}/\tilde{w}\} = P''$. Then since $\sigma : U \rightharpoonup U \cup V$ and $\tilde{w} \subseteq U \cup V$, by the hypothesis of the lemma $Q\sigma \stackrel{x'\tilde{w}}{\Longrightarrow} Q'''$ with $P'''\mathcal{S}Q'''$. So $Q\sigma \stackrel{x'\tilde{z}}{\Longrightarrow} Q''$ where $Q'' = Q'''\{\tilde{z}/\tilde{w}\}$. Then by the first part of the previous lemma $Q\theta \stackrel{x\tilde{y}}{\Longrightarrow} Q'$ where $Q' = Q''\rho$. So since $\mathcal{S}$ is closed under one-one substitutions and $\{\tilde{z}/\tilde{w}\}$ and ρ are one-one, $P'\mathcal{S}Q'$. □

Sangiorgi showed [10] that barbed $\mathbf{\Pi}$-congruence $\approx_b^{\mathbf{\Pi}}$ coincides with early congruence $\approx_e$ on Π. By Lemma 1, open bisimilarity is preserved by all contexts in $\mathbf{\Pi}^{\widehat{\nu}+}$. Moreover it is stronger than $\approx_e$ on $\Pi^{\widehat{\nu}}$. The following theorem states that open bisimilarity coincides with barbed $\mathbf{\Pi}^{\widehat{\nu}+}$-congruence on $\Pi^{\widehat{\nu}}$.

Theorem 1 Let $P, Q \in \Pi^{\widehat{\nu}}$. Then $P \approx Q$ iff $P \approx_b^{\mathbf{\Pi}^{\widehat{\nu}+}} Q$.

Proof: (a) We first show that $P \approx Q$ implies $P \approx_b^{\mathbf{\Pi}^{\widehat{\nu}+}} Q$. By Lemma 1, $P \approx Q$ implies $\mathcal{C}[P] \approx \mathcal{C}[Q]$ and hence $\mathcal{C}[P] \stackrel{\cdot}{\approx}_b \mathcal{C}[Q]$ for any context $\mathcal{C}[\cdot]$ in $\mathbf{\Pi}^{\widehat{\nu}+}$, and hence $P \approx_b^{\mathbf{\Pi}^{\widehat{\nu}+}} Q$.

(b) The proof of the converse involves modification and extension of ideas used by Sangiorgi [10] to show that on Π, barbed $\mathbf{\Pi}$-congruence is included in early congruence.

Given a finite set of names U choose a set F disjoint from U, infinite and coinfinite in each sort. Then let $V \subseteq F$ be finite and contain at least twice as many names of each sort as U. From the names not in F choose distinct $s : S_*$ and a_i, $b_i[\sigma]$, $c_i[z, \tilde{w}]$, $d_i[z]$ and $e_i[\tilde{w}]$ of a sort S with $\Sigma(S) = ()$ for each $i < \omega$, $z \in U \cup F$, finite $\tilde{w} \subseteq U \cup F$ and finite $\sigma : U \cup F \rightharpoonup U \cup F$. Now define agents $W_i^s(U, F)$ as follows:

$$\begin{aligned} W_i^s(U,F) &\stackrel{\text{def}}{=} a_i + \Sigma_{(1)}\overline{s}\,\overline{x}\tilde{y}.\overline{W}_i^s(U,F,\sigma) \\ \overline{W}_i^s(U,F,\sigma) &\stackrel{\text{def}}{=} b_i[\sigma] \\ &\quad + \Sigma_{(2)}\overline{z}\tilde{w}.(c_i[z,\tilde{w}] + \tau.W_{i+1}^s(U',F')) \\ &\quad + \Sigma_{(3)}z(\tilde{v}).(d_i[z] + \Sigma_{(4)}[\tilde{v} = \tilde{w}]e_i[\tilde{w}] + \tau.W_{i+1}^s(U',F')) \\ &\quad + \tau.W_{i+1}^s(U',F') \end{aligned}$$

where $U' = U \cup V$, $F' = F - V$, $\sigma = \{\tilde{y}/\tilde{x}\}$ and in the summations: (1) $\tilde{x} \subseteq U$ with the x_i distinct and $\tilde{y} \subseteq U \cup V$, (2) $z \in U \cup \tilde{y}$ and $\tilde{w} \subseteq U \cup V$, (3) $z \in U \cup \tilde{y}$ and $\tilde{v}$ are chosen from $V - \tilde{y}$, and (4) $\tilde{w} \subseteq U \cup \tilde{y}$.

Then define

$$\mathcal{C}_{i,s}^{U,F}[\cdot] \stackrel{\text{def}}{=} (s \lhd \cdot) \mid W_i^s(U,F)$$

Now set PSQ if for some finite U with $\mathrm{fn}(P,Q) \subseteq U$ and some F, s and i as above, $\mathcal{C}^{U,F}_{i,s}[P] \dot{\approx}_b \mathcal{C}^{U,F}_{i,s}[Q]$. We claim that $\mathcal{S}$ is an open bisimulation on $\Pi^{\widehat{\nu}}$. We check the sufficient condition given in Lemma 3. Suppose PSQ as $\mathcal{C}^{U,F}_{i,s}[P] \dot{\approx}_b \mathcal{C}^{U,F}_{i,s}[Q]$.

(a) First note that $\mathcal{S}$ is closed under one-one substitutions since if ρ is one-one then as $\dot{\approx}_b$ is closed under one-one substitutions, $\mathcal{C}^{U,F}_{i,s}[P]\rho \dot{\approx}_b \mathcal{C}^{U,F}_{i,s}[Q]\rho$, i.e. $\mathcal{C}^{U\rho,F\rho}_{i,s\rho}[P\rho] \dot{\approx}_b \mathcal{C}^{U\rho,F\rho}_{i,s\rho}[Q\rho]$. So since $\mathrm{fn}(P\rho, Q\rho) \subseteq U\rho$, $U\rho \cap F\rho = \emptyset$ and $s\rho \notin U\rho \cup F\rho$, $P\rho\, \mathcal{S}\, Q\rho$.

Now fix $\sigma : U \rightharpoonup U \cup V$ and suppose $P\sigma \xrightarrow{\alpha} P'$.

(b) Suppose $\alpha = \overline{z}\widetilde{w}$. Then

$$\begin{aligned} P_0 = \mathcal{C}^{U,F}_{i,s}[P] &\longrightarrow P_1 = (s \lhd P\sigma) \mid \overline{W}^s_i(U,F,\sigma) \\ &\longrightarrow P_2 = (s \lhd P') \mid (d_i[z] + e_i[\widetilde{w}] + \tau.\, W^s_{i+1}(U',F')) \\ &\longrightarrow P_3 = \mathcal{C}^{U',F'}_{i+1,s}[P']. \end{aligned}$$

So $Q_0 = \mathcal{C}^{U,F}_{i,s}[Q] \Longrightarrow Q_1 \Longrightarrow Q_2 \Longrightarrow Q_3$ with $P_j \dot{\approx}_b Q_j$ for each j. Since $Q_0 \downarrow_{a_i}$ but $P_1 \Uparrow_{a_i}$, i.e. $P_1 \Longrightarrow R$ implies not $R \downarrow_{a_i}$, the W-component must act in $Q_0 \Longrightarrow Q_1$. Moreover since $P_1 \downarrow_{b_i[\sigma]}$, the W-component must act exactly once performing the action $\overline{s}\,\widetilde{x}\widetilde{y}$ where $\sigma = \{\widetilde{y}/\widetilde{x}\}$. So $Q_1 = (s \lhd Q') \mid \overline{W}^s_i(U,F,\sigma)$ where for some Q^*, $Q \Longrightarrow Q^*$ and $Q^*\sigma \Longrightarrow Q'$ and so $Q\sigma \Longrightarrow Q'$. Further, since $Q_1 \downarrow_{b_i[\sigma]}$ but $P_2 \Uparrow_{b_i[\sigma]}$, the W-component must act in $Q_1 \Longrightarrow Q_2$. Moreover since $P_2 \downarrow_{d_i[z]}$ and $P_2 \downarrow_{e_i[\widetilde{w}]}$ the W-component must act exactly once performing the action $z\widetilde{w}$. So $Q_2 = (s \lhd Q'') \mid (d_i[z] + e_i[\widetilde{w}] + \tau.\, W^s_{i+1}(U',F'))$ where $Q' \xRightarrow{\alpha} Q''$. Finally, since $Q_2 \downarrow_{d_i[z]}$ and $P_3 \Uparrow_{d_i[z]}$, the W-component must act in $Q_2 \Longrightarrow Q_3$. Moreover since $P_3 \downarrow_{a_{i+1}}$ the W-component must act exactly once performing a τ-action and $Q_3 = \mathcal{C}^{U',F'}_{i+1,s}[Q''']$ where $Q'' \Longrightarrow Q'''$. So $Q\sigma \xRightarrow{\alpha} Q'''$ and $P'\mathcal{S}Q'''$ since $P_3 \dot{\approx}_b Q_3$.

(c) Suppose $\alpha = \tau$. Then

$$\begin{aligned} P_0 = \mathcal{C}^{U,F}_{i,s}[P] &\longrightarrow P_1 = (s \lhd P\sigma) \mid \overline{W}^s_i(U,F,\sigma) \\ &\longrightarrow P_2 = (s \lhd P') \mid \overline{W}^s_i(U,F,\sigma) \\ &\longrightarrow P_3 = \mathcal{C}^{U',F'}_{i+1,s}[P'] \end{aligned}$$

By a similar argument to that above, $Q\sigma \Longrightarrow Q'''$ with $P_3 \dot{\approx}_b \mathcal{C}^{U',F'}_{i+1,s}[Q''']$ and so $P'\mathcal{S}Q'''$.

(d) Suppose $\alpha = z\widetilde{w}$ where $\widetilde{w} \subseteq U \cup V$. Then

$$\begin{aligned} P_0 = \mathcal{C}^{U,F}_{i,s}[P] &\longrightarrow P_1 = (s \lhd P\sigma) \mid \overline{W}^s_i(U,F,\sigma) \\ &\longrightarrow P_2 = (s \lhd P') \mid (c_i[z,\widetilde{w}] + \tau.\, W^s_{i+1}(U',F')) \\ &\longrightarrow P_3 = \mathcal{C}^{U',F'}_{i+1,s}[P'] \end{aligned}$$

By a similar argument to that above, $Q\sigma \xRightarrow{\alpha} Q'''$ with $P_3 \dot{\approx}_b \mathcal{C}^{U',F'}_{i+1,s}[Q''']$ and so $P'\mathcal{S}Q'''$. Hence by Lemma 3, $\mathcal{S}$ is an open bisimulation. □

We now give another characterization of open bisimilarity on $\Pi^{\widehat{\nu}}$. The following definition combines the use on reduction and observability in the definition of barbed bisimilarity with the treatment of contexts in the *dynamic congruence* of [9] (which on $\Pi^{\widehat{\nu}}$ also coincides with open bisimilarity [11]).

Definition 5 Let $\mathbf{C}$ be a class of contexts. *Dynamic barbed* $\mathbf{C}$*-congruence* is the largest symmetric relation $\simeq_{\mathbf{C}}$ on $\Pi^{\widehat{\nu}+}$ such that whenever $P \simeq_{\mathbf{C}} Q$ and $\mathcal{C}[\cdot]$ is in $\mathbf{C}$,

1. if $\mathcal{C}[P] \downarrow_x$ then $\mathcal{C}[Q] \Downarrow_x$, and
2. if $\mathcal{C}[P] \longrightarrow P'$ then $\mathcal{C}[Q] \Longrightarrow Q'$ with $P' \simeq_{\mathcal{C}} Q'$.

The following result establishes that on $\Pi^{\widehat{\nu}}$, dynamic barbed $\mathbf{\Pi}^{\widehat{\nu}}$-congruence and dynamic barbed $\mathbf{\Pi}^{\widehat{\nu}+}$-congruence coincide with open bisimilarity.

Theorem 2 Let $P, Q \in \Pi^{\widehat{\nu}}$.

1. If $P \approx Q$ then $P \simeq_{\mathbf{\Pi}^{\widehat{\nu}+}} Q$.
2. If $P \simeq_{\mathbf{\Pi}^{\widehat{\nu}}} Q$ then $P \approx Q$.

Proof: 1. By Lemma 1, $P \approx Q$ implies that for each $\mathbf{\Pi}^{\widehat{\nu}+}$-context $\mathcal{C}[\cdot]$, $\mathcal{C}[P] \approx \mathcal{C}[Q]$ and hence if $\mathcal{C}[P] \downarrow_x$ then $\mathcal{C}[Q] \Downarrow_x$, and if $\mathcal{C}[P] \longrightarrow P'$ then $\mathcal{C}[Q] \Longrightarrow Q'$ with $P' \approx Q'$. Hence $\approx$ is a dynamic barbed $\mathbf{\Pi}^{\widehat{\nu}+}$-bisimulation.

2. We show that $\simeq_{\mathbf{\Pi}^{\widehat{\nu}}}$ is an open bisimulation. Suppose $P \simeq_{\mathbf{\Pi}^{\widehat{\nu}}} Q$ and $P\sigma \xrightarrow{\alpha} P'$ where $\sigma = \{\widetilde{y}/\widetilde{x}\}$ and $\alpha = \overline{z}\widetilde{w}$, $z\widetilde{w}$ or τ. Choose new names $a, b, c, d : S$ with $\Sigma(S) = ()$ and $s : S'$ with $\Sigma(S') = (\widetilde{S})$ where $\widetilde{x} : \widetilde{S}$, and set

$$\mathcal{C}[\cdot] = \begin{cases} (s(\widetilde{x}).\,\cdot) \mid (a + \overline{s}\widetilde{y}.\,(b + z(\widetilde{v}).\,(c + [\widetilde{v} = \widetilde{w}]d + \tau))) & \text{if } \alpha = \overline{z}\widetilde{w} \\ (s(\widetilde{x}).\,\cdot) \mid (a + \overline{s}\widetilde{y}.\,(b + \overline{z}\widetilde{w}.\,(c + \tau))) & \text{if } \alpha = z\widetilde{w} \\ (s(\widetilde{x}).\,\cdot) \mid (a + \overline{s}\widetilde{y}.\,(b + \tau)) & \text{if } \alpha = \tau \end{cases}$$

Suppose $\alpha = \overline{z}\widetilde{w}$. Then

$$\begin{aligned} P_0 = \mathcal{C}[P] \quad &\longrightarrow P_1 = P\sigma \mid (b + z(\widetilde{v}).\,(c + [\widetilde{v} = \widetilde{w}]d + \tau)) \\ &\longrightarrow P_2 = P' \mid (c + [\widetilde{w} = \widetilde{w}]d + \tau) \\ &\longrightarrow P_3 = P' \end{aligned}$$

so since $P \simeq_{\mathbf{\Pi}^{\widehat{\nu}}} Q$, $Q_0 = \mathcal{C}[Q] \Longrightarrow Q_1 \Longrightarrow Q_2 \Longrightarrow Q_3$ with $P_j \simeq_{\mathbf{\Pi}^{\widehat{\nu}}} Q_j$ for each j. Since $Q_0 \downarrow_a$ but $P_1 \Uparrow_a$ and $P_1 \downarrow_b$, $Q_1 = Q' \mid (b + z(\widetilde{v}).\,(c + [\widetilde{v} = \widetilde{w}]d + \tau))$ for some Q' with $Q\sigma \Longrightarrow Q'$. Since $Q_1 \downarrow_b$ but $P_2 \Uparrow_b$ and $P_2 \downarrow_{c,d}$, $Q_2 = Q'' \mid (c + [\widetilde{w} = \widetilde{w}]d + \tau)$ for some Q'' with $Q' \stackrel{\alpha}{\Longrightarrow} Q''$. Since $Q_2 \downarrow_c$ but $P_3 \Uparrow_c$, $Q_3 = Q'''$ where $Q'' \Longrightarrow Q'''$. Hence $P' \simeq_{\mathbf{\Pi}^{\widehat{\nu}}} Q'''$ for some Q''' with $Q\sigma \stackrel{\alpha}{\Longrightarrow} Q'''$.
The cases $\alpha = z\widetilde{w}$ and $\alpha = \tau$ are similar. □

From the two theorems we have:

Corollary 1 On $\Pi^{\widehat{\nu}}$, open bisimilarity, barbed $\mathbf{\Pi}^{\widehat{\nu}+}$-congruence, dynamic barbed $\mathbf{\Pi}^{\widehat{\nu}}$-congruence and dynamic barbed $\mathbf{\Pi}^{\widehat{\nu}+}$-congruence coincide.

4 The Full Calculus

We now consider how the above discussion is affected by the restriction operator. As mentioned in the Preliminaries, in its presence the definition of open bisimilarity must be modified to take into account that if $P \xrightarrow{\alpha} P'$ with $\alpha = \overline{x}(\nu\,\widetilde{z})\widetilde{y}$, the names $\widetilde{z}$ are not subject to arbitrary instantiation in P'. For example if $P = (\nu\,z)\overline{x}z.\,[z = y]y$ and $Q = (\nu\,z)\overline{x}z$, then P and Q should be open bisimilar since $P \xrightarrow{\overline{x}(\nu\,z)z} P' = [z = y]y$ and z

and y should not be subject to instantiation to the same name in P'. To achieve this a distinction-indexed family of relations is used. Writing $\Delta(F,\tilde{z})$ for the distinction

$$\{(w,z) \mid w \in F, z \in \tilde{z}\} \cup \{(z,z') \mid z,z' \in \tilde{z}, z \neq z'\}$$

where F and $\tilde{z}$ are disjoint sets of names, we have the following (in essence from [11]):

Definition 6 On Π, *indexed open bisimilarity* is the largest distinction-indexed family $\{\approx_D\}_D$ of symmetric relations such that whenever $P \approx_D Q$, ρ respects D and $P\rho \xrightarrow{\alpha} P'$ where the bound names of α are fresh, then from some Q', $Q\rho \stackrel{\widehat{\alpha}}{\Longrightarrow} Q'$ and $P' \approx_{D'} Q'$ where

$$D' = \begin{cases} D\rho & \text{if } \alpha \text{ is not an output action} \\ D\rho \cup \Delta(\mathrm{fn}(P\rho, Q\rho), \tilde{z}) & \text{if } \alpha = \overline{x}(\nu\,\tilde{z})\tilde{y}. \end{cases}$$

The members of the family $\{\approx_D\}_D$ differ from one another. Continuing the example above, $[z=y]y \approx_{\{(y,z)\}} \mathbf{0}$ but $[z=y]y \not\approx_{\emptyset} \mathbf{0}$. An immediate question is how dynamic barbed $\mathbf{\Pi}$-congruence is related to the open D-bisimilarities. The following theorem shows that $\simeq_{\mathbf{\Pi}}$ is not as discriminating as any $\approx_D$.

Theorem 3 On Π, $\simeq_{\mathbf{\Pi}} \not\subseteq \approx_D$ for any D.

Proof: Consider $P_x = (\nu\, y)\,\overline{x}y.\,x(z).\,(y+y.\,y+y.\,[z=y]\,y)$ and $Q_x = (\nu\, y)\,\overline{x}y.\,x(z).\,(y+y.\,y)$. It is simple to check that for any D, $P_x \not\approx_D Q_x$ as $[z=y]\,y \not\approx_{D'} \mathbf{0}$ and $[z=y]\,y \not\approx_{D'} y$ where $D' = D \cup \{(x,y)\}$ with y fresh. However, $P_x \simeq_{\mathbf{\Pi}} Q_x$ where $\simeq_{\mathbf{\Pi}}$ is *strong* dynamic barbed $\mathbf{\Pi}$-congruence. In brief outline the proof of this is as follows. Consider the agents $P'_{x,R} = (\nu\, y)\,(x(z).\,(y+y.\,y+y.\,[z=y]\,y) \mid R)$ and $Q'_{x,R} = (\nu\, y)\,(x(z).\,(y+y.\,y) \mid R)$. Define

$$\begin{aligned} \mathcal{S}_0 &= \{\langle \mathcal{C}[P_x], \mathcal{C}[Q_x]\rangle \mid x \in \mathsf{N}, \mathcal{C}[\cdot] \in \mathbf{\Pi}\}, \\ \mathcal{S}_1 &= \{\langle \mathcal{C}[P'_{x,R}], \mathcal{C}[Q'_{x,R}]\rangle \mid x \in \mathsf{N}, R \in \Pi, \mathcal{C}[\cdot] \in \mathbf{\Pi}\}, \text{ and} \\ \mathcal{S} &= \sim_{\emptyset} \cup \mathcal{S}_0 \cup \mathcal{S}_1 \end{aligned}$$

where $\sim_{\emptyset}$ is *strong* open $\emptyset$-bisimilarity. Then $\mathcal{S}$ is a strong dynamic barbed $\mathbf{\Pi}$-bisimulation. The proof, though fairly routine, is too long to include here. □

Thus in contrast to the restriction-free case, on Π dynamic barbed $\mathbf{\Pi}$-congruence is too weak to distinguish some agents which are not open D-bisimilar for any D. The proof of Theorem 2(2), which establishes that on $\Pi^{\widehat{\nu}}$ dynamic barbed $\mathbf{\Pi}^{\widehat{\nu}}$-congruence is an open bisimulation, can not be extended to the full calculus: it is impossible to achieve the effect of an arbitrary respectful substitution by name instantiation via an appropriate $\mathbf{\Pi}$-context.

On $\Pi^{\widehat{\nu}}$, barbed $\mathbf{\Pi}^{\widehat{\nu}+}$-congruence and dynamic barbed $\mathbf{\Pi}^{\widehat{\nu}+}$-congruence also coincide with open bisimilarity. But the $s \lhd \cdot$ operators do not preserve the indexed open bisimilarities:

Lemma 4 $P \approx_D Q$ does not imply $s \lhd P \approx_D s \lhd Q$.

Proof: Consider $P = (\nu\, z)\overline{x}z.\,[z=y]y$ and $Q = (\nu\, z)\overline{x}z$ and fix D. Then $P \approx_D Q$ as $P' \approx_{D'} \mathbf{0}$ where $P' = [z=y]y$ and $D' = D \cup \{(x,z),(y,z)\}$ with z fresh. But the derivation $s \lhd P \xrightarrow{\overline{x}(\nu\, z)z} s \lhd P' \xrightarrow{szy} s \lhd [y=y]y \xrightarrow{y}$ can not be matched by $s \lhd Q$. □

To characterize indexed open bisimilarity as a (dynamic) barbed congruence, some form of distinction-indexing of families of contexts would be expected. The example in the above proof suggests consideration of distinction-indexed operators, say $s \lhd_D \cdot$ with D serving to limit the substitutions which may be applied to P via s in $s \lhd_D P$. The appropriate definition of the indexed operators is not obvious. Corresponding to the two rules defining $s \lhd \cdot$ one might consider for $s \lhd_D \cdot$ the rules

1. $s \lhd_D P \xrightarrow{s\widetilde{xy}} s \lhd_{D\sigma} P\sigma$ provided $\sigma = \{\widetilde{y}/\widetilde{x}\}$ respects D, and
2. if $P \xrightarrow{\alpha} P'$ then $s \lhd_D P \xrightarrow{\alpha} s \lhd_D P'$.

But then the fact that if $\{\widetilde{y}/\widetilde{x}\}$ does not respect D, $s \lhd_D P$ has no $s\widetilde{x}\widetilde{y}$-transition is awkward; and is the second rule appropriate if α is an output action containing bound names?

Such considerations are of significance in relation to congruence properties of $\approx_D$. For example with the above definition, which denies that $s \lhd_D P$ has an $s\widetilde{x}\widetilde{y}$-transition if $\{\widetilde{y}/\widetilde{x}\}$ does not respect D, we have the following. Consider $P = (\nu\, z)\,\overline{x}z.\,[z = y]y$ and $Q = (\nu\, z)\,\overline{x}z.\,[z = w]w$. Taking over the definition of $\approx_D$ on Π we have $P \approx_\emptyset Q$. But $s \lhd_\emptyset P \not\approx_\emptyset s \lhd_\emptyset Q$ and setting $R = x(z).\,\overline{s}zy.\,v$, $(s \lhd_\emptyset P) \mid R \not\approx_\emptyset (s \lhd_\emptyset Q) \mid R$ as

$$(s \lhd_\emptyset P) \mid R \xrightarrow{\tau} (\nu\, z)\,((s \lhd_\emptyset [z=y]y) \mid \overline{s}zy.\,v) \xrightarrow{\tau} (\nu\, z)\,((s \lhd_\emptyset [y=y]y) \mid v) \xrightarrow{y}$$

and this derivation can not be matched by $(s \lhd_\emptyset Q) \mid R$.

One might attribute this difficulty to the fact that by virtue of the second transition rule, $s \lhd_\emptyset P \xrightarrow{\overline{x}(\nu\, z)z} s \lhd_\emptyset [z=y]y$ and consider changing that to

2′. if $P \xrightarrow{\alpha} P'$ then $s \lhd_D P \xrightarrow{\alpha} s \lhd_{D'} P'$ where

$$D' = \begin{cases} D & \text{if } \alpha \text{ is not an output action} \\ D \cup \Delta(\mathrm{fn}(P), \widetilde{z}) & \text{if } \alpha = \overline{x}(\nu\, \widetilde{z})\widetilde{y}. \end{cases}$$

Then we would have $s \lhd_\emptyset P \xrightarrow{\overline{x}(\nu\, z)z} s \lhd_{\{(x,z),(y,z)\}} [z = y]y$ (recording the distinctness of z from y and x, the free names of P), and according to the first transition rule this derivative has no szy-transition as $\{y/z\}$ does not respect the distinction; thus no τ-transition from $(\nu\, z)((s \lhd_{\{(x,z),(y,z)\}} [z = y]y) \mid \overline{s}zy.\,v)$ may be inferred. But that too is problematical as considering now $(s \lhd_\emptyset Q) \mid R$ we have the derivation

$$(s \lhd_\emptyset Q) \mid R \xrightarrow{\tau} (\nu\, z)\,((s \lhd_D [z=w]w) \mid \overline{s}zy.\,v) \xrightarrow{\tau} (\nu\, z)\,((s \lhd_{D'} [y=w]w) \mid v) \xrightarrow{v}$$

where $D = \{(x,z),(w,z)\}$ and $D' = \{(x,y),(w,y)\}$, and this can not be matched by $(s \lhd_\emptyset P) \mid R$.

The difficulty here is that with rules 1 and 2′, the transitions of $s \lhd_D P$ depend to some extent on which names occur free in P. However, it is worth noting in passing that something can be salvaged here. Adopting rules 1 and 2′ and altering the definition of indexed open bisimilarity slightly (so that for D-bisimilarity, an input action $s\widetilde{x}\widetilde{y}$ with $s : S_*$ need be matched only if $\{\widetilde{y}/\widetilde{x}\}$ respects D), it is possible to find an indexed family of sets of contexts for which a characterization result can be established.

To give a more satisfactory treatment we introduce instead operators $s \lhd_D^U \cdot$ for D a distinction and U a set of names with $\mathsf{dom}(D) \subseteq U$ by the rules

1. $s \lhd_D^U P \xrightarrow{s\widetilde{xy}} s \lhd_{D\sigma}^{U\sigma} P\sigma$ provided $\sigma = \{\widetilde{y}/\widetilde{x}\}$ respects D, and

2. if $P \xrightarrow{\alpha} P'$ then $s \lhd_D^U P \xrightarrow{\alpha} s \lhd_{D'}^{U'} P'$ where

$$(D',U') = \begin{cases} (D, U \cup \tilde{y}) & \text{if } \alpha = x\tilde{y} \text{ where } x \text{ is not of sort } S_* \\ (D \cup \Delta(U,\tilde{z}), U \cup \tilde{z}) & \text{if } \alpha = \overline{x}(\nu\,\tilde{z})\tilde{y} \\ (D, U) & \text{if } \alpha = \tau. \end{cases}$$

We decree that $s \lhd_D^U P$ is well-formed only if $\text{fn}(P) \subseteq U$. Note that any derivative of a well-formed agent is well-formed. For simplicity here we stipulate also that $s \lhd_D^U \cdot$ operators may not be nested. It may be useful for relax this prohibition. Doing so would require an extra clause in rule 2 above and in other definitions and arguments. We thus have $\text{fn}(s \lhd_D^U P) = U \cup \{s\}$ and for a substitution ρ, $(s \lhd_D^U P)\rho = s\rho \lhd_{D^*}^{U\rho} P\rho$ where $D^* = D\rho - \text{id}$ (so if ρ respects D then $D^* = D\rho$). The following notation is useful.

Definition 7

1. Π_D^+ (resp. $\mathbf{\Pi}_D^+$) is the set of agents (resp. contexts) built from the operators of the π-calculus together with the $s \lhd_D^U \cdot$ operators (and in which the latter are not nested).
2. $\Pi^+ = \bigcup\{\Pi_D^+ \mid D \text{ a distinction}\}$.

Then we have:

Definition 8 On Π^+, *indexed open bisimilarity* is the largest distinction-indexed family $\{\approx_D\}_D$ of symmetric relations such that whenever $P \approx_D Q$, ρ respects D and $P\rho \xrightarrow{\alpha} P'$ where the bound names of α are fresh, then from some Q', $Q\rho \overset{\widehat{\alpha}}{\Longrightarrow} Q'$ and $P' \approx_{D'} Q'$ where

$$D' = \begin{cases} D\rho\sigma & \text{if } \alpha = s\tilde{x}\tilde{y} \text{ with } s : S_* \text{ and } \sigma = \{\tilde{y}/\tilde{x}\} \\ D\rho \cup \Delta(\text{fn}(P\rho, Q\rho), \tilde{z}) & \text{if } \alpha = \overline{x}(\nu\,\tilde{z})\tilde{y} \\ D\rho & \text{otherwise.} \end{cases}$$

We first establish a congruence result analogous to Lemma 1.

Lemma 5 If $P \approx_D Q$ then $\mathcal{C}[P] \approx_D \mathcal{C}[Q]$ for $\mathcal{C}[\cdot] \in \mathbf{\Pi}_D^+$, provided $P, Q, \mathcal{C}[\cdot]$ are *compatible*, i.e. $\mathcal{C}[P]$ and $\mathcal{C}[Q]$ are well-formed and if $\cdot$ occurs in $\mathcal{C}[\cdot]$ in the scope of an input prefix $x(\tilde{y})$ then no name in $\tilde{y}$ occurs in D.

Proof: As for Lemma 1 the proof is by induction. We consider in detail the argument for the $s \lhd_D^U \cdot$ operators, but first note that if $P \approx_D Q$ then $(\nu\,x)P \approx_{D'} (\nu\,x)Q$ where D' is D with all pairs containing x removed, and if $P \approx_{D''} Q$ then $x(\tilde{y}).\,P \approx_D x(\tilde{y}).\,Q$ where D'' is D with all pairs containing a name in $\tilde{y}$ removed. Let

$$\mathcal{S}_D = \{\langle s \lhd_D^U P, s \lhd_D^U Q\rangle \mid P \approx_D Q,\ \text{fn}(P,Q) \subseteq U,\ s \in \mathsf{N}\}.$$

We show that $\{\mathcal{S}_D\}_D$ is an indexed open bisimulation. Suppose that ρ respects D and $(s \lhd_D^U P)\rho \xrightarrow{\alpha} R$. Then either (i) $\alpha = s\rho\,\tilde{x}\tilde{y}$ and $R = s\rho \lhd_{D\rho\sigma}^{U\rho\sigma} P\rho\sigma$ where $\sigma = \{\tilde{y}/\tilde{x}\}$ respects $D\rho$, or (ii) $R = s\rho \lhd_{D'}^{U'} P'$ where $P\rho \xrightarrow{\alpha} P'$ and

$$(D',U') = \begin{cases} (D\rho, U\rho \cup \tilde{y}) & \text{if } \alpha = x\tilde{y} \\ (D\rho \cup \Delta(U\rho,\tilde{z}), U\rho \cup \tilde{z}) & \text{if } \alpha = \overline{x}(\nu\,\tilde{z})\tilde{y} \\ (D\rho, U\rho) & \text{if } \alpha = \tau. \end{cases}$$

In case (i), $(s \lhd_D^U Q)\rho \xrightarrow{\alpha} R' = s\rho \lhd_{D\rho\sigma}^{U\rho\sigma} Q\rho\sigma$ and since ρ respects D and σ respects $D\rho$, $P\rho\sigma \approx_{D\rho\sigma} Q\rho\sigma$ and so $R\mathcal{S}_{D\rho\sigma}R'$. In case (ii), $Q\rho \stackrel{\widehat{\alpha}}{\Longrightarrow} Q'$ with $P' \approx_{D''} Q'$ where

$$D'' = \begin{cases} D\rho \cup \Delta(\mathrm{fn}(P\rho, Q\rho), \widetilde{z}) & \text{if } \alpha = \overline{x}(\nu\,\widetilde{z})\widetilde{y} \\ D\rho & \text{otherwise.} \end{cases}$$

Then $(s \lhd_D^U Q)\rho \stackrel{\widehat{\alpha}}{\Longrightarrow} R' = s\rho \lhd_{D'}^{U'} Q'$ and since $P' \approx_{D''} Q'$ and $D'' \subseteq D'$, $P' \approx_{D'} Q'$ and so $R\mathcal{S}_{D'}Q'$. □

In the previous section we saw that in the presence of the $s \lhd \cdot$ operators, in order to ensure that $P \xrightarrow{\alpha} P'$ implies $P\rho \xrightarrow{\alpha\rho} P'\rho$ a side condition is required. The condition given was that if $\alpha = s\,\widetilde{x}\widetilde{y}$ with $s : S_*$ then ρ is one-one on $\widetilde{x}$ and there is no $z \in \mathrm{fn}(P) - \widetilde{x}$ such that $z\rho \in \widetilde{x\rho}$. This condition is insufficient to guarantee the result in the presence of the $s \lhd_D^U \cdot$ operators. For suppose $P = s \lhd_{\{(x_1,x_2)\}}^{\{x_1,x_2,z\}} [x_1 = x_2]z$, $\alpha = s\,x_1 y_1 x_2 y_2$ and $\rho = \{ww/y_1y_2\}$. Then $\sigma = \{y_1y_2/x_1x_2\}$ respects $\{(x_1, x_2)\}$ so $P \xrightarrow{\alpha} P' = s \lhd_{\{(y_1,y_2)\}}^{\{y_1,y_2,z\}} [y_1 = y_2]z$. But $P\rho = P$, $\alpha\rho = s\,x_1 w x_2 w$ and $\sigma' = \{ww/x_1x_2\}$ does not respect $\{(x_1, x_2)\}$ so $P\rho$ has no $\alpha\rho$-transition. It is thus necessary to augment the condition. Note that if ρ is one-one then it satisfies the new condition.

Lemma 6

1. Suppose $P \xrightarrow{\alpha} P'$, that if $\alpha = s\,\widetilde{x}\widetilde{y}$ with $s : S_*$ then ρ is one-one on $\widetilde{x}$ and there is no $z \in \mathrm{fn}(P) - \widetilde{x}$ such that $z\rho \in \widetilde{x\rho}$, and that if $r \lhd_D^U \cdot$ occurs in P and σ respects D then ρ respects $D\sigma$. Then $P\rho \xrightarrow{\alpha\rho} P'\rho$.
2. Suppose $P\rho \xrightarrow{\beta} P''$ and ρ is one-one. Then for some α and P' with $\alpha\rho = \beta$ and $P'\rho = P''$, $P \xrightarrow{\alpha} P'$.

Proof: An extension of that of Lemma 2. □

The following analogue of Lemma 3 will be useful.

Lemma 7 Suppose that $\{\mathcal{S}_D\}_D$ is a family of relations on Π such that if $P\mathcal{S}_DQ$ and ρ is one-one then $P\rho\,\mathcal{S}_{D\rho}\,Q\rho$, and that whenever $P\mathcal{S}_DQ$ there are a finite U with $\mathrm{fn}(P, Q, D) \subseteq U$ and a finite V containing at least twice as many names of each sort as U with $V \cap U = \emptyset$, such that for each $\sigma : U \to U \cup V$ which respects D,

1. if $P\sigma \xrightarrow{\tau} P'$ then $Q\sigma \Longrightarrow Q'$ with $P'\mathcal{S}_{D\sigma}Q'$,
2. if $P\sigma \xrightarrow{x\widetilde{y}} P'$ with $\widetilde{y} \subseteq U \cup V$, then $Q\sigma \stackrel{x\widetilde{y}}{\Longrightarrow} Q'$ with $P'\mathcal{S}_{D\sigma}Q'$, and
3. if $P\sigma \xrightarrow{\overline{x}(\nu\,\widetilde{z})\widetilde{y}} P'$ then $Q\sigma \stackrel{\overline{x}(\nu\,\widetilde{z})\widetilde{y}}{\Longrightarrow} Q'$ with $P'\mathcal{S}_{D'}Q'$ where setting $G = \mathrm{fn}(P\sigma, Q\sigma)$ and $D^* = D\sigma \cup \Delta(G, \widetilde{z})$, $D^* \subseteq D'$ and $D'\lceil(G \cup \widetilde{z}) \subseteq D^*$ where $D\lceil X = \{(u, v) \in D \mid u, v \in X\}$.

Then $P\mathcal{S}_DQ$ implies $P \approx_D Q$.

Proof: An extension of that of Lemma 3. □

We can now establish the characterization result.

Theorem 4 Suppose $P, Q \in \Pi$. Then $P \approx_D Q$ iff $\mathcal{C}[P] \dot{\approx}_b \mathcal{C}[Q]$ for each $\mathcal{C}[\cdot]$ in $\mathbf{\Pi}_D^+$ such that $P, Q, \mathcal{C}[\cdot]$ are compatible.

Proof: If $P \approx_D Q$ then by Lemma 5, for each $\mathcal{C}[\cdot]$, $\mathcal{C}[P] \approx_D \mathcal{C}[Q]$ and hence $\mathcal{C}[P] \dot{\approx}_b \mathcal{C}[Q]$.

The argument for the converse is an extension of that in the proof of the corresponding result in the restriction-free case. Given a finite set of names U choose a set F disjoint from U, infinite and coinfinite in each sort. Then let $V \subseteq F$ be as in Lemma 7. From the names not in F choose distinct $s : S_*$ and a_i, $b_i[\sigma]$, $c_i[z, \widetilde{w}]$, $d_i[z]$, $e_i[h, z]$ and $f_i[g, h]$ of a sort S with $\Sigma(S) = ()$ for each $i < \omega$, $z \in U \cup F$, finite $\widetilde{w} \subseteq U \cup F$, $g, h \in \omega$ and finite $\sigma : U \cup F \rightharpoonup U \cup F$. Now define agents $W_i^s(D, U, F)$ as follows:

$$
\begin{aligned}
W_i^s(D,U,F) \stackrel{\text{def}}{=}\ & a_i \\
& + \Sigma_{(1)} \overline{s}\, \widetilde{x}\widetilde{y}.\ (b_i[\sigma] \\
& \qquad + \Sigma_{(2)} \overline{z}\widetilde{w}.\ (c_i[z,\widetilde{w}] + \tau.\, W_{i+1}^s(D\sigma, U\sigma \cup \widetilde{w}, F - (\widetilde{y} \cup \widetilde{w}))) \\
& \qquad + \Sigma_{(3)} z(\widetilde{v}).\ (d_i[z] \\
& \qquad\qquad + \Sigma_{(4)} [v_h = u] e_i[h,u] \\
& \qquad\qquad + \Sigma_{(5)} [v_g = v_h] f_i[g,h] \\
& \qquad\qquad + \tau.\, W_{i+1}^s(D\sigma \cup \Delta(U\sigma, \widetilde{v} - U\sigma), U\sigma \cup \widetilde{v}, F - (\widetilde{y} \cup \widetilde{v}))) \\
& \qquad + \tau.\, W_{i+1}^s(D\sigma, U\sigma, F - \widetilde{y}))
\end{aligned}
$$

where $\sigma = \{\widetilde{y}/\widetilde{x}\}$ and in the summations: (1) $\widetilde{x} \subseteq U$ with the x_i distinct and $\widetilde{y} \subseteq U \cup V$ are such that $\{\widetilde{y}/\widetilde{x}\}$ respects D, (2) $z \in U \cup \widetilde{y}$ and $\widetilde{w} \subseteq U \cup V$, (3) $z \in U \cup \widetilde{y}$ and $\widetilde{v}$ are chosen from $V - \widetilde{y}$, (4) $u \in U \cup \widetilde{y}$ and $h \in \{1, \ldots, j\}$ where $j = |\widetilde{v}|$, and (5) $g, h \in \{1, \ldots, j\}$ where $j = |\widetilde{v}|$.

Then define

$$\mathcal{C}_{i,s,D}^{U,F,\widetilde{u}}[\cdot] \stackrel{\text{def}}{=} (\nu\, \widetilde{u})((s \lhd_D^U \cdot) \mid W_i^s(D, U, F))$$

Now set $P \mathcal{S}_D Q$ if for some finite U and $\widetilde{u}$ with $\text{fn}(P, Q, D, \widetilde{u}) \subseteq U$ and F, s and i as above, $\mathcal{C}_{i,s,D}^{U,F,\widetilde{u}}[P] \dot{\approx}_b \mathcal{C}_{i,s,D}^{U,F,\widetilde{u}}[Q]$. Note that by the construction, $P, Q, \mathcal{C}_{i,s,D}^{U,F,\widetilde{u}}[\cdot]$ are compatible. We claim that $\{\mathcal{S}_D\}_D$ satisfies the hypothesis of Lemma 7 and hence that $P \mathcal{S}_D Q$ implies $P \approx_D Q$. Suppose $P \mathcal{S}_D Q$ as $\mathcal{C}_{i,s,D}^{U,F,\widetilde{u}}[P] \dot{\approx}_b \mathcal{C}_{i,s,D}^{U,F,\widetilde{u}}[Q]$.

(a) If ρ is one-one then since $\dot{\approx}_b$ is preserved by one-one substitutions, $\mathcal{C}_{i,s,D}^{U,F,\widetilde{u}}[P]\rho \dot{\approx}_b \mathcal{C}_{i,s,D}^{U,F,\widetilde{u}}[Q]\rho$, i.e. $\mathcal{C}_{i,s\rho,D\rho}^{U\rho,F\rho,\widetilde{u}}[P\rho] \dot{\approx}_b \mathcal{C}_{i,s\rho,D\rho}^{U\rho,F\rho,\widetilde{u}}[Q\rho]$. So since $\text{fn}(P\rho, Q\rho, D\rho, \widetilde{u}) \subseteq U\rho$, $U\rho \cap F\rho = \emptyset$ and $s\rho \notin U\rho \cup F\rho$, $P\rho\, \mathcal{S}_{D\rho}\, Q\rho$.

Now fix $\sigma : U \rightharpoonup U \cup V$ which respects D and suppose $P\sigma \xrightarrow{\alpha} P'$.

(b) Suppose $\alpha = \overline{z}(\nu\, \widetilde{v})\widetilde{w}$. Then

$$
\begin{aligned}
P_0 = \mathcal{C}_{i,s,D}^{U,F,\widetilde{u}}[P] &\longrightarrow P_1 = (\nu\, \widetilde{u})((s \lhd_{D\sigma}^{U\sigma} P\sigma) \mid (b_i[\sigma] + \ldots)) \\
&\longrightarrow P_2 = (\nu\, \widetilde{u}\widetilde{v})((s \lhd_{D'}^{U'} P') \mid (d_i[z] + \ldots + \tau.\, W_{i+1}^s(D', U', F')) \\
&\longrightarrow P_3 = (\nu\, \widetilde{u}\widetilde{v})((s \lhd_{D'}^{U'} P') \mid W_{i+1}^s(D', U', F'))
\end{aligned}
$$

where $U' = U\sigma \cup \widetilde{v}$, $D' = D\sigma \cup \Delta(U\sigma, \widetilde{v})$ and $F' = F - (\widetilde{y} \cup \widetilde{v})$ where $\sigma = \{\widetilde{y}/\widetilde{x}\}$. So $Q_0 = \mathcal{C}_{i,s,D}^{U,F,\widetilde{u}}[Q] \Longrightarrow Q_1 \Longrightarrow Q_2 \Longrightarrow Q_3$ with $P_j \dot{\approx}_b Q_j$ for each j. Since $Q_0 \downarrow_{a_i}$ but $P_1 \Uparrow_{a_i}$ the W-component must act in $Q_0 \Longrightarrow Q_1$. Moreover since $P_1 \downarrow_{b_i[\sigma]}$, the W-component must act exactly once performing the action $\overline{s}\, \widetilde{x}\widetilde{y}$. So $Q_1 = (\nu\, \widetilde{u})((s \lhd_{D\sigma}^{U\sigma} Q') \mid (b_i[\sigma] + \ldots))$ where for some Q^*, $Q \Longrightarrow Q^*$ and $Q^*\sigma \Longrightarrow Q'$ and so $Q\sigma \Longrightarrow Q'$. Further, since $Q_1 \downarrow_{b_i[\sigma]}$ but $P_2 \Uparrow_{b_i[\sigma]}$, the W-component must act in $Q_1 \Longrightarrow Q_2$. Moreover since $P_2 \downarrow_{d_i[z]}$ the W-component must act exactly once performing an input with subject z. Moreover the object of the action must contain the same free names and in the same positions as the action α, by virtue of the actions of the form $e_i[h, u]$ which are observable in P_2, and the pattern of bound names in the object of the action must be the same as in α by virtue of the actions of the form $f_i[g, h]$ which are observable in P_2. Hence $Q_2 = (\nu\, \widetilde{u}\widetilde{v})((s \lhd^{U'}_{D'} Q'') \mid (d_i[z] + \ldots + \tau.\, W^s_{i+1}(D', U', F')))$ where $Q' \overset{\alpha}{\Longrightarrow} Q''$. Finally, since $Q_2 \downarrow_{d_i[z]}$ and $P_3 \Uparrow_{d_i[z]}$, the W-component must act in $Q_2 \Longrightarrow Q_3$. Moreover since $P_3 \downarrow_{a_{i+1}}$ the W-component must act exactly once performing a τ-action and $Q_3 = (\nu\, \widetilde{u}\widetilde{v})((s \lhd^{U'}_{D'} Q''') \mid W^s_{i+1}(D', U', F'))$ where $Q'' \Longrightarrow Q'''$. So $Q\sigma \overset{\alpha}{\Longrightarrow} Q'''$ and $P' S_{D'} Q'''$ since

$$C^{U',F',\widetilde{uv}}_{i+1,s,D'}[P'] \equiv P_3 \dot{\approx}_b Q_3 \equiv C^{U',F',\widetilde{uv}}_{i+1,s,D'}[Q'''].$$

Hence the hypothesis of Lemma 7 is satisfied as setting $G = \mathrm{fn}(P\sigma, Q\sigma)$ and $D^* = D\sigma \cup \Delta(G, \widetilde{v})$, $D^* \subseteq D'$ and $D' \lceil (G \cup \widetilde{v}) \subseteq D^*$.

The cases $\alpha = \tau$ and $\alpha = z\widetilde{w}$ are similar but simpler. □

5 Conclusion

The main characterization results involve the $s \lhd \cdot$ and $s \lhd^U_D \cdot$ operators, and thus their significance depends to some extent on the pertinence of these operators. Their usefulness in describing systems remains to be examined. One direction of particular interest is their possible rôle in encodings of λ-calculus reduction strategies in π-calculus other than those treated in [4]. Connections between the work here, study of the presentation of the π-calculus using explicit substitutions [1], and work on action structures [2] should be examined. Moreover, it remains to give a fuller account of the theory of the $s \lhd^U_D \cdot$ operators.

A final technical point concerns the precise choice of observables in defining barbed bisimilarity. It is shown in [8] that to characterize strong bisimilarity in CCS, it suffices to employ a single observable: whether an agent can perform a visible action. The treatment here of weak equivalences in the π-calculus makes thoroughgoing use of an infinite set of observables, streamlining a construction of [10] which also uses infinitely-many observables in establishing that early congruence coincides with barbed **Π**-congruence. It remains open whether this apparent prodigality in the use of observables is necessary.

References

[1] G. Ferrari, U. Montanari and P. Quaglia, *A π-calculus with Explicit Substitutions*, extended abstract (1993).

[2] A. Mifsud, forthcoming PhD thesis, University of Edinburgh.

[3] R. Milner, **Communication and Concurrency**, Prentice Hall (1989).

[4] R. Milner, *Functions as Processes*, Math. Struct. in Comp. Science 2, 119–141 (1992).

[5] R. Milner, *The Polyadic π-calculus: a Tutorial*, in **Logic and Algebra of Specification** ed. F. Bauer et al., Springer (1993).

[6] R. Milner, J. Parrow and D. Walker, *A Calculus of Mobile Processes, Parts I and II*, Information and Computation 100, 1–40 and 41–77 (1992).

[7] R. Milner, J. Parrow and D. Walker, *Modal Logics for Mobile Processes*, Theoretical Computer Science 114, 149–171 (1993).

[8] R. Milner and D. Sangiorgi, *Barbed Bisimulation*, in Proc. ICALP'92, Springer LNCS vol. 623, 685–695 (1992).

[9] U. Montanari and V. Sassone, *Dynamic Congruence vs. Progressing Bisimulation for CCS*, Fundamenta Informaticae XVI(2), 171–199 (1992).

[10] D. Sangiorgi, *Expressing Mobility in Process Algebras: First-Order and Higher-Order Paradigms*, report ECS–LFCS–93–262, Department of Computer Science, University of Edinburgh (1992).

[11] D. Sangiorgi, *A Theory of Bisimulation for the π-calculus*, in Proc. CONCUR'93, Springer LNCS vol. 715, 127–142 (1993).

Characterizing Bisimulation Congruence in the π–Calculus* (Extended Abstract)

*Xinxin Liu***
School of Cognitive and Computing Sciences
University of Sussex

Abstract. This paper presents a new characterization of the bisimulation congruence and D–bisimulation equivalences of the π–calculus. The characterization supports a bisimulation–like proof technique which avoids explicit case analysis by taking a dynamic point of view of actions a process may perform, thus providing a new way of proving bisimulation congruence. The semantic theory of the π–calculus is presented here without the notion of α–equivalence.

1 Motivation

The π–calculus, introduced in [MPW92a], presents a model of concurrent computation based upon the notion of *naming*. It can be seen as an extension of the theory of CCS [Mil89] (and other similar process algebras) in that names (references) are the subject of communication. This introduces mobility into process algebras. Such an extension allows us to clearly express many fundamental programming features which could at best be described indirectly in CCS.

The theory of CCS has been quite successful for specifying and verifying concurrent systems. The success is due to a solid equality theory based on the notion of bisimulation [Par81, Mil89]. Bisimulation has many nice properties. It induces a congruence relation for CCS constructions, thus supporting compositionality. It admits a very pleasant proof technique based on fixed point induction [Par81]. The proof technique not only provides a means of establishing the equality theory but also opens up a direct way of program verification.

Corresponding to the bisimulation equivalence in CCS, there are two main equalities in the π–calculus: *ground bisimulation equivalence* and *bisimulation congruence*. The notion of ground bisimulation is a natural generalization of that of bisimulation in CCS with a pleasant proof technique. However, ground bisimulation equivalence is not a congruence relation for π–calculus constructions, because now names are subject to substitution and ground bisimulation equivalence is not preserved under substitution of names. To obtain a congruence relation, bisimulation congruence is defined such that two processes are

* This work has been supported by the SERC grant GR/H16537
** Present address: Department of Computer Science, University of Warwick, Coventry CV4 7AL, UK. email: xinxin@dcs.warwick.ac.uk

related just in case they are ground bisimilar under all substitutions. Although this immediately gives us a congruence relation, this definition does not suggest any direct proof technique to establish congruence between processes other than tedious exhaustive case analysis. Thus, in extending CCS to the π–calculus, the nice feature of proof technique is somewhat lost for bisimulation congruence — the more important relation between π–calculus processes. In fact there is a whole series of distinction bisimulation equivalences such that two processes are D–bisimilar just in case they are ground bisimilar under all substitutions respecting D, where D is the so called *distinction* which tells that some pairs of names should not be substituted into the same name. Here the general definition of D–bisimilarity again is quantified over certain substitutions, and therefore it does not provide any proof technique to check D–bisimilarity between processes. Notice that bisimulation congruence is a particular instance of D–bisimulation equivalence where D poses no constraint upon substitutions, and ground bisimulation equivalence is a particular instance of D–bisimulation equivalence where D distinguishes any pair of names.

The purpose of this paper is to introduce a proof technique for bisimulation congruence of π–calculus. We characterize bisimulation congruence by an alternative definition based directly on the operational behaviour of processes. The new definition is in a style of bisimulation without explicit case analysis, thus providing a bisimulation like proof technique for congruence. In general, we will find that we cannot do this for the bisimulation congruence alone, we have to do it for D–bisimulation equivalences all together. In this paper, we establish such a proof technique for arbitrary D–bisimulation equivalence of which bisimulation congruence is a particular instance.

Here we roughly illustrate the idea behind our approach. Let us write $\sim$ for bisimulation congruence, $\sim_D$ for D–bisimulation equivalence, and $\dot{\sim}$ for ground bisimulation equivalence. A basic fact we can exploit in proving congruence of two processes is the following:

$$P \sim Q \text{ if and only if } P \sim_{\{x,y\}} Q \text{ and } P\{y/x\} \sim Q\{y/x\}$$

where x, y are two different given names, $\{x, y\}$ is the distinction which tells that x and y must not be substituted into the same name, and $P\{y/x\}$ means the term obtained by substituting y for free occurrences of x in P. This fact holds for the following reason. Because $P \sim Q$ means $P\sigma \dot{\sim} Q\sigma$ for any substitution σ, $P \sim_{\{x,y\}} Q$ means $P\sigma \dot{\sim} Q\sigma$ for those substitution σ that $x\sigma \neq y\sigma$, and $P\{y/x\} \sim Q\{y/x\}$ means $P\{y/x\}\sigma \dot{\sim} Q\{y/x\}\sigma$ for any substitution σ or equivalently $P\sigma \dot{\sim} Q\sigma$ for any substitution σ that $x\sigma = y\sigma$. Thus for two given names x, y, $P \sim Q$ just in case $P \sim_{\{x,y\}} Q$ and $P\{y/x\} \sim Q\{y/x\}$. Using this fact, if we choose properly x and y, we can make a step forward by reducing the problem of proving $P \sim Q$ into two subproblems of proving $P \sim_{\{x,y\}} Q$ and $P\{y/x\} \sim Q\{y/x\}$.

As a simple example let us prove the following

$$x|\bar{y} + x|\bar{x} \sim x.\bar{y} + \bar{y}.x + x|\bar{x}$$

According to the above discussion, this can be reduced to proving both of the following

$$x|\bar{y} + x|\bar{x} \sim_{\{x,y\}} x.\bar{y} + \bar{y}.x + x|\bar{x}$$

and

$$x|\bar{x} + x|\bar{x} \sim x.\bar{x} + \bar{x}.x + x|\bar{x}$$

Now in the first equivalence, the distinction $\{x, y\}$ requires that any pairs of different free names of the processes must be distinct under substitution. So the first equivalence is guaranteed by $x|\bar{y}+x|\bar{x} \dot{\sim} x.\bar{y}+\bar{y}.x+x|\bar{x}$. A similar argument concludes that the second equivalence is guaranteed by $x|\bar{x}+x|\bar{x} \dot{\sim} x.\bar{x}+\bar{x}.x+x|\bar{x}$, and now we can use the proof technique for $\dot{\sim}$. In the general case, we may have to further reduce the subproblems before $\dot{\sim}$ would guarantee D–bisimilarity of two processes.

In fact here we are doing case analysis to divide the substitution set into smaller subsets until $\dot{\sim}$ can solve the subproblems. This cannot be a satisfactory proof strategy in the general case. Because on many occasions, in order to conclude congruence between processes, it is unnecessary to do case analysis until ground bisimulation can come into play. The most obvious example is to prove $P \sim P$ for whatever complicated P. The aim of the paper is to introduce a proof technique which allows us to do the necessary case analysis implicitly and to keep it to minimum. A key point is to adopt a dynamic point of view of names by introducing conditional commitment. The approach here is inspired by the work of *symbolic bisimulation* of [HL92], where the idea of dividing a value space is used in a proof technique to establish bisimulation equivalence between value passing processes. In fact this paper applies the main idea in [HL92] while taking advantage of the primitive structure of the π–calculus.

As another contribution, this paper demonstrates that the core of the theory of π–calculus can be presented without using the notion of α–equivalence. Traditionally, α–equivalence, or "syntactic identity modulo α–conversion", plays a very important role in theories in which variables can be bound. However it is also well known that proofs involving this notion are very tedious. A desirable approach is that the basic semantic results are worked out independent of this notion. Of couse, afterwards the semantics should be shown to behave properly in the presence of α–equivalence. Previous works on the theory of π–calculus, like [MPW92a, MPW92b, San93], all employ the notion of α–equivalence in the semantic definition, thus the following development of the semantic theory suffer from the complication caused by α–equivalence. In this paper, by using the notion of *simultanous substitution* introduced in [Sto88], we show that the semantics of π–calculus can be defined on the much simpler notion of syntactic identity instead of α–equivalence. This gives a considerable advantage in the development of the theory.

The next section presents the basic algegbraic theory of the π-calculus. The section follows that presents the alternative characterization of bisimulation congruence and D-bisimulation equivalence. Section 4 concludes with a short discussion about some related work.

2 The π–Calculus

This section is a presentation of the basic algebraic theory of the π–calculus developed in [MPW92a, Mil91]. The presentation here is tailored to fit the new characterization of bisimulation congruence to be introduced in the next section. A novelty of this presentation is the absence of α–equivalence. The reader is referred to the original papers for a general account of the motivation and background of the π–calculus.

2.1 Agents

The π–calculus presented here is a simplified version of that in [Mil91]. The primitive entity in the π–calculus is a *name* which has no structure. We assume that we have an infinite set of names $\mathcal{N}$, and we use $x, y, \ldots$ to range over it. The main entity in the π–calculus is an *agent*, which can be a *process*, an *abstraction*, or a *concretion*. We use $P, Q, \ldots$ to range over processes, $F, G, \ldots$ over abstractions, $C, D, \ldots$ over concretions, and $A, B, \ldots$ over agents. These are built from names by the syntax in Figure 1.

$$
\begin{aligned}
P &::= \mathbf{0} \mid \tau.P \mid x.P \mid \bar{x}.P \mid x.F \mid \bar{x}.C \mid P + P' \mid P|P' \mid\ !P \mid \nu x P \\
F &::= (x)P \mid F|P \mid P|F \mid \nu x F \\
C &::= [x]P \mid C|P \mid P|C \mid \nu x C \\
A &::= P \mid F \mid C
\end{aligned}
$$

Fig. 1. Agents of the π–calculus

We assume that the reader has some familiarity with CCS [Mil89]; here we give an informal description of the above constructions and the intended meaning by comparing the process constructions here with those in CCS. Roughly speaking, π–calculus is a generalization of value passing CCS in that names may be passed in communication between processes. $\mathbf{0}$, $\tau.P$, $x.P$, $\bar{x}.P$, $P+Q$, $P|Q$ are the constructions inherited from CCS. $\nu x P$ is $P\backslash x$ in CCS notation, which restricts the use of the name x to P. So, νx binds free occurrences of x in P. A concretion C consists of two parts: a process and a name. The name part of $[x]P$ is a free name x while that of $\nu x[x]P$ is a bound name x. These are the two standard or normal forms of concretion. Later we will see that any concretion can be *normalized* to one of these forms. A negative prefix $\bar{x}.C$ now corresponds to the output prefix in CCS, which outputs the name part of C at port x and then continue with the process part of C. In its standard form, an abstraction $(x)P$ is in fact a function which for each name y gives a process $P\{y/x\}$, where we use the notation $P\{y/x\}$ to describe the syntactic substitution of y for all free occurrences of x in P. Thus free occurrences of x in P are bound by (x). Also we will see later that any abstraction can be normalized to such a form. Now a positive prefix $x.(y)P$ corresponds to the input prefix in CCS, which receives a name z at port x and then behaves like $P\{z/y\}$. Finally the replication $!P$ means $P|P|\ldots$ which plays the role of recursion. The pure synchronization structures $x.P, \bar{x}.P$ are not essential. They are included for the benefit of writing simple expressions in examples. Moreover $\alpha.\mathbf{0}$ is often abbreviated to α (we have already used this abbreviation in the earlier examples).

To summarize whether a name is free or bound in an expression A, we give the following definition.

Definition 1. *We write* $\mathtt{fn}(A)$ *for the set of free names of* A *— names which are neither bound by abstraction nor by restriction.* $\mathtt{fn}(A)$ *is defined inductively on the structure of* A*:*

$$\begin{aligned}
&\mathtt{fn}(\mathbf{0}) = \emptyset,\\
&\mathtt{fn}(\tau.P) = \mathtt{fn}(!P) = \mathtt{fn}(P)\\
&\mathtt{fn}(P + P') = \mathtt{fn}(P) \cup \mathtt{fn}(P')\\
&\mathtt{fn}(P|A) = \mathtt{fn}(A|P) = \mathtt{fn}(P) \cup \mathtt{fn}(A)\\
&\mathtt{fn}(x.A) = \mathtt{fn}(\bar{x}.A) = \{x\} \cup \mathtt{fn}(A)\\
&\mathtt{fn}([x]P) = \{x\} \cup \mathtt{fn}(P)\\
&\mathtt{fn}((x)P) = \mathtt{fn}(P) - \{x\}\\
&\mathtt{fn}(\nu x A) = \mathtt{fn}(A) - \{x\}
\end{aligned}$$

Sometimes we will write $\mathtt{fn}(A, B)$ *as an abbreviation for* $\mathtt{fn}(A) \cup \mathtt{fn}(B)$.

2.2 Simultaneous Substitution

We have informally used notation $P\{y/x\}$ for the substitution of y for all free occurrences of y in P. It need to be clarified what this substitution exactly means, as there are possibley bound names in a term, we have to be careful to avoid name clash when making such substitutions. In this paper we take the approach of *simultaneous substitution* introduced by Alan Stoughton [Sto88] for the lambda calculus. The definition below is a specialized version of that in [Sto88] in the sense that a name may only be substituted by another name in the π–calculus while a variable may be substituted by a term in the lambda calculus.

We assume that there is a function $\mathtt{fresh}$ which for a given set N of names will produce a name $\mathtt{fresh}(N)$ such that $\mathtt{fresh}(N) \notin N$ (or we can assume some proper ordering on $\mathcal{N}$ and take $\mathtt{fresh}(N)$ to be the smallest one which is not in $\mathcal{N}$). Now, substitution and its application to agents is formally given by the following definition.

Definition 2. *A substitution is a function from $\mathcal{N}$ to $\mathcal{N}$. We use σ, ρ to range over substitutions, and postfix substitutions in application. For a given substitution σ, $\sigma\{y_i/x_i\}_{1\leq i\leq n}$ denotes the following updated substitution of σ:*

$$x\sigma\{y_i/x_i\}_{1\leq i\leq n} = \begin{cases} y_i & \text{if } x = x_i \text{ for } 1 \leq i \leq n \\ x\sigma & \text{otherwise} \end{cases}$$

For two substitutions σ, ρ, we write $\sigma \circ \rho$ for the composition of σ with ρ, which is the substitution such that for $x \in \mathcal{N}, x\sigma \circ \rho = (x\sigma)\rho$ (note since we postfix substitution in application, the order of composition is the reverse of that in normal function composition).

For any substitution σ and name x, as a convention we let $\bar{x}\sigma = \overline{x\sigma}$ and $\tau\sigma = \tau$, thus extending the domain and range of substitutions to the set of all actions. We write $A\sigma$ for the agent obtained by applying the substitution σ to agent A. It is defined on the structure of A:

$$\begin{array}{lll}
\mathbf{0}\sigma & \equiv \mathbf{0} & \\
(\alpha.A)\sigma & \equiv \alpha\sigma.A\sigma & \\
(P+P')\sigma & \equiv P\sigma + P'\sigma & \\
(P|A)\sigma & \equiv P\sigma|A\sigma & \\
(A|P)\sigma & \equiv A\sigma|P\sigma & \\
(!P)\sigma & \equiv !P\sigma & \\
(\nu x A)\sigma & \equiv \nu z A\sigma\{z/x\} & z = \mathtt{fresh}(\{y\sigma \mid y \in \mathtt{fn}(A) - \{x\}\}) \\
((x)P)\sigma & \equiv (z)P\sigma\{z/x\} & z = \mathtt{fresh}(\{y\sigma \mid y \in \mathtt{fn}(P) - \{x\}\}) \\
([x]P)\sigma & \equiv [x\sigma]P\sigma &
\end{array}$$

In the above, z is chosen to avoid name clash by using `fresh`.

As demonstrated in [Sto88], this simultaneous substitution is easier to work with than standard single substitution. The effect of single substitution of x for y in P is now obtained by applying simultaneous substitution $\iota\{x/y\}$ on P, where ι is the identity map. So, from now on, we will write $P\iota\{x/y\}$ for single substitution instead of $P\{x/y\}$. The following conventions are adopted to avoid ambiguity without writing too many brackets. We assume that substitution (postfixed) has the highest precedence. Prefixed operators $[x], (x), \nu x, !, \alpha.$ have higher precedence than infixed operators $+$ and $|$. And $|$ has higher precedence than $+$. Thus $\nu z[z]P\sigma\{z/x\}$ means $\nu z[z](P\sigma\{z/x\})$. Throughout the paper, $\equiv$ is used for syntactic identity. One of the main advantages of simultaneous substitution is to enable us to work with syntactic identity, avoiding the troublesome α–equivalence.

We state in the following some properties enjoyed by this approach of substitution. The proofs can be found in [Liu94].

Lemma 3. *Let A be an agent, σ, ρ be two substitutions. If σ and ρ agree on $\mathtt{fn}(A)$, that is $\forall x \in \mathtt{fn}(A).x\sigma = x\rho$, then $A\sigma \equiv A\rho$.*

Corollary 4. *Let A be an agent, σ, ρ be substitutions, w, x, z be names. If $z \notin \{y\sigma \mid y \in \mathtt{fn}(A) - \{x\}\}$ then $A(\sigma \circ \rho)\{w/x\} \equiv A\sigma\{z/x\} \circ \rho\{w/z\}$.*

This corollary will be repeatedly used in the rest of the paper, sometimes with $\sigma = \iota$ or $\rho = \iota$.

Lemma 5. $\mathtt{fn}(A\sigma) = \{x\sigma \mid x \in \mathtt{fn}(A)\}$.

By this lemma, it is easy to see that $\mathtt{fn}((A\sigma)\rho) = \mathtt{fn}(A\sigma \circ \rho)$, because the left hand side $\{y\rho \mid y \in \mathtt{fn}(A\sigma)\} = \{y\rho \mid y \in \{x\sigma \mid x \in \mathtt{fn}(A)\}\}$ equals to the right hand side which is $\{x\sigma \circ \rho \mid x \in \mathtt{fn}(A)\} = \mathtt{fn}(A\sigma \circ \rho)$. Using this fact, we can prove the following stronger result.

Lemma 6. *Let A be an agent, σ, ρ be two substitutions. Then $(A\sigma)\rho \equiv A\sigma \circ \rho$.*

2.3 Normalization and Pseudo–Application

We have said earlier that abstractions and concretions have certain standard (normal) forms. Now we define the standard form of an abstraction and that of a concretion. The idea to deal with standard forms first appeared in [Mil91].

Definition 7. *An abstraction is in normal form if it is of form $(x)P$. For any abstraction F, its normal form $\mathtt{norma}(F)$ is defined inductively on the structure of F as follows:*

1. $\mathtt{norma}((x)P) \equiv (x)P$,
2. *if* $\mathtt{norma}(F) \equiv (y)P$, *then*

$$\mathtt{norma}(F|Q) \equiv (z)(P\iota\{z/y\}|Q) \qquad \mathtt{norma}(Q|F) \equiv (z)(Q|P\iota\{z/y\})$$

$$\mathtt{norma}(\nu x F) \equiv \begin{cases} (y)P & x \notin \mathtt{fn}(F) \\ (x)\nu y P\iota\{x/y, y/x\} & x \in \mathtt{fn}(F) \end{cases}$$

where $z = \mathtt{fresh}(\mathtt{fn}(F, Q))$.

In clause 2. above, it seems that $(y)\nu x P$ would be a simpler definition for $\mathtt{norma}(\nu x F)$ when $x \in \mathtt{fn}(F)$. Our definition swaps x, y in $(y)\nu x P$, which obviously does not change the semantics of the abstraction. However, our choice here is essential for the equivalences in the following Lemma 10. If we use the simpler version, those equivalences will only hold for in the sense of α–equivalence.

Definition 8. *A concretion is in normal form if it is of form $[x]P$ or $\nu x[x]P$. For any concretion C, its normal form $\mathtt{normc}(C)$ is defined inductively on the structure of C as follows:*

1. $\mathtt{normc}([x]P) \equiv [x]P$,
2. *if* $\mathtt{normc}(C) \equiv [y]P$, *then*

$$\texttt{normc}(C|Q) \equiv [y](P|Q) \qquad \texttt{normc}(Q|C) \equiv [y](Q|P)$$

$$\texttt{normc}(\nu x C) \equiv \begin{cases} \nu x[x]P & x = y \\ [y]\nu x P & x \neq y \end{cases}$$

3. *if* $\texttt{normc}(C) \equiv \nu y[y]P$, *then*

$$\texttt{normc}(C|Q) \equiv \nu z[z](P\iota\{z/y\}|Q) \qquad \texttt{normc}(Q|C) \equiv \nu z[z](Q|P\iota\{z/y\})$$

$$\texttt{normc}(\nu x C) \equiv \begin{cases} \nu y[y]P & x \notin \texttt{fn}(C) \\ \nu x[x]\nu y P\iota\{x/y, y/x\} & x \in \texttt{fn}(C) \end{cases}$$

where $z = \texttt{fresh}(\texttt{fn}(C, Q))$.

Again we swap the places of x, y in clause 3. in order to be able to prove the following Lemma 10.

Lemma 9. *For any abstraction F, concretion C the following hold*

$$\texttt{fn}(F) = \texttt{fn}(\texttt{norma}(F)) \qquad \texttt{fn}(C) = \texttt{fn}(\texttt{normc}(C))$$

Proof It is easy by induction on the structure of F and C. □

Lemma 10. *For any abstraction F, concretion C, substitution σ the following hold*

$$\texttt{norma}(F\sigma) \equiv (\texttt{norma}(F))\sigma \qquad \texttt{normc}(C\sigma) \equiv (\texttt{normc}(C))\sigma$$

Proof See [Liu94]. □

In normal forms, it is clear that an abstraction is ready to receive a name, and a concretion is ready to give a name. In [Mil91], a *pseudo–application* operator $\cdot$ is introduced to describe the result of the action of passing the name part of a concretion to an abstraction.

Definition 11. *Pseudo–application $\cdot$ is a binary operator between abstractions and concretions defined as follows,*

1. *If* $\texttt{norma}(F) \equiv (x)P$ *and* $\texttt{normc}(C) \equiv [y]Q$ *then*
   $F \cdot C$ *is defined to be* $P\iota\{y/x\}|Q$
2. *If* $\texttt{norma}(F) \equiv (x)P$ *and* $\texttt{normc}(C) \equiv \nu y[y]Q$ *then*
   $F \cdot C$ *is defined to be* $\nu z(P\iota\{z/x\}|Q\iota\{z/y\})$

where $z = \texttt{fresh}(\texttt{fn}(F, C))$.

In the above, when the name part of the concretion is a free name, this name is passed by simply substituting all free occurrences of x in P. To pass a bound name means to let the internal name be known by the process which receives the name, but it should not be known by other processes. So by passing a bound name, the scope of the restriction is extended to include the process receiving it. This is called *scope extrusion*.

Lemma 12. *The following equivalence holds for any substitution* σ

$$(F \cdot C)\sigma \equiv F\sigma \cdot C\sigma$$

Proof See [Liu94]. $\square$

2.4 Commitments

To formally describe the semantics of agents, we adopt the notion of *commitment* introduced in [Mil91]. A commitment $\alpha.A$ consists of an *action* α and a *continuation* A which is an agent. There are three kinds of α's: internal action τ, input action x via a name x, and output action $\bar{x}$ via a name x. Now the behaviour of a process can be described by its commitments. The way it is formalized is to define the relation

$$P \succ \alpha.A$$

between processes and commitments. It is clear that the set of commitments of $P + Q$ should be the union of that of P and Q. The relation $\succ$ is defined by the rules shown in Figure 2. Most of the rules explain themselves. Communication happens between two parallel components only when one wants to output a name and the other wants to receive a name on the same name prot. The result of communication may "twist" the parallel components because of the definition of pseudo–application. We can avoid this by introducing another pseudo–application operator. But this is unnecessary since in any case $|$ will turn out to be a symmetric operator. Restriction νx disallows any communication on

Act $$\frac{}{\alpha.A \succ \alpha.A}$$

Sum $$\frac{P \succ \alpha.A}{P + Q \succ \alpha.A} \qquad \frac{Q \succ \alpha.A}{P + Q \succ \alpha.A}$$

Intl $$\frac{P \succ \alpha.A}{P|Q \succ \alpha.(A|Q)} \qquad \frac{Q \succ \alpha.A}{P|Q \succ \alpha.(P|A)}$$

Sync $$\frac{P \succ x.P' \quad Q \succ \bar{x}.Q'}{P|Q \succ \tau.(P'|Q')} \qquad \frac{P \succ \bar{x}.P' \quad Q \succ x.Q'}{P|Q \succ \tau.(P'|Q')}$$

Com $$\frac{P \succ x.F \quad Q \succ \bar{x}.C}{P|Q \succ \tau.(F \cdot C)} \qquad \frac{P \succ \bar{x}.C \quad Q \succ x.F}{P|Q \succ \tau.(F \cdot C)}$$

Rest $$\frac{P \succ \alpha.A}{\nu x P \succ \alpha.(\nu x A)\iota} \quad x \notin name(\alpha)$$

Rec $$\frac{P \,|\, !P \succ \alpha.A}{!P \succ \alpha.A}$$

Fig. 2. Inference Rules for Commitments

the name x. In the rule $name(\alpha)$ gives a singleton set $\{x\}$ when α is x or $\bar{x}$ and gives $\emptyset$ when α is τ. Note that in the rule, the identity substitution ι seems to be unnecessary. However ι may change bound names. Thus although A and $A\iota$ are α-equivalent they are not necessaryly identical. Use of ι here ensures that Rest will not spoil the following Lemma 14.

Lemma 13. *If $P \succ \alpha.A$ then $name(\alpha) \subseteq \mathtt{fn}(P)$ and $\mathtt{fn}(A) \subseteq \mathtt{fn}(P)$.*

Proof See [Liu94]. □

Lemma 14. *If $P \succ \alpha.A$ then $P\sigma \succ \alpha\sigma.A\sigma$ for any substitution σ.*

Proof See [Liu94]. □

2.5 Ground Bisimulation and Congruence

We now go on to define an equivalence relation for agents. Let us first look at some expected properties of this equivalence relation. For two equivalent processes, every commitment of a process should be matched by an *equivalent* commitment of the other process. Thanks to the normalization of abstraction and concretion, two equivalent abstractions should gave equivalent processes for any name. Two equivalent concretions should have equivalent name parts as well as equivalent process parts. Every thing is quite straightforward until we compare two concretions with bound name parts. In this case what particular bound names are used is not important. What is important is that each of them is always different from any free name. Thus in order for two such concretions to be equivalent, it would be sufficient for the process parts to be equivalent whenever the bound names are replaced by any name different from the free names occuring in the concretions. We can define such an equivalence by the standard notion of bisimulation.

Definition 15. *A strong simulation $\mathcal{S}$ is a binary relation between agents such that for all $(A, B) \in \mathcal{S}$, one of the following must hold:*

1. *(A, B) is a pair of processes (P, Q) such that whenever $P \succ \alpha.A'$ then $Q \succ \alpha.B'$ for some $(A', B') \in \mathcal{S}$,*
2. *$\mathtt{norma}(A) \equiv (x)P, \mathtt{norma}(B) \equiv (y)Q$, and for every name $z \in \mathcal{N}$*
$$(P\iota\{z/x\}, Q\iota\{z/y\}) \in \mathcal{S}$$
3. *$\mathtt{normc}(A) \equiv [x]P, \mathtt{normc}(B) \equiv [y]Q$, $x = y$, and*
$$(P, Q) \in \mathcal{S}$$
4. *$\mathtt{normc}(A) \equiv \nu x[x]P, \mathtt{normc}(B) \equiv \nu y[y]Q$, and for some $z \notin \mathtt{fn}(A, B)$*
$$(P\iota\{z/x\}, Q\iota\{z/y\}) \in \mathcal{S}$$

A binary relation $\mathcal{S}$ is a (strong) bisimulation if both $\mathcal{S}$ and its inverse are strong simulations. We say that A is strong ground bisimilar *to B if there exists a bisimulation $\mathcal{S}$ such that $(A, B) \in \mathcal{S}$. In this case we write $A \dot{\sim} B$.*

It is routine to show that $\dot{\sim}$ is an equivalence relation. However it is not preserved by substitution. As a simple counter–example

$$\bar{x}.\mathbf{0}|y.\mathbf{0} \dot{\sim} \bar{x}.y.\mathbf{0} + y.\bar{x}.\mathbf{0}$$

but obviously

$$(\bar{x}.\mathbf{0}|y.\mathbf{0})\iota\{y/x\} \not\dot{\sim} (\bar{x}.y.\mathbf{0} + y.\bar{x}.\mathbf{0})\iota\{y/x\}$$

because the process on the left has the commitment $\tau.\mathbf{0}$ while the process on the left has not. So

$$(x)(\bar{x}.\mathbf{0}|y.\mathbf{0}) \not\dot{\sim} (x)(\bar{x}.y.\mathbf{0} + y.\bar{x}.\mathbf{0})$$

Thus $\dot{\sim}$ is not a congruence.

Lemma 16. *If $A \dot{\sim} B$ and $w \notin \mathtt{fn}(A, B)$, then $A\iota\{w/z\} \dot{\sim} B\iota\{w/z\}$.*

Proof Similar to the proof in [MPW92a]. □

The following definition gives us a congruence.

Definition 17. *Two agents A, B are strongly congruent, written $A \sim B$, if $A\sigma \dot{\sim} B\sigma$ for all substitutions σ.*

Theorem 18. *For any abstraction F and any concretion C*

$$F \sim \mathtt{norma}(F) \qquad C \sim \mathtt{normc}(C)$$

Proof See [Liu94]. □

2.6 Distinctions

Now we will see that a spectrum of equivalences can be defined parameterized by *distinctions.*

Definition 19. *A distinction is a symmetric irreflexive relation between names. We shall let D range over distinctions. A substitution σ respects a distinction D, written $\sigma \models D$, if for all $(x, y) \in D$, $x\sigma \neq y\sigma$.*

By this definition, ι respects any distinction. Here we use some abbreviations introduced in [MPW92a]. We will sometimes write a set of names A for the distinction $\{(x, y) \mid x, y \in A, x \neq y\}$ which keeps all members of A distinct from each other. Also for a distinction D and a name x, we define

$$D\backslash x = D - (\{x\} \times \mathcal{N} \cup \mathcal{N} \times \{x\})$$

This removes any constraint in D upon the substitution for x. Also, for any set $A \subseteq \mathcal{N}$ of names, we define $D\lceil A = D \cap (A \times A)$, and for any substitution σ which respects D, we define $D\sigma = \{(x\sigma, y\sigma) \mid (x, y) \in D\}$.

Definition 20. *Two agents A and B are D–*bisimilar, *written $A \sim_D B$, if $A\sigma \stackrel{\cdot}{\sim} B\sigma$ for all substitutions σ respecting D.*

It is easy to see that $\sim_D$ is an equivalence relation for any D, and that $\sim_D \subseteq \sim_{D'}$ just in case $D' \subseteq D$. In this sense, ground bisimulation equivalence and bisimulation congruence are two extreme cases of D–bisimulations

$$\stackrel{\cdot}{\sim} = \sim_{\mathcal{N}} \text{ and } \sim = \sim_{\emptyset}$$

To finish this section, we prove some properties of D–bisimulation which are important later in finding an alternative characterization of it.

Lemma 21. *If $P \sim_D Q$ then $P \sim_{D\lceil \mathtt{fn}(P,Q)} Q$.*

Proof Along the lines in [MPW92a]. □

Proposition 22. *If $[x]P \sim_D [x]Q$ then $P \sim_D Q$.*

Proof See [Liu94]. □

The next two propositions show the different nature of the two binding operators (x) and νx. It is easy to see that if $(x)P \stackrel{\cdot}{\sim} (y)Q$ then for every name z, $P\iota\{z/x\} \stackrel{\cdot}{\sim} Q\iota\{z/y\}$. In terms of D–bisimulation, that is to say if $(x)P \sim_{\mathtt{fn}((x)P,(y)Q)} (y)Q$ then $P\iota\{z/x\} \sim_{\mathtt{fn}((x)P,(y)Q)} Q\iota\{z/y\}$, where z is a name not free in $(x)P$ and $(y)Q$. Note that here the distinction $\mathtt{fn}((x)P,(y)Q)$ poses no restriction on z because z is not free in $(x)P$ and $(y)Q$, and this captures " for every name $z\ldots$". For general D–bisimulation we have the following fact.

Proposition 23. *If $(x)P \sim_D (y)Q$ and $z \notin \mathtt{fn}((x)P,(y)Q)$, then*

$$P\iota\{z/x\} \sim_{D\setminus z} Q\iota\{z/y\}$$

Proof See [Liu94]. □

Intuitively, if $\nu x[x]P \sim_D \nu y[y]Q$ then what names used for x and y are not important, as long as the name is distinguished from other free names in $\nu x[x]P$ and $\nu y[y]Q$.

Proposition 24. *If $\nu x[x]P \sim_D \nu y[y]Q$ and $z \notin \mathtt{fn}(\nu x[x]P, \nu y[y]Q)$, then*

$$P\iota\{z/x\} \sim_{D\cup D'} Q\iota\{z/y\}$$

where $D' = \{z\} \times \mathtt{fn}(\nu x[x]P, \nu y[y]Q) \cup \mathtt{fn}(\nu x[x]P, \nu y[y]Q) \times \{z\}$.

Proof See [Liu94]. □

3 Symbolic D–Bisimulations

This section presents the proof technique for the bisimulation congruence. We introduce a notion of *symbolic D–bisimulation* supported by a proof technique. We then show that the symbolic D–bisimulation coincides with D–bisimulation. Thus the proof technique can be used to show D–bisimulation equivalence of processes, with bisimulation congruence as a special case. The symbolic D–bisimulation introduced here is inspired by *symbolic bisimulation* introduced in [HL92].

The operational semantics introduced in the last section treated free names as constants. This can be seen through the following example. Consider $P|Q$ when $P \succ x.F$ and $Q \succ \bar{y}.C$. If x and y are different names, then the rules of $\succ$ cannot infer any communication between the components (assuming that the components have no other actions). Thus the possibility of communication between these two components when x and y are substituted by the same name is not considered by the relation $\succ$. When names are subject to substitution, it is not sufficient to consider only the $\succ$ relation. To adjust this constant point of view of free names, we introduce *conditional commitment*. We write $P \succ_\sigma \alpha.A$ for conditional commitment which means a commitment under substitution σ. Conditional commitments are defined by the rules in Figure 3. The rules basically say that conditional commitments are caused by two complementary commitments of parallel components, and that they propagate over the constructions. In the side condition of C-Rest, x is σ clean means $\forall y \in \mathcal{N}. x = y\sigma \Leftrightarrow x = y$. This notation is taken from [Jef92].

C-Act
$$\frac{}{\alpha.A \succ_\iota \alpha.A}$$

C-Sum
$$\frac{P \succ_\sigma \alpha.A}{P + Q \succ_\sigma \alpha.A} \qquad \frac{Q \succ_\sigma \alpha.A}{P + Q \succ_\sigma \alpha.A}$$

C-Intl
$$\frac{P \succ_\sigma \alpha.A}{P|Q \succ_\sigma \alpha.(A|Q)} \qquad \frac{Q \succ_\sigma \alpha.A}{P|Q \succ_\sigma \alpha.(P|A)}$$

C-Sync
$$\frac{P \succ_\iota x.P' \quad Q \succ_\iota \bar{y}.Q'}{P|Q \succ_{\iota\{x/y\}} \tau.(P'|Q')} \qquad \frac{P \succ_\iota \bar{y}.P' \quad Q \succ_\iota x.Q'}{P|Q \succ_{\iota\{x/y\}} \tau.(P'|Q')}$$

C-Com
$$\frac{P \succ_\iota x.F \quad Q \succ_\iota \bar{y}.C}{P|Q \succ_{\iota\{x/y\}} \tau.(F \cdot C)} \qquad \frac{P \succ_\iota \bar{y}.C \quad Q \succ_\iota x.F}{P|Q \succ_{\iota\{x/y\}} \tau.(F \cdot C)}$$

C-Rest
$$\frac{P \succ_\sigma \alpha.A}{\nu x P \succ_\sigma \alpha.(\nu x A)\iota} \quad x \notin name(\alpha),\ x \text{ is } \sigma \text{ clean}$$

C-Rec
$$\frac{P \,|\, !P \succ_\sigma \alpha.A}{!P \succ_\sigma \alpha.A}$$

Fig. 3. Inference Rules for Conditional Commitments

Lemma 25. *If $P \succ_\sigma \alpha.A$ then $\sigma = \iota\{x/y\}$ for some $x, y \in \mathcal{N}$. Moreover, if $\sigma = \iota\{x/y\}$ where $x \neq y$ then $\alpha = \tau$.*

Proof Easy to check that all the rules in Figure 3 preserve this property. Notice that $\iota = \iota\{x/x\}$ for any $x \in \mathcal{N}$. □

This lemma shows checking for the side condition in rule C-Rest is not difficult at all; the relation $\succ_\sigma$ thus defined is not much more complex than $\succ$. Now we show some desired properties of this relation.

Lemma 26. *If $P \succ_\sigma \alpha.A$ then $P\sigma \succ \alpha\sigma.A\sigma$.*

Proof See [Liu94]. □

The following lemma shows that conditional commitments provide us with a means to analyze commitments of $P\sigma$.

Lemma 27. *For a process P and substitution σ, $P\sigma \succ \alpha.A$ if and only if $P \succ_\rho \beta.A'$ with $A \equiv A'\sigma$, $\alpha = \beta\sigma$, and for some ρ', $\sigma = \rho \circ \rho'$.*

Proof See [Liu94]. □

Let us now concentrate on how to characterize $P \sim_D Q$ operationally in terms of the commitments of P and Q. According to the above discussion, we have to consider all commitments of the form $P \succ_\sigma \alpha.A$ and $Q \succ_\sigma \beta.B$ where $\sigma \models D$. More specifically, suppose $P \succ_\sigma \alpha.A$ for some $\sigma \models D$ and A, according to Lemma 26 in this case $P\sigma \succ \alpha\sigma.A\sigma$. Follow the definition of bisimulation, one may want to say the following:

(1) Whenever $P \succ_\sigma \alpha.A$, then $Q\sigma \succ \alpha\sigma.B\sigma$ for some B such that $A\sigma \sim_{D\sigma} B\sigma$...

However this is too strong for D–bisimulation. Let us look at the following two processes P and Q

$$P \equiv \alpha.(x|\bar{y}) + \alpha.(x.\bar{y} + \bar{y}.x) + \alpha.(x|\bar{x})$$
$$Q \equiv \alpha.(x.\bar{y} + \bar{y}.x) + \alpha.(x|\bar{x})$$

It is easy to see that $P \sim Q$. But for $P \succ_\iota \alpha.(x|\bar{y})$ there is no Q' such that $Q \succ \alpha.Q'$ and $Q' \sim x|\bar{y}$. A closer look reveals that in this case $P \succ_\iota \alpha.(x|\bar{y})$ is actually matched by different commitments of Q according to whether x and y are the same name. Since $x|\bar{y} \sim_{\{x,y\}} x.\bar{y} + \bar{y}.x$, if $x \neq y$ then $P \succ_\iota \alpha.(x|\bar{y})$ can be matched by $Q \succ \alpha.(x.\bar{y} + \bar{y}.x)$. If $x = y$, then it can be matched by $Q \succ \alpha.(x|\bar{x})$. Thus Q can match $P \succ_\iota \alpha.(x|\bar{y})$ *indirectly* by using the fact that $x|\bar{y} \sim_{\{x,y\}} x.\bar{y} + \bar{y}.x$ and $x|\bar{x} \sim x|\bar{x}$. In the following, we will introduce a relation $\succ^D_\mathcal{S}$ to express this indirect match, where D is a (assumed) distinction and $\mathcal{S}$ includes some (presupposed, or to be established) D-bisimulation relation.

Thus in the case of P and Q here we will write $Q \succ_{\mathcal{S}}^{\emptyset} \alpha.(x|\bar{y})$, where $\mathcal{S} = \{x|\bar{y} \sim_{\{x,y\}} x.\bar{y} + \bar{y}.x, x|\bar{x} \sim x|\bar{x}\}$ and $\emptyset$ is the empty distinction. Then we give the characterization of $\sim_D$ with the help of $\succ_{\mathcal{S}}^{D}$. The relation $\succ_{\mathcal{S}}^{D}$ corresponds to the idea of "dividing value space" in symbolic bisimulation [HL92].

Definition 28. *Let $\mathcal{S}$ be a set of triples of the form (A, D, B) where A, B are agents, D is a distinction. Then $\succ_{\mathcal{S}}$ is the smallest set of triples of process, distinction, and commitment such that for $(P, D, \alpha.A) \in \succ_{\mathcal{S}}$, which we will write $P \succ_{\mathcal{S}}^{D} \alpha.A$ from now on, then P is a process, D is a distinction, and $\alpha.A$ is a commitment, and moreover, one of the following must holds:*

1. *$P \succ \alpha.B$ for some B with $(A, D, B) \in \mathcal{S}$, or*
2. *P has two free names x, y such that $(x, y) \notin D$ and $P \succ_{\mathcal{S}}^{D\cup\{x,y\}} \alpha.A$ and $P\iota\{y/x\} \succ_{\mathcal{S}}^{D\iota\{y/x\}} \alpha\iota\{y/x\}.A\iota\{y/x\}$.*

Lemma 29. *If $P \succ_{\mathcal{S}}^{D} \alpha.A$, then for every $\sigma \models D$ there exist D', B such that $P\sigma \succ \alpha\sigma.B\sigma, \sigma \models D'$ and $(A, D', B) \in \mathcal{S}$.*

Proof See [Liu94]. □

The relation $\succ_{\mathcal{S}}$ is not very easy to understand by its definition. The following theorem characterizes it in the important case when $\mathcal{S}$ is the largest distinction bisimulation.

Theorem 30. *When $\mathcal{S} = \{(A, D, B) \mid A \sim_D B\}$, the following conditions are equivalent*

1. *$P \succ_{\mathcal{S}}^{D} \alpha.A$*
2. *for all $\sigma \models D$, there exists B such that $P\sigma \succ \alpha\sigma.B$ and $B \dot{\sim} A\sigma$.*

Proof See [Liu94]. □

Now we can give the definition of symbolic D–bisimulation.

Definition 31. A symbolic simulation, $\mathcal{S}$, *is a set of triples of the form (A, D, B) where A, B are agents, D is a distinction, such that whenever $(A, D, B) \in \mathcal{S}$, one of the following must hold:*

1. *(A, B) is a pair of processes (P, Q) such that whenever $P \succ_{\sigma} \alpha.A'$ for $\sigma \models D$ then $Q\sigma \succ_{\mathcal{S}}^{D\sigma} \alpha\sigma.A'\sigma$,*
2. *$\mathtt{norma}(A) \equiv (x)P, \mathtt{norma}(B) \equiv (y)Q$, and for some $z \notin \mathtt{fn}(A, B)$*

$$(P\iota\{z/x\}, D\backslash z, Q\iota\{z/y\}) \in \mathcal{S}$$

3. *$\mathtt{normc}(A) \equiv [x]P, \mathtt{normc}(B) \equiv [y]Q, x = y$, and*

$$(P, D, Q) \in \mathcal{S}$$

4. $\mathtt{normc}(A) \equiv \nu x[x]P, \mathtt{normc}(B) \equiv \nu y[y]Q$, *and for some* $z \notin \mathtt{fn}(A, B)$

$$(P\iota\{z/x\}, D \cup \{z\} \times \mathtt{fn}(A, B) \cup \mathtt{fn}(A, B) \times \{z\}, Q\iota\{z/y\}) \in \mathcal{S}$$

A set $\mathcal{S}$ *of triples is a* symbolic bisimulation *if both* $\mathcal{S}$ *and its inverse* $\mathcal{S}^-$ *are symbolic simulations. Two agents* A, B *are said to be* symbolicly D–bisimilar *if there exists a symbolic bisimulation* $\mathcal{S}$ *such that* $(A, D, B) \in \mathcal{S}$.

In the above definition, we use a set of triples instead of a family of D–indexed sets in order to avoid dealing with set of sets. Theorem 30 suggests that $Q\sigma \succ_{\mathcal{S}}^{D\sigma} \alpha\sigma.A'\sigma$ matchs $P \succ_\sigma \alpha.A'$ in order that $P \sim_D Q$, hence clause 1. In clause 2. z should be viewed as a place holder for any name. A simpler solution would be to choose a z which does not appear free in A, B, and D. But sometimes we may have trouble in choosing such a z: consider $(x)\mathbf{0} \sim_{\mathcal{N}} (y)\mathbf{0}$, we cannot find $z \notin \mathcal{N}$. However, the set of free names of A and B is always finite and any name which appears in D but does not appear free in either A or B is immaterial (Lemma 21). With these consideration, clause 2. seems to be workable. Clause 3. is simple. Proposition 23 and Proposition 24 and the comments in the end of the last section may help to comprehend clause 2. and clause 4. in the definition.

Later we will prove that symbolic D-bisimulation coincides with D-bisimulation. The definition of symbolic D-bisimulation is based on the commitments of the processes. Thus it provides us a bisimulation like technique to prove D-bisimulation: in order to prove $P \sim_D Q$, trying to establish a symbolic D-bisimulation $\mathcal{S}$ such that $(P, D, Q) \in \mathcal{S}$. Take the following two processes as given in an earlier example,

$$P \equiv \alpha.(x|\bar{y}) + \alpha.(x.\bar{y} + \bar{y}.x) + \alpha.(x|\bar{x})$$
$$Q \equiv \alpha.(x.\bar{y} + \bar{y}.x) + \alpha.(x|\bar{x})$$

we can prove that $P \sim Q$ by verifying that the following relation $\mathcal{B}$ is a symbolic bisimulation

$$\{(P, \emptyset, Q), (x|\bar{y}, \{x, y\}, x.\bar{y}+\bar{y}.x), (\mathbf{0}|\bar{y}, \{x, y\}, \bar{y}), (x|\mathbf{0}, \{x, y\}, x), (\mathbf{0}|\mathbf{0}, \{x, y\}, \mathbf{0})\} \cup I$$

where $I = \{(A, D, A) \,|\, \text{agent } A \text{ and distinction } D\}$. In verifying that the above is indeed a symbolic bisimulation, an intersting case is to match $P \succ \alpha.(x|\bar{y})$ with $Q \succ_{\mathcal{B}}^{\emptyset} \alpha.(x|\bar{y})$ which is the consequence of $Q\iota\{y/x\} \succ_{\mathcal{B}}^{\emptyset} \alpha\iota\{y/x\}.(x|\bar{y})\iota\{y/x\}$ and $Q \succ_{\mathcal{B}}^{\{x,y\}} \alpha.(x|\bar{y})$.

In the rest of this section we will prove that the symbolic D–bisimulation indeed characterizes D–bisimulation equivalence.

Theorem 32. *If* A *and* B *are* D–*bisimilar, then they are symbolicly* D–*bisimilar.*

Proof Let

$$\mathcal{S} = \{(A, D, B) \mid A \sim_D B\}$$

Because $\sim_D$ is symmetric, in order to show $\mathcal{S}$ is a symbolic bisimulation it is sufficient to show that $\mathcal{S}$ is a symbolic simulation. Take $(A, D, B) \in \mathcal{S}$, that is to say $A \sim_D B$. Because $\iota \models D$, so $A \dot{\sim} B$. Thus there are the following four cases.

First consider the case that (A, B) is a pair of processes (P, Q). We will show that whenever $P \succ_\sigma \alpha.A'$ for $\sigma \models D$ then $Q\sigma \succ_{\mathcal{S}}^{D\sigma} \alpha\sigma.A'\sigma$. For that, suppose $P \succ_\sigma \alpha.A'$ and $\sigma \models D$, by Theorem 30, we show that for all $\rho \models D\sigma$ there exists B such that $(Q\sigma)\rho \succ (\alpha\sigma)\rho.B$ and $B \dot{\sim} (A'\sigma)\rho$. This is guaranteed by the following:

1. $\rho \models D\sigma$ implies $\sigma \circ \rho \models D$, and thus
2. $P\sigma \circ \rho \dot{\sim} Q\sigma \circ \rho$, and moreover
3. $P \succ_\sigma \alpha.A'$ implies $P\sigma \succ \alpha\sigma.A'\sigma$ by Lemma 26, which implies $P\sigma\rho \succ \alpha\sigma\rho.A'\sigma\rho$ by Lemma 14.

Now consider the case $\mathtt{norma}(A) \equiv (x)P, \mathtt{norma}(B) \equiv (y)Q$. We will show that in this case there exists $z \notin \mathtt{fn}(A, B)$ such that

$$(P\iota\{z/x\}, D\backslash z, Q\iota\{z/y\}) \in \mathcal{S}$$

By Theorem 18 $A \sim_D B$ implies $(x)P \sim_D (y)Q$, thus by proposition 23, $P\iota\{z/x\} \sim_{D\backslash z} Q\iota\{z/y\}$ for any $z \notin \mathtt{fn}(A, B)$. Thus take any $z \notin \mathtt{fn}(A, B)$ (such z certainly does exist) we have $(P\iota\{z/x\}, D\backslash z, Q\iota\{z/y\}) \in \mathcal{S}$.

Next for the case $\mathtt{normc}(A) \equiv [x]P, \mathtt{normc}(B) \equiv [x]Q$, we will show

$$(P, D, Q) \in \mathcal{S}$$

Again by Theorem 18 $[x]P \sim_D [x]Q$. Thus the above follows directly from proposition 22.

Now consider the case $\mathtt{normc}(A) \equiv \nu x[x]P, \mathtt{normc}(B) \equiv \nu y[y]Q$. We will show that there exists $z \notin \mathtt{fn}(A, B)$ such that

$$(P\iota\{z/x\}, D \cup D', Q\iota\{z/y\}) \in \mathcal{S}$$

where $D' = \{z\} \times \mathtt{fn}(A, B) \cup \mathtt{fn}(A, B) \times \{z\}$. Because in this case $\nu x[x]P \sim_D \nu y[y]Q$, and by proposition 24 $P\iota\{z/x\} \sim_{D \cup D'} Q\iota\{z/y\}$ for any $z \notin \mathtt{fn}(A, B)$. Thus such z can be found. □

Theorem 33. *If A and B are symbolicly D–bisimilar, then they are D–bisimilar.*

Proof Suppose $\mathcal{S}$ is a symbolic bisimulation. We will show that

$$\mathcal{B} = \{(A\sigma, B\sigma) \mid (A, D, B) \in \mathcal{S}, \sigma \models D\}$$

is a simulation. It is exactly the same to show that $\mathcal{B}^-$ is also a simulation. So it follows that $\mathcal{B}$ is a bisimulation.

Suppose $(A\sigma, B\sigma) \in \mathcal{B}$ with D as witness, i.e. $(A, D, B) \in \mathcal{S}$ and $\sigma \models D$. We have to cover the following cases.

If (A, B) is a pair of processes (P, Q), then $(A\sigma, B\sigma)$ is a pair of processes of the form $(P\sigma, Q\sigma)$. Suppose $P\sigma \succ \alpha.A'$, by lemma 27 $\sigma = \rho \circ \rho'$ such that $P \succ_\rho \beta.A''$ for some ρ, β, A'' with $\alpha = \beta\sigma$ and $A' \equiv A''\sigma$. Because $(P, D, Q) \in \mathcal{S}$, to match $P \succ_\rho \beta.A''$, by the definition of $\succ_\rho$, Q must satisfy $Q\rho \succ_{\mathcal{S}}^{D\rho} \beta\rho.A''\rho$.

Because $\rho \circ \rho' = \sigma \models D$, it is not difficult to see that $\rho' \models D\rho$. Then by Lemma 29, there exist D', B'' such that $Q\rho \circ \rho' \succ \beta\rho \circ \rho'.B''\rho', \rho' \models D'$ and $(A''\rho, D', B'') \in \mathcal{S}$. So we find $Q\sigma \succ \alpha.B''\rho'$ with $(A''\rho \circ \rho', B''\rho') \in \mathcal{B}$.

If $\mathtt{norma}(A) \equiv (x)P, \mathtt{norma}(B) \equiv (y)Q$, then $\mathtt{norma}(A\sigma) \equiv (u)P\sigma\{u/x\}$ and $\mathtt{norma}(B\sigma) \equiv (v)Q\sigma\{v/y\}$ by Lemma 10 and the definition of substitution, where $u = \mathtt{fresh}(\{z\sigma \mid z \in \mathtt{fn}(P) - \{x\}\})$ and $v = \mathtt{fresh}(\{z\sigma \mid z \in \mathtt{fn}(Q) - \{y\}\})$. In this case we have to show that for any name $w \in \mathcal{N}$

$$((P\sigma\{u/x\})\iota\{w/u\}, (Q\sigma\{v/y\})\iota\{w/v\}) \in \mathcal{B}$$

Now because $(A, D, B) \in \mathcal{S}$ and $\mathcal{S}$ is a symbolic bisimulation, so

$$(P\iota\{z/x\}, D\backslash z, Q\iota\{z/y\}) \in \mathcal{S}$$

for some $z \notin \mathtt{fn}(A, B)$. For $\sigma \models D$, it must be the case that $\sigma\{w/z\} \models D\backslash z$. Thus $((P\iota\{z/x\})\sigma\{w/z\}, (Q\iota\{z/y\})\sigma\{w/z\}) \in \mathcal{B}$.

If $\mathtt{normc}(A) \equiv [x]P, \mathtt{normc}(B) \equiv [x]Q$, then by Lemma 10 $\mathtt{normc}(A\sigma) \equiv [x\sigma]P\sigma$ and $\mathtt{norma}(B\sigma) \equiv [x\sigma]Q\sigma$. Because $(A, D, B) \in \mathcal{S}$, thus $(P, D, Q) \in \mathcal{S}$. In this case obviously $(P\sigma, Q\sigma) \in \mathcal{B}$.

If $\mathtt{normc}(A) \equiv \nu x[x]P, \mathtt{normc}(B) \equiv \nu y[y]Q$, then $\mathtt{normc}(A\sigma) \equiv \nu u[u]P\sigma\{u/x\}$ and $\mathtt{normc}(B\sigma) \equiv \nu v[v]Q\sigma\{v/y\}$ by Lemma 10 and the definition of substitution, where $u = \mathtt{fresh}(\{z\sigma \mid z \in \mathtt{fn}(P) - \{x\}\})$ and $v = \mathtt{fresh}(\{z\sigma \mid z \in \mathtt{fn}(Q) - \{y\}\})$. In this case we have to show that for some $w \notin \mathtt{fn}(A, B)$

$$((P\sigma\{u/x\})\iota\{w/u\}, (Q\sigma\{v/y\})\iota\{w/v\}) \in \mathcal{B}$$

Because $(A, D, B) \in \mathcal{S}$, it follows that

$$(P\iota\{z/x\}, D \cup \{z\} \times \mathtt{fn}(A, B) \cup \mathtt{fn}(A, B) \times \{z\}, Q\iota\{z/y\}) \in \mathcal{S}$$

by the definition of symbolic D–bisimulation. Now let $w \notin \{x\sigma \mid x \in \mathtt{fn}(A, B)\}$, then it is clear that $\sigma\{w/z\} \models D \cup \{z\} \times \mathtt{fn}(A, B) \cup \mathtt{fn}(A, B) \times \{z\}$. Thus $((P\iota\{z/x\})\sigma\{w/z\}, (Q\iota\{z/y\})\sigma\{w/z\}) \in \mathcal{S}$. □

4 Conclusion and Related Work

This paper presents a new characterization of the bisimulation congruence and D–bisimulation equivalences of the π–calculus. The new characterization supports a bisimulation like proof technique which avoids explicit case analysis, thus providing a new way of proving bisimulation congruence.

The proof technique resembles the symbolic bisimulation for value passing processes introduced by Hennessy and Lin [HL92]. In their work, symbolic bisimulation of value passing processes is defined in terms of *symbolic transition* of the form $T \xrightarrow{b,a} T'$, where T, T' are process terms (may have free variables), a is some action, b is a boolean expression. This can be read as "under condition b, T may perform a and ivolve into T'". Then in order to match a symbolic transition, a finite collection of boolean expression B is to be found such that $\vee B = b$

for some boolean b. However, there is not an effective method in general to find such B. In this paper, due to the simplicity of dealing with names which is a very simple form of value, similar thing is achieved by introducing the relation $\succ_S^D$ which is constructively defined.

In [Ama92], Amadio introduced *uniform strong bisimulation* for π-calculus. The definition of uniform strong bisimulation is very similar to the definition of symbolic D-bisimulation in this paper without the more involved part of $\succ_S^D$. The result is that the resulting equivalence get is strictly stronger than the bisimulation congruence.

In [San93], Sangiorgi introduced the notion of *open bisimulation*. The equivalence resulting from open bisimulation is a congruence for π-calculus, and it is strictly stronger than the bisimulation congruence in this paper. He then gave an effective characterization for open bisimulation. His characterization is very similar to the characterization of D-bisimulation by symbolic D-bisimulation, except that the complication of $\succ_S^D$ is not necessary for open bisimulation.

A different approach to prove bisimulation congruence is taken in [PS93], where an axiom system is presented for π–calculus processes. Unlike our approach where we work with all D–bisimulation equivalences at the same time, they stay within the bisimulation congruence by extending the conditional expression with negation and disjunction. This allows any general condition like *true* to be split into a logically equivalent disjunctive formula ψ, which achieves the effect similar to $\succ_S^D$.

The work carried out in the paper focuses on the the congruence induced by the *late* version of bisimulation equivalence. It would be interesting to see whether a similar characterization can be found for the early version. This is not obvious since in the symbolic definition is very close to that of late bisimulation. Also we leave out the match construction $[x = y]P$ of the π–calculus of [MPW92a]. The match construction does not give the π–calculus extra power. The theory developed here can cope with inclusion of this construction by introducing compound boolean expression in the conditional commitment. These could be a topic for further research.

Acknowledgements The author would like to thank Matthew Hennessy for reading a draft of the paper and for many insiteful comments and suggestions. The author would also like to thank Alan Jeffrey and Huimin Lin for inspiring discussions on the topic of the paper.

References

[Ama92] R. Amadio. A uniform presentation of chocs and π–calculus. Technical Report Rapport de recherche 1726, INRIA-Lorraine, Nancy, 1992.

[HL92] M. Hennessy and H. Lin. Symbolic bisimulation. Technical Report Technical Report 1/92, School of Congnitive and Computing Sciences, University of Sussex, 1992.

[Jef92] A. Jeffrey. Notes on a trace semantics for the π–calculus. 1992.

[Liu94] Xinxin Liu. Characterizing bisimulation congruence in the π–calculus. Technical Report 2/1994, University of Sussex, Computer Science, 1994.

[Mil89] R. Milner. *Communication and Concurrency.* Prentice–Hall, 1989.

[Mil91] R. Milner. The polyadic π–calculus: a tutorial. *The Proceedings of the International Summer School on Logic and Algebra of Specification*, 1991.

[MPW92a] R. Milner, J. Parrow, and D. Walker. A calculus of mobile processes, (parts i and ii). *Information and Computation*, 100, 1992.

[MPW92b] R. Milner, J. Parrow, and D. Walker. Modal logics for mobile processes. *Theoretical Computer Science*, 1992. to appear.

[Par81] D. Park. Concurrency and automata on infinite sequences. *Lecture Notes In Computer Science, Springer Verlag*, 104, 1981. Proceedings of 5th GI Conference.

[PS93] J. Parrow and Davide Sangiorgi. Algebraic theories for value–passing calculi. Technical report, Department of Computer Science, University of Edinburgh, 1993. Forthcoming.

[San93] D. Sangiorgi. A theory of bisimulation for π–calculus. Technical report, University of Edinburgh, 1993. Forthcoming.

[Sto88] Allen Stoughton. Substitution revisited. *Theoretical Computer Science*, 59:317–325, 1988.

The Limit View of Infinite Computations*

Nils Klarlund**

BRICS, Department of Computer Science,
University of Aarhus
Ny Munkegade, DK-8000 Århus, Denmark
klarlund@daimi.aau.dk

Abstract. We show how to view computations involving very general liveness properties as limits of finite approximations. This computational model does not require introduction of infinite nondeterminism as with most traditional approaches. Our results allow us directly to relate finite computations in order to infer properties about infinite computations. Thus we are able to provide a mathematical understanding of what simulations and bisimulations are when liveness is involved.
In addition, we establish links between verification theory and classical results in descriptive set theory. Our result on simulations is the essential contents of the Kleene-Suslin Theorem, and our result on bisimulation expresses Martin's Theorem about the determinacy of Borel games.

1 Introduction

It is generally believed that to model general liveness properties of concurrent systems, such as those expressed by infinitary temporal logics, we must use machines with infinite (countable) nondeterminism. Such models arise for example in program verification involving fairness, where transformations of programs induce nondeterminism.

But it is disturbing that countable nondeterminism, for which no physical implementation seems to exist, is introduced in our model of computation. In contrast, any conventional Turing machine can be implemented and we can observe its finite runs, although not all of them, of course, due to physical constraints. But how would a physical device carry out a nondeterministic choice among uncountably many possibilities at each computation step? Instead, it seems more reasonable to let the machine compute finite information about progress that somehow gives rise to an acceptance condition on infinite computations.

Another foundational problem we would like to address is the lack of general notions of simulation and bisimulation for programs that incorporate liveness

* This article is a revised and extended version of an earlier technical report ("Convergence Measures," TR90-1106, Cornell University), which was extracted from the author's Ph.D. thesis. Due to space limitations, all proofs have been omitted in this article.

** Partially supported by an Alice & Richard Netter Scholarship of the Thanks to Scandinavia Foundation, Inc. and NSF grant CCR 88-06979.

conditions. Since simulations are local equivalences, we also here need a better understanding of progress of finite computations towards defining infinite ones.

In this paper, we introduce a *limit concept* that allows deterministic machines to calculate *progress approximations* so that analytic or coanalytic sets[1] of computations are defined. Thus nondeterminism is not inherent to models of computations involving even very general liveness conditions, even those that are expressed by infinitary temporal logics.

Our concept is a natural generalization of Büchi or Rabin conditions, which define only sets very low in the Borel[2] hierarchy of properties. Our progress approximations generalize Büchi automata, where states are designated as accepting or non-accepting and the limit condition is that infinitely many accepting states are encountered.

Our main goal is to show that reasoning about the infinite behavior of our machines can be carried out directly in terms of progress approximations without transformations. Specifically, we turn our attention to two fundamental problems for programs with liveness conditions:

- finding a progress concept for showing that one program implements another program so that each step contributing to a live computation of the first program is mapped to a corresponding step of the second program; and
- finding a progress concept for showing that two programs can simulate each other so that each step of one corresponds to a step of the other equivalent with respect to making or not making progress towards a live computation.

Our results for these two problems are essentially the contents of the two perhaps most celebrated results of descriptive set theory: the Kleene-Suslin Theorem and Martin's Theorem about the determinacy of Borel games, respectively.

Previous Work

For certain kinds of specifications, such as those involving bounded nondeterminism or fairness, dozens of verification methods have been suggested; see [1, 2, 3, 4, 6, 7, 16, 17, 18, 24]. Yet the general problem has, to the author's knowledge, been addressed only in relatively few articles [5, 9, 28]. The

---

[1] The notion of *analytic* set can be defined in many ways. For example, M is analytic if there is a nondeterministic automaton (with a countable state space) such that M is the set of infinite sequences allowing an infinite run, see [28]. The class of analytic sets is denoted $\mathbf{\Sigma}^1_1$. The dual of an analytic set is said to be *coanalytic* or $\mathbf{\Pi}^1_1$.

[2] The *Borel hierarchy* is the least class of sets containing the class $\mathbf{\Sigma}^0_1$ of open sets and closed under countable intersection and union. For example, the Borel hierarchy contains the class $\mathbf{\Pi}^0_2$ of sets that are countable intersections of open sets. Every property defined by a Büchi automaton, including usual fairness conditions, is a finite Boolean combination of $\mathbf{\Pi}^0_2$ sets (and so is at the third level of the Borel hierarchy), see [27]. Every Borel set is analytic and coanalytic. Vice versa, the Kleene-Suslin Theorem states that any set that is both analytic and coanalytic is also Borel.

earlier proposals solve the verification problem by transformations that introduce infinite nondeterminism.

The most general such approach is that of Vardi [28]. Vardi uses a computational model corresponding to nondeterministic automata with infinite conjunctive branching for defining specifications. The apparent physical unrealizability of this concept motivated the limit view given in the present paper. Vardi's method can easily be reformulated as progress measures [29], i.e. as mappings from the states of the implementation. These progress measures, however, do not imply the ones presented here, since we use a different computational model. Together with the Boundedness Theorem for $\mathbf{\Pi}_1^1$ sets, Vardi's results amount to the Kleene-Suslin Theorem, although this was not noted in [28].

A few methods have appeared that more directly quantify progress [3, 13, 11, 22], but these methods only apply to sets at low levels of the Borel hierarchy, namely finite Boolean combinations of $\mathbf{\Pi}_2^0$ sets.

In [10], a simple progress measure based on a condition, called the *Liminf condition*, was proposed. This condition, however, can be used only to reason about specifications that are $\mathbf{\Sigma}_3^0$, i.e. at the third level of the Borel hierarchy. Other approaches to viewing computations as limits are based on metrics of mathematical analysis [21]. These approaches also deal with sets at the third level.

Recursion-theoretic aspects of relating automata with different kinds of acceptance conditions have been studied in [26].

In this paper we report on the most general measure proposed in [15]. In addition, we introduce here the new concept of progress bisimulation.

2 Overview

Our results are based on an abstract, graph-theoretic formulation of the verification problem. We represent the transitions of a program as a directed, countable graph $G = (V, E)$, where vertices V and edges E correspond to program states and transitions. Then the infinite paths in G correspond to all possible infinite computations.

To define live computations, we introduce *progress approximations* on V that assign a finite amount of information to each vertex. In turns out that if we let this information be a labeled tree, then very general properties can be expressed. Thus a progress approximation τ associates a finite tree $\tau(v)$ to each vertex v. A computation $v_0 v_1 \cdots$ defines an infinite sequence $\tau(v_0), \tau(v_1), \ldots$ of progress approximations and a *limit tree* $\lim \tau(v_i)$ that consists of the nodes that from a point on occur in every progress approximation. The computation is *live* if the limit tree has only finite paths, i.e. if it is *well-founded* (it may still be infinite). We call this condition the *well-foundedness condition* of τ and abbreviate it WF τ.

The WF condition is extraordinarily powerful. We prove that the sets specified by WF conditions constitute the class $\mathbf{\Pi}_1^1$ of coanalytic sets. This class includes all Borel sets as we show using progress approximations. In fact, we show that automata combined with temporal logics with infinite conjunctions and disjunctions express the class of Borel sets and can be coded as WF conditions.

The dual of the WF condition is the condition that requires the limit tree to contain some infinite path. This condition is called the *non-well-foundedness condition* and denoted ¬WF. The sets specified by ¬WF conditions constitute the class $\mathbf{\Sigma}^1_1$ of analytic sets.

In order to relate two programs with liveness conditions, we first study a simpler problem. We may view WF τ as a *specification* that every computation of G is live. Thus we say that G *satisfies* WF τ if every infinite path $v_0 v_1 \cdots$ of G satisfies WF τ. Note that this property seems to call for considering uncountably many infinite computations. Our first result is to show that G satisfies WF τ can be established by local reasoning about vertices and edges.

2.1 Progress Measures

For proving the property of program termination, we usually resort to mapping program states to some values, and we then verify that the value decreases with every transition. These values quantify progress toward the property of termination. Similarly for a property specified by a WF condition, we seek a relation on some set of progress values that the states with their progress approximations can be mapped to. The relation must ensure that the limit tree is well-founded.

To do this, we use tree embeddings as the set of progress values. We fix a well-founded tree T and a mapping μ such that $\mu(v)$ specifies an embedding of $\tau(v)$ in T. We then define the WF *progress relation* $\trianglerighteq_{\mathrm{WF}}$ on tree embeddings. Intuitively, it states that embedded nodes move forward in T according to a predefined ordering. If in addition μ satisfies the verification condition

(VC) for any transition from v to v', it is the case that $\mu(v) \trianglerighteq_{\mathrm{WF}} \mu(v')$,

then μ is a WF *progress measure*. Our first result is:

Graph Result

All infinite paths in G satisfy WF τ if and only if there is a progress measure μ for G and τ.

Thus the question of verifying that *all* infinite computations satisfy the specification is equivalent to finding *some* mapping that is a WF progress measure. In other words, the existence of a progress measure means that each step of a program contributes in a precise mathematical sense to bringing the computation closer to the specification.

2.2 Progress Simulations

To formulate our results on progress simulations, we turn to a generally accepted model of infinite computations. There is an alphabet Σ of letters representing *actions*, and a *program* $\mathcal{P}$ is a nondeterministic transition system or automaton over Σ. The *computations* or runs over an infinite word $a_0 a_1 \cdots$ are the sequences of states, beginning with an initial state, that may occur when the word is processed according to the transition relation. A word is *recognized* by $\mathcal{P}$ if it allows a run. The set of words recognized by $\mathcal{P}$ is called the *language* of $\mathcal{P}$ and denoted $L(\mathcal{P})$. (Note that in this model we have abstracted away the details of the machine structure and technical complications such as stuttering.)

Thanks to the countable nondeterminism present in such programs, they define the class of $\mathbf{\Sigma^1_1}$ of analytic sets[3]. Now given two programs $\mathcal{P}$ and $\mathcal{Q}$, called the *implementation* and *specification*, we say that $\mathcal{P}$ *implements* $\mathcal{Q}$ if every word recognized by $\mathcal{P}$ is also recognized by $\mathcal{Q}$, i.e. if $L(\mathcal{P}) \subseteq L(\mathcal{Q})$. The *verification problem* is to establish $L(\mathcal{P}) \subseteq L(\mathcal{Q})$ by relating the states of the programs without reasoning directly about infinite computations.

It is well-known that if we can find a *simulation*, also known as a homomorphism or refinement map, from the reachable states of $\mathcal{P}$ to the states of $\mathcal{Q}$, then $L(\mathcal{P}) \subseteq L(\mathcal{Q})$. (This method is not complete, however, since $L(\mathcal{P}) \subseteq L(\mathcal{Q})$ might hold while no simulation exists [1, 14, 24].)

The preceding discussion has ignored liveness, including common concepts such as starvation and fairness. So assume that $\mathcal{P}$ also defines a set $Live_{\mathcal{P}}$ of state sequences said to be *live*. For example, the set $Live_{\mathcal{P}}$ may be specified by a formula in temporal logic or by a WF condition. The *live language* $L^\circ(\mathcal{P})$ of $\mathcal{P}$ is the set of words that allow a live computation. We say that $\mathcal{P}$ *satisfies* $\mathcal{Q}$ if the words allowing a live computation of $\mathcal{P}$ also allow a live computation of $\mathcal{Q}$, i.e. if $L^\circ(\mathcal{P}) \subseteq L^\circ(\mathcal{Q})$. The verification problem is now to show that $\mathcal{P}$ satisfies $\mathcal{Q}$ without considering infinite computations.

To simplify matters, we assume that a simulation already exists from $\mathcal{P}$ to $\mathcal{Q}$ and that the set $Live_{\mathcal{Q}}$ is expressed as a WF condition of a progress approximation $\tau_{\mathcal{Q}}$ on $\mathcal{Q}$'s state space. The set $Live_{\mathcal{P}}$ cannot be expressed as a WF condition if the verification problem is to be reduced to only a well-foundedness problem [25]. Thus we instead specify $Live_{\mathcal{P}}$ by a $\neg$WF condition of a progress approximation $\tau_{\mathcal{P}}$ on $\mathcal{P}$'s state space.

We show that there is an operation $merge^{\vee}$ that merge progress approximations so as to express the condition $Live_{\mathcal{P}} \Rightarrow Live_{\mathcal{Q}}$, i.e. $\neg$WF $\tau_{\mathcal{P}} \Rightarrow$ WF $\tau_{\mathcal{Q}}$ or, equivalently, WF $\tau_{\mathcal{P}} \vee$ WF $\tau_{\mathcal{Q}}$. Thus we formulate a *progress simulation* from $\mathcal{P}$ to $\mathcal{Q}$ as a simulation h together with a progress measure for the progress approximation $merge^{\vee}(\tau_P(p), \tau_S(h(p)))$, which is defined on $\mathcal{P}$'s reachable states.

We use the Graph Result to derive

[3] If in addition the program $\mathcal{P}$ can be *effectively* or *recursively represented* (that is, the transition relation can calculated by a Turing machine, which on input (s, a, s') halts with the answer to whether (s, a, s') is in the transition relation), then the language recognized is said to be *analytical*. The class of such languages is denoted Σ^1_1. In general, the effective class corresponding to a class denoted by a boldface letter is denoted by the lightface letter.

General Progress Simulation Theorem

> If there is a simulation from $\mathcal{P}$ to $\mathcal{Q}$, then
> $\mathcal{P}$ satisfies $\mathcal{Q}$
> if and only if
> there is a progress simulation from $\mathcal{P}$ to $\mathcal{Q}$.

The General Progress Simulation Theorem in particular solves the verification problem for programs and specifications that are expressed using formulas in infinitary temporal logic (under the assumption that a simulation exists).

The theorem has an effective version, which we call the *Finite Argument Theorem*. It shows that there is a uniform way of obtaining a progress simulation. Thus there is an algorithm that calculates a Turing machine for calculating a progress simulation given as input Turing machines defining $\mathcal{P}$, $\mathcal{Q}$, and a simulation h with $L^\circ(P) \subseteq L^\circ(S)$. This is not a decidability result, but an explicit reduction of the Π^1_1-complete problem of establishing $L^\circ(P) \subseteq L^\circ(S)$ to the classic Π^1_1-complete problem of whether a recursive tree is well-founded.

There is a strong connection to descriptive set theory. In fact, we show that the Finite Argument Theorem expresses the Kleene-Suslin Theorem as a statement about the feasibility of program verification.

2.3 Progress Bisimulations

Consider a program $\mathcal{P}$ with state space P and transition relation $\rightarrow_{\mathcal{P}}$ and a program $\mathcal{Q}$ with state space Q and transition relation $\rightarrow_{\mathcal{Q}}$.

The notion of bisimulation stipulates that the programs are equivalent if there is a relation $R \subseteq P \times Q$ containing the pair of initial states such that:

- if $R(p,q)$ and $p \xrightarrow{a}_{\mathcal{P}} p'$, then there is q' such that $q \xrightarrow{a}_{\mathcal{Q}} q'$ and $R(p',q')$, and
- vice versa, if $R(p,q)$ and $q \xrightarrow{a}_{\mathcal{Q}} q'$, then there is p' such that $p \xrightarrow{a}_{\mathcal{Q}} p'$ and $R(p',q')$.

This definition is central to the algebraic treatment of concurrency. The essential result is that the existence of the bisimulation relation is equivalent to the impossibility of observing a difference in behavior of the two systems with respect to ability of carrying out actions.

Assuming now that $\mathcal{P}$ and $\mathcal{Q}$ are bisimilar in this traditional sense, can we then compare them also regarding liveness? That is, we would like to relate program states also with respect to how close they are to satisfying the liveness conditions so as to formalize the intuition: for any transition of one program there is a transition for the other program which is equivalent with respect to progress or non-progress towards the liveness condition.

To get an understanding of what observing liveness means, we formulate the process as an infinite game between an *observer* and a *responder*. The game is the same as the one that characterizes bisimilarity, although the winning conditions are different: bisimilar programs $\mathcal{P}$ and $\mathcal{Q}$ are *live equivalent* if no observer can devise bisimilar computations of $\mathcal{P}$ and $\mathcal{Q}$ so that one is live and the other is not.

More precisely, the observer is allowed to pick actions and transitions according to the following rules in order to produce corresponding computations.

First, the observer chooses an action and a transition on this action for one of the programs from its initial state. Then the responder lets the other program make a corresponding transition on the same action from its initial state. The new pair of states must belong to the bisimulation relation (the responder can always find a new state by definition of bisimulation relation).

Next, the observer chooses a second action and a transition for one of the programs. This transition is again matched by the responder who lets the other program make a corresponding step.

This process continues *ad infinitum* and produces an infinite word and computations of $\mathcal{P}$ and $\mathcal{Q}$ over this word. If it is not the case that some observer can choose actions and transitions so that however the responder matches the observer's moves, a live and a non-live computation are produced, then $\mathcal{P}$ and $\mathcal{Q}$ are said to be *live equivalent*.

The way an observer chooses actions and transitions is called a *testing strategy*. Generally, a strategy is a function of all previous choices made by the other player. In case a choice is solely dependent on a current pair of states, the strategy is said to be *memoryless*. Similarly, the responder's answers are described by a *response strategy*, which is also a function of the previous choices. The response strategy is memoryless if it is dependent only of the current pair of states and the name and action of the process picked by the observer.

For usual bisimulation, it can be shown for both players that having a winning strategy is equivalent to having a winning memoryless strategy. Also, a bisimulation relation encodes a class of memoryless response strategies.

Unfortunately, the two programs below show informally that even for simple liveness conditions, it may happen that neither player has a winning memoryless strategy.

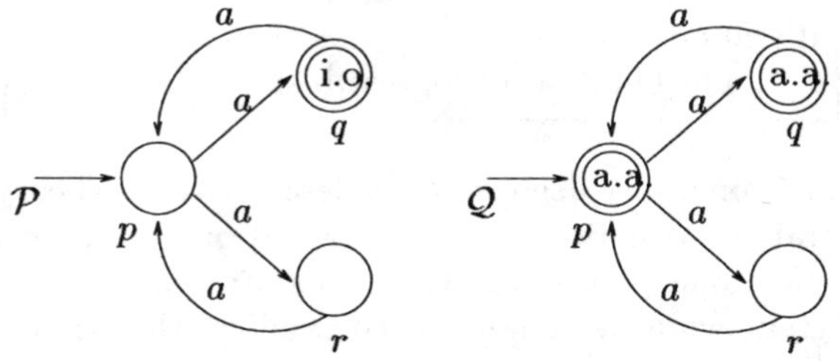

Here $\mathcal{P}$ and $\mathcal{Q}$ are the same program over a one letter alphabet except for the liveness condition: the program $\mathcal{P}$ accepts if the Büchi condition $\{q\}$ is satisfied, i.e. if the state q occurs infinitely often, and the program $\mathcal{Q}$ accepts if the states p and q occur almost always, i.e. if from some point on the state r is not encountered. It can be seen that neither the observer nor the responder has a winning memoryless strategy. In fact, the observer does have a winning strategy, namely "at p, pick the choice (q or r) that is the opposite of what the responder last did," but this is not a memoryless strategy.[4] Thus $\mathcal{P}$ and $\mathcal{Q}$ are not live equivalent.

For general systems that are live equivalent, we shall show that a natural notion of progress bisimilarity can be formalized for their finite computations if the liveness conditions are Borel. If finite computations u and v of $\mathcal{P}$ and $\mathcal{Q}$ are progress bisimilar, we must express by a progress value ρ how close they are to being either both live or both non-live. Since we assumed that $Live_P$ is Borel, it is both analytic and coanalytic. Thus there is a pair $\tau_P = (\tau'_P, \tau''_P)$ of progress approximations such that $Live_P$ is the set of infinite state sequences that satisfy WF τ'_P and also the set of sequences that satisfy $\neg$WF τ''_P. For notational simplicity, we assume that these approximations are defined on finite computations. We then define an operation $merge^{\Leftrightarrow}$ on progress approximations such that $merge^{\Leftrightarrow}(\tau_P, \tau_Q)$ specifies the joint state sequences that are both live or both non-live.

A progress bisimulation $R^*(u, v, \rho)$ is now a relation that for some fixed well-founded T relates a finite computation u of $\mathcal{P}$, a finite computation v of $\mathcal{Q}$, and an embedding ρ of $merge^{\Leftrightarrow}(\tau_P(u), \tau_Q(v))$ in T such that:

- if $R^*(u, v, \rho)$ and $u \rightarrow_P u'$, then there is v' and ρ' such that $v \rightarrow_Q v'$, $R^*(u', v', \rho')$, and $\rho \trianglerighteq_{\mathrm{WF}} \rho'$, and
- vice versa, if $R^*(u, v, \rho)$ and $v \rightarrow_Q v'$, then there is u' and ρ' such that $u \rightarrow_Q u'$, $R^*(u', v', \rho')$, and $\rho \trianglerighteq_{\mathrm{WF}} \rho'$.

Our second main result is :

General Progress Bisimulation Theorem

If Borel programs $\mathcal{P}$ and $\mathcal{Q}$ are bisimilar, then
  $\mathcal{P}$ and $\mathcal{Q}$ are live equivalent
if and only if
  $\mathcal{P}$ and $\mathcal{Q}$ allow a progress bisimulation.

This result follows from a very deep result in descriptive set theory by Martin [19] that all infinite games with Borel winning conditions are determined, i.e. it is always the case that one player has a winning strategy. Since determinacy of games with arbitrary winning conditions contradicts the Axiom of Choice [20], the General Progress Bisimulation Theory is hard to generalize. In fact, the study of the Determinacy Axiom is an important part of mathematical logic.

[4] Note however that only bounded memory about the past is necessary to specify the observer's moves. This is a general phenomenon: as shown in [8], games based on Boolean combinations of Büchi conditions have bounded-memory strategies, also known as forgetful strategies. For Rabin conditions, which are special disjunctive normal forms, memoryless strategies do exist [12].

3 Definitions

Programs and Simulations Assume a finite or countable alphabet Σ of *actions*. A program $\mathcal{P} = (P, \rightarrow, p^0, Live)$ over Σ consists of a *state space* P, a *transition relation* $\rightarrow \subseteq P \times \Sigma \times P$, an *initial state* p^0, and a liveness specification *Live*, which specifies a set of infinite state sequences. The program $\mathcal{P}$ is *deterministic* if for all p and a there is at most one p' such that $p \xrightarrow{a} p'$. A *computation* over an infinite word $a_0 a_1 \cdots$ is an infinite state sequence $p_0 p_1 \cdots$ such that $p_0 = p^0$ and $p_i \xrightarrow{a} p_{i+1}$, for all i. A computation is *live* if it satisfies *Live*. A *finite* computation $u \in P^*$ is a prefix of some infinite computation. The transition relation is extended to finite computations in the natural way: $u \xrightarrow{a} v$ if for some $\tilde{u}$, p, and p', $u = \tilde{u} \cdot p$, $v = u \cdot p'$, and $p \xrightarrow{a} p'$. The set of all words allowing some computation is denoted $L(\mathcal{P})$ and is called the *language* of $\mathcal{P}$. The subset of words in $L(\mathcal{P})$ that allow a live computation is denoted $L^{\circ}(\mathcal{P})$ and called the *live language* of $\mathcal{P}$.

A *simulation* $h : \mathcal{P} \hookrightarrow \mathcal{Q}$ is a partial function that maps the initial state of $\mathcal{P}$ to that of $\mathcal{Q}$ and respects the transition relation:

- $h(p^0) = s^0$, and
- $p \in \mathrm{dom}(h)$ and $p \xrightarrow{a}_{\mathcal{P}} p'$ implies $p' \in \mathrm{dom}(h)$ and $s \xrightarrow{a}_{\mathcal{Q}} s'$.

Note that if $\mathcal{P}$ and $\mathcal{Q}$ are deterministic with $L(\mathcal{P}) \subseteq L(\mathcal{Q})$, then a progress simulation exists (provided that $\mathcal{P}$ has no reachable state that has no successor). Also, h can be uniformly computed from effective representations of $\mathcal{P}$ and $\mathcal{Q}$.

Pointer Trees A *pointer tree* (or simply *tree*) T is a prefix-closed countable subset of ω^*, where ω is the set of natural numbers $0, 1, \ldots$ Each sequence $t = t^1 \cdots t^\ell$ in T represents a *node*, which has *children* $t \cdot d \in T$. Here $d \in \omega$ is the *pointer* to $t \cdot d$ from t. If t' is a prefix of $t \in T$, then t' is called an *ancestor* of t. We visualize pointer trees as growing upwards as in

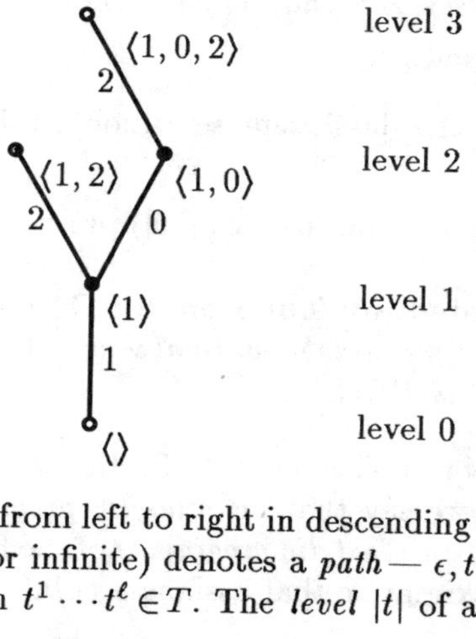

where children are depicted from left to right in descending order. Any sequence of pointers $t^1, t^2, \ldots$ (finite or infinite) denotes a *path*— $\epsilon, t^1, t^1 \cdot t^2, \ldots$ (finite or infinite) in T, provided each $t^1 \cdots t^\ell \in T$. The *level* $|t|$ of a node $t = t^1 \cdots t^\ell$ is the number ℓ; the level of ϵ is 0. T is *finite-path* or or *well-founded* if there are no infinite paths in T. This is also denoted WF T.

A well-founded tree T is *ν-rankable* if there is an assignment of ordinals to the nodes of T such that the root has rank ν and if a node t has rank γ then every child of t has rank less than γ.

4 WF Limit Representations

In this section we show how to represent analytic and coanalytic sets by limits. For a sequence $\tau_0, \tau_1, \ldots$ of pointer trees, we define $\lim_i \tau_i$ as:

$$t \in \lim_i \tau_i \text{ if and only if for almost all } i, t \in \tau_i.$$

It is not hard to see that $\lim_i \tau_i$ is a tree, which we call the *limit tree*. To characterize finite computations, we use a *progress approximation* τ that assigns a finite pointer tree $\tau(u)$ to each finite word $u \in \Sigma^*$. Thus we assume here that the underlying program is the transition system that has Σ^* as its state space and where the transition relation is defined so that the current state is the sequence of actions encountered. With this representation, the *live languages* $\lim_{\neg \mathrm{WF}} \tau$ and $\lim_{\mathrm{WF}} \tau$ are defined by: for a word $\alpha = a_0 a_1 \cdots$,

$$\alpha \in \lim_{\neg \mathrm{WF}} \tau \text{ if and only if } \neg \mathrm{WF} \lim_{u \to \alpha} \tau(u), \text{ and}$$

$$\alpha \in \lim_{\mathrm{WF}} \tau \text{ if and only if } \mathrm{WF} \lim_{u \to \alpha} \tau(u),$$

where $u \to \alpha$ denotes that u takes the values $\epsilon, a_0, a_0 a_1, \ldots$

The class $\mathbf{\Sigma}^1_1$ of analytic sets and the class $\mathbf{\Pi}^1_1$ of coanalytic sets can be described by limits:

Theorem 1. (Representation Theorem) *The limit operators* $\lim_{\neg \mathrm{WF}}$ *and* $\lim_{\mathrm{WF}}$ *define the classes* $\mathbf{\Sigma}^1_1$ *and* $\mathbf{\Pi}^1_1$, *i.e.* $S \in \mathbf{\Sigma}^1_1 \Leftrightarrow \exists \tau : S = \lim_{\neg \mathrm{WF}} \tau$ *and* $S \in \mathbf{\Pi}^1_1 \Leftrightarrow \exists \tau : S = \lim_{\mathrm{WF}} \tau$.

Proof The proof uses the classic representation involving projections of trees [20, p.77]. □

As with the usual representations (see [20]), we have:

Theorem 2. (Boundedness Theorem for $\mathbf{\Pi}^1_1$ sets) *Let* $C = \lim_{\mathrm{WF}} \tau$ *be a coanalytic set. If there is a countable ordinal* ν *such that for all* $\alpha \in C$, $\lim_{u \to \alpha} \tau(u)$ *is* ν*-rankable, then* C *is Borel.*

We postpone the proof of Theorem 2 to Section 7.

In the following, we say that an *analytic program* $\mathcal{P}$ is of the form $(P, \to, p^0, \neg \mathrm{WF}\ \tau)$ and that a *coanalytic program* is of the form $(P, \to, p^0, \mathrm{WF}\ \tau)$, where τ is a progress approximation that assigns a pointer tree to each state in P.

5 WF Relation and Measure

We use tree embeddings to measure progress of computations towards defining a finite-path tree in the limit. Let T be a fixed tree. An *embedding* of a tree τ in T is an injective mapping $\rho : \tau \to T$ such that $\rho(\epsilon) = \epsilon$ and for all $t \cdot d \in \tau$ there is d' with $\rho(t \cdot d) = \rho(t) \cdot d'$. Note that $|\rho(t)| = |t|$; in fact, ρ is just a structure-preserving relabeling of τ. Also note that $\mathrm{dom}(\rho)$ is the tree τ and that $\mathrm{rng}(\rho)$ is the image in T of τ.

We can now define the WF *relation*, which we denote by $\trianglerighteq_{\mathrm{WF}}$:

Definition 3. (WF Relation) $\rho \trianglerighteq_{\mathrm{WF}} \rho'$ if for all $s \in \mathrm{dom}(\rho) \cap \mathrm{dom}(\rho')$, $\rho(s) \succeq \rho'(s)$, where "$\succeq$" is defined by: $d^0 \cdots d^n \succeq e^0 \cdots e^n$ if either $d^0 \cdots d^n = e^0 \cdots e^n$ or there is a level $\lambda \leq n$ such that $d^\lambda > e^\lambda$ and for all $\ell < \lambda$, $d^\ell = e^\ell$.

Intuitively, $\rho \trianglerighteq_{\mathrm{WF}} \rho'$ holds if for any node s in both $\mathrm{dom}(\rho)$ and $\mathrm{dom}(\rho')$, the image in T of s under ρ' is the same as or to the right of the image under ρ (assuming that pointer trees are depicted as explained earlier). Although $\trianglerighteq_{\mathrm{WF}}$ is not a well-founded relation, it ensures well-foundedness in the limit provided T is well-founded.

Lemma 4. (WF Relation Lemma) *If* WF T *and* $\rho_0 \trianglerighteq_{\mathrm{WF}} \rho_1 \trianglerighteq_{\mathrm{WF}} \cdots$, *then* WF $\lim_i \mathrm{dom}(\rho_i)$.

This lemma is an immediate consequence of:

Proposition 5. *Let T be a fixed tree and let $\rho_0 \trianglerighteq_{\mathrm{WF}} \rho_1 \trianglerighteq_{\mathrm{WF}} \cdots$ be an infinite $\trianglerighteq_{\mathrm{WF}}$-related sequence of embeddings in T. Then there is an embedding ρ of* $\lim_i \mathrm{dom}(\rho_i)$ *in* $\lim_i \mathrm{rng}(\rho_i)$.

Hence if T is well-founded, $\trianglerighteq_{\mathrm{WF}}$ measures progress of pointer trees towards defining a well-founded tree. To state this more forcefully, we need some definitions.

Definition 6. Let $G = (V, E)$ be a countable, directed graph and let τ be a progress approximation on V. We say that an infinite path $v_0 v_1 \cdots$ satisfies the WF *condition* of τ, and write $v_0 v_1 \cdots \models \mathrm{WF}\tau$, if WF $\lim_i \tau(v_i)$. A graph G satisfies the WF condition of τ, and we write $G \models \mathrm{WF}\ \tau$, if every infinite path in G satisfies the WF condition.

Definition 7. A WF *progress measure* (μ, T) for (G, τ) is a finite-path tree T and a mapping $\mu : v \in V \to (\tau(v) \to T)$ such that

- $\mu(v)$ is an embedding of $\tau(v)$ in T; and
- μ respects the edge relation of G, i.e. $(u, v) \in E$ implies $\mu(u) \trianglerighteq_{\mathrm{WF}} \mu(v)$.

Theorem 8. (Graph Result) $G \models \mathrm{WF}\ \tau$ *if and only if* (G, τ) *has a* WF *progress measure.*

Proof "$\Leftarrow$" This follows from the WF Relation Lemma.
"$\Rightarrow$" The proof consists of a transfinite construction of μ and T. □

6 Progress Simulations

In this section, we present the General Progress Simulation Theorem. Let $\mathcal{P} = (P, \to_{\mathcal{P}}, p^0, \neg\text{WF } \tau_{\mathcal{P}})$ be an analytic implementation and $\mathcal{Q} = (Q, \to_{\mathcal{Q}}, q^0, \text{WF } \tau_{\mathcal{Q}})$ a coanalytic specification. To prove that $L^\circ(\mathcal{P}) \subseteq L^\circ(\mathcal{Q})$, we need to combine the progress approximations.

Definition 9. Given finite trees τ and τ', the set $\textit{merge}^\vee(\tau, \tau')$ consisting of nodes $d^0e^0 \cdots d^ne^n$ and $d^0e^0 \cdots e^{n-1}d^n$, where $n \geq -1$, $d^0 \cdots d^n \in \tau$, and $e^0 \cdots e^n \in \tau'$, is called the *or-merge* of τ and τ'.

It is not hard to see that $\textit{merge}^\vee(\tau, \tau')$ is a tree. The or-merge has the following properties:

Proposition 10. *Let τ_i and τ_i' be infinite sequences of trees.*

(a) $\text{WF} \lim_i \textit{merge}^\vee(\tau_i, \tau_i')$ *if and only if* $\text{WF} \lim_i \tau_i$ *or* $\text{WF} \lim_i \tau_i'$.
(b) *If* $\lim \textit{merge}^\vee(\tau_i, \tau_i')$ *is ν-rankable and* $\neg\text{WF} \lim_i \tau_i$, *then* $\lim_i \tau_i'$ *is ν-rankable.*

Given a simulation $h : \mathcal{P} \to \mathcal{Q}$, we measure progress towards $\textit{Live}_{\mathcal{P}} \Rightarrow \textit{Live}_{\mathcal{Q}}$ as follows.

Definition 11. A *progress simulation* (h, μ, T) from $\mathcal{P}$ to $\mathcal{Q}$ relative to h is a WF progress measure for $((V, E), p \mapsto \textit{merge}^\vee(\tau_{\mathcal{P}}(p), \tau_{\mathcal{S}}(h(p))))$, where $V \subseteq P$ are the states of $\mathcal{P}$ reachable by some finite computation and $(p, p') \in E$ if and only if $p \xrightarrow{a} p'$ for some a.

Theorem 12. (Progress Simulation Theorem) *Assume we have analytic $\mathcal{P} = (P, \to_{\mathcal{P}}, p^0, \neg\text{WF } \tau_{\mathcal{P}})$, coanalytic $\mathcal{Q} = (Q, \to_{\mathcal{Q}}, q^0, \text{WF } \tau_{\mathcal{Q}})$, and simulation $h : \mathcal{P} \to \mathcal{Q}$. Then $L^\circ(\mathcal{P}) \subseteq L^\circ(\mathcal{Q})$ if and only if there is a progress simulation from $\mathcal{P}$ to $\mathcal{Q}$ relative to h.*

Proof The proof follows from the WF Relation Lemma, Proposition 10, and Theorem 8. □

6.1 Suslin's Theorem

Corollary 13. (Suslin's Theorem) *Let L be a set of infinite sequences over ω that is both analytic and coanalytic. Then L is Borel.*

6.2 Finite Argument Theorem

A progress simulation can be viewed as an argument for why a program satisfies a specification. We show that for effective descriptions of program, specification, and simulation, there is an effective description of the progress measure. More precisely, let a WF *semi-measure* (μ, T) be a WF progress measure except that there is no requirement that T be well-founded. Then there is a total recursive function calculating an index of a WF semi-measure (μ, T) for $merge^{\vee}(\tau_P(p), \tau_S(h(p)))$ given indices for $\mathcal{P}$, $\mathcal{Q}$, and h; moreover, (h, μ, T) is a progress simulation, i.e. T is well-founded, if and only if $\mathcal{P}$ satisfies $\mathcal{Q}$.

Theorem 12′ (Finite Argument Theorem) A progress simulation can be obtained uniformly from indices of $\mathcal{P}$, $\mathcal{Q}$, and h.

Proof By analyzing the proof of Theorem 12 for computational contents, one can obtain an explicit algorithm for calculating μ and T. □

Intuitively, the Finite Argument Theorem shows that there is a systematic (in fact computable) way of getting a finite argument of correctness about finite computations from the program and the specification (if a simulation exists, for example by assuming that program and specification are deterministic).

The verification method based on WF progress measures is optimal in the following sense. For specifications that are Σ_1^1, it is Π_2^1-complete to determine whether a Σ_1^1 program satisfies the specification. For example, determining whether $L(\mathcal{P}) \subseteq L(\mathcal{Q})$, where $\mathcal{P}$ and $\mathcal{Q}$ are recursively represented nondeterministic transition systems is Π_2^1-complete [25]. It is hardly imaginable that a reasonable verification method would not be in Σ_2^1, which allows one to guess relations and verify that they are well-founded. But even a Σ_2^1 method cannot possible solve the Π_2^1-complete verification problem for Σ_1^1 sets. In this sense the preceding results are optimal.

Finally, we observe that, just as Suslin's Theorem is a consequence of Theorem 12, the Finite Argument Theorem implies Kleene's Theorem, which states that there is a uniform way of obtaining an index in the hyperarithmetical hierarchy of a set L from a Π_1^1 and a Σ_1^1 index of L [23].

7 Borel Programs

To describe Borel sets in terms that are useful for verification of programs, we introduce a class of programs whose acceptance conditions are infinitary temporal logic formulas. This will also allow us to prove the Boundedness Theorem for $\mathbf{\Pi_1^1}$ sets.

Definition 14. By transfinite induction, we define a *ranked formula* ϕ_γ, where γ is a countable ordinal, to be either a *temporal predicate* $\Box\Diamond\Phi$ ("infinitely often Φ") or $\Diamond\Box\Phi$ ("almost always Φ"), where Φ is a predicate on V, or a disjunction $\bigvee_{\gamma'<\gamma} \phi_{\gamma'}$ or a conjunction $\bigwedge_{\gamma'<\gamma} \phi_{\gamma'}$, where $\phi_{\gamma'}$ are ranked formulas.

A sequence $v_0 v_1 \cdots$ *satisfies* ϕ_γ, written $v_0 v_1 \cdots \models \phi_\gamma$, according to:

$$v_0 v_1 \cdots \models \Diamond\Box\Phi \text{ if and only if } \exists H : \forall h > H : v_h \models \Phi$$
$$v_0 v_1 \cdots \models \Box\Diamond\Phi \text{ if and only if } \forall H : \exists h > H : v_h \models \Phi$$
$$v_0 v_1 \cdots \models \bigwedge_{\gamma'<\gamma} \phi_{\gamma'} \text{ if and only if } \forall \gamma' < \gamma : v_0 v_1 \cdots \models \phi_{\gamma'}$$
$$v_0 v_1 \cdots \models \bigvee_{\gamma'<\gamma} \phi_{\gamma'} \text{ if and only if } \exists \gamma' < \gamma : v_0 v_1 \cdots \models \phi_{\gamma'}$$

Definition 15. A *Borel program* $\mathcal{P} = (P, \rightarrow, p^0, \phi_\nu)$ consists of a countable set of states P, a deterministic transition relation $\rightarrow \subseteq P \times \Sigma \times P$, an initial state p^0, and a ranked formula ϕ_ν.

Proposition 16. *The class of live languages accepted by Borel programs is the class of Borel sets.*

7.1 Proof of the Boundedness Theorem of Section 4

7.2 Borel Sets Are Analytic and Coanalytic

We show how to translate the temporal logic acceptance condition of a Borel program into a WF or $\neg$WF condition of a progress approximation defined on Σ^*. By this translation, program verification with temporal logic can take place by measuring progress using Theorem 8 or Theorem 12. The translation also proves that all Borel sets are analytic and coanalytic.

Theorem 17. *Let $\mathcal{P}$ be a Borel program. Then there exist progress approximations τ and τ' on Σ^* such that*

$$\lim_{\mathrm{WF}} \tau = L^\circ(\mathcal{P})$$
$$\lim_{\neg\mathrm{WF}} \tau' = L^\circ(\mathcal{P})$$

It is usually not possible to define τ as a function of the current state. Instead the whole history of states or actions must be used. In particular, a finite-state Borel program becomes infinite-state. (In contrast, note that Büchi conditions allow certain restricted third level properties to be expressed without going to infinite-state systems.)

In order to prove this theorem we need two lemmas. They show how to merge countably many sequences of finite trees into one such sequence that satisfies the WF condition if and only if all (respectively, one) of the original sequences satisfy the WF condition.

Lemma 18. *There is an operation merge$^\forall$ that merges any list of finite trees into a finite tree such that for any collection $(\tau_i^j)_i$, $j \in \omega$, of sequences of finite trees:*

$$\mathrm{WF}\lim_{i\to\omega} \mathit{merge}^\forall(\tau_0^i, \ldots, \tau_i^i)$$
if and only if
$$\forall j : \mathrm{WF}\lim_{i\to\omega} \tau_i^j$$

Lemma 19. *There is an operation merge$^\exists$ that merges any list of finite trees into a finite tree such that for any collection $(\tau_i^j)_i$, $j \in \omega$, of sequences of finite trees:*

$$\mathrm{WF}\lim_{i\to\omega} \mathit{merge}^\exists(\tau_0^i, \ldots, \tau_i^i)$$
if and only if
$$\exists j : \mathrm{WF}\lim_{i\to\omega} \tau_i^j$$

By Proposition 16, we have:

Corollary 20. *Borel sets are analytic and coanalytic.*

8 Progress Bisimulations

The full paper contains a formalization of the game outlined in Section 2.3. By Martin's result [19], one of the players has a winning strategy. If the responder has a winning strategy, then it can be described by a relation over finite computations and a progress measure for $Live_{\mathcal{P}} \Leftrightarrow Live_{\mathcal{Q}}$. This progress measure is formulated for the progress approximation $merge^{\Leftrightarrow}(\tau_{\mathcal{P}}(u), \tau_{\mathcal{Q}}(v))$, which is defined as $merge^{\wedge}(merge^{\vee}(\tau'_{\mathcal{P}}(u), \tau''_{\mathcal{Q}}(u)), merge^{\vee}(\tau''_{\mathcal{P}}(u), \tau'_{\mathcal{Q}}(u)))$.

9 Conclusion

We have used a limit view of finite computations to show that concepts of simulation and bisimulation can be be generalized to account also for very general liveness properties. The two generalized concepts establish a strong connection to two major theorems in descriptive set theory. The limit conditions presented here probably have only theoretical interest, however.

In practice, the mathematical challenge needed to establish even simple bisimulations for transitions systems with Büchi acceptance conditions seems quite difficult. Further investigation may reveal whether the concepts presented in this article may be sufficiently simplified for finite-state systems to be of use in practice.

Acknowledgements

Thanks to Dexter Kozen and Moshe Vardi for valuable comments on an earlier version of this article.

References

1. M. Abadi and L. Lamport. The existence of refinement mappings. *Theoretical Computer Science*, 82(2):253–284, 1991.
2. B. Alpern and F.B. Schneider. Recognizing safety and liveness. *Distributed Computing*, 2:117–126, 1987.
3. B. Alpern and F.B. Schneider. Verifying temporal properties without temporal logic. *ACM Transactions on Programming Languages and Systems*, 11(1):147–167, January 1989.
4. K.R. Apt and E.-R. Olderog. Proof rules and transformations dealing with fairness. *Science of Computer Programming*, 3:65–100, 1983.
5. I. Dayan and D. Harel. Fair termination with cruel schedulers. *Fundamenta Informatica*, 9:1–12, 1986.
6. N. Francez and D. Kozen. Generalized fair termination. In *Proc. 11th POPL, Salt Lake City*. ACM, January 1984.
7. O. Grumberg, N. Francez, J.A. Makowsky, and W.P. de Roever. A proof rule for fair termination of guarded commands. *Information and Control*, 66(1/2):83–102, 1985.

8. Y. Gurevich and L. Harrington. Trees, automata, and games. In *Proceedings 14th Symp. on Theory of Computing.* ACM, 1982.
9. D. Harel. Effective transformations on infinite trees with applications to high undecidability, dominos, and fairness. *Journal of the ACM*, 33(1):224–248, 1986.
10. N. Klarlund. Liminf progress measures. In *Proc. of Mathematical Foundations of Programming Semantics 1991.* LNCS.
11. N. Klarlund. Progress measures and stack assertions for fair termination. In *Proc. Eleventh Symp. on Princ. of Distributed Computing*, pages 229–240. IEEE, 1992.
12. N. Klarlund. Progress measures, immediate determinacy, and a subset construction for tree automata. In *Proc. Seventh Symp. on Logic in Computer Science*, 1992.
13. N. Klarlund and D. Kozen. Rabin measures and their applications to fairness and automata theory. In *Proc. Sixth Symp. on Logic in Computer Science.* IEEE, 1991.
14. N. Klarlund and F.B. Schneider. Proving nondeterministically specified safety properties using progress measures. *Information and Computation*, 107(1):151–170, 1993.
15. Nils Klarlund. *Progress Measures and Finite Arguments for Infinite Computations.* PhD thesis, TR-1153, Cornell University, August 1990.
16. D. Lehmann, A. Pnueli, and J. Stavi. Impartiality, justice and fairness: the ethics of concurrent termination. In *Proc. 8th ICALP.* LNCS 115, Springer-Verlag, 1981.
17. Z. Manna and A. Pnueli. Adequate proof principles for invariance and liveness properties of concurrent programs. *Science of Computer Programming*, 4(3):257–290, 1984.
18. Z. Manna and A. Pnueli. Specification and verification of concurrent programs by ∀-automata. In *Proc. Fourteenth Symp. on the Principles of Programming Languages*, pages 1–12. ACM, 1987.
19. D.A. Martin. Borel determinacy. *Ann. Math.*, 102:363–371, 1975.
20. Yiannis N. Moschovakis. *Descriptive Set Theory*, volume 100 of *Studies in Log. and the Found. of Math.* North-Holland, 1980.
21. L. Priese. Fairness. *EATCS Bulletin*, 50, 1993.
22. R. Rinat, N. Francez, and O. Grumberg. Infinite trees, markings and well-foundedness. *Information and Computation*, 79:131–154, 1988.
23. Hartley Rogers, Jr. *Theory of Recursive Functions and Effective Computability.* McGraw-Hill Book Company, 1967.
24. A.P. Sistla. A complete proof system for proving correctness of nondeterministic safety specifications. Technical report, Computer and Intelligent Systems Laboratory, GTE Laboratories Inc., 1989.
25. A.P. Sistla. On verifying that a concurrent program satisfies a nondeterministic specification. *Information Processing Letters*, 32(1):17–24, July 1989.
26. L. Staiger. Recursive automata on infinite words. In P. Enjalbert, A. Finkel, and K.W. Wagner, editors, *Proc. 10th Annual Symp. on Theoretical Computer Science (STACS), LNCS 665.* Springer Verlag, 1993.
27. W. Thomas. Automata on infinite objects. In J. van Leeuwen, editor, *Handbook of Theoretical Computer Science*, volume B, pages 133–191. MIT Press/Elsevier, 1990.
28. M. Vardi. Verification of concurrent programs: The automata-theoretic framework. *Annals of Pure and Applied Logic*, 51:79–98, 1991.
29. M. Vardi. Private communication, 1992.

Trace Refinement of Action Systems

R. J. R. Back and J. von Wright

Abo Akademi University, Turku, Finland

Abstract. Action systems provide a general description of reactive systems, capable of modeling terminating, aborting and infinitely repeating systems. Arbitrary sequential program statements can be used to describe the behavior of atomic actions. Action systems are used to extend program refinement methods for sequential programs to parallel and reactive system refinement. We give here a behavioral semantics of action systems in terms of execution traces, and define refinement of action systems in terms of this semantics. We give a simulation based proof rule for action system refinement in a reactive context, and illustrate the use of this rule with an example. The proof rule is complete under certain restrictions.

1 Introduction

An *action system* describes the behavior of a parallel system in terms of the atomic actions that can take place during the execution of the system. Action systems provide a general description of reactive systems, capable of modeling systems that may or may not terminate and where atomic actions need not terminate themselves. Arbitrary sequential program statements can be used to describe an atomic action. The action system approach to parallel and distributed systems was introduced by Back and Kurki-Suonio [5, 6], as a paradigm for describing parallel systems in a temporal logic framework. The same basic approach has later been used in other frameworks for distributed computing, notably UNITY [11] and TLA [14].

The *refinement calculus* was originally described by Back [2] to provide a formal framework for stepwise refinement of sequential programs. It extends Dijkstra's weakest precondition semantics [12] for total correctness of programs with a relation of refinement between program statements. This relation is defined in terms of the weakest preconditions of statements, and expresses the requirement that a refinement must *preserve total correctness* of the statement being refined. A lattice theoretic basic for the refinement calculus is described in [9]. A good overview of how to apply the refinement calculus in practical program derivations is given by Morgan [15].

By modeling parallel systems as action systems, which can be seen as special kinds of sequential systems, the refinement calculus framework can be extended to total correctness refinement of parallel systems [4, 7, 8]. Reactive system refinement can be handled by existing techniques for data refinement of sequential programs within the refinement calculus. The main extension needed is that *silent* or *stuttering* actions have to be considered explicitly. Data refinement methods for proving refinement of reactive and distributed systems are described by Back in [3].

Proving data refinement between program statements essentially amounts to proving a simulation relationship between the statements. Hence, data refinement does not only preserve total correctness but also the computation behavior of the action system. We will in this paper study this aspect of action system refinement more carefully. We will give a behavioral semantics of action systems in terms of execution traces. The notion of refinement of action systems is then described in terms of this semantics, i.e., refinement is required to preserve the behavior of action systems and not only their input-output behavior. We will give a very general simulation based proof rule for showing correctness of action system refinement in a reactive context. This proof rule is based on the explicit identification of stuttering actions in action systems. We show how both forward and backward simulation proof rules arise as special cases of this general notion of simulation. The general proof rules can be shown to be complete under certain rather reasonable restrictions. We will illustrate the use of the proof method with an example.

Related theories of distributed systems, but restricted to systems where only infinite computations are allowed, have been studied by a number of authors. We have been mostly influenced by the work of Abadi and Lamport [1] and Jonsson [13]. Butler [10] has studied similar kinds of simulation rules that we present here, but for a framework where action systems communicate by synchronized action rather than by shared variables, as they do in our approach.

2 Refinement calculus

The basic domains of refinement calculus arise by pointwise extension from the truth value lattice. The truth values

$$\mathsf{Bool} = \{\mathsf{F}, \mathsf{T}\}$$

form a complete boolean lattice under the *implication ordering*, $a \leq b$ iff $a \Rightarrow b$ for $a, b \in \mathsf{Bool}$. The bottom of this lattice is F, the top is T, complement is negation $\neg$, meet is conjunction $\wedge$ and join is disjunction $\vee$.

Let Σ be a set of *states* (called a *state space*). A *predicate over* Σ is a function $p : \Sigma \to \mathsf{Bool}$ which assigns a truth value to each state. Predicates can also be identified with subsets of Σ. The set of predicates on Σ is denoted $\mathsf{Pred}(\Sigma)$,

$$\mathsf{Pred}(\Sigma) = \Sigma \to \mathsf{Bool}.$$

The ordering on truth values is extended to an ordering on predicates by pointwise extension: for $p, q \in \mathsf{Pred}(\Sigma)$, we define $p \leq q$ as $(\forall \sigma \in \Sigma.\, p\,\sigma \Rightarrow q\,\sigma)$. Predicates on Σ also form a complete boolean lattices with this ordering. The identically false predicate false is the bottom in this lattice and the identically true predicate true is the top. Complement $\neg$, meet $\wedge$ and join $\vee$ are defined pointwise in this lattice, so that $(p \wedge q)\,\sigma = (p\,\sigma \wedge q\,\sigma)$ and so on. If we consider predicates as subsets of Σ, then the ordering is the subset ordering, false is the empty set, true is the universal set, $\neg p$ is set complement $(\Sigma - p)$, $\wedge$ is intersection and $\vee$ is union.

Let Σ and Γ be two state spaces. A *relation from Σ to Γ* is a function $P : \Sigma \to \mathsf{Pred}(\Gamma)$, that associates as set of *final states* in Γ with each initial state in Σ. We write

$$\mathsf{Rel}(\Sigma, \Gamma) = \Sigma \to \mathsf{Pred}(\Gamma)$$

for the set of relations from Σ to Γ. This view of relations is isomorphic to viewing relations as subsets of $\Sigma \times \Gamma$.

The ordering on predicates is extended to relations by pointwise extension: for $P, Q \in \mathsf{Rel}(\Sigma, \Gamma)$, we define $P \leq Q$ as $(\forall \sigma \in \Sigma . P\,\sigma \leq Q\,\sigma)$. The relations also form a complete boolean lattice under this ordering, and the lattice operations are the pointwise extensions of the corresponding operations on predicates. In addition, we can use relational composition, writing $P;\, Q$ for the composition of two relations $P \in \mathsf{Rel}(\Sigma, \Gamma)$ and $Q \in \mathsf{Rel}(\Gamma, \Delta)$.

Pointwise extension of predicates gives us predicate transformers. A *predicate transformer* is a function $S : \mathsf{Pred}(\Gamma) \to \mathsf{Pred}(\Sigma)$, where Γ and Σ are two state spaces. The set of predicate transformers of this type is denoted

$$\mathsf{Ptran}(\Sigma, \Gamma) = \mathsf{Pred}(\Gamma) \to \mathsf{Pred}(\Sigma)$$

Program statements are interpreted as weakest precondition predicate transformers, i.e., as predicate transformers that map a postcondition $q \in \mathsf{Pred}(\Gamma)$ to the weakest precondition $p \in \mathsf{Pred}(\Sigma)$ such that the program statement is guaranteed to terminate in a final state satisfying q whenever the initial state satisfies p. The reversal of state spaces in the definition of $\mathsf{Ptran}(\Sigma, \Gamma)$ is justified by this "backward" view of predicate transformers. Program statements are identified with their associated predicate transformers in the Refinement Calculus. Hence, we may reason about and manipulate statements as if they were predicate transformers.

Pointwise extension of the ordering of predicates to predicate transformers gives us the *refinement ordering* on predicate transformers. For $S, T : \mathsf{Ptran}(\Sigma, \Gamma)$, we define

$$S \leq T \quad \Leftrightarrow \quad (\forall q : \mathsf{Pred}(\Gamma) .\, S\, q \leq T\, q).$$

The refinement ordering models the notion of a *total correctness preserving program refinement*. Thus, if S and T are two specific program statements (predicate transformers), then $S \leq T$ will hold if and only if T satisfies any total correctness specification that S satisfies (a total correctness specification is typically given as a precondition-postcondition pair).

Predicate transformers again form a complete boolean lattice under the refinement ordering. The bottom of this lattice is the predicate transformer abort that maps each postcondition to false. The top of the lattice is the predicate transformer magic that maps each postcondition to true. The abort statement is never guaranteed to terminate, and can be implemented as, e.g., an infinite loop. The magic statement is *miraculous*, it is guaranteed to achieve any postcondition desired. It is an imaginary statement, that cannot be implemented on a real computer, but is often useful in formal calculations.

Meets and joins in the predicate transformer lattice are also defined pointwise, so that, $(S \wedge T)\, q = (S\, q) \wedge (T\, q)$ and so on. Meet models *demonic nondeterministic choice* between executing S or T, whereas join models *angelic nondeterministic choice* between S or T. As the predicate transformer lattice is complete, meet and join can be taken over an arbitrary set $\{S_i \mid i \in I\}$ of predicate transformers, and are then denoted $(\wedge i \in I.\, S_i)$ and $(\vee i \in I.\, S_i)$, respectively.

Predicate transformers are functions from predicates to predicates, so they can be combined using functional composition. Let $S \in \mathsf{Ptran}(\Sigma, \Gamma)$ and $T \in \mathsf{Ptran}(\Gamma, \Delta)$. We write $S;\, T$ for the functional composition $S \circ T : \mathsf{Ptran}(\Sigma, \Delta)$ of these two predicate transformers. Functional composition models sequential composition of the corresponding statements.

We define certain primitive predicate transformers directly. Given a predicate $p \in \mathsf{Pred}(\Sigma)$, the *guard* $[p] \in \mathsf{Ptran}(\Sigma, \Sigma)$ and the *assert* $\{p\} \in \mathsf{Ptran}(\Sigma, \Sigma)$ are defined by

$$\{p\}\, q = p \wedge q \qquad \text{and} \qquad [p]\, q = (\neg p \vee q).$$

The assert statement acts as a skip-statement if the predicate p holds and otherwise as abort. The guard statement also acts as a skip statement if the predicate p holds, but otherwise as magic.

Given a relation $P \in \mathsf{Rel}(\Sigma, \Gamma)$, we define the *angelic update statement* $\{P\}$ and the *demonic update statement* $[P]$, by

$$\{P\}\, q\, \sigma = (\exists \gamma \in \Gamma.\, P\, \sigma\, \gamma \wedge q\, \gamma) \quad \text{and} \quad [P]\, q\, \sigma = (\forall \gamma \in \Gamma.\, P\, \sigma\, \gamma \Rightarrow q\, \gamma).$$

The demonic update statement will change the initial state σ to some new state σ' such that $P\, \sigma\, \sigma'$ holds, if such a new state σ' exists. Otherwise it will behave as magic. The choice of the new state is done demonically, i.e., a postcondition is guaranteed to be established only if *every* possible new state satisfies the postcondition. The angelic update statement will also change the initial state to some final state that satisfies P, if such a state exists, but the choice is done angelically, i.e., a postcondition is guaranteed to be established if there is *some* new state that satisfies the postcondition. If there is no such new state, then the effect is that of an abort.

Ordinary statement constructors, such as recursion, conditional statements, blocks with local variables and iteration statements, can all be defined in term of these primitive lattice theoretic operations and sequential composition. For instance, a guarded command $g \rightarrow S$ in Dijkstra's language is defined as the statement $[g];\, S$ (the construct $[g]$ thus corresponds to a "naked guard"). A multiple assignment statement $x, y := e, f$ in a state space with components (x, y, z) can, e.g., be described as a demonic update statement $[\lambda(x, y, z).\, \lambda(x', y', z').\, x' = e \wedge y' = f \wedge z' = z)]$. A *nondeterministic assignment* $x := x'.P(x', x, y)$ again stands for the demonic update statement $[\lambda(x, y, z).\, \lambda(x', y', z').\, P(x', x, y) \wedge y' = y \wedge z' = z]$.

The predicate transformers that are constructed out of asserts, guards, angelic and demonic update statements, using only (arbitrary) meet and join and sequential composition, will all be *monotonic*: if $p \leq q$, then $S\,p \leq S\,q$. In the other direction, one can show that every monotonic predicate transformer can in fact be constructed in this way. Thus, the statement constructors above are sufficient to characterize the set of monotonic predicate transformers.

The *conjunctive* predicate transformers form a subset of the monotonic predicate transformers, satisfying the condition $S\,(\wedge i \in I.\, q_i) = (\wedge i \in I.\, S\,q_i)$ for any $I \neq \emptyset$. Disjunctive predicate transformers are defined dually. A predicate transformer is *universally conjunctive*, if the condition also holds for $I = \emptyset$. This is equivalent to requiring that $S\,\mathsf{true} = \mathsf{true}$. Considered as a program statement, this expresses the fact that the statement S is guaranteed to always terminate. Each universally conjunctive predicate transformer can be described as a demonic update statement $[R]$, for some relation R, whereas each conjunctive predicate transformer can be described as a statement $\{p\}$; $[R]$, for some predicate p and relation R.

3 Behavioral semantics of Action Systems

Identifying statements with their predicate transformers means that we only can consider the input-output behavior of statements. In reactive systems, this is not sufficient, because such a system can be placed in an environment where it reacts with other systems. Hence, the input-output behavior is influenced by the behavior of other systems during computation. Reactive systems cannot therefore be modeled as weakest precondition predicate transformers. However, a small extension of the predicate tranformer framework does give us the power to describe reactive systems and methods for refining such systems that preserve the notion of correctness that is natural for such systems. Moreover, the extension is such that the methods of the refinement calculus for sequential programs carry over to this extension, thus providing a pleasing unification of sequential and parallel/reactive program refinement.

The action systems provide the mechanism for achieving this unification. An *action system* is essentially an initialized block with a body that contains an iteration, i.e., a statement that is repeatedly executed. As we here are interested in the *reactive behavior* of an action system, we give action systems a semantics in terms of behaviors, rather than an input-output semantics. This semantics then permits us to define a composition operator (parallel composition) which models placing the action system in a reactive environment.

An *action system* **A** is a pair (A_0, A), where A_0 is an *initialization command*, of the form

$$A_0 = [\lambda\, u\, (a', u').\, p(a', u') \wedge (u' = u)],$$

and A is an *action*, a conjunctive statement on the two-component states (a, u). The predicate p is called the *initialization predicate*, and it is denoted pA_0.

The *enabledness guard* of action A is denoted gA and the *termination guard* of action A is denoted tA. These are defined as

$$gA = \neg\, A\,\mathsf{false} \qquad \text{and} \qquad tA = A\,\mathsf{true}. \tag{1}$$

We use the notation nA for the next-state relation of a conjunctive statement A. For A of the form $\{p\}$; $[R]$, with $\mathsf{dom}\, R \subseteq p$, the guard, termination and next state relation are

$$tA(a,u) = p(a,u) \tag{2}$$
$$gA(a,u) = \neg p(a,u) \vee \exists a', u' .\, nA(a,u)(x',u') \tag{3}$$
$$nA(a,u)(a',u') = p(a,u) \wedge R(a,u)(a',u'). \tag{4}$$

Intuitively, execution of an action system $\mathbf{A}$ (in isolation) should be interpreted as follows: Execution starts in some global state u_0. In the initialization phase, the local component is given a value a_0 such that the initialization predicate holds, i.e., such that $pA_0(a_0,u)$ holds. After this, the action A is executed repeatedly, as long as it is enabled (i.e., as long as gA holds). If the action is not enabled, the action system terminates and if the action aborts, then the whole action system aborts.

3.1 Behavioral semantics

A *behavior* is a sequence s of states with two components:

$$s = \langle (a_0,u_0),(a_1,u_1),\ldots\rangle \tag{5}$$

The first component is the *local state* while the second is the *global state*. Behaviors can be finite or infinite. Finite behaviors, in turn, can be terminated or aborted. We give the semantics of $\mathbf{A} = (A_0, A)$ as the set *beh*($\mathbf{A}$) of its behaviors.

The state sequence (5) is an *infinite behavior* of $\mathbf{A}$ if it is infinite and the following hold for all states (a_i, u_i) in the sequence:

$$pA_0(a_0,u_0) \tag{6}$$
$$nA(a_i,u_i)(a_{i+1},u_{i+1}) \tag{7}$$

A terminated behavior is one that ends in a state where the action is not enabled. Thus, the state sequence (5) is a *terminated behavior* of $\mathbf{A}$ if it is finite, condition (6) holds for the initial state and (7) hold for all but the last state in the sequence, and

$$\neg gA(a_n,u_n) \tag{8}$$

hold for the last state (a_n, u_n).

A behavior aborts if its last (proper) state is one where termination is not guaranteed. The state sequence (5) is thus an *aborted behavior* of $\mathbf{A}$ if it is finite, condition (6) holds for the initial state and (7) hold for all but the last state in the sequence, and

$$\neg tA(a_n, u_n) \tag{9}$$

hold for the last state (a_n, u_n).

The semantics of $\mathbf{A}$ is now the set $beh(\mathbf{A})$ of all its behaviors. If the initialization predicate is false, then this set is empty. We can think of $beh(\mathbf{A})$ as a disjoint union of the infinite behaviors, the terminated behaviors and the aborted behaviors. Alternatively, we can think of the aborted behaviors as having a special last state $\bot$, to distinguish them from terminated behaviors. However, this is not necessary, since we can always decide whether a finite state sequence is a terminated behavior or an aborted behavior by evaluating tA and gA in the last state.

3.2 Syntactic action systems

The action systems that we use in practice have more than one action. We use the syntax

$$\mathbf{A} = \mathsf{begin\ var}\ a.\, p;\ \mathsf{do}\ A_1 \parallel \ldots \parallel A_n\ \mathsf{od\ end} \tag{10}$$

for action systems. Semantically, we identify this action system with $\mathbf{A} = (A_0, A)$, where A_0 is as above and $A = A_1 \wedge \ldots \wedge A_n$. Thus the overall action is simply the demonic choice between all the separate actions.

Since the multiple action form is just a notation, we do not need to give a separate semantics to these action systems. Intuitively, the action system in (10) is executed in initial state u_0 as follows. First, the local component is initialized so that the initialization predicate p holds. Now we repeatedly choose (demonically) one of the enabled actions for execution. If no action is enabled, then execution terminates.

The demonic choice of action means that if an aborting action is enabled, then that action (or some other aborting action) is chosen.

Although we do not need to give a separate semantics to these action systems, we note that the behaviors can be characterized in terms of the separate actions. First, straightforward computation gives

$$tA = tA_1 \wedge \ldots \wedge tA_n \quad \text{and} \quad gA = gA_1 \vee \ldots \vee gA_n$$

Furthermore, the conditions for the next state all become

$$(\exists j.\, tA(a_i, u_i) \wedge nA_j(a_i, u_i)(a_{i+1}, u_{i+1})).$$

If the actions are written in such a form that no action is enabled in a state where some other action aborts, then we can drop the first conjunct, getting just the condition $(\exists j.\, nA_j(a_i, u_i)(a_{i+1}, u_{i+1}))$.

When reasoning about refinement of action systems, we will want to single out certain actions as stuttering actions. A *stuttering action* $A_\natural$ must satisfy the following conditions: it is universally conjunctive and

$$nA_\natural(a,u)(a',u') \Rightarrow (u'=u)$$

i.e., it terminates normally, leaving the global state unchanged.

The actions that are not singled out as stuttering actions are called *change actions*. Note that we put no restriction on change actions; a change action may well permit a state change where the global component is not changed at all.

3.3 Parallel composition of action systems

Parallel composition is the main operation on action systems; $\mathbf{A} \parallel \mathbf{B}$ models the action system $\mathbf{A}$ placed in the environment $\mathbf{B}$. We can also define other operations on action systems, such as *hiding*, *renaming* and *sequential composition* [3], but we will concentrate on parallel composition here.

Two action systems can be composed in parallel, provided that they work on compatible global state spaces. Given action systems $\mathbf{A} = (A_0, A)$ and $\mathbf{B} = (B_0, B)$, the parallel composition $\mathbf{A} \parallel \mathbf{B}$ is defined as follows. Its local state component (a, b) combines the local states a and b of $\mathbf{A}$ and $\mathbf{B}$. Its initialization predicate is the conjunction $pA_0 \wedge pB_0$ of the initialization predicates of $\mathbf{A}$ and $\mathbf{B}$ and its action is the demonic choice $A \wedge B$.

Parallel composition is easily shown to be commutative and associative (modulo a reordering of the local state components):

$$\mathbf{A} \parallel \mathbf{B} = \mathbf{B} \parallel \mathbf{A} \tag{11}$$
$$\mathbf{A} \parallel (\mathbf{B} \parallel \mathbf{C}) = (\mathbf{A} \parallel \mathbf{B}) \parallel \mathbf{C} \tag{12}$$

Operationally, an execution of $\mathbf{A} \parallel \mathbf{B}$ starts by assigning proper values to both local states and then arbitrarily interleaving A-actions and B-actions. However, we have to consider the questions of abortion and termination a bit more carefully.

Assume that execution reaches a state (a, b, u) where one of the two components, say $\mathbf{A}$, would terminate, i.e., where $\neg gA(a, u)$ holds. If $\mathbf{B}$ can continue, then execution continues with a B-action. The basic reason for this is that $\mathsf{magic} \wedge B = B$, and when $\neg gA$ holds, A is miraculous, i.e., it behaves like magic.

If $\mathbf{B}$ can continue, we may again get to a situation where $\mathbf{A}$-actions are possible. Thus, we may even get infinite behaviors when composing two systems that taken separately have only finite behaviors.

Now assume that execution of the parallel composition $\mathbf{A} \parallel \mathbf{B}$ reaches a state (a, b, u) where $\mathbf{A}$ would abort, i.e., where $\neg tA(a, u)$ holds. In this case, the parallel composition aborts. This is because aborting behavior pre-empts all other possibilities; $\mathsf{abort} \wedge B = \mathsf{abort}$. Thus aborting models the entire system being turned off or stopped.

We do not make any fairness assumptions for the execution of action systems, nor do we assume here that parallel composition is done with fair interleaving of actions from the component systems. It is possible to define action systems with fair execution and give refinement rules for such action systems. For instance, [6] contains a detailed study of fairness issues in action systems, within the temporal logic framework.

4 Trace refinement of action systems

Traditionally, a distributed system is defined to implement a specification if every trace (observable behavior) of the system is permitted by the specification. In our framework, both specifications and implementations are action systems. Thus the implementation relation is a relation of refinement; the refinement $\mathbf{A} \sqsubseteq \mathbf{C}$ holds when $\mathbf{C}$ is an implementation of $\mathbf{A}$. We shall now make this notion formal.

Assume that s is a behavior. An occurrence of two consecutive states in s with the same global component is called a *stuttering step*. By removing all *finite* stuttering, and the local state component in each state, we get the *trace* $tr(s)$ of s.

Since we do not remove infinite stuttering, the trace of a finite behavior is finite while the trace of an infinite behavior is infinite.

We define an *approximation relation* $\preceq$ on behaviors as follows: s approximates t (written $s \preceq t$) if either s is aborting and $tr(s)$ is a prefix of $tr(t)$, or neither s nor t is aborting, and $tr(s) = tr(t)$.

The refinement $\mathbf{A} \sqsubseteq \mathbf{C}$ holds if every behavior of $\mathbf{C}$ has an approximating behavior in $\mathbf{A}$:

$$\mathbf{A} \sqsubseteq \mathbf{C} \overset{\mathrm{df}}{=} \forall t \in beh(\mathbf{C}).\, \exists s \in beh(\mathbf{A}).\, s \preceq t$$

We call the refinement relation $\sqsubseteq$ *trace refinement.*

Lemma 1. *Trace refinement is reflexive and transitive.*

When considering a (proposed) trace refinement $\mathbf{A} \sqsubseteq \mathbf{C}$, we usually speak of $\mathbf{A}$ as the *abstract* and of $\mathbf{C}$ as the *concrete* action system.

4.1 Simulations between action systems

In practice it is not feasible to prove a trace refinement $\mathbf{A} \sqsubseteq \mathbf{C}$ by using the definition directly. Instead, we can use simulation methods, i.e., methods for constructing an abstract behavior which approximates a given concrete behavior. Simulation methods are closely connected with methods of data refinement.

Below we will use the following notation. The n-fold sequential composition of a command S is written S^n (formally, $S^0 = \mathsf{skip}$ and $S^{n+1} = S; S^n$ for $n \geq 0$). We will write S^* for the demonic choice of all n-fold sequential compositions of a statement, $S^* = (\wedge n \in \mathsf{Nat}.\, S^n)$. Finally, we let DO_S denote the termination guard of the iteration of S, $DO_S = (\mathsf{do}\, S\, \mathsf{od})\, \mathsf{true}$.

Assume that the action system $\mathbf{A} = (A_0, A)$ works on the "abstract" state space (a, u) and $\mathbf{C} = (C_0, C)$ on the "concrete" state space (c, u). Let γ be a statement from initial states (c, u) to final states (a, u). We say that γ is an *abstraction statement* if it does not change the value of the global variable u.

We say that abstraction statement γ is a *simulation* between $\mathbf{A}$ and $\mathbf{C}$ if there is a *decomposition* $A = A_\sharp \wedge A_\natural$ and $C = C_\sharp \wedge C_\natural$, where $A_\natural$ and $C_\natural$ are stuttering actions, such that the following conditions are satisfied:

$$A_0; A_\natural^* \leq C_0; C_\natural^*; \gamma \tag{13}$$

$$\gamma; A_\sharp; A_\natural^* \leq C_\sharp; C_\natural^*; \gamma \tag{14}$$

$$\gamma(tA \wedge gA) \leq gC \tag{15}$$

$$\gamma(tA \wedge DO_{A_\natural}) \leq DO_{C_\natural} \tag{16}$$

Figure 1 illustrates the first two of these conditions. The diagram is "subcommuting", in the sense that of two paths with the same end points, the one lower down represents a more refined command.

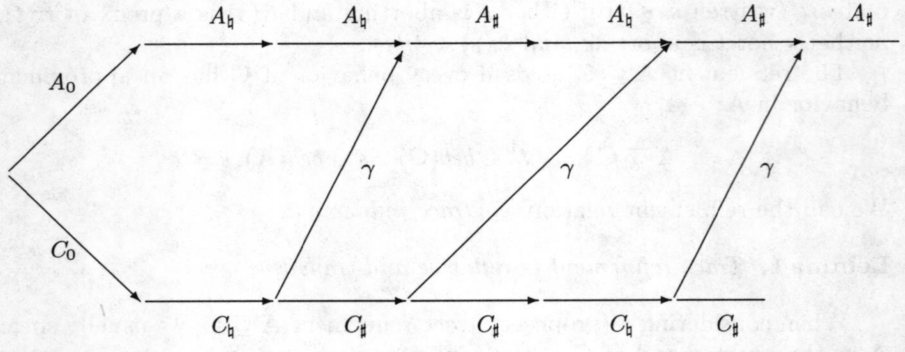

Fig. 1. Simulation: example case

4.2 Forward simulation

We consider the special case of simulation where the abstraction command is an angelic update statement. We assume that the abstraction relation $R = \lambda(a, c, u).R(a, c, u)$ is given. Let γ be the angelic abstraction command

$$\gamma = \{\lambda(c, u).\, \lambda(a, u').\, R(a, c, u) \wedge u' = u\}.$$

In this case (13)–(16) can be rewritten as

$$pC_0(c,u) \wedge nC_\natural^m(c,u)(c',u')$$
$$\Rightarrow \exists n, a, a'.\, R(a',c',u') \wedge pA_0(a,u) \wedge nA_\natural^n(a,u)(a',u') \qquad (17)$$
$$R(a,c,u) \wedge (nC_\sharp;\, nC_\natural^m)(c,u)(c',u')$$
$$\Rightarrow \neg tA(a,u) \vee (\exists n, a'.\, R(a',c',u') \wedge (nA_\sharp;\, nA_\natural^n)(a,u)(a',u')) \qquad (18)$$
$$R(a,c,u) \wedge \neg tC(c,u) \Rightarrow \neg tA(a,u) \qquad (19)$$
$$R(a,c,u) \wedge \neg gC(c,u) \Rightarrow \neg tA(a,u) \vee \neg gA(a,u) \qquad (20)$$
$$R(a,c,u) \wedge \neg DO_{C_\natural}(c,u) \Rightarrow \neg tA(a,u) \vee \neg DO_{A_\natural}(a,u) \qquad (21)$$

We get five conditions here, because condition (14) gives two conditions, (18) and (19). Using these equations, we can prove that **A** is trace refined by **C**.

Theorem 2. *Assume that* **A** *and* **C** *are as above and that conditions (17)–(21) hold. Then the trace refinement* $\mathbf{A} \sqsubseteq \mathbf{C}$ *is valid.*

This proof method is usually called *forward simulation.*

4.3 Backward simulation

Dually to forward simulation, we get a method of backward simulation if the abstraction command is demonic. In this section, we will need the notion of a continuous action system.

We say that the action system $\mathbf{A} = (A_0, A)$ is *continuous* if both the initialization command A_0 and the action A are continuous predicate transformers. This is equivalent to requiring that for all u, the set $\{a | pA_0(a,u)\}$ is finite, and that for all (a,u), the set $\{(a',u') | nA(a,u)(a',u')\}$ is also finite. To put this another way, we require that pA_0 (viewed as a relation between the states u_0 and (x_0, u_0)) and nA are both image-finite.

Let γ be the demonic abstraction command

$$\gamma = [\lambda(c,u).\, \lambda(a,u').\, R(a,c,u) \wedge u' = u].$$

In this case (13)–(16) can be rewritten as

$$R(a,c,u) \wedge pC_0(c,u) \wedge nC_\natural^m(c,u)(c',u')$$
$$\Rightarrow \exists n, a'.\, pA_0(a,u) \wedge nA_\natural^n(a,u)(a',u') \qquad (22)$$
$$R(a',c',u') \wedge (nC_\sharp;\, nC_\natural^m)(c,u)(c',u')$$
$$\Rightarrow \exists n, a.\, R(a,c,u) \wedge (\neg tA(a,u) \vee (nA_\sharp;\, nA_\natural^n)(a,u)(a',u')) \qquad (23)$$
$$\neg tC(c,u) \Rightarrow \exists a.\, R(a,c,u) \wedge \neg tA(a,u) \qquad (24)$$
$$\neg gC(c,u) \Rightarrow \exists a.\, R(a,c,u) \wedge (\neg tA(a,u) \vee \neg gA(a,u)) \qquad (25)$$
$$\neg DO_{C_\natural}(c,u) \Rightarrow \exists a.\, R(a,c,u) \wedge (\neg tA(a,u) \vee \neg DO_{A_\natural}(a,u)) \qquad (26)$$

Theorem 3. *Assume that* **A** *and* **C** *are action systems. Furthermore assume that* **A** *is continuous, that the abstraction relation R is total and that conditions (22)–(26) hold. Then the trace refinement* $\mathbf{A} \sqsubseteq \mathbf{C}$ *is valid.*

This method for proving refinement is known as *backward simulation.*

4.4 Compositional reasoning

A reactive system is generally composed from smaller components. The components can be modeled as action systems and the composition operator is parallel composition. We say that a method for proving trace refinement is *compositional* if $\mathbf{A} \parallel \mathbf{B} \sqsubseteq \mathbf{C} \parallel \mathbf{B}$ holds for all action systems $\mathbf{B}$ whenever we have proved $\mathbf{A} \sqsubseteq \mathbf{C}$ using the method in question.

The basic idea is that if the refinement $\mathbf{A} \sqsubseteq \mathbf{C}$ is proved using a compositional method, then $\mathbf{C}$ can replace $\mathbf{A}$ in any context (i.e., in any parallel composition).

In general, neither forward nor backward simulation is compositional. However, we do get compositionality under certain conditions.

Let R be a predicate over (a, c, u) and $\mathbf{B} = (B_0, B)$ an action system over state (b, u). We say that $\mathbf{B}$ *does not interfere with* R if the condition

$$tB(b,u) \wedge R(a,c,u) \;\Rightarrow\; B(\lambda(b,u).\, R(a,c,u))(b,u)$$

holds universally. Thus B does not interfere with R if B cannot make R false, when it is established.

Forward simulation is compositional under a noninterference condition.

Theorem 4. *Assume that* $\mathbf{A} \sqsubseteq \mathbf{C}$ *is proved by forward simulation with abstraction relation* R *and that* $\mathbf{B}$ *does not interfere with* R*. Then* $\mathbf{A} \parallel \mathbf{B} \sqsubseteq \mathbf{C} \parallel \mathbf{B}$.

An important special case is when the abstraction relation R is *local*, i.e., when $R(a,c,u) = R'(a,c)$ for some R' (syntactically, this is the case when R does not refer to the global component at all). In this case it is obviously impossible for $\mathbf{B}$ to interfere with R.

Corollary 5. *Assume that the trace refinement* $\mathbf{A} \sqsubseteq \mathbf{C}$ *is proved by forward simulation with a local abstraction invariant. Then* $\mathbf{A} \parallel \mathbf{B} \sqsubseteq \mathbf{C} \parallel \mathbf{B}$ *holds for arbitrary action system* $\mathbf{B}$.

For backward simulation, we do not have a compositionality theorem corresponding to Theorem 4. However, there is a result corresponding to Corollary 5.

Theorem 6. *Assume that the trace refinement* $\mathbf{A} \sqsubseteq \mathbf{C}$ *is proved by backward simulation with a local abstraction invariant. Then* $\mathbf{A} \parallel \mathbf{B} \sqsubseteq \mathbf{C} \parallel \mathbf{B}$ *holds for arbitrary action system* $\mathbf{B}$.

5 Using the simulation method

We shall now show how the simulation method is used in practice. Before we give an example of a trace refinement proof using simulation, we discuss a few ways of making the simulation method easier to use.

As already noted, we want to write action systems in a form that syntactically shows a number of distinct actions. We now assume that the action A of the action system $\mathbf{A} = (A_0, A)$ and action C of action system $\mathbf{C} = (C_0, C)$ are decomposed as

$$A = A_1 \wedge \ldots \wedge A_n \wedge A_\natural \quad \text{and} \quad C = C_1 \wedge \ldots \wedge C_m \wedge C_\natural$$

where $A_\natural$ and $C_\natural$ are stuttering actions.

We can prove a trace refinement $\mathbf{A} \sqsubseteq \mathbf{C}$ using the simulation method as before, but with the condition (14) replaced by a separate condition for each concrete change action C_i, as follows. For each C_i, there must exist a set of abstract actions $\{A_{i_j}\}$ such that

$$\gamma; (\wedge j.\, A_{i_j}); A_\natural^* \leq C_i; C_\natural^*; \gamma \tag{27}$$

Thus we check this condition for each concrete change action C_i, but we are free to choose a suitable combination of abstract change actions that should have the same effect as C_i. Note that we can group together abstract actions arbitrarily, when proving (27). The groupings for different C_i may overlap, and some abstract actions may not be used at all. In most practical cases, however, we are close to a one-to-one-correspondence between abstract and concrete actions.

The simulation method does not require stuttering to be present. Since $S \wedge \mathsf{magic} = S$ for all commands S, we can use the simulation method as such, setting $A_\natural = C_\natural = \mathsf{magic}$.

Straightforward calculations show that the simulation conditions (13)–(16) in this case reduce to

$$A_0 \leq C_0; \gamma, \qquad \gamma; A \leq C; \gamma \qquad \text{and} \qquad \gamma(tA \wedge gA) \leq gC$$

In this case, the verification conditions for both forward and backward simulation are simplified considerably.

5.1 A simpler simulation method

The treatment of concrete stuttering makes the proof rules of the simulation methods quite complicated. For example, the free (i.e., universally quantified) occurrence of m in the second verification condition of forward simulation (18) indicates that it can be quite difficult to find the right instantiations of n and a' on the right hand side. We shall now give a more useful (though slightly weaker) method that makes stuttering easier to handle.

We say that γ is a *weak simulation* between $\mathbf{A} = (A_0, A)$ and $\mathbf{C} = (C_0, C)$ if the actions can be decomposed as $A = A_\sharp \wedge A_\natural$ and $C = C_\sharp \wedge C_\natural$ where $A_\natural$ and $C_\natural$ are stuttering actions and γ is an abstraction command which satisfies the following conditions:

$$A_0; A_\natural^* \leq C_0; \gamma \tag{28}$$
$$\gamma; A_\sharp; A_\natural^* \leq C_\sharp; \gamma \tag{29}$$
$$\gamma(tA \wedge gA) \leq gC \tag{30}$$
$$\gamma; A_\natural^* \leq C_\natural; \gamma \tag{31}$$
$$\gamma(tA \wedge DO_{A_\natural}) \leq DO_{C_\natural} \tag{32}$$

Lemma 7. *If γ is a weak simulation between* **A** *and* **C**, *then γ is a simulation between* **A** *and* **C**.

In the forward case, i.e., when the abstraction command is angelic, the conditions for weak simulation can be rewritten into the following:

$$pC_0(c,u) \Rightarrow \exists n\; a'\; a.\; R(a,c,u) \wedge pA_0(a',u) \wedge nA_\natural^n(a',u)(a,u) \tag{33}$$

$$\begin{aligned} & R(a,c,u) \wedge nC_\sharp(c,u)(c',u') \\ & \quad \Rightarrow \neg tA(a,u) \vee (\exists n\; a'.\; R(a',c',u') \wedge (nA_\sharp;\, nA_\natural^n)(a,u)(a',u')) \end{aligned} \tag{34}$$

$$R(a,c,u) \wedge \neg tC(c,u) \Rightarrow \neg tA(a,u) \tag{35}$$

$$R(a,c,u) \wedge \neg gC(c,u) \Rightarrow \neg tA(a,u) \vee \neg gA(a,u) \tag{36}$$

$$R(a,c,u) \wedge nC_\natural(c,u)(c',u) \Rightarrow \exists n\; a'.\; R(a',c',u) \wedge nA_\natural^n(a,u)(a',u) \tag{37}$$

$$R(a,c,u) \wedge \neg DO_{C_\natural}(c,u) \Rightarrow \neg tA(a,u) \vee \neg DO_{A_\natural}(a,u) \tag{38}$$

From Lemma 7 and Theorem 2 we immediately see that the existence of a weak forward simulation implies that $\mathbf{A} \sqsubseteq \mathbf{C}$. In the next section we shall illustrate this method on an example refinement.

6 Example: a lossy queue

We give two specifications of a lossy FIFO-queue and show that they are equivalent (i.e., each system refines the other). This example is intended to illustrate the simulation method. It uses stuttering both in the abstract and the concrete system in an essential way.

The queue is internal (local) in both systems. The environment communicates with the queue in the following way. It can put values into the variable *in*, setting the *inf* flag and it can request values by setting the *outf* flag. The queue takes elements from *in* (resetting the *inf* flag) and returns values to *out* (resetting the *outf* flag). The difference between the two systems is the ways in which the queue loses values: System **C** can lose values anywhere in the queue while system **A** can lose only the value at the front of the queue.

System **A** is the action system $\mathbf{A} = (A_0, A_1 \wedge A_2 \wedge A_\natural)$, where the initialization and the actions are as follows:

$$\begin{aligned} A_0 &: a := [\,] \\ A_1 &: \mathit{inf} \;\rightarrow a, \mathit{inf} := a :: \mathit{in}, F \\ A_2 &: \mathit{outf} \wedge a \neq [\,] \rightarrow \mathit{out}, a, \mathit{outf} := \mathit{hd}\; a, \mathit{tl}\; a, F \\ A_\natural &: a \neq [\,] \rightarrow a := \mathit{tl}\; a \end{aligned}$$

Here $A_\natural$ is the stuttering action which loses a message from the front of the queue. The queue is modeled as a list ([ ] is the empty queue while *hd* and *tl* are the front and rest functions; $a :: x$ is the queue a with the element x added at the rear).

System $\mathbf{C} = (C_0, C_1 \wedge C_2 \wedge C_\natural)$ is almost the same, but the stuttering action is different:

$$\begin{aligned}
&C_0 : c := [\,] \\
&C_1 : inf \ \rightarrow c, inf := c :: in, F \\
&C_2 : outf \wedge c \neq [\,] \rightarrow out, c, outf := hd\ c, tl\ c, F \\
&C_\natural : c \neq [\,] \rightarrow c := c'.\ (\exists i < len\ c.\ c' = del(c, i))
\end{aligned}$$

Here, *len* c is the length of the list c and $del(c, i)$ is the result of deleting the ith element from c (the head is the 0th element)

The refinement $\mathbf{C} \sqsubseteq \mathbf{A}$ is easily proved by forward simulation using the abstraction relation

$$R(a, c) \quad = \quad (a = c)$$

This refinement only makes the stuttering action more deterministic.

The opposite refinement $\mathbf{A} \sqsubseteq \mathbf{C}$ requires more elaborate reasoning. The essential feature of the refinement is that any loss of an element in $\mathbf{C}$ can be mimicked in $\mathbf{A}$ by waiting until the element in question is at the front of the queue. If this waiting is infinite, then we need not bother at all, since in this case the loss of the element has no observable consequences.

The abstraction invariant R is local. It is defined by

$$R(a, c) \quad = \quad (hd\ a = hd\ c) \wedge c \prec a$$

where $c \prec a$ means that c is a sublist of a. The definition of R should be interpreted so that if either one of a and c is empty, then the other one is also empty.

We can now check the six conditions (33)–(38). We first note that

$$nA_\natural^n(a, u)(a', u') \quad = \quad (a' = rest(a, n)) \wedge (u' = u)$$

where $rest(a, n)$ is the result of removing the n first element from the list a. Here u represents the global state component containing (at least) the components $inf, outf, in, out$.

The initialization condition (33). This condition is

$$c = [\,] \ \Rightarrow\ \exists n\ a\ a'.\ R(a, [\,]) \wedge (a = [\,]) \wedge (a' = rest(a, n))$$

which is obviously satisfied by choosing $n = 0$ and $a = a' = [\,]$.

The action condition (29). We first show that C_1 implements A_1. Here no stuttering is needed; we show that

$$\begin{aligned}
&(hd\ a = hd\ c) \wedge c \prec a \wedge inf \wedge \neg inf' \wedge (c' = c :: in) \\
&\Rightarrow \exists a'.\ (hd\ a' = hd\ c') \wedge c' \prec a' \wedge inf \wedge \neg inf' \wedge (a' = a :: in)
\end{aligned}$$

(for readability, we have omitted the conjuncts $in' = in$ and other similar conjuncts on both sides). Choosing $a' = a :: in$ obviously works here.

Now we show that C_2 implements A_2. Intuitively, both actions give the front element to the environment, but we may need to lose some elements (some stuttering actions $A_\natural$) to keep up with earlier losses in **C**. The requirement is

$$\begin{aligned} &(hd\ a = hd\ c) \wedge c \prec a \wedge outf \wedge (c \neq [\,]) \wedge (out' = hd\ c) \wedge (c' = tl\ c) \wedge \neg outf' \\ \Rightarrow\ &\exists n\ a'\ a''.\ (hd\ a'' = hd\ c') \wedge c' \prec a'' \wedge outf \wedge (a \neq [\,]) \\ &\quad \wedge (out' = hd\ a) \wedge (a' = tl\ a) \wedge \neg outf \wedge (a'' = rest(a', n)) \end{aligned}$$

Obviously we must choose $a' = tl(a)$. If $c' = [\,]$, then choose $n = len\ a'$ and $a'' = [\,]$ and the condition is easily checked. If $c' \neq [\,]$, then choose $n = min\{k | a_k = hd\ c'\}$, where a_k is the kth element of a. This number n is well-defined, since $c \prec a$ implies $c' \prec a'$.

The abortion condition (35). This condition is trivially satisfied, since all actions involved are always terminating.

The termination condition (36). This condition is

$$R(a, c) \wedge \neg inf \wedge (c = [\,]) \ \Rightarrow \neg inf \wedge (a = [\,])$$

which is obviously true, by the definition of R.

The stuttering condition (37). We now show that the concrete stuttering action $C_\natural$ (loss of an element) implements skip. Intuitively, a loss of an element inside the queue is not reflected in **A**, but if the front element is lost, then stuttering in **A** is needed. We have to show that

$$\begin{aligned} &(hd\ a = hd\ c) \wedge c \prec a \wedge outf \wedge (c \neq [\,]) \wedge (c \neq [\,]) \wedge (c' = del(c, i)) \\ \Rightarrow\ &\exists n\ a'.\ (hd\ a' = hd\ c') \wedge c' \prec a' \wedge (a' = rest(a, n)) \end{aligned}$$

If $i > 0$, then choose $n = 0$ and $a' = a$. If on the other hand $i = 0$, then we have lost the front element in c. In this case, if $c' = [\,]$, then choose $n = len\ a'$ and $a' = [\,]$, otherwise choose $n = min\{k | a_k = hd\ c'\}$.

The infinite stuttering condition (38). This condition is trivially satisfied, since both systems permit only finite stuttering.

We have shown that the two specifications **A** and **C** refine each other, i.e., that they are equivalent. The refinement $\mathbf{A} \sqsubseteq \mathbf{C}$ is not a trivial result, since **C** permits behavior (loss of an element from the inside of the queue) that has no immediate counterpart in **A**. Since the abstraction relations were local, we can compose either specification with an arbitrary environment **B**, and the results are equivalent. This environment may feed the queue with new elements and remove them in arbitrary ways, or it may just add elements to the queue without ever removing them. It may even do nothing at all.

7 Soundess and Completeness of General Simulation

Forward and backward simulation are sound under some very general conditions. General simulation is also sound, but we need stronger assumptions in that case: action systems may neither have infinite stuttering nor terminating behaviors. The first restriction is not very severe, but the second one is a restriction we would not want to make. However, we have not found a soundness proof for the case when terminating behaviors are permitted.

We also have a completeness theorem for the restricted case. This theorem states that if the trace refinement $\mathbf{A} \sqsubseteq \mathbf{C}$ holds, then there is a simulation γ that proves it.

In the case with no terminating behaviors and no infinite stuttering the simulation conditions (13)–(16) reduce to the following:

$$A_0;\ A_\natural^* \leq C_0;\ C_\natural^*;\ \gamma \tag{39}$$

$$\gamma;\ A_\sharp;\ A_\natural^* \leq C_\sharp;\ C_\natural^*;\ \gamma \tag{40}$$

Theorem 8. *Assume that the action systems* $\mathbf{A} = (A_0, A)$ *and* $\mathbf{C} = (C_0, C)$ *are given, where* $\mathbf{A}$ *is continuous and where neither* $\mathbf{A}$ *nor* $\mathbf{C}$ *has any terminating or infinitely stuttering behaviors. Then the trace refinement* $\mathbf{A} \sqsubseteq \mathbf{C}$ *holds if and only if there exists an abstraction command* γ *and a decomposition of the actions* A *and* C *such that conditions (39) and (40) are satisfied.*

The completeness theorem shows that any trace refinement can be proved using simulation. In fact, the proof of the soundness theorem shows that any trace refinement $\mathbf{A} \sqsubseteq \mathbf{C}$ can be proved by a combination of backward and forward simulation, through an intermediate action system $\mathbf{B}$. The proof uses a power construction where the local state component of B ranges over sets of values of the local component of A. In practice, it seems that most trace refinements can be proved using forward simulation. However, in situations where the concrete action system postpones a nondeterministic choice backward simulation may be required. We are not aware of any non-pathological examples where both forward and backward simulation would fail.

Jonsson [13] consider two special situations in which the completeness question for refinement between distributed systems is simplified. He shows that his notion of forward simulation is complete if the abstract system is deterministic. Dually, backward simulation is complete if the concrete system is forest-like. This is true in our framework too, in the case when there are no stuttering actions.

8 Conclusions

We have above described the basic method for refining action systems, expressed as a refinement rule in the Refinement Calculus. This gives us a very general and powerful proof method for stepwise refinement of parallel and reactive systems. Forward and backward refinement methods were shown to be special cases of the general refinement rule. These rules can be shown to be sound under some very general conditions. We derived simplified versions of these rules, which are usually sufficient to establish refinement in practice. The general simulation rule is sound and complete for nonterminating systems with no infinite stuttering.

Acknowledgments We would like to thank Michael Butler and Rob Udink for comments on the paper, and Kaisa Sere for extensive discussions on the topics treated here.

References

1. M. Abadi and L. Lamport. The existence of refinement mappings. *Theoretical Computer Science*, 82:253–284, 1991.
2. R. Back. *Correctness Preserving Program Refinements: Proof Theory and Applications*, volume 131 of *Mathematical Center Tracts.* Mathematical Centre, Amsterdam, 1980.
3. R. Back. Refinement calculus, part II: Parallel and reactive programs. In *REX Workshop for Refinement of Distributed Systems,* volume 430 of *Lecture Notes in Computer Science*, Nijmegen, The Netherlands, 1989. Springer–Verlag.
4. R. Back. Refining atomicity in parallel algorithms. In *PARLE Conference on Parallel Architectures and Languages Europe*, Eindhoven, the Netherlands, June 1989. Springer Verlag.
5. R. Back and R. Kurki-Suonio. Decentralization of process nets with centralized control. In *2nd ACM SIGACT-SIGOPS Symp. on Principles of Distributed Computing*, pages 131–142. ACM, 1983.
6. R. Back and R. Kurki-Suonio. Distributed co–operation with action systems. *ACM Transactions on Programming Languages and Systems*, 10:513–554, October 1988.
7. R. Back and K. Sere. Stepwise refinement of action systems. *Structured Programming*, 12:17–30, 1991.
8. R. Back and K. Sere. Superposition refinement of parallel algorithms. In K. Parker and G. Rose, editors, *Formal Description Techniques IV*, pages 475–493. Elsevier Science Publishers (North-Holland), 1992.
9. R. Back and J. von Wright. Refinement calculus, part I: Sequential programs. In *REX Workshop for Refinement of Distributed Systems,* volume 430 of *Lecture Notes in Computer Science*, Nijmegen, The Netherlands, 1989. Springer–Verlag.
10. M. Butler. *Refinement and Decomposition of Value-Passing Action Systems.* In E. Best, editor, *CONCUR'93*, volume LNCS 715. Springer–Verlag, 1993.
11. K. Chandy and J. Misra. *Parallel Program Design: A Foundation.* Addison–Wesley, 1988.
12. E. Dijkstra. *A Discipline of Programming.* Prentice–Hall International, 1976.
13. B. Jonsson. Simulations between specifications of distributed systems. In *Proceedings of 2nd International Conference on Concurrency Theory (CONCUR '91),* volume 527 of *Lecture Notes in Computer Science*, Amsterdam, The Netherlands, 1991. Springer–Verlag.
14. L. Lamport. A Temporal Logic of Actions. Src report 57, Digital SRC, 1990.
15. C. Morgan. *Programming from Specifications.* Prentice-Hall, 1990.

Bisimulation for Models in Concurrency

Mogens Nielsen and Christian Clausen

BRICS**
Department of Computer Science
University of Aarhus
DK-8000 Aarhus C, Denmark

Abstract. Recently, Joyal, Nielsen and Winskel suggested a categorical definition of bisimulation, applicable to a wide range of models in concurrency with an accompanying notion af observations. The definition is in terms of span of open maps, and it coincides with Park and Milner's strong bisimulation for the standard model of labelled transition systems with sequential observations. Here, we briefly present the general set-up, and discuss its applications. For the model of transition systems with independence and nonsequential observations, the associated notion of bisimulation was shown to be a slight strengthening of the history preserving bisimulations of Rabinovich and Trakhtenbrot. Furthermore, it turns out that this bisimulation has game theoretic and logical characterizations in the form of pleasantly simple modifications of well-known characterizations of standard strong bisimulation.

1 Introduction

An important ingredient of the theory of concurrency is the notion of *behavioral equivalence* between processes; what does it mean for two systems to be equal with respect to their communication structures? There is no unique answer to this question, but, undoubtedly, one of the most popular and successful answers was given by Park [Par81]: Two processes (or states s and s' of two transition systems) are equivalent, or *bisimilar*, if for all actions a, every a-derivative of s is bisimilar to some a-derivative of s', and vice versa.

One of the measures of success for a behaviour equivalence is its accompanying *theory*. And here bisimulation is particularly rich in results. Let us mention just three examples of elegant and powerful characterizations.

The original definition is in terms of the existence of a bisimulation relation: Two transition systems are *bisimilar* iff there is a relation $\mathcal{S}$ over states such that the initial states are related, and

- whenever $s \; \mathcal{S} \; s'$ and $s \xrightarrow{a} s_1$, there is a transition $s' \xrightarrow{a} s_1'$ such that $s_1 \; \mathcal{S} \; s_1'$, and
- whenever $s \; \mathcal{S} \; s'$ and $s' \xrightarrow{a} s_1'$, there is a transition $s \xrightarrow{a} s_1$ such that $s_1 \; \mathcal{S} \; s_1'$.

** Basic Research in Computer Science, Centre of the Danish National Research Foundation.

Secondly, as shown by Stirling, the process of exploring whether two transition systems are bisimilar or not can be viewed as a *game* between two persons, Player and Opponent, taking turns [Sti93]. This provides an operational setting in which bisimulation may be understood experimentally. Player tries to prove the systems bisimilar, whereas Opponent intends otherwise. The game is opened by Opponent who chooses a transition from the initial state of one of the systems. This transition must be matched by Player with an equally labelled transition from the initial state of the other system. The new states form the starting point for the next pair of moves, and so forth. The play continues like this *forever*, in which case Player wins, or until either Player or Opponent is unable to move, in which case the opposition wins. This game is *characteristic* for bisimulation in the sense that two transition systems are bisimilar iff Player has a *winning strategy*, i.e. iff Player is able to win every game starting from the initial states.

And, thirdly, we have the characterization of bismulation in terms of *Hennessy-Milner logic* [HM85], a modal logic in which the modalities are indexed by actions: Two systems are bisimilar iff they satisfy the same logical assertions.

In the transition system model of CCS and CSP, parallelism is treated as *non-deterministic interleaving* of atomic actions. As a result, the CCS-processes $a \parallel b$, which can do the atomic actions a and b in parallel, is bisimilar to the process $a.b+b.a$, which non-deterministically chooses to do either *"a followed by b"* or *"b followed by a"*. In fact, the associated transition systems are isomorphic. Abstracting away from the names of the states, both transition systems are represented by the system of Fig. 1. Due to this identification, the transition system

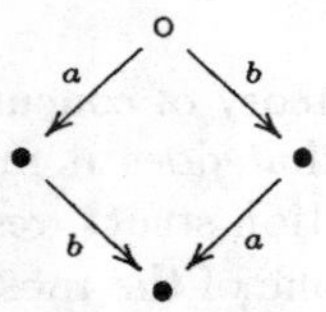

Fig. 1. A transition system representing both $a \parallel b$ and $a.b + b.a$.

model is usually called an *interleaving model*, and bisimulation is traditionally called *interleaving bisimulation* when confusion is possible.

Petri nets , on the other hand, model the *physical disjointness* of distributed processes. The processes $a \parallel b$ and $a.b + b.a$ are represented by the labelled nets of Fig. 1 [Old91].

The leftmost net consists of two independent events labelled a and b, whereas the rightmost net is a purely (nondeterministic) sequential net. The independence of the two events in the leftmost net is represented in net terms as disjointness of their neighbourhood of local states (conditions). Many other closely related formalizations of the same idea in *non-interleaving* models have been suggested, e.g. the *asynchronous transition systems* of [Bed88, Shi85] and the *transitions systems with independence* of [WN94]. For a survey of these, see [WN94].

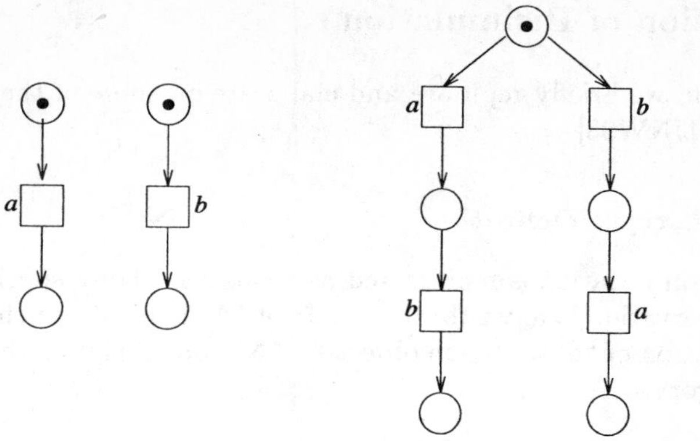

Fig. 2. Labelled Petri nets representing $a \parallel b$ and $a.b + b.a$.

What is now the appropriate generalization of bisimulation to these "independence models"? Many attempts have been made to answer this question. Unfortunately, with almost just as many different answers. Moreover, many of the proposed equivalences are incomparable. (See [GG89] and [GKP92] for definitions and comparisons of some of them.)

One reason behind these variations is that the step from interleaving models to independence models opens up for a variety of choices, when trying to define an equivalence at the concrete level. [JNW93] reports on an attempt to define bisimulation in a *uniform* way across a wide range of different models for concurrent computation with an associated notion of observations. As a first measure of success, it is observed in [JNW93] that the abstract definition specializes to interleaving bisimulation in the case of ordinary transition systems with sequential observations.

In the context of an independence model, [JNW93] suggested pomsets [Pra86] as appropriate observations, giving rise to an induced notion of $\mathbf{Pom}_L$-*bisimilarity*. In [JNW93], a concrete characterization of $\mathbf{Pom}_L$-bisimilarity is given in the model of *event structures*, which may be thought of as *unfoldings* of nets or transition systems with independence. Interestingly, the characterization is not equal to any previously published equivalence; in fact, it is a strengthening of the history-preserving bisimulation [GG89, RT88].

In this paper, we briefly survey the results of [JNW93], emphasizing the generality of the approach, and mentioning some applications of the theory. Furthermore we present in some detail concrete characterizations of $\mathbf{Pom}_L$-bisimilarity in the model of transition systems with independence.

It turns out that surprisingly small twists of the game theoretic [Sti93] characterization of interleaving bisimulation lead to characterizations of $\mathbf{Pom}_L$-bisimilarity. The twists consists in introducing a notion of backtracking, inspired by the idea behind the back and forth bisimulations of [DMV90]. On the logical side, the Hennessy-Milner logic extended with a past tense modality [HS85] turns out to be characteristic for $\mathbf{Pom}_L$-bisimilarity. These results are taken from [NC94], and stated here in a slightly simplified form.

2 A Notion of Bisimulation

In this section we briefly rephrase and elaborate on some of the definitions and results from [JNW93].

2.1 An Abstract Definition

A model of computation is represented as a category. For a specific model, **M**, a choice of observation is any subcategory **P** of **M**. Typically, a choice of observation is a selection of "observation objects" of **M**, and **P** is then the corresponding full subcategory.

Definition 1. Given a model **M** and a choice of observation **P**, where **P** is a subcategory of **M**, a morphism $f : X \to Y$ is said to be **P**-*open* in **M** iff whenever a square

$$\begin{array}{ccc} P & \xrightarrow{p} & X \\ {\scriptstyle m}\downarrow & & \downarrow{\scriptstyle f} \\ Q & \xrightarrow{q} & Y \end{array}$$

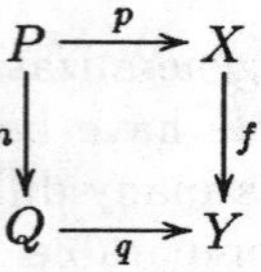

commutes, i.e. $f \circ p = q \circ m$, there is a morphism $p' : Q \to X$ such that the "triangles" in

$$\begin{array}{ccc} P & \xrightarrow{p} & X \\ {\scriptstyle m}\downarrow & \nearrow{\scriptstyle p'} & \downarrow{\scriptstyle f} \\ Q & \xrightarrow{q} & Y \end{array}$$

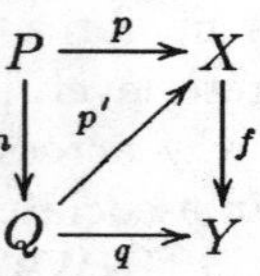

commute, i.e. $p' \circ m = p$ and $f \circ p' = q$. □

Fact: *In the familiar example of **M** being a category of transition systems and **P** being sequences of labels, it turns out that open maps correspond to the well-known zig-zag morphisms of [Ben84] - see [JNW93].*

Definition 2. Assume **P** is a subcategory of **M** and define two objects X and X' of **M** to be **P**-*bisimilar* iff there is a span of **P**-open morphisms f and f' with common domain Y:

□

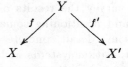

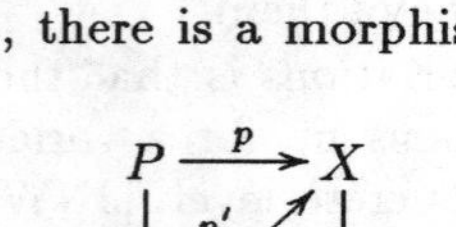

Fact: *Using that pullbacks of **P**-open maps are themselves **P**-open, it can be shown that **P**-bisimilarity is an equivalence relation provided that **M** has pullbacks. In all such cases, **P**-bisimilarity is simply the equivalence induced by being related by **P**-open maps - see [JNW93].*

Fact: *The category of transition systems turns out to have pullbacks, and the notion of* **P***-bisimilarity (***P** *again being sequences of labels) turns out to coincide precisely with (strong) bisimilarity in the sense of [Mil89] - see [JNW93].*

We would like the reader to appreciate the general set-up as a guideline for making the right choices in the search for generalizations of bisimulation to other models than standard transition systems. However, one also gets a number of properties "for free", by applying this abstract definition. One example is the second fact above, implying the property of being an equivalence. Another example is the following.

Theorem 3. *Let* **M** *be a coreflective subcategory of* **N** *with* J *right adjoint to the inclusion functor* I*:* $\mathbf{M} \hookrightarrow \mathbf{N}$ *and* **P** *a subcategory of* **M***. Then:*

(i) For all objects M *and* M' *of* **M***,* M *and* M' *are* **P***-bisimilar in* **M** *iff* $I(M)$ *and* $I(M')$ *are* **P***-bisimilar in* **N***.*
(ii) For all objects N *and* N' *of* **N***,* N *and* N' *are* **P***-bisimilar in* **N** *iff* $J(N)$ *and* $J(N')$ *are* **P***-bisimilar in* **M***.*

Proof. Follows from generalizations of the proof from [JNW93] of the concrete case of **M** being labelled event structures, **N** transition systems with independence, and **P** pomsets, or the corresponding proof from [NW94] of the case of **M** being labelled asynchronous transition systems, **N** labelled Petri nets, and **P** pomsets. □

Typical applications of this theorem are based on the fact that for many system models in concurrency, coreflective subcategories have been identified, where the right adjoint of the coreflection produces a representation of behaviour. Two example are the ones mentioned in the proof above. In such situations, the theorem allows you to conclude that two systems are bisimilar iff the same holds for their behaviour repesentations.

Both these examples of properties of any bisimulation based on the abstract definition in terms of span of open maps, are to be contrasted with the usual task of proving these highly desirable properties for notions of bisimulations defined on the concrete level.

To our knowledge the theory has mainly been applied to generalizations of bisimulation to so-called non-interleaving models like Petri nets [NW94] and transition systems with independence [JNW93]. The latter example is presented in the following section. But the set-up should find similar applications in the search for appropriate generalizations of bisimulation in other settings, e.g. timed transition systems, probabilistic transition systems, etc.

2.2 A Noninterleaving Bisimulation

In the following we present in some detail one complete example of the application of the abstract definition, the one for transition systems with independence and nonsequential obeservations from [JNW93]. Transition systems with independence are precisely what their name suggests, namely ordinary transition systems with an additional relation expressing when one transition is independent of another. The independence relation expresses which actions can happen in parallel.

Definition 4. A *transition system with independence* is a structure

$$X = (S, i, L, Tran, I)$$

where

- S is a set of *states* with a distinguished *initial state* i,
- L is a set of *labels*,
- $Tran \subseteq S \times L \times S$ is a set of *transitions*[3], and
- $I \subseteq Tran^2$ is an *independence relation* which is irreflexive and symmetric.

Moreover, we require the following axioms to hold:

1. $s \xrightarrow{a} s_1 \sim s \xrightarrow{a} s_2 \Rightarrow s_1 = s_2$
2. $s \xrightarrow{a} s_1 \; I \; s_1 \xrightarrow{b} u \Rightarrow \exists s_2 .\, s \xrightarrow{a} s_1 \; I \; s \xrightarrow{b} s_2 \; I \; s_2 \xrightarrow{a} u$
3. (a) $s \xrightarrow{a} s_1 \prec s_2 \xrightarrow{a} u \; I \; w \xrightarrow{b} w' \Rightarrow s \xrightarrow{a} s_1 \; I \; w \xrightarrow{b} w'$
   (b) $w \xrightarrow{b} w' \; I \; s \xrightarrow{a} s_1 \prec s_2 \xrightarrow{a} u \Rightarrow w \xrightarrow{b} w' \; I \; s_2 \xrightarrow{a} u$

where the relation $\prec$ between transitions is defined by

$$s \xrightarrow{a} s_1 \prec s_2 \xrightarrow{a} u \Leftrightarrow \exists b .\, s_1 \xrightarrow{b} u \; I \; s \xrightarrow{a} s_1 \; I \; s \xrightarrow{b} s_2 \; I \; s_2 \xrightarrow{a} u,$$

and $\sim$ is the least equivalence relation including $\prec$. □

The $\sim$-equivalence classes should be thought of as *events*. Thus, Axiom 1 asserts that the occurrence of an event at a state yields a unique state. Similarly, Axiom 3 asserts that independence respects events. Axiom 2 describes the intuitive property of independence that whenever two independent transitions occur consecutively, they can also occur in the opposite order. Hence, if $s \xrightarrow{a} s_1 \xrightarrow{b} u$ are independent transitions there is an "independence square"

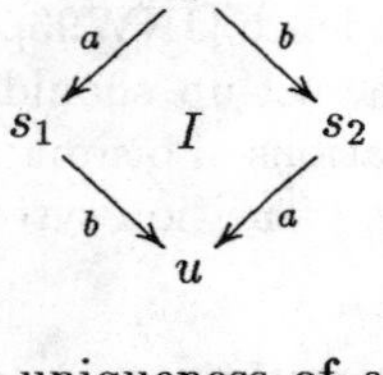

Moreover, Axiom 1 implies the uniqueness of s_2. So we are justified in saying that s_2 (or $s \xrightarrow{b} s_2 \xrightarrow{a} u$) is *the* completion of $s \xrightarrow{a} s_1 \xrightarrow{b} u$.

[3] As usual, a transition $(s, a, s_1) \in Tran$ is written as $s \xrightarrow{a} s_1$.

Notice that an ordinary labelled transition system can be viewed as a transition system with independence having empty independence relation. Furthermore, the standard labelled case graph of a labelled (safe) net, with two transitions being independent iff they represent firings of independent (in net terminology) events, is a transition system with independence [WN94]. As an example the transition system with independence above is the representation of the CCS-expression $a \parallel b$ or its corresponding net from 1 (following [WN94]).

For later use, we introduce some terminology. For a transition $t = (s \xrightarrow{a} s_1)$ we shall write $src(t)$, $tgt(t)$, and $\ell(t)$ for s, s_1, and a, respectively. The set $Seqs(X)$ consists of those transition sequences $\bar{t} = t_0 t_1 \cdots t_{n-1}$ in X beginning at the initial state ($src(t_0) = i$) which are consecutive ($src(t_{i+1}) = tgt(t_i)$). Transition sequences are always indexed from zero. We write $(\bar{t})_i$ or simply t_i for the i'th transition in $\bar{t}$. The length of $\bar{t}$ is referred to as $|\bar{t}|$. When nothing else is stated, a transition system with independence X is assumed to have components S, i, L, $Tran$, and I.

In stating the formal results in this paper, it is sometimes convenient to exclude systems having the property that the same action (label) has multiple independent occurrences. Formally, this phenomenon is captured in the following definition.

Definition 5. A transition system with independence is said to exhibit *auto-concurrency* iff it has two consecutive and independent transitions with equal labels. □

The category **TI** has transition systems with independence as objects. For the remaining part of this paper we fix a set L and restrict ourselves to those transition systems with independence that have labelling set L. As morphisms in the category $\mathbf{TI}_L$ we choose the fiber-morphisms of [WN94]:

Definition 6. Let $X = (S, i, L, Tran, I)$ and $X' = (S', i', L', Tran', I')$ be transition systems with independence. A *morphism* f from X to X' is a function $f : S \rightarrow S'$ such that

- $f(i) = i'$
- for all transitions $s \xrightarrow{a} s_1$ in X, $f(s) \xrightarrow{a} f(s')$ in X'
- $s \xrightarrow{a} s_1 \; I \; u \xrightarrow{b} u_1$ in X implies $f(s) \xrightarrow{a} f(s_1) \; I' \; f(u) \xrightarrow{b} f(u_1)$ in X' □

What should be the associated notion of (nonsequential) observations? One choice made in [JNW93] is Pratt's pomsets [Pra86], a smooth generalization of sequences of labelled actions to partially ordered labelled actions. We identify the category $\mathbf{Pom}_L$ of pomsets with its full and faithful embedding in $\mathbf{TI}_L$. For details we refer to [JNW93], but to illustrate the idea, we show the transition systems for two simple examples. Firstly, the totally ordered pomset $a_1 \cdots a_n ab$ is represented by the following "stick":

Secondly, the transition system for the slightly modified pomset, in which the final occurrences of a and b are unordered is represented by the following "lollipop":

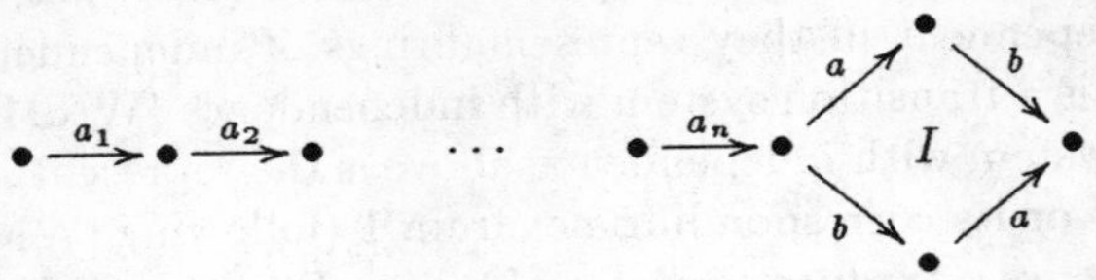

In general, the states of the transition system reprenting a pomset will be the downwards closed subsets of the given pomset, and the transitions are the (labelled) covering relations of the ordering under inclusion.

The following proposition characterizes $\mathbf{Pom}_L$-open morphisms in $\mathbf{TI}_L$ [JNW93].

Proposition 7. *A morphism $f : Y \to X$ in $\mathbf{TI}_L$ is $\mathbf{Pom}_L$-open iff it is* zig-zag *and* reflects consecutive independence, *i.e. iff it has the following properties:*

- *whenever r is reachable and $f(r) \xrightarrow{a} s_1$ there is a state r_1 in Y such that $r \xrightarrow{a} r_1$ & $f(r_1) = s_1$, and*
- *whenever r is reachable, $r \xrightarrow{a} r_1$ and $r_1 \xrightarrow{b} r_2$ are transitions in Y, and*

$$f(r) \xrightarrow{a} f(r_1)\ I\ f(r_1) \xrightarrow{b} f(r_2),$$

we also have $r \xrightarrow{a} r_1\ I\ r_1 \xrightarrow{b} r_2$.

The category $\mathbf{TI}_L$ has pullbacks, so $\mathbf{Pom}_L$-bisimilarity is an equivalence relation in $\mathbf{TI}_L$. Furthermore, from Theorem 3 it follows that two $\mathbf{TI}_L$-objects are $\mathbf{Pom}_L$-bisimilar iff their unfolded event structures are $\mathbf{Pom}_L$-bisimilar [JNW93]. And on event structures [JNW93] $\mathbf{Pom}_L$-bisimilarity turns out to be a slight strengthening of the history-preserving bisimilarity originally defined in [GG89, RT88]. In fact, the same strengthening has been studied in [Bed91] in which the equivalence is denoted *hereditary* history-preserving bisimilarity. The interested reader is referred to [JNW93] for details. Whatever this notion of history-preserving bisimulation is, a natural question is: Does $\mathbf{Pom}_L$-bisimilarity for $\mathbf{TI}_L$ also have characterizations in the spirit of e.g. the game-theoretic and logical characterizations of bisimulation for standard transition systems? This question is answered positively in the next sections.

But before we address these questions, we would like to comment on the robustness of $\mathbf{Pom}_L$-bisimilarity with respect to the exact choice of category of observations. The question of observability of pomsets has been an issue in concurrency for some time, and this motivates the question of exactly how dependent our notion of bisimilarity is on the choice of pomsets in their full generality. It might be thought that hereditary history-preserving bisimulation, presented as $\mathbf{Pom}_L$-bisimilarity, is affected by restricting the category $\mathbf{Pom}_L$ to smaller classes of objects. However, let us say that a pomset is *almost totally ordered* iff it is of one of the two simple forms illustrated above, i.e. either a "stick" or a "lollipop". The following theorem states a surprisingly strong robustness of our bisimulation.

Theorem 8. *Let $\mathbf{P}_L$ be any full subcategory of $\mathbf{Pom}_L$ containing all the almost totally ordered pomsets as objects. Then any two transition systems with independence are $\mathbf{P}_L$-bisimilar iff they are $\mathbf{Pom}_L$-bisimilar.*

Proof. Follows from small modifications of the proof in [NW94] for the case of Petri nets. □

3 Characteristic Games

We first present a general definition of games inspired by [AJ92], and then we provide an instance of a characteristic game for $\mathbf{Pom}_L$-bisimilarity.

3.1 Basic Definitions

A *game* is a structure $\Gamma = (C, c_0, \triangleright, \lambda)$ where

- C is a set of *configurations* with a distinguished *initial configuration* c_0,
- $\triangleright \subseteq C^2$ is a set of *moves*. Formally, a *play* of Γ is a (possibly infinite) sequence of moves

$$c_0 \cdot c_1 \cdot c_2 \cdot \ldots,$$

  such that $c_0 \triangleright c_1 \triangleright c_2 \triangleright \cdots$. The set $Pos(\Gamma)$ of *positions* consists of all finite plays. The meta-variable p ranges over positions.
- $\lambda : Pos(\Gamma) \to \{O, P\}$ is a function indicating whose *turn* it is to move in a given *position* (an element of $Pos(\Gamma)$, defined below) of a play.

We require all plays to be *alternating*, i.e. we require $\triangleright$ and λ together to satisfy that if $\lambda(p \cdot c) = Q$ and $c \triangleright c'$ then $\lambda(p \cdot c \cdot c') = \overline{Q}$, where $\overline{P} = O$ and $\overline{O} = P$. Furthermore, Opponent should start every play. This is expressed by demanding $\lambda(c_0) = O$.

In defining when a game is won we take Player's point of view: A *play p is won (by P)* if one of the following conditions hold: either p is infinite or p is finite and $\lambda(p) = O$. If p is not won, it is *lost*.

A *strategy* is a partial function $\sigma : Pos(\Gamma) \rightharpoonup C$ such that

$$\sigma(p \cdot c) = c' \text{ implies } c \triangleright c'.$$

We reserve the words strategy for Player and *counter-strategy* for Opponent and use σ and τ to range over strategies and counter-strategies, respectively. Player is said to *follow her strategy* σ in a play $c_0 \cdot c_1 \cdot \ldots \cdot c_n \cdot c_{n+1} \cdot \ldots$ iff $\lambda(c_0 \cdot c_1 \cdot \ldots \cdot c_n) = P$ implies $c_{n+1} = \sigma(c_0 \cdot c_1 \cdot \ldots \cdot c_n)$. Similarly, we can define when Opponent follows his strategy.

The set $Plays(\sigma, \tau)$ of plays in which both Player and Opponent follow their strategies is easily seen to be prefix-closed. This leads to the following definition of *the play of a strategy σ against a counter-strategy τ*:

$$\langle \sigma | \tau \rangle = \bigsqcup \{p \mid p \in Plays(\sigma, \tau)\},$$

where the least upper bound refers to the prefix-ordering. Finally, σ is said to be a *winning strategy* iff $\langle \sigma | \tau \rangle$ is won for any counter-strategy τ. Similarly, we define τ to be a *winning counter-strategy* iff $\langle \sigma | \tau \rangle$ is lost for any σ.

3.2 A Characteristic Game for Interleaving Bisimulation

The first game considered is a "sequence variant" of the game defined by Stirling [Sti93]. Given two ordinary transition systems X and X' we take as configurations (ordered) pairs of *transition sequences* with the pair consisting of empty sequences as initial configuration. Informally, a play progresses as follows. Opponent starts out by first choosing either X or X' and then a transition from the initial state of the system chosen. If Player can't match the move with an equally labelled transition from the initial state of the other system, she loses. Otherwise, she chooses such a matching transition, and it's again Opponent's turn to move. He chooses a system, not necessarily the same as before, and a transition of that system leading out of the state arrived at in the previous pairs of moves. Again, Player is required to match with an equally labelled transition in the other system. The play continues like this *forever*, in which case Player wins, or until either Player or Opponent is *stuck* (unable to move), in which case the other participant wins.

The above description is now formalized to fit the basic definitions of games. We define the *interleaving game* between transition systems X and X' to be $\Gamma(X, X') = (C, c_0, \triangleright, \lambda)$ where

- $C = \mathit{Seqs}(X) \times \mathit{Seqs}(X')$. As a convention, writing configurations $(\bar{t}, \bar{t}')$, $(\bar{t}t, \bar{t}')$, and $(\bar{t}, \bar{t}'t')$ implicitly means that $|\bar{t}| = |\bar{t}'|$.
- $c_0 = (\varepsilon, \varepsilon)$.
- $\lambda : \mathit{Pos}(\Gamma(X, X')) \to \{O, P\}$ is defined by taking

$$\lambda(\bar{t}, \bar{t}') = O \text{ and } \lambda(\bar{t}t, \bar{t}') = \lambda(\bar{t}, \bar{t}'t') = P.$$

- $\triangleright \subseteq C^2$ is defined by the rules

$$\begin{array}{rcll} (\bar{t}, \bar{t}') & \triangleright & (\bar{t}t, \bar{t}') & \text{if } \bar{t}t \in \mathit{Seqs}(X) \\ (\bar{t}, \bar{t}') & \triangleright & (\bar{t}, \bar{t}'t') & \text{if } \bar{t}'t' \in \mathit{Seqs}(X') \\ (\bar{t}t, \bar{t}') & \triangleright & (\bar{t}t, \bar{t}'t') & \text{if } \bar{t}'t' \in \mathit{Seqs}(X') \ \&\ \ell(t') = \ell(t) \\ (\bar{t}, \bar{t}'t') & \triangleright & (\bar{t}t, \bar{t}'t') & \text{if } \bar{t}t \in \mathit{Seqs}(X) \ \&\ \ell(t) = \ell(t') \end{array}$$

Just like Stirling's game, the game $\Gamma(X, X')$ is *characteristic* for interleaving bisimulation in the following sense.

Theorem 9. *Two transition systems X and X' are bisimilar iff Player has a winning strategy in $\Gamma(X, X')$.*

Proof. Small modifications of the reasoning of Stirling [Sti93]. □

3.3 Allowing Opponent to Backtrack

A natural notion of backtracking for the interleaving game is expressed by allowing Opponent to do backwards moves like

$$(\bar{t}t, \bar{t}'t') \triangleright (B, \bar{t}, \bar{t}'t'),$$

where the B is a directive to Player to play backwards on the longer of the sequences. Player must match with the move

$$(B, \bar{t}, \bar{t}'t') \rhd (\bar{t}, \bar{t}').$$

It is easy to see that these additional rules do *not* give Opponent more opportunities to beat Player, nor the other way around.

Proposition 10. *Two transition systems are bisimilar iff Player has a winning strategy in their associated game with backtracking.*

Backtracking in an independence model is much more interesting. Consider a simple transition system with independence X

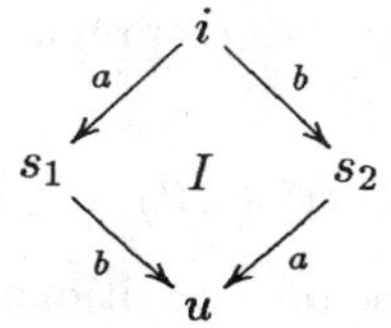

consisting of a single independence square. Since $i \xrightarrow{a} s_1$ and $s_1 \xrightarrow{b} u$ are independent, the sequence $\bar{t} = i \xrightarrow{a} s_1 \xrightarrow{b} u$ in X represents the observation "a and b in parallel". Another representative of this observation is the sequence $i \xrightarrow{b} s_2 \xrightarrow{a} u$. Following the intuiton behind independence, u represents the state in which a and b have just occurred, but it does not necessarily make any sense to ask in which order. So this gives us two ways to backtrack within $\bar{t}$: Either along $s_1 \xrightarrow{b} u$, leaving behind the sequence $i \xrightarrow{a} s_1$, *or* along $s_2 \xrightarrow{a} u$ leaving behind the sequence $i \xrightarrow{b} s_2$.

In terms of the net representation of $a \parallel b$ from Section 1 this amounts to the following: After firing the a-transition followed by the b-transition you may naturally backtrack on the a-transition, since the firing of the b-transition has in no way affected the post-conditions of the a-transition. In general, a transition t in a firing sequence $\bar{t}$ of a net is available for backtracking iff none of the transitions following t in $\bar{t}$ affects the postconditions of t. Let us formalize this intuition for transition systems with independence.

A transition t_i of a sequence $\bar{t}$ is said to be *backwards enabled* iff it by repeated use of Axiom 2 of Definition 4 can be "pushed to last position in $\bar{t}$." By Axiom 3, this is equivalent to requiring t_i to be independent of all transitions t_j in $\bar{t}$ with $j > i$. This leads to the following formal definition.

Definition 11. For $\bar{t} = t_0 \cdots t_{n-1}$, a sequence in a transition system with independence X, and $i \in \{0, \ldots, n-1\}$, we define

$$t_i \in BEn(\bar{t}) \text{ iff } \forall j \in \{i+1, \ldots, n-1\}.\, t_j \; I \; t_i,$$

where I is the independence relation in X. If $t_i \in BEn(\bar{t})$ we define $\delta(i, \bar{t})$ to be the result of deleting the event corresponding to t_i, i.e.

$$\delta(i, \bar{t}) = t_0 \cdots t_{i-1} s_{i+1} \cdots s_{n-1},$$

where $s_{i+1} \prec t_{i+1}, \ldots, s_{n-1} \prec t_{n-1}$ as in the following figure in which the squares are the unique completions defined in Section 2.

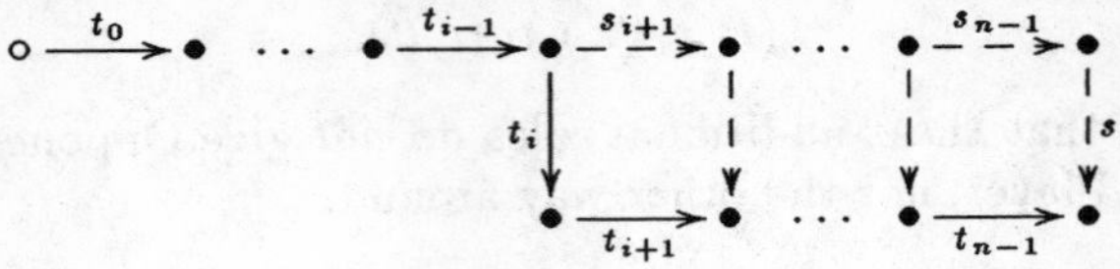

□

In [NC94] a backtrcking game is shown to be characteristic for **TI**-systems. For siplicity, we present here a version of this game, characteristic for systems without auto-concurrency. The backtracking game on transition systems with independence is a simple extension of the previously defined (forward) game. By introducing rules like

$$(\bar{t}, \bar{t'}) \rhd (t_i, \delta(i, \bar{t}), \bar{t'}) \text{ if } t_i \in BEn(\bar{t})$$

we allow Opponent to backtrack on transitions which are backwards enabled. The transition t_i is a request to Player to play backwards on an equally labelled transition of the longer of the sequences. So the only way Player can respond to such moves is to use the rule

$$(t_i, \delta(i, \bar{t}), \bar{t'}) \rhd (\delta(i, \bar{t}), \delta(j, \bar{t'})) \text{ if } t'_j \in BEn(\bar{t'}) \text{ and } l(t_i) = l(t'_j),$$

provided, of course, that t'_j is backwards enabled in $\bar{t'}$. Formally, we define the backtracking game $\Gamma(X, X')$ on transition systems with independence X and X' to be the structure $(C, c_0, \rhd, \lambda)$:

- $C = Seqs(X) \times Seqs(X') \cup (Tran \cup Tran') \times Seqs(X) \times Seqs(X')$. Conventionally, writing configurations $(t_i, \delta(i, \bar{t}), \bar{t'})$ and $(t'_i, \bar{t}, \delta(i, \bar{t'}))$ implicitly means that $|\bar{t}| = |\bar{t'}|$.
- $c_0 = (\varepsilon, \varepsilon)$.
- $\lambda : Pos(\Gamma(X, X')) \to \{O, P\}$ is defined by taking $\lambda(\bar{t}, \bar{t'}) = O$ and $\lambda(\bar{t}t, \bar{t'}) = \lambda(\bar{t}, \bar{t'}t') = \lambda(t_i, \delta(i, \bar{t}), \bar{t'}) = \lambda(t'_i, \bar{t}, \delta(i, \bar{t'})) = P$.
- $\rhd \subseteq C^2$ is defined by the following rules:

$$\begin{array}{rll}
(\bar{t}, \bar{t'}) & \rhd (\bar{t}t, \bar{t'}) & \text{if } \bar{t}t \in Seqs(X) \\
(\bar{t}, \bar{t'}) & \rhd (\bar{t}, \bar{t'}t') & \text{if } \bar{t'}t' \in Seqs(X') \\
(\bar{t}t, \bar{t'}) & \rhd (\bar{t}t, \bar{t'}t') & \text{if } \bar{t'}t' \in Seqs(X') \ \&\ \ell(t') = \ell(t) \\
(\bar{t}, \bar{t'}t') & \rhd (\bar{t}t, \bar{t'}t') & \text{if } \bar{t}t \in Seqs(X) \ \&\ \ell(t) = \ell(t')
\end{array}$$

$$\begin{array}{rll}
(\bar{t}, \bar{t'}) & \rhd (t_i, \delta(i, \bar{t}), \bar{t'}) & \text{if } t_i \in BEn(\bar{t}) \\
(\bar{t}, \bar{t'}) & \rhd (t'_i, \bar{t}, \delta(i, \bar{t'})) & \text{if } t'_i \in BEn(\bar{t'}) \\
(t_i, \delta(i, \bar{t}), \bar{t'}) & \rhd (\delta(i, \bar{t}), \delta(j, \bar{t'})) & \text{if } t'_j \in BEn(\bar{t'}) \ \&\ l(t_i) = l(t'_j) \\
(t'_i, \bar{t}, \delta(i, \bar{t'})) & \rhd (\delta(j, \bar{t}), \delta(i, \bar{t'})) & \text{if } t_j \in BEn(\bar{t}) \ \&\ l(t_j) = l(t'_i)
\end{array}$$

Definition 12. Two transition systems with independence X and X' are *Γ-equivalent* iff Player has a winning strategy in $\Gamma(X, X')$. □

With a simple example we will now illustrate how backtracking distinguishes parallelism from non-deterministic interleaving.

Example 1. Consider the transition systems with independence representing the CCS-processes $a \parallel b$ and $a.b + b.a$:

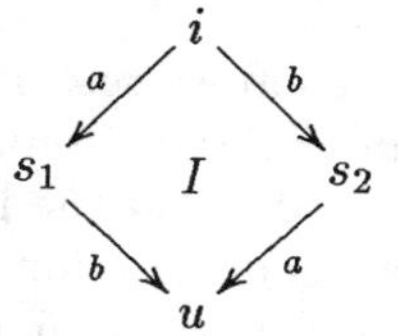

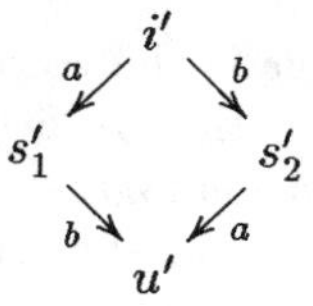

These systems are interleaving bisimilar but *not* Γ-equivalent, as we are able to define a winning counter-strategy τ as follows (here, p ranges over all appropriate positions):

$$\tau(\varepsilon, \varepsilon) = (i \xrightarrow{a} s_1, \varepsilon)$$
$$\tau(p \cdot (i \xrightarrow{a} s_1, i' \xrightarrow{a} s'_1)) = (i \xrightarrow{a} s_1 \xrightarrow{b} u, i' \xrightarrow{a} s'_1)$$
$$\tau(p \cdot (i \xrightarrow{a} s_1 \xrightarrow{b} u, i' \xrightarrow{a} s'_1 \xrightarrow{b} u')) = (i \xrightarrow{a} s_1, i \xrightarrow{b} s_2, i' \xrightarrow{a} s'_1 \xrightarrow{b} u')$$

The point is, of course, that Player is unable to backtrack on label a in the sequence $i' \xrightarrow{a} s'_1 \xrightarrow{b} u'$, as these transitions are dependent. □

Distinguishing the transition systems with independence of Example 1 is, in fact, a minimum demand on any reasonable generalization of bisimulation to independence models. And following the reasoning of Example 1, the reader should not be surprised that backtracking may be used by Opponent to detect the partial order structures of configurations. This property holds for many of the behavioural equivalences suggested for noninterleaving models, but amongst all those it turns out that Γ-equivalence coincides exactly with the abstractly derived $\mathbf{Pom}_L$-bisimilarity of Section 2:

Theorem 13. *For* **TI**-*systems witout auto-concurrency Γ-equivalence coincides with* $\mathbf{Pom}_L$*-bisimilarity.*

Proof. Follows from the proof of the corresponding theorem in [NC94], showing that a slightly modified game is characteristic for the full class of **TI**-objects. □

4 Characteristic Logics

Just as interleaving bisimulations can be characterized as a relation over paths, we can interpret the Hennessy-Milner logic over paths rather than states. Following [HS85], we may add a past tense modality ⓐ, where a is a label, and obtain a logic which still characterizes bisimulation for ordinary transition systems. However, interpreted over transition systems with independence, we obtain a logic which is characteristic for $\mathbf{Pom}_L$-bisimilarity. Again, for simplicity we present here a version of this logic, characteristic for systems without auto-concurrency.

4.1 Hennessy-Milner logics

Let **Assn** be the following language of assertions:

$$A ::= \neg A \mid \bigwedge_{j \in J} A_j \mid \langle a \rangle A \mid @A.$$

By convention, *true* is the conjunction over the empty set. The interpretations of negation, conjunction, and $\langle a \rangle A$ are like in ordinary Hennessy-Milner logic. For ordinary transition systems, $@A$ is interpreted as "at the last moment – just before a –it was the case that A" [HS85]. It seems natural for transition systems with independence to interpret $@A$ as "a could have been the last action, in which case at the last moment – just before a – it was the case that A". And this is exactly the interpretation we take.

In the formal definition of this interpretation we shall use the following notation:

Let X be a transition system with independence and suppose $\bar{t}, \bar{r} \in Seqs(X)$. Define

$$\bar{r} \xrightarrow{a} \bar{t} \;\text{ iff }\; \bar{r}(s \xrightarrow{a} s_1) = \bar{t}$$
$$\bar{r} \overset{a}{\rightsquigarrow} \bar{t} \;\text{ iff }\; \exists i. (t_i \in BEn(\bar{t}) \;\&\; \ell(t_i) = a \;\&\; \bar{r} = \delta(i, \bar{t}))$$

Let X be a transition system with independence and define the *satisfaction* relation $\models_X \subseteq Seqs(X) \times \textbf{Assn}$ by structural induction on assertions:

$$\begin{array}{rcl} \bar{t} \models_X \neg A & \text{iff} & \bar{t} \not\models_X A \\ \bar{t} \models_X \bigwedge_{j \in J} A_j & \text{iff} & \forall j \in J. \bar{t} \models_X A_j \\ \bar{t} \models_X \langle a \rangle A & \text{iff} & \exists \bar{r}. (\bar{t} \xrightarrow{a} \bar{r} \;\&\; \bar{r} \models_X A) \\ \bar{t} \models_X @A & \text{iff} & \exists \bar{r}. (\bar{r} \overset{a}{\rightsquigarrow} \bar{t} \;\&\; \bar{r} \models_X A) \end{array}$$

An assertion is *satisfied by* X, written $\models_X A$, iff $\varepsilon \models_X A$.

Definition 14. Two transition systems with independence X and X' are **Assn**-equivalent iff they satisfy the same assertions, i.e. iff

$$\forall A \in \textbf{Assn}. (\models_X A \Leftrightarrow \models_{X'} A).$$

□

For ordinary transition systems (without independence) this logic is characteristic for bisimulation.

Theorem 15. *Two transition systems are bisimilar iff they are* **Assn**-*equivalent.*

Proof. See [HS85]. □

Also, it is quite easy to see that the only-if part of this theorem carries over to the noninterleaving setting:

Proposition 16. *If two transition systems with independence are* **Pom**$_L$*-bisimilar, then they are also* **Assn***-equivalent.*

Proof. See [NC94]. □

However, the if part of the previous theorem does not generalize completely to transition systems with independence.

Example 2. Consider two systems X and X'

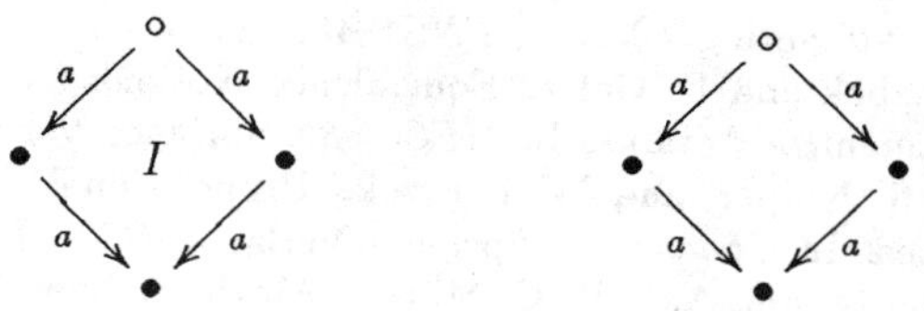

which are identical except that the square in X is an independence square, whereas the square in X' is not. These systems satisfy the same assertions, but are certainly *not* **Pom**$_L$-bisimilar. As a matter of fact, this example also show why our simple games with backtracking are not characteristic for the full class of systems with auto-concurrency. □

However, the characterization *does* carry over, if we restrict ourselves to systems without auto-concurrency.

Theorem 17. *Two* **PI***-systems without auto-concurrency are* **Pom**$_L$*-bisimilar iff they are* **Assn***-equivalent.*

Proof. See [NC94]. □

5 Conclusion

In this paper we hope to have conveyed the general applicability of the approach to bisimulation suggested by Joyal, Nielsen and Winskel. We expect this to be a useful guideline for transporting the important concept of bisimulation to many different settings. Here, we have provided some hopefully convincing arguments for the naturalness of the bisimulation obtained by applying the general set-up to one particular noninterleaving model studied in [JNW93]. We are currently investigating applications to a number of different models in concurrency, like models with time and probability.

The particular case studied above introduces some interesting open problems. One is the decidability of **Pom**$_L$-bisimilarity for finite state systems. Another is the usefulness of our characteristic logic as a specification logic for noninterleaving models. Both of these are being looked into.

References

[AJ92] S. Abramsky and R. Jagadeesan. Games and Full Completeness for Multiplicative Linear Logic. DoC 92/24, Imperial College of Science, Technology and Medicine, 1992.

[Bed88] M. A. Bednarczyk. *Categories of asynchronous systems.* PhD thesis, University of Sussex, 1988. Technical report no. 1/88.

[Bed91] M. A. Bednarczyk. Heredity History Preserving Bisimulations. Draft of 1991.

[Ben84] J. Van Bentham. Correspondence theory. In D. Gabbay and F. Guenthner, editors, *Handbook of Philosophical Logic*, volume 2. Reidel, 1984.

[DMV90] R. De Nicola, U. Montanari, F. Vaandrager. Back and forth bisimulations. In *Concur '90.* Springer-Verlag *LNCS* 458, 1990.

[GG89] R. van Glaabek and U. Goltz. Equivalence Notions for Concurrent Systems and Refinement of Actions. In *MFCS '89.* Springer-Verlag *LNCS* 379, 1989.

[GKP92] U. Goltz, R. Kuiper, and W. Penczek. Propositional Temporal Logics and Equivalences. In *Concur '92.* Springer-Verlag *LNCS* 630, 1992.

[HM85] M. C. Hennessy and A. J. R. G. Milner. Algebraic Laws for Non-determinism and Concurrency. *Journal of ACM*, 32(1), 1985.

[HS85] M. Hennessy and C. P. Stirling. The power of the future perfect in program logics. *Information and Control*, volume 67, 1985.

[JNW93] A. Joyal, M. Nielsen, and G. Winskel. Bisimulation and open maps. In *LICS '93*, 1993. Full version in *BRICS RS-94-7*, Computer Science Department, Aarhus University, 1994.

[NC94] M. Nielsen, C. Clausen. Bisimulations, games and logic. To appear in *New Results in Theoretical Computer Science*,Springer-Verlag *LNCS*. Full version in *BRICS RS-94-6*, Computer Science Department, Aarhus University, 1994.

[NW94] M. Nielsen, G. Winskel. Petri nets and bisimulations. *BRICS RS-94-15*, Computer Science Department, Aarhus University, 1994.

[Mil89] A. J. R. G. Milner. *Communication and Concurrency.* Prentice Hall, 1989.

[Old91] E.-R. Olderog. *Nets, Terms and Formulas.* Cambridge University Press, 1991.

[Par81] D. M. R. Park. Concurrency and Automata on Infinite Sequences. In *Theoretical Computer Science, 5th GL-conference.* Springer-Verlag *LNCS* 104, 1981.

[Pra86] V. R. Pratt. Modelling concurrency with partial orders. *International Journal of Parallel Programming*, 15(1), 1986.

[RT88] A. Rabinovich and B. Trakhtenbrot. Behaviour structures and nets. *Fundamenta Informatica*, 11(4), 1988.

[Shi85] M. W. Shields. Concurrent machines. *Computer Journal*, 88, 1985.

[Sti93] C. Stirling. Modal and Temporal Logics for Processes. Notes for Summer School in Logic Methods in Concurrency, Department of Computer Science, Aarhus University, 1993.

[WN94] G. Winskel and M. Nielsen. Models for Cuncurrency. To appear in S. Abramsky and D. Gabbay, editors, *Handbook of Logic in Computer Science*, volume 3. Oxford University Press, 1994.

Invariants in Process Algebra with Data

Marc Bezem
Jan Friso Groote

Department of Philosophy, Utrecht University
Heidelberglaan 8, 3584 CS Utrecht, The Netherlands
Email: Marc.Bezem@phil.ruu.nl, JanFriso.Groote@phil.ruu.nl

Abstract. We provide rules for calculating with invariants in process algebra with data, and illustrate these with examples. The new rules turn out to be equivalent to the well known Recursive Specification Principle which states that guarded recursive equations have at most one solution. In the setting with data this is reformulated as 'every *convergent* linear process operator has at most one fixed point' (CL-RSP). As a consequence, one can carry out verifications in well-known process algebras satisfying CL-RSP using invariants.

Note: The authors are partly supported by the Netherlands Computer Science Research Foundation (SION) with financial support of the Netherlands Organization for Scientific Research (NWO).

1 Introduction

Process algebra allows one to prove that certain processes are equal; typically, an abstraction of a (generally complicated) implementation and a (preferably compact) specification of the external behaviour of the same system are shown equal. Process algebra has been used to verify a variety of distributed systems such as protocols, systolic arrays and computer integrated manufacturing systems (see e.g. [1]). The main technique to prove such process identities consists of algebraic manipulation with terms, i.e. elementary calculations, which has been proven successful in major branches of mathematics.

However, current process algebraic techniques are considered unsuitable to verify large and complex systems. In particular, it appears that knowledge and intuition about the correct functioning of distributed systems can hardly be explicitly incorporated in the calculations. Since the algebraic proofs are usually long, many attempts to construct a proof smother into a large amount of undirected calculations.

Therefore, the need is felt to adapt the theory of process algebra in such a way that intuitions about the functioning of distributed systems can be expressed in a natural way and can be used in calculations. One of the most successful techniques in this respect is the use of invariants, as put forward prominently by Dijkstra and Hoare. Almost all existing verifications of sequential and distributed programs use relations between variables that remain valid during the course of the program. A comprehensive survey for distributed programs is [5]. The closest approximation of the techniques in this paper we could find in the classical literature is [13].

In process algebra — as far as we know — invariants are seldomly explicitly used. An early but incomplete attempt to verify a sliding window protocol in process algebra using invariants is [8]. A Hoare Logic based approach to invariants in process algebra has been elaborated in [10, 14]. Rudimentary, implicit use of invariants in process algebra, however, is quite common. For example, the set of accessible states of a process is an invariant of that process (modulo the identification of subsets of the state space with relations between the variables).

We investigate invariants in the setting of μCRL [9, 11, 12], in which process algebra is combined with data. It is straightforward to formulate invariants in μCRL as predicates. We first adapt the Recursive Specification Principle (RSP), which states that guarded recursive specifications have unique solutions, such that it can effectively be used in a setting with data. We introduce convergent linear process operators (CLPO's) and formulate the principle CL-RSP, which states that every convergent linear recursive operator has at most one fixed point. Then we provide several formulations of equivalent principles to allow smooth calculations using invariants. We illustrate almost all rules with examples, and provide two somewhat larger examples at the end. Remarkably, all new rules turn out to be equivalent to CL-RSP. As a consequence, any verification using invariants can be done with CL-RSP, not appealing to invariants. This means that invariants are in a sense not necessary.

But in spite of this unnecessariness of invariants the Concrete Invariant Corollary (Corollary 3.9) has been successfully applied to different sizable examples (see e.g. [3, 4, 6]), which up till now appeared unverifiable using process algebraic techniques. The reason for this is that proofs employing invariant techniques are considerable smaller than proofs that do without. Moreover, by first formulating and proving invariants, and then using them in the verification, one achieves a separation of concerns that makes verifications easier. Actually, we think that theorems such as the Concrete Invariant Corollary will conduce to process algebraic verifications of substantially larger distributed systems; but only time will tell.

Acknowledgements. We thank Jan Bergstra, Wim Hesselink, Tonny Hurkens, Jaco van de Pol, Alex Sellink, Jan Springintveld, Jos van Wamel and the referees for discussions on the topic of this paper and for their comments.

2 Preliminaries

We assume the existence of non-empty, disjoint sets with data elements, which are called *data types* and are denoted by letters D and E. Furthermore, we assume a set of many sorted operations on these sets, which are called *data operations*. There is one standard data type **Bool**, which consists of the elements t and f. We assume that the standard boolean operations are defined on **Bool**. We also assume the existence of a set *pAct* that contains parameterised atomic actions. Every element of *pAct* comes equipped with the data type of its parameter. The elements of *pAct* are regarded as mappings from data types to processes.

Definition 2.1. A *pCRL*^{1}*-algebra* is a set $\mathbb{P}$, disjoint from the data types, with operations

$$
\begin{array}{l}
a : D \to \mathbb{P} \;\; (\text{for all } a \in pAct,\ D \text{ the data type of } a) \\
\delta, \tau : \mathbb{P} \\
+, \cdot : \mathbb{P} \times \mathbb{P} \to \mathbb{P} \\
\Sigma : (D \to \mathbb{P}) \to \mathbb{P} \;\; (\text{for each data type } D) \\
\_ \lhd \_ \rhd \_ : \mathbb{P} \times \mathbf{Bool} \times \mathbb{P} \to \mathbb{P}
\end{array}
$$

satisfying the (conditional) equations A1–7, SUM1,3,4,5,11, Bool1,2, C1,2 from Table 1. If the algebra also satisfies the equations B1 and B2 for branching bisimulation [7] it is called a *pCRL*$^{1\tau}$*-algebra.*

The name pCRL stands for a pico Common Representation Language. The superscript 1 refers to the fact that, contrary to μCRL, all actions have exactly one parameter. By using the data type with one element and by using pairing, actions depending on zero or more than one data type can be simulated. Therefore, we use zero or more than one parameter whenever convenient.

A1 $x + y = y + x$	SUM1 $\Sigma_{d:D} x = x$
A2 $x + (y + z) = (x + y) + z$	SUM3 $\Sigma p = \Sigma p + p(d)$
A3 $x + x = x$	SUM4 $\Sigma_{d:D}(p(d) + q(d)) = \Sigma p + \Sigma q$
A4 $(x + y) \cdot z = x \cdot z + y \cdot z$	SUM5 $\Sigma_{d:D}(p(d) \cdot x) = (\Sigma p) \cdot x$
A5 $(x \cdot y) \cdot z = x \cdot (y \cdot z)$	SUM11 $(\forall d \in D\ p(d) = q(d)) \to \Sigma p = \Sigma q$
A6 $x + \delta = x$	
A7 $\delta \cdot x = \delta$	Bool1 $\neg(\mathsf{t} = \mathsf{f})$
	Bool2 $\neg(b = \mathsf{t}) \to b = \mathsf{f}$
B1 $c \cdot \tau = c$	C1 $x \lhd \mathsf{t} \rhd y = x$
B2 $c \cdot (\tau \cdot (x + y) + x) = c \cdot (x + y)$	C2 $x \lhd \mathsf{f} \rhd y = y$

Table 1. $x, y, z \in \mathbb{P}$, c is τ or $a(d)$ for $a \in pAct$, $d \in D$ and $p, q : D \to \mathbb{P}$, $b \in \mathbf{Bool}$

Table 1 specifies a subset of the axioms from the proof theory of μCRL [11, 12]. The operations $+$ and $\cdot$ and equations A1–7 and B1,2 are standard for process algebra (see [2]) and therefore not explained. The operation $\_ \lhd \_ \rhd \_$ is the *then-if-else* operation. The sum operation Σ over a data type D expresses that its argument $p : D \to \mathbb{P}$ may be executed with some data element d from D. Instead of $\Sigma(\lambda d{:}D.x)$ we generally write $\Sigma_{d:D} x$. Note that we use explicitly typed λ notation to denote mappings. If convenient we sometimes drop the explicit types.

We also use a meta-sum notation $\Sigma_{i \in I} p_i$ for $p_1 + p_2 + \cdots + p_n$ when $I = \{1, \ldots, n\}$. The difference between the notations is the use of the colon versus the use of the membership symbol. We use the convention that $\cdot$ binds stronger than Σ, followed by $\_ \triangleleft \_ \triangleright \_$, and $+$ binds weakest.

We call a mapping $p : D \rightarrow \mathbb{P}$ a *parameterised process* and a mapping $(D \rightarrow \mathbb{P}) \rightarrow (E \rightarrow \mathbb{P})$ a *process transformation* (*process operator* if $D = E$). Generally, letters p, q are used for parameterised processes and letters Φ, Ψ, Ξ (Θ) refer to process operators (transformations).

Definition 2.2. A process operator Ψ is called (pCRL-)*expressible* iff Ψ can be written as

$$\lambda p{:}D \rightarrow \mathbb{P}.\lambda d{:}D.t(p, d)$$

where $t(p, d)$ only consists of operations mentioned in Definition 2.1.

A process operator Ψ is called *linear* iff Ψ can be written as

$$\begin{aligned} \lambda p{:}D \rightarrow \mathbb{P}.\lambda d{:}D.\ & \Sigma_{i \in I} \Sigma_{e_i : D_i} c_i(f_i(d, e_i)) \cdot p(g_i(d, e_i)) \triangleleft b_i(d, e_i) \triangleright \delta + \\ & \Sigma_{i \in I'} \Sigma_{e_i : D'_i} c'_i(f'_i(d, e_i)) \triangleleft b'_i(d, e_i) \triangleright \delta \end{aligned}$$

for some finite index sets I, I', actions $c_i, c'_i \in pAct \cup \{\tau\}$, data types D_i, D'_i, D_{c_i} and $D_{c'_i}$, functions $f_i : D \rightarrow D_i \rightarrow D_{c_i}$, $g_i : D \rightarrow D_i \rightarrow D$, $b_i : D \rightarrow D_i \rightarrow \mathbf{Bool}$, $f'_i : D \rightarrow D'_i \rightarrow D_{c'_i}$, $b'_i : D \rightarrow D'_i \rightarrow \mathbf{Bool}$.

Definition 2.3. A linear process operator (*LPO*) Ψ written in the form above is called *convergent* iff there is a well-founded ordering $<$ on D such that $g_i(d, e_i) < d$ for all $d \in D$, $i \in I$ and $e_i \in D_i$ with $c_i = \tau$ and $b_i(d, e_i)$.

In this paper we restrict ourselves to *linear* process operators, thus excluding, for example, $\lambda pd.\, a \cdot b \cdot p(d)$. Note that the notion of a convergent linear process operator both specialises and generalises usual notions of a guarded recursive specification. First, $\lambda pd.\, a \cdot b \cdot p(d)$ is not a CLPO, but would be considered guarded. Second unguarded occurrences are allowed in a CLPO on the condition that the parameter decreases in the sense of some well-founded ordering. The latter seems an unnecessary complication, but is in fact crucial for applications such as in Subsection 4.3 and in [3, 4, 6]. We use convergent LPO's for the same reason as guarded recursive specifications are used, namely to uniquely determine (parameterised) processes. For this purpose, the *Recursive Definition Principle* (RDP) and the *Recursive Specification Principle* (RSP) were introduced in [2]. We reformulate these principles in the presence of data.

Definition 2.4. A pCRL-algebra is said to satisfy *RDP* iff every expressible process operator Ψ has at least one fixed point, i.e. there exists a $p : D \rightarrow \mathbb{P}$ such that $p = \Psi p$.

A pCRL-algebra is said to satisfy *CL-RSP* iff every convergent linear process operator (CLPO) has at most one fixed point.

In the sequel we assume that all algebras that we consider satisfy CL-RSP. RDP is only used in the examples, where it will be tacitly assumed, too.

If RDP and CL-RSP hold, we can use CLPO's to define (parameterised) processes. Generally, and conforming to μCRL [9] this is denoted as follows. If $\Psi : (D\rightarrow\mathbb{P})\rightarrow(D\rightarrow\mathbb{P})$ is a CLPO, we write

$$\textbf{proc} \quad p(x{:}D) = \Psi p x$$

This means that we define $p : D\rightarrow\mathbb{P}$ as the unique fixed point of Ψ.

Example 2.5. Consider the following two processes. We assume that the pCRL-algebra contains the data type of natural numbers $\mathbb{N}$ with the standard operations, as well as a data type $\mathbb{N}\times\mathbb{N}$ with pairing and projection operations. Here and below we simply write $q(m, n{:}\mathbb{N})$ to conform to standard notations, where actually $q(o : \mathbb{N}\times\mathbb{N})$ would be required, with m and n the first and, respectively, second projection of o.

$$\begin{array}{ll} \textbf{proc} & p(n{:}\mathbb{N}) = a(n)\cdot p(n) + \tau\cdot p(n-1) \lhd n > 0 \rhd \delta \\ & q(m, n{:}\mathbb{N}) = (\Sigma_{n':\mathbb{N}}\tau\cdot q(m-1, n') \lhd n = 0 \rhd \tau\cdot q(m, n-1)) \lhd m > 0 \rhd \tau \end{array}$$

It is obvious that the first process definition is convergent, using the standard ordering on natural numbers. In the second example, the right hand side should first be linearised into

$$\begin{array}{l} (\tau \lhd m = 0 \rhd \delta) + (\tau\cdot q(m, n-1) \lhd m > 0 \wedge n > 0 \rhd \delta) + \\ (\Sigma_{n':\mathbb{N}}\tau\cdot q(m-1, n') \lhd m > 0 \wedge n = 0 \rhd \delta) \end{array}$$

Taking the lexicographical ordering on $\mathbb{N}\times\mathbb{N}$ defined by $\langle m, n\rangle < \langle m', n'\rangle$ iff $(m < m')\vee(m = m' \wedge n < n')$, one easily sees that the second process definition is convergent. With CL-RSP it follows that both p and q are unique parameterised processes. (In the second example this can also be established by proving by transfinite induction that $q(m, n) = \tau$.)

3 Invariants

In this section we provide a number of equivalent versions of CL-RSP. Some of these are formulated to accommodate the convenient use of invariants. Due to the abstract setting of this section, the true content of the lemmas may be hard to grasp, although the proofs are very short and straightforward. Therefore, almost all lemmas are illustrated with examples.

Lemma 3.1. *(Symmetrical Lemma). Assume that the following diagram commutes, i.e.* $\Theta(\Phi p) = \Psi(\Theta p)$ *for all* p *and* $\Theta'(\Phi' p') = \Psi(\Theta' p')$ *for all* p'.

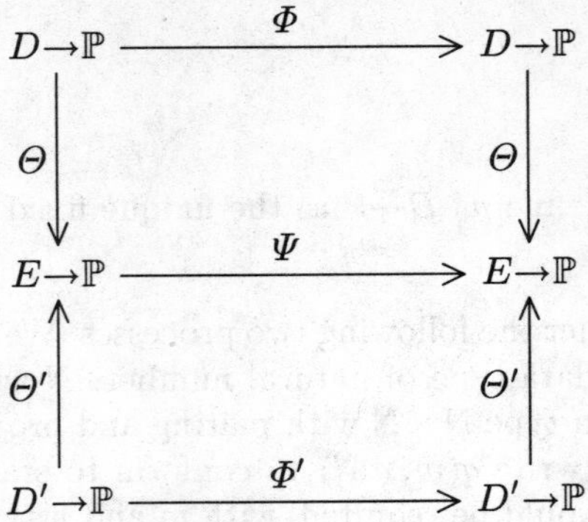

Let Ψ *be a CLPO. If* $\Theta p = \Theta(\Phi p)$ *and* $\Theta' p' = \Theta'(\Phi' p')$, *then* $\Theta p = \Theta' p'$. *In particular, if* $p = \Phi p$ *and* $p' = \Phi' p'$ *then* $\Theta p = \Theta' p'$.

Proof.

$$\left.\begin{array}{l} \Theta p = \Theta(\Phi p) = \Psi(\Theta p) \\ \Theta' p' = \Theta'(\Phi' p') = \Psi(\Theta' p') \end{array}\right\} \stackrel{\text{CL-RSP}}{\Longrightarrow} \Theta p = \Theta' p'.$$

□

An important special case of this lemma is $\Theta = \lambda p.\, p \circ \alpha$ for some $\alpha : E \to D$, where $\circ$ denotes function composition. Commutativity of the upper part of the diagram then boils down to $(\Phi p) \circ \alpha = \Psi(p \circ \alpha)$ for all p. Spelling this out leads to the well-known notion of *bisimulation mapping* α, as becomes apparent in the next example.

It should be noted that the proof above does not depend on the particular structure of CLPO's. The existence of unique fixed points is the only fact that is used in the proofs. Therefore the result in Lemma 3.1 and all subsequent lemmas carry over to all process operators assuming that they have unique fixed points.

Example 3.2. Consider the following two processes:

proc $q(x{:}D) = a(d(x)) \cdot q(f(x))$
$q'(y{:}D') = a(e(y)) \cdot q'(g(y))$

We prove by the Symmetrical Lemma that $q(x_0) = q'(y_0)$, provided $d(f^n(x_0)) = e(g^n(y_0))$ for all $n \in \mathbb{N}$. Take $E = \mathbb{N}$. Define $\Phi : (D \to \mathbb{P}) \to (D \to \mathbb{P})$ by $\Phi p = \lambda x.\, a(d(x)) \cdot p(f(x))$, $\Phi' : (D' \to \mathbb{P}) \to (D' \to \mathbb{P})$ by $\Phi' p' = \lambda y.\, a(e(y)) \cdot p'(g(y))$, and $\Psi : (\mathbb{N} \to \mathbb{P}) \to (\mathbb{N} \to \mathbb{P})$ by $\Psi r = \lambda n.\, a(d(f^n(x_0)))\, r(n+1)$. Then we have that Ψ is convergent and $q = \Phi q$, $q' = \Phi' q'$. Moreover, define bisimulation mappings $\alpha : \mathbb{N} \to D$, $\alpha' : \mathbb{N} \to D'$ by putting $\alpha n = f^n(x_0)$, $\alpha' n = g^n(y_0)$. Then the following diagram commutes.

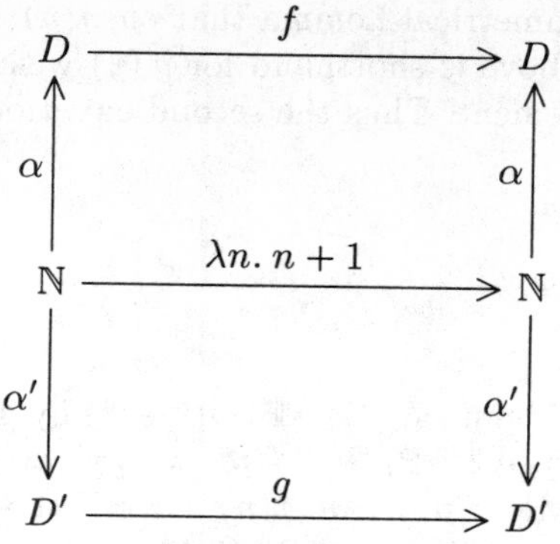

Since $d(f^n(x_0)) = e(g^n(y_0))$ for all $n \in \mathbb{N}$, α and α' are indeed bisimulation mappings. Define the transformations $\Theta : (D{\rightarrow}\mathbb{P}){\rightarrow}(\mathbb{N}{\rightarrow}\mathbb{P})$, $\Theta' : (D'{\rightarrow}\mathbb{P}){\rightarrow}(\mathbb{N}{\rightarrow}\mathbb{P})$ by $\Theta p = p \circ \alpha$, $\Theta' p' = p' \circ \alpha'$. Then it follows from the previous diagram that the diagram in the Symmetrical Lemma commutes. Hence $\Theta q = \Theta' q'$ and $q(x_0) = q'(y_0)$.

The following lemma facilitates calculating with invariants. A typical application is with $\Xi = \lambda px.p(x) \triangleleft I(x) \triangleright \delta$, where $I(x)$ is an invariant of $\Phi : (D{\rightarrow}\mathbb{P}){\rightarrow}(D{\rightarrow}\mathbb{P})$. We explain the intuition later.

Lemma 3.3. *(Asymmetrical Lemma). Assume that the following diagram commutes.*

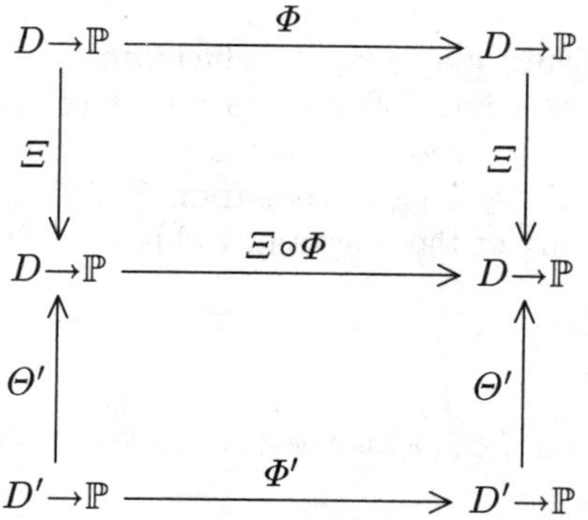

Assume also that $\Xi \circ \Phi$ is a CLPO. If $\Xi p = \Xi(\Phi p)$ and $\Theta' p' = \Theta'(\Phi' p')$ then $\Xi p = \Theta' p'$. In particular, if $p = \Phi p$ and $p' = \Phi' p'$ then $\Xi p = \Theta' p'$.

Proof. Take $\Psi = \Xi \circ \Phi$ in Lemma 3.1. □

Example 3.4. Consider the following two processes.

proc $q(x{:}\mathbb{N}) = a(even(x)){\cdot}q(x+2)$
$\quad\quad q' = a(\mathrm{t}){\cdot}q'$

We prove by the Asymmetrical Lemma that $even(n) \rightarrow q(n) = q'$. As stated in the preliminaries, q' above is shorthand for $q'(y)$ with y a variable of a type $\mathbb{1}$ containing only one element. Thus the second equation actually reads:

$$q'(y{:}\mathbb{1}) = a(\mathrm{t})\cdot q'(y)$$

Take $D = \mathbb{N}$, $D' = \mathbb{1}$. Define $\Phi : (\mathbb{N}\rightarrow\mathbb{P})\rightarrow(\mathbb{N}\rightarrow\mathbb{P})$ by $\Phi p = \lambda n.\, a(even(n))\cdot p(n+2)$, and $\Phi' : (\mathbb{1}\rightarrow\mathbb{P})\rightarrow(\mathbb{1}\rightarrow\mathbb{P})$ by $\Phi' p' = \lambda y.\ a(\mathrm{t})\cdot p'(y)$. Moreover, define $\Xi : (\mathbb{N}\rightarrow\mathbb{P})\rightarrow(\mathbb{N}\rightarrow\mathbb{P})$ by $\Xi p = \lambda n.\ p(n) \lhd even(n) \rhd \delta$ and, for given $y \in \mathbb{1}$, $\Theta' : (\mathbb{1}\rightarrow\mathbb{P})\rightarrow(\mathbb{N}\rightarrow\mathbb{P})$ by $\Theta' p' = \lambda n.\ p'(y) \lhd even(n) \rhd \delta$. Then we have that $\Xi \circ \Phi$ is convergent and $q = \Phi q$, $q' = \Phi' q'$. We verify the commutativity of the diagram. The lower part of the diagram requires that we prove the equation $(\Xi(\Phi(\Theta' p')))n = (\Theta'(\Phi' p'))n$. The LHS evaluates to $(a(even(n)\cdot(p'(y) \lhd even(n+2) \rhd \delta)) \lhd even(n) \rhd \delta$ and the RHS to $(a(\mathrm{t})\cdot p'(y)) \lhd even(n) \rhd \delta$. These are equal since $even(n) \rightarrow (a(even(n)) = a(\mathrm{t}) \wedge even(n+2))$. The upper part of the diagram requires proving the equation $(\Xi(\Phi(\Xi p)))n = (\Xi(\Phi p))n$. This equation is handled in a similar way, using $even(n) \rightarrow even(n+2)$ (in other words: $even(n)$ is an invariant of Φ). It follows by the Asymmetrical Lemma that $\Xi q = \Theta' q'$, i.e. $\lambda n.\ q(n) \lhd even(n) \rhd \delta = \lambda n.\ q'(y) \lhd even(n) \rhd \delta$, so $even(n) \rightarrow q(n) = q'(y)$.

Intuition. The following may help to elucidate the relation between an invariant and the commutativity of the upper part of the diagram in the Asymmetrical Lemma. Let $\Xi = \lambda px.\ p(x) \lhd I(x) \rhd \delta$, where $I(x)$ is an invariant of $\Phi : (D\rightarrow\mathbb{P})\rightarrow(D\rightarrow\mathbb{P})$. Expanding the equation $\Xi(\Phi(\Xi p)) = \Xi(\Phi p)$, which corresponds to the upper part of the diagram, yields the following equation:

$$\lambda x.\ \Phi(\lambda x'.\, p(x') \lhd I(x') \rhd \delta)x \lhd I(x) \rhd \delta = \lambda x.\ \Phi px \lhd I(x) \rhd \delta$$

Typically, Φ does a number of calls of the form $p(x')$. These are the so-called recursive calls when Φ is regarded as defining the process p by $p = \Phi p$. The equation expresses that at such a point the invariant must be valid, i.e. p in the RHS may be replaced by $\lambda x'.p(x) \lhd I(x) \rhd \delta$. The displayed equation is clearly satisfied when $I(x) \rightarrow I(x')$ for every x, x' such that $p(x')$ occurs in Φpx. This is exactly the case for an invariant I.

The following trivial consequence of the previous lemmas is useful in simplifying recursive processes using invariants.

Lemma 3.5. *(Simplifying Lemma). Assume that the following diagram commutes.*

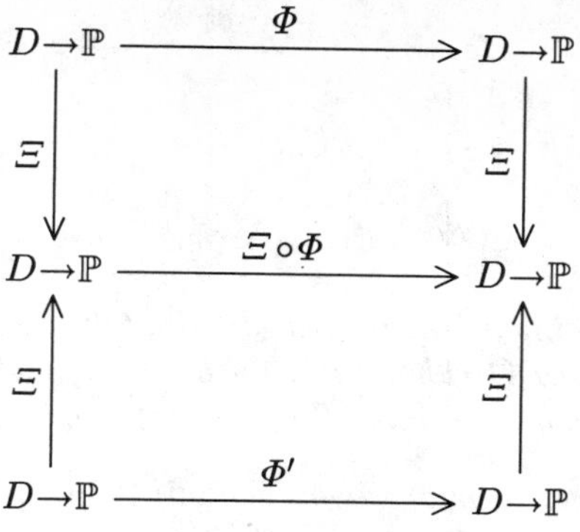

Assume that $\Xi\circ\Phi$ *is a CLPO. If* $\Xi p = \Xi(\Phi p)$ *and* $\Xi p' = \Xi(\Phi' p')$ *then* $\Xi p = \Xi p'$*. In particular, if* $p = \Phi p$ *and* $p' = \Phi' p'$ *then* $\Xi p = \Xi p'$.

Proof. Apply Lemma 3.3 with $\Theta' = \Xi$. □

Example 3.6. Consider the following two processes.

proc $q(x{:}\mathbb{N}) = a(x, even(x))\cdot q(x+2)$
$q'(x{:}\mathbb{N}) = a(x, \mathsf{t})\cdot q'(x+2)$

We prove by the Simplifying Lemma that $even(n) \rightarrow q(n) = q'(n)$. Take $D = \mathbb{N}$ and define $\Phi : (\mathbb{N}\rightarrow\mathbb{P})\rightarrow(\mathbb{N}\rightarrow\mathbb{P})$ by $\Phi p = \lambda n.\ a(n, even(n))\cdot p(n+2)$, and $\Phi' : (\mathbb{N}\rightarrow\mathbb{P})\rightarrow(\mathbb{N}\rightarrow\mathbb{P})$ by $\Phi' p = \lambda n.\ a(n,\mathsf{t})\cdot p(n+2)$. Moreover, define $\Xi : (\mathbb{N}\rightarrow\mathbb{P})\rightarrow(\mathbb{N}\rightarrow\mathbb{P})$ by $\Xi p = \lambda n.\ p(n) \lhd even(n) \rhd \delta$. Then we have that $\Xi\circ\Phi$ is convergent and $q = \Phi q$, $q' = \Phi' q'$. The commutativity of the diagram is easily proved in a way similar to Example 3.4. It follows by the Simplifying Lemma that $\Xi q = \Xi q'$, i.e. $\lambda n.\ q(n) \lhd even(n) \rhd \delta = \lambda n.\ q'(n) \lhd even(n) \rhd \delta$, so $even(n) \rightarrow q(n) = q'(n)$.

Lemma 3.7. *(Invariant Lemma). Assume that the following diagram commutes.*

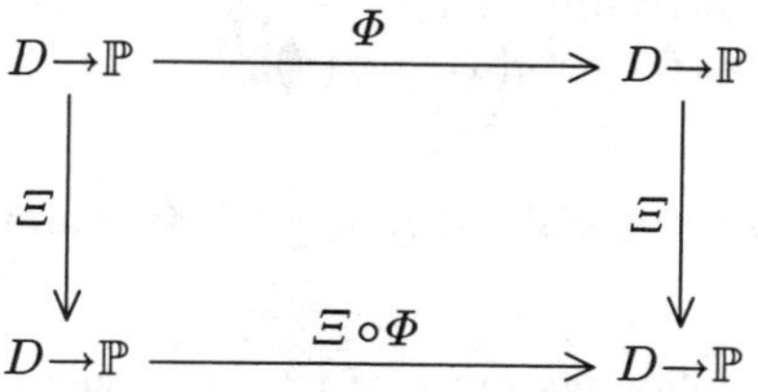

Assume also that $\Xi\circ\Phi$ *is a CLPO. If* $\Xi p = \Xi(\Phi p)$ *and* $\Xi p' = \Xi(\Phi p')$ *then* $\Xi p = \Xi p'$.

Proof. Apply Lemma 3.5 with $\Phi' = \Phi$. □

Corollary 3.8 *(Abstract Invariant Corollary). Assume that the following diagram commutes.*

$$
\begin{array}{ccc}
D{\rightarrow}\mathbb{P} & \xrightarrow{\quad \Phi \quad} & D{\rightarrow}\mathbb{P} \\
\Big\downarrow{\scriptstyle \Xi} & & \Big\downarrow{\scriptstyle \Xi} \\
D{\rightarrow}\mathbb{P} & \xrightarrow{\quad \Xi\circ\Phi \quad} & D{\rightarrow}\mathbb{P}
\end{array}
$$

Assume that Ξ is defined by an invariant I of Φ, i.e. $\Xi = \lambda px.\, p(x) \triangleleft I(x) \triangleright \delta$, and that $\Xi\circ\Phi$ is a CLPO. Then for all $q, q'{:}D{\rightarrow}\mathbb{P}$ such that $I(x) \rightarrow q(x) = \Phi qx$ and $I(x) \rightarrow q'(x) = \Phi q'x$ we have $I(x) \rightarrow q(x) = q'(x)$.

Proof. Note that $I(x) \rightarrow q(x) = \Phi qx$ is equivalent to $\Xi q = \Xi(\Phi q)$, and likewise for q'. □

Corollary 3.9 *(Concrete Invariant Corollary). Assume*

$$
\begin{aligned}
\Phi = \lambda p{:}D{\rightarrow}\mathbb{P}.\lambda d{:}D.\ & \Sigma_{j\in J}\Sigma_{e_j:D_j} c_j(f_j(d,e_j))\cdot p(g_j(d,e_j)) \triangleleft b_j(d,e_j) \triangleright \delta + \\
& \Sigma_{j\in J'}\Sigma_{e_j:D'_j} c'_j(f'_j(d,e_j)) \triangleleft b'_j(d,e_j) \triangleright \delta
\end{aligned}
$$

is a LPO. If for some predicate $I : D{\rightarrow}\mathbf{Bool}$

$\lambda pd.\Phi pd \triangleleft I(d) \triangleright \delta$ is convergent, and
$I(d) \wedge b_j(d,e_j) \rightarrow I(g_j(d,e_j))$ for all $j \in J$, $d \in D$ and $e_j \in D_j$,

i.e. I is an invariant of Φ, and for some $q : D{\rightarrow}\mathbb{P}$, $q' : D{\rightarrow}\mathbb{P}$ we have

$$
\begin{aligned}
I(d) &\rightarrow q(d) = \Phi qd, \\
I(d) &\rightarrow q'(d) = \Phi q'd,
\end{aligned}
$$

then

$$I(d) \rightarrow q(d) = q'(d).$$

Proof. We apply the Abstract Invariant Corollary. Let the conditions be as above. Define $\Xi = \lambda pd.p(d) \triangleleft I(d) \triangleright \delta$. By assumption $\Xi\circ\Phi$ is a CLPO. According to the intuition after Example 3.4 we can show that the diagram in Corollary 3.8 commutes. As by assumption $I(d) \rightarrow q(d) = \Phi qd$ and $I(d) \rightarrow q'(d) = \Phi q'd$, we may conclude that $I(d) \rightarrow q(d) = q'(d)$. □

Proposition 3.10. Lemmas 3.1, 3.3, 3.5, 3.7, Corollaries 3.8 and 3.9 are equivalent to CL-RSP.

Proof. Consider the following cycle of implications: CL-RSP $\rightarrow$ Lemma 3.1 $\rightarrow$ Lemma 3.3 $\rightarrow$ Lemma 3.5 $\rightarrow$ Lemma 3.7 $\rightarrow$ Corollary 3.8 $\rightarrow$ Corollary 3.9 $\rightarrow$ CL-RSP. All implications but the last have been established already. The last implication is obvious: take $I = \lambda x.\mathrm{t}$ in the Concrete Invariant Corollary 3.9. □

4 Two larger examples

We provide two examples that show how the results above can be applied. In the first example two queues are shown equal and in the second it is shown how two persons can play table tennis.

4.1 Two queues

Example 4.1. Consider the following two queues:

proc $q(old, new{:}\mathbb{N}, v{:}\,set, n{:}\mathbb{N}) =$
$$s(get(v, old))\cdot q(old+1, new, v - \langle old, get(v, old)\rangle, n) \lhd old \neq new \rhd \delta +$$
$$\textstyle\sum_{d:D} r(d)\cdot q(old, new+1, v + \langle new, d\rangle, n) \lhd old + n \neq new \rhd \delta$$

proc $q'(l{:}list, n{:}\mathbb{N}) =$
$$s(toe(l))\cdot q'(untoe(l), n) \lhd size(l) > 0 \rhd \delta +$$
$$\textstyle\sum_{d:D} r(d)\cdot q'(cons(d, l), n) \lhd size(l) < n \rhd \delta$$

In the definition of the process q, *set* is a data type defining sets, where $\emptyset$ is the empty set and $+$ and $-$ denote addition and deletion, respectively. Elements of the set v are pairs $\langle i, d\rangle$ consisting of an index i and a datum d, where the index uniquely determines the datum (intuition: the oldest datum has the smallest index). Moreover, $get(v, i)$ is the unique datum d such that $\langle i, d\rangle \in v$ (if v contains exactly one $\langle i, d\rangle$, otherwise $get(v, i)$ is arbitrary). In the definition of process q', *list* is the common data type of lists, with constructors *nil* and *cons*. For brevity, we denote lists with square brackets: $[]$ for the empty list and $[d, d_0, \ldots, d_{n-1}]$ for $cons(d, [d_0, \ldots, d_{n-1}])$. Moreover, $toe(l)$ is the last element of the list l and $untoe(l)$ is the result of deleting this element ($toe([])$ and $untoe([])$ are arbitrary). Finally, $size(l)$ is the length of the list l.

We want to prove $q(0, 0, \emptyset, n) = q'([], n)$ using the Concrete Invariant Corollary 3.9. We use the following CLPO Φ

$$\Phi = \lambda old, new{:}\mathbb{N}\, v{:}\,set\, n{:}\mathbb{N}.$$
$$s(get(v, old))\cdot q(old+1, new, v - \langle old, get(v, old)\rangle, n) \lhd old \neq new \rhd \delta +$$
$$\textstyle\sum_{d:D} r(d)\cdot q(old, new+1, v + \langle new, d\rangle, n) \lhd old + n \neq new \rhd \delta$$

which is exactly the CLPO defining q. Now we define the relation $I(old, new, v, n)$ by

$$old \leq new \leq old + n \;\wedge v = \{\langle old, get(v, old)\rangle, \ldots, \langle new - 1, get(v, new-1)\rangle\}.$$

This relation expresses the intuition about the correct functioning of the first queue: there can never be more than n elements in the list, i.e. *old* and *new* do not differ more than n, and all positions from *old* to *new* contain a datum. This relation is an invariant in the sense of Corollary 3.9 as it satisfies

(a1) $(I(x, y, v, n) \wedge x \neq y) \rightarrow I(x+1, y, v - \langle x, get(v, x)\rangle, n)$;
(a2) $(I(x, y, v, n) \wedge x + n \neq y) \rightarrow I(x, y+1, v + \langle y, d\rangle, n)$;

Next we show that q and $q'' = \lambda old, new{:}\mathbb{N}\, v{:}set\; n{:}\mathbb{N}.q'(\alpha(old, new, v), n)$ satisfy

$$I(x, y, v, n) \rightarrow q(x, y, v, n) = (\Phi q)(x, y, v, n),$$
$$I(x, y, v, n) \rightarrow q''(x, y, v, n) = (\Phi q'')(x, y, v, n).$$

If $new \geq old$, $\alpha(old, new, v)$ denotes $[get(v, new - 1), \ldots, get(v, old)]$. If $new < old$, we let $\alpha(old, new, v)$ denote $[]$. The parameterised process q is by definition a fixed point of Φ. We do not even need the invariant to show this. For the other implication we calculate

$$\begin{aligned} q''(old, new, v, n) &= q'(\alpha(old, new, v), n) = \\ &s(toe(\alpha(old, new, v)))\cdot q'(untoe(\alpha(old, new, v), n) \\ &\qquad \triangleleft size(\alpha(old, new, v)) > 0 \triangleright \delta + \\ &\Sigma_{d:D} r(d)\cdot q'(cons(d, \alpha(old, new, v)), n) \triangleleft size(\alpha(old, new, v)) < n \triangleright \delta. \end{aligned}$$

Now observe that the invariant $I(x, y, v, n)$ implies the following identities.

(b1) $(x \neq y) = (size(\alpha(x, y, v)) > 0)$;
(b2) $(x + n \neq y) = (size(\alpha(x, y, v)) < n)$;
(c1) $(x \neq y) \rightarrow get(v, x) = toe(\alpha(x, y, v))$;
(c2) $(x + n \neq y) \rightarrow d = d$;
(d1) $(x \neq y) \rightarrow \alpha(x + 1, y, v - \langle x, get(v, x)\rangle) = untoe(\alpha(x, y, v))$;
(d2) $(x + n \neq y) \rightarrow \alpha(x, y + 1, v + \langle y, d\rangle) = cons(d, \alpha(x, y, v))$.

As an example we prove d2:

$$(I(x, y, v, n) \wedge x{+}n \neq y) \rightarrow \alpha(x, y{+}1, v{+}\langle y, d\rangle) =^{\star} [d, get(v, y{-}1), \ldots, get(v, x)] =$$
$$cons(d, [get(v, y - 1), \ldots, get(v, x)]) = cons(d, \alpha(x, y, v)).$$

In $\star$ we use the invariant to show that $get(v + \langle y, d\rangle, y) = d$. From the identities above it easily follows that

$$\begin{aligned} &I(old, new, v, n) \rightarrow q'(\alpha(old, new, v), n) = \\ &\quad s(get(v, old))\cdot q'(\alpha(old + 1, new, v - \langle old, get(v, old)\rangle), n) \triangleleft old \neq new \triangleright \delta + \\ &\quad \Sigma_{d:D} r(d)\cdot q'(\alpha(old, new + 1, v + \langle new, d\rangle), n) \triangleleft old + n \neq new \triangleright \delta = \\ &\quad (\Phi q'')(old, new, v, n). \end{aligned}$$

Now it follows from the Concrete Invariant Corollary 3.9 that

$$I(old, new, v, n) \rightarrow q(old, new, v, n) = q'(\alpha(old, new, v), n).$$

Because $I(0, 0, \emptyset, n)$ is satisfied we find

$$q(0, 0, \emptyset, n) = q'([], n).$$

Remark 4.2. As Corollary 3.9 follows from CL-RSP, the proof can be done without using it. This would require calculating with an explicit Ξ as used in Corollary 3.8. There are two reasons why this is unpleasant. In the first place it leads to larger terms that must be manipulated. In the second place it mixes checking the invariant properties with proving that processes are fixed points. The use of Corollary 3.9 yields a better separation of these two concerns.

4.2 μCRL[1]-algebras

The example in the next subsection shows how invariants can be combined straightforwardly with parallelism. In this section we introduce the required operators. Besides the set *pAct* we now also assume a partial function $\gamma : pAct \to pAct \to pAct$ that defines how actions communicate. The function γ is commutative and associative and if $\gamma(a, b) = c$, then the data types of a, b and c are all equal.

Definition 4.3. A μCRL^1-*algebra* is a set $\mathbb{P}$ with the operations

$$
\begin{array}{l}
a : D \to \mathbb{P} \quad \text{(for all } a \in pAct \text{ and data type } D\text{)} \\
\delta, \tau : \mathbb{P} \\
+, \cdot : \mathbb{P} \to \mathbb{P} \to \mathbb{P} \\
\Sigma : (D \to \mathbb{P}) \to \mathbb{P} \quad \text{(for each data type } D\text{)} \\
\|, \mathbin{\lfloor\!\lfloor}, | : \mathbb{P} \to \mathbb{P} \to \mathbb{P} \\
\_ \lhd \_ \rhd \_ : (\mathbb{P} \times \textbf{Bool} \times \mathbb{P}) \to \mathbb{P} \\
\partial_H, \tau_I, \rho_R : \mathbb{P} \to \mathbb{P} \quad \text{(for all } H, I \subseteq pAct \text{ and } R \in pAct \to pAct \text{ such that} \\
\qquad\qquad\qquad\qquad\qquad \text{if } R(a) = b \text{ and } a : D \to \mathbb{P} \text{ then } b : D \to \mathbb{P}\text{)}
\end{array}
$$

that satisfies the (conditional) equations in Tables 1 through 3, except B1 and B2. If B1 and B2 are also satisfied, then we call $\mathbb{P}$ a μCRL$^{1\tau}$-*algebra*.

SUM6	$\Sigma_{d:D}(p(d) \mathbin{\lfloor\!\lfloor} z) = (\Sigma p) \mathbin{\lfloor\!\lfloor} z$	CF	$a(d) \mid b(e) = \begin{cases} \gamma(a,b)(d) & \text{if } d = e \text{ and } \gamma(a,b) \text{ defined} \\ \delta & \text{otherwise} \end{cases}$
SUM7	$\Sigma_{d:D}(p(d) \mid z) = (\Sigma p) \mid z$		
SUM8	$\Sigma_{d:D}(\partial_H(p(d))) = \partial_H(\Sigma p)$		
SUM9	$\Sigma_{d:D}(\tau_I(p(d))) = \tau_I(\Sigma p)$		
SUM10	$\Sigma_{d:D}(\rho_R(p(d))) = \rho_R(\Sigma p)$	CD1	$\delta \mid x = \delta$
		CD2	$x \mid \delta = \delta$
CM1	$x \parallel y = x \mathbin{\lfloor\!\lfloor} y + y \mathbin{\lfloor\!\lfloor} x + x \mid y$	CT1	$\tau \mid x = \delta$
CM2	$c \mathbin{\lfloor\!\lfloor} x = c \cdot x$	CT2	$x \mid \tau = \delta$
CM3	$c \cdot x \mathbin{\lfloor\!\lfloor} y = c \cdot (x \parallel y)$		
CM4	$(x + y) \mathbin{\lfloor\!\lfloor} z = x \mathbin{\lfloor\!\lfloor} z + y \mathbin{\lfloor\!\lfloor} z$	DD	$\partial_H(\delta) = \delta$
CM5	$c \cdot x \mid c' = (c \mid c') \cdot x$	DT	$\partial_H(\tau) = \tau$
CM6	$c \mid c' \cdot x = (c \mid c') \cdot x$	D1	$\partial_H(a(d)) = a(d)$ if $a \notin H$
CM7	$c \cdot x \mid c' \cdot y = (c \mid c') \cdot (x \parallel y)$	D2	$\partial_H(a(d)) = \delta$ if $a \in H$
CM8	$(x + y) \mid z = x \mid z + y \mid z$	D3	$\partial_H(x + y) = \partial_H(x) + \partial_H(y)$
CM9	$x \mid (y + z) = x \mid y + x \mid z$	D4	$\partial_H(x \cdot y) = \partial_H(x) \cdot \partial_H(y)$

Table 2. $x, y, z \in \mathbb{P}$, $a, b \in pAct$, $d, e \in D$ for data type D and c, c' are $a(d)$, τ or δ

The name of a μCRL^1-algebra is derived from the specification language μCRL [9], because the algebra contains the same process operators. The superscript 1

TID $\tau_I(\delta) = \delta$	RD $\rho_R(\delta) = \delta$
TIT $\tau_I(\tau) = \tau$	RT $\rho_R(\tau) = \tau$
TI1 $\tau_I(a(d)) = a(d)$ if $a \notin I$	R1 $\rho_R(a(d)) = R(a)(d)$
TI2 $\tau_I(a(d)) = \tau$ if $a \in I$	
TI3 $\tau_I(x + y) = \tau_I(x) + \tau_I(y)$	R3 $\rho_R(x + y) = \rho_R(x) + \rho_R(y)$
TI4 $\tau_I(x \cdot y) = \tau_I(x) \cdot \tau_I(y)$	R4 $\rho_R(x \cdot y) = \rho_R(x) \cdot \rho_R(y)$

Table 3. $x, y \in \mathbb{P}$, $a \in pAct$ and $d \in D$ for some data type D

refers to the fact that actions can have only one parameter. For an explanation of the new operators we refer to [2].

A process operator Ψ is called (μCRL^1-)*expressible* iff Ψ can be expressed with the operations mentioned in Definition 4.3. A μCRL^1-algebra is said to satisfy RDP iff every expressible process operator Ψ has at least one fixed point.

4.3 Table tennis

Example 4.4. We consider two persons playing table tennis. Person p_1 is a perfect player who always returns the ball properly. Person p_2 is a weak player who misses the ball when it is too far. The goal of the game is to get the ball into a square bucket that stands on the table.

When we assume that the players play rather rigidly, we can describe the behaviour of the players as follows:

$$
\begin{aligned}
\textbf{proc} \quad & p_1(l, v{:}\mathbb{R}) = \textstyle\sum_{x,y:\mathbb{R}} r_2(x, y)\,(in \lhd |x| < l \wedge |y| < l \rhd s_1(-x, y - v)\, p_1(l, v)) \\
& p_2(x_h, y_h, k, l{:}\mathbb{R}) = \textstyle\sum_{x,y:\mathbb{R}} r_1(x, y)\,(in \lhd |x| < l \wedge |y| < l \rhd \\
& \qquad (s_2(-\tfrac{1}{2}x, y)\, p_2(x, y, k, l) \lhd (x_h - x)^2 + (x_h - y)^2 < k^2 \rhd out))
\end{aligned}
$$

A referee throws the ball at position x_0, y_0. Player p_2 receives the ball (via the communication $\gamma(r_1, s_1) = c_1$) and sends it back to position $(-\frac{1}{2}x_0, y_0)$. Then player p_1 receives the ball (via communication $\gamma(r_2, s_2) = c_2$ and sends it back to position $(\frac{1}{2}x_0, y_0 - v_0)$. The game continues, except if the ball arrives in the square bucket, which is placed around position $(0, 0)$ with sides $2l$, or if player p_2 cannot move his hand far enough from position (x_h, y_h) to the ball, which he can only do over a distance k each time it is his turn.

The total system of players is described by the following expression, where all communication actions are hidden, because we are only interested in the question whether the ball will end up on the floor or in the bucket.

$$
\begin{aligned}
& Syst(x_0, y_0, v_0, x_h, y_h, k, l) = \\
& \tau_{\{c_1,c_2\}}(\partial_{\{r_1,r_2,s_1,s_2\}}(s_1(x_0, y_0) \cdot p_1(l, v_0) \parallel p_2(x_h, y_h, k, l))).
\end{aligned}
$$

We sketch the main steps towards an answer of the question above. Using the axioms above we first expand *Syst* to the following equation, referred to as (I).

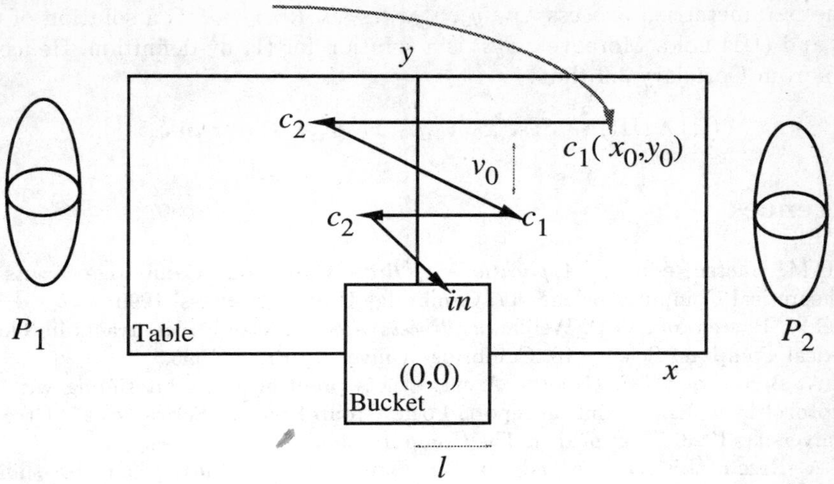

Fig. 1. Players p_1 and p_2 play table tennis

$$
\begin{aligned}
&\mathit{Syst}(x_0, y_0, v_0, x_h, y_h, k, l) = \\
&\quad \tau{\cdot}\mathit{in}{\cdot}\delta \lhd (|x_0| < l \wedge |y_0| < l) \vee \\
&\qquad\qquad ((x_h - x_0)^2 + (y_h - y_0)^2 < k^2 \wedge |\tfrac{1}{2}x_0| < l \wedge |y_0| < l) \rhd \delta + \\
&\quad \tau{\cdot}\mathit{out}{\cdot}\delta \lhd (|x_0| \geq l \vee |y_0| \geq l) \wedge (x_h - x_0)^2 + (y_h - y_0)^2 \geq k^2 \rhd \delta + \\
&\quad \tau{\cdot}\mathit{Syst}(\tfrac{1}{2}x_0, y_0 - v_0, v_0, x_0, y_0, k, l) \\
&\qquad\qquad \lhd (|\tfrac{1}{2}x_0| \geq l \vee |y_0| \geq l) \wedge (x_h - x_0)^2 + (y_h - y_0)^2 < k^2 \rhd \delta.
\end{aligned}
$$

Note that the definition of *Syst* cannot be seen as a guarded recursive specification in the usual sense, due to the unguarded occurrence of *Syst* on the right hand side. We develop sufficient conditions for a successful game. In order to guarantee that player p_2's hand is close enough to the place where the ball will land, and that the speed of the ball is within reasonable limits (otherwise the ball will end too far away in the y-direction), we formulate the following condition (II)

$$(x_h - x_0)^2 + (x_h - y_0)^2 < k^2 \wedge \tfrac{1}{4}x_0^2 + v_0^2 < k^2.$$

Moreover, the ball must end in the bucket. This is expressed by (III)

$$n \geq 0 \wedge 2^n l > x_0 \geq 0, \text{ where } n = \text{entier}(\frac{y_0 + l}{v_0}).$$

The variable n expresses how many turns it takes to get the ball in the bucket. It is easy to see that the conjunction of (II) and (III) is an invariant in the sense of Corollary 3.9.

Moreover, starting in a state where the invariant holds, a game only takes n turns. It follows that the convergence condition of Corollary 3.9 is satisfied.

The parameterised process $\lambda x_0, y_0, v_0, x_h, y_h, k, l{:}\mathbb{R}.\tau{\cdot}in{\cdot}\delta$ is a solution of (I) if (II) and (III) hold. Moreover, *Syst* is a solution for (I) by definition. Hence it follows from Corollary 3.9 that

$$(\mathrm{II}) \wedge (\mathrm{III}) \rightarrow Syst(x_0, y_0, v_0, x_h, y_h, k, l) = \tau{\cdot}in{\cdot}\delta.$$

References

1. J.C.M. Baeten, editor. *Applications of Process Algebra.* Cambridge Tracts in Theoretical Computer Science 17. Cambridge University Press, 1990.
2. J.C.M. Baeten and W.P. Weijland. *Process Algebra.* Cambridge Tracts in Theoretical Computer Science 18. Cambridge University Press, 1990.
3. M.A. Bezem and J.F. Groote. A correctness proof of a one bit sliding window protocol in μCRL. Technical report, Logic Group Preprint Series no. 99, Utrecht University, 1993. To appear in The Computer Journal.
4. M.A. Bezem, J.F. Groote and J.J. van Wamel. A correctness proof of a sliding window protocol in μCRL. Technical report, Logic Group Preprint Series, Utrecht University, 1994. To appear.
5. K.M. Chandy and J. Misra. *Parallel Program Design. A Foundation.* Addison-Wesley, 1988.
6. L. Fredlund, J.F. Groote and H. Korver. A verification of a leader election protocol in μCRL, 1994. To appear.
7. R.J. van Glabbeek and W.P. Weijland. Branching time and abstraction in bisimulation semantics (extended abstract). In G.X. Ritter, editor, *Information Processing 89*, pages 613–618. North-Holland, 1989. Full version available as Report CS-R9120, CWI, Amsterdam, 1991.
8. R.A. Groenveld. Verification of a sliding window protocol by means of process algebra. Report P8701, Programming Research Group, University of Amsterdam, 1987.
9. J.F. Groote and A. Ponse. The syntax and semantics of μCRL. Technical Report CS-R9076, CWI, Amsterdam, December 1990.
10. J.F. Groote and A. Ponse. Process algebra with guards. Combining Hoare logic and process algebra (Extended abstract). In J.C.M. Baeten and J.F. Groote, editors, *Proceedings CONCUR 91*, Amsterdam, volume 527 of *Lecture Notes in Computer Science*, pages 235–249. Springer-Verlag, 1991. Full version appeared as Technical Report CS-R9069, CWI, Amsterdam, 1990; and is to appear in *Formal Aspects of Computing.*
11. J.F. Groote and A. Ponse. Proof theory for μCRL. Technical Report CS-R9138, CWI, Amsterdam, August 1991.
12. J.F. Groote and A. Ponse. Proof theory for μCRL: a language for processes with data. In D.J. Andrews, J.F. Groote, and C.A. Middelburg, editors. *Proceedings of the International Workshop on Semantics of Specification Languages*, pages 231–250. Workshops in Computer Science, Springer Verlag, 1994.
13. E.C.R. Hehner. **do** Considered **od**: A contribution to the programming calculus. *Acta Informatica*, 11:287–304, 1979.
14. A. Ponse. Process expressions and Hoare's logic. *Information and Computation*, 95(2):192–217, 1991.

Testing-Based Abstractions for Value-Passing Systems

Rance Cleaveland* and James Riely**

[1] Dept. of Computer Science, N.C. State University, Raleigh, NC 27695-8206, USA
[2] Dept. of Computer Science, University of N.C., Chapel Hill, NC 27599-3175, USA
email: rance@csc.ncsu.edu, riely@cs.unc.edu

Abstract. This paper presents a framework for the abstract interpretation of processes that pass values. We define a process description language that is parameterized with respect to the set of values that processes may exchange and show that an abstraction over values induces an abstract semantics for processes. Our main results state that if the abstract value interpretation safely/optimally approximates the ground interpretation, then the resulting abstracted processes safely/optimally approximate those derived from the ground semantics (in a precisely defined sense). As the processes derived from an abstract semantics in general have far fewer states than those derived from a concrete semantics, our technique enables the automatic analysis of systems that lie beyond the scope of existing techniques.

1 Introduction

Research over the past decade points to the practical viability of automatically verifying concurrent finite-state systems. Algorithms have been proposed for determining whether such systems enjoy properties specified by formulas in various temporal logics [4, 5, 8, 25, 27, 28] and for computing whether or not two systems exhibit the same (or related) observable behavior [2, 6, 18, 21]. Tools built around implementations of these algorithms have been applied to the analysis of a variety of different kinds of systems [7, 11, 12, 22, 23, 24]. When communicating processes are capable of exchanging values taken from an infinite set, however, the resulting system is usually not finite-state, and the automatic analysis routines mentioned above, which rely to some extent on an enumeration of system states, are not directly applicable. Even when the set of values is finite (as is the case, for example, in communication protocols, where packets typically have a fixed width) automatic analysis rapidly becomes impractical as the size of the value set increases. On the other hand, many system properties are largely insensitive to the specific values that systems pass. Some, such as deadlock-freedom and fairness constraints, do not refer to specific values at all, while others are only sensitive to certain aspects of data. These observations suggest that it may be possible to reduce the analysis of value-passing systems to simpler systems that exchange more abstract values.

In this paper, we present a framework for generating *abstractions* of communicating systems based on abstractions of the values exchanged by processes. Such abstracted systems in general have many fewer states than the systems from which they are constructed while retaining some measure of information about the behavior of the original system. This last fact permits the analysis of a smaller, abstracted system in lieu of the original one, with results obtained from the former also guaranteed to be applicable to the latter.

---

* Research supported by NSF/DARPA Grant CCR-9014775, NSF Grant CCR-9120995, ONR Young Investigator Award N00014-92-J-1582, and NSF Young Investigator Award CCR-9257963.

** Research supported by ONR Contract N00014-92-C-0182.

Our work is inspired by that done in the *abstract interpretation* of sequential programming languages [9], which has led to the development of techniques that permit certain properties of sequential programs to be deduced automatically at compile-time. In particular, our approach is similar to work on *factored semantics* described in [17], although our setting is operational rather than denotational. More specifically, we give a semantics for a language similar to CSP [16] in which the core semantics is explicitly parameterized with respect to a *value interpretation* that defines the meaning of data. We also define the conditions under which an abstract value interpretation is *safe* relative to the original interpretation and under which a safe abstraction is said to be *optimal.* We then prove the main results of this paper: safe (optimal) abstract value interpretations yield safe (optimal) abstract process interpretations using our parameterized semantics.

The remainder of the paper is organized as follows. The next section formally introduces value interpretations. Section 3 then gives the syntax and semantics of processes and defines a preorder on processes, indicating when one process approximates another. The semantic relation is a variant of the testing/failures preorders [13], which we also argue preserves both liveness and safety properties of processes. In Section 4 we extend the abstraction functions defined in Section 2 to process terms (syntax) and labeled transition systems (semantics) so that the main results may be formally stated. The section following presents these results, while Section 6 contains a simple example illustrating how they may be applied to the analysis of concurrent systems. Section 7 contains our conclusions and directions for future work.

2 Values and value abstractions

In the next section we give the syntax and semantics of VPL_I—Value-Passing Language with value interpretation I. VPL_I is a simple variant of the language defined by Hennessy and Ingólfsdóttir in [14]; the difference lies in the fact that VPL_I is explicitly parameterized with respect to an interpretation I of values. In this section we introduce value interpretations and show how traditional notions from *abstract interpretation* may be adapted to our setting.

2.1 Value interpretations

In order to define the syntax of VPL_I, we first fix a syntax for constructing boolean and value expressions that is parameterized with respect to the values that may appear in these expressions. That is, the syntax of the expression language contains "holes" to be filled by members of the value set; changing the value set then simply changes the choices for filling the holes. In this setting, a *value interpretation* for a set of values should allow us to "evaluate" expressions.

To formalize these notions, let $(x, y \in)$ *Var* be a countable set of variable symbols (we write "$(x, y \in)$ *Var*" to indicate that the symbols x and y will range over the set *Var*), and let let Σ_{Expr} and Σ_{BExpr} be fixed signatures containing no 0-ary function symbols (constants). The idea is that Σ_{Expr} and Σ_{BExpr} contain constructors for building expressions and boolean expressions, respectively. Also let *Val* be a nonempty set of values that is disjoint from *Var*. Then $(e \in) Expr_{Val}$ contains the elements of the term algebra built from $\Sigma_{Expr} \cup Val \cup Var$, with the arity of elements in *Val* and *Var* taken to be 0, and $(be \in)$ $BExpr_{Val}$ represents the set of elements of the term algebra $\Sigma_{BExpr} \cup Val \cup Var$. $Expr_{Val}$ and $BExpr_{Val}$ comprise the set of value and boolean expressions, respectively, that may be built from variables and elements of *Val* using the constructors in Σ_{Expr} and Σ_{BExpr}.

We use $e_1[e_2/x]$ to represent the expression obtained by simultaneously replacing all (free) occurrences of x in e_1 by e_2 in the usual sense, and $CExpr_{Val}$ (resp. $CBExpr_{Val}$) to denote the subset of $Expr_{Val}$ ($BExpr_{Val}$) closed with respect to *Var*. Also let $\wp(S)$ denote the power set of set S. We may now define value interpretations as follows.

Definition 1. *A* value interpretation *is a triple* $I = \langle Val_I, \mathbb{B}_I[\![\cdot]\!], \mathbb{E}_I[\![\cdot]\!]\rangle$ *where* $(v \in) Val_I$ *is a countable set of values,* $\mathbb{B}_I[\![\cdot]\!]\colon CBExpr_{Val_I} \mapsto (\wp(Bool) - \{\emptyset\})$, *and*
$$\mathbb{E}_I[\![\cdot]\!]\colon CExpr_{Val_I} \mapsto (\wp(Val_I) - \{\emptyset\}).$$

We usually write $Expr_I$, $CExpr_I$, $BExpr_I$ and $CBExpr_I$ in lieu of $Expr_{Val_I}$, et cetera; we also do not distinguish between values and their syntactic representation.

One noteworthy aspect of this definition is that the "valuation" functions $\mathbb{E}_I[\![\cdot]\!]$ and $\mathbb{B}_i[\![\cdot]\!]$ may be nondeterministic; that is, $\mathbb{E}_i[\![e]\!]$ may return a set of possible values. The utility of this will be made apparent in Section 2.3.

The remainder of this section is devoted to a discussion of *abstractions* over value interpretations. In particular, we show how traditional concepts from abstract interpretation —abstraction, concretization, safety and optimality— may be adapted to our setting. We consider each of these in turn.

2.2 Abstraction and concretization

Abstract interpretation may be seen as the generalized theory of static analysis of programs. The motivation for its study arises from practical considerations in the design of compilers. One would like compilers to generate code that is as efficient and free of runtime errors as possible; however, many of the analyses required are undecidable in general. Abstract interpretation provides a basis for analyzing abstracted versions of programs in order to provide partial information about their behavior.

The formal foundations of abstract interpretation lie in the definition of *abstraction* and *concretization* functions between "concrete" and "abstract" domains. Intuitively, the concrete domain contains the meanings of "real" programs, while the abstract domain includes the meanings of programs obtained by abstracting away some of the detail from concrete programs. Formally, let $\langle C, \sqsubseteq_C\rangle$ and $\langle A, \sqsubseteq_A\rangle$ be preorders.[3]. C may be thought of as representing the possible concrete meanings a program might have, with $c_1 \sqsubseteq_C c_2$ holding if c_1 contains "less information" than c_2, while A represents the corresponding set of abstract meanings. Then an abstract interpretation of C in A may be given as a pair of functions, α and γ, that constitute a *Galois insertion.*

Definition 2. *Given preorders* $\langle C, \sqsubseteq_C\rangle$ *and* $\langle A, \sqsubseteq_A\rangle$, *we say that* α *and* γ *form a Galois insertion, written* $\langle C, \sqsubseteq_C\rangle \underset{\gamma}{\overset{\alpha}{\rightleftarrows}} \langle A, \sqsubseteq_A\rangle$, *when:*

- $\alpha\colon C \mapsto A$ *and* $\gamma\colon C \mapsto A$ *are monotonic,*
- $\forall c \in C\colon\ \gamma \circ \alpha(c) \sqsubseteq_C c$, *and*
- $\forall a \in A\colon\ \alpha \circ \gamma(a) =_A a$, *where* $a =_A a'$ *iff* $a \sqsubseteq_A a'$ & $a' \sqsubseteq_A a$.

Function α is usually called the *abstraction function*, while γ is called the *concretization function*. The Galois insertion requirements may be seen as an assertion that α and γ are compatible. In particular, the second condition indicates that α does not "add information" to its argument, while the third indicates that γ "preserves the information" of its argument. It should be noted that our use of the symbol $\sqsubseteq$ is contrary to tradition in abstract interpretation; thus, the second condition would usually be written as $\gamma \circ \alpha(c) \sqsupseteq_C c$. Our notation is chosen to be consistent with traditional information-theoretic orderings on processes.

[3] Traditionally, these are taken to be lattices, but we require this slightly weaker formulation in Section 4

In the setting of value interpretations there is no *a priori* notion of ordering on values; however, we can define still abstraction functions as follows. Given two sets of values, Val_C (for *concrete*) and Val_A (for *abstract*), we call a total surjection $\alpha \colon Val_C \mapsto Val_A$ an *abstraction* function. As an example, let Val_C be the set of natural numbers and Val_A be the set $\{\mathsf{neg}, 0, \mathsf{pos}\}$. Then we may define the usual abstraction $\alpha \colon Val_C \mapsto Val_A$ by taking $\alpha(c) = \mathsf{neg}$ if $c < 0$, $\alpha(0) = 0$, and $\alpha(c) = \mathsf{pos}$ if $c > 0$.

An abstraction function naturally generalizes to expressions: in $\alpha(e)$ each occurrence of a value c in e is replaced by $\alpha(c)$. When no confusion can arise, we abuse notation slightly by using α to refer any such "lifted" instance of α.

Definition 3. *The following functions are defined by induction on the structure of their domains:* $\alpha : Expr_C \mapsto Expr_A$, $\alpha : CExpr_C \mapsto CExpr_A$, $\alpha : BExpr_C \mapsto BExpr_A$, *and* $\alpha \colon CBExpr_C \mapsto CBExpr_A$.

We write $\alpha \colon C \mapsto A$ refer to the entire family of functions induced by $\alpha : Val_C \mapsto Val_A$ between value interpretations C and A.

In order to apply traditional abstract interpretation techniques to value interpretations, we also need a concretization function for each abstraction α. Values are unordered, however, and the inverse of α, a natural choice for γ, is not in general a function. The powerset of values, on the other hand, does have a natural information-theoretic ordering. Suppose $V_C \subseteq Val_C$; then V_C represents the potential results of evaluating an expression in the concrete interpretation C, and likewise for Val_A. The smaller the set, the more the information available about the actual value returned: indeed, usually we expect that $\mathbb{E}_C[\![\cdot]\!]$ is deterministic and total and thus maps each expression to a singleton set. So we take as our preorder $\langle \wp(C) - \{\emptyset\}, \supseteq \rangle$, where $V_C \supseteq V'_C$ means that V_C contains less information than V'_C as it contains more elements. We may now define abstraction and concretization functions on these domains as follows.

Definition 4. *For* $\alpha : Val_C \mapsto Val_A$, $V_C \subseteq Val_C$ *and* $V_A \subseteq Val_A$, *define the lifted abstraction and concretization functions as:* $\alpha(V_C) = \{a \mid \exists c \in V_C : \alpha(c) = a\}$, *and* $\gamma(V_A) = \{c \mid \exists a \in V_A \colon \alpha(c) = a\}$.

These functions turn out to form a Galois insertion.

Lemma 5.
$$\langle \wp(Val_C), \supseteq \rangle \underset{\gamma}{\overset{\alpha}{\rightleftarrows}} \langle \wp(Val_A), \supseteq \rangle$$

In a similar way we can define lifted abstractions and concretizations on all of the syntactic categories of VPL_I. In each case, the result is a Galois insertion on the preorder over sets induced by the superset relation. For example, we have that:

$$\langle \wp(CExpr_C), \supseteq \rangle \underset{\gamma}{\overset{\alpha}{\rightleftarrows}} \langle \wp(CExpr_A), \supseteq \rangle$$

2.3 Safety

In traditional abstract interpretation, after giving a Galois insertion $\langle S_C, \sqsubseteq_C \rangle \underset{\gamma}{\overset{\alpha}{\rightleftarrows}} \langle S_A, \sqsubseteq_A \rangle$ one then gives abstract versions $f_A : S_A \mapsto S_A$ for each operation $f_C : S_C \mapsto S_C$ used in defining the semantics of a language. Of course, one would wish that an abstraction f_A of f_C be compatible with f_C, in some sense. This notion is made precise by defining f_A to be a *safe* approximation of f_C if for all $c \in S_C$, $(f_A \circ \alpha)(c) \sqsubseteq (\alpha \circ f_C)(c)$. Intuitively, f_A is safe if it can never "add information" to the results produced by f_C; that is, $\alpha \circ f_C$ produces the most precise abstract information for any value $c \in S_C$.

In our setting, there are no specific operators with respect to which safety can be defined, since the exact syntax of expressions is not specified. Instead, our definition of safety uses the evaluation functions of the interpretation.

Definition 6. *A value abstraction* $\alpha : C \mapsto A$ *is* safe *iff for all* $e \in CExpr_C$ *and* $be \in CBExpr_C$,

$$\mathbb{B}_A[\![\alpha(be)]\!] \supseteq \mathbb{B}_C[\![be]\!] \ \ and \ \ \mathbb{E}_A[\![\alpha(e)]\!] \supseteq \alpha(\mathbb{E}_C[\![e]\!]).$$

In other words, one interpretation is *safe* relative to another if for all terms, the former yields no more precise a result than the former. Returning to our example, let $e = (1 + (-2))$. The most precise abstract information about e would be $\alpha(\mathbb{E}_C[\![e]\!]) = \{\mathsf{neg}\}$, whereas $\mathbb{E}_A[\![\alpha(e)]\!] = \{\mathsf{neg}, 0, \mathsf{pos}\}$. In this case, the abstract semantics can yield no more precise an answer; if it did, it would get at least some answer "wrong", since $\alpha(1 + (-2)) = \alpha(2 + (-1)) = \alpha(1 + (-1)) = \mathsf{pos} + \mathsf{neg}$.

2.4 Optimality

While safety is a necessary condition for an abstraction of an operator to be useful, it is not sufficient. For example, one can give an abstract operator that is trivially safe: just map each abstract value to a least value in the abstract domain. While safe, this operator does not convey useful information about the concrete operation it is supposed to approximate. In our previous example, the semantic function that maps all expressions to $\{\mathsf{neg}, 0, \mathsf{pos}\}$ would be an example of such a trivial, yet safe, semantics.

At the opposite extreme from the trivial semantics is the optimal (or *induced*) semantics. In the traditional setting, f_A is said to be *optimal* for f_C if f_A is the most precise safe approximation of f_C. Formally [17], we may say that f_A is optimal if $f_A(a) =_A \alpha \circ f_C \circ \gamma(a)$, where $=_A$ is the equivalence induced by $\sqsubseteq_A$.

In order to formalize this notion in our setting, we first must extend our semantic functions to operate over *sets* of terms.

Definition 7. *For* $BS \subseteq CBExpr_I$ *and* $ES \subseteq CExpr_I$ *define:*

$$\mathbb{B}_I[\![BS]\!] = \{v \mid \exists be \in BS\colon\ v \in \mathbb{B}_I[\![be]\!]\}, \ \ and$$
$$\mathbb{E}_I[\![ES]\!] = \{v \mid \exists e \in ES\colon\ v \in \mathbb{E}_I[\![e]\!]\}.$$

Given $\alpha\colon C \mapsto A$, *we say that* A *is* optimal *for* C *iff for all* $e \in CExpr_C$ *and* $be \in CBExpr_C$:

$$\mathbb{B}_A[\![be]\!] = \alpha(\mathbb{B}_C[\![\gamma(be)]\!]) \ \ and \ \ \mathbb{E}_A[\![e]\!] = \alpha(\mathbb{E}_C[\![\gamma(e)]\!]).$$

2.5 Preview

This section has introduced value interpretations and described the conditions under which an abstract value interpretation is considered safe and optimal. In the next section we present a process description language defined parametrically with respect to value interpretations. The semantics of the language is given as a mapping from process terms to labeled transition systems, and a preorder is defined on these semantic objects. In Section 4 we construct a Galois insertion between concrete and abstract labeled transition systems. Finally, in Section 5, we extend the definitions of safety and optimality to the process description language and prove the main results: if an abstract value interpretation is safe (optimal), then the process interpretation constructed using the abstract semantics will be safe (optimal).

3 Processes

This section introduces the syntax and semantics of VPL_I and defines a semantic preorder relating processes given in the language.

3.1 Syntax

In addition to the sets of value- and boolean-expression constructors mentioned in the previous section, the definition of process terms is parameterized with respect to countable sets $(P, Q \in)$ *PN* of process names and $(c \in)$ *Chan* of channel names. We use L to range over finite subsets of *Chan*. Given a value interpretation I, we define the set of possible *communications* as $(a, b \in) Comm_I = \{c?v, c!v \mid c \in Comm \ \& \ v \in Val_I\}$. The set of actions, $(\lambda \in) Act_I = Comm_I \cup \{\tau\}$, includes also the hidden action τ. Intuitively, $c?v$ represents the act of receiving value v on channel c, while $c!v$ corresponds to the output of v on c. The action τ represents an internal computation step. Finally, if $(f \in) Chan \mapsto Chan$ then $\hat{f} \in Act_I \mapsto Act_I$ is defined by $\hat{f}(\tau) = \tau$, $\hat{f}(c!v) = f(c)!v$, and $\hat{f}(c?v) = f(c)?v$. That is, $\hat{f}$ relabels the channel components of actions.

The syntax of $(t \in) VPL_I$ may now be given by the following grammar:

$$\begin{aligned} t ::= \mathsf{nil} \ \mid \ c?x.t \ \mid \ c!e.t \ \mid \ be \rhd t_1 \diamond t_2 \ \mid \ t_1 [\!] t_2 \ \mid \ t_1 \oplus t_2 \\ \mid \ t_1 | t_2 \ \mid \ t \backslash L \ \mid \ t[f] \ \mid \ P(\overline{e}) \ \mid \ (\mathsf{rec}\ P(\overline{x}).t)\,(\overline{e}) \end{aligned}$$

The notation $\overline{x}$ indicates a vector of variables, likewise $\overline{e}$ a vector of expressions. For term $(\mathsf{rec}\ P(\overline{x}).t)\,(\overline{e})$ to be well formed we require that $\overline{x}$ and $\overline{e}$ have the same number of elements and that each occurrence of P in t be applied to this same number of arguments. The term $c?x.t$ binds x in t, while the term $(\mathsf{rec}\ P(\overline{x}).t)\,(\overline{e})$ binds P and $\overline{x}$ in t. We assume the usual definitions of substitution (for process names and for variables) and closed terms; we denote the set of closed terms of VPL_I as $(p, q \in) Proc_I$ and call such terms *processes*.

3.2 Semantics

Before presenting the formal semantics of processes, we first give some intuition as to their behavior. Term nil represents the terminated process. The process $c?x.t$ is capable of receiving a value on channel c and subsequently behaves as t with the received value substituted for x. If the expression e is a constant (that is, $e \in Val_I$), then process $c!e.p$ will output e on channel c; otherwise, $c!e.p$ may spontaneously evolve to $c!v.p$ for any v in $\mathbb{E}_I[\![e]\!]$. We write the conditional as $be \rhd p \diamond q$; this process may have one or two possible internal moves, depending on the valuation of be. We use the symbol $[\!]$ to denote external choice and $\oplus$ to denote internal choice. $p|q$ denotes the parallel composition of p and q. The process $p \backslash L$ behaves as p with the exception that communication along channels in L is forbidden, and $p[f]$ behaves as p with the channels relabeling by f. Finally, $(\mathsf{rec}\ P(\overline{x}).p)\,(\overline{e})$ may spontaneously unfold, substituting $\overline{e}$ for $\overline{x}$.

This intuition is formalized in the transition relation $(\longrightarrow_I) \subseteq (Proc_I \times Act_I \times Proc_I)$, where $p \xrightarrow{\lambda}_I q$ holds if p is capable of executing action λ and evolving to q. To define this transition relation we first need some auxiliary notation. We use the overbar to indicate complementary communications; thus $\overline{c?v} = c!v$ and $\overline{c!v} = c?v$. Let the function name : $(Act \mapsto Chan \cup \{\tau\})$ map communications to the channels on which they occur and τ to itself; for example, $\mathrm{name}(c?v) = c$ and $\mathrm{name}(\tau) = \tau$. The formal definition of $\longrightarrow_I$ is given in Table 1. We write $p \xrightarrow{\lambda}_I$ to abbreviate $(\exists q : \ p \xrightarrow{\lambda}_I q)$ and $p \not\xrightarrow{\lambda}$ to abbreviate $\neg(p \xrightarrow{\lambda}_I)$. If $p \not\xrightarrow{\tau}$ we say that p is *stable*.

Using this operational semantics, we may now defined a mapping from process terms to *labeled transition systems* as follows.

Definition 8. *A (rooted)* labeled transition system *over value interpretation I is a triple $\langle \Sigma, \sigma^0, \rightarrowtail \rangle$, where Σ is a set of states, $\sigma^0 \in \Sigma$ is an initial state, and $(\rightarrowtail) \subseteq (\Sigma \times Act_I \times \Sigma)$ is a transition relation. Let $(\mathcal{M}, \mathcal{N} \in) LTS_I$ be the set of all such labeled transition systems.*

In)	$c?x.t \xrightarrow{c!v}_I t[v/x]$, for all $v \in Val_I$		
Out)	$c!e.p \xrightarrow{\tau}_I c!v.p$, if $e \notin Val_I \wedge v \in \mathbb{E}_I[\![e]\!]$	$c!v.p \xrightarrow{c!v}_I p$	
Rec)	$(\mathsf{rec}\ P(\overline{x}).t)(\overline{e}) \xrightarrow{\tau}_I (t[\mathsf{rec}\ P(\overline{x}).t/P])[\overline{e}/\overline{x}]$		
Int)	$p \oplus q \xrightarrow{\tau}_I p$	$p \oplus q \xrightarrow{\tau}_I q$	
Cond)	$be \rhd p \diamond q \xrightarrow{\tau}_I p$, if $tt \in \mathbb{B}_I[\![be]\!]$	$be \rhd p \diamond q \xrightarrow{\tau}_I q$, if $ff \in \mathbb{B}_I[\![be]\!]$	
Ext)	$\dfrac{p \xrightarrow{\tau}_I p'}{p [\!] q \xrightarrow{\tau}_I p' [\!] q}$ $\quad \dfrac{q \xrightarrow{\tau}_I q'}{p [\!] q \xrightarrow{\tau}_I p [\!] q'}$	$\dfrac{p \xrightarrow{a}_I p'}{p [\!] q \xrightarrow{a}_I p'}$ $\quad \dfrac{q \xrightarrow{a}_I q'}{p [\!] q \xrightarrow{a}_I q'}$	
Par)	$\dfrac{p \xrightarrow{\lambda}_I p'}{p \vert q \xrightarrow{\lambda}_I p' \vert q}$ $\quad \dfrac{q \xrightarrow{\lambda}_I q'}{p \vert q \xrightarrow{\lambda}_I p \vert q'}$	$\dfrac{p \xrightarrow{a}_I p' \quad q \xrightarrow{\overline{a}}_I q'}{p \vert q \xrightarrow{\tau}_I p' \vert q'}$	
Res)	$\dfrac{p \xrightarrow{\lambda}_I p'}{p \backslash L \xrightarrow{\lambda}_I p' \backslash L}$ name$(\lambda) \notin L$		
Ren)	$\dfrac{p \xrightarrow{\lambda}_I p'}{p[f] \xrightarrow{f(\lambda)}_I p'[f]}$		

Table 1. Transition Rules for VPL_I, where $I = \langle Val_I, \mathbb{B}_I[\![\cdot]\!], \mathbb{E}_I[\![\cdot]\!] \rangle$

We can now define the meaning of a process by mapping it to an element of LTS_I. Let $p \in Proc_I$; then $\mathbb{P}_I[\![p]\!] = \langle Proc_I, p, \longrightarrow_I \rangle$. We sometimes refer to $\mathbb{P}_I[\![p]\!]$ as the model *of p.*

As a matter of practical concern, we note that unreachable states and the edges connecting them may safely be eliminated $\mathbb{P}_I[\![p]\!]$.

3.3 Semantic ordering

In order to reason about the relative expressiveness of abstract process semantics, we need a preorder on transition systems that reflects the notion of approximation: if $\mathcal{M}$ is smaller than $\mathcal{N}$ in the preorder, then the behavior of $\mathcal{M}$ should approximate that of $\mathcal{N}$. For this purpose we use a variant of the *must preorder* of [14]. In addition to having a pleasing operational justification based on process testing, this preorder may be seen to relate processes on the basis of the safety and liveness properties that they enjoy. In order to define this relation, we first introduce the following definitions, which borrow heavily from [6, 13].

Definition 9. *Let I be an interpretation, let $\mathcal{M} = \langle \Sigma_\mathcal{M}, \sigma^0_\mathcal{M}, \rightarrowtail_\mathcal{M} \rangle$ be a transition system in LTS_I, let $\sigma, \varrho \in \Sigma_\mathcal{M}$, and let $s \in Comm^*_I$.*

- *The* trace relation, $(\Longrightarrow_\mathcal{M}) \subseteq (\Sigma_\mathcal{M} \times Comm^*_I \times \Sigma_\mathcal{M})$, *is defined inductively on the structure of $Comm^*_I$ as follows.*

(a) $(\overset{\epsilon}{\Longrightarrow}_{\mathcal{M}}) = (\overset{\tau}{\longrightarrow}_{\mathcal{M}})^*$, *where* $(\overset{\tau}{\longrightarrow}_{\mathcal{M}})^*$ *is the transitive and reflexive closure of* $\overset{\tau}{\longrightarrow}_{\mathcal{M}}$.
(b) $(\overset{as}{\Longrightarrow}_{\mathcal{M}}) = (\overset{\epsilon}{\Longrightarrow}_{\mathcal{M}}) \circ (\overset{a}{\longrightarrow}_{\mathcal{M}}) \circ (\overset{s}{\Longrightarrow}_{\mathcal{M}})$, *where* $\circ$ *denotes relational composition.*

- *The* convergence relation, $\downarrow^{\mathcal{M}} \subseteq (\Sigma_{\mathcal{M}} \times Comm_I^*)$, *is defined inductively as follows.*
  (a) $\sigma \downarrow^{\mathcal{M}} \epsilon$ *iff there is no infinite sequence* $\langle \sigma_i \rangle_{i \geq 1}$ *with* $\sigma \overset{\tau}{\longrightarrow}_{\mathcal{M}} \sigma_1$ *and* $\sigma_i \overset{\tau}{\longrightarrow}_{\mathcal{M}} \sigma_{i+1}$.
  (b) $\sigma \downarrow^{\mathcal{M}} as$ *iff* $\sigma \downarrow^{\mathcal{M}} \epsilon$ *and* ($\sigma \overset{a}{\Longrightarrow}_{\mathcal{M}} \varrho$ *implies* $\varrho \downarrow^{\mathcal{M}} s$).

- *Let* $Event = \{c?, c! \mid c \in Chan\}$ *be the set of* events *and* $\sigma \in \Sigma_{\mathcal{M}}$. *Then the set events in which a process may initially engage is given by*

$$\mathsf{init}_{\mathcal{M}}(\sigma) = \{c? \mid \exists v \in Val_I\colon\ \sigma \overset{c?v}{\longrightarrow}_{\mathcal{M}}\} \cup \{c! \mid \exists v \in Val_I\colon\ \sigma \overset{c!v}{\longrightarrow}_{\mathcal{M}}\}.$$

  The acceptance set *of* σ *after a trace* s *is defined as follows.*

$$\mathsf{acc}_{\mathcal{M}}(\sigma, s) = \{\mathsf{init}_{\mathcal{M}}(\varrho) \mid \sigma \overset{s}{\Longrightarrow}_{\mathcal{M}} \varrho \ \ \&\ \ \varrho \overset{\tau}{\not\longrightarrow}_{\mathcal{M}}\}$$

- *Let* $AS, BS \subseteq \wp(Event)$; *then* $AS \subset\subset BS$ *iff* $\forall A \in AS\colon\ \exists B \in BS\colon\ B \subseteq A$.

Thus $\sigma \overset{s}{\Longrightarrow}_{\mathcal{M}} \varrho$ holds if σ can perform the actions listed in s with any number of intervening τ actions and end up as ϱ. We abbreviate ($\exists \varrho\colon\ \sigma \overset{s}{\Longrightarrow}_{\mathcal{M}} \varrho$) as $\sigma \overset{s}{\Longrightarrow}_{\mathcal{M}}$. The predicate $\sigma \downarrow^{\mathcal{M}} s$ holds if σ is incapable of infinite internal computation at any point during its "executions" of s. The set $\mathsf{init}(\sigma)$ is the set of initial events of σ; we emphasize that this set includes no references to values. The acceptance set $\mathsf{acc}(\sigma, s)$ represents the set of "event capabilities" of σ after s. Note that the set of events does not depend on the value interpretation. Each set AS in $\mathsf{acc}(\sigma, s)$ corresponds to a state that σ may reach by executing s and contains the set of next possible events in that state. The fact that $\mathsf{acc}(\sigma, s)$ may contain more than one such set indicates that nondeterministic choices may occur during the execution of s; the more sets $\mathsf{acc}(\sigma, s)$ contains, the more nondeterministic σ is in its execution of s. Finally, the ordering $\subset\subset$ relates acceptance sets on the basis of their relative nondeterminism; intuitively, $AS \subset\subset BS$ if AS represents a "less nondeterministic" set of processes.

Notation. We write $\mathcal{M} \overset{s}{\Longrightarrow}$ for $\sigma^0_{\mathcal{M}} \overset{s}{\Longrightarrow}_{\mathcal{M}}$ and $\mathsf{lang}(\mathcal{M})$ for $\{s \mid \mathcal{M} \overset{s}{\Longrightarrow}\}$, the *language* of $\mathcal{M}$. We also write $\mathcal{M} \downarrow s$ for $\sigma^0_{\mathcal{M}} \downarrow^{\mathcal{M}} s$, and $\mathsf{acc}(\mathcal{M}, s)$ for $\mathsf{acc}_{\mathcal{M}}(\sigma^0_{\mathcal{M}}, s)$.

The *specification preorder* relates transition systems on the basis of their nondeterminism. Formally, it is defined as follows.

Definition 10. *Let* $\mathcal{M}, \mathcal{N} \in LTS_I$.

- $\mathcal{M} \sqsupseteq_I^{may} \mathcal{N}$ *iff* $\mathsf{lang}(\mathcal{N}) \subseteq \mathsf{lang}(\mathcal{M})$.
- $\mathcal{M} \sqsubseteq_I^{must} \mathcal{N}$ *iff for all* s $\mathcal{M} \downarrow s$ *implies* ($\mathcal{N} \downarrow s$ *and* $\mathsf{acc}(\mathcal{N}, s) \subset\subset \mathsf{acc}(\mathcal{M}, s)$).
- $\mathcal{M} \sqsubseteq_I \mathcal{N}$ *iff* $\mathcal{M} \sqsupseteq_I^{may} \mathcal{N}$ *and* $\mathcal{M} \sqsubseteq_I^{must} \mathcal{N}$.
- $\mathcal{M} \eqsim_I \mathcal{N}$ *iff* $\mathcal{M} \sqsubseteq_I \mathcal{N}$ *and* $\mathcal{N} \sqsubseteq_I \mathcal{M}$.

It is traditional to abbreviate $\mathbb{P}_I[\![p]\!] \sqsubseteq_I \mathbb{P}_I[\![q]\!]$, as $p \sqsubseteq_I q$.

We now compare our semantics with the one given in [14]. There, value interpretations are assumed to be deterministic. Table 2 gives their formulation of the semantics. This definition of $\hookrightarrow$ may be substituted into our definitions for $\mathbb{P}_I[\![\cdot]\!]$ to generate new transition systems for processes and hence a new preorder on processes that we denote $\ll_I$. If the valuation functions are deterministic, then the preorders relate exactly the same terms.

Theorem 11. *Let* I *be such that the range of* $\mathbb{E}_I[\![\cdot]\!]$ *is* $\{\{v\} \mid v \in Val_I\}$ *and the range of* $\mathbb{B}_I[\![\cdot]\!]$ *is* $\{\{tt\}, \{ff\}\}$. *Then* $p \sqsubseteq_I q$ *iff* $p \ll_I q$

All rules but (*Out*) and (*Cond*) from table 1 with $\hookrightarrow$ replacing $\longrightarrow_I$

$$Out')\quad c!e.p \overset{c!v}{\hookrightarrow} p \text{ if } \mathbb{E}_I[\![e]\!] = \{v\}$$

$$Cond')\quad \frac{p \overset{\lambda}{\hookrightarrow} p'}{be \rhd p \diamond q \overset{\lambda}{\hookrightarrow} p'}\ \mathbb{B}_I[\![be]\!] = \{tt\} \qquad \frac{q \overset{\lambda}{\hookrightarrow} q'}{be \rhd p \diamond q \overset{\lambda}{\hookrightarrow} q'}\ \mathbb{B}_I[\![be]\!] = \{ff\}$$

Table 2. Traditional semantics of value passing

We close this section by remarking on connections between $\sqsubseteq_I$ and safety and liveness properties. Olderog and Hoare [20] present a framework for the consideration of safety and liveness in the context of labeled transition systems; they define a preorder that is similar to the specification preorder and show that if one transition system is less than another, then the higher one enjoys all the safety and liveness properties satisfied by the lower one, where safety and liveness properties are expressed in terms of traces, acceptance sets, et cetera. It can be shown that very similar results hold for $\sqsubseteq_I$. For example, one may define a safety property $\mathcal{S}$ as any prefix-closed subset of $Comm_I^*$ (ie, the set of traces where the "bad thing" has not happened) and stipulate that a transition system $\mathcal{M}$ satisfies $\mathcal{S}$ iff $\mathsf{lang}(\mathcal{M}) \subseteq \mathcal{S}$. Then it follows that if $\mathcal{M} \sqsubseteq_I \mathcal{N}$ and $\mathcal{M}$ satisfies $\mathcal{S}$, then $\mathcal{N}$ must satisfy $\mathcal{S}$ also.

In a similar vein, Olderog and Hoare characterize liveness properties as sets of transition systems.[4] Then $\mathcal{M}$ satisfies liveness property $\mathcal{L}$ iff for all *deterministic behaviors* $\mathcal{D}$ of $\mathcal{M}$, there exists a transition system $\mathcal{L}_i \in \mathcal{L}$ such that $\mathcal{L}_i \sqsubseteq^{must} \mathcal{D}$. Here a deterministic behavior is a restriction of a transition system such that the acceptance set after each trace contains a single set of events. If $\mathcal{M} \sqsubseteq \mathcal{N}$ then one may show that the set of deterministic behaviors of $\mathcal{M}$ is also "less than" the deterministic behaviors of $\mathcal{N}$; this, along with the fact that the specification preorder is finer than the must preorder, allows us to conclude that if $\mathcal{M}$ satisfies a liveness property $\mathcal{L}$, then so does $\mathcal{N}$.

4 Abstractions of transition systems

In this section we show that, given a Galois insertion on sets of values, we may construct a Galois insertion on transition systems ordered by the specification preorder. As a consequence of this, we have (Corollary 16) that reasoning conducted on abstract transition systems carries over to their concretized counterparts. Corollary 17 then shows that abstractions may be composed, a result of practical importance in that it licenses the use of intermediate abstractions in reasoning about more abstract properties of systems.

Note first that Definitions 3 and 4 can be extended to define abstraction and concretization functions on all the sets of syntactic objects of VPL_I. Thus we have, for example:

$$\alpha\colon Comm_C^* \mapsto Comm_A^*,\quad \alpha\colon Act_C \mapsto Act_A,\quad \text{and}\quad \alpha\colon Proc_C \mapsto Proc_A.$$

Likewise we can extend Lemma 5 to cover process terms, so that

$$\langle \wp(Proc_C), \supseteq\rangle \underset{\gamma}{\overset{\alpha}{\rightleftarrows}} \langle \wp(Proc_A), \supseteq\rangle.$$

[4] It is worth noting that deadlock-freedom is expressed as a liveness property in this framework, which is also powerful enough to express concepts such as eventuality and boundedness.

The definition of appropriate "liftings" of α and γ to transition systems, however, is less immediate. We first define abstraction. Since states in arbitrary transition systems have no structure, the labels on transitions are the only natural candidates for abstraction.

Definition 12. *Let $\mathcal{N} = \langle \Sigma_{\mathcal{N}}, \sigma^0_{\mathcal{N}}, \rightarrowtail_{\mathcal{N}} \rangle$ be a transition system in LTS_C. The abstraction of $\mathcal{N}$ to LTS_A is the transition system $\alpha(\mathcal{N}) = \langle \Sigma_{\mathcal{N}}, \sigma^0_{\mathcal{N}}, \rightarrowtail_{\mathcal{M}} \rangle$, where*

$$\sigma \overset{\alpha(\lambda)}{\rightarrowtail}_{\mathcal{M}} \varrho \textit{ iff } \sigma \overset{\lambda}{\rightarrowtail}_{\mathcal{N}} \varrho.$$

Clearly this abstraction preserves as much of the original meaning of the process as possible; in fact, these abstractions will be used as the standard by which to judge the abstract semantics of processes presented in the next section.

The definition of concretization for transition systems is more difficult. We want to define γ so that $\langle LTS_C, \sqsubseteq_C \rangle \overset{\alpha}{\underset{\gamma}{\rightleftarrows}} \langle LTS_A, \sqsubseteq_A \rangle$. Our solution is to introduce new states into the concretization of a transition system. Each edge $\sigma \overset{\lambda}{\rightarrowtail} \varrho$ of the original system is replaced by two sets of edges: the first is a set of τ edges from σ to one of the new states; the second is a set of edges with labels from $\gamma(\lambda)$ that map back to ϱ. To ensure that the specification preorder is preserved, however, some care must be taken with the definitions. Throughout the remainder of this section, let $\mathcal{M} = \langle \Sigma_{\mathcal{M}}, \sigma^0_{\mathcal{M}}, \rightarrowtail_{\mathcal{M}} \rangle$ be a transition system over value interpretation A, and let $\sigma, \varrho \in \Sigma_{\mathcal{M}}$. We first introduce the concept of an image product.

Definition 13. *For each state σ, define the set of concretized consequents,* $\mathsf{con}(\sigma)$ *to be*

$$\mathsf{con}(\sigma) = \{\{\langle \sigma, \lambda, \varrho \rangle \colon \lambda' \in \gamma(\widehat{\lambda})\} \colon \langle \sigma, \widehat{\lambda}, \varrho \rangle \in (\rightarrowtail_{\mathcal{M}})\},$$

and let $X = \{\chi_1, \chi_2, \ldots\} = \mathsf{con}(\sigma)$. The image product *of σ is then defined:*

$$\mathsf{ip}(\sigma) = \{S \colon S \subseteq (\cup X) \textit{ and } |S \cap \chi_k| = 1\}$$

The image product of a state is the set of all possible combinations of concretized edges leaving the state. As an example of an image product, consider a state σ with two edges, $(\sigma \overset{a!\top}{\rightarrowtail}_{\mathcal{M}} \varrho_1)$ and $(\sigma \overset{b!\top}{\rightarrowtail}_{\mathcal{M}} \varrho_2)$. If $\gamma(\top) = \{0, 1\}$, then the image product of σ is the set

$$\begin{aligned}\{\, &\{\langle \sigma, a!1, \varrho_1 \rangle, \langle \sigma, b!0, \varrho_2 \rangle\}, \{\langle \sigma, a!1, \varrho_1 \rangle, \langle \sigma, b!1, \varrho_2 \rangle\},\\ &\{\langle \sigma, a!0, \varrho_1 \rangle, \langle \sigma, b!0, \varrho_2 \rangle\}, \{\langle \sigma, a!0, \varrho_1 \rangle, \langle \sigma, b!1, \varrho_2 \rangle\} \,\}.\end{aligned}$$

We can now formally define the concretization of a transition system as a bipartite graph. One set of states, including the root, is taken directly from the original system, while the other set of states is constructed using the image product.

Definition 14. *Let $\mathcal{M} = \langle \Sigma_{\mathcal{M}}, \sigma^0_{\mathcal{M}}, \rightarrowtail_{\mathcal{M}} \rangle$ be a transition system in LTS_A. The concretization of $\mathcal{M}$ to LTS_C is the transition system $\gamma(\mathcal{M}) = \langle \Sigma_{\mathcal{N}}, \sigma^0_{\mathcal{M}}, \rightarrowtail_{\mathcal{N}} \rangle$, where $\Sigma_{\mathcal{N}}$ and $\rightarrowtail_{\mathcal{N}}$ are defined as follows.*

$$\begin{aligned}\Sigma_{\mathcal{N}} &= \Sigma_{\mathcal{M}} \cup \left(\textstyle\bigcup_{\sigma \in \Sigma_{\mathcal{M}}} \mathsf{ip}(\sigma)\right)\\ \sigma &\overset{\tau}{\rightarrowtail}_{\mathcal{N}} \pi \textit{ iff } \pi \in \mathsf{ip}(\sigma)\\ \pi &\overset{\lambda}{\rightarrowtail}_{\mathcal{N}} \varrho \textit{ iff } (\exists \sigma \colon \langle \sigma, \lambda, \varrho \rangle \in \pi)\end{aligned}$$

From the definitions, we can derive the following.

$$\begin{aligned}&\forall s \in Comm^*_C, \mathcal{N} \in LTS_C \colon && s \in \mathsf{lang}(\mathcal{N}) && \textit{implies} && \alpha(s) \in \mathsf{lang}(\alpha(\mathcal{N})),\\ &\forall \widehat{s} \in Comm^*_A, \mathcal{M} \in LTS_A \colon && \widehat{s} \in \mathsf{lang}(\mathcal{M}) && \textit{iff} && \exists s \in \gamma(\widehat{s}) \colon s \in \mathsf{lang}(\gamma(\mathcal{M})).\end{aligned}$$

Similar results hold also for convergence and for acceptance sets, allowing us to conclude that α and γ do indeed form a Galois insertion over transition systems.

Theorem 15. $\langle LTS_C, \sqsubseteq_C \rangle \overset{\alpha}{\underset{\gamma}{\rightleftarrows}} \langle LTS_A, \sqsubseteq_A \rangle$.

The following corollary implies in essence that if an "abstract" property holds of an abstracted system then the corresponding "concretized" property holds for the original system. Corollary 17 then shows how abstractions may be composed.

Corollary 16. $\mathcal{M} \sqsubseteq_A \alpha(\mathbb{P}_C[\![p]\!])$ *iff* $\gamma(\mathcal{M}) \sqsubseteq_C \mathbb{P}_C[\![p]\!]$

Corollary 17. *Let* $\alpha = \delta \circ \beta$, *where* $\alpha : Val_C \mapsto Val_A$, $\beta : Val_C \mapsto Val_I$, *and* $\delta : Val_I \mapsto Val_A$. *Then for* $\mathcal{C} \in LTS_C$, $\mathcal{I} \in LTS_I$ *and* $\mathcal{A} \in LTS_A$, *we have* $\mathcal{I} \sqsubseteq_I \beta(\mathcal{C})$ *iff* $\delta(\mathcal{I}) \sqsubseteq_A \alpha(\mathcal{C})$. *Moreover, if there exists* $\gamma : A \mapsto I$ *such that* $\langle \wp(Val_I), \supseteq \rangle \overset{\delta}{\underset{\gamma}{\rightleftarrows}}$ *then* $\langle \wp(Val_A), \supseteq \rangle$,

$$\mathcal{A} \sqsubseteq_A \alpha(\mathcal{C}) \text{ iff } \gamma(\mathcal{A}) \sqsubseteq_I \beta(\mathcal{C}).$$

The significance of Corollary 17 is twofold. First, it states that intermediate abstractions can be used to prove more abstract properties. Second, it states that properties that hold for the most abstract model also hold for models at intermediate levels of abstraction. This suggests, for example, that an interpretation that distinguishes some values may be used to prove properties that ignore values altogether. Thus, in order to prove properties of a concrete system, users of our framework may employ many abstraction functions, starting with the most abstract; if the desired then can be proven at the most abstract level, then the task is done, otherwise more and more concrete models may be used.

5 Abstract semantics

In the previous section we showed how to abstract the model of a process in such a way that properties of the abstract model hold also for the original. This technique, however, requires that the concrete model be constructed, an impossibility in the case that the concrete model is infinite state. In this section we advocate an alternative method: rather than abstracting the concrete model, one simply constructs a model using the abstract semantics of Table 1. We show that if the value abstraction is *safe*, then properties of the resulting abstract model will also hold for the concrete model. The advantage of this approach is clear: the concrete model need never be constructed.

5.1 Safety

Theorem 18. *If* α *is a safe value abstraction from* C *to* A *(Definition 6), then for all* $p \in Proc_C$:

$$\mathbb{P}_A[\![\alpha(p)]\!] \sqsubseteq_A \alpha(\mathbb{P}_C[\![p]\!]).$$

Proof. By the definition of $\sqsubseteq$ it suffices to show that $\mathbb{P}_A[\![\alpha(p)]\!]$ is *may*-greater and *must*-less than $\alpha(\mathbb{P}_C[\![p]\!])$. Let $\mathcal{N} = \alpha(\mathbb{P}_C[\![p]\!])$ with transition relation $\rightarrowtail_{\mathcal{N}}$; by definition 8, the transition relation of $\mathbb{P}_A[\![\alpha(p)]\!]$ is $\longrightarrow_A$.

The *may*-inclusion requirement is satisfied iff iff $p \overset{s}{\Longrightarrow}_C$ implies $\alpha(p) \overset{\alpha(s)}{\Longrightarrow}_A$. We establish this last implication in Theorem 21 below.

Regarding the *must*-inclusion requirement, we have the following proof obligation.

$$\alpha(p) \downarrow^A \alpha(s) \text{ implies } p \downarrow^C s \;\;\&\;\; \mathrm{acc}_C(p,s) \subset\subset \mathrm{acc}_A(\alpha(p), \alpha(s))$$

Theorems 22 and 23, below, establish that this obligation is indeed met. □

In the rest of this subsection we sketch the proofs of Theorems 21-23. To begin with we must establish a relationship between the transition relations $\longrightarrow_C$ and $\longrightarrow_A$. Lemma 19 states that every edge in $\longrightarrow_C$ is matched by an edge in $\longrightarrow_A$. Lemma 20 shows that if p is a stable process under $\longrightarrow_C$, then $\alpha(p)$ can reach (via $\longrightarrow_A$) some stable state whose initial event capabilities are a subset of those available to p.

Lemma 19. $\forall p, q, \lambda$: $p \xrightarrow{\lambda}_C q$ *implies* $\alpha(p) \xrightarrow{\alpha(\lambda)}_A \alpha(q)$

Lemma 20. $\forall p$: $p \stackrel{\tau}{\not\longrightarrow}_C$ *implies* $(\exists \widehat{p}\colon \alpha(p) \stackrel{\epsilon}{\Longrightarrow}_A \widehat{p} \stackrel{\tau}{\not\longrightarrow}_A$ *and* $\mathsf{init}_A(\widehat{p}) \subseteq \mathsf{init}_C(p))$

Lemma 19 is proved by induction over the structure of process terms. The proof makes use of the safety of α and requires that substitution be well behaved with respect to abstraction. The proof of Lemma 20 also proceeds by structural induction and uses Lemma 19.

Theorem 21 establishes that every trace of p is matched by a trace of $\alpha(p)$. Note that the converse does not hold in general since the abstraction of the conditional may introduce new traces into the language of $\alpha(p)$. The proof is by induction on the length of the trace s; both the basis and induction steps follow immediately from Lemma 19.

Theorem 21. $\forall p, q, s$: $p \stackrel{s}{\Longrightarrow}_C q$ *implies* $\alpha(p) \stackrel{\alpha(s)}{\Longrightarrow}_A \alpha(q)$

Theorem 22 states that if the abstraction of a process converges on a trace then so must the original process. Again the converse does not hold in general, as can be seen by considering the process $((1 = 1) \triangleright \mathsf{nil} \diamond \mathsf{rec}\ P.P)$ under an abstraction that evaluates all boolean expressions to $\{tt, ff\}$. Theorem 23 provides the final piece of the puzzle.

Theorem 22. $\forall p, s$: $\alpha(p) \downarrow^A \alpha(s)$ *implies* $p \downarrow^C s$

Theorem 23. $\forall p, s$: $\alpha(p) \downarrow^A \alpha(s)$ *implies* $\mathsf{acc}_C(p, s) \subset\subset \mathsf{acc}_A(\alpha(p), \alpha(s))$

Assuming $\alpha(p) \downarrow^A \alpha(s)$, the proof obligation for Theorem 23 can be written as:

$$p \stackrel{s}{\Longrightarrow}_C q \stackrel{\tau}{\not\longrightarrow}_C \text{ implies } (\exists \widehat{q}\colon \alpha(p) \stackrel{\alpha(s)}{\Longrightarrow}_A \widehat{q} \stackrel{\tau}{\not\longrightarrow}_A \ \&\ \mathsf{init}_A(\widehat{q}) \subseteq \mathsf{init}_A(q)).$$

The proof is again by induction on s. The basis case ($s = \epsilon$) requires a further induction on the length of the longest initial τ-sequence of p. That there can be no infinite τ sequence is established by the premise and the fact that the model of a process is image finite (see [14]).

5.2 Optimality

In order to prove optimality, we must first lift $\mathbb{P}_I[\![\cdot]\!]$ to sets of process terms. To this end we introduce the following operator on transition systems.

Definition 24. *Given a set of transition systems* $\{\mathcal{M}_1, \mathcal{M}_2, \ldots\}$ *where* $\mathcal{M}_k = \langle \Sigma_k, \sigma_k^0, \rightarrowtail_k\rangle \in LTS_I$, *define the* internal sum *of the set to be:* $\bigoplus_k \mathcal{M}_k = \langle \Sigma, \sigma^0, \rightarrowtail\rangle$, *where* σ^0 *is a fresh state,* $\Sigma = \bigcup_k \{\langle k, \sigma\rangle \mid \sigma \in \Sigma_k\} \cup \{\sigma^0\}$, *and* $\rightarrowtail$ *is defined as follows.*

$$\sigma^0 \stackrel{\tau}{\rightarrowtail} \langle k, \sigma\rangle \text{ iff } \sigma = \sigma_k^0$$
$$\langle k, \sigma\rangle \stackrel{\lambda}{\rightarrowtail} \langle j, \varrho\rangle \text{ iff } k = j \ \&\ \sigma \stackrel{\lambda}{\rightarrowtail}_k \varrho$$

The internal sum of a set of processes is the greatest lower bound of these processes with respect to the specification preorder. The meaning of a set of process terms can now be defined, for $PS \subseteq Proc_I$, as follows.

$$\mathbb{P}_I[\![PS]\!] = (\bigoplus_{p \in PS} \mathbb{P}_I[\![p]\!])$$

The following theorem establishes that, given an optimal abstract value interpretation, $\mathbb{P}_A[\![\cdot]\!]$ is optimal for $\mathbb{P}_C[\![p]\!]$. It follows from Theorems 15 and 18.

Theorem 25. *If α is an optimal value abstraction from C to A (Definition 7), then for all $p \in Proc_A$:*

$$\mathbb{P}_A[\![p]\!] \eqsim_A \alpha(\mathbb{P}_C[\![\gamma(p)]\!]).$$

5.3 Exact analysis

Even if an abstract semantics is not optimal, there may still be processes for which the abstract semantics is "exact". To end the section, we give a sufficient condition for establishing that this is the case. The condition is a natural generalization of *data-independence* as studied by Wolper [29]. We need the following definitions.

Definition 26. *Let $\alpha: C \mapsto A$ and $f: Val_C \mapsto Val_C$. Then f* respects *α if for every v in Val_C, $\alpha(v) = \alpha(f(v))$. Extend f to process terms as for α in Definition 3. Then a process $p \in Proc_C$ is* α-independent *if for all f respecting α, $\alpha(\mathbb{P}_C[\![p]\!]) \eqsim_A \alpha(\mathbb{P}_C[\![f(p)]\!])$.*

Intuitively, p is α-independent if its behavior modulo α is independent of specific values, modulo α.

Theorem 27. *If $\alpha: C \mapsto A$ is safe and $p \in Proc_C$ is α-independent, then*

$$\mathbb{P}_A[\![\alpha(p)]\!] \eqsim_A \alpha(\mathbb{P}_C[\![p]\!]).$$

6 Example

In this section we give a small example illustrating the utility of our results. Consider the following system consisting of a router and two processing units. The router waits for a value, which is a natural number, to arrive on its in channel; it then routes the (halved) value to the "left" processing unit if the original value is even and to the right otherwise. (Thus the least significant bit of the value may be thought of as an "address".) Assume that the value interpretation C is the standard one for natural numbers. The VPL process describing this system may be given as follows.

$$\begin{aligned}
\mathsf{Router} &= \mathsf{in}?(v).((v \bmod 2) = 0) \rhd \mathsf{left}!(v/2).\mathsf{Router} \diamond \mathsf{right}!(v/2).\mathsf{Router} \\
\mathsf{Unit}_0 &= \mathsf{in}?(v).\mathsf{out}!(f(v)).\mathsf{Unit}_0 \\
\mathsf{Unit}_1 &= \mathsf{in}?(v).\mathsf{out}!(g(v)).\mathsf{Unit}_1 \\
\mathsf{System} &= (\mathsf{Router} \mid \mathsf{Unit}_0[\mathsf{left/in}] \mid \mathsf{Unit}_1[\mathsf{right/in}]) \backslash \{\mathsf{left}, \mathsf{right}\}
\end{aligned}$$

We would like to determine whether the above system is deadlock-free. Unfortunately, its state space is infinite, and naive state-space enumeration techniques would not terminate. The results in this paper suggest, however, that if we can come up with a safe abstraction on values and establish that the resulting abstracted process is deadlock-free, then so is the original system. That is, letting A be the abstract interpretation and α the abstraction from C to A, it follows from the fact that $\mathbb{P}_A[\![p]\!] \sqsubseteq_A \alpha(\mathbb{P}_C[\![p]\!])$ that $\mathbb{P}_C[\![p]\!]$ deadlocks if and only if $\alpha(\mathbb{P}_C[\![p]\!])$ does.

Consider the trivial abstract value space A in which all concrete values are collapsed into a single abstract value 0, every expression evaluates to 0, and every boolean evaluates to the set $\{ff, tt\}$. The abstraction function α that maps the concrete interpretation into this interpretation is clearly safe. When we apply this abstraction to the above system, we get a system that is semantically equivalent to the following.

$$\begin{aligned} \mathsf{Router}_A &= \mathsf{in?0.(left!0.Router} \oplus \mathsf{right!0.Router)} \\ \mathsf{Unit}_A &= \mathsf{in?0.out!0.Unit}_A \\ \mathsf{System}_A &= (\mathsf{Router} \mid \mathsf{Unit}_A[\mathsf{left/in}] \mid \mathsf{Unit}_A[\mathsf{right/in}]) \backslash \{\mathsf{left}, \mathsf{right}\} \end{aligned}$$

This system is finite-state, and using reachability analysis one may determine that it is deadlock-free. Accordingly, it follows that the original system is also deadlock-free.

7 Discussion

In this paper we have shown how abstractions on values may be used to generate abstractions on processes that pass values. We defined the semantics of processes parametrically with respect to a value interpretation and showed that safe value abstractions induce safe abstract semantic functions and optimal value abstractions likewise induce optimal semantic functions. We proved our results relative to the *specification preorder* which preserves not only safety properties, but also liveness properties.

One may use our technique to simplify the task of reasoning about value-passing systems as follows. Given a system and a safety or liveness property, one may first attempt to establish satisfaction using the most abstract value interpretation that is exact with respect to the specification. If satisfaction can be shown, the task is finished; otherwise, one can select a less abstract interpretation and repeat the analysis. The hope is that one finds a value interpretation that is concrete enough to prove the property desired, yet abstract enough so that satisfaction is (rapidly) computable. This process would be facilitated by an environment providing a library of interpretations, along with tools capable of analyzing processes to suggest which of the more concrete interpretations available should be chosen in the event that verification fails, and we would like to pursue the development of such an environment as future work. It would also be interesting to characterize the properties preserved by the specification preorder in terms of a temporal logic; one candidate would appear to be linear time temporal logic without a next operator. We also would like to investigate the addition of values with structure to our model. The extension to disjoint sums (for example, the set of integers and characters) is straight-forward. More challenging are sets of values whose elements are ordered, as are the denotations of functions in domain theory. A solution here, however, would open up the possibility of treating higher-order value passing languages. To this end it would be useful to cast our results in terms of *acceptance trees* [14]; this rephrasing should not present difficulties. Finally, we intend to further explore the connections between our approach and effect systems.

Related Work. Existing work on abstractions of concurrent systems has focused on the development of abstraction techniques that preserve certain classes of formulas in various temporal logics [1, 3, 10]. The frameworks of these papers differ in details, but each considers how to generate, from an abstraction on values, abstractions on Kripke structures that preserve various fragments of the temporal logic CTL^*. Their programming models have focused on shared memory, whereas our considers value-passing; in addition, their semantics are based on the *simulation* preorder, which is incomparable to the preorder used here [26]. Consequently, the "properties" that are preserved would in general be different. Characterizing these differences precisely remains a topic that needs to be addressed.

The goals of our work are also similar to those of Hennessy and Lin in their work on *symbolic bisimulations* [15]. Central to their work is the notion of a symbolic transition system, which is a transition system with sets of free variables as states and guarded expressions as edges. Symbolic transition systems are often finite, but even trivial recursive processes whose arguments vary from call to call may have infinite symbolic transition systems, rendering their technique ineffective. For example (rec $P(x).c!x.P(x+1)$)(0) has an infinite symbolic transition system; our method will produce a finite transition system for this process, given a finite abstract value set.

Our work is also related to that done by Nielson and Nielson on effect systems for CML [19]. An *effect system* is an extension of a conventional type system that describes the side-effects (in our case, events) that a program may have. In the case that the properties of interest can be described using the trivial abstraction, our method reduces to an effect system for process, in the spirit of the Nielsons' work. Their language is much more complex, supporting higher-order and structured values. However, our abstractions preserve more of the behavior of the original process than do theirs; for example, their abstractions reduce internal to external non-determinism.

As for more applied work, Yeh and Young [30] have used an approach that can be seen as an instance of ours to ours for verifying properties of Ada programs. Their success points to the practical importance of our technique.

References

1. S. Bensalem, A. Bouajjani, C. Loiseaux, and J. Sifakis. Property-preserving simulations. In *Proceedings of the Workshop on Computer-Aided Verification*, volume 663 of *LNCS*, pages 260—273. Springer-Verlag, June 1992.
2. B. Bloom and R. Paige. Computing ready simulations efficiently. In *Proceedings of the North American Process Algebra Workshop*, Workshops in Computing, pages 119–134, Stony Brook, New York, August 1992. Springer-Verlag.
3. Edmund M. Clarke, Orna Grumberg, and David E. Long. Model checking and abstraction. In *Proceedings ACM POPL*, pages 343–354, January 1992.
4. E.M. Clarke, E.A. Emerson, and A.P. Sistla. Automatic verification of finite-state concurrent systems using temporal logic specifications. *ACM TOPLAS*, 8(2):244–263, April 1986.
5. R. Cleaveland. Tableau-based model checking in the propositional mu-calculus. *Acta Informatica*, 27(8):725–747, September 1990.
6. R. Cleaveland and M.C.B. Hennessy. Testing equivalence as a bisimulation equivalence. *Formal Aspects of Computing*, 5:1–20, 1993.
7. R. Cleaveland, J. Parrow, and B. Steffen. The Concurrency Workbench: A semantics-based tool for the verification of finite-state systems. *ACM TOPLAS*, 15(1):36–72, January 1993.
8. R. Cleaveland and B. Steffen. A linear-time model-checking algorithm for the alternation-free modal mu-calculus. *Formal Methods in System Design*, 2:121–147, 1993.
9. P. Cousot and R. Cousot. Comparing the Galois connection and widening/narrowing approaches to abstract interpretation. In *PLILP '92*, volume 631 of *LNCS*, pages 269–295. Springer-Verlag, August 1992.
10. D. Dams, O. Grumberg, and R. Gerth. Abstract interpretation of reactive systems: Abstractions preserving ∀CTL*, ∃CTL* and CTL*. In *PROCOMET '94*, IFIP Transactions. North-Holland/Elsevier, June 1994. Full version available from Eindhoven University of Technology.
11. J. Goyer. Communications protocols for the B-HIVE multicomputer. Master's thesis, North Carolina State University, 1991.
12. E. Harcourt, J. Mauney, and T. Cook. Specification of instruction-level parallelism. In *Proceedings of the North American Process Algebra Workshop*, August 1993. Technical Report TR93-1369, Cornell University.
13. M.C.B. Hennessy. *Algebraic Theory of Processes*. MIT Press, Boston, 1988.
14. M.C.B. Hennessy and A. Ingólfsdóttir. A theory of communicating processes with value-passing. *Information and Computation*, 107:202–236, December 1993.

15. M.C.B. Hennessy and H. Lin. Symbolic bisimulations. Technical Report 1/92, Sussex University, 1992.
16. C.A.R. Hoare. *Communicating Sequential Processes*. Prentice-Hall, London, 1985.
17. N.D. Jones and F. Nielson. *Abstract Interpretation: a Semantics-Based Tool for Program Analysis*. Handbook of Theoretical Computer Science. Oxford, To appear.
18. P. Kanellakis and S.A. Smolka. CCS expressions, finite state processes, and three problems of equivalence. *Information and Computation*, 86(1):43–68, May 1990.
19. F. Nielson and H. Nielson. From CML to process algebras. In E. Best, editor, *Proceedings of CONCUR '93*, volume 715 of *LNCS*, pages 493–508, Hildesheim, Germany, August 1993. Springer-Verlag.
20. E.-R. Olderog and C.A.R. Hoare. Specification-oriented semantics for communicating processes. *Acta Informatica*, 23:9–66, 1986.
21. R. Paige and R.E. Tarjan. Three partition refinement algorithms. *SIAM Journal of Computing*, 16(6):973–989, December 1987.
22. J. Parrow. Verifying a CSMA/CD-protocol with CCS. In *Proceedings of the IFIP Symposium on Protocol Specification, Testing and Verification*, pages 373–387, Atlantic City, New Jersey, June 1988. North-Holland.
23. J. Richier, C. Rodgriguez, J. Sifakis, and J. Voiron. Verification in XESAR of the sliding window protocol. In *Proceedings of the IFIP Symposium on Protocol Specification, Testing and Verification*, pages 235–250, Zurich, May 1987. North-Holland.
24. V. Roy and R. de Simone. Auto/Autograph. In *Computer-Aided Verification '90*, pages 235–250, Piscataway, New Jersey, July 1990. American Mathematical Society.
25. C. Stirling and D. Walker. Local model checking in the modal mu-calculus. In *TAPSOFT '89*, volume 352 of *LNCS*, pages 369–383, Barcelona, March 1989. Springer-Verlag.
26. R. van Glabbeek. The linear time – branching time spectrum. In *Proceedings of CONCUR '90*, volume 458 of *LNCS*, pages 278–297. Springer-Verlag, August 1990.
27. M. Vardi and P. Wolper. An automata-theoretic approach to automatic program verification. In *Proceedings of the Symposium on Logic in Computer Science*, pages 332–344, Cambridge, Massachusetts, June 1986. Computer Society Press.
28. G. Winskel. A note on model checking the modal ν-calculus. In *Proceedings ICALP*, volume 372 of *LNCS*, pages 761–772, Stresa, Italy, July 1989. Springer-Verlag.
29. P. Wolper. Expressing interesting properties of programs in propositional temporal logic. In *Proceedings ACM POPL*, pages 184–193, January 1986.
30. W.J. Yeh and M. Young. Compositional reachability analysis using process algebra. In *TAV '91*, pages 49–59. ACM SIGSOFT, ACM Press, October 1991.

A congruence theorem for structured operational semantics with predicates and negative premises

C. VERHOEF

Department of Mathematics and Computing Science
Eindhoven University of Technology
P.O. Box 513, 5600 MB Eindhoven, The Netherlands
e-mail: chrisv@win.tue.nl

ABSTRACT. We proposed a syntactic format, the *panth* format, for structured operational semantics in which besides ordinary transitions also predicates, negated predicates, and negative transitions may occur such that if the rules are stratifiable, strong bisimulation equivalence is a congruence for all the operators that can be defined within the *panth* format. To show that this format is useful we took some examples from the literature satisfying the *panth* format but no formats proposed by others. The examples touch upon issues such as priorities, termination, convergence, discrete time, recursion, (infinitary) Hennessy-Milner logic, and universal quantification. Collation: pp. 16, ill. 2, tab. 5, ref. 25.

1. Introduction

In recent years, it has become a standard method to provide process algebras, process calculi, and programming and specification languages with an operational semantics in the style of Plotkin [22]. As a consequence, the Plotkin style rules themselves became an object of research. A number of so-called *formats* were proposed; a format is a syntactical constraint on the form of the rules. A central issue in the area of structured operational semantics is to define formats ensuring that some important property holds, for instance, that strong bisimulation equivalence is a congruence relation. Of course, we want such a format to be as general as possible.

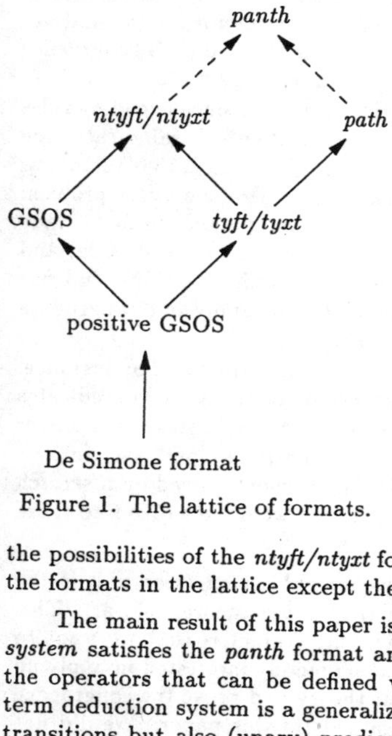

Figure 1. The lattice of formats.

In this way a whole lattice of formats came into being. We depict this lattice in figure 1. An arrow from one format to another indicates that all operators definable in the first format can also be defined in the second one. If there are no arrows connecting two formats they are (syntactically) incomparable. The most basic format originates from De Simone [23]. Yet it is already powerful enough to define all the usual operators of, for instance, *CCS* or *ACP*. The GSOS format of Bloom, Istrail and Meyer [8] allows negative premises but no lookahead and the *tyft/tyxt* format of Groote and Vaandrager [15] allows lookahead but no negative premises. They both generalize the format of De Simone. The positive GSOS format is, so the speak, the greatest common divisor of the GSOS and the *tyft/tyxt* format. The *ntyft/ntyxt* format of Groote [14] is, in fact, the least common multiple of the *tyft/tyxt* format and the GSOS format: it allows both lookahead and negative premises. The *path* format of Baeten and Verhoef [5] generalizes the *tyft/tyxt* format with predicates. In this paper we discuss the *panth* format, which stands for "predicates and *ntyft/ntyxt* hybrid format". The dashed arrows in figure 1 point to it. This format combines the possibilities of the *ntyft/ntyxt* format and the *path* format. We will not give the definitions of all the formats in the lattice except the definitions of the four formats in the upper diamond.

The main result of this paper is a congruence theorem stating that if a so-called *term deduction system* satisfies the *panth* format and is *stratifiable* then *strong bisimulation* is a congruence for all the operators that can be defined within the format. First, we will briefly explain the italics. A term deduction system is a generalization of a transition system specification [15]: it allows not only transitions but also (unary) predicates on states. The *panth* format is a syntactical constraint on a term deduction system; it still allows for occurrence of both transitions and predicates and their negations, in the premises. A term deduction system is stratifiable if the complexity of the conclusion of each rule is greater than the complexity of its premises. This notion is based on Groote [14]. The notion of strong bisimulation originates from Park [21] but we require in addition that bisimilar processes satisfy the same predicates; cf. [5]. Now that we have an idea of the significant notions occurring in the main result we briefly discuss its proof. Baeten and Verhoef [5] already conjectured that this result could be proved in the same way as their congruence theorem for the *path* format. Indeed, this turns out to be the case: we code each predicate as a binary relation and we apply the congruence theorem of Groote [14] to the coded system. This coding trick was first announced by Groote and Vaandrager [15] and independently found by others, most notably Baeten and Verhoef [5] and Wan Fokkink. As a consequence of this coding trick, all the operators that can be defined in the *panth* format can also be defined in Groote's *ntyft/ntyxt* format. This observation might give raise to the question if there is need for the *panth* format at all. Next, we will motivate the need for this new format.

An advantage of the *panth* format is that it provides simply more syntactic freedom than other formats for defining rules since we can use transitions and predicates and both their negations, whereas in other formats we either have predicates but no negative premises or negative premises but no predicates. This is not just an intrinsic advantage since there are examples of such operational semantics in the literature in which the combination of transitions and predicates with negative transitions and/or negated predicates occurs. We will sketch this in the next paragraph.

In the literature we see more and more that operational rules in the style of Plotkin are decorated with extra predicates on states to express matters like (un)successful termination, convergence, divergence [1], enabledness [7], maximal delay, side conditions [20], etc. Baeten and Verhoef give many examples of this kind of decorated transition rules in their paper on the *path* format [5] thereby showing that there is a need for a general format describing such decorated rules. Another phenomenon that we see in the literature is the use of negative premises in rules defining the operational semantics. We can find negative premises to operationally describe deadlock detection [18], sequencing [8], priorities [4], probabilistic behaviour [19], urgency [10], and various real [17] and discrete time [2] settings. Now it will not be very surprising that there are also hybrid rules using both decorations and negative premises (we will treat some of them in the applications). This is where the *panth* format comes into play, since these hybrid rules quite often turn out to satisfy the *panth* format and are stratifiable. Now the advantage is that we immediately have that strong bisimulation is a congruence for all the operators defined in this way; a property that we wish to hold in many cases.

The above advantage is not only of practical value but also of intuitive value since encoding rules to fit one of the known formats in order to get congruenceness in return often contraindicates the intuitive character of the original rules. Another disadvantage of such a coding trick is that there now are two transition systems that have to be shown equivalent. A fast solution to the latter problem is to throw away the original transition system, which is inadvisable in our opinion. In fact, many people prefer to use their own rules rather than encoded rules (that the reader has to decode) and choose to verify the congruence property without a general congruence theorem. We think that our *panth* format is very user-friendly in the sense that people immediately can apply our congruence result to their own rules instead of first having to become coding experts.

There are also theoretical advantages to adding predicates to known formats. For instance, Baeten and Verhoef observe that some negative premises can be expressed positively using predicates and pose the question which negative premises can be written positively with predicates. Vaandrager gives a partial answer: for any GSOS system there exists an equivalent positive GSOS system over the same language, extended with positive predicates. Vaandrager and Verhoef proved on a scratch paper that this result extends to the infinite case. However, in this paper we do not dive into these theoretical issues.

Now that we have given some motivation for this paper we discuss the organization of it in the remainder of this section. The paper consists of two parts: a practical and a theoretical part. This is due to the fact that we pursue two communicative targets. The first target is that we want to give rules of thumb accompanied with instructive examples for readers merely interested in applying our congruence theorem. The second target is to formally treat our theory and prove the congruence theorem; this part is for readers more interested in the theoretical side of this paper. We did not choose for a chronological ordering of our paper. In section 2 we start with the end: namely the applications. At first sight this may seem a bit illogical but there are good reasons for this ordering.

An important reason advocating this ordering is that (uninitiated) readers can see that it is not at all necessary to go through all the theory to be able to apply the congruence theorem and that mostly a few simple rules of thumb will do. Another reason justifying this ordering is that the area of application is operational semantics. Operational rules often are easy to read and, moreover, they can be understood without the theoretical part. The last and maybe most important reason for this ordering is that the reader immediately can see if his or her operational semantics has a good chance to fit our format. If this is the case the time has come to read on and enter the theoretical part of this paper. An additional advantage is that those readers already have a good impression of the notions that will be made precise in the second part. This part starts in section 3 where the notions stratifiable and term deduction system are made precise. Also in this section we do our very best not to loose the reader by interspersing a running example among the abstract definitions. Following Groote [**14**] we show that stratifiability is a sufficient condition on a term deduction system to guarantee that there exists a transition relation that agrees with it. In section 4, we define the *panth* format and the notion of strong bisimulation in the presence of predicates on states. Then we state and prove our main result: the congruence theorem. The last section contains concluding remarks and discusses future work.

2. Applications

In this section we give some examples that we (mostly) took from the literature. These examples turn out to satisfy the *panth* format and are stratifiable but do not satisfy formats proposed before. With the aid of our congruence theorem we then find that strong bisimulation is a congruence. The examples include issues such as priorities, termination, convergence, discrete time, recursion, (infinitary) Hennessy-Milner logic, and universal quantification (in particular, so-called weak predicates).

We use the first example to define the significant notions informally: the *panth* format and stratifiability.

Priorities

The first example is an operational semantics of a basic process algebra with priorities, BPA_θ, that originates from Baeten and Bergstra [**4**]; it can also be found in Baeten and Weijland [**6**]. In this language we have alternative and sequential composition and a priority operator (denoted $+$, $\cdot$, and θ resp.) and a set A of atomic actions. There is also a partial ordering $<$ on the set of atomic actions to express priorities. For instance, if $a < b$ and b and c are not related we have $\theta(a+b) = b$ and $\theta(b+c) = b+c$. We list the operational semantics of BPA_θ in table 1. This operational semantics is a small one; still it contains besides transitions $\cdot\xrightarrow{a}\cdot$ also (postfix) predicates $\cdot\xrightarrow{a}\surd$, for all $a \in A$, and both their negations $\cdot\overset{a}{\nrightarrow}$ and $\overset{a}{\nrightarrow}\surd$. So this example is particularly suitable to informally introduce our *panth* format. For completeness we recall that $x\overset{a}{\nrightarrow}$ means that there is no x' such that $x\xrightarrow{a}x'$ and $x\overset{a}{\nrightarrow}\surd$ if we do not have $x\xrightarrow{a}\surd$. Often, we will omit the centered dot: $x \cdot y = xy$.

$$a\xrightarrow{a}\surd \quad \frac{x\xrightarrow{a}x'}{x+y\xrightarrow{a}x'} \quad \frac{y\xrightarrow{a}y'}{x+y\xrightarrow{a}y'} \quad \frac{x\xrightarrow{a}\surd}{x+y\xrightarrow{a}\surd} \quad \frac{y\xrightarrow{a}\surd}{x+y\xrightarrow{a}\surd} \quad \frac{x\xrightarrow{a}x'}{xy\xrightarrow{a}x'y}$$

$$\frac{x\xrightarrow{a}\surd}{xy\xrightarrow{a}y} \quad \frac{x\xrightarrow{a}x',\ \{x\overset{b}{\nrightarrow}, x\overset{b}{\nrightarrow}\surd \mid b > a\}}{\theta(x)\xrightarrow{a}\theta(x')} \quad \frac{x\xrightarrow{a}\surd,\ \{x\overset{b}{\nrightarrow}, x\overset{b}{\nrightarrow}\surd \mid b > a\}}{\theta(x)\xrightarrow{a}\surd}$$

Table 1. A Transition system for BPA_θ.

There are two conditions that must hold for a transition system before we can apply our congruence theorem. They are that the rules have to be in *panth* format and that the system has to be stratifiable. We first list the conditions for the *panth* format.

Check for each rule the following. All the transitions in the premises must end in distinct variables; denote this set by Y. If the conclusion is a transition $t\xrightarrow{a}t'$ then either $t = x$ for a variable $x \notin Y$ or $t = f(x_1, \ldots, x_n)$ with $x_1, \ldots, x_n$ distinct variables not occurring in Y. If the conclusion is of the form Pt then we treat t as above (P is some unary predicate). Of course, f is an n-ary function symbol.

Now it is easy to verify that the rules of table 1 are in *panth* format but it will be even more easy if we also list the things that we do not have to worry about.

There is no restriction on the number of premises. There is also no restriction on terms occurring in predicates, negated predicates, and negated transitions in the premises. There is no restriction on a term occurring in the left-hand side of a transition in a premise or in the right-hand side of a conclusion.

As an example we treat the last but one rule of table 1. There is just one positive transition ending in a variable x', for the negated predicates and negative transitions there is nothing to check, since there are no restrictions on their terms. The conclusion begins with a term of the form $f(x)$ and $x \neq x'$. So this rule is in *panth* format. The other rules are treated the same only simpler.

Now we give the rules of thumb for the stratifiability. This condition is a bit more involved: we have to define a map, called a stratification, for which two conditions must hold for each rule instantiated with closed terms. If a stratification exists for a set of rules we call this set stratifiable. Roughly, a rule is stratifiable if the complexity of the conclusion is greater than the complexity of its premises. This complexity is measured with a stratification. The arguments that a stratification takes are positive transitions and predicates; we call them positive formulas. A stratification measures the complexity of its arguments in terms of numbers, so it ranges over numbers. We also have the following two conditions on a stratification S for every rule instantiated with closed terms to express that the complexity of the conclusion may not exceed the complexity of the premises. Let c be the conclusion of a closed instantiation of a rule and let h be a positive premise of it. Then we want that $S(h) \leq S(c)$. Now we treat the negative premises. Since S is only defined on positive formulas we have to turn the negative formulas into positive ones. There are two cases: first let $t \stackrel{a}{\not\longrightarrow}$ be a closed instantiation of a negative transition. Then we want that $S(t \stackrel{a}{\longrightarrow} s) < S(c)$ for all closed terms s. Secondly, let $\neg Pt$ be a closed instantiation of a negated predicate P then we want that $S(Pt) < S(c)$.

Next, we will give a recipe for finding a stratification. In most cases we can find a stratification (for which the two conditions hold) by measuring the complexity of a positive formula in terms of counting a particular symbol occurring in the conclusion of a rule with negative premises.

As an example we give a stratification for the rules in table 1. The rules containing negative premises have in their conclusion a θ. We define a map that counts the number of θ's as follows: let t be a closed term with n occurrences of θ's then $S(t \stackrel{a}{\longrightarrow} s) = S(t \stackrel{a}{\longrightarrow} \surd) = n$. Now we check the two conditions for the last but one rule. Replace each x and x' by closed terms t and t'. Since the number of θ's occurring in $\theta(t)$ is one greater than the number of θ's occurring in t we are done. The other rules are dealt with just as simply.

Termination and convergence

The next example is an operational semantics originating from Aceto and Hennessy [1]. It is an operational semantics of a *CCS* like process algebra extended with a successful termination predicate and a convergence predicate. Their approach is to first inductively define both predicates and then define the transition relation using one of the predicates. In this semantics they use a negative premise to express unsuccessful termination. Baeten and Verhoef [5] showed that this operational semantics can be written positively by explicitly defining a third unsuccessful termination predicate. This approach is sometimes* less work than our approach, which is finding a stratification. In table 2 we list their rules for the (postfix denoted) termination predicate $\surd$, for their convergence predicate $\downarrow$, and their rules for the non-deterministic choice $+$, the sequential composition ;, the parallel composition $|$, the binding constructor *recx*. _, and the encapsulation operator $\partial_H(\cdot)$. We treat recursion in the same way as Groote and Vaandrager [15] by adding process names *recx*. t to the signature for each $t \in O(\Sigma)$ (= open terms) to obtain that the recursion rules fit our format (we will do this in more detail in an example later on; see table 4). However, it would be a better idea to incorporate recursion within our format as is done for the GSOS format [8] and De Simone's format [23].

It is easy to see that the operational semantics consisting of the rules in table 2 satisfy the *panth* format. We will give a stratification. We already explained that the first thing to do is to look at the rules with negative premises. In this case there is just one such rule. In the conclusion we see the symbol $\downarrow$. Define a map S that counts the number of $\downarrow$'s occurring in a positive formula. It is easy to see that this map is a stratification. We check the two conditions for the negative rule. Replace each x and y by closed terms t and s respectively. Since $S(t\surd) = 0 < 1 = S((t;s)\downarrow)$ the

---

* Especially when only the negated predicate is important. See, for instance, [3] or [7].

$$nil\surd \qquad \frac{x\surd, y\surd}{(x+y)\surd} \qquad \frac{x\surd, y\surd}{(x;y)\surd} \qquad \frac{x\surd, y\surd}{(x \mid y)\surd} \qquad \frac{x\surd}{\partial_H(x)\surd} \qquad \frac{t[recx.\,t/x]\surd}{recx.\,t\surd}$$

$$\delta\downarrow \qquad nil\downarrow \qquad \mu\downarrow \qquad \frac{x\downarrow}{\partial_H(x)\downarrow} \qquad \frac{t[recx.\,t/x]\downarrow}{recx.\,t\downarrow} \qquad \frac{x\downarrow, y\downarrow}{(x+y)\downarrow}$$

$$\frac{x\downarrow, y\downarrow}{(x \mid y)\downarrow} \qquad \frac{x\surd, y\downarrow}{(x;y)\downarrow} \qquad \frac{\neg(x\surd), x\downarrow}{(x;y)\downarrow} \qquad \mu \xrightarrow{\mu} nil \qquad \frac{x \xrightarrow{\mu} x'}{x+y \xrightarrow{\mu} x'} \qquad \frac{x \xrightarrow{\mu} x'}{y+x \xrightarrow{\mu} x'} \qquad \frac{x \xrightarrow{\mu} x'}{x;y \xrightarrow{\mu} x';y}$$

$$\frac{x\surd, y \xrightarrow{\mu} y'}{x;y \xrightarrow{\mu} y'} \qquad \frac{x \xrightarrow{\mu} x'}{x \mid y \xrightarrow{\mu} x' \mid y} \qquad \frac{x \xrightarrow{\mu} x'}{y \mid x \xrightarrow{\mu} y \mid x'} \qquad \frac{x \xrightarrow{a} x', y \xrightarrow{\bar{a}} y'}{x \mid y \xrightarrow{\tau} x' \mid y'} \qquad \frac{x \xrightarrow{\mu} x'}{\partial_H(x) \xrightarrow{\mu} \partial_H(x')}, \mu \notin H \qquad \frac{t[recx.\,t/x] \xrightarrow{\mu} x'}{recx.\,t \xrightarrow{\mu} x'}$$

Table 2. The rules of Aceto and Hennessy for $\surd$, $\downarrow$, and their action relations.

negative condition holds. For the positive condition we have $S(s\downarrow) = 1 \le 1 = S((t;s)\downarrow)$. The other rules are also very simple.

Aceto and Hennessy are interested in rooted weak bisimulation instead of strong bisimulation, so our theorem will not directly apply to their situation. However, Baeten and Verhoef [5] show for an operational semantics of Van Glabbeek [13] for *ACP* with abstraction that rooted *weak* bisimulation is a congruence with the aid of their congruence theorem for *strong* bisimulation. We leave as an open problem whether a similar trick can also be applied for the *CCS* like process algebra of Aceto and Hennessy.

$$\underline{\underline{a}} \xrightarrow{a} \surd \qquad \frac{x \xrightarrow{a} x'}{xy \xrightarrow{a} x'y} \qquad \frac{x \xrightarrow{\sigma} x'}{xy \xrightarrow{\sigma} x'y} \qquad \frac{x \xrightarrow{a} \surd}{xy \xrightarrow{a} y} \qquad \sigma_d(x) \xrightarrow{\sigma} x$$

$$\frac{x \xrightarrow{a} x'}{x+y \xrightarrow{a} x' \xleftarrow{a} y+x} \qquad \frac{x \xrightarrow{a} \surd}{x+y \xrightarrow{a} \surd \xleftarrow{a} y+x} \qquad \frac{x \xrightarrow{\sigma} x', y \xrightarrow{\sigma} y'}{x+y \xrightarrow{\sigma} x'+y'} \qquad \frac{x \xrightarrow{\sigma} x', y \not\xrightarrow{\sigma}}{x+y \xrightarrow{\sigma} x' \xleftarrow{\sigma} y+x}$$

Table 3. *BPA* with discrete time.

Discrete time

The next example is an operational semantics of Baeten and Bergstra [2] describing a basic process algebra with relative discrete time. In table 3 we list their rules. The $\underline{\underline{a}}$ stands for the action a in the current time slice and σ_d stands for the discrete time unit delay. A transition $\xrightarrow{\sigma}$ denotes the passage to the next time slice. It is easy to see that the rules of table 3 satisfy the *panth* format. Baeten and Bergstra apply a coding trick to obtain that their rules satisfy the *ntyft/ntyxt* format of Groote and give a stratification S with $S(t \xrightarrow{a} t') = n$ if the number of function symbols of t equals n. If we just add $S(t \xrightarrow{a} \surd) = n$ with the number of function symbols of t equals n (and not encode the rules) we are done. Note that according to our recipe it suffices to only count the number of $+$ signs in t. Baeten and Bergstra still have to show that their system is equivalent to the encoded one.

$$\frac{\langle t_X|E\rangle \xrightarrow{a} y}{\langle X|E\rangle \xrightarrow{a} y} \qquad \frac{\langle t_X|E\rangle \xrightarrow{\sigma} y}{\langle X|E\rangle \xrightarrow{\sigma} y} \qquad \frac{\langle t_X|E\rangle \xrightarrow{a} \surd}{\langle X|E\rangle \xrightarrow{a} \surd} \qquad \frac{\langle t_X|E\rangle \xrightarrow{\sigma} \surd}{\langle X|E\rangle \xrightarrow{\sigma} \surd}$$

Table 4. Recursion rules for *BPA* with discrete time.

Discrete time and recursion

We extend the last operational semantics with rules concerning recursion. The resulting example will be particularly interesting, since it deepens our insight in the notion of a stratification. Before we continue, we briefly explain some recursion terminology. We extend the signature with a set of constants called process names with typical elements $X, Y, Z, \ldots$. A recursive specification E over a set N of process names is a set of equations of the form $X = t$ such that t is a closed term that may only contain guarded occurrences of process names in N and $X \in N$. An occurrence of a process name in a term is guarded if it occurs in a subterm of the form $a \cdot s$ or $\sigma_d(s)$. The intention of a recursive specification is to (uniquely) specify the behaviour of infinite processes. The guardedness demand is to exclude specifications that specify more than one process like $X = X$. Now $\langle X|E\rangle$

denotes the X component of a solution of the recursive specification E. The expression $\langle t_X|E\rangle$ is short-hand for the right-hand side of the equation belonging to X with every process name Y replaced by $\langle Y|E\rangle$. So, for example, if $E = \{X = aX + \sigma_d(X)\}$ the expression $\langle aX + \sigma_d(X)|E\rangle$ is short-hand for $a\langle X|E\rangle + \sigma_d(\langle X|E\rangle)$. It is easy to see with the rules of tables 3 and 4 that $\langle X|E\rangle \xrightarrow{a} \langle X|E\rangle$ and $\langle X|E\rangle \xrightarrow{\sigma} \langle X|E\rangle$.

Our recipe for finding a stratification was to count the function symbol occurring in the conclusion of a rule with a negative premise. In this case it is the + symbol. Since there can be any finite number of + symbols in the premise of a recursion rule whereas in its conclusion there is not a single + symbol our approach no longer works; so a fortiori the stratification of Baeten and Bergstra will not work. We solve this by assigning to these dangerous conclusions the ordinal number $\omega = \omega_0$. Define a stratification S as follows. Let n be the number of unguarded occurrences of process names in t and let m be the number of + symbols that occur in t. Let $S(t \xrightarrow{\alpha} t') = S(t \xrightarrow{\alpha} \surd) = \omega \cdot n + m$ with α either a or σ. Now it is not hard to check that the two conditions hold for S. As an example, we check a recursion rule: $S(\langle t_X|E\rangle \xrightarrow{a} y) = \omega \cdot 0 + m$, since we have forbidden unguarded occurrences in right-hand sides. Now $S(\langle X|E\rangle \xrightarrow{a} y) = \omega \cdot 1 + 0$. The other rules are also simple.

The reader can easily see that S could be chosen more minimally: it suffices to define S only on σ-transitions and let $S(t \xrightarrow{a} t') = 0$. However, the above stratification also works for all the extensions that Baeten and Bergstra discuss in their paper whereas the minimal version only works for this example. So also for all their extensions we have that bisimulation equivalence is a congruence.

The above recursion problem also arises if we add recursion to our first example concerning priorities. Fortunately, it can be solved in the same way; for more information on the combination of priorities and recursion we refer to Groote **[14]**. In fact, we did not have this problem with the example of Aceto and Hennessy since we there counted the rare symbol $\downarrow$. This illustrates that it is wise not to count too much. For, if we had counted all function symbols we immediately ran into the recursion problem above.

Hennessy-Milner logic

The next example concerning Hennessy-Milner logic **[16]** is due to Frits Vaandrager **[24]**. The set of Hennessy-Milner logic formulas over a given alphabet $A = \{a, b, \ldots\}$ is given by the following grammar: $\varphi ::= T|\varphi \wedge \varphi|\langle a\rangle\varphi|\neg\varphi$. Suppose that we have a positive transition system specification, in say *tyft/tyxt* format, defining transition relations $\xrightarrow{a}$ for each $a \in A$. With the four simple rules in table 5 we can define the satisfaction relation $\models$ within the *panth* format by defining postfix predicates $\_ \models \varphi$ for all formulas φ.

With the aid of the fundamental result of Hennessy and Milner saying that two processes are bisimilar if and only if they satisfy the same Hennessy-Milner logic formulas we also have that this extension does not change the definition of bisimulation in the presence of the satisfaction predicates.

$$x \models T \qquad \frac{x \xrightarrow{a} x',\ x' \models \varphi}{x \models \langle a\rangle\varphi} \qquad \frac{x \models \varphi,\ x \models \psi}{x \models \varphi \wedge \psi} \qquad \frac{\neg(x \models \varphi)}{x \models \neg\varphi}$$

Table 5. The satisfaction relation $\models$ as postfix predicates $\_ \models \varphi$.

Let S be a stratification given by $S(t \xrightarrow{a} t') = 0$ and $S(t \models \varphi) = n$ $(t, t' \in C(\Sigma) = \text{closed terms})$ with n the number of $\neg$ symbols occurring in φ. It is easy to see that the rules of table 5 together with our positive operational semantics defining $\cdot \xrightarrow{a} \cdot$ satisfy the *panth* format and that they are stratifiable.

We can do the same with infinitary Hennessy-Milner logic formulas. We restrict ourselves to index sets of a size bounded by some regular cardinal, since otherwise the hypotheses do not necessarily form a set (and thus not obey the *panth* format). Only the third rule of table 5 changes to the following rule (I an index set)

$$\frac{\{x \models \varphi_i : i \in I\}}{x \models \bigwedge_{i \in I} \varphi_i}.$$

It is easy to see that this rule satisfies the *panth* format. We have to be careful with our choice of a stratification. The one above will no longer work, since addition of ordinals is not commutative.

The stratification that we now need measures maximal nesting of $\neg$ symbols within a formula. For instance $S(x \models \neg T \wedge \neg\neg T) = 2$. We inductively define S on the postfix predicates $\_ \models \varphi$:

$$S(x \models T) = 0, \quad S(x \models \langle a \rangle \varphi) = S(x \models \varphi),$$
$$S(x \models \bigwedge_{i \in I} \varphi_i) = \sup_{i \in I} S(x \models \varphi_i), \quad S(x \models \neg\varphi) = S(x \models \varphi) + 1.$$

Note that this stratification also works for the finite case.

Universal quantification

Some predicates that we find in the literature are defined with a universal quantifier in their hypotheses. The purpose of this last example is to show that it is often possible to define such predicates within our format. We illustrate this with the weak termination predicate $\surd\!\!\!\surd$ of Aceto and Hennessy [1]. A process p is weakly terminating ($p\surd\!\!\!\surd$) if for all q that cannot perform any silent moves but are reachable from p with only silent steps (zero or more) we have that $q\surd$; see table 2 for the termination predicate $\surd$. Or in a Plotkin style rule:

$$\frac{\forall q : p \xrightarrow{\epsilon} q, q \stackrel{\tau}{\not\rightarrow} \Longrightarrow q\surd}{p\surd\!\!\!\surd}.$$

Clearly, this rule does not fit our format. This is due to the fact that our format is of an existentional nature. However, the combination of an existentional quantifier and negation leads to a universal quantifier. With this we can define the weak termination predicate $\surd\!\!\!\surd$ of Aceto and Hennessy within our format. We mention that $p \xrightarrow{\epsilon} q$ means that p evolves into q by performing zero or more silent actions, which can be easily defined within our format. We need an auxiliary predicate to define the weak termination predicate. The first rule below defines this auxiliary predicate which holds if the negation of the hypothesis of the above rule holds. The second rule defines the weak termination predicate by simply negating the auxiliary predicate.

$$\frac{p \xrightarrow{\epsilon} q, q \stackrel{\tau}{\not\rightarrow}, \neg(q\surd)}{p\overline{\surd\!\!\!\surd}}, \quad \frac{\neg p\overline{\surd\!\!\!\surd}}{p\surd\!\!\!\surd}.$$

We can find a stratification with a cumulative application of our recipe: count the number of $\overline{\surd\!\!\!\surd}$ symbols plus two times the number of $\surd\!\!\!\surd$ symbols in a positive formula.

In this way we can also define Aceto and Hennessy's weak convergence predicate and its parameterized version (and the resulting operational semantics is stratifiable). We recall that Aceto and Hennessy are interested in rooted weak bisimulation instead of strong bisimulation. Moreover, we think it would be a better idea to study a format that allows universal quantification.

3. Term deduction systems

The examples that we discussed in section 2 are term deduction systems. In this section we will define this notion, which generalizes the concept of a transition system specification [15]. We will also define the notion of stratifiability, which is due to Groote [14]. Following Groote, we prove that being stratifiable is a sufficient condition to define a transition relation in the presence of predicates and negative premises. We intersperse a running example among the abstract definitions so that the reader immediately has a concrete idea about them.

Before we continue with the definitions we will list some preliminaries for completeness sake.

We assume that we have an infinite set V of variables with typical elements $x, y, z, \ldots$. A (single sorted) signature Σ is a set of function symbols together with their arity. If the arity of a function symbol $f \in \Sigma$ is zero we say that f is a constant symbol. We restrict ourselves to signatures that contain at least one constant symbol. The notion of a term (over Σ) is defined as expected: $x \in V$ is a term; if $t_1, \ldots, t_n$ are terms and if $f \in \Sigma$ is n-ary then $f(t_1, \ldots, t_n)$ is a term. A term is also called an open term; if it contains no variables we call it closed. We denote the set of closed terms by $C(\Sigma)$ and the set of open terms by $O(\Sigma)$ (note that a closed term is also open). We also want to speak about the variables occurring in terms: let $t \in O(\Sigma)$ then $var(t) \subseteq V$ is the set of variables occurring in t.

A substitution σ is a map from the set of variables into the set of terms over a given signature. This map can easily be extended to the set of all terms by substituting for each variable occurring in an open term its σ-image.

Definition (3.1) A term deduction system is a structure (Σ, D) with Σ a signature and D a set of deduction rules. The set $D = D(T_p, T_r)$ is parameterized with two sets, which are called respectively the set of predicate symbols and the set of relation symbols. Let s, t, and $u \in O(\Sigma)$, $P \in T_p$, and $R \in T_r$. We call expressions $Ps, \neg Ps, tRu$, and $t\neg R$ formulas. We call the formulas Ps and tRu positive and $\neg Ps$ and $t\neg R$ negative. If S is a set of formulas we write $PF(S)$ for the subset of positive formulas of S and $NF(S)$ for the subset of negative formulas of S.

A deduction rule $d \in D$ has the form

$$\frac{H}{C}$$

with H a set of formulas and C a positive formula; to save space we will also use the notation H/C. We call the elements of H the hypotheses of d and we call the formula C the conclusion of d. If the set of hypotheses of a deduction rule is empty we call such a rule an axiom. We denote an axiom simply by its conclusion provided that no confusion can arise. The notions "substitution", "*var*", and "closed" extend to formulas and deduction rules as expected.

Definition (3.2) Let T be a term deduction system. Let $F(T)$ be the set of all closed formulas over T. We denote the set of all positive formulas over T by $PF(T)$ and the negative formulas by $NF(T)$. Let $X \subseteq PF(T)$. We define when a formula $\varphi \in F(T)$ holds in X; notation $X \vdash \varphi$.

$X \vdash sRt$ if $sRt \in X$,
$X \vdash Ps$ if $Ps \in X$,
$X \vdash s\neg R$ if $\forall t \in C(\Sigma) : sRt \notin X$,
$X \vdash \neg Ps$ if $Ps \notin X$.

The purpose of a term deduction system is to define a set of positive formulas that can be deduced using the deduction rules. For instance, if the term deduction system is a transition system specification then a transition relation is such a set. For term deduction systems without negative formulas this set comprises all the formulas that can be proved by a well-founded proof tree. If we allow negative formulas in the premises of a deduction rule it is no longer obvious which set of positive formulas can be deduced using the deduction rules. Bloom, Istrail, and Meyer [8] formulate that a transition relation must agree with a transition system specification. We will use their notion; it is only adapted to the framework of this paper.

Definition (3.3) Let $T = (\Sigma, D)$ be a term deduction system and let $X \subseteq PF(T)$ be a set of positive closed formulas. We say that X agrees with T if a formula $\varphi \in X$ if and only if there is a deduction rule instantiated with a closed substitution such that the instantiated conclusion equals φ and all the instantiated hypotheses hold in X. More formally: X agrees with T if

$$\varphi \in X \iff \exists H/C \in D \text{ and } \sigma : V \longrightarrow C(\Sigma) \text{ such that } \sigma(C) = \varphi \text{ and } \forall h \in H : X \vdash \sigma(h).$$

Not every term deduction system defines a set of positive formulas that agrees with it. A term deduction system can define more than one set of positive formulas that agrees with it. We show this in the following two examples. Groote [14] gives similar examples with relations instead of predicates.

Example (3.4) Let T_1 be the term deduction system that consists of one constant symbol c and one deduction rule $\neg Pc/Pc$. For all $X \subseteq PF(T_1)$ that agree with T_1 we have $Pc \in X \iff Pc \notin X$. Clearly, such an X does not exist.

Let T_2 be the term deduction system that consists of one constant symbol c and one deduction rule Pc/Pc. Then $\emptyset$ and $\{Pc\}$ both agree with T_2.

Groote [14] formulates a sufficient condition for the existence of a transition relation that agrees with a given transition system specification. We essentially follow Groote by formulating a similar condition: we incorporate predicates in his notion. Indeed, this condition is sufficient for the existence of a set of positive formulas for a given term deduction system. We obtain this result in a similar way as Groote by extending his notions with predicates and by proving his results for these extended notions.

Definition (3.5) Let $T = (\Sigma, D)$ be a term deduction system. The formula dependency graph G of T is a labelled directed graph with as nodes positive formulas. For all deduction rules $H/C \in D$ and for all closed substitutions σ we have the following edges in G: for all $h \in PF(H)$ there is an edge $\sigma(h) \xrightarrow{p} \sigma(C)$; for all $s\neg R \in NF(H)$ there is for all $t \in C(\Sigma)$ an edge $\sigma(sRt) \xrightarrow{n} \sigma(C)$; for all $\neg Ps \in NF(H)$ there is an edge $\sigma(Ps) \xrightarrow{n} \sigma(C)$. If e is an edge of G we denote this by $e \in G$. An edge labelled with a p is called positive and if it is labelled with an n it is called a negative edge. A set of edges is called positive if all its elements are positive and negative if they are all negative.

Example (3.6) We depict in figure 2 the formula dependency graphs of the term deduction systems T_1, T_2 of example (3.4), and the formula dependency graph of a new one: T_3. The last term deduction system consists of a constant symbol c and for all $n \geq 0$ a deduction rule $\neg P_n c / P_{n+2} c$ and for all odd n a deduction rule $\neg P_n c / P_0 c$. The term deduction system T_3 is based on an example of Groote **[14]**.

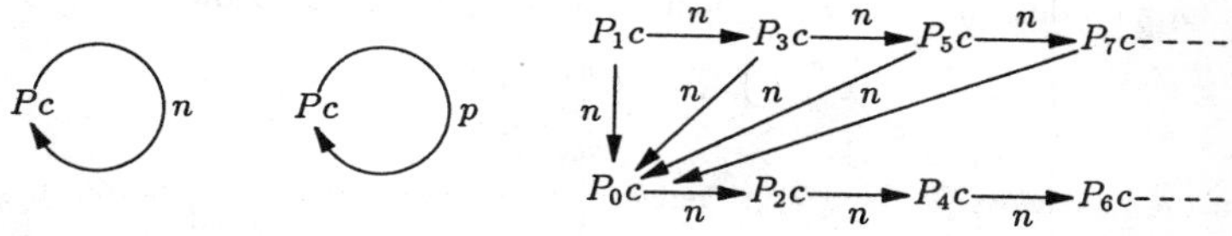

Figure 2. Three formula dependency graphs.

Definition (3.7) A term deduction system is stratifiable if there is no node in its formula dependency graph that is the start of a backward chain of edges containing an infinite negative subset.

A term deduction system is called strictly stratifiable if there is no node in its formula dependency graph that is the start of an infinite backward chain of edges.

Definition (3.8) Let $T = (\Sigma, D)$ be a stratifiable term deduction system and let G be its formula dependency graph. We inductively define a mapping $|\cdot|$ from the set of positive formulas of T to an ordinal α that calculates the number of negative edges in G that can be reached with a backward chain of edges beginning in φ. Note that if G contains a cycle with a negative edge we cannot define this mapping. However, we can define this mapping if G only contains positive cycles. Two formulas φ and ψ are equivalent if they occur in a cycle of the formula dependency graph G or if they are identical; notation $\varphi \sim \psi$. We write $[\varphi]$ for the equivalence class containing φ. Note that since T is stratifiable there are only positive cycles. Define $|\cdot| : PF(T)/\!\sim \longrightarrow \alpha$ as follows

$$|[\varphi]| = \sup\big(\{|[\psi]| + 1 : \psi \xrightarrow{n} \chi \in G,\ [\chi] = [\varphi]\} \cup \{|[\psi]| : \psi \xrightarrow{p} \chi \in G,\ [\psi] \neq [\varphi] = [\chi]\} \big).$$

We assume that $\sup(\emptyset) = 0$. Now define $|\varphi| = |[\varphi]|$.

Example (3.9) With the aid of figure 2 we see that T_1 is not stratifiable and that T_2 and T_3 are stratifiable. It is not hard to see that for the term deduction system T_3 we have $|P_{2n+1}c| = n$ and $|P_{2n}c| = \omega + n$ for all $n \geq 0$.

Definition (3.10) Let $T = (\Sigma, D)$ be a term deduction system. A mapping $S : PF(T) \longrightarrow \alpha$ for an ordinal α is called a stratification for T if for all deduction rules $H/C \in D$ and closed substitutions σ the following conditions hold. For all $h \in PF(H)$ we have $S(\sigma(h)) \leq S(\sigma(C))$; for all $s\neg R \in NF(H)$ we have for all $t \in C(\Sigma) : S(\sigma(sRt)) < S(\sigma(C))$; for all $\neg Ps \in NF(H)$ we have $S(\sigma(Ps)) < S(\sigma(C))$. A stratification is called strict if we in addition have that $S(\sigma(h)) < S(\sigma(C))$ for all $h \in PF(H)$.

Lemma (3.11) A term deduction system is (strictly) stratifiable if and only if there exists a (strict) stratification for it.

Proof. Essentially the proof of Lemma 4.2.12 in Groote **[14]**.

We need the next definition to construct a set of positive formulas that agrees with a given term deduction system. We define a mapping, called the degree, that assigns to a term deduction system an ordinal number with a property called regularity. We assume that the axiom of choice holds for this definition, since we assume that the only cardinal numbers that exist are the natural numbers or $\aleph_\alpha$ for all ordinal numbers $\alpha \geq 0$. We recall that an ordinal number is a transitive set of transitive sets and that for all ordinal numbers $\alpha \geq 0$ the cardinality of the (initial) ordinal number ω_α equals $\aleph_\alpha$ (by definition). We also recall that $\aleph_0$ and $\aleph_{\alpha+1}$ are regular for all $\alpha \geq 0$ (if we assume the axiom of choice).

Definition (3.12) Let V be a set. If $0 \leq |V| < \aleph_0$ we define $d(V) = \omega_0$. If $|V| = \aleph_\alpha$ for an ordinal $\alpha \geq 0$ we define $d(V) = \omega_{\alpha+1}$. Let $T = (\Sigma, D)$ be a term deduction system. The degree $d(H/C)$ of a deduction rule $H/C \in D$ is the degree of its set of positive premises: $d(H/C) = d(PF(H))$. Let $\omega_\alpha = \sup\{d(H/C) : H/C \in D\}$. The degree $d(T)$ of a term deduction system T is ω_0 if $\alpha = 0$ and $\omega_{\alpha+1}$ otherwise.

Example (3.13) Let T_3 be as in example (3.6). It is easy to see that $d(T_3) = \omega_0$.

Next, we will define a set of positive formulas from which we will show that it agrees with a given term deduction system.

Definition (3.14) Let $T = (\Sigma, D)$ be a term deduction system and let $S : PF(T) \longrightarrow \alpha$ be a stratification for an ordinal number α. We define a set $T_S \subseteq PF(T)$ as follows.

$$T_S = \bigcup_{i<\alpha} T_i^S, \quad T_i^S = \bigcup_{j<d(T)} T_{i,j}^S.$$

We will often use unions over T_i^S and $T_{i,j}^S$; therefore, we define the following notations

$$U_i^S = \bigcup_{i'<i} T_{i'}^S \ (i \leq \alpha), \quad U_{i,j}^S = \bigcup_{j'<j} T_{i,j'}^S \ (j \leq d(T)).$$

We drop the superscripts S, provided that no confusion arises. Now we define for all $i < \alpha$ and for all $j < d(T)$ the set $T_{i,j} = T_{i,j}^S$:

$$T_{ij} = \Big\{\varphi \mid S(\varphi) = i, \exists H/C \in D \text{ and } \sigma : V \longrightarrow C(\Sigma) \text{ with } \sigma(C) = \varphi,$$
$$\forall h \in PF(H) : U_{i,j} \cup U_i \vdash \sigma(h) \text{ and } \forall h \in NF(H) : U_i \vdash \sigma(h)\Big\}.$$

Example (3.15) Let $T = T_3$ be the term deduction system of example (3.6). Let $S : PF(T) \longrightarrow \omega_0 \cdot 2$ be the strict stratification that we defined in lemma (3.11). Note that $S = |\cdot|$ in this example; see definition (3.8). We will calculate T_S; so it suffices to calculate $T_{i,j}$ for all $i < \alpha$ and $j < d(T)$. Since there are no positive premises we have that $T_{i,0} = T_{i,j}$ for all $j < d(T)$. So $T_i = T_{i,0}$. It is not hard to verify that for all $n \geq 0$ we have $T_{2n} = T_{\omega_0+2n+1} = \emptyset$, $T_{2n+1} = \{P_{4n+3}c\}$, and $T_{\omega_0+2n} = \{P_{4n}c\}$. So we find that $T_S = \{P_0c, P_3c, P_4c, P_7c, P_8c, P_{11}c, \ldots\}$.

Next, we state a number of results of Groote [14] that transpose effortlessly to our situation. The proofs of these statements can be given along the same lines as was done in Groote [14].

Theorems (3.16) Let $T = (\Sigma, D)$ be a term deduction system and let $S : PF(T) \longrightarrow \alpha$ be a stratification for an ordinal number α. Then T_S agrees with T. If S' is also a stratification for T then $T_S = T_{S'}$.

If T is strictly stratifiable then there is at most one set of closed positive formulas that agrees with T. If S is a strict stratification for T, then this set is T_S.

Theorem (3.17) There exists a term deduction system with an agreeing set of positive formulas that is not stratifiable.

Proof. See Bol and Groote [9]. They show that this is already the case for a term deduction system without predicates.

Definition (3.18) Let T and T' be stratifiable term deduction systems. Let S and S' be stratifications for T and T'. If T and T' have the same signature and if $T_S = T'_{S'}$ we say that T and T' are equivalent.

4. The congruence theorem

In this section we will formally define the *panth* format and other notions necessary to state the congruence theorem and then we will prove it. We expect that this result can be proved by adapting the proof of the congruence theorem of Groote to our situation. However, we prove a stronger result since we moreover show that every term deduction system in *panth* format can be reduced to a term deduction system in *ntyft/ntyxt* format. Apart from that, our proof contains an interesting argument (which is not present in Groote's proof) that can also be applied to prove other meta theorems; see Verhoef [**25**].

Although the idea behind the proof of our congruence theorem is natural, it turns out that we need a lot of bookkeeping. Therefore, the proof may be difficult reading. For convenience sake, we intersperse the formal proof with informal intuitions.

Definition (4.1) Let $T = (\Sigma, D)$ be a term deduction system with $D = D(T_p, T_r)$. Let in the following K, L, M, and N be index sets of arbitrary cardinality, let $s_k, t_l, u_m, v_n, t \in O(\Sigma)$ for all $k \in K$, $l \in L$, $m \in M$, and $n \in N$, let $P_k, P_m, P \in T_p$ be predicate symbols for all $k \in K$ and $m \in M$, and let $R_l, R_n, R \in T_r$ be relation symbols for all $l \in L$ and $n \in N$.

A deduction rule $d \in D$ is in *pntyft* format if it has the form

$$\frac{\{P_k s_k : k \in K\} \cup \{t_l R_l y_l : l \in L\} \cup \{\neg P_m u_m : m \in M\} \cup \{v_n \neg R_n : n \in N\}}{C} \tag{1}$$

with $C = f(x_1, \ldots, x_n)Rt$, $f \in \Sigma$ an n-ary function symbol and $X \cup Y = \{x_1, \ldots, x_n\} \cup \{y_l : l \in L\} \subseteq V$ a set of distinct variables. If $var(d) = X \cup Y$ we call d pure. A variable in $var(d)$ that does not occur in $X \cup Y$ is called free.

A deduction rule $d \in D$ is in *pntyxt* format if it has the form (1) and $C = xRt$. $X \cup Y = \{x\} \cup \{y_l : l \in L\} \subseteq V$ is a set of distinct variables. If $var(d) = X \cup Y$ we call d pure. A variable in $var(d)$ that does not occur in $X \cup Y$ is called free.

A deduction rule is in *pntyf* format if $C = Pf(x_1, \ldots, x_n)$ and it is in *pntyx* format if $C = Px$ with $X \cup Y \subseteq V$ distinct variables. The notions pure and free are defined as expected.

We explain the names of the deduction rules. The *p* in the phrases *pntyft*, *pntyxt*, *pntyf*, and *pntyx* refers to the predicates occurring in the rules, the *n* refers to the presence of negative formulas in the premises, the *ty* refers to the positive relation part in the set of hypotheses, and the *ft*, *xt*, *f*, and *x* refer to the various conclusions. The names *ntyft* and *ntyxt* are taken from Groote [**14**].

If a deduction rule $d \in D$ has one of the above forms we say that this rule is in *panth* format, which stands for "predicates and *ntyft/ntyxt* hybrid format". A term deduction system is in *panth* format if all its rules are. A term deduction system is called pure if all its rules are pure.

A term deduction system is in *ntyft/ntyxt* format if it is in *panth* format and its set of predicate symbols is empty. The *ntyft/ntyxt* format originates from Groote [**14**]. A term deduction system is in *path* format if it is in *panth* format and there are no negative formulas in the rules. The *path* format originates from Baeten and Verhoef [**5**]. A term deduction system is in *tyft/tyxt* format if it is in *path* format and its set of predicate symbols is empty. The *tyft/tyxt* format originates from Groote and Vaandrager [**15**].

We need the technical notion of well-foundedness of a term deduction system, which will be used in the proof of the congruence theorem. The notion of well-foundedness is taken from Groote and Vaandrager [**15**], where it is also used in the proof of their congruence theorem. The same phenomenon occurs in Groote's paper [**14**] and in Baeten and Verhoef [**5**]. Fokkink [**12**] shows that the well-foundedness is not necessary for the congruence theorem of Groote and Vaandrager [**15**] and that this generalizes to our format. Therefore, we omitted the well-foundedness demand in the examples we discussed in section 2 (but all these examples are well-founded).

Definition (4.2) Let $T = (\Sigma, D)$ be a term deduction system and let F be a set of formulas. The variable dependency graph of F is a directed graph with variables occurring in F as its nodes. The edge $x \longrightarrow y$ is an edge of the variable dependency graph if and only if there is a positive relation $tRs \in F$ with $x \in var(t)$ and $y \in var(s)$.

The set F is called well-founded if any backward chain of edges in its variable dependency graph is finite. A deduction rule is called well-founded if its set of hypotheses is so. A term deduction system is called well-founded if all its deduction rules are well-founded.

Lemma (4.3) For every well-founded stratifiable term deduction system in *panth* format there is an equivalent pure well-founded term deduction system in *panth* format.

Proof. Essentially the proof of Lemma 4.4.9 in Groote [14].

Next, we will define the notion of strong bisimulation, which is based on Park [21].

Definition (4.4) Let $T = (\Sigma, D)$ be a stratifiable term deduction system with stratification S and let $D = D(T_p, T_r)$. A binary relation $B \subseteq C(\Sigma) \times C(\Sigma)$ is called a (strong) bisimulation if for all $s, t \in C(\Sigma)$ with sBt the following conditions hold. For all $R \in T_r$

$$\forall s' \in C(\Sigma)\ (T_S \vdash sRs' \Rightarrow \exists t' \in C(\Sigma) : T_S \vdash tRt' \wedge s'Bt'),$$
$$\forall t' \in C(\Sigma)\ (T_S \vdash tRt' \Rightarrow \exists s' \in C(\Sigma) : T_S \vdash sRs' \wedge s'Bt'),$$

and for all $P \in T_p$

$$T_S \vdash Ps \Leftrightarrow T_S \vdash Pt.$$

The first two conditions are known as the transfer property. Two states $s, t \in C(\Sigma)$ are bisimilar if there exists a bisimulation relation containing the pair (s, t). If s and t are bisimilar we write $s \sim t$. Note that bisimilarity is an equivalence relation.

Theorem (4.5) Let $T = (\Sigma, D)$ be a well-founded stratifiable term deduction system in *panth* format then strong bisimulation is a congruence for all function symbols occurring in Σ.

Proof. The structure of this proof resembles the proof of the congruence theorem of Baeten and Verhoef [5].

Groote [14] proved this theorem in the case that the set of predicate symbols is empty, that is, if the term deduction system is in *ntyft/ntyxt* format. Our strategy to prove the non-empty case is to construct from a term deduction system a new one without predicates with the property that two terms are bisimilar in the old term deduction system if and only if they are bisimilar in the new one. We make the new term deduction system from the old one by coding each predicate symbol in the old system as a special relation symbol in the modified one.

To begin with, we construct from a term deduction system a new one by extending the original signature with a xenoconstant and moving the predicates of the original system to xenorelations.

Let $T = (\Sigma, D)$ be a well-founded stratifiable term deduction system in *panth* format and suppose that $D = D(T_p, T_r)$ with $T_p \neq \emptyset$. In accordance with lemma (4.3) we may assume that T is pure. We define a new term deduction system $T' = (\Sigma', D')$. Let ξ be a constant function symbol that is strange to Σ and define $\Sigma' = \Sigma \cup \{\xi\}$. Let $D' = D'(\emptyset, T'_r)$ with $T'_r = T_r \cup \{R_P \mid P \in T_p\}$ (disjoint union). A relation symbol R_P for $P \in T_p$ is defined as follows. For two terms s and t over Σ' we have sR_Pt if and only if Ps and $t = \xi$. The set of deduction rules is $D' = \{d' \mid d \in D\}$ and a deduction rule d' is constructed from an old rule $d \in D$ as follows. Let $d = H/C$. The set of hypotheses of d' is the set H but with the positive predicates $\{P_k s_k : k \in K\}$ replaced by $\{s_k R_{P_k} z_k : k \in K\}$ with $\{z_k : k \in K\}$ a set of distinct variables disjoint with $var(d)$ and the negative predicates $\{\neg P_m u_m : m \in M\}$ replaced by $\{u_m \neg R_{P_m} : m \in M\}$. If the conclusion of the old rule is of the form Pt then the conclusion of the new rule is $tR_P\xi$. Otherwise C remains the same. Note that T' is pure, well-founded and in *ntyft/ntyxt* format.

Next, we stratify the xenosystem by assigning to each positive xenoformula the ordinal that a stratification for the original system assigns to this positive formula with every ξ replaced by a fixed closed original term.

We verify that T' is stratifiable. Let $S : PF(T) \longrightarrow \alpha$ be a stratification for T and let c be a closed term over Σ. For all $s \in O(\Sigma')$ we inductively define a term $s[\xi/c] \in O(\Sigma)$ as follows. Let $\xi[\xi/c] = c$. If $x \in V$ is variable then $x[\xi/c] = x$. Let $f \in \Sigma$ be n-ary, and let $t_1, \ldots, t_n \in O(\Sigma')$ then $f(t_1, \ldots, t_n)[\xi/c] = f(t_1[\xi/c], \ldots, t_n[\xi/c])$. Now we can define $S' : PF(T') \longrightarrow \alpha$ as follows. Let $s, t \in C(\Sigma')$ and let $R \in T_r$ and $P \in T_p$ then

$$S'(sRt) = S(s[\xi/c]Rt[\xi/c]), \quad S'(sR_Pt) = S(Ps[\xi/c]).$$

For all $\sigma' : V \longrightarrow C(\Sigma')$ we define a substitution $\sigma'[\xi/c] : V \longrightarrow C(\Sigma)$ as follows. Define $\sigma'[\xi/c](x) = \sigma'(x)[\xi/c]$ for all $x \in V$. Note that the following holds for all $s \in O(\Sigma)$ and $t \in O(\Sigma')$

$$s[\xi/c] = s, \quad \sigma'(t)[\xi/c] = \sigma'[\xi/c](t[\xi/c]). \qquad (2)$$

To show that S' is a stratification for T' we have to check the conditions of definition (3.10). Let $d' = H'/C' \in D'$ be a rule and let $d = H/C \in D$ be its corresponding rule in the original system T. The deduction rule d' is of the form

$$\frac{\{s_k R_{P_k} z_k : k \in K\} \cup \{t_l R_l y_l : l \in L\} \cup \{u_m \neg R_{P_m} : m \in M\} \cup \{v_n \neg R_n : n \in N\}}{C'}. \quad (3)$$

Let $\sigma' : V \longrightarrow C(\Sigma')$ be a closed substitution and let $\sigma = \sigma'[\xi/c]$. Note that with (2) we have for all $s, t \in O(\Sigma)$ and $u \in O(\Sigma')$

$$S'(\sigma'(sRt)) = S(\sigma(sRt)), \quad S'(\sigma'(sR_P u)) = S(\sigma(Ps)).$$

So for each type of conclusion we have $S'(\sigma'(C')) = S(\sigma(C))$. We have four cases. First, we treat the case $s_k R_{P_k} z_k$.

$$S'(\sigma'(s_k R_{P_k} z_k)) = S(\sigma(P_k s_k)) \leq S(\sigma(C)) = S'(\sigma'(C'))$$

since S is a stratification. The case $t_l R_l y_l$ is treated analogously. We treat the negative premises. Let $u'_m \in C(\Sigma')$

$$S'(\sigma'(u_m R_{P_m} u'_m)) = S(\sigma(P_m u_m)) < S(\sigma(C)) = S'(\sigma'(C'))$$

since S is a stratification. We treat the last case. Let $v'_n \in C(\Sigma')$.

$$S'(\sigma'(v_n R_n v'_n)) = S(\sigma(v_n R_n v'_n[\xi/c])) < S(\sigma(C)) = S'(\sigma'(C')).$$

Again, we used that S is a stratification. So S' is a stratification and we find that T' is stratifiable.

Now we will prove that two closed Σ-terms u and v are bisimilar in the xenosystem T' if and only if they are bisimilar in the original system T. In order to do this we use a number of properties that are listed below.

Let $P \in T_p$, $R \in T_r$, and $u, v \in C(\Sigma') \supseteq C(\Sigma)$ (unless otherwise specified) then the following properties hold for all $i < \alpha$ and $j < d(T') = d(T)$. (We denote the bisimulation relation in T by $\sim$ and in T' by $\sim'$.)

(i)	$T'_{i,j} \vdash uR_P v \Longrightarrow v = \xi$	(ii)	$u \in C(\Sigma), T'_{i,j} \vdash uRv \Longrightarrow v \in C(\Sigma)$
(iii)	$u, v \in C(\Sigma), T'_i \vdash uRv \Longrightarrow T_i \vdash uRv$	(iv)	$u \in C(\Sigma), T'_i \vdash uR_P\xi \Longrightarrow T_i \vdash Pu$
(v)	$u \in C(\Sigma), T_i \vdash Pu \Longrightarrow T'_i \vdash uR_P\xi$	(vi)	$u, v \in C(\Sigma), T_i \vdash uRv \Longrightarrow T'_i \vdash uRv$
(vii)	$u \in C(\Sigma), T_i \vdash \neg Pu \Longrightarrow T'_i \vdash u\neg R_P$	$(viii)$	$u \in C(\Sigma), T'_i \vdash u\neg R_P \Longrightarrow T_i \vdash \neg Pu$
(ix)	$u \in C(\Sigma), T_i \vdash u\neg R \Longrightarrow T'_i \vdash u\neg R$	(x)	$u \in C(\Sigma), T'_i \vdash u\neg R \Longrightarrow T_i \vdash u\neg R$

(xi) $\quad u, v \in C(\Sigma) \Longrightarrow (u \sim v \iff u \sim' v)$

The proof of (i) follows directly from the definitions of $T'_{i,j}$ and the deduction rules in D'.

We prove (ii) with transfinite induction on i. So suppose that (ii) holds for all $i' < i$. We show the induction step for i with transfinite induction on j. So suppose that it is valid for all $j' < j$; we prove it for j. By definition of $T'_{i,j}$ there is a rule $d' = H'/C' \in D'$ as in (3) with $C' = sRt$ and a closed substitution σ with $\sigma(s) = u$ and $\sigma(t) = v$. In particular, for all $l \in L$ we have $U'_i \cup U'_{i,j} \vdash \sigma(t_l R_l y_l)$. Since the deduction rules are pure we have that $var(t) \subseteq var(s) \cup \{y_l : l \in L\}$. So it suffices to show that $\sigma(y_l) \in C(\Sigma)$ for all $l \in L$ since $\sigma(s) \in C(\Sigma)$. We denote the set of all y_l by Y. Suppose that there is a $y_{l_0} \in Y$ with $\sigma(y_{l_0}) \in C(\Sigma') \setminus C(\Sigma)$. This contradicts the well-foundedness of the rule d', for $T'_{i'} \vdash \sigma(t_{l_0}) R_{l_0} \sigma(y_{l_0})$ for an $i' < i$ or $T'_{i,j'} \vdash \sigma(t_{l_0}) R_{l_0} \sigma(y_{l_0})$ for a $j' < j$ so with the induction hypotheses for i or j we find that $\sigma(t_{l_0}) \in C(\Sigma') \setminus C(\Sigma)$. Since t_{l_0} is a Σ-term, this must be the result of a substitution. This can only be due to a variable $y_{l_1} \in Y$. With induction on the subsubscript we find an infinite backward chain of edges $y_{l_0} \longleftarrow y_{l_1} \longleftarrow \ldots$ in the variable dependency graph of d'. This concludes the induction step for j so by definition of T'_i we find that (ii) holds for i, which concludes the induction step for i.

A simple example due to Fokkink [11] shows that for property (ii) the well-foundedness cannot be missed. Suppose that we have a signature that consists of a single constant a. We have two rules: the axiom xRx and the rule xRx/aSx. Clearly, this system is not well-founded. The xenosystem has the same rules; only the signature is extended with the xenoconstant ξ. It is easy to see that we can derive in this new system that $aS\xi$.

We simultaneously verify (iii)–(x) with transfinite induction on i. Suppose that they hold for all $i' < i$; we prove them for i by verifying the following four properties for all $j < d(T) = d(T')$.

$$u, v \in C(\Sigma), T'_{i,j} \vdash uRv \Longrightarrow T_{i,j} \vdash uRv \tag{4}$$

$$u \in C(\Sigma), T'_{i,j} \vdash uR_P\xi \Longrightarrow T_{i,j} \vdash Pu \tag{5}$$

$$u \in C(\Sigma), T_{i,j} \vdash Pu \Longrightarrow T'_{i,j} \vdash uR_P\xi \tag{6}$$

$$u, v \in C(\Sigma), T_{i,j} \vdash uRv \Longrightarrow T'_{i,j} \vdash uRv \tag{7}$$

We prove (4)–(7) with transfinite induction on j, so assume that they are valid for all $j' < j$ then we check them for j.

We begin with equation (4). Let $u, v \in C(\Sigma)$ and suppose that $T'_{i,j} \vdash uRv$. By definition of $T'_{i,j}$ there is a deduction rule $d' = H'/C' \in D'$ of the form displayed in (3) with $C' = sRt$, $s, t \in O(\Sigma)$ and a closed substitution σ with $\sigma(s) = u$ and $\sigma(t) = v$. Moreover, we have $U'_i \cup U'_{i,j} \vdash \sigma(s_k R_{P_k} z_k), \sigma(t_l R_l y_l)$ for all $k \in K$ and $l \in L$ and we have $U'_i \vdash \sigma(u_m \neg R_{P_m}), \sigma(v_n \neg R_n)$ for all $m \in M$ and $n \in N$. In order to use induction we have to know that terms like $\sigma(s_k), \sigma(t_l), \ldots \in C(\Sigma)$. It suffices to show that $\sigma(y_l) \in C(\Sigma)$ for all $l \in L$. With (ii) we find for all $l \in L$ that $\sigma(y_l) \in C(\Sigma)$ just like in the proof of (ii). Now we find using (i) and the induction hypotheses on i or j that $U_i \cup U_{i,j} \vdash \sigma(P_k s_k), \sigma(t_l R_l y_l)$ for all $k \in K$ and $l \in L$. We find using the induction hypothesis on i that $U_i \vdash \sigma(\neg P_m u_m), \sigma(v_n \neg R_n)$ for all $m \in M$ and $n \in N$. The deduction rule $d = H/C \in D$ with $C = sRt$ that corresponds with d' takes the form

$$\frac{\{P_k s_k : k \in K\} \cup \{t_l R_l y_l : l \in L\} \cup \{\neg P_m u_m : m \in M\} \cup \{v_n \neg R_n : n \in N\}}{C}. \tag{8}$$

Define $\rho : V \longrightarrow C(\Sigma)$ with $\rho(z_k) = z_k$ for all $k \in K$ and $\rho(x) = \sigma(x)$ otherwise; in particular, we have $\rho(s) = u$ and $\rho(t) = v$. By definition of $T_{i,j}$ we find that $T_{i,j} \vdash uRv$; use (2) to see that $S'(uRv) = S(uRv)$. Equation (5) is treated analogously.

Now we treat equation (6). Let $u \in C(\Sigma)$ and assume $T_{i,j} \vdash Pu$. By definition of $T_{i,j}$ there is a deduction rule $d = H/C \in D$ of the form (8) with $C = Ps$ for some $s \in O(\Sigma)$ and there is a closed substitution σ with $\sigma(s) = u$ and $U_i \cup U_{i,j} \vdash \sigma(P_k s_k), \sigma(t_l R_l y_l)$ for all $k \in K$ and $l \in L$ and $U_i \vdash \sigma(\neg P_m u_m), \sigma(v_n \neg R_n)$ for all $m \in M$ and $n \in N$. Since $\sigma : V \longrightarrow C(\Sigma)$ we immediately find with the induction hypotheses on i or j that $U'_i \cup U'_{i,j} \vdash \sigma(s_k R_{P_k} \xi), \sigma(t_l R_l y_l)$ for all $k \in K$ and $l \in L$ and $U'_i \vdash \sigma(u_m \neg R_{P_m}), \sigma(v_n \neg R_n)$ for all $m \in M$ and $n \in N$. Let $d' = H'/C' \in D'$ be the deduction rule that corresponds with d. It takes the form displayed in (3) with $C' = sR_P\xi$. Define $\sigma' : V \longrightarrow C(\Sigma')$ by $\sigma'(z_k) = \xi$ for all $k \in K$ and $\sigma'(x) = \sigma(x)$ otherwise; note that $\sigma'(s) = u$. Since $S(Pu) = S'(uR_P\xi)$ (use (2)) we find by definition of $T'_{i,j}$ that $T'_{i,j} \vdash uR_P\xi$.

Equation (7) is verified in the same way. Now (4)–(7) are valid for all $j < d(T)$, which implies that (iii)–(vi) are valid for i. With this we can show that (vii)–(x) also hold for i.

We only treat (vii) since the cases $(viii)$–(x) are treated in the same way. Suppose that $u \in C(\Sigma)$ and $T_i \neg Pu$. Suppose that $T'_i \not\vdash u \neg R_P$ then there is a $u' \in C(\Sigma')$ with $T'_i \vdash uR_P u'$. With (i) we find that $u' = \xi$ so with (iv) for i we find that $T_i \vdash Pu$, which is a contradiction.

This concludes the induction step (on i), so (iii)–(x) are valid for all $i < \alpha$.

Now we verify (xi). Firstly, let $u \sim v$. Then there is a bisimulation relation B with uBv. Define $B' = B \cup \Delta'$, with $\Delta' = \{(t, t) : t \in C(\Sigma')\}$ the diagonal. We show that B' is a bisimulation with $uB'v$ in the new system T'. Clearly, $uB'v$. Now let $sB't$. We distinguish two cases: $s = t$ and $s \neq t$. We verify that the conditions in definition (4.4) hold for the second case since the first case is trivial. Since $s \neq t$ we have $s, t \in C(\Sigma)$ and sBt. Since there are no predicates in T' we only have to verify both transfer properties of definition (4.4). For each transfer property we have two cases: R and R_P. Now let $R \in T_r$ and suppose $T'_{S'} \vdash sRs'$ for some $s' \in C(\Sigma')$. We find with (ii) that $s' \in C(\Sigma)$ and with (iii) that $T_S \vdash sRs'$. Since sBt there is a $t' \in C(\Sigma)$ with $T_S \vdash tRt'$ and $s'Bt'$. So we obtain $s'B't'$ and with (vi) that $T'_{S'} \vdash tRt'$. The second condition in definition (4.4) is verified analogously. We check the first condition for R_P. Let $P \in T_p$ and suppose that $T'_{S'} \vdash sR_Ps'$ for some $s' \in C(\Sigma')$. We find with (i) that $s' = \xi$. So with (iv) we get $T_S \vdash Ps$. Since sBt we find $T_S \vdash Pt$ and with (v) that $T'_{S'} \vdash tR_P\xi$. Clearly $\xi B'\xi$. The second condition in (4.4) is checked analogously.

Secondly, let $u \sim' v$. Then there is a bisimulation relation B' containing the pair (u, v). Let $B = B' \cap (C(\Sigma) \times C(\Sigma))$. We show that B is a bisimulation with uBv in the original system T. Since $u, v \in C(\Sigma)$ we clearly have uBv. Let sBt. We check the conditions of definition (4.4). Let $R \in T_r$ and suppose that $T_S \vdash sRs'$ for some $s' \in C(\Sigma)$. With (vi) we find $T'_{S'} \vdash sRs'$. Since $sB't$ there is a $t' \in C(\Sigma')$ with $T'_{S'} \vdash tRt'$ and $s'B't'$. With (ii) we find $t' \in C(\Sigma)$ so $s'Bt'$. With (iii) we have $T_S \vdash tRt'$. The second condition in definition (4.4) is verified analogously. Next, we show that the last condition of (4.4) from left to right holds. The other direction can be shown analogously. Let $P \in T_p$ and suppose that $T_S \vdash Ps$. With (v) we find $T'_{S'} \vdash sR_P\xi$ so since $sB't$ there is a $t' \in C(\Sigma')$ with $T'_{S'} \vdash tR_Pt'$. With (i) we find $t' = \xi$ so with (iv) we find $T_S \vdash Pt$. This concludes the proof of (xi).

Now we are in a position to prove the congruence theorem. Let $f \in \Sigma$ be an n-ary function symbol. Let $u_i, v_i \in C(\Sigma)$ and $u_i \sim v_i$ for $1 \leq i \leq n$. With (xi) we find $u_i \sim' v_i$ for all $1 \leq i \leq n$. Since the term deduction system T' is well-founded stratifiable and in *ntyft/ntyxt* format we can apply the congruence theorem of Groote [**14**] so $f(u_1, \ldots, u_n) \sim' f(v_1, \ldots, v_n)$. Since $f(u_1, \ldots, u_n)$ and $f(v_1, \ldots, v_n)$ are Σ-terms we find with (xi) that $f(u_1, \ldots, u_n) \sim f(v_1, \ldots, v_n)$. This concludes the proof of (4.5).

Corollary (4.6) Every term deduction system in *panth* format can be reduced to a transition system specification in *ntyft/ntyxt* format. If the term deduction system is moreover well-founded and stratifiable then bisimulation equivalence is preserved: two terms are bisimilar in the *panth* system iff they are bisimilar in the *ntyft/ntyxt* system.

5. Conclusions and future work

In this paper we presented a syntactical format, the *panth* format, for structured operational semantics with predicates and negative premises such that if the rules are stratifiable we have that strong bisimulation is a congruence for all the operators that can be defined within this format. With operational semantics mostly taken from the literature we showed that our format is useful: the examples satisfy our format but no formats proposed by others. Moreover, with these examples we informally explained the notions necessary to use our result thereby showing that it can be easily applied without scrutinizing the abstract definitions. The examples include issues such as priorities, termination, convergence, discrete time, recursion, (infinitary) Hennessy-Milner logic, and universal quantification (in particular, so-called weak predicates).

We will briefly discuss future work. Since the stratification technique is not always satisfactory (cf. (3.17)), Bol and Groote [**9**] proposed the more general reduction technique (for the less general *ntyft/ntyxt* format). A first possibility for future work could be to use their methods to generalize our work. A second possibility is to incorporate recursion within our framework as is done for the GSOS format [**8**] and De Simone's format [**23**]. A third generalization could be to allow universal quantification in the hypotheses.

We conclude that the *panth* format is useful, and that our congruence theorem is practical.

Acknowledgements Thanks to Jos Baeten, Inge Bethke, Frank de Boer, Roland Bol, Jan Friso Groote, Hans Mulder, and Frits Vaandrager for valuable comments and interesting discussions. Thanks to the referees for their valuable comments.

6. References

[1] L. Aceto, M. Hennessy, *Termination, deadlock and divergence*, JACM, **39**(1):147–187, Januari 1992.

[2] J. C. M. Baeten, J. A. Bergstra, *Discrete Time Process Algebra*, Report P9208b, Amsterdam, 1992. An extended abstract appeared in: W. R. Cleaveland, editor, Proceedings CONCUR 92, Stony Brook, LNCS **630**, pp. 456–471, Springer-Verlag, 1992.

[3] J. C. M. Baeten, J. A. Bergstra, *Process algebra with a zero object*, in: J. C. M. Baeten and J. W. Klop, editors, Proceedings CONCUR 90, Amsterdam, LNCS **458**, pp. 83–98, Springer-Verlag, 1990.

[4] J. C. M. Baeten, J. A. Bergstra, *Processen en Procesexpressies*, Informatie, **30**(3), pp. 177–248, 1988.

[5] J. C. M. Baeten and C. Verhoef, *A congruence theorem for structured operational semantics with predicates*, in: E. Best (ed.), Proceedings CONCUR 93, LNCS **715**, pp. 477–492, Springer-Verlag, 1993.

[6] J. C. M. Baeten, W. P. Weijland, *Process algebra*, Cambridge Tracts in Theoretical Computer Science **18**, Cambridge University Press, 1990.

[7] J. A. Bergstra, A. Ponse, J. J. van Wamel, *Process algebra with backtracking*, Report P9306, Programming Research Group, University of Amsterdam, 1993.

[8] B. Bloom, S. Istrail, and A. R. Meyer, *Bisimulation can't be traced: preliminary report*, In: Proceedings 15*th* POPL, San Diego, California, pp. 229–239, 1988.

[9] R. N. Bol and J. F. Groote, *The meaning of negative premises in transition sytem specifications*, Report CS-R9054, CWI, Amsterdam, 1990 An extended abstract appeared in J. Leach Albert, B. Monien, and M. Rodríguez Artalejo, editors, Proceedings 18*th* ICALP, Madrid, pp. 481–494, 1991

[10] T. Bolognesi and F. Lucidi, *Timed process algebras with urgent interactions and a unique powerful binary operator*, In J. W. de Bakker, C. Huizing, W. P. de Roever, and G. Rozenberg, editors, Proceedings of the REX Workshop "Real-time: Theory in Practice", LNCS **600**, pp. 124–148, 1992.

[11] W. J. Fokkink, *personal communication*, January 1993.

[12] W. J. Fokkink, *The tyft/tyxt format reduces to tree rules*, in TACS'94, Masami Hagiya, John C. Mitchell, eds., pp. 440–453, LNCS **789**, Sendai, Japan.

[13] R. J. van Glabbeek, *Bounded nondeterminism and the approximation induction principle in process algebra*, In: Proceedings STACS **87** (F. J. Brandenburg, G. Vidal-Naquet, M. Wirsing, eds.), LNCS **247**, Springer Verlag, pp. 336–347, 1987.

[14] J. F. Groote, *Transition system specifications with negative premises*, Report CS-R9850, CWI, Amsterdam, 1989. An extended abstract appeared in J. C. M. Baeten and J. W. Klop, editors, Proceedings CONCUR 90, Amsterdam, LNCS **458**, pp. 332–341, Springer-Verlag, 1990.

[15] J. F. Groote and F. W. Vaandrager, *Structured operational semantics and bisimulation as a congruence*, I & C **100**(2), pp. 202–260, 1992.

[16] M. Hennessy, R. Milner, *Algebraic laws for nondeterminism and concurrency*, JACM **32**(1), pp. 137–161.

[17] A. S. Klusener, *Completeness in real time process algebra*, Technical Report CS-R9106, CWI, Amsterdam, 1991. An extended abstract appeared in J. C. M. Baeten and J. F. Groote, editors, Proceedings CONCUR 91, Amsterdam, LNCS **527**, pp. 376–392, 1991.

[18] K. G. Larsen, *Modal Specifications*, Technical Report R89-09, Institute for Electronic Systems, The University of Aalborg, 1989.

[19] K. G. Larsen, A. Skou, *Compositional Verification of Probabilistic Processes*, in: W. R. Cleaveland, editor, Proceedings CONCUR 92, Stony Brook, LNCS **630**, pp. 456–471, Springer-Verlag, 1992.

[20] F. Moller and C. Tofts, *A Temporal Calculus of Communicating Systems*, in: J. C. M. Baeten and J. W. Klop, editors, Proceedings CONCUR 90, Amsterdam, LNCS **458**, pp. 401–415 Springer-Verlag, 1990.

[21] D. M. R. Park, *Concurrency and automata on infinite sequences*, In P. Duessen (ed.) 5*th* GI Conference, LNCS **104**, pp. 167–183, Springer-Verlag, 1981.

[22] G. D. Plotkin, *A structural approach to operational semantics*, Report DAIMI FN-19, Computer Science Department, Aarhus University, 1981.

[23] R. de Simone, *Higher-level synchronising devices in* MEIJE-SCCS, TCS **37**, pp. 245–267, 1985.

[24] F. W. Vaandrager, *personal communication*, April 1993.

[25] C. Verhoef, *A general conservative extension theorem in process algebra*, Report CSN 93/38, Eindhoven University of Technology, 1993. Note: to appear in the Proceedings of the IFIP Working Conference on Programming Concepts, Methods and Calculi, San Miniato, Italy, 1994.

Deriving Complete Inference Systems for a Class of GSOS Languages Generating Regular Behaviours

Luca Aceto *

School of Cognitive and Computing Studies,
University of Sussex,
Falmer, Brighton BN1 9QH, England
email: luca@cogs.sussex.ac.uk

Abstract. In this paper I characterize a class of *infinitary* GSOS specifications, obtained by relaxing some of the finiteness constraints of the original format of Bloom, Istrail and Meyer, which generate regular processes. I then show how the techniques of Aceto, Bloom and Vaandrager can be adapted to give a procedure for converting any such language definition to a complete equational axiom system for strong bisimulation of processes which does not use infinitary proof rules. Equalities between recursive, regular processes can be established in the resulting inference systems by means of standard axioms to unwind recursive definitions, and the so-called *Recursive Specification Principle* (RSP).

1 Introduction

Since de Simone's pioneering work on the expressivity of the calculi SCCS and MEIJE (see, e.g., [19]), there has been considerable interest in the meta-theory of process algebras. As many process algebras are defined by structural operational semantics (SOS) [18], this way of giving semantics to programming and specification languages has been a natural handle for proving results for classes of languages. In particular, several formats for SOS rules have emerged in the literature (see, e.g., [19, 7, 10, 8]) and a wealth of properties that hold for *all* languages specified in terms of rules which fit these formats have been established.

In [3] I gave a contribution to this line of research by presenting, together with B. Bloom and F. Vaandrager, a procedure for converting any language definition in the GSOS format of Bloom, Istrail and Meyer [7] to a finite complete equational axiom system which precisely characterizes strong bisimulation of processes. Such a complete equational axiom system included, in general, one infinitary induction principle — essentially a reformulation of the Approximation Induction Principle (AIP) [4]. An infinitary proof rule like AIP is indeed necessary to obtain completeness for arbitrary GSOS systems because, as shown in [3], testing bisimulation over GSOS systems is Π^0_1-complete. However, it is well-known that AIP and other infinitary

* The work reported in this paper was partly carried out during a stay at Aalborg University Centre, 9220 Aalborg Ø, Denmark, and was partially supported by the Danish Natural Science Research Council under project DART. Additional funding was received by the HCM project EXPRESS.

proof rules are not necessary for the axiomatization of, e.g., strong bisimulation over regular behaviours (see the classic references [14, 6]). Thus it should be possible to fine tune the methods of [3] to produce complete inference systems for strong bisimulation over classes of GSOS systems that generate regular behaviours which do not rely on infinitary proof rules like AIP. This is the aim of this paper.

In this paper, I give a procedure for extracting from a GSOS specification that generates regular processes a complete axiom system for strong bisimulation equivalence. This axiom system is equational, except for one conditional equation, and does not rely on infinitary proof rules.

First of all, following [2], I characterize a class of *infinitary* GSOS specifications, obtained by relaxing some of the finiteness constraints of the original format of Bloom, Istrail and Meyer [7], which has some of the basic sanity properties of the original GSOS format. For example, it will ensure that the transition relation induced by the rules will be finitely branching. Syntactic restrictions are then imposed on the rules in these infinitary GSOS specifications to ensure that the semantics of processes is given by finite process graphs. The result is a class of infinitary GSOS systems that includes most of the standard operations used in the literature on process algebras. I then show how the techniques of [3] can be adapted to give a procedure for converting any such language definition to a complete equational axiom system for strong bisimulation of processes which does not use infinitary proof rules. Equalities between recursive, regular processes can be established in the resulting inference systems by means of standard axioms to unwind recursive definitions, and the so-called *Recursive Specification Principle* (RSP) [4].

Interestingly, it turns out that not all the infinitary GSOS systems from [2] which generate finite labelled transition systems are amenable to the development of a corresponding equational theory à là [3]. In particular, operations that use their arguments in unboundedly many different ways can still generate finite process graphs, but cannot be axiomatized in finitary fashion — at least not using the techniques of [3]. As an example, consider the operation f with rules (one such rule for each $i \in \omega$ and $j \leq i$):

$$\frac{x \xrightarrow{a_i} y}{f(x) \xrightarrow{a_j} 0} \qquad (1)$$

For each process P that can initially perform only a finite number of different actions, the semantics of $f(P)$ is given by a finite process graph. However, such an operation cannot be axiomatized in finitary fashion using the techniques of [3] because there is no upper bound on the number of different rules for it which have the same hypothesis. (See Proposition 26). Similarly, operations that have no upper bound on the number of positive hypotheses for their arguments, i.e. antecedents like $x \xrightarrow{a_i} y$ in rule (1), do not lend themselves to a clean algebraic description using the methods of [3]. (See Proposition 28). However, for GSOS systems whose operations are defined by rules without negative hypotheses, it is possible to give a reasonably aesthetic axiomatization of operations like the one given by the rules (1). A revised strategy that can be used to axiomatize these operations is presented in the full version of this paper [1]. When applied to the operation f described by the rules (1), the revised strategy produces the following natural equations:

$$f(0) = 0$$

$$f(x+y) = f(x) + f(y)$$
$$f(a_i.x) = \sum_{1 \leq j \leq i} a_j.0 \quad (a_i \in \mathsf{Act})$$

The paper is organized as follows. Section 2 is devoted to a review of background material from the theory of structural operational semantics and process algebras that will be needed in this study. Section 3 introduces the class of regular infinitary GSOS systems that will be axiomatized in Section 5. This is a subclass of the infinitary simple GSOS systems from [2] which afford a clean algebraic treatment. Section 5 presents an adaptation of the techniques from [3] to regular infinitary GSOS systems and two simple impossibility results which motivate the restriction to the class of systems under consideration. The algorithm of Section 5 produces an equational theory which is strongly head normalizing for all processes, i.e., that allows one to prove that a process P is equivalent to the sum of its initial derivatives. In Section 5.3, I discuss the completeness of the inference system obtained by extending the resulting equational theory with the recursive specification principle. Finally, in Section 6, I discuss some directions for further research. Familiarity with [3, 2] will be helpful, but not necessary, in reading the paper. As this is not an introductory paper on deriving complete axiomatizations from SOS rules, I shall often refer the reader to the literature for examples and motivations. Precise pointers to the literature will be given wherever necessary. For lack of space, all proofs have been omitted from this presentation—they may be found in [1], together with many more references to related studies in this fast growing research area.

2 Preliminaries

I assume that the reader is familiar with the basic notions of process algebra and structural operational semantics; see, e.g., [9, 11, 15, 4, 18, 10, 7] for more details and extensive motivations.

Let Var be a denumerable set of *process variables* ranged over by x, y. A *signature* Σ consists of a set of *operation symbols*, disjoint from Var, together with a function *arity* that assigns a natural number to each operation symbol. The set $\mathbb{T}(\Sigma)$ of *terms* over Σ is the least set such that

1. Each $x \in \mathsf{Var}$ is a term.
2. If f is an operation symbol of arity l, and $P_1, \ldots, P_l$ are terms, then $f(P_1, \ldots, P_l)$ is a term.

I shall use $P, Q, \ldots$ to range over terms and the symbol $\equiv$ for the relation of syntactic equality on terms. $\mathrm{T}(\Sigma)$ is the set of *closed* terms over Σ, i.e., terms that do not contain variables. Constants, i.e. terms of the form $f()$, will be abbreviated as f. A (closed) Σ-substitution is a mapping σ from the set of variables Var to the set of (closed) terms over Σ. The notation $\{P_1/x_1, \ldots, P_n/x_n\}$, where the P_is are terms and the x_is are distinct variables, will often be used to denote the substitution that maps each x_i to P_i, and leaves all the other variables unchanged. A Σ-*context* $C[\mathbf{x}]$ is a term in which at most the variables in the vector $\mathbf{x}$ appear. $C[\mathbf{P}]$ is $C[\mathbf{x}]$ with x_i replaced by P_i wherever it occurs.

Besides terms I have *actions*, elements of some given countable set Act, which is ranged over by a, b, c.

Definition 1 (GSOS Rules and Infinitary GSOS Systems). Suppose Σ is a signature. A *GSOS rule* ρ over Σ is an inference rule of the form[2]:

$$\frac{\bigcup_{i=1}^{l}\left\{x_i \xrightarrow{a_{ij}} y_{ij} \mid 1 \leq j \leq m_i\right\} \ \cup\ \bigcup_{i=1}^{l}\left\{x_i \stackrel{b_{ik}}{\not\rightarrow} \mid 1 \leq k \leq n_i\right\}}{f(x_1, \ldots, x_l) \xrightarrow{c} C[\mathbf{x}, \mathbf{y}]} \tag{2}$$

where all the variables are distinct, $m_i, n_i \geq 0$, f is an operation symbol from Σ with arity l, $C[\mathbf{x}, \mathbf{y}]$ is a Σ-context, and the a_{ij}, b_{ik}, and c are actions in Act. An *infinitary GSOS system* is a pair $G = (\Sigma_G, R_G)$, where Σ_G is a countable signature and R_G is a countable set of GSOS rules over Σ_G.

It is useful to name components of rules of the form (2). The operation symbol f is the *principal operation* of the rule, and the term $f(\mathbf{x})$ is the *source*. $C[\mathbf{x}, \mathbf{y}]$ is the *target*; c is the *action*; the formulas above the line are the *antecedents*; and the formula below the line is the *consequent*. If, for some i, $m_i > 0$ then I say that ρ *tests its i-th argument positively*. Similarly if $n_i > 0$ then I say that ρ *tests its i-th argument negatively*. An operation f *tests its i-th argument positively (resp. negatively)* if it occurs as principal operation of a rule that tests its i-th argument positively (resp. negatively).

GSOS systems have been introduced and studied in depth in [7]. The reader familiar with those references may have noticed that infinitary GSOS systems, unlike the GSOS systems in [7], are not required to consist of a finite signature and a finite set of GSOS rules. This slight generalization of the original definition will allow me to deal with calculi which, like, e.g., CCS [15], postulate an infinite action set. In the setting of this paper, it will also be natural to treat languages with a denumerable set of operations. (See, e.g., the language RCCS in Sect. 4).

Intuitively, an infinitary GSOS system gives a language, whose constructs are the operations in the signature Σ_G, together with a Plotkin-style structural operational semantics [18] for it defined by the set of conditional rules R_G. Informally, the intent of a GSOS rule is as follows. Suppose that we are wondering whether $f(\mathbf{P})$ is capable of taking a c-step. We look at each rule with principal operation f and action c in turn. We inspect each positive antecedent $x_i \xrightarrow{a_{ij}} y_{ij}$, checking if P_i is capable of taking an a_{ij}-step for each j and if so calling the a_{ij}-children Q_{ij}. We also check the negative antecedents; if P_i is *in*capable of taking a b_{ik}-step for each k. If so, then the rule *fires* and $f(\mathbf{P}) \xrightarrow{c} C[\mathbf{P}, \mathbf{Q}]$. Roughly, this means that the transition relation associated with an infinitary GSOS system, notation $\rightarrow_G$, is the one defined by structural induction on terms using the rules in R_G. This essentially ensures that a transition $f(\mathbf{P}) \xrightarrow{a}_G Q$ exists between the closed terms $f(\mathbf{P})$ and Q iff there exist a closed substitution σ, and a rule for f whose antecedents hold when instantiated with σ, and whose instantiated conclusion yields $f(\mathbf{P}) \xrightarrow{a}_G Q$. The interested reader is referred to [7] for the details of the formal definition of $\rightarrow_G$. As usual, the operational

[2] The format for GSOS rules considered in this paper is the original one of Bloom, Istrail and Meyer. However, all the results in this paper hold for a generalized version of GSOS rule in which an infinite number of negative antecedents is allowed.

semantics for the closed terms over Σ_G will be given in terms of the notion of labelled transition system.

Definition 2 (Labelled Transition Systems and Process Graphs). Let A be a set of labels. A *labelled transition system (lts)* is a pair $(S, \rightarrow)$, where S is a set of *states* and $\rightarrow \subseteq S \times A \times S$ is the *transition relation*. As usual, I shall write $s \xrightarrow{a} t$ in lieu of $(s, a, t) \in \rightarrow$. A state t is *reachable* from state s if there exist states $s_0, \ldots, s_n$ and labels $a_1, \ldots, a_n$ such that $s = s_0 \xrightarrow{a_1} s_1 \xrightarrow{a_2} \cdots \xrightarrow{a_n} s_n = t$. A *process graph* is a triple $(r, S, \rightarrow)$, where $(S, \rightarrow)$ is an lts, $r \in S$ is the *root*, and each state in S is reachable from r. If $(S, \rightarrow)$ is an lts and $s \in S$ then $\mathsf{graph}(s, (S, \rightarrow))$ is the process graph obtained by taking s as the root and restricting $(S, \rightarrow)$ to the part reachable from s. I shall write $\mathsf{graph}(s)$ for $\mathsf{graph}(s, (S, \rightarrow))$ whenever the underlying lts $(S, \rightarrow)$ is understood from the context.
An lts $(S, \rightarrow)$ is *finite* iff S and $\rightarrow$ are finite sets. A process graph $\mathsf{graph}(s, (S, \rightarrow))$ is finite if the restriction of $(S, \rightarrow)$ to the part reachable from s is.

The lts specified by an infinitary GSOS system G, denoted by $\mathsf{lts}(G)$, is then given by $(\mathrm{T}(\Sigma_G), \rightarrow_G)$ and the process graph defining the operational semantics of a closed term P is $\mathsf{graph}(P, \mathsf{lts}(G))$ (abbreviated to $\mathsf{graph}(P)$ when the infinitary GSOS system G is clear from context).

The basic notion of equivalence among terms of an infinitary GSOS system I shall consider in this paper is that of *bisimulation* [17].

Definition 3. Suppose G is an infinitary GSOS system. A binary relation $\sim \subseteq \mathrm{T}(\Sigma_G) \times \mathrm{T}(\Sigma_G)$ over closed terms is a *bisimulation* if it is symmetric, and $P \sim Q$ implies, for all $a \in \mathsf{Act}$,

If $P \xrightarrow{a}_G P'$ then, for some Q', $Q \xrightarrow{a}_G Q'$ and $P' \sim Q'$.

I write $P \leftrightarrows_G Q$ if there exists a bisimulation $\sim$ relating P and Q. The subscript G is omitted when it is clear from context.

Lemma 4. *Suppose G is an infinitary GSOS system. Then $\leftrightarrows_G$ is an equivalence relation and a congruence for all operation symbols f of G,* i.e., $(\forall i : P_i \leftrightarrows_G Q_i) \Rightarrow f(\mathbf{P}) \leftrightarrows_G f(\mathbf{Q})$.

For an infinitary GSOS system G, I shall write $\mathsf{Bisim}(G)$ for the quotient algebra of closed Σ_G-terms modulo bisimulation. That is, for $P, Q \in \mathbb{T}(\Sigma_G)$,

$$\mathsf{Bisim}(G) \models P = Q \quad \Leftrightarrow \quad (\forall \text{ closed } \Sigma_G\text{-substitutions } \sigma : P\sigma \leftrightarrows_G Q\sigma) \ .$$

Definition 5 ([3]). An infinitary GSOS system H is a *disjoint extension* of an infinitary GSOS system G, notation $G \sqsubseteq H$, if the signature and rules of H include those of G, and H introduces no new rules for operations of G.

Note that if H disjointly extends G then H introduces no new outgoing transitions for terms of G. In this paper, I shall be interested in equations which are preserved by taking disjoint extensions of infinitary GSOS systems. Following [3], I thus introduce, for G an infinitary GSOS system, the class $\mathsf{BISIM}(G)$ of all algebras $\mathsf{Bisim}(G')$, for G' a disjoint extension of G. Thus we have, for $P, Q \in \mathbb{T}(\Sigma_G)$,

$$\mathsf{BISIM}(G) \models P = Q \quad \Leftrightarrow \quad (\forall G' : G \sqsubseteq G' \Rightarrow \mathsf{Bisim}(G') \models P = Q) \ .$$

3 Regular Infinitary GSOS Systems

In this section, I shall show how to impose syntactic restrictions on the format of rules in an infinitary GSOS system G which ensure that $\mathsf{graph}(P)$ is a finite process graph for each $P \in \mathrm{T}(\Sigma_G)$. Some of the results to follow are from [2], and I refer the reader to that reference for intuition and examples. The class of infinitary GSOS systems which will be considered in this paper will be a subclass of the simple GSOS systems of [2] which allows for the development of a clean algebraic theory à là [3].

In order to obtain that $\mathsf{graph}(P)$ is a finite process graph for each closed term P, it is necessary to impose restrictions on the class of infinitary GSOS systems under consideration, ensuring that the transition relation be finitely branching and that the set of states reachable from P be finite. Finite branching of the transition relation $\rightarrow_G$ is one of the basic sanity properties of the original GSOS format of Bloom, Istrail and Meyer [7]. However, in the presence of a possibly infinite action set and signature, it is easy to specify operations which give rise to infinitely branching process graphs, and explicit constraints ruling out this pathology must be imposed on infinitary GSOS systems.

Definition 6. The *positive trigger* of rule (2) is the l-tuple over 2^{Act} $\langle e_1, \ldots, e_l \rangle$, where $e_i = \{a_{ij} | 1 \leq j \leq m_i\}$.

Definition 7 (Boundedness and Uniform Boundedness). An operation f in an infinitary GSOS system is *bounded* iff for each positive trigger, the corresponding set of rules for f is finite. An infinitary GSOS system is *bounded* iff each of its operations is.

An operation in an infinitary GSOS system is *uniformly bounded* iff there exists an upper bound n_f on the number of distinct rules for f having the same positive trigger. An infinitary GSOS system is *uniformly bounded* iff each of its operations is.

The notion of bounded infinitary GSOS system is from [2], and is inspired by ideas developed by Vaandrager [20, Definition 3.2] for de Simone systems. The notion of uniform boundedness is new in this paper, and will play an important role in Sect. 5.1. (In particular, it will be crucial in the proof of Proposition 25). Of course, every uniformly bounded operation is also bounded. The following example shows that the converse is not true.

Example: Let $\mathsf{Act} = \{a_i \mid i \geq 1\}$ be a denumerable set of actions. Consider an infinitary GSOS system G comprising a unary operation f and constant $\mathbf{0}$, with rules (one such rule for each $i \in \omega$ and $j \leq i$):

$$\frac{x \xrightarrow{a_i} y}{f(x) \xrightarrow{a_j} \mathbf{0}} \qquad (3)$$

Then f is bounded, as there are exactly i rules with trigger a_i for each $i \geq 1$. However, f is not uniformly bounded.

Lemma 8 ([2]). *For each infinitary, bounded GSOS system G, the transition relation $\rightarrow_G$ is finitely branching.*

In order to characterize an interesting class of infinitary GSOS systems which generate finite process graphs, I shall now introduce a further restriction on infinitary GSOS systems that ensures that processes have a finite set of states. The following notions are from [2].

Definition 9. A GSOS rule of the form (2) is *simple* iff $C[\mathbf{x}, \mathbf{y}]$ is either a variable in $\mathbf{x}, \mathbf{y}$ or it is of the form $g(z_1, \ldots, z_n)$ where each z_i is a variable in $\mathbf{x}, \mathbf{y}$. An operation is *simple* iff all the rules for it are. An infinitary GSOS system $G = (\Sigma_G, R_G)$ is *simple* iff each operation in Σ_G is.

Definition 10. Let $G = (\Sigma_G, R_G)$ be a simple, infinitary GSOS system. The *operator dependency graph* associated with G is the directed graph with Σ_G as set of nodes, and set of edges E given by: $(f, g) \in E$ iff there exists a rule $\rho \in R_G$ with f as principal operation and target $g(z_1, \ldots, z_n)$, for some $z_1, \ldots, z_n \in \mathsf{Var}$. I shall write $f \prec_G g$ iff $fE^{\star}q$ in the operator dependency graph for G, where $E^{\star}$ denotes the reflexive and transitive closure of E.

Definition 11 (Very Simple GSOS Systems). Let $G = (\Sigma_G, R_G)$ be a simple, infinitary GSOS system. An operation $f \in \Sigma_G$ is *very simple* iff it is uniformly bounded and $\{g \mid f \prec_G g\}$ is finite. A simple, infinitary GSOS system is *very simple* iff every operation in its signature is.

Proposition 12. *Let $G = (\Sigma_G, R_G)$ be a very simple GSOS system. Then, for all $P \in \mathrm{T}(\Sigma_G)$, $\mathsf{graph}(P)$ is a finite process graph.*

The following definition introduces the subclass of very simple GSOS systems that I shall study in the remainder of this paper. The following definition is new in this paper, and will play an important role in Sect. 5.2. (In particular, it will be crucial in the proof of Proposition 27).

Definition 13 (Regular GSOS Systems). Let $G = (\Sigma_G, R_G)$ be an infinitary GSOS systems. An operation $f \in \Sigma_G$ has *limited fan-in* iff for every argument i for f there exists an upper bound $m_{(f,i)}$ on the number of distinct positive antecedents for argument i in the rules for f in R_G. I say that an operation $f \in \Sigma_G$ is *regular* iff it is very simple, and has limited fan-in. An infinitary GSOS systems is *regular* iff every operation in its signature is.

Most of the standard operations used in the literature on process algebras are regular. An example of a very simple operation which is *not* regular is presented below.

Example: Let $\mathsf{Act} = \{a_i \mid i \geq 1\}$ be a denumerable set of actions. Consider the very simple GSOS operation g with rules (one such rule for each $i \in \omega$):

$$\frac{\left\{x \xrightarrow{a_j} y_j \mid 1 \leq j \leq i\right\}}{g(x) \xrightarrow{a_i} 0} \tag{4}$$

Then g is not regular as it has a rule with n positive antecedents for its one argument for each $n \in \omega$.

4 The Problem

The main problem addressed in [3] was to find a complete axiomatization of bisimulation on closed terms – that is, equality in $\mathsf{Bisim}(G)$ – for an arbitrary GSOS system specification G. In that reference it was shown how to find a finite (conditional) equational theory T such that for all closed terms $P, Q \in \mathrm{T}(\Sigma_G)$, $T \vdash P = Q \Leftrightarrow \mathsf{Bisim}(G) \models P = Q$. The theory T generated by the methods in [3] was purely equational, apart from the presence of one infinitary conditional equation which is a reformulation of the *Approximation Induction Principle* (AIP) familiar from the literature on ACP [4]. Indeed, by recursion theoretic considerations spelled out in [3], it is not possible to do without an infinitary proof rule like AIP for general GSOS specifications. However, for classes of GSOS systems generating regular behaviours, it should be possible to obtain complete axiomatizations of bisimulation on closed terms that do not rely on infinitary proof rules. In the remainder of this paper, I shall present a way of obtaining such complete axiomatizations of bisimulation for the regular GSOS specifications introduced in Definition 13. The presentation will follow [3] quite closely, and the reader will be referred to that paper for examples of applications of the theory.

In [3], it was shown how to reduce the completeness problem for arbitrary GSOS specifications to that for FINTREE, a simple fragment of CCS suitable for expressing finite trees, which was solved by Hennessy and Milner in [12]. Here I shall follow the same approach, by showing how to reduce the completeness problem for *regular* GSOS specifications to that for finite process graphs, which was solved by Milner in [14].

The infinitary GSOS system FINTREE has a constant symbol $\mathbf{0}$ denoting the null process; unary operation symbols $a(\cdot)$, one for each action in Act, denoting action prefixing; and a binary symbol $+$ for nondeterministic choice. The null process is incapable of taking any action, and consequently has no rules. For each action a there is a rule $ax \xrightarrow{a} x$. The operational semantics of $P + Q$ is defined by the rules (one pair of rules for each $a \in \mathsf{Act}$):

$$\frac{x \xrightarrow{a} x'}{x + y \xrightarrow{a} x'} \qquad \frac{y \xrightarrow{a} y'}{x + y \xrightarrow{a} y'} \tag{5}$$

A *recursive specification* E is a set of equations $\{x = P_x \mid x \in V_E\}$ with V_E a finite set of variables and every P_x a guarded FINTREE term with variables in V_E of the form $\sum_{i \in I} a_i.x_i$, where I is a finite index set. (The summation notation is justified by axioms (S1)–(S2) in Fig. 1. As usual, an empty sum is identified with $\mathbf{0}$.)

The infinitary GSOS system RCCS is obtained by disjointly extending FINTREE with constants of the form $\langle x \mid E \rangle$ for each recursive specification E and variable $x \in V_E$. The variables in V_E are bound in $\langle x \mid E \rangle$. Intuitively, $\langle x \mid E \rangle$ denotes the x-component of a solution of E. Let $E = \{x = P_x \mid x \in V_E\}$ be a recursive specification, and P be an RCCS term. Then, following the standard ACP practice (see, e.g., [4]), $\langle P \mid E \rangle$ denotes the term obtained by replacing each free occurrence of $x \in V_E$ in P by $\langle x \mid E \rangle$, i.e., $\langle P \mid E \rangle$ stands for $P\{\langle x \mid E \rangle / x \mid x \in V_E\}$. The operational semantics of each constant $\langle x \mid E \rangle$ is given by the (finite) set of axioms, one such axiom for each summand $a_i.x_i$ in P_x:

$$\langle x \mid E\rangle \xrightarrow{a_i} \langle x_i \mid E\rangle \ .$$

The following fact is well-known (see, e.g., [14, 6]), and, as RCCS is easily seen to be a very simple GSOS system, is, in fact, a corollary of Proposition 12:

Lemma 14. *For every $P \in \mathrm{T}(\Sigma_{\mathsf{RCCS}})$, $\mathsf{graph}(P)$ is finite.*

Bisimulation equivalence over regular processes has been completely axiomatized by Milner [14], and Bergstra and Klop [6] without the use of infinitary proof rules like AIP. To pave the way to the extension of these results to regular GSOS systems, I shall now show that the axioms in Fig. 1 are complete for equality in Bisim(RCCS) by adapting Milner's proof to the language RCCS.

$$x + y = y + x \qquad \text{(S1)}$$
$$(x+y)+z = x+(y+z) \qquad \text{(S2)}$$
$$x + x = x \qquad \text{(S3)}$$
$$x + 0 = x \qquad \text{(S4)}$$

$$\langle x \mid E\rangle = \langle P_x \mid E\rangle \qquad \text{(REC)}$$
$$\frac{E}{x \;=\; \langle x \mid E\rangle}\; E \text{ guarded} \quad \text{(RSP)}$$

Fig. 1. The theory T_{RCCS}

The following notion from [14] will be important in the remainder of the paper.

Definition 15. Let G be an infinitary GSOS system that disjointly extends RCCS, and T be an collection of Σ_G-equations. A term $P \in \mathrm{T}(\Sigma_G)$ T-provably satisfies a recursive specification $E = \{x = P_x \mid x \in V_E\}$ in the variable $x_0 \in V_E$ iff there are terms Q_x for $x \in V_E$ with $P \equiv Q_{x_0}$, such that for all $x \in V_E$, $T \vdash\ Q_x = P_x\{Q_y/y \mid y \in V_E\}$

Proposition 16. *For all $P, Q \in \mathrm{T}(\Sigma_{\mathsf{RCCS}})$, $\mathsf{Bisim(RCCS)} \models P = Q \Leftrightarrow T_{\mathsf{RCCS}} \vdash P = Q$.*

The completeness of the theory T_{RCCS} can be proven, following Milner, in three steps:

1. For each $P \in \mathrm{T}(\Sigma_{\mathsf{RCCS}})$, it is possible to prove a strong head normalization property for T_{RCCS}, namely $T_{\mathsf{RCCS}} \vdash\ P = \sum\left\{a.Q \mid P \xrightarrow{a}_{\mathsf{RCCS}} Q\right\}$.
2. Following Milner [14, 16], one shows that if $P \leftrightarrows_{\mathsf{RCCS}} Q$ then P and Q T_{RCCS}-provably satisfy a common recursive specification $E = \{x = P_x \mid x \in V_E\}$ in some variable $x_0 \in V_E$.
3. Finally, using (RSP), it is possible to show that if P and Q T_{RCCS}-provably satisfy a common recursive specification E in the variable $x_0 \in V_E$, then $T_{\mathsf{RCCS}} \vdash P = Q$.

In the reminder of this paper, I shall mimic the strategy outlined above to derive complete inference systems for regular GSOS specifications that do not rely on an infinitary conditional equation like the AIP. The inference systems derived using the methods presented in the remainder of this paper will be equational, apart from the conditional equation (RSP). The equational part of the proof system will allow me to prove an analogue of the strong head normalization result stated in step 1 of the aforementioned proof sketch. This will require a variety of methods that will be presented in the following section.

5 Axiomatizing Regular GSOS Operations

As mentioned in the previous section, the core of the derivation of complete inference systems for regular GSOS systems will be the generation of a set of equations which allow one to prove an analogue of the strong head normalization result stated in the proof of Proposition 16, viz., that each closed term is provably equal to the sum of its initial derivatives. Following [3], I shall first show how to axiomatize a class of well-behaved regular GSOS operations, the smooth operations of [3]. Secondly, I shall extend these results to arbitrary regular GSOS operations.

5.1 The Axiomatization of Regular Smooth Operations

The following definition is from [3], where motivation and examples of smooth operations can be found.

Definition 17. A GSOS rule is *smooth* if it takes the form

$$\frac{\left\{x_i \xrightarrow{a_i} y_i \mid i \in I\right\} \cup \left\{x_i \stackrel{b_{ij}}{\not\rightarrow} \mid i \in K, 1 \leq j \leq n_i\right\}}{f(x_1, \ldots, x_l) \xrightarrow{c} C[\mathbf{x}, \mathbf{y}]} \qquad (6)$$

where I, K are disjoint sets such that $I \cup K = \{1, \ldots, l\}$, and no x_i with $i \in I$ appears in $C[\mathbf{x}, \mathbf{y}]$. An operation from an infinitary GSOS system G is *smooth* if all the rules for this operation are smooth. G is *smooth* if it contains smooth rules only.

In order to obtain a strongly head normalizing equational theory for regular, smooth operations, I shall first show how to obtain equations that describe the interplay between such operations and the FINTREE combinators. Examples of the laws that can be derived using the results below may be found in [3]. Lemmas 18–22 hold for arbitrary infinitary GSOS systems, and will be stated in full generality even though, in the remainder of the paper, I shall only apply them to obtain equations for regular operations. The following lemma describes how smooth operations interact with the summation operation of FINTREE, and is a slightly sharpened version of [3, Lemma 4.3].

Lemma 18 (Distributivity Laws). *Let f be an l-ary smooth operation of an infinitary GSOS system G that disjointly extends* FINTREE, *and suppose that i is an argument of f for which each rule for f has a positive antecedent. Then the equation:*

$$f(x_1, \ldots, x_i + y_i, \ldots, x_l) = f(x_1, \ldots, x_i, \ldots, x_l) + f(x_1, \ldots, y_i, \ldots, x_l) \qquad (7)$$

is valid in BISIM(G).

The following lemma, that extends [3, Lemma 4.6] to infinitary GSOS systems, gives *inaction laws* to describe the interaction between arbitrary operations and the FINTREE constant $\mathbf{0}$; that is, laws which say when a term $f(\mathbf{P})$ is bisimilar to $\mathbf{0}$.

Lemma 19 (Inaction Laws). *Suppose f is an l-ary smooth operation of an infinitary GSOS system G that disjointly extends* FINTREE, *and suppose that, for $1 \leq i \leq l$, term P_i is of the form $\mathbf{0}$, x_i, ax_i or $ax_i + y_i$. Suppose further that for each rule for f of the form (6) there is an index i such that either (1) $i \in I$ and $P_i \equiv \mathbf{0}$ or $P_i \equiv ax_i$ for some $a \neq a_i$, or (2) $i \in K$ and $P_i \equiv b_{ij}x_i + y_i$ for some $1 \leq j \leq n_i$. Then:*

$$\mathsf{BISIM}(G) \models f(\mathbf{P}) = \mathbf{0} \ . \tag{8}$$

To complete the series of results giving equations dealing with the interplay between smooth operations and the FINTREE combinators, I shall now present results corresponding to the action laws of [3]. In particular, I shall follow the "alternative" approach given in [3, Sect. 6] in which the interplay between prefixing and smooth operations is described by means of so called "peeling" and "action laws".

Definition 20 ([3]). A smooth operation f from an infinitary GSOS system G is *distinctive* if, for each argument i, either all rules for f test i positively or none of them does, and moreover for each pair of different rules for f there is an argument for which both rules have a positive antecedent, but with a different action.

The following lemma gives the so-called peeling laws. These are laws that can be used to reduce the arguments that are tested negatively by a smooth and distinctive operation to a form in which either action laws or inaction laws can be applied.

Lemma 21 (Peeling Laws). *Suppose f is a distinctive smooth operation of a disjoint extension G of* FINTREE, *with a rule ρ of the form*

$$\frac{\left\{x_i \xrightarrow{a_i} y_i \,|\, i \in I\right\} \cup \left\{x_i \overset{b_{ij}}{\not\rightarrow} \,|\, i \in K, 1 \leq j \leq n_i\right\}}{f(\mathbf{x}) \xrightarrow{c} C[\mathbf{x}, \mathbf{y}]}$$

Let $k \in K$ be such that x_k does not occur in $C[\mathbf{x}, \mathbf{y}]$, and $b \notin \{b_{kj} | 1 \leq j \leq n_k\}$. Take

$$P_i \equiv \begin{cases} a_i y_i & i \in I \\ bx'_k + x''_k & i = k \\ x_i & i \in K \wedge i \neq k \end{cases} \quad \textit{and} \quad Q_i \equiv \begin{cases} a_i y_i & i \in I \\ x''_k & i = k \\ x_i & i \in K \wedge i \neq k \end{cases}$$

Then:

$$\mathsf{BISIM}(G) \models f(\mathbf{P}) = f(\mathbf{Q}) \ . \tag{9}$$

Lemma 22 (Action Laws). *Suppose f is a distinctive smooth operation of a disjoint extension G of* FINTREE, *with a rule ρ of the form*

$$\frac{\left\{x_i \xrightarrow{a_i} y_i \,|\, i \in I\right\} \cup \left\{x_i \overset{b_{ij}}{\not\rightarrow} \,|\, i \in K, 1 \leq j \leq n_i\right\}}{f(\mathbf{x}) \xrightarrow{c} C[\mathbf{x}, \mathbf{y}]}$$

Let

$$P_i \equiv \begin{cases} a_i y_i & i \in I \\ \mathbf{0} & i \in K \wedge n_i > 0 \\ x_i & otherwise \end{cases}$$

Then:

$$\mathsf{BISIM}(G) \models f(\mathbf{P}) = c.C[\mathbf{P}, \mathbf{y}] \ . \tag{10}$$

The combination of peeling laws (9), instantiated action laws (10), distributivity laws (7), and inaction laws (8), gives a theory that is head normalizing for terms built from distinctive smooth operations that are *discarding* [3, Definition 6.2].

Definition 23 (Discarding and Good Operations). A smooth GSOS rule like (6) is *discarding* if for no argument i that is tested negatively, x_i occurs in the target. A smooth operation is *discarding* if all the rules for this operation are. A smooth operation is *good* if it is both discarding and distinctive.

Theorem 24. *Suppose G is an infinitary GSOS system with* $\mathsf{RCCS} \sqsubseteq G$. *Let* $\Sigma \subseteq \Sigma_G - \Sigma_{\mathsf{RCCS}}$ *be a collection of good operations of G. Let T be the equational theory that extends* $\{(\mathrm{S1}), \ldots, (\mathrm{S4}), (\mathrm{Rec})\}$ *with the following axioms, for each operation f from Σ:*

1. *for each argument i of f that is tested positively, a distributivity axiom (7),*
2. *for each rule for f of the form (6), for each argument i that is tested negatively, and for each action* $b \notin \{b_{ij} | 1 \leq j \leq n_i\}$, *a peeling law (9),*
3. *for each rule for f, an action law (10),*
4. *all the inaction laws (8) for f.*

Then $\mathsf{BISIM}(G) \models T$ *and, for each* $P \in \mathrm{T}(\Sigma \cup \Sigma_{\mathsf{RCCS}})$,

$$T \vdash P = \sum \left\{ a.Q \mid P \xrightarrow{a}_G Q \right\} .$$

The next proposition shows how to handle general smooth and discarding operations by expressing them as a *finite* sum of good operations, in very much the same way as the merge operation of ACP is expressed as a sum of the auxiliary operations of left-merge and communication merge (see, e.g., [4] for a textbook presentation). In particular, the following proposition allows for the "discovery" of the auxiliary operations of ACP. See [3] for examples.

Proposition 25. *Let G be a regular infinitary GSOS system which disjointly extends* $\mathsf{FINTREE}$. *Assume that f is an l-ary smooth and discarding operation of G. Then there exists a disjoint extension G' of G with l-ary good, regular operations* $f_1, \ldots, f_n$ *such that G' is a regular GSOS system, and*

$$\mathsf{BISIM}(G') \models f(\mathbf{x}) = f_1(\mathbf{x}) + \cdots + f_n(\mathbf{x}) \ . \tag{11}$$

It is interesting to note that the above proposition would *not* hold if regular operations were allowed to be bounded, but not uniformly so. As an example, consider the operation f on page 6 given by the rules (3). This operation is bounded, but not uniformly bounded. I shall now show that, under mild assumptions, it is impossible to express f as a finite sum of unary smooth, distinctive operations.

Proposition 26. *Let* Act $= \{a_i \mid i \geq 1\}$ *be a denumerable set of actions, and* G *be an infinitary GSOS system which disjointly extends* FINTREE *comprising the smooth, discarding unary operation* f *given by the rules (3). Then there does not exist a disjoint extension* G' *of* G *with a family of unary smooth and distinctive operations* $f_1, \ldots, f_n$ *such that*

$$\mathsf{Bisim}(G') \models f(x) = f_1(x) + \cdots + f_n(x) \ .$$

Proposition 25 is the only result in this paper which would not hold if I allowed regular operations to be bounded, rather than uniformly bounded.

5.2 General Regular Operations

In this subsection I show how to axiomatize GSOS operations that are not both smooth and discarding. The technical development parallels the results presented in [3, Sect. 4.2].

Proposition 27. *Suppose* G *is a regular GSOS system containing an operation* f *with arity* l *that is not both smooth and discarding. Then there exists a regular disjoint extension* G' *of* G *with a smooth and discarding operation* f' *with arity* l' *(possibly different from* l*), and there exist vectors* $\mathbf{z}$ *of* l *distinct variables, and* $\mathbf{v}$ *of* l' *variables in* $\mathbf{z}$ *(possibly repeated), such that:*

$$\mathsf{BISIM}(G') \models f(\mathbf{z}) = f'(\mathbf{v}) \ . \tag{12}$$

It is interesting to note that the above proposition would *not* hold for very simple GSOS operations that are not regular. As an example, consider the operation g on page 7 given by the rules (4). This operation is very simple, but not regular. I shall now show that, under mild assumptions, it is impossible to express g as a finite sum of smooth operations.

Proposition 28. *Let* Act $= \{a_i \mid i \geq 1\}$ *be a denumerable set of actions, and* G *be an infinitary GSOS system which disjointly extends* FINTREE *comprising the very simple unary operation* g *given by the rules (4). Then there does not exist a disjoint extension* G' *of* G *with a family of smooth operations* $g_1, \ldots, g_n$ *with arities* $l_1, \ldots, l_n$*, respectively, such that*

$$\mathsf{Bisim}(G') \models g(x) = g_1(\underbrace{x, \ldots, x}_{l_1\text{-times}}) + \cdots + g_n(\underbrace{x, \ldots, x}_{l_n\text{-times}}) \ .$$

Proposition 27 is the only result in this paper that does not hold in general for very simple GSOS systems which contain operations that do not have limited fan-in.

The theory that has been developed so far gives a strongly head normalizing equational theory for all regular GSOS operations.

Theorem 29. *Let* G *be a regular GSOS system. Then the regular GSOS system* G' *and the equational theory* T *produced by the algorithm of Fig. 2 have the property that* $\mathsf{BISIM}(G') \models T$ *and, for all* $P \in \mathrm{T}(\Sigma_{G'})$, $T \vdash P = \sum \left\{ a.Q \mid P \xrightarrow{a}_{G'} Q \right\}$.

Input	A regular GSOS system G.
Output	A regular infinitary GSOS system G' that disjointly extends G, and an equational theory T, such that $\text{BISIM}(G') \models T$ and T is strongly head normalizing for all terms of G'.

Step 1. Add to G a disjoint copy of RCCS.

Step 2. For each regular operation $f \in \Sigma_G$ that is not both smooth and discarding, apply the construction of Proposition 27 to extend the system with a regular smooth and discarding version f', in such a way that law (12) holds. Add all the resulting instances of law (12) to $\{(\mathrm{S1}), \ldots, (\mathrm{S4}), (\mathrm{REC})\}$.

Step 3. For each smooth, discarding and non-distinctive operation $f \notin \Sigma_{\mathsf{RCCS}}$ in the resulting system, apply the construction of Proposition 25 to generate good, regular operations $f_1, \ldots, f_n$ in such a way that law (11) is valid. The system so-obtained is the infinitary GSOS system G' we were looking for. Add to the equational theory all the resulting instances of law (11).

Step 4. Add to the equational theory obtained in Step 3 the equations given by applying Theorem 24 to all the good operations in $\Sigma_{G'} - \Sigma_{\mathsf{RCCS}}$. The result is the theory T we were looking for.

Fig. 2. The algorithm

5.3 Completeness

For any regular GSOS system G, the algorithm presented in Fig. 2 allows for the generation of a disjoint GSOS extension G' with a strongly head-normalizing equational theory. The reader might recall that this was the first step in the proof of completeness of T_{RCCS} for Bisim(RCCS). I shall now show how to mimic the remaining two steps in the proof of Proposition 16 to obtain completeness for arbitrary regular GSOS specifications.

The following proposition plays the role of step 2 of the proof of Proposition 16 in this setting.

Proposition 30. *Suppose that G is a regular GSOS system. Let G' and T denote the disjoint extension of G, and the strongly head normalizing equational theory constructed by the algorithm in Fig. 2, respectively. Then, for all $P, Q \in \mathrm{T}(\Sigma_{G'})$ such that $\mathsf{Bisim}(G') \models P = Q$, there exists a recursive specification E T-provably satisfied in the same variable x_0 by both P and Q.*

The promised completeness result now follows easily from the previous theory.

Theorem 31 (Completeness). *Suppose that G is a regular GSOS system. Let G' and T denote the disjoint extension of G, and the strongly head normalizing equational theory constructed by the algorithm in Fig. 2, respectively. Then, $T \cup \{(\mathrm{RSP})\}$ is complete for equality in $\mathsf{Bisim}(G')$.*

6 Further Work

The developments of this paper suggest several interesting topics for further research. Below I list some directions for further work that I plan to explore. The class of regular operations that has been axiomatized in this paper is quite large, and includes most of the standard operations found in the literature on process algebras. Notable exceptions are, e.g., the desynchronizing operation Δ present in the early versions of Milner's SCCS [13], and the Kleene star operation considered in [5]. It is a challenging open problem to extend the class of regular GSOS operations considered in this paper to include operations like Milner's Δ and Kleene star.

In this paper, I have not considered issues related to the effectiveness of regular infinitary GSOS languages, and of the resulting axiomatizations. Standard GSOS languages à là Bloom, Istrail and Meyer enjoy pleasant recursion-theoretic properties, and any proper extension of their work to infinitary languages ought to possess at least some of them. In future work I plan to investigate a class of infinitary, recursive GSOS languages and study the resulting axiomatizations produced by the methods of [3]. Finally, it would be interesting to find alternative ways of axiomatizing general GSOS operations that, like the one presented in [1, Sect. 7.1], do not use the full power of the technical notion of distinctiveness used in [3] and in this study.

Acknowledgements: Many thanks to Bard Bloom and Frits Vaandrager for the joint work [3] which formed the main inspiration for this paper. Y.S. Ramakrishna provided much needed terminological assistance.

References

1. L. Aceto, *Deriving complete inference systems for a class of GSOS languages generating regular behaviours*, Report IR 93–2009, Institute for Electronic Systems, Department of Mathematics and Computer Science, Aalborg University, Aalborg, November 1993. Also available as Computer Science Report 1/94, University of Sussex, January 1994.
2. ——, *GSOS and finite labelled transition systems*, Report 6/93, Computer Science, University of Sussex, Brighton, 1993. To appear in *Theoretical Computer Science*.
3. L. Aceto, B. Bloom, and F. Vaandrager, *Turning SOS rules into equations*, Report CS-R9218, CWI, Amsterdam, June 1992. To appear in *Information and Computation* 111(1/2), May/June 1994.
4. J. Baeten and W. Weijland, *Process Algebra*, Cambridge Tracts in Theoretical Computer Science 18, Cambridge University Press, 1990.
5. J. Bergstra, I. Bethke, and A. Ponse, *Process algebra with iteration and nesting*, Report P9314b, University of Amsterdam, Amsterdam, February 1994.
6. J. Bergstra and J. Klop, *A complete inference system for regular processes with silent moves*, in Proceedings Logic Colloquium 1986, F. Drake and J. Truss, eds., Hull, 1988, North-Holland, pp. 21–81. First appeared as: Report CS-R8420, CWI, Amsterdam, 1984.
7. B. Bloom, S. Istrail, and A. Meyer, *Bisimulation can't be traced: preliminary report*, in Conference Record of the Fifteenth Annual ACM Symposium on Principles of Programming Languages, 1988, pp. 229–239. Full version available as Technical Report 90-1150, Department of Computer Science, Cornell University, Ithaca, New York, August 1990. To appear in the *Journal of the ACM*.
8. R. Bol and J. Groote, *The meaning of negative premises in transition system specifications (extended abstract)*, in Proceedings 18th ICALP, Madrid, J. Leach Albert,

B. Monien, and M. Rodríguez, eds., vol. 510 of Lecture Notes in Computer Science, Springer-Verlag, 1991, pp. 481–494. Full version available as Report CS-R9054, CWI, Amsterdam, 1990.

9. S. Brookes, C. Hoare, and A. Roscoe, *A theory of communicating sequential processes*, J. Assoc. Comput. Mach., 31 (1984), pp. 560–599.
10. J. Groote and F. Vaandrager, *Structured operational semantics and bisimulation as a congruence*, Information and Computation, 100 (1992), pp. 202–260.
11. M. Hennessy, *Algebraic Theory of Processes*, MIT Press, Cambridge, Massachusetts, 1988.
12. M. Hennessy and R. Milner, *Algebraic laws for nondeterminism and concurrency*, J. Assoc. Comput. Mach., 32 (1985), pp. 137–161.
13. R. Milner, *On relating synchrony and asynchrony*, Tech. Report CSR–75–80, Department of Computer Science, University of Edinburgh, 1981.
14. ——, *A complete inference system for a class of regular behaviours*, J. Comput. System Sci., 28 (1984), pp. 439–466.
15. ——, *Communication and Concurrency*, Prentice-Hall International, Englewood Cliffs, 1989.
16. ——, *A complete axiomatisation for observational congruence of finite-state behaviors*, Information and Computation, 81 (1989), pp. 227–247.
17. D. Park, *Concurrency and automata on infinite sequences*, in 5th GI Conference, P. Deussen, ed., vol. 104 of Lecture Notes in Computer Science, Springer-Verlag, 1981, pp. 167–183.
18. G. Plotkin, *A structural approach to operational semantics*, Report DAIMI FN-19, Computer Science Department, Aarhus University, 1981.
19. R. d. Simone, *Higher-level synchronising devices in* MEIJE–*SCCS*, Theoretical Comput. Sci., 37 (1985), pp. 245–267.
20. F. Vaandrager, *Expressiveness results for process algebras*, in Proceedings REX Workshop on Semantics: Foundations and Applications, Beekbergen, The Netherlands, J. de Bakker, W. de Roever, and G. Rozenberg, eds., vol. 666 of Lecture Notes in Computer Science, Springer-Verlag, 1993, pp. 609–638.

Process Algebra with Partial Choice

J.C.M. Baeten
Department of Computer Science, Eindhoven University of Technology
P.O.Box 513, 5600 MB Eindhoven, The Netherlands

J.A. Bergstra
Programming Research Group, University of Amsterdam
Kruislaan 403, 1098 SJ Amsterdam, The Netherlands, and
Department of Philosophy, Utrecht University,
Heidelberglaan 8, 3584 CS Utrecht, The Netherlands

The objective of this paper is to bridge the gap between ACP and TCSP. To this end, ACP is extended with two non-deterministic choice operators in a setting of bisimulation semantics. With these operators, we can express safety properties of systems without the use of silent steps, and we can verify safety properties in a setting in which no assumption on fairness (or unfairness) has been made.

Note: This research was supported in part by ESPRIT basic research action 7166, CONCUR2. The second author is also partially supported by ESPRIT basic research action 6454, CONFER.

1. INTRODUCTION.

The objective of this paper is to bridge the gap between ACP [BEK84, BAW90] and TCSP [BRHR84, HOA85]. Earlier, in [BEKO88] and [BABK87], ready, failure and ready trace semantic models have been provided for ACP. However, these models do not take into account TCSP's rather sophisticated views on non-determinism versus choice. We agree with the observation underlying TCSP that externally influencible choice and non-determinism are to be distinguished and that more than one operator is needed.

After many experiments, we have concluded that it may be useful to extend ACP with two more operators:

$\sqcup\!\!\!\!+$ *static* or *partial* alternative composition

$\sqcup$ *collecting* alternative composition.

These operators exist together with the usual alternative composition operator

$+$ called *dynamic* alternative composition here.

A choice $p + q$ is made exactly when the first action of p or q is executed, so the choice is made at the root of the system. On the other hand, a choice $p \sqcup q$ is made a long time ago, before any action is executed in the system whatsoever. Finally, a choice $p \sqcup\!\!\!\!+ q$ is somewhere in between the previous actions, but we don't know where; $p \sqcup\!\!\!\!+ q$ behaves somewhere between $p \sqcup q$ and $p + q$.

The choice $p \sqcup\!\!\!\!+ q$ is called static because when control arrives at its root state probably just one option is left; the choice $p \sqcup q$ is called collecting because it represents $\{p, q\}$ (with the notational convention in mind that $p = \{p\}$). The choice $p \sqcup\!\!\!\!+ q$ is called partial because only partial information about the timing of the choice is available.

In [BAB94] we have provided a connection between the communication mechanisms of CCS (see [MIL80]) and ACP. This paper complements that one. It deviates from [BKO88] by being based on bisimulation entirely. In this way we hope to have it both ways: combine TCSP's sophistication concerning choice and non-determinism with the mathematical clarity of bisimulations, the cornerstone of CCS.

Further we find that the introduction of partial choice and collecting choice allows us in many cases to express safety properties of systems without the use of silent steps and to verify safety properties in a setting in which no assumption about fairness (or unfairness) has yet been made. Avoiding silent steps as well as fairness considerations are virtues of TCSP that we consider advantages indeed. We hope to have extended ACP in such a way that these virtues have become available in the ACP setting as well.

Moreover, our introduction of partial choice may shed new light on probabilistic choice (see [BABS92]) and the combination of probabilistic choice with other choice operators (cf. [JON93]).

Finally, our development is such that in the absence of silent steps, a model can also be found along the lines of the projective limit model of [BEK84], which is in fact an alternative presentation of the metric space model of [BAZ82].

2. PROCESS ALGEBRA WITH PARTIAL CHOICE.

We start by extending process algebra with the partial choice operator $\uplus$.

2.1 BASIC PROCESS ALGEBRA.

Assume that we have a (finite) set of constants A = {a,b,c,...} and a special constant $\delta \notin A$. Further, we have the binary operators + (dynamic choice), $\uplus$ (partial choice), · (sequential composition). The axioms for +,· are the standard axioms for BPA_δ, except that axiom A3 (X + X = X) is restricted to atomic actions. See table 1 ($a \in A$). A3 is restricted, because it does not hold anymore for processes involving the new choice operator. Note that the axioms in table 1 still provide a complete axiomatisation of the standard model of BPA_δ. This is a consequence of the following lemma.

$X+Y=Y+X$	A1
$(X+Y)+Z=X+(Y+Z)$	A2
$a+a=a$	AA3
$(X+Y)\cdot Z=X\cdot Z+Y\cdot Z$	A4
$(X\cdot Y)\cdot Z=X\cdot(Y\cdot Z)$	A5
$X+\delta=X$	A6
$\delta\cdot X=\delta$	A7

TABLE 1. BPA_δ with restricted A3.

2.2 LEMMA. Let t be a closed term over BPA_δ. Then A1,2,4,6, AA3 $\vdash t+t=t$.

PROOF: We use induction on the structure of basic terms (see e.g. [BAW90]).

i. Constants: for atoms, this is AA3, for δ it follows from A6.

ii. Prefix multiplication: $a\cdot x + a\cdot x = (a+a)\cdot x = a\cdot x$.

iii. Dynamic sum: $(x+y)+(x+y) = x+(y+(x+y)) = x+((x+y)+y) = x+(x+(y+y)) =$ $= (x+x)+(y+y) = x+y$.

2.3 PARTIAL SUM.

The partial alternative composition operator has the same laws as the dynamic alternative composition operator, except that we have the full analogue of axiom A3 of BPA ($X + X = X$), but no A6. As far as mutual distributivity of alternative composition operators is concerned, partial sum comes before dynamic sum. The partial sum operator obeys exactly the laws of the sum operator in [BABS92]. Thus it is the partial sum operator that can be extended to a probabilistic sum.

We call the basic theory with the two alternative composition operators $BPA_{\boxplus}$.

$X \boxplus Y = Y \boxplus X$	PAC1
$(X \boxplus Y) \boxplus Z = X \boxplus (Y \boxplus Z)$	PAC2
$X \boxplus X = X$	PAC3
$(X \boxplus Y) \cdot Z = X \cdot Z \boxplus Y \cdot Z$	PAC4
$(X \boxplus Y) + Z = (X + Z) \boxplus (Y + Z)$	PAC5

TABLE 2. Partial alternative composition.

2.4 REALISATION.

Now we want to express a notion of realisation or implementation. We use a partial order $\leq$ in order to express this. Thus, if $X \leq Y$, then X *realises* Y, i.e. X has less static non-determinism than Y. The central law is PAC6 in table 3.

$X \leq X \boxplus Y$	PAC6

TABLE 3. Realisation.

Thus, our axiom system contains equations and inequalities. We assume the standard properties of equality in reasoning about systems of equations. Similarly, we have the following properties for reasoning about inequalities:

$X \leq X$ reflexivity

$X \leq Y \wedge Y \leq X \Leftrightarrow X = Y$ antisymmetry

$X \leq Y \wedge Y \leq Z \Rightarrow X \leq Z$ transitivity

$X \leq Y \Rightarrow C[X] \leq C[Y]$ closed under contexts

$X \leq Y \Rightarrow \rho(X) \leq \rho(Y)$ substitutivity (ρ a mapping from variables to terms), i.e. we have a *partial order algebra* in the terminology of [HEN88].

2.5 LEMMA. For all closed terms t over $BPA_{\boxplus}$ we have $t \leq t + t$.

PROOF: For terms over BPA_{δ}, this is a consequence of lemma 2.2. It remains to consider the partial sum operator. By induction, assume the lemma holds for x, y, then:

$$x \boxplus y \leq x \boxplus y \boxplus (x + y) \boxplus (y + x) \leq (x + x) \boxplus (y + x) \boxplus (x + y) \boxplus (y + y) =$$
$$= ((x \boxplus y) + x) \boxplus ((x \boxplus y) + y) = (x + (x \boxplus y)) \boxplus (y + (x \boxplus y)) = (x \boxplus y) + (x \boxplus y).$$

We can give an intuition for this inequality as follows: t+t has more non-determinism than t, because different non-deterministic choices can have been made in the different copies of t.

2.6 SEMANTICS.

We define a process graph model, similar in spirit to the stratified model of [HAJ90, HAN91]. This model can also be seen as a special case of the modal transition systems of [LAT88]. We distinguish between a partial sum branching and a dynamic sum branching.

We define a *p-graph* to be a quintuple $\langle S, D, \rightarrow, \twoheadrightarrow, r\rangle$ such that:

- S is the set of *static* or *partial states*
- D is the set of *dynamic states*; S and D are disjoint
- $\rightarrow \subseteq D \times A \times S$ is the *labeled transition relation*, denoting dynamic choice
- $\twoheadrightarrow \subseteq S \times D$ is the *unlabeled transition relation*, denoting partial or static choice
- $r \in S$ is the *root node.*

Define $\mathbb{PG}$ to be the set of all p-graphs that satisfy the following restrictions:

i. S and D are countable
ii. the root node has at least one outgoing transition.

A static state without outgoing transitions is called an *end node*. A dynamic state without outgoing transitions is called a *deadlock node*. We write $s \twoheadrightarrow d$ iff $\langle s,d\rangle \in \twoheadrightarrow$, and $d \xrightarrow{a} s$ iff $\langle d,a,s\rangle \in \rightarrow$. The names of the states do not matter, so actually we are considering equivalence classes of p-graphs under graph isomorphism. This assumption enables us to assume that state sets are disjoint whenever this is convenient.

The interpretation function will assign a p-graph from $\mathbb{PG}$ to each process. We proceed to define the interpretation. First, constants.

$[\![a]\!] = \langle\{0,2\}, \{1\}, \{\langle 1,a,2\rangle\}, \{\langle 0,1\rangle\}, 0\rangle$

$[\![\delta]\!] = \langle\{0\}, \{1\}, \varnothing, \{\langle 0,1\rangle\}, 0\rangle.$

Fig. 1 illustrates these definitions. We use the following pictorial conventions: closed circles denote static states, open circles dynamic states, and a small incoming arrow denotes the root node.

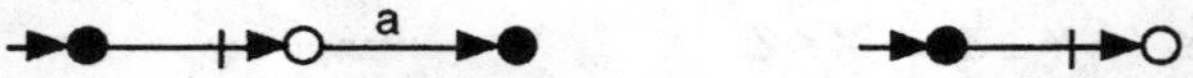

FIGURE 1. Constants.

<u>Partial sum.</u> We define $g \mathbin{+\!\!\!+} h$, for two p-graphs g,h. Let g,h be given with disjoint state sets. Then $g \mathbin{+\!\!\!+} h$ is obtained by creating a new root node r, and adding, for each unlabeled transition $s \twoheadrightarrow d$ where s is the root of g or h, a new unlabeled transition $r \twoheadrightarrow d$.

<u>Dynamic sum.</u> Let two p-graphs g,h be given with disjoint state sets. We obtain g+h by creating a new root node r, and creating a new dynamic node $\langle d,e\rangle$ for each pair consisting of a dynamic node d in g reachable from the root by an unlabeled arrow, e a similar node in h. We have unlabeled transitions $r \twoheadrightarrow \langle d,e\rangle$ for each such new dynamic node, and a labeled transition $\langle d,e\rangle \xrightarrow{a} s$ whenever there is a transition $d \xrightarrow{a} s$ or $e \xrightarrow{a} s$. As an example, we show $(a \mathbin{+\!\!\!+} b) + c$ in fig.2 (omitting unreachable nodes).

<u>Sequential composition.</u> Let two p-graphs g,h be given with disjoint state sets. We obtain g·h by appending a copy of h to each endnode of g.

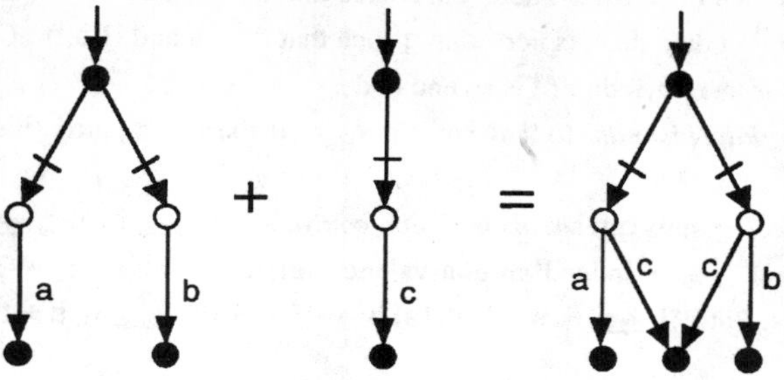

FIGURE 2. Dynamic sum.

2.6 STRUCTURED OPERATIONAL SEMANTICS.

We can also obtain a p-graph for each closed term by means of a structured operational semantics. We show the rules in table 4. Static states are given by terms (over $BPA_{\boxplus}$), dynamic states by boxed terms (over BPA_δ). Modulo the definition of bisimulation that follows, the structured operational semantics yields the same graphs as the definitions above. We will omit the proof of this fact.

$$a \nrightarrow \boxed{a} \qquad \boxed{a} \xrightarrow{a} \surd \qquad \delta \nrightarrow \boxed{\delta}$$

$$\frac{x \nrightarrow \boxed{x'}}{x \cdot y \nrightarrow \boxed{x' \cdot y}} \qquad \frac{\boxed{x} \xrightarrow{a} x'}{\boxed{x \cdot y} \xrightarrow{a} x' \cdot y} \qquad \frac{\boxed{x} \xrightarrow{a} \surd}{\boxed{x \cdot y} \xrightarrow{a} y}.$$

$$\frac{x \nrightarrow \boxed{x'},\ y \nrightarrow \boxed{y'}}{x + y \nrightarrow \boxed{x' + y'}}$$

$$\frac{\boxed{x} \xrightarrow{a} x'}{\boxed{x+y} \xrightarrow{a} x',\ \boxed{y+x} \xrightarrow{a} x'} \qquad \frac{\boxed{x} \xrightarrow{a} \surd}{\boxed{x+y} \xrightarrow{a} \surd,\ \boxed{y+x} \xrightarrow{a} \surd}$$

$$\frac{x \nrightarrow \boxed{x'}}{x \boxplus y \nrightarrow \boxed{x'},\ y \boxplus x \nrightarrow \boxed{x'}}$$

TABLE 4. Operational semantics of closed terms over $BPA_{\boxplus}$.

2.7 PARTIAL BISIMULATION.

Let two p-graphs g,h be given, and let R be a relation between nodes of g and nodes of h. R is a *partial bisimulation* if:

i. the roots are related
ii. if R(s,t) and s $\twoheadrightarrow\!\!\!\!/$ d then there is node e in h such that t $\twoheadrightarrow\!\!\!\!/$ e and R(d,e)
iii. if R(d,e) and d $\xrightarrow{a}$ s then there is node t in h such that e $\xrightarrow{a}$ t and R(s,t)
iv. if R(d,e) and e $\xrightarrow{a}$ t then there is node s in g such that d $\xrightarrow{a}$ s and R(s,t)
v. if R(s,t) then s is an end node iff t is an end node.

We say that g is *partially bisimilar* to h, denoted $g \underline{\leftarrow\!\!\!\leftrightarrow} h$, if there is a partial bisimulation from g to h.

We say that two p-graphs g,h are *bisimulation equivalent* , $g \underline{\leftarrow\!\!\!\leftrightarrow\!\!\!\rightarrow} h$, if $g \underline{\leftarrow\!\!\!\leftrightarrow} h$ and $h \underline{\leftarrow\!\!\!\leftrightarrow} g$. It is easy to see that $\underline{\leftarrow\!\!\!\leftrightarrow\!\!\!\rightarrow}$ is indeed an equivalence relation. Denote by $\mathbb{PG}/\underline{\leftarrow\!\!\!\leftrightarrow\!\!\!\rightarrow}$ the set of equivalence classes. Put $\mathbb{PG}/\underline{\leftarrow\!\!\!\leftrightarrow\!\!\!\rightarrow} \models s \le t$ iff $[\![s]\!] \underline{\leftarrow\!\!\!\leftrightarrow} [\![t]\!]$ and $\mathbb{PG}/\underline{\leftarrow\!\!\!\leftrightarrow\!\!\!\rightarrow} \models s = t$ if $[\![s]\!] \underline{\leftarrow\!\!\!\leftrightarrow\!\!\!\rightarrow} [\![t]\!]$.

2.8 THEOREM (SOUNDNESS). Let s,t be closed terms. Then $BPA_{\boxplus} \vdash s \le t \Rightarrow [\![s]\!] \underline{\leftarrow\!\!\!\leftrightarrow} [\![t]\!]$.
HINT OF PROOF: First we need to prove that $\mathbb{PG}/\underline{\leftarrow\!\!\!\leftrightarrow\!\!\!\rightarrow}$ is a partial order algebra. Then, it is sufficient to check each axiom separately.

We proceed to investigate the converse of theorem 2.8, i.e. the completeness of our axiomatisation. In order to do this, we first need the notion of a basic term.

2.9 DEFINITION. We define the set of basic terms $\mathcal{B}$ inductively, with the help of an intermediary set $\mathcal{B}_+$. In $\mathcal{B}$, the top operator is a partial sum and in $\mathcal{B}_+$ a dynamic sum.

i. $A \cup \{\delta\} \subseteq \mathcal{B}_+ \subseteq \mathcal{B}$
ii. $a \in A, t \in \mathcal{B} \Rightarrow a \cdot t \in \mathcal{B}_+$
iii. $t, s \in \mathcal{B}_+ \Rightarrow t + s \in \mathcal{B}_+$
iv. $t, s \in \mathcal{B} \Rightarrow t \boxplus s \in \mathcal{B}$.

An example of a basic term: $(a \cdot (b \boxplus (c + d)) + b) \boxplus \delta$.

Let p be a process in $BPA_{\boxplus}$. We say p has a *dynamic head normal form* ($p \in HNF+$) if there are $n,m \in \mathbb{N}$ with $n + m > 0$, $a_1, ..., a_n \in A$, $b_1, ..., b_m \in A \cup \{\delta\}$ and processes $p_1, ..., p_n$ such that

$$BPA_{\boxplus} \vdash p = a_1 \cdot p_1 + ... + a_n \cdot p_n + b_1 + ... + b_m.$$

We say a process q has a *partial head normal form* ($q \in HNF\boxplus$) if there is $k > 0$ and processes $q_1, ..., q_k$ in dynamic head normal form such that

$$BPA_{\boxplus} \vdash q = q_1 \boxplus ... \boxplus q_k.$$

Note that $\mathbb{PG}/\underline{\leftarrow\!\!\!\leftrightarrow\!\!\!\rightarrow} \models p = p + p$ holds for all $p \in HNF+$. It is easy to see that this law does not hold for all processes, as the counterexample $p \equiv a \boxplus b$ shows.

2.10 THEOREM: Let s be a closed term. Then there is a basic term t such that $BPA_{\boxplus} \vdash s = t$.
HINT OF PROOF: By term rewrite analysis. It is straightforward to show that the term rewrite system shown in table 5 is confluent and normalising. Thus, each term has a unique normal form. Each normal form is a basic term. The reduction to normal form constitutes a proof in $BPA_{\boxplus}$.

$(X+Y)\cdot Z \to X\cdot Z+Y\cdot Z$	RA4
$(X\cdot Y)\cdot Z \to X\cdot(Y\cdot Z)$	RA5
$\delta\cdot X \to \delta$	RA7
$(X \boxplus Y)\cdot Z \to X\cdot Z \boxplus Y\cdot Z$	RPAC4
$(X \boxplus Y) + Z \to (X+Z) \boxplus (Y+Z)$	RPAC5
$X + (Y \boxplus Z) \to (X+Y) \boxplus (X+Z)$	RPAC5'

TABLE 5. Rewrite system.

2.11 THEOREM (COMPLETENESS). Let s,t be closed terms. Then $[\![s]\!] \leftrightarrow\!\!\!\!\!\!\!\!\;{-} [\![t]\!] \Rightarrow BPA_{\boxplus} \vdash s \le t$

HINT OF PROOF: By 2.10, it is enough to consider basic terms. Using the structured operational semantics of 2.6, we show that for each basic term t we have:

- $t \nrightarrow \xrightarrow{a} t' \Leftrightarrow t' \in \mathcal{B} \wedge \exists t'' \in \mathcal{B}\, \exists s,s' \in \mathcal{B}_{+}\ ((PAC1,2 \vdash t = t'' \boxplus s \vee PAC1,2 \vdash t = s)$
  $\wedge (A1,2 \vdash s = s' + a\cdot t' \vee A1,2 \vdash s = a\cdot t'))$
- $t \nrightarrow \xrightarrow{a} \surd \Leftrightarrow \exists t'' \in \mathcal{B}\, \exists s,s' \in \mathcal{B}_{+}\ ((PAC1,2 \vdash t = t'' \boxplus s \vee PAC1,2 \vdash t = s)$
  $\wedge (A1,2 \vdash s = s' + a \vee A1,2 \vdash s = a))$

On the basis of these equivalences, the theorem follows easily.

2.12 ADDITIONAL OPERATORS.

$X \parallel Y = X \mathbin{|\!\!\lfloor} Y + Y \mathbin{|\!\!\lfloor} X$	
$a \mathbin{|\!\!\lfloor} X = a\cdot X$	
$a\cdot X \mathbin{|\!\!\lfloor} Y = a\cdot(X \parallel Y)$	
$(X \square Y) \mathbin{|\!\!\lfloor} Z = X \mathbin{|\!\!\lfloor} Z \;\square\; Y \mathbin{|\!\!\lfloor} Z$	for $\square \in \{+, \boxplus\}$

TABLE 6. Additional axioms for $PA_{\boxplus}$.

$a \mid b = b \mid a$	
$(a \mid b) \mid c = a \mid (b \mid c)$	
$a \mid \delta = \delta$	
$X \parallel Y = X \mathbin{|\!\!\lfloor} Y + Y \mathbin{|\!\!\lfloor} X + X \mid Y$	
$a \mathbin{|\!\!\lfloor} X = a\cdot X$	
$a\cdot X \mathbin{|\!\!\lfloor} Y = a\cdot(X \parallel Y)$	
$(X \square Y) \mathbin{|\!\!\lfloor} Z = X \mathbin{|\!\!\lfloor} Z \;\square\; Y \mathbin{|\!\!\lfloor} Z$	for $\square \in \{+, \boxplus\}$
$a\cdot X \mid b = (a \mid b)\cdot X$	
$a \mid b\cdot X = (a \mid b)\cdot X$	
$a\cdot X \mid b\cdot Y = (a \mid b)\cdot(X \parallel Y)$	
$(X \square Y) \mid Z = X \mid Z \;\square\; Y \mid Z$	for $\square \in \{+, \boxplus\}$
$X \mid (Y \square Z) = X \mid Y \;\square\; X \mid Z$	for $\square \in \{+, \boxplus\}$
$\partial_H(a) = a$	if $a \notin H$
$\partial_H(a) = \delta$	if $a \in H$
$\partial_H(X \square Y) = \partial_H(X) \;\square\; \partial_H(Y)$	for $\square \in \{+, \cdot, \boxplus\}$

TABLE 7. Additional axioms for $ACP_{\boxplus}$.

We sketch the extension of $BPA_{\sqcup\!\!+}$ with additional operators. First, free merge is presented in table 6. Next, in table 7, we have merge with communication and encapsulation. In both cases, $a \in A \cup \{\delta\}$.

2.13 RECURSION.

Finally, we will consider systems of recursive equations. Treatment of these is standard, see e.g. [BAW90]. We will only consider completely guarded equations in the sequel. As an open question, we leave the formulation of axioms or proof rules in order to deal with such systems. Thus, we will only use semantic reasoning, where infinite processes are concerned.

2.14 GRAPH MODEL.

Definition of parallel composition on the graph model is not so straightforward. We give the definition of merge with communication only for a restricted subset, for graphs in which each dynamic state has exactly one incoming transition. We can do this because each p-graph is bisimulation equivalent with such a graph (proof omitted). Then the definition goes as follows: let two p-graphs $g = \langle S_1, D_1, \rightarrow_1, \twoheadrightarrow_1, r_1\rangle$, $h = \langle S_2, D_2, \rightarrow_2, \twoheadrightarrow_2, r_2\rangle$ be given with disjoint state sets and with exactly one incoming transition for each dynamic node. The set of static nodes of $g \| h$ is $S_1 \times S_2$, the set of dynamic nodes $D_1 \times D_2$, the root is $\langle r_1, r_2\rangle$, we have $\langle s,t\rangle \twoheadrightarrow \langle d,e\rangle$ iff $s \twoheadrightarrow_1 d$ and $t \twoheadrightarrow_2 e$ and $\langle d,e\rangle \xrightarrow{a} \langle s,t\rangle$ if

- $d \xrightarrow{a}_1 s$ and $t \twoheadrightarrow_2 e$, or
- $e \xrightarrow{a}_2 t$ and $s \twoheadrightarrow_1 d$, or
- $d \xrightarrow{b}_1 s$, $e \xrightarrow{c}_2 t$ and $b \mid c = a \neq \delta$.

Next, the definition of encapsulation is straightforward. Let p-graph g be given. $\partial_H(g)$ is obtained from g by erasing all transitions $d \xrightarrow{a} s$ with $a \in H$.

We give a structured operational semantics for the additional operators in table 8 ($a,b,c \in A$). Since after a static step in a parallel composition, the component not chosen has to "take back" the static step, we have to remember the static nodes. This requires an operator with four arguments: $\_\boxed{\_\|\_}\_$, the inner arguments denoting the dynamic states, the outer ones the static states they came from. The last line gives an operational semantics for recursion: here $X = t_X$ is an equation in a recursive specification E.

$$\frac{x \nrightarrow \boxed{x'},\ y \nrightarrow \boxed{y'}}{x \| y \nrightarrow x\boxed{x' \| y'}y} \qquad \frac{\boxed{x'} \xrightarrow{a} x''}{x\boxed{x' \| y'}y \xrightarrow{a} x'' \| y,\ y\boxed{y' \| x'}x \xrightarrow{a} y \| x''}$$

$$\frac{\boxed{x'} \xrightarrow{a} \surd}{x\boxed{x' \| y'}y \xrightarrow{a} y,\ y\boxed{y' \| x'}x \xrightarrow{a} y} \qquad \frac{\boxed{x'} \xrightarrow{b} x'',\ \boxed{y'} \xrightarrow{c} y'',\ b \mid c = a}{x\boxed{x' \| y'}y \xrightarrow{a} x'' \| y''}$$

$$\frac{\boxed{x'} \xrightarrow{b} \surd,\ \boxed{y'} \xrightarrow{c} \surd,\ b \mid c = a}{x\boxed{x' \| y'}y \xrightarrow{a} \surd} \qquad \frac{\boxed{x'} \xrightarrow{b} x'',\ \boxed{y'} \xrightarrow{c} \surd,\ b \mid c = a}{x\boxed{x' \| y'}y \xrightarrow{a} x'',\ y\boxed{y' \| x'}x \xrightarrow{a} x''}$$

$$\frac{x \nrightarrow \boxed{x'}}{\partial_H(x) \nrightarrow \boxed{\partial_H(x')}} \qquad \frac{\boxed{x} \xrightarrow{a} x',\ a \notin H}{\boxed{\partial_H(x)} \xrightarrow{a} \partial_H(x')} \qquad \frac{\boxed{x} \xrightarrow{a} \surd,\ a \notin H}{\boxed{\partial_H(x)} \xrightarrow{a} \surd}$$

$$\frac{t_X \nrightarrow \boxed{y}}{X \nrightarrow \boxed{y}} \qquad \frac{\boxed{t_X} \xrightarrow{a} y}{\boxed{X} \xrightarrow{a} y} \qquad \frac{\boxed{t_X} \xrightarrow{a} \surd}{\boxed{X} \xrightarrow{a} \surd}$$

TABLE 8. Operational semantics of additional operators.

2.14 EXAMPLE. We illustrate the definition of parallel composition. We assume there is no communication.

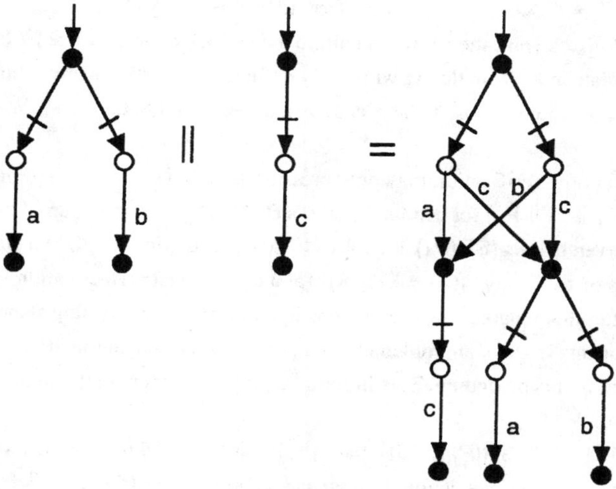

FIGURE 3.

3. IMPLEMENTATION.

If a process P can be written without the $\sqcup\!\!\sqcup$ operator, we call P *total*. If $P \le Q$, we say that P is a *realisation* of Q. If moreover P is total and P is computable, then we say that P is an *implementation* of Q.

3.1 STANDARD REALISATION.

We define the standard realisation function SR inductively ($a \in A \cup \{\delta\}$):

i. $SR(a) = a$

ii. $t \in HNF+ \Rightarrow SR(a \cdot t) = a \cdot SR(t)$

ii. $SR(a \cdot (t \sqcup\!\!\sqcup s)) = SR(a \cdot t) + SR(a \cdot s)$

iii. $SR(t + s) = SR(t) + SR(s)$

iv. $SR(t \sqcup\!\!\sqcup s) = SR(t) \sqcup\!\!\sqcup SR(s)$.

Note that since $a \cdot (t \sqcup\!\!\sqcup s) = (a + a) \cdot (t \sqcup\!\!\sqcup s) = a \cdot (t \sqcup\!\!\sqcup s) + a \cdot (t \sqcup\!\!\sqcup s) \ge a \cdot t + a \cdot s$, we always have $SR(p) \le p$. Moreover, if t is in dynamic head normal form, then SR(t) is total.

EXAMPLE: an unreliable channel, that may corrupt messages is given by the recursive equation

$$K = \sum_{d \in D} r_1(d) \cdot i \cdot (s_2(d) \sqcup\!\!\sqcup s_2(\perp)) \cdot K$$

The standard realisation satisfies $SR(K) = \sum_{d \in D} r_1(d) \cdot (i \cdot s_2(d) + i \cdot s_2(\perp)) \cdot SR(K)$.

3.2 DEFINITION. We call a process P *deadlockfree* iff P has a p-graph without a deadlock node.

3.3 PROPOSITION. Let $Y \le X$. If X is deadlockfree, then Y is deadlockfree.

HINT OF PROOF: Suppose not, then Y has a path to a deadlock node s. Since $[Y] \underline{\Leftrightarrow} [X]$, there is also a dynamic state in X bisimulating with s. By definition of partial bisimulation, this state can have no outgoing transitions. Thus, X has a deadlock node, contradiction.

3.4 NOTE. A method for verification may now proceed as follows. First, a system is described in the form $P = \partial_H(P_1 \parallel ... \parallel P_n)$ for certain processes P_i that might contain partial choice operators. Then, a proof is given that $\partial_H(SR(P_1) \parallel ... \parallel SR(P_n))$ is a solution for X, in a specification that is usually in terms of $\tau_I(X)$, say $\tau_I(X) = E(\tau_I(X))$ for a certain recursive equation E (here, τ_I is the abstraction operator, that renames internal actions into the silent step). Using standard realisation, each of the components is given an implementation, so that we get an automaton model. Often, the first step is skipped in this procedure. This introduces philosophical complications about the states of the specification.

If $\partial_H(SR(P_1) \parallel ... \parallel SR(P_n))$ fails the specification, we know that a very plausible implementation fails, so we are warned about the validity of $\partial_H(P_1 \parallel ... \parallel P_n)$. Often, that $\partial_H(SR(P_1) \parallel ... \parallel SR(P_n))$ satisfies the specification is proven under a general overall fairness assumption (which is quite reasonable in case of finite state systems). Then, if implementations $Q_i \le P_i$ are considered which are sometimes not fair, we must be careful: process $\partial_H(Q_1 \parallel ... \parallel Q_n)$ may contain an I-livelock that $\partial_H(SR(P_1) \parallel ... \parallel SR(P_n))$ does not show. An example of this is given by the unreliable channel in 3.1, used in an alternating bit protocol (as in 3.5), taking the implementation

$$Q = \sum_{d \in D} r_1(d) \cdot i \cdot s_2(\perp) \cdot Q$$

of the channel. Even in other cases, the proof of $\tau_I(X) = E(\tau_I(X))$ may use a kind of combined fairness which the Q_i cannot be supposed to have.

3.5 ALTERNATING BIT PROTOCOL.

Let D be a finite set of data. We use the standard read/send communication function given by $r_k(x) \mid s_k(x) = c_k(x)$ for communication port k and message x (and δ otherwise). We specify sender S, unreliable channels K,L and receiver R as in [BAW90].

$$S = S0 \cdot S1 \cdot S$$

$$Sb = \sum_{d \in D} r_1(d) \cdot Sb_d \qquad \text{for } b = 0,1.$$

$$Sb_d = s_2(db) \cdot ((r_6(1-b) + r_6(\perp)) \cdot Sb_d + r_6(b)) \qquad \text{for } b = 0,1,\ d \in D.$$

$$K = \sum_{d \in D, b \in B} r_2(db) \cdot i \cdot (s_3(db) \sqcup\!\!\!\!+ s_3(\perp)) \cdot K$$

$$L = \sum_{b \in B} r_5(b) \cdot i \cdot (s_6(b) \sqcup\!\!\!\!+ i \cdot s_6(\perp)) \cdot L$$

$$R = R1 \cdot R0 \cdot R$$

$$Rb = \Big(\sum_{d \in D} r_3(db) + r_3(\perp)\Big) \cdot s5(b) \cdot Rb \;+ \sum_{d \in D} r_3(d(1-b)) \cdot s_4(d) \cdot s_5(1-b) \qquad \text{for } b=0,1$$

$$ABP = t_I \circ \partial_H(S \parallel K \parallel L \parallel R),$$

where $H = \{r_k(x), s_k(x) : k \in \{2,3,5,6\}, x \in D \cup (D \times B) \cup B \cup \{\perp\}\}$ is the set of communication actions, $I = \{c_k(x) : k \in \{2,3,5,6\}, x \in D \cup (D \times B) \cup B \cup \{\perp\}\} \cup \{i\}$ is the set of internal actions, and t_I is the *pre-abstraction* operator (from [BAB88]), that renames all internal actions into t.

ABP is a partial process specifying the alternating bit protocol. Constructing the transition system for this process, we can derive the following recursive specification for ABP:

$$X = \sum_{d \in D} r_1(d) \cdot Y_d$$

$$Y_d = t \cdot t \cdot (t \cdot t \cdot t \cdot t \cdot t \cdot t \cdot Y_d \sqcup\!\!\!\!+ t \cdot s_4(d) \cdot Z) \qquad \text{for } d \in D.$$

$$Z = t \cdot t \cdot (t \cdot t \cdot t \cdot t \cdot t \cdot t \cdot Z \sqcup\!\!\!\!+ t \cdot X).$$

Adding more non-determinism, we can simplify this specification considerably. Consider the following recursive specification, and let process BUF1 be a solution for this specification:

$$X' = t \cdot X' \sqcup\!\!\!\!+ \sum_{d \in D} r_1(d) \cdot Y'_d \qquad Y'_d = t \cdot Y'_d \sqcup\!\!\!\!+ s_4(d) \cdot X' \qquad \text{for } d \in D.$$

By considering the p-graphs of these processes, we can derive ABP $\leq$ BUF1 holds in our model. It is an open question, how to derive this inequality on the basis of algebraic calculations.

3.6 FIFO QUEUES.

BUF1 is a general specification of a one-place buffer. It has many different realisations. We think that every one-place buffer described will be a realisation of this process. We can generalise even further, and present (without further comment) a specification (with input port 1 and output port 2) such that every unbounded or bounded buffer or queue will be a realisation of it. The variables are parametrised by sequences of data elements from D.

$$Q_{\varepsilon} = Q_{\varepsilon}^{t} \uplus Q_{\varepsilon}^{r} \uplus Q_{\varepsilon}^{rt} \qquad (\varepsilon \text{ empty sequence})$$

$$Q_{\sigma d} = Q_{\sigma d}^{t} \uplus Q_{\sigma d}^{r} \uplus Q_{\sigma d}^{rt} \uplus Q_{\sigma d}^{s} \uplus Q_{\sigma d}^{sr} \uplus Q_{\sigma d}^{st} \uplus Q_{\sigma d}^{srt} \qquad (\sigma \in D^*, d \in D)$$

$$Q_{\sigma}^{t} = t \cdot Q_{\sigma} \qquad (\sigma \in D^*)$$

$$Q_{\sigma}^{r} = \sum_{d \in D} r_1(d) \cdot Q_{d\sigma} \qquad (\sigma \in D^*)$$

$$Q_{\sigma}^{rt} = t \cdot Q_{\sigma} + \sum_{d \in D} r_1(d) \cdot Q_{d\sigma} \qquad (\sigma \in D^*)$$

$$Q_{\sigma d}^{s} = s_2(d) \cdot Q_{\sigma} \qquad (\sigma \in D^*, d \in D)$$

$$Q_{\sigma d}^{sr} = s_2(d) \cdot Q_{\sigma} + \sum_{e \in D} r_1(e) \cdot Q_{e\sigma d} \qquad (\sigma \in D^*, d \in D)$$

$$Q_{\sigma d}^{st} = s_2(d) \cdot Q_{\sigma} + t \cdot Q_{\sigma d} \qquad (\sigma \in D^*, d \in D)$$

$$Q_{\sigma d}^{srt} = s_2(d) \cdot Q_{\sigma} + t \cdot Q_{\sigma d} + \sum_{e \in D} r_1(e) \cdot Q_{e\sigma d} \qquad (\sigma \in D^*, d \in D).$$

4. PROCESS ALGEBRA WITH COLLECTING CHOICE.

In a setting where we also have collecting sum ⊔, some things change. The main difference is, that all axioms that involve a duplication of a variable turn into inequalities.

4.1 BASIC PROCESS ALGEBRA.

We start with BPA, so we have a (finite) set of constants A = {a,b,c,...}, a special constant $\delta \notin A$, and binary operators +, ⊔, $\uplus$, ·. Axioms A4, PAC3,4,5 are not valid anymore. The axioms in table 9 replace the ones of $BPA_{\uplus}$ in tables 1 and 2. Notice that the inequality version of PAC3, $X \leq X \uplus X$, is a direct consequence of PAC6.

$X + Y = Y + X$	A1
$(X + Y) + Z = X + (Y + Z)$	A2
$a + a = a$	AA3
$(X + Y)\cdot Z \leq X\cdot Z + Y\cdot Z$	A4≤
$(X\cdot Y)\cdot Z = X\cdot(Y\cdot Z)$	A5
$X + \delta = X$	A6
$\delta\cdot X = \delta$	A7
$X \boxplus Y = Y \boxplus X$	PAC1
$(X \boxplus Y) \boxplus Z = X \boxplus (Y \boxplus Z)$	PAC2
$(X \boxplus Y)\cdot Z \leq X\cdot Z \boxplus Y\cdot Z$	PAC4≤
$(X \boxplus Y) + Z \leq (X + Z) \boxplus (Y + Z)$	PAC5≤
$X \leq X \boxplus Y$	PAC6

TABLE 9. Axioms replacing $BPA_{\boxplus}$ in the presence of collecting sum.

Next, we show the axioms for the collecting alternative composition in table 10. This operator distributes both ways over sequential composition. This is an important difference with dynamic and partial choice. Replacing all + operators by $\sqcup$ operators gives us the traces of a process. Thus, we do not view trace theory as a homomorphic image of a bisimulation based process algebra, but rather obtain a set of traces by using collecting choice only. Note that dynamic and partial choice distribute over $\sqcup$ but not the other way around, thus the collecting choice has precedence (comes before) other forms of choice. In TCSP there is distribution both ways. We think that this two-way distribution is incompatible with the bisimulation model, and forces the use of failure semantics. Therefore, we do not include the other distributive law here.

As for partial choice, $X \sqcup \delta = X$, does not hold. This is because the choice has already been made, and so deadlock cannot be avoided if the wrong choice has been made. CAC8 expresses the idea that realisation reduces collecting non-determinism.

The axioms in tables 9 and 10 together give the theory $BPA_{\sqcup}$. If a process P can be written without the $\sqcup$ operator, we call P *connected*. Thus, in section 2 we treated the theory of the connected processes. Consistent with the terminology in section 3, if P can be written without $\boxplus$ and $\sqcup$, we call P *total*.

$X \sqcup Y = Y \sqcup X$	CAC1
$(X \sqcup Y) \sqcup Z = X \sqcup (Y \sqcup Z)$	CAC2
$X = X \sqcup X$	CAC3
$(X \sqcup Y)\cdot Z = X\cdot Z \sqcup Y\cdot Z$	CAC4
$X\cdot(Y \sqcup Z) = X\cdot Y \sqcup X\cdot Z$	CAC5
$(X \sqcup Y) + Z = (X + Z) \sqcup (Y + Z)$	CAC6
$(X \sqcup Y) \boxplus Z = (X \boxplus Z) \sqcup (Y \boxplus Z)$	CAC7
$X \leq X \sqcup Y$	CAC8

TABLE 10. Collecting alternative composition.

4.2 SEMANTICS.

In a setting with collecting sum, our semantic domain now consists of nonempty sets of p-graphs. Let $\mathbb{PPG}$ be the set of nonempty sets of p-graphs from $\mathbb{PG}$. The interpretation of the constants now becomes the singleton set consisting of the earlier interpretation.

For collecting sum, we simply put $[\![P \sqcup Q]\!] = [\![P]\!] \cup [\![Q]\!]$. For all other binary operators $\Box$ (so $\Box \in \{+, \cdot, \mathbin{\#}\}$) we put $[\![P \Box Q]\!] = \{g \Box h : g \in [\![P]\!], h \in [\![Q]\!]\}$.

We define partial bisimulation on $\mathbb{PPG}$ as follows: $G \underline{\leftarrow\!\!\!\rightarrow} H$ iff $\forall g \in G\ \exists h \in H\ g \underline{\leftarrow\!\!\!\rightarrow} h$. We can still obtain soundness as before. For basic terms, we need an extra layer for collecting sum at the top.

4.3 DEFINITION. We define an extended set of basic terms $\mathcal{B}_{\sqcup}$ by adding the following clauses to definition 2.9: i. $\mathcal{B} \subseteq \mathcal{B}_{\sqcup}$ ii. $t, s \in \mathcal{B}_{\sqcup} \Rightarrow t \sqcup s \in \mathcal{B}_{\sqcup}$.
An example of an extended basic term: $((a\cdot(b \mathbin{\#} (c + d)) + b) \mathbin{\#} \delta) \sqcup (a\cdot b \mathbin{\#} a\cdot(b \mathbin{\#} c))$.

4.4 THEOREM: Let s be a closed term. Then there is a basic term t such that $BPA_{\sqcup} \vdash s = t$.
SKETCH OF PROOF: By term rewrite analysis. We do this in two stages. First, we rewrite using the rules in table 11 below. This gives us a $\sqcup$-normal form, i.e. a term where all $\sqcup$-operators appear at the top level only (i.e. there is no operator other than $\sqcup$ above $\sqcup$ in the parse tree). Then, on the subterms below the $\sqcup$ operators, we use the rewrite rules of table 5, in 2.10.

$(X \sqcup Y)\cdot Z \to X\cdot Z \sqcup Y\cdot Z$	RCAC4
$X\cdot(Y \sqcup Z) \to X\cdot Y \sqcup X\cdot Z$	RCAC5
$(X \sqcup Y) + Z \to (X + Z) \sqcup (Y + Z)$	RCAC6
$X + (Y \sqcup Z) \to (X + Y) \sqcup (X + Z)$	RCAC6'
$(X \sqcup Y) \mathbin{\#} Z \to (X \mathbin{\#} Z) \sqcup (Y \mathbin{\#} Z)$	RPAC6
$X \mathbin{\#} (Y \sqcup Z) \to (X \mathbin{\#} Y) \sqcup (X \mathbin{\#} Z)$	RPAC6'

TABLE 11. Rewrite system.

4.5 LEMMA: For all closed $BPA_{\sqcup}$-terms t we have $BPA_{\sqcup} \vdash t \le t + t$.
PROOF: By 4.4, we may suppose $t \in \mathcal{B}_{\sqcup}$. We use induction on the structure of basic terms. All cases except the following are handled in lemma 2.5. Suppose the lemma holds for x, y, then:

$$x \sqcup y \le x \sqcup y \sqcup (x + y) \sqcup (y + x) \le (x + x) \sqcup (y + x) \sqcup (x + y) \sqcup (y + y) =$$
$$= ((x \sqcup y) + x) \sqcup ((x \sqcup y) + y) = (x + (x \sqcup y)) \sqcup (y + (x \sqcup y)) = (x \sqcup y) + (x \sqcup y).$$

4.6 THEOREM (COMPLETENESS). Let s,t be closed terms. Then $[\![s]\!] \underline{\leftarrow\!\!\!\rightarrow} [\![t]\!] \Rightarrow BPA_{\sqcup} \vdash s \le t$.

4.7 ADDITIONAL OPERATORS.

We show the axioms for $ACP_{\sqcup}$. The ones for $PA_{\sqcup}$ can be obtained easily from these. We see that the full expansion theorem is no longer valid. The way to expand the merge is to first get all collecting sums to the top level, factor them out, and then use the full expansion theorem on the connected subterms.

$a \mid b = b \mid a$	
$(a \mid b) \mid c = a \mid (b \mid c)$	
$a \mid \delta = \delta$	
$X \parallel Y \leq X \mathbin{\|\!\!\lfloor} Y + Y \mathbin{\|\!\!\lfloor} X + X \mid Y$	
$a \mathbin{\|\!\!\lfloor} X = a \cdot X$	
$a \cdot X \mathbin{\|\!\!\lfloor} Y = a \cdot (X \parallel Y)$	
$(X \square Y) \mathbin{\|\!\!\lfloor} Z \leq X \mathbin{\|\!\!\lfloor} Z \ \square\ Y \mathbin{\|\!\!\lfloor} Z$	for $\square \in \{+, \uplus\}$
$(X \sqcup Y) \mathbin{\|\!\!\lfloor} Z = X \mathbin{\|\!\!\lfloor} Z \sqcup Y \mathbin{\|\!\!\lfloor} Z$	
$X \mathbin{\|\!\!\lfloor} (Y \sqcup Z) = X \mathbin{\|\!\!\lfloor} Y \sqcup X \mathbin{\|\!\!\lfloor} Z$	
$(X \sqcup Y) \parallel Z = X \parallel Z \sqcup Y \parallel Z$	
$X \parallel (Y \sqcup Z) = X \parallel Y \sqcup X \parallel Z$	
$a \cdot X \mid b = (a \mid b) \cdot X$	
$a \mid b \cdot X = (a \mid b) \cdot X$	
$a \cdot X \mid b \cdot Y = (a \mid b) \cdot (X \parallel Y)$	
$(X \square Y) \mid Z \leq X \mid Z \ \square\ Y \mid Z$	for $\square \in \{+, \uplus\}$
$X \mid (Y \square Z) \leq X \mid Y \ \square\ X \mid Z$	for $\square \in \{+, \uplus\}$
$(X \sqcup Y) \mid Z = X \mid Z \sqcup Y \mid Z$	
$X \mid (Y \sqcup Z) = X \mid Y \sqcup X \mid Z$	
$\partial_H(a) = a$	if $a \notin H$
$\partial_H(a) = \delta$	if $a \in H$
$\partial_H(X \square Y) = \partial_H(X) \square \partial_H(Y)$	for $\square \in \{+, \cdot, \sqcup, \uplus\}$

TABLE 12. Axioms for $ACP_{\sqcup}$.

5. CONCLUSION.

We have extended ACP, in a setting of bisimulation semantics, with two additional choice operators: partial sum and collecting sum. This serves to bridge the gap between ACP and TCSP: we can combine TCSP's distinction between choice and non-determinism with the operational structure of bisimulations.

Further we found that the introduction of partial choice and collecting choice allows us, in some cases, to express safety properties of systems without the use of silent steps and to verify safety properties in a setting in which no assumption about fairness (or unfairness) has been made. These verifications take place in the model; an algebraic style of verification has not been proposed here. Avoiding silent steps as well as fairness considerations are virtues of CSP that we consider advantages indeed. We think we have extended ACP in such a way that these virtues have become available in the ACP setting as well.

We found that it is the partial sum operator, that extends nicely to a probabilistic sum operator. Thus, the theory presented here forms a possible basis for a theory involving probabilistic choice together with other forms of choice. This allows one to describe systems where we know the probability of some choices, but not of all choices.

REFERENCES.

[BAB88] J.C.M. BAETEN & J.A. BERGSTRA, *Global renaming operators in concrete process algebra,* I&C 78, 1988, pp. 205-245.

[BAB94] J.C.M. BAETEN & J.A. BERGSTRA, *On sequential composition, action prefixes and process prefix,* to appear in FAC 6 (3), 1994.

[BABK87] J.C.M. BAETEN, J.A. BERGSTRA & J.W. KLOP, *Ready trace semantics for concrete process algebra with priority operator,* The Computer Journal 30 (6), 1987, pp. 498-506.

[BABS92] J.C.M. BAETEN, J.A. BERGSTRA & S.A. SMOLKA, *Axiomatizing probabilistic processes: ACP with generative probabilities,* in Proc. CONCUR'92, Stony Brook (W.R. Cleaveland, ed.), LNCS 630, Springer Verlag 1992, pp. 472-485.

[BAW90] J.C.M. BAETEN & W.P. WEIJLAND, *Process algebra,* Cambridge Tracts in Theoretical Computer Science 18, Cambridge University Press 1990.

[BAZ82] J.W. DE BAKKER & J.I. ZUCKER, *Processes and the denotational semantics of concurrency,* I&C 54, pp. 70-120.

[BEK84] J.A. BERGSTRA & J.W. KLOP, *Process algebra for synchronous communication,* Inf. & Control 60, pp. 109-137.

[BEKO88] J.A. BERGSTRA, J.W. KLOP & E.-R. OLDEROG, *Readies and failures in the algebra of communicating processes,* SIAM J. of Comp. 17 (6), 1988, pp. 1134-1177.

[BRHR84] S.D. BROOKES, C.A.R. HOARE & W. ROSCOE, *A theory of communicating sequential processes,* JACM 31, 1984, pp. 560-599.

[HAN91] H. HANSSON, *Time and probability in formal design of distributed systems,* Ph.D. thesis, DoCS 91/27, Univ. of Uppsala 1991.

[HAJ90] H. HANSSON & B. JONSSON, *A calculus for communicating systems with time and probabilities,* in Proc. RTSS90, Orlando, IEEE Computer Society Press 1990.

[HEN88] M. HENNESSY, *Algebraic theory of processes,* MIT Press 1988.

[HOA85] C.A.R. HOARE, *Communicating sequential processes,* Prentice Hall 1985.

[JON93] B. JONSSON, *Probabilistic processes,* notes of a tutorial at CONCUR'93, Hildesheim 1993.

[LAT88] K.G. LARSEN & B. THOMSEN, *A modal process logic,* in Proc. LICS'88, 1988.

[MIL80] R. MILNER, *A calculus of communicating systems,* LNCS92, Springer 1980.

Probabilistic Simulations for Probabilistic Processes *

Roberto Segala and Nancy Lynch

MIT Laboratory for Computer Science
Cambridge, MA 02139

Abstract. Several probabilistic simulation relations for probabilistic systems are defined and evaluated according to two criteria: compositionality and preservation of "interesting" properties. Here, the interesting properties of a system are identified with those that are expressible in an untimed version of the Timed Probabilistic concurrent Computation Tree Logic (TPCTL) of Hansson. The definitions are made, and the evaluations carried out, in terms of a general labeled transition system model for concurrent probabilistic computation. The results cover weak simulations, which abstract from internal computation, as well as strong simulations, which do not.

1 Introduction

Randomization has been shown to be a useful tool for the solution of problems in distributed systems [1, 2, 12]. In order to support reasoning about probabilistic distributed systems, many researchers have recently focused on the study of models and methods for the analysis of such systems [3, 5, 7, 19–21]. The general approach that is taken is to extend to the probabilistic setting those models and methods that have already proved successful for non-probabilistic distributed systems.

In the non-probabilistic setting, labeled transition systems have become well accepted as a basis for formal specification and verification of concurrent and distributed systems. (See, e.g., [16, 17].) A transition system is an abstract machine that represents either an implementation (i.e., a physical device or software system), or a specification (i.e., a description of the required properties of an implementation). In order to extend labeled transition systems to the probabilistic setting, the main addition that is needed is some mechanism for representing probabilistic choices as well as nondeterministic choices [7, 19, 21].

In the non-probabilistic setting, there are two principal methods that are used for analyzing labeled transition systems: temporal logic (e.g. [18]), which is used to establish that a system satisfies certain properties, and equivalence or preorder relations (e.g., [8, 16, 17]), which are used to establish that one system "implements" another, according to some notion of implementation. Each equivalence or preorder preserves some of the properties of a system, and thus the use of a relation as a notion of implementation means that we are interested only in the properties that such a relation preserves.

Among the equivalences and preorders that have proved most useful are the class of *simulation* relations, which establish step-by-step correspondences between two systems. Bisimulation relations are two-directional relations that have proved fundamental in the process algebraic setting. Unidirectional simulations, such as refinement mappings and forward simulations, have turned out to be quite successful in formal verification of non-probabilistic distributed systems [10, 15, 16]. Thus, it is highly desirable to extend the use of simulations to the probabilistic setting.

---

* Supported by NSF grant CCR-89-15206, and CCR-92-25124, by DARPA contracts N00014-89-J-1988 and N00014-92-J-4033, and by ONR contract N00014-91-J-1046.

In this paper, we define several extensions of the classical bisimulation and simulation relations (both in their strong and weak versions), to the probabilistic setting. There are many possible extensions that could be made; it is important to evaluate the various possibilities according to objective criteria. We use two criteria: compositionality and preservation of "interesting" properties. The first requirement, compositionality, is widely accepted since it forms the basis of many modular verification techniques.

To make sense of the second requirement, it is necessary to be specific about what is meant by an "interesting" property. Here, we identify the interesting properties of a system with those that are expressible in an untimed version (PCTL) of the Timed Probabilistic concurrent Computation Tree Logic (TPCTL) of Hansson [7]; as discussed in [7], this logic is sufficiently powerful to represent most of the properties of practical interest. Thus, our second evaluation criterion is based on the types of PCTL formulas that a relation preserves. For the weak relations, i.e., the ones that abstract from internal computation, we use a new version of PCTL, called WPCTL, which abstracts from internal computation as well.

We define and evaluate our simulation relations in terms of a new general labeled transition system model for concurrent probabilistic computation, which borrows ideas from [7, 21]. The model distinguishes between probabilistic and nondeterministic choices but, unlike the Concurrent Markov Chains of [7, 21], does not distinguish between probabilistic and nondeterministic states. A *probabilistic automaton* is a labeled transition system whose transition relation is a set of pairs $(s, (\Omega, \mathcal{F}, P))$, where $(\Omega, \mathcal{F}, P)$ is a discrete[2] probability distribution over (action,state) pairs and a special symbol δ, representing deadlock. If δ is not an element of Ω and all the pairs of Ω have the same action, then a step is called *simple* and can be denoted by $s \xrightarrow{a} (\Omega', \mathcal{F}', P')$, where $(\Omega', \mathcal{F}', P')$ is a discrete probability distribution over states. The separation between nondeterministic and probabilistic behavior is achieved by means of *adversaries* (or schedulers), that, similar to [7, 19, 21], choose a next step to schedule based on the past history of the automaton. In our case, differently from [7, 19, 21], we allow an adversary to choose the next step randomly. Indeed, an external environment that provides some input essentially behaves like a randomized adversary.

Our first major result is that randomized adversaries do not change the distinguishing power of PCTL and WPCTL. Intuitively, the main reason for this result is that PCTL and WPCTL are concerned with probability bounds rather than exact probabilities.

We then redefine the *strong bisimulation* relation of [7, 13] in terms of our model, and also define a *strong simulation* relation that generalizes the simulation relation of [11], strengthening it a bit so that some liveness is preserved. We show that strong simulation preserves PCTL formulas without negation and existential quantification, and we show that the kernel of strong simulation preserves PCTL formulas without existential quantification. Next, we generalize the strong relations by making them insensitive to probabilistic combination of steps, i.e., by allowing probabilistic combination of several transitions in order to simulate a single transition. The motivation for this generalization is that the combination of transitions corresponds to the ability of an adversary to choose the next step probabilistically. Our second main result is that the new relations, called *strong probabilistic bisimulation* and *strong probabilistic simulation*, are still compositional and preserve PCTL formulas and PCTL formulas without negation and existential quantification, respectively.

Similar to the strong case, we define new relations that abstract from internal computation and we show that they preserve WPCTL. However, the straightforward generalization of the strong probabilistic relations, although compositional, does not guarantee that

[2] Discreteness is needed because of measurability issues.

WPCTL is preserved. For this reason we introduce other two relations, called *branching probabilistic bisimulation* and *branching probabilistic simulation*, which impose new restrictions similar to those of branching bisimulation [6]. Our third main result is that branching probabilistic bisimulation and branching probabilistic simulation are compositional and preserve PCTL formulas and PCTL formulas without negation and existential quantification, respectively, up to a condition about divergences.

We conclude with a discussion about some related work in [11]. In particular we show how the idea of *refinement* of [11] applies to our framework. We define a refinement preorder in the style of [11] for each simulation relation of this paper, and, surprisingly, we show that none of the new refinements is compositional. However, the counterexample that we present gives some insight for possible solutions to the problem.

The rest of the paper is organized as follows. Section 2 defines the standard automata of non-probabilistic systems; Section 3 introduces our probabilistic model; Section 4 introduces PCTL, defines its semantics in terms of our model, and shows that the distinguishing power of PCTL does not change by using randomized adversaries; Sections 5 and 6 study the strong and weak relations, respectively, on our probabilistic model, and show how they preserve PCTL formulas; Section 7 contains some concluding remarks concerning the refinement-based preorders of [11] and further work.

2 Automata

An *automaton* A consists of four components: a set $states(A)$ of states, a nonempty set $start(A) \subseteq states(A)$ of start states, an action signature $sig(A) = (ext(A), int(A))$ where $ext(A)$ and $int(A)$ are disjoint sets of external and internal actions, respectively, and a transition relation $steps(A) \subseteq states(A) \times acts(A) \times states(A)$, where $acts(A)$ denotes the set $ext(A) \cup int(A)$ of actions. Thus, an automaton is a state machine with labeled steps (also called transitions). Its action signature describes the interface with the external environment by specifying which actions model events that are visible from the external environment and which ones model internal events.

An *execution fragment* α of an automaton A is a (finite or infinite) sequence of alternating states and actions starting with a state and, if the execution fragment is finite, ending in a state, $\alpha = s_0 a_1 s_1 a_2 s_2 \cdots$, where each $(s_i, a_{i+1}, s_{i+1}) \in steps(A)$. Denote by $fstate(\alpha)$ the first state of α and, if α is finite, denote by $lstate(\alpha)$ the last state of α. Furthermore, denote by $frag^*(A)$ and $frag(A)$ the sets of finite and all execution fragments of A, respectively. An *execution* is an execution fragment whose first state is a start state. Denote by $exec^*(A)$ and $exec(A)$ the sets of finite and all execution of A, respectively. A state s of A is *reachable* if there exists a finite execution that ends in s. A finite execution fragment $\alpha_1 = s_0 a_1 s_1 \cdots a_n s_n$ of A and an execution fragment $\alpha_2 = s_n a_{n+1} s_{n+1} \cdots$ of A can be *concatenated*. In this case the concatenation, written $\alpha_1 \frown \alpha_2$, is the execution fragment $s_0 a_1 s_1 \cdots a_n s_n a_{n+1} s_{n+1} \cdots$. An execution fragment α_1 of A is a *prefix* of an execution fragment α_2 of A, written $\alpha_1 \leq \alpha_2$, if either $\alpha_1 = \alpha_2$ or α_1 is finite and there exists an execution fragment α_1' of A such that $\alpha_2 = \alpha_1 \frown \alpha_1'$.

3 The Basic Probabilistic Model

3.1 Probabilistic Automata

Definition 1. A *probability space* is a triplet $(\Omega, \mathcal{F}, P)$ where Ω is a set, $\mathcal{F}$ is a collection of subsets of Ω that is closed under complement and countable union and such that

$\Omega \in \mathcal{F}$, and P is a function from $\mathcal{F}$ to $[0,1]$ such that $P[\Omega] = 1$ and for any collection $\{C_i\}_i$ of at most countably many pairwise disjoint elements of $\mathcal{F}$, $P[\cup_i C_i] = \sum_i P[C_i]$.

A probability space $(\Omega, \mathcal{F}, P)$ is *discrete*[3] if $\mathcal{F} = 2^{\Omega}$ and for each $C \subseteq \Omega$, $P[C] = \sum_{x \in C} P[\{x\}]$. It is immediate to verify that for every discrete probability space there are at most countably many points with a positive probability measure.

The Dirac distribution over an element x, denoted by $\mathcal{D}(x)$, is the probability space with a unique element x.

The product of two discrete probability spaces $(\Omega_1, \mathcal{F}_1, P_1)$ and $(\Omega_2, \mathcal{F}_2, P_2)$, denoted by $(\Omega_1, \mathcal{F}_1, P_1) \otimes (\Omega_2, \mathcal{F}_2, P_2)$, is the discrete probability space $(\Omega_1 \times \Omega_2, 2^{\Omega_1 \times \Omega_2}, P)$, where $P[(x_1, x_2)] = P_1[x_1]P_2[x_2]$ for each $(x_1, x_2) \in \Omega_1 \times \Omega_2$. □

Definition 2. A *probabilistic automaton* M is an automaton whose transition relation $steps(M)$ is a subset of $states(M) \times Probs((acts(M) \times states(M)) \cup \{\delta\})$, where $Probs(X)$ is the set of discrete probability spaces $(\Omega, \mathcal{F}, P)$ where $\Omega \subseteq X$.

A probabilistic automaton M is *simple* if for each step $(s, (\Omega, \mathcal{F}, P)) \in steps(M)$ there is an action $a \in acts(M)$ such that $\Omega \subseteq \{a\} \times states(M)$. In such a case a step can alternatively be represented as $(s, a, (\Omega, \mathcal{F}, P))$ where $(\Omega, \mathcal{F}, P) \in Probs(states(M))$, and it is called a *simple step with action a*.

A probabilistic automaton is *fully probabilistic* if it has a unique start state and from each state there is at most one step enabled. □

Thus a probabilistic automaton differs from an automaton in that the action and the next state of a given transition are chosen probabilistically. The symbol δ that can appear in the sample space of each transition represents those situations where a system deadlocks. Thus, for example, it is possible that from a state s a probabilistic automaton performs some action with probability p and deadlocks with probability $1-p$.

A simple probabilistic automaton does not allow any kind of probabilistic choice on actions. Once a step is chosen, then the next action is determined and the next state is given by a random distribution. Several systems in practice can be described as simple probabilistic automata; indeed our analysis will focus on simple probabilistic automata and we will use general probabilistic automata only for the analysis of probabilistic schedulers.

A fully probabilistic automaton is a probabilistic automaton without nondeterminism; at each point only one step can be chosen..

The generative model of probabilistic processes of [5] is a special case of a fully probabilistic automaton; simple probabilistic automata are partially captured by the reactive model of [5] in the sense that the reactive model assumes some form of nondeterminism between different actions. However, the reactive model does not allow nondeterministic choices between steps involving the same action. By restricting simple probabilistic automata to have finitely many states, we obtain objects with a structure similar to that of the Concurrent Labeled Markov Chains of [7]; however, in our model we do not need to distinguish between nondeterministic and probabilistic states. In our model nondeterminism is obtained by means of the structure of the transition relation. This allows us to retain most of the traditional notation that is used for automata.

Definition 3. Given a probabilistic automaton M, its *nondeterministic reduction* $\mathcal{N}(M)$ is the automaton A obtained from M by transforming each transition $(s, (\Omega, \mathcal{F}, P))$ into the set of transitions (s, a, s') where $(a, s') \in \Omega$. In other words $\mathcal{N}(M)$ is obtained from M by transforming all the probabilistic behavior into nondeterministic behavior. □

[3] If we accept the Axiom of Choice, then the requirement $\mathcal{F} = 2^{\Omega}$ is sufficient.

The execution fragments and executions of a probabilistic automaton M are the execution fragments and executions of its nondeterministic reduction $\mathcal{N}(M)$. However, for the study of the probabilistic behavior of a probabilistic automaton, some more detailed structure is needed. Such a structure, which we call an *execution automaton*, is introduced in Section 3.2.
The next definition shows how it is possible to combine several steps of a probabilistic automaton into a new one. It plays a fundamental role for the definition of probabilistic adversaries and the definition of our probabilistic simulations.

Definition 4. Given a probabilistic automaton M, a finite or countable set $\{(\Omega_i, \mathcal{F}_i, P_i)\}_i$ of probability distributions of $Probs((acts(M) \times states(M)) \cup \{\delta\})$, and a positive weight p_i for each i such that $\sum_i p_i \leq 1$, the combination $\sum_i p_i(\Omega_i, \mathcal{F}_i, P_i)$ of the distributions $\{(\Omega_i, \mathcal{F}_i, P_i)\}$ is the probability space $(\Omega, \mathcal{F}, P)$ such that

- $\Omega = \begin{cases} \cup_i \Omega_i & \text{if } \sum_i p_i = 1 \\ \cup_i \Omega_i \cup \{\delta\} & \text{if } \sum_i p_i < 1 \end{cases}$
- $\mathcal{F} = 2^{\Omega}$
- for each $(a, s) \in \Omega$, $P[(a, s)] = \sum_{(a,s)\in\Omega_i} p_i P_i[(a, s)]$
- if $\delta \in \Omega$, then $P[\delta] = (1 - \sum_i p_i) + \sum_{\delta\in\Omega_i} p_i P_i[\delta]$.

A pair $(s, (\Omega, \mathcal{F}, P))$ is a *combined step* of M if there exists a finite or countable family of steps $\{(s, (\Omega_i, \mathcal{F}_i, P_i))\}_i$ and a set of positive weights $\{p_i\}_i$ with $\sum_i p_i \leq 1$, such that $(\Omega, \mathcal{F}, P) = \sum_i p_i(\Omega_i, \mathcal{F}_i, P_i)$ □

For notational convenience we write $s \xrightarrow{a} (\Omega, \mathcal{F}, P)$ whenever there is a simple step $(s, a, (\Omega, \mathcal{F}, P))$ in M, and we write $s \xrightarrow{a}_{\mathrm{P}} (\Omega, \mathcal{F}, P)$ whenever there is a simple combined step $(s, a, (\Omega, \mathcal{F}, P))$ in M. We extend the arrow notation to weak arrows ($\stackrel{a}{\Longrightarrow}$ and $\stackrel{a}{\Longrightarrow}_{\mathrm{P}}$) to state that $(\Omega, \mathcal{F}, P)$ is reached through a sequence of steps, some of which are internal. Formally, $s \stackrel{a}{\Longrightarrow} (\Omega, \mathcal{F}, P)$ ($s \stackrel{a}{\Longrightarrow}_{\mathrm{P}} (\Omega, \mathcal{F}, P)$) iff there exists a (combined) step $(s, (\Omega', \mathcal{F}', P'))$ such that $(\Omega, \mathcal{F}, P) = \sum_{(b,s')\in\Omega'} P'[(b, s')](\Omega_{(b,s')}, \mathcal{F}_{(b,s')}, P_{(b,s')})$, where, for each $(b, s') \in \Omega'$, if $b = a$ then $s' \Longrightarrow (\Omega_{(b,s')}, \mathcal{F}_{(b,s')}, P_{(b,s')})$ ($s' \Longrightarrow_{\mathrm{P}} (\Omega_{(b,s')}, \mathcal{F}_{(b,s')}, P_{(b,s')})$), and if $b \neq a$ then b is internal and $s' \stackrel{a}{\Longrightarrow} (\Omega_{(b,s')}, \mathcal{F}_{(b,s')}, P_{(b,s')})$ ($s' \stackrel{a}{\Longrightarrow}_{\mathrm{P}} (\Omega_{(b,s')}, \mathcal{F}_{(b,s')}, P_{(b,s')})$). The relation $\Longrightarrow$ ($\Longrightarrow_{\mathrm{P}}$) differs from $\stackrel{a}{\Longrightarrow}$ ($\stackrel{a}{\Longrightarrow}_{\mathrm{P}}$) in that it is also possible not to move from s, i.e., it is possible that $s \Longrightarrow \mathcal{D}(s)$ ($s \Longrightarrow_{\mathrm{P}} \mathcal{D}(s)$).
We now turn to the parallel composition operator for simple probabilistic automata, which is defined in the CSP style [9]. As outlined in [7], the definition of a parallel composition operator for general probabilistic automata is problematic. We will address the issue of a general parallel composition operator in further work.

Definition 5. Two simple probabilistic automata M_1, M_2 are *compatible* if

1. $int(M_1) \cap acts(M_2) = \emptyset$, and
2. $int(M_2) \cap acts(M_1) = \emptyset$.

The *parallel composition* $M_1 \| M_2$ of compatible simple probabilistic automata M_1, M_2 is the simple probabilistic automaton M such that

1. $states(M) = states(M_1) \times states(M_2)$
2. $start(M) = start(M_1) \times start(M_2)$
3. $ext(M) = ext(M_1) \cup ext(M_2)$
4. $int(M) = int(M_1) \cup int(M_2)$

5. $((s_1, s_2), a, (\Omega, \mathcal{F}, P)) \in \mathit{steps}(M)$ iff $(\Omega, \mathcal{F}, P) = (\Omega_1, \mathcal{F}_1, P_1) \otimes (\Omega_2, \mathcal{F}_2, P_2)$, where $\otimes$ denotes the product of probability spaces, such that
   (a) if $a \in \mathit{acts}(M_1)$ then $(s_1, a, (\Omega_1, \mathcal{F}_1, P_1)) \in \mathit{steps}(M_1)$, else $(\Omega_1, \mathcal{F}_1, P_1) = \mathcal{D}(s_1)$, and
   (b) if $a \in \mathit{acts}(M_2)$ then $(s_2, a, (\Omega_2, \mathcal{F}_2, P_2)) \in \mathit{steps}(M_2)$, else $(\Omega_2, \mathcal{F}_2, P_2) = \mathcal{D}(s_2)$. □

3.2 Schedulers and Adversaries

Several papers in the literature use schedulers, sometimes viewed as adversarial entities, to resolve the nondeterminism in probabilistic systems [4, 7, 14, 21]. An adversary is an object that schedules the next step based on the past history of a probabilistic automaton.

Definition 6. An *adversary* for a probabilistic automaton M is a function $\mathcal{A}$ taking a finite execution fragment α of M and returning a probability distribution over $\perp$ and a subset of the steps enabled from $\mathit{lstate}(\alpha)$. Formally, $\mathcal{A} : \mathit{frag}^*(M) \rightarrow \mathit{Probs}(\mathit{steps}(M) \cup \{\perp\})$, such that if $\mathcal{A}(\alpha) = (\Omega, \mathcal{F}, P)$ and $(s, (\Omega', \mathcal{F}', P')) \in \Omega$, then $s = \mathit{lstate}(\alpha)$. An adversary is *deterministic* if it returns only Dirac distributions, i.e., the next step is chosen deterministically. Denote the set of adversaries and deterministic adversaries for a probabilistic automaton M by $\mathit{Advs}(M)$ and $\mathit{DAdvs}(M)$, respectively. □

The symbol $\perp$ in Definition 6 is used to express the fact that an adversary is allowed not to schedule anyone at any point. Such an option is useful when some specific actions are meant to model input from the external environment.

Definition 7. An *adversary schema* for a probabilistic automaton M, denoted by Advs, is a subset of $\mathit{Advs}(M)$. If Advs is a proper subset of $\mathit{Advs}(M)$ then Advs is a *restricted adversary schema*, otherwise Advs is a *full adversary schema*. □

Adversary schemas are used to reduce the power of a class of adversaries. Note, for example, that the set of deterministic adversaries $\mathit{DAdvs}(M)$ is an example of a restricted adversary schema whenever M is not fully probabilistic. Throughout the rest of this paper we denote by $\mathit{Probabilistic}(M)$ the adversary schema where each adversary can choose $\perp$ on input α iff there is no step enabled in M from $\mathit{lstate}(\alpha)$, and we denote by $\mathit{Deterministic}(M)$ the set of deterministic adversaries of $\mathit{Probabilistic}(M)$.

The next step is to define what it means for a probabilistic automaton to run under the control of an adversary. Namely, suppose that M has already performed some execution fragment α and that an adversary $\mathcal{A}$ starts resolving the nondeterminism at that point. The result of the interaction between M and $\mathcal{A}$ is a fully probabilistic automaton, called an *execution automaton*, where at each point the only step enabled is the step due to the choice of $\mathcal{A}$. A similar construction appears in [21]. Unfortunately, the definition of an execution automaton is not simple since each state contains the past history of M.

Definition 8. An *execution automaton* H of a probabilistic automaton M is a fully probabilistic automaton such that

1. $\mathit{states}(H) \subseteq \mathit{frag}^*(M)$.
2. for each step $(\alpha, (\Omega, \mathcal{F}, P))$ of H there is a combined step $(\mathit{lstate}(\alpha), (\Omega', \mathcal{F}', P'))$ of M, called the *corresponding combined step*, such that $\Omega' = \{(a, s) | (a, \alpha a s) \in \Omega\}$, $\mathcal{F}' = 2^{\Omega'}$, and $P'[(a, s)] = P[(a, \alpha a s)]$ for each $(a, s) \in \Omega'$. If $q = \mathit{lstate}(\alpha)$, then denote $(\Omega, \mathcal{F}, P)$ by $(\Omega_q, \mathcal{F}_q, P_q)$.

3. each state of H is reachable, i.e., for each $\alpha \in states(H)$ there exists an execution of $\mathcal{N}(H)$ leading to state α. □

Now we can define formally what it means for a probabilistic automaton M to run under the control of an adversary $\mathcal{A}$.

Definition 9. Given a probabilistic automaton M, an adversary $\mathcal{A} \in Advs(M)$, and an execution fragment $\alpha \in frag^*(M)$, the execution $H(M, \mathcal{A}, \alpha)$ of M under adversary $\mathcal{A}$ with starting fragment α is the execution automaton of M whose start state is α and such that for each state q there is a step $(q, (\Omega, \mathcal{F}, P)) \in steps(H(M, \mathcal{A}, \alpha))$ iff $\mathcal{A}(q) \neq \mathcal{D}(\perp)$ and the corresponding combined step of $(q, (\Omega, \mathcal{F}, P))$ is obtained from $\mathcal{A}(q)$. □

3.3 Events

We define a probability space $(\Omega_H, \mathcal{F}_H, P_H)$ for each execution automaton H, so that it is possible to analyze the probabilistic behavior of an automaton once the nondeterminism is removed. The sample space Ω_H is the set of maximal executions of H, where a maximal execution of H is either infinite or finite and not extendible. Specific kinds of not extendible executions are finite executions α whose last state enables a step where δ has a positive probability. Those executions are denoted by $\alpha\delta$. Note that an execution of H can be uniquely denoted by the corresponding execution fragment of M. Thus, to ease the notation, we define an operator $\alpha\uparrow$ that takes an execution fragment of M and gives back the corresponding execution of H, and $\alpha\downarrow$ that takes an execution of H and gives back the corresponding execution fragment of M.

For each finite execution α of H, possibly extended with δ, let R_α, the rectangle with prefix α, be the set $\{\alpha' \in \Omega_H \mid \alpha \leq \alpha'\}$, and let $\mathcal{R}_H$ be the class of rectangles for H. The probability $\mu_H(R_\alpha)$ of the rectangle R_α is the product of the probabilities associated with each edge that generates α in H. This is well defined since the steps of H are described by discrete probability distributions. Formally, if $\alpha = q_0 a_1 q_1 \cdots q_{n-1} a_n q_n$, where each q_i is an execution fragment of M, then $\mu_H(R_\alpha) \triangleq P_{q_0}[(a_1, q_1)] \cdots P_{q_{n-1}}[(a_n, q_n)]$. If $\alpha = q_0 a_1 q_1 \cdots q_{n-1} a_n q_n \delta$, then $\mu_H(R_\alpha) \triangleq P_{q_0}[(a_1, q_1)] \cdots P_{q_{n-1}}[(a_n, q_n)] P_{q_n}[\delta]$. Standard measure theory results assert that there is a unique measure $\bar{\mu}_H$ that extends μ_H to the σ-algebra $\sigma(\mathcal{R}_H)$ generated by $\mathcal{R}_H$. $\mathcal{F}_H$ is then obtained from $\sigma(\mathcal{R}_H)$ by extending each event with any set of executions taken from 0-probability rectangles, and P_H is obtained by extending $\bar{\mu}_H$ to $\mathcal{F}_H$ in the obvious way. With this definition it is possible to show that any union of rectangles (even uncountable) is measurable. In fact, at most countably many rectangles have a positive measure.

In our analysis of probabilistic automata we are not interested in events for single execution automata. Whenever we want to express a property, we want to express it relative to any execution automaton. This is the purpose of event schemas.

Definition 10. An *event schema* e for a probabilistic automaton M is a function that associates an event of $\mathcal{F}_H$ with each execution automaton H of M. □

4 Probabilistic Computation Tree Logic

In this section we present the logic that is used for our analysis, and we give it a semantics based on our model. It is a simplification of the *Timed Probabilistic concurrent Computation Tree Logic* (TPCTL) of [7], where we do not consider time issues. Then, we show that randomized adversaries do not change the distinguishing power of the logic.

Consider a set of actions ranged over by a. The syntax of PCTL formulas is defined as follows:

$$f ::= a \mid \neg f \mid f_1 \wedge f_2 \mid \mathcal{IA}f \mid f_1\ EU_{\geq p}\ f_2 \mid f_1\ AU_{\geq p}\ f_2 \mid f_1\ EU_{>p}\ f_2 \mid f_1\ AU_{>p}\ f_2$$

Informally, the atomic formula a means that action a is the only one that can occur during the first step of a probabilistic automaton; the formula $\mathcal{IA}f$ means that f is valid for a probabilistic automaton M after making the first transition invisible; the formula $f_1\ EU_{\geq p}\ f_2$ means that there exists an adversary such that the probability of f_2 eventually holding and f_1 holding till f_2 holds is at least p; the formula $f_1\ AU_{\geq p}\ f_2$ means that the same property as above is valid for each adversary. For the formal semantics of PCTL we need two auxiliary operators on probabilistic automata.

Let M be a probabilistic automaton, a an action of M, and s a state of M. Then $M[(a,s)]$ is a probabilistic automaton obtained from M by adding a new state s', adding a new step $(s', a, \mathcal{D}(s))$, and making s' into the unique start state. In other words $M[(a,s)]$ forces M to start with action a and then reach state s.

Let M be a probabilistic automaton. Then $\overrightarrow{M}$ is obtained from M by adding a duplicate of each start state, by making the duplicate states into the new start states, and, for each step $s \xrightarrow{a} (\Omega, \mathcal{F}, P)$ of M, by adding a step $s' \xrightarrow{\tau} (\Omega, \mathcal{F}, P)$ from the duplicate s' of s, where τ is an internal action that cannot occur in any PCTL formula. In other words $\overrightarrow{M}$ makes sure that the first step of M is invisible.

Let M be a probabilistic automaton, and let α be an execution of M. Let $\sqsupseteq$ denote either $\geq$ or $>$. Then we define the satisfaction relations $M \models f$ and $\alpha \models_M g$ as follows

$M \models a$	iff each step leaving from a start state is a simple step with action a,
$M \models \neg f$	iff not $M \models f$,
$M \models f_1 \wedge f_2$	iff $M \models f_1$ and $M \models f_2$,
$\alpha \models_M f_1\ U\ f_2$	iff there exists $n > 0$ such that $\alpha = s_0 a_1 s_1 \cdots a_n s_n \frown \alpha'$, $M[(a_n, s_n)] \models f_2$, and for each i, $1 \leq i < n$, $M[(a_i, s_i)] \models f_1$,
$M \models \mathcal{IA}f$	iff $\overrightarrow{M} \models f$,
$M \models f_1\ EU_{\sqsupseteq p}\ f_2$	iff there exists an adversary $\mathcal{A}$ and a start state s_0 such that $P_H[e_{f_1 U f_2}(H)] \sqsupseteq p$, where $H = H(M, \mathcal{A}, s_0)$, and $e_{f_1 U f_2}(H)$ is the set of executions α' of Ω_H such that $\alpha' \downarrow \models_M f_1\ U\ f_2$,
$M \models f_1\ AU_{\sqsupseteq p}\ f_2$	iff for each adversary $\mathcal{A}$ and each start state s_0, $P_H[e_{f_1 U f_2}(H)] \sqsupseteq p$, where $H = H(M, \mathcal{A}, s_0)$, and $e_{f_1 U f_2}(H)$ is the set of executions α' of Ω_H such that $\alpha' \downarrow \models_M f_1\ U\ f_2$.

Note that for each execution automaton H the set $e_{f_1 U f_2}(H)$ can be expressed as a union of rectangles, and thus it is an element of $\mathcal{F}_H$. This guarantees that the semantics of PCTL is well defined. In the definition above we did not mention explicitly what kind of adversaries to consider for the validity of a formula. In [7] the adversaries are assumed to be deterministic. However, the semantics does not change by adding randomization to the adversaries. The intuitive justification of this claim is that if we are just interested in upper and lower bounds to the probability of some event to happen, then any probabilistic combination of events stays within the bounds. Moreover, deterministic adversaries are sufficient to observe the bounds.

Theorem 11. *For each probabilistic automaton M and each PCTL formula f, $M \models f$ relative to Deterministic(M) iff $M \models f$ relative to Probabilistic(M).*

Proof sketch. The proof is by induction on the structure of the formula f, and most of it is simple routine checking. Two critical points are the following: if $M \models f_1\ EU_{\sqsupseteq p}\ f_2$ relative to randomized adversaries, then we need to make sure that there exists at least a deterministic adversary that can be used to satisfy $f_1\ EU_{\sqsupseteq p}\ f_2$; if $M \models f_1\ AU_{\sqsupseteq p}\ f_2$ relative to deterministic adversaries, then we need to make sure that no probabilistic adversary would lead to a violation of $f_1\ AU_{\sqsupseteq p}\ f_2$. In both cases the idea is to convert a probabilistic adversary $\mathcal{A}$ for a probabilistic automaton M into a deterministic one such that the probability of $e_{f_1 U f_2}$ is increased (first case) or decreased (second case). □

We now show how to change the syntax and semantics of PCTL to abstract away from internal computation. The new logic is denoted by WPCTL. The syntax of WPCTL is the same as that of PCTL with the additional requirement that no internal action can occur in a formula. For the semantics of WPCTL, there are three main changes.

$M \models a$ iff each weak step leaving from a start state is labeled with action a,
$\alpha \models_M f_1\ U\ f_2$ iff there exists $n > 0$ such that $\alpha = s_0 a_1 s_1 \cdots a_n s_n \frown \alpha'$,
a_n is external, $M[(a_n, s_n)] \models f_2$, and for each $i, 1 \le i < n$,
if a_i is external, then $M[(a_i, s_i)] \models f_1$,
$M \models \mathcal{JA} f$ iff $\overset{\Rightarrow}{M} \models f$,

where $\overset{\Rightarrow}{M}$ hides the first external steps of M, i.e., it is obtained from M by duplicating all its states (and then removing the non-reachable ones at the end), by making the duplicates of the old start states into the new start states, by reproducing all the internal transitions in the duplicated states, and, for each external step $(s, a, (\Omega, \mathcal{F}, P))$ of M, by adding an internal step $(s', \tau, (\Omega, \mathcal{F}, P))$ from the duplicate s' of s, where τ is a new internal action. Note that the satisfaction relation for an execution is defined solely in terms of its external steps.

Theorem 12. *For each probabilistic automaton M and each WPCTL formula f, $M \models f$ relative to Deterministic(M) iff $M \models f$ relative to Probabilistic(M).* □

5 Strong Relations

In this section we analyze relations that are sensitive to internal computation. We formalize the bisimulations of [7] (strong bisimulation) and the simulations of [11, 13] (strong simulation) in our model, and we show that the kernel of strong simulation, which is coarser than strong bisimulation, preserves PCTL formulas that do not contain $EU_{\sqsupseteq p}$. We then introduce other two coarser relations that allow probabilistic combination of steps and continue to preserve PCTL formulas without $EU_{\sqsupseteq p}$. For convenience, throughout the rest of this paper we assume that no pair of probabilistic automata has any state in common.

Definition 13. Let $\mathcal{R}$ be an equivalence relation over a set X. Two probability spaces $(\Omega_1, \mathcal{F}_1, P_1)$ and $(\Omega_2, \mathcal{F}_2, P_2)$ of *Probs*(X) are $\mathcal{R}$-equivalent, written $(\Omega_1, \mathcal{F}_1, P_1) \equiv_{\mathcal{R}} (\Omega_2, \mathcal{F}_2, P_2)$, iff for each $[x_1]_{\mathcal{R}} \in \Omega_1/\mathcal{R}$ there exists an $[x_2]_{\mathcal{R}} \in \Omega_2/\mathcal{R}$ such that $x_1\ \mathcal{R}\ x_2$, for each $[x_2]_{\mathcal{R}} \in \Omega_2/\mathcal{R}$ there exists an $[x_1]_{\mathcal{R}} \in \Omega_1/\mathcal{R}$ such that $x_2\ \mathcal{R}\ x_1$, and for each $[x_1]_{\mathcal{R}} \in \Omega_1/\mathcal{R}$, $[x_2]_{\mathcal{R}} \in \Omega_2/\mathcal{R}$ such that $x_1\ \mathcal{R}\ x_2$, $\sum_{x \in \Omega_1 \cap [x_1]_{\mathcal{R}}} P[x] = \sum_{x \in \Omega_2 \cap [x_2]_{\mathcal{R}}} P[x]$. In other words $(\Omega_1, \mathcal{F}_1, P_1)$ and $(\Omega_2, \mathcal{F}_2, P_2)$ are $\mathcal{R}$-equivalent if they assign the same probability measure to each equivalence class of $\mathcal{R}$. □

Definition 14. A *strong bisimulation* between two simple probabilistic automata M_1, M_2 is an equivalence relation $\mathcal{R}$ over $states(M_1) \cup states(M_2)$ such that

1. each start state of M_1 is related to at least one start state of M_2, and vice versa;
2. for each $s_1 \mathcal{R} s_2$ and each step $s_1 \xrightarrow{a} (\Omega_1, \mathcal{F}_1, P_1)$ of either M_1, M_2, there exists a step $s_2 \xrightarrow{a} (\Omega_2, \mathcal{F}_2, P_2)$ of either M_1, M_2 such that $(\Omega_1, \mathcal{F}_1, P_1) \equiv_{\mathcal{R}} (\Omega_2, \mathcal{F}_2, P_2)$.

We write $M_1 \simeq M_2$ whenever $acts(M_1) = acts(M_2)$ and there is a strong bisimulation between M_1 and M_2. □

Condition 2 of Definition 14 is stated in [7, 13] in a different but equivalent way, i.e., for each equivalence class $[x]$ of $\mathcal{R}$, the probabilities of reaching $[x]$ from s_1 and s_2 are the same. The next definition is used to introduce strong simulations. It appears in a similar form in [11]. Informally, $(\Omega_1, \mathcal{F}_1, P_1) \sqsubseteq_{\mathcal{R}} (\Omega_2, \mathcal{F}_2, P_2)$ means that there is a way to split the probabilities of the states of Ω_1 between the states of Ω_2 and vice versa, expressed by a weight function w, so that the relation $\mathcal{R}$ is preserved. In other words the left probability space can be embedded into the right one up to $\mathcal{R}$.

Definition 15. Let $\mathcal{R} \subseteq X \times Y$ be a relation between two set X, Y, and let $(\Omega_1, \mathcal{F}_1, P_1)$ and $(\Omega_2, \mathcal{F}_2, P_2)$ be two probability spaces of $Probs(X)$ and $Probs(Y)$, respectively. Then $(\Omega_1, \mathcal{F}_1, P_1)$ and $(\Omega_2, \mathcal{F}_2, P_2)$ are in relation $\sqsubseteq_{\mathcal{R}}$, written $(\Omega_1, \mathcal{F}_1, P_1) \sqsubseteq_{\mathcal{R}} (\Omega_2, \mathcal{F}_2, P_2)$, iff there exists a weight function $w : X \times Y \to [0, 1]$ such that

1. for each $x \in X$, $\sum_{y \in Y} w(x, y) = P_1[x]$,
2. for each $y \in Y$, $\sum_{x \in X} w(x, y) = P_2[y]$,
3. for each $(x, y) \in X \times Y$, if $w(x, y) > 0$ then $x \mathcal{R} y$. □

Definition 16. A *strong simulation* between two simple probabilistic automata M_1, M_2 is a relation $\mathcal{R} \subseteq states(M_1) \times states(M_2)$ such that

1. each start state of M_1 is related to at least one start state of M_2;
2. for each $s_1 \mathcal{R} s_2$ and each step $s_1 \xrightarrow{a} (\Omega_1, \mathcal{F}_1, P_1)$ of M_1, there exists a step $s_2 \xrightarrow{a} (\Omega_2, \mathcal{F}_2, P_2)$ of M_2 such that $(\Omega_1, \mathcal{F}_1, P_1) \sqsubseteq_{\mathcal{R}} (\Omega_2, \mathcal{F}_2, P_2)$.
3. for each $s_1 \mathcal{R} s_2$, if $s_2 \xrightarrow{a}$, then $s_1 \xrightarrow{a}$.

We write $M_1 \sqsubseteq_{\mathrm{SS}} M_2$ whenever $acts(M_1) = acts(M_2)$ and there is a strong simulation between M_1 and M_2. The kernel of strong simulation is denoted by $\equiv_{\mathrm{SS}}$. □

The third requirement in the definition of a strong simulation is used to guarantee some minimum liveness requirements. It is fundamental for the preservation of PCTL formulas; however it can be relaxed by requiring s_1 to enable some step whenever s_2 enables some step.

Proposition 17. *$\simeq$ and $\sqsubseteq_{\mathrm{SS}}$ are compositional That is, for each M_1, M_2 such that $acts(M_1) = acts(M_2)$, and for each M_3 compatible with both M_1 and M_2, if $M_1 \simeq M_2$, then $M_1 \| M_3 \simeq M_2 \| M_3$, and if $M_1 \sqsubseteq_{\mathrm{SS}} M_2$, then $M_1 \| M_3 \sqsubseteq_{\mathrm{SS}} M_2 \| M_3$.* □

Lemma 18. *Let X, Y be two disjoint sets, $\mathcal{R}$ be an equivalence relation on $X \cup Y$, and let $(\Omega_1, \mathcal{F}_1, P_1)$ and $(\Omega_2, \mathcal{F}_2, P_2)$ be probability spaces of $Probs(X)$ and $Probs(Y)$, respectively, such that $(\Omega_1, \mathcal{F}_1, P_1) \equiv_{\mathcal{R}} (\Omega_2, \mathcal{F}_2, P_2)$. Then $(\Omega_1, \mathcal{F}_1, P_1) \sqsubseteq_{\mathcal{R}'} (\Omega_2, \mathcal{F}_2, P_2)$, where $\mathcal{R}' = \mathcal{R} \cap X \times Y$.* □

Lemma 18 can be used to prove directly that bisimulation is finer than simulation. The same observation applies to all the other pairs of relations that we define in this paper.

Theorem 19. *Let M_1 and M_2 be two simple probabilistic automata, and let f be a PCTL formula.*

1. *If $M_1 \simeq M_2$, then $M_1 \models f$ iff $M_2 \models f$.*
2. *If $M_1 \sqsubseteq_{SS} M_2$ and f does not contain any occurrence of $\neg$ and $EU_{\sqsupseteq p}$, then $M_2 \models f$ implies $M_1 \models f$.*
3. *If $M_1 \equiv_{SS} M_2$ and f does not contain any occurrence of $EU_{\sqsupseteq p}$, then $M_1 \models f$ iff $M_2 \models f$.*

Proof sketch. The proofs are by induction on the structure of f, where the nontrivial step is the analysis of $f_1\ AU_{\sqsupseteq p}\ f_2$. In this case it is enough to show that for each execution automaton H_1 of M_1 there exists an execution automaton H_2 of M_2 such that $P_{H_2}[e_{f_1 U f_2}(H_2)] \leq P_{H_1}[e_{f_1 U f_2}(H_1)]$. The execution automaton H_2 is built by reproducing the structure of H_1 via $\mathcal{R}$. We also need to ensure that H_2 is obtainable from some adversary, and for this part we need Condition 3 of Definition 16. We do not need to show that H_2 can be generated by a deterministic adversary (indeed this is false in general) because of Theorem 11. □

Example 1. PCTL formulas with occurrences of $EU_{\sqsupseteq p}$ are not preserved in general by $\equiv_{SS}$. Consider the two simple probabilistic automata below.

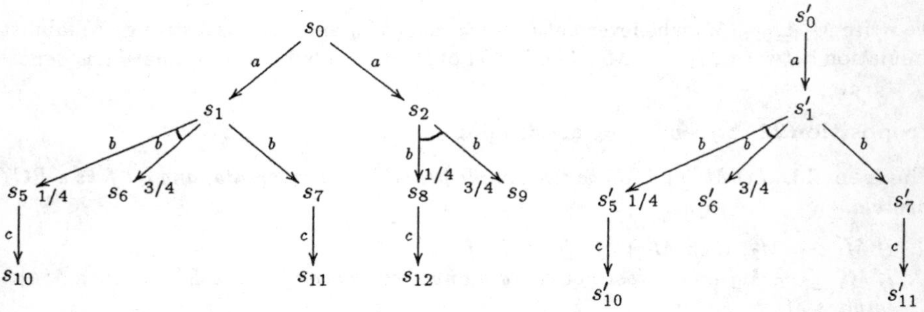

The two automata are strong simulation equivalent by matching each s_i with s_i' and by matching s_2, s_8, s_9, s_{12} to $s_1', s_5', s_6', s_{10}'$, respectively. However, the right automaton satisfies $true\ AU_{\geq 1}\ (a \wedge (true\ EU_{\geq 1/2}\ c))$, whereas the left automaton does not. □

Example 2. Consider the two probabilistic automata

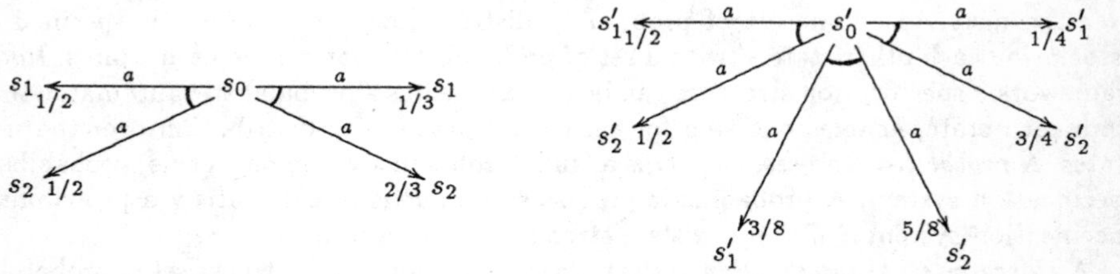

where s_0, s_0' are the start states, s_1, s_1' enable some step with action b, and s_2, s_2' enable some step with action c. The difference between the left and right automata is that the right automaton enables an additional step which is obtained by combining the two steps of the left automaton. Thus, the two automata satisfy the same PCTL formulas; however, there is no simulation from the right automaton to the left one since the middle step cannot be reproduced. □

Example 2 suggests two coarser relations where it is possible to combine several steps into a unique one. Note that the only difference between the new preorders and the old ones is the use of $\stackrel{a}{\longrightarrow}_{\mathrm{P}}$ (combined steps) instead of $\stackrel{a}{\longrightarrow}$ (regular steps) in Condition 2.

Definition 20. A *strong probabilistic bisimulation* between two simple probabilistic automata M_1, M_2 is an equivalence relation $\mathcal{R}$ over $states(M_1) \cup states(M_2)$ such that

1. each start state of M_1 is related to at least one start state of M_2, and vice versa;
2. for each $s_1 \; \mathcal{R} \; s_2$ and each step $s_1 \stackrel{a}{\longrightarrow} (\Omega_1, \mathcal{F}_1, P_1)$ of either M_1, M_2, there exists a combined step $s_2 \stackrel{a}{\longrightarrow}_{\mathrm{P}} (\Omega_2, \mathcal{F}_2, P_2)$ of either M_1, M_2 such that $(\Omega_1, \mathcal{F}_1, P_1) \equiv_{\mathcal{R}} (\Omega_2, \mathcal{F}_2, P_2)$.

We write $M_1 \simeq_{\mathrm{P}} M_2$ whenever $acts(M_1) = acts(M_2)$ and there is a strong probabilistic bisimulation between M_1 and M_2. □

Definition 21. A *strong probabilistic simulation* between two simple probabilistic automata M_1, M_2 is a relation $\mathcal{R} \subseteq states(M_1) \times states(M_2)$ such that

1. each start state of M_1 is related to at least one start state of M_2;
2. for each $s_1 \; \mathcal{R} \; s_2$ and each step $s_1 \stackrel{a}{\longrightarrow} (\Omega_1, \mathcal{F}_1, P_1)$ of M_1, there exists a combined step $s_2 \stackrel{a}{\longrightarrow}_{\mathrm{P}} (\Omega_2, \mathcal{F}_2, P_2)$ of M_2 such that $(\Omega_1, \mathcal{F}_1, P_1) \sqsubseteq_{\mathcal{R}} (\Omega_2, \mathcal{F}_2, P_2)$.
3. for each $s_1 \; \mathcal{R} \; s_2$, if $s_2 \stackrel{a}{\longrightarrow}$, then $s_1 \stackrel{a}{\longrightarrow}$.

We write $M_1 \sqsubseteq_{\mathrm{SPS}} M_2$ whenever $acts(M_1) = acts(M_2)$ and there is a strong probabilistic simulation between M_1 and M_2. The kernel of strong probabilistic simulation is denoted by $\equiv_{\mathrm{SPS}}$. □

Proposition 22. $\simeq_{\mathrm{P}}$ and $\sqsubseteq_{\mathrm{SPS}}$ are compositional. □

Theorem 23. *Let M_1 and M_2 be two simple probabilistic automata, and let f be a PCTL formula.*

1. *If $M_1 \simeq_{\mathrm{P}} M_2$, then $M_1 \models f$ iff $M_2 \models f$.*
2. *If $M_1 \sqsubseteq_{\mathrm{SPS}} M_2$ and f does not contain any occurrence of $\neg$ and $EU_{\sqsupseteq p}$, then $M_2 \models f$ implies $M_1 \models f$.*
3. *If $M_1 \equiv_{\mathrm{SPS}} M_2$ and f does not contain any occurrence of $EU_{\sqsupseteq p}$, then $M_1 \models f$ iff $M_2 \models f$.* □

Remark. Our strong probabilistic simulations provides us with a simple way to represent the closed interval specification systems of [11]. A *probabilistic specification system* of [11] is a state machine where each state is associated with a set of probability distributions over the next state. The set of probability distributions for a state s is specified by associating each other state s' with a set of probabilities that can be used from s. In our framework a specification structure can be represented as a probabilistic automaton that, from each state, enables one step for each valid probability distribution over the next states. A *probabilistic process system* is a "fully probabilistic" (in our terms) probabilistic specification system. A probabilistic process system P is said to satisfy a probabilistic specification system S if there exists a strong simulation from P to S.

A *closed interval specification system* is a specification system whose set of probability distributions are described by means of a lower bound and an upper bound, for each pair (s, s'), on the probability of reaching s' from s. Thus, the set of probability distributions that are allowed from any state form a polytope. By using our strong probabilistic simulation as satisfaction relation, it is possible to represent each polytope by means of its corners only. Any point within the polytope is then given by a combination of the corners. □

6 Weak Relations

The relations of Section 5 do not abstract from internal computation, whereas in practice a notion of implementation should ignore the internal steps of a system as much as possible. In this section we study the weak versions of the relations of Section 5, and we show how they relate to WPCTL. We introduce only the probabilistic version of each relation, since the others can be derived subsequently in a straightforward way. We start by presenting the natural extension of the probabilistic relations of Section 5; then, in order to preserve WPCTL, we introduce a branching version of the new relations using the basic idea of branching bisimulation [6].

Weak probabilistic bisimulations and weak probabilistic simulations can be defined in a straightforward manner by changing Condition 2 of Definitions 20 and 21 so that each step $s_1 \xrightarrow{a} (\Omega_1, \mathcal{F}_1, P_1)$ of an automaton can be simulated by a weak combined step $s_2 \overset{a\lceil ext(M_2)}{\Longrightarrow_{\mathrm{P}}} (\Omega_2, \mathcal{F}_2, P_2)$ of the other automaton, and by using weak steps in Condition 3. However, although the two weak relations are compositional, WPCTL formulas are not preserved by weak bisimulations and weak simulations. The key problem is that weakly bisimilar executions do not satisfy the same formulas. Consider the diagram below.

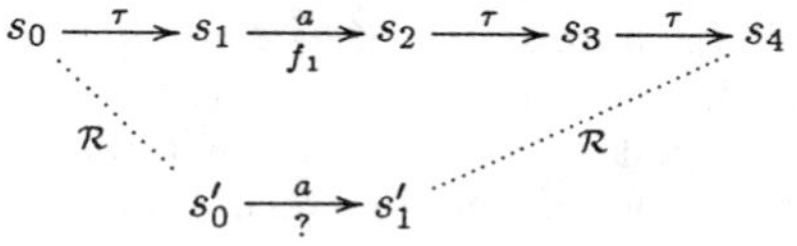

Since s_1' and s_2 are not necessarily related, it is not possible to deduce $M[(a, s_1')] \models f_1$ from $M[(a, s_2)] \models f_1$. To solve the problem we need to make sure that s_1' and s_2 are related, and thus we introduce the branching versions of our weak relations.

Definition 24. A *branching probabilistic bisimulation* between two simple probabilistic automata M_1, M_2 is an equivalence relation $\mathcal{R}$ over $states(M_1) \cup states(M_2)$ such that

1. each start state of M_1 is related to at least one start state of M_2, and vice versa;
2. for each $s_1 \mathcal{R} s_2$ and each step $s_1 \xrightarrow{a} (\Omega_1, \mathcal{F}_1, P_1)$ of either M_1, M_2, there exists a weak combined step $s_2 \overset{a\lceil ext(M_2)}{\Longrightarrow_{\mathrm{P}}} (\Omega_2, \mathcal{F}_2, P_2)$ of either M_1, M_2 such that $(\Omega_1, \mathcal{F}_1, P_1) \equiv_{\mathcal{R}} (\Omega_2, \mathcal{F}_2, P_2)$ and $s_2 \overset{a\lceil ext(M_2)}{\Longrightarrow_{\mathrm{P}}} (\Omega_2, \mathcal{F}_2, P_2)$ satisfies the branching condition, i.e., for each path α in the step $s_2 \overset{a\lceil ext(M_2)}{\Longrightarrow_{\mathrm{P}}} (\Omega_2, \mathcal{F}_2, P_2)$, and each state s that occurs in α, either $s_1 \mathcal{R} s$, $a\lceil ext(M_2)$ has not occurred yet, and each state s' preceding s in α satisfies $s_1 \mathcal{R} s'$, or for each $s_1' \in \Omega_1$ such that $s_1' \mathcal{R}\ lstate(\alpha)$, $s_1' \mathcal{R} s$.

We write $M_1 \simeq_{\mathrm{P}} M_2$ whenever $ext(M_1) = ext(M_2)$ and there is a branching probabilistic bisimulation between M_1 and M_2. □

Let a be an external action. Informally, the weak step $s_2 \overset{a\lceil ext(M_2)}{\Longrightarrow_{\mathrm{P}}} (\Omega_2, \mathcal{F}_2, P_2)$ in Definition 24 is obtained by concatenating several combined steps of M_2. Such a combination can be visualized as a tree of combined steps. The branching condition says that all the states of the tree that occur before action a are related to s_1, and that whenever a state s_2' of Ω_2 is related to some state s_1' of Ω_1, then all the states in the path from s_1 to s_2' that occur after action a are related to s_1' as well. In other words, each maximal path in the tree satisfies the branching condition of [6].

Definition 25. A *branching probabilistic simulation* between two simple probabilistic automata M_1, M_2 is a relation $\mathcal{R} \subseteq states(M_1) \times states(M_2)$ such that

1. each start state of M_1 is related to at least one start state of M_2;
2. for each $s_1 \mathrel{\mathcal{R}} s_2$ and each step $s_1 \xrightarrow{a} (\Omega_1, \mathcal{F}_1, P_1)$ of M_1, there exists a weak combined step $s_2 \overset{a\lceil ext(M_2)}{\Longrightarrow}_{\mathrm{P}} (\Omega_2, \mathcal{F}_2, P_2)$ of M_2 such that $(\Omega_1, \mathcal{F}_1, P_1) \sqsubseteq_{\mathcal{R}} (\Omega_2, \mathcal{F}_2, P_2)$, and $s_2 \overset{a\lceil ext(M_2)}{\Longrightarrow}_{\mathrm{P}} (\Omega_2, \mathcal{F}_2, P_2)$ satisfies the branching condition.
3. for each $s_1 \mathrel{\mathcal{R}} s_2$, if $s_2 \overset{a}{\Longrightarrow}$, then $s_1 \overset{a}{\Longrightarrow}$.

We write $M_1 \sqsubseteq_{\mathrm{BPS}} M_2$ whenever $ext(M_1) = ext(M_2)$ and there is a branching probabilistic simulation between M_1 and M_2. The kernel of branching probabilistic simulation is denoted by $\equiv_{\mathrm{BPS}}$. □

Proposition 26. *$\simeq_{\mathrm{P}}$ and $\sqsubseteq_{\mathrm{BPS}}$ are compositional.* □

To show that a WPCTL formulas are preserved by the different simulation relations, we need to guarantee that a probabilistic automaton is free from divergences with probability 1. The definition below allows a probabilistic automaton to exhibit infinite internal computation, but it requires that such a behavior can happen only with probability 0.

Definition 27. A probabilistic automaton M is *probabilistically convergent* if for each execution automaton H of M and each state q of H, the probability of diverging (performing infinitely many internal actions and no external actions) from q is 0, i.e., $P_H[\Theta_q] = 0$, where Θ_q is the set of infinite executions of H that pass through state q and that do not contain any external action after passing through state q. Note that Θ_q is measurable since it is the complement of a union of rectangles. □

Theorem 28. *Let M_1 and M_2 be two probabilistically convergent, simple probabilistic automata, and f be a WPCTL formula.*

1. *If $M_1 \simeq_{\mathrm{P}} M_2$, then $M_1 \models f$ iff $M_2 \models f$.*
2. *If $M_1 \sqsubseteq_{\mathrm{BPS}} M_2$ and f does not contain any occurrence of $\neg$ and $EU_{\sqsupseteq p}$, then $M_2 \models f$ implies $M_1 \models f$.*
3. *If $M_1 \equiv_{\mathrm{BPS}} M_2$ and f does not contain any occurrence of $EU_{\sqsupseteq p}$, then $M_1 \models f$ iff $M_2 \models f$.*

Proof sketch. Similar to the proof of Proposition 19. Here the construction of H_2 is much more complicated than in the proof of Proposition 19 due to the fact that we need to combine several weak steps. Moreover, we need to show that the branching requirement guarantees the preservation of properties between bisimilar executions. □

7 Concluding Remarks

7.1 Summary

We have extended some of the classical simulation relations to a new probabilistic model that distinguishes naturally between probabilistic and nondeterministic choice and that allows us to represent naturally randomized and/or restricted forms of scheduling policies. Our method of analysis was based on compositionality issues and preservation of PCTL and WPCTL formulas. We have observed that the distinguishing power of PCTL does not change if we allow randomization in the schedulers. Based on that, we have introduced a new set of relations whose main idea is that an automaton may combine probabilistically some of its steps in order to simulate another automaton.

7.2 Refinement-Based Preorders

In [11] there is a notion of refinement between probabilistic specification systems stating (up to a notion of image-finiteness that is not important here) that S_1 refines S_2 if each probabilistic process system that satisfies S_1, also satisfies S_2. The notion of refinement of [11] suggests a new set of preorders based on the relations of Sections 5 and 6. Namely, given a preorder $\sqsubseteq_X$, where X ranges over SS, SPS, WS, WPS, BS, BPS, we can define a new preorder $\preceq_X$ as

$$M_1 \preceq_X M_2 \text{ iff for each fully probabilistic } M_3, \text{ if } M_3 \sqsubseteq_X M_1 \text{ then } M_3 \sqsubseteq_X M_2.$$

Note, for example, that by restricting ourselves to the non-probabilistic case, $\preceq_{SS}$ reduces to complete trace inclusion (including internal actions), while $\preceq_{WS}$ and $\preceq_{BS}$ reduce to complete external trace inclusion. Moreover, by removing Condition 3 in the refinements of Sections 5 and 6, $\preceq_{SS}$ reduces to trace inclusion, while $\preceq_{WS}$ and $\preceq_{BS}$ reduce to external trace inclusion. Thus, we do not expect these preorders to be very strong. Unfortunately, none of the preorders above is compositional.

Example 3. Consider the three probabilistic automata

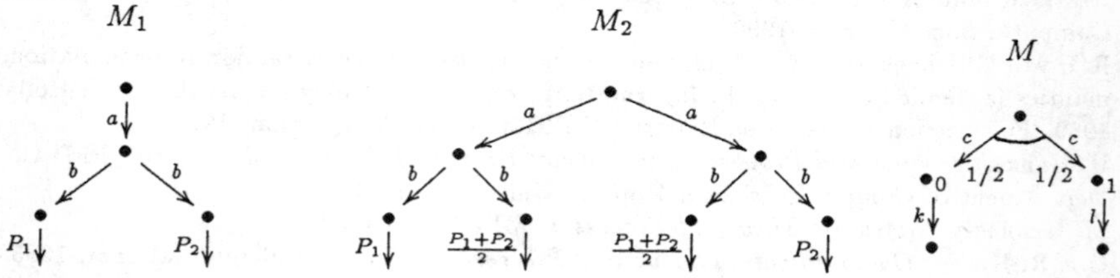

where the P_1-branch performs an action d and reaches a state enabling a new action z with probability 1/2, the P_2-branch performs an action d and reaches a state enabling a new action u with probability 1/2, and the $(P_1+P_2)/2$ branch is a combination of P_1 and P_2. It is easy to see that $M_1 \preceq_X M_2$ and $M_2 \preceq_X M_1$ for any X since any combination of steps of M_1 can be obtained from M_2 and vice versa; however, it is not the case that $M_1 \| M \preceq_X M_2 \| M$. Consider the following execution automaton H of $M_1 \| M$: perform action a followed by action c; if state $\bullet_0$ is reached then perform the left b in M_1, perform d, k and possibly z, else, perform the right b in M_1, perform d, l and possibly u. Clearly H satisfies $M_1 \| M$; however, H does not satisfy $M_2 \| M$ since in $M_2 \| M$ there is no state that corresponds to the state reached in H after the occurrence of action a. In other words H correlates the occurrence of action k with action z, and the occurrence of action l with action u, whereas such a correlation is not possible in $M_2 \| M$. □

Based on Example 3 we may conclude that the preorders $\preceq_X$ are not suitable for the compositional analysis of probabilistic systems. In reality it is still possible to use similar preorders if we make some additional assumptions. If we view a scheduler as an adversary, then we can say that an adversary chooses the next step based on the past history of the system. In Example 3 we have allowed the adversary to solve an internal choice of M_1 based on an internal condition of M. However, our counterexample would not work if the internal choices of each probabilistic automaton cannot be resolved by looking at the internal structure of other automata. A similar assumption is common for cryptographic systems.

7.3 Further Work

We are currently working on the definitions of adversary schemas that view other automata as black boxes, so that refinement-based preorders are compositional. Other further work includes finding some good notion of external behavior for probabilistic automata, studying applications of our results to the task of verifying probabilistic distributed systems, and extending our model and our results to handle real-time systems.

References

1. J. Aspnes and M.P. Herlihy. Fast randomized consensus using shared memory. *Journal of Algorithms*, 15(1):441–460, September 1990.
2. M. Ben-Or. Another advantage of free choice: completely asynchronous agreement protocols. In *Proceedings of the* 2nd *PODC*, August 1983.
3. I. Christoff. Testing equivalences for probabilistic processes. Technical Report DoCS 90/22, Ph.D. Thesis, Department of Computer Science, Uppsala University, Sweden, 1990.
4. M. Fischer and L. Zuck. Reasoning about uncertainty in fault tolerant distributed systems. In *Proceedings of the Symposium on Formal Techniques in Real-Time and Fault-Tolerant Systems*, LNCS 331, pages 142–158, 1988.
5. R.J. van Glabbeek, S.A. Smolka, B. Steffen, and C.M.N. Tofts. Reactive, generative, and stratified models of probabilistic processes. In *Proceedings* 5th *LICS*, pages 130–141. IEEE Computer Society Press, 1990.
6. R.J. van Glabbeek and W.P. Weijland. Branching time and abstraction in bisimulation semantics (extended abstract). In *Information Processing 89*, pages 613–618. North-Holland, 1989. Full version available as Report CS-R9120, CWI, Amsterdam, 1991.
7. H. Hansson. *Time and Probability in Formal Design of Distributed Systems.* PhD thesis, Department of Computer Science, Uppsala University, 1991.
8. M. Hennessy. *Algebraic Theory of Processes.* MIT Press, 1988.
9. C.A.R. Hoare. *Communicating Sequential Processes.* Prentice-Hall International, 1985.
10. B. Jonsson. Simulations between specifications of distributed systems. In *Proceedings CONCUR 91*, LNCS 527, pages 346–360, 1991.
11. B. Jonsson and K. G. Larsen. Specification and refinement of probabilistic processes. In *Proceedings of the 6th LICS*, July 1991.
12. E. Kushilevitz and M. Rabin. Randomized mutual exclusion algorithms revisited. In *Proceedings of the* 11th *PODC*, pages 275–284, 1992.
13. K. G. Larsen and A. Skou. Bisimulation through probabilistic testing. *Information and Computation*, 94(1):1–28, September 1992.
14. D. Lehmann and M. Rabin. On the advantage of free choice: a symmetric and fully distributed solution to the dining philosophers problem. In *Proceedings of the* 8th *POPL* pages 133–138, January 1981.
15. N.A. Lynch and M.R. Tuttle. Hierarchical correctness proofs for distributed algorithms. In *Proceedings of the* 6th *PODC*, pages 137–151, Vancouver, Canada, August 1987. A full version is available as MIT Technical Report MIT/LCS/TR-387.
16. N.A. Lynch and F.W. Vaandrager. Forward and backward simulations for timing-based systems. In *Proceedings of the REX Workshop "Real-Time: Theory in Practice"*, LNCS 600, pages 397–446, 1991.
17. R. Milner. *Communication and Concurrency.* Prentice-Hall International, 1989.
18. A. Pnueli. The temporal semantics of concurrent programs. *TCS*, 13:45–60, 1982.
19. A. Pnueli and L. Zuck. Verification of multiprocess probabilistic protocols. *Distributed Computing*, 1(1):53–72, 1986.
20. K. Seidel. Probabilistic communicating processes. Technical Report PRG-102, Ph.D. Thesis, Programming Research Group, Oxford University Computing Laboratory, 1992.
21. M. Y. Vardi. Automatic verification of probabilistic concurrent finite-state programs. In *Proceedings of 26th FOCS*, pages 327–338, Portland, OR, 1985.

Fully Abstract Characterizations of Testing Preorders for Probabilistic Processes

Shoji Yuen*
Dept. of Information Engineering
Nagoya University
Chikusa, Nagoya 464-01
Japan
yuen@nuie.nagoya-u.ac.jp

Rance Cleaveland** Zeynep Dayar
Dept. of Computer Science
North Carolina State University
Raleigh, NC 27695
USA
rance@csc.ncsu.edu
gr-zd@druid.csc.ncsu.edu

Scott A. Smolka***
Dept. of Computer Science
SUNY at Stony Brook
Stony Brook, NY 11794-4400
USA
sas@cs.sunysb.edu

Abstract. We present alternative characterizations of the testing preorders for probabilistic processes proposed in [CSZ92]. For a given probabilistic process, the characterization takes the form of a mapping from *probabilistic traces* to the interval $[0, 1]$, where a probabilistic trace is an alternating sequence of actions and probability distributions over actions. Our results, like those of [CSZ92], pertain to divergence-free probabilistic processes, and are presented in two stages: probabilistic tests without internal τ-transitions are considered first, followed by probabilistic tests with τ-transitions. In each case, we show that our alternative characterization is *fully abstract* with respect to the corresponding testing preorder, thereby resolving an open problem in [CSZ92]. In the second case, we use the alternative characterization to show that the testing preorder is actually an equivalence relation.

Finally, we give *proof techniques*, derived from the alternative characterizations, for establishing preorder relationships between probabilistic processes. The utility of these techniques is demonstrated by means of some simple examples.

1 Introduction

Communicating systems often exhibit behavior that is probabilistic or statistical in nature. For example, one may observe that a faulty communication link drops a message 2% of the time or that a site in a network is down with probability 0.05. Analyzing such behavior can thus lead to characterizations of the relative reliability of systems.

---

* Research performed while on leave at SUNY Stony Brook.

** Research supported in part by NSF/DARPA grant CCR-9014775, NSF grant CCR-9120995, ONR Young Investigator Award N00014-92-J-1582, and NSF Young Investigator Award CCR-9257963.

*** Research supported in part by NSF Grants CCR-9120995 and CCR-9208585, and AFOSR Grant F49620-93-1-0250DEF.

In [CSZ92], Cleaveland et al. proposed a testing preorder for probabilistic processes based on the probabilities with which a process passes tests. The basic idea is the following: probabilistic processes $\mathcal{P}$ and $\mathcal{Q}$ are related by the preorder if for all probabilistic tests $\mathcal{T}$, the probability by which $\mathcal{P}$ passes $\mathcal{T}$ is no greater than the probability by which $\mathcal{Q}$ passes $\mathcal{T}$.

The testing preorder of [CSZ92] ($\sqsubseteq$) can be viewed as an extension of the testing preorder of DeNicola and Hennessy [DH83, Hen88] for nondeterministic processes ($\sqsubseteq_{test}$) as follows. Let h be the homomorphism that maps probabilistic processes and tests onto nondeterministic processes and tests by erasing probabilities. Then, for probabilistic process $\mathcal{P}$ and probabilistic test $\mathcal{T}$, if $\mathcal{P}$ passes $\mathcal{T}$ with probability 1 (respectively a non-zero probability) in the probabilistic setting, then $h(\mathcal{P})$ *must* (respectively *may*) pass $h(\mathcal{T})$ in the nondeterministic setting. It follows that $\mathcal{P} \sqsubseteq \mathcal{Q}$ implies $h(\mathcal{P}) \sqsubseteq_{test} h(\mathcal{Q})$.

While intuitively appealing, the operational definition of $\sqsubseteq$ can be difficult to reason about. In particular, establishing that one process is related to another requires a consideration of the behavior of both processes in the context of all possible tests. Accordingly, it would be useful to have an alternative, more denotational characterization of $\sqsubseteq$ to ease the task of establishing relationships between probabilistic processes. Moreover, this characterization should be *fully abstract*, relating probablistic processes in exactly the same manner as $\sqsubseteq$.

In this paper, we present such a fully abstract characterization of $\sqsubseteq$, thereby resolving an open problem in [CSZ92]. For a given probabilistic process, our characterization takes the form of a mapping from *probabilistic traces* to the interval $[0,1]$, where a probabilistic trace is a sequence of pairs, with the first component of each pair being a probability distribution over actions and the second being an action.

Our results, like those of [CSZ92], pertain to divergence-free probabilistic processes, and are presented in two stages: probabilistic tests without internal τ-transitions are considered first, followed by probabilistic tests with τ-transitions. This two-tier presentation allows us to isolate the impact of τ-transitions in tests on the theory. In both cases, we show that our alternative characterization is fully abstract with respect to the corresponding testing preorder.

Using the alternative characterizations, we also show that the preorder in which tests may perform τ's is a strict refinement of the one in which tests are τ-free and, more importantly, that the finer preorder is actually an equivalence relation, a fact that went unnoticed in [CSZ92]. Finally, we give *proof techniques*, derived from the alternative characterizations, that further simplify the task of establishing the preorders. The utility of these techniques is demonstrated by means of some simple examples.

In terms of related work, Wu et al. [WSS94] propose a testing equivalence for *probabilistic I/O automata* and present a fully abstract characterization of the equivalence. In I/O automata [LT87], a distinction is made between *input* actions, which come from the environment and are always enabled, and *output* actions, which are locally controlled. Accordingly, in probabilistic I/O automata, separate probability distributions are associated with each input action and a single distribution with all locally controlled actions. Moreover, a *delay parameter*, which plays a key role in probabilistic I/O automata composition, is associated with each automaton state. Probabilistic I/O automata are thus a kind of hybrid of the reactive and generative models of probabilistic processes [vGSST90]. In contrast, processes and tests in our model are strictly generative and our approach is grounded in the testing theory of [DH83, Hen88].

Yi and Larsen [YL92] add an internal probabilistic choice operator to CCS in order to model processes that exhibit both nondeterministic and probabilistic behavior. They then develop a theory of probabilistic testing in which tests are processes that can perform a distinguished action to report success. In this framework a process passes a test with a set of probabilities, with each probability representing a possible resolution of the nondeterministic (i.e. nonprobabilistic) behavior of the process and the test. They also define testing preorders based on DeNicola and Hennessy's [DH83] testing preorder.

In [Chr90], Christoff also considers testing preorders for probabilistic processes and their fully abstract characterizations. His approach, however, differs from our own on a number of key points. Christoff's tests are deterministic and there is no notion of a success state; instead he defines testing preorders based on the probabilities induced by the interaction of a process and a test on L^*, where L is a set of observable actions. In our setting, tests are just probabilistic processes with a set of success states, and the testing preorder is defined in terms of the probability of a process successfully passing a test. Christoff's fully abstract models are defined in terms of "probabilistic functions" that map $(2^L - \emptyset)^* \times L^*$ to $[0,1]$. In our case, instead of using elements of $(2^L - \emptyset)^*$ we use sequences of probability distributions.

In [LS92a], Larsen and Skou introduce probabilistic bisimulation and a characterization of the probabilistic bisimulation as a form of probabilistic testing. In [LS92b], they define a calculus of reactive processes and an accompanying probabilistic modal logic. The latter is used to investigate compositional verification of probabilistic processes. Complete axiomatizations of both the calculus and logic are given. [HJ90] axiomatizes a calculus of *alternating processes* whose behavior alternates between nondeterministic and probabilistic states.

The structure of the rest of this paper is as follows. Section 2 reviews the testing theory of probabilistic processes put forth in [CSZ92]. Section 3 presents the alternative characterization of the testing preorder for tests without τ-transitions, and a proof technique derived from the characterization. Section 4 extends the results of the previous section to tests with τ-transitions and proves that the testing preorder is an equivalence relation. Section 5 concludes and contains our directions for future work.

2 Testing Preorders for Probabilistic Processes

In this section, we briefly review the testing theory of probabilistic processes from [CSZ92].

Definition 1 (Probabilistic Process). A *probabilistic process* is a 4-tuple (P, Act, μ, p_0) where

- P is a countable set of *states*;
- Act is a countable set of *observable actions* not containing the distinguished *silent action*, τ (we write Act_τ for $Act \cup \{\tau\}$);
- $\mu : P \times Act_\tau \times P \to [0,1]$, the *transition probability distribution function*, satisfies: for all $p \in P$, $\sum_{p' \in P, \alpha \in Act_\tau} \mu(p, \alpha, p') \in \{0,1\}$;
- $p_0 \in P$ is the *start state*.

We write **PP** for the class of all probabilistic processes; $p \xrightarrow{\alpha, \pi} p'$ if $\pi = \mu(p, \alpha, p') > 0$; and $\mu(p, \alpha)$ for $\sum_{p' \in P} \mu(p, \alpha, p')$. We refer to $p \xrightarrow{\alpha, \pi} p'$ as a *transition* of $\mathcal{P}$.

We require that probabilistic processes be *finite-branching* and *divergence-free*. A probabilistic process $\mathcal{P} = (P, Act, \mu, p_0)$ is finite-branching if for all $p \in P$ the set $\{\langle \alpha, p \rangle \mid \mu(p, \alpha, p') > 0\}$ is finite, while $\mathcal{P}$ is divergence-free if for no $p \in P$ is there an infinite sequence of states $p_0, p_1, \ldots$ with $p = p_0$ and $\mu(p_i, \tau, p_{i+1}) > 0$.

If A is a set then we call $d : A \to [0, 1]$ a *distribution over* A if $\sum_{a \in A} d(a) \in \{0, 1\}$; note the (slight) departure from traditional terminology. We denote the set of all distributions over A by D_A; thus, D_{Act_τ} represents the set of all distributions over Act_τ. If p is a state in process (P, Act, μ, p_0) then we write $\mu(p)$ for the distribution that satisfies $\mu(p)(\alpha) = \mu(p, \alpha)$ for all $\alpha \in Act_\tau$.

A *probabilistic test* is defined as a probabilistic process with a set of *successful* states.

Definition 2 (Probabilistic Test). A *probabilistic test* is a 5-tuple (T, Act, μ, t_0, S), where (T, Act, μ, t_0) is a probabilistic process and $S \subseteq T$. We write **T** for the class of all probabilistic tests.

Herewith, we restrict probabilistic tests to be *finite* in the sense that there exists no infinite sequence of transitions from any state. We also drop the adjective "probabilistic" when no confusion arises.

The preorder studied in this paper relates processes on the basis of the probabilities with which they pass tests. To define this probability formally, we introduce *interaction systems*.

Definition 3 (Interaction System). Let $\mathcal{P} = (P, Act, \mu_P, p_0)$ be a process and $\mathcal{T} = (T, Act, \mu_T, t_0, S)$ be a test. The *interaction system* for $\mathcal{P}$ and $\mathcal{T}$, $\mathcal{P} \| \mathcal{T}$, is of the form $(P \times T, Act, \mu_I, \langle p_0, t_0 \rangle)$ where μ_I is defined as follows. First let the *normalization function* $\nu : P \times T \to [0, 1]$ be given by:

$$\nu(p, t) = \Big(\sum_{\alpha \in Act} \mu_P(p, \alpha) \cdot \mu_T(t, \alpha)\Big) + \mu_P(p, \tau) + \mu_T(t, \tau) - \mu_P(p, \tau) \cdot \mu_T(t, \tau).$$

Then:

$$\mu_I(\langle p, t \rangle, \alpha, \langle p', t' \rangle) = \begin{cases} 0 & \text{if } \nu(p, t) = 0 \\ \frac{\mu_P(p, \alpha, p') \cdot (1 - \mu_T(t, \tau))}{\nu(p, t)} & \text{if } t = t',\ \nu(p, t) \neq 0, \text{ and } \alpha = \tau \\ \frac{\mu_P(t, \alpha, t') \cdot (1 - \mu_P(p, \tau))}{\nu(p, t)} & \text{if } p = p',\ \nu(p, t) \neq 0, \text{ and } \alpha = \tau \\ \frac{\mu_P(p, \alpha, p') \cdot \mu_T(t, \alpha, t')}{\nu(p, t)} & \text{otherwise} \end{cases}$$

Note that an interaction system has the same form as a process, and hence all the notation defined for processes may also be applied to interaction systems. Intuitively, we wish to view processes and tests as *reactive systems*; thus, if in the course of applying a test to a process an interaction between the two is possible, then some interaction is guaranteed to take place. The definition of interaction system captures this notion: the normalization factor may be seen as the total probability that an interaction happens, and this probability is used to condition the probabilities of individual interactions.

An interaction system can also be interpreted in terms of a coin-flipping game. $\mathcal{P}$ and $\mathcal{T}$, in states p and t, flip Act-labeled coins weighted according to $\mu_P(p)$ and $\mu_T(t)$, respectively. If the actions, which can be τ, indicated by the coins are same, then the test and the process synchronize on the action and the interaction system performs a transition. If the coin of the process indicates τ and the coin of the test does not, then the process does its τ independently, and vice versa. Finally, if the actions are different, and neither is τ, then the coins are flipped again.

In order to define the probability with which a process passes a test, we first introduce the notion of a computation in an interaction system.

Definition 4. Let $\mathcal{P} = (P, Act, \mu_P, p_0)$ be a process and $\mathcal{T} = (T, Act, \mu_T, t_0, S)$ a test, with $\mathcal{P}||\mathcal{T}$ the associated interaction system.

- We call $\langle p, t \rangle \in P \times T$ a *configuration*. A configuration $\langle p, t \rangle$ is *successful* if $t \in S$.
- A *computation* from a configuration $\langle p, t \rangle$ is a maximal sequence of the form
$$\langle p, t \rangle \xrightarrow{\alpha_1, \pi_1} \langle p_1, t_1 \rangle \xrightarrow{\alpha_2, \pi_2} \cdots \xrightarrow{\alpha_n, \pi_n} \langle p_n, t_n \rangle$$
where no configuration $\langle p_i, t_i \rangle$ is successful for $0 \le i < n$. Such a computation is *successful* if $\langle p_n, t_n \rangle$ is successful. For a configuration $\langle p, t \rangle$, let $\mathcal{C}_{\langle p,t \rangle}$ be the set of all computations beginning with $\langle p, t \rangle$, and let $\mathcal{S}_{\langle p,t \rangle} \subseteq \mathcal{C}_{\langle p,t \rangle}$ represent the set of all such successful computations. In addition, we use $\mathcal{C}_{\mathcal{P}||\mathcal{T}}$ and $\mathcal{S}_{\mathcal{P}||\mathcal{T}}$ to denote the sets $\mathcal{C}_{\langle p_0,t_0 \rangle}$ and $\mathcal{S}_{\langle p_0,t_0 \rangle}$, respectively.
- Let C be the above computation from $\langle p, t \rangle$. The the sequence F of transitions given by
$$F = \langle p, t \rangle \xrightarrow{\alpha_1, \pi_1} \langle p_1, t_1 \rangle \xrightarrow{\alpha_2, \pi_2} \cdots \xrightarrow{\alpha_m, \pi_m} \langle p_m, t_m \rangle$$
is said to be a *prefix* of C, written $F \preceq C$, if $m \le n$. (Note that F is not necessarily a computation.)
- Let C be a computation. Then $Pr(C) \in [0, 1]$ may be defined inductively as follows.
$$Pr(\langle p, t \rangle) = 1$$
$$Pr(\langle p, t \rangle \xrightarrow{\alpha, \pi} C') = \pi \cdot Pr(C')$$
If $\mathcal{C} \subseteq \mathcal{C}_{\langle p,t \rangle}$ for some $\langle p, t \rangle$ then we define $Pr(\mathcal{C}) = \sum_{C \in \mathcal{C}} Pr(C)$.

Intuitively, $Pr(C)$ records the probability that the process and test engage in computation C, starting from the initial configuration of C. It is straightforward to establish that for any configuration $\langle p, t \rangle$, Pr is a probability distribution over $\mathcal{C}_{\langle p,t \rangle}$. The probability with which a process passes a test then becomes the cumulative probability of the successful computations in the interaction system.

Definition 5. Let $\mathcal{P} = (P, Act, \mu_P, p_0)$ be a process and $\mathcal{T} = (T, Act, \mu_T, t_0, S)$ be a test. For $\pi \in [0, 1]$ we define the following predicates:

- p $\textit{pass}_\pi$ t if $Pr(\mathcal{S}_{p||t}) \ge \pi$
- $\mathcal{P}$ $\textit{pass}_\pi$ $\mathcal{T}$ if p_0 $\textit{pass}_\pi$ t_0

$\mathcal{P}\ pass_\pi\ \mathcal{T}$ holds if $\mathcal{P}$ has successful computations from $\langle p_0, t_0 \rangle$ in $\mathcal{P}||\mathcal{T}$ with total probability at least π. We now may define the testing preorder with respect to a set of tests as follows.

Definition 6 (Testing Preorder for Probablistic Processes). Let $\mathcal{E}$ be a class of probabilistic tests, and let $\mathcal{P} = (P, Act, \mu_P, p_0)$ and $\mathcal{Q} = (Q, Act, \mu_Q, q_0)$. Then $\mathcal{P} \sqsubseteq^{\mathcal{E}} \mathcal{Q}$ if for all $\mathcal{T} \in \mathcal{E}$ and $\pi \in [0,1]$, $\mathcal{P}\ pass_\pi\ \mathcal{T}$ implies $\mathcal{Q}\ pass_\pi\ \mathcal{T}$.

Intuitively, $\mathcal{P} \sqsubseteq^{\mathcal{E}} \mathcal{Q}$ means that $\mathcal{P}$ is "more reliable" with respect to $\mathcal{E}$ than $\mathcal{Q}$. In [CSZ92], $\mathcal{E}$ is taken to be the class of all tests; in this paper, we first consider a restricted class of tests in which no τ's are present before examining all tests.

3 Alternative Characterization for Tests without τ

In this section, we investigate the testing preorder for tests without τ-transitions. A test $\mathcal{T} = (T, Act, \mu_T, t_0, S)$ is called *τ-free* if $\mu_T(t, \tau, t') = 0$ for all $t, t' \in T$. We write $\mathbf{T_0}$ for the set of all τ-free tests. For notational convenience, we denote the preorder for τ-free tests as $\sqsubseteq_0$ instead of $\sqsubseteq^{\mathbf{T_0}}$.

3.1 The Alternative Characterization

The alternative characterization for $\sqsubseteq_0$ relies on *probabilistic traces* and the probabilities with which processes may execute probabilistic traces.

Definition 7 (Probabilistic Trace). A *probabilistic trace* over *Act* is an element of $(D_{Act} \times Act)^*$, where in each $\langle d, \alpha \rangle$ the set $\{\beta \mid d(\beta) > 0\}$ is finite. We use Tr_{Act} to denote the set of all probabilistic traces over *Act*.

A probabilistic trace consists of a sequence of pairs, with the first component of each pair being a probability distribution over actions and the second being an action. Intuitively, a trace represents a possible "interaction session" with a probabilistic process; each distribution defines the probabilities with which different actions are enabled by the environment, while the action component specifies the action that the environment and process agree to execute. Given such a trace, our goal is to define the probability that the process "executes" the trace to completion. Before doing this, however, we introduce some useful notation on traces.

Definition 8. Let $s = \langle d_1, \alpha_1 \rangle \cdots \langle d_i, \alpha_i \rangle \cdots \langle d_n, \alpha_n \rangle$ be an element of Tr_{Act}. Then $\delta(s) = d_1 \cdots d_i \cdots d_n$ and $\lambda(s) = \alpha_1 \cdots \alpha_i \cdots \alpha_n$, and $\delta(s, i) = d_i$ and $\lambda(s, i) = \alpha_i$. The length of s is denoted $|s|$; here $|s| = n$. We also use ε to represent the empty probabilistic trace.

We now turn to defining the probability with which a process exhibits a given probabilistic trace. We begin by introducing probabilistic analogues of *weak transitions*. Function $W_{\mathcal{P},\varepsilon} : P \times P \times D_{Act} \rightarrow [0,1]$ is intended to reflect the probability with which, beginning in one state, process $\mathcal{P}$ may silently evolve via some number of τ-transitions to another state, given a particular probability distribution describing the actions the environment is enabling. To define this function, we first give a function $W_{\mathcal{P}} : P \times N \times P \times D_{Act} \rightarrow [0,1]$, which describes the probability that $\mathcal{P}$ evolves from one state to another using the specified number of τ-transitions.

$$W_{\mathcal{P}}(p,0,p',d) = \begin{cases} 1 & \text{if } p = p' \\ 0 & \text{otherwise} \end{cases}$$

$$W_{\mathcal{P}}(p,i+1,p',d) = \begin{cases} \frac{1}{\nu(p,d)} \cdot \sum_{p'' \in P} \mu_P(p,\tau,p'') \cdot W_{\mathcal{P}}(p'',i,p',d) \\ \qquad \text{if } \nu(p,d) \neq 0 \\ 0 \quad \text{otherwise} \end{cases}$$

where $\nu(p,d) = (\sum_{\alpha \in Act} \mu_P(p,\alpha) \cdot d(\alpha)) + \mu_P(p,\tau)$.

$W_{\mathcal{P},\varepsilon}(p,p',d) = \sum_{i=0}^{\infty} W_{\mathcal{P}}(p,i,p',d)$

Note that the fact that $\mathcal{P}$ is divergence-free ensures that $W_{\mathcal{P},\varepsilon}(p,p',d)$ is well-defined.

We now introduce the analogue of a weak visible transition. Function $N_{\mathcal{P}} : P \times Act \times P \times D_{Act}$ represents the probability that in one state, process $\mathcal{P}$ may perform some internal transitions, and then the given action, to arrive at another state, given a probability distribution describing the actions enabled by the environment.

$$N_{\mathcal{P}}(p,\alpha,p',d) = \sum_{\{q|\nu(q,d)>0\}} W_{\mathcal{P},\varepsilon}(p,q,d) \cdot \frac{d(\alpha)}{\nu(q,d)} \cdot \mu_P(q,\alpha,p')$$

We define a function $M_{\mathcal{P}}$ for process $\mathcal{P}$ that, given a state p and a probabilistic trace s, returns the probability of the process "accepting" s starting at p.

Definition 9. Function $M_{\mathcal{P}} : P \times Tr_{Act} \rightarrow [0,1]$ may be defined as follows.

$$M_{\mathcal{P}}(p,\varepsilon) = 1$$
$$M_{\mathcal{P}}(p,\langle d,\alpha \rangle s') = \sum_{p' \in P} N_{\mathcal{P}}(p,\alpha,p',d) \cdot M_{\mathcal{P}}(p',s')$$

The alternative characterization for τ-free tests, written $\ll_0$, is now given in terms of $M_{\mathcal{P}}$.

Definition 10. $\mathcal{P} \ll_0 \mathcal{Q}$ if for all $s \in Tr_{Act}$ $M_{\mathcal{P}}(p_0,s) \leq M_{\mathcal{Q}}(q_0,s)$.

3.2 Full Abstraction

The rest of this section is devoted to showing that $\ll_0$ coincides with $\sqsubseteq_0$, in other words, that $\ll_0$ is *fully abstract* with respect to $\sqsubseteq_0$. We break this proof into two pieces. We first establish that $\ll_0$ is an *abstraction* of $\sqsubseteq_0$; then we show that $\ll_0$ is *adequate* for $\sqsubseteq_0$.

3.2.1 Abstraction

The theorem we wish to establish in this section is the following.

Theorem 1 (Abstraction). *$\mathcal{P} \sqsubseteq_0 \mathcal{Q}$ implies $\mathcal{P} \ll_0 \mathcal{Q}$.*

To prove this result, we show how to construct a probabilistic test from a probabilistic trace with the property that the probability with which a process passes the test is the same as the probability with which it executes the sequence. Given a sequence s, the definition of this test $\mathcal{T}(s)$ is the following.

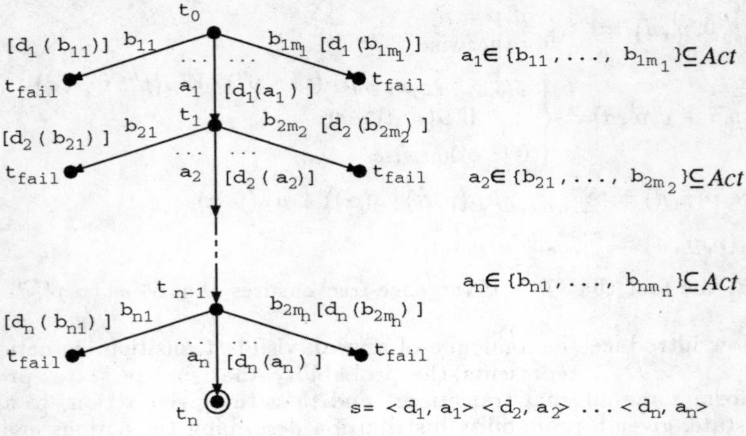

Fig. 1. Structure of $\mathcal{T}(s)$

Definition 11. For $s \in Tr_{Act}$, the test $\mathcal{T}(s)$ is defined by $(T, Act, \mu_s, t_0, \{t_{|s|}\})$ where $T = \{t_i | 0 \leq i \leq |s|\} \cup \{t_{fail}\}$ and

$$\mu_s(t, \alpha, t') = \begin{cases} \delta(s,i)(\alpha) & \text{if } t = t_{i-1},\ t' = t_i \text{ and } \alpha = \lambda(s,i) \\ \delta(s,i)(\alpha) & \text{if } t = t_{i-1},\ t' = t_{fail} \text{ and } \alpha \neq \lambda(s,i) \\ 0 & \text{otherwise} \end{cases}$$

Intuitively, $\mathcal{T}(s)$ has a "spine" labeled by the actions of s which is the unique path leading to the only successful state. The paths that are not on the spine lead to the failure state. Figure 1 depicts a typical $\mathcal{T}(s)$. We are now able to prove the following.

Lemma 1. *Let* $\mathcal{P} = (P, Act, \mu_P, p_0)$. *Then for all* $s \in Tr_{Act}$, $Pr(\mathcal{S}_{\mathcal{P}\|\mathcal{T}(s)}) = M_{\mathcal{P}}(p_0, s)$.

Proof. We prove, by induction on the length of s, a stronger result; namely, that for all $p \in P$, $Pr(\mathcal{S}_{p\|\mathcal{T}(s)}) = M_{\mathcal{P}}(p, s)$.

Given this lemma, the proof of Theorem 1 follows in a straightforward manner. Let s be a probabilistic trace; we want to show that $M_{\mathcal{P}}(p_0, s) \leq M_{\mathcal{Q}}(q_0, s)$. This follows from the fact that since $\mathcal{P} \sqsubseteq_0 \mathcal{Q}$, $Pr(\mathcal{S}_{\mathcal{P}\|\mathcal{T}(s)}) \leq Pr(\mathcal{S}_{\mathcal{Q}\|\mathcal{T}(s)})$. Then Lemma 1 gives the desired result.

3.2.2 Adequacy

We now wish to establish that $\ll_0$ is adequate for $\sqsubseteq_0$; that is, our task is to prove the following theorem.

Theorem 2 (Adequacy). $\mathcal{P} \ll_0 \mathcal{Q}$ *implies* $\mathcal{P} \sqsubseteq_0 \mathcal{Q}$.

To prove this result, we in essence argue that in order to understand how a process interacts with tests, it suffices to consider tests of a very restricted form—namely, tests that can be constructed from probabilistic traces. We refer to these tests as *essential* tests, since they expose all relevant aspects of process behavior.

In order to see why essential tests suffice to characterize processes with respect to $\sqsubseteq_0$, consider the factors that determine the probability with which a process passes an arbitrary test. In general, such a test has some number of "successful transition sequences" that lead from the start state of the test to an accepting state and do not pass through an accepting state along the way. When a process interacts with such a test, each successful computation exercises exactly one of these successful sequences; by summing up the probabilities of these computations, we may speak of the probability with which a process exercises a given successful sequence. Then the sum of the probabilities over all such sequences yields the probability with which the process passes the test. Thus, if we can construct an appropriate essential test for each such successful path, we may characterize the behavior of a process with respect to the test by looking only at the relevant essential tests.

To formalize these intuitions, let $\mathcal{P} = (P, Act, \mu_P, p_0)$ be a process and $\mathcal{T} = (T, Act, \mu_T, t_0, S)$ be a test, and let F be of the form:

$$\langle p, t \rangle \xrightarrow{\alpha_1, \pi_1} \langle p_1, t_1 \rangle \xrightarrow{\alpha_2, \pi_2} \cdots \xrightarrow{\alpha_m, \pi_m} \langle p_m, t_m \rangle$$

We use $F\lceil_{\mathcal{T}}$ to denote the transition sequence in $\mathcal{T}$ that interacts with a transition sequence in $\mathcal{P}$ to produce F. Thus, $F\lceil_{\mathcal{T}}$ is of the form:

$$t \xrightarrow{\alpha_1, \rho_1} t_1 \xrightarrow{\alpha_2, \rho_2} \cdots \xrightarrow{\alpha_m, \rho_m} t_m$$

Suppose that $F_{\mathcal{T}}$ is a transition sequence in $\mathcal{T}$ that starts from state t. Then we define $\mathcal{C}_{\langle p,t \rangle}\lceil_{F_{\mathcal{T}}} = \{F \mid F\lceil_{\mathcal{T}} = F_{\mathcal{T}} \text{ and } F \preceq C \text{ for some } C \in \mathcal{C}_{\langle p,t \rangle}\}$. Intuitively, $\mathcal{C}_{\langle p,t \rangle}\lceil_{F_{\mathcal{T}}}$ is the set of computation prefixes from $\langle p, t \rangle$ that exercise the transition sequence $F_{\mathcal{T}}$ in $\mathcal{T}$.

Now suppose that $F_{\mathcal{T}}$ is the transition sequence $t \xrightarrow{\alpha_1, \rho_1} t_1 \cdots \xrightarrow{\alpha_m, \rho_m} t_m$ in test $\mathcal{T}$, and let $F_{\mathcal{T}}(i)$ denote the ith state of $F_{\mathcal{T}}$, i.e. $F_{\mathcal{T}}(0) = t$ and $F_{\mathcal{T}}(i) = t_i$ for $i > 0$. We may define a probabilistic trace $tr(F_{\mathcal{T}}) = \langle d_1, \alpha_1 \rangle \cdots \langle d_m, \alpha_m \rangle$, where $d_i = \mu_T(F_{\mathcal{T}}(i-1))$ is the probability distribution on actions induced by $\mathcal{T}$'s transition relation at state $F_{\mathcal{T}}(i)$. Note that the fact that $\mathcal{T}$ is finite-branching ensures that each d_i returns 0 for all but a finite number of actions.

In general, because of potential nondeterminism in $\mathcal{T}$, $d_i(\alpha_i)$ will exceed $\mu_T(t_{i-1}, \alpha, t_i)$, and hence the probabilistic trace does not accurately reflect the probabilities in the transition sequence. However, the next lemma shows a strong relationship between the two.

Lemma 2. *Let $\mathcal{P} = (P, Act, \mu_P, p_0)$ be a process and $\mathcal{T} = (T, Act, \mu_T, t_0, S)$ be a test, and let $F_{\mathcal{T}}$ be a transition sequence in $\mathcal{T}$ starting from t_0. Then $Pr(\mathcal{C}_{\mathcal{P}\|\mathcal{T}}\lceil_{F_{\mathcal{T}}}) = v \cdot M_{\mathcal{P}}(p_0, s)$ where $s = tr(F_{\mathcal{T}})$ and $v = \prod_{1 \le i \le |F_{\mathcal{T}}|} \frac{\mu_T(t_{i-1}, \alpha_i, t_i)}{\mu_T(t_{i-1}, \alpha_i)}$ such that $t_i = F_{\mathcal{T}}(i)$ with $\alpha_i = \lambda(s, i)$.*

Proof. We prove a stronger fact; namely $Pr(\mathcal{C}_{\langle p,t \rangle}\lceil_{F_{\mathcal{T}}}) = v \cdot M_{\mathcal{P}}(p, s)$ for all $p \in P$ and $u_0 \in T$, where $v = \prod_{1 \le i \le |F_{\mathcal{T}}|} \frac{\mu_T(u_{i-1}, \beta_i, u_i)}{\mu_T(u_{i-1}, \beta_i)}$ with $u_i = F_{\mathcal{T}}(i)$ and $\beta_i = \lambda(s, i)$. This follows by induction on the length of $F_{\mathcal{T}}$.

In the statement of this lemma, note that v and s only depend on $F_{\mathcal{T}}$. Thus, once $F_{\mathcal{T}}$ is fixed then so are v and s. This fact and Lemma 1 enable us now to prove the following.

Lemma 3. *Let $F_{\mathcal{T}}$ be a non-empty transition sequence in $\mathcal{T}$ starting from t_0. Then $\mathcal{P} \ll_0 \mathcal{Q}$ implies $Pr(\mathcal{C}_{\mathcal{P}\|\mathcal{T}}\lceil_{F_{\mathcal{T}}}) \leq Pr(\mathcal{C}_{\mathcal{Q}\|\mathcal{T}}\lceil_{F_{\mathcal{T}}})$.*

The proof of the adequacy theorem now follows from the following fact. Fix a test $\mathcal{T}$, and let $\mathcal{T}_S$ be the set of successful transition sequences in $\mathcal{T}$. Then $Pr(\mathcal{S}_{\mathcal{P}\|\mathcal{T}}) = \sum_{F_{\mathcal{T}} \in \mathcal{T}_S} Pr(\mathcal{C}_{\mathcal{P}\|\mathcal{T}}\lceil_{F_{\mathcal{T}}})$ and $Pr(\mathcal{S}_{\mathcal{Q}\|\mathcal{T}}) = \sum_{F_{\mathcal{T}} \in \mathcal{T}_S} Pr(\mathcal{C}_{\mathcal{Q}\|\mathcal{T}}\lceil_{F_{\mathcal{T}}})$. Since $\mathcal{P} \ll_0 \mathcal{Q}$, Lemma 3 ensures that for each $F_{\mathcal{T}} \in \mathcal{T}_S$, $Pr(\mathcal{C}_{\mathcal{P}\|\mathcal{T}}\lceil_{F_{\mathcal{T}}}) \leq Pr(\mathcal{C}_{\mathcal{Q}\|\mathcal{T}}\lceil_{F_{\mathcal{T}}})$, and it therefore follows that $Pr(\mathcal{S}_{\mathcal{P}\|\mathcal{T}}) \leq Pr(\mathcal{S}_{\mathcal{Q}\|\mathcal{T}})$.

3.3 A Proof Technique

We close this section by giving a result that eases the task of showing $\mathcal{P} \ll_0 \mathcal{Q}$. Let *traces*$(\mathcal{P})$ be the set of the sequences of the observable actions (without probabilities) that $\mathcal{P}$ can execute from its start state. The following is immediate.

Lemma 4. *If $\lambda(s) \notin traces(\mathcal{P})$, then $M_{\mathcal{P}}(p_0, s) = 0$*

It also follows that if $\mathcal{P} \ll_0 \mathcal{Q}$ then any trace of $\mathcal{P}$ is a trace of $\mathcal{Q}$.

Lemma 5. *$\mathcal{P} \ll_0 \mathcal{Q}$ implies $traces(\mathcal{P}) \subseteq traces(\mathcal{Q})$*

Now suppose that $S \subseteq Tr_{Act}$. We write $\mathcal{P} \ll_0^S \mathcal{Q}$ if $M_{\mathcal{P}}(p_0, s) \leq M_{\mathcal{Q}}(q_0, s)$ for all $s \in S$. The next theorem shows that to check whether $\mathcal{P} \ll_0 \mathcal{Q}$ holds, we can limit the probabilistic traces that need checking as follows.

Theorem 3. *Let $S_{\mathcal{P}} = \{s \in Tr_{Act} \mid \lambda(s) \in traces(\mathcal{P})\}$. Then $\mathcal{P} \ll_0 \mathcal{Q}$ if and only if $\mathcal{P} \ll_0^{S_{\mathcal{P}}} \mathcal{Q}$ and $traces(\mathcal{P}) \subseteq traces(\mathcal{Q})$.*

On the basis of this theorem and the full abstractness result, then, we have the following proof technique for showing that $\mathcal{P} \sqsubseteq_0 \mathcal{Q}$.

- Check if $traces(\mathcal{P}) \subseteq traces(\mathcal{Q})$.
- Check if $M_{\mathcal{P}}(p_0, s) \leq M_{\mathcal{Q}}(q_0, s)$ for $s \in Tr$ such that $\lambda(s) \in traces(\mathcal{Q})$.

Example 1. We prove that $\mathcal{P}_1 \sqsubseteq_0 \mathcal{Q}_1$, where $\mathcal{P}_1$ and $\mathcal{Q}_1$ are depicted in the following.

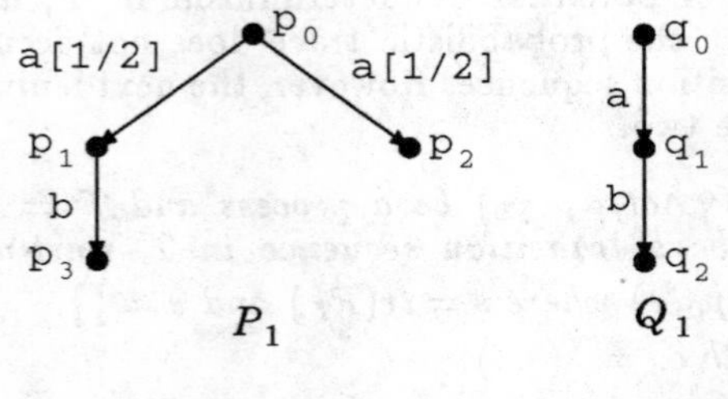

Since $traces(\mathcal{P}_1) = traces(\mathcal{Q}_1) = \{\epsilon, a, ab\}$, we must check the probabilistic traces $\langle d_1, a \rangle$ and $\langle d_1, a \rangle \langle d_2, b \rangle$.

(Case 1): $s = \langle d_1, a \rangle$. Then $M_{\mathcal{P}_1}(p_0, s) = M_{\mathcal{Q}_1}(q_0, s) = 1$

(Case 2): $s = \langle d_1, a \rangle \langle d_2, b \rangle$. Then $M_{\mathcal{P}_1}(p_0, s) = \frac{1}{2} \leq 1 = M_{\mathcal{Q}_1}(q_0, s)$

Example 2. We establish that $\mathcal{P}_2 \sqsubseteq_0 \mathcal{Q}_2$.

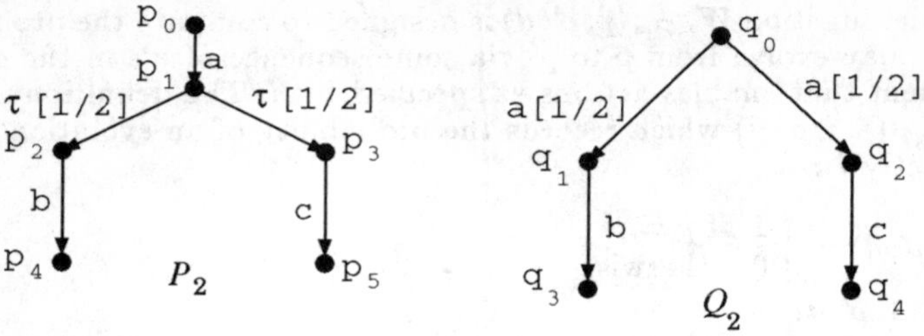

Since $traces(\mathcal{P}_2) = traces(\mathcal{Q}_2) = \{\varepsilon, a, ab, ac\}$, we check the following cases.

(Case 1): $s = \langle d_1, a \rangle$. $M_{\mathcal{P}_2}(p_0, \langle d_1, a \rangle) = M_{\mathcal{Q}_2}(q_0, \langle d_1, a \rangle) = 1$

(Case 2): $s = \langle d_1, a \rangle \langle d_2, b \rangle$.

$$M_{\mathcal{P}_2}(p_0, \langle d_1, a \rangle \langle d_2, b \rangle) = M_{\mathcal{Q}_2}(q_0, \langle d_1, a \rangle \langle d_2, b \rangle) = \frac{1}{2}$$

(Case 3): $s = \langle d_1, a \rangle \langle d_2, c \rangle$. Similar to Case 2.

We can show $\mathcal{Q}_2 \sqsubseteq_0 \mathcal{P}_2$ in a similar way. Consequently, we have that $\mathcal{P}_2$ and $\mathcal{Q}_2$ are equivalent.

4 Alternative Characterization for General Tests

We next investigate $\sqsubseteq^{\mathbf{T}}$, the testing preorder induced by the general tests, which may include transitions labeled by τ. (In the sequel, we simply write $\sqsubseteq^{\mathbf{T}}$ as $\sqsubseteq$.) As the set of tests is now larger, one might expect this new preorder to be strictly finer than $\sqsubseteq_0$, and this is indeed the case. For instance, in Example 1, the processes are related with respect to τ-free tests, but they are not related if τ-transitions are possible in tests. Let $\mathcal{T}_1$ and $\mathcal{T}_2$ be the following tests, where $t_{1,2}$ and $t_{2,2}$ are the successful states.

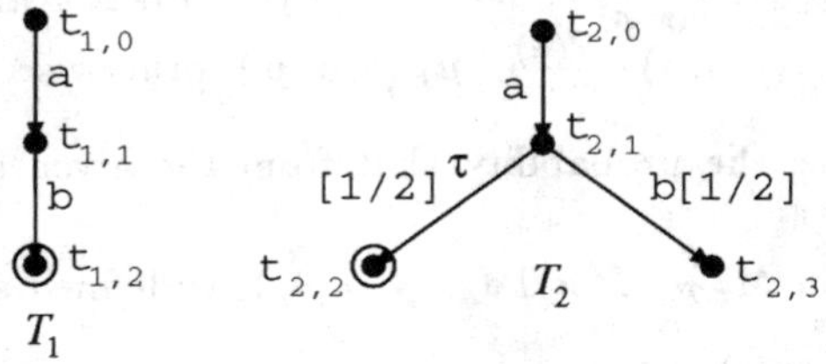

$Pr(\mathcal{S}_{\mathcal{P}_1 \| \mathcal{T}_1}) = \frac{1}{2}$ and $Pr(\mathcal{S}_{\mathcal{Q}_1 \| \mathcal{T}_1}) = 1$, but $Pr(\mathcal{S}_{\mathcal{P}_1 \| \mathcal{T}_2}) = \frac{3}{4}$ and $Pr(\mathcal{S}_{\mathcal{Q}_1 \| \mathcal{T}_2}) = \frac{1}{2}$, showing these processes are not related.

4.1 The Alternative Characterization

In order to define the alternative characterization of $\sqsubseteq$ we first introduce τ's into probabilistic traces.

Definition 12 (Probabilistic Trace with τ). A sequence $s \in (D_{Act_\tau} \times Act_\tau)^*$ is called a *probabilistic trace* of Act_τ where in each $\langle d, \alpha \rangle$ the set $\{\beta \mid d(\beta) > 0\}$ is finite. The set of all probabilistic traces of Act_τ is denoted by Tr_{Act_τ}.

Again we define a function to give the probability with which a process exhibits a given trace. Since probabilistic traces may include τ's, we must modify the functions defined in the previous section.

As before, the function $W_{\tau,\mathcal{P},\varepsilon}(p, p', d)$ is designed to compute the probability that process $\mathcal{P}$ may evolve from p to p' via some sequence of τ's in the context of an environment that enables actions as specified by d. The definition is given in terms of $W_{\tau,\mathcal{P}}(p, i, p', d)$ which records the probability of an evolution from p to p' using exactly i τ's.

$$W_{\tau,\mathcal{P}}(p, 0, p', d) = \begin{cases} 1 & \text{if } p = p' \\ 0 & \text{otherwise} \end{cases}$$

$$W_{\tau,\mathcal{P}}(p, i+1, p', d)$$

$$= \begin{cases} \frac{1}{\nu(p,d)} \cdot \sum_{p'' \in P} (1 - d(\tau)) \cdot \mu_P(p, \tau, p'') \cdot W_{\tau,\mathcal{P}}(p'', i, p', d) \\ \qquad \text{if } \nu(p, d) \neq 0 \\ 0 \qquad \text{otherwise} \end{cases}$$

where $\nu(p, d) = (\sum_{\alpha \in Act} \mu_P(p, \alpha) \cdot d(\alpha)) + \mu_P(p, \tau) + d(\tau) - \mu_P(p, \tau) \cdot d(\tau)$.

$$W_{\tau,\mathcal{P},\varepsilon}(p, p', d) = \sum_{i=0}^{\infty} W_{\tau,\mathcal{P}}(p, i, p', d)$$

Note that this definition changes the normalization factor $\nu(p, d)$ to take into account the probability that the environment enables τ's and that d is not allowed to "execute" its τ when determining $W_{\tau,\mathcal{P}}(p, i, p', d)$. Also in this case, $W_{\tau,\mathcal{P}}(p, p', d)$ is well-defined since $\mathcal{P}$ is divergence-free.

We now define $N_{\tau,\mathcal{P}}(p, \alpha, p', d)$, which computes the probability that $\mathcal{P}$ evolves from p to p' using internal computation followed by α, given d. When $\alpha = \tau$, we must account for two possibilities, one in which the environment executes its τ and one in which it does not.

$$N_{\tau,\mathcal{P}}(p, \alpha, p', d)$$

$$= \begin{cases} \sum_{\{q \mid \nu(q,d) > 0\}} W_{\tau,\mathcal{P},\varepsilon}(p, q, d) \cdot \frac{d(\tau)}{\nu(q,d)} \cdot \mu_P(q, \tau, p') \\ \quad + W_{\tau,\mathcal{P},\varepsilon}(p, p', d) \cdot \frac{d(\tau)}{\nu(p',d)} \cdot (1 - \mu_P(p', \tau)) & \text{if } \alpha = \tau \text{ and } \nu(p', d) \neq 0 \\ \sum_{\{q \mid \nu(q,d) > 0\}} W_{\tau,\mathcal{P},\varepsilon}(p, q, d) \cdot \frac{d(\alpha)}{\nu(q,d)} \cdot \mu_P(q, \alpha, p') & \text{otherwise} \end{cases}$$

Function $M_{\tau,\mathcal{P}}$ computes the probability that from the given state process $\mathcal{P}$ completes the given trace.

Definition 13. Function $M_{\tau,\mathcal{P}} : P \times Tr_{Act_\tau} \to [0, 1]$ is defined as follows.

$$M_{\tau,\mathcal{P}}(p, \varepsilon) = 1$$

$$M_{\tau,\mathcal{P}}(p, \langle d, \alpha \rangle s') = \sum_{p' \in P} N_{\tau,\mathcal{P}}(p, \alpha, p', d) \cdot M_{\tau,\mathcal{P}}(p', s')$$

The alternative characterization for general tests is given in terms of $M_{\tau,\mathcal{P}}$.

Definition 14. $\mathcal{P} \ll \mathcal{Q}$ if for all $s \in Tr_{Act_\tau}$ $M_{\tau,\mathcal{P}}(p_0, s) \leq M_{\tau,\mathcal{Q}}(q_0, s)$

4.2 Full Abstraction

In this section we establish that $\ll$ is equivalent to $\sqsubseteq$. To do this, we first show that $\ll$ is an abstraction of $\sqsubseteq$, and then we show that $\ll$ is adequate for $\sqsubseteq$.

4.2.1 Abstraction

Theorem 4 (Abstraction). *$\mathcal{P} \sqsubseteq \mathcal{Q}$ implies $\mathcal{P} \ll \mathcal{Q}$.*

The construction of probabilistic tests from probabilistic traces is the same as in Section 3, the only difference being that the action alphabet is Act_τ. Namely, $\mathcal{T}(s) = (T, Act_\tau, \mu_s, t_0, \{t_{|s|}\})$ for $s \in Tr_{Act_\tau}$. The proof of Theorem 4 follows directly from the next lemma.

Lemma 6. *Let $\mathcal{P} = (P, Act, \mu_P, p_0)$. Then for all $s \in Tr_{Act_\tau}$, $Pr(\mathcal{S}_{\mathcal{P}\|\mathcal{T}(s)}) = M_{\tau,\mathcal{P}}(p_0, s)$.*

4.2.2 Adequacy

Theorem 5 (Adequacy). *$\mathcal{P} \ll \mathcal{Q}$ implies $\mathcal{P} \sqsubseteq \mathcal{Q}$.*

The proof of adequacy is essentially identical to the case of τ-free tests.

Lemma 7. *Let $\mathcal{P} = (P, Act, \mu_P, p_0)$ be a process and $\mathcal{T} = (T, Act, \mu_T, t_0, S)$ be a test, and let $F_\mathcal{T}$ be a transition sequence in $\mathcal{T}$ starting from t_0. Then $Pr(\mathcal{C}_{\mathcal{P}\|\mathcal{T}}\lceil F_\mathcal{T}) = v \cdot M_{\tau,\mathcal{P}}(p_0, s)$ where $s = tr(F_\mathcal{T})$ and $v = \prod_{1 \le i \le |F_\mathcal{T}|} \frac{\mu_T(t_{i-1}, \alpha_i, t_i)}{\mu_T(t_{i-1}, \alpha_i)}$ such that $t_i = F_\mathcal{T}(i)$ with $\alpha_i = \lambda(s, i)$.*

As before, s and v are dependent only on $F_\mathcal{T}$. Thus the following lemma holds.

Lemma 8. *Let $F_\mathcal{T}$ be a non-empty transition sequence in $\mathcal{T}$ starting from t_0. Then $\mathcal{P} \ll \mathcal{Q}$ implies $Pr(\mathcal{C}_{\mathcal{P}\|\mathcal{T}}\lceil F_\mathcal{T}) \le Pr(\mathcal{C}_{\mathcal{Q}\|\mathcal{T}}\lceil F_\mathcal{T})$.*

Theorem 5 follows from the fact that $Pr(\mathcal{S}_{\mathcal{P}\|\mathcal{T}}) = \sum_{F_\mathcal{T} \in \mathcal{T}_S} Pr(\mathcal{C}_{\mathcal{P}\|\mathcal{T}}\lceil F_\mathcal{T})$, where $\mathcal{T}_S$ is the set of successful transition sequences in $\mathcal{T}$.

4.3 Equivalence Property

Somewhat surprisingly, it turns out that $\sqsubseteq$ is in fact an equivalence relation. To prove this result, we first show that $\sqsubseteq$ is in fact characterized by *non-blocking* probabilistic traces.

Definition 15 (Non-blocking probabilistic trace). Probabilistic trace s is *non-blocking* if for all $i \le |s|$, $d_i(\tau) > 0$.

Definition 16. $\mathcal{P} \ll^{NB} \mathcal{Q}$ if $M_{\tau,\mathcal{P}}(p_0, s) \le M_{\tau,\mathcal{Q}}(q_0, s)$ for all non-blocking s.

We say that a probabilistic trace is "blocking" if it is not non-blocking. We also call an essential test "non-blocking" if it is generated from a non-blocking probabilistic trace, and "blocking" if it is generated from a blocking probabilistic trace.

We show that $\sqsubseteq$ is is actually characterized by $\ll^{NB}$. We first prove the following lemma.

Lemma 9. *$\mathcal{P} \ll^{NB} \mathcal{Q}$ implies $\mathcal{P} \ll \mathcal{Q}$*

Proofsketch. Suppose $M_{\tau,\mathcal{P}}(p_0, s) \le M_{\tau,\mathcal{Q}}(q_0, s)$ for all non-blocking s and $\mathcal{P} \not\ll \mathcal{Q}$. Then, there exists a blocking s_0 such that $M_{\mathcal{P}}(p_0, s_0) > M_{\mathcal{Q}}(q_0, s_0)$. We can show that there exists a non-blocking s'_0 such that $M_{\tau,\mathcal{P}}(p_0, s'_0) > M_{\tau,\mathcal{Q}}(q_0, s'_0)$, deriving a contradiction.

To build s'_0, we modify any "blocking" distribution d in s_0 to d', where $d'(\tau) > 0$ in such a way that $M_{\tau,\mathcal{P}}(p_0, s'_0) > M_{\tau,\mathcal{Q}}(q_0, s'_0)$. Such d' always exist due to the fact that a process is finite-branching and has a lower bound on its transition probabilities.

That $\mathcal{P} \ll \mathcal{Q}$ implies $\mathcal{P} \ll^{NB} \mathcal{Q}$ is trivial; thus we can conclude that the non-blocking essential tests give the same preorder as do the essential tests.

Corollary 1. *$\mathcal{P} \ll \mathcal{Q}$ if and only if $\mathcal{P} \ll^{NB} \mathcal{Q}$*

An essential feature of non-blocking essential tests is that they can be "inverted"; from a given nonempty non-blocking essential test we may construct a set of non-blocking essential tests with the property that the cumulative probability with which any process passes the derived tests is 1 minus the probability that the process passes the original test. On the basis of the alternative characterization, then, we may conclude that if $\mathcal{P} \sqsubseteq \mathcal{Q}$ holds, then so does $\mathcal{Q} \sqsubseteq \mathcal{P}$. The reason that this inversion is possible is that unsuccessful computations can only end in configurations of the form $\langle p, t_{fail} \rangle$; that is, it is impossible to fail by getting "stuck" on the spine.

Definition 17 (Inverse Set of Non-blocking Probabilistic Traces). For a nonempty non-blocking s, a set of non-blocking probabilistic traces, denoted by s^{-1}, is inductively constructed as follows:

$$\langle d, \alpha \rangle^{-1} = \{\langle d, \beta \rangle \mid \beta \ne \alpha, d(\beta) > 0\}$$
$$(\langle d, \alpha \rangle s)^{-1} = \langle d, \alpha \rangle^{-1} \cup \{\langle d, \alpha \rangle s' \mid s' \in s^{-1}\}$$

The basic idea for the inverse set is to flip the failure state and the success state in an essential test. By simply flipping the states, the test has many successful paths. Therefore, we decompose the test again into a set of essential tests. The property is formally stated as follows.

Lemma 10. *If s is non-blocking, $M_{\tau,\mathcal{P}}(p_0, s) + \sum_{s' \in s^{-1}} M_{\tau,\mathcal{P}}(p_0, s') = 1$.*

Proof. We prove, by induction on the length of s, the slightly stronger fact: for a non-blocking probabilistic trace s, $M_{\tau,\mathcal{P}}(p, s) + \sum_{s' \in s^{-1}} M_{\tau,\mathcal{P}}(p, s') = 1$ for all $\mathcal{P}$ and for all $p \in P$.

Due to the existence of the inverse set, $\ll^{NB}$ is shown to be commutative. Namely, it forms an equivalence relation.

Lemma 11. *$\mathcal{P} \ll^{NB} \mathcal{Q}$ implies $\mathcal{Q} \ll^{NB} \mathcal{P}$*

Proof. By the definition of a non-blocking s, $M_{\tau,\mathcal{P}}(p_0, s) \le M_{\tau,\mathcal{Q}}(q_0, s)$. And for all $u \in s^{-1}$, $M_{\tau,\mathcal{P}}(p_0, u) \le M_{\tau,\mathcal{Q}}(q_0, u)$ since u is non-blocking. Thus

$$\sum_{u \in s^{-1}} M_{\tau,\mathcal{P}}(p_0, u) \le \sum_{u \in s^{-1}} M_{\tau,\mathcal{Q}}(q_0, u)$$
$$1 - M_{\tau,\mathcal{P}}(p_0, s) \le 1 - M_{\tau,\mathcal{Q}}(q_0, s)$$
$$M_{\tau,\mathcal{Q}}(q_0, s) \le M_{\tau,\mathcal{P}}(p_0, s)$$

The identity of $\ll$ and $\ll^{NB}$ and the full abstractness of $\ll$ with respect to $\sqsubseteq$ lead to the equivalence property of the preorder.

Theorem 6. *$\mathcal{P} \sqsubseteq \mathcal{Q}$ implies $\mathcal{Q} \sqsubseteq \mathcal{P}$*

4.4 A Proof Technique

We now provide a proof technique that is similar to the technique for τ-free tests. We first show that the traces of processes are identical if they are related by the testing preorder.

Lemma 12. *$\mathcal{P} \ll \mathcal{Q}$ implies $traces(\mathcal{P}) = traces(\mathcal{Q})$*

This follows from the fact that $\ll$ is an equivalence relation and $\ll$ implies $\ll_0$. It also turns out that if the "visible content" of a probabilistic trace is not a (nonprobabilistic) trace of a process, then the process is incapable of executing the probabilistic trace. Formally, if $\sigma \in Act_\tau^*$, then let $\widehat{\sigma}$ be σ with all τ's removed. We now have the following.

Lemma 13. *If $\widehat{\lambda(s)} \notin traces(\mathcal{P})$, then $M_{\tau,\mathcal{P}}(p_0, s) = 0$*

Theorem 7. *Let $S = \{s \mid \widehat{\lambda(s)} \in traces(\mathcal{P})\}$. Then, $\mathcal{P} \ll \mathcal{Q}$ if and only if $traces(\mathcal{P}) = traces(\mathcal{Q})$ and $\mathcal{P} \ll^S \mathcal{Q}$.*

This theorem and the full abstraction result imply the following proof technique for $\mathcal{P} \sqsubseteq \mathcal{Q}$.

- Check if $traces(\mathcal{P}) = traces(\mathcal{Q})$
- Check if $M_\mathcal{P}(p_0, s) = M_\mathcal{Q}(q_0, s)$ for all s such that $\widehat{\lambda(s)} \in traces(\mathcal{P})$.

Example 3. We use the proof technique to show that $\mathcal{P}_3 \sqsubseteq \mathcal{Q}_3$ where $\mathcal{P}_3$ and $\mathcal{Q}_3$ are given by:

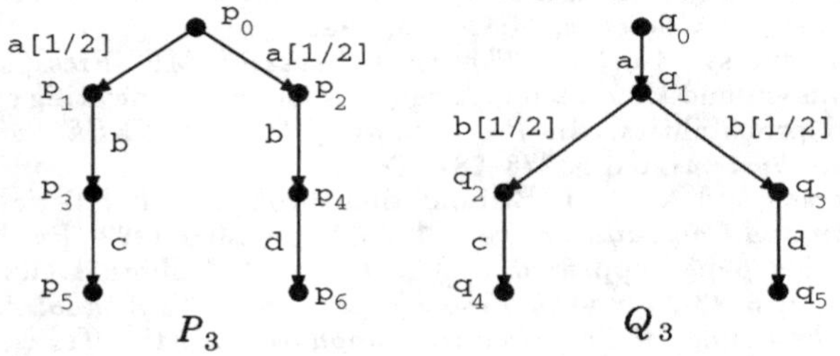

Since $traces(\mathcal{P}_3) = traces(\mathcal{Q}_3) = \{\varepsilon, a, ab, abc, abd\}$, we only need consider s such that $\widehat{\lambda(s)} \in \{\varepsilon, a, ab, abc, abd\}$. The details are left to the reader.

5 Concluding Remarks and Future Work

We have presented alternative characterizations of the testing preorders for probabilistic processes put forth in [CSZ92]. Specifically, we have investigated two preorders, distinguished on the basis of whether or not tests are allowed to make τ-transitions. In each case, we have proven the characterization to be fully abstract with respect to the corresponding testing preorder and given a proof technique that eases the task of establishing the preorder. Moreover, we have shown the second preorder to be an equivalence relation, a fact that went unnoticed in [CSZ92].

Our results are also applicable to *substochastic processes* [CSZ92], where the sum of the probabilities of outgoing transitions from a state may be strictly less than one. The deficit represents the process's capacity for *undefined behavior*.

Our present characterizations rely on succinctly encoding essential tests as probabilistic traces. As future work, we seek to establish more denotational characterizations based entirely on the structure of probabilistic processes. The acceptance tree model of [Hen88] for nondeterministic processes offers an appealing starting point for such an investigation.

We would also like to extend our testing preorder to handle time as well as probability. This would enable, for example, reasoning about "soft" real-time systems in which deadlines may be missed but not "too often."

Acknowledgement. The first author would like thank Prof. Yasuyoshi Inagaki of Nagoya University who provided support for his stay at SUNY Stony Brook.

References

[Chr90] I. Christoff. Testing equivalences and fully abstract models for probabilistic processes. In J. C. M. Baeten and J. W. Klop, editors, *Proceedings of CONCUR '90 – First Intl. Conf. on Concurrency Theory,* volume 458 of *Lecture Notes in Computer Science*, pages 126–140. Springer-Verlag, 1990.

[CSZ92] R. Cleaveland, S. A. Smolka, and A. E. Zwarico. Testing preorders for probabilistic processes. In *Proceedings of the 19th ICALP*, volume 623 of *Lecture Notes in Computer Science*, pages 708–719. Springer Verlag, July 1992.

[DeN87] R. DeNicola. Extensional equivalences for transition systems. *Acta Informatica*, 24:211–237, 1987.

[DH83] R. DeNicola and M.C.B. Hennessy. Testing equivalences for processes. *Theoretical Computer Science*, 34:83–133, 1983.

[Hen88] M.C.B. Hennessy. *Algebraic Theory of Processes.* MIT Press, 1988.

[HJ90] H. A. Hansson and B. Jonsson. A calculus for communicating systems with time and probabilities. In *Proceedings of the 11th IEEE Symposium on Real-Time Systems*, pages 278–287, 1990.

[LS92a] K. G. Larsen and A. Skou. Bisimulation through probabilistic testing. *Information and Computation*, 94(1):1–28, September 1992. Preliminary versions of this paper appeared as University of Aalborg technical reports R 88-18 and R 88-29, and in *Proceedings of the 16th Annual ACM Symposium on Principles of Programming Languages*, Austin, Texas, 1989.

[LS92b] K. G. Larsen and A. Skou. Compositional verification of probabilistic processes. In *Proceedings of CONCUR '92*, volume 630 of *Lecture Notes in Computer Science*, pages 456–471. Springer-Verlag, 1992.

[LT87] N.A. Lynch and M. Tuttle. Hierarchical correctness proofs for distributed algorithms. In *Proceeding the 6th Annual ACM symposium on Principles of Distributed Computing*, pages 137–151, 1987.

[Mil89] R. Milner. *Communication and Concurrency.* Prentice Hall, 1989.

[vGSST90] R. J. van Glabbeek, S. A. Smolka, B. Steffen, and C. M. N. Tofts. Reactive, generative, and stratified models of probabilistic processes. In *Proceedings of the 5th IEEE Symposium on Logic in Computer Science*, pages 130–141, Philadelphia, PA, 1990.

[WSS94] S. Wu, S.A. Smolka, and E.W. Stark. Composition and behaviors of probabilistic I/O automata. In *Proceedings of CONCUR '94*, Lecture Notes in Computer Science. Springer Verlag, 1994.

[YL92] W. Yi and Kim G. Larsen. Testing probabilistic and nondeterministic processes. In *Protocol Specification, Testing and Verification XII*, pages 47–61, 1992.

Composition and Behaviors of Probabilistic I/O Automata

Sue-Hwey Wu*, Scott A. Smolka*, Eugene W. Stark**

Department of Computer Science
State University of New York at Stony Brook
Stony Brook, NY 11794 USA***

Abstract. We augment the I/O automaton model of Lynch and Tuttle with probability, as a step toward the ultimate goal of obtaining a useful tool for specifying and reasoning about asynchronous probabilistic systems. Our new model, called *probabilistic I/O automata*, preserves the fundamental properties of the I/O automaton model, such as the asymmetric treatment of input and output and the pleasant notion of asynchronous composition. For the class of probabilistic I/O automata without internal actions, we show that *probabilistic behavior maps*, which are an abstract representation of I/O automaton behavior in terms of a certain expectation operator, are compositional and fully abstract with respect to a natural notion of probabilistic testing.

1 Introduction

I/O automata are a kind of state machine that have been proposed by Lynch and Tuttle [LT87] as a tool for specifying and reasoning about asynchronous systems. The distinguishing features of the I/O automaton model are: an asymmetric treatment of input and output actions, a notion of asynchronous composition that takes a "compatible" collection of I/O automata and produces a new I/O automaton as a result, a simple correspondence between computations of a composite I/O automaton and certain collections of computations of its component automata, the treatment of liveness properties through the introduction of a "fairness partition" on the action set of an automaton, and the use of simulation-based techniques for proving that the set of action sequences that can be produced by one I/O automaton is a subset of the set of action sequences that can be produced by another. In this paper, we consider the problem of augmenting I/O automata with probability information, as a step toward the ultimate goal of obtaining a useful tool for specifying and reasoning about asynchronous probabilistic systems. As much as possible, we would like to preserve the characteristic features of the I/O automaton model, especially the

* Research supported in part by NSF Grants CCR-9120995 and CCR-9208585, and AFOSR Grant F49620-93-1-0250DEF.

** Research supported in part by NSF Grant CCR-8902215.

*** E-mail: suewu@cs.sunysb.edu, sas@cs.sunysb.edu, stark@cs.sunysb.edu

asymmetric treatment of input and output and the associated pleasant notion of composition.

There are some interesting issues that arise when one attempts to add probability to I/O automata. These issues derive from the input/output dichotomy and also from the asynchronous notion of composition for such automata, in which for any given state of a composite automaton there can be a number of component automata "competing" with each other to control the execution of the next action. It is inadequate simply to introduce, for each state q, a single probability distribution μ on the set of all transitions from state q, because intuitively there is no good reason why the choice between input transitions (which are "externally controlled" by the environment of the automaton) and output or internal transitions (which are "locally controlled" by the automaton itself) should admit a meaningful probabilistic description independent of any particular environment. So, instead of one probability distribution for *all* transitions for state q, we introduce several probability distributions: one distribution over all the locally controlled transitions from state q, and separate distributions for each input action e. Our model is thus a kind of hybrid between the "reactive" and "generative" approaches described in [vGSST90].

The introduction of multiple probability distributions on transitions still does not solve all problems, however. Although within a single automaton we do not wish to ascribe probabilities to choices between externally controlled and locally controlled transitions, when automata are composed we do wish to have a natural probabilistic description of the outcome of the competition between component automata for control of the next action. To this end we introduce the concept of the *delay parameter* $\delta(q)$ associated with each state q. The idea is as follows: when a component automaton in a composite system arrives in state q, it draws a random delay time from an exponential distribution with parameter $\delta(q)$. This time describes the length of time the automaton will remain in state q before executing its next locally controlled action. The competition between several component automata vying for control of the next locally controlled action is won by the automaton having the least amount of delay time left. If we assume that the delay time distributions of component automata are independent, we can assign a definite probability to the event that any given component automaton will win the competition in any given system state. The "memoryless" property of the exponential distribution makes it irrelevant whether the component automata draw one delay time when they first enter their local state, or whether each component draws a new delay time after each global transition. This last feature makes it possible to give a simple definition of composition for probabilistic I/O automata.

Having obtained definitions for probabilistic I/O automata and their composition, it becomes interesting to consider their "external behaviors." The external behavior of an ordinary I/O automaton is the set of all sequences of external actions that can be produced in the various executions of the automaton. Lynch and Tuttle show that the mapping from I/O automata to external behaviors respects composition, in the sense that the external behavior of a composite automaton is determined in a natural way by the external behaviors of the component automata. Since ordinary I/O automata have sets of action sequences as their external behaviors, one might expect probabilistic I/O automata to have probability distributions on action sequences as their external behaviors. Although this intuition can be validated to a certain extent, if one wishes the mapping from probabilistic I/O automata to external behaviors to respect composition, then the situation requires a bit more finesse than simply using probability distributions on action sequences as external behaviors. The reason is this: to compute the probability distribution on action sequences determined by a composite automaton, it is necessary to have information about the internal delays of each of the component automata as well as the probability distribution they each induce on action sequences.

Our notion of external behavior for probabilistic I/O automata is obtained as follows: Let A be a probabilistic I/O automaton having no input or internal actions, and satisfying certain finite branching conditions. Then the automaton A induces a probability distribution on the set of all its executions, and, given an action sequence $\alpha = e_0 e_1 \dots e_{n-1}$, a conditional distribution on the subset X_α of all executions whose action sequences extend α. We may view the sequences $d_0 d_1 \dots d_n$ of delay parameters associated with the states in such an execution as the values of an $(n+1)$-dimensional random variable D defined on X_α. We define $\mathcal{E}_\alpha^A$ to be the functional that takes each real-valued function $g : \mathcal{R}^{n+1} \to \mathcal{R}$ to its expectation, weighted by the probability of the set X_α. Since the formal summation formula that defines $\mathcal{E}_\alpha^A$ makes sense even when A is allowed to have input actions, we can use the same formula to associate a functional $\mathcal{E}_\alpha^A$ with an arbitrary probabilistic I/O automaton A. We show that, for probabilistic I/O automata with no internal actions, a compositional notion of behavior is obtained if one takes the external behavior of an automaton A to be the mapping $\mathcal{E}^A$ that assigns to each action sequence α of length n the associated functional $\mathcal{E}_\alpha^A$ on $\mathcal{R}^{n+1} \to \mathcal{R}$.

Besides showing that our notion of behavior is compositional, we are also able to show that it is "fully abstract," in the sense that any two automata having distinct behaviors can be distinguished by a certain kind of probabilistic test. The key idea in the proof is that the success probability of tests in a certain class gives us the expectations of certain rational functions of the delay parameters. Using the uniqueness of partial fraction expansions of rational functions [Lan84], we can recover full information about the functionals $\mathcal{E}_\alpha^A$ from these expectations.

The recent research literature contains a plethora of proposals for probabilistic models. Each of these proposals addresses different issues, and introduces probability in a different way. In *reactive processes* [Rab63, LS92], for each state q and action e, a separate probability distribution is associated with the set of e-labeled transitions leaving state q. In contrast, in *generative processes* [vGSST90], for each state q a single probability distribution is associated with the set of all transitions leaving state q. The *stratified processes* [vGSST90] model refines the generative model with a multi-level probabilistic choice mechanism. *Alternating processes* [HJ90, Han91] are a mixture of strictly alternating probabilistic and nondeterministic states. The *stochastic processes* of [Mol82, GHR92, Hil93] associate a stochastic delay, represented as a random variable, with the firing of transitions. In *probabilistic specifications* [JL91] transitions are labeled by *sets* of probabilities, rather than single probabilities. Finally, the model of *probabilistic communicating processes* [Sei92] contains both an external (deterministic) and internal (probabilistic) choice operator, and processes are defined as conditional probability measures. There are a number of other probabilistic models worth mentioning, but are omitted due to space limitations.

The main contribution of our work is a compositional semantics for asynchronous probabilistic systems, which is fully abstract with respect to probabilistic testing. To our knowledge, we are the first to give such a result. The closest earlier work is that of Christoff [Chr90], although his approach differs from our own on a number of key aspects: Christoff considers only purely generative processes, whereas our model captures both generative and reactive processes. Christoff's tests are deterministic and there is no notion of success state or success action; instead, he introduces testing equivalences based on the probabilities induced by the interaction of a process and a test on L^*, where L is a set of observable events. In our model, tests are just probabilistic I/O automata with a distinguished "success action" ω, and testing equivalence is defined in terms of the probability of a process successfully passing a test. Christoff's denotational models, which he shows to be fully abstract with respect to testing, are defined in terms of "probability functions" that map $(2^L - \emptyset)^* \times L^*$ to $[0,1]$. No composition operator on processes is defined in [Chr90] and thus the issue of compositionality of his denotational semantics is left untreated. On the other hand, our model is compositional, and to obtain this result we find it necessary to include information about the probability of internal delays in the abstract representation of a process.

The rest of this paper is organized as follows: In Section 2, we review some basic definitions and results pertaining to ordinary I/O automata and the composition operation on such automata. In Section 3, we define our probabilistic version of I/O automata, and show how the notion of composition for ordinary I/O automata extends to the probabilistic case. In Section 4, we define our notion of probabilistic behavior, and we show that the map taking each automaton to its behavior respects composition. In Section 5, we show that our notion of behavior is fully abstract with respect to probabilistic testing. Finally, in Section 6, we summarize what we have accomplished and outline plans for future investigation.

2 I/O Automata

In this section, we review some basic definitions and results pertaining to ordinary I/O automata. For further details, the reader is referred to [Tut87].

An *I/O automaton* is a quadruple $A = (Q, q^{\mathrm{I}}, E, \Delta)$, where

- Q is a set of *states*

- $q^{\mathrm{I}} \in Q$ is a distinguished *start state.*
- E is a set of *actions*, partitioned into disjoint sets of *input*, *output*, and *internal* actions, which are denoted by E^{in}, E^{out}, and E^{int}, respectively. The set $E^{\mathrm{loc}} = E^{\mathrm{out}} \cup E^{\mathrm{int}}$ of output and internal actions is called the set of *locally controlled* actions, and the set $E^{\mathrm{ext}} = E^{\mathrm{in}} \cup E^{\mathrm{out}}$ is called the set of *external* actions.
- $\Delta \subseteq Q \times E \times Q$ is the *transition relation*, which satisfies the following *input-enabled* property: for any state $q \in Q$ and input action $e \in E^{\mathrm{in}}$, there exists a state $r \in Q$ such that $(q, e, r) \in \Delta$.

It will sometimes be convenient for us to use the notation $q \xrightarrow{e} r$ to assert that $(q, e, r) \in \Delta$.

The original definition of I/O automaton [Tut87] included an additional piece of data: a partition of the set of locally controlled actions. Such partitions are used to define a notion of *fair execution* for I/O automata, which is essential if one wishes to establish liveness properties for such automata. We do not treat liveness properties in this paper. Even so, to treat liveness in a probabilistic setting it would seem more natural to bypass fairness altogether, and instead use probability information to define a notion of "satisfies a liveness property with probability one." We shall therefore ignore the partition component of I/O automata in our discussion.

Lynch and Tuttle define a *finite execution fragment* of an I/O automaton A to be an alternating sequence of states and actions of the form

$$q_0 \xrightarrow{e_0} q_1 \xrightarrow{e_1} \cdots \xrightarrow{e_{n-1}} q_n,$$

such that $(q_k, e_k, q_{k+1}) \in \Delta$ for $0 \leq k < n$. In this paper, we find it convenient to use a slightly more liberal definition of execution fragment, to allow such fragments to contain actions not in E. We use the term *native* to refer to an execution or execution fragment of A in which only actions from E appear. We also impose the technical condition that the set E of actions of an I/O automaton be a subset of a fixed, countable *universe of actions* U. This is not really much of a restriction in practice, since in practical situations we have to be able to explicitly denote all actions by a finite sequence of symbols. For us, then, a *finite execution fragment* is an alternating sequence of states and actions as above such that $(q_k, e_k, q_{k+1}) \in \Delta$ whenever $e_k \in E$ and such that $q_{k+1} = q_k$ whenever $e_k \in U \setminus E$. An execution fragment with $q_0 = q^{\mathrm{I}}$ (the distinguished start state) is called an *execution.*

If σ denotes an execution fragment as above, then we will use $\sigma(k)$ to denote the state q_k, for $0 \leq k \leq n$. We use the term *trace* to refer to a sequence of actions. If σ is an execution fragment as above, then the *trace* of σ, denoted $\mathrm{tr}(\sigma)$, is the sequence of actions $e_0 e_1 \ldots e_{n-1}$ appearing in σ.

A collection $\{A_i : i \in I\}$ of I/O automata, where $A_i = (Q_i, q_i^{\mathrm{I}}, E_i, \Delta_i)$, is called *compatible* if for all $i, j \in I$, $E_i^{\mathrm{out}} \cap E_j^{\mathrm{out}} = \emptyset$ and $E_i^{\mathrm{int}} \cap E_j = \emptyset$. We define the *composition* $\prod_{i \in I} A_i$ of such a collection to be the I/O automaton $(Q, q^{\mathrm{I}}, E, \Delta)$, defined as follows:

- $Q = \prod_{i \in I} Q_i$.
- $q^{\mathrm{I}} = \langle q_i^{\mathrm{I}} : i \in I \rangle$.
- $E = \bigcup_{i \in I} E_i$, where $E^{\mathrm{out}} = \bigcup_{i \in I} E_i^{\mathrm{out}}$, $E^{\mathrm{int}} = \bigcup_{i \in I} E_i^{\mathrm{int}}$ and $E^{\mathrm{in}} = (\bigcup_{i \in I} E_i^{\mathrm{in}}) \setminus E^{\mathrm{out}}$.
- Δ is the set of all $(\langle q_i : i \in I \rangle, e, \langle r_i : i \in I \rangle)$ such that for all $i \in I$, if $e \in E_i$, then $(q_i, e, r_i) \in \Delta_i$, otherwise $r_i = q_i$.

With our more liberal definition of execution fragments, we have a simple correspondence between computations of a composite I/O automaton and the computations of its component automata. Suppose σ is an execution fragment for a composite automaton $\prod_{i \in I} A_i$, of the form

$$q_0 \xrightarrow{e_0} q_1 \xrightarrow{e_1} \dots \xrightarrow{e_{n-1}} q_n,$$

where $q_k = \langle q_{k,i} : i \in I \rangle$. Then for each $i \in I$, the execution fragment σ projects in an obvious way to an execution fragment $\sigma | A_i$ for A_i by replacing each state q_k by its projection $q_{k,i}$. Suppose $\mathrm{tr}(\sigma) = \alpha$, then $tr(\sigma | A_i) = \alpha$ for each $i \in I$. This mapping, taking each execution fragment σ of $\prod_{i \in I} A_i$ to indexed collections of execution fragments $\langle \sigma | A_i : i \in I \rangle$, is invertible, in the sense made precise by the following proposition.

Proposition 1. *Suppose $A = \prod_{i \in I} A_i$. Then for each action sequence α of the form $e_0 e_1 \dots e_{n-1}$, the map, that takes each execution fragment σ of $\prod_{i \in I} A_i$ with $\mathrm{tr}(\sigma) = \alpha$ to the collection of execution fragments $\{\sigma | A_i : i \in I\}$, is a bijection, from the set of execution fragments ρ of A having trace α to the set of indexed collections $\{\rho_i : i \in I\}$, where each ρ_i is an execution fragment of A_i with trace α.*

3 Probabilistic I/O Automata

A *probabilistic I/O automaton* is a sextuple $A = (Q, q^{\mathrm{I}}, E, \Delta, \mu, \delta)$, where

- $(Q, q^{\mathrm{I}}, E, \Delta)$ is an I/O automaton, called the *underlying* I/O automaton. The transition relation Δ is required to satisfy the following properties:
  1. The *local finite-branching* property:
     for all $q \in Q$, the set $\{(q, e, r) \in \Delta : e \in E^{\mathrm{loc}}\}$ is finite.
  2. The *input image-finiteness* property:
     for all $q \in Q$ and all $e \in E^{\mathrm{in}}$, the set $\{r \in Q : (q, e, r) \in \Delta\}$ is finite.
- $\mu : (Q \times E \times Q) \to [0, 1]$ is the *transition probability* function, which is required to satisfy the following conditions:
  1. $\mu(q, e, r) > 0$ iff $(q, e, r) \in \Delta$.
  2. $\sum_{r \in Q} \mu(q, e, r) = 1$, for all $q \in Q$ and all $e \in E^{\mathrm{in}}$.
  3. For all $q \in Q$, if there exist $e \in E^{\mathrm{loc}}$ and $r \in Q$ such that $(q, e, r) \in \Delta$, then $\sum_{r \in Q} \sum_{e \in E^{\mathrm{loc}}} \mu(q, e, r) = 1$,
- $\delta : Q \to [0, \infty)$ is the *state delay* function, which is required to satisfy the following condition: for all $q \in Q$, we have $\delta(q) > 0$ if and only if there exist $e \in E^{\mathrm{loc}}$ and $r \in Q$ such that $(q, e, r) \in \Delta$.

The local finite-branching condition on the transition relation Δ is imposed so that in Section 3.1 we can obtain a probability distribution on the set of all native executions of an automaton A with an empty set of input actions. This condition is also needed so that we can obtain discrete probability distributions in key situations in Section 4; thereby avoiding technical problems of measurability that would arise in a more general setting. Once we have imposed the local finite-branching condition, the input image-finiteness condition is required in order for the class of probabilistic I/O automata to be closed under the composition operation defined in Section 3.2.

The transition probability function μ describes the probability, for each state q, of choosing one transition from state q as opposed to another. As discussed in the introduction, we do not ascribe any probability to the choice between an input transition and an output or internal transition, since any such probability will be determined by the environment. Similarly, the choice between a transition for one input action and a transition for a different input action is also under the control of the environment, so we do not attempt to assign probabilities in this case either. The stochastic conditions (2) and (3) on μ reflect this point of view: Condition (2) states that for each state q and input action e, the function μ determines a probability distribution on the set of states r such that $q \xrightarrow{e} r$. Condition (3) states that if there is some locally controlled action enabled in state q, then μ determines a probability distribution on the set of all pairs (e, r) such that e is locally controlled and $q \xrightarrow{e} r$.

The state delay function δ assigns to each state q a nonnegative real number $\delta(q)$. As discussed in the introduction, the intuitive interpretation of $\delta(q)$ is as the parameter of an exponential distribution describing the length of a random "delay period" from the time state q is entered by the automaton until the time it executes its next locally controlled action. The condition on δ corresponds to the intuition that if no locally controlled action is available in state q, then the delay period will be infinite.

Function δ can be extended to finite execution fragments as follows. Let σ be a finite execution fragment of the form

$$q_0 \xrightarrow{e_0} q_1 \xrightarrow{e_1} \cdots \xrightarrow{e_{n-1}} q_n,$$

and d_i denote the value $\delta(q_i)$ for $0 \leq i \leq n$. Then let $\delta(\sigma)$ denote the sequence $d_0 d_1 \ldots d_n$. We call $\delta(\sigma)$ the *delay sequence* of σ. We use d, d' to denote delay sequences. Let $d = d_0 d_1 \ldots d_n$ and $d' = d'_0 d'_1 \ldots d'_n$ be two arbitrary delay sequences. Then $d + d'$ is the componentwise sum of d and d'. This notation is used extensively in Sections 4 and 5.

To simplify notation in the sequel, it will be convenient for us to adopt the following convention regarding the application of μ to triples (q, e, r) where e is not in the set E of actions of A: we define $\mu(q, e, r) = 1$ if $q = r$, and we define $\mu(q, e, r) = 0$ if $q \neq r$.

3.1 Probability Distributions on Executions and Traces

Suppose $A = (Q, q^I, E, \Delta, \mu, \delta)$ is a probabilistic I/O automaton. In this section, we consider the problem of assigning probabilities to sets of executions of A. If A is an arbitrary probabilistic I/O automaton, it does not make much sense to ask about the probability of sets of executions of A, since we lack any sort of probabilistic description of when input actions will occur and which ones they will be. However, in case $E^{\text{in}} = \emptyset$, we do not lack any such information, and the question becomes a meaningful one. We shall likewise restrict our attention to sets of native executions of A (those that contain only actions in E) since actions outside E are under the control of the environment.

In any discussion of probability, it is necessary to begin by describing the probability space. In our case, the set of basic outcomes is the set of all native executions of A (both finite and infinite). If

$$\sigma = q_0 \xrightarrow{e_0} q_1 \xrightarrow{e_1} \dots \xrightarrow{e_{n-1}} q_n$$

is a finite native execution, then define the set $[\sigma]$ to be the set of all finite and infinite native executions of the form

$$\rho = q_0 \xrightarrow{e_0} q_1 \xrightarrow{e_1} \dots \xrightarrow{e_{n-1}} q_n \xrightarrow{e_n} q_{n+1} \dots$$

In other words, for any finite native execution σ, the set $[\sigma]$ is the set of all finite and infinite native executions ρ that extend σ. Define a set of native executions of A to be *basic measurable* if it is the union (possibly empty) of a finite disjoint collection of sets of the form $[\sigma]$ and singleton sets of the form $\{\rho\}$, where ρ is a finite native execution with $[\rho] \neq \{\rho\}$. A basic measurable set of the form $\{\rho\}$ or of the form $[\sigma]$ is called *simple*.

Lemma 2. *The collection of basic measurable sets of executions of A is nonempty, and is closed under pairwise union, pairwise intersection, and complement. That is, it forms an algebra of sets.*

We now show how to assign probability to basic measurable sets of executions. Suppose

$$\sigma = q_0 \xrightarrow{e_0} q_1 \xrightarrow{e_1} \dots \xrightarrow{e_{n-1}} q_n$$

is a finite native execution. To a simple basic measurable set $[\sigma]$ we assign probability as follows:

$$\Pr([\sigma]) = \prod_{k=0}^{n-1} \mu(q_k, e_k, q_{k+1}).$$

In particular, if q^I denotes the unique execution with one state and no actions, then $\Pr([q^I]) = 1$. To a simple basic measurable set $\{\rho\}$ with $[\rho] \neq \{\rho\}$ we assign probability 0.

To extend the above assignment of probability to all basic measurable sets, we need the following result:

Lemma 3. *Suppose* $B = \bigcup_{i=1}^{m} S_i$ *and* $B = \bigcup_{j=1}^{n} S'_j$ *are two representations of* B *as a finite disjoint union of simple basic measurable sets. Then*

$$\sum_{i=1}^{m} \Pr(S_i) = \sum_{j=1}^{n} \Pr(S'_j)$$

To each basic measurable set $B = \bigcup_{i=1}^{n} S_i$ represented as a finite disjoint union of simple basic measurable sets S_i, we assign probability as follows:

$$\Pr(B) = \sum_{i=1}^{n} \Pr(S_i).$$

The preceding lemma shows that this definition is independent of the particular choice of representation.

Lemma 4. Pr *is a measure (a countably additive set function) on the algebra of basic measurable sets.*

Proof Sketch – It is obvious from the definitions that Pr is finitely additive. A König's Lemma argument shows that if a basic measurable set B is a countable union of basic measurable sets S_i, then at most finitely many of the sets S_i can be nonempty. Hence for the class of basic measurable sets, countable additivity reduces to finite additivity. □

Proposition 5. Pr *extends to a complete measure (which we also denote by* Pr*) on a* σ*-algebra containing the algebra of basic measurable sets. Moreover, since* $\Pr([q^{\mathrm{I}}]) = 1$, *it follows that* Pr *is a probability measure.*

Proof Sketch – This is a corollary of the Extension Theorem for measures ([Wei74], Theorem 2, p. 97) which states that any measure defined on a ring $\mathcal{R}$ extends to a complete measure on a σ-algebra containing $\mathcal{R}$. □

We can also assign probabilities to sets of traces. Still working with respect to a probabilistic I/O automaton A, we define a set V of traces of A to be *measurable* if $\mathrm{tr}_A^{-1}(V)$ is a measurable set of executions of A. To each such set we assign probability as follows:

$$\Pr(V) = \Pr(\mathrm{tr}^{-1}(V)).$$

It is easy to check that these definitions determine a probability space on the set of traces.

3.2 Composition

A collection $\{A_i : i \in I\}$ of probabilistic I/O automata, where

$$A_i = (Q_i, q_i^{\mathrm{I}}, E_i, \Delta_i, \mu_i, \delta_i),$$

is called *compatible* if the corresponding collection of underlying I/O automata is compatible. The *composition* $\prod_{i \in I} A_i$ of a *finite* compatible collection of probabilistic I/O automata is defined to be the sextuple $(Q, q^{\mathrm{I}}, E, \Delta, \mu, \delta)$, where

1. Q, q^{I}, E, and Δ are defined as for composition of ordinary I/O automata.
2. $\delta(\langle q_i : i \in I\rangle) = \sum_{i\in I} \delta_i(q_i)$.
3. If $e \in E^{\mathrm{in}}$, then

$$\mu(\langle q_i : i \in I\rangle, e, \langle r_i : i \in I\rangle) = \prod_{\{i\in I: e\in E_i\}} \mu_i(q_i, e, r_i).$$

If $e \in E_k^{\mathrm{loc}}$ for some k, then

$$\mu(\langle q_i : i \in I\rangle, e, \langle r_i : i \in I\rangle) = \frac{\delta_k(q_k)}{\sum_{i\in I} \delta_i(q_i)} \prod_{\{i\in I: e\in E_i\}} \mu_i(q_i, e, r_i).$$

In this paper, we restrict our attention to the composition of finite collections only. The finiteness assumption ensures that the sum in (2) converges, and that the products appearing in the definition of μ are nonzero.

The definition of composition can be motivated as follows: In any given state $q = \langle q_i : i \in I\rangle$ of a composite automaton $A = \prod_{i\in I} A_i$, the component automata A_i participate in a race to see which one will be the next to execute a locally controlled action. Conceptually, when each component automaton A_i enters its local state q_i, it chooses a random "delay period" from an exponential distribution with parameter $\delta_i(q_i)$. It then delays for this amount of time before executing its next locally controlled action. The winner of the race from state q will be that component automaton A_i with the least amount of time to wait. Because of the "memoryless" property of the exponential distribution, it is not necessary for us to keep track in the composite automaton of how long each component automaton A_i has already delayed in state q_i—the amount of time A_i has left to delay in state q_i is described by the same exponential distribution with parameter $\delta_i(q_i)$, regardless of how long A_i has already delayed. This fact simplifies the definition of composition considerably, and would also be important if we wished to construct a real-world implementation of the probabilistic behavior modeled by these automata.

Assuming that the random delay periods associated with the component automata A_i are independent, the probability that the winner of the race from state q will be a particular component A_k will be the probability that the random delay period chosen by A_k is the minimum among all the delay periods chosen by the A_i. This probability is the ratio $\delta_k(q_k)/\sum_{i\in I} \delta_i(q_i)$. The distribution of the time that composite automaton A delays in state q before executing its next locally controlled action is the distribution of the minimum of the delay times of each of the components. Here the situation is simplified by another property of the exponential distribution: the distribution of the minimum of a finite collection $\langle x_i : i \in I\rangle$ of independent random variables, where x_i is exponentially distributed with parameter $\delta_i(q_i)$, is again exponentially distributed with parameter $\sum_{i\in I} \delta_i(q_i)$ [Tri82]. This explains the definition of δ.

The definition of μ can now be explained as follows: If it has already been determined that the next action to be executed is a particular input action e, then the probability of choosing a particular transition (q, e, r), where $q = \langle q_i : i \in I\rangle$

and $r = \langle r_i : i \in I \rangle$ is simply the joint probability that component A_i executes (q_i, e, r_i), for all $i \in I$ such that $e \in E_i$. Assuming independence, this joint probability is just the product of the individual probabilities $\mu_i(q_i, e, r_i)$. On the other hand, if it has been determined that the next action to be executed is not an input action, but rather a locally controlled action, then which locally controlled action is actually executed depends on the outcome of the race for control between the component automata. The probability that the transition executed will be (q, e, r), where $q = \langle q_i : i \in I \rangle$ and $r = \langle r_i : i \in I \rangle$, and $e \in E_k^{\mathrm{loc}}$ is locally controlled by A_k, is the joint probability that each A_i will execute transition (q_i, e, r_i), times the probability that A_k will win the race. Assuming independence, the former is just the product of the individual probabilities $\mu_i(q_i, e, r_i)$. As already discussed, the latter probability is the ratio $\delta_k(q_k)/\sum_{i \in I} \delta_i(q_i)$.

Proposition 6. *If $\{A_i : i \in I\}$ is a finite compatible collection of probabilistic I/O automata, then $\prod_{i \in I} A_i$ is also a probabilistic I/O automaton.*

4 Behaviors of Probabilistic I/O Automata

In this section and the next section, we consider the restricted class of probabilistic I/O automata $A = (Q, q^{\mathrm{I}}, E, \Delta, \mu, \delta)$ for which the set E^{int} of internal actions is empty. We call probabilistic I/O automata satisfying this condition *restricted* probabilistic I/O automata. We wish to associate with such an automaton a more abstract representation in which we ignore the details of the particular state set and transition relation of the automaton, and focus instead on externally observable aspects of its probabilistic behavior.

Suppose A is a restricted probabilistic I/O automaton. Given a trace $\alpha = e_0 e_1 \ldots e_{n-1}$, for each delay sequence $d = d_0 d_1 \ldots d_n$ define the quantity $p_\alpha^A(d)$ by:

$$p_\alpha^A(d) = \sum_\sigma \prod_{k=0}^{n-1} \mu_A(\sigma(k), e_k, \sigma(k+1)),$$

where the summation is taken over all executions σ of A having trace α and delay sequence d. Observe that convergence of the summation is automatic, since by the local finite-branching and input image-finiteness properties of A, the set $\{\sigma : tr(\sigma) = \alpha\}$ is finite. The same reasoning also shows that, for a fixed α, the set of all d for which $p_\alpha^A(d)$ is nonzero, is finite. In case the set of input actions of A is empty, and α contains only actions in E_A, the quantity $p_\alpha^A(d)$ is the probability of the set of all native executions of A having α as a prefix of their trace and d as a prefix of their delay sequence.

Now, if $g : \mathcal{R}^{n+1} \to \mathcal{R}$ is a real-valued function, define

$$\mathcal{E}_\alpha^A[g(D)] = \sum_d g(d) p_\alpha^A(d),$$

where the sum ranges over all $(n+1)$-tuples $d = (d_0, d_1, \ldots, d_n)$ of nonnegative real numbers. We may view $\mathcal{E}_\alpha^A$ as a functional

$$\mathcal{E}_\alpha^A : (\mathcal{R}^{n+1} \to \mathcal{R}) \to \mathcal{R}.$$

In case the set of input actions of A is nonempty, we may regard the sequences d as the values of an $(n+1)$-dimensional random variable $D = (D_0, D_1, \ldots, D_n)$ defined on the conditional probability space X_α of native executions of A whose traces extend α. In this case, the quantity $\mathcal{E}_\alpha^A[g(D)]$ is just the expectation of $g(D)$, times the probability p_α^A of the set X_α.

Our abstract representation for probabilistic I/O automata assigns, to each restricted probabilistic I/O automaton A, the mapping $\mathcal{E}^A$ that takes each trace $\alpha \in U^*$ of length n to the functional $\mathcal{E}_\alpha^A$ on $\mathcal{R}^{n+1} \to \mathcal{R}$. We call the mapping $\mathcal{E}^A$ the *probabilistic behavior map* associated with A.

The compositionality of the representation of automata by probabilistic behavior maps is established in Theorem 1 below. In this theorem, $D^{A|B}$, D^A, and D^B denote $(n+1)$-dimensional random variables representing the random sequences of delays in an execution of $A|B$, A, and B, respectively. These symbols are used (as is conventional in probability theory) as dummies indicating the variables over which the summations are to be taken; thus the notation $\mathcal{E}^{A|B}$ denotes a summation over $D^{A|B}$, the notation $\mathcal{E}^A$ denotes a summation over D^A, and the notation $\mathcal{E}^B$ denotes a summation over D^B.

Theorem 1. *Suppose A and B are compatible probabilistic I/O automata and $\alpha = e_0 e_1 \ldots e_{n-1}$. Then*

$$\mathcal{E}_\alpha^{A|B}[g(D^{A|B})] = \mathcal{E}_\alpha^B[\mathcal{E}_\alpha^A[g(D^A + D^B) \cdot h(D^A, D^B)]],$$

where

$$h(D^A, D^B) = \left(\prod_{k \in K_A^{\text{loc}}} \frac{D_k^A}{D_k^A + D_k^B} \right) \left(\prod_{k \in K_B^{\text{loc}}} \frac{D_k^B}{D_k^A + D_k^B} \right)$$

$$K_A^{\text{loc}} = \{k : 0 \le k < n,\ e_k \in E_A^{\text{loc}}\} \quad \textit{and} \quad K_B^{\text{loc}} = \{k : 0 \le k < n,\ e_k \in E_B^{\text{loc}}\}$$

Proof Sketch – Write out the summation that defines $\mathcal{E}_\alpha^{A|B}$, then use the definition of $\mu_{A|B}$ to rewrite this expression in terms of μ_A and μ_B. By Proposition 1 and the definition of composition for probabilistic I/O automata, the executions σ of $A|B$ with trace α and delay sequence d are in bijective correspondence with pairs (σ_A, σ_B), where σ_A is an execution of A having α as its trace and d_A as its delay sequence, σ_B is an execution of B having α as its trace and d_B as its delay sequence, and $d = d_A + d_B$. Finally, apply the definitions of $\mathcal{E}_\alpha^A$ and $\mathcal{E}_\alpha^B$. □

5 Testing Equivalence and Full Abstraction

In this section we show that probabilistic behavior maps are fully abstract with respect to a notion of probabilistic testing equivalence. That is to say, probabilistic I/O automata A and B determine the same probabilistic behavior map if and only if in a certain sense they cannot be distinguished by any probabilistic test.

Formally, a *test* is simply a probabilistic I/O automaton T that has a distinguished output action ω. We interpret the occurrence of ω in a computation of

T as an indication that the test has succeeded. A test is called *closed* if its set of input actions is empty. For closed tests T, it makes sense (see Section 3.1) to talk about the probability of sets of native executions of T. Lemma 7 shows that the set of all successful native executions of a closed test T is measurable. We call the probability of this set the *success probability* of T.

Lemma 7. *Suppose T is a closed test. Then the set of all successful native executions of T is measurable. The probability of this set is given by the formula*

$$\sum_{\alpha \in \bar{\Omega}} \mathcal{E}^T_{\alpha\omega}[1],$$

where $\bar{\Omega}$ is the set of all traces that do not contain ω.

Suppose $A = (Q_A, q^{\mathrm{I}}_A, E_A, \Delta_A, \mu_A, \delta_A)$ is a probabilistic I/O automaton. A *proper test* for A is a test $T = (Q_T, q^{\mathrm{I}}_T, E_T, \Delta_T, \mu_T, \delta_T)$ such that $E^{\mathrm{in}}_T \subseteq E^{\mathrm{out}}_A$, $E^{\mathrm{in}}_A \subseteq E^{\mathrm{out}}_T \setminus \{\omega\}$, and $E^{\mathrm{loc}}_A \cap E^{\mathrm{loc}}_T = \emptyset$. If T is a proper test for A, then the collection $\{A, T\}$ is compatible. Let $A|T$ denote its composition, then $A|T$ is a closed test.

If A and B are probabilistic I/O automata with the same set of actions, then we call A and B *testing equivalent* if for all proper tests T for A and B, the success probability of $A|T$ equals the success probability of $B|T$.

We now define a particular class of tests that will be useful for distinguishing probabilistic I/O automata. Let a set of actions $E = E_0 \cup E_1$ be fixed. For each trace $\alpha = e_0 e_1 \dots e_{n-1}$ with $e_k \in E$ for $0 \le k < n$, and for each sequence $x = x_0, x_1, \dots, x_n$ of positive real numbers, we define a test $T_{\alpha,x} = (Q, q^{\mathrm{I}}, E_T, \Delta, \mu, \delta)$ as follows:

- $Q = \{0, 1, 2, \dots, n, n+1\}$.
- $q^{\mathrm{I}} = 0$.
- $E_T = \{e_0, e_1, \dots, e_{n-1}\} \cup \{\omega, *\}$, with $E^{\mathrm{in}}_T = E_1$ and $E^{\mathrm{out}}_T = E_0 \cup \{\omega, *\}$.
- Δ is the union of the following sets:
  1. $\{(k, e_k, k+1) : 0 \le k < n\}$
  2. $\{(n, \omega, n+1)\}$
  3. $\{(k, *, n+1) : 0 \le k < n\}$
  4. $\{(k, e, n+1) : 0 \le k < n, e \in E^{\mathrm{in}}_T, e \ne e_k\}$
  5. $\{(n, e, n+1) : e \in E^{\mathrm{in}}_T\}$.
  6. $\{(n+1, e, n+1) : e \in E^{\mathrm{in}}_T\}$.
- μ is defined as follows:
  1. If $0 \le k < n$, then $\mu(k, e_k, k+1) = \begin{cases} 1, & \text{if } e_k \in E^{\mathrm{in}}_T \\ 1/2 & \text{otherwise.} \end{cases}$
  2. $\mu(n, \omega, n+1) = 1$.
  3. If $0 \le k < n$, then $\mu(k, *, n+1) = \begin{cases} 1, & \text{if } e_k \in E^{\mathrm{in}}_T \\ 1/2 & \text{otherwise.} \end{cases}$
  4. If $0 \le k < n$, $e \in E^{\mathrm{in}}_T$, and $e \ne e_k$, then $\mu(k, e, n+1) = 1$.
  5. If $e \in E^{\mathrm{in}}_T$, then $\mu(n, e, n+1) = 1$, and $\mu(n+1, e, n+1) = 1$.
- $\delta(k) = x_k$ for $0 \le k \le n$ and $\delta(n+1) = 0$.

Intuitively, the test $T_{\alpha,x}$ succeeds when it manages to produce the trace $\alpha\omega$ by passing successively through states $0, 1, 2, \ldots, n$ and finally to $n+1$. For $0 \leq k \leq n$, the state k has delay parameter x_k, so the delay sequence $\delta(\sigma)$ associated with a successful execution σ of $T_{\alpha,x}$ is the sequence $x_0 x_1 \ldots x_n 0$. This is the only way executions of $T_{\alpha,x}$ can succeed; executions that deviate from α in the initial section cause $T_{\alpha,x}$ to enter the state $n+1$ without performing the success action ω. In each state k, where $0 \leq k < n$, the test $T_{\alpha,x}$ has a nonzero chance of failing by performing the action $*$ and going directly to state $n+1$. This gives $T_{\alpha,x}$ a certain sensitivity to the delays of its environment.

Lemma 8. *Suppose A is a probabilistic I/O automaton. Then for each trace $\alpha = e_0 e_1 \ldots e_{n-1} \in E_A^*$, and for each sequence $x = x_0, x_1, \ldots, x_n$ of positive real numbers, the test $T_{\alpha,x}$ (with $E_0 = E_A^{\text{in}}$ and $E_1 = E_A^{\text{out}}$) is a proper test for A. Moreover, the success probability of $A|T_{\alpha,x}$ is given by:*

$$2^{-c} \cdot \mathcal{E}_{\alpha\omega}^{A}\Big[\prod_{k=0}^{n} \frac{y_k}{x_k + D_k^A}\Big],$$

where for all $0 \leq k < n$ we have

$$y_k = \begin{cases} D_k^A, & \text{if } e_k \in E_A^{\text{out}} \\ x_k & \text{otherwise,} \end{cases}$$

$y_n = x_n$, and c is the number of $k \in \{0, 1, \ldots, n-1\}$ for which $e_k \in E_A^{\text{in}}$.

The following lemma is a uniqueness theorem for partial fraction expansions of rational functions in several variables. It is a key component of the proof of full abstraction (Theorem 2).

Lemma 9. *Suppose f and f' are two rational functions of $n \geq 0$ variables $x_0, x_1, \ldots, x_{n-1}$, defined as follows:*

$$f = \sum_{i \in I} \frac{c_i}{\prod_{k=0}^{n-1}(x_k + d_{i,k})} \qquad\qquad f' = \sum_{i' \in I'} \frac{c'_{i'}}{\prod_{k=0}^{n-1}(x_k + d'_{i',k})},$$

where I and I' are finite sets, $c_i \in (0, \infty)$ for $i \in I$, $c'_i \in (0, \infty)$ for $i \in I'$, and for each distinct $i, j \in I$ the sets $\{(k, d_{i,k}) : 0 \leq k < n\}$ and $\{(k, d_{j,k}) : 0 \leq k < n\}$ are distinct. If $f = f'$, then there exists a bijection $(\text{ - })' : I \to I'$ such that $c_i = c'_{i'}$ and $d_{i,k} = d'_{i',k}$ for all $i \in I$ and $0 \leq k < n$.

Proof Sketch – The proof is by induction on n. □

Theorem 2. *Suppose A and B are restricted probabilistic I/O automata with the same set of actions. Then A and B are testing equivalent if and only if the associated probabilistic behavior maps $\mathcal{E}^A$ and $\mathcal{E}^B$ are equal.*

Proof Sketch – If $\mathcal{E}^A = \mathcal{E}^B$, then the fact that A and B are testing equivalent follows directly from Theorem 1 and Lemma 7.

Conversely, suppose A and B are testing equivalent. For each trace $\alpha \in U^*$ of length n that contains no occurrences of the special action ω, Lemma 8 shows that the tests $T_{\alpha,x}$ are proper tests for A and B, and that the success probability of $A|T_{\alpha,x}$ is given by an expression $\mathcal{E}^A_{\alpha\omega}[g(D^A, x)]$, where g is a certain rational function of the $n+1$ random variables D^A and the $n+1$ unknowns x. The expression $\mathcal{E}^A_{\alpha\omega}[g(D^A, x)]$ is thus a rational function of x alone. The success probability of $B|T_{\alpha,x}$ is given by a similar rational function. Since A and B are testing equivalent, these two rational functions must have the same values for all positive x, hence they are the same rational function. Using Lemma 9, we show that the quantities $p^A_{\alpha\omega}(d)$ and $p^B_{\alpha\omega}(d)$, used in the definitions of $\mathcal{E}^A_\alpha$ and $\mathcal{E}^B_\alpha$, can be recovered uniquely from these rational functions, thus showing that $\mathcal{E}^A_\alpha = \mathcal{E}^B_\alpha$ for all traces α that do not contain ω. A final step in the proof removes the restriction on α, thus showing that $\mathcal{E}^A = \mathcal{E}^B$. □

6 Summary and Conclusion

In this paper, we have presented a framework in which probability can be added to I/O automata. To capture the asymmetric treatment of input and output indigenous to I/O automata, a separate distribution is associated with each input action, in the reactive style, and a single distribution is associated with all locally controlled actions, in the generative style. No relative probabilities are defined among different input actions nor between input and locally controlled actions. Moreover, the pleasant notion of I/O automaton asynchronous composition is retained, in part, through the introduction of state delay parameters. Delay parameters admit a natural probabilistic description of the outcome of the competition between automata vying for control of the next action.

As is the practice with ordinary I/O automata, we introduced a more abstract representation of the external behaviors of probabilistic I/O automata (without internal actions), *probabilistic behavior maps*. This representation maps finite action sequences to a set of expectation functionals which give information not only about the probabilities of action sequences but also delay sequences. This latter information is essential for achieving compositionality. We also showed that probabilistic behavior maps are fully abstract with respect to a natural notion of probabilistic testing.

As future work, we plan to generalize probabilistic behavior maps to probabilistic I/O automata with internal actions. We have obtained preliminary results in this direction for the subclass of probabilistic I/O automata in which the internal transitions do not change the state delay parameters. Additionally, we would like to extend our I/O automaton model to handle time as well as probability. The presence of the state delay function in our model provides a convenient mechanism on which to base this work.

References

[Chr90] I. Christoff. Testing equivalences and fully abstract models for probabilistic processes. In J. C. M. Baeten and J. W. Klop, editors, *Proceedings of CONCUR '90 – First International Conference on Concurrency Theory*, Lecture Notes in Computer Science, Volume 458, pages 126–140. Springer-Verlag, 1990.

[GHR92] N. Götz, U. Herzog, and M. Rettlebach. TIPP — a language for timed processes and performance evaluation. Technical Report 4/92, University of Erlangen-Nürnberg, Germany, November 1992.

[Han91] H. A. Hansson. *Time and Probability in Formal Design of Distributed Systems.* PhD thesis, Department of Computer Systems, Uppsala University, 1991.

[Hil93] J. Hillston. PEPA: Performance enhanced process algebra. Technical Report CSR-24-93, Department of Computer Science, University of Edinburgh, Edinburgh, Great Britain, March 1993.

[HJ90] H. A. Hansson and B. Jonsson. A calculus for communicating systems with time and probabilities. In *Proceedings of the 11th IEEE Symposium on Real-Time Systems*, 1990.

[JL91] B. Jonsson and K. G. Larsen. Specification and refinement of probabilistic processes. In *Proceedings of the 6th IEEE Symposium on Logic in Computer Science*, Amsterdam, July 1991.

[Lan84] S. Lang. *Algebra.* Addison-Wesley, Menlo Park, California, 1984.

[LS92] K. G. Larsen and A. Skou. Bisimulation through probabilistic testing. *Information and Computation*, 94(1):1–28, September 1992. Preliminary versions of this paper appeared as University of Aalborg technical reports R 88-18 and R 88-29, and in *Proceedings of the 16th Annual ACM Symposium on Principles of Programming Languages*, Austin, Texas, 1989.

[LT87] N. A. Lynch and M. Tuttle. Hierarchical correctness proofs for distributed algorithms. In *Proceedings of the 6th Annual ACM Symposium on Principles of Distributed Computing*, 1987.

[Mol82] M. K. Molloy. Performance analysis using stochastic Petri nets. *IEEE Trans. Comput.*, C-31(9), September 1982.

[Rab63] M. O. Rabin. Probabilistic automata. *Information and Control*, 6:230–245, 1963.

[Sei92] K. Seidel. *Probabilistic CSP.* PhD thesis, Oxford University, 1992.

[Tri82] K. S. Trivedi. *Probability & Statistics with Reliability, Queuing, and Computer Science Applications.* Prentice Hall, Englewood Cliffs, New Jersey, 1982.

[Tut87] M. Tuttle. Hierarchical correctness proofs for distributed algorithms. Master's thesis, MIT, April 1987.

[vGSST90] R. J. van Glabbeek, S. A. Smolka, B. Steffen, and C. M. N. Tofts. Reactive, generative, and stratified models of probabilistic processes. In *Proceedings of the 5th IEEE Symposium on Logic in Computer Science*, pages 130–141, Philadelphia, PA, 1990.

[Wei74] A. J. Weir. *General Integration and Measure.* Cambridge University Press, 1974.

Author Index

Springer-Verlag and the Environment

We at Springer-Verlag firmly believe that an international science publisher has a special obligation to the environment, and our corporate policies consistently reflect this conviction.

We also expect our business partners – paper mills, printers, packaging manufacturers, etc. – to commit themselves to using environmentally friendly materials and production processes.

The paper in this book is made from low- or no-chlorine pulp and is acid free, in conformance with international standards for paper permanency.

Lecture Notes in Computer Science

For information about Vols. 1–759
please contact your bookseller or Springer-Verlag

Vol. 760: S. Ceri, K. Tanaka, S. Tsur (Eds.), Deductive and Object-Oriented Databases. Proceedings, 1993. XII, 488 pages. 1993.

Vol. 761: R. K. Shyamasundar (Ed.), Foundations of Software Technology and Theoretical Computer Science. Proceedings, 1993. XIV, 456 pages. 1993.

Vol. 762: K. W. Ng, P. Raghavan, N. V. Balasubramanian, F. Y. L. Chin (Eds.), Algorithms and Computation. Proceedings, 1993. XIII, 542 pages. 1993.

Vol. 763: F. Pichler, R. Moreno Díaz (Eds.), Computer Aided Systems Theory – EUROCAST '93. Proceedings, 1993. IX, 451 pages. 1994.

Vol. 764: G. Wagner, Vivid Logic. XII, 148 pages. 1994. (Subseries LNAI).

Vol. 765: T. Helleseth (Ed.), Advances in Cryptology – EUROCRYPT '93. Proceedings, 1993. X, 467 pages. 1994.

Vol. 766: P. R. Van Loocke, The Dynamics of Concepts. XI, 340 pages. 1994. (Subseries LNAI).

Vol. 767: M. Gogolla, An Extended Entity-Relationship Model. X, 136 pages. 1994.

Vol. 768: U. Banerjee, D. Gelernter, A. Nicolau, D. Padua (Eds.), Languages and Compilers for Parallel Computing. Proceedings, 1993. XI, 655 pages. 1994.

Vol. 769: J. L. Nazareth, The Newton-Cauchy Framework. XII, 101 pages. 1994.

Vol. 770: P. Haddawy (Representing Plans Under Uncertainty. X, 129 pages. 1994. (Subseries LNAI).

Vol. 771: G. Tomas, C. W. Ueberhuber, Visualization of Scientific Parallel Programs. XI, 310 pages. 1994.

Vol. 772: B. C. Warboys (Ed.),Software Process Technology. Proceedings, 1994. IX, 275 pages. 1994.

Vol. 773: D. R. Stinson (Ed.), Advances in Cryptology – CRYPTO '93. Proceedings, 1993. X, 492 pages. 1994.

Vol. 774: M. Banâtre, P. A. Lee (Eds.), Hardware and Software Architectures for Fault Tolerance. XIII, 311 pages. 1994.

Vol. 775: P. Enjalbert, E. W. Mayr, K. W. Wagner (Eds.), STACS 94. Proceedings, 1994. XIV, 782 pages. 1994.

Vol. 776: H. J. Schneider, H. Ehrig (Eds.), Graph Transformations in Computer Science. Proceedings, 1993. VIII, 395 pages. 1994.

Vol. 777: K. von Luck, H. Marburger (Eds.), Management and Processing of Complex Data Structures. Proceedings, 1994. VII, 220 pages. 1994.

Vol. 778: M. Bonuccelli, P. Crescenzi, R. Petreschi (Eds.), Algorithms and Complexity. Proceedings, 1994. VIII, 222 pages. 1994.

Vol. 779: M. Jarke, J. Bubenko, K. Jeffery (Eds.), Advances in Database Technology — EDBT '94. Proceedings, 1994. XII, 406 pages. 1994.

Vol. 780: J. J. Joyce, C.-J. H. Seger (Eds.), Higher Order Logic Theorem Proving and Its Applications. Proceedings, 1993. X, 518 pages. 1994.

Vol. 781: G. Cohen, S. Litsyn, A. Lobstein, G. Zémor (Eds.), Algebraic Coding. Proceedings, 1993. XII, 326 pages. 1994.

Vol. 782: J. Gutknecht (Ed.), Programming Languages and System Architectures. Proceedings, 1994. X, 344 pages. 1994.

Vol. 783: C. G. Günther (Ed.), Mobile Communications. Proceedings, 1994. XVI, 564 pages. 1994.

Vol. 784: F. Bergadano, L. De Raedt (Eds.), Machine Learning: ECML-94. Proceedings, 1994. XI, 439 pages. 1994. (Subseries LNAI).

Vol. 785: H. Ehrig, F. Orejas (Eds.), Recent Trends in Data Type Specification. Proceedings, 1992. VIII, 350 pages. 1994.

Vol. 786: P. A. Fritzson (Ed.), Compiler Construction. Proceedings, 1994. XI, 451 pages. 1994.

Vol. 787: S. Tison (Ed.), Trees in Algebra and Programming – CAAP '94. Proceedings, 1994. X, 351 pages. 1994.

Vol. 788: D. Sannella (Ed.), Programming Languages and Systems – ESOP '94. Proceedings, 1994. VIII, 516 pages. 1994.

Vol. 789: M. Hagiya, J. C. Mitchell (Eds.), Theoretical Aspects of Computer Software. Proceedings, 1994. XI, 887 pages. 1994.

Vol. 790: J. van Leeuwen (Ed.), Graph-Theoretic Concepts in Computer Science. Proceedings, 1993. IX, 431 pages. 1994.

Vol. 791: R. Guerraoui, O. Nierstrasz, M. Riveill (Eds.), Object-Based Distributed Programming. Proceedings, 1993. VII, 262 pages. 1994.

Vol. 792: N. D. Jones, M. Hagiya, M. Sato (Eds.), Logic, Language and Computation. XII, 269 pages. 1994.

Vol. 793: T. A. Gulliver, N. P. Secord (Eds.), Information Theory and Applications. Proceedings, 1993. XI, 394 pages. 1994.

Vol. 794: G. Haring, G. Kotsis (Eds.), Computer Performance Evaluation. Proceedings, 1994. X, 464 pages. 1994.

Vol. 795: W. A. Hunt, Jr., FM8501: A Verified Microprocessor. XIII, 333 pages. 1994.

Vol. 796: W. Gentzsch, U. Harms (Eds.), High-Performance Computing and Networking. Proceedings, 1994, Vol. I. XXI, 453 pages. 1994.

Vol. 797: W. Gentzsch, U. Harms (Eds.), High-Performance Computing and Networking. Proceedings, 1994, Vol. II. XXII, 519 pages. 1994.

Vol. 798: R. Dyckhoff (Ed.), Extensions of Logic Programming. Proceedings, 1993. VIII, 362 pages. 1994.

Vol. 799: M. P. Singh, Multiagent Systems. XXIII, 168 pages. 1994. (Subseries LNAI).

Vol. 800: J.-O. Eklundh (Ed.), Computer Vision – ECCV '94. Proceedings 1994, Vol. I. XVIII, 603 pages. 1994.

Vol. 801: J.-O. Eklundh (Ed.), Computer Vision – ECCV '94. Proceedings 1994, Vol. II. XV, 485 pages. 1994.

Vol. 802: S. Brookes, M. Main, A. Melton, M. Mislove, D. Schmidt (Eds.), Mathematical Foundations of Programming Semantics. Proceedings, 1993. IX, 647 pages. 1994.

Vol. 803: J. W. de Bakker, W.-P. de Roever, G. Rozenberg (Eds.), A Decade of Concurrency. Proceedings, 1993. VII, 683 pages. 1994.

Vol. 804: D. Hernández, Qualitative Representation of Spatial Knowledge. IX, 202 pages. 1994. (Subseries LNAI).

Vol. 805: M. Cosnard, A. Ferreira, J. Peters (Eds.), Parallel and Distributed Computing. Proceedings, 1994. X, 280 pages. 1994.

Vol. 806: H. Barendregt, T. Nipkow (Eds.), Types for Proofs and Programs. VIII, 383 pages. 1994.

Vol. 807: M. Crochemore, D. Gusfield (Eds.), Combinatorial Pattern Matching. Proceedings, 1994. VIII, 326 pages. 1994.

Vol. 808: M. Masuch, L. Pólos (Eds.), Knowledge Representation and Reasoning Under Uncertainty. VII, 237 pages. 1994. (Subseries LNAI).

Vol. 809: R. Anderson (Ed.), Fast Software Encryption. Proceedings, 1993. IX, 223 pages. 1994.

Vol. 810: G. Lakemeyer, B. Nebel (Eds.), Foundations of Knowledge Representation and Reasoning. VIII, 355 pages. 1994. (Subseries LNAI).

Vol. 811: G. Wijers, S. Brinkkemper, T. Wasserman (Eds.), Advanced Information Systems Engineering. Proceedings, 1994. XI, 420 pages. 1994.

Vol. 812: J. Karhumäki, H. Maurer, G. Rozenberg (Eds.), Results and Trends in Theoretical Computer Science. Proceedings, 1994. X, 445 pages. 1994.

Vol. 813: A. Nerode, Yu. N. Matiyasevich (Eds.), Logical Foundations of Computer Science. Proceedings, 1994. IX, 392 pages. 1994.

Vol. 814: A. Bundy (Ed.), Automated Deduction—CADE-12. Proceedings, 1994. XVI, 848 pages. 1994. (Subseries LNAI).

Vol. 815: R. Valette (Ed.), Application and Theory of Petri Nets 1994. Proceedings. IX, 587 pages. 1994.

Vol. 816: J. Heering, K. Meinke, B. Möller, T. Nipkow (Eds.), Higher-Order Algebra, Logic, and Term Rewriting. Proceedings, 1993. VII, 344 pages. 1994.

Vol. 817: C. Halatsis, D. Maritsas, G. Philokyprou, S. Theodoridis (Eds.), PARLE '94. Parallel Architectures and Languages Europe. Proceedings, 1994. XV, 837 pages. 1994.

Vol. 818: D. L. Dill (Ed.), Computer Aided Verification. Proceedings, 1994. IX, 480 pages. 1994.

Vol. 819: W. Litwin, T. Risch (Eds.), Applications of Databases. Proceedings, 1994. XII, 471 pages. 1994.

Vol. 820: S. Abiteboul, E. Shamir (Eds.), Automata, Languages and Programming. Proceedings, 1994. XIII, 644 pages. 1994.

Vol. 821: M. Tokoro, R. Pareschi (Eds.), Object-Oriented Programming. Proceedings, 1994. XI, 535 pages. 1994.

Vol. 822: F. Pfenning (Ed.), Logic Programming and Automated Reasoning. Proceedings, 1994. X, 345 pages. 1994. (Subseries LNAI).

Vol. 823: R. A. Elmasri, V. Kouramajian, B. Thalheim (Eds.), Entity-Relationship Approach — ER '93. Proceedings, 1993. X, 531 pages. 1994.

Vol. 824: E. M. Schmidt, S. Skyum (Eds.), Algorithm Theory – SWAT '94. Proceedings. IX, 383 pages. 1994.

Vol. 825: J. L. Mundy, A. Zisserman, D. Forsyth (Eds.), Applications of Invariance in Computer Vision. Proceedings, 1993. IX, 510 pages. 1994.

Vol. 826: D. S. Bowers (Ed.), Directions in Databases. Proceedings, 1994. X, 234 pages. 1994.

Vol. 827: D. M. Gabbay, H. J. Ohlbach (Eds.), Temporal Logic. Proceedings, 1994. XI, 546 pages. 1994. (Subseries LNAI).

Vol. 828: L. C. Paulson, Isabelle. XVII, 321 pages. 1994.

Vol. 829: A. Chmora, S. B. Wicker (Eds.), Error Control, Cryptology, and Speech Compression. Proceedings, 1993. VIII, 121 pages. 1994.

Vol. 830: C. Castelfranchi, E. Werner (Eds.), Artificial Social Systems. Proceedings, 1992. XVIII, 337 pages. 1994. (Subseries LNAI).

Vol. 831: V. Bouchitté, M. Morvan (Eds.), Orders, Algorithms, and Applications. Proceedings, 1994. IX, 204 pages. 1994.

Vol. 832: E. Börger, Y. Gurevich, K. Meinke (Eds.), Computer Science Logic. Proceedings, 1993. VIII, 336 pages. 1994.

Vol. 833: D. Driankov, P. W. Eklund, A. Ralescu (Eds.), Fuzzy Logic and Fuzzy Control. Proceedings, 1991. XII, 157 pages. 1994. (Subseries LNAI).

Vol. 834: D.-Z. Du, X.-S. Zhang (Eds.), Algorithms and Computation. Proceedings, 1994. XIII, 687 pages. 1994.

Vol. 835: W. M. Tepfenhart, J. P. Dick, J. F. Sowa (Eds.), Conceptual Structures: Current Practices. Proceedings, 1994. VIII, 331 pages. 1994. (Subseries LNAI).

Vol. 836: B. Jonsson, J. Parrow (Eds.), CONCUR '94: Concurrency Theory. Proceedings, 1994. IX, 529 pages. 1994.

Vol. 837: S. Wess, K.-D. Althoff, M. M. Richter (Eds.), Topics in Case-Based Reasoning. Proceedings, 1993. IX, 471 pages. 1994. (Subseries LNAI).

Vol. 838: C. MacNish, D. Pearce, L. Moniz Pereira (Eds.), Logics in AI. Proceedings, 1994. IX, 413 pages. 1994. (Subseries LNAI).

Vol. 839: Y. G. Desmedt (Ed.), Advances in Cryptology - CRYPTO '94. Proceedings, 1994. XII, 439 pages. 1994.